THE GREAT FOLK DISCOGRAPHY

VOLUME 2
THE NEXT GENERATION

MARTIN C. STRONG

This edition published in Great Britain in 2011 by
Polygon, an imprint of Birlinn Ltd
West Newington House
10 Newington Road
Edinburgh
EH9 1QS

www.polygonbooks.co.uk

ISBN 978 1 84697 177 8

British Library Cataloguing-in-Publication Data
A catalogue record for this book is available on request from the British Library

The publisher acknowledges investment from
Creative Scotland towards the publication of this book

Typeset by Brinnoven, Livingston
Printed and bound by Bookwell, Finland

This book is dedicated to ...

my mother Jean Fotheringham
(born: 6th of January 1929,
died of cancer:
31st of August 1985)

Still missing you
and thanks for still
guiding me through all
the hard times.

my dad Gerry/Geoff Strong
(born: 28th of July 1930,
died of a heart attack:
20th October 1998)

Will miss you always
You were also a great friend,
inspiration and someone who
could make me laugh

Hope you're both getting on up there
If only ...

Contents

Acknowledgements

Putting my family first (as one should always do), lots of love and a very special mention go to my daughters, Samantha (7), Suzanne (28) and Shirley (30), my grandkids Lyla (4), Jade (8) and Ivor (13), plus my auntie Joyce, the McElroy cousins Kevin, Brian, Stephen (and Nina), Paul (who recently passed away) and Maureen (who died in May 2003), uncle Frank and family from Australia, auntie Isobel and uncle Danny, and cousins Daniel & Jennifer.

All the best and cheers go to Allan and Elaine Brewster (and family), Andy Risk, Stan Lyon (and Linda), Peter McGuckin, Tony and Claire Hughes, Vic Zdzieblo, George Main, Brian and Margaret Hunter, Alan Duncan, Bernie Harkins, Davie Blair, Mark Robertson (former LIST man and GFD contributor MR), former GRD series contributor Adam Stafford (Y'all Is Fantasy Island mainman), Elaine Brown, Eileen Scott-Moncrieff, Michael Fletcher, Edward 'Kip' Hannan, James Zdzieblo, Iain McLean, Martin McDermott, Laurie Doolan, Stefan Lewandowski (and Marie), Sandy and Caroline McCrae, Kevin Goodman, Paul Hughes, Billy and Ann Ross, Brian McKerracher, Bobby Callaghan, Brian Vause, Derek Clarkin, Cliff Pattenden, Johnny Parker, John Cassidy, George Dickson, Martin McKenna, Scott McKean, Billy Pate, Barry and Katriona Moore, Jock and Linda McLeish, Davie and Vi Seath, Graeme and Doreen, Scott Honeyman, Gary Friel, Lynn and Stewart Aitchison, Jimmy Muir, Graeme Minto (my accountant), Ray Morton, Tony Weir, Russell Mayes, Sheridar and Mitch, Malky Farrell, John Merilees, Gizmo, Peter Sharp, Jamie Mullan, Watty Morrison, Alan White, Davie Galloway, Barry Devlin, Rab Bell, Tich, Mando Notrangelo, Jim Hunter, Derek Fleming, Calum and Julie, Peter Rankine, Des Kerr, Matt Wotherspoon, John 'Tubby' Walker, Arthur Jack, Geoff Irvine, Pat Kelly, Francis McKenzie, Dennis Devlin, Peter Moffat, Wladyslaw "Willie" and Isabel Waledzik, Cheerz pub (Neil and all the staff) and anyone whom I've inadvertently left out. Good luck to Megan Adam (pop artist) – couldn't get a commission for you or even myself – sorry.

Major websites (www) that were sourced for bits'n'pieces, recordings, etc. were: eBay, wikipedia, spotify, amazon, all music guide, rate your music, discogs, galactic ramble, time has told me, gemm, eil, and a handful of others. The NME, Mojo, Uncut and Record Collector were (and still are) my fave periodical rags. Books that inspired me to do a little better in a folk-music sense were the much-thumbed: The Guinness Who's Who Of Folk Music, Rare Record Price Guide series, British Hit Singles & Albums, Joel Whitburn's Top Pop Albums (& Singles), Electric Folk, The Tapestry Of Delights, Turn! Turn! Turn!: The '60s Folk-Rock Revolution, Eight Miles High: Folk-Rock's Flight From Haight-Ashbury To Woodstock (both by Richie Unterberger) and my own Great Rock Discography series.

Also, I'd like to thank my publishers Birlinn (Neville, Hugh, Alison, Kenny, Jim etc.) and typesetter Bill Murray.

Thanks to the multitude of folk stars et al who emailed back details and sent on a few of the worthy CDs, notably: Alasdair Roberts (see Foreword), Terry Friend, Martin Joseph, Felicity Buirski, Geoff Davis (of Probe Plus), Stanley Greenthal, Robb Johnson, Stanley Accrington, Steve Gillette and Cindy Mangsen, Erica Wheeler, Ilene Weiss, Kate MacLeod and Kat Eggleston, Emily White, Simone White, Scott Alarik, Jim Post, Cliff Eberhardt, Catie Curtis, Carrie Newcomer, Wally Pleasant, Judy Dunlop, Ken Nicol, Charlotte Greig, Dave Cartwright, Dave Evans, David Jaycock, Jana Hunter, Damien (and Sarah) Jurado, David Francey, Ed Hamell (On Trial), Paul Downes, Josephine Foster, Kieran Halpin, Paul James, Jo Freya, Cindy Lee Berryhill, Mick Ryan, The Amazing Mr. Smith, Jim Bisgood, Leo Abrahams, Kenny Anderson, Roger Wilson, Bram Taylor, Tom Rose, Dick Miles, The Bushwackers, Clive Harvey, O'Hooley and Tidow, David Delarre, Kris Delmhorst, Orion Dommisse, Cindy Kallett, Sally Rogers, Ora Cogan, Adem, Simon Mayor, Richard Bishop, Duck Baker, Ed Alkalay, Gareth Turner, Paul Alan Taylor, Gary Wilcox, Brian Bell, Georgina Boyes, Doug Hudson, and Robin and Bina Williamson – and I hope I've not missed anyone out.

Foreword

This thing called 'folk music' – what is it? It's a hoary old question. One that's been around for as long as there have been folk to ask it. One that has had in the past, has now and will continue to have as many answers as there are folk to provide answers to it. Answers innumerable as the grains of sand in the Sahara. So many answers, in fact, as to render the very question redundant. You see, in these post-post-postmodern times, it's all relative – your answer isn't the same as mine. Yesterday's answer isn't the same as today's. Hell, if you ask me again tomorrow, my answer will be different than it is right now!

To some, it's the creative expression of an entire people's soul in musical form, wherever in the world that people might be found: it's about internationalism and commonalities between cultures – the voice of all people. To others, it's the music that emanates from their own particular territory: it's about nationalism and what makes their own culture distinctive – the voice of *a* people. To some, it's communal – raising voices together, dancing, sharing tunes, songs and good times. To others, it's about a strong single voice with a message of protest or a story to tell. For some, it's a case of pastoral whimsy, psychedelic nostalgia, romantic mysticism – a rose-tinted stroll through some bygone Arcadia. For others, it's about something more grounded – the realities and difficulties of people's everyday working lives, urban and rural. Some believe that folk music is one of the most noble, glorious and sophisticated achievements of human creativity; on the other hand, one of my late fellow countrymen, a cantankerous man of letters – who declared himself a socialist! – is on record describing folksong as nothing but 'the braying of unlettered peasants'!

At this stage in the game, perhaps it's best not to ask that vexed question, 'What is folk music?' at all. All there really is to know is that folk, wherever they are to be found and for as long as they have existed, have made music. It seems certain that they will continue to do so until they either evolve into another species or become extinct (let's hope it's the former – I'm sure whatever music the next species of hominid makes will be fascinating).

The impulse to create music is universal. As I write, millions – nay, billions – of people worldwide are engaged in it: folk of all ages, races, creeds, genders and sexual orientations. Some are doing it alone and others in groups; some professionally and others for fun. Some are singing and playing the ancient traditional songs and ballads of their various nations; some are making new music of their own devising. Some are strumming instruments of wood and string, blowing through tubes of metal and pounding on taut animal skins; others are using the latest hi-tech sound-generating equipment – synthesisers and the like. This, by one very wide definition, is 'folk music', and thankfully it will never stop happening.

A relatively small percentage of all the folk who create sound do so in front of recording equipment; an even smaller fraction of those go on to have the resultant recordings pressed onto a vinyl record or burned onto a CD and made commercially available. The volume you are holding in your hands now, dear reader, attempts to document recent developments in this vast field – the field of recorded 'folk music' in all its forms.

'Who are you anyway?' I hear you ask. Well, I'm a musician myself – a Scot, these days mainly a guitarist, a singer of auld ballads and a creator of new songs. A couple of weeks ago, in early August, I was fortunate enough to land a couple of gigs in the sunshine at Sidmouth Folk Week in Devon, England. There was an astounding range of tremendously skilled musicians there, both professionals on stage and amateurs in pub sessions. After I played, it was a simple yet profound and life-affirming joy to sit in the bar and listen to all kinds of folk playing, on accordion, fiddle and guitar, the traditional tunes of that region (and beyond), and then to sit in a room full of people singing the songs of that region (and further afield) together in glorious heterophony, all for the sheer pleasure of it. As a foreigner in those parts, it was a great education for me!

But traditional tunes and songs are only a part of what 'folk music' is about nowadays. For many of the contemporary artists you'll read about between these pages, the kind of traditional music-making I have just described is but the starting point for their own music – a forward-thinking, exploratory, challenging music; music which draws on sources beyond those which have commonly been understood as 'folk music'; a music with eyes firmly on the future but with respect for the past.

I can't claim to be even vaguely familiar with a lot of the sonic treats that Mr Strong is bringing to our attention here, but I am certain that it'll be well worth your time and effort to explore them. It's a huge and complex field of endeavour: take your time, savour it; take pleasure in the journey, make your own connections.

Whatever potential answers the troublesome question at the beginning of this foreword might have, at a certain point it's time to stop asking and start enjoying, start creating. That's what the artists you'll encounter in the following pages have done – in their own new, unique, multi-faceted, surprising, exciting, bizarre, moving, terrifying and beautiful ways.

Alasdair Roberts
Glasgow, September 2011

Introduction by Martin C. Strong

Not only is this the second volume of the GREAT FOLK DISCOGRAPHY (subtitled on this occasion THE NEXT GENERATION), this is also my eighteenth book and my thirtieth year as a writer, although for the past months, due to circumstances out of my control, I've had to downsize my life's mission impossible to just a hobby.

Whether the recession (or someone/something else) will finally kill off my GREAT ROCK DISCOGRAPHY series, time will tell. One thing is clear, that, if I can survive on 'scraps' and living off the proverbial begging bowl for the last couple of years – like so many of the artists I've recently written about – I can maybe squeeze out a few more. But this might not be with Birlinn Books, who thought it relevant to tell me halfway through Volume Two that part three of the trilogy (THE GREAT FOLK DISCOGRAPHY: CELTIC CONNECTIONS) would now not be forthcoming in January 2013. Stop press: if this book sells they will publish it. But it might be, for the first time ever, there will only be two volumes in a trilogy – I'm proud to say another first for the GRD series. I'll make available iconic Celtic acts The Chieftains, Battlefield Band, Clannad, Shooglenifty etc. in another form or medium.

Pulping large remainder stocks of my worthy GREAT SCOTS MUSICOGRAPHY (published by Mercat Press in 2002) also didn't help my goals and ambitions. Apart from totally demoralising me while I was getting around to scribing the blood, sweat and tears biogs/discogs it takes to produce this book, it nearly made me just give up the ghost. This was not the only gremlin that would niggle away at my brain, there were of course financial problems (banks, debts/debtors and day-to-day crises); if it hadn't been for my many friends and my own street-cred ingenuity, one might've been out with the bin-bags. If I'm not touting for work, I still sit at my computer(s) nearly every day on my old rickety office chair as described last year – it's just lost two castors and I've never been able to afford a new £40 one, or a new printer for that matter. Basic food and having the fares to see my wee bairn comes first. Not for the first time (and probably not for the last) I've sold all my records and CDs to give you the reader another book. Nothing left to sell apart from myself.

Despite it being late to hit the shops (due to heavy snow in November and December), the GREAT FOLK DISCOGRAPHY: VOLUME 1 – PIONEERS & EARLY LEGENDS received a maximum 5* in the April 2011 edition of Record Collector monthly mag. I and thousands of folk fans haven't seen much of a review before or since, even the internet (my discography books and my name produce nearly 30,000 hits!) has seen little in terms of promotion. Yes, sales were poor and it seems it's 'nobody's fault but mine' as the old folk-blues song would suggest. If you've purchased the second volume, why not buy the 600-page companion piece first volume – available directly from www.birlinn.co.uk. Other books – if still in print as all rights have reverted back to me – can be found at www.canongate.net.

Anyway, that'll all be in the past and swept under the carpet, until of course I find another publisher for either Volume 3, the ninth edition of The Great Rock Discography (new title and all) or my warts'n'all novel. Any takers?

It must be said as, well, my publishers (and others) have been kind and gracious over the years and will probably get this book and the previous one out and into your homes or at least the local library. A big thanks to Kenny Redpath at Birlinn who persevered and garnered me a spot at the prestigious Edinburgh International Book Festival on 27th August; I just hope I can live up to all the hype. Stop press: I was nervous but I managed to get through it all without a wine or ciggy in sight.

I have now 20,000 rock/pop/folk/metal/indie/psychedelic/country/Celtic/country/blues/Scots and movie artists in my ever-expanding database and there must be some Dragon out there that would like to get all my work online – before it goes to cyberspace or Wikipedia for free. Would be a waste of millions of facts if nothing happened. Incidentally, you can look me up in the Wiki pages, and hopefully it'll be updated (and linked) by the time you read this.

When I first started my 'proper' discographies many moons ago there were only a handful of other writers doing similar work, now if one looks on online websites (and the odd book) there are tens of thousands publishing simple discographies. Ironic then that the master of ceremonies (the MC himself) gets hardly any monies while others who've done far less get all the wongas.

I'm currently getting my own websites up and running at www.mcstrong.com and www.greatrockbible.com and although they may still be under construction by the time your read this, it'll be worth going back to check their progress. It'll be hard to get going – as will my music site – but grit and determination should see them win through. The positive side is that each discography/biography will be available individually very soon and, by all accounts, very cheap. One will also find them on my own site(s).

Folk music has become my passion over the last several years (and beyond) – and from an old prog-meets-punk fan of the '70s, that's some admission. Okay, I still love Beefheart, Mogwai and early Genesis, plus The Fall, Pink Floyd and Popol Vuh. But on a folk-rock diet of DYLAN, The INCREDIBLE STRING BAND, FAIRPORT CONVENTION and NICK DRAKE (all of course from the first volume), I've been transported back in time, while my new folk buddies have been from the '80s (The POGUES) to the '00s (FLEET FOXES). This is the timescale we concentrate on here in this second volume.

I would think this would be a good time to reveal my 'Best of' list, a list that you could also try to put together yourself. I had no response from letters in my last book – no letters when I used to get around five a week. Maybe it's the medium thing – why not try my email address at mcstrong@btinternet.com.

In the previous volume I separated my lists in North American and British acts (as depicted in the book itself); this time I'm clumping them together. I've picked five tracks from my best 1–5 modern-day acts, three each from the next best 5 (i.e. Nos 6–10) and one each from the next best (Nos 11–20) – (albums in brackets); yes, I do love freak-folk music.

So here's my recommended playlist:

1. ESPERS: 1. Flowery Noontide ('Espers') / 2. Dead Queen ('Espers II') / 3. Caroline ('Espers III') / 4. Hearts & Daggers ('Espers') / 5. Voices ('Espers')

2. CIRCULUS: 1. Transmuting Power ('Thought Becomes Reality') / 2. Michael's Garden ('Thought Becomes Reality') / 3. Sumer Is Incumen In ('Thought Becomes Reality') / 4. My Body Is Made Of Sunlight ('The Lick On The Tip Of An Envelope Yet To Be Sent') / 5. Song Of Our Despair ('Clocks Are Like People')

3. FLEET FOXES: 1. Your Protector ('Fleet Foxes') / 2. Sun It Rises ('Fleet Foxes') / 3. White Winter Hymnal ('Fleet Foxes') / 4. Bedouin Dress ('Helplessness Blues') / 5. Helplessness Blues ('Helplessness Blues')

4. The POGUES: 1. Sally MacLennane ('Rum, Sodomy And The Lash') / 2. Thousands Are Sailing ('If I Should Fall From Grace With God') / 3. Boys From The County Hell ('Red Roses For Me') / 4. Navigator ('Rum, Sodomy And The Lash') / 5. Dirty Old Town ('Rum, Sodomy And The Lash')

5. The PROCLAIMERS: 1. Letter From America [acoustic] ('This Is The Story') / 2. I'm Gonna Be (500 Miles) ('Sunshine On Leith') / 3. Sunshine On Leith ('Sunshine On Leith') / 4. Make My Heart Fly ('This Is The Story') / 5. Love Can Move Mountains 'Note & Rhymes')

6. GORKY'S ZYGOTIC MYNCI: 1. Sometimes The Father Is The Son ('Barafundle') / 2. Diamond Dew ('Barafundle') / 3. Patio Song ('Barafundle')

7. ALASDAIR ROBERTS: 1. Carousing ('Farewell Sorrow') / 2. Riddle Me This ('The Amber Gatherers') / 3. I Had A Kiss Of The King's Hand ('The Amber Gatherers')

8. 10,000 MANIACS: 1. My Mother The War ('Secrets Of The I-Ching') / 2. Can't Ignore The Train ('The Wishing Chair') / 3. Hey Jack Kerouac ('In My Tribe')

9. IN GOWAN RING: 1. One Silver Ring ('The Twin Trees') / 2. Lady Beyond The River ('The Twin Trees') / 3. Spindle Tree ('Love Charms')

10. CURRENT 93: 1. The Teeth Of The Winds Of The Sea ('Of Ruine Or Some Blazing Starre') / 2. Black Ships In The Sky ('Black Ships Ate The Sky') / 3. Then Kill Caesar ('Black Ships Ate The Sky')

11. NATALIE MERCHANT: Crazy Man Michael ('The House Carpenter's Son')

12. JOSEPHINE FOSTER AND THE SUPPOSED: Well-Heeled Man ('All The Leaves Are Gone')

13. ELLIOTT SMITH: Ballad Of Big Nothing ('Either/Or')

14. EX REVERIE: Cedar ('The Door Into Summer')

15. The IMAGINED VILLAGE: 'Ouses, 'Ouses, 'Ouses ('The Imagined Village')

16. BILLY BRAGG: 1. The Milkman Of Human Kindness ('Life's A Riot With Spy Vs. Spy')

17. The UNTHANKS: Starless ('Last')

18. STEVE FORBERT: Thinkin' ('Alive On Arrival')

19. MUMFORD & SONS: Little Lion Man ('Sigh No More')

20. The MEN THEY COULDN'T HANG: The Green Fields Of France (No Man's Land) ('Night Of A Thousand Candles')

21. [wild card] – The HANDSOME FAMILY: Weightless Again ('Through The Trees')

A Brief History of Folk Music (Part 2)

In 1977 and the ensuing few years, folk music had the stuffing kicked out of it by the advent of punk and new wave, although many critics had reported its death-knell when major international artists such as JONI MITCHELL and BOB DYLAN had deviated from its roots into jazz and Jesus respectively. Many other '60s/'70s Brit-folk legends had seen – or were about to see – their contracts expire; former Island Records stalwarts FAIRPORT CONVENTION and The INCREDIBLE STRING BAND were two prime examples, while there were a raft of one-time giants of folk who also branched out into the mainstream (AL STEWART, JOHN MARTYN et al), or were basically left out in the cold. The tragic and untimely death of SANDY DENNY in April 1978 proved to be yet another major setback.

The electro-'80s, the poseur pop new romantics and NWOBHM literally stuck the knife into the very heart and soul of folk music, but underneath, and with the same ethos of DIY/punk independence, new traditional labels began to sprout up, while pioneering company Topic Records (who'd been responsible for kickstarting the careers of many folk artists: The WATERSONS, SHIRLEY COLLINS etc.) were sticking to their guns and looking ahead as well as keeping their footing in the past; singing talents such as MARTIN CARTHY, DICK GAUGHAN and a young JUNE TABOR showcased this approach. I have already covered these monumental and pioneering acts in Volume 1.

Yes, it was time to see the genre moving on. This came about during the mid-'80s, and ironically enough it was instigated by the splintered remnants of former London-based punks The Nips (i.e. The Nipple Erectors), who were to surface in The POGUES and The MEN THEY COULDN'T HANG. The former's Irish slant (featuring 'mouthy genius' SHANE MacGOWAN at the helm) would of course rejuvenate Celtic music as well as sea shanties et al, while crusty folk outfits emerged every other week.

Woolly-eared purists from any side of the tracks might be up in arms, but it was here that the kids – just like in the '50s, '60s and '70s – made folk exciting and riveting once again. Out of their shadows filtered acts such as The OYSTER BAND, BILLY BRAGG, The WATERBOYS, The PROCLAIMERS, EDDI READER and inevitably the LEVELLERS.

Over the pond there had also been a lull in proceedings when country music was king, but even through this, there emerged at least one true crossover act: NANCI GRIFFITH; not yer conventional Nashville/Grand Ole Opry star like Dolly, Tammy or Patsy, but an unassuming beauty with a sense of amiable tranquillity and sentimentality much in line with the Joni's, the Joan's and the Judy's. The '80s broke new ground for Nanci, and a plethora of mainly female folk stars transpired, while the 'Fast Folk' mag/imprint led the way via its cult/underground scene. Artists such as JANE SIBERRY, SUZANNE VEGA, PHRANC, LUCINDA WILLIAMS, MICHELLE SHOCKED, SHAWN COLVIN, TRACY CHAPMAN, INDIGO GIRLS, ANI DIFRANCO and even NATALIE MERCHANT (from outlanders 10,000 MANIACS) would be party to the new revival of folk in North America; new guys on the block such as GREG BROWN and JOHN GORKA were a tad overshadowed by their prettier female counterparts. These artists were still going strong into the '90s and '00s, while British singer-songwriters like DAVID GRAY, Irishman DAMIEN RICE, SETH LAKEMAN, ELIZA CARTHY (daughter of Martin), KATE RUSBY and teen-pop-folkie KT TUNSTALL were beginning to emerge from the pack and into the post-millennium mainstream; one guy in particular ALASDAIR ROBERTS [see his foreword] combined all angles of folk: the traditional, the Celtic and the singer-songwriter elements; one would have to travel way back in time and memoriam for anything similar.

During a period when folk music was taking off in all manner of wyrd and wonderful tangents (drawing inspiration from psych-folk outfits COMUS, The INCREDIBLE STRING BAND and a potpourri of the avant-garde), freak-folk was reborn sometime in the mid-'90s. It indeed had a terrestrial feel about it taking in global (formerly experimental) acts, namely CURRENT 93 (part-timers from industrial sources), IN GOWAN RING, FAUN FABLES, JOANNA NEWSOM, FERN KNIGHT, CIRCULUS and its biggest exponent so far, ESPERS.

Over the years with the ever-evolving nature of folk, acts have dipped their big toe into the genre (not counting anti-folkers The MOLDY PEACHES, COCOROSIE, REGINA SPEKTOR and others), one could safely file indie stars including ELLIOTT SMITH (sadly deceased in 2003), CHUMBAWAMBA, JAH WOBBLE, MIDLAKE, SUFJAN STEVENS, DEVENDRA BANHART, BRIGHT EYES and ANIMAL COLLECTIVE in this moonlighting category.

Nowadays, student-kids and their parents could revel at the thought of playlisting the likes of top global acts like FLEET FOXES, The DECEMBERISTS, BON IVER, MUMFORD & SONS, NOAH AND THE WHALE and even folk-blues pensioner SEASICK STEVE without alienating the other generation. It seems now that folk music in all its glorious foibles and follies, has come full circle and into the charts – a poignant time then for reading this book and its pioneering predecessor. *MCS*

How To Read The Book

If you're struggling in any way how to comprehend some of the more complex parts of each discography, here are some examples to make it easier. Read below for around ten minutes, taking a step at a time. The final lines/examples you see will give you a good guide before you proceed with the actual chronological discographies. However, I think that once you've read your own favourites you'll have a good idea. There have been no complaints so far, although this book might have a few queries regarding the introduction of catalogue numbers.

FOLK GROUP/ARTIST

Born where and when/Formed where and when, plus biography including style/analysis/reviews/ album rating, songwriters, cover versions, trivia etc. *MCS* = Martin Charles Strong / *BG* = former biographer Brendon Griffin

SINGER(born: day/month/year, town/city, country) – vocals, whatever (ex-GROUP; if any) / **MUSICIAN** (b. birth name/day/place) – instruments / **OTHER MUSICIANS** – other instruments, vocals etc.

US/UK date. (album) *<US cat.no.>* *(UK cat.no.)* **THE TITLE** [chart no.] [ ] alt-date [ ] — US or UK label / UK or US label

note: UK label – might be a foreign label if not released in UK.

also: Labels only mentioned when the group signs a new contract.

note: UK date – might also be a foreign release, even an American/ Canadian one, if not issued in Britain.

note: (UK catalogue number; in curved brackets) <US cat.no.; in jagged brackets>

note: chart positions UK and US are in the boxes under the labels.

also: the boxes in the above example have been left blank, indicating they did not hit either UK or US charts.

note: US date after the boxes indicates a variation from its UK counterpart.

also: Any other info after the boxes (e.g. German) indicates it was not issued in the US.

UK date. (7") *(UK cat.no.)* A-SIDE. / B-Side [ ] [–]
US date. (7") *<US cat.no.>* A-SIDE. / Different B-Side [–] [ ]

note: The two examples above show that the UK and US release do not have an identical A-side and B-side, thus the chart boxes are marked with a – to indicate it was not released in either the UK or the US.

UK date. (7"/c-s) *(CATNO 1/+C)* A-SIDE. / B-Side [ ] [–]

note: above had two formats with the same tracks (i.e. 7"/c-s). However, catalogue numbers will always vary among different formats – often only slightly (e.g. CATNO 1/+C). Each cat.no. would read thus: (7")=(CATNO 1) and (c-s)=(CATNO 1C). To save space the (/) slash comes into effect. The (/) means 'or' and in this case it is prefixed with a + sign for the equivalent cassette (c-s).

UK date. (7"/c-s) *(example same as above)* SEE ABOVE [ ] [–]
(12"+=/cd-s+=) *(CATNO 1-12/1-CD)* – Extra tracks.

note: If there are more formats with extra or different tracks, a new line would be used. Obviously there would also be alternative catalogue numbers utilising the '(/)' as before. Extra tracks would therefore mean the addition of the sign '(+=)' to each format.

UK date. (lp/c/cd) *(CATNO 200/+MC/CD)* *<US cat.no.4509>*
ALBUM TITLE [ ] [–]
– Track listing/Track 2/and so on. *(re-issued = re-iss. A later date, and other 'Label' mentioned, if different from original; new cat.no.) (could be re-iss. many times and if '(+=)' sign occurs there will be extra tracks from the original) <could also apply to the US release if in pointed brackets>*

note: Album above released in three formats, thus three catalogue numbers are necessary. The 'long-player' lp *(CATNO 200)* is obvious. The 'cassette' c = +MC *(CATNO 200MC)* or 'compact disc' cd *(CATNO 200CD)*. The US *<cat.no.>* will normally be just one set of numbers (or see further below for other details).

UK date. (cd/c/lp) *(CD/TC+/CATNO 200)* *<US cat.no.4509>*
ALBUM TITLE [ ] US date [ ]

note: This time a prefix is used instead of a suffix, thus the differentials appear before the standard lp catalogue number. For instance, the cd would read as *(CDCATNO 200)*.

Jun 97. (cd/c/lp) *<(5557 49860-2/-4/-1)>* **ALBUM TITLE** [1] May 97 [1]

note: Some catalogue numbers don't include any letters, but instead consist of a number sequence followed by one digit which universally corresponds with the format (i.e. 2 = cd / 4 = c / 1 = lp). also: If the US numbers are identical, there would be no need to list them separately, i.e. *<(the numbers)>*

note: I've also marked down an actual date of release and its variant in the US (you'll find this fictitious album also hit No.1 in both charts 'and Ah've no' even heard it yet, man!')

—— **NEW MUSICIAN/SINGER** (b. whenever etc.) – instruments (ex-GROUP(s) replaced = repl. DEPARTING MUSICIAN/SINGER, who joined whatever.

note: Above denotes a line-up change.

GROUP or ARTIST with change of name

US label / UK label

Jun 11. (cd/c/lp; GROUP or ARTIST with minor change of name)
<(cat.no.)> **ALBUM TITLE** [1] May 11 [1]

note: the 11 in question is 2011.

– compilations etc. (section) –

UK date. (cd) *compilation label only*; *(cat.no.)* **ALBUM TITLE** [100] [–]
– Track listing etc.

for comparison, here's an example of a real entry ... (from the Cult section in Volume 1)

CALLINAN-FLYNN

An Irish psych-folk duo from the early 70s, CALLINAN-FLYNN comprised bit-part actor and English-raised singer/guitarist David Callinan (who'd appeared in movies The Lion In Winter & Sinful Davey), plus fellow songwriter Mick Flynn; they'd been in local Limerick acts the Spalpeens and Urban Clearway, touring with such pop luminaries as Elton, Rod, BERT JANSCH and BILLY CONNOLLY).

Joined by a host of session players and friends, the underground label Mushroom delivered one rare and mighty 45, 'We Are The People (The Road To Derry Town)', a track taken from their equally collectable album (both are worth around £300 mint). The album itself, **FREEDOM'S LAMENT** (1972) {*6}, consisted of over a dozen songs, nine penned themselves, and surely worthy of a CD re-issue; check out 'The Old Man And The Flower' and 'Ballad Of Belfast'.

Returning to his first love, acting, although still scribing the odd song (a few covered by newbie chanteur Sean Tyrrell), Callinan subsequently authored a handful of novels, including Fortress Manhattan and The Ten Minute Miracle. Flynn, it seemed, went off the musical radar. *MCS*

DAVID CALLINAN (b.10 Jan '45) – vocals, guitar / **MICK FLYNN** – vocals, guitar / + session players

UK Mushroom / US not issued

1972. (ltd-7") *(50MR 17)* **WE ARE THE PEOPLE (THE ROAD TO DERRY TOWN)** / The Old Man And The Flower [ ] [–]

1972. (ltd-lp) *(150MR 18)* **FREEDOM'S LAMENT**
– Puckaree / Freedom's lament / Paddy's green shamrock shore / Moon coin reel / The old man and the flower / The banks of Newfoundland / Beyond the pale / Ballad of Belfast / Marion's song / Paddy's delight (tinker's polka) / London NW12 / Fortune for the finder / We are the people (the road to Derry Town) / A woman is a woman. *(re-iss. on 'Dolphin'; DOLM 5007)*

Section 1
Britain and Beyond

Leo ABRAHAMS [folk part]

Something of an all-rounder in the music business, Royal Academy of Music alumnus and guitarist LEO ABRAHAMS (born London, October 16, 1977) has played for Imogen Heap, ED HARCOURT, Brian Eno, movie composer David Holmes and over a hundred others in session (having been introduced to them all in the early 2000s). The experimental artist has been behind the controls to produce/arrange the likes of David Byrne, Starsailor, Brett Anderson, Paolo Nutini, Carl Barat, etc.

For the purposes of this book, his first three albums ('Honeytrap' 2005, 'Scene Memory' 2006 and 'The Unrest Cure' 2007) were ambient-laptop excursions with little or nothing to do with folk music. The last-named was nearly getting there, featuring as it did KT TUNSTALL, FOY VANCE and ED HARCOURT; Leo's time spent moonlighting with ALELA DIANE and others in HEADLESS HEROES just might have swayed him to find a folk niche.

But then, out of the blue, arrived **THE GRAPE AND THE GRAIN** (2009) {*7}, his first record to use mediaeval lutes, hurdy-gurdys, cellos, etc on a predominantly "folk" album. There was a foreboding ambience, mainly in its sparse backdrop, but the set was bright as a midsummer night's dream, performed with panache by Leo, a modern-day Harold Budd-cum-JOHN RENBOURN player. Prime tracks are 'Masquerade', 'The Northern Jane', 'Spring Snow' and finale 'Daughter Of Persuasion'. Please note: discography below is selective and folk-biased. *MCS*

Leo Abrahams - guitars (+ session people)

UK Just Music / US not issued

Mar 09. (cd) *(TAO 026)* **THE GRAPE AND THE GRAIN** ☐ ⊟
- Masquerade / Come the morning / From here / Spring snow / Blind / The grape and the grain / New wine / Ends meet / A ghost on every corner / The northern Jane / Daughter of persuasion.

The ACCIDENTAL (⟹ The MEMORY BAND)

Stanley ACCRINGTON

Google this man and you're likely to be bombarded with info about a legendary lower-division English football team, Accrington Stanley; there was also an indie outfit from the mid-1990s, if one has to be pedantic.

But we don't want to give you this, we want to give you singer-songwriter, raconteur and all-round funny bloke STANLEY ACCRINGTON (also known as Mike Bray, born August 7, 1951, Wyken, Coventry, Warwickshire), a man introduced to folk music in the 1960s by his brother Roger. While a student in London in the 1970s Mike expanded his influences into the sounds of CROSBY, STILLS & NASH, while a certain JAKE THACKRAY was also a later inspiration.

Having moved to Lancaster at this point, Bray would write many a witty ballad down on paper but was too shy to perform them. That was rectified on August 4, 1979, when he plucked up enough courage to knock out a song or two at the buffet bar in Stalybridge railway station. He was subsequently booked (not red-carded, though) to play his first gig that December at the Ring O' Bells in Middleton, near Manchester. He appeared on Radio Piccadilly's folk music programme the following night.

Encouraged by this promising start, STANLEY ACCRINGTON (as he was now known) built up a solid local reputation from Lancashire to Yorkshire in the early 1980s. A succession of cassette-only albums was kick-started by the weird but wonderful **SICK AS A PARROT** (1981) {*7}; his subsequent above-par sets were football-themed in the folk-comic tradition, although his lengthier, "serious" songs earned a poorer reception than his topically funny efforts.

Over the course of the 1980s he performed constantly, highlights being the Whitby Week and Fylde Festivals – perennial annuals for him to the present day – plus stints in Hong Kong in 1988 and 1992. Among his non-humorous songs, one might like to start with 'Lesley' or 'The Last Train Has Gone', respectively protest and nostalgia songs about Sellafield nuclear power station and the demise of the local railway lines.

ACCRINGTON's material is often satirical, topical, and often very silly. He likes to confuse audiences with a ragbag of songs of many different type, reflecting his own disorganisation and relentlessness. He has composed some instant songs to fit sudden situations, and is constantly writing new stuff to the detriment of the older material that he leaves behind.

Stanley is generally accepted into the mainstream of folk music because his self-written material usually pays homage to traditional or accepted folk songs. He is also a useful MC and plays guitar and keyboards. Now married with three kids and still living in Oldham (and keeping up a day job), the poet and storyteller that is STANLEY ACCRINGTON is, alas, one of folk music's almost forgotten men. In 2008, having released over 20 albums over a 30-year span, he was a big part of live act Doc Harvey and The Philistans, alongside Chris Harvey and Phil Brown. *MCS & SA himself*

Stanley Accrington - vocals, acoustic guitar

UK own label / US not issued

1981. (ltd-c) *(none)* **SICK AS A PARROT** ⊟ mail-o ⊟
- [alphabetical order]: Abattoir / All in remembrance / 'Arry the dog / As big as that / Black holes in Failsworth / Curse of the clown / Cynthia / February morning / Gordon [trad] / Guinness / Mat Groves / No iron horses / Norwegian song / Rochdale canal.

1982. (ltd-c) *(none)* **OVER THE BALL** ⊟ mail-o ⊟
- [first half]: The great Walenda / As I walked out… / 'erbert / Cameroons World Cup squad song / Cap'n Noah / Good times gone / [second half]: O'Hara's truss / Hawaiian love song / Queen of the South / Thomas More's prayer / Common Market song / Pinball wizard.

1983. (ltd-c) *(none)* **OFFSIDE TRAP** ⊟ mail-o ⊟
- [first half]: Lady Di / Princess and the frog / Penalty aria / Burglar Bill / Whitworth Morris / KX313 / [second half]: Redundant vampire / Castleton coven / Twas on a May morning / Drop the bomb / Lesley / History of England.

1984. (ltd-c) *(none)* **CYNICAL FOUL** ⊟ mail-o ⊟
- [alphabetical]:- 7 TV nights / Chanson de tunnel / Couldn't happen here / Darien / Lancashire Fusiliers / Love over logic / Nosmo king / Onion bhaji / Quintinshill / Road tonight / Safari / Sheep that glow.

1985. (ltd-c) *(none)* **A GAME OF TWO HALVES** ⊟ mail-o ⊟
- [alphabetical]:- 11th May / Bridget O / El falla / Eric Blair / Join the masons / Last train / Log of MHS Conqueror / Mat rap / Pieces / S&M / Stan and the art of motorcar maintenance / Tag.

1986. (ltd-c) *(none)* **YELLOW CARD** ⊟ mail-o ⊟
- [alphabetical order]:- A clown retires / Ballad of Cecil P / Blackstone light / Draculaid / Drongos / E, by gum / Franklin II / Hello little stranger / One day…. / Richard Kirkman / Special trains / Tut tut.

1988. (ltd-c) *(none)* **JUST ANOTHER GAME** ⊟ mail-o ⊟
- [first half]: Abattoir / Hunting the slug / Rochdale canal / Devil in Chesterfield / No iron horses / 1588 / Stanley's heros / Buddy / Green and yellow / [second half]: Streets revisited / Call me crazy / Trees screaming / Crows above the wheatfield / Cajamarca / As you are.

1990. (ltd-c) *(none)* **90 MINUTES** [live] ⊟ mail-o ⊟
- [alphabetical]:- 12 days / 3 steps – Raindrops / A day in the life / Ballad of Cecil P / Boris B – Guy G / Cap'n Maggie / Couldn't happen here / Di – Norwegian / Eddie E / Green and yeller / Penalty aria / Sheep that glow – Nosmo / This old town.

1991. (ltd-c) *(none)* **HOME BANKER** ⊟ mail-o ⊟
- [alphabetical order]:- A desert song / All in remembrance / Bits in between / Circles in the corn / Crib / End of an earache / Fathom the poll-tax / Gulf War songs / Heart / Johnny's gone to war / Sweet Kate Adie / Widnes bound / Wounded knee.

1992. (ltd-c) *(none)* **EAST FIFE 5 FORFAR 4** ⊟ mail-o ⊟
- [first half]: Cynthia / Battle of Maldon / Dirty tricks / Cap'n Bob / Dizzy / I do feel awful / King Tut trots / Bread and Albert / Vole / [second half]: 39 over again / Best man / Handbag / Pasha moon / Pharoah / Hitting / P.L.U.

1993. (ltd-c) *(none)* **ON A HAT TRICK** [-] mail-o [-]
- [first half]: The player / Krikkit / Th' olympics / Perip rap / Roots 66 / Th' Royals / Don't let… / I could believe / [second half]: Aviators / Rio / Play the game / Sarajevo / Ozymandias 2 / Corridors.

1995. (ltd-c) *(none)* **GOING FOR THE DOUBLE** [-] mail-o [-]
- [no track listings available].

1998. (ltd-c) *(none)* **THROUGH THE TURNSTILE** [-] mail-o [-]
- [alphabetical order]: All gone quiet / Beef / Change / Cromarty / Dancing in a line / Farewell, Tories / Goldsmith / Guinness / Hong Kong / Kilkenny / Muraroa / Pillar box / Real Sgt Pepper.

1999. (ltd-cd) *(none)* **SEMI FINAL REPLAY** [-] mail-o [-]
- Black holes in Failsworth / Sheep that glow / History of England / Matty G / 1980s medley / Twas on a May morning / 'Arry the dog / 1980s medley part 17 / Buddy H / Onion bhaji / Muraroa (the musical) / Nosmo / Battle of Maldon / 1990s medley / Handbag / Millennium dome.

1999. (ltd-cd) *(none)* **SEMI FINAL SECOND LEG** [-] mail-o [-]
- The great Walenda / Last train / It couldn't happen here / Lesley / A day in the life of the world / Call me crazy / The last Beyer-Garrett / Horizon / Darien / Crib / Thin blue line / Crows above the wheatfield / O'Neill's war / A clown retires.

2003. (ltd-cd) *(none)* **GROUND: ZERO** [-] mail-o [-]
- Magnificent / Guinness / Perip rap / Seven TV nights / Sicknote: the reply / Three wise women / Head end / Flatpack blues / Song #182 / Johnny's gone to war / Trees screaming / Ozymandias 2 / Cavern in the ground.

2005. (ltd-cd) *(none)* **VERSES WHITBY … VERSES FLEETWOOD** [-] mail-o [-]
- Introduction to Whitby / Whitby alphabet / Whitby prayer / Pubs of old Whitby / Ghost walks / Carnival day / Red sparrers / The good ship Gordon Tyrrell / Introduction to Fleetwood / Blackpool tram / Mrs Miggins / Knott End ferry / Fleetwood prayer / Last train / Sam Sherry / The big one.

Mar 06. (ltd-cd) *(none)* **PROMOTION/RELEGATION** [-] mail-o [-]
- 1969 / Carmen Miranda / Cockles / Belfast city / Saddleworth seasons / Night watch / Pharaoh's chariot / Special trains / Saddest moon / Katrina / Red wine Friday night / Sorry for… / Magdala street / Gloriana.

2010. (ltd-cd) *(none)* **INTO ADMINISTRATION** [-] mail-o [-]
- Census / Piggies / Workhouse … Poverty knock / Canoe / Apple day girl / … Country song / Monopoly / Colin Kemp / Bethlehem / Newfoundland reel / Spell … / Nothing.

- (5-7*) compilations, etc.-

1990. (ltd-c) *(none)* **SLOW ACTION REPLAY** [-] mail-o [-]

ADEM

Adem Ilhan was equally known for playing bass alongside Kieran Hebden in the post-rock outfit Fridge, while, with Johnny Lynch (of The PICTISH TRAIL), the electro duo Silver Columns was also included on his CV around the mid-2000s. And who could forget his part in Brit-folk supergroup The MEMORY BAND on their 2006 set 'Apron Strings'?

Born November 20, 1977, Roehampton in south-west London (of Turkish descent), his acoustic solo works were of the nu-folk/folktronica persuasion. Signed to Domino Records (home to Franz Ferdinand and JAMES YORKSTON), ADEM's debut album **HOMESONGS** (2004) {*8} was a magical abstract offering, best tracks being the mournful 'Statued' (subsequently used in the movie 'Dead Man's Shoes'), the banjo-led 'One In A Million' and the singles 'These Are Your Friends' and 'Ringing In My Ear'.

Having set the template for his brand of indie-folk, **LOVE AND OTHER PLANETS** (2006) {*7} marked the man as no one-trick pony. Augmented this time around by drummer Alex Thomas (ex-Groop Dogdrill) and backing vocalist Emma MacFarlane, and mixed by Fridge leader Hebden, ADEM's miserabilist aesthetic shone through 'Launch Yourself' (very different to the Four Tet remix 7" also available), 'Crashlander' (his own 'Space Oddity' of sorts) and the opener 'Warning Call'.

Just to prove acoustic folk music could move in the same circles as alt/indie-rock, ADEM's third project, **TAKES** (2008) {*6}, was a set of mainly 1990s alt-rock. Having earlier covered Jeff Buckley's 'Mojo Pin' (for tribute CD 'Dream Brother') and Johnny Cash's 'I Walk The Line' (for a Levi Jeans commercial), he had some experience in this field. For completists everywhere, the set list and originals comprised:- Bedhead ('Bedside Table'), PJ Harvey ('Oh My Lover'), Lisa Germano ('Slide'), Pinback ('Loro'), Deus ('Hotellounge'), The Aphex Twin ('To Cure A Weakling Child' + 'Boy/Girl Song'), Yo La Tengo ('Tears Are In Your Eyes'), Smashing Pumpkins ('Starla'), Tortoise ('Gamera'), Bjork ('Unravel' – a star track here), The Breeders ('Invisible Man') and Low ('Laser Beam'). Stripped of their grungy heritage and back to their bare bones, one could vouch on every level for each new arrangement. Of late, ADEM has been conspicuous by his absence, surfacing only on the Silver Columns' 'Yes, And Dance' set in 2010 and the 'Lau Vs. Adem' EP of 2011 with Scottish folkies LAU. *MCS*

Adem Ilhan - vocals, acoustic guitar, banjo, etc. (of Fridge)

UK Domino — US Domino

Mar 04. (cd/lp) *(WIG CD/LP 129)* *<DNO 33>* **HOMESONGS** [ ] Jul 04 [ ]
- Statued / Ringing in my ear / Gone away / Cut / These are your friends / Everything you need / Long drive home / Pillow / One in a million / There will always be.

May 04. (10"/cd-s) *(RUG 178 T/CD)* THESE ARE YOUR FRIENDS / After The Storm / [tunnel interlude] / Let It Burn [ ] [-]

Sep 04. (7") *(RUG 183CD)* RINGING IN MY EAR. / I Can Give You A Reason (cd-s+=) *(RUG 183CDP)* - Friends, beware / Wake up lullaby. [ ] [-]

Apr 06. (cd/lp) *(WIG CD/LP 160)* *<DNO 98>*
LOVE AND OTHER PLANETS [ ] Aug 06 [ ]
- Warning call / Something's going to come / X is for kisses / Launch yourself / Love and other planets / Crashlander / Sea of tranquility / You and moon / Last transmission from the lost mission / These lights are meaningful / Spirals / Human beings gather 'round.

Jul 06. (7") *(RUG 231)* LAUNCH YOURSELF [Four Tet mix]. / [Thomas Eriksen mix] [ ] [-]
(7"/cd-s+=/12"+=) *(RUG 231 X/CD/TP)* - [Hot Chip mix] / [original].

May 08. (cd/d-lp) *(WIG CD/LP 177)* **TAKES** [covers] [ ] [-]
- Bedside table / Oh my lover / Slide / Loro / Hotellounge / To cure a weakling child/ Boy/girl song / Tears are in your eyes / Starla / Gamera / Unravel / Invisible man / Laser beam.

ADMIRAL FALLOW

The missing link between Del Amitri, KING CREOSOTE and MIDLAKE, but influenced by SPRINGSTEEN, Waits and Wainwright (Rufus, not Loudon) Glasgow-based ADMIRAL FALLOW are centred around Edinburgh-born singer-songwriter Louis Abbott. Formed as Brother Louis Collective in 2007 (his other band is The Moth And The Mirror), the group's debut release was the sparklingly bright 'These Barren Years' for Jen Anderson's Euphonious Records. With a name change to nu-folksters ADMIRAL FALLOW and a call to ex-Delgados drummer Paul Savage for production duties, Abbott (also acoustic guitar), Sally Hayes (harmony vocals, flute and piano), Gordon Skene and/or Tom Stearn (on guitars), Kevin Brolly (clarinet and drums), Joe Rattray (double bass) and Phil Hague (field drum/drums) issued their debut set, **BOOTS MET MY FACE** (2010) {*7}, a record that boasted at least three gems: 'Squealing Pigs', a fresh version of 'These Barren Years', 'Dead Leg' and 'Subbuteo' – not depicting the "flick to kick" football game but a lyrical exploration of inner-city life. *MCS*

Louis Abbott - vocals, acoustic guitar / **Sally Hayes** - vocals, flute, piano / **Gordon Skene** - guitar, vocals; (or) Tom Stearn / **Kevin Brolly** - clarinet, drums, vocals / **Joe Rattray** - double bass, vocals / **Phil Hague** - field drum, drums, vocals

UK Euphonious — US not issued

Mar 09. (cd-s; as BROTHER LOUIS COLLECTIVE) *(-)*
THESE BARREN YEARS / Gypsy Girl [ ] [-]

Lo-Five — not issued

Apr 10. (dl-s) *(-)* SQUEALING PIGS [ ] [-]

Apr 10. (cd) *(LO 5033)* **BOOTS MET MY FACE** [ ] [-]
- Dead against smoking / Squealing pigs / Subbuteo / Delivered / These barren years / Old balloons / Bomb through the town / Four bulbs / Taste the coast / Dead leg. *(re-prom. Ma r11 +=; same)* - The sad clown cast.

ALESSI'S ARK

With no hint of a 'Oh Lori' about this Alessi and her Ark, then-teenager Alessi Laurent-Marke (born June 30, 1990, Hammersmith, London) sang and strummed in her own inimitable blend of dreamy, squeaky-clean folk-pop. Her father, Alan Marke, is a high-up television producer/MD, while her influences include Graham Nash (ex-CSN&Y) and Meg White (of The White Stripes); the latter inspired her to take up the drums at the age of 11. Having produced her own fanzine (Brain Bulletin) for a GCSE course before she left school at 16, the singer-songwriter's ('Glendora' was one of her first compositions) self-released demo EP 'Bedroom Bound' led her to sign for Virgin Records, apparently on the eve of her 17th birthday. At the turn of 2009 two classy singles surfaced: 'The Horse' and 'Over The Hill' – both included on her sparklingly fresh debut set **NOTES FROM THE TREEHOUSE** (2009) {*7}.

With a voice that could encapsulate Bjork, Catatonia's Cerys Matthews and American JOANNA NEWSOM, Alessi had class in leaps and bounds, while the album was produced in the US by session man and new-found friend Mike Mogis (of BRIGHT EYES); also in the studio were Nate Walcott, Shane Aspegren and Ian Aeillo. Other highlights featured on this evergreen set were 'Magic Weather', 'Constellations', 'Memory Box' and 'Ribbon Lakes'; a Lynyrd Skynyrd cover, 'Simple Man' featured on the Rough Trade shops' bonus cuts.

By the time album number two (**TIME TRAVEL** {*7}) arrived in 2011, ALESSI'S ARK were the property of Robin Guthrie's Bella Union imprint. With a dozen songs but a running time of less than half an hour, the record was nevertheless value for money, highlighted as it was by 'On The Plains', 'Wire', the title track and a version of the perennial 'Maybe I Know' (a hit for Lesley Gore in 1964); session help was headed by multi-instrumentalist Marcus Hamblett. *MCS*

Alessi Laurent-Marke - vocals, acoustic guitar, autoharp (with session people)

UK Zooey / US not issued

Sep 07. (cd-ep) *(none)* BEDROOM BOUND □ –
- My bedroom / The horse / For one year / The crown / Let's race.

Virgin / not issued

Dec 08. (7"ep) *(VUS 1982)* THE HORSE EP □ –
- The horse (radio mix) / Neighbour's birds / Let's race.
(cd-ep) *(VSD 1982)* - Patchwork of dreams.

Jan 09. (ltd-7") *(VUS 1983)* OVER THE HILL. / The Crown □ –

Jan 09. (cd-ep; shared w/ Thunder Power) *(MSK 0940)* FRIEND SHIPS □ –
- [TP track] / Witch / [TP] / Hummingbird / [TP].

(above issued on EMI)

Apr 09. (cd) *(CDV 3054)* **NOTES FROM THE TREEHOUSE** □ –
- Magic weather / The horse / Over the hill / Ribbon lakes / Constellations / The asteroids collide / Woman / Memory box / Hummingbird / The dog / Glendora / Cotton and the thread. *(Rough Trade +=)* - Witch / Pinewoods / Money / Simple man.

Bella Union / not issued

Mar 10. (cd-ep) *(BELLACD 237)* SOUL PROPRIETOR □ –
- The robot / Shovelling / Dancing feet / The bird song.

Apr 11. (cd) *(BELLACD 281)* **TIME TRAVEL** □ –
- Kind of man / Wire / On the plains / Must have grown / Time travel / The fever / Blanket / Maybe I know / Stalemate / The robot / Run / The bird song.

ALIANZA (⟹ SHOW OF HANDS)

ALIAS RON KAVANA (⟹ KAVANA, Ron)

ALL ABOUT EVE

Not necessarily an out-and-out folk-rock act, ALL ABOUT EVE nevertheless had their acoustic-rock moments. Named after a Bette Davis film, and formed in 1985 in London by singing music journalist Julianne Regan and ex-Aemotti Crii songwriter Tim Bricheno, the group released four indie hits on their own Eden Records before landing a contract with Mercury in mid-1987.

Their major-label debut (a remix of their second indie 45, 'In The Clouds') hit the UK Top 50 and paved the way for many more to come. Playing prog-folk and acid-tinged hippie-goth, and influenced by early-1970s acoustic LED ZEPPELIN and even Curved Air (at least in imagery and mysticism), ALL ABOUT EVE were, for a brief period in the late 1980s, something of an alluring alternative to the disposable pop clogging up the charts.

A follow-up single, 'Wild Hearted Woman', cracked the Top 40 in 1988, although the band really broke through that summer with the ethereal 'Martha's Harbour', a single that crossed over to rock/pop fans and made the UK Top 10. Its success fuelled further sales of their eponymous debut album (**ALL ABOUT EVE** (1988) {*8}), which included all their hits so far and achieved a similar chart position.

The tricky business of simultaneously balancing goth/indie and mainstream fanbases came undone with a more morose follow-up album, **SCARLET AND OTHER STORIES** (1989) {*6}. Though it made the Top 10, it failed to hit the heights of its predecessor, the record's downbeat sound possibly attributable to the internal ructions taking place.

Bricheno finally left for Sisters Of Mercy in 1990, his replacement being Marty Willson-Piper of The Church, initially on a temporary basis and subsequently full-time. Despite being touted as a return to form, **TOUCHED BY JESUS** (1991) {*6} failed to meet commercial expectations, and the band split from their label shortly after. Despite a comeback with a set for MCA, **ULTRAVIOLET** (1992) {*5}, the band finally called it a day early in the following year.

Regan subsequently formed Harmony Ambulance (who released a one-off 45 for Rough Trade) before going on to work with Bernard Butler and later to form Mice. In 2000/2001 the acoustic ALL ABOUT EVE toured alongside The Mission on their Resurrection tour. Subsequent concert sets **FAIRY LIGHT NIGHTS** (in two volumes {*6} & {*6}) showcased their long-awaited return. Bricheno also joined The Mission for a time after his relationship with Regan floundered. *MCS*

Julianne Regan (b.30 Jun '62, Coventry, England) - vocals, acoustic guitar, bass, (some) keyboards / **Timothy Bricheno** (b. 6 Jul '63, Huddersfield, England) - guitar / **Andy Cousin** - bass / **Manuela Zwingmann** - drums (ex-X-Mal Deutschland)

UK Eden / US not issued

Jul 85. (12") *(1 EDEN)* D FOR DESIRE. / Don't Follow Me (March Hare) □ –

—— group now augmented by a drum machine

Apr 86. (12") *(2 EDEN)* IN THE CLOUDS. / End Of The Day / Love Leads Nowhere □ –

Apr 87. (7") *(EVEN 3)* OUR SUMMER. / Lady Moonlight □ –
(ext.12"+=) *(EVENX 3)* - Shelter from the rain.

Jul 87. (7") *(EVEN 4)* FLOWERS IN OUR HAIR. / Paradise □ –
(12"+=) *(EVENX 4)* - Devil woman.

—— added **Mark Price** - drums

Mercury / Mercury

Oct 87. (7") *(EVEN 5)* IN THE CLOUDS. / She Moves Through The Fair 47 –
(12"+=) *(EVENX 5)* - Calling your name.

Jan 88. (7") *(EVEN 6)* WILD HEARTED WOMAN. / Apple Tree Man 33 –
(c-s+=/12"+=) *(EVEN M/X 6)* - Like Emily.
(12" box++=) *(EVENX 6-22)* - What kind of fool (live).
(cd-s+=) *(EVNCD 6)* - Like Emily / In the clouds.

Feb 88. (lp/c)(cd) *(MERH/+C 119)(<834 260-2>)* **ALL ABOUT EVE** 7 □
- Flowers in our hair / Gypsy dance / In the clouds / Martha's harbour / Every angel / Like Emily / Shelter from the rain / She moves through the fair / Wild hearted woman / Never promise (anyone forever) / What kind of fool. *(c+=/cd+=)*- Apple tree man / In the meadow / Lady Moonlight. *(cd re-iss.Aug95; same)*

Mar 88. (7"/7" g-f) *(EVEN/+G 7)* EVERY ANGEL. / Wild Flowers 30 –
(12"+=) *(EVENX 7)* - Candy tree.
(10"++=)(cd-s++=) *(EVEN 710)(EVNCD 7)* - More than this hour.

Jul 88. (7") *(EVEN 8)* MARTHA'S HARBOUR. / Another Door 10 –
(12"+=) *(EVENX 8)* - In the meadow (live).
(c-s++=) *(EVENM 8)* - Never promise (anyone forever) (live).
(cd-s+=) *(EVNCD 8)* - She moves through the fair (live) / Wild flowers (live).
(12"+=) *(EVENXB 8)* - In the clouds (live) / Shelter from the rain (live).

Nov 88. (7") *(EVEN 9)* WHAT KIND OF FOOL. / Gold And Silver 29 –
(12"+=) *(EVENX 9)* - The garden of Jane Delawney.
(12"box++=/cd-s++=) *(EVN XB 9/CD 99)* - ('A'-Autumn rhapsody mix).
(10"+=) *(EVEN 9-10)* - Every angel (live).

Sep 89. (7"/c-s) *(EVEN/EVNMC 10)* ROAD TO YOUR SOUL. / Pieces Of Our Heart 37 –
(ext.12"+=)(pic-cd-s+=) *(EVNXP/EVCDX 10)* - Hard Spaniard.

Oct 89. (lp/c/cd) *(<838 965-1/-4/-2>)* **SCARLET AND OTHER STORIES** 9 □
- Road to your soul / Dream now / Gold and silver / Scarlet / December / Blind lemon Sam / More than the blues / Tuesday's child / Pieces of our heart (**) / Hard Spaniard (*) / The empty dancehall / Only one reason / The pearl fisherman. *(c+=*)(cd+=**)*

Dec 89. (7"/c-s) *(EVEN/+MC 11)* DECEMBER. / Drowning 34 –
(7"pic-d+=/10"+=) *(EVEN P/B 11)* - Paradise ('89 remix).
(c-s+=/12"+=/cd-s+=) *(EVE MC/NX/NCD 11)* - The witches' promise.

Apr 90. (7"/c-s) *(EVEN/+MC 12)* SCARLET. / Our Summer (live) 34 –
(12"+=/cd-s+=) *(EVENX/EVNCD 12)* - Candy tree (live) / Tuesday's child (live).

—— (Aug'90) - when Bricheno went off to join Sisters Of Mercy (also later Tin Star), **Marty Willson-Piper** (of The Church) came in temp. at first, then full-time

Jun 91. (7") *(EVEN 14)* FAREWELL MR SORROW. / Elizabeth Of Glass 36 –
(12"+=/cd-s+=) *(EVENX/EVNCD 14)* - All the rings round Saturn.

Vertigo / Mercury

Aug 91. (7"/7"pic-d/c-s) *(EVEN/+P/MC 15)* STRANGE WAY. / Drawn To Earth 50 –
(pic-cd-s+=) *(EVNCD 15)* - Share it with me.
(10"+=) *(EVENB 15)* - Share it with me / Nothing without you.
(12"+=) *(EVENX 15)* - Nothing without you / Light as a feather.

Aug 91. (cd/c/lp) *(<51046-2/-4/-1>)* **TOUCHED BY JESUS** 17 □
- Strange way / Farewell Mr. Sorrow / Wishing the hours away / Touched by Jesus / The dreamer / Share it with me (*) / Rhythm of life / The mystery we are / Hide child / Ravens / Are you lonely. *(c/cd+= *) (re-iss.Feb93; same)*

Oct 91. (7") *(EVEN 16)* THE DREAMER (remix). / Frida Of Blood And Gold 41 –

(12"+=) *(EVENX 16)* - Road to Damascus / Strange way (demo).
(cd-s+=) *(EVNCD 16)* - Road to Damascus / ('A'-nightmare mix).
MCA. MCA.

Sep 92. (7" ep/c-ep/cd-ep/10" blue-ep) *(MCS/+C/CD/T 1688)*
PHASED EP [38] [–]
- Phased / Mine / Infrared / Ascent-descent.

Oct 92. (cd/c/lp) *(<MCD/MCC/MCA 10712>)* **ULTRAVIOLET** [46] [ ]
- Phased / Yesterday goodbye / Mine / Freeze / Things he told her / Infrared / I don't know / Dream butcher / Some finer day / Blindfolded visionary / Outside the sun.

Nov 92. (7"/c-s) *(MCS/+CS 1706)* SOME FINER DAY. / Moodswing [57] [–]
(10"+=/cd-s+=) *(MCS T/CD 1706)* - Dive in.

—— disbanded early 1993, Regan formed Harmony Ambulance and released one-off 45 for Rough Trade. In 1994 she began working with Bernard Butler (ex-Suede), signing solo to Permanent ...

MICE

Regan - vocals / with **Cousin** + **Price** and **Bic** - guitar (ex-Cardiacs)
Permanent Permanent

Nov 95. (7" yellow/c-s) *(7/CA SPERM 30)* MAT'S PROZAC. / Bang Bang [ ] [–]
(cd-s+=) *(CDSPERM 30)* - Julie Christie.

Apr 96. (7"/c-s/cd-s) *(7/CA/CD SPERM 31)* THE MILKMAN (semi-skimmed version) / The Milkman (full-cream version) / Martian Man / Die Ubermaus [ ] [–]

Jul 96. (7" colrd/c-s) *(7/CA SPERM 033)* DEAR SIR. / ('A'-mix) [ ] [–]
(cd-s+=) *(CDSPERM 033)* - Pyjamadrama / Tiny window.

Aug 96. (cd/c/lp) *(<PERM CD/MC/LP 035>)* **BECAUSE I CAN** [ ] [ ]
- Mat's prozac / Star / Dear sir / Bang bang / The milkman / Trumpet song / Blue sonic boy / Julie Christie / Miss World / Battersea / Messed up.

ALL ABOUT EVE

re-formed in 1999: **Regan, Cousin, Willson-Piper + Robin Guy**
Yeaah Yeaah

Jun 00. (cd) *(<YEAAH 8>)* **FAIRY LIGHT NIGHTS** (live acoustic) [ ] Aug 00 [ ]
- What kind of fool? / In the clouds / Forever / Share it with me / Will I start to bleed? / Miss World / Martha's harbour / Shelter from the rain / Are you lonely? / Apple tree man. *(re-iss. Dec 01 as UNPLUGGED on Brilliant!; 33076) (re-iss. Jan 02 as MARTHA'S HARBOUR on Dressed To Kill; MIDRO 850) (re-iss. Sep 03 on Jam Tart; AAEVP 9CD) (d-cd re-iss. Aug '03 as ACOUSTIC NIGHTS on Snapper+=; SMDCD 464)- FAIRY LIGHT NIGHTS TWO - LIVE ACOUSTIC*

—— **Toni Haimi** - guitar (ex-Lowdown Shakin' Chills, ex-Malluka, Nozzle) repl. Marty

Dec 01. (cd) *(YEAAH 24)* **FAIRY LIGHT NIGHTS TWO** - LIVE ACOUSTIC [ ] [–]
- Scarlet / The mystery we are / You bring your love to me / Freeze / Mine / More than the blues / Never promise (anyone forever) / Yesterday goodbye / Wild hearted woman / Every angel. *(re-iss. Apr 02 on Jam Tart; AAEVP 1CD)*
Castle Music not issued

Oct 01. (cd) *(CMRCD 332)* **LIVE & ELECTRIC AT THE UNION CHAPEL** [live December 9 2000] [ ] [–]
- Lady moonlight / Freeze / Wishing the hours away / Martha's harbour / Wild hearted woman / In the clouds / Miss World / Are you lonely / December / Forever / More than the blues / You bring your love to me / Shelter from the rain / What kind of fool / Outshine the sun. *(re-iss. d-cd Nov 01 on Jam Tart+=; AAEVP 4)* - Never promise anyone forever / Scarlet / Farewell Mr. Sorrow.

—— now trimmed to a duo of **Regan** + **Cousin**
Jam Tart not issued

Dec 02. (cd-ep) *(AAEVP 7)* ICELAND [ ] [–]
- Last Christmas / Walking in the air / December revisited / Melting / Cold / A winter's tale / December (amnesia mix).

Mar 03. (cd) *(AAEVP 8)* **CINEMASONIC** [live May 31 2002 at Shepherds Bush Empire] [ ] [–]
- Let me go home / The dreamer / Somebody said / Blue sonic boy / Daisychains / I don't know / Phased / Ctrl-alt-delete / Sodium / Touched by Jesus / Life on Mars.

- (8-10*) compilations -

Mar 06. (d-cd) *Mercury; (9837331)* **KEEPSAKES: A COLLECTION** [ ] [–]
- Flowers in our hair (extended) / In the clouds / Calling your name / Paradise (1988 remix) / Martha's harbour / Every angel (7" remix) / What kind of fool (autumn rhapsody) / Wild flowers (1988 BBC session) / Candy tree (live) / Wild hearted woman (live) / Our summer (live) / In the meadow (live) / Gold and silver / Scarlet / Road to your soul / Drowning / December / What kind of fool (2006) / The empty dancehall - revisited // Farewell Mr. Sorrow / Strange way / Rhythm of life / Wishing the hours away / The dreamer (Tim Palmer mix) / Touched by Jesus / Are you lonely / See Emily play (demo) / Phased / Freeze / I don't know (alt. mix) / Some finer day / Infrared / Outside the sun / Let me go home / Keepsakes / Raindrops. *(ltd-editions have free DVD)*

- (5-7*) compilations, others, etc.-

Feb 91. (cd-ep) *Mercury; (EVCDX 13)* THIRTEEN [live] [ ] [–]
- In the clouds / Never promise (anyone forever) / Scarlet / More than the blues / Road to your soul.

Nov 92. (cd/c/lp) *Vertigo; (<514 154-2/-4/-1>)* **WINTER WORDS: HITS AND RARITIES** [ ] Jun 98 [ ]
- Our summer / Flowers in our hair / In the clouds / Martha's harbour / Every angel / Wild hearted woman / What kind of fool / Road to your soul / Scarlet / December / Farewell Mr Sorrow / Strange way / The dreamer / Paradise / Candy tree / Drowning / Wild flowers / Theft / Different sky. *(re-iss. Apr '95 cd/c; same)*

Nov 93. (cd) *Windsong; (WINCD 044)* **BBC RADIO 1 LIVE IN CONCERT - GLASTONBURY FESTIVAL** [live 1989] [ ] [–]
- Every angel / Candy tree / Wild hearted woman / Gold and silver / What kind of fool / Tuesday's child / Martha's harbour / In the clouds / Road to your soul / Only one reason / Flowers in our hair / In the meadow / Paradise / Our summer.

Dec 01. (cd; by JULIANNE REGAN & MICE) *Jam Tart; (AAEVP 3)*
NEW & IMPROVED [ ] [–]
- Dear sir / Miss World / Star as bright as you are / Trumpet song / The milkman / Mat's prozac / Blue sonic boy / Bang bang / Battersea / Messed up / Star / Tiny meadow / Pyjamadrama / Martian man / Unborn angel / Dumb girl / A dark place / Hit or miss / Julie Christie.

Jul 02. (cd) *Jam Tart; (AAEVP 5) / United States Dist.; <USD 134>*
RETURN TO EDEN - VOLUME ONE THE EARLY RECORDINGS [ ] Nov 02 [ ]
- D for Desire / Don't follow me (March hare) / Suppertime / End of the day / Love leads nowhere / In the clouds / Apple tree man (demo) / Shelter from the rain / Every angel (demo) / In the meadow (demo) / Our summer / Lady moonlight / Our summer (extended) / Flowers in our hair / Paradise / Devil woman / Flowers in our hair (extended).

Mar 07. (cd) *Voiceprint; (VP 6012CD)* **SIXTY MINUTES WITH ...** [ ] [–]
- In the clouds (first version) / Let me go home / Touched by Jesus / Flowers in our hair (extended) / Martha's harbour / Outside the sun / Every angel (demo) / Scarlet / Melting / D for desire / What kind of fool / Wild hearted woman / Shelter from the rain.

- budget compilations, etc.-

Aug 99. (cd) *Spectrum; (544 153-2)* **THE BEST OF ALL ABOUT EVE** [ ] [–]
- Our summer / Lady moonlight / Flowers in our hair / Paradise / Gypsy dance / In the meadow / Every angel / Martha's harbour / What kind of fool / Gold and silver / Candy tree / Road to your soul / Tuesday's child / Different sky / Farewell Mr Sorrow / Wishing the hours away / Are you lonely / Share it with me.

Martin/Maartin ALLCOCK

Maart – as he was called for short – was born January 5, 1957, Middleton in Lancashire. He has become something of a multi-tasking folk+ producer and a workhorse sessionman. Of course, many music buffs with recognise his name as that of a one-time player with Celtic-folkers The BULLY WEE BAND (in the early 1980s), a stalwart of FAIRPORT CONVENTION (from autumn 1985 to winter 1996) and holder of a moonlight job with both JETHRO TULL (as keyboard player from early 1988 to late 1991) and ... er... The Mission (in 1991). His aforementioned session work – he's played on over a hundred albums – has seen him feature for bands from PLEXUS to RALPH McTELL and DAN AR BRAZ to SWARBRICK to Celtic Visions – one could go on ad infinitum.

Multi-instrumentalist ALLCOCK first came to the attention of fellow Lancashire minstrel MIKE HARDING (a comic folk singer and now a BBC Radio Two DJ), who invited the student on tour in 1977. Martin soon moved to Brittany, where he met ROBIN WILLIAMSON, although a subsequent job as a trainee chef in Shetland kept him out of the limelight. A brief stint with The BULLY WEE BAND and a tour in Europe alongside KIERAN HALPIN set up his FAIRPORTs venture, and he played with bands concurrently until 1992.

Finally, his solo album **MAART** {*6} was issued in 1991, a cocktail of traditional cuts which were more akin to his work with the FAIRPORTs; Beverley Craven, Robert Plant and a host of others summoned up the talented ALLCOCK to join them.

In 1998, Maartin was the middle man (and the letter A) with old pals act Dave Whetstone and Pete Zorn in the short-lived WAZ! A second set, **OX15** {*6} – referring to his Oxfordshire home postcode – finally found its way out in 2000, a record which proved to be rockier than his previous effort, due probably to the inclusion of old JETHRO TULL mates Ian Anderson and Clive Bunker, FAIRPORT's Gerry Conway and Chris Leslie, Troy Donockley (of IONA and The MADDY PRIOR BAND), Indian singer Najma Akhtar (of Page & Plant fame) and Gill Allcock. From The Allman Brothers' 'Jessica' (segued with 'The Wind That Shakes The Barley') to other instrumentals including the inspirational 'Crash Polka', the set works well in the context of a folk-rock album. Two further covers appear: KIERAN HALPIN's 'Simple' and ALLAN TAYLOR's 'Chimes At Midnight'.

Of late, ALLCOCK has become bass player and tour manager with Nashville/bluegrass singer-songwriter Beth Nielsen Chapman, while also becoming something of an all-rounder with his part in comic actor Adrian Edmondson's punk-folk supergroup project The BAD SHEPHERDS. *MCS*

Martin Allcock - vocals, guitar, fiddle, keyboards, mandolin, etc.

UK Woodworm / US not issued

Apr 91. (c/cd) *(WRC/+D 012)* **MAART**
- Milltown maid – Jenny's wedding / Minosegi boro / Yow Diddley / North country girl / Planxty Madam Crofton / Con Casey's jig – Tripping up the stairs / The reluctant barman / Why did I leave my home? / The overseer's reply / On the floor / Flaherty's hornpipe – The eight pints of Guinness / The Lowlands of Holland. *(cd re-iss. Oct 97 on Amara; 109)*

A New Day / not issued

Feb 00. (cd) *(ANDCD 38)* **OX15**
- Daichovo chara / Whenever we see the dark / Crash polka / Watermarks / Chimes at midnight / Jessica – The wind that shakes the barley / Untitled / Simple / Bean a 'ti ar lar / Sand dancer / A dream / Elementary.

Squiggle / not issued

Apr 04. (cd) *(CD1)* **SERVING SUGGESTION** mail-o

WAZ!

Allcock with **Dave Whetstone** - accordion (ex-COCK & BULL BAND) + **Pete Zorn** - vocals, saxophone

Cooking Vinyl / not issued

Mar 98. (cd) *(COOKCD 143)* **WAZ!**
- It goes high / Rhythm of the time / The swallow / Alfredo's / Journey / One man travelling success / Step this way / Old shoes / Sway with me / Bernie's wish – Le grand fromage / You're my honey / Ladies in waiting / Scent of romance / Winding to you / Is there a wheeze now?

—— **STEVE TILSTON** - guitar, vocals; repl. WHETSTONE

Waz / not issued

Apr 99. (cd) *(WAZCD 2)* **FULLY CHROMATIC**

—— Maartin has since helped form The BAD SHEPHERDS with comic actor Adrian Edmondson

AMALGAMATED SONS OF REST (⟹ ROBERTS, Alasdair)

The Amazing Mr. SMITH (⟹ SMITH, The Amazing Mr.)

ANCIENT BEATBOX (⟹ BLOWZABELLA)

APPENDIX OUT (⟹ ROBERTS, Alasdair)

Olof ARNALDS

Co-existing alongside her more ambitious and ambient neo-classical outfit Olafur Arnalds, Iceland's OLOF ARNALDS (together with a host of her country's finest exports including Slowblow, Mugison, Kjartan Sveinsson of Sigur Ros, and Skuli Sverrisson and Eirikur Orri Olafsson, both of Mum) released the surprisingly enterprising and plucky **VID OG VID** (2007) {*7} and found a niche in the nu-folk market.

Born in 1980, the sultry Olof embarked on exporting her music further afield in Britain and the continent; the aforementioned debut finally hit the UK in 2009 when she signed a deal with One Little Indian Records. Songs such as 'Englar Og Darar' showed off her pixieish voice to fine effect, while the Megas-penned 'Orfeus Og Everidis' was simply and minimalistically delicious, her voice somewhat akin to an alt-Celtic Bjork.
The fact that Bjork (on the track 'Surrender') was roped in to guest on her dreamy follow-up **INNUNDIR SKINNI** (2010) {*7} attested her twee, heart-on-sleeve inspirations. The LEONARD COHEN-like 'Crazy Car', 'Madrid' and 'Jonathan' were flights of freak-folk fancy, the last more leprechaun-like than elfin, while the first became a single that deserved greater rewards. *MCS*

Olof Arnalds - vocals, multi / with guests

UK/Ice 12 Tonar / US not issued

Aug 07. (cd) *(12T 041)* **VID OG VID** Ice
- Englar og Darar / I nyju husi / Klara / Vid og vid / Orfeus og Everidis / Vittu af mer / Moldin / Nattsongur / Skjaldborg / Aevagomul orkupula. *(<UK/US-iss. Nov '09/Jan '10 on One Little Indian; TPLP 959CD>)*

One Little Indian / not issued

Jun 10. (7") *(1078 TP7)* INNUNDIR SKINNI. / Close My Eyes
Sep 10. (7") *(1083 TP7)* CRAZY CAR. / (Sukiyaki)
Sep 10. (lp/cd) (TPLP 1065/+CD) **INNUNDIR SKINNI**
- Vinur minn / Innundir skinni / Crazy car / Vinkonur / Svif birki / Jonathan / Madrid / Surrender / Allt I Guddi.
Mar 11. (7") *(1086 TP7)* SURRENDER. / Instants

The ASKEW SISTERS

Formed as a neo-classical-inspired trad-folk vocal duo, Guildhall graduates Emily (on violin and cello) and Hazel (on melodeon) created atmospheric folk inspired by greats like SHIRLEY (& DOLLY) COLLINS, JACQUI McPHEE or even The UNTHANKS.
Initially part of The Hampshire Recorder Sinfonia, The ASKEW SISTERS combined aspects of Morris medievalism, baroque and chamber/ contemporary Celtic-folk on a trio of sets for Wild Goose Records, culminating in 2010 with the gracious **THROUGH LONESOME WOODS** {*7}.

As on **ALL IN A GARDEN GREEN** (2007) {*6} and **THE AXFORD FIVE** (2009) {*6} (the latter a collaboration with Craig Morgan Robson), the sisters excelled on new arrangements of perennial traditionals, this time around with 'Henry Martin', 'The Bonny Bows Of London Town', 'Lord Bateman' and the medley of 'Valentine' and 'The Turtle Dove'. Keeping Bright Young Folk fare alive and kicking into the second post-millennial decade, it harked back to the halcyon days of the folk revival scene of the 1960s and 1970s – Sandy Denny and Maddy Prior would be proud. *MCS*

Hazel Askew - vocals, melodeon / **Emily Askew** - violin, cello, vocals

UK Wild Goose / US not issued

Feb 06. (cd-ep; as EMILY & HAZEL ASKEW) *(WGS 329EP)* SIX BY TWO
- Chasse pain / Robin Wood and the pedlar / Little Polly Polka - Dick Iris's hornpipe / Hanter dro / Sovay / Glorishears – Eleanor Rigby.
Aug 07. (cd) *(WGS 345CD)* **ALL IN A GARDEN GREEN**
- Adieu to old England / All in a garden green – Horses bransle / The old Virginia lowlands / Fare thee well my dearest dear / High Germany / Dorrington lads / The lover's ghost / The banks of the sweet primroses / Blenheim House – Malt has come down / Bedlam city / A noble riddle wisely expounded / The unfortunate tailor – Shaalds of Foula / Three drunken maidens.
Aug 09. (cd; by The ASKEW SISTERS & CRAIG MORGAN ROBSON) *(WGS 364CD)* **THE AXFORD FIVE**: songs collected from five Hampshire women
- The gypsy laddie / He was under my window / Long Lankle / Down in Fleet Street / Bold William Taylor / Lord Derwentwater / An old man came courting me / The Lowlands of Holland / Abroad as I was walking / Beautiful Nancy / Tarry trousers / Down the lane / A famous farmer / Sweet lovely Joan / The trooper's horse.
May 10. (cd) *(WGS 372CD)* **THROUGH LONESONE WOODS**
- Saturday night – Through lonesome woods / The blue eyed strange – Goddesses – Mrs Casey / Henry Martin / The bonny bows of London town / The dusty miller – The Presbyterian hornpipe / Lord Bateman / Sweet Lemaney / Mundesse – Paddy Carey's / Jack the jolly tar / If I was a blackbird / Valentine – The turtle dove.

ATTILA THE STOCKBROKER

A ranting Oi!/punk-poet turned hey-nonny-nonny folk bard, ATTILA THE STOCKBROKER (b. John Baine, October 21, 1957 in Southwick, West Sussex) has flitted between these genres, and more besides, from the 1980s to the present day.

He initially trained to be a real stockbroker, but the lure of show business proved too strong, and Baine set himself up as a performance poet, fiddler and mandolin player under the title in which he now rejoices. Brief stints in obscure Harlow-based punk bands English Disease and Brighton Riot Squad ensued, and he was also briefly part of the Belgian band Contingent. The last-named outfit released one single, 'Police Control' (1979).

Following a Radio 1 session for John Peel, ATTILA secured a deal with independent label Cherry Red, who issued his debut album, **RANTING AT THE NATION** {*7}, in 1983. Some tracks, including 'A Bang And A Wimpy', were recycled from his earlier 'ranting' EPs, and if you're partial to songs about Russians, England, Albania and fish, this set will be just your cup of tea.

Sometimes described as the alternative Les Dawson, his ranting was light relief to the Oi! music scene as he took up where John Cooper Clarke left off. Shot through with typically barbed humour, his state-of-the-nation commentaries were well observed, if something of an acquired taste. Critical opinion wasn't exactly favourable, and, perhaps as a result of that, ATTILA was increasingly developing the musical aspect of his work.

Moving on from the sparse mandolin backing which had accompanied his earlier work, the release of **SAWDUST AND EMPIRE** (1984) {*7} found the man moving in folkier circles alongside the likes of fellow former punk and general space cadet John Otway. Tracks such as the minstrel-like 'March Of The Levellers' (an instrumental) prefigured New Model Army's brash take on radical Roundhead times, while Baine and his two female accompanists excelled on the title track. His collaboration with Otway (what, no Wild Willy Barrett?) on **CHERYL - A ROCK OPERA** (1991) {*6} remains the stuff of legend.

With album titles like **LIBYAN STUDENTS FROM HELL** (1987) {*5} and **SCORNFLAKES** (1988; also a book) {*6}, you knew what to expect from this un-PC performer. Combining punk rock with mediaeval music in mid-1990s outfit Barnstormer, ATTILA has now passed the 2,500-gig mark and celebrated 30 years in the trade. A glance at his expanding discography will reveal where he's at these days; few outsiders would have recognised him in his one-off appearance for Brighton & Hove Albion FC (as Seagulls Ska) in their greatest achievement of 2005, the Top 20 hit 'Tom Hark (We Want Falmer)'. *MCS*

Attila The Stockbroker - vocals, fiddle, mandolin

UK / US

No Wonder / not issued

1981. (c-ep) *(E 1)* PHASING OUT CAPITALISM

Radical Wallpaper / not issued

1982. (7" ep; shared) *(Rad Wall 003)* ROUGH, RAW AND RANTING
- A bang and a Wimpy / Pap music for wreck people / Andy is a corporatist / I don't talk to popstars / Foyer bar / They must be Russians / Russians in the DHSS // [SEETHING WELLS tracks].

Cherry Red / not issued

Oct 82. (7" ep) *(CHERRY 46)* COCKTAILS EP
- Cocktails / Contributory negligence / The night I slept with Seething Wells / Fifth column / The oracle.

Apr 83. (lp) *(ARED 46)* **RANTING AT THE NATION** [live // studio]
- Awayday / The night I slept with Seething Wells / Contributory negligence / Nigel wants to go to C&A's / Albanian football / The perils of stealing half a bottle of wine / They must be Russians / Russians in the DHSS / Russians in McDonald's / The oracle / Death in Bromley / A bang and a Wimpy / Nigel wants to go and see Depeche Mode / Russians at the Henley Regatta / Russians on the centre court / Fifth column // The fall of King Zog / Holiday in Albania (for Jello) / Burn it down / England are back (Luxembourg where are you?) / Where are you goin' with that flounder? / Hands off our halibuts! / Flappin' in the wind / Gentlemen on the wrist / Eros products commercial / The Spencers' croft cat (dead cat strut) / A very silly East European propaganda station / The fall of King Zog (reprise).

——next with **Red Fruth** - flute + **Lynne** - melodeon

Anagram / not issued

Mar 84. (lp) *(GRAM 13)* **SAWDUST AND EMPIRE**
- March of the levellers / Sawdust and empire / Alone in the disco / Recession / Dies irae (World War 3) / Spare a thought / Nigel's revenge... / Holiday in Albania [Gjirokastra folk festival version] / Boadicea uber alles / Factory gods / Midas the grand / Ghosts of the levellers. *(cd-r iss. 2006; CDGRAM 13)*

Cherry Red / not issued

Aug 84. (12" ep) *(12CHERRY 82)* RADIO RAP! EP
- Radio rap! [lobotomised wombat mix] / Everytime I eat vegetables... / Let the drain take the strain / Vomit on a Viking / Take a leak on a green / Albanian rifle poem / Nigel wants to join the SAS / I don't talk to pop stars / Love and herpes... / A letter from Nigel's mum / Russians versus the Tetley Bittermen / Poetry requiem / Radio dub [traumatised turbot mix].

Plastic Head / not issued

Mar 87. (m-lp) *(PLASLP 009)* **LIBYAN STUDENTS FROM HELL**
- Libyan students from hell / I'm so miserable / Airstrip one / The ballad of Comrade Enver / Pedi dies / The rapping mole / Another country / Glenzendes empire / The green fields of France.

Probe Plus / not issued

Sep 88. (lp/c) *(PROBE 20/+C)* **SCORNFLAKES**
- [Wordside]:- Introduction / Slough (the quagmire strikes back) / Freedom of the press? / Livingstone rap '88 (the salamander Sandinista!) / Short sharp shock identity card mergermania / Radio rap! / Vegetables / Unification BBC / Rappin' mole! [Russian] / Fiddle thrash 1 / Tell Sid... / Andy is a corporatist / N-N-N-Nineteen [Selhurst Park mix] / Love poems: Rain / River poem / On the beach at Worthing / To Slough and sanity / Bedtime / Grand finale: Bogies from his nose / [Thrashside]:- Libyan students from hell / Ayatollah wallah / The Spencers' croft cat [special 7th anniversary 'still dead' mix] / Airstrip one [roots version] / Echoes of Rhodesia [live in Berlin, GDR] / Fiddle thrash 2 / Factory gods (an atheist gospel song) / Outroduction. *(c+=)* - [live in East Germany]:- Fifth column / World War Three / Forty years.

Musidisc / not issued

Apr 91. (m-cd/m-lp) *(10789-2/-1)* **DONKEY'S YEARS**
- Jingo bells / Tyler smiles (22.10.90) / Roll up for the donkey derby... / The iron men of rap / This is free Europe / Mountaineering in Belgium / Market sektor one (for Jorg Wolter) / The ligger's song / Tammy's song [feat. Sarah Subservient] / The bible according to Rupert Murdoch. *(cd+=)* - Retrospective abortion / Dustbin poem / The pen and the sword [pre-con-version] / Sawdust and empire / Libyan students from hell! [mega city Paris mix].

(next set + a subsequent single credited with John Otway)

Strikeback / not issued

Oct 91. (cd; by ATTILA & OTWAY) *(SBR 46CD)* **CHERYL - A ROCK OPERA**
- Overture / A Wembley Central encounter / The sensitivity of the broken-hearted / The sympathetic response / Cheryl / The penny drops / Our room / Cheryl's decline / A more romantic view / Cheryl's going home / She's gone! but who's this? / Boys in the hood (trainspotter rap) / A misunderstanding / A solitary tune / Train information / The Starlight Express / The unsympathetic response / Finale / Overture reprise / The last word.

Terz / not issued

1992. (lp) *(terz 71011)* **THIS IS FREE EUROPE** German
- This is free Europe / The iron men of rap! / Market sektor one / Jingo bells / Tyler smiles / Holiday in Albania revisited / Libyan students from hell / The pen and the sword / Washington bullets / The ligger's song / Retrospective abortion / The bible according to Rupert Murdoch / Sawdust and empire.

ATTILA THE STOCKBROKER'S BARNSTORMER

with **Martin Fish** - guitar / **Dan Woods** - bass / **Tim O'Tay** - recorders / **M. M. McGhee** - drums

Mad Butcher / not issued

1995. (7"; as BARNSTORMER) *(none)* SARAJEVO

Aug 96. (cd/c) *(HELMET CD/CAS 1)* **THE SIEGE OF SHOREHAM**
- Bombarde (parts 1 & 2) / The one that got away / The Blanford forum / Cheering the plough / Sarajevo / Worms / March of the levellers - The diggers' song / Tyler smiles / Tirana / Old teenagers / The siege of Shoreham / Camelot by numbers / Horns / The torchbearer / And I won't run away / The zen Stalinist manifesto / Joseph Porter's sleeping bag / Victoria road / (untitled).

Townsend / not issued

Aug 00. (cd) *(none)* **JUST ONE LIFE...**
- Haider! / The ghost road / Game boy rude boy / Scumball Pinochet (for Marc Bolan) / The worm and the archer / Cero - His master's voice / Another country / The ballad of Comrade Enver / 20 years / Just one life.

May 04. (cd) *(6)* **ZERO TOLERANCE**
- Death of a salesman / Baghdad ska / Baghdad dub / Hey celebrity / Guy Fawkes table / Mohammed the Kabul Red / Song for the defeated / Comandante Joe / Valentine's day (Hans Blix and The Clash) / Blood for oil / Oil power / Abramovich's donkey sanctuary / What's the difference / Bunter's revolution / A nasal appraisal / Marktsektor one.

ATTILA THE STOCKBROKER

Back... / not issued

2007. (cd) *(BACK2CGRCD 002)* **LIVE IN NORWAY [live]** Norway
- Intro / My poetic licence / Russians in the DHSS / New world order rap / Spam / Every time I eat vegetables... / Punk night at the Duck's Nuts / Supermodel / Comandante Joe / Blood for oil / Tyler smiles / Maggots 1 Maggie 0.

- (8-10*) compilations -

Sep 10. (cd) *Mad Butcher; (MBC 012)* **DISESTABLISHED 1980** German
- Baghdad ska / The Blandford forum / Blood for oil / Sarajevo / Old teenagers / This is free Europe / Tyler smiles / Scumball Pinochet / The ghost road / His master's voice / Game boy - Rude boy / Sawdust and empire / Haider! / March of the levellers - The liggers' song - The world turned upside down / Market sektor one / Just one life / Death of a salesman / Fifth column / And I won't run away.

- (5-7*) compilations, others, etc.-

Jul 93. (cd/c) *Larrikin; (LRF CD/C 264)* **666: NEIGHBOUR OF THE BEAST** Austra
- The bible according to Rupert Murdoch / The iron men of rap! / The beatification of Paul Keating / Jingo bells / Save the whale / Privatisation (explained to the stupid) / Iraqi invaders from hell! / Somewhere under the rainbow / Australian decomposition / Contributory negligence - A bang and a Wimpy.

Apr 99. (cd) *Roundhead - Mad Butcher; (HELMET CD2 - MBR 021)* **POEMS ANCIENT & MODERN: A LIVE ANTHOLOGY 1981–1999**
- The bible according to Rupert Murdoch / Designated areas / Comic in a basket / The zen Stalinist manifesto / Xenophobia / A sugared dish / The iron men of rap! / Andy is a corporatist / Nature poems: The maggot / The rat-tailed maggot / The don't care bear / The slug / The lemming / Trainspotter rap! / Southwich / Slough / Worthing / Belgium / Stornoway / New world order rap! / Russians in the DHSS / Awayday / A bang and a Wimpy / Nigel wants to go to C&A's / Joseph Porter's sleepinge bagge / The final ablution / And Smith must score... / Goldstone ghosts / Veronica / Contributory negligence.

Apr 99. (cd) *Roundhead - Mad Butcher; (HELMET CD3 - MBR 003)* **THE PEN & THE SWORD: SELECTED SONGS 1981–1995**
- This is free Europe / Sawdust and empire / Factory goods / Tyler smiles / The pen and the sword / Market sektor one / The iron men of rap! / Recession / Libyan students from hell! / Holiday in Albania revisited / Fifth column / Forty years / The diggers' song / Roll up for the donkey derby / Tammy's song / Midas the grand / Airstrip one.

B

BABY WHALE

Definitely one for the connoisseur and collector of folk oddities, BABY WHALE's one and only record almost didn't see the light. Recorded in 1973 for DJM Records, it was shelved due to a vinyl shortage at the pressing plant and the energy restrictions imposed in the three-day week that was the government's response to the coalminers' work-to-rule.

The band can truly thank the people at Kissing Spell, who delivered it some three decades later. Comprising Nick Barraclough (now a top DJ for BBC Radio 2), Pennsylvania-born singer-songwriter/artist Annie Baker, Steve Brooks, Adrian Kendon, and fiddlers Brian Wren and Lindsey Scott, soft-folk-rockers BABY WHALE produced some terrific harmonies on **THE DOWNHILL CLIMB** {8*} (2002).

The Cambridge-formed sextet can be traced back to a contract-baiting Edinburgh Fringe Festival show in 1972 and subsequent gigs supporting FAIRPORT CONVENTION, Curved Air, MC5 and Mud, with songs such as trad cuts 'The Cuckoo' and 'The Cuckoo's Nest' (each segued with Baker and Brooks compositions) hitting the right note. Check out the Ernest Hemingway-inspired opener 'The Old Man And The Sea'; elsewhere on the album, 'Cabin Town' and 'Easy Feeling' are of the post-bluegrass/pre-alt-country persuasion. *MCS*

Annie Baker - vocals, acoustic guitar / **Steve Brooks** - vocals, guitar (ex-Toby Jug Band) / **Nick Barraclough** - vocals, bass, harmonium / **Adrian Kendon** - double bass, vocals / **Lindsey Scott** - fiddle / **Brian Wren** - fiddle

UK Kissing Spell — US not issued

Apr 02. (cd) *(KSCD 931)* **THE DOWNHILL CLIMB** [rec. 1973] ☐ ⊟
- The old man and the sea / The downhill climb – The cuckoo's nest / Cornfields – The cuckoo / This time / Circles and circuses / Dependable spokes / Things are not free / Evening song / This ain't my life / Cabin town / Easy feeling / Strangler.

—— Barraclough would later be part of Telephone Bill & The Smooth Operators

Miriam BACKHOUSE

Born May 8, 1948, at Lewes, Miriam was active in folk circles during the latter half of the 1970s, a time when the genre was finding it difficult to compete commercially with the all-encompassing New Wave scene.

In 1976, two traditional songs ('The Recruited Collier' and 'Cuckoo's Nest') appeared on the freebie Bill Leader-produced V/A folk fundraiser LP 'The Second Folk Review Record', while the collaborative 'Fortuna' set (with DAVE GOULDER, Irvine Hunt and Brian Miller) was issued the same year.

GYPSY WITHOUT A ROAD (1977) {*8} was a solo near-breakthrough for Miriam – or it should've been – a strong acoustic-ballad-type record that featured Brian Etheridge (keys and bass) and Stephen Delft (dulcimer) on two ROSIE HARDMAN songs ('The Dark Side Of The Moon' and the title track), Will Williams' 'The Farmers Have Gone East', DAVE GOULDER's 'Far Away Tom' and Jeremy Taylor's `Nasty Spider', plus a few sourced songs.

Around the turn of the decade Miriam emigrated to Durban, South Africa, where for nearly three decades she worked and performed part-time; in the mid-1990s she released two CDs, 'Over Africa' and 'African Rose – Folk Songs'. In 2008 she was back living in the UK. *MCS*

Miriam Backhouse - vocals, guitar / with session people

UK Mother Earth — US not issued

May 77. (lp) *(MUM 1203)* **GYPSY WITHOUT A ROAD** ☐ ⊟
- Far away Tom / The widow / The farmers have gone east / Long Lankin / Nasty spider / The dark side of the moon / John Riley / Keys of Canterbury / Gypsy without a road. *(re-iss. 1994 on Vinyl Tab; DORIS 001) (cd-iss. Feb 98 +=; CDDORIS 001)* - Veera vata (live) / I'll lay ye doon love (live).

—— Miriam emigrated to South Africa.

The BAD SHEPHERDS

This really shouldn't work, but somehow they pull it off. Whether it's the surprise (and unmistakable) voice of former Young Ones and Bottom sit-comic Adrian/Ade Edmondson and his thrash mandolin, or the dexterity and musicianship of folk veterans MAARTIN ALLCOCK, arranger Troy Donockley, All-Ireland fiddler Andy Dinan and fifth member Mark Woolley, it just does.

The brainwave of Edmondson, who'd attempted a parody-rock coup many moons ago with heavy-rock act Bad News, he hatched his plan after buying a mandolin in Soho after a liquid Christmas lunch in 2007. Meeting up with said musicians, and after numerous beers, they formed the fun folk-punk group initially to tour the UK and play the 2009 Cropredy Festival.

Recorded "as live" at the Blue Moon studios in Banbury, its title meaning "one, two, three, four!" in the old Cumbrian dialect,**YAN, TYAN, TETHERA, METHERA!** {*8} caused quite a stir when released in 2009, described in one quarter as 'the Ramones living in Cumbria'. Whether John Lydon would raise a smile at their reinterpretations of 'God Save The Queen' [No Future] and 'Rise', the jury was out. New wave classics were nu-folked up beyond belief, examples including The Jam's 'Down In The Tube Station At Midnight', The Undertones' 'Teenage Kicks' (would Peely have approved?), Squeeze's 'Up The Junction' and Talking Heads' 'Once In A Lifetime'. Kraftwerk's 'The Model' was also in there.

In round two, **BY HOOK OR BY CROOK** (2010) {*7}, the trio (without Maartin) gave another batch of worthy punk-rock contenders the folk treatment. 'Anarchy In The UK' – complete with uillean pipes – will never be the same, and their revamps of The Ramones (medley), The Clash, Buzzcocks, XTC, The Members, The Specials, The Smiths and Motorhead also turn bemusement and then hilarity into crusty headbanging. A few could be in the running to be the theme tune for the new BBC series of One Man And His Dog. *MCS*

Adrian Edmondson - vocals, mandolin (ex-Bad News) / **Maartin Allcock** - guitars, bass (ex-BULLY WEE BAND, ex-FAIRPORT CONVENTION, ex-JETHRO TULL) / **Troy Donockley** - uillean pipes, cittern, pipes (ex-IONA, ex-MADDY PRIOR BAND) / **Andy Dinan** - fiddle (ex-TOSS THE FEATHERS); fifth member **Mark Woolley** - bodhran, percussion

UK Monsoon — US not issued

May 09. (cd) *(MONMUCD 002)* **YAN, TYAN, TETHERA, METHERA!** ☐ ⊟
- I fought the law – Cockers at Pockers / Down in the tube station at midnight / Rise / Whole wide world – Hag with the money / The model / Humours of Tullah – Teenage kicks – Whiskey in the jar – The merry blacksmith / Once in a lifetime – Pinch of snuff / London calling – Manchester calling – The Monaghan jig / Up the junction / Yan, tyan, tethera, methera!: Fraher's jig – Coppers and brass – The old bush – Rip the calico / God save the Queen – Mountain road.

—— now without ALLCOCK + Woolley

Nov 10. (cd) *(MONMUCD 005)* **BY HOOK OR BY CROOK** ☐ ⊟
- Anarchy in the UK / Sound of the suburbs / Making plans for Nigel / Friday night, Saturday morning / Ramones medley / Panic / Ace of spades / Ever fallen in love with someone (you shouldn't've) / White riot.

The BAND OF HOLY JOY

Coming across as a folky Euro-cabaret outfit, inspired by sources from Bertolt Brecht and Jacques Brel to Dexy's and The WATERBOYS, these lads and lassies (led by North Shields-born Jonny Brown) from bases in London gave indie music a little boost by way of a couple of great sets either side of the 1990s.

They formed in New Cross and Soho in the summer of 1982 as Jonny and his sister Maxine gathered up a host of friends including Brett Turnbull and proceeded to record two privately released cassettes. The following year, the BoHJ signed to South London indie Flim Flam, who issued their debut single, 'Had A Mother Who Was Proud'.

POGUES-like in their make-up and approach, this extended musical family traded in a similar raucous folk sound, although based on carousel cabaret and macabre and unpredictable lyrics. A debut mini-lp, **THE BIG SHIP SAILS** (1986) {*6}, appeared the following year, while a more stabilised line-up (Jonny recruiting a whole new cast including Adrian Bailey, Bill Lewington, Big John, Karel Van Bergen, Alfie Thomas and Jub Jenkins) worked on 1987's debut album proper, **MORE TALES FROM THE CITY** {*&}.

Rough Trade Records subsequently signed them and issued two acclaimed sets, **MANIC, MAGIC, MAJESTIC** (1989) {*8} and **POSITIVELY SPOOKED** (1990) {*8}, before the band headed off on a tour of the Soviet Union. Clipping their name to HOLY JOY, the ensemble made one further set, **TRACKSUIT VENDETTA** (1992) {*6}, before splitting. As a freelance journalist, Brown found work with various music rags, but was happier when again taking frontman position with Superdrug, alongside Lewington.

Reactivated in the early 2000s, the BoHJ (i.e. Jonny, Alfie Thomas and Chris Brierley) were back in fine form with comeback set **LOVE NEVER FAILS** (2002) {*6}. The band returned to the fore in 2007 for live gigs, while 2008 saw them perform live in New York, basically to promote and give away the gig-only mini-CD 'Punklore'. **PARAMOUR** (2010) {*8} kept Brown and the band's profiles reasonably high and showed their indie ethos hadn't deserted them. *MCS*

Jonny Brown - vocals / **Brett Turnbull** - organ, etc. / **Maxine** - accordion, vocals

UK US
self-rel. not issued

1982. (ltd-c) *(none)* **FAVOURITE FAIRYTALES FOR JUVENILE DELINQUENTS**

1983. (ltd-c) *(none)* **TALES FROM THE CITY**
- Liquid lunch / Children come out to play / Theme 1 / A glorious morning in Orton Street / Ill gotten gain / Things that speak in tongues / Rosemary Smith / Nylon rose / Frank's place / Theme 2 / Theme 3 / Scrut / This tune will haunt me / Sick on the rides (city of tales) / Fishwives / Soho Square / Ininerant St. thing / A great binge / Theme 4 / Helen / Nylon rose 2 / Disgust / Drug virgin #3 / The tide of life / One child.

Pleasantly Surprised not issued

Jun 84. (c) *(PS 004)* **MORE FAVOURITE FAIRY TALES**
- First hour of the day / Today smashes down! / The only thing thats working in this town / Liquid lunch / I'd dream if I could sleep / Violence, adolescence, nightmare / Maybe one day? / Peter's playground / Consumption / Mental / Snow white / Drug virgin / Anticipation / Bedtime again.

Flim Flam not issued

Oct 85. (12" ep) *(HARP 1T)* HAD A MOTHER WHO WAS PROUD: AND LOOK AT ME NOW
- Disgust / Consumption / Nylon rose.

May 86. (10" m-lp) *(HARP BABY 1)* **THE BIG SHIP SAILS**
- Prams, piers and bitter tears / Rosemary Smith / First hour of the day / Living legends / The boy sailor / Maybe one day.

—— added **Adrian Bailey** - trombone

Oct 86. (7") *(HARP 4)* WHO SNATCHED THE BABY? / A Great Binge / One Child
(12") *(HARP 4T)* - ('A') / One child / Yo!

—— **Jonny** + **Adrian** recruited new members **Bill Lewington** - drums / **Big John** - keyboards, banjo / **Karel Van Bergen** - violin / **Alfie Thomas** - accordion, keyboards / **Jub (John) Jenkins** - bass

Apr 87. (7") *(HARP 6)* ROSEMARY SMITH. / Aspidistra House
(12"+=) *(HARP 6T)* - Hanging Jonny.

May 87. (lp) *(HARPLP 1)* **MORE TALES FROM THE CITY**
- Who snatched the baby? / Mad Dot / When stars come out to play / The aspidistra house / The tide of life / Don't stick knives (in babbies' heads) / Leaves that fall in spring / Cities / Fishwives / Goodnight, god bless and goodbye.

Bye Bye Baby not issued

Dec 87. (lp) *(ByeBye 1)* **WHEN STARS COME OUT TO PLAY**
- Don't stick knives (in babbies' heads) / Mad Dot / Janis - this one's for you / Nico - this is the way out / Tide of life / One child / Amsterdam / North Shields / Fishwives / Who snatched the baby? / Yo!

Cause For Concern not issued

1988. (lp) *(CFC 003)* **THE DEVIL AND THE DEEP BLUE SEA**

—— **Mark Cavener** - double bass; repl. Jub

—— now with guests **Miss Adele Winter** + **David Coulter**

Rough Trade Rough Trade

Sep 88. (7") *(RT 223)* TACTLESS. / Butterfly Beauty Burns
(12"+=) *(RTT 223)* - Zombie.

Jun 89. (lp/c/cd) *(ROUGH/+C/CD 125) <ROUGH-US 69/+C/CD>* **MANIC, MAGIC, MAJESTIC**
- Route to love / Baubles, bangles, emotional tangles / Nightjars / Tactless / You've grown so old in my dreams / Killy car thieves / Bride / Manic, magic, majestic / What the moon saw / You're not singing anymore / Blessed joy. *(cd+=)* - Where it hurts.

Nov. 89. (7") *(RT 233)* EVENING WORLD HOLIDAY SHOW. / Broken Hearts Battered Minds
(12"+=) *(RTT 233)* - Jack Mark II.

Apr 90. (lp/c/cd) *(ROUGH/+C/CD 155)* **POSITIVELY SPOOKED**
- Real beauty passed through / Evening world holiday show / Because it was never resolved / Unlikely girl / Shadows fall / Bitten lips / Here it comes / Hot little hopes / Freda Cunningham / Torch me / Positively spooked / Look who's changed with the times.

Jun 90. (12" ep/cd-ep) *(RTT 243/+CD)* REAL BEAUTY PASSED THROUGH / Chantal. / Happy Go Lucky
(cd-ep+=) *(RTT 243CD)* - Lonely Cottage (instrumental).

The HOLY JOY

Jonny, Bill, Adrian, Alfie, Big John + Howard, Emmet, Chess + Chris

Ecuador not issued

Jul 92. (12"m/cd-s) *(EQ 3 T/CD)* CLAUDIA DREAMS. / Well You've Met This Boy / Jelly Baby

Jul 92. (cd/lp) *(EQ CD/LP 4)* **TRACKSUIT VENDETTA**
- Ragman / Casual 983 / Well you've met this boy / Suit vendetta / 0898 intermission / Claudia dreams / By the light of a magical moon / Kitchen emigre / Marvin in Ostende / Soulstress / Trafalgar Square.

Rough Trade Singles Club not issued

Aug 92. (7") *(45REV 11)* IT'S LOVEBITE CITY. / Sleepy Time Donald

—— split in 1993 - Brown + Lewington subsequently formed Superdrug

The BAND OF HOLY JOY

re-formed with **Brown, Thomas, Bailey + Hacker**

Rough Trade not issued

May 02. (cd) *(RTRADECD 044)* **LOVE NEVER FAILS**
- Capture my soul / Wilfred Owen / City trams / The death of love / Refugee / Hugh Grant / The laughter on Ganton Street / Someone shares my dreams / Grace darling / Love never fails / And then the real thing comes along.

—— In 2008 the band released 'Punklore', given away at gigs.

—— **Brown** + **Hewington** with **Chris Brierley** - violin / **Paul O'Donnell** - bass / **Andy Astle** - guitar

Radio Joy not issued

Jul 10. (cd) *(CD 02)* **PARAMOUR**
- We were the best of friends / Memory counts / Troubled sleep / I propose / Roadwork / I dreamed the city was on fire / And yea, I made it through the night / There is a bluebird on your shoulder.

- (5-7*) compilation -

Nov 07. (cd) *Cherry Red; (CDM RED 341)* **LEAVES THAT FALL IN SPRING ... - SEMINAL MOMENTS 84-04**
- Rosemary Smith / First hour of day / Manic, magic, majestic / Leaves that fall in spring / And then the real thing comes along / Prams piers bitter tears / It's lovebite city / Who snatched the baby? / Tactless / Consumption / Capture my soul / What the moon saw / You've grown so old in my dreams / Real beauty passed through / The death of love / Maybe one day.

The BAND OF RACK & RUIN (⟹ BISIKER & ROMANOV)

Damien BARBER

Splitting releases of solo sets with recordings by his band The DEMON BARBERS, Bright Young Folkie DAMIEN BARBER and his English concertina have kept up traditional fare throughout his home roots of Norfolk and beyond.

From 1996's solo offering **BOXED** {*8} to his group's celebratory **THE ADVENTURES OF CAPTAIN WARD** (2010) {*8}, his records (not forgetting the gigs that won him Best Live Act at the 2009 BBC Radio 2 Folk Awards) have brought plaudits from peers and critics. Featuring the odd sea shanty with impressive quick-fire arrangements, Damien and his merry band of gentlefolk (including stalwart Bryony Griffith on fiddle, Will Hampson on melodeon, Lee Sykes on bass, recent acquisition Ben Griffith on drums, and some fine clog dancers) struck a golden chord on the latter collection with tracks like 'Bonny Boy', 'Captain Ward', 'Three Drunken Maids' (all together now – "oi oi oi!") and a version of Grateful Dead's 'Friend Of The Devil'. It certainly had the wow! factor.

A collaboration between BARBER and Mike Wilson, **UNDER THE INFLUENCE** (2009) {*6}, veered into Celtic-meets-sea shanty territory, examples including works established by PETER BELLAMY, EWAN MacCOLL, MIKE WATERSON, DICK GAUGHAN, STAN HUGILL, etc.

From his solo debut, the pick of the bunch were BELLAMY's 'The Black And Bitter Night', AL STEWART's 'Nostradamus' and the perennial 'The Foggy Dew'. Featuring The Wilson Family, Grace Notes (with MAGGIE BOYLE) and STEVE TILSTON, **THE FURROWED FIELD** (2000) {*6} furthered the Demon Barber's solo CV. **UNCUT** (2002) {*6} and **WAXED** (2005) {*6} were complemented by Child ballads and works by 18th-century fiddler Joshua Jackson and modern-day folk star PETE MORTON. *MCS*

Damien Barber - vocals, English concertina, accordion, guitar / with Denny Bartley (guitar), Alistair Russell (guitar) + Chris Sherburn (Anglo concertina)

UK Nof — US not issued

May 96. (cd) *(NOF 002)* **BOXED**
- All around the world – Cooley's reel – O'Rourke's reel / The Newmarket polka – A Finnish polka – Jim Keefe's polka / Early to rise / The willow Runnell – Charming the cuckoo / Nostradamus / Bucks of Oranmore – The Earl's chair / Ready for the dance / Confidence / The black and bitter night / Out of the ocean – A jig – Calliope House / A reel – Stenson's reel – The convenience reel / The foggy dew. *(re-iss. Dec 00 on DJC; DJC 012)*

—— next with **The WILSON FAMILY, GRACE NOTES & STEVE TILSTON**

DJC — not issued

Dec 00. (cd) *(DJC 011)* **THE FURROWED FIELD**
- On board a "98" / The gypsy poacher – The eavesdropper – Apples in winter / Bold Reynolds / My enemy / Bill Norrie / The turtle and the asp / Hares on the mountain / The golden glove – The Munster cloak / Kilroy was here / Our ship / Three jolly butchers / Down the moor.

The DEMON BARBERS

Damien Barber with **Bryony Griffith** - fiddle, vocals / **Will Hampson** - melodeon, harminica / **Lee Sykes** - bass / **Rich Ashby** - drums

Sep 02. (cd) *(DJC 019)* **UNCUT** [live at Haworth Parish Hall, 26-27 April 2002]
- Willie Goggin / Ready for the dance / Companion of a mile – Three around tree / Way down town / Van Diemen's land / One thing better than sex / The grumbling old man – Katy Cruel – Tom and Jerry / Ruins by the shore / Kielder Castle – Sir Richard's song / The drunken sailor – Three maidens a-milking did go / The coalowner and the pitman's wife – I'll tousle your kurchy.

—— **Ben Griffith** - drums; repl. Ashby

Aug 05. (cd) *(DJC 026)* **WAXED**
- Edward / The ballad of Minepit Shaw – Idbury hill / A noble riddle wisely expounded – Brana's polka / The werewolf / John Riley / The creel – Doorus mill – Winnie Hayes – Spindle shanks – The musical priest – The pope's toe / Two brothers / Sir Richard's song – Brest knot / The famous flower of serving men – En passant la riviere – Kost ar c'hoat.

Demon Barbers Sound — not issued

Aug 08. (cd-ep; as DEMON BARBERS) *(DBS 001)* +24db
- The good old days / Friend of the Devil / The gallant frigate Amphridite / Betsy Bell and Mary Gray / Pit boots / Death and the lady – Under the rock.

Apr 09. (cd; by DAMIEN BARBER & MIKE WILSON) *(DBS 002)* **UNDER THE INFLUENCE** [covers]
- The green linnet / On board a "98" / The joy of living / Shiny O / My old man / Jim Jones at Botany Bay / Down the moor / On board a man of war / Andrew Rose / A fable from Aigge / Now westlin winds / Nostradamus.

Jun 10. (cd) *(DBS 009)* **THE ADVENTURES OF CAPTAIN WARD**
- Captain Ward / Munchen fest / Bonny boy / Rise up / Harry's hornpipe / Soul cake / Pound a week rise / The magpie / Three drunken maids / Calling-on song / Friend of the Devil / Kiss me quick my mammy's coming – The queen of sluts / Three ravens.

The BARELY WORKS

The resurgent interest in traditional Brit-folk during the latter half of the 1980s (in the shape of The POGUES, The MEN THEY COULDN'T HANG, et al) helped pave the way for some of the unlikeliest contenders on the scene, The BARELY WORKS.

Formed in London in 1988, the septet comprised seasoned folk/indie stalwarts Chris Thompson (ex-BOOTHILL FOOT-TAPPERS, vocals and banjo), fellow songwriter Sarah Allen (accordion and flute), her former Happy End bandmate Richard Avison (also ex-Dead Can Dance; trombone and vocals), Welshwoman Alison Jones (fiddle and vocals), Keith Moore (tuba), Mat Fox (hammer dulcimer and percussion) and former Redskins drummer Paul Hookham; the last-named left just prior to their well-received debut album for Cooking Vinyl Records, **THE BIG BEAT** (1990) {*7}. He was replaced by Tim Walmsley (also ex-Happy End).

An off-kilter cocktail of classical Celtic country, funky folk and brassy bluegrass, the album achieved a modicum of praise, none more enthusiastic than from FolkRoots (fRoots), who named the group Best Newcomer of 1990. From their high-end jigs 'n' reels such as 'As A Thoiseach (Keep It Up)', 'The White Cockade – Bonaparte's Retreat – Flop-Eared Mule' and 'Liberty – Blackberry Blossom – The Cuckoo's Nest', to the ska-flavoured 'Byker Hill' and the fiddle-infused 'Let's Go And Have A Good Time', The BARELY WORKS grafted very hard indeed. For many folk purists, their reworking of Captain Beefheart's 'Tropical Hot Dog Night' perhaps stretched their musical elasticity a little too far.

Stepping down in class but without changing the pop formula too much, the follow-up, **DON'T MIND WALKING** (1991) {*5}, shifted intermittently between their lively renditions of traditional pieces (e.g. the medley of 'The Flowers Of Edinburgh – Miss McCleod's Reel – The "Groove Is So Mighty" Reel') and originals such as Thompson's 'This Fire'. This album was Mat's swansong, and he and Keith were replaced by tuba player Alice Kinloch.

1992's **GLOW** {*5} saw the band cross over ever so slightly into the pop field, with only two traditional segment pieces ('Swinging On A Gate' and 'The Moving Cloud') being included. Sounding more like Madness and Modern Romance respectively, Avison's contributions 'Big River' and 'The Bell') were throwaway tunes, and only Jones's Kirsty MacColl-like 'Pull Me Up' lifted the beat. Thompson's best was 'Sitting Out The Back There'.

It was no big surprise when, shortly after a final gig at York Arts Centre, The BARELY WORKS broke up in 1993. Sarah Allen has since become an integral member of the award-winning Celtic-folk quartet FLOOK. *MCS*

Chris Thompson (b. Mar 19, '57, Ashford, Middlesex) - vocals, banjo (ex-BOOTHILL FOOT-TAPPERS) / **Sarah Allen** (b. Jul 22, '64, Tiverton, Devon) - accordion, flute, tin whistle / **Keith Moore** - tuba (of John Hegley's Popticians) / **Richard Avison** (b. Jul 19, '58, Rothbury, Northumberland) - trombone, vocals (ex-Happy End, ex-Dead Can Dance) / **Alison Jones** (b. Apr 6, '65, Sketty, Swansea, Wales) - fiddle, vocals (ex-Di's New Outfit) / **Mat Fox** (b. Nov 8, '56) - hammer dulcimer, percussion / **Tim Walmsley** (b. Mar 29, '56, Paddington, London) - drums (ex-Happy End) repl. Paul Hookham (ex-Redskins)

UK Cooking Vinyl — US Green Linnet

Jul 90. (lp/c/cd) *(COOK/+C/CD 024)* **THE BIG BEAT**
- The white cockade – Bonaparte's retreat - Flop-eared mule / Byker hill / Big old road / Let's go and have a good time / Liberty - Blackberry blossom - The cuckoo's nest / I'm not that bad anymore / The inventor / As a thoiseach (keep it up) / Tropical hot dog night / Growling old man and old woman. *(cd re-iss. Feb 03; same)*

Oct 91. (lp/c/cd) *(COOK/+C/CD 045) <GLCD 3071>* **DON'T MIND WALKING** — 1992
- Something'll have to change / Staten Island - No place two step - My love is but a lassie yet / Bread and water / This fire / The kindled flame / Back to the mountains / Petronella - Banbury breakdown - Mississippi Sawyer / Old Joe Clarke / The flowers of Edinburgh - Miss McCleod's reel - The 'groove is so mighty' reel / Stand together.

—— **Alice Kinloch** - tuba; repl. Moore + Fox

Aug 92. (cd/c) *(COOK CD/C 050)* **GLOW**
- Riddle me wry / Run out of loving / Swinging on a gate - Hornpipe for Snappy / Big river / Maybe I'm a fool - June / Pull me up / The bell / The moving cloud - Cliff - Treen beach / Sitting out the back there.

—— disbanded the following year; Chris and Sarah continued to work on the circuit as a duo; the latter had a brief stint in Celtic-folkers Bigjig (album 'Feet To The Floor' in 1994) before she joined FLOOK [see forthcoming Celtic-Folk Discography]

- (5-7*) compilations, etc.-

Feb 95. (cd) *Cooking Vinyl; (COOKCD 079)* **THE BEST OF THE BARELY WORKS**
- Byker Hill / As a thoiseach (Keep it up) / This fire / Liberty - Blackberry blossom - The cuckoo's nest / Big river / Bread and water / Maybe I'm a fool - June / Back to the mountains / The moving cloud - Cliff - Treen beach / Pull me up / Old Joe Clarke / Riddle me wry / Stand together.

Emily BARKER & THE RED CLAY HALO

From the depths of rural Bridgetown, Western Australia, rootsy acoustic singer-songwriter EMILY BARKER (born December 2, 1980) has the distinctive accolade of having two recent award-winning BBC TV drama theme songs to her name: 'Nostalgia' from Wallander and 'Pause' from The Shadow Line.

Landing in London for 2002's Cambridge Folk Festival, she duly took up residence as she performed further gigs as half of the duo The Low Country alongside guitarist Rob Jackson. The Low Country were exactly that, releasing two independent sets 'Welcome To The Low Country' (2003) and 'The Dark Road' (2004). Having influences ranging from JONI MITCHELL to SANDY DENNY and a few C&W artists in between, Emily embraced the nu-country-folk market by way of her solo debut album **PHOTOS FIRES FABLES** (2008) {*7}. Self-financed on her own Everyone Sang imprint and backed by The Red Clay Halo trio (Gill Sandell, Jo Silverston and Anna Jenkins), emotive ballads such as 'Under These Bruised Skies', 'The Suitcase', 'The Photo' and 'On A Train' gave a sense of desert-bowl solitude, sounding somewhere between LUCINDA WILLIAMS, EDDI READER and NATALIE MERCHANT.

The freshly-billed EMILY BARKER & THE RED CLAY HALO were officially up and running for the 2009-issued **DESPITE THE SNOW** {*7}, recorded live in four days at the Granary studios in Norfolk. One thinks the MP3 was on sale from Walking Horse the previous September. Premiering the aforementioned Wallander gem, the set was more chamber-folk-orientated, with old-timey country not far away. Disappear', 'The Greenway' and a reading of LAL & MIKE WATERSON's 'Bright Phoebus' were all worthy semi-classics.

Touring on the same bill as fellow folkies FRANK TURNER, The WAIFS (also from Australia) and JOSE GONZALEZ, the EMILY BARKER crew were poised to take all the honours at the prestigious Radio 2 Folk Awards with third album **ALMANAC** (2011) {*8}. A cleverly-thought-out set that combined all the rootsy elements to garner a wider audience, the record (featuring further augmentation by Ali Friend, Ted Barnes, Nat Butler, Liz Jones and Ben Eshmade) was best served by the ethereal 'Pause', 'Openings' and 'Witch Of Pittenweem', the latter based on the early 18th-century witch trials centred around the Fife fishing village – freak-folk it was not. *MCS*

Emily Barker - vocals, acoustic guitar, banjo (ex-Low Country) / with The Red Clay Halo: **Gill Sandell** - accordion, piano, flute, percussion, vocals / **Jo Silverston** - cello, saw, vocals / **Anna Jenkins** - violin, vocals

UK Everyone Sang — US not issued

Mar 08. (cd; as EMILY BARKER) *(ES 2007)* **PHOTOS FIRES FABLES**
- This is how it's meant to be / Blackbird / Home / Orlando / Under these bruised skies / Fields of June / The suitcase / The photo / Mystery / On a train / On a winter's day / If love could save.

—— same musicians as previous set; added guests Tom Mason (double bass) + Dan See (drums)

Apr 09. (7") *(ES 2009-7)* DESPITE THE SNOW. / This Is How It's Meant To Be [live]

May 09. (cd) *(ES 2010)* **DESPITE THE SNOW**
- Nostalgia [main theme for Wallander] / All love knows / Disappear / If it's all night long / Bloated, blistered, aching heart / Bright Phoebus / Storm in a teacup / The greenway / Sideline / Breath / Serendipity / Oh journey.

Feb 11. (cd) *(ES 2011)* **ALMANAC**
- Billowing sea / Reckless / Ropes / Little deaths / Dancers / Pause / Openings / Calendar / Light / Witch of Pittenweem / Bones.

Les BARKER

Lying somewhere in between trad/Brit-folk and music-hall pastiche, the work of LES BARKER and his alter-ego MRS ACKROYD'S BAND will surely go down in the annals of modern-day folklore as one of the genre's more eccentric characters. Mrs Ackroyd was the name of his beloved mongrel dog, who died around 1975/76 but lived on in the mind of Les and his band of followers.

Born January 30, 1947 in Manchester, England, his debut LP, **MRS ACKROYD SUPERSTAR!** (1977) {*7}, featured parodies of MIKE HARDING, VIN GARBUTT, JAKE THACKRAY, Bob Williamson and Noel Murphy with assistance from SAFFRON SUMMERFIELD and others. Books of poetry and monologues duly appeared to accompany each set, and he was the mind behind Cosmo The Fairly Accurate Knife Thrower and Jason And The Arguments. **DOGMATIC** (1980) {*6} featured a host of name folk stars including MARTIN SIMPSON, MAGGIE HOLLAND, PHIL BEER, IAN A. ANDERSON and American singer Bill Zorn.

Numerous guests featured on many of BARKER's folk operas. Quiet Riot (no, not that one but a band from Coventry) aided and abetted **THE MRS ACKROYD ROCK'N'ROLL SHOW** (1985) {*6}. **DOGOLOGUES** (1986) {*6} was his first of many live albums.

The 1988 set EARWIGO (recorded at the Bromyard Folk Festival the previous September) credited musicians/singers Lesley Davies, Steve Davies, Ian Blake, Barry Parkes and Eric Pressley, among others. **THE STONES OF CALLANISH** (1989) {*7} was the first to feature the WATERSON: CARTHY family contingent, plus folk stars not known for comedy-folk routines – JUNE TABOR, Fiona Simpson and Celtic-styled Scots Rod Paterson, Jim Sutherland, Cathy-Ann McPhee and PHIL CUNNINGHAM. And who could forget album titles such as **UP THE CREEK WITHOUT A POODLE** (1997) {*6} and **GNUS AND ROSES** (1994) {*6}.

With many albums and more than 50 published books, poet laureate-in-waiting LES BARKER is folk music's Jasper Carrott or Max Boyce. Mainly by word of mouth his comic genius has spread all over the world from North America to Australasia; he's now settled in Wales, where he has mastered the language. All together now: 'Llanfairpwllgwyngyllgogery ...' *MCS*

Les Barker - vocals (with many guests)

UK Free Reed — US not issued

1977. (7") *(FRY 1)* HOLLAND'S MEAT PIES. / Sparky's Magic Contraceptive

Aug 77. (lp) *(FRR 015)* **MRS ACKROYD SUPERSTAR!**
- Mrs Ackroyd / My granny's a wild flying dove / The rise and fall of Ghenghis Ackroyd / Vincent / Where do you go to, my Doris? / Candlelight and wine / Holland's meat pies / The fastest accountant in the west / Kippers for tea / Sparky's magic contraceptive / The curse of the house of the Baskervilles. *(cd-iss.Jun07 +=; FRRR 06)* - Three beasts / Breaking wind suddenly / The last inch of freedom / A murder ballad / I'm a loony from Manchester way / Inconsonants / The Queen's corgis / I will love you in the setting of the sun / The civilised world.

Avada — not issued

Nov 80. (lp) *(AVA 111)* **DOGMATIC**
- Pulling a hat out of a rabbit / Quasi B Goode / The Peking swallow / When Joneses ale caught fire / The Irish tune / Napoleon at your service / The undersea world of Jacques Cousteau / The Heckmondwike rapist / Nashnul Front song / Flat earth / Moby Nigel / Nigel's blues / Dream / Beware of young ladies who have three breasts / Eval Schmeval.

Apr 81. (7") *(AVS 112)* QUASI B GOODE. / Dream

Mrs Ackroyd — not issued

Jun 84. (7") *(MRS 001)* NIGEL'S BLUES. / Chicken Biriani Conga

1985. (lp) *(DOG 001)* **THE MRS ACKROYD ROCK'N'ROLL SHOW**
- The Mrs Ackroyd rock'n'roll show (part I) / I've got a hunch you don't love me, Esmeralda / Bones and booze and sex / Chicken biriani conga / Saudi Sidney / Hell's alsatians / Ted Crum / Nigel's blues / Morecambe Bay-o bayou gumbo / Weddell Waddle penguins-o / Do the hunch / The Mrs Ackroyd rock'n'roll show (part II). *(cd-iss. Jun 99; DOG 001CD)*

Feb 86. (lp/c) *(DOG 002/+C)* **DOGOLOGUES** (live at Stockport Grammar School, March 29 and October 11 1985)
- Dan Dare / Nelson / Scott of East Acton / Butterflies / Roy of the Rovers is gay / Eval Schmeaval / Lorna the library book burglar / Quasimodo / King Harold was a ventriloquist / Sparky's magic contraceptive. *(cd-iss.Sep94; DOG 002CD)*

May 88. (lp/c) *(DOG 004/+C)* **EARWIGO** (live at Bromyard Folk Festival, 18-19 September 1987)
- In the dark around the table / It Eppinged long ago / Pony and crap / Cohen the Barbarian / Holland's meat pies / The nose of Allan Dale / Earwigo. *(cd-iss. Apr 95; DOG 004CD)*

—— Barker words only; accompanied by singers **Rod Paterson** [the man] + guitar, **Lesley Davies** [the girl], **Janet Russell** [Hebridean woman], **Nick Dow** + **Bernard Wrigley** [lorry driver] + guitars, latter bass concertina, **June Tabor** [the Stones of Callanish], **Fiona Simpson** [the Towers of London], **Cathy-Ann MacPhee** [Gaelic singer] plus other musicians: **Savourna Stevenson** - harp / **Phil Cunningham** - synthesizer, accordion / **John Martin** - fiddle, viola, cello / **Jack Evans** - harmonica, whistles / **Neil Hay** - fretless bass / **Jim Sutherland** - perc.

1989. (d-lp/cd) *(DOG 005-006/+CD)* **THE STONES OF CALLANISH**: a folk opera by Les Barker
- The stones on the hill [JT] / Crucified on your old broken cross [RP] / Don't say goodbye [LD] / Across the wide ocean [JR] / Latha dhomh 's mi gabhail a' mhonaidh [CM] / Going down to Metal Bridge [ND & BW] / You ebb and flow [JR] / I stand here alone on the beach [LD] / On me way to Dover [ND] / The stones on the hill [JT] / Towers of London [RS] // You ebb and flow [RP] / Tasdan a'righ 's feileadh an t-saighdeir [CM] / Down from the hills [RP, FS & CM] / Sleep on, my darling [LD] / The stones on the hill [JT] / Another pint [RP] / Reconciliation [RP & LD] / Take me back to Lewis [LD].

The MRS ACKROYD BAND

Les Barker - vocals / **Martin Carthy** - vocals / **Lesley Davies** - vocals, tambourine / **Chris Harvey** - keyboards, guitar, mandolin, etc. / **June Tabor** - vocals / **Norma Waterson** - vocals, triangle / **Bernard Wrigley** - bass / **Alison Younger** - vocals / plus others incl. **Eliza Carthy** - vocals

1990. (c) *(DOG 007C)* **ORANGES AND LEMMINGS**: A CELEBRATION OF OUR MUSICAL HERITAGE
- Tortoise from hell / The trains of Waterloo / Steven and Stella / Nancy and Willie / She moves through the fair / In the snow of deep midwinter / Quasi B. Goode / Hunting the Cutty Wren / Jehovah's Witness at the door /

Llanfairpwllgwyngyllgogerychwyrndrobwllllantysiliogogogoch / The hard cheese of old England / My snails have not yet arrived / The William Patel ouverture. *(cd-iss. Sep '94; DOG 007CD)*

1991. (lp) *(DOG 008)* **AN INFINITE NUMBER OF OCCASIONAL TABLES** (live at Bromyard Folk Festival)
- An infinite number of occasional tables / Jason and the arguments / Waste not, want not / The hypochondria kid / Nobody hugs a hedgehog / I can't find my camouflage net / Spot, the eternal dalmatian / Reg was a lonely glow worm / The dwarf / Moses. *(cd-iss. Sep 94 & Apr 00; DOG 008CD)*

—— next sung by **Fiona Simpson, June Tabor, Roy Bailey, Pete Morton, Lesley Davies, Eliza Carthy, Alison Younger, Norma Waterson, Keith Hancock, The MRS ACKROYD BAND, Martin Carthy, Hilary Spencer, Chris While** with **Chris Harvey** (keyboards) + **Ken Nicol** (guitar)

1992. (cd/c; songs by LES BARKER) *(DOG 009 CD/C)* **SOME LOVE**
- This love / Wall of death / Saigon 1989, Hong Kong 1997 / Hostage / Minding the store / Everything glows / I'll bring you my song / I have blown it all away / Home fit for heroes / All one nation / Remember, all those years ago / BCCI / Elephant / Bolero.

—— **Maartin Allcock** - guitar; repl. Wrigley

—— added **Nick Fairclough** - drums (**Eliza** now f/t)

Jun 94. (cd/c) *(DOG 010 CD/C)* **GNUS AND ROSES**
- Down with the sausage roll / The seven years' Franco-Prussian war of the Spanish succession / My husband's got no porridge in him / Johnny, you're so peculiar / The Schwarzenegging song / Send in the cones / Ilkley d'amour / Leader of the treens / The January June / Dachshunds with erections can't climb stairs / Across the plains of Africa / Belle's bonnie bogey / Nobody hugs a hedgehog / Born under a road sign / Tam Lin / Blessed are the peacemakers.

LES BARKER

Dec 95. (cd/c) *(DOG CD/C 011)* **A CARDI AND BLOKE** [live at Towersey Folk Festival, August 27/28, 1995]
- Deja vu / Cosmo, the fairly accurate knife thrower / The one-legged horse / The author's story / The shipping forecast / The Guillemot / Heavy plant crossing / Irrational neutscene / Spot of the Antarctic / Orifice was an Italian composer / Cosmo, Prince of Denmark / The blood donor.

Feb 97. (cd) *(DOG 012)* **UP THE CREEK WITHOUT A POODLE** [live at Bromyard Folk Festival, September 1996]
- Go, stay and fetch / Odd socks / Have you got any news of the iceberg? / An admission / Why do cafes close at teatime? / The lonely little lemming / Administerium and the science of unclear physics / My snails have not yet arrived / I don't like my boomerang / The book of Kevin (chapter one) / Travel iron / BSA / Monologue '87 / Dachshunds with erections can't climb stairs / The phoenix.

The MRS ACKROYD BAND

Oct 99. (cd; Various Artists) *(DOG 013)* **THE WINGS OF BUTTERFLIES**: Songs by Les Barker
- Chaos (PETE MORTON) / Earth (NORMA WATERSON & MARTIN CARTHY) / Cortez (FIONA SIMPSON & CHRIS HARVEY) / The child (JUNE TABOR & CHRIS HARVEY) - Lead kindly light (The Choir) / Two per cent (PHIL BEER) / They make the laws (HILARY SPENCER & CHRIS HARVEY) / Spheres of influence (The Choir) / Safe haven (DAVE BURLAND) / Unnecessary people (The Choir) / I have blown it all away (LESLEY DAVIES, ALISON YOUNGER & CHRIS HARVEY) / Soldier (COOPE, BOYES and SIMPSON) / War horse town (STEVE TILSTON & FIONA SIMPSON) / All one nation (ALISON YOUNGER, The Choir & CHRIS HARVEY) - The flowers of the field (CHRIS HARVEY) - Earth (The Choir).

—— **Barker, Spencer, Younger + Harvey** were joined by **David Knutson** - vocals, guitar / **Eileen McGann** - vocals / **Bill Caddick** - vocals, guitar / **June Tabor, Cyril Tawney + Harvey Andrews**

Dec 99. (cd) *(DOG 014)* **TUBULAR DOGS**
- Sloop John A / O sole mio / Nolans / Grey tunnel line / Have you got any news of the iceberg? / Custard creams / Techno notice / Breaking winds suddenly / Krill / Get a long little dogie / Will the turtle be unbroken? / I live not near the Louvre / Harvey Andrews chorus.

Jul 01. (cd; by LES BARKER) *(DOG 015)* **AROVERTHERAPY** (live 1999–2001)
- Spot the zebra / The weakest link / Reinstalling windows / Chronology / Arnold / Blessed are the meek / Guide cats for the blind / Haiku / Mono / ancientmariner.com / The last but one of the Mohicans / Inconsonants / Stamped addressed antelope / The Y files / Voicemail / Detritus.

—— (see below for associated singers/musicians)

Sep 01. (cd; Les Barker's Works sung slowly) *(DOG 016)* **AIRS OF THE DOG**
- Hebrides (ALISON YOUNGER & CHRIS HARVEY) / Queen Cruelty (ANNETTE BATTY, STEVE TILSTON & JOHN NIELSON) / Another life (CINDY MANGSEN ...) / The place of the wolf (EILEEN McGANN & LES BARKER) / Foolish dreams (LESTER SIMPSON & CHRIS HARVEY) / Turn of the road (ARTISAN) / Waltz for nobody (DAVID KNUTSON & CHRIS HARVEY) / The flowers of the field (ALISON YOUNGER & CHRIS HARVEY) / In the dark of night (FIONA SIMPSON) / Heart of the heartland (EILEEN McGANN & DAVID KNUTSON) / If rivers turned and flowed upstream (CHRIS LESLIE) / Blackbird (HILARY SPENCER & CHRIS HARVEY) / I will love you in the setting of the sun (FIONA SIMPSON & MIKE SILVER) / The special light of lonely islands (JUNE TABOR & MARK EMERSON).

—— **Barker, Younger, Spencer, Harvey** plus **Roy Bailey, Steve Tilston, June Tabor, Clare Alexander, Pete Morton + Bill Zorn**

Nov 03. (cd) *(DOG 017)* **YELP!**
- Lots of oil / The lemmings' reunion / A murder ballad / David Beckham's groin / Dipstick and seals / Spencer's dog Rover / Detritus / There's a hole in my bodhran / Ben Kenobi / The Unigate milkman / Another train / Manzanasol / Auntie Beryl's new PC / Lord Franklin / Roseville fair / Ode to Joy Beverley / Roseville fair (JUNE TABOR outtake).

Oct 04. (cd; by LES BARKER) *(DOG 018)* **THE WAR ON TERRIER** (live at Stroud Fringe Festival 2004)
- A very English thing / The stealth comma / Amnesia / It was the surprise more than anything / An odd kind of ultimatum / Ode to joy / David Beckham's groin / The church of the wholly undecided / Nobody's as old as Derek Brimstone / The diphthong / Gladys / The inflatable boy / Disaster at sea / Sex is better than poetry / The civilised world.

May 06. (cd; by Various Artists) *(DOG 019)* **TWILIGHT OF THE DOGS**: SONGS OF LES BARKER
- The ashes of time (HILARY SPENCER) / Nathan and Garrett and Cody (NONNY JAMES) / The railways of New York (JACK HUDSON) / All the souls on Earth (FIONA SIMPSON) / Debate (LES BARKER) / Distant hills (NONNY JAMES) / The top of the world (STEVE TILSTON) / My blessings on Barra (ALISON YOUNGER) / The morning road (ALISON YOUNGER & HILARY SPENCER) / Angels of the north (PHIL BEER & JACKIE OATES) / The dawning of the day (ROY BAILEY & MARTIN SIMPSON) / Turn me round (MICHAEL KENNEDY) / First love (FIONA SIMPSON) / The last inch of freedom (PETE MORTON).

—— next MRS ... set featured **Chris Harvey** plus (acts)

Jan 08. (cd; by MRS ACKROYD BAND *) *(DOG 020)* **DARK SIDE OF THE MONGREL**
- The verb to be (LES BARKER) / I drive a Mitsubishi Brick Shogun (ALISON YOUNGER & HILARY SPENCER) / Mrs Groves (CLOUDSTREET) / The Marie Depreste (*) / You won't like Tom Jones (JEZ LOWE) / The house of the rising what? (HILARY SPENCER) / The can't can't (*) / Sensodyne (PINT & DALE) / My stock of Ovaltine (ALISON YOUNGER) / I can't believe it's not beef dripping (*) / Non-dairy creamer (HILARY SPENCER) / Rhubarb (*) / The maid of Melrose town (JUNE TABOR) / The cruel motherboard (CLOUDSTREET) / Hip hop Hamlet (*) / On and on (JOHN TAMS with COOPE, BOYES & SIMPSON) / Sam Lithgow's fleas (*) / The farting lass (ALISON YOUNGER) / Cariad ar goll (LES BARKER).

- (8-10*) compilations -

Jul 97. (cd; as LES BARKER) *Terra Nova; (TERRCD 007)* **PROBABLY THE BEST ALBUM EVER MADE BY ANYBODY IN OUR STREET**
- Cosmo revisited / Dachshunds with erections can't climb stairs / Jason and the arguments / Weddell Waddle penguins-o / The hard cheese of old England (MARTIN CARTHY) / King Harold was a ventriloquist / Everything glows (ELIZA CARTHY) / Stay, go and fetch / Earwigo.

- (Various Artists) tribute sets -

Sep 03. (d-cd) *Osmosys; (OSMOCD 020-21)* **GUIDE CATS FOR THE BLIND**: songs and poems of Les Barker
- Guide cats for the blind (LES BARKER) / Across the plains of Africa (KEN BRUCE) / The curse of the House of the Baskervilles (MIKE HARDING) / Stamped addressed antelope (NED SHERRIN) / Sprouts (SARAH KENNEDY) / Reg the vegetable gardener (SIR JIMMY YOUNG) / Custard creams (BILL CADDICK) / Waste not, want not (GERARD McDERMOTT) / Shipping forecast (BRIAN PERKINS) / Crawl of the Light Brigade (SALLY BOAZMAN) / The man next door's a burglar (JOHNNIE WALKER) / Git a long little dogie (JUNE TABOR) / Administerium and the science of unclear physics (HEINZ WOLFF) / Nobody hugs a hedgehog (NONNY JAMES) / Jehovah's Witness at the door (ALLAN BESWICK) / Blessed are the meek (RYAN KELLY) / Sammy's Bar revisited (CYRIL TAWNEY) / Amnesia (NICHOLAS PARSONS) / The last but one of the Mohicans (PAUL GAMBACCINI) / Detrius - Tu haiku (DAVE CASH + FIVE GUIDE CATS OF ARIJABA) // Sidney (SIC TRANSIT) / Have you got any news of the iceberg? (TERRY WOGAN) / Spot of the Antarctic (NONNY JAMES) / An infinite number of occasional tables (ROY HUDD) / The man who was eaten by his own bum (BERNARD WRIGLEY) / Voicemail (CHARLOTTE GREEN) / It was the surprise more than anything (BILLY BUTLER) / Hard cheese of old England (MARTIN CARTHY) / I can't find my camouflage net (PETER WHITE) / Detrius (DAVE CASH) / The dog formerly known as Prince (BRIAN MATTHEW) / The Unigate milkman (GALLIARD) / Captain Indecisive (TREVOR PEACOCK) / One legged horse (ROGER LLOYD PACK) / Lassie free and easy (CYRIL TAWNEY) / ancientmariner.com (IAN MacMILLAN) / The phoenix (NICKY CAMPBELL) / Everything glows (GENEVIEVE TUDOR) / Jason and the arguments (MARK and LARD) / Deja vu (LES BARKER).

Sep 05. (cd) *Osmosys; (OSMOCD 032)* **MISSING PERSIANS FILE**: Guide Cats For The Blind Vol 2
- The stealth comma (JOHN HUMPHREYS) / If (JOSS ACKLAND) / Missing Persians file (HARVEY ANDREWS & JOHN SHEPHERD) / A Crufts conversion (PRUNELLA SCALES) / Cosmo the fairly accurate knife thrower (LES BARKER) / I don't like my boomerang (EMMA CHAMBERS) / Will the turtle be unbroken (TOM PAXTON) / My snails have not yet arrived (TIMOTHY WEST & PRUNELLA

SCALES) / Napoleon's circular retreat from Reading (JEREMY VINE) / Lorna the library book burglar (NONNY JAMES) / Travel iron (GENEVIEVE TUDOR) / Spot was not like the rest (ED STEWART) / Dipsticks and seals (STEVE TILSTON) / Death by daffodils (FRANK HENNESSY) / Self knowledge (RYAN KELLY) / Non sequiturs (ROGER LLOYD PACK) / One-way cul-de-sac (RODNEY BEWES) / The King of Rome (SIC TRANSIT) / The undead parrot (DESMOND CARRINGTON) / King Harold was a ventriloquist (GERARD McDERMOTT) / A very English thing (TREVOR PEACOCK) / The lemmings' reunion (The MRS ACKROYD BAND).

Aug 07. (cd) *Osmosys; (OSMOCD 041)* **TOP CAT, WHITE TIE & TAILS:** Guide Cats for the blind - Volume 3
- The Franco-Prussian war of the Spanish succession (DAVE CASH) / Top cat, white tie and tails (NONNY JAMES) / Knot (ROGER LLOYD PACK) / An admission (JOSS ACKLAND) / The mask of Mono (ROBERT LINDSAY) / The church of the wholly undecided (LES BARKER) / Bungee jumping for lemmings (JENNY AGUTTER) / Mute swan (TIM BROOKE-TAYLOR) / Disaster at sea (EDWARD DE SOUZA) / No May (PRUNELLA SCALES) / Inconsonants (TREVOR PEACOCK) / I used to be a singer in a rock band (TONY HAWKS) / Acupuncture (TESSA PEAKE-JONES) / The author's story (TIM BROOKE-TAYLOR) / On performing poetry (ANDREW SACHS) / Garden waste (JENNY AGUTTER) / Home improvement (MICHAEL COCHRANE) / My phone's out of order (PETER DONALDSON) / Go stay and fetch (JUDI SPIERS) / Leonardo Da Thingy (ANDREW SACHS) / McPherson's lament (KEN BRUCE) / Reg was a lonely glow worm (NORMA DIXIT) / The Y files (GERARD McDERMOTT) / Oh Lord when I die (JOSS ACKLAND) / Chronology (CHRISTOPHER CAZENOVE) / The charge of the late brigade (CLARE BALDING & JIMMY McGRATH) / The secret (DEWARD DE SOUZA).

KASHMIR

Lesley Davies (b. Mar 23 '59, Stockport, Cheshire, England) - vocals, guitar / **Steve Davies** (b. Stephen Glynn Davies, Feb 17 '64, Romiley, Cheshire) - piano, synths, vocals / plus **Fiona Simpson** - vocals

Mrs Ackroyd — not issued

1986. (lp/c) *(DOG-003/+C)* **STAY CALM**
- Feed the stranger / Case of you / Better lying down / Time waits for no-one / Magic voice / Iceberg one Titanic nil / Uncle Bob says goodbye / One more chance / Easy way out / Stay calm / Hay una mujer desaparecida / Mow cop / Niago and Irvana.

—— **Steve** left and was repl. by **Jon Gibbons** - guitar

—— split; Lesley joined MRS ACKROYD BAND, LES BARKER, plus MIKE SILVER, Paul Metser's Cave Canem and George Borowski; she now teaches singing (mainly rock, pop and jazz) to students in the north-west of England.

Sally BARKER

Born September 19, 1959, at Barrow upon Soar in Leicestershire, England, Sally's inspirations and influences included MARY HOPKIN, Bessie Smith, Aretha Franklin, Bonnie Raitt and JOHN MARTYN. Throughout the first half of the 1980s she performed regularly with bassist Chris Watson (as Sally & Chris), supporting the likes of GORDON GILTRAP and STEELEYE SPAN, although it wouldn't be until 1986, after taking top prize at the Kendal Songsearch Competition, that her breakthrough arrived.

With acoustic guitar in hand the singer-songwriter found work supporting FAIRPORT CONVENTION, Wishbone Ash, Taj Mahal, RICHARD THOMPSON and ROY HARPER, which helped her gain the necessary kudos to compete in the fickle world of Brit-folk-blues. Her first, self-released LP, the live **IN THE SPOTLIGHT** (1988) {*6} – later to be re-issued and revamped as **SALLY BARKER** (1993) {*7}, was reasonably well received and comprised a handful of rootsy cover versions (TOWNES VAN ZANDT's 'Poncho And Lefty', The Rolling Stones' 'Honky Tonk Women', T-Bone Walker's 'Stormy Monday', Rickie Lee Jones's 'Chuck E's In Love' and Joan Armatrading's 'Love And Affection') alongside several of her own compositions.

Signing a deal with Hannibal Records, her sophomore set **THIS RHYTHM IS MINE** (1990) {*7} continued her rise to stardom, while slots supporting the likes of Robert Plant and BOB DYLAN helped her CV no end. The album itself featured some of her finest songs so far ('Money's Talking' and 'Lay Your Body Down' among them), while the cajun/folk-meets-country/bluegrass feel was provided by session players Martin Allcock, DANNY THOMPSON, Dave Mattacks and her soon-to-be POOZIES chums Patsy Seddon and Mary MacMaster (of Scottish outfit SILEAS). Completed by accordionist Karen Tweed, The POOZIES were depicted as the country's premiere all-women Celtic roots supergroup, although after a few sets Sally (who had been married since 1984 to dairy farmer Chris Wakeford and had two sons) made way for KATE RUSBY.

Meanwhile, Hypertension Records continued to issue the odd EP, mini-set and full album, her early 1990s work crediting The Rhythm, alongside Boris Carlin and Les Sampson. Following on from **TANGO!** (1992) {*5}, her third album proper, **BEATING THE DRUM** (1992) {*6}, kept her profile high. Combining family life with that of her solo and POOZIES career took its toll on her vocal cords, and while there were still a few recordings here and there, problems with tonsillitis curtailed her activities slightly until she had a successful operation.

From **FAVOURITE DISH** (1996) {*6} to her most recent solo set **MAID IN ENGLAND** (2003) {*6}, BARKER has graduated from torch folk-singer to a leading light in the folk fraternity; sadly, her husband died in 2003. Having earlier featured on a 'Live At The Royal Albert Hall' SHOW OF HANDS set, she's also worked with PETE MORTON (she'd once covered his 'Another Train' ballad) and JANET RUSSELL, while in 2006 she reunited with the revamped POOZIES as the replacement for EILIDH SHAW. Taking four years out from performing, she gained her Music Technology degree from de Montfort University in June 2007; just over a year later she presented her stage show "Joni Mitchell Project", and one low-key CD was released as 'Conversation: The Joni Mitchell Tapes (Vol. 1) in 2010. Over the years Sally has covered many outsider folk songs, none more rivetingly than Genesis's 'I Know What I Like (In Your Wardrobe)' and Xtc's 'Farmboy's Wages'. *MCS*

Sally Barker - vocals, acoustic guitar

UK Old Dog — US not issued

Aug 88. (lp) *(PUP 1)* **IN THE SPOTLIGHT** (live at Bangor, Wales, 23-5-88)
- Crazy way to feel / Sugar daddy / The worry / Chuck E's in love / The river / Nocturnal visions / Stormy Monday / Strange ways / Poncho and Lefty / (I don't wanna be) Your woman no more / Alexis Korner (still sings the blues in Heaven) / Honky tonk woman / Love and affection. *(cd-iss. Aug 89 +=; PUP 1CD)* - Hunting the buffalo / Companion / Dirty work. *(re-iss. Sep 93 as 'SALLY BARKER' on Hypertension UK cd) (c/lp; HYCD 200103) (HY 200103 C/LP)*- Hunting the buffalo / Nocturnal visions / The worry / Companion / Sugar daddy / Crazy way to feel / The river / Strange ways / Dirty work / (I don't wanna be) Your woman no more / Alexis Korner (still sings the blues in Heaven) / Poncho and Lefty / Honky tonk woman / Stormy Monday / Chuck E's in love / Love and affection.

Hannibal — not issued

Mar 90. (cd/c/lp) *(HBCD/HNBC/HNBL 1356)* **THIS RHYTHM IS MINE**
- Money's talking / This rhythm is mine / Angry women / Lay your body down / While you sleep / Big world / Chinese whispers / Or did you jump / Married man / The simple life. *(re-iss. Sep 93 on Hypertension cd+=) (lp/c; HYCD 200106) (HY 200106 LP/C)*- Chains / Another train.

SALLY BARKER & THE RHYTHM

with **Boris Carlin** - fretless bass, vocals / **Les Sampson** - drums, vocals

Old Dog — not issued

Nov 90. (cd-ep) *(???)* MONEY'S TALKING — German
- Money's talking / Another train / Alexis Korner (still sings the blues in Heaven) / Honky tonk woman. *(UK cd-iss. Mar 95 on Hypertension+=; HYCD 200149)* - TANGO!

1992. (m-cd) *(HYCD 200118)* **TANGO!** — German
- Tango! / Bed's too big / The golden glove / Who knows where the time goes / Don't you lie to me / Last train home / Chains / Tango! (normal version). *(cd-iss.+=)* - MONEY'S TALKING

1992. (cd)(c) *(HYCD 200124)<HY 200124C>* **BEATING THE DRUM**
- Let's play the game / Elephants / The female rambling sailor (Rebecca's rig) / Iguana waltz / Tango! / Sad man's tears / Larger than life / Me and my big mouth / Happy days and lonely nights / A thousand faces / Beating the drum. *(UK-iss. Mar 95; same)*

—— In the early 1990s, BARKER was part of The POOZIES (alongside SILEAS's Scots members Mary MacMaster and Patsy Seddon) on two sets, 'Dansoozies' (1993) and 'Chantoozies' (1995).

SALLY BARKER

Hypertension — not issued

1996. (cd) *(HYCD 296 165)* **FAVOURITE DISH** — German
- Moses / Favourite dish / Blue moon / Landing light / The honeymoon is over / Hold on / Good woman / I know what I like (in your wardrobe) / Sleepy eyes / The wind, she carries.

Rideout — not issued

1998. (cd; by SALLY BARKER & KEITH RICHARD BUCK) *(098)* **PASSION AND THE COUNTESS:** A LIVE ALBUM
- Mr Bang / We built fires / Money's talking / Farmboy's wages / Hold on / Married man / Landing light / The honeymoon is over / Favourite dish / I know what I like (in your wardrobe) / Moses / Good woman / Female rambling sailor - Rebecca / Another train.

Old Dog — not issued

2003. (cd) *(none)* **MAID IN ENGLAND**
- Sirens / Sleep's descending / Maid in England / The ballad of Mary Rose

(incorporating Roger's tune) / Old horses / Comrades in arms / Fall from grace / ·Captains / Hauls away / Bird / The farm.

—— In 2006, she returned to join The POOZIES (see SILEAS ⟹ Celtic-folk book); see biog above; 2011 will see her return to the stage as a fully-fledged solo artist

- (8-10*) compilations -

Sep 00. (cd) *Hypertension; (HYCD 200 192)* **ANOTHER TRAIN** [ ] [–]
- Another train / Favourite dish / Money's talking / Sleepy eyes / American car / Hunting the buffalo / Angry women / We built fires / Elephants / Nocturnal visions / While you sleep / Chinese whispers / Moses / I know what I like (in your wardrobe) / Alexis Korner (still sings the blues in Heaven) / Die sorge.

Steffen BASHO-JUNGHANS

Born Steffen Junghans, 1953, in Saxony in what was then East Germany (GDR), Steffen was of course inspired by the great American guitar virtuoso ROBBIE BASHO, although one could add PETER WALKER, LEO KOTTKE and JOHN FAHEY to the list.

From his heady days in Wacholder (a cajun/folk group, but note that sets 'Crystal Palace' (1978) and 'Gin-phonic' (1984) were by a jazz outfit of the same name), painter Steffen settled on the meditative approach to his bottleneck textures. With more than a nod to country-blues, one of their best efforts was the 1983 release 'Herr Witt ...'

Overtly experimental and increasingly intense and metaphysical, his best work came with **WATERS IN AZURE** (2002) {*8}, **SONG OF THE EARTH** (2000) {*7}, **LATE SUMMER MORNING** (2006) {*7} – featuring the 22-minute title track – and the live-in-concert **IN THE MORNING TWILIGHT** (2006) {*7}. Tour de force ragas were carried out in hypnotic formulae, and nearly all his work can be vouched for if one is in a sombre but relaxed Sunday-morning mood. Truly out there, and reaching out to the galactic stars rather than to purist folk fans. *MCS*

Steffen Basho-Junghans - guitars

Ger/UK US
Blue Moment Arts not issued

1989. (c) *(BMA 001)* **12 STRING SOLO** [–] German [–]
- a) Opener - Nur ein moment - Funny und der wind - Traumland (Basho-suite) / b) Manchmal – Franzl's lacheln - Voices - Am abend nach dem fest - Konig Artus' letzter abend.

1995. (cd) *(BMA 003)* **IN SEARCH OF THE EAGLE'S VOICE** [–] German [–]
- In search of the eagle's voice / Legend of Mount Shasta / The four directions / Sweet silence / Wild horse rambler / Rolling thunder / Mighty echoes / Purple mountain raga / Nightbird's song / The moon chant.

1996. (cd) *(BMA 004)* **FLEUR DE LIS 1** [–] German [–]
- Il furioso / Omar Khayyam garden / Nuages d'azur / Little flower fantasy / A short story / Gudrun / Classical rites / Song of the river princess / Highlander 2 / Camelot fair / Three willows / Chinese rose / Easter.

1996. (cd) *(BMA 005)* **FLEUR DE LIS 2** [–] German [–]
- Bohemian overture / Little water suite / Variations on Van Gogh / Springwalk / Highlander 1 / Fantasia de Catalunya / The golden sumsaidad / Lotus interlude / Friedersdorfer walzer / New Shakespeare variations / Azur return.

not issued Sublingual

2000. (cd) <*SLR 008*> **SONG OF THE EARTH** [–] [ ]
- The grand entry / Red in the rainbow / Song of the Earth / Sweet moonlight revelations / The gates of delight / Warrior's lullaby / Silent skies.

Strange Attractor Audio House — Strange Attractorss Audio House

2001. (cd) *(<SAAH 002>)* **INSIDE** [–] German [ ]
- 1st movement / 2nd movement parts 1-3 / 3rd movement. *(UK-iss. Mar 03; same)*

Feb 02. (cd) *(<SAAH 005>)* **WATERS IN AZURE** [ ] [ ]
- Waters (parts I-III) / Inside the rain / One No.1 (parts I-III) / Azure No.1. *(UK-iss. Mar '03; same)*

Feb 03. (cd) *(<SAAH 010>)* **RIVERS AND BRIDGES** (live) [–] German [ ]
- The river suite / Hear the winds coming / The Takoma Bridge incident / Rainbow dancing / Autumn II / Epilogue. *(UK-iss. Mar 03; same)*

Apr 04. (d-cd) *(<SAAH 20-21>)* **7 BOOKS** (live) [ ] [ ]
- I / II / III // IV / V / VI / VII.

2006. (ltd-cd) *(KD 007)* **IN THE MORNING TWILIGHT** (live 25th July 2005 at Hagateatern, Goteberg, Sweden) [–] Sweden [–]
- In the morning twilight / (Excerpt) from 7 Books (I-II) / Last days of the dragons / Charlette / Wild horse ramble / (Excerpt) Waters I-III.

(above issued on Kning Disk) (below on Locust Records)

Aug 06. (cd) *(<L 82>)* **LAST DAYS OF THE DRAGONS** [ ] [ ]
- The immortal chimes (Azure No.12) / A lost moment / Days of the dragon / A secret song / Dance of the young spirits / Southern crossings / And only the stars know... / The end's waltz.

Oct 06. (cd) *(<SAAH 045>)* **LATE SUMMER MORNING** [ ] [ ]
- Late summer morning / In a secret garden / Woodland orchestra / Azure No.3 / Northern winds / Sky dreamer's gold.

Architects Of Harmonic Rooms not issued

Nov 09. (lp) *(AOHRAR 01)* **IS** [–] German [–]
- When the plains are singing / Changes / Azure No.8 / Waiting for the clouds / Leaving Eden / ... And like wind we go.

Beartown not issued

Nov 09. (ltd-c-90) *(none)* **O SOM NAHA** [–] German [–]
- Parts 1-9b.

- (5-7*) compilations, others, etc.-

2001. (cd) *(BMA 006)* **LANDSCAPES IN EXILE** (recorded late 1998) [–] German [–]
- Filling the skies / Hundred birds courting the phoenix A/B / Landscapes in exile 1 / Landscapes in exile 2 / Wild geese alighting on the sandy shore / Flowery moonlight.

2005. (cd) *Sillyboy; (008CD)* **UNKNOWN MUSIC 1: ALIEN LETTER** [–] Italy [–]
- I / II (Kottke on Mars 1) / III / IV / V / VIa / VIb (Kottke on Mars 1) / VII / VIII / IX / X.

Oct '05. (cd) *Preservation Hall; (PRE 007)* **UNKNOWN MUSIC II: TRANSWARP MEDITATION** [–] Austra [–]
- I / Out of the time / III / IV / V / Nothing but nice / VII.

Jenny BEECHING

Born September 19, 1950 in Romford, Essex, this multi-talented folk artist (who played piano and guitar) was something a child prodigy, while her family had aspired to the stage. Inspired by the work of DYLAN, BAEZ and the Greenwich Village scene of the mid-1960s, Jenny performed in the London-based trad duo Lorelei with Christina Williamson; she subsequently teamed up with fellow musician Dave Cooper.

Throughout the 1970s (while adding the banjo to her CV), BEECHING established herself both as a solo artist and in a duo alongside equally gifted pianist/guitarist Tony Cliff. In fact, he was one of the sidemen (and writer of 'Onion Tears') on her debut LP alongside Steve Keith (violin) and Derek Simpson (melodeon). **A RIGHT SONG AND DANCE** (1979) {*6} was a collection of beautifully sung blues, jazz and swing-style tracks (Duke Ellington's 'I Got It Bad' was one such cut) delivered in a folk fashion.

Her second set, **NO MORE SAD GOODBYES** (1983) {*6}, featured top-notch guitarists PHIL BEER (also mandolin & violin), BERT JANSCH and Stan Gordon, alongside bassist Alan Morgan and drummer Roger Edgeson, while the record (yet to be issued on CD!) was released only in Italy.

1984/5 saw Jenny collaborate with ZUMZEAUX fiddler Chris Haigh (and the band Hotline), and one LP, **HOTLINE FROM LONDON** {*5} – issued only in Yugoslavia – made it out in 1986. Unusual in that she also busked and did a bit of teaching, Jenny would earn a BA in anthropology and geography. Her thesis went under the title: 'Buskers: Good For Nothing Or Good For Business?' One might think she could still be a teacher. *MCS*

Jenny Beeching - vocals, piano, acoustic guitar, banjo

UK US
MKS not issued

1979. (lp) *(MKS 001)* **A RIGHT SONG AND DANCE** [ ] [–]
- Rain / Love is pleasing / I got it bad / Onion tears / Never swat a fly / etc.

Appaloosa not issued

1983. (lp) *(AP 029)* **NO MORE SAD GOODBYES** [–] Italy [–]
- Susie's one night stand / In Cyprus / A leaf must fall / Taking the good with the bad / If you knew what it does to my heart / Breakaway / No more sad goodbyes / Sitting in a bar / Weather man / Pass the hat around / My man o' war / We can't get along.

A Soska-Jugoton not issued

1986. (lp; by JENNY BEECHING & CHRIS HAIGH) *(ULP-1787)* **HOTLINE FROM LONDON** [–] Yugo [–]
- Busking bebop / That's what friends are for / No strings attached / Trouble in mind / Flat broke / Frankie and Johnny / Lover man / Marco / The wedding on the Isle of Skye / Norwegian wood.

—— Jenny went back to education to study for her BA.

Phil BEER (⟹ SHOW OF HANDS)

Helen BELL

For a time in the early half of the 2000s, the name of HELEN BELL (and her trio OLA) looked a certainty to be folk's next big thing. Squeezing time in between her studies at York University, the year 2000 saw the fiddle and viola player release two albums, the solo **AUDIERNE** {*6} – featuring guitarist Ed Pritchard – and **THE ANIMALS ARE IN THE WEST** {*7}, the latter with BBC Radio Young Folk Award nominees OLA (Bell, Sarah Wright and Michael Jary); the self-released group follow-up **BE PREPARED FOR WEATHER** (2003) is rather rare.

One of her best-known compositions, 'Broken Town' found its way to being covered on JACKIE OATES's eponymous debut set in 2006, while an interview with Dr. Lindsay Aitkenhead on folk viola exponents, part of Dr Aitkenhead's research for her own thesis, conferred some academic prestige.

Along with singer/songwriter Tom Drinkwater (on guitar and bouzouki), she was part of PILLOWFISH, an eclectic duo with a penchant for prog-folk recalling the quirkiness of ROBIN WILLIAMSON or Tymon Dogg. **COMMON KNOWLEDGE** (2006) {*7} was a cocktail of political seriousness and OTT ditties of whimsical interplay; it's a pity it didn't include their version of ANDY IRVINE's 'Never Tire Of The Road', which has seen light only on a subsequent promo EP. *MCS*

Helen Bell - viola, fiddle / with Ed Pritchard (guitar)

UK: Little Acorn — US: not issued

2000. (cd) *(LACRCD 1)* **AUDIERNE** [ ] [–]

OLA

Helen Bell plus **Sarah Wright** - bodhran, flute, vocals / **Michael Jary** - English concertina

Green Fingers — not issued

2000. (cd) *(GFMCD 25)* **THE ANIMALS ARE IN THE WEST** [ ] [–]
- Fly up the hill to Beverly / Rosebud in June / Trip to Brittany / Reynard the fox – Clumsy lover / Si beg si mor / Rosie and Jim / Bold Riley / Catharsis – Tongadale / Toby / Harrison's moggis / Blue murder – Reel Beatrice / Kissing animals is better.

self-rel. — not issued

2003. (cd) *(none)* **BE PREPARED FOR WEATHER** [ ] [–]

PILLOWFISH

Tom Drinkwater - vocals, bouzouki, acoustic guitar / **Helen Bell** - viola, fiddle

Pillowfish — not issued

2006. (cd) *(PFCD 0601)* **COMMON KNOWLEDGE** [ ] [–]
- Seven stolen stars / The revolution will be in colour / The first bonfire – Pillowfish / Addiction / The ice sculptor / The world to mend / Cruel sea / Move your money / Hunting the off-licence – Trip to Heligoland / She's so dark / Fingerprints and smudges.

—— in 2007, they released a promo EP.

BELLOWHEAD

A Brit-folk supergroup, 10-piece BELLOWHEAD (featuring SPIERS & BODEN, DR FAUSTUS members BENJI KIRKPATRICK and Paul Sartin, Rachael McShane, Pete Flood, Giles Lewin, Andy Mellon, Brendan Kelly and Justin Thurgur) kicked off their folk-musical campaign with a well-received mini-set of sorts, **E.P.ONYMOUS** (2004) {*6}. Comprising five tracks over more than 25 minutes, this was country-dance goes gypsy-folk via 'Copshawholme Fair', 'Rochdale Coconut Dance' and the uplifting 'Prickle-Eye Bush'.

Initially showcased when invited to perform at the first Oxford Folk Festival in April 2004, BELLOWHEAD were a breath of fresh air for a revived English folk scene, and rewards were just around the corner when they won Best Live Act at the Radio 2 Folk Awards in 2005.

2006 saw the addition of Gideon Juckes on their debut set **BURLESQUE** {*7}. An hour long, it featured mostly traditional numbers performed on conventional folk instruments: SPIERS and main vocalist BODEN played fiddle and anglo-concertina/melodeon respectively, while others provided chaotic, fairground-like exotic brass and string accompaniment, and even bagpipes. McShane sang on a handful of tracks including 'Jordan', while other highlights were opener 'Rigs Of The Time', 'The Outlandish Knight' and 'London Town'.

Equally exciting, **MATACHIN** (2008) {*8} proved the ensemble were no one-trick pony. Songs such as 'Fakenham Fair', 'Cholera Camp' (a Rudyard Kipling poem set to music by PETER BELLAMY), the eerie 'Widow's Curse' and 'Bruton Town' were executed with tight precision for such a large group. Note that Sam Sweeney had now superseded Lewin.

Credited to BELLOWHEAD, but basically pieced together under an umbrella for various individual members, **UMBRELLOWHEAD** (2009) {*6} was next in line. Apart from group opener 'Unclothed Nocturnal Manuscript Crisis', the rest of the cuts were a rummage through the repertoires of associated bands including CHAVO (Mellon's outfit), BELSHAZZAR'S FEAST (Sartin & Co.), Setsubun Bean Unit (Kelly and Flood's act) and solo/duo offerings from SPIERS & BODEN and FAUSTUS (Kirkpatrick, Sartin and outsider Saul Rose).

With incomer Ed Neuhauser replacing Juckes, **HEDONISM** (2010) {*7} hoisted the band to new heights, once again setting sea-shanty stylings alongside big-trad-band folk. From sprightly Celtic opener 'New York Girls' to a reading of Jacques Brel's 'Amsterdam', no other group was as ambitious and adventurous as BELLOWHEAD. *MCS*

Jon Boden - vocals, fiddle, bagpipes (of SPIERS & BODEN) / **John Spiers** - melodeon, vocals (of SPIERS & BODEN) / **Benji Kirkpatrick** - mandolin, bouzouki, banjo, guitar (of DR FAUSTUS) / **Giles Lewin** - fiddle, bagpipes (ex-MADDY PRIOR CARNIVAL BAND) / **Paul Sartin** - fiddle, oboe (of DR FAUSTUS, of BELSHAZZAR'S FEAST) / **Brendan Kelly** - saxophones (of Setsubun Bean Unit) / **Andy Mellon** - trumpet / **Justin Thurgur** - trombone / **Rachael McShane** - cello, vocals / **Pete Flood** - percussion, cutlery (of Setsubun Bean Unit)

UK: Megafone — US: Megafone

Oct 04. (m-cd) *(<111>)* **E.P.ONYMOUS** [ ] Apr 95 [ ]
- Rambling sailor / Jack Robinson / Copshawholme fair / Rochdale coconut dance / Prickle-eye bush.

—— added **Gideon Juckes** (of Setsubun Bean Unit) - sousaphone, tuba, helicon, vocals

Westpark — not issued

Oct 06. (cd) *(87132)* **BURLESQUE** [ ] [–]
- Rigs of the time / Jordan / Across the line / London town / Sloe gin: a) Frozen gin, b) The vinegar reel, c) The sloe / Courting too slow / Flash company (the yellow handkerchief) / Hopkinson's favourite / One May morning early (by the green grove) / The outlandish knight (child 4) / Frog legs (or Fete du village) – Dragon's teeth / Fire marengo / Death and the lady.

—— **Sam Sweeney** (of KERFUFFLE) - fiddle, pipes; repl. Lewin

Navigator — not issued

Sep 08. (cd/lp) *(NAVIGATOR 017 CD/LP)* **MATACHIN** [ ] [–]
- Fakenham fair / Roll her down the bay / Vignette I / I drew my ship across the harbour / Kafoozalum - The priest's miss / Cholera camp / Vignette II / Whiskey is the life of man / Spectre review / Widow's curse / Bruton town / Trip to Bucharest - The flight of the folk mutants parts 1 & 2 / Vignette III.

Nov 09. (cd) *(112)* **UMBRELLOWHEAD** [ ] [–]
- Unclothed nocturnal manuscript crisis (BELLOWHEAD) / Ganka's song (Gankino) (CHAVO) / The fisherman (RACHAEL McSHANE) / Master Kilby (PETE FLOOD) / Rondo a la turkey: Rondo a la turka - Turkey in the straw - Yakety sax (BELSHAZZAR'S FEAST) / Wallbreaker (BENJI KIRKPATRICK) / Beating the bounds (JON BODEN) / Gujo ondo (SETSUBUN BEAN UNIT) / The beginning (JUSTIN THURGUR) / The new deserter (FAUSTUS) - Gaol song (HANNAH JAMES & SAM SWEENEY) / Tom Padget (SPIERS & BODEN) / Marunouchi (FARMYARD ANIMALS TRIO feat. PETE FLOOD, BRENDAN KELLY & GIDEON JUCKES) / Psalm 143 (The CHOIR OF CHRISTCHURCH CATHEDRAL, DUBLIN).

(above issued on Megaphone Records)

—— **Ed Neuhauser** - sousaphone, helicon, tuba; repl. Juckes

Oct 10. (cd/lp) *(NAVIGATOR 042 CD/LP)* **HEDONISM** [86] [–]
- New York girls / A-begging I will go / Cross-eyed and chinless / Broomfield hill / The hand weaver and the factory maid / Captain Wedderburn / Amsterdam / Cold blows the wind / Parson's farewell / Little Sally Racket / Yarmouth town.

BELSHAZZAR'S FEAST

Their name taken from a 17th-century biblical painting by Rembrandt, fiddler Paul Sartin (also of BELLOWHEAD and DR. FAUSTUS) and accordionist Paul Hutchinson were two of the growing legion of Bright Young Folk things. Formed in 1995 in Cornwall, England, this chamber-folk partnership combined playful humour and melancholy virtuoso instrumentation over several albums from **ONE TOO MANY** (1996) {*6}, their first for Wild Goose Records, to **FIND THE LADY** (2010) {*7}after moving to One Little Indian Records. Traditionalists in every sense of the word, they augmented the latter set with percussionist Pete Flood (of BELLOWHEAD), viola player JACKIE OATES and guitarist JIM MORAY. Medley tracks such as 'Widows Shall All Have Husbands – Hey Boys Up Go We', 'Royal Flush – Elephant Stairs', 'Queen Of Hearts – Well Done Jack' and 'Bloomsbury Market – Bloomsbury Hypermarket' fared best of all, their exacting "Captain Pugwash" template more or less set on other albums like **DROP THE REED** (1998) {*6}, **MR KYNASTON'S FAMOUS DANCE** (2000) {*6}, **JOHN PLAYFORD'S SECRET BALL** (2001) {*7}, **MR KYNASTON'S FAMOUS DANCE VOL.2** (2002) {*6}, the comeback double studio/live set **THE FOOD OF LOVE** (2008) {*7} and the festive **FROST BITES** (2009) {*6}. These recordings were a long way away from Sartin's time at the Purcell School of Music and his choral scholarship at Magdalen College, Oxford, and from Hutchinson's time as a choirmaster/organist and with dance band The Old Pull And Push. *MCS*

Paul Sartin - vocals, fiddle, oboe / **Paul Hutchinson** - accordion

UK Wild Goose — US not issued

1996. (cd) *(WGS 276CD)* **ONE TOO MANY** ☐ ⊟
- One too many / Boda waltz – Far away / Doll thy ale – Romanian dance / Museum hornpipe / Midnight on the water – Molly Rankin's / Cold frosty morn – Dancing bear / Wedding dance – Wild horseman / Hills of the north / Barbara Allen – Copper pipe polka / Fairy reel – Dick Gossip's. *(re-iss. 2010 on Terra Nova; TERRCD 022)*

1998. (cd) *(WGS 293CD)* **DROP THE REED** ☐ ⊟
- The May reels / Half Hannikin – The recruiting officer / The miller of Dee – La belle Jardiniere – Ebenezer / La petite nette – Fransk Morgenstjerne / Ffarwell Ned Pugh – Mae Mwhn Dwedyd / Mister Costa – Beggars roost / Auvergne polka – Cafouilee / Four babies rants / Twenty eighteen / Air / Brouillard – Les cloches. *(re-iss. Oct 05; same)*

2000. (cd) *(WGS 298CD)* **MR KYNASTON'S FAMOUS DANCE** ☐ ⊟
- Merry conclusion / Blenheim House / Queen of hearts / Lille / Count Leon / Wou'd you have a young virgin / Paston's maggot / Old Simon the king / Neat Mr John / Cupid disarm'd / Bonny grey ey'd morn / Woodstock park. *(d-cd-iss. Aug 03 +=; WGS 314CD)* - VOL.2

2001. (cd) *(WGS 304CD)* **JOHN PLAYFORD'S SECRET BALL** ☐ ⊟
- Maiden lane / Parsons farewell / Goddesses / The garland / Mundesse / Bobbing Joe / Jennie pluck pears / Cuckolds all a row / The fits come on me now / London gentlewomen / The maid peeped out at the window / Parson upon Dorothy / Gathering peascods / The old mole.

2002. (cd) *(WGS 310CD)* **MR KYNASTON'S FAMOUS DANCE VOL.2** ☐ ⊟
- Softly good tummas / Whiskers / The she favourite / Deil take the warr / Vaughans ramble / Whitsun holidays / Bickerstaffes prophesie / Evans delight / Fops fancy / Dudmason hall / The gay young squire / Old hob / Orange nan / Well done Jack. *(d-cd-iss.+=)* - MR KYNASTON'S FAMOUS DANCE

—— the duo was put on hold while Sartin moonlighted with BELLOWHEAD

May 08. (d-cd) *(WGS 353CD)* **THE FOOD OF LOVE** ☐ ⊟
- Mundesse – Gathering peascods / Twenty, eighteen / Softly good tummas – Shropshire lass / Doll thy ale – Rumanian dance / Rondo a la Turkey / Calne – Be careful in choosing a wife / Best of friends – Bishop of Chester's jig / Gentle Diana – Navvy man / Cal / Back and sides / Music for a found harmonium // [live]: Introduction / Boda waltz – Miss Love's waltz / Tommy Jenkins – Hunt the squirrel / La belle jardiniere – Ebenezer / Goliath of Gath / Ffarwell Ned Pugh – Something unpronounceable / Eine kleine nachtmusik – Spring from The Four Seasons / Hashbaz.

Nov 09. (cd) *(WGS 366CD)* **FROST BITES** [festive] ☐ ⊟
- Cherry tree carol – Yuleogy / King Herod and the cock – Parson's farewell / Tomorrow shall be my dancing day / Masquerade Royal – As Joseph was a-walking / Lonesome scenes of winter / Gerald road mazurkas – Sans day carol / One cold morning in December / Hampshire mummers' song.

One Little Indian — not issued

Sep 10. (cd) *(TPLP 1080CD)* **FIND THE LADY** ☐ ⊟
- Wild rover / Widows shall all have husbands / Thresherman / Queen of hearts – Well done Jack / Primus hornpipe / Lull me beyond thee / Turtle dove / Bloomsbury market – Bloomsbury hypermarket / Circle of biscuits / Queen of the May / Royal flush – Elephant stairs / Home lad, home.

BIG EYES

One of the new breed of neo-folk outfits, BIG EYES were led by singer/accordionist James Green, accompanied by fellow songwriters Mark Rimmer (guitar) and Katherine Wood (violin and vocals); there were places too for bassist Neil Shumsky and melodica player Elodie Ginsbourg. Unconventional to say the least, their blend of "freak folk" combined elements of eastern exotica, psychedelia and the avant-garde.

Hailing from Leeds but signing to Leicester's small independent Pickled Egg Records, their first studio outing was the mini-set **SONGS** (2000) {*7}, a record with each track clocking in at only a minute or two.

Receiving Radio 1 airplay from John Peel, their debut album proper, **CLUMSY MUSIC** (2001) {*8}, spread further afield, independent radio stations in Belgium making it an end-of-year near-poll-topper. With a guest spot from cellist Bela Emerson and pieces about cats ('Tibbs' and 'Sammy'), the album of 29 songs was definitely on the fringes of folk, or on the dark side rather than in the heart of the genre. Examples include the conversational (and longest item) 'Boots Locked'.

For the follow-up, **LOVE IS GONE MAD** (2002) {*7}, Mark was replaced by percussionist Andrew Brown. An even darker effort than its predecessor, it flitted between the melodramatic ('Big Eyes At Sea', 'Jeffrey's Teeth' and 'Country Bust') and the minimalistic ('Magic Sparks' and 'Baby Wing').

Following the addition of songwriter/musician David A. Jaycock, James Green and group were back after a short break. For the self-explanatory **WE HAVE NO NEED FOR VOICES WHEN OUR HEARTS CAN SING** (2004) {*6}, their sound was stripped back, leaving cinematic acoustics (and several vocal spots) splintered with moody and ambitious string "undertures". Terry Edwards of Gallon Drunk/Tindersticks featured as a guest, while highlights came courtesy of 'Spidersong', 'David's Lovesong' and 'Bugle Junior'.

To reflect the adjustments to the group, the basic duo settled on the new title of The BIG EYES FAMILY PLAYERS. This was a collaborative act that had room for such indie luminaries as JAMES YORKSTON (from The Fence Collective), Rachel Grimes (of Rachel's), Jeremy Barnes (of A HAWK AND A HACKSAW), James William Hindle (Track And Field), Suzy Mangion (of George), and a host of others to augment the 2006 comeback set **DO THE MUSIKING** {*6}.

Released a few months after an album with YORKSTON ('Folk Songs'), **WARM ROOM** (2009) {*6} featured only James (JAYCOCK was now a solo artist), his ever-evolving band included drummer Chris Boyd, Ellie Bond (violin), Gemma Green (harmoniflute) and Heather Ditch (vocals). Though at times far removed from the folk genre, there was still the odd minstrel piece, namely 'White Bones', 'Striptease' and 'False True Love'. Green's/BIG EYES' second cd-r, **FAMILY FAVOURITES** {*6}, released in 2011, was basically reworkings of earlier pieces such as 'Otto', 'The Chattering Lady', etc. *MCS*

James Green - vocals, guitars, accordion, keyboards, cello / **Mark Rimmer** - guitar, harmonium / **Katherine Wood** - violin, vocals / **Neil Shumsky** - bass / **Elodie Ginsbourg** - melodica

UK Pickled Egg — US not issued

May 00. (10" m-lp/m-cd) *(EGG 21/+CD)* **SONGS** ☐ ⊟
- Red tricycle / The boo girl / Dog eared / Big eyes / Long song / Gin head / Bad dream / Brain cell / Curled up / Feathers / Puppet show / Reprise of the big eyes.

Feb 01. (cd) *(EGG 29CD)* **CLUMSY MUSIC** ☐ ⊟
- Tibbs (cat song 1) / Cruisers / The optimist / Back seat / Llandysul / Odd company / The chattering lady / Life rattle / Loom / Heavy heart / Sleep / Becherovka / Samba sedation / Three left feet / Don't be shy / Pappy / Fuzzy felts / Le bonheur urbain / Sammy (cat song 2) / Carpet sleepers / Mohair / Boots locked / Night night.

2001. (ltd-7" shared) *(Delilah/Whiskey 33)* BIG EYES // EMPRESS ☐ ⊟
- Dead wood / Casper // [two tracks by Empress].

(above issued on Jonathon Whiskey)

—— **Andrew Brown** - percussion, drums; repl. Mark

Mar 02. (cd) *(EGG 36CD)* **LOVE IS GONE MAD** ☐ ⊟
- Magic sparks / Fast, loose and lovely / Big eyes at sea / Country dust / Mr Spy / Conway / Lovers leap / Lament for the lost ones / The victim / Amateur dramatics / Baby swing / Jeffrey's teeth / Lucha de Gatos / Inside / 1901 / Someone's dozin'.

—— added (guest on previous set) **David A. Jaycock** - vocals, guitar, harmonium

Mar 03. (7" ep) *(EGG 45)* I SEE CREATURES ☐ ⊟
- Gentle neck / Blackbeak / Death dance.

Mar 04. (cd) *(EGG 49CD)* **WE HAVE NO NEED FOR VOICES WHEN OUR HEARTS CAN SING** ☐ ⊟
- Otto / Spidersong / Exercise No.1 / David's love song / Lonesome pouch / Daedalus / Iceman / A second heavy heart / Bugle junior / Exercise No.2 / Laughing gas / Drunken ghost dance / On twigs / At Claydon Point / Podsley's lullaby / A stalker's song.

—— In Sep 05, James William Hindle & JAMES GREEN released the CD 'The Goat'.

The BIG EYES FAMILY PLAYERS

Jaycock + **Green** added **Katherine Jackson** (violin), **Gemma Green** (clarinet), **Rachel Grimes** (piano), **Jamie Crewe** (harp), **Jeremy Barnes** (percussion, drums), **Shaun Alcock** (drums), **Lindsay Aitkenhead** (viola, violin), **James William Hindle, Suzy Manion** + **James Yorkston** (vocals)

May 06. (cd) *(EGG 61)* **DO THE MUSIKING** ☐ ⊟
- Golden / Mr. Laurel's lapse / Absolute endings / For Gorecki / Owlet moth / Aquatopiate / For cognac / Doreen / Cuckoo without a clock / Prankyar / Sunday jacket / Bobo square / I just don't understand / Ballad of the blue lantern / Bear and butterfly / Die nacht / Shanty for Darty / Tresaith / A dream of fires / Olive / Going home / Lapping / Eight wrong choices / The printmaker's dilemmas / Cloak / And as you ask for trouble / The night jar / The two men who was one / Diweddglo.

—— **Jaycock** + **Green** added **Chris Boyd** - drums

2008. (cd-r) *(none)* DONKEYSONGS ⊟ Ire ⊟
- Snowflake runt / Lavinia / Donkeys disturbed by a meteor shower / Clunk orm / The orange miller / Yellow bird march / Leave your memories in the past / An improvised drowning.

(above was issued on Rusted Nail Records)

—— Green and co. also augmented JAMES YORKSTON on the 'Folk Songs' (2009) set

—— **James** + **Chris** added **Heather Ditch** - vocals / **Ellie Bond** - violin / + **Gemma Green** - harmoniflute (JAYCOCK had already gone solo)

Nov '09. (cd) *(EGG 72)* **WARM ROOM**
- Worried go / Striptease / Woodenwheel / A lick and a promise / White bones / Galapagos / Rojo / The green pin dance / False true love / Song for Newborough warren.

Apr '11. (cd-r) *(none)* **FAMILY FAVOURITES** [retakes of early work]
- Amateur dramatics / Jack / The boo girl / Otto / Three wheels / Bunny / The chattering lady / Fast, loose and lovely / For Gorecki / Lewis. waltz (reprise).

BISIKER & ROMANOV

Formed as a duo in the summer of 1987, Mick Bisiker and Al Romanov released only one record together (the eponymous **BISIKER & ROMANOV** (1988) {*7}), but it was held in such high esteem that it won the Music Retailers Association award for the best folk album of the year.

Classical guitarist and pianist Mick had cut his teeth running the university folk club in Birmingham and subsequently performing with early-1980s folk acts Cogglers Awl (alongside guitarist Roger Huckle) and Falstaff (adding flautist Clair Davenport and bassist John Davis); of the existence of any independent LPs is uncertain.

Fellside Records maintained their faith in BISIKER after Romanov attempted a career in classical/chamber music. His solo **HOME AGAIN** (1991) {*6} was a nice enough effort but sadly overlooked by the folk majority. BISIKER was back in business in the mid-1990s with The BAND OF RACK & RUIN. Other original members were John Davis, Keith Butterfield, Phil Wright and John Large, but only mail-order CDs were issued. *MCS*

Mick Bisiker (b. July 3 1958, Redhill, Surrey) - vocals, acoustic guitar, bouzouki / **Al Romanov** (b. Ralph Allin, February 29 1964, Halesowen, Birmingham) – fiddle

UK Fellside — US not issued

Nov 88. (lp/c) *(FE 068/+C)* **BISIKER & ROMANOV**
- The Wey and Arun canal / Hungarian dance / When the wind blows / The kid on the mountain / The fox / Josika / Down the moor / Jarrow march / Czardas / The eve's end.

—— the pair split, Romanov venturing into classical music

MICK BISIKER

1991. (cd/c) *(FE 083 CD/C)* **HOME AGAIN**
- Home again / Don't you go / Jigs / Katy Jane / Si beag si mor – Rose of Allendale / Maid from the shore / Mossy green banks of the Lea / Jigs and reels / Downhills of life / Rainbow's end. *(cd re-iss. Oct '99; same)*

—— Mick augmented Davey Slater on 'One More Curtain Call' (1994)

The BAND OF RACK & RUIN

Bisiker plus **John Davis** - bass / **Keith Butterfield** + **Phil Wright** + **John Large**

own label — not issued

1996. (cd/c) *(none)* **BALL & CHAIN** — mail-o
- Benjamin Bowmaneer / Back in your arms / The nightingale / Kid on the mountain - Silver spear / Maid from the shore / Greyhound / The two magicians / Ball and chain / Gypsy dancer / Condemned man's jig - Merry blacksmith - Reel of rack and ruin / The rover's lament.

—— new line-up: **Bisiker** plus **Nigel Ward** - fiddle, guitar / **Chris Radley** - bass, vocals (ex-The Trial, ex-Dead After Dark, of Firedaze) / **Duncan Arrow** - drums

1999. (cd) *(none)* **BOTH ENDS OF THE STREET** — mail-o
- Both ends of the street / Restless sea / Hullican jig - Dukes delight - Maid behind the bar / Nothing's changed / Where I'd rather be (tonight) / Hold me girl / Langstrom's pony - Nine points of roguery / Curse of the traveller / Wild mountain thyme.

2000. (d-cd) *(none)* **HARD TIMES** (live at The Fiddle and Bone, Birmingham) — mail-o
- Athol Highlanders / Nothing's changed / The nightingale / Restless sea / Where I'd rather be (tonight) / Maid from the shore / Farmer's boy / Back in your arms / The two magicians / Mick's reels / Dublin, you're breakin' my heart / Love on the street / Both ends of the street / The hard times of old England / Step it out Mary / The rover's lament / Time's a healer / Star of the County Down / Merry blacksmith - Reel of rack and ruin / London road / My young man.

—— Ward also divided his time with The Oddsods and Bailey & Ward

2005. (cd; as RACK AND RUIN) *(none)* **GONE TO ...** — mail-o
- Kesh jig / Livin' in the city / Bonnie light horseman / Calum Donaldson - The windlass / McMahon's - Killarney boys of pleasure / Love on the streets / Star of the County Down / Langstrome pony - Far from home / Mossy green banks of the Lea / Time's a healer / You can dance / Tell her I am - Lady Anne Montgomery - Knotted cord / Sheebag Sheemore - Rose of Allendale.

—— BISIKER & WARD have also issued 'The Hard Working Boater' (2005); Ward, solo, has released 'Cosmic Rhymes'(2008) and 'Destiny' (2009).

BLACK FLOWERS (⟹ TREMBLING BELLS)

James BLACKSHAW

On a mission to recreate the 12-string guitar wizardry of 1960s/70s blues-folk icons LEO KOTTKE, PETER LANG, JOHN FAHEY, ROBBIE BASHO and SANDY BULL, while standing tall amongst newbie modern-day contemporaries GLENN JONES and JACK ROSE, the youthful JAMES BLACKSHAW brings innovation and experimental skill to the acoustic musical table.

Born late 1981 in London, his mainly limited-edition, self-released CD-r albums have created quite a storm since the hypnotic **CELESTE** {*7} mini-set was released early in 2004. Combining guitar with Farfisa organ and cymbals, BLACKSHAW finger-picks his way through spiritual Eastern ragas with melody and flair. In two parts of around a quarter-hour each, each rhythm shapeshifts towards an almost mantra-rush climax. Thanks to New York imprint Tompkins Square, the album would be officially released to an ever-increasing fanbase.

The same outlet was responsible for BLACKSHAW's second effort proper, **LOST PRAYERS AND MOTIONLESS DANCES** (2004) {*7}, initially available to only 200 lucky aficionados (there was a split LP, White Goddess, with Davenport). Unlike his previous folk LP, harmonium drones suffused the first quarter of this lengthy 34-minute display of technical diversity, while the chords of C F C F C F maintained the infectious balance of free-form rhythm and master-class picking. The aforementioned WHITE GODDESS was added to the CD re-issue update.

Bells and bowed cymbals shrouded the opening of JB's third CD-r, **SUNSHRINE** (2005) {*7}, another release in limited form, although this time it stretched to 1000 copies (Tompkins Square was again behind the re-issue proper). Tuning twelve-string and six-string to C G C G C F, the multi-textured, 26-minute title track is the showpiece here. BLACKSHAW simply transcends the spirit and ethos of Brit-folkers BERT JANSCH and DAVY GRAHAM, moving the 1960s to the 2000s. Playing a six-string, the guitarist gets back to basics on the second and final track, 'Skylark Herald's Dawn', a rather shorter piece at just over three minutes but exquisite nevertheless.

His first official, proper CD release (not a CD-r), **O TRUE BELIEVERS** (2006) {*7}, was another giant step into acoustic instrumental territory (try C E C E C D). Ranging from the eighteen-minute 'The Elk With Jade Eyes' (complete with Indian tanpura and harmonium), via the eleven-minute 'Transient Life In Twilight', to the five-minute title-track finale, BLACKSHAW twists and turns with every joyous and meticulous note. More G-factor than X-Factor (G for guitar of course), James would win any such TV contest by a country mile, or maybe a folkie furlong.

An out-of-step live-in-Sweden set, **WAKING INTO SLEEP** (2006) {*5}, was thankfully overshadowed by the fifth studio album, **THE CLOUD OF UNKNOWING** (2007) {*7}, his first to gain a US release. Now in his mid-20s, BLACKSHAW showed signs of real maturity while finally breaking out into his own spiritual strum-storm. Opening with the multi-layered title track, his rhythmic fingerpicking offer endless possibilities. The two instrumentals that shine, 'Running To The Ghost' and the glorious fifteen-minute 'Stained Glass Windows' (both featuring accomplished violinist Fran Bury), are without question exemplary in craft and complexity. The Middle Eastern-meets-Morricone-styled 'The Mirror Speaks', has melodious moments of blissed-out, breakneck 12-string guitar that would make even Mike Oldfield envious. If music were a period building, BLACKSHAW would be its architect.

Again using Fran Bury on violin (and viola), **LITANY OF ECHOES** (2008) {*7} at times deviated from the alt-folk line and into the world of avant-classical, the examples being piano-led bookend tracks 'Gate Of Ivory' and 'Gate Of Horn' (think Philip Glass or Terry Riley). Pushing the boundaries of his own ambitious soundscapes, JB sets his sights on Eastern/Western transcendalisms in emotional and earthy pieces such as 'Past Has Not Passed', 'Echo And Abyss', 'Shroud' and his piece de resistance, 'Infinite Circle'.

Other projects such as BRETHREN OF THE FREE SPIRIT (alongside lute player Jozef Van Wissem), inspired by a heretical Christian order, made it a busy year for Blackshaw.

Two sets appeared in 2008, the lo-fi/ambient, Belgian-only set **ALL**

THINGS ARE FROM HIM, THROUGH HIM, AND IN HIM {*5} and **THE WOLF ALSO SHALL DWELL WITH THE LAMB** {*6}, the latter record a relaxing half-hour of 12-string (tuning D A D E A D) and baroque masterclass comprising experimental compositions rooted strictly in 13th/ 14th -century music.

With a move to Michael Gira's Young God imprint, **THE GLASS BEAD GAME** (2009) {*8} – named after a Hermann Hesse novel – was another dazzling display of acoustic atmospherics, including the nineteen-minute finale 'Arc'. Introducing vocalist Lavinia Blackwell (of TREMBLING BELLS) plus Current 93 newbies celloist John Contreras and violinist Joolie Wood (James had guested on the group's most recent recording, 'Aleph At Hallucinatory Mountain'), BLACKSHAW released yet another oblique-folk set, a suite in eight parts called **ALL IS FALLING** (2010) {*6}. *MCS*

James Blackshaw - 12-string acoustic guitar, Farfisa organ, cymbala, tamboura, harmonium, percussion

UK: Celebrate Psi Phenomenon — US: not issued

Jan 04. (cd-r) *(none)* **CELESTE**
- Celeste pt1 / Celeste pt2. *(ltd-re-iss. 2004 on Bark Fire; (BF 001) <(re-iss. Mar 08 on Tompkins Square; TSQ 1837)>*

UK: Bo' Weavil — US: Digitalis Industries

Nov 04. (ltd-cd-r) *<Digi 08>* **LOST PRAYERS AND MOTIONLESS DANCES**
- Lost prayers and motionless dances. *<(re-iss. Mar '08 on Tompkins Square+=; TSQ 1851)>* - WHITE GODDESS

Apr. '05. (ltd-cd-r) *<Digi 017>* **SUNSHRINE**
- Sunshrine / Skylark herald's dawn. *<(re-iss. Apr '08 on Tompkins Square; TSQ 1844)>*

May '05. (ltd-lp) *(Weavil 08)* **SUNSHRINE / CELESTE**

a split cd-r, White Goddess as DAVENPORT VS. JAMES BLACKSHAW, was issued on Static Records

UK: Important — US: Important

Feb '06. (cd) *(<IMPREC 084>)* **O TRUE BELIEVERS**
- Transient life in twilight / The elk with jade eyes / Spiralling skeleton memorial / O true believers. *(lp-iss. Sep '06 on Bo' Weavil; Weavil 13)*

UK: Kning Disk — US: not issued

Sep '06. (ltd-cd) *(KD 015)* **WAKING INTO SLEEP** (live Goteborg May 27, 2006) — Sweden
- Sunshrine / Celeste I / Transient life in twilight / Spiralling skeleton memorial.

UK: Tompkins Square - Fontana — US: Tompkins Square - Fontana

Jul 07. (cd/lp) *(<SQ 1967/TSQ 1974>)* **THE CLOUD OF UNKNOWING** — Jun 07
- The cloud of unknowing / Running to the ghost / Clouds collapse / The mirror speaks / Stained glass windows.

Jul 08. (cd) *(<TSQ 1783>)* **LITANY OF ECHOES** — Jun '08
- Gate of ivory / Past has not passed / Echo and abyss / Infinite circle / Shroud / Gate of horn.

UK: Young God — US: Young God

May 09. (cd/lp) *(<YG 40>)* **THE GLASS BEAD GAME**
- Cross / Bled / Fix / Key / Arc.

Aug 10. (cd) *(<YG 42>)* **ALL IS FALLING**
- (parts 1-8).

BRETHREN OF THE FREE SPIRIT

next was James's collaboration with **Jozef Van Wissem** - lute

UK: Incunabulum — US: not issued

2008. (ltd; m-cd/m-lp) *(AUDIOMER 001)* **ALL THINGS ARE FROM HIM, THROUGH HIM AND IN HIM** — Belg
- Attoka … wig - The lifting of the veil / All things are from him, through him and in him / How the unencumbered soul advises that one not refuse the calls of a good spirit / In him is no sin.

UK: Important — US: Important

Nov 08. (cd/lp) *(IMPREC 222)* **THE WOLF ALSO SHALL DWELL WITH THE LAMB**
- The sun tears itself from the heavens and comes crashing down from the mult… / The wolf also shall dwell with the lamb / Into the dust of the earth / I am a flower of Sharon and a rose in the valley.

Luka BLOOM

Born Kevin Barry Moore on May 23, 1955 in Newbridge, Ireland, he is the youngest sibling of Celtic-folk star CHRISTY MOORE. BLOOM was surrounded by music and musicians from an early age and began performing in his teens, his brother inviting him to play in his trad outfits PLANXTY and MOVING HEARTS. Initially recording under his real name of Barry Moore, he cut three obscure albums (**THE TREATY STONE** (1978) {*5}, **IN GRONINGEN** (1981) {*5} and **NO HEROES** (1982) {*5}) before relocating to the US (briefly in Washington DC, then more permanently in New York City) and adopting the name LUKA BLOOM. 'Luka' was taken from the SUZANNE VEGA song of the same name, and 'Bloom' after the protagonist of James Joyce's novel Ulysses. As these reference points might suggest, LUKA BLOOM purveys a highly articulate, intelligent strain of acoustic/electric folk. A tendon problem forced him to develop a strumming rather than finger-picking style. His eponymous debut as **LUKA BLOOM** (1988) {*4} was recorded in Dublin, and although it featured Leo Barnes of HOTHOUSE FLOWERS on sax, it failed to generate much interest, which led to its being withdrawn soon afterwards.

Securing a deal with Reprise Records at the turn of the decade, BLOOM released to all intents and purposes his debut album proper, the entirely self-written **RIVERSIDE** (1990) {*7}. Coming across like a more poetic, more precisely enunciated cross between Lloyd Cole and JACKIE LEVEN, one of BLOOM's guiding strengths was his way with arresting lyrical imagery, the echoes of his Celtic heritage sounding clearly through every chord and phrase. Classy tracks 'Dreams Of America' (revisited two decades later), 'An Irishman In China', 'Over The Moon' and 'The Man Is Alive' were certainly on the fringes of folk, sitting somewhere astride rock and rootsy pop.

1992's **THE ACOUSTIC MOTORBIKE** {*7} was just as good if not better, a perfectly conceived rap recital of LL Cool J's 'I Need Love' as wryly amusing as it was earnest, while his Celtic-ish reading of Elvis's 'Can't Help Falling In Love' was endearing at least.

In an attempt to capture the sound and atmosphere of his live show, BLOOM recorded **TURF** (1994) {*7} in a studio kitted out with stage, PA, etc. Diversions included the traditional song 'Black Is The Colour' and a cover of MIKE SCOTT's 'Sunny Sailor Boy', while social/political pieces 'Freedom Song' and 'Background Noise' showed he hadn't forgotten the troubles of his native country.

Without a label when Reprise let him go, almost half a decade went by without a release. He returned to Ireland, moving, via Dublin, to the village of Birr in County Offaly. Comeback set **SALTY HEAVEN** (1998) {*5} was a one-off for Sony (Shanachie in Ireland). His Irishness fully restored, the themes of 'Rainbow Warrior', the single 'Holy Ground' and 'Water Ballerina' showed exactly where his Celtic heart truly lay.

If his integration of pop-rock and Celtic-folk wasn't yet obvious to the naked ear, then covers set **KEEPER OF THE FLAME** (2000) {*6} laid the doubts to rest. Alongside tunes from The Cure ('In Between Days'), Radiohead ('No Surprises'), U2 ('Bad'), Bob Marley ('Natural Mystic'), Abba ('Dancing Queen'), Rose Royce ('Wishing On A Star'), Robbie Robertson ('Golden Feather') and Hunters And Collectors ('Throw Your Arms Around Me'), there were a handful from the folk-rock fraternity – DYLAN's 'Make You Feel My Love', JONI MITCHELL's 'Urge For Going', TIM HARDIN's 'If I Were A Carpenter' and the jazzy Charles Derringer-written title track.

BETWEEN THE MOUNTAIN AND THE MOON (2001) {*6} returned Luka to singer-songwriter status, and Sinead O'Connor was roped in to accompany him on 'Love Is A Place I Dream Of', while 'Perfect Groove' broadened his musical horizons with a strum-friendly jig-a-jig.

Following on from live set **AMSTERDAM** (2003) {*6}, BLOOM delivered the short and sweet (27-minute) **BEFORE SLEEP COMES** (2004) {*6}, a lilting mini-record comprising four self-penned ballads on Spanish guitar (he was recovering from a particularly bad bout of tendonitis) alongside traditional songs 'Singing Bird', 'She Moved Through The Fair', 'The Water Is Wide' and 'Nora'. The odd one out, 'I'll Walk Beside You', was an old Celtic-cross nugget.

Setting up his own Big Sky imprint at the age of fifty (Cooking Vinyl Records in the States), Luka the contemporary folk artist was back to his best with **INNOCENCE** (2005) {*7}, an introspective and intimate album highlighted by 'First Light Of Spring', 'City Of Chicago', 'Miracle Cure' and the VAN MORRISON-ish title track. Written with Simon O'Reilly, **TRIBE** {*5} surfaced in 2007, a blend of melodious and meditative material that incorporated aspects of country and rock. The NICK DRAKE-esque 'I Am A River' sat nicely alongside the devotional 'Peace Rains'.

More upbeat than usual (balanced with some quieter moments), and certainly taking a leaf from LEONARD COHEN's obvious-album-title book, **ELEVEN SONGS** (2008) {*6} found BLOOM in fine fettle, highlights including 'I'm On Your Side', 'Fire' and the uplifting, WATERBOYS-ish finale 'Don't Be Afraid Of The Light That Shines Within You'. If you'd missed

Luka's finest tracks, 2010's **DREAMS IN AMERICA** {*6} reprised and re-worked all his personal faves. *MCS*

Luka Bloom - vocals, acoustic guitar / with session people

UK Mulligan — US not issued

Sep 78. (lp; as BARRY MOORE) *(LUN 022)* **THE TREATY STONE** — Ire
- Girl / Black is the colour / Little martha and me (instrumental) / It's not good enough / Deep is the night / Jenny of the sun / Bury me at Wounded Knee / Sweet for Sue (instrumental) / Lonesome robin / The treaty stone.

—— next with Dutch session men + Eamon Murray - harmonicas, sax

Kloet — not issued

1981. (lp; by BARRY MOORE & EAMON MURRAY) *(KLOET 001)* **IN GRONINGEN** — Dutch
- Snowbird / The dog amongst the bushes / (a) One last cold kiss (b) The cold wind / Groningen / They're milking again / Our land / (a) The cliffs of Moher (b) Willy Coleman's / (a) I'll need your love (b) Between the sheets (c) Danny boy.

Ruby — not issued

1982. (lp; as BARRY MOORE) *(???)* **NO HEROES** — Ire
- German girl / Tired of here / Nothing new under the sun / Remember the brave ones / Isolation / Newbridge town / Winona / Our love / Feeling inside me / Mother, father, son.

Mystery — not issued

1988. (lp) *(MRLP 008)* **LUKA BLOOM** (rec. 1986) — Ire
- Wildlife / Parisienne / Gone to Pablo / Second skin / Rodrigo is home / Te adoro (instrumental) / It's a passion / Little boy / The way you talk to me / Delirious / Over the moon / Riding waves.

Reprise — Reprise

Feb 90. (cd/c/lp) *(<7599 26092-2/-4/-1>)* **RIVERSIDE**
- Delirious / Dreams in America / Over the moon / Gone to Pablo / The man is alive / An Irishman in Chinatown / Rescue mission / The one / Hudson lady / This is for life / You couldn't have come at a better time / The hill of Allen.

Jan 92. (cd) *(<7599 26670-2>)* **THE ACOUSTIC MOTORBIKE**
- Mary watches everything / You / I believe in you / I need love / Exploring the blue / This is your country / The acoustic motorbike / Can't help falling in love / Bones / Bridge of sorrow / Listen to the hoofbeat / Be well. *(re-iss. Jul 94; same)*

Feb 92. (c-s) <18989> I NEED LOVE

Warners — Warners

Jun 94. (cd/c) *(<9362 45608-2/-4>)* **TURF**
- Cold comfort / True blue / Diamond mountain / Right here, right now / Sunny sailor boy / Black is the colour / To begin to / Freedom song / Holding back the river / Background noise / The fertile rock / I did time / Sanctuary.

Sony — Shanachie

1998. (cd) *(491294-2) <SHCD 5739>* **SALTY HEAVEN** — 1999
- Blackberry time / The hungry ghost / Don't be so hard on yourself / Ciara / Rainbow warrior / Water ballerina / Holy ground / Cool breeze / The shape of love to come / Sanas / Forgiveness.

1999. (cd-s) <992> HOLY GROUND / I'm A Bogman

Evangeline — Bar/None

Nov 00. (cd) *(GEL 4015) <AHAON 119>* **KEEPER OF THE FLAME** — May 01
- Make you feel my love / In between days / Throw your arms around me / Bad / Keeper of the flame / Urge for going / No surprises / Wishing on a star / Golden feather *[US-only]* / Natural mystic / If I were a carpenter / Dancing queen.

Oct 01. (cd) <BRNCD 124> **BETWEEN THE MOUNTAIN AND THE MOON** — Jan 02
- Monsoon / Here and now / Perfect groove / Love is a place I dream of / Gabriel / Soshin / Moonslide / As I waved goodbye / I'm a bogman / Rainbow day / Hands of a farmer.

Big Sky — Evolver

Apr 03. (cd) *(BSCD 001) <2014>* **AMSTERDAM** (live February 11, 2002) — Ire
- Exploring the blue / Sunny sailor boy / Gone to Pablo / Natural mystic / You / Don't be so hard on yourself / Make you feel my love / Diamond mountain / Perfect groove / Monsoon / The fertile rock / Delirious / Gabriel. *(re-iss. Jun. 05 as 4xlp+=; 9035)* - If I were a carpenter / Ciara / Lily in the garden.

Big Sky — Bar/None

Sep 04. (m-cd) *(BSCD 002) <BRNCD 161>* **BEFORE SLEEP COMES** — Ire
- My singing bird / Before sleep comes / She moved through the fair (instrumental) / I'll walk beside you / Camomile / Be still now / Nora (instrumental) / The water is wide / She sings her songs with open eyes.

Big Sky — Cooking Vinyl

Feb 05. (cd) *(BSCD 003) <COOKCD 3367>* **INNOCENCE** — Mar 06
- Primavera / First light of spring / Innocence / Venus / Miracle cure / Peace on earth (instrumental) / Gypsy music / City of Chicago / June / Salvador / No matter where you go, there you are / Thank you for bringing me here / Larry Redicon's bow (instrumental). *<US+=>- Doing the best I can / I am not at war with anyone.*

Sep 07. (cd) *(BSCD 004) <COOKCD 4819>* **TRIBE** — Jul 07
- Tribe / Sound / I am a river / Change / Early morning (instrumental) / Out there / Dead of night / Star of Doolin (instrumental) / Homeless / Lebanon / Peace rains / Beara (instrumental).

Oct 08. (cd) *(BSCD 005)* **ELEVEN SONGS** — Ire
- There is a time / I'm on your side / I hear her, like Lorelei / I love the world I'm in / Sunday / Fire / When your love comes / See you soon / Eastbound train / Everyman / Don't be afraid of the light that shines within you.

Big Sky — Compass

Mar 10. (cd) *(BSCD 006) <557>* **DREAMS IN AMERICA** [acoustic re-takes] — Apr 10
- Dreams in America / Bridge of sorrow / Love is a place I dream of / Don't be so hard on yourself / Blackberry time / Lord Franklin / See you soon / Ciara / The acoustic motorbike / Cold comfort / Be still now / Black is the colour / I hear her, like Lorelei / Love is a monsoon / Sunny sailor boy.

- (5-7*) compilations -

Feb 07. (cd) *Warner Platinum; (8122 79993-2)* **THE PLATINUM COLLECTION**
- Delirious / Dreams in America / The fertile rock / Gone to Pablo / You couldn't have come at a better time / The hill of Allen / I believe in you / I need love / This is your country / The acoustic motorbike / I can't help falling in love / Be well / Diamond mountain / Black is the colour / Holding back the river / Background noise / Sanctuary.

BLOWZABELLA

The brainchild of Jon Swayne and Bill O'Toole, who were studying in Whitechapel, London, late in 1978, BLOWZABELLA (the name lifted from an 18th-century bawdy English jig, 'Blowzabella, My Bouncing Doxie') was a combination of all things folk music – generally trad/dance, world/eastern and Celtic/ceilidh.

Made up of various London college students from all over the country and beyond (original bagpiper Bill O'Toole was from Sydney, Australia), the embryonic line-up settled into place by 1980, comprising Swayne, Paul James, Chris Gunstone, Cliff Stapleton, Sam Palmer and Dave Roberts. Early members Juan Wijngaard and Dave Armitage left to take up their profession as instrument-makers.

Debut **BLOWZABELLA** (1982) {*7} saw the band's strengths go from colourful live festival attraction to establishing a tight and structured BLOWZABELLA sound. The line-up, however, was never stable too long: Dave Shepherd (ex-Dr. Cosgill's Delight fiddler) and the returning Dave Armitage (melodeon, bombarde) replaced Gunstone before a second instalment, **IN COLOUR** (1983) {*7}. Featuring Terry Chimes (ex-Clash), Max Johnson, Dave Mitchell and John Spires (of the Dead Sea Surfers), it dug deeper into the annals of English, European and Balkan folk heritage, marking the band out as similar in some respects to 1970s/80s (and onwards) Morris pioneers The ALBION DANCE BAND.

Striking up a long-lasting friendship with folk-singing stalwart FRANKIE ARMSTRONG (plus Brian Pearson and Jon Gillaspie), they featured on the collaborative LP 'Tam Lin' (1984). Successive albums by the widely-travelled band, **BOBBITYSHOOTY** (1984) {*6}, **THE BLOWZABELLA WALL OF SOUND** (1986) {*6} and **THE B TO A OF BLOWZABELLA** (1987) {*6} danced a pretty tune around their rivals. The latter two introduced Nigel Eaton and Ian Luff to take over from the outgoing Stapleton and Armitage.

Adding the returning Swayne (who had been off-duty on the "live in Brazil" LP **PINGHA FRENZY** (1988) {*6}, **A RICHER DUST** (1988) {*7} grew from music the group had written marking the 500th anniversary of the Battle of Stoke Field. They had now added Jo Fraser (ex-OLD SWANN BAND and soon-to-be Jo Freya). To mark Eaton and James's moonlighting project, an eponymous album was released in 1989. **ANCIENT BEATBOX** (1989) {*5} – featuring special guest vocals by SHEILA CHANDRA – highlighted the one-off single 'Raining (My Eyes Are Filled With Clouds)'.

The inclusion of young Andy Cutting on BLOWZABELLA's **VANILLA** (1990) {*6} was short-lived (Dave Roberts himself died in 1996) when the ensemble split. Although they periodically reunited for the odd gig, most became involved with other projects: Cutting joined forces with CHRIS WOOD, Freya went solo and formed Tanteeka for one set with Cutting too.

However, all was not lost, as Paul James got the band together for a 25th-anniversary shindig in 2003, resulting in himself, Swayne, Shepherd, Freya and Cutting regrouping in 2006 with newcomers Gregory Jolivet (hurdy-gurdy) and Barn Stradling (bass) for the recording of comeback set **OCTOMENTO** {*6}. A live concert set, **DANCE** (2010) {*6}, stood the long-serving BLOWZABELLA in good stead with their ever-growing folk-dance fanbase. *MCS*

Jon Swayne (b. Jonathan, Jun 26 '40, Glastonbury, Somerset) - bagpipes, flutes / **Paul James** (b. Apr 4 '57, Southampton, England) - bagpipes, saxophones, percussion (ex-Dr. Cosgill's Delight) repl. Juan Wijngaard (hurdy-gurdy, Flemish bagpipes) / **Chris Gunstone** - bouzouki, tapan / **Sam Palmer** - hurdy-gurdy / **Cliff Stapleton** - hurdy-gurdy; repl. Dave Armitage / **Dave Roberts** - melodeon, darabuka; repl. Australian Bill O'Toole

UK Plant Life / US not issued

1982. (lp) *(PLR 038)* **BLOWZABELLA** ☐ ☐
- Blowzabella – Marriage marches / L'enfant de dieu – Faerie dance / Kolomtanz / Bourree de sologne – Ai vist lou loup / Two Scottishes / Yane Sandanski / Bourree de brand – Valce sauteuse de rett / Jenny pluck pears – Half Hannikin / Cotillon – Drops of brandy / Three polka piquees / The sun from the east – Laura / Bourree a huit – Bourree tournante / Bourree (anon) – Bourree de cusset.

—— **Dave Shepherd** (b. Apr 7 '54, Sheffield, England) - violin (ex-Dr. Cosgill's Delight) + the returning **Dave Armitage** - melodeon, bombarde; repl. Gunstone

May 83. (lp) *(PLR 051)* **IN COLOUR** ☐ ☐
- Polka pique / Masters of war / Rutchenitsa / Captain Lemo – Robin's in the green – Epic branle / Queen Adelaide – Bricks and mortar / Epping Forest – The rolling of the stones – Dans-tro Plinn / Bourrees one and two / Faradole Tarascaire – Trip to Lincoln / Dorset four hand reel – Twin sisters – Sidbury four hand reel / Spanish jig / The French assembly / Bourrees three and four.

—— In mid-84 the band collaborated on FRANKIE ARMSTRONG, BRIAN PEARSON & JON GILLASPIE's LP 'Tam Lin' (now without Palmer)

Jul 84. (lp) *(PLR 064)* **BOBBITYSHOOTY** ☐ ☐
- Shave the monkey - Boys of the mill / The Presbyterian hornpipe - The Red Lyon / La ronde de milloraines / Branle de Borgoyne - Horses blanle / Bobbityshooty / Carl Wark / Eglantine - Man in the brown hat / The topman and the afterguard / The savage hornpipe - The Gloucestershire miner - William Taylor's table-top hornpipe / Scaramouche - Kathryn Arwen's march / Blowzabella – Jon's jig. *(cd-iss. Mar 98 on Osmosys; OSMOCD 015)*

—— **Nigel Eaton** (b. Jan 3 '66, Lyndhurst, Hampshire, England) - hurdy-gurdy + **Ian Luff** (b. Jan 4 '56, Brighton, England) - cittern, bass; repl. Stapleton + Armitage

Sep 86. (lp/c) *(PLR/PLC 074)* **THE BLOWZABELLA WALL OF SOUND** ☐ ☐
- Kopentisa / Eight step waltz - Lisa - Stukka gruppa / Hallowed ground / Newbury jig - Moll in the wood - Sword dance (ghost tune) - Old wi / Sideways glance / Roger de Coverley / Trip o'er Tweed / Lyke wake dirge / Finnish Scottish / Last chance bouree - Glass island / Sinfonia. *(cd-iss. Jul 96 on Osmosys; OSMOCD 005)*

Blowzabella / not issued

Jan 87. (c) *(BZB 01)* **THE B TO A OF BLOWZABELLA** ☐ ☐
- Jig: Spanish jig / Polka: The 48 bar polka / Hornpipes: The savage hornpipe – The Gloucestershire miner / William Taylor's table top hornpipe / 2-4 bourrees: Carree de Vouvray – D'aurore sand – Frederic Paris's bourree / Waltz: The café waltz / Polkas: The knife edge – Cafouillee / Mazurka: Fubu mazurka / 3-8 bourrees: Les poules huppees – Fil et bobine / Jigs: Shave the monkey – Boys of the mill / Waltz: Bouffard's waltz / Hornpipes: The new hornpipe – Polka: Kolomtanz / Schottisches: Derriere les carreaux – Mominette / Polkas: Pas d'ete / Jigs: The marriage marches / Laride / Jigs: Tarascaire – Trip to Lincoln – Epic branle.

—— Swayne was temporarily absent from live set below

Some Bizzare / not issued

Jul 88. (lp/cd) *(BIGH/+CD 001)* **PINGHA FRENZY** (live in Brazil 1987) ☐ ☐
- 3-8 bourrees / Lady Diamond - Spanish jig / Fanitullen / New hornpipes / Poolside polka / Behind our house / Kopenitsa / Scottishes / Glass island / 2-4 bourrees / Northern lass / 8 step waltz - Stukka gruppa.

—— added the returning **Swayne** plus **Jo Fraser** (b. Jo-Anne Fraser, Dec 4 '60, St. Albans, England) - sax, vocals, whistles (ex-OLD SWAN BAND); she became Jo Freya in '89

Plant Life / not issued

Jul 88. (lp/c/cd) *(PLR/PLC/PLCD 080)* **A RICHER DUST** ☐ ☐
- The war of the roses: Introduction - The willow runnel - The new jigs - The rose of Raby - Reprise - Finale / Death in a fen - Bruton town - Our captain cried / The moth / The man in the brown hat / The diamond / The new hornpipes / All the things are quite silent. *(cd re-iss. Jan 97 on Osmosys; OSMOCD 010)*

—— **Andy Cutting** (b. Mar 18 '69, West Harrow, Middlesex, England) repl. Roberts (who died in 1996)

Special Delivery / Green Linnet

Jun 90. (lp/c/cd) *(SPD/+C/CD 1028)* *<SIF/CSIF/GLCD 3050>* **VANILLA** ☐ ☐
- Spaghetti panic / La belle c'est endormir - Famous wolf / Jan Mijne man - Go mauve / Fulmine / Beanfield - Monster cafe / I wish, I wish / Down side – Solveig's song - Doctor Feg / Horizonto / In continental mood - Old queen - Flatworld / The lover's ghost / R.S.B. and the hobb / Spaghetti panic (live).

—— after they split (and although they periodically reunited for the odd gig), most became involved with other projects: Cutting joined forces with CHRIS WOOD (among other things), FREYA went solo and formed Tanteeka for one set (with Andy)

—— **Swayne, James, Shepherd, Freya + Cutting** regrouped in 2006 with newcomers **Gregory Jolivet** (hurdy-gurdy) + **Barn Stradling** (bass)

Blowzabella / not issued

Jul 07. (cd) *(Blowzabella 1)* **OCTOMENTO** ☐ ☐
- Oliver's and two beers / De Montford and Magaloufou / The origin of the world / New pneus / Tanteeka and round the corner / L'ance / Black lake and the duck / One for sorrow / Ham street / Le galant indiscret / Jackie tar / The new road to Alston and Lottie's / To the edges and Robin's / Hostilite.

Oct 10. (cd) *(Blowzabella 2)* **DANCE** [live] ☐ ☐
- Jan Mijne man – Go mauve / Molton – Sur la rance / The bay tree – Molinara / Penda's fen – The white rose – Epic branle / The rose of Raby / Man in the brown hat – Spring dance / Derriere les Carreaux – Mominette / In continental mood – The old queen – Flatworld / Horizonto / Il n'est plus temps – Famous wolf / The new hornpipes / The A minor mazurka – Motorway mazurka / Blowzabella – Shave the monkey – Boys of the mill.

- (5-7*) compilations, etc.-

Oct 95. (cd) *Osmosys; (OSMOCD 001)* **COMPILATION** ☐ ☐
- Blowzabella - Marriage marches / L'enfant de dieu - Faerie dance / Jenny pluck pears - Half Hannikin / Polka piquee / Bourees three & four / Shave the monkey - Boys of the mill / Eglantine - Man in the brown hat - Schottische Fran Havero - Minah / Eight step waltz - Lisa - Gruppa, stukka / Glass island / Newbury jig - Moll in the wood - Sword dance - Old wife of Coverdale / The new jigs / Death in a fen - Bruton town - Our captain cried / Spaghetti panic / Jan Mijne man - Go mauve / Horizonto.

ANCIENT BEATBOX

Paul James, Nigel Eaton + Ian Luff

Cooking Vinyl / not issued

Jun 89. (lp/c/cd) *(COOK/+C/CD 021)* **ANCIENT BEATBOX** ☐ ☐
- Laride / Raining (my eyes are filled with clouds) / Wooden box / I'll wait for you / Bouree a Pichon / Diamond / The many lives of Diana / All we live for.

Jan 90. (7") *(FRY 014)* RAINING (MY EYES ARE FILLED WITH CLOUDS) [bagpipe mix]. / Wooden Box ☐ ☐
(12"+=) *(FRY 014T)* - ['A'-DJ mix] / Bouree a Pichon [original].

BLUE ROSES

The musical alter-ego of Laura Groves (b. 1987, Shipley, West Yorkshire) and a few handpicked chums, BLUE ROSES and her Salvia imprint were quickly picked up by XL Recordings in 2008. Under her own name she'd released the ltd-edition 7" 'I Am Leaving'.

With folk music on a resurgence in the latter half of the 2000s (LAURA MARLING, JOANNA NEWSOM, etc.), Laura's dreamy versions of the genre lay somewhere between Kate Bush, JONI MITCHELL and, dare I say it, Julienne Regan of ALL ABOUT EVE.

The eponymous **BLUE ROSES** (2009) {*6} showed promise even if it didn't set the music world alight. Her template folk-ish, pastoral ballads blackballed her, thankfully, from the growing legions of the freak-folk fraternity. Tracks like 'Greatest Thoughts', 'I Wish I …', 'Doubtful Comforts' and a revamp of 'I Am Leaving' had a certain charm, while Groves was equally adept on both finger-picking acoustic guitar and piano. Let's hope there's some more soon. *MCS*

Laura Groves - vocals, acoustic guitar, piano (w/ sessioners/friends)

UK Salvia / US not issued

Oct 07. (ltd-7"; as LAURA GROVES) *(TIC 001)* I AM LEAVING. / Bridges ☐ ☐

XL-Salvia / XL

Mar 09. (ltd-7") *(XLS 412)* DOUBTFUL COMFORTS. / Untitled ☐ ☐

Apr 09. (cd) *(XLCD/XLLP 411)* *<92902-2/-1>* **BLUE ROSES** ☐ ☐
- Greatest thoughts / Cover your tracks / I am leaving / Can't sleep / I wish I … / Coast / Does anyone love me now? / Doubtful comforts / Rebecca / Imaginary flights.

Jun 09. (7") *(XLS 440)* I AM LEAVING / Moments Before Sleep ☐ ☐

BOB DELYN

Could be misleading to Zimmerman fans thinking they might be getting a Welsh-language version of a DYLAN album – condescending as it seems, this must have happened a few times!

Anyway, formed in Wales, BOB DELYN the folk-rock duo was instigated by poet/harpist Twm Morys (son of travel writer Jan Morris, CBE) and his French/Breton-singing girlfriend Nolwenn Korbell. The former was actually an English-born Welsh-language student at Aberystwyth University whose Celtic studies degree would stand him in good stead for his career in poetry and music. After working as a lecturer at Rennes University, he relocated to Brittany, where he met Nolwenn in 1988. The pair released a couple of decent albums: **SGWARNOGOD BACH BOB** (1990) {*6} – which means Bob's Little Hares – and **GEDON** (1992) {*6}, both fusions of weird Welsh-spoken folk-rock with roots reggae. If one were to pick their best tunes from this period, 'Pontypridd', 'Blewyn Glas', 'Ffair Y Bala', 'Poeni Dim' and the neo-classical-cum-Celtic 'Séance Watcyn Wyn'.

Morys continued without solo-bound Korbell for the remainder of the 1990s and early 2000s, his newest BOB DELYN A'R EBILLION ensemble completing two sets, **GWBADE BACH COCHLYD** (1996) {*6} – which means Little Red Faces – and **DORE** (2004) {*5}. Morys could well have taken the GORKY'S ZYGOTIC MYNCI or even the Super Furry Animals route to indie stardom, but instead BOB DELYN hoisted the Welsh and Breton flags above the ever-changing tides. Morys achieved the honour of Bardd Plant Cymru (children's poet laureate for Wales) for the years 2009-2010. *MCS*

Twm Morys (b. 1961, Oxford, England) - vocals, harp / **Nolwenn Korbell** (b. Feb 3 '68, Quimper, Finistere) – vocals, guitar

UK Crai — US not issued

Dec 90. (lp/c) *(CRAI/+C 005)* **SGWARNOGOD BACH BOB**
- Un bore / Asu Jo Pontypridd / Lisa Ian / Gwyddel yn y dre (A'r crac cymraeg) / Morgan Jones / Sgwarnogod bach Bob / Dyff Llun, dydd Mawrth / Dacw 'nghariad / Cardotyn / Blewyn glas. *(cd-iss. Jan 04 on Sain+=; SCD 2429)* - BOB DELIG

1991. (c-ep) *(CRAIC 011E)* BOB DOLIG
- Y swn / Dolig del / Dacw 'nghariad (Yn gwneud dyb remix: i lawr yn y berlian) / Caset bach arall i ddathlu'r dolig.

1992. (cd/c) *(CRAI CD/C 021)* **GEDON**
- Gortoz pell zo gortoz gwell / Poeni dim / Llys lfor haul / Ffair y bala / Corsydd fyrjinia / Mil harddach wyt / Beaj iskis / Seance watcyn wyn / Y swn / Tr n bach y sgwarnogod / Blosau haearn blodau glo / Y clerwr olaf / Llewg zotrog oz llep zotrog (kig ejen c'hoazh). *(cd re-iss. Jul 94 as BOB DELYN A'R EBILLION; same)*

—— Nolwenn subsequently released solo sets (one with Soig Siberil, 'Red')

BOB DELYN A'R EBILLION

Morys added **Gorwel Roberts, Edwin Humphries, Clare Jones, Tim Jackson, Einion Gruffudd, Gwyn Jones, Sharon James, Rhydwyn Michell, Gwilym Hannaby Ap Lonas**

Sep 96. (cd) *(CRAICD 049)* **GWBADE BACH COCHLYD**
- Yr angau / Pwy fedar olchi / Pa oan yaouank / Dacw dir / Dwedais fy chwedl I / Deuit ta bugale / Y teithiwr / Os ymadael / Dyman un newydd / Si hei lwli / Adar man.

Bos — not issued

2001. (cd-ep) *(R 002)* BENDIGEDIG — Welsh
- Angel bach gwyn / Walio / Yr afon / Blin.

Sain — not issued

Jan 04. (cd) *(SCD 2421)* **DORE**
- Can yr haul / Breuddwyd pysgod yr ucheldir / Gwely pres / Bugeilio'r Gwenith Gwyn / Hen wr mywn / Pethau bychain dewi sant / Lle mae dy dad di? / Y chwedl hon / Yr afon / Mynydd du / Yr haul yn mynd i lawr / Y llanw mawr hallt.

Jon BODEN (⟹ SPIERS AND BODEN)

Eric BOGLE

Born September 23, 1944, in Peebles in the Scotttish Borders, son of a bagpipe player, ERIC BOGLE's name has become synonymous with the resurgence of the 1980s folk scene while keeping the traditions (whether British or Australian) strictly in line with his music and manners of old. One of his songs in particular (written in the early 1970s), the epic 'The Band Played Waltzing Matilda', was a biting anti-war commentary adapted from a traditional Australian folk song and inspired by an Anzacs (Australian and New Zealand war veterans) march in Canberra. It remains his most famous work and his signature tune, and BOGLE has consistently followed a songwriting agenda centred on political and humanitarian issues, especially anti-war themes. Which isn't to say he lacks a sense of humour – far from it, as a cursory listen to any of his live efforts will attest.

At the age of 25, BOGLE, like so many Scots before him, emigrated to Australia, where he initially lived in the city of Canberra. After a period working as an accountant, he eventually took up singing, writing and performing full-time. The strength of his work, and of course his aforementioned classic (but no official recordings as yet), resulted in a few unofficial bootlegs (eg the **ERIC BOGLE LIVE IN PERSON** series).

However, **NOW I'M EASY** (1980) {*7} was issued as his domestic debut album proper, a record that contained both 'No Man's Land' (better known as 'Green Fields Of France' when first recorded by the MEN THEY COULDN'T HANG) and 'The Band Played Waltzing Matilda'. While Larrikin Records in Australia released several subsequent sets, Topic Records, Plant Life, Sonet and Flying Fish were responsible for his overseas material. With sidekick guitarist and mandolinist John Munro always in tow, BOGLE's 1980s albums were a somewhat hit-and-miss affair, but each had a foothold on folk's finest ground. **PLAIN AND SIMPLE** (1981) {*5}, **SCRAPS OF PAPER** (1982) {*6}, **WHEN THE WIND BLOWS** (1984) {*6}, **IN CONCERT** (1985) {*6}, **SINGING THE SPIRIT HOME** (1986) {*6} and **SOMETHING OF VALUE** (1988) {*7} – out of these one must listen at least to the penultimate LP's title track, a harrowing yet uplifting true story about a black prisoner's execution in South Africa.

VOICES IN THE WILDERNESS (1991) {*5} highlighted further evidence of his political awareness and featured songs by Andy McGloin ('It's Only Tuesday') and Bruce Watson ('Amazon'). 1993's **MIRRORS** {*5}railed against both the modern-day horrors of Brazil's murdered street children and the ghosts of Nazi Germany, while double live set **I WROTE THIS WEE SONG...** (1994) {*7} is as good a starting point as any for BOGLE beginners, featuring a clutch of his most enduring songs and heavy doses of between-songs banter.

A contemporary folk protest singer in the mould of WOODY GUTHRIE, PHIL OCHS, etc rather than a purely folk traditionalist, BOGLE rarely relies on anything other than an acoustic guitar for accompaniment, although he regularly performs and records with longstanding friends John Munro and Brent Miller. Almost all of BOGLE's 1990s and 2000s recordings were released in the UK on Scottish label Greentrax (more often home to folk-dance acts), the most enduring being **THE EMIGRANT AND THE EXILE** with Munro (1997) {*6}, **SMALL MIRACLES** (1997) {*6}, **ENDANGERED SPECIES** (2000) {*5}, **THE COLOUR OF DREAMS** (2002) {*5}, **OTHER PEOPLE'S CHILDREN** (2005) {*5} and **THE DREAMER** (2009) {*5}. *MCS*

Eric Bogle - vocals, acoustic guitar / with **John Munro** - guitar, mandolin, vocals / plus others

Aus/UK Larrikin — US not issued

1980. (lp) *(LRF 041)* **NOW I'M EASY**
- Now I'm easy / Leaving Nancy / I hate wogs / No man's land / Leaving in the morning / Since Nancy died / War correspondent / Song of the whale / Front row cowboy / The band played Waltzing Matilda. *(UK-iss. 1988 on Plant Life; PLR 042) (re-iss. Mar 89 on 'Larrikin' cd/lp; CD+/LRF 041) (cd-iss. Dec 97 on Celtic; CMCD 004)*

—— below features **John Munro** + **Brent Miller**

1981. (lp) *(none)* **PLAIN AND SIMPLE**
- Lady from Bendigo / Dan / The Aussie bar-b-q / Glasgow lullaby / Belle of Broughton / Mary and me / No man's land / Queensland whalers / No use for him / Bloody rotten audience / Gentle Annie. *(UK-iss. 1988 on Plant Life; PLR 033) (cd-iss. Nov 97 on Greentrax; CDTRAX 147)*

(above issued on Grass Roots Records)

1982. (lp) *(LRF 104)* **SCRAPS OF PAPER**
- Scraps of paper / No man's land / Front row cowboy / A reason for it all / He's nobody's moggy now / And the band played Waltzing Matilda / Now I'm easy / Just not coping / The ballad of Henry Holloway / If wishes were fishes. *(UK-iss. 1988 on Plant Life; PLR 046) (re-iss. Oct 88; same as Aus) <US-iss. Mar 89 on Flying Fish lp/cd; FF/+90/70 311> (re-iss. Jun '94 on 'Larrikin' cd/c; LARR CD/C 104) (cd re-iss. Mar 97 on Flying Fish; same)*

1982. (7") *(none)* IF WISHES WERE FISHES. / He's Nobody's Moggy Now

1984. (lp) *(LRF 144)* **WHEN THE WIND BLOWS**
- When the wind blows / Hard hard times / Birds of a feather / Lock keeper / Soldier soldier / Bushfire / Shining river / The enigma / Little Gomez / Safe in the harbour. *(UK-iss. Mar 85 on Topic; 12TS 437) <US-iss. Mar 89 on Flying Fish lp/cd; FF/+90 354> (re-iss. Jun 94 on 'Larrikin' cd/c; LARR CD/C 144)*

—— next set also features **Munro** + **Miller**

1985. (lp/c) *(LRF/TC-LRF 160)* **IN CONCERT** (live at The Octagon Theatre, Perth and W.A.)
- Hard hard times / Now I'm easy / Birds of a feather / A reason for it all / Nobody's moggy now / No man's land / Front row cowboy / When the wind blows / Lock keeper / Little Gomez / If wishes were fishes / Leaving Nancy / Wee China pig. *(re-iss. Aug 05 as 'AT THE STAGE: THE LIVE COLLECTION' on Greentrax d-cd+=; CDTRAX 286)* - Safe in the harbour / Do you know any Dylan? / And the band played Waltzing Matilda / As if he knows / The Dalai Lama's candle / One small star / Introduction song / At risk / The law / Refugee / Eric and the informers.

Nov 86. (7") *(none)* LIFELINE. / Shelter

Dec 86. (lp/c/cd) *(LRF 186/+C/CD)* **SINGING THE SPIRIT HOME**
- An old song / Lifeline / Singing the spirit home / Twenty years ago / All the fine young men / Leaving the land / Australian through and through / Lancelot and Guinevere / Silo / Shelter. *(UK-iss. Jun 87 on Sonet; SNTF 983) <US-iss. 1990 on Flying Fish; FF 447>*

Apr 87. (7") *(SON 2320)* SINGING THE SPIRIT HOME. / Australian Through And Through

(above issued on Sonet UK)

Jul 88. (cd/lp) *(CD+/LRF 220)* **SOMETHING OF VALUE**
- Something of value / Katie and the dreamtime land / Harry's wife / A change in the weather / Poor bugger Charlie / Rosie / Going back to Dublin / Them old songwritin' blues / Two strong arms / Across the hills of home (Jimmy's song). *(UK-iss. Sep 88 on Sonet lp/cd; SNT F/CD 1004) <US-iss. Mar '00 on Philo cd/lp; CD+/PH 1125>*

Apr 91. (cd/c) *(none)* **VOICES IN THE WILDERNESS** [-] [-]
- Peace has broken out / The lily and the poppy / Blues for Alex / What kind of man / Wilderness / Feed the children / Amazon / Silly slang song / Fences and walls / It's only Tuesday / The gift of years. *(UK-iss. Apr 91 on Greentrax cd/c; CD/C TRAX 040)* *<Canada cd-iss. on Alcazar;115>*

(above issued on Festival, below on ABC in Australia)

1993. (cd/c) *(CD/TC LRF 282)* **MIRRORS** [-] [-]
- Refugee / One small life / Plastic Paddy / Welcome home / Flat stony broke waltz / Vanya / Don't you worry about that / Mirrors / The song / Short white blues / At risk / Never again - Remember / Somewhere in America / Wouldn't be dead for quids / Wishing is free. *(UK-iss. Nov 93 on Greentrax cd/c; CD/C TRAX 068)*

1994. (d-cd/d-c) *(none)* **I WROTE THIS WEE SONG ...** (live) [ ] [-]
- Sound of singing / Leaving the land / Silly slang song / Mirrors / A reason for it all / Flying finger filler / Vanya / Don't you worry about that / Somewhere in America / Them old songwriting blues / Rosie // Feed the children / Singing the spirit home / Leaving Nancy / Now I'm easy / Plastic Paddy / No man's land / Never again - Remember / Short white blues / Welcome home / Daniel smiling / Eric and the informers / Shelter / The gift of years. *(UK-iss. Nov 94 on Greentrax d-cd/d-c; CD/C TRAX 082D)*

Greentrax — not issued

Feb 97. (cd/c; by ERIC BOGLE & JOHN MUNRO) *(CD/C TRAX 121)*
THE EMIGRANT AND THE EXILE [ ] [-]
- Poacher's moon / Were you there? / The strangers / World Cup fever / The ballad of Charles Devonport / Progress / Marking time / Campbell's daughter / One small star / Listen to the old ones / The end of an auld song / Cuddy river reverie / Kissing English arses talking blues / Standing in the light.

Jun 97. (cd) *(CDTRAX 130)* **SMALL MIRACLES** [ ] [-]
- Small miracles / The diggers' legacy / Dedication day / Ekka's silver jubille song / Always back to you / The blessing / Here in the green / Sayonara Australia / The golden city / Somebody's daughter / Keeper of the flame / Romeo and Juliet in Sarajevo / The red heart / Troy's song / Unsung hero / Heart of the land / One small star.

Jul 00. (cd) *(CDTRAX 196)* **ENDANGERED SPECIES** [ ] [-]
- Our national pride / The sign / Just here for the money / Jingle jangle / No gods at all / Robin's rant - Tom O'Neill's tantrum / The road to El Dorado / You've got nothing I need / Journeys / Turning circles / Beam me up, Scotty / Endangered species / The Waltzing Matilda waltz / Jimmy Dancer / The river of time.

Oct 02. (cd) *(CDTRAX 237)* **THE COLOUR OF DREAMS** [ ] [-]
- The colour of dreams / No resurrection / The Koala kafe / As if he knows / Reconciliation / Elvis 'n' me / Global economy / Daniel smiling / Care for the land / One morning in Bar Harbor / The Dalai Lama's candle / Homecoming / Ibrahim / Elizabeth's song / Cradle to the grave / Soaring free.

Nov 05. (cd) *(CDTRAX 287)* **OTHER PEOPLE'S CHILDREN** [ ] [-]
- Tambourine mountain / Hallowed ground / True believers / The last of the old timers / The promise / Tired / Other people's children / A good man / The demon / The last rodeo / Thou shalt not / To an athlete dying young / While I am here.

May 09. (cd) *(CDTRAX 337)* **THE DREAMER** [ ] [-]
- Bringing Buddy home / Standing in the light / Nothing worth saving / Snowdrop / The dreamer / Flying away / Canadian Christmas song / Someone else's problem / Lost soul / An Australian prayer for rain / The last note.

- (8-10*) compilations -

Aug 89. (cd/c/lp) *Greentrax; (<CD/C+/TRAX 028>)*
THE ERIC BOGLE SONGBOOK [ ] [ ]
- A reason for it all / Nobody's moggy now / Hard hard times / Scraps of paper / If wishes were fishes / Front row cowboy / And the band played Waltzing Matilda / Little Gomez / The Aussie bar-b-q / When the wind blows.

May 92. (cd/c) *Greentrax; (CD/C TRAX 051)*
THE ERIC BOGLE SONGBOOK 2 [ ] [-]
- Now I'm easy / Glasgow lullaby / No man's land / Do you know any Bob Dylan? / My youngest son came home today / Belle of Broughton / Leaving Nancy / Singing the spirit home / Wee china pig / Leaving the land / Rosie / All the fine young men / Across the hills of home (Jimmy's song).

Mar 01. (cd) *Greentrax; (<CDTRAX 210>)* **BY REQUEST**
(original Aus-title 'THE GIFT OF YEARS') [ ] [ ]
- Santa bloody Claus / Shelter / Leaving Nancy / He's nobody's moggy now / No man's land / Singing the spirit home / If wishes were fishes / Now I'm easy / Safe in the harbour / It's not cricket / One small star / Silly slang song / Big (in a small way) / And the band played Waltzing Matilda.

- essential boxed sets -

Jun 05. (5xcd-box) *Greentrax; (CDTRAX 40018)*
SINGING THE SPIRIT HOME [ ] [-]
- Now I'm easy / No man's land / Front row cowboy / Song of the whale / Dan / Aussie bar-b-q / Singing river / Lady from Bendigo / I hate wogs / Leaving Nancy (live) / And the band played Waltzing Matilda / Belle of Broughton // Scraps of paper / He's nobody's moggy now / If wishes were fishes / Bushfire / The enigma / Hard hard times / Do you know any Dylan? (live) / Safe in the harbour / Little Gomez / A reason for it all / Glasgow lullaby / My youngest came home today // When the wind blows / Wilderness / Silly slang song / Harry's wife / Shelter / What kind of man / Feed the children / Blues for Alex / Leaving the land / Something of value / Rosie (live) / Peace has broken out // Singing the spirit home / Katie and the dreamtime land / Welcome home / Don't you worry about that / Plastic daddy / Somewhere in America / One small life / Short white blues / Vanya / Mirrors / The gift of years / Wouldn't be dead for quids // Small miracles / Keeper of the flame / Standing in the light / The diggers' legacy / Dedication day / The golden city / Troy's song / Ekka's silver jubilee song / Romeo and Juliet in Sarajevo / The blessing / One small star / The end of an auld song.

- early exploitation releases -

1980. (lp) *Autogram; (ALLP 211)* **ERIC BOGLE vol.1: LIVE IN PERSON** (live in 1976) [-] German [-]
- Now I'm easy / The band played Waltzing Matilda / Belle of Broughton / Glasgow lullaby / Mansion hoose on the hill / Leavin' Nancy / No man's land / Mary and me / No use for him / Traditional folksinger's lament / The hero's return (Belfast song).

1981. (bootleg-lp) *Autogram; (ALLP 220)*
ERIC BOGLE vol.2: DOWN UNDER (live in 1976) [-] German [-]
- Shining river / Poor wee Billy MacMahon / She's be right / For king and country / No man's land / Homeless man / Wee pot stove / Queensland whalers / Owd zither / Island in the river / Death of Ben Hall.

1982. (bootleg-lp) *Autogram; (ALLP 253)*
ERIC BOGLE vol.3: PURE (live in 1976) [-] German [-]
- Seasons / Simple man's love song / Leavin' in the morning / Little fishy / Ice queen / My little darling / Sandy is a soldier / Why should I care / Suffer the children / Whisky-wine / I hate wogs (Oriental gentleman) / Belfast song.

- (5-7*) compilations, etc.-

Jan 94. (cd; ERIC BOGLE & JOHN MUNRO) *Wundertute; (TUT 72162CD) <55222>* **HARD HARD TIMES** (recorded 1984) [ ] Mar 97 [ ]
- Lady from Bendigo / Glasgow lullaby / Hard hard times / A reason for it all / Shining river / Song of the whale / Mary and me / Twenty years ago / When the wind blows / Never again / Belle of Broughton / Safe in the harbour.

Polly BOLTON

Once the voice of folk-rockers DANDO SHAFT (although not an original member), she'll be best remembered for her time spent in the mid-1980s line-up of the ASHLEY HUTCHINGS band on 'By Gloucester Docks I Sat Down And Wept' (1987). Hutchings's ALBION DANCE BAND also featured Polly on their 'I Got New Shoes' (1987) set, while his "All-Stars" almost immediately invited her to sing on the 'As You Like It' album.

Born February 27, 1950 in Coventry, England, her first solo outing came in 1979 with the Christmassy 'The Year Of The Child', assisted by the city's cathedral choir. Having worked with the likes of BERT JANSCH/Conundrum and Kevin Dempsey (with the latter in soul-fusion act Blue Aquarius), the singer/songwriter with a degree in botany finally delivered her debut solo set, **NO GOING BACK** (1990) {*6}. A collaborative cassette, (**WOODBINE AND IVY** {*5}), with John Shepherd and Steve Dunachie, followed soon afterwards, while Polly sang (mostly backing) on ALAIN STIVELL's 'The Mists Of Avalon' (1991) album.

1993 saw a second release with The POLLY BOLTON BAND (i.e. Shepherd and Dunachie), **SONGS FROM A COLD OPEN FIELD** {*6}, this time adopting a jazzier sound.

Her subsequent contributions to a SHOW OF HANDS "live" album and The ALBION BAND/guests' set 'The Gov'nor's Big Birthday Bash' kept her profile reasonably high, while there were also collaborative CDs such as the PB band outing **LOVELIEST OF TREES** (1996) {*6} – with English-gentleman actor Nigel Hawthorne – and **VIEW ACROSS THE BAY** (1998) {*6}, with Paul Dunmall. Conspicuous by her absence, although her music workshop in Shropshire has kept her busy, Polly finally unleashed a new trad-folk CD in 2009 entitled **THE MAGIC OF SONG** {*6}. It featured two tracks ('Rwanda' and 'Ethiopia') written by her long-time friend Kevin Dempsey. *MCS*

Polly Bolton - vocals (with session people)

UK MCA — US not issued

Dec 79. (7") *(MCA 547)* THE YEAR OF THE CHILD. / Do You Hear What I Hear [ ] [-]

—— in the mid-late 1980s, Polly was a member of the ASHLEY HUTCHINGS team

Making Waves — not issued

May 90. (lp/c/cd) *(SPIN/SPIC/SPINCD 134)* **NO GOING BACK** [ ] [-]
- When I get home / Don't ask me why / Alexander Graham Bell / Foxtrotting / Rainforest lament / The drowned lover / Exile / Licence to kill / The silver swan / Love needs a heart / Madness of love.

Polly Bolton — not issued

1991. (c; by POLLY BOLTON, JOHN SHEPHERD, STEVE DUNACHIE) *(PBB 01)* **WOODBINE AND IVY** [ ] [-]

- A week before Easter / Spencer the rover / The female rampling sailor / The blacksmith / Lovely Joan / Searching for lambs / Sovay / Bonny light horseman / Died for love / etc.

—— next with The POLLY BOLTON BAND (see below)

May 93. (cd/c; by POLLY BOLTON, STEVE DUNACHIE, JOHN SHEPHERD) *(PBB CD/C 02)* **SONGS FROM A COLD OPEN FIELD** ▭ ⊟
- Gypsy laddie / Banks of the Bann / Clerk Saunders / I love my love / The lake side of Innisfree / The grenadier and the lady / Salley gardens / Blackwaterside / The cruel mother / Brigg fair.

Aug 96. (cd; as The POLLY BOLTON BAND and NIGEL HAWTHORNE) *(SHEPCD 01)* **LOVELIEST OF TREES** ▭ ⊟
- Loveliest of trees / O see how thick / When smoke stood up / Farewell to barn and stack and tree / On moonlit heath and lonesome bank when I was one and twenty / Bredon / The lads in their hundreds / The new mistress / White in the moon / Into my heart an air that kills / Far in a western brookland / When I last came to Ludlow / With rue my heart is laden.

(above issued on Shepherd Records)

Mar 98. (cd; by POLLY BOLTON and PAUL DUNMALL) *(PBB 03CD)* **VIEW ACROSS THE BAY** ▭ ⊟
- Waterfalls / Bird dance / Mountain air / Forest talk / The oldest tree / Maguire's jig / Prayer wheel / Chasing / View across the bay / Fox's revenge / Brown bear dance / Mayflies' last dance / When will you return / Desert ice.

—— she's since set up her own workshop centre in Shropshire

		Polly Bolton	not issued
2009.	(cd) *(none)* **THE MAGIC OF SONG**	⊟ web	⊟

- You won't always feel / Searching for lambs / There is not one truth / Oh holy Lord / A stor mo choar / Rwanda / Barbara Allen / Ethiopia / Green willow / Fox song / Lagan love / The magic of song.

The BOOTHILL FOOT-TAPPERS

Working around London from 1982, frontman/leader Chris Thompson and his toe-tapping compadres (Kevin Walsh, Slim/Clive Pain, Wendy May/ Billingsley, Marnie Stephenson, and Merrill Heatley and her brother Danny) combined elements of country cow-punk and skiffle-folk, genres that set them apart from their run-of-the-mill rivals such as Helen And The Horns and Yip Yip Coyote.

Blessed with the courage to mix-and-match their own brand of funky fun-folk (check out the Kirsty MacColl-ish debut 45 'Get Your Feet Out Of My Shoes') with a handful of handpicked covers from luminaries such as Bob Marley and The Wailers ('Love And Affection'), Curtis Mayfield ('People Get Ready') and Flatt & Scruggs ('Bringing In The Georgia Mail'), The BOOTHILL FOOT-TAPPERS proved a breath of fresh air for critics and public alike.

With Simon Edwards (on melodeon) taking up where Slim left off (he continued with his Blubbery Hellbellies), the large group delivered only one LP in their time. **AIN'T THAT FAR FROM BOOTHILL** (1985) {*7} was toured around the country, while counterparts such as The POGUES and The Shillelagh Sisters shared a stage with them on a London Weekend TV special presented by Ben Elton. However, when certain members went off to do their own thing (Wendy May was running a disco in Kentish Town), Thompson found he was better at ease with The BARELY WORKS. A reformation early in 2011 was sadly without former Thompson sidekick and fellow songwriter Walsh, who died before the timely expanded CD re-issue of their album. *MCS*

Chris Thompson (b. Mar 19 '57, Ashford, Middlesex, England) - vocals, banjo / **Kevin Walsh** - acoustic guitar, vocals / **Wendy May (Billingsley)** - vocals / **Merrill Heatley** - vocals / **Marnie Stephenson** - washboard, vocals / **Slim** (b. Clive Pain) - accordion / **Danny Heatley** - drums

		UK Go! Discs	US not issued
Jul 84.	(7"/7" pic-d) *(TAP/+P 1)* GET YOUR FEET OUT OF MY SHOES. / Milk Train / True Blues	64	⊟
	(12"+=) *(TAPX 1)* - People get ready / Chasing women.		

—— **Simon Edwards** - melodeon; repl. Slim (to Blubbery Hellbellies)

		Phonogram	not issued
Mar 85.	(7") *(PH 33)* JEALOUSY. / A Bowl Of Porridge	▭	⊟
	(12"+=) *(PH 33-12)* - Bringing in the Georgia mail / Come see about me.		
May 85.	(7") *(PH 35)* TOO MUCH TIME. / How's Jack? (part 1)	▭	⊟
	(12"+=) *(PH 35-12)* - New river train / Coloured aristocracy.		
Aug 85.	(7") *(PH 37)* LOVE AND AFFECTION. / There's A Melody In Our Madness	▭	⊟
	(12"+=) *(PH 37-12)* - I ain't broke / Sue Bailey's diary.		
		Mercury	not issued
Oct 85.	(lp) *(MERH 76)* **AIN'T THAT FAR FROM BOOTHILL**	▭	⊟

- Love and affection / Jealousy / Pride takes a fall / Nothing ventured / Feelings / Sunday evening / Get your feet out of my shoes / Have you got the confidence for the trick? / Stand or fall / What's the matter? / There's no way (I can leave you alone) / Too much time. *(cd-iss. Nov 08 on Cherry Red+=; cdmred 379)*- Get your feet out of my shoes [7" version] / Milk train / True blues / People get ready / Chasing women / Bringing in the Georgia mail / A bowl of porridge / Come see about me / Too much time [7" version] / How's Jack? / Coloured aristocracy / New river train.

—— disbanded early '86; Thompson formed The BARELY WORKS, while Edwards formed K-Passa in the early 1990s (cassette, '2 From The Front')

Jim BOYES (⟹ COOPE BOYES & SIMPSON)

Maggie BOYLE

The name of MAGGIE BOYLE (born December 24, 1956 in Battersea, London) would be synonymous with her involvement in JOHN RENBOURN's Ship Of Fools, a band and project album (1988) that also featured her husband and solo folk minstrel STEVE TILSTON. From traditional Irish stock (her father was ballad singer Paddy Boyle from County Donegal), she sang at an early age under the guidance of her Monaghan tutor Oliver Mulligan, while her siblings Paul (fiddle) and Kevin Boyle (mainly banjo and guitar) were session men.

Maggie came to light in 1984 when her vocals and flute-playing were an integral part of the folk-based production of the ballet Sergeant's Early Dream, staged and choreographed by the Rambert Dance Company. Her husband Steve was also in attendance, and with him she set up the Run River imprint, making BOYLE's debut LP, **REACHING OUT** (1987) {*7}. Combining traditional ballads with songs from contemporary artists (including ROBIN WILLIAMSON's 'October Song'), the album should have been a platform to launch a burgeoning solo career. Instead, though, she chose to collaborate with or accompany her husband on subsequent albums, plus the Ship Of Fools project/set, and did a lot of session work. Records by BERT JANSCH, John McCormick, PETER BELLAMY, DAMIEN BARBER, among others, featured Maggie's vocals.

The 1990s saw Maggie take up a position in female folk trio GRACE NOTES (alongside Lynda Hardcastle and Helen Hockenhull), and four majestic sets have since become available, while her soundtrack commissions have included songs on 'Patriot Games' (1992) and 'Legends Of The Fall' (1994).

Just over a decade from her last previous solo outing, **GWEEBARRA** (1998) {*8} was a welcome return to the fold, a record that fused folk heritage with digital technology. Of late she's put together a couple of folk/ jazz hybrid supergroups – one with DUCK BAKER and Ben Paley for a 2005 album, **THE EXPATRIATE GAME** {*5}, featuring "Traditional Irish and American Music" - and the eponymous SKETCH (2008), with Gary Boyle and a guy called Dave Bowie (no, not that one!) *MCS*

Maggie Boyle - vocals, flute, bodhran (with session people)

		UK Run River	US not issued
Feb 87.	(lp) *(RRA 003)* **REACHING OUT**	▭	⊟

- Proud man / Quiet land of Erin / Joe's in bed / Mountain streams where the moorcocks / October song / Lowlands of Holland / Has sorrow thy young days shaded / Busk busk bonnie lassie / Pancake Tuesday / Reaching out / Road to Ballinamuck. *(cd/c-iss. Feb 90; RRA CD/MC 003)*

—— In 1988, Boyle was part of Ship Of Fools alongside JOHN RENBOURN and her husband STEVE TILSTON; with the latter she collaborated on two sets, 'Of Moor And Mesa' (1992) and 'All Under The Sun' (1996).

		Pure	not issued
Nov 98.	(cd) *(PRCD 05)* **GWEEBARRA**	▭	⊟

- Gweebarra shore / My generous lover / Lady Margaret / Ao tea roa / The bloody gardener / Deathairin o mo chroi / Paddy's rambles through the park / Harry Eddom / Blackbird / Lord Gregory / Little thatched cabin / If you walk away.

—— In 2005 she collaborated with DUCK BAKER & BEN PALEY on the album/project 'THE EXPATRIATE GAME' (rel. 2009)

—— next comprised **Maggie, Gary Boyle** (guitar) and **Dave Bowie** (double bass)

		Dagama	not issued
May 08.	(cd; as SKETCH) *(DCD 123)* **SKETCH**	▭	⊟

GRACE NOTES

Maggie Boyle - vocals, flute, bodhran / **Lynda Hardcastle** - vocals, recorder / **Helen Hockenhull** - vocals, keyboards

		Grace Notes	not issued
Dec 93.	(cd/c) *(GN 001 CD/C)* **DOWN FALLS THE DAY**	▭	⊟

- Roll around Heaven all day / A stitch in time / How can I keep from singing /

Trouble in mind / Sometime / The black and bitter night / Reynardine / Down falls the day / Gathering mushrooms / Bread and roses / River / Tom's song / The bramble and the rose.

Fellside — not issued

Mar 98. (cd) *(FECD 126)* **RED WINE & PROMISES**
- All that is gold / Spirit song / Magdalen laundry / Gypsy Davey / Lies / Finistere / Red wine and promises / Banks of the sweet Dundee / The goose / In the light tonight / Hubrisity / Welcome sailor / The quiet land of Erin / Witch of the Westmorelands / Withered and died - I'll follow the sun.

Oct 01. (cd) *(FECD 163)* **ANCHORED TO THE TIME**
- Blue Jay - Migrating bird / The oak and the laurel / Long way from home / Two sisters / Siobhan's lament - Reaching out / John Ball / King Sun / Cockleshells / Stockinger / Bone lace weaver / Dying of thirst / Don't come the cowboy with me sonny Jim! / Lullaby.

Jan 08. (cd) *(FECD 209)* **NORTHERN TIDE**
- When the ship comes in / The gardener / Rosa / The dewy ones / The power / Once I loved a sailor / Mrs. Rita / Rue / Song of the naturalist's wife - Widow without shawl (a portrait) - The wind that shakes the barley / The briar and the rose / White winos / The old man from Lee / Best wishes / Northern tide - Mingulay boat song.

Paul BRADY

From modest beginnings playing piano in a hotel in Donegal, to becoming a renowned international singer-songwriter switching to acoustic guitar, PAUL BRADY (born May 19, 1947 in Strabane, County Tyrone in Northern Ireland) has become one of his country's greatest exports alongside fellow PLANXTY star CHRISTY MOORE.

Following a stint in mid-1960s local R&B outfit The Kult, and on to celebrated Irish traditional and contemporary covers band The JOHNSTONS (superseding Michael Johnston in May '67), Paul performed with PLANXTY after his return to Ireland in the mid-1970s. He was initially credited on fiddler Tommy Peoples's cassette album 'The High Part Of The Road' in 1977. A period of time he enjoyed immensely, it was a productive year (and a bit) that saw him team up with old JOHNSTONS/PLANXTY bandmate ANDY IRVINE on the LP 'Andrew I & Paul B', and deliver his solo debut **WELCOME HERE KIND STRANGER** (1978) {*6}, Melody Maker's Folk Album Of The Year.

Formerly steeped in tradition like his aforementioned peers and Celtic-folk rivals, BRADY chose to take the pop-rock route to success, signing a lucrative deal with Warner Bros. His change of style was rewarded when 'Crazy Dreams' topped the Irish charts, while its parent album **HARD STATION** (1981) {*6} sold in vast quantities. Now mixing with rock gentry such as Dire Straits, Eric Clapton, Mark Knopfler, Santana and Dave Edmunds (the last two covering his songs), in the 1980s he recorded a series of fair-to-middling AOR studio albums, from 1983's **TRUE FOR YOU** {*5} to 1987's **PRIMITIVE DANCE** {*5}.

Described as being as close to VAN MORRISON as Steely Dan are to The Doobie Brothers, BRADY continued to create his own blend (or bland) of horizontal folk. Albums like **TRICK OR TREAT** (1991) {*6}, **SPIRITS COLLIDING** (1995) {*6}, **OH WHAT A WORLD** (2000) {*5} and **SAY WHAT YOU FEEL** (2005) {*5} fitting into a niche on the outer fringes of folk rather than being an integral part of it. BRADY received an honorary D.Litt degree in 2009 from the University of Ulster, while his tenth solo album, **HOOBA DOOBA** (2010) {*6}, marked another decade in the music business. *MCS*

Paul Brady - vocals, guitar (with session players)

Ire/UK Mulligan — US Green Linnet

Sep 78. (c/lp) *(C+/LUN 24)* *<C+/SIF 3015>*
WELCOME HERE KIND STRANGER
- Don't come again / I am a youth that's inclined to ramble / Jackson and Jane / The lakes of Pontchartrain / The creel / Out the door and over the wall / Young Edmund in the lowlands low / Boy on the hilltop - Johnny goin' to ceilidh / Paddy's green shamrock shore. *(cd-iss. Aug 94; LUNCD 24)*

WEA — not issued

Oct 80. (7") *(K 18355)* CRAZY DREAMS. / Something In The Atmosphere

May 81. (7") *(K 18779)* BUSTED LOOSE. / Road To The Promised Land

Jun 81. (lp/c) *(K/K4 58312)* **HARD STATION**
- Crazy dreams / The road to the promised land / Busted loose / Cold cold night / Hard station / Dancer in the fire / Night hunting time / Nothing but the same old story.

Polydor — Twenty One

Jun 82. (7") *(POSP 498)* CRAZY DREAM. / Something In The Atmosphere

Aug 82. (re; lp/c) *(POLS/+C 1072)* HARD STATION
(re-iss. 1988 on Mercury lp/c; PRICE/PRIMC 122) (re-iss. Feb. 90 on Mercury cd/c/lp; 834996-2/-4/-1) (<cd re-mast. May 99 on Rykodisc; RCD 10482>) <cd re-iss. 2001 on Compass; COM 4307>

May 83. (lp/c) *(POLS/+C 5091)* *<90504-1/-4>* **TRUE FOR YOU**
- The great pretender / Let it happen / Helpless heart / Dance the romance / Steel claw / Take me away / Not the only one / (interlude) / Trouble round the bend. *(re-iss. May '89 on Mercury lp/c/cd; 810893-1/-4/-2) (<cd re-mast. May '99 on Rykodisc; RCD 10483>) <cd re-iss. 2001 on Compass; COM 4327>*

Jun 83. (7") *(POSP 616)* THE GREAT PRETENDER. / Trouble Round The Bend

Demon — not issued

Nov 84. (lp) *(FIEND 34)* **FULL MOON** (live at the Half Moon, London)
- Hard station / Not the only one / Take me away / Busted loose / Dance the romance / Crazy dreams / Helpless heart / Steel claw. *(cd-iss. Nov 89 and Jan 93; CDFIEND 34)*

—— In 1986, the collaborative 'Molloy, Brady & Peoples' was released in Ireland (Mulligan Records).

Mercury — not issued

Mar 86. (7") *(MER 216)* DEEP IN YOUR HEART. / Follow On
(12"+=) *(MERX 216)* - Cold cold night.

Apr 86. (lp/c) *(MERH/+C 86)(826809-2)* **BACK TO THE CENTRE**
- Walk the white line / Wheel of heartbreak / Deep in your heart / To be the one / Follow on / The soulbeat / Airwaves / The island / The homes of Donegal. *(<cd re-mast. May 99 on Rykodisc; RCD 10484>) <cd re-iss. 2001 on Compass; COM 4314>*

Jun 86. (7") *(MER 224)* BACK TO THE CENTRE (WALK THE WHITE LINE). / Airwaves
(12"+=) *(MERX 224)* - The lakes of Pontchartrain.

Sep 86. (7") *(MER 232)* THE ISLAND. / The Great Pretender
(12"+=) *(MERX 232)* - Dance the romance.

Mar 87. (7") *(MER 241)* EAT THE PEACH. / In Case Of Accidents
(12"+=) *(MERX 241)* - ('A'-extended).
(cd-s++=) *(888464-2)* - The loving of a stranger.

Apr 87. (lp/c)(cd) *(MERH/+C 106)(832133-2)* **PRIMITIVE DANCE**
- Steal your heart away / The soul commotion / Paradise is here / It's gonna work out fine / The awakening / Eat the peach / Don't start knocking / Just in case of accidents / The game of love. *(<cd re-mast. May 99 on Rykodisc; RCD 10485>) <cd re-iss. 2001 on Compass; COM 4328>*

Jun 87. (7") *(MER 247)* STEAL YOUR HEART AWAY. / The Soul Connection
(12"+=) *(MERX 247)* - The awakening.

Fontana — not issued

Apr 91. (cd/c/lp) *(848454-2/-4/-1)* **TRICK OR TREAT**
- Soul child / Blue world / Nobody knows / Can't stop wanting you / You and I / Trick or treat / Don't keep pretending / Solid love / Love goes on / Dreams will come. *(<cd re-mast. May 99 on Rykodisc; RCD 10486>) <cd re-iss. Mar 01 on Compass; COM 4313>*

May 95. (cd/c/lp) *(526829-2/-4/-1)* **SPIRITS COLLIDING**
- I want you to want me / Trust in you / The world is what you make it / Marriage made in Hollywood / Help me to believe / I will be there / After the party's over / Just in time / Love made a promise / Beautiful world.

Rykodisc — Compass

May 00. (cd) *(RCD 10490)* *<COM 4304>* **OH WHAT A WORLD** — Feb 01
- Sea of love / I believe in magic / Love hurts / Oh what a world / The long goodbye / The law of love / Believe in me / Good love / Travellin' light / Minutes away, miles apart / Try me one more time.

Hypertension — Compass

Feb 04. (cd) *(HYP 3225)* *<COM 4358>* **SONGBOOK** (live for RTE at Marlay House, Rathfarnham, Dublin in August 2002) — German
- Oh what a world / The long goodbye / I will be there / Nobody knows / I believe in magic / Blue world / Crazy dreams / Nothing but the same old story / Helpless heart / Follow on / The world is what you make it / The homes of Donegal / The Hawana way.

Compass — Compass

Feb 05. (cd) *(<COM 4396>)* **SAY WHAT YOU FEEL**
- Smile / Don't try to please me / Love in a bubble / I only want you / Living for the corporation / Say what you feel / Locked up in heaven / Sail, sail on / The you that's really you / Doin' it in the dark / Beyond the reach of love / The man I used to be / Finally it's the right time.

Proper — not issued

Mar 10. (cd) *(PRPCD 056)* **HOOBA DOOBA**
- Cry it out / Rainbow / The price of fame / One more today / The winners' ball / Luck of the draw / Follow that star / Mother and son / Money to burn / You won't see me / Over the border / Living the mystery.

- (8-10*) compilations -

Sep 99. (cd) *Rykodisc; (RCD 10491) / Compass; <COM 4329>*
NOBODY KNOWS: THE BEST OF PAUL BRADY — Jan 02
- Nobody knows / The world is what you make it / Paradise is here (alt.) / Nothing but the same old story / The lakes of Pontchartrain (new recording) / Trick or treat / Trust in you / Not the only one (new vocal) / The island / Crazy dreams / Follow on / Just in time / The homes of Donegal / Arthur McBride (new recording).

- (5-7*) compilations, others, etc.-

Jun 92. (cd/c/lp) *Mercury; (512397-2/-4/-1)*
SONGS AND CRAZY DREAMS [ ] [–]
- Paradise is here / Dancer in the fire / Nothing but the same old story / Deep in your heart / The homes of Donegal / Walk the white line / The road to the promised land / The island / Steal your heart away / Follow on / Helpless heart.

Mar 02. (cd) *Compass; <COM 4335>* **THE MISSING LIBERTY TAPES** (live July 1978) [–] [ ]
- Paddy's green shamrock shore / I am a youth that's inclined to ramble / The creel - Out the door and over the wall / The jolly soldier - The Blarney pilgrim / Mary and the soldier / Jackson and Jane / Don't come again / The lakes of Pontchartrain / The crooked road to Dublin - The bucks of Oranmore / Arthur McBride and the sergeant.

Billy BRAGG

A stalwart of the third-generation British folk scene of the mid-1980s, BILLY BRAGG (born Steven William Bragg, December 20, 1957, at Barking in Essex) has incorporated punk-rock elements from his days as a Clash fan and the leader of new wave/pub-rock outfit Riff Raff.

Not considered to be a high point of his illustrious career, this Peterborough-based quintet nevertheless released a string of obscure indie 7" singles, including the wonderfully titled 'I Wanna Be A Cosmonaut'. They split in 1981, leaving Billy ill-at-ease with the music business.

Putting a spell in the Army behind him (he bought himself out after 90 days), BRAGG kick-started his solo career, busking around the streets of London complete with electric guitar and amplifier. His friend and roadie (they're still friends) Andy Kershaw has since gone on to bigger and better things at the BBC as a much-revered radio DJ; however, it was along the corridor at the John Peel Show that Billy received his first airplay, albeit played at the wrong speed.

That was in 1983, when Peter Jenner (an A&R man with Charisma Records) furnished busker Billy with some studio time, the resulting **LIFE'S A RIOT WITH SPY VS SPY** {*7} duly appearing on indie subsidiary Utility Records. With the help and distribution of new label Go! Discs the mini-LP hit the UK Top 30 in early 1984.

BRAGG's stark musical backdrop (for the most part, a roughly strummed electric guitar) and even starker vocals belied a keen sense of melody and passionate, deeply humane lyrics. 'The Milkman Of Human Kindness' was a love song of the most spirited variety, demonstrating that BRAGG approached politics from a humanist perspective rather than from a soapbox. After seeing first-hand how Thatcher had destroyed the mining communities, Billy's songs became more overtly political.

BREWING UP WITH BILLY BRAGG (1984) {*8} opened with the fierce 'It Says Here', but again the most affecting moments were to be found on heartfelt love songs like the wistful 'St. Swithin's Day'. A minor hit in Europe, it was surpassed by his first UK Top 20 entry, 'Between The Wars' (not on the album), while 'A New England' (from his mini-LP debut) strolled into the Top 10 when covered by Kirsty MacColl (daughter of EWAN MacCOLL).

Under the banner of "Red Wedge", a well-intentioned but unsuccessful campaign to engage music fans with the Labour Party cause in 1986/87 (Margaret Thatcher's Conservatives would romp home again in 1987), BRAGG toured alongside The Style Council, Madness, The Communards and Morrissey. His third album, **TALKING WITH THE TAXMAN ABOUT POETRY** (1986) {*8}, was his most successful and accomplished release yet, highlighted by the classic single 'Levi Stubbs' Tears' and 'Greetings To The New Brunette', on which Johnny Marr of The Smiths played guitar. And who could argue with the sentiments of 'Help Save The Youth Of America'?

Not content with saving our transatlantic cousins, BRAGG also did his bit for children in Britain, recording a cover of Lennon/McCartney's 'She's Leaving Home' (with Cara Tivey) for the flipside of Wet Wet Wet's chart-topping cover of the same composers' 'With A Little Help From My Friends' – the considerable proceeds went to the charity Childline.

BRAGG's next album, **WORKERS PLAYTIME** (1988) {*7}, saw a move away from the sparse accompaniment of old, while lyrically the record focused more on matters of the heart than of the ballot box. **THE INTERNATIONALE** (1990) {*5}, a mini-set released on Utility, was BB's most political work to date, featuring covers and rewrites of songs such as Carlos Mejia Godoy's 'Nicaragua Nicaraguita' and Jim Connell's socialist anthem 'The Red Flag'. The modern folk songs of the left, also including ERIC BOGLE's 'My Youngest Son Came Home Today' and EARL ROBINSON's 'I Dreamed I Saw Phil Ochs Last Night', were somewhat upstaged by (William) 'Blake's Jerusalem'. Note that the bonus-CD versions included extra readings of DICK GAUGHAN's 'Think Again', Bernice Johnson Reagon's 'Chile Your Waters Run Red Through Soweto', PHIL OCHS's 'Joe Hill', WOODY GUTHRIE's 'This Land Is Your Land' and Sam Cooke's 'A Change Is Gonna Come'.

Billy has covered a number of songs written by or associated with other acts, among them 'Walk Away Renee' (a hit for The Four Tops), 'Jeane' and 'Never Had No One Ever' (The Smiths), 'Seven And Seven Is' (Love), 'Dolphins' (RED NEIL), 'Everywhere' (Sid Griffin-Greg Trooper), 'When Will I See You Again' (The Three Degrees), 'Fear Is A Man's Best Friend' (John Cale), 'She Smiled Sweetly' (The Rolling Stones), 'Route 66' (BRAGG anglicised Bobby Troup's standard as 'A13, Trunk Road To The Sea') and `Dry Bed' (WOODY GUTHRIE).

On **DON'T TRY THIS AT HOME** (1991) {*8}, BRAGG enlisted a cast of musicians to flesh out the sound (including sidekick/roadie Wiggy from Riff Raff), a tactic that brought mixed results.

With **WILLIAM BLOKE** (1996) {*6}, Billy was now a bona-fide alt-folk artist, songs like 'A Pict Song' (a setting of a poem by Rudyard Kipling) fitting in neatly alongside 'Northern Industrial Town' and 'King James Version'. **BLOKE ON BLOKE** (1997) {*5} was a rather disappointing mini-collection of out-takes.

In 1998, Billy and alt-country group Wilco decided to do a tribute album dedicated to their dustbowl hero, WOODY GUTHRIE. In the collection {*8} **MERMAID AVENUE** (named after the street in Coney Island where the folk legend lived with his family in the late 1940s and early 1950s), BRAGG and Wilco set to music some of the unpublished lyrics Woody wrote there. From the bawdy, singalong raucousness of opener 'Walt Whitman's Niece' to the gorgeous, yawning back-porch swing of 'California Stars' and the desolate fragility of 'Birds And Ships' (featuring a heart-stopping guest vocal by Natalie Merchant), this ranked among the cream of both BRAGG's and Wilco's work. While each act interpreted the material in their own way – BRAGG obviously fitting more closely the mould of GUTHRIE's worldly, open-hearted troubadour – both Wilco and Billy brought their own personality to bear on Woody's words of wisdom.

As well as being a great record in its own right (surely a contender for album of the year) this collection underlined just how unceasingly prolific and inventive a songwriter GUTHRIE was. The spirit of this work cut to the heart of popular music. Inevitably, **MERMAID AVENUE VOL. II** (2000) {*6} couldn't quite match that high standard, but was nevertheless an enjoyable companion piece to its predecessor.

Credited to BILLY BRAGG AND THE BLOKES, **ENGLAND, HALF ENGLISH** (2002) {*5}, was again courting controversy, its obvious themes including the nation's (or its tabloid newspapers') backlash against immigration and multiculturalism. Sadly, it seemed to backfire against Billy, who was apparently living in a posh house in the Dorset suburb of Burton Bradstock – hardly a crime if you've made good from a working-class background and still have the time and the bottle to march alongside the dispirited of Britain and beyond.

Like its predecessor, **MR LOVE & JUSTICE** (2008) {*7} took its title from a book by Colin MacInnes, and again was augmented by The Blokes (Ben Mandelson, Lu Edmonds, Ian McLagan, Simon Edwards, Martyn Barker). BRAGG was now pigeonholed as an "anti-folk" artist, a weird term indeed for someone with folk so much in mind. One of his many recent successes outside his sparse solo work has been his part in the worldly-folk collective, The IMAGINED VILLAGE. *MCS & BG*

Billy Bragg - vocals, guitars (with various personnel)

Utility not issued

Jun 83. (m-lp) *(UTIL 1)* **LIFE'S A RIOT WITH SPY VS. SPY** [30] [–]
- The milkman of human kindness / To have and have not / Richard / A new England / The man in the iron mask / The busy girl buys beauty / Lovers town revisited. *(re-iss. Jan 84 on Go! Discs lp/c; UTIL/+C 1) (cd-iss. Sep 96 as 'LIFE'S A RIOT BETWEEN THE WARS' on Cooking Vinyl+=; COOKCD 106)* - BETWEEN THE WARS (EP tracks)

Go! Discs Elektra

Oct 84. (lp/c) *(A/Z GOLP 4)* **BREWING UP WITH BILLY BRAGG** [16] [–]
- It says here / Love gets dangerous / The myth of trust / From a Vauxhall Velox / The Saturday boy / Island of no return / St. Swithin's Day / Like soldiers do / This guitar says sorry / Strange things happen / A lover sings. *(cd-iss. Sep 96 on Cooking Vinyl; COOKCD 107)*

Feb 85. (7") *(???)* ST. SWITHIN'S DAY. / A New England [–] Euro [–]

Mar 85. (7"ep) *(AGOEP 1)* BETWEEN THE WARS [15] [–]
- Between the wars / The world turned upside down / Which side are you on? / It says here. *(cd+=)* - LIFE'S A RIOT ...

Dec 85. (7"m) (GOD 8) DAYS LIKE THESE. / I Don't Need This Pressure, Ron / Scholarship Is The Enemy Of Romance [43] [–]

Jun 86. (7"m) *(GOD 12)* LEVI STUBBS' TEARS. / Think Again / Walk Away Renee (version) [29] [–]
(12"+=) *(GODX 12)* - Between the wars (live).

Sep 86. (lp/c) *(A/Z GOLP 6)* **TALKING WITH THE TAXMAN ABOUT POETRY** [8] [ ]
- Greetings to the new brunette / Train train (*) / The marriage / Ideology / Levi Stubbs' tears / Honey, I'm a big boy now / There is power in a union / Help save the youth of America / Wishing the days away / The passion / The warmest room / The home front. *(cd-iss. May 87; AGOCD 6) (cd re-iss. Sep '96 on Cooking Vinyl; COOKCD 108)*

Nov 86. (7" m) *(GOD 15)* GREETINGS TO THE NEW BRUNETTE. / Deportees / The Tatler [58] [–]
(12"+=) *(GODX 15)* - Jeane / There is power in a union (instrumental).

—— In Oct 87, BRAGG was credited with The OYSTER BAND backing LEON ROSSELSON on his 45 Ballad Of A Spycatcher.

—— In May 88, Billy is credited with Cara Tivey on 'She's Leaving Home', the B-side of Wet Wet Wet's No.1 'With A little Help From My Friends'.

Go! Discs — Elektra

May 88. (m-lp/m-cd) *(A/ZA GOLP 1) <960-787-2>* **HELP SAVE THE YOUTH OF AMERICA** (LIVE AND DUBIOUS) [ ] [ ]
- Help save the youth of America / Think again / Chile your waters run red through Soweto / Days like these (DC mix) / To have and have not / There is power in a union (with The PATTERSONS).

Aug 88. (7" m) *(GOD 23)* WAITING FOR THE GREAT LEAP FORWARD. / Wishing The Days Away / Sin City [52] [–]

Sep 88. (lp/c/cd) *(AGOLP/ZGOLP/AGOCD 15) <60824>* **WORKERS PLAYTIME** [17] [ ]
- She's got a new spell / Must I paint you a picture / Tender comrade / The price I pay / Little timb-bomb / Rotting on demand / Valentine's Day is over / Life with the lions / The only one / The short answer / Waiting for the great leap forward. *(cd re-iss. Sep 96 on Cooking Vinyl; COOKCD 109)*

Nov 88. (7") *(GOD 24)* SHE'S GOT A NEW SPELL. / Must I Paint You A Picture [ ] [–]

—— In Jul 89, BB feat. on Norman Cook's single, 'Won't Talk About It'.

May 90. (m-lp/m-c/m-cd) *(UTIL/+C/CD 011) <60960>* **THE INTERNATIONALE** [34] Jun 90 [ ]
- The internationale / I dreamed I saw Phil Ochs last night / The marching song of the convert battalions / Blake's Jerusalem / Nicaragua Nicaraquita / The red flag / My youngest son came home today. *(<cd+dvd-iss. Feb 06 on Yep Roc+=; 2604>)* - (HELP SAVE THE YOUTH OF AMERICA tracks) / Joe Hill / This land is your land / Never cross a picket line / A change is gonna come / A miner's life. // (DVD live tracks).

(above was initially issued on Utility Records UK)

Jun '91. (7"/c-s) *(GOD/+MC 56)* SEXUALITY. / Bad Penny [27] [–]
(12"+=/cd-s+=) *(GOD X/CD 56)* - Sexuality (Manchester remix) / Sexuality (London remix).

Aug 91. (7"/c-s) *(GOD/+MC 60)* YOU WOKE UP MY NEIGHBOURHOOD. / Ontario Quebec And Me [54] [–]
(12"+=/cd-s+=) *(GOD X/CD 60)* - Bread and circuses / Heart like a wheel.

Sep 91. (cd/c/d-lp)(8x7" box) *(828279-2/-4/-1)(???) <61121>* **DON'T TRY THIS AT HOME** [8] [ ]
- Accident waiting to happen / Moving the goalposts / Everywhere / Cindy of a thousand lives / You woke up my neighbourhood / Trust / God's footballer / The few / Sexuality / Mother of the bride / Tank park salute / Dolphins / North Sea bubble / Rumours of war / Wish you were her / Body of water. *(re-iss. Nov 93 & Apr 98 on Cooking Vinyl lp/c/cd; COOK/+C/CD 062) (cd re-iss. Sep 96; COOKCD 110)*

Feb 92. (7"ep) *(GOD 67)* ACCIDENT WAITING TO HAPPEN (Red Star version) / Revolution / Sulk / The warmest room (live) [33] [–]
(12"+=/cd-s+=) *(GOD X/CD 67)* - live:- ('A') / Levi Stubbs' tears / Valentine's day is over / North Sea bubble.

Cooking Vinyl — Elektra

Aug 96. (7"/c-s) *(FRY/+C 051)* UPFIELD. / Thatcherites [46] [–]
(cd-s+=) *(FRYCD 051)* - Rule nor reason.

Sep 96. (lp/c/cd) *(COOK/+C/CD 100) <61935>* **WILLIAM BLOKE** [16] [ ]
- From red to blue / Upfield / Everybody loves you babe / Sugardaddy / A Pict song / Brickbat / The space race is over / Northern industrial town / The fourteenth of February / King James version. *(lp+=)* - Goalhanger.

May 97. (7") *(FRY 064)* THE BOY DONE GOOD. / Sugardaddy (re-mix) [55] [–]
(cd-s+=) *(FRYCDX 064)* - Never had no one ever / Run out of reasons.
(c-s/cd-s) *(FRY MC/CD 064)* - ('A') / Just one victory / Qualifications.

Jun 97. (m-cd) *(COOKCD 127)* **BLOKE ON BLOKE** [72] [–]
- The boy done good / Qualifications / Sugardaddy (Smokey gets in your ears mix) / Never had no one ever / Sugarduddy / Rule nor reason / Thatcherites.

BILLY BRAGG & WILCO

Elektra — Elektra

Jun 98. (cd/c) *(<7559 62204-2/-4>)* **MERMAID AVENUE** [34] [90]
- Walt Whitman's niece / California stars / Way over yonder in the minor key / Birds and ships / Hoodoo voodoo / She came along to me / At my window sad and lonely / Ingrid Bergman / Christ for President / I guess I planted / One by one / Eisler on the go / Hesitating beauty / Another man's done gone / The unwelcome guest.

Nov 98. (7"/c-s) *(E 3798/+C)* WAY OVER YONDER IN THE MINOR KEY. / My Thirty Thousand [ ] [–]
(cd-s+=) *(E 3798CD)* - Bug-eye Jim.

May 00. (cd/c) *<(7559 62522-2/-4)>* **MERMAID AVENUE VOL.II** [61] [88]
- Airline to Heaven / My flying saucer / Feed of man / Hot rod hotel / I was born / Secret of the sea / Stetson Kennedy / Remember the mountain bed / Blood of the lamb / Against th' law / All you fascists / Joe DiMaggio done it again / Meanest man / Black wind blowing / Someday, some morning, sometime.

BILLY BRAGG AND THE BLOKES

with **Ian McLagan** - keyboards, accordion / **Martyn Barker** - drums, percussion / **Simon Edwards** - bass / **Ben Mandelson** - bouzouki, mandolin, guitars / **Dave Woodhead** - trumpet / **Lu (Edmunds)** - guitars

Cooking Vinyl — Elektra

Feb 02. (cd-s) *(FRYCD 120)* ST. MONDAY / ENGLAND, HALF ENGLISH [ ] [–]

Mar 02. (lp/cd) *(COOK/+CD 222) <62743>* **ENGLAND, HALF ENGLISH** [51] [ ]
- St. Monday / Jane Allen / Distant shore / England, half English / NPWA / Some days I see the point / Baby Faroukh / Take down the Union Jack / Another kind of Judy / He'll go down / Dreadbelly / Tears of my tracks.

May 02. (cd-s) *(FRYCD 131)* TAKE DOWN THE UNION JACK / Mystery Shoes / England, Half English (7" remix) [22] [–]
(cd-s) *(FRYCD 131X)* - ('A'-Band version) / Yarra song / England, half English (12" remix).
(cd-s) (FRYCD 131XX) - ('A') / You pulled the carpet out / England, half English (ambient remix) / ('A'video).

Oct 05. (cd-s; as ROSETTA LIFE featuring BILLY BRAGG) *(FRYCD 252)* WE LAUGHED (Maxine Edgington and Billy Bragg) / The Light Within (Lisa Payne and Billy Bragg) / My Guiding Star (Veronica Barfoot & Billy Bragg) [ ] [–]

BILLY BRAGG

Cooking Vinyl — Anti

Mar 08. (7"/dl-s) *(FRY 341)* I KEEP FAITH. / Like Soldiers Do (acoustic) [ ] [–]

Mar 08. (cd) *(COOKCD 452) <86712-2>* **MR LOVE & JUSTICE** [ ] [ ]
- I keep faith / I almost killed you / M for me / The beach is free / Sing their souls back home / You make me brave / Something happened / Mr Love & Justice / If you ever leave / O freedom / The Johnny Carcinogenic show / Farm boy. *<d-cd+=; 86946-2>* - (solo equivalents of his band songs).

- (8-10*) compilations -

Jun 87. (d-lp/d-c/cd) *Go! Discs; (AGOLP/ZGOLP/AGOCD 8) / Elektra; <60726-1/-4/-2>* **BACK TO BASICS** [37] [ ]
- (LIFE'S A RIOT WITH SPY VS SPY tracks) / (BREWING UP WITH BILLY BRAGG tracks) / (BETWEEN THE WARS EP tracks). *(re-iss. Apr 98 on Cooking Vinyl d-lp/c/cd; COOK/+C/CD 060)*

Oct 03. (d-cd) *Cooking Vinyl; (COOKCD 266) / Rhino; <R2 73993>* **MUST I PAINT YOU A PICTURE?: THE ESSENTIAL BILLY BRAGG** [49] [ ]
- A new England / The man in the iron mask / The milkman of human kindness / To have and to have not / A lover sings / St. Swithin's Day / The Saturday boy / Between the wars / The world turned upside down / Levi Stubbs' tears / Walk away Renee / Greetings to the new brunette / There is power in a union / Help save the youth of America / The warmest room / Must I paint you a picture? / She's got a new spell / The price I pay / Valentine's Day is over / Waiting for the great leap forward // Sexuality / Cindy of a thousand lives / Moving the goalposts / Tank park salute / You woke up my neighbourhood / Accident waiting to happen (red stars version) / Sulk / Upfield / The fourteenth of February / Brickbat / The space race is over / The boy done good / Ingrid Bergman (with WILCO) / Way over yonder in the minor key (with WILCO) / My flying saucer (with WILCO) / All you fascists bound to lose (Blokes version) / NPWA / St. Monday / Some days I see the point / Take down the Union Jack (band version). *(ltd t-cd+=; COOKCD 266X)* - A13, trunk road to the sea / Fear is a man's best friend / Cold and bitter tears (live with TED HAWKINS) / Seven and seven is / When will I see you again / Rule nor reason (live) / Debris (live) / My bed (demo) / She smiled sweetly / Take down the Union Jack.

- essential boxed sets -

Mar 06. (7xcd-box+2xdvd) *Cooking Vinyl; (BRAGGBOX 001) / Yep Roc; <YEP 2600>* **VOLUME I** [ ] [ ]
- (LIFE'S A RIOT WITH SPY VS SPY tracks) // Strange things happen (alt.) / The cloth / Love lives here / Speedway hero / Loving you too long / This guitar says sorry (alt.) / Love gets dangerous (alt.) / The cloth / The man in the iron mask (alt.) / A13, trunk road to the sea / Fear is a man's best friend // (BREWING UP WITH BILLY BRAGG tracks) // It must be a river / Won't talk about it / Talking wag club blues / You got the power / The last time / Back to the old house / A lover sings (alt.) / Which side are you on? / It says here (alt.) / Between the wars / The world turned

upside down // (TALKING WITH THE TAXMAN ABOUT POETRY tracks) // Sin city / Deportees / There is power in a union (instrumental) / The tracks of my tears / Wishing the days away (alt.) / The clashing of ideologies (alt.) / Greetings to the new brunette (demo) / A nurse's life is full of woe / Only bad signs / Hold the fort // (THE INTERNATIONALE tracks) / Joe Hill / This land is your land / Never cross a picket line / A change is gonna come / A miner's life // (HERE AND THERE live dvd) // (FROM THE WEST DOWN TO THE EAST live DVD).

Oct 06. (8xcd-box+dvd) *Cooking Vinyl; (BRAGGBOX 002) / Yep Roc; <YEP 2605>* **VOLUME II**
- (WORKERS PLAYTIME tracks) // The only one (demo) / The price I pay (demo) / Love has no pride / That's entertainment / She's got a new spell (demo) / The short answer (demo) / Little time bomb (demo) / Bad penny (demo) / Reason to believe (live) / Must I paint you a picture (extended) / Raglan road (live) // (DON'T TRY THIS AT HOME tracks) // Party of God / North Sea bubble (demo) / Sexuality (demo) / Just one victory (alt.) / Everywhere (alt.) / Trust (demo) / Cindy of a thousand lives (demo) / The few (demo) / Revolution / Tighten up your wig / MBH / This gulf between us / Piccadilly rambler // (WILLIAM BLOKE tracks) // As long as you hold me (demo) / Who's gonna shoe your pretty little feet (demo) / Sugardaddy (demo) / The space race is over (demo) / Goalhanger (demo) / Upfield (demo) / The fourteenth of February (demo) / Qualifications / Never had no one ever / Thatcherites / All fall down // (ENGLAND, HALF ENGLISH tracks) // (BILLY BRAGG & THE BLOKES):- Billericay Dickie / Mansion on the hill / Glad and sorry / He'll go down (demo) / Yarra song / You pulled the carpet out / Mystery shoes / Tears of my tracks (demo) / Take down the Union Jack (band version) / England, half English (7" remix) / 1 2 3 4 5 6 7 8 / Dry bed (band version) / Danny Rose / She smiled sweetly // (IF YOU'VE GOT A GUESTLIST live DVD).

- (5-7*) compilations, others, etc.-

May 87. (12"ep) *Strange Fruit; (SFPS 027)* THE PEEL SESSIONS (rec. 1983)
- A new England / Strange things happen / This guitar says sorry / Love gets dangerous / A13 trunk road to the sea / Fear ... *(cd-iss. May 88; SFPSCD 027)*

Feb 92. (cd/c/lp) *Strange Fruit; (SFR CD/MC/LP 117)* **THE PEEL SESSIONS ALBUM**
- Lovers town / Between the wars / Which side are you on? / A lover sings / Days like these / The marriage / Jeane / Greetings to the new brunette / Chile your waters run red / She's got a new spell / Valentine's Day is over / The short answer / Rotting on demand. *(cd+=)* - A new England / Strange things happen / This guitar says sorry / Love gets dangerous / Fear is a man's best friend / A13 trunk road to the sea.

Nov 93. (d-lp/c/cd) *Cooking Vinyl; (COOK/+C/CD 061)* **VICTIM OF GEOGRAPHY**
- (TALKING WITH THE TAXMAN ABOUT POETRY tracks; 'Train train' d-lp-only) / (WORKERS PLAYTIME tracks). *(re-iss. Apr 98 cd/c; same)*

Aug 99. (cd/c/lp) *Cooking Vinyl; (COOK CD/MC/LP 186) / Rhino; <R2 75962>* **REACHING TO THE CONVERTED** (MINDING THE GAPS) 14
- Shirley / Sulk / Accident waiting to happen / Boy done good / Heart like a wheel / Bad penny / Ontario, Quebec and me / Walk away Renee / Rule nor reason / Days like these (UK version) / Think again / Scholarship is the enemy of romance / Wishing the days away (ballad version) / The tatler / Jeane / She's leaving home / I don't need this pressure, Ron.

BRANDYWINE BRIDGE

First there were The Brandywine Singers from the US (harmony-pop with a smidgen of trad), then there was the trio BRANDYWINE BRIDGE, a proper folk act from Britain. Formed in late 1974 by husband and wife Sheila and Stuart Hague with another multi-instrumentalist, Dave Grew, the group straddled trad and Celtic folk on two rare and quite collectable long-players, **THE GREY LADY** (1977) {*6} and **AN ENGLISH MEADOW** (1978) {*7}. Turning their musical inclinations to renaissance-period classical-folk, the team released another obscurity, **APERITIF** (1981) {*4}, and much later **AND SO TO THE FAIR** (1996) {*5}. *MCS*

Sheila Hague - vocals, acoustic guitar, recorders / **Stuart Hague** - vocals, bodhran, acoustic guitar, concertina, mandolin, etc / **Dave Grew** - vocals, banjo, fiddle, acoustic guitar, mandolin

UK Cottage — US not issued

1977. (lp) *(COT 311)* **THE GREY LADY**
- Bodhran jigs / The grey lady / Evening airs / New jigs: Clancy's fancy – Western lilt – Jackson's favourite jig / King Richard III / Forced duty / Quorn dollies / Fisherman's night song / Barrow bumps / Jack Hall. *(cd-iss. Mar 04 on Kissing Spell; KSCD 949)*

1978. (lp) *(COT 321)* **AN ENGLISH MEADOW**
- An English meadow / Dreamwater / Three lovers / Congreve's rockets / Hickory house tunes / Bonnie prince / Black Anna's bower / Sea wife's lament / Set of tunes / Toss your pennies / Billy the budgie / The ox. *(cd-iss. Feb 03 on Kissing Spell; KSCD 937)*

—— added one male musician

Q — not issued

1981. (lp) *(qs 001)* **APERITIF**
- Raven / Chasing rainbows / Kelly May / Mr Chaplin / A buffalo in New York City / The apartment / Unknown warrior / Barry Lee's fancy / A woman who needs loving / Out of the clouds.

Sound Alive — not issued

Nov 96. (cd) *(SAMLSCD 503)* **AND SO TO THE FAIR**: Brandywine Bridge play Music of Warwick Castle
- Horses brawle / Lavender's blue / The ballad of Moll Bloxham / Jaunty John / An English meadow / Dancing boy / Donkey riding / Bobby Shaftoe, folksong / Weekend in Warwick / Bernard of Clairvaux / Salisbury plain / The beggar's song / When a knight won his spurs / Over the hills. Folksong / The Boar's Head carol / The rose of Allendale / Lorna of Wychwood / Unto the fair.

BRASS MONKEY (⟹ volume one: under CARTHY, Martin)

BRETHREN OF THE FREE SPIRIT (⟹ BLACKSHAW, James)

Felicity BUIRSKI

Born December 9, 1952, in Kent, England, Felicity was a surprise to the folk fraternity when she arrived on the scene in 1987/88, having been an international Page Three model and, in 1978, one of the cheesecake girls on the Benny Hill Show. She had also released a disco-pop single in 1980.

Presumably no one took much notice of her musical background (her father was a concert pianist, her mother a classical singer) while she was being chased around the set by Benny Hill to the tune of 'Yakety Sax', or appearing in the soft-porn film The Stud; Felicity was also a roving reporter for the Beckenham Record in the early 1970s.

In 1988, as a singer-songwriter in the manner of LEONARD COHEN (whom she had met), Felicity released her debut album, **REPAIRS AND ALTERATIONS** {*7}. It was a great avant-folk record, but unfortunately TANITA TIKARAM, SUZANNE VEGA and even MARIANNE FAITHFULL were also around at the time. Recorded on the Greek island of Hydra and released by Run River (a label founded by celebrity folk couple STEVE TILSTON and MAGGIE BOYLE), it won a hi-fi magazine's Best Folk Album award in 1989, no doubt thanks to classy tracks 'Heartless Hotel' and 'Executioner's Song'. Session players included Bill Lovelady (on mandolin and guitars) and Mike Hug (on synths and piano).

It would be a decade before Felicity delivered another set, but **INTERIOR DESIGN** (1998) {*6} was certainly worth waiting for. However, yet another decade went by before the promised third set ('Committed To The Fire', scheduled for April '09 release) was premiered at a Glastonbury gig on November 27, 2008. Tragically, a near-fatal car crash the following March left Felicity housebound for two years, resulting in the record being put on hold. Fans could at least download one of the tracks, the environmental anthem 'Up Where The Eagles Fly'.

Stop press May 2011: With producer Michael Klein, Felicity is just about to start work on tracks for her fourth set ('Wayfarer'), which she assures me will be released, hopefully under the grandiose auspices of a four-CD boxed set comprising all her albums past and present. She describes the set as "one woman's journey from illusion to light". *MCS*

Felicity Buirski - vocals, acoustic guitar / (+ session people)

UK Philips — US not issued

Feb 80. (7") *(6006 623)* ANGEL. / Let It Be Me

Run River — not issued

Jan 88. (lp/c) *(RRA/+MC 004)* **REPAIRS AND ALTERATIONS**
- Dream on / Marilyn / Heartless hotel / Travelling home / The Aha song (I am the Lord) / Rumpelstiltskin / Executioner's song / Let there be light / Come to me darling. *(cd-iss. Sep 89; RRACD 004)*

May 88. (7") *(RRAS 002)* HEARTLESS HOTEL. / Travelling Home

Sep 89. (7"/12") *(RRAS 003/+T)* EXECUTIONER'S SONG. / Let There Be Light

Rhiannon — not issued

Aug 98. (cd) *(RHYCD 5005)* **INTERIOR DESIGN**
- Strange and familiar / Warrior woman / The window and me / Soldiers of the spirit / More than a lover / Fortitude of pain / Is it over? / Interior design / Blow the bridges. *(bonus +=)- Repairs and alterations / Woman (I;m back).*

i-Tunes — ...

Apr 09. (dl-s) *(-)* UP WHERE THE EAGLES FLY

2009. (cd) *(-)* **COMMITTED TO THE FIRE** [unreleased as yet]

BURGUNDY GRAPES

For the foundations of this Athens-based Greek freak-folk/alt-country duo (originally a trio), one has to reach back to 1994, when high-school friends Alexandros Miaoulis and Alexis Papaioannou teamed up with Melbourne-born songwriter/musician George Kolyvas.

Diagnosed with leukaemia in 1997, Alexis abandoned the project (he died in 2002), leaving the remaining pair to start recording at home in 2000. With the aid of Nikos Veliotis (cello) and Yiorgos Tsiatsoulis (accordion), they slowly but surely pieced together what was to become their long-awaited album, **BURGUNDY GRAPES** (2005) {*7}. Further guest spots were filled by Vassiliki Papandonopoulou (violin) and Nicholas Miaoulis (jew's harp).

Released by Outlandish Records of Greece, it was all instrumental (highlighted by 'Straight Line Blues', 'Red And Black' and 'In Search Of Morpheus'). It was promoted with a handful of choice gigs, accompanied by stalwart Yiorgos, Julia Kent (of Antony And The Johnsons), Carole Zweifel (of IN GOWAN RING) and Fabrizio Modonese Palumbo (of Larsen).

Following a stop-gap EP for Triple Bath Records, the duo pulled another set out of the hat by way of **MAN IN THE LIGHTHOUSE** (2010) {*7}, described as a meeting of Ry Cooder, Yann Tiersen and Ennio Morricone in a timeless Greenwich Village coffeehouse/folk bar. Prime cuts were 'Home Of No Return', 'Letters In A Shoe-Box' and 'Hint Of A Smile'. *MCS*

George Kolyvas - guitars, accordion, mandolin / **Alexandros Miaoulis** - guitars, mandolin, bass, metallophone, accordion, melodica, percussion

UK Outlandish — US not issued

Feb 05. (cd) *(001)* **BURGUNDY GRAPES** [–] Greek [–]
- Prelude / There and not there, and there again – April 9, '01 / Homes y muyeres / Semiramis / In search of Morpheus / Vineyard's sway / Red and black / Straight line blues / Even when you're gone / Outlandish / Long-forgotten accordion / Jim White should've played the drums on this one / Morning waltz.

Triple Bath — not issued

Feb 09. (cd) *(TRB.016)* LAGERO [–] Greek [–]
- Intro [condensed tango version of "Idalina"] / Sorrow in your bliss ["Spaghetti Western take"] / Straight line blues ["the straight version"] / Every march the 3rd at Idalina's / Diminishing scene.

Inner Ear — not issued

Jun 10. (cd) *(none)* **MAN IN THE LIGHTHOUSE** [–] Greek [–]
- Sorrow in your bliss / Home of no return / On the train to Berlin / Letters in a shoe-box / Hint of a smile / Took those troubles for a ride / Fine blossoming day / Time doesn't seem to be healing it / Old bridge / Sun trapped in the luminous room / The wind blew her in and then blew her out / The man in the lighthouse / At sea, the biggest danger is land / Anticipation song.

The BURNS UNIT (⟹ KING CREOSOTE)

R. CAJUN & THE ZYDECO BROTHERS (⟹ forthcoming GFD Vol.3: Celtic & Cajun Connections)

Simon CARE

English-born melodeon maestro SIMON CARE has been around the English Country Dance/folk scene for nigh-on three decades, having passed through the many line-ups of The ALBION BAND/ASHLEY HUTCHINGS, EDWARD II/E2K etc, WHAPWEASEL, The Morris On Band and his most diverse venture, TICKLED PINK.

Enlisting the help of musicians Mark Jolley, Gerald Claridge, Mark Hutchinson, Rob Kay, Trevor Landen and Guy Fletcher, this original "dance" outfit scored high with every release. The eponymous **TICKLED PINK** (1993) {*7} was jig'n'reel-friendly, taking trad tunes and turning them into wilder-than-wild arrangements. A dozen years in the wilderness, the group delivered their long-awaited second effort, **TERPSICHORE POLYHYMNIA** (2005) {*7}, for Talking Elephant Records, a must-listen record featuring a ceilidh-folk take of Kraftwerk's 'The Model'. With anticipation rife, **CEILIDH** (2011), a yet-to-be-certified release, resurrected the band for one final push. *MCS*

TICKLED PINK

Simon Care - melodeons / **Mark Jolley** - violin / **Gerald Claridge** - guitar / **Mark Hutchinson** - guitar / **Rob Kay** - keyboards / **Trevor Landen** - bass / **Guy Fletcher** - drums

UK: Pink Kitten — US: not issued

Nov 93. (cd/c) *(PINK 9301 CD/C)* **TICKLED PINK** ☐ ⊟
- Dutch "S" / The king / Upton Park jig / Tam lin / Strawberry-flavoured hornpipe / Blackleg / Saw jig / Green potato [Bombay mix] / Cape Horn / Mrs Foster's / The tube cowboy. *(re-iss. May 05 on Talking Elephant+=; TECD 075)* - Saw jig [live] / Need for speed [live] / Upton Park jig [acoustic].

Talking Elephant — not issued

Feb 05. (cd) *(TECD 074)* **TERPSICHORE POLYHYMNIA** ☐ ⊟
- My son John / La roulante / Japs and English / Postman's polka / Let the bullgine run – Johnny come home to Hilo / Need for speed / The model / Davy Lowston / The regatta / Apathy / Soldier's joy.

Rocksmere — not issued

May 11. (cd) *(RRCD 101)* **CEILIDH** ☐ ⊟
- Tip top polka / Dutch hornpipe / Uncle Bernard's / Drops of brandy / Burning bridges / The hogmanay / Three jolly sheepskins / Michael Turner's / Seneca square dance / Fretful porcupine / Buttered peas / Italian jig / Horse's brawl.

- (SIMON CARE) (8-10*) compilations –

Aug 02. (cd) *Talking Elephant; (TECD 044)* **THE BOX SET** ☐ ⊟
- Plough the speed / Shepherds hey – Orange in bloom – The Quaker / Reels [unreleased] / New St. George / Horseshoe hornpipe / Threats medley / Brilliant pebbles [live] / Let the bullgine run – Johnny come down to Hilo / Belltower polka / Fall back on top / Les mystere des box Vulgaire / Thomas' morris – Postman's polka / Fireman's song / Blairs / Wessex medley / Dutch "S".

Sep 08. (cd; as Various Artists) *Talking Elephant; (TECD 130)* **OH WHAT A CAPER** ☐ ⊟
- Sulgrave air – Shepherds hey / Moll in the wad / Til we meet again / Poteen / One way ticket / Good in everyone / You never know where we have been / Clackety melodeon / First Christmas waltz / Princess Royal / Matty Groves / Heathrow dawn / Go list for a sailor / Old Tom of Oxford – Wembley twizzle – Soldiers joy.

Kev CARMODY

Thee most popular Native Australian folk singer ever, Kevin Daniel Carmody (born 1946 at Cairns in Queensland) has been at the forefront of his country's heritage and culture with his widely-acclaimed protest music, and it's a pity his recordings don't stretch to a British or American release. Kev had every right to be an embittered Aboriginal in song: when he was ten, he and his little brother were removed from his drover parents by official government/Christian legislators who stuck him in with white foster guardians. His "stolen generation" struggles were intensified as he tried to better himself through education – he had been a labourer for 17 years, and was married with three children, when he enrolled at the Darling Downs Institute of Advanced Education.

Despite his lack of formal schooling (reading and writing were not his strengths at the time), CARMODY would subsequently complete his Bachelor of Arts degree and take his Ph.D in history.

Having taken up the acoustic guitar to help him with word assimilation in his adult education, Kev took up performing professionally and signed his first recording contract in 1987, having just turned 40. A year later, his debut LP was unleashed. **PILLARS OF SOCIETY** (1988) {*9} dealt with the hypocrisy of British settlers against his indigenous peoples in songs like 'Thou Shalt Not Steal', the DYLANesque 'Jack Deelin', 'Black Deaths In Custody', 'Black Bess' and other classics. All dealt with the injustices he had witnessed both first-hand and via his historical scholarship.

Mixing folk, country, blues and reggae into the melting pot, he released further albums for Festival Records. 1990's **EULOGY (FOR A BLACK PERSON)** {*7} described Kev's battles with poverty and racism, and 'Elly' and 'Blood Red Rose' were pitched together as a double-edged single release – one that got away, chart-wise.

In 1991 CARMODY teamed up with fellow folkie PAUL KELLY (and his Messengers) to write 'From Little Things Big Things Grow', a song about the drovers' walk-out at Gurindji that sparked off the indigenous land rights movement of the 1960s. His third album, **BLOODLINES** (1993) {*7}, contained his version of the track (first released on KELLY's 'Comedy' set), and the record inspired a musical TV documentary, 'Blood Brothers'.

Co-produced with Steve Kilbey of The Church, **IMAGES AND ILLUSIONS** (1995) {*6} found CARMODY reassessing his compliance with the mainstream music industry, and he would later take time to act as a speaker and activist for the Aboriginal peoples. Kev and other friends (Mairead Hannan for one) assisted his friend PAUL KELLY on the 2001-released OST/score for the film 'One Night The Moon'.

A rare self-financed album, **MIRRORS** {*6}, finally saw the light of day in 2004, but despite a tribute/best of double-CD a few years later, this has been Kev's last solo release so far. Always busy on the political front, CARMODY supported charities fighting poverty and cancer, and battled incessantly for Aboriginal rights (his country officially apologised for its appalling deeds in 2008). He and KELLY also contributed guest vocals to the hit Get Up Mob revamp of their 'From Little Things…' anthem, and he was inducted into the ARIA (Australian Recording Industry Association) Hall of Fame in 2009. *MCS*

Kev Carmody - vocals, guitar, didgeridoo / + session people

UK/Aus: Larrikin — US: not issued

Nov 88. (7") *(???)* JACK DEELIN. / [second version] ⊟ Austra ⊟

Nov 88. (lp) *(RBLP 88001)* **PILLARS OF SOCIETY** ⊟ Austra ⊟
- Pillars of society / Jack Deelin / Flagstone creek / Attack attack / Thou shalt not steal / Black deaths in custody / Black Bess / Comrade Jesus Christ / Twisted rail / White bourgeois woman. *(cd-iss. Feb 89 on Larrikin; CDLRF 237) (cd re-iss. 2007 on Song Cycles)*

Feb 90. (7") *(???)* THOU SHALT NOT STEAL. / Pillars Of Society ⊟ Austra ⊟

Festival — not issued

Nov 90. (7") *(???)* EULOGY (FOR A BLACK PERSON). / Cannot Buy My Soul ⊟ Austra ⊟

Nov 90. (cd) *(???)* **EULOGY (FOR A BLACK PERSON)** ⊟ Austra ⊟
- Elly / I've been moved / Eulogy (for a black person) / Cannot buy my soul / Sexual teaser / Tom Shane / Blood red rose / River of tears / Droving woman. *(cd re-iss. May 99; ???) (re-iss. 2007 on Song Cycles)*

Jul 91. (7") *(???)* FROM LITTLE THINGS BIG THINGS GROW ⊟ Austra ⊟

Apr 92. (7") *(PRK 929)* BLOOD RED ROSE / Elly ⊟ Austra ⊟

Oct 92. (cd-s) *(???)* LIVING SOUTH OF THE FREEWAY ⊟ Austra ⊟

Dec 92. (cd-ep) *(???)* STREET BEAT Austra
- Living south of the freeway / Darkside / Street beat / Rider in the rain.

Jul 93. (cd-s) *(???)* FREEDOM / Freedom [radio edit] / Thou Shalt Not Steal Austra

Jul 93. (cd) *(D 30954)* **BLOODLINES** Austra
- Freedom / Asbestosis / Rider in the rain / Messenger / Bloodlines / Darkside / Sorry business / BDP [Bourgeois Drop-out Progeny] / Living south of the freeway / On the wire / Earth mother [instrumental] / Bloodlines (return) [instrumental] / From little things big things grow / Revelations addendum chapter 23 verses 1-35. *(re-iss. 2007 on Song Cycles)*

May 94. (cd-s) *(???)* ON THE WIRE / The Messenger / Sorry Business Austra

Aug 95. (cd-s) *(D 901)* THE YOUNG DANCER IS DEAD / Eulogy / On The Wire Austra

Sep 95. (cd) *(D 31380)* **IMAGES AND ILLUSIONS** Austra
- Some strange strange people / Images of London / Needles in the nursery / Travellin' north / Fire and wind / River road / Jessica / The young dancer is dead / The anti-Christ / Sistem an' you / I'm still in love with you / Blue you / Solar wind / Shades of violet / Eulogy. *(re-iss. 2007 on Song Cycles)*

—— In 2001, Kev was credited on PAUL KELLY's soundtrack to 'One Night The Moon'

Song Cycles not issued

May 04. (cd) *(none)* **MIRRORS** Austra
- Dirty dollar / Are you connected? / Moonstruck / Refugees / Dubya love ya? / Who are they? / Campfire rain / El diablo blanco / Georgina river / Milky way / You beautiful / Comin' home.

- (8-10*) compilations -

2000. (cd) *Song Cycles; (none)* **MESSAGES (SONGS FROM THE FIRST FOUR ALBUMS)** Austra
- Pillars of society / Flagstone creek / Comrade Jesus Christ / Twisted rail / Thou shalt not steal / Elly / Travellin' north / I've been moved / The messenger / I'm still in love with you / On the wire / Freedom / From little things big things grow / Images of London / Jessica / Eulogy.

Feb 07. (d-cd) *Virgin; (0946 3 77741 2)* **CANNOT BUY MY SOUL: THE SONGS OF KEV CARMODY** Austra
- I've been moved (DAN KELLY) / Thou shalt not steal (JOHN BUTLER TRIO) / Elly (BERNARD FANNING) / The young dancer is dead (The LAST KINECTION) / From little things big things grow (The WAIFS) / River of tears (The DRONES) / On the wire (TROY CASSAR-DALEY) / Cannot buy my soul (ARCHIE ROACH) / Moonstruck (SARA STORER) / This land is mine (SCOTT WILSON & DAN SULTAN) / Darkside (TEX PERKINS) / Blood red rose (CLARE BOWDITCH) / Comrade Jesus Christ (The HERD) / Images of London (STEVE KILBEY) / Droving woman (PAUL KELLY, AUGIE MARCH AND MISSY HIGGINS) / Eulogy for a black man (The PIGRAM BROTHERS) // [equivalent KEV CARMODY versions].

Eliza CARTHY

Coming from a celebrity folk family (her father MARTIN CARTHY, her mother NORMA WATERSON) but looking like some adolescent pop-pixie princess, multi-talented child prodigy ELIZA "Liza" CARTHY was quite a prospect to behold. Born August 23, 1975, at Scarborough in North Yorkshire, she's disappointed no one since her youthful days fronting the Waterdaughters alongside auntie LAL WATERSON and cousin Maria Knight. Her musical latchkey-kid fame came through her trad/ceilidh-styled band The Kings Of Calicutt.

Award after award has garlanded her ever since she stepped up to the mic: whether for singing, fiddling or just being her hard-working self, Eliza has swept the board as one of folk music's most enduring and loveable characters. Solo albums, collaborative albums, family albums and a great many sessions have kept her busy over the past two decades.

The eponymous **ELIZA CARTHY & NANCY KERR** (1993) {*6}, and the pair's second release **SHAPE OF SCRAPE** (1995) {*7}, sandwiched Liza's introduction into the WATERSON: CARTHY family folk troupe on their eponymous 1994 album. Both contained enough traditional fare and sea shanties to shiver anybody's timbers.

On the solo front, but with the same panache and sophistication, **HEAT LIGHT AND SOUND** (1996) {*7} showed that no prisoners would be taken in her ambitious interpretations of hearty trad ballads and jigs. Session players included Barnaby Stradling, Olly Knight, James Fagan, Dan Plews and Hazel Wrigley, to name a handful. Her voice as sweet as her virtuoso fiddle playing, songs like 'Ten Thousand Miles' and the acappella 'Clark Saunders' rubbed shoulders with dance tunes from 'Cold, Wet And Rainy Night' to 'Jacky Tar'. Marking time a little, she released an album recorded three years earlier, **ELIZA CARTHY AND THE KINGS OF CALICUTT** (1997) {*6}. It was a little overshadowed by a second WATERSON: CARTHY effort 'Common Tongue', issued at the same time. Incidentally, the Kings were Barnaby, Saul Rose, Andi Wells and Maclaine Colston, with Celtic-folk producer John McCusker on guest violin.

Hailed by fans and critics alike, the masterful double set **RED RICE** (1998) {*8} saw her working with the usual suspects, while it also introduced a few Celtic musicians and song types to the fold (Andy Thorburn was one). She also covered BEN HARPER's 'Walk Away'.

Moving up to the majors after signing to Warner Bros, and with an array of seasoned session players to compete with her Brit-folk friends (and dad Martin on board), **ANGELS & CIGARETTES** (2000) {*7} had a contemporary folktronica, BETH ORTON-meets-Kirsty MacColl feel. Without a sourced song in sight, most of the tracks were written or co-written by CARTHY, the exception being her rendition of Paul Weller's 'Wild Wood'.

Eliza stepped back to her comfort zone courtesy of her trad-friendly collaboration with Martin Green on 2001's **DINNER** {*5}, a record that paved the way for her reunification with "proper" folk music (and Topic Records) in the shape of **ANGLICANA** (2002) {*7}. Like Red Rice before it, the set was nominated for a Mercury Music Prize. Meanwhile she had also guested notably on albums by BILLY BRAGG & Wilco ('Mermaid Avenue' Vols.I & II), BLUE MURDER ('No One Stands Alone') and of course, anything that her immediate family took part in around that time, including further WATERSON: CARTHY records.

ROUGH MUSIC (2005) {*7} brought in The Ratcatchers, including SPIERS & BODEN and the ever-ready Ben Ivitsky, all helping on trad arrangements of varied material, some of it from the pens of BILLY BRAGG and SCAN TESTER.

After her part in The IMAGINED VILLAGE collective, it was back to basics for Eliza on 2008's **DREAMS OF BREATHING UNDERWATER** {*6}, a record composed by CARTHY and Ivitsky except for Rory McLeod's 'Hug You Like A Mountain'. The promotional tour was cancelled when Eliza was diagnosed with a cyst in her throat, followed later in the year by the birth of her daughter. Two sets followed in relatively quick succession: **GIFT** (2010) {*6}with NORMA WATERSON and the self-composed solo outing **NEPTUNE** (2011) {*6}. *MCS*

Eliza Carthy - fiddle, vocals, one-row accordion, keyboards, etc. (with various session players)

UK Mrs. Casey — US not issued

Nov 93. (cd/c; ELIZA CARTHY & NANCY KERR) *(MCR 3991 CD/C)* **ELIZA CARTHY & NANCY KERR**
- Waterloo fair - Speed the plow / Lucy's waltz – Liza's favourite / Alistair's / The unquiet grave / The march of the kings of Laiose / An old man came courting / Swedish wedding march / Whittingham fair / Brushes and briars / Tune / The wrong favour / Prague - Polly Bishop's slip jig - The storyteller - Black and white rag.

—— In Oct 94 Eliza collaborated with her mother and father, MARTIN CARTHY and NORMA WATERSON, on the album cd/c 'Waterson: Carthy'.

Jul 95. (cd/c; ELIZA CARTHY & NANCY KERR) *(MCR 5992 CD/C)* **SHAPE OF SCRAPE**
- Edward Corcoran - Black joke / I know my love / Low down in the broom - The sukebind / The downfall of Paris / The ride in the creel / Mary custy air / Growling (the trees they do grow high) / The poor and young single sailor / Balter Svens Parapolkett / Bonny light horseman - Michael Turner's waltz / Wanton wife of Castlegate - Princess Royal / The gypsy hornpipe - The hawk - Indian queen.

Topic — Big Easy

Feb 96. (cd/c) *(TSCD/KTSC 482)* <52232> **HEAT LIGHT AND SOUND**
- Cold, wet and rainy night - The grand hornpipe / Cumberland waltz - Petit homme - Miss Bowls / What a beau your granny is - Stone steps / Ten thousand miles - Bacca pipes / Clark Saunders / Stamps for the dog / Peggy / Blind fiddler / Lady Barnsley's fancy - Trip to Cartmel – Hardy's crow / By then / Sheath and knife / Jacky tar.

—— In 1997, a second WATERSON: CARTHY set, 'Common Tongue' was issued.

Topic — Topic

Jul 97. (cd) *(<TSCD 489>)* **ELIZA CARTHY AND THE KINGS OF CALICUTT** (rec.1994) Aug 97
- Trip to Fowey - Cuckold came out of the Amery - Indian queen / Whirly whorl / Bonaparte's retreat / Little bear - Wobbly cat - Upton stick dance / Mother, go make my bed - Flower of Swiss Cottage / Good morning, Mr. Walker / Holm Band tune - Dave Roberts' tune – Jemima's jig / Sheffield Park - Polly Bishop's slip jig - Roger de Coverley / Fisher boy / If you will not have me, you may let me go - The pullet - The storyteller.

May 98. (2xcd) *(TSCD 493+494)* *<TSCDD 2001>* **RED RICE**
- RED: Accordion song (accidental Saturday night kitchen mix) / 10,000 miles / Billy boy - The widow's wedding / Time in the son / Stumbling on / Stingo - The stacking reel / Greenwood laddie - Mrs Capron's reel - Tune / Walk away / Adieu, adieu / Russia (call waiting) / Red rice. // RICE: Blow the winds - The game of draughts / The snow it melts the soonest / Picking up sticks - The old mole - Felton Lonnin - Kingston girls / Miller and the lass / Herring song / Mons Meg / Tuesday morning / Haddock and chips / The Americans have stolen my true love away / Zycanthos jig – Tommy's foot / Quebecois / The sweetness of Mary - Holywell hornpipe - Swedish

/ Benjamin Bowmaneer / Commodore Moore - The black dance - A Andy O. *<cd 'RED' / cd 'RICE' re-iss. Jun 01; TSCD 493 / TSCD 494>*

Warners Warners

Sep 00. (cd) *(<9362 47698-2>)* **ANGELS & CIGARETTES** □ □
- Whispers of summer / Train song / Beautiful girl / Whole / Poor little me / The company of men / Perfect / Wild wood / Breathe / Fuse.

Heroes Of Edible Music not issued

Dec 01. (cd; MARTIN GREEN & ELIZA CARTHY) *(none)* **DINNER** □ ⊟
- Fen / Mr. Preston's hornpipe / Stephen's leaving - The jolly f*cker - Rorospols / Abe's retreat - Kielder castle / Jack Warrel's hornpipe / Daniel Wright's hornpipe - A bagpipe hornpipe - Lemady / Saul's shoes - Prescott's punch / Presbyterian hornpipe - Game of draughts / Young Collins.

Topic Topic

Oct 02. (cd) *(<TSCD 539>)* **ANGLICANA** □ Nov 02 □
- Worcester city / Just as the tide was flowing / Limbo / Little gypsy girl / No man's jig - Hanoverian dance - Three jolly sheepskins / Pretty ploughboy / Bold privateer / Dr McMbe / In London so fair / Willow tree.

Apr 05. (cd) *(<TSCD 554>)* **ROUGH MUSIC** □ Jun 05 □
- Turpin hero / King James version / Cobbler's hornpipe / Gallant hussar / Upside down: Double lead through - Highland Mary - Dear tobacco / Mohair / The unfortunate lass / Scan tester's country stepdance - Lemmy Brazil's No.2 / Maid on the shore / Mr. McCusker and Mr. McGoldrick's English choice / Tom Brown.

Jun 08. (cd) *(<TSCD 571>)* **DREAMS OF BREATHING UNDERWATER** □ □
- Follow the dollar / Two tears / Rows of angels / Rosalie / Mr. Magnifico / Like I care (wings) / Lavenders / Little bigman / Simple things / Hug you like a mountain / Oranges and sea salt.

Jul 10. (cd; by ELIZA CARTHY & NORMA WATERSON) *(<TSCD 579>)* **GIFT** □ Aug 10 □
- Poor wayfaring stranger / Little grey hawk / Boston burglar / The nightingale – For Kate / Bonaparte's lament / The rose and the lily / Bunch of thyme / Ukulele lady – (If paradise is) Half as nice / Psalm of life / Prairie lullaby / Shallow brown.

Hem Hem not issued

May 11. (cd/lp) *(HHR 001 CD/LP)* **NEPTUNE** □ ⊟
- Blood on my boots / War / Write a letter / Tea at five / Monkey / Revolution / Britain is a carpark / Romeo / Hansel (breadcrumbs) / Thursday.

- (8-10*) compilation -

Jan 04. (cd) *Highpoint; <HPO 6005>* **THE DEFINITIVE COLLECTION** ⊟ □
- The light dragoon / Greenwood laddie - Mrs. Capron's reel - Tune / Mother, go make my bed - Flower of Swiss Cottage / Cold, wet and rainy night - The grand hornpipe / Fisher boy / Billy boy - The widow's wedding / French stroller / Stumbling on / Blow the winds - The game of draughts / Mons Meg / Diego's bold shore / Go from my window / Child among the weeds.

- (5-7*) compilation -

Feb 02. (cd; ELIZA CARTHY & NANCY KERR) *Mrs. Casey; (MCRCD 1003) / Gadfly; <512>* **ON REFLECTION** □ Sep 02 □
- The gypsy hornpipe - The hawk - Indian queen / Whittingham fair - For Whittingham fair / 3-2 hornpipes / Bushes and briars / Waterloo fair - Speed the plough / The keek in the creel / Dance to your daddy - The flaming drones / Prague – Eliza's favourites / Fen / Port 'n' brandy / I know my love / Paddy's rambles through the park / Growing (the trees they do grow high) / Reel du pendu / Bonnie light horseman.

Dave CARTWRIGHT

Somewhat overlooked by many music writers until recently, singer-songwriter DAVE CARTWRIGHT was born in April 1943 in Haslemere, Surrey, but grew up in Amblecote, West Midlands. Inspired by rock 'n' roll as a teenager, he founded his first band, The Crossfires, a short-lived late-1950s act that he abandoned for Kidderminster boppers The Clippers. His love of folk music came about after listening to the likes of DYLAN, PETER, PAUL & MARY, TOM PAXTON and their ilk.

At the turn of the 1960s/70s he played with Bev Pegg and his Goin' Nowhere Band on a couple of harmony-folk LPs, personnel comprising Bev Pegg (lead guitar and bass), Paul Davenport (piano), Ken Wright or Paul Mackreath or Peter Burkes (drums), Terry Clarke (bass), backing vocals Jan Lawson, Kate Mulraney and Annie Norris. It is thought this band turned up a little later as Away From The Sand. With possibly most of the above on board, DAVE CARTWRIGHT AND FRIENDS released **in the MIDDLE OF THE ROAD** (1971) {*4}.

Turning professional around this period, CARTWRIGHT almost immediately signed to Nat Joseph's burgeoning Transatlantic imprint, releasing his debut album proper, **A LITTLE BIT OF GLORY** {*7,} in 1972. 'Song For Susan' and '50 Miles Of Blue' (the latter a precursor to 'Grandad' or 'Matchstalk Men And Matchstalk Cats And Dogs'), among others, have diverse appeal; it's just a pity there was a certain Clifford T. Ward – also from Kidderminster – breaking through at the same time. CARTWRIGHT was to write a top-selling and critically acclaimed biography of the man ('Bittersweet – The Clifford T. Ward Story'), published in 2008.

BACK TO THE GARDEN (1973) {*6}, featuring the thought-provoking 'To Make Tomorrow Green', and **DON'T LET YOUR FAMILY DOWN** (1974) {*5} followed the same path, and he was better known for his local BBC radio shows and for being a regular on the BBC's Pebble Mill At One TV programme. A switch to DJM Records when times were more than tough for Transatlantic resulted in his swansong 1970s pop set, **MASQUERADE** (1977) {*5}.

Later in 1977, after an ecstatically-receivered support slot to Celtic-folk labelmates HORSLIPS, Dave retired to Hertfordshire, his radio shows (Folkus and The Rock 'n' Roll Years) keeping him busy for a while. With his hundreds of songs written in the wilderness years (over 700 was an estimate) Dave began his resurgence, issuing a handful of nice-and-easy acoustic CDs from his converted basement. As of spring 2011 he's touring Holland, where his career is going through a bit of a renaissance. It's well deserved – he's a thoroughly nice guy. *MCS*

Dave Cartwright - vocals, acoustic guitar, harmonica / + session players

UK US
Beaujangle not issued

1971. (ltd-lp; as DAVE CARTWRIGHT AND FRIENDS) *(DB 0001)* **in the MIDDLE OF THE ROAD** □ ⊟
- Middle of the road / Sweet Angeline / When summer comes to Susan / Friends and fools / Weekend / Miss never know how you feel / Maggie my dear / Nottingham town / Song to Joanie / Peaceful mind / Come along girl / I can move so sad. *(cd-iss. 2000s; same)*

Transatlantic not issued

1972. (lp) *(TRA 255)* **A LITTLE BIT OF GLORY** □ ⊟
- Song for Susan / Rainbow green / Blue-eyed Jean / We all need a king / Tom all-alone / Song of Davy / It hardly ever rains / Oh sweet momma / Fifty miles of blue / Middle of the road / Good times are coming again.

1973. (lp) *(TRA 267)* **BACK TO THE GARDEN** □ ⊟
- Night of magic / My delicate skin / Cobweb broom / To make tomorrow green / A little bit of glory / Dark eyed sailor / Shepherd's return / Chains / Angeline / Dance of the seasons / Back to the garden.

Sep 74. (lp) *(TRA 284)* **DON'T LET YOUR FAMILY DOWN** □ ⊟
- Travelling show / Don't let your family down / England / Joanna / Do you remember? / It isn't easy / Court of the queen / Maggie my dear / When love comes home / Song and dance man.

DJM. not issued

Jan 77. (lp) *(DJF 20489)* **MASQUERADE** □ ⊟
- Masquerade / Have you seen Sophie dance? / Queen of the May / Star movie / So you want to be a ballerina? / All the world's a stage / Band of hope / Love's own lady / Stage fright / Isabella / Starship Enterprise / When the lights go out at the fair.

Feb 77. (7") *(DJS 10750)* BAND OF HOPE. / Queen Of The May □ ⊟

Luna not issued

Aug 09. (cd) *(245)* **HONESTY** ⊟ mail-o ⊟
- Early morning / Jesus sleeps in Memphis / The white owl / Under siege / Hope (an English spiritual) / It all depends on you / Blood on the moon / Do nothing 'til you hear from me / I love the rain / I just want more (of what you've got) / God alone / Ad lib / Down among the dead men / You (the sun) / Midwinter / Zenobia.

May 10. (cd) *(246)* **STRANGE NEWS** ⊟ mail-o ⊟
- Amblecote / Just another day / You know me much too well / Purify / The cold light of day / In your dreams / Love is all we need / Songbirds / Cathedrals / Johnny Dean / For my country / Coimbra / When I die / Moon of sighs / The mirror / Cats don't care / Ned o' the hill.

Aug 10. (cd) *(247)* **WILLOW PATTERNS** ⊟ mail-o ⊟
- Isle Ornsay / Dark-haired girl / The last unicorn / Song of the dove / Under English skies / Big boy now / Willow pattern / Living on dreams / Quicksand / Urlecchina / Boston moon / Thief of love / Wonderful life / Nothing left to say / To put you in the picture / Faraway land.

- (8-10*) compilations –

2011. (cd) *Luna; (255)* **THE TRANSATLANTIC YEARS** 1972–1974 □ ⊟
- Song for Susan / To make tomorrow green / Maggie my dear / Middle of the road / Nights of magic / England / 50 miles of blue / The shepherd's return / Do you remember? / Tom-all-alone / Chains / The court of the queen / Oh sweet momma / Dark-eyed sailor / Travelling show / It hardly ever rains / Angeline / It isn't easy / Song of Davy / My delicate skin / Song and dance man.

CAUGHT ON THE HOP

From Wigan in England's north, theirs was a musical meeting of electric/acoustic folk and electronics. Headed by Mick Burrows and co-starring fellow strummer Bernie Forkin, fiddler Steve Padget and synth/keys player Steve

Jackman, this line-up produced one LP (**FROZEN FLAMES** (1986) {*5}) for Dragon Records before going back underground. Judging by some original titles (e.g. 'The Road To Kashmajiro') and a handful of sea shanty/trad tunes (including opener 'Admiral Benbow'), the band had been a hairsbreadth from staying on the dole. Although they'd never stopped playing pubs and festivals throughout, the band resurfaced in the early 1990s with new female member Terri (surname unknown) on programming/synths (Jackman had left). Second set **A NATION OF HOPKEEPERS** (1993) {*5} was probably a pun too far – think OYSTERBAND sitting in with The Shamen. However, they did succeed in wowing a few audiences, including a 12,000 crowd at Belgium's Dranouter Festival and a private-party gig for the Manchester United squad of the mid-1990s (Giggs, Keane, Cantona, Schmeichel, et al). *MCS*

Mick Burrows - vocals, mandolin, bouzouki / guitar / **Bernie Forkin** - bass, bouzouki, acoustic guitar / **Steve Jackman** - synthesizer, keyboards, flute / **Steve Padget** - fiddles

UK Dragon — US not issued

Nov 86. (lp) *(DRGN 863)* **FROZEN FLAMES**
- Admiral Benbow / Icy acres / The consolation prize / Sleep sound in the morning + The galley watch / Chase the buffalo / Adieu to all judges and juries / The prison ship / Edward / The road to Kashmajiro / Erin's lovely Lee / Galopede – Flowers of Edinburgh / The New York trader.

—— it is thought there were also two ltd-edition cassettes, 'The Lamb' and 'St Helens'

—— **Terri** - synthesizers, programming; repl. Jackman

Harbourtown — not issued

Oct 93. (cd) *(HARCD 024)* **A NATION OF HOPKEEPERS**
- Drill ye tarriers drill / The jolly thresherman / The floating bloater / The last of the dancing bears / The Diamantina drover / Da slockit light / The banks of the Nile / Honey in the rock / The Watford explosion / Donahoe Downs / The bonny ship the Diamond / Sinner man.

—— disbanded in 1995, and an album was more than likely shelved

Jim CAUSLEY (⟹ The DEVIL'S INTERVAL)

Mark CHADWICK (⟹ LEVELLERS)

Sheila CHANDRA [folk times]

Born March 14, 1965 in Waterloo, London, of Indian ancestry, teenage CHANDRA (and her husband Steve Coe) burst on to the music scene in 1982 through worldbeat pop duo Monsoon and their UK Top 20 one-hit-wonder 'Ever So Lonely'. With help from Coe she established herself in the ethnic dance-pop world with the quickfire string of albums 'Out On My Own' (1984), 'Quiet' (1984), 'The Struggle' (1985) and 'Nada Brahma' (1985).

The chant of CHANDRA was next heard on BLOWZABELLA's offshoot ANCIENT BEATBOX on a single, 'Raining (My Eyes Are Filled With Clouds)', lifted from their eponymous techno-folk set of 1989.

But who could have known the route (or roots) she'd take thereafter? Like some cocktail of Dead Can Dance and ethereal world/folk mantras, the groundbreaking **ROOTS AND WINGS** {*7} was unleashed on an unsuspecting world at the turn of the decade, her first album for five years. From the percussive and evocative Indian-ness of 'Shanti, Shanti, Shanti' to the breathtaking cinematic soundscape of the set's title track, the record juxtaposed culture and crossed borders. Her love of Celtic-folk was evident on her stark reinterpretation of the Scots traditional ballad 'Lament Of McCrimmon' (interpolated with 'Song Of The Banshee'), bringing to mind CLANNAD, ENYA or a reinvented Peter Gabriel. Multi-instrumentalist Steve Coe was on hand to augment proceedings, co-writing around 50% of the record (including the seven-minute 'The Struggle – The Dream' and the multi-layered 'One') with CHANDRA.

Proving it wasn't a one-off, **WEAVING MY ANCESTORS' VOICES** (1992) {*7} once again combined Eastern rhythms with world and Celtic-folk, the record even reprising 'Ever So Lonely' (in medley form). The vocal gymnastics of 'The Enchantment', 'Sacred Stones' and 'Dhyana And Donalogue' were reminiscent of the Cocteau Twins escaping the Highlands.

The trilogy was completed with **THE ZEN KISS** (1994) {*6}, CHANDRA's voice now taking on a sort of JUNE TABOR role, although transmeditational mantras echoed through the tracks 'Waiting', 'Shehnai Song' and 'A Sailor's Life'.

From 1996 onwards she reverted to experimental/drone-type sets, reviving her folk-world passport only with 'Breath Of Life', a song lifted from the Howard Shore score/OST to 'The Lord Of The Rings: The Two Towers' (2002). In 2007, CHANDRA was an integral part of the BBC award-winning The IMAGINED VILLAGE folk/worldbeat collective, her voice on 'The Welcome Sailor' a highlight. *MCS*

—— (below only concentrates on her folk sets)

Sheila Chandra - vocals / with backing musicians

UK Indipop — US not issued

Jan 90. (lp/c/cd) *(SCH/+MC/CD 5)* **ROOTS AND WINGS**
- One / Shanti, shanti, shanti / Roots and wings (traditional mix) / The struggle (Slagverks mix) / Lament of McCrimmon - Song of the banshee / Mecca / Roots and wings (original Madras mix) / Konnokol al dente / Escher's triangle / The struggle - The dream / Shanti, shanti, shanti. *<US cd-iss. 1995 on Caroline; CAR 1779> <re-iss. Apr 00 on Narada; 49086>*

Real World — Real World

May 92. (cd/c) *(CDRW/RWMC 24)* *<62322>* **WEAVING MY ANCESTORS' VOICES** — Jan 93
- Speaking in tongues I / Dhyana and Donalogue / (a) Nana (b) The dreaming / Ever so lonely - Eyes - Ocean / The enchantment / The call / Bhajan / Speaking in tongues II / Sacred stones / Om namaha shiva.

May 94. (cd/c) *(CDRW/RWMC 45)* *<62342>* **THE ZEN KISS**
- La Sagesse (women, I'm calling you) / Speaking in tongues III / Waiting / Shehnai song / Love it is a killing thing / Speaking in tongues IV / Woman and child / En mireal del penal / A sailor's life / Abbess Hildegard / Kafi noir.

—— subsequent solo albums:- 'ABoneCroneDrone' (1996), 'This Sentence Is True'.

- corresponding compilation -

Apr 99. (cd) *Real World; (CDRW 77)* *<47184>* **MOONSUNG: A RealWorld Retrospective**
- Ever so lonely - Eyes / Ocean / Dhyana and Donalogue / Shehnai song / The enchantment / Speaking in tongues III / ABoneCroneDrone 3 (excerpt) / Nana / Waiting / Sacred stones / AboneCroneDrone 1 (excerpt) / Lagan love - Nada Brahma / Blacksmith. *<re-iss. Jul 08 +=; 80076>* - Ever so lonely - Eyes - Ocean.

—— other compilations:- 'Silk 1983–1990' (1990) on Indipop and 'The Indipop Retrospective' (2003) on Narada World Records.

The CHARTISTS

Named after the early-Victorian radical reform movement, this group was founded by Welsh songwriter, Wynford Jones and based around the Islwyn Folk Club. Other members included Geri Thomas, Laurence Eddy, Geoff Cripps, Remo Lusardi and multi-instrumentalist Russell Jones. Showcasing their concept LP from their live beginnings in 1979, **THE CHARTISTS** (1982) {*5}, finally reached independent outlets three years later. A confident piece of electric folk-opera, the limited-edition album was akin to 1970s work by LOUDEST WHISPER and HORSLIPS. After a sabbatical of five years, the group returned, without Remo and Russell, with **CAUSE FOR COMPLAINT** (1987) {*6}, taking up social issues and the odd industrial dispute as their inspiration. Guests included fiddler BRIAN McNEILL of the BATTLEFIELD BAND, drummer Nick Lewis, flautist Nigel Hodge (later a full-time member in 2007) and cornet player Julian Harris. *MCS*

Wynford Jones - vocals, guitar / **Geri Thomas** - narrator, vocals, whistle / **Remo Lusardi** - vocals, guitars / **Russell Jones** - multi / **Laurence Eddy** - vocals, guitar, synths / **Geoff Cripps** - vocals, mandolin, guitars, autoharp, bass

UK Steam Pie — US not issued

1982. (ltd-lp) *(SPR 1001S)* **THE CHARTISTS**
- The miners' hard times / The charter / Frost Williams and Jones / Bogey, bogey, one pound ten / The march - part one / The march - part two / Fare thee well to Newport / These brave men.

—— now without Remo + Russell

1987. (ltd-lp) *(SPR 1004S)* **CAUSE FOR COMPLAINT**
- We regret to inform / Those were the days / The band / Dic Penderyn / Cause for complaint / Jack of all trades / The blue and the green / Summer comes rolling around / Er cof am / 1984. *(re-iss. 1990s as 'IT'S NOT RIGHT' on Hypertension, Germany)*

—— they split in August 1990; Jones + Eddy later formed Lawford; Cripps was in Allan Yn Y Fan

—— **Jones, Eddy, Thomas + Nigel Hodge** re-formed in 2007, but the group has been put on hold for now

Mic CHRISTOPHER

But for his tragic death on November 29, 2001, MIC CHRISTOPHER would, judging by a posthumous set put together around a year later, surely have been a major star.

Born September 21, 1969 in the Bronx, New York City to Irish parents, young Mic moved back with them to the Emerald Isle in 1972. His interest in Irish traditional and contemporary sounds evolved throughout his schooldays, although he left at fifteen to be a banjo-playing busker in Dublin. There he met up with Glen Hansard and Frames buddy David Odlum; the latter's brother Karl (on bass) would help Mic form his first proper folk band, The MARY JANES (adding guitarist Simon Good and their first drummer, Steven Hogan).

A publishing deal with Warner-Chappell was behind the Irish-only release of their drummerless debut set, **BORED OF THEIR LAUGHTER** (1994) {*6}.

The addition of Australian drummer Mark Stanley saw the release of a second set, **SHAM** (1998) {*6}, while tours of the festival circuit (including Glastonbury, Feile and the Fleadh) helped promote it beyond its indie status. In 1999 the band split, leaving CHRISTOPHER to take on a solo tour of Australia.

Things looked brighter for Mic in 2001, with a projected tour supporting The WATERBOYS just over the horizon. However, this was to come to an abrupt end when, having fallen from a motorcycle a few months previously, he took a tumble after a gig on November 18 in Groningen, the Netherlands. Falling into a coma, Mic never recovered, and 11 days later he died in hospital. Recorded with an array of session friends including Glen Hansard, Karl Odlum, David Odlum (of The Frames) Colm Mac Con Iomaire, LISA HANNIGAN and Gemma Hayes, Meteor Irish Music winner **SKYLARKIN'** (2002) {*8} showed what just might have been. Songs like 'Heyday' (now featured on a Guinness TV ad), 'Listen Girl', 'Looking For Jude' and 'Kid's Song' (all lifted from the 'Heyday' EP released before his death) paved the way for fan and soon-to-be major-label folkie DAMIEN RICE. *MCS*

The MARY JANES

Mic Christopher - vocals, acoustic guitar / **Karl Odlum** - bass (ex-KILA) / **Simon Good** - guitar / **Steven Hogan** - drums (left before debut set)

Ire/UK Hunter S. — US not issued

1994. (cd) *(HSTCD 03)* **BORED OF THEIR LAUGHING** — Irish
- Taken in / Short a few / Lyin' down / Diamonds / Story so far / Friends / Talkin' war / Talkin' war (II) / H.U.M.F.R.E.A. / Nearly dead.

—— added **Mark Stanley** (b. Australia) – drums

Loza — not issued

1998. (cd) *(MJCD 002)* **SHAM** — Irish
- Sham / Winesong / Simple times / Queen of hearts / Part of me / Bones / Cut me loose / Come what may / Friends / Begging / Party game / Centurian.

—— split in 1999; Mic went solo

MIC CHRISTOPHER

Sep 01. (cd-ep) *(none)* HEYDAY / — own
- Heyday / Listen girl / Looking for Jude / Kid's song. *(re-iss. Dec 02; mic 002CD)*

—— tragically Mic died on November 29, 2001

- posthumous releases -

Loza — not issued

Nov 02. (cd) *(mic 001D)* **SKYLARKIN'** — Irish
- Heyday / Kid's song / Listen girl / Looking for Jude / That's what good friends do / The loneliest man in town / Wide eyed and lying / What a curious notion / I've got your back / Skylarking / Daydreamin'.

CHUMBAWAMBA [folk period]

A meeting of anarcho-punk minds in the mid-1980s (based in a communal squat somewhere in Armley, Leeds), CHUMBAWAMBA were inspired by long-time indie stalwarts Crass and everyone who railed against the day's Thatcher government, etc., etc. The miners' strike of 1984-85, and what they saw as the hypocrisy of 1985's Live Aid project, were among the subjects of the band's agitprop approach. It was appropriate and indeed inevitable that the group (Danbert Nobacon, Alice Nutter, Boff Whalley, Lou Watts, Mavis Dillon, Dunstan Bruce, Harry Hamer, et al) would succumb to delivering a folk album.

With only voices a cappella to be heard (instruments had been abandoned for the time being), **ENGLISH REBEL SONGS 1381-1914** (1988) {*6}, was exactly what it said on the tin.

In a dozen traditional songs and a finale ('Coal Not Dole', from the pen of unknown songwriter Kay Sutcliffe), CHUMBAWAMBA re-imagined ye olde protest songs of the downtrodden and oppressed and turned them into become post-Orwellian anthems, like some fusion of The WATERSONS and Crass. Highlights included 'The Cutty Wren', 'The Collier's March' and 'Chartist Anthem'. But there were other political unrests throughout the world, and the Chums could fight the good fight in other musical forms and shapes.

Discovering the subversive possibilities in the emerging rave culture, CHUMBAWAMBA turned in the dancefloor-friendly `Slap!' set (1990), while the rest of the 90s looked commercially hopeful for a group of their anti-Establishment outlook. Their 1994 album 'Anarchy' (their first on One Little Indian) broke into the UK Top 30, while no one could have foreseen the British (and American!) success of both the single 'Tubthumping' and its accompanying EMI-released pop album 'Tubthumper' (1997). Things took a commercial nosedive soon afterwards, a ice-bucket of water thrown over deputy prime minister John Prescott at the 1998 Brit Awards probably not helping their cause, while a parting of the ways with EMI a few years later left the Chumbas out to dry.

So they got knocked down, but they got up again, although their return to anarcho-folk was greeted with a little disdain at first, as 'Readymades' (2002) and 'Un' (2004) – as an eight-piece – were of the folk-tronic variety, the latter shading partly into bona-fide folk music. Examples, with accordionist ANDY CUTTING on board, included 'A Man Walks Into A Bar' (by activist ROBB JOHNSON), the part-salsa 'Buy Nothing Day' and 'Rebel Code'.

Trimmed to a neat quartet (Boff Whalley, Lou Watts, former sound engineer Neil Ferguson and recent acquisition Jude Abbott), plus guests Winkie Thin on accordion, Jones and Telfer from OYSTERBAND and the COOPE, BOYES AND SIMPSON triumvirate, they recorded **A SINGSONG AND A SCRAP** (2006) {*7}, the group's inaugural release for agit-folk label No Masters. Listen out for their cover of The Clash's 'Bankrobber'.

A retrospective of sorts, combining songs old and new (or olde and nu), **GET ON WITH IT: LIVE** (2007) {*7} – with new accordionist Phil Moody – perfectly matched the trad 'Hard Times Of Old England' and LAL WATERSON's 'A Stitch In Time' with 'Timebomb' and 'Homophobia', etc.

Following a Glastonbury performance the previous summer, **THE BOY BANDS HAVE WON** (2008) {*7} (the short version of a very long full title) continued their folk march, crediting some repeat prescriptions from OYSTERBAND, ROY BAILEY, ROBB JOHNSON, RAY HEARNE, and BARRY COOPE & JIM BOYES. Production work for labelmate JO FREYA (who'd worked with them on the LAL WATERSON Project) led to album number 15, **ABCDEFG** (2010) {*7}. Simple but confrontational songs and themes were always at the heart of the group's repertoire, such as 'Torturing James Hetfield' (in response to the Metallica man allowing his music to be used for torture at Guantanamo Bay) and 'You Don't Exist', in support of veteran German group (originally East German, and banned there) the Klaus Renft Combo. *MCS*

—— [folk discography only]

Alice Nutter - vocals / **Boff Whalley** (b. Allan Mark Whalley) - guitar, vocals, clarinet / **Lou Watts** - vocals, guitar / **Mavis Dillon** - bass, trumpet, French horn / **Harry Hammer** (b. Darren) - drums / **Danbert Nobacon** (b. Nigel Hunter) - vocals / with **Simon Commonknowledge** - keyboards, accordion, piano

UK Agit Prop — US not issued

Oct 88. (10"m-lp) *(PROP 003)* **ENGLISH REBEL SONGS 1381–1914**
- The Cutty wren / The diggers' song / Colliers march / The triumph of General Ludd / Chartist anthem / The bad squire (*) / Song on the times / Smashing of the van / World turned upside down / Poverty knock / Idris strike song / Hanging on the old barbed wire / Coal not dole (*). *(re-iss. Feb 93 lp/cd; PROP 3/+CD) (re-iss. Feb 95 on One Little Indian lp/c/cd; TPLP 64/+C/CD) <US cd-iss. Jun 98 on Imprint; 8769> (cd re-iss. Jun 03 as ENGLISH REBEL SONGS 1381-1984 on Mutt+= *; MUTT 004)*

—— now trimmed to a quartet (**June Abbott, Boff Whalley, Lou Watts** + **Neil Ferguson** ; Neil from '91)

No Masters — Trade Root

Feb 06. (cd) *(NMCD 23)* *<TRCD 3>* **A SINGSONG AND A SCRAP**

- Laughter in a time of war / William Francis / By and by / You can (mass trespass, 1932) / Walking into battle with the Lord / When Alexander met Emma / Fade away (I don't want to) / Bankrobber / Learning to love / The land of do what you're told / Bella ciao / Smith & Taylor / Untitled. *(iss. also on Edel; 0165512ERE)*

—— added **Phil Moody** - accordion, vocals

Jan 07. (cd) *(NMCD 26)* **GET ON WITH IT: LIVE** (live)
- Buy nothing day / A stitch in time / Song on the times / Hard times of old England / By and by / Jacob's ladder / Timebomb / Homophobia / William Francis / Learning to love / Diggers' song / On eBay / Hanging on the old barbed wire / Bella ciao.

Mar 08. (cd) *(NMCD 28)* <TRCD 6> **... THE BOY BANDS HAVE WON**
- When an old man dies / Add me / Words can save us / Hull or Hell / El fusilado / Unpindownable / I wish that they'd sack me / Word bomber / All fur coat and no knickers / Fine line / Lord Bateman's motorbike / A fine career / To a little radio / (Words flew) Right around the world / Sing about love / Bury me deep / You watched me dance / Compliments of your waitress / Rip RP / Charlie / The ogre / Refugee / Same old same old / Waiting for the bus / What we want. *(iss.also on Westpark; WP 87154)*

Mar 10. (cd) *(NMCD 33)* **ABCDEFG**
- Introduction / Voices, that's all / Pickle / Wagner at the Opera / Underground / Torturing James Hetfield / The Devil's interval / Hammer stirrup and anvil / Puccini said / That same so-so tune / Singing out the days / You don't exist / The song collector / Missed / Ratatatay / New York song / Dance, idiot, dance. *(also on Westpark; WP 87186)*

CIRCULUS

If The INCREDIBLE STRING BAND, FAIRPORT CONVENTION and Gong had evolved into one band, then acid/prog-folkers CIRCULUS might have been the outcome of that wyrd-to-the-moon faerie fantasy league. Hailing from South London, the brainchild of frontman Michael Tyack, the outfit had been on the go since the late 1990s. Signed to Rise Above Records, Tyack and his band of medieaval minstrels (Will Summers, Oliver Parfitt, George Parfitt, Lo Polidoro, Sam Kelly and Victor Hugo) recreated subliminal spaced-out folk-rock for a whole new generation, while also inviting retro-buff hippies to their pixie party.

Debut set **THE LICK ON THE TIP OF AN ENVELOPE YET TO BE SENT** (2005) {*7} embraced the resurgence of freak-folk and claimed it back from the likes of ESPERS and their American cousins. To reconnect to the past, although not quite back to mediaeval times, track six 'Swallow' (also a single) featured the delightful sunny vocals of MARIANNE SEGAL, one-time member of early-1970s cult-folk act JADE. Getting a two-page spread in the NME was extraordinary for the period, but the beauty of songs like 'My Body Is Made Of Sunlight', 'The Scarecrow', 'Candlelight' and 'Power To The Pixies' couldn't be allowed to go unrecognised.

Close on its heels, **CLOCKS ARE LIKE PEOPLE** (2006) {*7} dropped the ISB influences, replacing them with a lighter, PENTANGLE-meets-Barclay James Harvest approach. The power of CIRCULUS was in their chameleon-like skill to echo a host of prog and folk figures from Genesis and JETHRO TULL to GRYPHON in tracks like 'Wherever She Goes', 'To The Fields', Bouree' and 'Velocity Races'.

Taking time out to accompany SEGAL on her solo venture 'The Gathering' (2007), a revised CIRCULUS (on their own Mythical Cake imprint) were back in town for album number three, **THOUGHT BECOMES BEAUTY** (2009) {*9}. Were we witnessing a second (or third) coming of prog-folk? Yes, if tracks like the classy Michael's Garden', 'Guide Our Way', 'Transmuting Power' and the crumhorn-friendly 'Fortunate Ones' were anything to go by; ditto the AMAZING BLONDEL-esque 'Packington's Pound' and 'Sumer Is Icumen In'. Now if the GORKY'S had taken this route ... *MCS*

Michael Tyack - vocals, guitar, baglama, lute / with **Will Summers** - flute, recorder, crumhorn / **Oliver Parfitt** - keyboards, synths / **George Parfitt** - bass / **Lo Polidoro** - vocals, harmonium (also Solo Artist) / **Victor Hugo** - bongos / **Sam Kelly** - drums, percussion

UK Instant Farma — US not issued

1999. (cd-ep) *(none)* GIANTISM — demo
- Little big song / The true lover's farewell / My Lady Carey's dompe / Everglade / Sombrero fallout / All you people.

Rise Above — Candlelight

Jul 05. (cd/ltd-colrd-lp) *(RISE CD/LP 063)* <CDL 0226> **THE LICK ON THE TIP OF AN ENVELOPE YET TO BE SENT** — Aug 05
- Miri it is / My body is made of sunlight / The scarecrow / Orpheus / We are long lost / Swallow / The aphid / Candlelight / La rotta *[lp-only]* / Power to the pixies.

Jul 05. (ltd-7") *(RISE7-064)* MIRI IT IS (Moog up mix). / (other by Witchcraft)

Oct 05. (7") *(RISE7-065)* SWALLOW. / My Body Is Made Of Sunlight
(cd-s+=) *(RISEMCD 65)* - La rotta.

Aug 06. (cd/ltd-colrd-lp) *(RISECD 093)* **CLOCKS ARE LIKE PEOPLE**
- Dragon's dance / Song of our despair / Willow tree / Wherever she goes / Velocity races / To the fields / Bouree / This is the way / Reality's a fantasy. *(lp w/free 7")* - Tapestry.

Oct 06. (7"/cd-s) *(RISE 7/CD 94)* SONG OF OUR DESPAIR. / Tapestry / Honeycomb

—— in 2007, MARIANNE SEGAL invited them to collaborate on the album 'The Gathering'.

—— **Tom Goldsmith** - bass + **Holly-Jane Shears** - vocals; repl. George, Oliver + Lo

—— **Alan French** - drums + **Anthony Elvin** - percussion; repl. Sam + Hugo

Mythical Cake — not issued

Jun 09. (cd) *(MYTHCAKE 001)* **THOUGHT BECOMES REALITY**
- Transmuting power / Fortunate ones / Guide our way / Michael's garden / Trotto / Packington's pound / Sumer is icumen in / Tristan's lament / Kalenda Maya / Within you is the sun.

—— **Tyack** recruited near-new outfit: **Holly-Jane Shears** - vocals / **Joe Woolley** - guitars, vocals / **Tali Trow** - bass, vocals / **Mike Farmer** - keyboards, synths / **Paul Wale** - mandolin, vocals / **Pat Kenneally** - drums, keyboards, vocals

The CLAN (⟹ WE FREE KINGS)

CLAYHILL

If Joe Cocker had whispered his way into folk-rock in the 1960s, he just might have sounded like CLAYHILL's raspy frontman Gavin Clark – a modern-day GERRY RAFFERTY or DAVID GRAY. A former member of the short-lived Sunhouse (from Nottingham) and a friend of film director and screenwriter Shane Meadows (the group contributed to the soundtrack of his indie film 'Twenty Four Seven'), Clark helped form London-based CLAYHILL with former BETH ORTON alumni Ali Friend and Ted Barnes in 2002.

By 2004, after supporting Aqualung at the Queen Elizabeth Hall (it seems that their earliest release, **AFTERLIGHT** , went unnoticed in some quarters), songs from their debut mp3 began to find their way on to film scores. 'Please Please Please Let Me Get What I Want', a DRAKE-ian reading of the Smiths song, soundtracked Meadows' 'This Is England' and 'Afterlight' the same director's 'Dead Man's Shoes'. A year later, a Tim Buckley tribute record included their take on 'The River'.

Full sets **SMALL CIRCLE** (2004) {*7} and **MINE AT LAST** (2006) {*8} produced a stir (if nothing else) from record executives, while songs like 'End Refrain', 'Moon I Hide', 'Northern Soul' and virtually everything from the latter record should have seen them acclaimed as acoustic-folk's new saviours. While Barnes and Clark supplied the score to another Shane Meadows film, 'Somers Town', CLAYHILL called it a day after a gig on September 5, 2009. *MCS*

Gavin Clark - vocals (ex-Sunhouse) / **Ali Friend** - bass, keyboards (ex-Beth Orton, ex-Red Snapper) / **Ted Barnes** - guitar, keyboards (ex-Beth Orton, ex-solo artist) / + additional musicians

UK Eat Sleep — US not issued

May 03. (mp3) *(none)* **AFTERLIGHT**
- Figure of eight / Hourglass / Grasscutter / Even enough / Moon I hide / Northern soul / One nerve / Afterlight / Please please please let me get what I want.

Feb 04. (m-cd) *(EAT 009CD)* **CUBAN GREEN**
- Figure of eight / Face of the sun / Hour glass / Grasscutter / Kind of man / So far out.

Jun 04. (7") *(EAT 010S)* GRASSCUTTER. / Grasscutter (M Craft mix)

Sep 04. (cd) *(EAT 011CD)* **SMALL CIRCLE**
- Alpha male / Northern soul / Moon I hide / Human trace / Even though / Rushes of blonde / Mystery train / Grasscutter / Afterlight / End refrain. *(ltd-cd+=; EAT 011CDX)*

Sep 04. (7") *(EAT 012S)* NORTHERN SOUL. / Figure Of Eight (acoustic)

Aug 05. (cd) *(EAT 050CD)* **CLAYHILL (ACOUSTIC)**
- Figure of eight / Northern soul / Mystery train / Face of the sun / Grasscutter / Funny how / Please please please let me get what I want / Disscordents.

Apr 06. (7") *(EAT 053S)* HALFWAY ACROSS. / Gutter

May 06. (cd) *(EAT 052CD)* **MINE AT LAST**
- Beard / Suffer not / One nerve / Hector's laugh / Hang on / Halfway across / Buy me a suit / Mari-Sol / Dying breed / Fortress / Whites of the eyes / After the slaughter.

—— CLAYHILL split in 2009

Vikki CLAYTON

Until the past decade or so, Vikki was largely ignored by most journals and critics outside the folk fraternity, her love of other musical interests such as trad-jazz and classical music probably alienating her from the fickle folk industry.

Born December 12, 1952, in Paddington, London (she later relocated with her family to Lincolnshire), Vikki's passion for the Anglo-Australian folk-revivalist composer Percy Grainger had evolved from listening to the works of Vaughan Williams, Benjamin Britten, et al, while theatre/film cast musicals and ye olde folksongs of traditional Morris dancing also took her fancy. When folk-rock struck gold in the late 1960s and FAIRPORT CONVENTION were all the rage, Vikki took new inspiration from SANDY DENNY, although she was not the only one to echo her vocal style throughout the 1970s and 1980s.

After a time in the short-lived Kelsay and Ragged Heroes (the latter a septet/octet with one LP in 1983, 'Annual'), CLAYTON finally delived some solo recordings. The cassette-only **HONOR-TOKENED** (1987) {*5} and **LOST LADY FOUND** (1988) {*7}, the latter featuring her first cover of a SANDY DENNY song, evoked memories of folk's halcyon days, while Vikki's voice possessed a purity and soul all on its own. On the CD re-issues for her A New Day imprint, there were a few bonus FAIRPORT-inspired nuggets, including 'Crazy Man Michael' and 'Matty Groves'.

Subsequently working with FAIRPORT's Ric Sanders (on the set 'Carried Away', alongside Fred A. Baker) and **MIDSUMMER CUSHION** (1991) with GORDON GILTRAP, Tony Moore, etc, VIKKI CLAYTON also delivered a number of fine folk-orientated records. Two of these stand out from the pack: the self-explanatory **IT SUITS ME WELL: The Songs Of Sandy Denny** (1994) {*6} and the **MOVERS AND SHAKERS** (1997) {*6} set, which showcased her all-star folk band of Ric Sanders, Gerry Conway, JOHN KIRKPATRICK and JETHRO TULL's Martin Barre. She currently lives in England and New Zealand. *MCS*

Vikki Clayton - vocals, acoustic guitar

UK: Vikki — US: not issued

1987. (c) *(VIKKI 1)* **HONOR - TOKENED**
- The blacksmith / Missing you / The birth of Robin Hood / Horncastle fair / The banks of the Nile / Is your love in vain / Peggy on the sea / Yarmouth town / George Collins. *(cd re-mast. Mar 98 on 'A New Day'+=; ANDCD 18)* - Crazy man Michael / Africa was calling / Beguiled / The girlie press gang / My Donald.

1988. (c) *(VIKKI 2)* **LOST LADY FOUND**
- Lisbon / The mermaid / The false bride / Africa calling version one / Lost lady found / Wanton Mary / Bushes and briars / Lady Margaret / Two magicians / The passing of a queen. *(cd re-mast. Jan 99 on 'A New Day'+=; ANDCD 19)* - White dress / I want something / Matty Groves / Movers and shakers / My bonny light horseman / Sir Hugh of Lincoln.

Prestige — not issued

Sep 91. (c) *(CASSGP 008)* **MIDSUMMER CUSHION**
- The gardener's bonny daughter / Mad Meg / Dolly's mistake / Wanton Mary / Lucy's lament / Singing Jinny / Proud Betsy / I love thee / The badger. *(cd-iss. Jun 94; CDGSP 008)*

Road Goes On Forever — not issued

Sep 93. (cd) *(RGFCD 013)* **IN FLIGHT**
- The birth of Robin Hood / Crazy man Michael / Ranzo / Grandma's hands / Lovely Joan / Loving Hannah / Ain't misbehaving / Squadron leader / Sailing / She belongs to me / Georgia / Bonneville blues / The hiring fair / Hen hoe down / Matty! *(re-iss. Mar 94 on 'Terrapin Truckin'; TRUCKCD 013) (re-iss. May 96 on Silver Vinyl; SIVCD 0006)*

Terrapin Truckin' — Terrapin Truckin'

Sep 94. (cd/c) *(<TRUCK CD/MC 021>)* **IT SUITS ME WELL:**
The Songs Of Sandy Denny — 1995
- Who knows where the time goes / It suits me well / No end / Fotheringay / Tomorrow is a long time / A sailor's life / I'm a dreamer / Rising of the moon / The banks of the Nile / White dress / John the gun. *(cd re-iss. May 96 on Silver Vinyl; SIVCD 0007) (cd re-iss.2000 on HTD+=; HTDCD 083)* - One way donkey ride / Like an old fashioned waltz / The sea.

A New Day — not issued

Apr 97. (cd) *(ANDCD 15)* **MOVERS AND SHAKERS**
- Pilgrim / Ten years / Africa calling / My Donald / Kisses in the dark / Movers and shakers / Wild nights / The payback / I want something / The girlie press gang / Bonny light horseman / Sir Hugh of Lincoln / Beguiled.

Nov 01. (cd) *(ANDCD 50)* **LOOKING AT THE STARS**
- These are my people / Last love / Shackleton's song / Bewitched / The ballad of Pearl and Deene / Too beautiful / Looking at the stars / The present / Snakebite / Coming soon / The awakening / Anne of Lochroyan / Stars.

Rod CLEMENTS

This is a sort of addendum to the LINDISFARNE entry in GFD Vol.1. An original and re-formation band member on and off since the late 1960s, bassist/singer Roderick Parry Clements (born November 17, 1947, North Shields in Tyne and Wear) wrote the group's classic breakthrough single 'Meet Me On The Corner' in 1972.

From his early days in the latter half of the 1960s with the Downtown Faction, to the proto-LINDISFARNE outfit Brethren, the shift from blues to folk came about after the release of FAIRPORT CONVENTION's 'Liege and Lief'. Meeting lead singer Alan Hull also helped to cement LINDISFARNE as one of England's finest folk-rock bands. Clements was also a session man of note (Van Der Graaf's Peter Hammill enlisted him for his 'Fools Mate' album), and the initial break-up of LINDISFARNE led to him forming splinter group JACK THE LAD.

Connections with BERT JANSCH and JACQUI McSHEE resulted in a brief spell with the resurgent PENTANGLE, while Mark Knopfler, MICHAEL CHAPMAN, RALPH McTELL and others requested his session-work talents.

ROD CLEMENTS solo was more of a rootsy, country-folk affair. His rare debut **ONE TRACK MIND** (1994) {*6} – featuring Ray Laidlaw and Steve Cunningham – combined his own songs ('Meet Me On The Corner' and a reprised 'Leather Lauderette' with BERT JANSCH) with covers from the pens of WOODY GUTHRIE ('Hard Travellin''), LEADBELLY ('Bourgeois Blues'), DYLAN ('Down In The Flood'), Oscar Woods ('Evil Hearted Woman'), Frank Hutchison ('The Train That Carried My Girl From Town') and Dr. Feelgood ('Sneaky Suspension').

Subsequent studio albums **STAMPING GROUND** (2000) {*6} and **ODD MAN OUT** (2006) {*6} saw Clements co-write some tunes with Nigel Stonier (husband of rootsy English/Irish singer-songwriter Thea Gilmore), a solo artist in his own right. ROD CLEMENTS and the Ghosts of Electricity (alongside long-time collaborators Dave Hull-Denholm and Ian Thompson) were behind **LIVE GHOSTS** (2004) {*6}, a retrospective that came full circle with a simple finale take of 'Meet Me On The Corner'. *MCS*

Rod Clements - vocals, bass, guitar, keyboards (with session people)

UK: self-rel. — US: not issued

1994. (ltd-cd) *(none)* **ONE TRACK MIND**
- Hard travellin' / The train that carried my girl from town / Bourgeois blues / Train in G major / Ain't no more cane / Down in the flood / Road to kingdom come / Evil hearted woman / Meet me on the corner / Leather launderette / No turning back. *(re-iss. Aug 02 on Siren+=; 02) <US-iss. May 03 on United States Dist.+=; USD 225>* - Sneaky suspension / Piston broke again / Long vehicle / No turning back [home version]. *(re-iss. May 08 as 'ONE TRACK MIND: 1994 2001 2008' on Batsville ++=; none)* - A dream within a dream (LINDISFARNE) / Blues for a dying season (DOWNTOWN FACTION).

Market Square — United States Dist.

Sep 00. (cd) *(MSMCD 107)* **STAMPING GROUND**
- Stamping ground / Whisky highway / Blue interior / Hattie McDaniel at the Oscars 1939 / Whole lifestyle thing / Charity man / Roads of East Northumberland / Black rain / We have to talk / Cowboy in the rain / One more night with you / Old blue goose.

—— now as **Rod Clements and the Ghosts of Electricity**: with Dave Hull-Denholm (guitars and vocals) + Ian Thomson (bass and vocals)

Nov 04. (ltd-cd) *(none)* **LIVE GHOSTS** [live at Market Bosworth Rugby Football Club in Leicestershire on March 5-7 2004]
- Stamping ground / Why can't I be satisfied? / Blue interior / Charity man / Roads of East Northumberland / When Jones gets back to town / Candlelight / Whole lifestyle thing / Remember tomorrow / Can't do right for doing wrong / Lost highway / Meet me on the corner.

(above issued on Batsville Records)

Jun 06. (cd) *(MSMCD 143)* **ODD MAN OUT**
- All grown up and nowhere to go / Existentially yours / Taking the back road home / Dead man's karaoke / Odd man out / Touch-me-not / Ragtown / New best friend / September sunrise / Morocco bound.

The COCK AND BULL BAND

London traditional quartet the HEMLOCK COCK & BULL BAND (Paul Martin and former ALBION BAND multi-instrumentalists Dave Whetstone, John Maxwell and Jean-Pierre Rasle) had their origins in 1978 as a trio comprising Dave, Paul and Brad Bradstock.

ALL BUTTONED UP (1981) {*7} was a classic trad-Brit-folk album with edge and excitement, featuring cutting-edge polkas, jigs, schottisches, hornpipes, songs and waltzes including their highly un-Wicker Man-like version of 'Corn Riggs'. Reuniting after time spent at the HUTCHINGS ranch, **EYES CLOSED AND ROCKING** (1985) {*6} was just what the doctor ordered. It was the last set with WHETSTONE, who went off to a solo career and subsequently to form WAZ! alongside (Maartin) ALLCOCK and Pete Zorn; Pete Lockwood was now a fully-fledged member of The COCK & BULL BAND.

Controlled by Frenchman Rasle (who had now added lead vocals to his array of instrumentation), their third set, **CONCRETE ROUTES, SACRED COWS** (1989) {*5}, was produced by additional percussionist Nigel Pegrum (ex-STEELEYE SPAN). The band found female accompaniment in 1993 with Vanda Sainsbury and turned to a Celtic-folk sound for another three CDs: **BELOW THE BELT** (1993) {*6}, **PUMPED UP AND LOADED** (1996) {*6} and **ENCORE DU VINGT** (1999) {*5}. Jean-Pierre also played with Jah Wobble's Invaders Of The Heart, Ex-Cathedra, Gabriel Yacoub, etc. In 1995 he joined up with Chalemie (Sara Stowe and Matthew Spring) – and that's just the half of it. *MCS*

Paul Martin - acoustic bass, dulcimer, mandola / **Dave Whetstone** - melodeons, Anglo concertina, guitars / **Jean-Pierre Rasle** - bagpipes, crumhorn, recorders, harmonica, rauschpfeife / **John Maxwell** - drums, percussion, washboard, vocals

UK Topic — US not issued

Jul 81. (lp; as The HEMLOCK COCK & BULL BAND) *(12TS 421)* **ALL BUTTONED UP** □ ⊟
- Donkey riding – Buffalo girls / Portabello – Briggham / Berger, bergere – Bourree berrichonne / Tit for tat – Princess Amelia's birthday / Mon reve – William Irwin's quickstep / The cockade – Corn riggs – The twin sisters / Latrigg side – The Dorsetshire hornpipe / Needle-cases / A trip to Shorts – Lewis Castle / Huzza, cock and bull.

—— all except Martin joined up with ASHLEY HUTCHINGS in The ALBION DANCE BAND

May 85. (lp) *(12TS 440)* **EYES CLOSED AND ROCKING** □ ⊟
- One for Dan / Valse villageoise – Bouree a ruols / The banister / Sugar on the doughnut – Advice to the ladies / The wonder – Ridotta rock / Prince Frederick's – Suky's delight / Les violettes roses – Hop and skip – Circle / William Irwin's I, II & III / The welch rabbit – Hotfoot.

—— WHETSTONE left to go solo and form WAZ! alongside MAARTIN ALLCOCK and Pete Zorn; Dave was repl. by **Pete Lockwood** - keyboards, sax, percussion, sequences

Rogue — not issued

Apr 89. (lp/c; as COCK AND BULL) *(FMSL 2015/+C)* **CONCRETE ROUTES, SACRED COWS** □ ⊟
- Lunch in the pub / Green park – Camargo – The noggin / Miss Kitty's delight – Irish Vauxhall – A new dance – Anthony's courtship / Fine companions – The Rhine – Ronde du Quercy / Stony brawl / Modal hornpipe – Beau Nash / Purcell's march – Le topinambour / Sun hall – Bad joke – Monsieur Pantin / The white cottage.

Cock & Bull — not issued

1991. (cd/c) *(C&B 103 CD/C)* **A COCK AND BULL STORY** [compilation] □ ⊟
- Monkey riding / Speed the plough / The cockade – Corn riggs – The twin sisters / William Irwin's I, II & III / Horse's brawl / One for Dan / Lunch in the pub / Prince Frederick's – Suky's delight / Mon reve – William Irwin's quickstep / Modal hornpipe – Beau Nash / Advice to the ladies / The white cottage – La conterie – High street, high time / Portabello – Briggham / Donkey riding – Buffalo girls.

—— **Rasle** (now on added lead vocals), **Martin** + **Lockwood** recruited **Vanda Sainsbury** - clarinet, piano, recorders

Dec 93. (cd/c) *(C&B 104 CD/C)* **BELOW THE BELT** □ ⊟
- L'hesitante / Villeneuve / La Mal Mariee – St Martin's isle – The bryhar / Below the belt / Trip to Sainburys – L'androgyne – La souris – La penible / Trip to the lawndry / Banle du pinguin – Pauve laboureur – Penguin brawl / 8.30 trop tot – Mrs Waghorn – K.B.S.M. / The R.S.J. / L'accidentelle – Andronov-o.

Mrs. Casey — not issued

Jun 96. (cd) *(MCRCD 6992)* **PUMPED UP & LOADED** □ ⊟
- Stony move / Fille d'Orleans / L'escalier / La paresse – Montmiral / Le jaywalker / Jeanneton / Leo-Leon – Panique couscous / The watchmaker – The reaper / Broken nights / Voici la St Jean / Cajun bypass / La route d'Edinbourg / Cantona / The dealer – Stony haze / The polekat / Little wonder / Peartree bridge.

Apr 99. (cd) *(MCRCD 9993)* **ENCORE DU VINGT** □ ⊟
- Encore du vingt / N'y faites pas l'amour / Le petit coin / Chamaliere / Branle de Normandie / Peaslake maffia / Le gros orteil – L'auriculaire / Abeille et bourdon – Catovsky's march / Voyage / Nifty thrifty / Broomfield House / La Mariolle – Tunbridge frisk – The Strickland / Kus mijn kloten / Valse haute / The ridotta.

—— split post-millennium; Rasle formed Monsieur Pantin (album 'Ma Rosalie' in 2004)

COCOON

Formed in Clermont-Ferrand, France in 2006, COCOON (multi-instrumentalist Mark Daumail and co-songsmith Morgane Imbeaud) arrived on the UK scene a year later when **MY FRIENDS ALL DIED IN A PLANE CRASH** (2007) {*8} found its way across the Channel, having been a hit in their native country. Relying on their command of the English language, the couple sang twee-folk in a manner not unlike SIMON & GARFUNKEL, although clearly inspired by the likes of PENTANGLE, FAIRPORT CONVENTION and DEVENDRA BANHART.

Produced by Ian Caple and arranged by Dickon Hinchliffe (of Tindersticks), album number two, **WHERE THE OCEANS END** (2010) {*7}, featured the sunny delights of summer songs 'Comets', Sushi' and 'Oh My God'. Uplifting and sugary-sweet, the album should appeal to new folk fans who have yet to raid their parents' old record collections in the attic. *MCS*

Morgane Imbeaud (b. 14 Apr' 87) - keyboards, tambourine, vocals / **Mark Daumail** (b. 6 Dec '84) - vocals, guitar, ukulele / with **Denis Clavaizolle** - bass / **Yann Clavaizolle** - drums / **Davy Sladek** - flute

UK Sober and Gentle — US not issued

Apr 07. (cd-ep) *(SOBEP 02)* FROM PANDA MOUNTAINS ⊟ French ⊟
- On my way / Tell me / June / I don't give a shit / Hummingbird.

Oct 07. (cd) *(SOBCD 005)* **MY FRIENDS ALL DIED IN A PLANE CRASH** ⊟ French ⊟
- Take off / Vultures / On my way / Seesaw / Christmas song / Tell me / Owls / Paper boat / Cliffhanger / Chupee / Hummingbird / Microwave. *(re-iss. Nov 08 on Discograph; 613573-2) (UK-iss. Jan 10; same as original)*

Aug 09. (cd+dvd) *(SOBDVD 001)* **BACK TO PANDA MOUNTAINS** [live concert] ⊟ French ⊟
- Hummingbird / Vultures / Owls / Seesaw / 84 / On my way / Babyseal / Microwave / Cliffhanger / Take off / Chupee / Hey ya! / Tell me // [DVD concert].

Barclay — not issued

Oct 10. (cd/lp) *(275 134/146-0)* **WHERE THE OCEANS END** ⊟ French ⊟
- Sushi / Comets / Dee doo / Yum yum / Mother / Oh my god / Super powers / Cathedral / Sea lion II (I will be gone) / Dolphins / Baby seal / In my boat. *(UK-iss. Mar 11 on V2)*

Lee COLLINSON

Born January 15, 1965, at Dorking in Surrey, he incidentally shares the same birth name as the late Dr. Feelgood singer Lee Brilleaux. His formative years found him performing in rock acts Cloud Nine, Richard III and Typically Max. That aside, Lee's vocation in life was as a jazz-folk-blues guitarist (and singer), having almost won BBC Radio Folk On 2's prestigious Young Tradition Award.

Subsequent broadcasts led to a chance meeting with the boss of the new independent Spiv Records, and the final results **LIMBO** {*7} saw light in 1990. Scansfolk magazine named it Folk Album of 1991. Among its cocktail of traditional and pop items, several tracks received select airplay, while solo tours of the UK (and of Germany, with KEITH HANCOCK) showed that Lee meant business. He also sidelined with Hancock the latter on his Hokey Pokey set 'Circle Dance'.

Borrowing one of HANCOCK's tracks ('Purple Pas De Deux'), he set about finding a record label to release a second set. Finally delivered on Fledg'ling in 1995, **SLIP THE DRIVER A FIVER** {*7} was graciously reviewed by The Listening Post. It also boasted a handful of big folk players including CHRISTINE COLLISTER, BARB JUNGR and fiddler TOM McCONVILLE, while Lee's best efforts were on a cover of Joe Ely's 'Me And Billy The Kid' and some traditional-sourced material.

Another five years or so passed before the release of album three, **BREATHLESS**, but whether it was good or bad, this obscure record has been hard to track down, and so indeed has Lee himself. *MCS*

Lee Collinson - vocals, guitar

UK Spiv — US not issued

Jul 90. (lp/c) *(SPIV 102/+C)* **LIMBO** □ ⊟
- Moreton Bay / Witch at the wheel – Flowers of Edinburgh / Limbo / Wild hills of Wanning – J.R. Pigg / Roof is leaking / Song for Bowdoin / Roger's courtship / Here comes the night / Dusty windowsills – Tie the bonnet / Fanny Blair.

Fledg'ling — not issued

1995. (cd) *(FLED 3003)* **SLIP THE DRIVER A FIVER** □ ⊟
- Never been to Texas / People of the heavens / The purple pas de deux / The reflex waltz / Fair Sally / Driving wheel / One out of three - Slip the driver a fiver / Me and Billy The Kid / Lord Mayor's march / The beautiful waitress.

Chama — not issued

2000s. (cd) *(none)* **BREATHLESS** □ ⊟
- Breathless / Morning blues / Small town talk / Pretty little dog / The widow / Chocolate Jesus / Grey eagle - Salt river / Blue eyed Suzie / Shiver me timbers / One fine morning.

Christine COLLISTER (⟹ GREGSON, Clive & ...)

COOPE BOYES & SIMPSON

Much like the WATERSONS, The COPPER FAMILY and PETER BELLAMY in a previous generation, this English a cappella folk trio from the north have hit all the right notes since their (and their Rotherham-based label No Masters Co-operative's) inception in 1990.

Balancing their act between political folk tunes (several penned by themselves) and sacred Classic FM festive songs, this glorious triumvirate has been heralded as the musical second coming in post-millennium popular folk.

With over a dozen albums since **FUNNY OLD WORLD** (1993) {*6}, Barry Coope, Jim Boyes (ex-SWAN ARCADE) and Lester Simpson have engaged in a string of collaborations, none mightier than with the WATERSON: CARTHY family contingent and supergroup BLUE MURDER (the former act plus offspring and Dave and Heather Brady). Christmastime has been celebrated with their 'Gaudete'-type collective, featuring Fi Fraser (Barry's wife), her sister JO FREYA (ex-BLOWZABELLA) and Jim's wife Georgina, while other acts from Europe (Panta Rhei, Wak Maar Proper, etc) have celebrated in concert with the trio.

More recently CHUMBAWAMBA, once the catalyst among the indie pigeons and pop stars to boot, have invited the lads to combine resources on 'A Singsong And A Scrap' (2005), 'Get On With It' (2006) and 'The Boy Bands Have Won' (2008). If you're looking for a good place to start on the prolific trail of CB&S, you wouldn't be disappointed with **FALLING SLOWLY** (1996) {*7}, **HINDSIGHT** (1998) {*6}, **TWENTY-FOUR SEVEN** (2002) {*7}, **TRIPLE ECHO** (2005) {*8}, **VOICES AT THE DOOR** (2006) {*7} – with Fi, Jo and Georgina – and **AS IF ...** (2010) {*7}. *MCS*

Barry Coope - vocals / **Jim Boyes** - vocals (ex-SWAN ARCADE) / **Lester Simpson** - vocals / with sparse accompaniment

UK No Masters Voice — US not issued

Nov 93. (cd) *(NMVCD 3)* **FUNNY OLD WORLD** □ ⊟
- Unison in harmony / Down upon the dugout floor / Polly on the shore / Remembrance day – Coal not dole / One hand on the radio / The humble heart (Shaker hymn) / Roll me in your arms / Sweet Evelina / Bound for Van Diemen's island / Bringing in the sheaves / Only remembered / Welcome to the west / Funny old world. *(c-iss. Feb 96; NMMC 3)*

—— next with Flemish musicians: Willem Vermandere, Norbert Detaeye, etc.

No Masters — not issued

Nov 95. (cd/c; as w/ Various Artists) *(NMCD/NMMC 8)* **WE'RE HERE BECAUSE WE'RE HERE** [CONCERT PARTY *: PASSCHENDAELE] □ ⊟
- We're here because we're here [*] / Duizend soldaten (WILLEM VERMANADERE) / Chorus line (BOYES) / Concert party: Passchendaele [*] / Chorus line (BOYES) / When this blasted war is over (NORBERT DETAEYE) / Down upon the dugout floor (CB&S) / In Flanders (ND) / Mijn land (WV) / Flanders (BOYES) / De vluchteling (WV) / I want to go home (CB&S) / Standing in line (SIMPSON) / Vladslo (WV) / Het slagveld van boesinghe (ND) / Mendingem (SIMPSON) / Good old General Haig [*] / Duits kerkhof (WV) / Abide with me (ND) / Only remembered (CBS & D) / Roses of Picardy (ND) / Beethoven – Who are we [*] / The burning mill at Messines [*].

Aug 96. (cd) *(NMCD 9)* **FALLING SLOWLY** □ ⊟
- The forward march / Falling slowly / Little man you've had a busy day – Standing in line / So sincere / Weekend girl / Since the exodus began / Rufford park poachers / Farewell to England / Shuffling Jack / Spinning in the sky / Thurnscoe rain / The way of the world / The ship.

—— **Coope** (added piano) + **Simpson** (added bagpipes)

Nov 96. (cd; by PANTA RHEI / COOPE, BOYES AND SIMPSON) *(NMCD 10)* **PASSCHENDAELE SUITE and PASSCHENDAELE TERMINUS** [music from The Peace Concerts] □ ⊟
- Dodendans (PANTA RHEI) / The land of the long white cloud (SIMPSON) / Een ship (PANTA RHEI) / Ao tea roa / Robin's song (PANTA RHEI & BARRY COOPE) / Lay me low / The bloody fields of Flanders (PANTA RHEI & SIMPSON) / Still in the night (BOYES, COOPE & FABIEN DEGRYSE) / Ein schottisch tantz (PANTA RHEI) / (Mad old, sad old) Shuffling Jack (w/ PANTA RHEI) / Tyne cot at night – I want to go home / Largo (LUC PILARTZ, AURELIE DORZEE, KATHY ADAM) / The new Jerusalem (w/ PANTA RHEI).

Feb 98. (cd) *(NMCD 11)* **HINDSIGHT** □ ⊟
- Shallow brown / John Barleycorn / Sprig of thyme / Pleasant and delightful / She's like a swallow / Six jolly miners / Dog and gun / Henry's downfall / Jerry Brandreth's plaint – Said the master to me / The bold Princess Royal / Reynardine / Low down in the broom / Wild goose shanty / The Coppers' Christmas song / Ten thousand miles.

Nov 98. (cd) *(NMCD 13)* **A GARLAND OF CAROLS** [festive] □ ⊟
- Shepherds arise / Down in yon forest / Coventry carol / As I sat on a sunny bank / While shepherds watched (Lyngham) / Nowell and Nowell / In Bethlehem city / Christmas is now drawing near at hand / The carnal and the crane / Here we come a-wassailing / The three harks / The moon shines bright / The boar's head carol / The Dunstan lullaby / While shepherds watched their flocks by night.

Jul 99. (cd) *(NMCD 15)* **WHERE YOU BELONG**: a song cycle for Belper □ ⊟
- The river flows / The valley / Where you belong / The ballad of Samuel Slater / Ghost mail / The Belper militia / The levelution / The nailer's song / Under the apple tree / Fairground attraction / Pulling down song / Homeland / The river flows.

Oct 99. (cd) *(NMCD 50)* **WHAT WE SING IS WHAT WE ARE** [compilation] □ ⊟
- Make it mend it / Rufford Park poachers / Broken hearted among the pines / The levelution / Like another rolling stone / Homeland / Unison in harmony / Hush my babe / Lay me down / Falling slowly / Lloyd George's beer / The sprig of thyme / Who will blow the candle out / Polly on the shore / Only remembered / Jerusalem revisited / Ten thousand miles.

—— next with Wak Maar Proper

Nov 99. (cd) *(NMCD 14)* **CHRISTMAS TRUCE / KERSTBESTAND** [live festive] □ ⊟
- The rhyme of No Man's Land / Nu zijt wellekome / The Dunstan lullaby / While shepherds watched (Pentonville) / The boar's head / Onward Christian soldiers / The Coventry carol / The Christmas truce / O kerstnacht, schoner dan de dagen / Living it up / Allah O'Akhbar / When this blasted war is over / Minuit chretien / Peace on earth / Blood and gold / The Meadowhill carol / Senzenina / The Wiltshire carol / Jerusalem of gold / Reconciliation.

—— In 2002, the trio were part of BLUE MURDER alongside WATERSON: CARTHY

Jul 02. (cd) *(NMCD 20)* **TWENTY-FOUR SEVEN** □ ⊟
- Twenty-four seven / Present friends / Privatise / Man of double deed / Uttoxeter souling song / January lullaby / Sounding rafters / Raise your voices / Heaven's waiting room / The sea must have an ending / Cold coasts of Iceland – Three ships / In the name of God / Waiting by the road.

—— next as BARRY COOPE – JIM BOYES – LESTER SIMPSON – FI FRASER – JO FREYA – GEORGINA BOYES

Nov 03. (cd) *(NMCD 21)* **FIRE AND SLEET AND CANDLELIGHT** [regional and historical carols] □ ⊟
- Hark, hark what news (good news) / While shepherds watched their flocks by night (sweet chiming bells) / Drive the cold winter away / Diadem / Gloucestershire wassail / Personent hodie / Clementsing / I saw three ships / King Pharim / Hail smiling morn / The cherry tree carol / Peace o'er the world (the Bradda' anthem) / Shepherds rejoice / Down in yon forest.

Jun 05. (cd) *(NMCD 22)* **TRIPLE ECHO**: songs collected by Ralph Vaughan Williams, George Butterworth and Percy Grainger □ ⊟
- Bushes and briars / The ploughman's dream / New garden fields / The cuckoo / Ward the pirate / Lovely on the water / The turtle dove / Riding down to Portsmouth / Riley the fisherman / Lovely Joan / Shanties: Santa Anna – Dollar and a 'alf day – Storm along / Banks of green willow / It hails, it rains / New Christmas / Horkstow Grange.

—— next with former children's laureate and storyteller MICHAEL MORPURGO [*], with COOPE BOYES & SIMPSON plus FI FRASER, JO FREYA, GEORGINA BOYES

Jun 06. (cd) *(NMCD 24)* **PRIVATE PEACEFUL: THE CONCERT** [live] □ ⊟
- Bandaghem [SIMPSON] / [*] / Hares on the mountains / [*] / Little man you've had a busy day / [*] / England to her sons / [*] / Standing in line / Good old General Haig – The Sergeant Major's having a time – Hanging on the old barbed wire / [*] / Down upon the dugout floor / [*] / Only remembered / [*] / Oranges and lemons [COOPE] / [*] / Lay me low / Mendinghem – Dozinghem [SIMPSON].

—— next set also credited FI FRASER, JO FREYA, GEORGINA BOYES

Nov 06. (cd) *(NMCD 25)* **VOICES AT THE DOOR**: MIDWINTER SONGS AND CAROLS [festive] □ ⊟
- How beautiful upon the mountains / While shepherds watched – Hail chime on / Curly Hark-Newton's / While shepherds were watching / The holy well / Bodmin wassail / Barwell old Hark / Time to remember the poor / While shepherds watched – Liverpool / Wexford carol / Innocent's song / George Dunn's wassail / The first good joy our Mary had / Star of Bethlehem / Adam lay ybounden – deo gracias / Jacob's well / Ding dong merrily on high.

May 10. (cd) *(NMCD 35)* **AS IF ...** □ ⊟
- Now is the cool of the day / Silence / A hill of little shoes / Keep your distance / Float in dreams / Haven / The slave's lament – Goal song / The emperor's new clothes / Golden bird / Under a stone / Spring 1919 / We got fooled again.

JIM BOYES

No Masters Voice — not issued

Feb 93. (cd/c) *(NMV 1 CD/C)* **OUT OF THE BLUE** ☐ ⊟
- Bringing in the sheaves / Dark in the daylight / Down upon the dugout floor / We know what your game is / Will I see your face again / Pilot and the bomb aimer / Under a stone / Carousel / Acres of gladness / Caged lions / Subtle song / Meadowhall carol / Goodnight song. *(cd re-iss. Mar 00; same)*

LESTER SIMPSON

Simpson - vocals, melodeons, pipes, harmonica / with Nigel Corbett (guitar, mandolin, violin), Wendy Weatherby (cellos, vocals) , Nigel Jardine (drums)

No Masters — not issued

Jul 00. (cd) *(NMCD 16)* **ONE** ☐ ⊟
- Singing the ages down / The schooner set: The Malcolm Miller's farewell – The old Winston Churchill – The steamboat / The rhyme of No Man's Land / Polly on the shore / Potato waltz – Galician jigs / Wallis / She moved through the fair / Fairground attraction waltzes: The land of the long white cloud – Waltz clog – La chapka / Hard and stubbled field / Standing in line / Dozinghem / Weekend girl / Shearwaters / Homeland.

Pete COOPER

Known for his virtuoso fiddle playing (having taken violin lessons from the age of nine), PETE COOPER is one of the leading lights in the field of old-timey folk music, although Irish, American, Scandinavian and Eastern European music take precedence. That's not to say his music is of the Celtic-folk persuasion, but it does have connections to that genre and falls under the world-music umbrella. Born November 18, 1951, at Gnosall in Staffordshire, Pete learned his trade while winning a scholarship to Oxford University, graduating in 1973.

Before a spell in West Virginia (where he collaborated on a 1979 album, 'Frosty Morning', with dulcimer player HOLLY TANNEN), busker COOPER spent some time living in a "political squat" in Brixton, south London, where the radical theories of LEON ROSSELSON and others were taking shape. Pete's Villa Road band, The Cuckoo's Nest, supported The 101'ers, a pub-rock act led by future Clash singer Joe Strummer.

In 1981/82, having split with girlfriend TANNEN, Pete returned to his London folk-club roots, and between Norwegian bar-gig residencies alongside Lawrie Wright (guitar and piano) in 1983-86, he found time to work for several years in a duo with fellow folk artist PETA WEBB. The album 'The Heart Is True' was released to wide acclaim in 1986, and DICK GAUGHAN was a big fan.

1986 also saw the founding of his Fiddling From Scratch teaching project, and over the years his workshops brought out the best in artists from Lucy Farr to KATHRYN TICKELL. Solo albums were a rare event for Pete, but the early 1990s saw at least two surface, the cassette-only **ALL AROUND THE WORLD** (1990) {*6} and Irish CD **THE WOUNDED HUSSAR** (1993) {*6}. The musicians who performed on the latter set (Kathryn Locke, Geoff Coombs and former ZUMZEAUX fiddler Neti Vaandrager) emerged on Pete's subsequent Celtic-meets-Eastern project and demo-type tape **VIVANDO** (1995) {*5}.

Spreading his teaching and songbook-writing to all parts of the globe (his published tutorial works are available via his website), COOPER has enriched England and the world with at least two collaborative albums with Richard Bolton. He has also worked with grassroots outfit RATTLE ON THE STOVEPIPE, featuring banjo players DAVE ARTHUR and Chris Moreton; young Dan Stewart took the place of the latter in 2007 (see discography for further details). *MCS*

Pete Cooper - fiddle, vocals

UK: Fiddling From Scratch — US: not issued

Feb 90. (c) *(FFS 001)* **ALL AROUND THE WORLD**: Fiddle Music from IRELAND, SCANDINAVIA, EASTERN EUROPE and the USA ☐ ⊟
- Maggie Pickens - Molly, will you marry me? / Swallow's tail / Reinlender / Ducks on the pond / Yellow rose of Texas / Hungarian songs / All around the world - Buttermilk Mary - Green fields of Ross Beigh / The Blarney pilgrim / Little rabbit / Lucy Farr's polkas / The chancellor - Galway Bay / Norwegian bridal march / Three Rucenitsas / Waltz from Vaqrmland / Bessarabian wedding dance / The Arkansas traveller.

Oct 93. (cd/c) *(FFS 002 CD/C)* **THE WOUNDED HUSSAR** ☐ ⊟
- Reel of Mullinavat - Dr Gilbert / Chicago jig - Tom Billy's / Julia Clifford's - Din Tarrant's / O'Carolan's draught / Garret Barry's - Pipes on the hob / Donegal mazurkas / Jug of punch - Eddie Kelly's / The wounded hussar / Toormore - Cullen slide / Musical priest - Salamanca - Morning dew - Heart is true / Ace and deuce of pipering / Donegal Highlands / Bryan O'Lynn – Connachtman's rambles - Paddy Clancy's / Lad O'Beirne's - Paddy Ryan's dream / McGlinchey's hornpipe.

—— VIVANDO were formed by **Cooper** - fiddle / **Neti Vaandrager** - fiddle, vocals (ex-ZUMZEAUX) / **Geoff Coombs** - mandola / **Kathryn Locke** - cello

Glenthorn — not issued

Nov 95. (c; as VIVANDO) *(GLN 001C)* **VIVANDO** ☐ ⊟
- Alpenherd / One extraordinary Friday / Viva Laredo / The L&N don't stop here anymore / The likely wood jig / The ornament / The architect's waltz - Bella Napoli / The carrot / Cool of the day - The green garden / Farewell to Islington – Jenny's chickens - Bonny Kate / Let's sing - The silver wedding.

—— next with **Richard Bolton** (cello and guitar)

Big Chain — not issued

Jan 02. (cd; as PETE COOPER & RICHARD BOLTON) *(BC 101)* **TURNING POINT**: FIDDLE & CELLO DUETS ☐ ⊟
- Chip / Lorna / Molly / Melting / Buzz / Peace / Hackney / Thirteen / Heartbeat / Louise / August / Islington.

Apr 05. (cd) *(BC 102)* **LONDON SESSIONS**: NEW AND TRADITIONAL FOLK TUNES (compilation from 1988–2001) ☐ ⊟
- Little rabbit / Bank of turf / Spanish point / August / Waltz from Varmland / Reinlander / Donegal Highlands / Before the blossom / Devil - Hackney / Incitement / The wounded hussar / Rainy island / Take the 'A'-tune / Toormore - Cullen / Arkansas traveller / Coming home / Lorna.

Oct 06. (cd; as COOPER & BOLTON) *(BC 103)* **THE SAVAGE HORNPIPE** ☐ ⊟
- Roadrage - Berserk / Persian Ricardo / Maiden lane / The world turned upside down / Synapse - Hod the lass / The cuckoo's nest / Ashley's - The savage / The sleeper / Snicket - G for Gnosall / Acton township / The lover's ghost / Katya / Ironlegs - The sportsman's / Salisbury plain / Wilbye's lament / The galopede.

—— Cooper also released instructional book/CDs including 'English Fiddle Tunes', 'Eastern European Fiddle Tunes', 'Irish Fiddle Solos', 'Mel Bay's Complete Irish Fiddle Player', etc.

DAVE ARTHUR with PETE COOPER / CHRIS MORETON

Wild Goose — not issued

Aug 03. (cd) *(WGS 311CD)* **RETURN JOURNEY** ☐ ⊟
- Shepherds' hey – Old Molly Hare / Harrison Brady – Winder slide / Dan O'Keefe's No.2 – Ducks in the pond / I wish I had someone to love me / Georgia girl / Little Margaret / Rattle on the stovepipe – Cuckoo's nest / Sherman's march / When he cometh – Michael Turner's waltz / Napoleon crossing the Alps / The two sisters / Did-na-do / Oh death / Downfall of Richmond / Pushboat.

—— the trio evolved into …

RATTLE ON THE STOVEPIPE

Apr 06. (cd) *(WGS 333CD)* **EIGHT MORE MILES** ☐ ⊟
- Tennessee mountain fox-chase / Eight more miles to Louisville / The boatman – Cuffy / The new rigged ship – Green Willis / The light dragoon – Downfall of Paris / The lakes of Pontchartrain / Over the waterfall / Willie's ghost / Fred Pidgeon's No.1 – Jenny Lind polka / Footmarks in the snow / Father, father, build me a boat / Nancy – Nancy Clough / Sail away ladies.

—— (2007) **Dan Stewart** - banjo, guitar; repl. Moreton

Nov 09. (cd) *(WGS 371CD)* **NO USE IN CRYIN'** ☐ ⊟
- Elzick's farewell / Short jacket and white trousers / Sadie at the back door / Willie Moore / Red apple juice / Old John Peel – Rock that cradle, Joe / You've been a friend – Frisky Jenny / Princess Royal / Monday morning go to school ('The two brothers', Child ballad 49) / Ways of the world / Damned old piney mountains / Sally in the garden / Dillard Chandler / Roll, Alabama, roll!

Sep 10. (cd) *(WGSCD 374)* **SO FAR, SO GOOD**: THE BEST OF RETURN JOURNEY AND EIGHT MORE MILES (compilation) ☐ ⊟
- The new-rigged ship – Green Willis / The boatman – Cuffy / The two sisters / Tennessee mountain fox-chase / The light dragoon – Downfall of Paris – Mississippi sawyer / When he cometh – Michael Turner's waltz / Did-na-do / The lakes of Pontchartrain / Napoleon crossing the Alps / Eight more miles to Louisville / Shepherd's hey – Old Molly Hare / Father, father, build me a boat / Oh death / Fred Pidgeon's No.1 – Jenny Lind polka / Sail away ladies / Dan O'Keefe's No.2 – Ducks in the pond / I wish I had someone to love me.

Ray COOPER (⟹ OYSTERBAND)

COSMOTHEKA

A bit of an overlooked oddity here. COSMOTHEKA, named after a mid-19th-century concert venue, "Cosmotheca", in Marylebone, London – the Greek word is loosely translatable as "the world's a stage") – were perched somewhere between modern-day music-hall comedy and trad-folk. It was formed in 1972 by Redditch-born brothers Dave and Al Sealey, who both had roots in pop music. Dave was a singer with The Chances Are, who used to be backed by a certain Reginald Dwight.

For more than 25 years the Sealeys flitted between radio, television and the recording studio by way of Radio 4's 'A Postcard From Cosmotheka', TV's Pebble Mill At One and several recorded sets such as opening salvo **A LITTLE BIT OFF THE TOP** (1974) {*6}.

Appearing on The Good Old Days, Roy Hudd's Halls Of Fame, The Bob Monkhouse Show and a Chas'n'Dave Christmas special, and recording material from the post-war and even pre-war variety stage, Dave and Al took their comic heritage all over the world. Dave continued to work as a solo artist after the death of his brother Al in 1999. *MCS*

Dave Sealey (b. 20 Feb '46, Redditch, Worcestershire) – vocals / **Al Sealey** (b. Alan Sealey, 18 May '40) – vocals / (+ session men)

UK Highway — US not issued

1974. (lp) *(SHY 6002)* **A LITTLE BIT OFF THE TOP**
- You don't want to keep on showing it, Mary / Wait till the work comes round / Let's all go mad / 'Arry, 'Arry, 'Arry / A little bit off the top / Ragtime waltz / Robin Redbreast / 'E dunno where 'e are / Mrs Carter / Riding on a motor car / Little Billy's wild Woodbines / The other department, please.

1977. (lp) *(SHY 7001)* **WINES & SPIRITS**
- Good little girl / The 'ouses in between / The baby's name / Little Dolly Daydream / Down the road / Up went my umberella / The golden dustman / The ragtime ragshop / The kangaroo hop / Hitchy coo / Johnny / Robin Redbreast / Music box tune / Only come down for the day / Timothy, let's have a look at it / Just like the ivy.

1981. (lp) *(SHY 7015)* **A GOOD TURN-OUT**
- Never let your braces dangle / The night began to fall / The skipper of the Mercantile Marine / Don't do it again, Matilda / Love, love, love / I can't do my bally bottom button up / It's a great big shame / The grizzly bear / Back answers / Proper cup o' coffee.

Dambuster — not issued

Dec 85. (lp) *(DAM 008)* **COSMOTHEKA**
- In a little Wigan garden / Alabama band / Down the road / Liarty / Thuthie / I like little people / Wot a mouth / Three ha'pence a foot / It's a pity to waste the cake / Bread and marmalade / Just like the ivy, I'll cling to you / Brahn boots.

BBC — not issued

Aug 89. (lp/c) *(REH/ZCR 746)* **KEEP SMILING THROUGH**: THE HIT SONGS OF WORLD WAR II
- Smiling through / Follow the white line / Wish me luck as you wave me goodbye / I get along without you very well / I love to sit with Sophie in the shelter / Hey little hen / I did what I could with my gasmask / Dig dig dig to victory / Whitehall warriors / I'm dreaming of a white Christmas / White cliffs of Dover / They're all under the counter / Lili Marlene – D-Day dodgers / I'm gonna get lit up when the lights go up in London / Roll me over / Knees up Mother Brown / We'll meet again / Medley. *(cd-iss. Aug 90; BBCCD 746) (cd/c re-iss. Apr 94 on Empire; EMPR CD/MC 509)*

—— sadly, Al died in 1999

- (5-7*) compilations, etc.-

May 02. (cd) *Folksound; (FSCD 55)* **YOU ONLY HAD TO ASK**
- Wot a mouth / Don't do it again, Matilda / Mrs Carter / It's a pity to waste the cake / It's a great big shame / Love, love, love / Little Billy's wild Woodbines / The kangaroo hop / The other department, please / Thuthie / I can't do my bally bottom button up / Wot I want is a proper cup of coffee.

Adrian CROWLEY

Born 1979 in Sliema, Malta, but raised in Barna, County Galway, Ireland (via Cameroon), sadcore singer and multi-instrumentalist CROWLEY has become one of the finds of his generation. Having spent time writing songs in Toulouse, France, he returned in 1997 to a new location of Rathmines on the outskirts of Dublin. Between autumn 1997 and autumn 1998 he laid down tracks for his self-produced debut set **A STRANGE KIND** (1999) {*7}.

With material recalling the golden days of the 1970s - NICK DRAKE, AL STEWART, et al - and augmented by the ever-faithful Thomas Haugh on percussion and Clifford Rees on cello (guest percussionist Rabada and engineer Donal O'Mahonny were also present), the unashamedly melancholic album displayed enough quality to get a remastered reissue on New Jersey's Ba Da Bing! Records in 2002. With haunting orchestral soundscapes dramatising the mood (check out instrumentals 'Trilogy' and 'Introduction'), the downbeat tracks give off an air of expectation – expectation that comes good on highlights such as 'The Cage Of My Ribs', 'Emotional Playground', 'Sister Of Mine' and closing piece de resistance 'Safe House', all slightly echoing the late Jeff Buckley or even bedsit crooner LEONARD COHEN.

With the aid of an Arts Council grant and an invitation from Chicago's top producer, Steve Albini, CROWLEY, Haugh and cellist Kate Ellis flew to the States to record his second set, **WHEN YOU ARE HERE YOU ARE FAMILY** (2002) {*7}.

Its title taken from graffiti that Crowley spotted in a photograph he'd taken in New York, the plaintive set once again displayed aching emotions set to mellow musak. From lush orchestral opener 'Tall Ships', to the blissfully mournful 'Solitary Diving' and 'Over The Waterway', each poetic piece gets the listener moping empathetically. How much Albini's magic adds to the tempered, lo-fi decorum one can't say, but it certainly reaches its emotional potential – in spades. 'North Shore Song' and 'Only Daughter – Sweet Sorrow' are another two worthy tearjerkers.

Moving at funereal pace, and sedately as only a NICK DRAKE clone could be, **A NORTHERN COUNTRY** (2004) {*8} was another slice of fragile folk sung in whispered monotones; it was afforded very little publicity at the time. If you get a chance, playlist 'Great Salt Lake', 'Brake Lines' and 'Birthday'.

Recorded over a week at his sister's house in Dublin – hence its UK-only release – **LONG DISTANCE SWIMMER** (2007) {*7} became an instant hit among the lo-fi-folk fraternity and was subsequently nominated as Irish Album of the Year. Of the dozen Smog-meets-Red House Painters creations, opener 'Bless Our Tiny Hearts', 'Electric Eels' and the title track are worth of the admission fee.

Maintaining a Celtic connection of sorts, CROWLEY signed a deal with Scotland's top indie-pendent, Chemikal Underground. **SEASON OF THE SPARKS** (2009) {*8} was another delightful set, the artist finally breaking free of the NICK DRAKE and folk-rock tags. This batch delivered in buckets, highlights including 'Summer Haze Parade', 'The Wishing Seat' and 'Squeeze Bees' (the latter once the priceless property of the eccentric Ivor Cutler). *MCS*

Adrian Crowley - vocals, guitar, piano, harmonium, saxophone, melodica / + session people incl. Thomas Haugh (percussion)

UK own label — US not issued

Jul 99. (cd) *(none)* **A STRANGE KIND** — Irish
- Capricorn / Slow fuse / Emotional playground / Introduction / The cage of my ribs / Trophies / Trilogy / Sister of mine / Safe house. <*(re-iss. Sep 02 + UK Aug 05 on Ba Da Bing!+=; BING-035)*> - Trilogy [video].

—— added Kate Ellis (cello)

Road Relish — Ba Da Bing!

Jan 02. (cd) <*BING-032*> **WHEN YOU ARE HERE YOU ARE FAMILY**
- Tall ships / Over the waterway / Girl from the estuary / North shore song / Starlings / Only daughter - Sweet sorrow / For the last time / Solitary diving / The devil's at the piano / Tonight I can see. *(UK-iss. Aug 05; same as US)*

May 02. (ltd-7") *(RR7-010)* FICKLE LIGHT. / (other by Nina Hynes) — Irish

Misplaced — Ba Da Bing!

Jul 04. (cd) *(MM 106)* <*BING 043*> **A NORTHERN COUNTRY**
- One hundred words for snow / Dark anvil skies / Morning frost / A northern country / Photographing lightning strikes / Cassiopeia / Harmonium song / Great Salt Lake / Brake lines / Piano song / Happiness came to my door / Birthday.

—— added Stephen Shannon (bass), Marja Tuhkanen (violin and viola)

Fence — not issued

Jun 07. (7" pink/cd-r) *(FNC-SECRET7-001)* BLESS OUR TINY HEARTS. / Star Of The Harbour

Tin Angel — not issued

Oct 07. (cd) *(TAR 003)* **LONG DISTANCE SWIMMER**
- Bless our tiny hearts / These ley waters / Star of the harbour / Temporary residence / Walk on part / Victoria / Harmony row / Theft by starlight / Electric eels / Leaving the party / Brother at sea / Long distance swimmer.

Chemikal Underground — not issued

Nov 09. (cd) *(Chem 124cd)* **SEASON OF THE SPARKS**
- Summer haze parade / The beekeeper's wife / The wishing seat / The three sisters / Squeeze bees / Liberty stream / Horses like to dream all night / Season of the sparks / Swedish room / Pay no mind (to the dawn cryer).

CROWS (⟹ RYAN, Mick)

Nancy Elizabeth CUNLIFFE(⟹ ELIZABETH, Nancy)

CURRENT 93 [folk part]

Formed in London in 1982, CURRENT 93 was initially an offshoot of 23 Skidoo, with ex-members David Tibet and Fritz Haaman along with John Balance (ex-Psychic TV and a member of Coil) and former members of Crisis, who evolved into Death In June.

Obscure but influential early players on the UK experimental/industrial scene, CURRENT 93 combined mediaeval-style choral chants with unsettling samples and hypnotic electronic percussion on their early albums. Recording alternately for the tiny Laylah and Maldorer labels at a prolific rate throughout the latter half of the 1980s, Tibet worked with whoever was available, mainly Steven Stapleton (of Nurse With Wound), Hilmar Orn Hilmarsson (of Psychic TV) and Rose McDowell (ex-Strawberry Switchblade). They gradually evolved a stark, folky sound no less spooky than his earlier work.

Come the 1990s, CURRENT 93 began a new chapter in their career on the newly established Durtro imprint, releasing new, vinyl-only material and re-issuing their rare and extremely collectable 1980s work on CD. The addition of Michael Cashmore was crucial in taking the band into toned-down, poetic acoustics.

For the purposes of this book, a handful of folk-orientated works have been picked out from Tibet and friends' at least 93 releases. Mixing up the mediaeval medicine, **THUNDER PERFECT MIND** (1992) {*7} introduced CURRENT 93 to the world of freak-folk, probably the first act to arrive there from industrial drone. A forerunner of IN GOWAN RING, ESPERS and a raft of like-minded souls, Tibet read his way through such derivative items as 'The Descent Of Long Satan And Babylon', 'A Sadness Song', 'A Lament For My Suzanne' and 'A Song For Douglas After He's Dead'.

The uplifting **OF RUINE, OR SOME BLAZING STARRE** (1994; cd 1996) {*8} was a poetic beauty that seemed to channel a long-gone time, producing golden tracks like 'Steven And I In The Field Of Stars' and 'The Teeth Of The Winds Of The Sea', 'Let Us Go To The Rose' and 'Moonlight, You Will Say'.

Also part of Tibet and Stapleton's folk phase, **ALL THE PRETTY LITTLE HORSES** (1996) {*7} (re-issued as a boxed set in 2007 and re-titled after one of its short songs, 'The Inmost Light'), was another climactic, mystical album, with guest vocals from Nick Cave on the last two songs. Tibet shines on 'The Frolic' and 'The Bloodbells Chime', but be warned, folkies, there are clusters of noise. The title track of CURRENT 93's next folkish venture, **SLEEP HAS HIS HOUSE** (2000) {*5}, was a 24-minute 'Metal Machine Music'-like drone, but that was countered by 'The Magical Bird In The Magical Woods', an eight-minute dirge that surpassed the derivative remainder.

With guest singers Marc Almond, Bonnie 'Prince' Billy, Baby Dee, Antony, Cosey Fanni Tutti, Clodagh Simonds, PANTALEIMON and SHIRLEY COLLINS performing versions of Charles Wesley's 18th-century hymn 'Idumaea', **BLACK SHIPS ATE THE SKY** (2006) {*8} was just the ticket. Almond's vocal comes off like a fusion of 'Amazing Grace' and Nine Inch Nails's 'Hurt', and Will Oldham's sadcore banjo rendition is an almighty tearjerker, but the limelight is stolen by SHIRLEY COLLINS' concluding box-accordion version. 'Then Kill Caesar' is seminal 1980s indie (think Fad Gadget), and the title track has a couple of eerie, un-folk variations that would do credit to Van Der Graaf Generator or Public Image Ltd.

Tibet is a master of the subliminal and nihilistic, and in folk music, however minimal and out-there, he shows a side that many acolytes may not have discovered. *MCS*

David Tibet - vocals / **Steven Stapleton** - multi / **Michael Cashmore** - multi / + guests

UK Durtro — US not issued

Jun 92. (d-lp) *(DURTRO 011)* **THUNDER PERFECT MIND**
- A beginning / The descent of Long Satan and Babylon / A sadness song / A song for Douglas after he's dead / In the heart of the wood and what I found there / Mary waits in silence / A silence song / A lament for my Suzanne / Riverdeadbank / All the stars are dead now / Rosy star tears from heaven / When the May rain comes / Thunder perfect mind I / Thunder perfect mind II / Hitler as Kalki (SDM) / A sad sadness song. *(cd-iss. Oct 96; DURTRO 011CD) (<d-cd iss. Nov03//2005 +=; DURTRO 069CD//DURTRO JNANA 1979CD>)* - [out-takes]: Suzanne: She and I in darkness we lay and lie / Red house / Our lady or horsies / Anyway, people die / Silence as Christine / Maldorer is ded ded ded ded / They return to their earth / In sadness sang / [live in Amiens, 15 XIII 1990]: Khor ba' I nyes dmigs / Lament for her / A song for Douglas after he's dead / They return to their earth (for my Christ thorn) / A song for Douglas after he's dead (rebirth).

1994. (ltd-blue-lp) *(DURTRO 018)* **OF RUINE, OR SOME BLAZING STARRE**
- A voice from Catland / Steven and I in the field of stars / The teeth of the winds of the sea / Moonlight, you will say / Into the bloody hole I go / The darkly splendid world / The cloud of unknowing / Let us go to the rose / All the world makes great blood / The great, bloody and bruised veil of the world / Into the menstrual night I go / Dormition and dominion / So: this empire is nothing / This shining shining world. *(cd-iss. Oct 96; DURTRO 018CD) <cd re-iss. Jun 07; DURTRO JNANA 1961>*

1995. (12"/cd-s) *(DURTRO 025/+CD)* TAMLIN. / How The Great Satanic Glory Faded

Feb 96. (ltd-clear-lp) *(DURTRO 026)* **ALL THE PRETTY LITTLE HORSES**
- The long shadows fall / All the pretty little horsies / Calling for vanished faces I / The inmost night / The carnival is dead and gone / The bloodbells chime / Calling for vanished faces II / The frolic / The inmost light / Twilight twilight, nihil nihil / The inmost light itself / All the pretty little horses [feat. NICK CAVE] / Patripassian [feat. NICK CAVE]. *(cd-iss. Oct 96 +=; DURTRO 026CD)* - Reading by Thomas Ligotti [hidden track]. *(3-cd-box-iss. Apr 07 as THE INMOST LIGHT+=; DURTRO 033)*- [disc 1]:- WHERE THE LONG SHADOWS FALL // [disc 3]:- THE STARS ARE MARCHING SADLY HOME

2000. (cd; as CURRENT NINETY THREE) *(DURTRO 051)* **SLEEP HAS HIS HOUSE**
- Love's young dream / Good morning, great Moloch / The magical bird in the magical woods / Red hawthorn tree / Immortal bird / Niemanswasser / Lullaby / Sleep has his house / The god of sleep has made his house. *(d-cd re-iss. Mar 06 +=; DURTRO 1925)* - Sleep has his house / Poppy / Go to sleep / Sky end / Hypnagogic Christ.

May 06. (cd) *(DURTRO 211)* **BLACK SHIPS ATE THE SKY**
- Idumaea [vocals: MARC ALMOND] / Sunset (the death of Thumbelina) / Black ships in the sky / Then kill Caesar / Idumaea [vocals: BONNIE 'PRINCE' BILLY] / This autistic imperium is nihil reich / The dissolution of 'the boat millions of years' / Idumaea [vocals: BABY DEE] / Bind your tortoise mouth / Idumaea [vocals: ANTONY] / Black ships seen last year south of heaven / Babylon destroyer / Idumaea [vocals: CLODAGH SIMONDS] / Black ships were sinking into Idumaea [vocals: COSEY FANNI TUTTI] / The beautiful dancing dust [vocals: ANTONY] / Idumaea [vocals: PANTALEIMON] / Black ships in the harbours / Idumaea / Black ships ate the sky / Why Caesar is burning (part 2) / Idumaea [vocals: SHIRLEY COLLINS].

Andy CUTTING (⟹ WOOD, Chris)

DAPHNE'S FLIGHT (⟹ MUCKRAM WAKES)

DARWIN SONG PROJECT

Whether this ensemble will prove a one-off project only time will tell, but the live album that does exist is immaculate in conception from start to finish.

The album of the same name, marking the bicentenary of Shrewsbury icon Charles Darwin's birth (2009) {*8}, featured an array of celebrated Brit-folk stars including RACHAEL McSHANE, Stu Hanna, Celtic-folkie EMILY SMITH, CHRIS WOOD, KARINE POLWART, JEZ LOWE and Americans MARK ERELLI and KRISTA DETOR. Written and rehearsed in seven days in a farmhouse in Shropshire in March 2009, the youthful folk enterprise was almost immediately the subject of a BBC Radio 4 documentary and was championed on the airwaves by comic-folkie MIKE HARDING. Each biographical track features a permutation of duets, trios, quartets and quintets (except finale 'You May Stand Mute'), but the predominant voice is that of Rachael's, while Karine comes in a close second. The velvet tones of CHRIS WOOD on the sublime `Turtle Soup' are a definite highlight, as are the contrasting, DYLAN-esque ERELLI on 'Kingdom Come' and SMITH on 'Thinking Path'. Although it didn't quite match the earlier collective of The IMAGINED VILLAGE (of which Chris was also a part), the father of evolution might be gratified to know he had been celebrated as a man, husband and father as well as one of the country's greatest scientists. *MCS*

Rachael McShane - vocals (of BELLOWHEAD) / **Stu Hanna** - vocals, guitar, mandolin (of MEGSON) / **Emily Smith** - vocals / **Mark Erelli** - vocals, guitar / **Chris Wood** - vocals / **Krista Detor** - vocals, piano / **Karine Polwart** - vocals / **Jez Lowe** - vocals, guitar

UK: Shrewsbury Folk Festival — US: not issued

Aug 09. (cd) *(SFFCD 001)* **DARWIN SONG PROJECT** [live]
- Trust in the rolling ocean / Heavy in my hand / Turtle soup / Kingdom come / The merchant's question / Thinking path / Jemmy Button / From Miss Emily Brawley / The Earl of Darwin's farewell – Save a place / Emma's lullaby / We're all leaving / Mother of mysteries / Will you be waiting? / Mother of my soul / Clock of the world / We'll hunt him down / You may stand mute.

DEAF HEIGHTS CAJUN ACES (⟹ forthcoming Vol.3: Celtic Connections)

The DEIGHTON FAMILY

Yorkshire was the base for this husband-wife-and-children collective, who created an eclectic array of pop and country tunes and turned them into Cajun-styled folk songs. It was the brainchild of multi-instrumentalist and vocalist Dave Deighton, who organised his immediate family into one tight ensemble. His Indonesian-born wife Josie equally nurtured and guided children Kathleen, Arthur, Rosalie, Maya and Angelina through their formative years, all of them keen musicians on instruments from fiddle to drums.

Described as "The Carter Family of the global village" in one journal, their talent was obvious, and more obviously still was that it was better served up to North Americans. They toured in Canada and the US in 1990. The suitably-titled **ACOUSTIC MUSIC TO SUIT MOST OCCASIONS** (1987) {*7} and their follow-up **MAMA WAS RIGHT** (1990) {*6} secured a niche with lovers of country, Creole and Celtic-folk, while audiences found them endearing to both eye and ear. However, the ambitious and slightly off-kilter **ROLLING HOME** (1992) {*5}, featuring covers of anything and everything (from Jim Reeves's hit 'I Love You Because' to Johnny Nash's 'I Can See Clearly Now' via RICHARD THOMPSON's 'Has He Got A Friend For Me'), produced mixed results.

As a musical unit, the parents decided to call it a day, and Kathleen and Rosalie joined up with JULIE MATTHEWS, KATHRYN ROBERTS, KATE RUSBY and Pat Shaw for the one-off album project INTUITION in 1993. ROSALIE DEIGHTON eventually went solo, but The DEIGHTON FAMILY reunited for Glasgow's Celtic Connections festival on Burns' Night (January 25) 2009. Sadly, Kathleen Deighton-Cousins died in 2010. *MCS*

Dave Deighton - vocals, melodeon, guitar, fiddle, harmonica / **Josie Deighton** (b. South Moluccan Islands, Indonesia) – acoustic guitar, bodhran / **Kathleen Deighton** - fiddle / **Arthur Deighton** - guitar, mandolin / **Rosalie Deighton** - vocals, mandolin, percussion / **Maya Deighton** - flute, tin whistle / **Angelina Deighton** - drums, percussion

UK: Rogue — US: Philo

Jul 87. (lp) *(FMSL 2010) <PH 1120>* **ACOUSTIC MUSIC TO SUIT MOST OCCASIONS** — Dec 88
- Travelling light / Matchbox / Two little boys / Muddy roads – Give the fiddler a dram / Bo weevil / Keep that candle burning / All shook up / Tennessee wig walk / Money / Handsome Molly / Tin whistle / Blue suede shoes / Going down the road. *(cd-iss. 1989; FMSD 5010) (cd re-iss. Mar 00; CDPH 1120)*

1990. (cd/c) *<CDPH/CPH 1130>* **MAMA WAS RIGHT**
- Wonderful tonight / Soldier's joy / Mama was right / When you're smiling (the whole world smiles with you) / In my time of dyin' / Cotton-eyed Joe – Magpie / Farther along / Castle Kelly / Bonaparte's retreat / Many good men / The miser – Taxman / Cotton patch rag / Salvation railroad / Slow air (the little field of barley) / Freight train blues. *(UK-iss. Mar 00; same as US)*

UK: Green Linnet — US: Green Linnet

Feb 92. (cd/c) *(<GLCD/CSIF 1116>)* **ROLLING HOME**
- I love you because / I can see clearly now / Save the last dance for me / The road to Newcastle / The green rolling hills of West Virginia / Reuben's train / Under the boardwalk / I forgot to remember to forget / When I get home / Leather britches / Rollin' home / Has he got a friend for me / Gilbert Clancy's reel.

—— The DEIGHTON FAMILY issued nothing more (Rosalie and Kathleen joined INTUITION)

ROSALIE DEIGHTON

UK: Independiente — US: not issued

Oct 01. (cd) *(ISOM 22CD)* **TRUTH DRUG**
- Bruised / Infinitely high / Send me an angel / Be easy on me / Rain love / Instant fix / I believe / Crazy world tomorrow / Lie to me / Instinct / Ideal me / Silver lining.

UK: Echo — US: not issued

Apr 07. (cd) *(ECSCD 73)* **21 DAYS**
- Sing to me / Wagon wheel (these days) / Fairweather friend / Turn down the light / Where do you go when you dream? / Pilgrim / Don't / Favour / Bruised / 21 days / Second best.

Matt DEIGHTON

He's worked with such luminaries as Paul Weller, Oasis (as fill-in for Noel Gallagher) and the latter-day Wolfhounds, but most acid-jazz aficionados will recall MATT DEIGHTON as the frontman for influential 1990s London outfit Mother Earth. Fewer will probably know of his NICK DRAKE/BILL FAY-like acoustic soul-folk of the 2000s, and one low-key set, **VILLAGER** {*6}, that goes as far back as 1995.

YOU ARE THE HEALER (2000) {*7}, featuring Brian Auger, Tim Harris and Liam Genockey, and **THE COMMON GOOD** (2001) {*6}, with Weller and Mick Talbot on board, showed a man with promise, while 2005's **WAKE UP THE MOTHS** {*7} set saw him take on Brian Protheroe's 'Pinball' and no less than three BILL FAY nuggets: 'Release Is In The Eye', ''Til The Christ Come Back' and 'I Hear You Calling'. DEIGHTON is currently recording his comeback set. *MCS*

Matt Deighton - vocals, acoustic guitar / + session players

UK Apex Ent... US not issued

Jun 95. (cd) *(none)* **VILLAGER**
- Good for us / Stones around the candle / Villager – Bone dry boat / Jesus loves the rain / Get out of the road / Hey, my mind / Pure English honey / The windmills of Norfolk / Two piece jigsaw puzzle / Hiding in the breeze. *(re-iss. Aug 97 and Jun 00 on Focus; FOCUSCD 1)*

Barley Wheel not issued

Mar 00. (cd/lp) *(WHEELCD 1)* **YOU ARE THE HEALER**
- Five years in pieces / Easy times / Twisted wheel / You are the healer / Lay down your weary light / The garden grows / 72 minutes to Switzerland / In the finish / Little lost / Tannis roots / So are you / Next year. *(re-iss. Jan 02 on Yeaah; YEAAH 55)*

Alfafame not issued

Jun 01. (cd) *(YEAAH 54)* **THE COMMON GOOD**
- Large as life / 'Til Monday / The populator / The rolling bus / The common good / Before and after / All the above / Just remember / Back to the meantime / Finger of rain / A saint coming home / Evensong / Tumbling free / With everyone.

Jul 01. (cd-s) *(YEAAH 1)* 'TIL MONDAY / THE POPULATOR / The Populator [acoustic] / Just An Ordinary

Barley Wheel not issued

Mar 05. (cd) *(WHEELCD 2)* **WAKE UP THE MOTHS**
- If you get swayed in the night time… / I just can't face the world etc / Feeling that I'm falling / Release is in the eye / Pinball / Over my head / Austin the twice born / Be without / 'Til the Christ come back / In the manner we choose / I hear you calling / Don't turn around, look ahead / Wake up the moths / Am I song.

—— Matt would form The Bench Connection with Chris Sheehan, releasing one set, 'Around The House In 80 Days' (2007)

The DEMON BARBERS (⟹ BARBER, Damien)

Damien DEMPSEY

Mixing up a heady cocktail of contemporary Irish balladeering and traditional Celtic/Irish folk-rock reggae, singer-songwriter DAMIEN DEMPSEY (born 1975, Donaghmede in Dublin) has all the promise of a young CHRISTY MOORE. Over the past decade or so, DEMPSEY's unique urban approach to the folk genre has won him many star admirers, including Sinead O'Connor, Morrissey and DYLAN.

It all started back in 1995 when Damien graduated from a "rock school"-type afterclass run by Dublin's Ballyfermot College of Further Education, and brought an early taste of success for DEMPSEY (then billed by surname only) by way of underground hit 'Dublin Town'. Tipped as the next big thing by Irish music magazine Hot Press, the track was showcased on Damien's hippie-hop-folk debut album **THEY DON'T TEACH THIS SHIT IN SCHOOL** (2000) {*8}. Others worth checking out are 'Seanchai' (a Celtic trance ballad), 'Colony', 'Jealousy' and the Bob Marley-esque title track.

Produced by veteran John Reynolds, **SEIZE THE DAY** (2003) {*6} made room for guests Brian Eno and Sinead O'Connor. Contrasting songs such as the reggaefied 'Negative Vibe' and the folky 'Ghosts Of Overdoses' gave the cloth-capped Dubliner a certain maturity and his first of two Meteor Ireland music awards. 2005's **SHOTS** {*7} was the other (for Best Male Artist), a record that went straight to No.1 in his homeland and led to a major-label contract. The concert set **LIVE AT THE OLYMPIA** (2006) {*6}, his fourth studio album **TO HELL OR BARBADOS** (2007) {*6} (also a chart-topper) and covers set **THE ROCKY ROAD** (2008) {*6}, featuring The DUBLINERS' John Sheahan and Barney McKenna, all depicted a man of ambition and tradition in equal measure. *MCS*

Damien Dempsey - vocals, guitar / + band

UK Rockhall US not issued

1995. (cd-ep; as DEMPSEY) *(RHCD 002)* CONTENDER EP — Irish
- Alright tonight / Bottle talk / Rollercoaster / Cardboard city.

Treasure Island Discs not issued

Feb 97. (cd-s; as DEMPSEY) *(TIDCD 012)* DUBLIN TOWN [mixes: ska / dub linn / acoustic] — Irish

Zinc not issued

Mar 00. (cd) *(ZINC 001)* **THEY DON'T TEACH THIS SHIT IN SCHOOL**
- Jealousy / NYC Paddy / Colony / Seanchai / I've no alibi / Chillin' / It's important / Bad time garda / It's all good / They don't teach this shit in school / Dublin town / Beside the sea. *(re-iss. Oct 05 on Independent Records …; IRL 024)*

Apr 00. (cd-s) *(ZINC 002)* CHILLIN' / I've No Alibi / Some Of These Girls Are Crazy / Bottle Talk [live] — Irish

self-rel. not issued

Oct 02. (cd-ep) *(none)* NEGATIVE VIBES EP — gigs
- Negative vibes [radio] / Negative vibes / Ghosts of overdoses / Jar song / Factories.

Clear Attack

May 03. (cd-s) *(CLE 001)* NEGATIVE VIBES / Industrial School / Negative Vibes [album version] — Irish

May 03. (cd) *(CLR 001)* *<86010>* **SEIZE THE DAY** — Oct 04
- Negative vibes / Ghosts of overdoses / It's all good / Factories / Jar song / Celtic tiger / Apple of my eye / Industrial school / Great Gaels of Ireland / Marching season siege / Seize the day. *(UK-iss. May 04 on Independent Records…; IRL 018)*

Sep 03. (cd-ep) *(CLE 002)* IT'S ALL GOOD — Irish
- It's all good / Party on / Beside the sea / You were always on my mind.

(above featured Sinead O'Connor)

Jun 04. (cd-s) *(IRLCDS 001)* IT'S ALL GOOD / [version] / Industrial School

Aug 04. (cd-s) *(IRLCDS 002)* APPLE OF MY EYE / Beside The Sea [live] / You Were Always On My Mind [live]

Clear United For Opportunity

Feb 05. (cd-s) *(CLE 003)* ST. PATRICK'S DAY / [album version] / Anywhere You Go — Irish

Mar 05. (cd) *(CLR 002 - IRL 022)* *<UFO 1007>* **SHOTS** — Jun 06
- Sing all our cares away / Not on your own tonight / St. Patrick's Day / Cursed with a brain / Party on / Colony / Patience / Hold me / Choctaw nation / Spraypaint backalley.

Apr 05. (cd-s) *(IRLCDS 005)* HOLD ME / [album version] / NYC Paddy

May 05. (cd-s) *(CLE 004)* PATIENCE [mixes: single / Eno / desert / album] — Irish

Sony - BMG United For Opportunity

Jun 06. (cd) *(82876 85665-2 – IRL 028)* **LIVE AT THE OLYMPIA** [live] — Irish
- Patience / Party on / Hold me / Seize the day / Not on your own tonight / Apple of my eye / Sing all our cares away / Negative vibes / Industrial school / It's all good / [encores]: Factories / Colony.

May 07. (cd-s) *(88697 10798-2)* YOUR PRETTY SMILE / Celtic Tiger [live] — Irish

Jun 07. (cd) *(88697 10051-2 – IRL 034)* *<UFO 1010>* **TO HELL OR BARBADOS**
- Maasai / Kilburn stroll / How strange / Chase the light / Your pretty smile / Serious / Teachers / Summer's in my heart / To Hell or Barbados / The city. *(d-cd-ss. Nov 07 +=; ???)* - Not on your own tonight (part 2) / Saturday finally comes / Wild one / Schooldays are over / Fly me to the moon / Taobh leis an muir [Beside the sea] / The rhythm of time / Holy night.

Aug 07. (cd-s) *(88697 15035-2)* THE CITY / Jealousy — Irish

Nov 07. (cd-s) *(88697 20431-2)* KILBURN STROLL Fly Me To The Moon — Irish

Feb 08. (dl-s) *(-)* THE BALLAD OF RONNIE DREW — Irish

May 08. (cd-s) *(88697 32440-2)* A RAINY NIGHT IN SOHO / Johnny Jump Up — Irish

Jun 08. (cd) *(88697 32116-2 – IRL 038)* *<UFO 1014>* **THE ROCKY ROAD**
- The rocky road to Dublin / Schooldays over / A rainy night in Soho / The twang man / Sullivan John / Kelly from Killan – The teetotaler / The foggy dew / Hot asphalt / Night visiting song / The hackler from Grouse Hall – The Monaghan jig / Madam I'm a darlin'.

Dec 10. (cd-s; by DAMIEN DEMPSEY & GLEN HANSARD) *(88697 82443-2)* THE AULD TRIANGLE / Raglan Road / Not On Your Own Tonight (part 2) — Irish

Kevin Dempsey (⟹ WHIPPERSNAPPER)

The DEVIL'S INTERVAL

Friends since meeting in 2002 while studying traditional music at Newcastle University, singers and musicians Jim Causley, Lauren McCormick and Emily Portman formed their Bright Young Folk trio a few years later. Supported by former folk soloists turned tutors SANDRA KERR and CHRIS COE, the group performed at a number of festivals from Sidmouth to Oxford while finding time to record their debut set, **BLOOD & HONEY** (2006) {*7}. Readers will recognize most of the trad tunes, including the perennials 'The Cuckoo', 'Silver Dagger' (Dolly Parton, eat your heart out), 'Long Lankin' and 'Two Crows'.

Their obvious talent was rewarded with a Best New Act award at the 2007 BBC Folk On Two night, when they had already completed a guest spot for the ritual festive record by WATERSON: CARTHY, 'Holy Heathens And The Old Green Man'.

Meanwhile, MAWKIN-bound JIM CAUSLEY produced a threesome of his own with the release of solo sets, **FRUITS OF THE EARTH** (2005) {*6}, **LOST LOVE FOUND** (2007) {*6} and **DUMNONIA** (2011) {*7}. After a one-off with RUBUS by way of the anglo-quintessential **NINE WITCH KNOTS** (2008) {*7}, PORTMAN's career took off with her choice solo effort **THE GLAMORY** (2010) {*8}. Past master SHIRLEY COLLINS was added to her growing fanbase, quoted as saying "she was born to sing". *MCS*

Jim Causley (b. 31 Oct '80, Exeter, England) – vocals, accordion, concertina, etc. / **Lauren McCormick** (b. Derbyshire, England) – vocals, piano, flute / **Emily Portman** (b. Somerset, England) - vocals, concertina

UK Wild Goose — US not issued

Aug 06. (cd) *(WGS 335CD)* **BLOOD & HONEY**
- Green valley / Silver dagger / Studying economy / The leaves of life / The well below the valley / Two crows / The bonfire carol / A May carol / Down among the dead men / The cuckoo / Long Lankin / The midsummer carol / Blow me Jack.

JIM CAUSLEY

Jul 05. (cd) *(WGS 326CD)* **FRUITS OF THE EARTH**
- John Barleycorn / Arsott of Tetcott / Tan yard side / The pricklie brush / Old Riverside / Harvest song / Rewind / The carnal and the crane / The lusty young smith / Sing Ivy / The whimple wassail / Yonders hill / Unwind. *(re-iss. 2010; same)*

Oct 07. (cd) *(WGS 348CD)* **LOST LOVE FOUND**
- Polly Vaughn / Cupid the ploughboy / Wild rover / Loving Hannah / Shule rune / Lady all skin and bone / Traitor's love / Oxford city / Autumn days / Rolling of the stones.

—— it was at this stage CAUSLEY joined forces with MAWKIN

—— Causley subsequently joined DAVID ROTHERAY (ex-Beautiful South, ex-HOMESPUN)

Mar 11. (cd) *(WGS 377CD)* **DUMNONIA**
- When I was young / Little ball of yarn / Georgie / Old Uncle Whiteway / The old threshing mill / Sidbury to Stockland set / The Earl of Totnes / Royal comrade / Exeter town / She moved through the fair – German clockmaker / Tamar Valley requiem / Exmoor anthem / Honiton lace / The game of cards / In the sidings / Larkbeare / The Tythe pig / Wailey wailer.

RUBUS

Emily Portman - vocals, concertina / **Christi Andropolis** (b. USA) – fiddle, viola, vocals / **Dave Newey** - guitar / **Will Schrimshaw** - drums, percussion

Wild Goose — not issued

Aug 08. (cd) *(WGS 356CD)* **NINE WITCH KNOTS**
- Cecilia / Cornish young man / Golden ball / Willie's lady / Greenwood sidey / She's like the swallow / Watchet sailor / Sheep crook black dog / Rolling of the stones / My son David / Sowing song.

EMILY PORTMAN

Furrow — not issued

Mar 10. (cd) *(FUR 002)* **THE GLAMOURY**
- Bones and feathers / Tongue-tied / Fine silica / Grey stone / Mossycoat / Hide / Stick stock / Little longing / Pretty skin / Sirens / Two sisters / Three gold hairs.

Cara DILLON

The voice of an angel is a term overused in the world of entertainment, but for Northern Ireland chanteuse CARA DILLON it's a description well earned. Born July 21, 1975 in Dungiven, County Londonderry, Cara's introduction into music came at the age of 14, when she won the prestigious All-Ireland Singing Trophy. Her sister is Mary Dillon of Celtic-folk act Deanta.

Living up to the hype, Cara soon led out Irish traditional outfit OIGE (pronounced "Oy-ga") – basically schoolkid brothers Ruadhrai and Murrough O'Kane – and finally released CDs in Scotland for Lochshore Records. Paul McLaughlin (guitars) also features on these albums, **LIVE** (1994) {*6} and **BANG ON** (1996) {*6}, the latter retaining her only as a guest. Joining young super-trad-folk-group EQUATION (alongside SETH LAKEMAN and his brothers) and performing on Mike Oldfield's 'Tubular Bells III' in 1998, things looked bright for the rising star. She and Sam Lakeman (her partner and future husband) formed the short-lived Polar Star.

Retaining Sam on production and songwriting, she signed a lucrative deal with Rough Trade Records, who released the predominantly trad-sourced set **CARA DILLON** {*8} in 2001. The album won the Hot Press Irish Music Award and two BBC Radio 2 Folk Awards (opening track 'Black Is The Colour' won Best Song), and Cara promoted its dreamscape gems, such as 'I Am A Youth That's Inclined To Ramble', 'The Maid Of Culmore' and 'Green Grows The Laurel', on a global tour.

With more of an emphasis on their songwriting talents (from 'High Tide' to 'Everywhere'), the classic **SWEET LIBERTY** (2003) {*9} – recorded at her and Sam's Somerset home in Frome – was the album to bring her the attention she deserved. Alongside Tommy Sands's tale of a couple battling the sectarian troubles of Ireland ('There Were Roses'), the best traditional songs showcased were 'Bonny Bonny' and 'Erin The Green'.

AFTER THE MORNING (2006) {*7} completed her spell at Rough Trade with another gorgeous but derivative set of songs that was Celtic in tone, featuring as it did PAUL BRADY on 'The Streets Of Derry', DOUGIE MACLEAN's composition 'Garden Valley', Mary Ann Kennedy's 'Walls' and a fine arrangement of sourced delight 'Brockagh Braes'. It seemed the name of CARA DILLON was finally filtering into the minds of a wider audience when her own self-financed fourth album, **HILL OF THIEVES** (2009) {*7} cracked the UK Top 75. *MCS*

OIGE

Cara Dillon - vocals, fiddle / **Ruadhrai O'Kane** - fiddle, bodhran / **Paul McLaughlin** - guitars / **Murrough O'Kane** - flute, whistles

UK Lochshore — US not issued

Dec 94. (cd) *(LDLCD 1225)* **LIVE** (live)
- Dunga: Coughlan's jig - Castlebar jig - Old Leitrum / The flower of Margherallyo / The clumsy lover reels: The clumsy lover - Ships are sailing - Michael Dwyer's reel - Laurel tree / P. stands for Paddy / Liz Carroll's reels: Boys of the lough (in D) - Boys of the lough (in A) – Mother's delight / Girls put the fags out: Ashplant - Red haired lass / Green grasses grow bonnie / Slow boat to China reels: Miss McGuiness - Swallow tail / The weaver / The mountain road reels: The mountain road - Concertina reel / Bushes and briars.

Jun 96. (cd) *(CDLDL 1242)* **BANG ON**
- Silver spear reels: Silver spear - Victory reel - The boys of Malin / The banks of the Bann / The maid of Culmore / Touch me if you dare reels: The North Sea Chinaman - Boys of the lough - Touch me if you dare / My bonnie labouring boy / The hot rock set: The sea horse - The hot rock reel / Bonnie blue eyed lassie / Fergal O'Gara's reels: Fergal O'Gara's - Tarbolton - Leslie's / The flower of Magherally, O! / Roaring Mary reels: Swinging on the gate - Roaring Mary / Maids of Michaeltown.

—— Cara joined folk supergroup EQUATION (until 1996)

CARA DILLON

Cara Dillon - vocals / with **Sam Lakeman** - instruments

Rough Trade — Sanctuary

Jul 01. (cd) *(RTRADECD 019)* <83202> **CARA DILLON** — Feb 02
- Black is the colour / Donald of Glencoe / Craigie Hill / Green grows the laurel / Lark in the clear air / The lonesome scenes of winter / Blue mountain river / I wish I was / The maid of Culmore / She's like the swallow / I am a youth that's inclined to ramble.

Sep 03. (cd) *(RTRADECD 123)* <83233> **SWEET LIBERTY** — Mar 04
- High tide / The winding River Roe / Everywhere / There were roses / Whare are you / The gem of the roe / Bonny bonny / Erin the green / Broken bridges / Falling like a star / Standing on the shore / The emigrant's farewell.

Rough Trade — Compass

Feb 06. (cd) *(RTRADECD 198)* <COM 74439>
AFTER THE MORNING — Sep 06
- Never in a million years / I wish you well / Here's a health / Brockagh braes / Garden valley / October winds / Bold Jamie / The streets of Derry / This time / The snow they melt the soonest / Walls / Grace.

Aug 06. (cd-s) *(RTRADSCD 359)* THIS TIME / I WISH YOU WELL

—— in Apr '07, Dillon and 2Dev issued 'Black Is The Colour' for Anjuna Beats

Charcoal — not issued

May 08. (dl-s/cd-s; as CARA DILLON & JOHN SMITH) *(001)*
IF I PROVE FALSE / If I Prove False (live DVD version)

Jan 09. (cd) *(002)* **HILL OF THIEVES** — [69]
- The hill of thieves / Johnny, lovely Johnny / The parting glass / Spencer the rover / False, false / Jimmy mo' mhile stor / She moved through the fair / P stands for Paddy (lament for Johnny) / The verdant braes of Skreen / The lass of Glenshee / Fil, fil a run o.

Leslie DOWDALL (⟹ IN TUA NUA)

Paul DOWNES

A classical guitarist playing folk music: there aren't many to file under this category. GORDON GILTRAP and JOHN RENBOURN are possibly the only prime exponents, but the incisive technique of PAUL DOWNES (born August 2, 1953 in Exeter) was almost unique in this field. Paul first came to the attention of the folk world in the mid-1970s through two collaborative LPs with long-time songwriting buddy PHIL BEER, **LIFE AIN'T WORTH LIVING** (1973) {*6} and **DANCE WITHOUT MUSIC** (1976) {*6}.

DOWNES' debut solo LP, **STILL LIFE** (1978) {*6}, featured vocalist BEER and another friend, guitarist/song-contributor STEVE KNIGHTLEY; others playing on the set were brothers Warwick Downes (bass and congas) and Len Downes (violin/viola), plus Mick Candler (drums), Ken Byng (pedal steel). There were covers of songs by Dik Cadbury, BOB PEGG, EWAN MacCOLL and LEON ROSSELSON. Second set **LIFE GOES ON** (1980) {*6} also credited songsmith KNIGHTLEY, as well as GARY & VERA ASPEY, Bill Boazman, O'Carolan and PETER BELLAMY, while his new band (except Warwick) comprised Paul Simmonds, Martyn Bradley, Martin Angell, Stuart Reed and Chris Billings. Both records are now on a combined CD.

Discovering a love of bluegrass while former New KINGSTON TRIO plucker Bill Zorn was in London in the early 1980s, DOWNES helped found The Arizona Smoke Revue. They released three sets: 'Arizona Smoke Revue' (1980), 'A Thunder In The Horizon' (1981) and 'The Blackwater Boys'. On a similarly rootsy theme, Paul was behind Irish-trad/mod-jazz outfit The Joyce Gang (with David McKeown and John Redmond) for many gigs and the albums 'Sober For A Week' (1991), 'Deadheads Don't Dance' (1994), 'In Yer Face – Live' (1996) and 'No True Road' (2000).

Maintaining his low-key but effective solo career, DOWNES (an avid Exeter rugby supporter) released two sadly underrated folk albums in the 1990s, **DIRECTLY** (1992) {*7} and **OVERDUE** (1996) {*6}. The latter a little closer to his traditional roots, courtesy of a few sourced songs including 'Black Is The Colour'. Of late Paul has teamed up with singer-songwriter and Wild Goose Records artist MICK RYAN on two collaborative albums, 'Grand Conversation' (2008) and 'Away In The West' (2010). *MCS*

Paul Downes - vocals, guitar / with session people/guests

UK Sweet Folk — US not issued

1973. (lp; by PAUL DOWNES & PHIL BEER) *(SFA 016)* **LIFE AIN'T WORTH LIVING (IN THE OLD FASHIONED WAY)** ☐ ⊟
- Peggy and the soldier / The hunting of Arscott of Tetcott / The bonny bunch of roses / Helen's and Jan's favourites / The snow it melts the soonest / The banks of Newfoundland / Spanish ladies / Low down in the broom / Marrowbones / McCleod's lament / Both sexes / Tabhair dom do lamh [Give me your hand] / Life ain't worth living.

1976. (lp; by PAUL DOWNES & PHIL BEER) *(SFA 046)* **DANCE WITHOUT MUSIC** ☐ ⊟
- Dance without music / Song / Let me play / Somewhere in green / Sunday supplement / Five-poster bed / Take back your pictures / Flower girl / Born again / Friends.

1978. (lp) *(SFA 086)* **STILL LIFE** ☐ ⊟
- Same old friends of mine / I could not take my eyes off her / Some words / Did you like the battle / The first time ever I saw your face / Still life / Puss in boots / Changeless story / You'll be next / Sweet air season / Across the hills. *(cd-r iss. Jan 02 as 'LIFE RESTORED' +=; LRCDR 1)* - LIFE GOES ON

Avada — not issued

Nov 80. (lp) *(AVA 109)* **LIFE GOES ON** ☐ ⊟
- Tall ships / My true love / The price of coal / The plains of Waterloo / Life goes on / The worm forgives the plough / Planxty Hewlett / Sir Richard's song / The friar in the well / Sit you down. *(cd-r iss.+=)- STILL LIFE*

—— Downes and Beer teamed up with American Bill Zorn in Arizona Smoke Revue for three sets, 'Arizona Smoke Revue' (1981), 'A Thunder In The Horizon' and 'The Blackwater Boys'. Downes would join The Joyce Gang for four albums

Rola — not issued

Mar 82. (d-lp; by DOWNES AND BEER) *(R 004/005)* **LIVE IN CONCEPT** [live & part-compilation] ☐ ⊟
- Passed you by / List for a sailor – Teetotaler reel / Pavanas / Andalusian gypsies / Cursed Anna / Things we said today / Across the hills / Rough with the smooth / Did you like the battle // Let me play / Both sexes / Them toad suckers / Ode to Billy Joe / Life goes on / Old fiddler / My canary's got circles under his eyes / Nuages – Sweet Georgia Brown / Half asleep / Fox on the run.

HTD. — not issued

1992. (cd) *(HMCD 16)* **DIRECTLY** ☐ ⊟
- Long way to go / Driving at the moon / I am the foe / Robert and the cowboys / The rose in the thorn / She sits alone / The brook / Call it a loan / Watch the sun go down / Dancing with Nancy / When the boys are on parade / Angi – Cocaine / The moth / The ballad of Cursed Anna.

Mar 96. (cd/c) *(HTD CD/MC 55)* **OVERDUE** ☐ ⊟
- I thought you'd come / Black is the colour / Closer / For whom the bell tolls / Lovers / Overdue / Losing the fight / Lark above the downs / Go to work on Monday / Tomorrow if not today / Come and be a soldier / Sheath and knife / Real old style.

—— In the late 2000s, DOWNES teamed up with MICK RYAN on two CDs, 'Grand Conversation' and 'Away In The West'.

- (5-7*) compilations, extras, etc.-

Sep 08. (cd; by DOWNES & BEER) *Talking Elephant; (TECD 131)* **LIVE AT NETTLEBED** (recorded late 1970s) ☐ ⊟
- Bruce - Coming rains / Nancy's - A tune set / Call it a loan / Life goes on / Honour and praise / Opinion on love / Sir Richard's song / Both sexes / Blues in D / Sheath and knife / There but for fortune / Go to work on Monday.

DR FAUSTUS

Formed in 1998 by traditional English musicians and vocalists Tim Van Eyken, Robert Harbron, Benji Kirkpatrick and Paul Sartin. Kirkpatrick and Sartin were also key members of large ensemble BELLOWHEAD. Kirkpatrick was an award-winning solo artist and a member of the WATERSON: CARTHY collective.

Steeped in traditional waters, they signed a deal with Rotherham-based Cumbrian label Fellside. The quartet were a much-touted prospect (comic-folkie and J MIKE HARDING was one patron). **THE FIRST CUT** (2003) {*7} went deep into the sources, their obvious talents spreading over the likes of 'Newry Town', 'Young Henry Martin' and 'The Cambric Shirt' (also known as 'Scarborough Fair'). **WAGER** (2005) {*6} was met with similar enthusiasm. Eight-minute opener 'Broomfield Wager' was typical of their inventive approach while keeping their musical template intact. Sadly, an appearance at the Towersey Village Festival brought the curtain down, at least on this collective.

Minus VAN EYKEN and Harbron, but with WATERSON: CARTHY sidekick Saul Rose, Kirkpatrick and Sartin stepped up to the mark again with the undoctored FAUSTUS. Described as a harmony-fuelled trio with genuine chemistry, their accessible Elizabethan folk and mediaeval musical jousts flowed freely on the likes of the part-a-cappella opener 'Brisk Lad' on their eponymous **FAUSTUS** (2008) {*7} set. 'Ballina Whalers' and ‚Acre Of Land' are worth the admission price alone. *MCS*

Tim Van Eyken - vocals, melodeon, guitar (of WATERSON: CARTHY) / **Robert Harbron** - English concertina, guitar, fiddle, vocals / **Benji Kirkpatrick** - vocals, bouzouki, banjo, harmonica, guitar (of BELLOWHEAD, of SETH LAKEMAN) / **Paul Sartin** - vocals, fiddle, oboe (of BELLOWHEAD, of BELSHAZZAR'S FEAST)

UK Fellside — US not issued

Aug 03. (cd) *(FECD 177)* **THE FIRST CUT** ☐ ⊟
- Newry town / Dr Faustus set - The peacock followed the hen - The old woman tossed up in a blanket / The trooper and the maid / The thresherman / May reel set No.1 - Bacca pipes jig / The cambric shirt / Captain Ward / Salisbury plain / Tantalus set - Young Joe / The Lincolnshire poacher - Dr Fausters' tumblers / Young Henry Martin.

Apr 05. (cd) *(FECD 189)* **WAGER** ☐ ⊟
- Broomfield wager / Grey mare (Crossed couple - Grey mare - Legacy) / The disdainful lady / The dawn - The Glafis hornpipe / Peter's Schottische - T stands for Thomas / Lord Ellenwater / Shepherds' song / A bed between friends - The two rascals / Jack Williams the boatswain / Spanish ladies.

FAUSTUS

Benji + **Paul** with **Saul Rose** (of WATERSON: CARTHY)

Navigator — not issued

May 08. (cd/d-lp) *(NAVIGATOR 5 CD/LP)* **FAUSTUS** ☐ ⊟
- Brisk lad / The hostess daughter / Ballina whalers / Next stop: Grimsby – The three rascals – Aunt Crisps / The new deserter / The old miser / The green willow tree / Will the weaver / Acre of land. *(d-lp+=)* - (BENJI KIRKPATRICK): Boomerang. *(cd re-iss. 2010 +=; ???)* - Temperley hornpipe – Oxford University voluntary quickstep / The betrayed maiden.

Kris DREVER (⟹ Celtic-Folk Discography)

The DRUIDS

Formed 1969 in Derby, the initial trio comprised ex-pop lad John Adams plus folk acolytes Keith Kendrick and Mick Hennessy, all vocalists and talented strummers. Almost immediately supplemented by fiddler Dave Broughton and singer Judi Longden (whom they met on the set of a folk documentary film), the DRUIDS raided the vaults of A.L. LLOYD and Ralph Vaughan Williams for a couple of decent LPs for Decca offshoot Argo Records. The first of these, **BURNT OFFERING** (1971) {*7}, featured sleeve artwork depicting "The Wicker Colossus of the Druids, whereas Malefactors of War and sometimes innocent persons (where there was a deficiency of the former) were Burnt as sacrifices to their Deities" (as it said on the tin) – nice idea for the film The Wicker Man, then. The second and final instalment, **PASTIME WITH GOOD COMPANY** (1973) {*5}, demonstrated that their archaic approach to trad-folk music of old was somewhat dated. STEELEYE SPAN and others had attempted such musical manoeuvres, and indeed failed until they turned the volume dial up to an electric-folk 11. However, the DRUIDS were the stamping ground for Adams, who with his wife, Suzie Adams, found further folk fame in MUCKRAM WAKES. The rest of the DRUIDS (though probably not Kendrick) combined with others from St George's Canzona and Trevor Crozier's Broken Consort to release a one-off set as GILES FARNABY'S DREAM BAND. *MCS*

Keith Kendrick - vocals, guitar, banjo / **John Adams** - vocals, mandolin, bass / **Mick Hennessy** - vocals, bass / with **Dave Broughton** - fiddle, accordion / **Judi Longden** - vocals

UK Argo — US not issued

May 71. (lp) *(ZFB 22)* **BURNT OFFERING**
- Thursday night - Brian Borouhme - Frost is all over / The trooper and his horse / A sailor's life / General Taylor / Salvation band / Hunting the hare – Exile's jig / The castle of Dramore / Our captain cried 'all hands' / Fare thee well, Enniskillen / The cuckoo's nest / The boar's head carol / The Christmas hare / A brisk young widow / The prickly bush / Madame Bonaparte - Roxburgh Castle / The farmer's three sons / Gabriel John / The butcher and the parson.

— In 1971, The DRUIDS (Kendrick, Adams + Hennessy) teamed up with MARTIN WYNDHAM-READ ⟹, Gerry Fox and The Band Of The Scots Guards to release 'SONGS AND MUSIC OF THE REDCOATS' (on Argo).

Mar 73. (lp) *(ZFB 39)* **PASTIME WITH GOOD COMPANY**
- Rollicking Irishman / All's dear but poor man's labour / Leaves of life / Sally gardens / Irish girl / White cockade / Flowers of Edinburgh / Come let us dance and sing.

— split after above; some of the DRUIDS (probably not KENDRICK, who went solo) teamed up with Trevor Crozier's Broken Consort and St George's Canzona to form ...

GILES FARNABY'S DREAM BAND

added **Jeff Clyne** - bass / **Dave MacRae** - electric piano / **Trevor Tompkins** - drums

Argo — not issued

Apr 73. (7") *(AFW 112)* NEWCASTLE BROWN. / 29th Of May

1973. (lp) *(ZDA 158)* **GILES FARNABY'S DREAM BAND**
- The hare's maggot / Rufty tufty - Beau stratagem - Appley House / The hole in the wall - The chirping of the nightingale / Pastime with good company / Daphne - Nonsuch – Jack's maggot - Childgrove / Shrewsbury lasses / Newcastle Brown / Helston furry dance - Picking of sticks - The butterfly / The Indian queen / The happy clown / Ratcliffe highway / The twenty ninth of May / The black nag - Poor robins' nest - Greensleeves / Portabella / The draper's maggot - Tower hill / Mr. Beveridge's maggot - The British toper – London's glory. *(cd-iss. 2004 on Walhalla; WH 90324)*

— Adams, meanwhile, joined MUCKRAM WAKES; Hennessy joined ROARING JELLY

Judy DUNLOP

Over the years dancer and singer JUDY DUNLOP (born 27th August 1955), of Brampton in Cumbria, has been associated with folk music's greatest names. Her husband ASHLEY HUTCHINGS (along with his ALBION BAND ensembles) was at the top of a tree whose other branches included DAVE SWARBRICK, MARTIN CARTHY and her first collaborative partner Steve Marsh, a classical guitarist introduced to Judy by Alan James (father of Hannah James).

From her time in Appalachian dance team Feet First (with Hannah's mother Julie James) to her 1990s work with HUTCHINGS on **SWAY WITH ME** (1991) {*7} – "a celebration of the tree and its offspring" – to her time with his LARK RISE BAND in 1998, she's not wavered from her purist folk principles.

Of her own sparse but worthy recording efforts, these can safely be recommended: her joint album with Jon Scaife (**I WANT SOMETHING** (2001) {*7}), a new set with Steve Marsh (**PAINTING SHOULD BE FUN** (2008) {*6}) and MICK RYAN's outstanding and enterprising concept sets 'The Navvy's Wife' and 'The Pauper's Path'. *MCS*

Judy Dunlop - vocals / (+ session people)

UK Albino — US not issued

Dec 91. (cd; by JUDY DUNLOP and ASHLEY HUTCHINGS) *(ALB 007)*
SWAY WITH ME: A celebration of the Tree and its offspring
- Tree / The oak / Pierce the screen / Thirlmere, February 1922 / Morning of high silence / Achren's riddle / Hanging tree / The fallen elm (excerpt) / The woodlands of England / Hazel-nutting / Green city / Dialogue from 'A Canterbury Tale' / Turn the lathe gently / Wood-burning rhyme / The charcoal burner - Burning up / The willow / Mannikins / The bee and the butterfly / Thanks trees! / Sway with me / Apple pie. *(re-iss. Feb 92 on Road Goes On Forever; RGFCD 008) (re-mast. Jun 05 on Talking Elephant; TECD 080)*

HTD — not issued

Dec 99. (cd) *(HTDCD 106)* **MY ARMS ARE A CRADLE**: A collection of traditional and modern lullabies
- Gaelic lullaby / Threats medley / The sun and the moon / Logan braes / Go to sleep bonny babe / Hush little baby / Leave-talking / Fairy boy / All fall down / Hebron / The crow and the cradle / Tomorrow may come / Coulter's candy / Cuddle doon / My arms are a cradle / Daylight is fading. *(re-iss. Nov 06 on Talking Elephant; TECD 104)*

Talking Elephant — not issued

Nov 01. (cd; by JUDY DUNLOP & JON SCAIFE) *(TECD 029)*
I WANT SOMETHING...
- Mary and the soldier / Bare-faced lies / Raven / What has happened to Lulu? / I'm a woman / Merchant's son / Star o' the bar / Poem – I want something / Boza girls / The Sheffield grinder / Strange fruit / Waltz for Jonathan and Stephen / The L & N don't stop here any more / Silence and tears / The olive trees – Hanging tree.

Jump — not issued

Apr 08. (cd; as JUDY DUNLOP / STEVE MARSH) *(none)*
PAINTING SHOULD BE FUN
- Kerry is no more / Angel in deep shadow / The well / Flowers are red / Amazing grace / Too late love comes / Buffalo jump / And so it goes / Wolfe / Evening star / Burning times / Captain, my captain / The leaves turn to brown / Anachie Gordon / Albatross.

E

EDWARD II

A fusion of Morris-folk (think The ALBION BAND), reggae and worldbeat music (think Afro Celt Sound System), the band were formed in 1984 as EDWARD II & THE RED HOT POLKAS in Cheltenham, Gloustershire, featuring an initial line-up of guitarist Tom Greenhalgh, bassist John Gill, drummer Steve Goulding (the first on a moonlight shift from the Mekons; Gill and Goulding would later join that band), second guitarist Jon Moore (ex-TIGER MOTH), brothers Barney, Rod and Danny Stradling (on guitar, melodeon and percussion respectively) and Dave Haines (melodeon). The band issued their debut Cooking Vinyl Records LP **LET'S POLKA STEADY!** (1987) {*7} with the help of dub producer Mad Professor. Certainly adventurous for its day but probably better served up live in concerts and festivals, the high spots were 'The 79th Highlanders' Farewell To Gibraltar', 'Sophie Bourbon's Hornpipe' and opener 'Dawn Run'.

When Rod departed, the group expanded and added drummer Alton Zebby, a brass section of Neil Yates, John Hart and Gavin Sharp, and vocalist Lorna Bailey. They released a second album, **TWO STEP TO HEAVEN** (1989) {*7}, once again with Mad Professor at the controls for the "odd" polka, jig and hornpipe.

Radically trimming their title to EDWARD II and changing personnel drastically (the Mekons moonlighters returned to their day jobs), Moore, Yates, Hart and Zebby hired newcomers Rees Wesson (on melodeon, accordion and vocals), Glen Latouche (vocals and percussion), Tee Carthy (bass) and McKilla the rapper. **WICKED MEN** (1991) {*6} showed they'd lost none of their eccentricities or bite, even if Moore was the only original member remaining. Traditional lines might be recognized in best tunes 'Dashing Away', 'She's Gone To California' and 'List For A Sailor'. Regrouping in the mid-1990s with the added attraction of former ALBION BAND melodeon player Simon Care on board, EDWARD II surfaced twice more with **ZEST** (1997) {*6} and **THIS WAY UP** (1999) {*6}.

Splitting up after one of their many Cropredy appearances, Moore, Yates and Care, along with Kwame Yeboah, Kellie While (another stray from The ALBION BAND/ASHLEY HUTCHINGS set-up), Neil Fairclough, Pat Illingworth and Andy Morel, reunited as e2k. Signed to the illustrious folk imprint Topic Records, the ensemble delivered two further long-players, **SHIFT** (2001) {*6} and **IF NOT NOW** (2003) {*6}, the latter demonstrating yet again their collective disarray. Fairclough, Illingworth, Morel and solo-bound Simon Care making way for Simon Katz, Nana Yaa, Paul Francis, BATTLEFIELD BAND fiddler John McCusker and bright young piper Michael McGoldrick, e2k were re-formed for several reunion concerts in 2009. *MCS*

Tom Greenhalgh - vocals, guitar (of Mekons) / **Jon Moore** - guitar, fiddle, vocals (ex-TIGER MOTH) / **Barney Stradling** - guitar / **Rod Stradling** - melodeon (ex-TIGER MOTH) / **Dave Haines** - melodeon / **Danny Stradling** - percussion (ex-IAN A. ANDERSON) / **John Gill** - bass (future Mekons) / **Steve Goulding** - drums (future Mekons, ex-The Rumour, etc)

UK Cooking Vinyl — US not issued

Oct 87. (7"; as EDWARD II & THE RED HOT POLKAS) *(CHEF 001)* DAWN RUN. / [B-side by The OYSTER BAND]

Oct 87. (lp/c; as EDWARD II & THE RED HOT POLKAS) *(COOK/+C 007)* **LET'S POLKA STEADY!**
- Dawn run / Little left Lew / Swiss boy / The 79th Highlanders' farewell to Gibraltar / Blue blue morning / Another fine mess / The walls of Butlin's / Mr. Prime's polka / Three hand reel / Sophie Bourbon's hornpipe. *(cd-iss. Feb 03; COOKCD 007)*

—— Rod departed for solo set 'Rhythms Of The World'; group added **Alton Zebby** - percussion, drums / **Neil Yates** - trumpet / **John Hart** - bass trombone, organ, guitar, vocals / **Gavin Sharp** - tenor trombone / **Lorna Bailey** - vocals

Jan 89. (lp/c/cd; as EDWARD THE SECOND AND THE RED HOT POLKAS) *(COOK/+C/CD 019)* **TWO STEP TO HEAVEN**
- Bjorn again polka / Lovers' two step / Swing easy / Staffordshire hornpipe / Jenny Lind / Pomp and pride / Untitled polka / The Queen's jig / The steamboats / Cliffhanger / Stack of wheat / Brimfield hornpipe / Swedish polka / Two step to heaven. *(cd re-iss. Jul 96; same)*

Feb 89. (7"; as EDWARD II & THE MAD PROFESSOR) *(FRY 007)* SWEDISH POLKA (the paid in krona mix). / Swedish Polka (Bjorn again polka)
(12"+=) *(FRY 007T)* - ('A'-Smorgasbord mix).

—— (when Greenhalgh, Gill + Goulding returned to Mekons) **Moore, Yates, Hart** + **Zebby** recruited **Rees Wesson** - melodeon, accordion, vocals / **Glen Latouche** - vocals, percussion / **Tee Carthy** - bass / **McKilla** - rapper

Pure Bliss — Priority

Nov 91. (cd) *(BLISSCD 001)* **WICKED MEN**
- Miles away / Dashing away / The rondo mondo / Brilliant pebbles / My love (the horizontal polka) / Real world / She's gone to California / OK bayou / Shepherd's hey / List for a sailor.

Jul 92. (12"/cd-s) *(BLISS X/CD 002)* *<57009-2>* WICKED FOURPLAY — Apr 92
- Dashing away / +3

—— added **Simon Care** - melodeon (ex-ALBION BAND)

Ock — not issued

Jan 97. (cd) *(004-2)* **ZEST**
- People get ready / What if? / Make a change / Special kind of woman / Night nurse / Live together / La russe / I'll help you fly / Justice / The wild mountain thyme / Home / The old and the new.

Oct 99. (cd) *(005-2)* **THIS WAY UP**
- More than a song / Rocky road / Come and buy / Daring to dream / The soldier / Radio / Early one morning / Things we have in common / It's worth a try / Plough the speed / Don't let the fire go out / Farewell to Clusone.

—— split after a Cropredy gig in 1999, but re-formed as ...

e2k

Moore, Yates + Care plus **Kwame Yeboah** - vocals, multi / **Kellie While** - vocals, guitar (of The ALBION BAND / ASHLEY HUTCHINGS) / **Neil Fairclough** - bass / **Pat Illingworth** - drums / **Andy Morel** - saxophones

Topic — Topic

Feb 01. (cd) *(TSCD 522)* **SHIFT**
- The water is wide / Something left behind / The blackthorn stick - The rakes of Kildare - The rocks of Penrhyn / Love for a season / Everdance / The farmer's cursed wife / A life less hard to bear / You bring me joy / The wind in the trees / Fair and tender ladies / Itue, stitue, statue / Take me home.

—— **Simon Katz** - percussion + **Nana Yaa** ; repl. Fairclough

—— **Paul Francis** - drums; repl. Illingworth

—— **John McCusker** - fiddle (ex-BATTLEFIELD BAND) repl. Morel

—— **Michael McGoldrick** - Uillean pipes, guitar, mandolin; repl. Simon Care who subsequently went solo

Oct 03. (cd) *(<TSCD 538>)* **IF NOT NOW** — Jan 04
- Come and join us / The shepherd and the crows / Dealing with history / Chance melody: Custy's - The rolling waves - Chance melody / Common ground / Gye wani - The mountain lark / Holding on / He moved through the fair - Out the other side / St. George's quay - The new-rigged ship / Be sure your lover - Noon lassies / A lullaby for everyone - Stormy blues.

—— split for the final time late 2003; re-formed mid-2009

- (8-10*) compilation -

Jul 09. (d-cd) *E2 Music; (E2CD 1001)* **EDWARD II: THE DEFINITIVE COLLECTION**
- Johnny Mickey Barry's / The 79th Highlanders' farewell to Gibraltar / Dawn run / Sophie Bourbon's hornpipe / Staffordshire hornpipe / Swing easy / Untitled polka / Swedish polka (the paid in krona mix) / Just as the tide was a-flowing / Brilliant pebbles / Miles away / Dashing away / People get ready / The wild mountain thyme / La russe / Rocky road / Plough the speed / Chance melody / Let a thousand blossoms bloom.

The EIGHTEENTH DAY OF MAY

Only one album for this cosmopolitan London-based folk-rock outfit, but the eponymous **EIGHTEENTH DAY OF MAY** (2006) {*7}, for the resurgent Hannibal Records (via Rykodisc), established the sextet as one of England's brightest prospects.

With a line-up centred around American and Swedish songwriters, singers and musicians Allison Brice and Richard Olsen respectively (Ben Phillipson, Alison Cotton and Mark Nicholas and Karl Sabino of Arrowe Hill made up the numbers), the album recalled the vintage days of FAIRPORT CONVENTION, JEFFERSON AIRPLANE and PENTANGLE. The band even went so far as to revamp BERT JANSCH's 'Deed I Do', and there are two trad songs 'Lady Margaret' and 'Flowers Of The Forest'. It's a pity they split in 2008. *MCS*

Allison Brice (b. US) - vocals, flute, dulcimer, harmonium / **Richard Olsen** (b. Sweden) - vocals, guitar, sitar, harmonica / **Ben Phillipson** - vocals, guitar, mandolin / **Alison Cotton** - viola (of Saloon) / **Mark Nicholas** - bass, guitar, vocals (of Arrowe Hill) / **Karl Sabino** - drums, percussion, autoharp, glockenspiel, vocals (of Arrowe Hill)

UK Transistor — US not issued

Jun 05. (7") *(TR6 45003S)* THE HIGHEST TREE. / Sir Casey Jones

Feb 06. (7") *(TR6 45006S)* COLD EARLY MORNING. / Strings / Dawn

UK Hannibal - Rykodisc — US Hannibal - Rykodisc

May 06. (cd) *(<HNCD 1496>)* **THE EIGHTEENTH DAY OF MAY**
- Eighteen days / Sir Casey Jones / The highest tree / Deed I do / Hide + seek / Twig folly close / Lady Margaret / Cold early morning / Monday morning's no good coming down / The waterman's song to his daughter / Flowers of the forest / The mandrake screams.

May 06. (7"/cd-s) *(HN/+CD 1523)* HIDE + SEEK. / Mary Anne / Codine

—— the band split in 2008

the ELECTROPATHICS

The English Country Dance revival of the 1980s (featuring The OLD SWAN BAND, The VICTORY BAND, et al) wouldn't have been as relevant without the eccentricities of The ELECTROPATHICS. Formed in 1979 as The Electropathic Battery Band by Alan Rawlinson, John "Grog" Gregson, John Lewis, Nick Tamblin, Maggie Andrew and Moira and Dave Hanvey, the playful outfit would take stage attired in Edwardian-period costumes. By 1984, and without Nick, Dave and Moira, melodeon players KEITH HANCOCK and Howard Jones (not the 1980s pop star) were invited into the fold, while Maggie would also make way for new drummer Pierce Butler. As the ELECTROPATHICS they released one solitary set, **(BATTERIES NOT INCLUDED)** (1988) {*7}, a weird, whacky and fairly wonderful record by all accounts (as stated in fRoots), with a fair share of brass-laden music-hall/folk tracks sourced from various places. 'Russia', 'Rochdale Nutters' and 'The Old Bazaar In Cairo' were certainly worth a listen. It's worth noting that they contributed a track to a various-artists "Children In Need" double-cassette; their version of the Kinks' 'Harry Rag' is worth finding, but where and how is something of a mystery.

The music-hall ensemble continued to perform throughout the north-east, but as members tailed off (HANCOCK for one went solo) they gradually disappeared from the scene. With only original Alan Rawlinson remaining from the pack (Tim Kenny, Dave Manley, Tim Veitch, Ian Sherwood and Chris Bartram were all members at various times), and everyone moving to pastures new, the ELECTROPATHICS split in 1994, reforming sporadically for the occasional reunion gig. *MCS*

Alan Rawlinson (b. May '55, Scholes, Leeds) – vocals, cornet, trumpet, flute, trombone, sousaphone / **John "Grog" Gregson** - vocals, guitar / **John Lewis** - clarinet, banjo, tenor sax, mandolin / **Jackie Rawlinson** (b. Jackie Hamilton, May '65, Wilmslow, Cheshire) – fiddle, vocals / **Howard Jones** - vocals, melodeon, anglo concertina, hammered dulcimer / **Keith Hancock** (b. Oct '53, Audenshaw, Lancashire) – melodeon, hammer dulcimer, vocals / **Pierce Butler** - drums, percussion, vocals; Moira Hanvey (vocals, whistles), Dave Hanvey (melodeon, vocals), Nick Tamblin (harmonica, glockenspiel, percussion, vocals/caller) and Maggie Andrew (percussion) were early members until leaving at various times in the mid-1980s

UK Sticky Label — US not issued

Oct 88. (lp/c) *(GUM 001/+C)* **(BATTERIES NOT INCLUDED)**
- Helter skelter / Very shy / Lost at sea / Russia / Stonecracker John / Rochdale nutters / Never swat a fly / Jam up the nuts – Jump at the sun / Whitsun dance – The bloody fields of Flanders / The deviation – Gertrude's villa / Northfield / Gaddafi's gallop – The old bazaar in Cairo.

—— **Dave Manley** (b. Feb '57, Warwickshire) – flute, sax, vocals; repl. Lewis

—— **Tim Veitch** (b. May '62) – cello, vocals; repl. live temp. Alistair Gillies

—— HANCOCK went solo soon afterwards; repl. by **Tim Kenny** (b. Aug '60) – vocals, guitar (in 1989); (in 1991) **Chris Bartram** (b. Dec '46, Yorkshire) – percussion, vocals; repl. Gregson, leaving **Alan Rawlinson** the only original until they split in 1994

Nancy ELIZABETH

Born Nancy Elizabeth Cunliffe, December 5, 1983, this talented multi-instrumentalist and singer-songwriter from the village of Billinge Higher End (near Wigan, Lancashire) is the epitome of ethereal folk. Her formative years were spent learning the piano and guitar, and by the time she was eighteen – while attending Liverpool's Institute for Performing Arts – she'd sent a demo album and EP to publishers. Later she would take on more exotic instrumentation, such as the khim (a hammered dulcimer from Thailand) and the Celtic harp.

Before she dropped the Cunliffe from her name, NANCY ELIZABETH released her first proper EP in 2006 for Manchester's Timbreland. Entitled 'The Wheel Turning King' and comprising six tracks including the brief title number, it was recorded in a nearby church and took its concept from ancient Indian mythology.

BATTLE AND VICTORY (2007) {*8} was to follow, a hybrid of 1960s/70s folk styles such as JONI MITCHELL and SANDY DENNY, while she also attracted comparisons with American freak-folk contemporaries JOANNA NEWSOM, MEG BAIRD and SHARRON KRAUS. The singles 'I Used To Try' and 'Hey Son' in particular showed why she was received with such great affection by folk in-the-know, while 'Off With Your Axe', 'The Remote Past' and 'Weakened Bow' were equally acclaimed.

The **WROUGHT IRON** (2009) {*7} set seemed to be dug out from deep in some secluded Narnia-like woodland, and the tension and drama on such pieces as 'Feet Of Courage', 'The Act' and `Canopy' promised that this artist can go as far as she wants in today's pedestrian music business. *MCS*

Nancy Elizabeth - vocals, guitars, multi / (+ session people/guests)

UK Timbreland — US not issued

Jun 06. (ltd-10" ep/cd-ep; as NANCY ELIZABETH CUNLIFFE) *(TMBR 004/006)* THE WHEEL TURNING KING
- Place to shelter / Waiting for cars / Sense / Wildfire / The moving sand / The wheel turning king.

UK Leaf — US not issued

Jul 07. (ltd-7") *(Dock 48)* HEY SON. / Live By The Sea

Sep 07. (ltd-7") *(Dock 49)* I USED TO TRY. / In The Morning

Oct 07. (cd/red-lp) *(BAY 60 CD/V)* **BATTLE AND VICTORY**
- I'm like the paper / I used to try / Off with your axe / The remote past / Coriander / Eight brown legs / Electric / Hey son / Weakened bow / What is human / Lung / How can I stop? / Battle and victory.

Oct 09. (cd/lp) *(BAY 68 CD/V)* **WROUGHT IRON**
- Cairns / Bring on the hurricane / Tow the line / Feet of courage / Divining / Cat bells / Canopy / Lay low / The act / Ruins / Winter, baby.

Mike ELLIOTT

Possibly an oversight from the first edition, all-round entertainer and comic-folk star MIKE ELLIOTT (born July 17, 1946, Sunderland) found fame on the live circuit as warm-up act for Geordie folk band LINDISFARNE.

A teacher of drama and part-timer with the trad-folk trio Northern Front (alongside Ed Pickford and Nick Fenwick), he released two solo LPs for Rubber Records: **OUT OF THE BROWN** (1977) {*6} and **AT LAST IT'S MIKE ELLIOTT** (1983) {*5}, the second of which was also the title of a subsequent TV series for the then recently founded Channel 4. A one-hour special, 'Meet Mike Elliott', had been broadcast in 1982 and featured old friends LINDISFARNE. One claim to fame was that Elliott became the first professional UK act to perform in China, beating Wham! in the process.

Always a man who courted controversy (an earlier flipside, 'Talkin' Crap', had been banned by the BBC), and a regular at the Cambridge Folk Festival, "Mike The Mouth" was re-launched in 1995 as host of a late night Century FM radio talk show. More than once he was sacked for swearing at caller, but duly reinstated. An actor with over a dozen minor roles behind him (including TV series 'Crocodile Shoes', 'Byker Grove' 'Spender' and the film 'Billy Elliott'), Mike was still a popular presenter in the 2000s for North East Magic Radio, Sun FM, etc. In 2001 he helped create a new board game, Social Insecurity, which apparently is a cross between Monopoly and the comic 'Viz'. *MCS*

Mike Elliott - vocals, acoustic guitar

UK Rubber — US not issued

1977. (lp) *(RUB 025)* **OUT OF THE BROWN**
- Just a word in your ear / Talkin' crap / Cushie butterfield / A true and woeful story of a woman undone / Thank you Lord / A red badge of carrots / Brown ale crazy / He was a rover / Ferret's magic / Lav story / Joseph / Mary and the bairn / Commercial break.

May 83. (7") *(ADUB 18)* MAKIN' ME HAPPY. / Talkin' Crap

Jul 83. (lp/c) *(RUB/+C 044)* **AT LAST IT'S MIKE ELLIOTT!**
- Pseudosciences / Bio-rhythms / Willy trapping / TV adverts / Breasts for men / Trip to France / Grammar schoolboy / St. Tupperware / Cow turd pie / Makin' me happy.

—— Mike retired from solo studio work but contined with live comedy

EMMY THE GREAT

Emma-Lee Moss, who performs as EMMY THE GREAT, was born in 1984 in Hong Kong but later moved with her parents to Oxford, England. Bursting on to London's anti-folk scene in 2006 with her debut single 'Secret Circus', girly singer-songwriter Emma was immediately filed alongside anti-folk heroine KIMYA DAWSON (ex-MOLDY PEACHES) and MARTHA WAINWRIGHT.

Augmented by main players Euan Hinshelwood, Ric Hollingbery, Pete Baker and Euan Robinson, a string of singles materialised (premiered at Glastonbury and other festivals), leading up to her debut album **FIRST LOVE** (2009) {*6}. The record was graced by the aforementioned 45s, 'We Almost Had A Baby' and the title track, plus COHEN-esque songs 'Absentee', 'Dylan' and '24'. June 2011 will see the release of her second set, **VIRTUE**. *MCS*

Emmy/Emma - vocals, acoustic guitar / **Euan Hinshelwood** - guitar (of Younghusband) / **Euan Robinson** - backing vocals (of Stars Of Sunday League) / with **Ric Hollingbery** - violin, viola (of Pengilly's) / **Pete Baker** - drums, percussion

UK Drowned In Sound — US not issued

Apr 06. (7") *(DIS 002)* SECRET CIRCUS. / The Hypnotist's Son

own label — not issued

2006. (cd-ep) *(none)* TAKE ME I'M FREE
- Edward is dedward / My party is better than yours / The hypnotist's son / Gloria.

Close Harbour — Close Harbour

Sep 07. (ltd-7"ep) *(CH 01)* MY BAD
- The Easter parade / M.I.A. / City song / The woods.

Dec 07. (ltd-7") *(CH 02)* GABRIEL. / If Had Known The Last Time Was Going To Be The Last Time I Would Have Let You Enjoy It

Nov 08. (ltd-7") *(CL 0130)* WE ALMOST HAD A BABY. / Short Country Song

Feb 09. (ltd-7") *(CH 0002X)* FIRST LOVE. / Burn Baby Burn (vs Younghusband)

Feb 09. (cd) *(CH 0307CD)* *<0075758>* **FIRST LOVE**
- Absentee / 24 / We almost had a baby / The Easter parade / Dylan / On the museum island / War / First love / M.I.A. / The Easter parade (part 2) / Bad things coming, we are safe / Everything reminds me of you / City song.

Aug 09. (12"ep) *(CH 003)* EDWARD E.P. (first songs)
- Edward is dedward / Bowl collecting blood / Two steps forward / Canopies and drapes.

Capitol — Capitol

Jun 11. (cd) *(5380 0124-2)* **VIRTUE**
- Dinosaur sex / A woman, a woman, a century of sleep / Iris / Paper forest (in the afterglow of rapture) / Cassandra / Creation / Sylvia / Exit night – Juliet's theme / North / Trellick tower.

ENGLISH ACOUSTIC COLLECTIVE (⟹ WOOD, Chris)

EQUATION

Notable as the stamping ground for bright young violinist SETH LAKEMAN and his brothers Sean and Sam, traditional folk outfit EQUATION were formed in 1995 in Dartmoor, Devon; former INTUITION singers KATHRYN ROBERTS and KATE RUSBY made up the quintet. The LAKEMAN BROTHERS had produced one set under their own steam, **THREE PIECE SUITE** (1994), but it went virtually unnoticed.

Dubbed "the leaders of the folk bratpack", EQUATION went through a few personnel shuffles over the next few years. KATE RUSBY chose a solo career (to be replaced by Sam's Derry-born wife CARA DILLON), and Sam and Cara made way for rhythm section Darren Edwards and Iain Goodall.

Sounding something akin to Fleetwood Mac juxtaposed with The Corrs or FAIRPORT CONVENTION, **HAZY DAZE** (1998) {*7} and **THE LUCKY FEW** (1999) {*8} trod a thin line between folk-rock and contemporary Celtic-pop. James Croker joined on the latter album. While 'Strange Love' stood out on their first effort, 'Mother And Child', 'Autumn Tune', 'Paper Bag' and 'Sheffield Park' were certainly outstanding on their second.

With Seth and Sam taking a back seat (Sean was always the main songwriter, and Roberts and newcomer Reggie Brown now took supporting credits), third album **FIRST NAME TERMS** {*6} was finally in the shops by 2002. Apart from some of the acoustics and instrumentation, the folk part was lost on this album. Comparing tracks like 'Jack And Suzanne' and 'Wild Card' with songs on their trad-covers EP 'The Dark Ages' (e.g. 'The Cuckoo's Nest', 'Lord Gregory' and 'Lovely Nancy'), EQUATION sounded like two different groups. This surely led to dissent within the group, and only long-lost second-line-up recordings from 1995/96 emerged on **RETURN TO ME** (2003) {*6} as Geoff Travis (who had originally signed them to Blanco Y Negro) moved them across the corridor to Rough Trade. A schmaltzy and clean-cut set, it remained a favourite with fans of CARA DILLON and co.

Meanwhile, Barnsley-born KATHRYN ROBERTS and partner SEAN LAKEMAN retrieved their trad-folk credentials by way of a couple of sets, **1.** (2002) {*7} and **2.** (2004) {*6}. They've since had twin daughters, Poppy and Lily, born in July 2007. *MCS*

The LAKEMAN BROTHERS

Sean Lakeman (b. 1974) - guitar / **Seth Lakeman** (b. Mar '77) - violin / **Sam Lakeman** (b. Nov '75) - keyboards

UK Crapstone — US not issued

1994. (cd) *(???)* **THREE PIECE SUITE**
- Hot for Clarence - Parsley in the ears / Rookeries nook / Francois - Henenbihen / Seven gypsies / Tom's wood / Leg o' mutton - The yellow tinker / And so it goes / The drift – Nobody's fool / Emonan / Cahoots.

EQUATION

Kathryn Roberts - vocals, piano, clarinet (ex-INTUITION) / **Kate Rusby** - vocals, fiddle (ex-INTUITION) / **Sean Lakeman** - guitars / **Seth Lakeman** - violin, vocals, mandolin / **Sam Lakeman** - keyboards

—— (1995–96) **Cara Dillon** - vocals; repl. RUSBY who went solo

—— added **Darren Edwards** - bass

1996. (cd-s) *(???)* HE LOVES ME / Seven Wonders ("In Session" re-recording) / Sad The Girl (Real World demo version)

—— **Iain Goodall** - drums, percussion; repl. Sam + solo-bound CARA DILLON

Blanco Y Negro — Putumayo

Feb 98. (cd) *(3984 20824-2)* **HAZY DAZE**
- Safe and sound / My world / Sister / What did you do today? / Kissing crime / Communion / Ataxia / Sad the girl / Clueless / Choose your moves / Myself.

1999. (cd) *<155>* **HAZY DAZE** (shuffled)
- Kissing crime / Sister / Myself / What did you do today? / Communion / Ataxia / Strange love / Safe and sound / My world / Sad the girl / Choose your moves.

—— added **James Croker** - guitar (Sam Lakeman + Reggie Brown guested)

1999. (cd) *(???)* *<176>* **THE LUCKY FEW** — Jul 00
- Not the man / Mother and child / Paper bag / Autumn tune / Too much to say / Picture the change / The prize / No change likely / Sheffield park / Hard underground / A better view / Squeeze and hide. *(re-iss. Nov 03 on Black Burst; BLACKCD 003)*

—— Seth + Sam were now always credited as guests only; **Brown** now permanent

I Scream — not issued

2001. (cd-ep) *(001)* THE DARK AGES EP
- Sailor boy / Lord Gregory / The cuckoo's nest / Lovely Nancy / A drummer won my love.

—— (Brown was again a guest and co-writer)

2002. (cd) *(ISCD 003)* **FIRST NAME TERMS**
- Wild card / Cry wolf / Rise up and deny / Clare / Speak your thoughts / Full speed / For Carrie / The end of May / Drowning man / Coming around again / Jack and Suzanne / Lost all feeling. *(re-iss. Jun 04; EQCD 003)*

- (5-7*) compilations, others, etc.-

Mar 03. (cd) *Rough Trade; (RTRADECD 083)* **RETURN TO ME** [shelved from 1995–96]
- He loves me / Golden bird / Strange love / Cloths of heaven / Song of the well / Return to me / Cross the river / Let him cry / Sad the girl / Can't cry hard enough / No goodbyes / Wake up.

KATHRYN ROBERTS AND SEAN LAKEMAN

I Scream — not issued

2002. (cd) *(ISCD 002)* **1.**

- Granite mill / Joe Peel / Lord Gregory / Once I had a sweetheart / Georgia Lee / Spring / The lambs on the green hills / The drowned lovers / Lovely Nancy / The maid with the bonny brown hair. *(re-iss. Jun 04; EQCD 002)*

Jun 04. (cd) *(ISCD 005)* **2.**
- Rosie Ann / Sir Arthur / Lifetime of tears / The buxom lass / Willow tree / The red barn / 20 million things / Rule and bant / The Whitby maid / Rosie Anderson.

e2k (⟹ EDWARD II)

Dave EVANS

Somewhat overlooked by many folk buffs, probably because there was another Dave Evans around at the time, albeit an American bluegrass player, this Bristolian finger-pickin' guitarist (tunng CGDGAD) was surely another in the mould of JANSCH, GRAHAM, RENBOURN and DRAKE.

EVANS's debut set **THE WORDS IN BETWEEN** (1971) {*7} – recorded on a two-track and featuring some harmony vocals by Adrienne Webber, harmonica by Keith Warrington and second guitar by Pete Airey – was independently released by Village Thing boss IAN A. ANDERSON, a solo artist himself. Many might recognise the lyrical genius of the opener 'Rosie' (subsequently covered by a handful of artists), while 'Doorway', 'Magic Man' and 'Sailor' were also worthy period pieces.

EVANS's second effort, **ELEPHANTASIA** (1972) {*5}, was a disappointment by comparison, a bluesy set co-produced with label owner ANDERSON (guests this time around were Steve Swindells, John Merrett, Rodney Matthews and Warrington). Check out 'Lady Portia', the excellent title track and three more of the best on the CD re-issue of his debut.

Psychedelic bluegrass was a term never used around the time of his instrumental third album, **SAD PIG DANCE** (1974) {*6}, but it should have cropped up if anyone had taken the time to listen to Dave's sliding licks; Kicking Mule Records and new boss/producer STEFAN GROSSMAN had always been an inspiration. **TAKE A BITE OUT OF LIFE** (1977) {*5} was the guitarist's swansong before he disappeared from the music scene – where is he now?

MAGGIE HOLLAND (former wife of IAN A. ANDERSON) covered a handful of Dave's songs on her subsequent sets, and others too have offered up their takes on a very underrated artist who grows in stature as the years go by. *MCS*

Dave Evans - vocals, acoustic guitar / + guests

UK: The Village Thing — US: not issued

Dec 71. (lp) *(VTS 6)* **THE WORDS IN BETWEEN**
- The words in between *[track 2 on CD]* / Rosie *[track 1 on CD]* / Grey lady morning / Insanity rag / Magic man / Now is the time / Doorway / City road / Circular line / Sailor. *(cd-iss. Jun 01 on Weekend Beatnik+=; WEBE 9039)* - Beauty queen / St Agnes park / Lady Portia / Only blue / Elephantasia.

Dec 72. (lp) *(VTS 14)* **ELEPHANTASIA**
- Only blue / Elephantasia / Lady Portia / That's my way / On the run / St. Agnes park / Beauty queen / Ten ton Tasha / Earth, wind, sun and rain / Take me easy.

UK: Kicking Mule — US: Kicking Mule

1974. (lp) *(SNKF 107)* **SAD PIG DANCE**
- Stagefright / Chaplinesque / The train and the river / Veronica / Captain / Knuckles and busters / Medley: Mole's moan (the gentle man trap) / Sad pig dance / Raining cats and dogs / Braziliana / Sun and moon / Steppenwolf / Morocco John / Sneaky. *<US-iss. Mar 89; KM-120> <cd-iss. Aug 99 +=; KMCD-3912>* - Whistling milkman / Insanity rag / Willie me / Tear away / Jessica / Grey hills / Ugly duckling / Jolymont / Cold feet.

Dec 76. (7") *(SOK 37)* TAKE A BITE OUT OF LIFE. / Sad Pig Dance

Jan 77. (lp) *(SNKF 122)* **TAKE A BITE OUT OF LIFE**
- Keep me from the cold / Whistling milkman / Illustrated man / You and me / Insanity rag / Every bad dog / Take a bite out of life / Willie me / You're wrong / Sunday is beautiful / Tear away / Lucky me / I'm all right. *<US-iss.Mar89; KM-134>*

—— In 1978 (but recorded 1975) EVANS provided five tracks ('Jessica', 'Grey Hills', 'Ugly Duckling', 'Jolymont' and 'Cold Feet') on Grossman's 'Contemporary Guitar Workshop'.

—— where is Dave now?

F

James FAGAN (⟹ KERR, Nancy & ...)

FAIRGROUND ATTRACTION (⟹ READER, Eddi)

The FAMOUS POTATOES

From Rochford in Essex and unearthed (sorry!) in the early 1980s as The FOLK PISTOLS, Richard Baxter, his brother Keith, Paul "Prof" McDowell and Melanie Johnson performed at the odd barn dance, releasing two privately pressed cassette albums: **GET YOUR SKATES ON!** (1981) {*6} and **TWIST WITH KEN** (1982) {*5} during their early phase.

Radically changing the group name to The FAMOUS POTATOES and enhancing their line-up with the rhythm section of Nigel Blackaby and Paul Collier, these Essex hillbillies produced a third cassette-only album, **DIG** (1983) {*6}, literally labelled as "sweet soil music", although folk-dance (a pot-pourri of Cajun, skiffle, C&W/swing, gospel and celtic/ceilidh) was the order of day.

Instrumentally, all eight – yes, eight, with the addition of Nick Pynn and Rikki Reynolds – were adept musicians, using washboard, accordion, fiddle and recorder among the more conventional instrumentation. The latter half of the 1980s produced no less than three LPs: **IF IT WAS GOOD FOR MY OLD MOTHER ...** (1985) {*6}, **THE SOUND OF THE GROUND** (1986) {*6} and **BORN IN A BARN** (1989) {*6}, all comprising fine musical fodder for festivals, parties and weddings. With new recruits Charlie Skelton (Pynn joined Steve Harley & Cockney Rebel) and Tony "Please Sir" Littman (he replaced Reynolds), 1999 saw the Potatoes return in swing courtesy of **BARNDANCING** {*6}; Johnson subsequently became Melanie Derbyshire. *MCS*

Richard Baxter (b. Aug '59, Westcliff-on-Sea, Essex) - vocals, melodeon, saxophone, mouth organ / **Keith Baxter** (b. Oct '57) - caller, banjo, trombone, washboard / **Paul "Prof" McDowell** (b. Sep '58) - accordion, percussion, vocals / **Melanie Johnson** (b. Feb '61, Swindon, Wiltshire) - clarinet, recorder, vocals

UK Private — US not issued

1981. (c; as The FOLK PISTOLS) *(none)* **GET YOUR SKATES ON!**
- All the way to Galway – Winster galop – Rakes of mallow / Queen Victoria's – Under the greenwood tree – Won't go home / Young woodland rebels / Unemployed sweetheart / Cassette – Pig's trotter – New Year's day / Soldier's joy – Fairy dance – Rose tree / Johnny comes marching – Runaway trains / Star polka - Schottische / Bread and butter – Tarpaulun jacket – Bonnie Dundee / Young Collins (dub).

1982. (c; as The FOLK PISTOLS) *(none)* **TWIST WITH KEN**
- Monck's march (folkfinger) / Lady in the boat – Fiery clockface – Blaydon races / Arkansas traveller – Rose tree / News of victory – Little burnt potato / Young woodland rebels – Brighton camps – Nutty girls / Smash the window – Major Mackie's – Last straw / Foot in the puddle – St Ann's skip / The party – Shetland Boston two-step.

—— added **Nigel Blackaby** (b. Nov '58) - bass, double bass, vocals + **Paul Collier** (b. Feb '59) - drums, vocals

1983. (ltd-c) *(none)* **DIG**
- Johnny's down the river - Sugar in my coffee-o / Crow black chicken / (The) Trout sisters / Two-step de bayou teche / Vandals of Hammerwich / (There's) No hell in Georgia - Rattler treed a possum / Cold kale in Aberdeen - Miss Forbes' farewell (to Banff) / Seneca square dance - Un, deux, trois / Saturday night waltz / Going down the river / I'm gonna leave old Arkansas - (Where the) Irish potatoes (grow) / Monk's march.

—— added **Nick Pynn** - fiddle, mandolin, banjo, viola + **Rikki Reynolds** - guitar

Waterfront — not issued

Aug 84. (7") *(WFS 8)* I LIKE CHICKEN PIE. / Chicken Reel Stomp (part 1 & 2)

Sep 85. (lp) *(WF 018)* **IT WAS GOOD FOR MY OLD MOTHER ...**
- Johnson boys / Mashed potato blues / Silly Bill / Jealous hearted me / Lookin' for money / Old time religion / I don't mind / Peach pickin' time / Yes sir! / Honey I'm ramblin' away. *(c-iss. Jun '86 +=; WF 018C)* - I like chicken pie / Chicken reel stomp. *(cd-iss. 06 on Sweet Soil Music mail-o; SSMCD 2)*

Sep 86. (lp/c) *(WF 028/+C)* **THE SOUND OF THE GROUND**
- Are you ready? / Nothin' shakin' / Famous potatoes / Hold that critter down / (She's a) Runaround / You're pouring water on a drowning man / Going down the river / Drinking wine spo-dee-o-dee / Nightingale stomp / That's right / I saw the light / El sonido del soelo / Roll in my sweet baby's arms / Wait till the cows come home. *(cd-iss. 06 on Sweet Soil Music mail-o; SSMCD 3)*

Sep 89. (lp/c) *(WF 046/+C)* **BORN IN A BARN**
- The women go wild over me / Seven nights to rock / Truck driving man / My heart cracked / Too hot to handle / Jericho / Uncle Pynn / Who stole the train / Bloodshot eyes / Snowdeer / Crazy arms / What kind of man / Eight more miles to Leigh-on-Sea. *(cd-iss. 06 on Sweet Soil Music mail-o; SSMCD 4)*

—— split in 1990; re-formed for gigs/concerts, etc.

—— **Charlie Skelton** (b. Feb '63, Enfield, Middlesex, England) - fiddle; repl. Pynn who joined Steve Harley & Cockney Rebel

—— **Tony "Please Sir" Littman** (b. Jul '51, Westcliff-on-Sea) - guitar; repl. Reynolds

—— Johnson subsequently became Melanie Derbyshire

Sweet Soil Music — not issued

Apr 99. (cd/c) *(SSM CD/MC 1)* **BARNDANCING**
- Cherokee shuffle - Paddy won't you drink some cider / Newton grove - George Washington / Choupique two-step / All the way to Galway - Winster galop - The rakes of Mallow / Rakes of Kildare - The railway / Blue moon of Kentucky / Thirty pound waltz / Springfield girl - Sourwood mountain / Viva seguin / Jambalaya / Maxwell Smart / Lament for the death of the Rev. Archie Beaton / Eighth of January – Elzic's farewell / Hindustan / The repeal of the licensing laws.

—— still going strong, but no further releases (as of 2011)

The FASTEST BAT

Formed in Birmingham, West Midlands in the summer of 1984 by Keith Slater, Ian Peters, Paul Douglas and Martin Hankin, the FASTEST BAT played good-time electric-folk in the mould of SPUD or LINDISFARNE offshoot JACK THE LAD.

For their one and only set (worth around £30), **COLD HAILY WINDY NIGHT** (1985) {*6}, The FASTEST BAT "combined the richness of folk melody and lyrics with the techniques of the 80s". Drinking songs such as 'Standing Down In New York' (performed many times at the local Bat Cave) featured additional guitar work by Tony "Bundle" Kelsey, while the best on show was 'P Stands For Paddy'. *MCS*

Martin Hankin - bass, vocals / **Paul Douglas** - guitar / **Ian Peters** - acoustic guitar, mandolin, keyboards, vocals / **Keith Slater** - drums, fiddle, vocals

UK Human — US not issued

1985. (lp) *(HUMANLP 002)* **COLD HAILY WINDY NIGHT**
- Corn rigs / Roll the woodpile / The shores of Old Blighty / Jim Jones / The leaking whippet (immortal at last!) / P stands for Paddy / Cold haily windy night / Brisk young widow / Standing down in New York / Jig - Four poster bed.

—— disappeared from sight after above set; Slater tried his hand on the solo circuit

FAUSTUS (⟹ DR FAUSTUS)

David FERRARD

Born in Edinburgh in 1977 and raised partly by his American mother in the States and his Scottish father here in Britain – hence his half 'n' half accent – David returned to his Caledonian roots from a folk fact-finding mission in the Blue Ridge mountains of North Carolina to the Celtic Connections festival in 2006; he won the Danny Kyle Award for his show. Not particularly prolific in the studio (he gets his message across by way of small intimate gigs), FERRARD has still managed to release a few albums; **BROKEN SKY** (2008) {*6} was his debut.

The softly-spoken, cherub-faced troubadour wrote all the songs on the set except Karen Deitz's 'This Heart'. 'Hills Of Virginia' (about the Iraq war) and 'The Hour Of Plenty' probably give a good insight into where he's coming from, while one of his best, 'One Hell Of A Ride', is about country-folk's favourite subjects: murder and trains.

On stage, FERRARD can sing his way through many a guid Scottish traditional song ('Ye Jacobites', 'Parcel Of Rogues', 'Peg And Awl' and 'Green Grow The Rashes-O' among them), his style very close to the pioneering folk masters JOHN DENVER, EWAN MacCOLL and his mentor/tour guide ROY BAILEY. David has guested on Bailey's 2009 set `Below The Radar'.

Many of these sourced songs found their way on to David's second set, **ACROSS THE TROUBLED WAVE** (2010) {*6}, a charming recording featuring multi-instrumentalist Josh Goforth and two ballads by Dunbar songwriter Kenny Brill: 'Gilmartin' (about the Highland Clearances) and 'S09 Monktonhall' (depicting life in the mines). In a favourite live staple, 'The Slave's Lament', David bravely tackles one of Burns's more obscure songs. A new album is on its way for summer 2011. *MCS*

David Ferrard - vocals, acoustic guitar

UK: Flamingo West — US: not issued

Mar 08. (cd) *(010)* **BROKEN SKY**
- Broken sky / Rain / Dmitri's pocket radio / One hell of a ride / Hills of Virginia / Visions of our youth / The hour of plenty / Radio blues / This heart / Take me out waltzing tonight / Never let go.

UK: Alter Road — US: not issued

Jan 10. (cd) *(ARRCD 001)* **ACROSS THE TROUBLED WAVE**
- Peg and awl / The slave's lament / Gilmartin / Jackaro / Once I knew a pretty girl / Calling my children home / My dearest dear / S09 Monktonhall / Follow the drinking gourd / A-rovin' on a winter's night / The jute mill song / Pretty Saro / Hard times come again no more.

FIDDLER'S DRAM (⟹ OYSTERBAND)

FIELDWORK (⟹ RYAN, Mick)

FIRST AID KIT

Who said woolly cardigans were old hat? Certainly not cutesy country-pie sisters Klara and Johanna Soderberg, who'd arrived on the London folk scene via Enskede, a suburb of Stockholm, Sweden. Not too dissimilar to the dulcet tones of JOANNA NEWSOM, the teenagers signed a deal with Wichita Records, their first release for that label an earlier Swedish mini-cd, **DRUNKEN TREES** {*6}, in 2009. Featuring the rather twee 'You're Not Coming Home Tonight' (a single flipped with 'Tangerine') and the bluesy 'Jagadamba, You Might', there seemed plenty for indie-folk kids to revel in. The UK version of the record added their take on FLEET FOXES' 'Tiger Mountain Peasant Song'.

With a sound not too dissimilar to the latter US act, **THE BIG BLACK AND THE BLUE** (2010) {*7} had several strum-friendly sweet and sour moments, the most compelling being 'Heavy Storm', 'Ghost Town', 'I Met Up With The King' and the old-timey 'Waltz For Richard'.

Be careful to avoid confusion with a completely different First Aid Kit (*c.*2006–08), who released electronica sets 'first' and 'Plaits'. *MCS*

Klara Soderberg (b. 1989) - vocals / **Johanna Soderberg** (b. 1992) - vocals / with session players

UK: Wichita — US: Third Man

Feb 09. (m-cd/m-lp) *(WEBB 201 CD/LP)* **DRUNKEN TREES**
- Little moon / You're not coming home tonight / Tangerine / Jagadamba, you might / Our own pretty ways / Perviglio / Cross oceans / Tiger mountain peasant song *[not on orig. Apr 08 on Rabid, Sweden; RABID 036]*

Feb 09. (ltd-7") *(WEBB 206S)* YOU'RE NOT COMING HOME. / Tangerine

Oct 09. (ltd-7") *(WEBB 234S)* HARD BELIEVER. / Waltz For Richard

Feb 10. (cd/lp) *(WEBB 222 CD/LP)* **THE BIG BLACK AND THE BLUE**
- In the morning / Hard believer / Sailor song / Waltz for Richard / Heavy storm / Ghost town / Josefin / A window opens / Winter is all over you / I met up with the king / Wills of the river. *(cd+=; WEBB 222CDL)* - All my trials.

Apr 10. (shared-7") *(WEBB 248STEN)* JOSEFIN. / [Peggy Sue track]

Oct 10 (7") *(WEBB 278S)* GHOST TOWN. / When I Grow Up

Mar 11. (7") *<TMR 074>* UNIVERSAL SOLDIER. / It Hurts Me Too

FISHBAUGH, FISHBAUGH & ZORN (⟹ ZORN, Pete)

FIT & LIMO

Post-1980s psych-folk from Germany is as rare as hen's teeth, but FIT & LIMO (Petra and Stefan Lienemann) fit the bill. Formed in Altdorf, Bavaria, the husband-and-wife duo released mainly cassettes during their early primitive-psychedelic days (see discography below), and have worked under many pseudonyms, including the psych-pop Kannibalen & Missionare (find their eponymous tape album from 1983) and Pure Luege (with a third party, Repp), on several collections under the Servil imprint from 1983 onwards. FIT & LIMO was their acid-folk identity; the Shiny Gnomes was their indie-pop alter-ego.

At times very INCREDIBLE STRING BAND/CLIVE PALMER, at others devoted to fuzz-rock and spacey experimental drones, F & L really got under way with the release of **THAT TOTALLY TORE MY HEAD OFF** (1991) {*6}. The folk sounds on that album were 'Pretty Distracted', 'Kiss My Crown', 'Seven Rings' and 'Fish In A Glass'; unless you're a fan of Neil Young in 'Weld' mode, you might want to avoid the lengthy live finale 'Bed Peace'.

ANGEL GOPHER (1993) {*8} and the ISB tribute EP 'This Moment' (the title track plus 'Come With Me', 'Three Is A Green Crown' and 'Chinese White') defined the duo's settled cosmic-folk years. Glockenspiel, tabla and other exotic instruments were the high spots. **AUTRE MONDE** (1995) {*8}, meanwhile, was hidden inside a bonus double-CD re-issue of 'Angel' as Volume III of **FOLLY IS AN ENDLESS MAZE**; think Barrett, Bolan and Mike HERON rolled into one. Ditto FIT & LIMO's first set for September Gurls Records, **THE SERPENT UNROLLED** {*7}, a record of a dozen originals and a couple of covers of Grateful Dead ('Dark Star') and PEARLS BEFORE SWINE/TOM RAPP ('Images Of April') material.

AS ABOVE SO BELOW (2000) {*6}, **GINNISTAN** (2002) {*6}, **TERRA INCOGNITA** (2004) {*6} and **ASTRALIS** (2007) {*6} continued their mission to revive psych-folk and take it into the 21st century. Their growing legion of loyal fans will have their covers of Richard Berry's 'Louie Louie', The Beachnuts' 'I've Got A Tiger In My Tank', The Rolling Stones' 'The Last Time', The Velvet Underground's 'Sunday Morning' and Syd Barrett's 'Wined And Dined'. Limo was also part of psychedelic outfit Discolor, who released 'III' in 2001. *MCS*

Fit (Petra Lienemann) – vocals, multi / **Limo** (Stefan Lienemann) - vocals, multi

UK: Servil — US: not issued

1982. (c) *(none)* KLEINE SCHIFFCHEN — German

1983. (c) *(none)* ROTE BLUMEN — German

1984. (c) *(none)* **GOLDEN TRASH** — German
- Blop!!! / Popular girl / D.C. affairs / De plus en plus / Sunday morning / Happy birthday / Jane and Serge / Chocolat kiss / Singapore sling / Wined and dined.

1984. (ltd-c; shared) *(none)* **IM BLICKPUNKT** — German
- [Stratis side] // Fotoliebe / Kurts schachtelhaus / Der elefant / Rote blumen / Gold und silber / Nous sommes les secret / Kleine schiffchen / Freibeuter / Je n'ais pas de plan.

(above on IRRE Tapes)

1985. (c) *(none)* **PUT ON THE FLIPSIDE** — German
- I've got a tiger in my tank / Daddy's stroboscope / Louie Louie / Tripping mind / I know a land / Winner of your heart / Last time / Welshman of sorts / Dear monster tentacles / Love torture / Don't fall down.

UK: Bouncing Corporation — US: not issued

1989. (lp) *(Head 10)* **REVISITED** — German
- Everybody is / Feather and dust / Eyelet / Ivan Pawle / Sailing girls / The fear of the world / Bed peace revisited.

UK: Hurdy Gurdy Beat — US: not issued

Nov 91. (cd) *(HGBCD 21015)* **THAT TOTALLY TORE MY HEAD OFF** — German
- Seven rings / Family jam / Dumb angel / Mountain of dub / Fish in a glass / Sense of Saturday / You live in a dream / Pretty distracted / Kiss my crown / Upstairs / Sounds from the purple house / Bed peace [soundtrack/live at Forum Enger, November 1988].

UK: Kickside — US: not issued

Feb 93. (ltd-cd) *(numbered)* **ANGEL GOPHER** — German
- Fortune seller / Gopher hat / Mystery / Baby song / September 13th / Not from the world / The carpet / Stony glory / Panaelonia themes / Black berry / Mrs. Child / A sigh about time / Late summer / Snake king / Goddess / The little girl lost / Broken strings.

UK: Ruhra Pente — US: not issued

1993. (7" ep) *(RP 001)* THIS MOMENT [Fit & Limo play The Incredible String Band] — German
- This moment / Come with me / Three is a green crown / Chinese white.

UK: Strange Ways — US: not issued

May 95. (d-cd) *(WAY 107-2)* **FOLLY IS AN ENDLESS MAZE** — German
- (VOL.I) / (THIS MOMENT EP) // (VOL.III: AUTRE MONDE):- - Lux / The life and times of Pan / Fairy ring / Pillow mine / Working in my garden / Curiosity / Nutshell / Old hob / Scented / Tranceweg / All to see / God's press / Three dances / I know you / Introducing the colours / The world.

		September Gurls		Hand/Eye
1998.	(cd) *(SGCD 20)* **THE SERPENT UNROLLED**	▭	German	▭

- Morgenrore / Born in the eleventh month / Dark star / Walking the labyrinth / Song of the Basilisk / Florence's birthday / Images of April / Salad day / Marry me / I'll be clay / Mondisch / Traumtur / The dew / Her ancient theme.

2000. (ltd-7" ep; shared) *<h/e 005>* THE SILENCE OF A MILLION TONGUES [w/ STONE BREATH] ▭ ▭
- [SB track] / Lapis theme / Stein / [SB track].

2000. (cd/lp) *(SGCD 26)* **AS ABOVE SO BELOW** ▭ German ▭
- Owsley blues / Measured tides / The highest mountain / Stormcows and thunderclouds / Haga's painting / Christian alchemy / Mondwasser / Glockenspiel / My sweetheart's voice / Before Babylon / World in a grain / Open scene / Umarmurgen.

2002. (cd/d-lp) *(SGCD 28)* **GINNISTAN** ▭ German ▭
- Sub rosa / Here's the place / A girl named Fabel / I stood in the streams / Graser / Indica / By water fair / Mermaid / Dear Ginnistan / Sternenklar / Wonnberg / Der komische pfad / Swiss bliss / Upper and lower Ginnistan.

Dec 04. (cd/lp) *(SGCD 31)* **TERRA INCOGNITA** ▭ German ▭
- Seraph / Will you / Lass uns auf die reise gehn / Golden floor / Wende dich her / The weaving song / Unknown world / Morning wake / Mary of Malibran / In den garten Salomos / Cantiamo / Weisse asche.

Mar 06. (ltd-cd-r) *<h/e-moon 13>* INDIAN WORM MOON ▭ ▭
- Powwowpsy / Is it true? / Take me to that place.

Jun 07. (cd) *(SGCD 38)* **ASTRALIS** ▭ German ▭
- Dem neuen jahr / The lovers / Sweet imagination / Wind whispers / Drift away / The moon shines bright / Sing the forest temple / Around the fount / The snow it melts the soonest / Been on the road so long / With the river / Down in yon forest / Chinese firebird / Lucky boat / A swamp room lullabye / Nebula / Prelenglanz / Astralis.

- (5-7*) compilations, others, etc.-

1988. (lp) *Bouncing Corporation; (Head 4)* **RETROSPECTIVE 1983–1988** ▭ German ▭
- Tripping mind / Days of glasnost / Dear monster tentacles / Jane and Serge / Coming home / Rote blumen / Welshman of sorts / Chocolate kiss / Daddy's stroboscope / Porridge.

1995. (ltd-lp) *Catweezle; (CW 002)* **FEATHER AND DUST** [early material] ▭ German ▭
- Feather and dust / Porridge / Daddy's stroboscope / Eyelet / I know a land / Rote blumen / Dear monster tentacles / Ivan Pawle / Bed peace revisited. *(w/ 7"+=)* - She took a long cold look [wild wood version] / She took a long cold look ['95 version].

Jul 06. (ltd d-lp//cd) *September Gurls; (SGLPCD 37)* **A GARLAND OF FLOWERS // A BUNCH OF HERBS** ▭ German ▭
- September 13th / Three is a green crown / The life and times of Pan / Scented / Not from this world / Nutshell / The carpet / Snake king / Goddess / Gopher hat / Mystery / God's press / Come with me // Lapis theme / The wizard and the dragonfly / The calm whirl / Christian alchemy [alt.] / Mountain of dub / When the world began / Nocturnal / Stein / The surrealist waltz / She took a long cold look / Oh Sphinx / Mantra / Humpty Dumpty [alt.ext.] / Wer hat die schonsten schafchen.

FLOWERS & FROLICS

Formed in London in 1974 by Australian musician Graeme Smith (who returned to his home country before they made any recordings), the essence English country-dance and music-hall folk group came from musicians and singers Mike Bettison, Roger Digby, Bob King, Dan Quinn, Ted Stevens and Alex West. No doubt taking inspiration from former FAIRPORT bassist ASHLEY HUTCHINGS and his ever-evolving ALBION (COUNTRY) BAND, **BEES ON HORSEBACK** (1977) {*7} was a fine example of traditional fare with the exception of 'Two Little Girls In Blue', which featured JUNE TABOR on vocals. BOB DAVENPORT made his entrance in part three of the opening medley. By 1984 both King and West had departed, although **SOLD OUT** {*5} took on newcomers, Trevor Bennett, Rob Gifford and Nick Havell before it was decided that a re-organisation was needed.

GAS MARK 5 would be the project of the three newcomers and Dan Quinn, although their time would come later in the 1980s (see forthcoming second edition). *MCS*

Mike Bettison (b. Jun 3, '51, Chiswick, London) - melodeon, vocals / **Roger Digby** (b. Apr 19, '49, Colchester, Essex) - Anglo concertina, piano, vocals / **Bob King** (b. Mar 27, '52, Eastbourne, Sussex) - banjo, guitar / **Dan Quinn** (b. Oct 11, '49, Grimsby, South Humberside) - melodeon, vocals / **Ted Stevens** (b. Sep '52, Redruth, Cornwall) - percussion / **Alex West** (b. Nov 8, '54) - tuba, brass / + guest vocalists

		UK Free Reed	US not issued
1977.	(lp) *(FRR 016)* **BEES ON HORSEBACK**	▭	▭

- Grandfather's tune - He played his ukulele (as the ship went down) - Mickey Mouse's son and daughter / Down the road - See me dance the polka / Everybody knows me by my old brown hat / Tommy make room for your uncle Nos.1 & 2 - Ned Kelly's fancy / The Ratcliffe highway / Shufflin' Sam / Galopede - Dorset four-hand reel - Shepton Mallet hornpipe / Woodland revels – Alexander's rag-time band / Whistling prince - The Mudgee Schottische - Harry Cotter's Schottische / Wotcher / Huntsman's chorus - John Ryan's – Broom's reel / Silverton polka / (My name it is) McCarty - Cunnamulla stockman's jig - Manchester gallop / Two little girls in blue. *(cd re-mast. Jun 08 +=; FRRR 18)* - Manferrina - The Glakey hornpipe / By the time I get to Phoenix - The dock of the bay / Scan Tester's quadrilles / unknown / Rue the day - The Mudgee waltz / The Queensland drovers / The shores of Botany Bay / Shepton Mallet hornpipe - In the toyshop - Whistle-at-her.

—— **Trevor Bennett** (b. Aug 4, '45, Grantham, Lincolnshire) - trombone, flugelhorn / **Rob Gifford** (b. Mar 1, '55, Wansted, London) - percussion / **Nick Havell** (b. Jan 7, '51, Stratford, London) - bass trombone; repl. King + West

		EFDSS	not issued
Nov 84.	(lp) *(BR 6)* **SOLD OUT**	▭	▭

—— all three newcomers would form GAS MARK 5, taking with them Dan Quinn

——the original line-up re-formed in 1999 + Davenport + PETA WEBB

		Hebe Music	not issued
2000.	(cd) *(HEBECD 002)* **REFORMED CHARACTERS**	▭	▭

- Grandfather's tune - He played his ukulele (as the ship went down) - Mickey Mouse's son and daughter / Ned Kelly's fancy - The Woolloomooloo lair - The Cunnamulla stockman's jig - The Manchester gallop / Bill Bailey - Woodland revels / Wotcher / Hot punch - Family jig – Uncle's jig / Silverton polka / Two little girls in blue / Down the road - See me dance the polka / Martin / A starry night for a ramble - The watercress girl - The Mudgee waltz / Whistling prince - The Mudgee schottische - Harry Cotter's schottische / Sunny afternoon / Shufflin' Sam / The shores of Botany Bay / Walter Bulwer's polkas / After you've gone / Shepton Mallet hornpipe - In the toyshop - Whistle-at-her.

——With Will Duke, Quinn also released two sets for the same company: 'Wild Boys' (1996) and 'Scanned' (2001)

Johnny FLYNN

Not exactly a Celtic-folk artist, although his band The PICTISH TRAIL showed a modicum of promise, actor/poet/singer-songwriter FLYNN was actually born in South London in 1982 and now, via the US, lives in Cellardyke, Fife. The multi-instrumentalist also runs the Fence Collective label with Kenny Anderson (also known as King Creosote).

Inspired by Yeats and Shakespeare, FLYNN and his band The Sussex Wit (Adam Beach, Matt Edmonds, Joe Zeitlin, and Lillie Flynn) burst on to the Brit-folk-blues scene in 2008 with **A LARUM** {*7}. With more than a dozen cuts on board (check out 'The Wrote And The Writ', 'Tickle Me Pink' and 'Shore To Shore'), FLYNN's witty lyrics and the group's melodious backing take centre stage. **BEEN LISTENING** (2010) {*6} introduces a lot of brass, both instrumentally and attitude-wise, songs such as 'Howl' and 'The Water' (with nu-folkster LAURA MARLING in attendance) competing with new-folk-kids-on-the-block MUMFORD & SONS and NOAH AND THE WHALE. If folk's not your bag, Flynn also branched out with ADEM in the New Order-styled Silver Columns, while the PICTISH TRAIL have released several limited-edition and rare CD-rs. *MCS*

JOHNNY FLYNN AND THE SUSSEX WIT

Johnny Flynn - vocals, acoustic guitar, mandolin, violin, etc. / with The Sussex Wit: **Adam Beach** - bass, banjo, organ, percussion / **Matt Edmonds** - drums, keyboards, banjo, vocals / **Joe Zeitlin** - cello / **Lillie Flynn** - backing vocals

		UK Young And Lost Club	US not issued
Feb 07.	(ltd-7") *(YALC 0013)* TICKLE ME PINK. / Cold Bread	▭	▭
Jul 07.	(ltd-7") *(YALC 0016)* ODE TO A MARE TROD DITCH	▭	▭

- Eyeless in Holloway / Oh to eat an apple.

		Vertigo	Lost Highway
Nov 07.	(cd-ep) *(175 308-9)* JOHNNY FLYNN AND THE SUSSEX WIT EP	▭	▭

- Tickle me pink / Cold bread / Eyeless in Holloway / Oh to eat an apple.

Nov 07.	(ltd-7") *(174 823-0)* THE BOX. / The Wrote And The Writ	▭	▭

JOHNNY FLYNN

credited solo although still backed by The Sussex Wit

Mar 08.	(ltd-7") *(176 097-1)* LEFTOVERS. / Dusty Fingers	▭	▭
May 08.	(7"pink) *(176 664-5)* TICKLE ME PINK. / Old Tricks	▭	▭
	(cd-s) *(176 664-2)* - *['A'] / The ghost of O'Donahue.*		
May 08.	(cd/d-lp) *(176 113-2/-0) <B0011433-02/-01>* **A LARUM**	▭	▭

- The box / The wrote and the writ / Tickle me pink / Brown trout blues / Eyeless in Holloway / Shore to shore / Cold bread / Wayne Rooney / Leftovers / Sally / Hong Kong cemetry / Tunnels / All the dogs are lying down / Shore to shore (reprise).

Jul 08. (cd-ep) *<778070>* HONG KONG CEMETRY EP
- Cold bread / Tickle me pink / Hong Kong cemetry / The box.

Transgressive not issued

Jun 10. (7") *(TRANS 112)* KENTUCKY PILL. / [MPC demo]

Jun 10. (cd/d-lp) *(TRANS 113 S/X)* **BEEN LISTENING**
- Kentucky pill / Lost and found / Churlish May / Been listening / Barnacled warship / Sweet William (part 2) / The water / Howl / Agnes / Amazon love / The prizefighter and the heiress. *(cd [some]w/cd+=)* - The water [alt.] / [demos]: Been listening / Lost and found / Churlish May / Howl / The prizefighter and the heiress. *(d-lp+=)* - [SWEET WILLIAM ep promo]: The mountain is burning / Trains (Rose, Mary and time) / Sweet William (part 1) / Drums / [alt.]: The water.

Aug 10. (7"m) *(TRANS 119)* BARNACLED WARSHIP. / The Break In The Line / The Triumph Of Hellenism

Nov 10. (7") *(TRANS 121)* THE WATER. / Chimney Sweepers

The PICTISH TRAIL

aka **Johnny Flynn**

Fence not issued

Mar 03. (cd-r) *(none)* THE PICTISH TRAIL
- Orange soil / Filthy mucky / You've found a start / Chinese whispers / Same old / The best thing to do / Going down to the water / I must try / Lazy day / For anything.

2004. (cd-ep) *(none)* PICK @ PICTISH
- Intro / I know (you're going to want to leave, now) / Misery guts / Everyone and everything / Spider on a train / You into view / Cocks / Ortni / Cheating (at hide and seek).

Nov 07. (ltd-7" clear-green) *(FNC-SECRET7-002)* WORDS FAIL ME NOW. / [track by Found] gig

Sep 08. (cd) *(FNC 904)* **SECRET SOUNDZ VOL.1**
- Secret sound #2 / All I own / I don't know where to begin / Secret sound #1 / Words fail me now / Ribbon (the twist) / Winter home disco / The lighthouse / Into the smoke / Secret sound #5.

Dec 08. (ltd-7" clear-white) *(FNC-SECRET7-007)* WINTER HOME DISCO [Hot Chip remix]. / [Found remix]

Jan 11. (m-lp; w/m-cd) *(FNC 907)* **IN ROOMS**
- I've been set upon / In rooms / Barbara wire fence / The Lemsip tonsil rap / Drip feed blink #1 / Fishface / A final snap / My fizzy bitz / No, rattlesnake / Time bomb / Not to be / Even if you didn't pass that way / 13 pillars / Ladders / Brain freeze / Please yourself / Waiting #3 (Michelle) / House arrest / Plain to set / To your health / Hymn for her / Bubbalicious / Stay to your side / Tell me what is on your mind / Wavelengths / A summoning high / Sweating battery acid / Prequels / Tied to the seat / Two way mirror / Afraid – Dead / Well, I never … / Werewolf who / Birds / Promise me / Cover ears and eyes up / Waiting #2 (Stanley) / It's not happening / Arm in / Our school of ties / Headfirst legend / Roof / Bubbles / Waiting #1 / G.U.I.L.L.O.T.I.N.E.P.A.G.E.S. / Fool tilt / My icecream / Drip feed blink #2 / Let me get drunk with you / You are in my dreams.

FRASER SISTERS (⟹ FREYA, Jo)

Jo FREYA

Born Jo-Anne Rachel Newmarch Fraser, December 4, 1960 at St. Albans in Hertfordshire, JO FREYA (her surname taken to appease the actors' union Equity) has been a stalwart of several classy trad-folk outfits. With her sister Fi Fraser, and at the age of 13, she'd been part of The OLD SWAN BAND and BLOWZABELLA, two outfits that rejuvenated the English country-dance scene during the 1970s and 1980s respectively. As a clarinettist and tenor saxophonist she's more than competent, and as a singer she's a breath of fresh air, acceding to the gracious throne once occupied by her idols LAL WATERSON, SHIRLEY COLLINS and MADDY PRIOR.

Her first solo album, **TRADITIONAL SONGS OF ENGLAND** (1993) {*7}, was basically what it said on the sleeve – a folk-meets-olde chamber-pot-pourri with credits for Fi (on harmony), Paul Burgess (violin and recorders) and Flos Headford (violin) – all friends from her OLD SWAN BAND days – and Nick Hooper (guitar), Dave Townsend (concertina, accordion and violin), Kathryn Locke (cello), Nigel Eaton (hurdy gurdy) and the Rose Consort of Viols.

The collaboration **LUSH** (1994) {*7} with fellow songsmith Kathryn Locke (and her/their debut for the No Masters Co-operative) showcased choice covers of songs by TRACY CHAPMAN ('Baby Can I Hold You') and Joan Armatrading ('The Weakness In Me').

TOKEN WOMEN (Jo, Fi, Alice Kinloch from The BARELY WORKS, Jackie Allen, Heather Vigar-Horsley and Jo May) released their first of three CDs in 1993, **THE RHYTHM METHOD** {*6}. 1995's **OUT TO LUNCH** {*6} and 2001's **ELSA** {*6} showed the versatility and ambition of an artist who had been in the business for two decades and was only in her mid-thirties.

Without sister Fi, her sextet FREYJA released a few jazz-folk albums either side of her sole TANTEEKA outing, **A NEW TRADITION** (1997) {*6}, alongside long-time colleagues Alice Kinloch, Andy Cutting and Oliver Knight.

Augmented by Barry Coope (of COOPE BOYES & SIMPSON, whom both sisters had guested for on a couple of festive sets) on keyboards, Andy on accordion again, Ralph Jordan and Karen Tweed, Fi Fraser and Jo Freya issued the trad-friendly set **THE FRASER SISTERS** (1998) {*6}. A second batch, **GOING AROUND** {*7}, with Ralph still in tow, was released in 2001: CHERYL WHEELER's 'Summer Fly' and Tom Waits's 'The Briar And The Rose' were particularly noteworthy.

A return to BLOWZABELLA in the latter half of the 2000s was matched with a resurrection of FREYA's solo career, albeit through a **LAL** (WATERSON) {*7} tribute in 2007 featuring a galaxy of talent (sister Fi, Jim Boyes, Jude Abbott and Neil Ferguson of CHUMBAWAMBA, MARY McMASTER of The POOZIES and Harry Hamer of the Sex Patels). Jude and Neil were partly responsible for the near-flawless, protest-friendly **FEMALE SMUGGLER** (2008) {*7} set, a record that triumphed on tracks such as 'Roses' (about domestic violence), `Little 'O" (about emails) and the quirky title-track broadside. Of late, she's once again combined with her CHUMBAWAMBA friends on **GET WELL SOON** (2011) {*6}, having earlier completed the collaboration **MEET** (2010) {*6} with Maalstroom. *MCS*

Jo Freya - vocals, tenor sax, clarinet, etc. / with session people

UK Saydisc US not issued

Mar 93. (cd/c) *(CD/C SDL 402)* **TRADITIONAL SONGS OF ENGLAND**
- All things are quite silent / As I set off to Turkey / As Sylvie was walking / General Wolfe / Though I live not where I love / A sailor's life / Rounding the Horn / Lord Franklin / The unquiet grave / The Broomfield wager / There was a lady all skin and bone / Geordie / Maids when you're young never wed an old man / Bold William Taylor / Lovely Joan / A blacksmith courted me / The carnal and the crane / The green cockade / Fourpence a day / The streams of lovely Nancy / Sweet England. *(cd re-iss. Mar 05; same)*

No Masters Voice not issued

Jan 94. (cd/c; by JO FREYA AND KATHRYN LOCKE) *(NMV 5 CD/C)* **LUSH**
- Yeta / Autumn leaves – Hoozberg / Fish frenzy / Baby can I hold you / Never mind the Pollocks / Maids of Coolmore / Nimbus / Drowned in your eyes / Special tea / Sorry – Naylor's / Rufus / The weakness in me / Road rissole. *(cd re-iss. Feb 96; same)*

TOKEN WOMEN

Jo + Fi plus **Alice Kinloch** - brass (ex-BARELY WORKS) / **Jackie Allen** - violin / **Heather Vigar-Horsley** - flute, keyboards / **Jo May** - percussion

Feb 93. (cd/c) *(NMV 2 CD/C)* **THE RHYTHM METHOD**
- The gypsy's hornpipe – Sleep sound in in the morning / Tiennet – Les poules huppet / J.J. / Alimony run / Schottische de lande – Polka d'Avignon / Harvey's – Finnish / Somewhere the sun is shining – The rainbow waltz / Nechells – Sac du The / Walter Bulwer's No.2 & 1 / London schottische – Horizonto / Once in a while / Nuttella / The lawnmower and the hippo – Reels des jeune maries – Grumbling old man and the cackling old woman / Haunt. *(cd re-iss. Feb 96; same)*

Nov 95. (cd) *(NMCD 6)* **OUT TO LUNCH**
- Grommet – Fragrant vagrant / The lost elephant / Jo's jig – Vertigo / Tarlo – Ghost guardian / Bad / Beasting pudden wi' legs on / 'Ippy merde / The Silverton polka / The paddocks – The shrew's bouree / I can dream, can't I? / Oppning – Synapse collapse / Max Baxter's.

Jul 01. (cd) *(NMCD 18)* **ELSA**
- Spootiskerry – Battle of Aughrim / Bantry Bay – President Garfield's / Cuckoo's nest – Danish / Foula reel – Da new rigged ship / Earl of Mansfield / Wychwood – Glorious thirteenth / Mikenda one / Gerry O'Connor's – Cleveland park / Scottish set / An dro / Godmother – Il est bien temps / Calliope House – Juniper jig / Dubuque – Bill Cheetham's.

FREYJA

Jo Freya - vocals, sax / **Gabrielle Meyer** - violin, vocals / **Belen de Benito** - guitars, vocals / **Anne-Lise Foy** - hurdy gurdy, vocals / **Eva Vavrinecz** - double bass, vocals / **Nicola Marsh** - percussion

Osmosys not issued

Jul 96. (cd) *(OSMOCD 006)* **FREYJA**
- Entradilla / Freylech / Csardas / Le moulin des deux roues / Snieder danz – Reelin'

over the rooftops / Krummshots / Rossignolet / Lost papers / Setalos kopogos tusszentos csardas / Vecinos.

—— **Jo May** - vibraphone, percussion + **Marria Johnson** - violin, vocals; repl. Gabrielle + Nicola

Apr 01. (cd) *(OSMOCD 016)* **ONE BATHROOM**
- Gravel walks to granny / Kara min moder – Kallebiten / La belle endormie / Hajnal nota – Green cockade / Siete mujeres and one bathroom / La borderie / Magas hegyen / Todora – More sojkp – Susko / Leksandslat – A sailor's life / Amnesia.

TANTEEKA

Jo Freya - vocals, saxophones, clarinets, whistles / **Alice Kinloch** - vocals, brass / **Andy Cutting** - accordions (of CHRIS WOOD & ...) / **Oliver Knight** - guitars

Osmosys not issued

Sep 97. (cd) *(OSMOCD 013)* **A NEW TRADITION**
- A laxity of morals / Pierre de Grenoble / Midnight feast / Ouvrez la porte / Day to day (up to here) / Mikenda / Claire Conner's lament / Laurel's retreat / Rossignolet / Thing / Watching the grass grow / Broomfield wager / Steel works / Le soir venu.

FRASER SISTERS

Jo + Fi with friends and session people

No Masters not issued

Jul 98. (cd; as FI & JO FRASER) *(NMCD 12)* **THE FRASER SISTERS**
- Garden of love / The lowlands of Holland / The rose of Raby – Fim / A stitch in time / Bonny light horseman / Man of passion / Hold back the tide / Friday the 12th – Havero polka – Friday the 13th / Hug you like a mountain / Tiennet – Tourdion / The coldness of winter / Bird in cage / All the way with you / Jumper song / Bramble and the rose / Swedelska.

Oct 01. (cd) *(NMCD 19)* **GOING AROUND**
- Going to leave this country / Sansonnette – Coridinio / Summerfly / Half in love with you / Watercress girl / Sault the groom / Yorkshire romance / Seamstress / Laughing in her sleep – Grinding her teeth / Briar and the rose / La Fontaine – Time will end / Monday morning.

JO FREYA

Oct 07. (cd; as JO FREYA'S LAL WATERSON PROJECT) *(NMCD 27)*
LAL
- Midnight feast / Dazed / Wilson's arms / Song for Thirza / Together / Long vacation / The bird / May butterfly / Party games / Flight of the pelican / Same old Salty / Bath time / Foolish one / Stumbling on / Migrating bird.

Aug 08. (cd) *(NMCD 29)* **FEMALE SMUGGLER**
- Female smuggler / Different shades of meaning / Lynedoch place – Pardon Kolloreg / Roses / A thief can too / Chasing water / Marvellous companion / Boris Tortu – Gavotte Montagne / Little 'O' / Edwin in the lowlands low / Josephine Butler / Claire Connor's lament – Diary diary / Oh America.

Oct 10. (cd; by MAALSTROOM & JO FREYA) *(NMCD 36)* **MEET**
- Musicport / Rattling roof tiles / Everybody has a tale / Thyroid jig / Waltzing up the stairs / Green grow the rushes oh / Song for Leon / No better friends / Braw sailing / Gorges du Dailley / Closing of the day.

—— next with **Jude Abbott** + **Neil Ferguson** (of CHUMBAWAMBA)

Mar 11. (cd; by FREYA ABBOTT FERGUSON) *(NMCD 37)*
GET WELL SOON
- Real men can wear pink / The piper's path / Betsy Walton / Bold William Brigg / Old community / Mirrors / Cornwall / Glass house mazurka / Entre le boeuf – Food and donkeys / Two sisters / Dear God / My life with Margarita / San Fran.

GARMANA (⟹ Great Celtic-folk/World-music Discography)

GAS MARK 5

The five in question comprised four former members (Dan Quinn, Nick Havell, Trevor Bennett and Rob Gifford) of mid-1970s English ceilidh-dance outfit FLOWERS & FROLICS plus one refugee (Chris Taylor) from The OYSTER BAND. Jumping at the chance to establish themselves in and around the burgeoning but splintered festival folk scene, GAS MARK 5 blew away the opposition on their trad-sourced eponymous debut in 1988; the earlier release 'In The Kitchen' may have been a limited-edition demo. **GAS MARK 5** {*6} juxtaposed ye olde tunes with a few of Taylor's attempts at ringing the changes, while there were modern-day covers of material by SI KAHN ('What You Do With What You've Got') and BOB DAVENPORT ('Policeman Prowl').

Without Quinn on board (Terry Mann was his replacement), **JUMP!** (1991) {*5} was served up as the band's second set, and although each polka, fling and hornpipe had its appeal, JOHN KIRKPATRICK's 'Jump At The Sun' stood out. Further personnel upheavals (Michael Davidson for Mann and Dave Blackmore for Havell) led to an eventual implosion after album number three, **GUIZERS** (1994) {*4}, went virtually unnoticed. *MCS*

Dan Quinn - melodeon / **Nick Havell** - bass, trombone / **Trevor Bennett** - trombones and flugelhorn / **Rob Gifford** - percussion (all four ex-FLOWERS & FROLICS) / **Chris Taylor** - melodeon, guitar, mouth organ (ex-OYSTER BAND)

UK Festival — US not issued

1987. (c) *(Festival C1)* IN THE KITCHEN

Oct 88. (lp/c) *(Festival 2/C2)* **GAS MARK 5**
- Mad Moll / The Lafayette two-step / The weasel in the grass - Policeman prowl / The bog road - Blackwall tunnel - Bad boys of Dunkirk - Martin O'Connor's / The lads in their hundreds - Battle of the Somme / Margaret's waltz - Tell her I am - Mr Crow's jig - Joseph Taylor's favourite / Dogma / William Kimber's / Lena - What you do with what you've got / Drummond castle / The Hogmanay.

—— **Terry Mann** (b. Oct 6, '63, Barking, London) - saxophones, guitar, bass, wind, synths; repl. Quinn who moved to Brighton; later he reunited with FLOWERS & FROLICS

Regular — not issued

Oct 91. (cd/c) *(REGUL 02 CD/MC)* **JUMP!**
- The Waterloo dance - Knocknaburragh polka / Cognac au Poivre - Anything for JohnJo / Jump at the sun / Bromsberrow heath reel - Pigtown fling / Star above the garter - My love is gone and I care not / Marigold / Hasty marriage / The rent rebate / Kippers in the post / Dill Pickles rag / Pheasant in the coal shed - Gypsy hornpipe / Jackie Daley's - The last chance.

—— **Michael Davidson** - bass, guitar, mandolin; repl. Mann

—— **Dave Blackmore** - saxophones, keyboards; repl. Havell

Oct 94. (cd/c) *(REGUL 03 CD/MC)* **GUIZERS**
- The runaway pig / Orlando's return - Farewell my ugly / Rory's kip / The rat's whiskers - Nights at the circus / Banks of the Ching - The kitchen girl / That's the rain on again - Camping weather / The tempest - Vilnius tanze / Not a penny left - The last bus home / The Duke of Perth - The battle of Aughrim / Breton gavotte - The Aireys' regret / A rock and a wee pickle too - Andy McGann's - Billy the fish / Nobody cares for me.

—— split in 1996

The GENTLE GOOD

Basically the brainchild of singer-songwriter Gareth Bonello from Cardiff, The GENTLE GOOD come across as very NICK DRAKE, at least in the orchestration, although comparisons will be made (thanks to several Welsh-language songs) to nearly-man MEIC STEVENS.

In 2008, with Seb Goldfinch (violin), Harriet Earis (cello) and producer Llion Robertson (keyboards), Bonello released the non-album single 'Dawel Disgyn' and his debut album **WHILE YOU SLEPT I WENT OUT WALKING** {*6}j, a rather simplistic and relaxed bunch of ballads led by 'A Man Made Of Moss', with 'Waiting For Jane' and 'Winterberries' as sedate as a Sunday morning.

The long-awaited **TETHERED FOR THE STORM** (2011) {*7} – also with Llion and Harriet – was another sprinkling of fireside folk songs, with solo vocalist CATE LE BON (as dual vocalist on some), Lisa Jen (of '9Bach'), Dewi Parri (bass), Steven Goundrey (guitar) and drummer Jack Egglestone all on hand to provide some needed depth to rainy-day songs such as 'Aubade' (very Camel), 'Pamela' and 'Ocean Is King'. *MCS*

Gareth Bonello - vocals, acoustic guitar, banjo, glockenspiel / + guests + orchestra

UK self-rel. — US not issued

2005. (ltd-cd-r) *(none)* FIND YOUR WAY BACK HOME EP
- Y deryn du / Back to the forest / Can y fari / Fish out of water.

Gwymon — not issued

Nov 07. (ltd-7" ep) *(GWYMONCD 002)* DAWEL DISGYN
- Dawel disgyn / The hitcher / Amser / Waiting for Jane.

Nov 08. (cd) *(GWYMONCD 004)* **WHILE YOU SLEPT I WENT OUT WALKING**
- A man made of moss / Baled y conflict / Waiting for Jane / Titrwm tatrwm / Let your light be your guide / Cri'r adar main / Gwel yr adeilad / Hiraeth am feirion / Winterberries / Crwydro'r caeau glas.

Mar 11. (cd) *(GWYMONCD 013)* **TETHERED FOR THE STORM**
- Aubade / Colled / Pamela / Deuawd / Holly blue / Old window song / Llosgi Pontydd / Tethered for the storm / Ocean is king / Cysgod y dur.

GILES FARNABY'S DREAM BAND (⟹ The DRUIDS)

The GLOWORMS

Working in the tradition of Morris On/English country-dance giants such as The ALBION DANCE BAND and The OLD SWAN BAND, musicians Laurel Swift, Jon Brenner and Colin Cotter (collectively The GLOWORMS) will be better known to fans of The IMAGINED VILLAGE as the trio who contributed 'Kit White's I & II' to The IMAGINED VILLAGE's groundbreaking debut set in 2007.

The GLOWORMS' first outing, LAUREL SWIFT's part-solo trad set **BEAM** {*6} (2005), credited a host of guests on the sleeve, including: The GLOWORMS of course, fiddlers JACKIE OATES (also vocals), John Dipper (of CHRIS WOOD's English Folk Collective), Miranda Rutter (also viola) and Fiona Taylor, melodeon player Saul Rose (of BELSHAZZAR'S FEAST, etc), tuba player Nic Hurst, clarinettist Glyn Hawke, trumpeter Chantel Nappen and singer Lauren McCormick. Track eight, 'Midsummer Carol' also featured added vocalists Judy Hardman, Mal Ricketts, Frances Watt, Sue Swift and Robert Harbron.

RUNNING JOAK (2007/08) {*7} was described by many critics and pundits as the future of English folk – but the jury is still out on that, the band having been conspicuous by their absence ever since. Still, the medleys on show had equal shares of fire and fun to be heard on the likes of 'The Tank – Mr Cosgill's Delight' and 'Llama Riding' – Dr Faustus's Tumblers'. *MCS*

Laurel Swift - vocals, fiddle, dancer / **Jon Brenner** - piano accordion / **Colin Cotter** - tenor banjo

UK Necta Arts — US not issued

Apr 05. (cd; as Laurel Swift and the Gloworms, etc ...) *(NECTACD 001)* **BEAM**
- Willie of Winsbury / Return of the bourree – The bourree strikes back – Bourree a boscatel (JOHN DIPPER & LAUREL SWIFT) / Barham down – The yellow joak (The

GLOWORMS) / The meeting of minds / An awhesyth – An dufunyans (QUARTET) / Glorishears – All the world – The willow tree – Banks of the Dee (LAUREL SWIFT & SAUL ROSE) / Reilly the fisherman (The GLOWORMS) / Midsummer carol / Old Minehead hobby horse tune – French tune – Sweet Jenny Jones (JOHN DIPPER & LAUREL SWIFT) / The bold fisherman (The GLOWORMS) / Battered hake – Jon O'Groats (The GLOWORMS).

EFDSS — not issued

Jan 08. (cd) *(EFDSS 14)* **RUNNING JOAK**
- The battered hake polka – Jon O'Grouts / The tank – Mr Cosgill's delight / Kit White's I – Kit White's II / Don Juan one – William Taylor's tabletop hornpipe / Serpentiner och konfetti / Barham down – The yellow joak – The go! Of London city / Horses never smile / Cuddly house / Llama riding – Dr Faustus's tumbler / Trip to nobody's – Herbert the sherbet / Julian and Sandy are bronze – The battery hornpipe.

GOD'S LITTLE MONKEYS

The mid-1980s threw together some weird and wonderful genre hybrids, but punk-folk was surely the ultimate contradiction in terms: spiky mops, ripped army trousers and bovver boots were without question a fashion folk-pas. GLM's earlier life as MALCOLM'S INTERVIEW was typical of the time.

Hailing from York and consisting of vocalists Josephine Swiss and Jon Townend, plus David Allan and Martin Appleby (David Wall was installed after debut 45 'You Don't Listen'), **BREAKFAST IN BEDLAM** (1987) {*6} was their only collection for Special Delivery (i.e. indie/folk imprint Cooking Vinyl). The album featured Northumbrian piper KATHRYN TICKELL on two cuts ('Blue And Yellow' and Ed Pickford's 'Crime'), and group compositions seemed to be overshadowed by choice covers of EWAN MacCOLL ('Moving On'), BILLY BRAGG ('It Says Here') and DICK GAUGHAN ('Which Side Are You On?').

A radical name change to GOD'S LITTLE MONKEYS resulted in a resurgence in the quartet's fortunes as Cooking Vinyl kept the faith and unleashed their next offering, **NEW MAPS OF HELL!** (1989) {*8}. Reasonably big in Europe and Canada (where they'd signed a deal with Alias Records), the band's OYSTERBAND-like political themes were appreciated across many borders, tracks such as 'Hangman Botha', 'Tory Heart', 'New Year's Honours' and 'New Statesman' finding a niche on other shores.

However, riled by some unworthy, upbeat pop mixes on follow-up album **LIP** (1991) {*4}, Swiss and Townend decided not to pursue that direction any further. On reflection, the decision to revamp the Temptations' soul classic 'Ball Of Confusion' was certainly ill-advised, but there was some meat and balls in the Who-meets-Bangles-ish 'The Greed Creed' – it wasn't exactly folk music, though. Ditto the un-foxy 'Reynard', which in the name alone promised a lot more. *MCS*

MALCOLM'S INTERVIEW

Jo/Josephine Swiss - vocals, keyboards, accordion / **Jon Townend** - vocals, guitar, fiddle, harmonica / **Martin Appleby** - bass, accordion, vocals / **David Allan** - drums, percussion, bass

UK Eggs Will Walk — US not issued

Jun 85. (12") *(EGG 1)* YOU DON'T LISTEN. / Cruel Mother

—— **David Wall** - bass, accordion, harmonica, vocals; repl. Appleby

Special Delivery — not issued

Sep 87. (7") *(SPEC45 002)* FINER POINTS OF FEELING. / BLOW THE MAN DOWN

Oct 87. (lp/c) *(SPD 1006/+C)* **BREAKFAST IN BEDLAM**
- Moving on / A hundred years / Blue and yellow / Sea never dry / Finer points of feeling / Mood must change / Blow the man down / It says here / Which side are you on? / Crime / Pound a week rise / Edge of darkness.

GOD'S LITTLE MONKEYS

retained the same line-up

Cooking Vinyl — Alias

Aug 89. (7") *(FRY 010)* SOUND OUT THE SYMBOLS. / Sea Never Dry

Oct 89. (lp/c/cd) *(COOK/+C/CD 022)* <A 005/+C/CD> **NEW MAPS OF HELL!**
- Pay that money down / Hangman Botha / Underneath the arches / Sound out the symbols / Minister for motivation / New Year's honours / Sea never dry / Tory heart / Where were you? / New statesman / Gas town / Whistle, daughter, whistle.

Feb 90. (7") *(FRY 013)* WHISTLE, DAUGHTER, WHISTLE. / Where Were You

Aug 91. (7") *(FRY 018)* YOU WIN SOME BUT LOSE MORE. / Too Many Flesh Suppers

Aug 91. (lp/c/cd) *(COOK/+C/CD 043)* <A 017/+C/CD> **LIP**
- Hollywood or the Humber / You win some but lose more / True colour / Too many flesh suppers / Reynard / Ball of confusion (that's what the world is today) / Defense of the wicked / Bare floor blues / Calgary cross / The greed creed.

—— split when remaining members Jo + Jon couldn't find a US deal

GOLDOOLINS

Acid-folk could be either dark and eerie or light and bubblegum-breezy, and it was very rarely a group could fit into both camps: GOLDOOLINS were in that small musical family.

Formed by former high school chums and Israeli nu-progsters E.T. Doolin (of Lord Flimnap) and O.D. Goldbart (you can see where the band name comes from), this English-language outfit was out there. (Multi-instrumentalist E.T. Doolin had released an eponymous CD in 2003 – think acoustic-Beatles.)

E.T. subsequently phoned home to invite wife Tadlik N. Doolin into the fold, and the trio became the Middle East equivalent of PETER, PAUL & MARY, with a healthy dose of PENTANGLE to boot. **GOLDOOLINS** (2004) {*6} flirted between the songs of O.D. ('Be My Friend', 'Ocean Song' and 'My Only Home') and those of E.T. ('I Know You're Not Alone' and 'Better Things'). 'Fain Would I Wed' was "lute-d" from 16th-century English composer Thomas Campion.

SONGS OF THE TURLY CRIO (2005) {*7} and **THE WORLD IS SOMEWHERE ELSE** (2006) {*7}, ventured further into their Beatles-meets-ESPERS sound, the latter also appealing to fans of lengthier FAIRPORT/DENNY-like songs with 'Ah! I See Horizons' and the title track. What are they up to now? *MCS*

O.D. Goldbart - vocals, multi / **E.T. Doolin** - vocals, multi / **Tadlik N. Doolin** - vocals, multi

UK Earsay — US not issued

Oct 04. (cd) *(ES 035)* **GOLDOOLINS** — Israel
- Be my friend / Better things / Fain would I wed / My only home / I'm doin' something / I know you're not alone / Twilight queen / Ooh phitome hashavti (and suddenly I thought) / Man (is light as a feather) / Ocean song / Waiting for the rain / Tishan habibi (Sleep dear boy).

Goldoolins — not issued

Nov 05. (cd) *(none)* **SONGS OF THE TURLY CRIO** — Israel
- Pretender's lament / Bed of wood / Fantasies / Find her / (Till then it's just) You and me in this world / Sheva shanin (Seven years) / The man he killed / Country traveler / Dusty / Song for Dodo.

Turly Crio — not issued

Dec 06. (cd) *(003)* **THE WORLD IS SOMEWHERE ELSE** — Israel
- 'Nother day / Ah! I see horizons / Buky, where art thou? / I am the grass / Yet to come / Green / One shot / Buky, lead the way to Highway 40 / My song / The world is somewhere else.

- (5-7*) compilations, others, etc.-

2008. (cd) *Turly Crio; (004)* **WE B GD'S U B U** — Israel
- I know you're not alone / Be my friend / My only home / Ocean song / Waiting for the rain / Tishan habibi (Sleep dear boy) / Twilight queen / Country traveler / Sheva shanim / 'Nother day / Ah! I see horizons / One shot / The world is somewhere else / Hackdasha / Gargir avack / Susei ha-parashim / Musings of a young sergeant major / Average midaged couple / Hackdasha nosephet / One day.

GONE TO EARTH

A thoroughly unique indie-thrash-punk-celtic-folk outfit formed in Manchester in 1984, GONE TO EARTH kicked off as a six-piece consisting of singer-songwriter/guitarist Dave Robinson, vocalist Jane Alexander, manic fiddler Dave Clarke, bassist Dave Thom (also on mandolin), electric guitarist Tudor (Sam Davis) and drummer Harry Hutchinson. After only a handful of gigs, Liverpool-based vinyl imprint Probe Plus offered them a contract, releasing their first of a handful of 12" EPs, 'Dogs Went Out The Window', in 1985. Like some East Of Eden tune ('Jig-A-Jig', possibly), or PLANXTY-meets-STEELEYE SPAN at their most raucous, their trad-esque reels ('Three Drummers', 'Magician' and 'Liverpool Hornpipe' were primeval examples) could virtually blow the roof off any gig.

Always filed behind The POGUES and MEN THEY COULDN'T HANG,

GONE TO EARTH (Jane had now made way for Brenda Kenny) tried everything to be different from their folk-pop-friendly peers, but drinking songs were hardly the solution. Subsequent full sets **FOLK IN HELL** (1986) {*7} and **VEGETARIAN BULLFIGHTER** (1987) {*6} were met with a muted response outside the indie fraternity. Half Man Half Biscuit had become the kingpins of the Probe stable, but GONE TO EARTH also had claims to a place among the big boys, especially as a live act. Their second album (featuring classy, fiddle-friendly opener 'Salford Rumble') was without Robinson, Kenny and Tudor, remaining members Clarke, Thom (now on vocals) and Hutchinson enlisting new bassist Andrew Wright Williams. Sadly, it was RIP for GTE in 1991. Not to be confused with the Australian guitar-pop act who worked under the same name from the late 1990s. *MCS*

Dave Robinson - guitar, vocals (lead after debut) / **Jane Alexander** - vocals / **Dave Clarke** - fiddle, vocals / **Tudor** (b. Sam Davis) - electric guitar / **Dave Thom** - bass, mandolin / **Harry Hutchinson** - drums

		UK Probe Plus	US not issued
Sep 85.	(12" ep) *(PP 14)* DOGS WENT OUT THE WINDOW	[ ]	[–]
	- Three drummers / Magician [live party version - Bombay mix] / Rose red / Liverpool hornpipe.		
	—— **Brenda Kenny** - vocals, percussion; repl. Jane		
	—— added guest Daz (spoons)		
Nov 85.	(12" ep) *(PP 15)* LIVE & BURIED	[ ]	[–]
	- Tippin' it up to Nancy / Rose of York / John Ryan's polka / Home by Bearna / Endbit.		
Sep 86.	(7") *(PP 20)* BLINDED IN LOVE. / Martin's One Horned Cow (live)	[ ]	[–]
	(12"+=) *(PP 20T)* - Never come back (version Viadukt magic mix).		
Nov 86.	(lp/c) *(probe 6/+c)* **FOLK IN HELL**	[ ]	[–]
	- No work today / Rose red / Wily old bachelor / Rendezvous / Snafu jig / Never come back / Three drummers (live) / Guns of love / Lubyanka stomp / B2 (live) / Gates of Heaven / Johnny stopped the tide. *(c+=)* - Blinded in love (long version) / Never come back (dub).		
	—— now without Robinson, Kenny + Tudor (**Clarke + Thom** now on vox) with **Hutchinson** plus **Andrew Wright Williams** - bass)		
Nov 87.	(lp/c) *(PROBE 15/+c)* **VEGETARIAN BULLFIGHTER**	[ ]	[–]
	- Salford rumble / Dear John / Did you really? / Foreign animals / Kelly's tractor / Only our rivers / Lie so well / Someday / Eh'la! / Be yourself.		

—— split in the late 1980s; Thom (and GONE TO EARTH newbie drummer Gavin Whelan, ex-James) would later join John Donaldson (ex-Levellers 5) in the band Calvin Party. Clarke turned up in mid-1990s outfit The She (one set, 'Penance'). Thom also played with Sonnenberg, who released 'Fishing In The Pool' (2006).

Jose GONZALEZ

Born in 1978 and raised by Argentinean parents, Jose grew up playing classical guitar and Brazilian bossa nova in the chilly environs of Gothenburg, Sweden. Although influenced by punk/hardcore (he released a single with Renascence for the label Destination in the 1990s), the JOSE GONZALEZ whom people raved over in the mid-2000s was an entirely different proposition, laid-back to the point of being horizontal.

Post-millennium, GONZALEZ was still concentrating on the domestic market, initially recording as JUNIP (with Tobias Winterkorn and Elias Araya) before striking out as a solo artist with a series of singles and his debut album **VENEER** (2003) {*8}. With a voice so unobtrusive as to be beyond low-key, the focus was on GONZALEZ's close-mic'd, heavy-fingered and engagingly ragged acoustic picking, a post-modern update of 1970s avant-folkies NICK DRAKE, AL STEWART, ELLIOTT SMITH and Mark Kozelek (Red House Painters).

The record finally saw a UK release in spring 2005 on prog-techno label Peacefrog, although it never really took off until Jose's sublime cover of The Knives' 'Heartbeats' was used on a striking Sony Bravia TV ad (the one with the coloured balls bouncing around a San Francisco street). Both the single and the album went UK Top 10 in early 2006, making him one of the most unlikely indie pop stars of his sadcore generation.

Clocking in at just over 30 minutes, the album achieved its effect through songs like 'Remain', 'Crosses', 'Lovestain', 'Deadweight On Velveteen' and 'Stay In The Shade'. One cut not included on this watershed neo-folk album was a reading of Kylie Minogue's 'Hand On Your Heart' – not his only cover, as he's also essayed such perennial gems as Joy Division's 'Love Will Tear Us Apart' and Bruce Springsteen's 'Born In The USA' and 'The Ghost Of Tom Joad'

Having churned out the odd vocal for electro kids Zero 7, Savath & Savalas and Plan B, it was time for GONZALEZ, once touted as a one-man SIMON & GARFUNKEL, to get back to solo singer-songwriter ground. **IN OUR NATURE** (2007) {*6}, his first on Mute US, was another restrained and introspective set. Soothing, melancholy and a little more passionate than its predecessor, the UK Top 20 album featured the anti-war/political 'How Low' and the singles 'Down The Line', 'Killing For Love' and his acoustic take on Massive Attack's 'Teardrop'.

Regaining indie status with JUNIP once again, Jose, Tobias and Elias were back in the limelight once again with their long-awaited debut set **FIELDS** (2010) {*6}. Not exactly building on GONZALEZ's folk credentials (it could be termed folktronica), the album touched on melancholy but upbeat jazz rhythms and Krautrock, the exceptions being 'Always', 'Without You' and 'Don't Let It Pass'. *MCS*

Jose Gonzalez - vocals, classical guitar, percussion

		UK	US
		Kakafoni	not issued
2003.	(7") *(KAKAFONI 2)* DEADWEIGHT ON VELVETEEN	[–]	Sweden [–]
		Imperial	not issued
2003.	(7") *(IMP 004S)* CROSSES. / Storm	[–]	Sweden [–]
	(cd-s+=) *(IMP 005CDS)* - Hints / Deadweight on velveteen.		
2003.	(cd) *(IMP 007CD)* **VENEER**	[–]	Sweden [–]
	- Slow moves / Remain / Lovestain / Heartbeats / Crosses / Deadweight on velveteen / All you deliver / Stay in the shade / Hints / Save your day / Broken arrows.		
2003.	(12") *(IMP 008T)* CROSSES (remix)	[–]	Sweden [–]
2004.	(7") *(IMP 010)* REMAIN. / Suggestions	[–]	Sweden [–]
	(cd-ep+=) *(IMP 009CDS)* - Lovestain / Love will tear us apart.		
2004.	(7") *(IMP 011S / SERV 012)* HAND ON YOUR HEART. / (other by JENS LEKMAN)	[–]	Sweden [–]
2004.	(cd-ep) *(IMP 016CDS)* STAY IN THE SHADE	[–]	Sweden [–]
2004.	(7") *(IMP 019S)* DOWN THE HILLSIDE	[–]	Sweden [–]
		Peacefrog	Hidden Agenda
Mar 05.	(7"/cd-s+=) *(PFG 065/+CD)* CROSSES. / Storm	[ ]	[–]
Apr 05.	(lp/cd) *(PFG 066/+CD)* <74> **VENEER**	[ ]	Aug 05 [ ]
Oct 05.	(cd-ep) *(PFG 069CD)* <81> STAY IN THE SHADE	[ ]	Jan 06 [ ]
	- Stay in the shade / Down the hillside / Sensing owls / Hand on your heart / Instr.		
Jan 06.	(7"/cd-s) *(PFG 076/+CD)* HEARTBEATS. / Suggestions	9	[–]
	(dvd-s) *(PFG 076DVD)* - ('A') / ('A'-live) / (live in London video documentary) / ('A'-Colour Like No Other video).		
Jan 06.	(lp/cd; re-) *(as prev)* **VENEER**	7	[–]
Apr 06.	(7"/cd-s; re-) *(PFG 065/+CDX)* CROSSES	[ ]	[–]
Jul 06.	(cd-s; re-) *(PFG 083CD)* HAND ON YOUR HEART / Down By The Hillside / Sensing Owls	29	[–]
		Peacefrog	Mute
Sep 07.	(7"/cd-s) *(PFG 112/+CD)* DOWN THE LINE. / Smalltown Boy	[ ]	[–]
Sep 07.	(cd/lp) *(PFG 114 CD/LP)* <69367-2/-1> **IN OUR NATURE**	19	[ ]
	- How low / Down the line / Killing for love / In our nature / Teardrop / Abram / Time to send someone away / The nest / Fold / Cycling trivialities.		
Nov 07.	(cd-s) *(PFG 116CD)* TEARDROP / Four Forks Ache	[ ]	[–]
Apr 08.	(cd-s) *(PFG 119CD)* KILLING FOR LOVE / Neon Lights	[ ]	[–]
Jul 08.	(12"ep) *(PFG 120-0)* IN OUR NATURE: remixes	[ ]	[–]
	- Killing for love / How low / Killing for love / In our nature / Fall on your knees - Madam (2).		

JUNIP

Jose's side-project with **Tobias Winterkorn** - keys / **Elias Araya** - drums

		Kakafoni	not issued
Oct 00.	(ltd-7") *(KAKAFONI 1)* STRAIGHT LINES	[–]	Sweden [–]
	- HC / Cut the rope / Dilettante / Straight lines.		
		Teme Shet	not issued
2005.	(10"ep/cd-ep) *(TEME 001 T/CD)* BLACK REFUGEE	[–]	Sweden [–]
	- Black refugee / Turn to the assassin / Official / Chugga-chugga / The ghost of Tom Joad.		
		City Slang	Mute
Jun 10.	(12"ep) *(SLANG 9550070)* ROPE & SUMMIT EP	[–]	Sweden [–]
	- Rope and summit / Far away / At the doors / Loops.		
Sep 10.	(cd/d-lp) *(SLANG 747888)* <9448-2/-1> **FIELDS**	[ ]	[ ]
	- In every direction / Always / Rope and summit / Without you / It's alright / Howl / Sweet and bitter / Don't let it pass / Off point / To the grain / Tide. *(3xcd-box-iss.+=; SLANG 748061)* - ROPE AND SUMMIT EP / Chickens / Azaleadalen / BLACK REFUGEE EP		

GORKY'S ZYGOTIC MYNCI

[folk part]

The Fontana folk years 1996-1998 proved to be GORKY'S ZYGOTIC MYNCI most commercially productive and enduring era. Welsh psych-progsters Euros Childs, Richard James and John Lawrence, plus relative newcomers

Megan Childs (on violin) and Osian Evans had had a hard time competing with their country's indie-pop counterparts Super Furry Animals – who, incidentally, could turn in the odd Welsh-speaking ditty.

Now more akin to another iconic valleys hero, MEIC STEVENS, or the sunny side of Scottish acid-folkers The INCREDIBLE STRING BAND, the Gorkys hit paydirt (and the Top 50) when trippy singles 'Patio Song' and the pixieish 'Diamond Dew' reached new heights. Parent set **BARAFUNDLE** (1997) {*9} was duly given the thumbs up: a slow burner in folk circles, apparently, though its original folk appeal and future freak-folk acceptance have deservedly come in time. If you're looking for evidence, set your controls for the heart of 'Starmoonsun', 'Heywood Lane', 'Cursed, Coined And Crucified', 'The Wizard And The Lizard' and the truly PLANXTY-like 'Sometimes The Father Is The Son'.

GORKY 5 (1998) {*5} was a let-down in comparison, with few signs of psych-folk within its grooves. The singles 'Sweet Johnny' and 'Let's Get Together (In Our Minds)' were more countryfied, although by the lilting finale 'Catrin' one was asking the question: why? *MCS*

Euros Childs - vocals, keys, synthesizer / **Richard James** - guitars, bass / **John Lawrence** - bass, guitars, keys / **Megan Childs** - violin / **Osian Evans** - drums

UK Fontana — US Fontana

Oct 96. (7"m/cd-s) *(GZM X/CD 1)* PATIO SONG. / No One Looked Around / Morwyr O Hyd Yn Lladd Eu Hun Ar Y Tir [41] [–]

Mar 97. (7"m/c-s/cd-s) *(GZM/+MC/CD 2)* DIAMOND DEW. / Queen Of Georgia / Tears In Disguise [42] [–]

Apr 97. (cd/c) *(<534 769-2/-4>)* **BARAFUNDLE** [46] [ ]
- Diamond dew / The Barafundle bumbler / Starmoonsun / Patio song / Better rooms ... / Heywood lane / Pen gwag glas / Bola bola / Cursed, coined and crucified / Sometimes the father is the son / Meirion Wylit / The wizard and the lizard / Miniature kingdoms / Dark night / Hwyl fawr i pawb / Wordless song.

Jun 97. (7"/c-s) *(GZM/+MC 3)* YOUNG GIRLS AND HAPPY ENDINGS. / DARK KNIGHT [49] [–]
(cd-s) *(GZMCD 3)* - Marching ants.

May 98. (7") *(GZM 4)* SWEET JOHNNY. / Un Hogyn Trist, Un Hogan Drist [60] [–]
(cd-s+=) *(GZMCD 4)* - Mifi mihafan.

Aug 98. (7"/cd-s) *(GZM/+CD 5)* LET'S GET TOGETHER (IN OUR MINDS). / Billy And The Sugarloaf Mountain / Hwiangerdd Mair [43] [–]

Aug 98. (cd/c/lp) *(558 822-2/-4/-1)* **GORKY 5** [67] [–]
- The tidal wave / Dyle fi / Let's get together (in our minds) / Tsunami / Not yet / Only the sea makes sense / Softly / Frozen smile / Sweet Johnny / Theme from Gorky 5 (Russian song) / Hush the warmth / Catrin.

GRACE NOTES (⟹ BOYLE, Maggie)

Richard GRAINGER

Born May 21, 1949, in Middlesbrough, Richard's earliest musical memories were of listening to his father playing the ukulele George Formby-style to his mother's singing.

Inspired by TV programmes such as 'Hallelujah' and 'Hullabaloo' in the first half of the 1960s, and by folk stars such BOB DYLAN, MARTIN CARTHY and DAVY GRAHAM, Richard began performing in clubs as a member (and writing partner of Ron Angel) in the Teesside Fettlers. The 1970s seemed to whizz by in Whitby, North Yorkshire, where he lived, only regular work in pubs and at the odd festival (with best friend Charles O'Connor of HORSLIPS) keeping the wolf from the door. GRAINGER's songs (especially 'Whitby Whaler' and 'Teesside And Yorkshire') were starting to attract attention, some of them gracing a handful of various-artists LPs.

Turning pro in 1984/85, Richard signed for Cumbrian-based independent Fellside Records, which produced his debut album **HERBS ON THE HEART** (1985) {*6}. A second set, **DARKLANDS** (1989) {*6}, dealt with rising unemployment in the north-east, while the collaboration **HOME ROUTES** (1990) {*6} cassette – with DICK MILES – featured some easy-going traditional ballads.

Nine years on, and having produced only one further set, **THUNDERWOOD** (1994) {*6}, with The HOUSE BAND's Chris Parkinson as sidekick, GRAINGER returned to his roots in Middlesbrough to record its history in **TOWN IN TIME** (1999) {*6}.

Following 2002's **WINGS OF ANGELS** {*5}, the release of his sea-shanty stage opera from 1997, **EYE OF THE WIND** (2004) {*6}, was a landmark achievement, marking the arrival of HM Bark Endeavour, a replica of Captain Cook's ship, on its trip from Australia. MIKE WATERSON, Jill Pidd, The Wilson Family, Stormalong John and The Keelers were all present and correct. Of late, GRAINGER has taken time to record and release (mail order only) a couple of CDs, **ON HEATHER AND CLARTY MOOR** (2006) {*5} and **WAR HORSE** (2008) {*6}. *MCS*

Richard Grainger - vocals, acoustic guitar

UK Fellside — US not issued

May 85. (lp/c) *(FE 038/+C)* **HERBS ON THE HEART** [ ] [–]
- Whitby whaler / Princess to a beggarman / Death of Nelson / The weaver and the factory maid / The isles of Shetland / Teeside and Yorkshire / Faithful sailor boy / Every time / Willie O'Reilly / Days at the end.

Folksound — not issued

Dec 89. (lp) *(FSLP 8)* **DARKLANDS** [ ] [–]
- Give us a job / Farewell to Angus / The whalerman's lament / Evergreen / The grey cock / The chemical workers' song / Born today / Barricades / Lowlands of Holland / The old pubs - The last light on the row / Darklands.

Brewhouse — not issued

Nov 90. (c; by RICHARD GRAINGER & DICK MILES) *(BHC 9008)* **HOME ROUTES** [ ] [–]
- The alimony run / Farewell to Angus / Our sheepshearing's done / Sir John Fenwick's the flower among them a' - Miss Maydell Armstrong / Rap 'er t bank - Farewell to the Monty - Celebrated working man / The Whitby whaler / The cot – Archie's fancy / Flying high / Cornish wassail / The buffalo skinners.

Folksound — not issued

Aug 94. (cd) *(FSCD 27)* **THUNDERWOOD** [ ] [–]
- Silent spring / Old Whitby town / Golden grove / Mallaig moorings / Northern town bay / Foxhunting song / Streets of Kings Cross / The mermaid / Polly on the shore / Glasgow wedding / Far from home / Grove fisherman / Ghost of old Solem / From Mulgrave to Eskside / Thunderwood.

self-rel. — not issued

1999. (cd) *(none)* **TOWN IN TIME** [–] mail-o [–]
- Middlesbrough / The Klondike song / The Linthorpe reel - Middlehaven / The ballad of James Readman / Trying hard to make ends meet / Come along by / The procession / Ring of iron / Cleveland brew / Teesside and Yorkshire / Teesside bridges / A day in Redcar / The chemical workers' song / Steelmen / Last night on the row / Give me a job / Football songs medley / Mujhe apni sharan mein - Ayresome march - Middlesbrough mela / The Evening Gazette / Roll river flow. *(re-iss. Jan 09 on Klondike; KCD 006)*

Klondike — not issued

2002. (cd) *(KCD 001)* **WINGS OF ANGELS** [–] mail-o [–]
- Zetland / My love is on board / Anchor up / Pity the poor / Sailor / Eastscar rocks.

(below narrated by Sir David Attenborough)

Feb 04. (cd) *(KCD 002)* **EYE OF THE WIND** [–] mail-o [–]
- Blake's endeavour / Farmers' toast / Come along by' / Eye of the wind / Brave Wolfe / James Cook of Cleveland / My Jimmy lad / Jack's maggot / Keel Row / College hornpipe / The resolution / Haul away / Rio lasses / Endeavour shanty.

Nov 04. (cd) *(KCD 003)* **ON HEATHER AND CLARTY MOOR** [–] mail-o [–]
- Teeside and Yorkshire / Mary of the Dale / Willy went to Westerdale / Iron miner's testimonial / Foxhunting song / Lyke wake dirge / T' auld wife of Coverdill / Cleveland home / The last coble fisherman / Ghost of old Solem / Lass o' Dalogill / Come along by Darklands / Lass o' Dalogill (reprise).

Jan 08. (cd) *(KCD 004)* **WAR HORSE** [–] mail-o [–]
- John the miller / Land and sea / The bold Trincomalee / Rockin' the cradle / Celebrated working man / Scarborough fair / Like the snow / The whaleboat Essex / Brigg fair / The wild goose / Haulin' the nets / Dark eyes.

David GRAY

Born David Peter Gray, June 13, 1968, at Sale in Manchester, GRAY has gone from backstreet singer-songwriter to international star, a modern-day folk-poet for a whole new bedsitter-to-coffeehouse generation.

As a boy of nine, David moved to Solva (in Pembrokeshire, Wales) with his family, where he discovered the joys of guitar-strumming while taking in the local punk-folk scene. In 1992, through manage and A&R man Rob Holden, he signed to Virgin offshoot Hut and issued his debut set **A CENTURY ENDS** (1993) {*6}, which displayed his tender and emotional songwriting skills. Check out 'Living Room', 'Wisdom' and the title track.

FLESH {*7} appeared one year later. Featuring Neill MacColl (son of EWAN MacCOLL) on slide guitar, the ten songs teeter between angst ('What Are You?') and romance ('Mystery Of Love', 'Falling Free' and the title track).

By now GRAY had made a promising name for himself, attracting a huge cult following around Britain and Europe. The two albums were not bad for someone who was still learning his trade, and comparisons to DYLAN, MIKE SCOTT, VAN MORRISON and even Eddie Vedder were bandied about like confetti at a wedding. The acoustic guitars, bouncing pedal steel and occasional piano made the stand-out tracks levitate above some contemporaries' attempts at melancholic music, proving GRAY to be one of Britain's best-kept secrets and filing him alongside Yorke and Ashcroft.

SELL, SELL, SELL (1996) {*6} was perhaps too melancholic for its own good, and didn't gain enough exposure to hit the shops in the UK. Nevertheless, it received some airplay from Radio One's Steve Lamacq (at least for opener 'Faster, Sooner, Now' and 'Gutters Full Of Rain'), and it went on to sustain GRAY's reputation in the alt-music world.

It was 1999's **WHITE LADDER** {*9}, on new imprint IHT, that caught the attention of critics and audiences alike. It was a fine album in which GRAY took us into the underworld of his soul, with tracks 'Sail Away' and Soft Cell's 'Say Hello Wave Goodbye' bringing something delicate and strangely human to the work.

Easily the highlight of the set was 'Babylon', a chart flop first time around, although album opener 'Please Forgive Me' compensated a little for this, clocking in at No.72. But what a difference a year can make: duly licensed to East West Records, 'Babylon' was re-promoted to a wider audience, and after massive playlisting it peaked at No.5. The resurrected parent album also climbed the charts post-millennium, rising to No.1 a whole year later. A newcomer of sorts despite his thirtysomething years and long paying of dues, GRAY proceeded to have three more major hits in 2001 with 'Please Forgive Me', 'This Years Love' and 'Sail Away'.

The sombre singer/songwriter returned in 2002 with **A NEW DAY AT MIDNIGHT** {*6}, an altogether more thoughtful and intimate set than his preceding classic. It included the soaring piano lament 'See You On The Other Side', a deep but uplifting exploration of GRAY's psyche. Another surefire hit with fans was the song 'Be Mine', a slight hark-back to his early days. It was the bitterly bitter-sweet sound of his piano on the frosty ballad 'December', though, that set him apart from many copyists.

UK chart-topper **LIFE IN SLOW MOTION** (2005) {*6}, featuring the hits 'The One I Love' and the talismanic 'Hospital Food', didn't bring much extra colour to GRAY's signature sound, a sound which had already spawned the pedestrian Daniel Blunt and James Powter.

Taking a sabbatical of sorts and signing with Mercer Street Records, GRAY returned with a new backing band (including American neo-traditionalist JOLIE HOLLAND and Annie Lennox) on his seventh studio album, **DRAW THE LINE** (2009) {*6}. **FOUNDLING** (2010) {*6} was another universal Top 20 hit, an ambitious double that had its origins as a projected side set from the same sessions as its predecessor. *MCS*

David Gray - vocals, guitar, keyboards / with session people

UK Hut — US Caroline

Nov 92. (12"ep/cd-ep) *(HUT/+CD 23)* BIRDS WITHOUT WINGS. / L's Song / The Light [ ] [–]
Mar 93. (12"ep/cd-ep) *(HUT/+CD 27)* SHINE. / Brick Walls / The Rice [ ] [–]
Apr 93. (cd/c/lp) *(CDHUT/HUTMC/HUTLP 9)* *<CAROL 1739>* **A CENTURY ENDS** [ ] Nov 93 [ ]
- Shine / A century ends / Debauchery / Let the truth sting / Gathering dust / Wisdom / Lead me upstairs / Living room / Birds without wings / It's all over. *(cd re-iss. Jul 01; CDHUTX 9) (d-cd-iss. Oct 02 on EMI+=; 543413-0)* - FLESH
Jul 93. (12"ep/cd-ep) *(HUT/+CD 32)* WISDOM. / Lovers / 4am [ ] [–]
Sep 94. (cd/c) *(CDHUT/HUTMC 17)* **FLESH** [ ] [–]
- What are you? / The light / Coming down / Falling free / Mystery of love / Lullaby / New horizons / Love's old song / Flesh. *<US cd-iss. Jul 00 on Vernon Yard; 39770>* *(cd re-iss. Jul 01; CDHUTX 17) (d-cd-iss.+=)* - A CENTURY ENDS

EMI — not issued

Apr 96. (cd) *(7243 8 37357)* **SELL, SELL, SELL** [–] Europe [–]
- Faster, sooner, now / Late night radio / Sell, sell, sell / Hold on to nothing / Everytime / Magdalena / Smile / Only the lonely / What am I doing wrong? / Gutters full of rain / Forever is tomorrow is today / Folk song. *(UK-iss. Jul 00; CDEMC 3755) <US-iss. Sep 00 on Nettwerk; ???>*

iht — ATO

Mar 99. (cd) *(ihtcd 001)* **WHITE LADDER** [ ] [–]
- Please forgive me / Babylon / My oh my / We're not right / Nightblindness / Silver lining / White ladder / This year's love / Sail away / Say hello wave goodbye.
Mar 99. (cd-s) *(ihtcds 001)* THIS YEAR'S LOVE / Nightblindness / Over My Head [ ] [–]
Jul 99. (cd-s) *(ihtcds 002)* BABYLON / Lead Me Upstairs (live) / New Horizons (live) [ ] [–]
Nov 99. (12")(cd-s) *(ihtv 001)(ihtcds 003)* PLEASE FORGIVE ME. / Please Forgive Me (Paul Hartnoll remix) [72] [–]
Apr 00. (re-cd) *(8573 82983-2)* *<21539>* **WHITE LADDER** [1] Jan 00 [ ]
Jun 00. (c-s/cd-s) *(EW 215 C/CD1)* *<radio cut>* BABYLON / Tell Me More Lies / Over My Head [5] Nov 00 [57]
(cd-s+=) *(EW 215CD2)* - ('A'-video).

eastwest — RCA

Aug 00. (re-cd) *<69351>* **WHITE LADDER** [–] [35]
Oct 00. (c-s) *(EW 219C)* PLEASE FORGIVE ME / (Paul Hartnoll remix) [18] [–]
(cd-s+=) *(EW 219CD)* - Babylon (live at the Point) (video).
Mar 01. (c-s/cd-s) *(EW 228 C/CD1)* THIS YEAR'S LOVE (strings remix) / Flame Turns Blue / The Lights Of London [20] [–]
(cd-s) *(EW 228CD2)* - ('A'-live) / Roots of love / Tired of me.
Jul 01. (c-s) *(EW 234C)* SAIL AWAY / (club mix) [26] [–]
(cd-s+=) *(EW 234CD)* - ('A'-Rae & Christian remix).
Dec 01. (cd-s) *(EW 244CD)* SAY HELLO WAVE GOODBYE (edit) [26] [–]
Oct 02. (cd) *(5046 61658-2)* *<68154>* **A NEW DAY AT MIDNIGHT** [1] 17 Nov 02 [ ]
- Dead in the water / Caroline / Long distance call / Freedom / Kangaroo / Last boat to America / Real love / Knowhere / December / Be mine / Easy way to cry / The other side.
Dec 02. (cd-s) *(EW 259CD)* THE OTHER SIDE / Lorelei / Decipher [35] [–]
Apr 03. (cd-s) *(EW 264CD)* BE MINE / Loverboy / Falling Down From The Mountainside (live 2002) [23] [–]

Atlantic — ATO

Sep 05. (7"/cd-s) *(ATUK 013/+CD)* THE ONE I LOVE. / Going In Blind (piano and strings version) [8] [–]
(cd-s) *(ATUK 013CDX)* - ('A'-acoustic) / With open arms / Everybody's leaving town.
Sep 05. (cd) *(5046 79766-2)* *<71068>* **LIFE IN SLOW MOTION** [1] [16]
- Alibi / The one I love / Lately / Nos da cariad / Slow motion / From here you can almost see the sea / Ain't no love / Hospital food / Now and always / Disappearing world.
Nov 05. (7"/cd-s) *(ATUK 018/+CD)* HOSPITAL FOOD. / Smile Like You Mean It (BBC Radio 1 live version) [34] [–]
(cd-s) *(ATUK 018CDX)* - ('A') / Baltimore (live at V2003) / Crimson lightning / ('A'-live at the Church studios 26.07.05).
Mar 06. (7") *(ATUK 027)* ALIBI. / Golden Ray [71] [–]
(cd-s) *(ATUK 027CD)* - ('A') / Tracer.
(cd-s) *(ATUK 027CDX)* - ('A'-live) / Long gone now / Sacred ground / ('A'-video).
Nov 07. (cd-s) *(ATUK 071CD1)* YOU'RE THE WORLD TO ME [53] [–]
(cd-s+=) *(ATUK 071CD2)* - Song to the siren.

Polydor — Mercer Street

Sep 09. (cd-s) *(2715673)* FUGITIVE / Jitterbug [ ] [–]
Sep 09. (cd) *(2712298)* *<DWT 70109>* **DRAW THE LINE** [5] [12]
- Fugitive / Draw the line / Nemesis / Jackdaw / Kathleen / First chance / Harder / Transformation / Stella the artist / Breathe / Full steam. *(d-cd+=; 2716841)* - (Live at the Roundhouse):- World to me / Sail away / Ain't no love / Babylon / Slow motion / The one I love / The other side / Nightblindness.
Dec 09. (dl-s) *(-)* FULL STEAM [ ] [–]
Jul 10. (dl-s) *(-)* A MOMENT CHANGES EVERYTHING [ ] [–]
Aug 10. (cd/lp) *(2745353)* *<DWT 70193-2/-1>* **FOUNDLING** [18] [9]
- Only the wine / Foundling / Forgetting / Gossamer thread / The old chair / In God's name (for Bryan part 1) / We could fall in love again tonight / Holding on / When I was in your heart / A new day at midnight / Davey Jones' locker. *(w/ free cd+=)* - Fixative (for Bryan part 2) / Morning theme / The dotted line / A million years / Who's singing now / Old Father Time / Indeed I will / A moment changes everything.

- (8-10*) compilations -

Nov 07. (cd) *Atlantic; (5144 24164-2) / ATO; <21591-2>* **GREATEST HITS** [11] [96]
- You're the world to me / Babylon / The one I love / Please forgive me / Be mine / Hospital food / This year's love / Alibi / Sail away / Shine (live at the Hammersmith Apollo) / Caroline / The other side / Flame turns blue / Destroyer.

- (5-7*) compilations, etc.-

Jul 00. (cd) *iht; (IHTCD 002) / ATO; <69375>* **LOST SONGS 95–98** [ ] Apr 01 [ ]
- Flame turns blue / Twilight / Hold on / As I'm leaving / If your love is real / Tidal wave / Falling down the mountainside / January rain / Red moon / A clean pair of eyes / Wurlitzer.
Feb 01. (re;cd/c) *eastwest; (<8573 86953-2/-4>)* **LOST SONGS 95–98** [7] [ ]
Jul 01. (cd) *Hut; (CDHUT 67)* **THE EP'S 1992-1994 ALBUM** [68] [ ]
Oct 02. (d-cd) *Hut; (543414-0)* **SELL, SELL, SELL / THE EP'S 1992–1994 ALBUM** [ ] [–]
Mar 07. (cd) *Hut; (CDHUT 88)* *<88479>* **SHINE: THE BEST OF THE EARLY YEARS** [ ] [ ]
- Shine / Late night radio / Coming down / Birds without wings / The light / Everytime / A century ends / Lullaby / Faster, sooner, now / Wisdom / Falling free / Sell, sell, sell / Debauchery / Flesh / Hold on to nothing.

Clive GREGSON and Christine COLLISTER

Often compared to sometime folk former celebrity duo RICHARD & LINDA THOMPSON, CLIVE GREGSON & CHRISTINE COLLISTER were prominent over a timespan that covered many years with mixed results.

Clive's roots were firmly planted in power-pop/pub-rock outfit

Any Trouble (from 1976 to 1984), a quartet reaching out to post-new wave audiences in the wake of labelmate star attraction Elvis Costello. Underachievers by the era's standards, the upbeat group managed to slip under the chart radar with four studio LPs, two for Stiff Records – 'Where Are All The Nice Girls?' (1980) and 'Wheels In Motion' (1981) – and a couple for EMI America, 'Touch And Go' (1983) and 'Wrong End Of The Race' (1984). Ironically, album two revamped RICHARD THOMPSON's 'Dimming Of The Day'.

GREGSON had dipped a toe into folk via his studio work with promising act TICKAWINDA, but nothing was cast in stone until 1985's solo debut, **STRANGE PERSUASIONS** {*6}. Not too far removed from the sound of his mentor/boss THOMPSON (or a polished RALPH McTELL backed by Squeeze), the record straddled singer-songwriter folk and FM-friendly AOR, examples including 'Home Is Where The Heart Is' (a rare single) and 'Jewel In Your Crown'. Subsequent production work for GREGSON included records by OYSTERBAND, KEITH HANCOCK and Irish-Canadian STEPHEN FEARING.

Catching a performance by Christine at a bar in Manchester (she had previously sung and strummed in Italy), Clive was quick to see the potential of the young singer, who soon joined him in session work for RICHARD THOMPSON. As CLIVE GREGSON & CHRISTINE COLLISTER, the duo first surfaced on live set **HOME AND AWAY** (1986) {*7}. A shoestring-budget, cassette-only release initially sold at gigs, it featured a handful of Any Trouble retreads alongside covers of Merle Haggard's 'Mama Tried', Carl Perkins's 'Matchbox', Whitfield-Strong's 'I Heard It Through The Grapevine', Larry Williams's 'Slow Down', Eric Kaz's 'I'm Blowin' Away' and his friend HANCOCK's 'Chase The Dragon'. That same year, the sensuous and unmistakable voice of COLLISTER was heard on the theme tune ('Warm Love Gone Cold') of TV drama series 'The Life And Loves Of A She-Devil'.

Often regarded as their official debut, although the previous set had already been served up on Cooking Vinyl (Flying Fish in America), **MISCHIEF** (1987) {*6} kicked off with the bluesy 'I Wouldn't Treat A Dog' (another rare 45), while their blend of Brit-folk-pop was squarely stuck in the middle between Fleetwood Mac harmonies and Delta blues on tracks like 'Everybody Cheats On You' and 'This Tender Trap'.

A CHANGE IN THE WEATHER (1989) {*7}, which featured an interpretation of the 1950s McCoy-Singleton nugget 'Tryin' To Get To You', and covers set **LOVE IS A STRANGE HOTEL** (1990) {*4}, carried the couple into a new decade, although the latter departure was a shade self-indulgent, retreading material from the unlikeliest of sources including 10cc ('The Things We Do For Love'), Del Amitri ('Move Away Jimmy Blue'), Aztec Camera ('How Men Are'), Bruce Springsteen ('One Step Up'), and Paul Carrack ('Always Better With You').

With their relationship coming to an abrupt but dignified end, **THE LAST WORD** (1992) {*7} was similar in many respects to the THOMPSONs' parting/farewell album of a decade earlier, 'Shoot Out The Lights'. Ex-Bible songsmith BOO HEWERDINE was roped in for three songs (a cool blend of all things roots), although real heartache and emotion shine through on 'This Broken Home', 'I Don't Want To Lose You' and the countrified 'Close Down This Bar'. COLLISTER went on to perform alongside The Jailbirds, a part-time outfit comprising BARB JUNGR and Heather Joyce.

Taking time to brush themselves down, both finally emerged as full-fledged solo artists in the mid-1990s, GREGSON with a couple of fair-to-middling albums, **PEOPLE AND PLACES** (1995) {*4} and **I LOVE THIS TOWN** (1996) {*6}. COLLISTER's two studio sets for Fledg'ling Records, **BLUE ACONITE** (1996) {*5} and **THE DARK GIFT OF TIME** (1998) {*7}, featured a wealth of choice covers in 'How Far To The Horizon?' (Jesse Winchester), 'Private Storm' (Sam Phillips), 'Can't Win' (RICHARD THOMPSON), 'Paper Wings' (GILLIAN WELCH & DAVE RAWLINGS), 'Heart Like A Wheel' (ANNA McGARRIGLE), 'Midnight Feast' (LAL WATERSON & OLIVER KNIGHT), 'Blue Moon On The Rise' (JULIE MATTHEWS & CHRIS WHILE), 'Harvest For The World' (The Isley Brothers), 'Broken Bicycles' + 'Dirt In The Ground' (Tom Waits), 'The Whole Night Sky' (BRUCE COCKBURN), 'Deeper Well' (Emmylou Harris), 'I Want To Vanish' (Elvis Costello), 'Black Eyed Dog' (NICK DRAKE), 'God Bless The Child' (Billie Holiday), 'Lowish Time' (HELEN WATSON), 'Free Will And Testament' (Robert Wyatt) and 'Sad And Beautiful World' (Colin Linden).

COLLISTER also joined forces with another four of the best modern-day Brit-folk females in supergroup DAPHNE'S FLIGHT (featuring HELEN WATSON, MELANIE HARROLD, JULIE MATTHEWS and CHRIS WHILE) for a one-off CD in 1995.

Moving from Demon to Fellside Records (and now based in Nashville), the reflective and brooding GREGSON delivered a series of decent albums in the form of **HAPPY HOUR** (1999) {*6}, **COMFORT AND JOY** (2002) {*7} and **LONG STORY SHORT** (2004) {*7}. Comeback set **BITTERSWEET** (2011) {*7} confirms the singer-songwriter is back to his best.

COLLISTER, meanwhile, found her way on to the roster of stalwart folk imprint Topic, delivering a couple of part-original, part-covers albums, **AN EQUAL LOVE** (2001) {*6} – interpreting Sarah McLachlan's 'Full Of Grace' and Henry Mancini's 'Moon River' – and **INTO THE LIGHT** (2002) {*5}. The latter featured songwriting by BARB JUNGR and readings of U2's 'I Still Haven't Found What I'm Looking For' (very Alison Moyet), Paul Simon's 'Quiet', Roddy Frame's 'Hymn To Grace' and Kit Hain's 'Lost And Found'.

Of late, Christine has self-released a few solo CDs, while the Beat Goes On label documented her **LIVE** (2008) {*6} set with bluesman Dave Kelly & The Travelling Gentlemen. A torch-folk record of sorts, this collection reprises SANDY DENNY's 'Who Knows Where The Time Goes?', TOWNES VAN ZANDT's 'Pancho And Lefty', Jackson Browne's 'World In Motion' and a few select Brill Building numbers. *MCS*

CLIVE GREGSON

Clive Gregson (b. Jan 4, 1955, Ashton-under-Lyne, Manchester, England) - vocals, guitar, keyboards (ex-Any Trouble) / with **Christine Collister** (b. Dec 28, 1961, Douglas, Isle Of Man) - guitar, percussion, vocals

UK Demon — US not issued

Apr 85. (7") *(D 1036)* HOME IS WHERE THE HEART IS. / Could This Be The One [ ] [–]

Apr 85. (lp/c) *(FIEND/+CASS 45)* **STRANGE PERSUASIONS** [ ] [–]
- Summer rain / Jewel in your crown / I still see her face / Home is where the heart is / Play the fool / Poor relation / This town / The safety net / Could this be the one? [US cd-only*] / American car / I fall apart. *(cd-iss. Jan 90; FIENDCD 45) (<US cd-iss. 1995 & UK Jan 04 on Compass+=; 4229-2>)*

CLIVE GREGSON & CHRISTINE COLLISTER

self-rel. — not issued

Nov 86. (c) *(none)* **HOME AND AWAY** (live Feb-Mar 86) [–] gigs [–]
- It's all just talk / Mama tried / Home is where the heart is / All the time in the world / Unlucky in love / Matchbox / When my ship comes in / I heard it through the grapevine / Chase the dragon / As lovers do / All because of you / Northern soul / Touch and go / Slow down / I'm blowing away. *(re-iss. Jan 87 on 'Cooking Vinyl'; COOK 003) <US-iss.1987 on Flying Fish; FF-473> (cd-iss. Jul 89; COOKCD 003) (re-iss. May 90 lp/c/cd; BAKE/+C/CD 002) <cd-iss. 1995; FF 90-473> (cd re-iss. Jul 06 on Gott Discs; 044) (cd re-iss. May 09 on Beat Goes On; BGOCD 880)*

Special Delivery — Rhino

Sep 87. (lp/c/cd) *(SPD/+C/CD 1010)* *<R1/R4/R2-70842>* **MISCHIEF** [ ] 1990 [ ]
- I wouldn't treat a dog / Everybody cheats on you / That same mistake / I specialise / We're not over yet / Not a day passes / Rain on your parade / I wonder what went wrong / This tender trap / I will be there / Wash me away / No word of a lie. *(cd re-mast. May 07 on Gott Discs+=; 061)* - Lost at sea / Farewell note / I wouldn't treat a dog. *(cd re-iss. May 09 on Beat Goes On; BGOCD 881)*

— re-recruited **Phil Barnes** + **Martin Hughes** (ex-Any Trouble)

Feb 88. (12"ep) *(SPET12 003)* I WOULDN'T TREAT A DOG / I Wonder What Went Wrong. / The Tender Trap / Everybody Cheats On You [ ] [–]

Feb 89. (lp/c/cd) *(SPD/+C/CD 1022)* *<R1/R4/R2-70914>* **A CHANGE IN THE WEATHER** [ ] [ ]
- This is the deal / Blessing in disguise / (Don't step in) My blue suede shoes / Tryin' to get to you / How weak I am / Temporary sincerity / Blues on the run / Voodoo doll / Standing in your shadow / Jumped up madam / Talent will out. *(cd re-iss. May 09 on Beat Goes On; BGOCD 883)*

GREGSON & COLLISTER

Oct 90. (lp/c/cd) *(SPD/+C/CD 1035)* *<R4/R2-70961>* **LOVE IS A STRANGE HOTEL** [ ] Nov 90 [ ]
- The things we do for love / Move away Jimmy Blue / How men are / Love is a strange hotel / Even a fool would let go / One step up / For a dancer / (I heard that) Lonesome whistle / Same situation / Always better with you / Today I started loving you again / The most beguiling eyes.

Mar 92. (cd/c) *(SPD CD/C 1045)* *<R2/R4-70282>* **THE LAST WORD** [ ] [ ]
- I know something / Here I go again / This broken home / Snow in Philadelphia / I could be happy / I shake / I don't want to lose you / She's meeting a man / Last man alive / Close down this bar / Could this be the one?

- (8-10*) compilations, etc.-

Oct 06. (cd) *Gott Disc; (054)* **THE BEST OF CLIVE GREGSON & CHRISTINE COLLISTER**
- This is the deal / It's all just talk / I shake / Home is where the heart is / I wouldn't treat a dog / All the time in the world / I specialise / Love is a strange hotel / How weak I am / Here I go again / We're not over yet / (Don't step in) My blue suede shoes / Touch and go / Wash me away / Tryin' to get to you / Northern soul / Could this be the one? *(re-iss. May 09 on Beat Goes On; BGOCD 882)*

Dec 06. (cd-s) *Gott Disc; (056)* HOME IS WHERE THE HEART IS / (Don't Step In) My Blue Suede Shoes / Could This Be The One

CLIVE GREGSON

Demon Compass

Apr 95. (cd) *(FIENDCD 764) <4227-2>* **PEOPLE & PLACES** Mar 95
- Camden Town / Feathers / Mary's divorce / Gabriel / My eyes gave the game away / Medicine house / Black train coming / Box number / Blue rose / My favourite lies / Restless / Lily of the valley / When this war is over. *(re-iss. Jan 04; same as US)*

Sep 96. (cd) *(FIENDCD 786) <4234-2>* **I LOVE THIS TOWN** Aug 96
- I love this town / Tattoo / Love casts a long shadow / Jericho junction / Lonely street / Things I didn't do / Geography / Secondhand car / Rumour factory / The cross I bear / Ramshackle road / My brilliant past. *(re-iss. Jan 04; same as US)*<i>(dl re-iss. 2010 on Gregsongs+=; CGCD 1001)* - Jericho junction (reprise).

Fellside Compass

Mar 99. (cd) *(FECD 141) <4266-2>* **HAPPY HOUR**
- I get what I deserve / Fred Astaire / Nothing ever lasts / Cause for complaint / Melody / True beauty / Firefly / Come home soon / Salt / I would have walked away / How could I resist? / Until we meet again / There comes a time.

Jan 02. (cd) *(FECD 164) <4336-2>* **COMFORT AND JOY** Mar 02
- Frances O'Connor / Antidote / Fingerless gloves / I'm there for you / It's you I want to hold / If I was your lover / Catholic girl / White suit of notes / Riding on a bus / Pretty Peggy-o / String of pearls / Comfort and joy.

Fellside Gadfly

May 04. (cd) *(FECD 184) <GAD 288>* **LONG STORY SHORT** Sep 04
- Cornerstone / Over the garden wall / Ghosts / Wintertime / My bitter half / Paper dolls / I never learned a thing about you / My other life / All my stories / Jenny / Your love / Joan of Arkansas / I remember you / Goldfish bowl / Cool cool rain.

Full Fill not issued

May 11. (cd) *(ffcd 133)* **BITTERSWEET**
- Bittersweet / Come around / Julianne / A little more love / Sunny left town / Till you get home / One for the trees / The door is open / Back where I belong / I think I am falling in love / Start again / Daisy chain / That's the thing about love / Without you. *(d-cd+=; ffcd 133s)* - Pay no never mind / As long as there is love / Rings / Everything will be fine / The other side of love / Right back to you.

- (8-10*) compilations -

Jan 90. (lp/c/cd) *Special Delivery; (SPD/+C/CD 1026)* **WELCOME TO THE WORKHOUSE** [solo recordings from 1980–85]
- Standing in your shadow / No idea / First time behind the wheel (please don't stop) / Time does not heal / Trouble with love / Human heart / I'll be your man / This tender trap / You'd better go home / Give me a chance / She'll belong to me / She's out of my life.

Apr 09. (cd) *Gregsongs; (CGCD 12287)* **THE BEST OF CLIVE GREGSON**
- I love this town / Antidote / Home is where the heart is / Trouble with love / Fred Astaire / Cornerstone / Touch and go / Camden Town / Fingerless gloves / Jericho junction / Jewel in your crown / Cool, cool rain / Feathers / Summer rain / Tattoo / Black train coming / Comfort and joy / There comes a time.

- (5-7*) compilations, etc.-

May 95. (cd) *Gregsongs; (CGCD 9401)* **CAROUSEL OF NOISE** [live/unreleased]
- I shake / Second choice / Telephone lines / Cozac - Hinxworth / The queen's head / Peggy Sue / Lonesome whistle / Dead man's shoes / That same mistake / The minute you're gone / Stay another day / Highlands in January - Kiss the girls / I'm gonna take my own advice / Learning the game / It doesn't take much / I was in chains / It's all just talk. *(re-iss. Aug 02 on Fellside; FECD 169)*

Aug 10. (mp3) *Gregsongs; (-)* **FORWARD INTO REVERSE**
- I'm still rockin' / My front door / I lost you / Hey Ginnie / Forget me not / Fortune teller / Beck and call / Mojo / Turn ugly overnight / Insecurity / Ragamuffin / If I thought for one moment / You don't love me no more.

CHRISTINE COLLISTER

BBC not issued

Sep 86. (7") *(RESL 199)* WARM LOVE GONE COLD. / Cavatina (from Act 2 of The Marriage of Figaro)
(12"+=) *(12RESL 199)* - ['A'-extended] / For Lucille.

Fledg'ling Green Linnet

Sep 94. (cd) *(FLECD 1004) <GLCD 3106>* **LIVE** (at The Gaiety Theatre, Douglas, Isle Of Man) 1995
- Last chance Texaco / Starting all over / The bird that I held in my hand / Trying to get to you / Easy terms / Outside myself / I keep forgettin' / Human nature / Guilty / Two time tango / Warm love gone cold / Twenty-nine ways to my baby's door / Ruby / Shades of Scarlett conquering / Love me like a man.

Oct 96. (cd) *(FLED 3010)* **BLUE ACONITE**
- How far to the horizon? / Private storm / Can't win / Paper wings / Kicking in my stall / Heart like a wheel / Forever he said / Midnight feast / Blue moon on the rise / Harvest for the world / Broken bicycles.

Mar 97. (cd-ep) *(CING 4001)* HORIZON EP
- How far to the horizon / Harvest for the world / How will I ever be simple again / Guilty / Mirage.

Fledg'ling Koch Int.

Apr 98. (cd) *(FLED 3016) <KOC-CD 8022>* **THE DARK GIFT OF TIME** Sep 98
- The whole night sky / Dirt in the ground / Deeper well / I want to vanish / Black eyed dog / Point Scarlett / God bless the child / Lowish time / Always there / Free will and testament / Sad and beautiful world.

Topic Topic

May 01. (cd) *(<TSCD 1001>)* **AN EQUAL LOVE** Aug 02
- Waiting for my prayer / Can't cry hard enough / Full of grace / Venus proud / An equal love / It's raining everyday / Give it up / Motherless child / Extra care / In the beginning / Moon river.

Sep 02. (cd) *(<TSCD 1002>)* **INTO THE LIGHT** Mar 03
- Ashlands / Hymn to grace / Lost and found / Act of kindness / A kinder heart / Brittle man / Fallen angel / Like mercury / Endlessly / Little bird / I still haven't found what I'm looking for / Quiet.

Stereoscout not issued

Apr 04. (cd) *(none)* **HOME** (live) own
- Lowish time / Kicking in my stall / Act of kindness / Broken bicycles / Waiting for my prayer / Sad and beautiful world / Vincent / Deeper well / God bless the child / It's all just talk / Warm love gone cold / Extra care / I still haven't found what I'm looking for / Songbird.

Jan 06. (cd) *(none)* **LOVE ...** own
- Time in a bottle / Mad, mad me / I've got you under my skin / Hallelujah / The man with the child in his eyes / Amelia / Lighter than air / The moon's a harsh mistress / The air that I breathe / Who knows where the time goes? / For all we know.

Beat Goes On not issued

Jul 08. (cd; as CHRISTINE COLLISTER, DAVE KELLY & THE TRAVELLING GENTLEMEN) *(BGOCD 823)* **LIVE** [live May 2005]
- Mockingbird / Pancho and Lefty / Boulder to Birmingham / World in motion / Sad and beautiful world / Who knows where the time goes? / Anyhow, I love you / 110 in the shade / Kicking in my stall / Guilty / Baby what you want / Lost and found / Private number / Clapping song / Let it be me.

- (5-7*) compilations, etc.-

Sep 99. (cd) *Fledg'ling; (<FLED 3025>)* **SONGBIRD** Feb 00
- Kicking in my stall / How far to the horizon? / Guilty / Can't cry hard enough / Black eyed dog / Driving past / How will I ever be simple again / Starting all over / Free will and testament / Broken bicycles / Cornfield / Point Scarlett / I keep forgetting / Track of my tears / Songbird.

Charlotte GREIG

Born August 10, 1954 in Malta (her father was in the Navy), Charlotte's youth was spent in Charsfield in Suffolk, Luccombe in Somerset and a convent boarding school in Broadstairs, Kent, where she was taught piano. She went on to study philosophy at Sussex University.

A career in journalism in the 1980s led to her having books published, one of which, 'Will You Still Love Me Tomorrow' (about girl groups in pop music), was made into a six-part series for BBC Radio One, which she presented. Many may recognise her name as a reviewer of roots music for Mojo magazine around the late 1990s, and she continues to write novels, plays, and of course music.

Recording five CDs in total, the traditionally-biased singer-songwriter (who had relocated to Cardiff) performed mainly on harmonium, although dulcimer and acoustic guitar played a part in her recordings too. Her 1998 debut was **NIGHT VISITING SONGS** {*6}, and, inspired by folk legend LAL WATERSON and gothic-folkie NICO (after her time with the Velvet Underground), Charlotte and her trusty multi-instrumentalist sidekick Julian Hayman produced four more solo sets – **DOWN IN THE VALLEY** (2000) {*6}, **AT LLANGENNITH** (2001) {*6}, **WINTER WOODS** (2003) {*6} and **QUITE SILENT** (2005) {*7}.

The last-named album included a musical adaptation of W.B. Yeats's poem 'The Lake Isle of Innisfree' and several mediaeval ballads such as 'Under The Leaves', 'Rosemary Lane', 'The Lark In The Morning' and 'All Things Are Quite Silent'.

Sadly for folk fans, since her last album Charlotte has concentrated mainly on literary work, but there is something in the pipeline to do with 'Dr Freud's Cabaret', her 2010 musical theatre play in collaboration with Anthony Reynolds (ex-Jack, ex-Jacques). *MCS*

Charlotte Greig - vocals, harmonium, dulcimer, acoustic guitar

UK Harmonium — US not issued

Oct 98. (cd) *(HM 713)* **NIGHT VISITING SONGS** ☐ ⊟
- Vine leaves / Lucky in love / Gathering rushes / Bury me / Seven seas / The grey cock / A passenger / Lucy Wan / Searching for lambs / Crows.

—— added **Julian Hayman** - multi + **Edward James** - guitar, vocals

Mar 00. (cd) *(HM 719)* **DOWN IN THE VALLEY** ☐ ⊟
- Trees / The cruel mother / Down in the valley / Black name / Take me home / The wondrous cross / House of pain / Here I stand / To make you stay / The bells of paradise / All through the night / Shadow in a dream.

May 01. (cd) *(HM 840)* **AT LLANGENNITH** ☐ ⊟
- At Llangennith / Willie O'Winsbury / That man / Free fall / Perfect wave / Walk on / The snows / Gotta get you home / Over the water / Leave it blue.

Apr 03. (cd) *(HM 725)* **WINTER WOODS** ☐ ⊟
- Oh novelty / Stained glass window / Wind on the river / Cotton crown / Shallow brown / Winter woods / Twin stars / Wychanger / The cuckoo / Heaven.

Jul 05. (cd) *(HM 208)* **QUITE SILENT** ☐ ⊟
- Under the leaves / Bury me here / Go from my window / I wish, I wish / Makeless / On a virgin plain / The garden at dawn (interlude) / The generous lover / Rosemary Lane / The lark in the morn / Blowing wind / All things are quite silent / Innisfree.

Sara GREY

Born March 22, 1940, in Boston, Massachusetts, but raised in New England and New Hampshire, SARA GREY is an honorary Brit, having subsequently lived in Scotland for nearly forty years and in England for four. Her omission from Volume I was not accidental.

For a good decade across the late 1950s and the 1960s, Sara studied the fine arts and achieved a BFA with honours in theatre, art and speech. Integrating life as a teacher with an acting career, she travelled to areas of America (from Ohio and Montana to New York and Pennsylvania) that specialised in mountain music. She'd explored their folklore and old-timey history while collating a host of recordings in her various banjo-plucking safaris throughout the States.

In 1970, with the help of friend ED TRICKETT, she completed her first and only American release. **SARA GREY** {*6} was met with a muted response from a country in transition from folk to country music. Falling in love with Britain (her son Kieron Means's father Andrew was once a Melody Maker journalist), Sara established herself in the UK, where a string of collaborative albums with Ellie Ellis was issued by Cumbrian-based imprint Fellside. **A BREATH OF FRESH AIR** (1982) {*6}, **MAKING THE AIR RESOUND** (1985) {*5} and **YOU GAVE ME A SONG...** (1988) {*5} – the latter for Greenwich Village Records – showed her pride in bringing the traditional roots of America and beyond to British shores.

With her accompanists The Lost Nation Band (ROGER WILSON and DAVE BURLAND – the latter a replacement for BRIAN PETERS), the 1990s were just as enlightening, with solo albums **PROMISES TO KEEP** (1990) {*6}, **SARA** (1994) {*6} and **BACK IN THE AIRLY DAYS** (1998) {*6} coming out through the Harbourtown and Waterbug imprints.

In 2002, GREY teamed up with her son Kieron and fiddler Kate Lissauer on a back-to-basics set,

BOY, SHE'S A DAISY: NORTH AMERICAN SONGS & BALLADS {*6}. Sara and Kate were credited on Kieron's 'Run Mountain' set the same year, while Grey also supported Kieron on another album, 'Far As My Eyes Can See'. He returned the favour on mum's subsequent works, including two Fellside comebacks, **A LONG WAY FROM HOME** (2005) {*6} and the excellent Appalachian-trail set **SANDY BOYS** (2009) {*7}. *MCS*

Sara Grey - vocals, banjo, dulcimer, autoharp / first with **Ed Trickett**

UK not issued — US Folk Legacy

1970. (lp) *<FSI-38>* **SARA GREY** ⊟ ☐
- Rigs of rye / The two sisters / The horse trader's song / Few days / Open the door softly / Fair flower of Northumberland / Fiddlers green / The Texas rangers / Raspberry lane / Boatman / Grey funnel line / Cobweb of dreams. *<cd-iss. Oct 10; CD-38>*

SARA GREY & ELLIE ELLIS

Fellside — not issued

1982. (lp) *(FE 031)* **A BREATH OF FRESH AIR** ☐ ⊟
- Going to Little Creek - Big Liza / Wintry winds / Freighting from Wilcox to Globe / Jolly raftsman, O - Lake of the Caogama boatman - Sandy river belle / Going out west this fall / Turtle dove / Train on the island / Cole Younger / Sally in the garden - Frosty morning / Rowley's tax list / Lonesome roving wolves / Some little bug / Parting friends.

May 85. (lp) *(FE 039)* **MAKING THE AIR RESOUND** ☐ ⊟
- The bayou Sara / The goodnight loving trail / Dear honey / Little birdie – Washington's march - Waiting for Nancy / Love was the price / The old granite state / Knoxville girl / Aragon mill - New wood / Cobweb of dreams / Bull at the wagon / Let your light from the lighthouse shine on me / Friends and neighbours.

Greenwich Village — Greenwich Village

May 88. (lp) (*<GVR 231>*) **YOU GAVE ME A SONG...** ☐ 1987 ☐
- Mae Smith / Why do you stand there in the rain / Shoes and stockings - Old Mother Flanagan / I'd like to go home / Ground so poor / 40s medley: I'll be seeing you - Where or when / Go to work on Monday / Pinwherry dip / If I could be the rain / Will you miss me / Her bright smile haunts me still / Shady grove - Kitchen girl / Quiet people.

SARA GREY

Harbourtown — not issued

Jul 90. (lp/c) *(HAR/+C 011)* **PROMISES TO KEEP** ☐ ⊟
- I love you well / Lakes of Champplain / La belle Riviere / Sweet William's ghost / Jenny's gone to Ohio - Cider mill / Oh death / Dry stone walls / Lady of Carlisle / Mervin Barr / The sky / Going away / Sunrise / Nice like that. *(cd-iss. 2000; HARCD 011)*

1994. (cd) *(HARCD 028)* **SARA** ☐ ⊟
- Prodigal son / State of Arkansas / Banks of Kilrea / Unfortunate rake / As I roved out / Miss Julia - The day I fought Dwyer - The kissing song / Sweet William / My God he is a rock / Betsy liken - Sadie at the back door / The lady gay / Johnny Barden / Going to leave this country / High toned dance / The milliner's daughter / Last winter was a hard one / Across the bridge.

Waterbug — not issued

Oct 98. (cd) *(WBG 0044CD)* **BACK IN THE AIRLY DAYS** ☐ ⊟
- Dry stone walls / A tale of the airly days / Another man's wedding / The frog's wedding / Gosford's fair desmene / The Pinery boys / William Hall / The bass viol / A&F reel / Fair Fanny Moore / Republicans and democrats / Goodbye my lover I'm gone / Disheartened ranger / Going to Kansas / Loch Maree / Johnny Doyle / I'll sell my hat, I'll sell my coat / Cranberry song / Texans in Maine / Down the road.

The Living Tradition — not issued

Sep 02. (cd; as SARA GREY with Kieron Means and Kate Lissauer) *(LTCD 1301)* **BOY, SHE'S A DAISY**: NORTH AMERICAN SONGS AND BALLADS ☐ ⊟
- Rosianne / Meet her when the sun goes down / Parting hand / The silk merchant's daughter / Say darlin' say / War medley: Dear honey - Poor soldier - The southern girl's reply - The dying legionnaire / Bucking bronco / The little carpenter / Blue mountain lake / Gone solid gone / Hop high my Lulu girl / The scow on Cowdens shore / The house carpenter.

—— Sara and Kate were also credited on Kieron's 'Run Mountain' set (2002)

—— While Grey also supported Kieron on his album 'Far As My Eyes Can See', he returned the favour on her simultaneously-issued set below.

Fellside — not issued

Aug 05. (cd) *(FECD 196)* **A LONG WAY FROM HOME** ☐ ⊟
- Lazy John / Pretty crowin' chicken / Barbara Allen / Derry dens of Arrow / Last chance / Down in Mississippi / I'm so lonesome I could cry / The prodigal son / Nellie was a lady / Five nights drunk / Black water / Sweet sunny south / Pretty Saro / Old Smokey / Ducks on the millpond.

Sep 09. (cd) *(FECD 225)* **SANDY BOYS** ☐ ⊟
- Sandy boys / Goodnight-loving trail / Resurrection day / Sheep, sheep don't you know the road / East Virginia blues / Molly Cottontail and Jeremy Taylor-o / The cruel Lowland maid / Fine times at our house / Old Paint / The jealous brothers / Rake and rambling boy / Black is the colour / Walkin' down the road / Young Hunting / Train on the island.

Vernon HADDOCK's JUBILEE LOVELIES

Britain's answer to the JIM KWESKIN JUG BAND, folky schoolmates Vernon Haddock (on mandolin), David Elvin, Sid "Piles" Lockhart and co. were an up-and-coming act on the roster of EMI's Columbia Records (and DONOVAN's managers Peter Eden and Geoff Stephens) who released a one-off long-player in 1965.

The eponymous **VERNON HADDOCK'S JUBILEE LOVELIES** {*6} was not at all bad, but it sold only around 400 copies, which led the band's break-up early in 1967. The album itself was a cocktail of old-timey, pre-Bonzo Dog Doo-Dah Band ditties and novelty folk-rock compositions, the best of which were 'Viola Lee Blues', 'Don't Let Your Deal Go Down' and Lockhart's 'Vickyandal'. We await its overdue CD release – and yes, the band should have been in section 3 of Volume I. *MCS*

David Elvin - vocals, guitar, banjo, kazoo / **Sid "Piles" Lockhart** - vocals, guitar / **Vernon Haddock** - mandolin, swanee whistle, jug / **Alan Woodward** - guitar / **Alan "Little Bear" Sutton** - percussion, washboard / **David Vaughn** - harmonica, vocals

UK Columbia — US not issued

Dec 65. (lp) *(SX 6011)* **VERNON HADDOCK'S JUBILEE LOVELIES**
- Coney Island washboard / Don't let your deal go down / Clementine / Coloured aristocracy / Mandy, make up your mind / Boodle-am shake / Viola Lee blues / Vickyandal / Stealin' / Little whitewashed chimney / I wish I could shimmy like my sister Kate.

—— only Elvin was to resurface; he guested live for the Bonzo Dog Doo-Dah Band

Gerry HALLOM

Born December 24, 1950, at Richmond in Surrey, HALLOM spent some of his young adult years in the outback of Australia, where he refined his bushwhacker themes in concert.

Returning to Britain in the late 1970s, he signed up with Cumbrian-based Fellside Records, who issued his first LP, **TRAVELLIN' DOWN THE CASTLEREAGH** (1981) {*7}. Praised lavishly by the press (The Guardian called it "the best debut in years"), it contained at least three Banjo Paterson songs alongside RALPH McTELL's 'Gypsy' and Henry Lawson's trad find 'Andy's Gone With Cattle'. Session players comprised JEZ LOWE (banjo, whistles, etc), NIC JONES (fiddle) and John Bowden (melodeon).

A RUN A MINUTE (1984) {*6} was formulaic in approach, with covers of songs by EWAN MacCOLL ('My Old Man'), JEZ LOWE ('Black Diamond'), and Thomas E. Spencer ('The Outside Track'). With guests Bowden, JONES and LOWE again on board, and after time spent studying for a degree, **OLD AUSTRALIAN WAYS** (1989) {*6} was a sort of tribute to Paterson and another national bard of Australia, Will Ogilvie. **ON THE PERIPHERY** (1997) {*6} marked his time in the studio with producer Oliver Knight and a host of folk stars including PETE COOPER, ANDY IRVINE, Keith Jackman, John Bowden, NIC JONES, LAL WATERSON, and Steve Thompson *MCS*

Gerry Hallom - vocals, acoustic guitar

UK Fellside — US not issued

Jun 81. (lp) *(FE 026)* **TRAVELLIN' DOWN THE CASTLEREAGH**
- The overlander / Streets of Forbes / Jog along till shearing / Andy's gone with cattle / Mowing down the barley / Bonnie house o' Airlie / Song of artesian waters / Shearing at Castlereagh / 'Ard tac / The bushman's song (travellin' down the Castlereagh) / Gypsy.

May 84. (lp) *(FE 036)* **A RUN A MINUTE**
- The free selector's daughter / My old man / Bond Street swell / Bright fine gold / With the cattle / General Leeds clock meeting / Black diamond / New chum shearer / How McDougal topped the score / The outside track.

1989. (lp/c) *(FE 074/+C)* **OLD AUSTRALIAN WAYS**
- Where the dead men lie / The lights of Cobb and Co. / Where the brumbies come to water / Clancy of the overflow - Old Australian ways / No more boomerang / Song of the wheat / Down the river / The first surveyor / Northward to the shed / The grey gulf water.

William Boyd — not issued

Dec 97. (cd) *(WBMCD 001)* **ON THE PERIPHERY**
- All down the days / The rider / The calm before the storm / Taoist tales / Come down days / Lisbon story / Myra's children / City lights city limits / The fizzer / Hey rain / I don't know why / Early.

- (5-7*) compilations, etc.-

Feb 98. (cd) *Musica Pangaea; (MP 10003CD)* **UNDISCOVERED AUSTRALIA II**
- The overlander / Streets of Forbes / Jog along till shearing / Andy's gone with cattle / The bushman's song (travellin' down the Castlereagh) / Song of artesian waters / Shearing at Castlereagh / The free selector's daughter / With the cattle / New chum shearer / The outside track / Where the dead men lie / The lights of Cobb and Co. / Clancy of the overflow - Old Australian ways / No more boomerang / Song of the wheat / Northward to the shed / The grey gulf water.

Mary HAMPTON

So many neo-folk artists have been said to sound like SANDY DENNY that a disorderly queue has been formed, and leading the line is Brighton-born MARY HAMPTON, a young woman whose early CV has included work with ELIZA CARTHY (on CARTHY's 'Rough Music' album in 2005), and a year later as part of Stereolab side-project Imitation Electric Piano on their 'Blow It Up, Burn It Down, Kick It 'Til It Bleeds' set. Mainly trad songs featured on Mary's first two CD-rs, 'Book One' (2006) and 'Book Two' (2007).

If you needed to test the waters and confirm her whispering, Sandy-esque traits, you could track down her gloriously nostalgic debut album **MY MOTHER'S CHILDREN** (2008) {*8}. Peeling petal after pastoral petal from each blossoming bud in her garden of dainty delights, but with a certain fragility and freak-folk frailty, the flowers in question include 'Because You're Young', 'Free Grace', 'Pygmalion' (very ALASDAIR ROBERTS) and the finale, 'Exeunt'.

A subsequent appearance at the Green Man Festival in 2008 and a joint tour with American DIANE CLUCK raised her profile, while with her band, the Mary Hampton Cotillion (Seth Bennett, Alice Eldridge, Alistair Strachan and Jo Burke), she performed some unaccustomed concert dates in 2011 – at Bristol's Blaise Castle and on a rooftop above the Queen Elizabeth Hall – to promote her second set, **FOLLY** (2011) {*7}, and her recent signing to Rough Trade. *MCS*

Mary Hampton - vocals, acoustic guitar / with various personnel

UK Teaspoon — US not issued

2006. (cd-r) *(none)* BOOK ONE [live *] — self
- Silver dagger (*) / Love me little (*) / The gardener (*) / Let no man steal your thyme (*) / Eros / Fare thee well (*).

2007. (cd-r) *(none)* BOOK TWO [live *] — self
- Silver pebble (*) / Sweet dreams of Nancy / Pretty Polly (*) / Bonny boy (*) / Hares in the old plantation / Song of wandering Aengus (*).

Navigator — not issued

Aug 08. (cd/lp) *(NAVIGATOR 15/+LP)* **MY MOTHER'S CHILDREN**
- Because you're young / Free grace / Honey / Concerning a frozen sparrow / Ballad of the talking dog / Pygmalion / Meanwhile? / The bell they gave you / Island / Exeunt.

Teaspoon — not issued

Jun 11. (cd) *(TSR 001)* **FOLLY**
- The man behind the rhododendron / Benjamin Bowmancer / Forget-me-not / Kiss V / Hoax and benison / Honey in the rock / No.32 / Lullaby for the beleaguered.

Rough Trade — not issued

Jul 11. (7") *(RTRADS 626)* HONEY IN THE ROCK. / Hoax And Benison

Keith HANCOCK

Born October 28, 1953, at Audenshaw in Greater Manchester, Keith's formative musical background was with 1970s dance outfits including the Grimsby Morris Men. His father had played the banjo with the Manchester Kentucky Minstrels in the 1960s.

Forsaking a brief musical liaison with his wife Janet, HANCOCK went professional in 1983. A subsequent cassette/LP, **THIS WORLD WE LIVE IN** (1986) {*6}, contained at least one gem, 'Chase The Dragon' (about drug addiction), which was passed on to the newly-formed CLIVE GREGSON & CHRISTINE COLLISTER. Backed and produced by GREGSON (plus Martin Hughes, Mick Doonan, Howard Lees and John Hobson), his second solo album, **MADHOUSE** (1988) {*6}, was another with edgy lyrics, for example in the acerbic anti-tabloids track 'Headline News'.

Splitting his time between solo gigs and working with The ELECTROPATHICS (with whom he recorded 'Batteries Not Included' in 1987), melodeonist HANCOCK also contributed various song to benefit albums such as the 'Children In Need Album' (1987), 'Squires Fancy' (1988), 'Choices, Rights And Liberties' (1989), 'Hard Cash' (1990) and 'The Circle Dance' (1990).

Although never quite getting off the ground, The KEITH HANCOCK BAND (with MARTIN CARTHY, DAVE SWARBRICK and bassist Ruari McFarlane) scraped together enough studio time for a couple of out-takes, a handful available on retrospective CD **BORN BLUE** (1999) {*6}. Album number three **COMPASSION** (1993) {*6} – featuring LEE COLLINSON (on slide guitar), Terry Mann (bass) and Dave Swan (drums) – found its way to the record shops through German outlet Hypertension. What Keith's up to nowadays is uncertain. *MCS*

Keith Hancock - vocals, melodeon (with session people)

UK KJK — UK not issued

1986. (c) *(KJK 101)* **THIS WORLD WE LIVE IN**
- Fruit of the loom – The shuttle / Chase the dragon / etc. *(lp-iss. Oct 88 on Greenwich Village; GVR 237)*

Spiv — not issued

Aug 88. (lp/c) *(SPIV 101/+C)* **MADHOUSE**
- Headline news / Helter skelter / The bad loser / The strangest of lands / Sunk without a trace / Chase the dragon / Workhorse / Lousy timing / Life in the system / Boys of the old brigade / The bloodletting game / South Africa. *(cd-iss. Sep 90 on Hypertension German/UK Sep 93; HYCD 200 107/+C)*

Hypertension — not issued

Feb 93. (cd/c) *(HYCD 200 133/+C)* **COMPASSION** German
- Funerals today, skips tomorrow / I believe in magic / Dear Angie / The man who pulls the trigger / Half measures won't do it / Panacea / The purple pas de deux / Out of fashion / Child of tomorrow / These weary days. *(UK-iss. Feb 95; same)*

- (5-7*) compilations, others, etc.-

1999. (cd) *Nico's; (NRC 4046-2)* **BORN BLUE** Dutch
- Fruit of the loom – The shuttle / Gadaffi's gallop – The old bazaar in Cairo / Jam up the nuts – Jump at the sun / Harry Rag / Workhorse / Coventry caper – Second Wednesday / Porton Down / Half measures won't do it / I believe in magic / Man who pulls the trigger / Lads' night / Sunk without a trace / Everybody knows.

Lisa HANNIGAN

Born February 12, 1981, at Kilcloon, County Meath in Ireland. Most people who are into nu-folk music will recall her days as vocal partner to DAMIEN RICE. From her days as his regular sidekick at the Temple Bar in Dublin and at the Glastonbury Festival in 2003, multi-instrumentalist HANNIGAN proved her dexterity on his groundbreaking sets 'O' and '9'. Whether it was her work moonlighting with the pseudonymous Daisy Okell Quartet, or a rare solo outing at the 2006 Electric Picnic Festival in Stradbally, County Laois, that prompted RICE to fire her the following March, no one has yet found out.

Anyway, it couldn't have worked out better, as Lisa's star started to ascend after the release of her solo debut, **SEA SEW** (2008) {*8}, a record hailed one of Ireland's best albums of the year and subsequently nominated for the Mercury Prize. A surprise chartbreaker at No.58, the set was described in reviews as "charmingly idiosyncratic" and "exquisitely ethereal", its best cuts being 'Venn Diagram', 'Lille', the rockier 'Keep It All', 'Ocean And A Rock' and a violin version of BERT JANSCH's Courting Blues'. Tours supporting Jason Mraz and DAVID GRAY, and appearances on the Jay Leno and Stephen Colbert TV shows in the US, boosted her CV no end. *MCS*

Lisa Hannigan - vocals, harmonium, guitar, banjo, piano (with session people)

UK Lisa Hannigan — US ATO

Aug 08. (dl-s) *(-)* LILLE

Sep 08. (cd) *(lh 001) <88088 21643-2>* **SEA SEW** 58 Feb 09
- Ocean and a rock / Venn diagram / Sea song / Splishy splashy / I don't know / Keep it all / Courting blues / Pistachio / Teeth / Lille. *(d-cd-iss. Sep 10 +=; ihcd 002)* - (LIVE AT FINGERPRINTS EP tracks).

Dec 09. (cd-ep) *<ATOEP 007>* LIVE AT FINGERPRINTS [live in Long Beach, California on November 1, 2008]
- Sea song / Splishy splashy / Ocean and a rock / Venn diagram / I don't know / Lille.

John Wesley HARDING

Born Wesley Harding Stace, October 22, 1965, at Hastings in East Sussex, HARDING took his stage name from a 1968 DYLAN album named for the Wild West outlaw.

The son of an opera-singing mother and jazz-pianist father, John Wesley was an early starter in the rock stakes, performing locally while at high school. A self-taught guitarist who took up music professionally after completing his university studies, his influences during this spell were LOUDON WAINWRIGHT III, JOHN PRINE and of course DYLAN. Supporting John Hiatt, he attracted the attention of re-issue specialist Demon Records, and his debut/live set, **IT HAPPENED ONE NIGHT** (1988) {*8}, was blessed with enough literate wit and musical talent to attract the interest of American label Sire. He recorded 'God Made Me Do It: The Christmas EP', featuring a reading of Madonna's 'Like A Prayer' and a Viv Stanshall fun promo interview, the following year.

Wesley's best moments on the album were the namecheck tracks 'July 13th 1985' (the date of Live Aid), 'Roy Orbison Knows (The Best Man's Song)', 'Phil Ochs, Bob Dylan, Steve Goodman, David Blue And Me' and a cover of PRINCE's 'Kiss'.

Time and again though, reviewers fell back on veterans such as Costello, Nick Lowe and Dave Edmunds as reference points; that the Attractions (Pete Thomas and Bruce Thomas as The Good Liars, with Andy Paley, Peter Case, etc.) actually played on his follow-up album only encouraged the comparisons. **HERE COMES THE GROOM** (1990) {*8} was another collection of quintessentially English songwriting, HARDING achieving a fine balance between emotional expressiveness and clever-clever wordplay. The best examples are 'Cathy's New Clown' (not exactly the Everlys), 'The Devil In Me' and the title track.

It's a balance he somehow managed to maintain, with varying degrees of success, through a further two albums, **THE NAME ABOVE THE TITLE** (1991) {*6} and **WHY WE FIGHT** (1993) {*7}, but HARDING has never quite managed to break out of the cult-appeal ghetto and into the mainstream.

Rhino Records kept the faith with JWH for at least one more effort, 1997's **JOHN WESLEY HARDING'S NEW DEAL** {*6}, while **AWAKE** (1998) {*7} – billed under the faux multi-instrumentalist disguise of the Gangsta Folk – was his first for Zero Hour. **TRAD ARR JONES** (1999) {*6} was HARDING's most ambitious album to date, acknowledging the timeless interpretations of under-the-radar traditionalist Brit-folk star NIC JONES.

For many musos and listeners this still didn't shake off the Elvis Costello albatross from around his neck. Wes's smooth yet acerbic vocals were unfettered on album number seven (not counting the **DYNABLOB** series), **THE CONFESSIONS OF ST. ACE** (2000) {*7}, a record that starred at least three more gems, 'She's A Piece Of Work', 'I'm Wrong About Everything' and 'Humble Bee'.

ADAM'S APPLE (2004) {*7} was richer in production than previous sets, while his balladeering folk had expanded to accommodate some funk or folktronica on 'Protest Protest Protest' and 'Sluts'. The retrograde 'Sussex Ghost Story' and 'While You Smile' maintained the early promise without really trying too hard.

To create a musical companion piece to his novel 'Misfortune' (published under his real name), 2005 saw Wesley Stace turn a cappella in The LOVE HALL TRYST, a medieval/trad quartet featuring friends Kelly Hogan (ex-Jody Grind), Edinburgh-based comic actor and baritone singer Brian

Lohmann and Nora O'Connor (ex-Blacks). Alongside several HARDING and sourced numbers, **SONGS OF MISFORTUNE** {*6} –reminiscent of The WATERSONS and The COPPER FAMILY – featured a cover of LEONARD COHEN's 'Joan Of Arc'.

Not exactly prolific post-millennium, JWH marked a comeback of sorts with **WHO WAS CHANGED AND WHO WAS DEAD** (2009) {*6}, long-time friends and musical accomplices Scott McCaughey and Peter Buck (both of Minus 5) possibly responsible for taking him out of the confines of folk and into the realms of AOR. Check out 'Daylight Ghosts' and 'A Very Sorry Saint'. *MCS*

John Wesley Harding - vocals, acoustic guitar

UK Demon / US Rhino

Dec 88. (lp/cd) *(L-FIEND/+CD 137)* <*R1/R2-70764*> **IT HAPPENED ONE NIGHT** [live November 5, 1988]
- Headful of something - The Devil in me / Who you really are / Famous man / July 13th 1985 / One night only / Affairs of the heart / Humankind / Phil Ochs, Bob Dylan, Steve Goodman, David Blue and me / The night he took her to the fairground / The biggest monument / Save a little room for me / Kiss – Lover's society / Careers service / Pound pound pound / Roy Orbison knows (the best man's song) / Bastard son. *(<d-cd-iss. Oct 04 on Appleseed+=; APRCD 1083>)*- IT NEVER HAPPENED AT ALL: Every sunrise is another sunset / Three legged man / Love's sacrifice / Roy Orbison knows / The Devil in me / Same thing twice / Browning road / Lovers society / Scared of guns / Who you really are / Bad fruit / Pound pound pound / One night only / The night he took her to the fairground / Save a little room for me / You can't take it with you.

Sire / Sire

Nov 89. (12"ep/cd-ep) <*1-/2-26093*> **GOD MADE ME DO IT: THE CHRISTMAS EP**
- Here comes the groom / Talking Christmas goodwill blues / Like a prayer / The rent / (a cosy promotional chat: Viv Stanshall free-associates with John Wesley Harding).

Jun 90. (cd/c/lp) *(<7599 26087-2/-4/-1>)* **HERE COMES THE GROOM**
- Here comes the groom / Cathy's new clown / Spaced cowgirl / Scared of guns / You're no good / When the sun comes out / The devil in me / An audience with you / Dark dark heart / Same thing twice / Affairs of the heart / Nothing I'd rather do / Things snowball / The red rose and the briar / Bastard son. *<d-cd-iss. Jul 03 on Collectables+=; COL 7482>* - THE NAME ABOVE THE TITLE

Jul 90. (7") *(W 9749)* THE DEVIL IN ME. / The Rent
(12"+=) *(W 9749T)* - Covered up in aces / Like a prayer.

Nov 90. (7") *(W 9531)* DARK DARK HEART. / Scared Of Guns

Feb 91. (cd/c) *(<7599 26532-2/-4>)* **THE NAME ABOVE THE TITLE**
- Movie theme / The world (and all its problems) / Fifty-fifty split / The people's drug / The movie of your life / I can tell (when you're telling lies) / Bridegroom blues / Save a little room for me / Anonymous 1916 / The person you are / Long dead gone / The facts of life / Driving in the rain / Backing out / Crystal blue persuasion. *<d-cd-iss.+=>- HERE COMES THE GROOM*

Apr 91. (7") *(W 0007)* THE PERSON YOU ARE. / Patron Saint Of Losers
(12") *(9362-40015)* - ('A') / The Devil in me (live) / Dark dark heart (live) / Scared of guns (live).

Apr 93. (cd/c) *(<9362 45032-2/-4>)* **WHY WE FIGHT**
- Kill the messenger / Ordinary weekend / The truth / Dead centre of town / Into the wind / Hitler's tears / Get back down / Me against me / The original Miss Jesus / Where the bodies are / Millionaire's dream / Come gather round.

Jul 93. (cd-ep) <*45331-2*> PETT LEVELS: THE SUMMER EP
- Summer single / Your new clothes / One shot / When the sun comes out (acoustic version) / The end of something.

Kingfisher / Rhino

Jan 97. (cd) *(JWHCD 1)* <*R2 72250*> **JOHN WESLEY HARDING'S NEW DEAL** — Feb 96
- To whom it may concern / Other people's failure / The secret angel / Kiss me, Miss Liberty / Heart without a home / God lives upstairs / Infinite combinations / The king is dead boring / The triumph of trash / Cupid and psycho / Still photo / In paradise / The speed of normal.

Zero Hour / Zero Hour

May 98. (cd) *(<ZHCD 1210>)* **AWAKE** — Mar 98
- Good morning (I just woke up) / Your ghost (don't scare me no more) / Window seat / Burn / It's all my fault / Sweat... tears, blood and come / Poor heart / Miss Fortune / Song I wrote myself in the future / Something to write home about / You're looking at me / You so and so / I'm staying here (and I'm not buying a gun) / Good bye (late o'clock). *(re-iss. Feb 01 on Appleseed+=; APRCD 1040)* - Wooden overcoat / Jackson Cage / Punch 'n' Judy / I just woke up / Wreck on the highway.

Mar 99. (cd) *(<ZHCD 2210>)* **TRAD ARR JONES** — Feb 99
- The singer's request / Little Musgrave / The golden glove / Annachie Gordon / The Flandyke shore / William and Nancy's parting / William Glenn / The bonny bunch of roses / Master Kilby / Annan water / Isle of France. *(re-iss. Mar 01 on Appleseed+=; APRCD 1041)* - Canadee-i-o / Billy don't you weep for me / Edward / The humpback whale.

not issued / Mammoth

Aug 00. (cd) <*0125503MAM*> **THE CONFESSIONS OF ST. ACE**
- Humble bee / She's a piece of work / People love to watch you die / I'm wrong about everything / Same piece of air / Old girlfriends / Bad dream baby / Goth girl / You in spite of yourself / Our lady of the highways / After the fact / Too much into nothing.

not issued / DRT

Jan 04. (cd) <*DRT 406*> **ADAM'S APPLE**
- Nothing at all / Monkey and his cat / Negative love / Sleeper awake / Pull / Sussex ghost story / It stays / Hard / Sluts / Protest protest protest / She never talks / When you smile.

Rebel Group / Rebel Group

May 09. (cd) *(<RBG 0125>)* **WHO WAS CHANGED AND WHO WAS DEAD** — Mar 09
- My favourite angel / Love or nothing / Oh! Pandora / A very sorry saint / Sleepy people / Daylight ghosts / The end / Sick organism / Congratulations (on your hallucinations) / Top of the bottom / Someday son / Your mind's playing tricks on you / Wild boy. *(w/ free live cd+=)* - Kiss me Miss Liberty / The person you are / The people's drug / Still photo / The top of the bottom / Negative love / Monkey and his cat / Kill the messenger / The truth / Our lady of the highways / Window seat / The devil in me.

- (5-7*) compilations, others, etc.-

May 98. (cd) *Mod Lang;* **DYNABLOB** *[live]*
- Phil Ochs, Bob Dylan, Steve Goodman, David Blue and me / The man with two surnames / The wrong goodbye / Peeling bark / Dead on arrival / The devil in me / Save a little room for me / Build me a coffin / Idiot's delight / Eating each other's babies / Ask why / The person you are / The celestial shuttle / Talkin' return of the great gangsta folk scare blues / Election night. *<re-iss. 2007 on Wow; none>*

Oct 03. (cd) *DRT; <none>* **DYNABLOB 2**: IT HAPPENED EVERY NIGHT [live]
- Handful of sand / Elvis has left the building / Hostile two party system / Gentleman's dream / Star struck banner / A fan speaks – Famous man / Skyscrapers of Memphis / The brain of Britain / When dreams come true / No more / When all the bad things in your life turn to worth it / Election night – You will be cured / Robert Frost rag / I just wanna talk / $55.

Oct 03. (cd) *DRT; <none>* **DYNABLOB 3**: 26th MARCH 1999
- The singer's request / Things snowball / Isle of France / Save a little room for me / William Glenn / Talkin' return of the great gangsta folk scare blues / Little Musgrave / The red rose and the briar / Miss fortune / Window seat / Annan water.

Oct 03. (cd) *DRT; <none>* **D4: SWINGS AND ROUNDABOUTS**
- Merry-go-round / The governess / The common kiss / Dreamfader / Darwin / Love's reign of terror / Meet the sheep / For an actress / Don't rain on me today / Thank you, you're welcome / The fall of the house of Harding / World of light.

The LOVE HALL TRYST

Wesley Stace + Kelly Hogan + Nora O'Connor + Brian Lohmann

Appleseed / Appleseed

Aug 05. (cd) *(<APRCD 1089>)* **SONGS OF MISFORTUNE**
- Do not fear the dark / Joan of Arc (the ballad of La Pucelle) / Lord Bateman / Female rambling sailor / Lord Lovel / The sanguinary butcher / Shallow brown / Lambkin / The lady dressed in green / The abandoned baby / Jack in the green / Do not fear the dark (electric) / Lord Bateman (electric).

Bella HARDY

Born at Edale in the Peak District of Derbyshire, Bright Young Folk thing Bella (singer and virtuoso violinist) fuelled her promising career by attended the renowned Folkworks Youth Summer School at the tender age of 13. Her interest in traditional-dance music prompted her and some likeminded teens from the school to form folk orchestra The PACK, mainly to gain free entry to festivals at Warwick, Sidmouth and Cambridge. Around a dozen members strong (see discography), the ensemble released one set in 2002, **12 LITTLE DEVILS** {*6} – kind of KATHRYN TICKELL meets SHARON SHANNON. Four of their troupe (Sophy and Emily Ball, Sam Pirt and Joey Oliver) were also active in the folk/ceilidh band 422.

Enjoying an abundant spell of honours, HARDY was nominated for three BBC Radio 2 Folk Awards, and she also collected a BA in English Literature in 2005 and a master's degree in music in 2007.

Her solo debut, **NIGHT VISITING** (2007) {*8}, received lavish praise everywhere from fRoots to Mojo, and tracks such as 'Down In Yon Forest', 'All Things Are Quite Silent' and the Celtic-esque 'Bonny Susie Cleland' rivalled in mood and character the work of The UNTHANKS.

IN THE SHADOW OF MOUNTAINS (2009) {*8} continued her rise to semi-stardom, many critics at the time comparing her songs ('Mary Mean' and 'Sylvie Sovay' included) to the style of Lennon- McCartney, although traditional songs such as 'The Cruel Mother' proved where her bread was buttered. Guest spots on DAVID ROTHERAY's 'The Life Of Birds' set (on

'The Digital Cuckoo', 'Living Before The War' and 'The Hummingbird') preceded Bella's first CD for Navigator Records, **SONGS LOST AND STOLEN** (2011) {*7}. Entirely self-penned, and again produced by Mattie Foulds (of The BURNS UNIT), the highlights this time around were 'Jenny Wren', 'Rosabel' and 'Full Moon Over Amsterdam'. *MCS*

The PACK

Bella Hardy - vocals, violin / **Emma Hardy** - fiddle, viola / **Lucy Nelson** - bodhran, clarinet / **Michael Jary** - concertina (of Ola) / **Matt Nelson** - saxophone (of Niblik) / **Ian Stephenson** - guitar / **Chantel Noppen** - concertina, trumpet / **Talei Edwards** - fiddle / **Sophy Ball** - fiddle (of 422) / **Emily Ball** - fiddle (of 422) / **Sam Pirt** - piano-accordion (of 422) / **Joey Oliver** - whistles, oboe (of 422)

UK Selwyn — US not issued

2002. (cd) *(SYNMCD 0005)* **12 LITTLE DEVILS**
- Catharsis – Frenchies' reel / Ringen – The wizard walk / The golden keyboard – Noon lasses / Peterman / Reunion jig – Morrison's jig / Kaytagi / The football match / The congress reel – Hommage a Edmond Parizeau – Farmor's brudspolska / Bette mct / The devil came down to Yorkshire / Margaret's waltz – Itchy fingers – Clumsy lover.

BELLA HARDY

Noe — not issued

Sep 07. (cd) *(01)* **NIGHT VISITING**
- Three black feathers / Dog and gun / Young Edmund / Down in yon forest / Heart hill / Searching for lambs / All things are quite silent / Maying song / Molly Vaughan / Alone, Jane? / Bonnie Susie Cleland.

Aug 09. (cd) *(02)* **IN THE SHADOW OF MOUNTAINS**
- Mary mean / Rosebud in June / Broadlee bank / Smoke and ashes / Sylvie Sovay / Low down in the broom / Ten thousand miles / Cruel mother / All in the morning / Island boy / The trawlerman's wife.

Navigator — not issued

Apr 11. (cd) *(NAVIGATOR 045)* **SONGS LOST AND STOLEN**
- Labyrinth / Flowers of May / Walk it with you / Bridge of Dean / The herring girl / Full moon over Amsterdam / Written in green / Jenny Wren / Promises / Rosabel.

Nick HARPER

Being the son of esteemed folk singer-songwriter ROY HARPER was never going to be plain sailing, although it must have had a few perks. Born June 2, 1965, in Wiltshire, Nick was inspired by his dad and several class acts who visited his family, including David Gilmour, Robert Plant and Jimmy Page. He would make his recording debut with his father and the latter guitarist/icon on 1985's 'Whatever Happened To Jugula?'.

As with his father, pundits were unable to pigeonhole him into one genre or category, but Nick's sound was either acoustic-rock or singer-songwriter folk. Self-released on his own Sangraal imprint, mini-set **LIGHT AT THE END OF THE KENNEL** (1994) {*6} was particularly well-received (as was 1995's **SEED** {*7}), and almost immediately led to Glenn Tilbrook taking him on under his newly-formed Quixotic umbrella.

With the former Squeeze man at the controls, accomplished finger-picking guitarist HARPER was unintentionally competing against his father on two subsequent albums, **SMITHEREENS** (1998) {*5} and **HARPERSPACE** (2000) {*6}, the latter faring a tad better than his previous overproduced collection. The double-live **DOUBLE LIFE** (2002) {*8}, which ended his tenure with Quixotic, was a marriage of hard-driven rock (check out 'Guitarman' and 'Headless') and the acoustic delicacies of 'The Verse That Time Forgot'.

Reverting to issuing records on his own Sangraal imprint, HARPER has delivered a string of thought-provoking sets: **BLOOD SONGS** (2004) {*6}, **TREASURE ISLAND** (2006) {*6}, **MIRACLES FOR BEGINNERS** (2007) {*6} and **THE LAST GUITAR** (2010) {*6}; the latter featured a guest spot for his teenage daughter. Probably one of Nick's career highs was when he climbed Mount Snowdon in October 2007 to perform a concert, and on the back of that, his 14-day expedition for the Love Hope Strength Foundation charity, ascending Mount Everest, raised over £250,000. *MCS*

Nick Harper - vocals, guitars (with session people)

UK Sangraal — US Griffin

1994. (m-cd) *(SGCD 094)* <*GCD 458*> **LIGHT AT THE END OF THE KENNEL** — Jul 95
- 100 things / Is this really me? / Shadowlands / Flying dog / Headless / Riverside. *(re-iss. Nov 96 on Terra Nova; TERRCD 003)*

Sangraal — not issued

Oct 95. (cd) *(SGCD 095)* **SEED**
- Glittering eye / The Kilty stone / Radio silence / Crazy boy / Three magpies / Big Jim and the twins / Thanks for the miracle / Building our own temple / Pendle's choice / Mr. Grey / Peace, love and happiness / Janet and John.

Quixotic — not issued

May 98. (cd) *(QRCD 0098)* **SMITHEREENS**
- Smithereens / Ghost of her touch / In our time / My baby / The tyger / Twisted / Out of it / Two way thing / No truth up in the mountains / The magnificent G-Seven / She really was / Everything's better / Acoustic smithereens.

1999. (cd-ep) *(SGCD 099)* INSTRUMENTAL — mail-o
- Swansong / The sky goes all the way home / The whack 'n' riddle tree / Harperspace / Like punk never happened / Riverside (revisited) / Instrumental.

(above issued on Sangraal)

Jun 00. (cd) *(QUIXCD 004)* **HARPERSPACE**
- The verse time forgot / Happy man / Aeroplane / Karmageddon / Roomspin / There is magic in this world / Nothing but love / Watching the stars / Kettledrum heart / She rules my world / Song of madness / Before they put me in the ground.

May 02. (d-cd) *(QUIXCD 008)* **DOUBLE LIFE** [live]
- She rules my world / Karmageddon / The verse time forgot / The Magnificent G7 / Aeroplane / The Kilty stone / Flying dog / The galaxy song / Headless [official string break version] // Building our own temple / In our time / Janet and John / Crazyboy / Guitarman [whole lotta love mix] / Out of it / Watching the stars [7-string version] / Kettledrum heart / The consumer meets the wolfman.

Sangraal — Sangraal

Feb 04. (cd) (<*SR 0003CD*>) **BLOOD SONGS**
- Foreplay / Love junky / Lily's song / Love is music / Imaginary friend / Stronger / Vampire song / The wanderer and his shadow / The kissing gate / Boy meets planet / My little masterpiece / Blood song.

Jan 06. (cd) *(SR 0004CD)* **TREASURE ISLAND**
- By my rocket comes fire / Treasure Island / Underground stream / Good bus / Intelligent design? / Knuckledraggers / Sleeper cell / Real life / Bloom / Around the sun / 365 / A Wiltshire tale.

Jun 07. (dl-s) *(-)* BLUE SKY THINKING

Jun 07. (cd) *(SR 0007CD)* **MIRACLES FOR BEGINNERS**
- Miracles for beginners / Blue sky thinking / The field of the cloth of gold / Magic feather / Evo / Two secs / Always / Your love has saved me from myself / Communication / Simple.

2010. (cd) *(SR 0010CD)* **THE LAST GUITAR**
- One of the 38 / For you / The story of my heart / Ama dablam / Passing chord / Hey bomb / Freestyle / Pop fiction / On / Jim Crow is dead / The last guitar / Silly daddy.

Pete HARRIS (⟹ RYAN, Mick &...)

Sue HARRIS

Born May 17, 1949, in Coventry, original oboeist turned hammered-dulcimer exponent SUE HARRIS is better known in folk circles for her collaborations with husband JOHN KIRKPATRICK. Formerly an oboeist with IAN A. ANDERSON's ENGLISH COUNTRY BLUES BAND and ASHLEY HUTCHINGS's The ALBION COUNTRY BAND, the latter's 1973 set 'The Battle Of The Field' was significant in that she played both instruments on that record. The oboe was the more tiring as she was pregnant with her first son, BENJI KIRKPATRICK (also of BELLOWHEAD and DR. FAUSTUS) later to become a star in his own right.

While the hammered dulcimer took over as her main instrument in 1975, her recordings (some co-credited) with melodeon maestro JOHN KIRKPATRICK included some of the couple's best work. 'The Rose Of Britain's Isle' (1974), 'Among The Many Attractions…' (1976), 'Shreds And Patches' (1977), 'Facing The Music' (1980), 'Ballad Of The Black Country' (1981), 'English Canals' (1981) and 'Stolen Ground' (1985) were favourites of folk buffs in the know.

Not content with husband-and-wife project sets, HARRIS was credited alongside MARTIN WYNDHAM-READ and MARTIN CARTHY on 'The Old Songs' (1984).

Her album with Tufty Swift and brother Alan Harris, **HOW TO MAKE A BAKEWELL TART** (1977) {*6}, was soon followed by **HAMMERS AND TONGUES** (1978) {*7}, a solo LP featuring Swift (on one-row four-stop melodeon), Martin Brinsford (mouth organ, etc), JOHN KIRKPATRICK (button accordion, Anglo concertina, etc), Alan Harris (tenor banjo, etc) and Jenny Harris (harmony).

On a part-time basis while bringing up Benji, she was independently working as session player for Gerry Rafferty ('Night Owl'), Pere Ubu ('The Tenement Years') and The RICHARD & LINDA THOMPSON Band.

Alongside John again, she appeared with The UMPS AND DUMPS on 'The Moon's In A Fit' (1980) and The ALBIONs' 'Lark Rise To Candleford' (1980). A trio with DAVE WHETSTONE (ex-COCK AND BULL BAND) was projected in the early 1990s.

HARRIS's first completely solo CD was **PASTORELA** (2002) {*7}, a record with traditional fare and centuries-old tunes from James Scott Skinner, Turlough O'Carolan and others of the Celtic kind. Still grafting among the folk community, she lends her natural voice to choirs and orchestras. *MCS*

Sue Harris - vocals, hammered dulcimer / with **Tufty Swift** - melodeon, fiddle, mouth organ / **Alan Harris** - banjo, double bass, piano

UK Free Reed — US not issued

Nov 77. (lp; by TUFTY SWIFT with ALAN HARRIS & SUE HARRIS) *(FRR 017)* **HOW TO MAKE A BAKEWELL TART: COUNTRY DANCE TUNES AND SONGS** ☐ ⊟
- Winter processional – Blue-eyed stranger No.2 / Kit White's square eight / Father's whiskers / Mr Gubbin's bicycle / The officer's polka / Sam Steel's waltz and schottische / Buttered pease – Mulberry bush / Boatman's dance / Rig-a-jig / Old Mother Casey / Herbert Smith's four-hand reel / Swedish tune / Gaspe reel / Tip-top polka / Waltz me, Willy / Brass nuts / Winster Morris gallop – The miner's standard / Miss Baker's hornpipe / Lady of the lake – Buffalo girls. *(cd-iss.+=)* - HAMMERS AND TONGUES

—— she added **John Kirkpatrick** - button accordion, Anglo concertina, two-row melodeon / **Martin Brinsford** - mouth organ, skulls bass, tambourine / **Jenny Harris** - harmony

Nov 78. (lp) *(FRR 020)* **HAMMERS AND TONGUES** ☐ ⊟
- Perry gutter – All asiden / The donkey's death *[not on re-cd]* / Old man in a wood – Gay ladies' polka / McCaffery *[not on re-cd]* / Put on your ta-ta, little girl / Just watch the ivy / Pottings polka / In the midst of night / Green grow the laurels / All the months of the year – All the year round. *(cd-iss. 2007 as 'HAMMERS, TONGUES AND A BAKEWELL TART'+=; FRRR 02)* - HOW TO MAKE A BAKEWELL TART

—— HARRIS went into session work and continued to partner KIRKPATRICK until …

Beautiful Jo — not issued

May 02. (cd) *(BEJOCD 37)* **PASTORELA**: Music of the Hammered Dulcimer ☐ ⊟
- O'Carolan's cup – In the shadow of the king's hill / Fair maid on the shore / Parson's farewell – Indian queen / John's jaunt / Caractacus medley / Pastorela / Sprig of thyme / The Whetstone – McColl's jig / Gypsies' lullaby – Billy Pigg's hornpipe / Lamento di Tristan / Scott Skinner tunes / Bill Charlton's hornpipe.

Ray HEARNE

Born in Rotherham, South Yorkshire, to Irish parents, Ray combines both brogues to, as he puts it, "give voice to communal dreams and aspirations". With his own lyrical balladeering, often set to traditional Irish tunes, the tracks on his debut album **BROAD STREET BALLADS** (2001) {*7} were placed firmly in his native South Yorkshire countryside. With No Masters label stars JO FREYA, BARRY COOPE and JIM BOYES (on chorus) on board, plus further augmentation from jazz saxophonist Tim Garland, Uilleann piper Steafan Hannigan (of Sin E), melodeon player Luke Daniels and former FAIRPORT/JETHRO TULL bassist Martin Allcock, songs such as 'Rother Sing A Don Song', 'Yorkshire Colliery' and 'Mild Imaginings' found favour among his growing fan base.

His songs have subsequently been recorded by COOPE BOYES & SIMPSON, ROY BAILEY and KATE RUSBY. The latter interpreted Ray's 'Curtains', broadcast on BBC Radio 2's ballad series in 2006. HEARNE is an advocate of helping others in his community, and he volunteers in learning disabilities projects and regeneration schemes throughout Yorkshire.

Several years in the making (he is chairman of the No Masters Co-operative), **THE WRONG SUNSHINE** (2009) {*7} was another well-crafted work, with songs rooted in his Northern community such as 'Pudding Burner', 'The Long Song Line' and 'Baghdad-on-Dearne'. *MCS*

Ray Hearne - vocals, acoustic guitar

No Masters — not issued

Apr 01. (cd) *(NMCD 17)* **BROAD STREET BALLADS** ☐ ⊟
- The merry music of the minstrel man / Calling Joe Hill / Rother sing a Don song / Along the Don water / Valleys of virtue / Mild imaginings / Yorkshire colliery / The last of the alley gaters / Harry Appleblossom / Dark disbelief / The balladmaker's apprentice / Thurnscoe rain.

Oct 09. (cd) *(NMCD 31)* **THE WRONG SUNSHINE** ☐ ⊟
- Manvers Island bound / The long song line / Baghdad-on-Dearne / Song for David / The melting shop chaps / The navvy boys / Things to say / March of the daffodils / Pudding burner / Young and easy / Point the finger at the emperor / Well / I know why the caged bird sings / The fields of Foggydew / The collier's elegy.

Lynne HERAUD & Pat TURNER

Formed in 2002 by a cappella singers LYNNE HERAUD (from Stanstead Abbotts in Hertfordshire) and PAT TURNER. HERAUD arrived on the folk scene in the 1970s as part of a semi-successful duo with Sue Ashby. In the following decade she sang alongside Frank Lee and John Lambert in Tom, Dick & Harry, but her first recordings were with vocal sparring partner (and former DRUIDS muso) KEITH KENDRICK on 2001's 'Stars In My Crown'. Pat's CV included time spent with vocal harmony act Filigree, and like Lynne (a folk club owner in Hoddesdon and Waltham Abbey) she had been a member of the Cityfolk team.

Having gotten under way on their own steam with debut set **PARALLEL** (2003) {*5}, these near-forgotten ladies of trad-folk signed to Wild Goose for **THE MOON SHINES BRIGHT** (2005) {*6}. Combining sourced material (including Burns's 'There'll Never Be Peace Until Jamie Comes Home') with their own individual songs, Lynne and Pat revived many a good tune. With **SEPTEMBER DAYS** (2007) {*6} and **TICKLED PINK** (2010) {*6}, it was clear they'd lost none of their confrontational wit and humour, as witness Lynne's 'Pheromones' and In Praise Of The Menopause'. *MCS*

Lynne Heraud - vocals / **Pat Turner** - vocals

UK own label — US not issued

2003. (cd) *(none)* **PARALLEL** ☐ ⊟
- May carol / The sheep are 'neath the snow / Black is the colour / In the gloaming / Affair on 8th Ave / English puddings / Perhaps / Poor lonely widow / Outlaws / John Reilly / Get away old man / I wish I wish / Snowmaiden / Sheep stealer / The working man.

Wild Goose — not issued

Feb 05. (cd) *(WGS 321CD)* **THE MOON SHINES BRIGHT** ☐ ⊟
- The moon shines bright / Autumn is down / There'll never be peace until Jamie comes home / Odd sock / Where the seeds of love grew / Cupid's garden / Man in grey / Fair maid of Islington / Regret / The golden wheat / Spanish dancer / My bonnie bonnie boy / Bright fine gold / Bonnie labouring boy / No more / I just want to be like the other girls.

Jul 07. (cd) *(WGS 342CD)* **SEPTEMBER DAYS** ☐ ⊟
- The collier laddie / The little turtle dove / Twa corbies / Pheromones / Whitsuntide carol / Where is my boy tonight? / The harper / Off for the op / Lovely Susan the milkmaid / Reres hill / September days / The bonny Irish maid / Lament of the flither girls / Foreign fields.

May 10. (cd) *(WGS 373CD)* **TICKLED PINK** ☐ ⊟
- Bonny George Campbell / Oxfam girls / Back in the game / Rosemary lane / Distant rumblings / Time you old gypsy man / Small fish / The smear test / Green grows the laurel / The wife of Ushers Well / The black ship / In praise of the menopause / Braw sailing / The sweetman / Imimb.

HERMAN DUNE

Sitting perilously close to the border separating neo-folk music from avant-indie-rock (also known as anti-folk), Swedish trio/duo HERMAN DUNE really cut a rug when the Herman Dune brothers David-Ivar and Andre, plus original drummer Ome, relocated to Paris. It was there that the brothers' recordings found a home, but a shared 7" alongside The Stars At My Desk in 1998, a cassette and another single were the whole of their output. One record in particular, **TURN OFF THE LIGHT** (2000) {*6}, was the band's first proper UK despatch, a simplistic NEIL YOUNG-meets-David Byrne affair that found favour with UK radio DJ John Peel. The strengths of twin guitarists (and singers) David-Ivar/Yaya and Andre were their lo-fi structure and their finger-picking interplay, much in display on their rush-released follow-up **"THEY GO TO THE WOODS"** (2001) {*7}, as on 'The Right Path Lays Open Before Me' and 'By The Door Of The Temple'.

Enlisting new drummer 'Cosmic' Neman Herman Dune to replace Ome, HD continued their prolific recording schedule with **SWITZERLAND HERITAGE** (2001) {*7} and a split release with American indie-rockers Cerberus Shoal, **THE WHYS AND HOWS OF…** (2002) {*6}. 2003 saw the release of two further Pavement-meet-Belle-And-Sebastian sets, one, **MASH CONCRETE METAL MUSHROOM** {*5}, for American listeners, and one for the Brits (but recorded in New York), **MAS CAMBIOS** {*6}. At some point they had moved to Portland, Oregon.

Having toured with former Eric's Trip starlet Julie Doiron, HERMAN DUNE invited the singer/bassist into their inner circle (however briefly) for album number whatever, **NOT ON TOP** (2005) {*7}. Marking their first appearance on the French-based Source Etc imprint, and their last with Stanley Brinks-bound Andre, the Richard Formby-produced **GIANT** (2006) {*6} was a definite push for indie superstardom and hardly a set that constituted folk per se. Ditto **NEXT YEAR IN ZION** (2008) {*6} – their debut on their Everloving label – and 2011's **STRANGE MOOSIC** {*6}. *MCS*

David-Ivar "Yaya" Herman Dune - vocals, guitars / **Andre Herman Dune** - vocals, guitars, fiddle / **Ome** - organ, vocals

UK/Fr self-rel. — US not issued

1997. (ltd-c) *(none)* MONEY MAKERS ON MY BACK [–] French [–]

RuminanCe — not issued

1998. (ltd; white-7"ep) *(RUM 005)* GLOW IN THE DARK [shared w/ The STARS AT MY DESK] [–] French [–]
- What do you know (about my philosophy)? / SkinHead / Carnival of souls (the red nose deer and the mountain goat) / Sitting beside you // [The STARS AT MY DESK tracks].

Prohibited - Atmospheriques — Shrimper

Jul 00. (7"/cd-s) *(PRO 017/+CD – ATM 20010)* BETWEEN THE LITTLE HOUSES [ ] [–]
- Shakespeare And North Hoyne / I do the crabwalk.

Aug 00. (cd/lp) *(PRO 014/015 – 2362-2/-1)* **TURN OFF THE LIGHT** [ ] [–]
- Our smell lingers / Drug-dealer in the park / You're so far from me / I do the crabwalk / Shakespeare and North Hoyne / World of workers / Ulrika's body / A hundred times better / As long as fakers rule / From that night [@ the Lounge Ax] / Slight miscalculation. *(UK re-iss. Jan 03; same)*

Dec 00. (cd-ep) *(PRO 021CD)* FIRE EP [ ] [–]
- The backyard berries / Just like that / Fire / It's better asunder.

May 01. (cd) *<SHR 121>* **"THEY GO TO THE WOODS"** [–] [ ]
- The right path lays open before me / They go to the woods / By the door of the temple / Heed the wrath / From German streets / I look at you at night / Strange plot / I'll come back when I come back / Deer wild baby / For the night / Black dog.

—— **'Cosmic' Neman Herman Dune** - drums, percussion; repl. Ome

Oct 01. (cd) *(PRO 024CD)* **SWITZERLAND HERITAGE** [ ] [–]
- Two crows / HD rider / The speed of a star / Blinded / Black cross / Little architect / Martin Donovan in trust / Going to Everglades / Not knowing / Pukka / With a tankful of gas / Coffee and fries / After Y2K / Expect the unexpected.

North East Indie — North East Indie

Jul 02. (cd) *(<NEI 25>)* **THE WHYS AND HOWS OF HERMAN DUNE AND CERBERUS SHOAL** [shared w/ CERBERUS SHOAL] [ ] [ ]
- I want a woman / Garaje #1 / A sight for soul eyes / Garaje #2 / If someone loves you / Garaje #3 / That woman is a murderess // [CERBERUS SHOAL tracks].

below is a David-Ivar offshoot featuring Etienne Greib + Nicolas Galina

Intercontinental — not issued

Oct 02. (7"ep; by TEMPLE TEMPLE) *(itc 9)* HEY … WE ARE … TEMPLE TEMPLE … HAIL TEMPLE TEMPLE… [–] French [–]
- Bring your passion / Cubs vs Yankees / Radio on / Next time.

Track and Field — Shrimper

Nov 02. (ltd-cd-r; by DAVID-IVAR HERMAN DUNE & EL BOY DIE) *<SHR 131>* **DI-DIE LIVE** [live] [–] [ ]
- My girl / The kingdom is not here at all / All the night / Semi-automatic baby / Tell me why / I lost the control / Blue train / You're the winner tonight / Going down / Strong as iron man.

Aug 03. (cd) *<SHR 142>* **MASH CONCRETE METAL MUSHROOM** [–] [ ]
- Introduction – New Jersey cross concrete / On the knick / Monkey song / Let me pry / All about you / Not that big a story / Futon song / Metal mash / Why would that hurt? (if you never loved me) / Taking taxis in winter clothes.

Oct 03. (cd) *(heat 16)* **MAS CAMBIOS** [ ] [–]
- With a fistful of faith / Red blue eyes / Show me the roof / My friends kill my folks / In the summer camp / In August / You stepped on sticky fingers / Sunny sunny cold cold day / At your Luau night / Winners lose / The static comes from my broken heart / So not what I needed.

Nov 04. (cd; by DAVID-IVAR HERMAN DUNE) *(<SHR 145>)* **YA YA** [ ] [ ]
- Time of glory – NYC / Song for the family / Take me to your country house / Do the swimming dragon / From the richest planet / Your properties / Coming from the attic window / New Jersey fake ID / My brand new bike / These arms of mine.

Jan 05. (m-cd; by DAVID-IVAR HERMAN DUNE) *(GUN 4)* **DEMENTED ABDUCTION: NOVASCOTIA RUNS FOR GOLD** [ ] [–]
- Nova Scotia / Loneliest man / In the house / Sheer wonder / Burn baby / Little baby cubs / Whatever burns / Mud cubes will melt anyway.

(above issued on Smoking Gun)

—— added **Julie Doiron** - bass, vocals

Apr 05. (cd/lp) *(heat 33/+lp)* **NOT ON TOP** [ ] [–]
- Little wounds / Not on top / Had I not known / Walk, don't run / Slow century / This will never happen / German green / Recording Farfisa / You could be a model, goodbye / Seven cities / Good for no one / Orange hat / Whatever burns the best baby / Eleven stones / Warning spectrum.

Jun 05. (cd-ep; mono) *(lane 22cd)* JACKSON HEIGHTS [ ] [–]
- Jackson Heights / Suburbs with you / Pet rabbit / Evil umpire / Big thing / The enemy's gone but you can't go home for shelter.

—— now without Doiron

Source Etc — not issued

Oct 06. (cd/d-lp) *(SOUR 125/+LP)* **GIANT** [ ] [–]
- I wish that I could see you soon / Nickel chrome / 1-2-3 – Apple tree / Bristol / Pure hearts / No master / Take time back to New York City / Baby bigger [instrumental] / This summer / Your name – My game / By the light of the moon / When the water gets cold and freezes on the lake / Giant / I'd rather walk than run / Glory of old / Mrs Bigger [instrumental] / Evidence here.

Feb 07. (7"green-ep) *(SOUR 126)* I WISH THAT I COULD SEE YOU SOON / I Wish That I Could See You Soon [version]. / Song Of Samuel [ ] [–]
(cd-s) *(SOURCD 126)* - ['A'] / I Wish I Had Someone That I Loved Well.

—— now w/out Andre, who had his own one-man group Stanley Brinks (one set 'Dank U' in 08)

City Slang — Everloving

Apr 08. (cd-ep) *<EVE 022>* I WISH THAT I COULD SEE YOU SOON [–] [ ]
- I wish I could see you soon / When the water gets cold (and freezes on the lake) / Take him back to New York City / I'd rather walk than run / I wish I had someone that I loved well.

Jun 08. (cd-ep) *<EVE 023>* 1.2.3 – APPLE TREE [–] [ ]
- 1.2.3 – Apple tree / Your name – My game / Song for Golda / Pure hearts / Song for Samuel.

Sep 08. (cd/lp) *(SLANG 105177-2/-1) <EVE 027>* **NEXT YEAR IN ZION** [ ] [ ]
- My home is nowhere without you / Try to think about me (don't worry a bit) / When the sun rose up this morning / When we were still friends / On a Saturday / My baby is afraid of sharks / Lovers are waterproof / Next year in Zion / Someone knows better than me / My best kiss / Baby baby you're my baby / (Nothing left but) Poison in the rain.

City Slang — Fortuna Pop

May 11. (cd/lp) *(SLANG 50003/+LP) <FPOP 119CDBK>* **STRANGE MOOSIC** [ ] Jun11 [ ]
- Tell me something I don't know / I hear strange moosic / Be a doll and take my heart / Where is the man? / Lay your head on my chest / Monument park / In the long long run / Your love is gold / The rock / Just like summer / My joy / Magician.

Boo HEWERDINE

Mark Hewerdine (born 1961 in London) started his musical life as leader of The Bible, a mildly underachieving if distracting indie-pop outfit in the mid-to-late 1980s. Formed in Norwich out of Cambridge outfit The Great Divide (the latter combo released a handful of singles), The Bible in their latter years featured Neil MacColl (brother of Kirsty) and were probably most famous for their 'Eureka' set in 1987. HEWERDINE left the band in 1989 to embark on a solo career, the first fruits of which were actually a joint album with Texan country singer Darden Smith, **EVIDENCE** (1989) {*7}, in which Boo expanded his songwriting style beyond the knowing pop of his former band.

IGNORANCE (1992) {*6} took the lessons learned working with Smith and struck out in a spare, singular style, which highlighted the genteel sadness that peppers HEWARDINE's work, bringing to mind a softer, more spiritual version of Squeeze's Chris Difford. Boo subsequently found time to briefly re-form The Bible in 1994 for an EP, 'Dreamlife', and an album which eventually surfaced as 'Dodo' in 1999.

With comparisons being drawn with the likes of Aztec Camera's Roddy Frame, **BAPTIST HOSPITAL** (1996) {*6} showcased more thoughtful if unsurprising downbeat strummage from HEWERDINE. It was the first of two of his albums to be produced by former NICK DRAKE producer John Wood, and was perhaps also notable for k.d. lang's cover of the album's 'Last Cigarette' for her 2004 smoking-themed set 'Drag'.

Another dose of heartfelt acoustica, **THANKSGIVING** (1999) {*7}, followed as HEWERDINE was beginning to gain the reputation of an unsung hero of British folk-pop. In another eventful twist, Boo was asked to re-record that album's 'Bell, Book And Candle' in 2004 for a climactic death scene in UK TV soap 'Emmerdale'. While this didn't set the singer up with a legion of new fans, it brought his songs back to a deservingly broader audience, and he was asked to contribute songs to the soundtrack/score of 'High Fidelity', the film of Nick Hornby's novel. A long-time fan, Hornby also wrote about one of The Bible's songs in his book '31 Songs'.

ANON (2002) {*5} followed in the same vein as its predecessors but made little impression, while the imaginately titled **A LIVE ONE** (2003) {*7} brought together highlights from his pre- and post-Bible career in stark clarity, and is arguably the best representation of his work in an intimate live setting.

HEWERDINE has also written songs for artists as diverse as EDDI READER, CLIVE GREGSON, former Spice Girl Mel C, Natalie Imbruglia and Madness frontman Suggs. One of his most famous songs is the EDDI READER hit 'The Patience Of Angels', which he recorded himself for

HARMONOGRAPH (2006) {*7}, an album that displayed the same ethereal qualities as were making multi-platinum stars of indie bods Elbow at the same time. He also produced READER's 'Sings The Songs Of Robert Burns' album in 2003. Recorded in Glasgow, the simple acoustic vibe on the songs of **GOD BLESS THE PRETTY THINGS** (2009) {*6} showcased more of HEWERDINE's clean, expressive songwriting. *MR*

BOO HEWERDINE and DARDEN SMITH

both vocals and all guitars (with session people)

Ensign not issued

Jul 89. (7") *(ENY 625)* ALL I WANT (IS EVERYTHING). / South By South West
(cd-s+=) *(ENYCD 625)* - My Doreen / Tell me why.
(12") *(ENYX 625)* - ('A') / Tell me why / My Doreen / ('A'-demo).

Aug 89. (lp/c) *(CHEN/ZCHEN 11)* **EVIDENCE**
- All I want (is everything) / Under the darkest moon / Reminds me (a little of you) / South by southwest / These chains / The first chill of winter / Out of this world / Love is a strange hotel / Evidence / Oil on the water / Tell me why [*] / Who, what, where and why? / A town called Blue. *(cd on Chrysalis+= *; CCD 1726) (cd re-iss. Nov 95 on Haven+= *; HAVENCD 6)* - My Doreen. *<US cd-iss. May 96 on Compass+=; 7 4232 2>*

BOO HEWERDINE

Ensign not issued

Feb 92. (cd)(c/lp) *(CCD 1930)(Z+/CHEN 24)* **IGNORANCE**
- I remember - The ship song / 59 yds / Sweet invisible / Swan silvertone / Touched / Little bits of zero / 16 miles / Gravity / Ignorance / A slow divorce / History. *(cd re-iss. Nov 95 on Haven+=; HAVENCD 007)* - Talk me down / The ghost of Johnny Ray / Liberty horses / The ghost of summer walking. *<US cd-iss. Sep 96 on Compass+=; 7 4235 2>*

Mar 92. (12"ep/cd-ep) *(ENY X/CD 653)* HISTORY / Little Bits Of Zero / Talk Me Down / The Ghost Of Johnny Ray

May 92. (12"ep/cd-ep) *(ENY X/CD 654)* 59 YDS / Liberty Horses / The Ghost Of Summer Walking / 16 Miles (version 2)

—— In 1994, Boo briefly re-formed The Bible for a one-off EP and (released 1999) album.

Blanco Y Negro Discovery

Nov 95. (cd-s) *(NEG 83CDX)* WORLD'S END / One Sad Cowboy / Another Mess Of Blues

Jan 96. (cd)(c) *(0630 12045-2)(WE 491) <77042>* **BAPTIST HOSPITAL** Sep 96
- World's end / The love thieves / Last cigarette / Dreamlife / Joke / Baptist hospital / A song for a friend / Candyfloss / Sycamore fall / Holy water / Junk / Greedy. *(cd re-iss. 2002 on Haven+=; ???)* - Firedogs / One sad cowboy / Another mess of blues / Black cat.

Feb 96. (c-s) *(NEG 86C)* JOKE / Auctioneers
(cd-s+=) *(NEG 86CD)* - Black cat / Firedogs.
(cd-s) *(NEG 86CDX)* - ('A') / First day in Hell / Buzz Aldrin / I miss you - Sha la la.

Black Burst Compass

Apr 99. (cd) *(BLACKCD 002) <7 4267-2>* **THANKSGIVING**
- The birds are leaving / Swansong / Hope is a name / Lazy heart / Water song / 'Our boy' / Bell, book and candle / Thanksgiving / Footsteps fall / Homesick son / Eve / A long winter / Murder in the dark / Please don't ask me to dance. *(re-iss. Jan 02; same)*

Haven not issued

Oct 01. (cd-ep) *(HAVENT 6CD)* EXTRAS
- Sweet on the vine / Extras / Dream baby / A cloud no bigger than your hand.

Jun 02. (cd) *(HAVENCD 15)* **ANON**
- Kite / Anon / Dream baby / A cloud no bigger than your hand / Apple tree / The Devil takes care of his own / Extras / Peacetime / Roundabout / Hunger / Looking for a light on the rails / Mapping the human heart.

Madan not issued

Mar 03. (cd) *(LIVE 001)* **A LIVE ONE** (live at The Ram Folk Club, Claygate, 21st September 2001) gigs
- Bell, book and candle / Sweet on the vine / Joke / Wings on my wheels / Murder in the dark / Graceland / Please don't ask me to dance / The border / Patience of angels / World's end / The birds are leaving / Lucky penny / Soul / Paper planes. *(re-iss. Sep 04; same)*

mVine not issued

Nov 05. (cd-ep) *(MVBHCD 01)* ONTARIO EP
- Ontario / White lies / Hummingbird / Sleeping beauty.

Jan 06. (cd) *(MVBHCD 02)* **HARMONOGRAPH**
- The girl who fell in love with the moon / Weatherman / Ontario / Butterfly (on a pin) / Sugar on the pill / Slow learner / Sing to me / Patience of angels / Submarines / Nameless / Mountains / I felt her soul move through me.

Navigator not issued

May 08. (m-cd) *(Navigator 13)* **TOYBOX NO.1**
- Koh-i-noor / Ellis Island blues / Dragonflies / Taxi dancer / Bible pages / Sunset.

Oct 08. (m-cd) *(Navigator 26)* **TOYBOX NO.2**
- White lilies / Follow my tears / Harvest gypsies / Limelight / Stone in your shoe / Amen.

Oct 09. (cd) *(Navigator 11)* **GOD BLESS THE PRETTY THINGS**
- Geography / Muddy water / Sleeping lions / New year's eve / Rags / It's a beautiful night / In Paris after the war / Soul mate / Silver wings / I almost said goodbye / You and me.

Fay HIELD (⟹ The WITCHES OF ELSWICK)

Geoff HIGGINBOTTOM

Born February 13, 1959, in Stockport, Cheshire, this multi-instrumentalist (six-string and 12-string guitars, bodhran and Appalachian dulcimer) first came to light when he took third place in a competition at the Warwick Folk Festival in 1985. Almost immediately, sporting a designer beard (now just a moustache), he released his debut LP **SONGS FROM THE LEVENSHULME TRIANGLE** {*6}, promoting songs such as 'Farmer's Toast' at consecutive Sidmouth International festivals.

Performing the occasional shanty as well as his own numbers and some covers, the now Manchester-based singer/songwriter delivered the more accessible **FLOWERS TOMORROW** (1987) {*7}, its topical themes including South Africa ('Nelson And Winnie'). He contributed the song 'Spare The Child' to 1987's various-artists Children In Need album. He took a break after his third album, **MORE THAN POUNDS AND PENCE** (1990) {*6}, although you could still see Geoff on TV (blink and you'd miss him), playing bit parts in soaps from 'Brookside' to 'Emmerdale' and 'Coronation Street'. He continues to perform around Manchester and beyond, still going strong as of 2009. Fan favourites include his interpretations of RICHARD THOMPSON's '1952 Vincent Black Lightning' and Bob Marley's 'No Woman No Cry', reportedly changing the words to "No rum and no pies" after the third verse. *MCS*

Geoff Higginbottom - vocals, acoustic guitar, Appalachian dulcimer, bodhran

UK unknown US not issued

Nov 85. (lp) *(???)* **SONGS FROM THE LEVENSHULME TRIANGLE**

Dragon not issued

1987. (lp) *(DRGN 871)* **FLOWERS TOMORROW**
- Here I am amongst you / The hard times of old England / Tommy's lot / A poor old man / The wizard of Alderley / Nelson and Winnie / The battle of Sowerby Bridge / The man of the Sandune / Johnny jump up / A week before Easter / Shallow brown / Flowers tomorrow.

Dec 90. (lp) *(DRGN 903)* **MORE THAN POUNDS AND PENCE**

own label not issued

2001. (cd) *(none)* **LIVE AT GREGSON LANE** [live May 4, 2000]
- Here I am amongst you / Do ray me / July wakes / Johnny jump up / Peter Green / The Leish Young buy a broom / 1952 Vincent black lightning / Now I'm easy / The blind lead the blind / Gay fusilier / I want to see the bright lights tonight.

Maggie HOLLAND

Born December 19, 1949, at Alton in Hampshire, folk singer MAGGIE HOLLAND has played in several roots acts. As bass player and eventually vocalist with bluesy duo HOT VULTURES (alongside then husband IAN A. ANDERSON), she performed numerous gigs around Britain and Europe while releasing the albums 'Carrion On' (1975), 'The East Street Shakes' (1977) and 'Up The Line' (1979).

Expanding and evolving the group into The ENGLISH COUNTRY BLUES BAND (with Rod Stradling, SUE HARRIS and later Chris Coe), this outfit delivering two more sets, 'No Rules' (1982) and 'Home And Deranged' (1984). Meanwhile HOLLAND carved out a solo career with **STILL PAUSE** (1983) {*7}, a blend of traditional British/American ballads and covers from the pens of DAVE EVANS ('Time To Kill'), Peter Rowan ('Mad Lydia's Waltz'), DYLAN ('Just Like Tom Thumb's Blues'), Tom Yates ('Bye Bye Bohemia'), RICHARD THOMPSON ('The Great Valerio'), Jimmie Rodgers ('Peach Picking Time In Georgia'), Anne Lister ('Icarus'), Jesse Winchester ('Black Cat') and CHRIS SMITHER ('Homunculus'). Guests included JOHN KIRKPATRICK and IAN A. ANDERSON.

The 12" EP/mini-set **A SHORT CUT** (1986) {*5} was a collaboration with TIGER MOTH colleague Jon Moore, this time around covering songs by RICHARD THOMPSON ('For Shame Of Doing Wrong'), Tymon Dogg ('Locks And Bolts And Hinges'), DYLAN ('My Back Pages'), AL STEWART ('Accident On Third Street'), BRUCE COCKBURN ('If I Had A Rocket Launcher') and Graham Larkbey ('Your Husband Didn't Like It').

TIGER MOTH in all its shapes and forms delivered a string of LPs, including one as ORCHESTRE SUPER MOTH, while HOLLAND toured with The Vacant Lot (a country dance band) and, reflecting her fascination with DYLAN, Maggie's Farm. Tours of Bangladesh, Nepal, Thailand and the Philippines are among her most cherished memories, as is her role as lead singer in Tony Harrison's 'Mysteries' trilogy, in a three-month run for the National Theatre at London's Lyceum in 1985.

Virtually unaccompanied, **DOWN TO THE BONE** (1992) {*7} featured her own compositions (some with Jon Moore), two each by DYLAN ('Is Your Love In Vain' and 'Most Of The Time') and ROBB JOHNSON ('Overnight' and 'Little Sister's Gone'), plus one each from BILLY BRAGG ('Levi Stubbs' Tears'), Stewart McGregor ('Coshieville'), Steve Earle ('My Old Friend The Blues'), Danny Kortchmar ('You're Not Drinking Enough') and MARTIN CARTHY ('Company Policy').

HOLLAND subsequently relocated to Leith, a suburb of Edinburgh, and recorded **BY HEART** (1995) {*6}, covering OYSTERBAND's 'Oxford Girl', DAVE EVANS's 'Rosie', ROBB JOHNSON's 'Cathy Come Home' and 'Evergreen', Debby McClatchy's 'The Colorado Song', MICHAEL CHAPMAN's 'Postcards From Scarborough', BILLY BRAGG's 'Tank Park Salute', Tom Waits's 'Invitation To The Blues' and Tucker Zimmerman's 'Taoist Tale'.

Signing up with Irregular Records, her 1999 solo set **GETTING THERE** {*6} featured label boss ROBB JOHNSON (guitar), Terry Mann (on melodeon, sax, whistle and harmonica) and Fiona Larcombe (fiddle) on a record with more than a few of JOHNSON's own songs, including 'Tourists And Casualties', 'Hancock In Australia', 'Good At Heart', 'Love In Another Language' and 'How Much I Miss You'.

Of course, the inevitable DYLAN songs cropped up ('Visions Of Johanna' and 'Not Dark Yet'), plus one each by AL STEWART ('Accident On Third Street'), RALPH McTELL ('Peppers And Tomatoes') and DICK GAUGHAN ('Childhood's End'). Her own 'A Place Called England' (winner, the following February, of Best Song at the BBC Radio 2 folk awards) and the eight-minute 'All Alone' were also worthy additions to any set.

Scots musicians Malcolm Ross (formerly of Josef K and Orange Juice) and cellist Wendy Weatherby were involved in **CIRCLE OF LIGHT** (2003) {*6}, and there were of course covers of songs by the usual suspects. JOHNSON was the source of another five ('St Ives End Lane', 'Night Café', 'Texas Prison Songs', 'Permanent Free Zone' and 'Sunlight And Snow'), rubbing shoulders with BRAGG ('Between The Wars'), AL STEWART ('Manuscript'), DYLAN ('Bob Dylan's Dream'), EVANS ('Time To Kill') and Alan Tunbridge ('Time Is Flying'). Of late, Maggie has been a little conspicuous by her absence, but she's already achieved more than most folk stars could dream of. *MCS*

Maggie Holland - vocals, guitars, banjo, bass, etc. (ex-HOT VULTURES, ex-ENGLISH COUNTRY BLUES BAND, of TIGER MOTH) / with session people

UK Rogue — UK not issued

Jun 83. (lp) *(FMSL 2002)* **STILL PAUSE** ☐ ⊟
- Time to kill / Vandy / Mad Lydia's waltz / Just like Tom Thumb's blues / Bye bye bohemia / The banks of the Nile / If he's gone / The great Valerio / Peach picking time in Georgia / Icarus / The house carpenter / Black cat / Homunculus.

Sep 86. (m-lp; by MAGGIE HOLLAND & JON MOORE) *(FMST 4008)* **A SHORT CUT** ☐ ⊟
- For shame of doing wrong / Locks and bolts and hinges / My back pages / Accident on third street / If I had a rocket launcher / Your husband didn't like it.

—— Maggie rejoined TIGER MOTH and helped form ORCHESTRE SUPER MOTH

1989. (ltd-c) *(none)* **THE CASSETTE** ⊟ demo ⊟
- No good at love / Sandy hill / Old man / etc.

1992. (cd) *(FMSD 5022)* **DOWN TO THE BONE** ☐ ⊟
- Overnight / Black crow / Levi Stubbs' tears / A proper sort of gardener / Salt of the earth / Little sister's gone / Coshieville / My old friend the blues / Sir Galahad / Is your love in vain / You're not drinking enough / Sandy hill / Never too late / Company policy / Perfumes of Arabia / Most of the time / Change in the air.

Rhiannon — not issued

Sep 95. (cd) *(RHYD 5008)* **BY HEART** ☐ ⊟
- Oxford girl / Rosie / Only dreaming / Smokey's bar / Cathy come home / Catherine of Aragon's song / The rowan tree / May morning dew / Evergreen / The Colorado song / Postcards from Scarborough / Tank park salute / Jack Haggerty / Company of strangers / Seven gypsies / Invitation to the blues / Taoist tale.

Irregular — not issued

Apr 99. (cd) *(irr 035)* **GETTING THERE** ☐ ⊟
- Planet of the clowns / Visions of Johanna / Tourists and casualties / Accident on 3rd Street / Peppers and tomatoes / Fair Rosamund / All alone / Not dark yet / Hancock in Australia / Childhood's end / Good at heart / Love in another languange / How much I miss you / A place called England.

Nov 03. (cd) *(irr 040)* **CIRCLE OF LIGHT** ☐ ⊟
- St Ives end lane / Roving on a winter's night / Cold night on Bernard Street / Between the wars / The shepherds' song / Manuscript / Time to kill / Number 4071, Private Bennett / Night café / World turned upside down / Bob Dylan's dream / Texas prison songs / Time is flying / Permanent free zone / Sunlight and snow.

- (8-10*) compilations -

Jul 07. (cd) *Weekend Beatnik; (WEBE 9044)* **BONES** ☐ ⊟
- A place called England / Levi Stubbs' tears / Mad Lydia's waltz / Black crow / Most of the time / Living a lie / No good at love / Bye bye bohemia / A proper sort of gardener / Sandy hill / If I had a rocket launcher / Vandy / Coshieville / Locks and bolts and hinges / The great Valerio / Never too late / Banks of the Nile / Perfumes of Arabia / Change in the air / Time to kill / Overnight / Homunculus / Look up look up / Old man.

The HOLY JOY (⟹) The BAND OF HOLY JOY)

HOME SERVICE

A folk-rock supergroup of sorts, HOME SERVICE were formed from stray former ALBION DANCE BAND members JOHN TAMS (also ex-MUCKRAM WAKES), BILL CADDICK and ex-GRYPHON Graeme Taylor. Joined by Michael Gregory, Malcolm Bennet and BRASS MONKEY alumni Roger Williams and Howard Evans (trumpeter Colin Rae left in 1980), the ensemble abandoned their original name The First Eleven for one less numerically inflexible.

With a few personnel tweaks along the way (Jonathan Davie, another GRYPHON refugee, superseded Bennet and Steve King was introduced), HOME SERVICE went from appearing at the 1982 Cambridge Folk Festival to bona-fide album recording artists, their debut **THE HOME SERVICE** (1984) {*6} meeting with favourable reviews. Adding neo-classical saxophonist Andy Findon and guest singer LINDA THOMPSON, their work on the National Theatre project **THE MYSTERIES** (1985) {*6} was brought to life for an album.

Disgruntled with their lack of live work, CADDICK resumed his solo career in 1985, leaving the band to piece together album number three, **ALRIGHT JACK** (1986) {*7}, a record formed around half a dozen Percy Grainger folk songs side by side with traditional tunes. JOHN TAMS's compositions 'Sorrow /Babylon', 'Scarecrow' and the title track came off best.

With TAMS bailing out for solo work and the rest of the group concentrating more on outside projects, the group split. A reformation for the Hokey Pokey charity set 'All Through The Year' in 1991 led HOME SERVICE (without TAMS) to try once more, but after several live shows, recorded for the concerts album **WILD LIFE** (1995) {*6}, they called it a day again.

TAMS was already carving out a considerable career as musical director and actor at the National Theatre ('Lark Rise To Candleford' was one of many projects he'd undertaken), while soundtrack work came his way for ITV's action-adventure series 'Sharpe' (he also played the role of Rifleman Daniel Hagman). In 1996 he and Dominic Muldowney released their music for the series as **OVER THE HILLS AND FAR AWAY: The Music Of Sharpe** {*6}. His solo career for Topic Records got under way in 2000 with **UNITY** {*7}; two other sets have since surfaced, **HOME** (2002) {*7} and **THE RECKONING** (2005) {*8}, the latter a Best Album winner at the BBC Radio 2 Folk Awards, where he also won Best Folk Singer of the Year and Best Traditional Track, for 'Bitter Withy'.

TAMS also became musical director of the BBC Radio 2 programme 'Radio Ballads', a 2006 update of the legendary EWAN MacCOLL series of the 1950s. In 2007 and 2009 John was awarded honorary doctorates by Sheffield Hallam University and Derby University respectively, while an album of music for the National Theatre production 'WarHorse' was released in 2008. The show, which picks up awards year after year, is now on Broadway. *MCS*

John Tams (b. Feb 16 '49) - vocals, acoustic guitar, melodeon (ex-MUCKRAM WAKES, ex-ALBION BAND) / **Bill Caddick** (b. Jun '44, Wolverhampton, Midlands) - vocals, guitar, dobro (ex-ALBION BAND) / **Graeme Taylor** (b. Feb 2 '54, Stockwell, London) - vocals, guitar (ex-GRYPHON) / **Malcolm Bennet** - bass / **Michael Gregory** (b. Nov 16 '49, Gower, Wales) - drums, percussion / **Roger Williams** (b. Jul 30 '54, Cottingham, Yorkshire) - trombone (of BRASS MONKEY) / **Howard Evans** (b. Feb 29 '44, Chard, Somerset) - trumpet (of BRASS MONKEY) / Colin Rae (trumpet) left before recording

UK Luggage — US not issued

Aug 81. (7") *(LUG 1)* DOING THE INGLISH. / Bramsley ☐ ⊟

—— **Jonathan Davie** (b. Sep 6 '54, Twickenham, Middlesex) - bass (ex-GRYPHON, ex-Banned) repl. Malcolm Bennet / added **Steve King** - keyboards

Jigsaw not issued

Jun 84. (lp) *(SAW 3)* **THE HOME SERVICE**
- Don't let 'em grind you down / One more day / Never gonna be a cowboy now / Peat bog soldiers / Chaconne / The old man's song / Doin' the best I can / She moves among men / Walk my way. *(cd-iss. May 96 as 'EARLY TRANSMISSIONS' on Road Goes On Forever+=; RGFCD 028)- Doing the Inglish / Bramsley.*

—— added **Andy Findon** - sax, flutes, clarinet (ex-Michael Nyman Band)

Coda not issued

Jan 85. (lp/c) *(NAT/+C 1)* **THE MYSTERIES**
- The Nativity: God - Creation - Serpents dance - Cain and Abel – Don't be an outlaw / The Nativity II: Appearance of the archangel - Shay fan yan ley - Journey to Bethlehem - The nativity - Lay me low - Herod / The Nativity III: The kings - Shepherds arise / The Passion: Entry to Jerusalem - Betrayal and denial - All in the morning (part 1) - The arrest - Scourging - All in the morning part II - The trial - Lewk up lewk up / The Passion II: The road to Calvary - Crucifixion - The moon shines bright - We sing allelujah / Doomsday: God - Wonderous love - The death of Mary / Doomsday II: The coronation of the virgin - Lyke wake dirge - Judgement - The wheel. *(cd-iss. May 98 on Fledg'ling; FLED 3014)*

Jan 86. (7"ep) *(CODS 15)* THE MYSTERIES
- Shey fan yah ley / We sing allelujah / Shepherds arise / Lewk up lewk up.

—— now without BILL CADDICK (he continued solo)

Making Waves not issued

Apr 86. (lp/c) *(SPIN/SPIC 119)* **ALRIGHT JACK**
- Alright Jack / Rose of Allendale / Radstock jig / Sorrow-Babylon / The Duke of Marlborough fanfare / A Lincolnshire posy: a. Dublin Bay, b. Horkstow Grange, c. Rufford Park poachers, d. The brisk young sailor, e. Lord Melbourne, f. The lost lady found / Look up look up / Scarecrow. *(re-iss. Feb 87 on Hobsons Choice; HCM 001) (cd-iss. Jul 91 on Fledg'ling; FLY 1001CD) (cd re-iss. 1997; FLED 3011) (cd re-iss. Jun 05; FLED 3015)*

Jun 86. (7") *(SURF 114)* SORROW. / Rose Of Allendale

—— split the following year, although they re-formed for Hokey Pokey charity set 'All Through The Year' (1991); HOME SERVICE (without Tams) re-formed in 1991

Fledg'ling not issued

Jun 95. (cd) *(FLED 3001)* **WILD LIFE** [live August 1992]
- Chaconne / The reaper – Scarecrow – Battle of the Somme / Lili Marlene walks away – Pappa Joe's polka / Born a dog, died a gentleman / Napoleon's grande marche / Summer is a' coming in / The encounter / She moves among men / Never gonna be a cowboy now / One more whiskey / Battle Pavanne – Peat bog soldiers / Stay on the line / Rainbow waistcoat.

JOHN TAMS

Crucible not issued

1987. (7") *(MEK 005)* I'LL FLY AWAY. / Rolling Home

—— Tams rejoined The ALBION BAND (also ASHLEY HUTCHINGS)

Virgin not issued

Apr 96. (cd; as JOHN TAMS & DOMINIC MULDOWNEY) *(VTCD 81)* **OVER THE HILLS AND FAR AWAY**: The Music Of SHARPE (TV Soundtrack)
- The overture: a) Sharpe's theme, b) Prelude / I'm ninety five (The BAND AND BUGLES OF THE LIGHT DIVISION) / Over the hills and far away / The Spanish sword / Rogue's march / The collier recruit (KATE RUSBY) / The bird in the bush - The colours / The Spanish bride / The shilling / Gentleman soldier / Bugle call - Moneymusk (The BAND BUGLES ...) / Broken-hearted I will wander (KATE RUSBY) / Badajoz / The rambling soldier / The huntsman chorus - The Italian song (The BAND AND BUGLES ...) / Johnny is gone for a soldier / The forlorn hope / Love farewell / Sunset (The BAND AND BUGLES ...) / Sharpe's song – Sharpe's theme.

Topic Topic

Jul 00. (cd) *(<TSCD 508>)* **UNITY** Apr 01
- Whole new vision / American dream (girl in Texas) / From where I lie - Sheepcounting / Unity (raise your banners high) / Spanish bride / Somewhere the sun is shining - Hold back the tide / Winds of change (Yalta beach-bonfire night) / Harry Stone (hearts of coal) / Who will blow the candle out tonight?

Oct 02. (cd) *(<TSCD 533>)* **HOME** Feb 03
- You don't know me anymore / Another grey and grim old grimy day / Yonder (down the winding road) / The ballroom / Hugh Stenson and Molly Green / Right on line / The traveller / Red gown / Bound east for Cardiff / When this song is ended there's no more.

Sep 05. (cd) *(<TSCD 551>)* **THE RECKONING** Nov 05
- Written in the book / Safe house / Amelia / How high the price? / Bitter withy / A man of constant sorrow / The sea: Pretty Nancy - A sailor's life - One more day - As I looked east, as I looked west / Including love.

—— In 2008, Tams provided songs for the CD of music by Adrian Sutton for the National Theatre production of 'WarHorse'; a year later he was behind The Band And Bugles Of The Rifles' "Help For Heroes" single 'Love Farewell'.

- (8-10*) compilation -

Nov 07. (cd) *Highpoint; (<HPO 6015>)* **THE DEFINITIVE COLLECTION** Jan 08
- Doing time to fit your crime (ASHLEY HUTCHINGS) / Harry Stone (hearts of coal) / Yonder (down the winding road) / Sweet rose of Allendale (HOME SERVICE) / Spanish bride / Evona (OLIVER KNIGHT) / Polska (the clunch) - The traveller / Bitter withy / Lay me low / Hugh Stenson and Molly Green / Unity (raise your banners high) / Scarecrow (HOME SERVICE).

HOMESPUN

Initially intended to be a spin-off from David Rotheray's long-time Beautiful South association, HOMESPUN, a countrified folk-pop outfit including former session singer-turned-pop star Sam Brown (daughter of 1960s R'n'R skiffler Joe Brown), produced three sets during a tidy tenure in the mid-2000s.

HOMESPUN (2003) {*7}, **EFFORTLESS COOL** (2005) {*7} and **SHORT STORIES FROM EAST YORKSHIRE** (2008) {*8} combined some steely twangs over rootsy ballad-folk and was certainly a million miles away from sultry Sam's solo hit days of the late 1980s (remember 'Stop'?), or for that matter the music of The Beautiful South. One thing that was clear was that Sam's voice had never been better, and it seemed she'd thrown it away on years of singing pop-inflected songs. The HOMESPUN collective was an inspired decision by both artists: check out especially the third-album songs 'The Screen Goes Black', 'My Sorrows Learned To Swim' and 'Short Story' from album three.

DAVID ROTHERAY's solo project **THE LIFE OF BIRDS** (2010) {*7} featured collaborations with folk stars JIM CAUSLEY ('The Sparrow, The Thrush And The Nightingale'), BELLA HARDY ('Living Before The War', 'The Digital Cuckoo' and 'The Hummingbird', with Jim), ELIZA CARTHY ('The Road To The South' and 'Cover Your Garden Over'), KATHRYN WILLIAMS ('Crows, Ravens And Rooks'), nu-trad-folk lord ALASDAIR ROBERTS ('Draughty Old Fortress'), and others from Camille O Sullivan, FERNHILL's Julie Murphy, Celtic-folkie ELEANOR McEVOY, NAT(alie) JOHNSON and JACK L(ukeman). *MCS*

David Rotheray (b. Feb 9 '63, Hull) – guitar, bass (ex-Beautiful South) / **Sam Brown** (b. Samantha Brown, Oct'64, London) – vocals / with **Melvin Duffy** - pedal steel / **Tony Robinson** - keyboards, brass / **Clare MacTaggart** - violin, banjo, mandolin / **Gary Hammond** - percussion

UK Music Vision / US not issued

Aug 03. (cd) *(BHCCD 001)* **HOMESPUN**
- Unfortunately young / Did you ever? / Don't force me to be free / Anniversary rag / Let me be good / I'm in your head / Lonely together / Days / Your radio / Footsteps / Sundial. *(re-iss. Mar 08 on Active Media; BH1)*

Feb 05. (cd) *(BHCCD 002)* **EFFORTLESS COOL**
- Sweetness / If we're so happy / Love will come around / Italy / Effortless cool / Rubber duck / A minute / Whistlestop blues / Cosy island lullaby / The reluctant sailor / If God was a girl / You are here. *(re-iss. Mar 08 on Active Media; BH2)*

Feb 05. (cd-s) *(BHSCD 003)* EFFORTLESS COOL / Unfortunately Young / We Can Swing Together [live]

May 05. (cd-s) *(BHSCD 004)* IF WE'RE SO HAPPY / Whistlestop Blues / Lonely Together

Active Media not issued

Feb 08. (cd) *(BHSCD 005)* **SHORT STORIES FROM EAST YORKSHIRE**
- Short story / My sorrows learned to swim / Happiness passes / Driver (with MARY COUGHLAN) / First people on earth / Memo to self / Magician's daughter / Yorkshire ghost / Watching / Lover's chapel (with ELEANOR McEVOY) / Screen goes black / Rendezvous roulade.

DAVID ROTHERAY

with guest spots from various sources

Proper not issued

Aug 10. (cd) *(PRPCD 061)* **THE LIFE OF BIRDS**
- The sparrow, the thrush and the nightingale / Living before the war / The road to the south / Crows, ravens and rooks / Draughty old fortress / Sweet forgetfulness / The hummingbird / Taller than me / Almost beautiful / Flying lessons / The best excuse in the world (is the truth) / The digital cuckoo / Cover your garden over / The sparrow, the thrush and the nightingale (part II).

HORSES BRAWL

The Norfolk-based team of fiddle/recorder/crumhorn player Laura Cannell and guitarist Adrian Lever (initially a trio with cellist Jonathan Manton) have been described as a contemporary folk and early music group, recalling ye olde days of GRYPHON and AMAZING BLONDEL

Self-taught Laura had graduated with a first from the London College of Music in 2001, and a subsequent masters degree helped her with further studies and projects; bursaries and grants were awarded in 2005/2006. Meanwhile, her baroque/chamber-folk group with Adrian and Jonathan was beginning to garner plaudits from audiences at their many promotional festival appearances.

The trio's debut album **HORSES BRAWL** (2005) {*7} procured tunes from as far afield as Bulgaria and Romania and gave modern-day makeovers to the odd renaissance and Elizabethan jig.

Equally exciting and vibrant, their second set, **DINDIRIN** (2007) {*8} – without the departing Jonathan – stoked the mediaeval hearth, containing another dollop of improv Mediterranean music from the twelfth century to the nineteenth. **WILD LAMENT** (2009) {*7} continued the young duo's fascination with formal, foot-tapping folk, best examples including 'Maggots' and 'Merula'. *MCS*

Laura Cannell - fiddle, crumhorn, recorder / **Adrian Lever** - acoustic guitar / **Jonathan Manton** - cello

UK Brawl — US not issued

Oct 05. (cd) *(BRAWL 001)* **HORSES BRAWL** □ ⊟
- Mofo / Stampanasa / Hobo / Douce dame / Inspiration / Galliard / Frisk / A bruxa / Chara / Istanbul.

—— now without Manton

Dec 06. (cd-s) *(BRAWL 002)* SHAVE THE DONKEY / Mai / La Gamba □ ⊟

Jun 07. (cd) *(BRAWL 003)* **DINDIRIN** □ ⊟
- Passim estampie / Brannells / Fawrhoro / Misdelight / Bibit / La gamba / Alca / Shave the donkey / Mai / Dindirin.

Jun 09. (cd) *(BRAWL 004)* **WILD LAMENT** □ ⊟
- Tourdion / Maggots / Merula / Loyaute / Ave Maria / L'ymage / Psalm 23 / Pase el agoa / The bonny miller / In aeternum.

HOT RATS (⟹ TUNDRA)

HOUSE BAND (⟹ forthcoming Celtic-Folk Discography)

HOVEN DROVEN (⟹ Great Celtic-Folk/World-Music Discography)

Doug HUDSON (⟹ TUNDRA)

Alistair HULETT

Born October 15, 1951 in Glasgow, Scotland, Alistair was one of that rare breed of Scots musicians who embraced both Celtic-folk and acoustic singer-songwriter territory. Sadly, he died aged 59 on January 28, 2010, during the writing of this book.

By the time the teenaged ALISTAIR HULETT had like many Scots before him moved to New Zealand, he had already developed a serious taste for folk music. He made a natural progression from fan to performer, subsequently relocating to Australia, where he honed his skills on the folk-club circuit. By the time punk made its way down under in 1979 the expatriate Scot had already begun to exercise his own songwriting talent, eventually marrying punk and folk in ROARING JACK.

Formed in the early 1980s, the band's debut set, **STREET CELTABILITY** (1986) {*6}, topped the Australian indie chart and set the pace for other young bands of their kind. The Celtic connection central to their music found HULETT and co. supporting British and Irish brethren such as The POGUES, BILLY BRAGG and The MEN THEY COULDN'T HANG, while second set **THE CAT AMONG THE PIGEONS** (1988) {*7} was nominated for the Australian equivalent of a Brit Award. Despite similar plaudits for a third set, **THROUGH THE SMOKE OF INNOCENCE** (1990) {*6}, the band called it a day in 1992. Those who had never caught the likes of 'Buy Us A Drink', 'We Don't Play No Elton Fucking John' and the anti-sectarian 'The Old Divide And Rule' had certainly missed out. HULETT resumed the solo career he'd begun in his teens.

Unsurprisingly perhaps, the singer-songwriter gravitated back towards more traditional folk with his acclaimed debut album **DANCE OF THE UNDERCLASS** (1991) {*6}. In contrast, **IN THE BACKSTREETS OF PARADISE** (1994) {*6} was a harder-hitting (at least musically) affair, comprising songs originally written for a fourth ROARING JACK album and recorded by HULETT's newly formed Hooligans. Although the Scotsman proceeded to tour the record's harder material with this acoustic outfit, he simultaneously maintained a concert schedule geared towards the purists.

Although originally intended as a solo venture, **SATURDAY JOHNNY AND JIMMY THE RAT** (1995) {*6} ended up as a collaboration with English folk veteran DAVE SWARBRICK, at that time a fellow expatriate. A tribute to the original folk revival, the record revealed a natural chemistry that also translated to the stage. A hugely popular Australian tour was followed by long-awaited UK gigs, and the duo went on to cut a second set together, 1998's **THE COLD GREY LIGHT OF DAWN** {*6}. The whole experience eventually led to Alistair once again living in Glasgow, where he created a series of politically motivated workshop projects concentrating on popular protest.

In 2005, after another collaboration with SWARBRICK on **RED CLYDESIDE** (2002) {*6}, HULETT was truly back to his best with **RICHES AND RAGS** (2005) {*7} – check out his sublime version of The INCREDIBLE STRING BAND's golden nugget 'First Girl I Loved'. Sadly, he was to pass away five years later.

Many fellow musicians attended his funeral, and it was decided to record a various-artists tribute set. 'Love, Loss And Liberty' (2011) featured tracks by JUNE TABOR, NIAMH PARSONS, ROY BAILEY, ALISTAIR ROBERTS, Sheena Wellington, and blues lover HULETT himself on 'The Internationale'. *MCS*

ROARING JACK

Alistair Hulett - vocals, acoustic guitar / **Rab Mannell** - guitar, bouzouki / **Davey Williams** - bass / **Hunter Owens** - accordion, mandolin, vocals / **Steve Thompson** - drums

UK Mighty Boy — US not issued

1986. (m-lp) *(MBEP 0002)* **STREET CELTABILITY** ⊟ Austra ⊟
- The old divide and rule / Buy us a drink / Wild rover again / Yuppietown / Ballad of 1975 / Shell shocked crowd.

—— **Steph/Steven Miller** - accordion; repl. Owens

—— **Rob Gilchrist** - drums; repl. Thompson (who died in the 1990s, as did Rob)

Nov 88. (lp/c/cd) *(MBLP/MBTC/MBCD 7007)* **THE CAT AMONG THE PIGEONS** ⊟ Austra ⊟
- Uisge beatha / Love in the modern age / Lights of Sydney town / The day that the boys came down / The lass behind the beertaps / Go leave / Destitution road / The swaggies have all waltzed Matilda away / Moving on / Playing for the traffic / The thin red line / The cat among the pigeons / Lads of the BLF. *(cd+=)* - Yuppietown / The old divide and rule / Shell shocked crowd / Honky tonks in Heaven.

Jun 89. (7") *(MB 20247)* THE SWAGGIES HAVE ALL WALTZED MATILDA AWAY [new version]. / Song Of A Drinking Man's Wife (No Half Measures) ⊟ Austra ⊟

Nov 90. (cd/c/lp) *(MBCD/MBTC/MBLP 7016)* **THROUGH THE SMOKE OF INNOCENCE** ⊟ Austra ⊟
- Girl on a gate / Song of choice / Her latest affectation / Ways of a rover / Lass from Yarrow / October wind / Polythene flowers / Child's play / The bonny wee well / Take-away love / A stranger and a friend / Shot down in flames. *(cd+=)* - Just like cigarettes / The ball of yarn.

Jan 91. (7") *(???)* FRAMED. / Criminal Justice ⊟ Austra ⊟

(above was a benefit single for the campaign exposing the frame-up of Tim Anderson)

- (8-10*) compilations, etc.-

Nov 02. (d-cd) *Jump Up; (none)* **THE COMPLETE WORKS** ⊟ German ⊟
- (STREET CELTABILLITY tracks) / (THE CAT AMONG THE PIGEONS tracks) / Honky tonks in Heaven // (THROUGH THE SMOKE OF INNOCENCE cd tracks) / Framed / Criminal justice.

ALISTAIR HULETT

Red Rattler — not issued

1991. (cd) *(RATCD 001)* **DANCE OF THE UNDERCLASS** ⊟ Austra ⊟
- Among Proddy dogs and Papes / Yuppietown / After the smoke cleared / Destitution road / He fades away / Suicide town / No half measures / Farewell to whisky / The swaggies have all waltzed Matilda away / Plains of Maralinga / Dictatorship of capital / The internationale. *(re-iss. Aug 00 on Jump Up (Germany); JUMPUP 001)*

1994. (cd) *(RATCD 002)* **IN THE BACK STREETS OF PARADISE** ⊟ Austra ⊟
- New age of the fist / Everyone I know / Militant red / She's got no conscience / John Maclean's march / Good morning Bouganville / Victor Jara of Chile / Almost unintentional / Out in the danger zone / Kick it over. *(re-iss. May 01 on Jump Up (Germany); JUMPUP 002)*

1995. (cd; by ALISTAIR HULETT & DAVE SWARBRICK) *(RATCD 003)* **SATURDAY JOHNNY AND JIMMY THE RAT** ⊟ Austra ⊟
- Saturday Johnny and Jimmy the rat / In the days of '49 / An bunan buidhe (The yellow bittern) / Blue murder / The earl of Errol / The tattie howkin' / A migrant's lullabye / Ways of a rover / The Forfar sodger / Behind barbed wire / The old divide and rule. *(re-iss. Jun 04 on Jump Up (Germany); JUMPUP 007)*

Apr 98. (cd; by ALISTAIR HULETT & DAVE SWARBRICK)
(MFCD 513) **THE COLD GREY LIGHT OF DAWN**
- The siege of Union Street / Chylde Owlett / Among Proddy dogs and Papes / Sons of liberty / Suicide town / The days that the boys came down / The merchant's son / When the wee birds start leaving / Harold's best men / The swaggies have all waltzed away.

—— (above issued on Musikfolk)

2000. (cd) *(RATCD 004)* **IN SLEEPY SCOTLAND** — Austra
- Waterman's hornpipe / Geordie / Tam Lin / In sleepy Scotland / The overgate / Tinker in the lum / The weaver and the factory maid / Brown Adam / By Ibrox Park / The dark loch / Battle of Waterloo - John D. Burgess.

Aug 02. (cd; by ALISTAIR HULETT & DAVE SWARBRICK)
(RATCD 005) **RED CLYDESIDE** — Austra
- The Red Clydesiders / The lassies of Neilston / Mrs. Barbour's army / Don't sign up for war / The granite cage / When Johnny came hame tae Glesga / Around George Square / John Maclean and Agnes Wood / The ghosts of Red Clyde.

2005. (cd) *(RATCD 006)* **RICHES AND RAGS** — Austra
- The fair flower of Northumberland / Criminal justice / Riches and rags / The recruited collier / The dark eyed sailor / Stealing back to my same old used to be / Shot down in flames / Militant red / Old King Coal / The first girl I loved / Trouble in mind.

—— Alistair died in 2010

Phil HULSE (⟹ The QUEENSBERRY RULES)

Sophie HUNGER

You could easily draw a line through BETH ORTON and LAURA MARLING to find where Sophie's sound comes from. Born Emilie Jeanne-Sophie Welti Hunger, March 31, 1983, at Bern in Switzerland, and later raised in London and Bonn, she was impressed by jazz music first (courtesy of her music-buff dad), and then hip-hop, R&B, country and bluegrass. Finally folk became her staple diet. A graduate in German and English, HUNGER subsequently teamed up with Supersterz before taking the lead role (as Emilie Welti) in one-album indie band Fisher; they disbanded in 2007.

Together with her backing band (Christian Prader, Michael Flury, Simon Gerber and Marc Erbetta), HUNGER gave a concert in July 2008 at the prestigious Montreux Jazz Festival. By the end of that year, she had delivered two Switzerland-only albums, **SKETCHES ON SEA** (2007) {*6} and **MONDAY'S GHOST** (2008) {*7}. Purists could argue about the folk credibility of the majority of the tracks, but each had its rootsy, Billie Holiday-esque moments: 'A Protest Song', 'Drainpipes' and 'Shape' were proof enough.

Her 2010 album **1983** {*7} – the year of her birth – was caught between blues and singer-songwriter folk, though it also saw her cover French band Noir Desir's gem 'Le Vent Nous Portera'. 'Lovesong To Everyone', 'Your Personal Religion' and the sombre 'Train People' take the honours as music that somewhat expanded her musical horizons without putting her nu-breed style of fragile-folk at risk. In the same year, Sophie featured on two tracks ('Let Me Go!' and 'Dirge') on Erik Truffaz's set 'In Between'. *MCS*

Sophie Hunger - vocals, acoustic guitar, piano (with session players)

UK Gentlemen — US not issued

Sep 07. (cd) *(GTL 044-2)* **SKETCHES ON SEA** — Swiss
- Mr. Porter's wedding / Zuri / Sad fisherman / Marketplace / Leaving Tehran / Beauty above all / Before you say … / Hello? / Dr Stummi / Nashville / The tourist / Die Fahrende / Lies fur zwarge / Flucht nach obe.

Two Gentlemen — Manimal

Oct 08. (cd) *(twogt! 001-2)* **MONDAY'S GHOST** — Swiss
- Shape / The boat is full / A protest song *[track 10 on re-cd]* / [*] / Walzer fur niemand / Birth-day / Sophie Hunger blues / Round and round / The tourist / Teenage spirit / Rise and fall *[track 12 on re-cd]* / Drainpipes *[track 12 on re-cd]* / Monday's ghost *[track 11 on re-cd]* / House of gods / Spiegelbild *[not on re-cd]*. *(UK-iss. Feb 09 on Universal; 531 495-2)* - Beauty above all [insert *]

Mar 10. (cd) *(twogt! 009-2)* **1983** — Swiss
- Leave me with the monkeys / Lovesong to everyone / 1983 / Headlights / Citylights forever / Your personal religion / Le vent nous portera / Travelogue / Breaking the waves / D'red / Approximately gone / Invisible / Broken English / Train people. *(UK-iss. Jun 10 cd/d-lp; same)*

May 11. (cd) *<none>* **SOPHIE HUNGER** [collection]

I

The IMAGINED VILLAGE

Imagined and produced by Simon Emmerson, leader of the AFRO CELT SOUND SYSTEM world-folk collective/supergroup, the IMAGINED VILLAGE is less a band than a project. Their introductory Various Artists album was part story, part traditional and part neo-folk, with a multi-cultural, star-studded guest list.

Ambitious, and revered in all the right circles, **THE IMAGINED VILLAGE** (2007) {*8} harked back to the days of The COPPER FAMILY as storyteller John Copper – son of Bob – opened the set with ''Ouses, 'Ouses', 'Ouses', supported in chant by SHEILA CHANDRA. Once a favourite with the FAIRPORTs, TRAFFIC and countless folk acts from England and beyond, 'John Barleycorn' this time around drew on the talents of ELIZA and her father MARTIN CARTHY, with a verse or two by Paul Weller. Eliza was prominent on further re-inventions such as her solo 'Acres Of Ground', the Benjamin Zephaniah rap/poem reprise of 'Tam Lyn Retold', 'Cold Haily Rainy Night' (with MARTIN CARTHY, CHRIS WOOD, the Young Coppers and Trans-Global Underground) and 'Hard Times Of Old England' (with BILLY BRAGG, the Young Coppers and dhol drumming by Johnny Kalsi).

Post-millennium indie-folktronica outfit TUNNG (Sam Genders and Mike Lindsay) had arguably the strangest trad effort here, 'Death And The Maiden Retold', while CHANDRA and WOOD took on 'The Welcome Sailor'. Emmerson's folk orchestra performed the instrumental 'Pilsden Pen', while The GLOWORMS (akin to a ceilidh Penguin Café) called the listener to dance on 'Kit White's I & II'. IAN A. ANDERSON and his TIGER MOTH crew (featuring Eliza) produced the rousing finale, 'Sloe On The Uptake'.

Album number two, **EMPIRE AND LOVE** {*7} (2010), was a record de-cluttered of celebrity guest spots, now down to the core of Emmerson, WOOD, the CARTHYs and a select group of musicians. With Eastern rhythms in the backdrop, Eliza once again shines on the venturesome 'Space Girl', her father achieving mixed results on the atmospherically spacey 'Scarborough Fair' (SIMON & GARFUNKEL's version will never sound the same) and the ill-advised revamp of Slade's 'Cum On Feel The Noize'. *MCS*

Various Artists (see biog above and track listing below)

UK Real World / US Real World

Sep 07. (cd) *(CDRW 147)* <80142> **THE IMAGINED VILLAGE** [ ] Jul 08 [ ]
- 'Ouses, 'ouses, 'ouses (JOHN COPPER and SHEILA CHANDRA with SIMON EMMERSON) / John Barleycorn (PAUL WELLER, MARTIN CARTHY and ELIZA CARTHY) / Tam Lyn retold (BENJAMIN ZEPHANIAH and ELIZA CARTHY with TRANS-GLOBAL UNDERGROUND and SIMON EMMERSON) / Death and the maiden retold (TUNNG) / Cold haily rainy night (CHRIS WOOD, ELIZA CARTHY, MARTIN CARTHY and The YOUNG COPPERS with TRANS-GLOBAL UNDERGROUND) / The welcome sailor (SHEILA CHANDRA and CHRIS WOOD) / Acres of ground (ELIZA CARTHY) / Pilsdon pen (The VILLAGE BAND) / Hard times of old England retold (BILLY BRAGG and The YOUNG COPPERS with ELIZA CARTHY and SIMON EMMERSON) - Worms meet moths (English ceilidh medley) / Kit white's I & II (The GLOWORMS) / Sloe on the uptake (TIGER MOTH).

— on the second set, the performers were **Emmerson, Eliza, Martin, Chris Wood, Sheema Mukherjee, Simon Richmond, Ali Friend, Andy Gangadeen, Barney Morse-Brown, Johnny Kalsi** + friends

ECC / not issued

Jan 10. (cd) *(ECC 002)* **EMPIRE AND LOVE** [ ] [-]
- My son John / Sweet Jane / Space girl / Byker hill / Scarborough fair / Mermaid / The hand weaver and the factory maid / The lark in the morning / Rose buds in June – Mrs. Preston's hornpipe / Cum on feel the noize / Scarborough fair (string reprise).

IN TUA NUA

Too celtic for folk-rock or too folk-pop for celtic (Sinead O'Connor was said to have rehearsed with the band early on), IN TUA NUA's sound lay somewhere between The WATERBOYS and HOTHOUSE FLOWERS.

Formed in Howth, Dublin around 1982, the group originally comprised lead singer Leslie Dowdall, guitarists Ivan O'Shea and Martin Clancy (also keyboards), piper Vinny Kilduff, violinist Steve Wickham, bassist Jack Dublin and drummer Paul Byrne, IN TUA NUA (which means "in the new world or tribe" in Gaelic) found a supporter in Bono, who signed them to U2's newly-founded Mother label. Recognising their obvious talent (and after only a one-off 45, 'Coming Thru'), mothership Island Records invited them on board, although all too briefly. A version of JEFFERSON AIRPLANE's 'Somebody To Love' bombed, as did 'Take My Hand', co-written by Sinead, and personnel diversions (Brian O'Briain came in for Kilduff and Aingeala de Burca for WATERBOYS-bound Wickham) interrupted proceedings slightly.

Finally delivered in the spring of 1987 for Virgin Records, **VAUDEVILLE** {*6} contained a couple of ones-that-got-away including a Sinead duet, 'Heaven Can Wait'. Personnel changes continued as violinist Lovely Previn replaced de Burca and Matt Spalding replaced O'Shea. Second set **THE LONG ACRE** (1988) {*6} was produced by American Don Dixon (more famous for having worked with R.E.M.), but only the minor hit 'All I Wanted' gave the septet any credibility or hope. A further 45, 'Don't Fear Me Now' was interesting for its covers of Television's 'See No Evil', Jimi Hendrix's 'Burning Of The Midnight Lamp' and David Bowie's Boys Keep Swinging'. Although there were a few reunions after their split in 1990, it was left to solo LESLIE DOWDALL to keep the flag flying. *MCS*

Leslie Dowdall - vocals / **Martin Clancy** - keyboards, guitar / **Ivan O'Shea** - guitar / **Steve Wickham** - violin / **Jack Dublin** - bass / **Vinnie Kilduff** - piper / **Paul Byrne** - drums

UK Mother / US not issued

Jul 84. (7") *(MOTHER 1)* COMING THRU. / Laughing At The Moon [ ] [-]

Island / Island

Jan 85. (7") *(IS 211)* TAKE MY HAND. / Fire In My Heart [ ] [-]
(12"+=) *(12IS 211)* - Coming thru.

Apr 85. (7") *(IS 223)* SOMEBODY TO LOVE. / Into The Dark [ ] [-]
(12"+=) *(12IS 223)* - Sleeping tide.

Aug 85. (7") *(IS 254)* BLUE EYES AGAIN. / No Love, No Pain [-] Ire [-]
(12"+=) *(12IS 254)* - King of kings / Stop, turn.

— **Aingeala De Burca** - violin; repl. Wickham who joined The WATERBOYS

— **Brian O'Briain** - saxophone, Uillean pipes; repl. Vinnie

Virgin / Atlantic

Jun 86. (7") *(VS 855)* SEVEN INTO THE SEA. / Ballad Of Irish Love [ ] [-]
(12"+=) *(VS 855-12)* - ['A'-extended].

Mar 87. (7") *(VS 939)* HEAVEN CAN WAIT. / Belt Me [ ] [-]
(12"+=) *(VS 939-12)* - The man.

Apr 87. (cd/c/lp) *(CD/TC+/V 2421)* **VAUDEVILLE** [ ] [-]
- Seven into the sea / Right road to Heaven / Love / No solution / Valuable lessons / Heaven can wait / Voice of America / Rain / Pearl of dreams / Walking on glass. *(cd+=)* - Vaudeville.

Oct 87. (12") *(VS 1023)* SOME THINGS NEVER CHANGE / Vaudeville. // Ballad Of St. Patrick / Alternative Voice Of America [ ] [-]

— **Matt Spalding** - bass; repl. O'Shea

— **Lovely Previn** - violin; repl. de Burca

Apr 88. (7") *(VS 1072)* ALL I WANTED. / The Word Punishment [69] [-]
(12"+=) *(VST 1072)* - (Holy hour) At the beggar's bush.
(cd-s++=) *(VSCD 1072)* - An inch of an acre.

May 88. (cd/c/lp) *(CD/TC+/V 2526)* <90948-2/-4/-1> **THE LONG ACRE** [ ] [ ]
- Woman on fire / All I wanted / Wheel of evil / Meeting of the waters / The innocent and the honest ones / World wired up *[UK-only]* / Seven into the sea *[US-only]* / Some things never change / Don't fear me now / Emotional barrier / The long acre / Sweet lost soul.

Jun 88. (7") *(VS 1091)* DON'T FEAR ME NOW (KISS YOU ONCE MORE). /Everybody's Darling [ ] [-]
(12"+=) *(VST 1091)* - See no evil / Burning of the midnight lamp.
(cd-s+=) *(VSCD 1091)* - Boys keep swinging / All I wanted.
Oct 88. (7") *(VS 1118)* WHEEL OF EVIL. / The Innocent And The Honest Ones (live) [ ] [ ]
(12"+=) *(VST 1118)* - Heaven can wait (live).
(3" cd-s++=) *(VSCD 1118)* - Molloy.
—— after recording a third album (see below), IN TUA NUA disbanded early 1990; they re-formed briefly for gigs in 2004; DOWDALL went solo

iTunes iTunes
Sep 07. (cd) *(none)* **WHEN NIGHT CAME DOWN ON SUNSET** [-] net [-]

LESLIE DOWDALL

with Ronan Hardiman, Jimmy Smith, Graham Henderson, Dave Early, Pat Fitzpatrick, etc.

Solid - Grapevine not issued
1997. (cd) *(???)* **NO GUILT, NO GUILE** [-] Irish [-]
- Everything / Spiral moon / Saturday night / Ride the storm / Wonderful thing / I can't take anymore / Torn inside / It's too late / Deeper - In my life / If you want me to stay / Wonderful thing (orchestral version).
—— singles from album: Wonderful Thing, Everything
—— next with Brendan Murphy, Tony Molloy, Bill Shanley, etc.

LD not issued
1998. (cd) *(none)* **OUT THERE** [-] net [-]
- Out there / Coming up roses / Secret garden / This time next year / 8,000 miles / Freedom / Miss you / Angel / Sun rays / How can I tell / Sparkle / Lift me up.
—— singles from album: Freedom, 8,000 Miles, Angel
—— DOWDALL subsequently featured on sets by Ronan Hardiman

J

Hilary JAMES (⟹ MAYOR, Simon &…)

David A. JAYCOCK

Not particularly the biggest or best "folk" star, but David is most certainly up there (or out there) with experimental players like SIR RICHARD BISHOP and JAMES BLACKSHAW, a family-tree extention of FAHEY and his ilk.

Formerly of BIG EYES FAMILY PLAYERS and currently in Manchester psych-rock act Bingo Jesus, Cornwall-born JAYCOCK (05/02/74) finger-picks and rambles his way through 14 free-flowing vignettes on his debut mini-set, **THE IMPROVISED KILLING OF UNCLE FAUSTUS AND OTHER MYTHOLOGIES** (2007) {*7} just over half an hour of pastoral, bleak or macabre Morricone-meets-Williams, soundtrack-type fare. Check out 'Tremolo Party', ''56-'57' and 'Hood Faire'.

Certainly not for the purist folk fan, album number two **THE COLEOPTEROUS CUCKOOS COLLUDE** (2008) {*7} – named after a Hitchcockian nightmare – carries on in JAYCOCK's sinister-Segovia-versus-FAHEY-in-a-fairground manner. The dark vocal of 'A New Love Song' is a treasure, breaking free of post-trad boundaries but keeping the spirit (or even the ghosts) of old-timey stylists.

Delivered only on vinyl and limited to 250 copies, **PRESETS** (2010) {*6} finds JAYCOCK more laid-back than on previous sets, and has been described as something akin to American cousins SIX ORGANS OF ADMITTANCE. Who'll be fast and lucky enough to pick up one of the 100 copies of fourth album/cd-r **A MAGNIFYING GLASS FOR THE ANTS** (2011) {*6} is a matter for speculation: one hates to drone on, but a wider release would be nice. *MCS*

David A. Jaycock - vocals, guitars (ex-BIG EYES)

UK / US
Early Winter / not issued

Jan 07. (ltd; m-cd-r) *(EWR 4)* **THE IMPROVISED KILLING OF UNCLE FAUSTUS AND OTHER MYTHOLOGIES** — own
- A cocktail party / Lost in a bear pit / George's square kite / Es cortinas para usted / Tremolo study / Hood Faire / Ruben / Waltz for Sadie / Reeleel / The improvised killing of Uncle Faustus / '56-'57 / Bonny Jaycock Turner / Twentieth century dance (a dance to decadence) / Basking.

Red Deer Club / not issued

Mar 08. (cd) *(RDC 010)* **THE COLEOPTEROUS CUCKOOS COLLUDE**
- Prelude in the minor / A third waltz / A new love song / That warm feeling in my belly / Spilling the beans at St. Neot / Knots on the tide / Woodcutter's lapse / Bontempi waltz / Inside out / Monica's lament / The coleopterous cuckoos collude / Tiger moths' descent / A dream of falling / There be killer bees in them there trees / Half cut but moving swiftly / Zither song.

Great Pop Supplement / not issued

May 09. (ltd-7") *(none)* A NEW LOVE SONG. / That Warm Feeling In My Belly

Blackest Rainbow / not issued

Aug 10. (ltd-lp) *(BRR 193)* **PRESETS**
- Prelude / Beach combing / Soup dragons / Starling / Under the stairs / Winnie the wince / Wedding dress rag & lost in space / Blackest cat waltz / God's own toys / Philip's trumpet / Wolves on trains / Blackest cat.

Feb 11. (ltd-cd-r) *(BRRCDR)* **A MAGNIFYING GLASS FOR THE ANTS**
- Bowed stuff / The murderous magician / Horses 4 / Frenzy / The jazz police are all asleep / The beautiful beast / A magnifying glass for the ants / Prelude in E minor / Regressing into a dance / In the middle of a triptych / Three quarters fool / Courses.

Nat JOHNSON AND THE FIGUREHEADS

Formed by singer Natalie and her MONKEY SWALLOWS THE UNIVERSE colleague Kevin Gori, NAT JOHNSON AND THE FIGUREHEADS are one part acoustic-folk to two parts indie-pop/rock. Her honey-layered vocals on their debut set **ROMAN RADIO** (2009) {*7} lie somewhere between the Delgados' Emma Pollack and Kirsty MacColl, while the album itself carries the weight of The Smiths playing alt-country – check out 'Dirty Rotten Soul', 'Watching For Life' and 'Agnes'.

JOHNSON's previous outfit, the rootsy Sheffield-based MONKEY …, released two albums in their short timespan, **BRIGHT CARVINGS** (2006) {*6} and **THE CASKET LETTERS** (2007) {*7}. Described in some quarters as Britain's answer to The HANDSOME FAMILY (the spotlight being on the sparring vocals of Nat and Kevin on tragi-country 'The Ballad Of The Breakneck Bride'), the second collection comes up trumps. Of late, Nat has taken time out to be part of DAVID ROTHERAY's (ex-Beautiful South) project/collective The Life Of Birds. *MCS*

MONKEY SWALLOWS THE UNIVERSE

Nat Johnson - vocals, acoustic guitar / **Kevin Gori** - acoustic guitar, mandolin, piano / **Catherine Tully** - violin / **Andy George** - bass / **Rob Dean** - drums

UK / US
Thee Sheffield Phonographic Corporation / not issued

Feb 06. (cd) *(SPCLP 004)* **BRIGHT CARVINGS**
- Sheffield shanty / Martin / Jimmy down the well / The chicken fat waltz / Down / You yesterday / Wallow / 22 / Fonz you! / Still / Beautiful never. *(bonus +=)* - Untitled.

Jul 06. (ltd-7" blue) *(SPC 013S)* SCIENCE. / Happiness
(cd-s+=) *(SPC 013)* - Florence.

Loose / not issued

Apr 07. (7") *(VJS 9)* LITTLE POLVIER. / Hemingway

Aug 07. (cd) *(VJCD 173)* **THE CASKET LETTERS**
- Statutory rights / Bloodline / Science / Matterhoney / Gravestones / Little Polvier / Elizabeth and Mary / Ballad of the breakneck bride / Paper, scissors, stone / When the work is done.

NAT JOHNSON AND THE FIGUREHEADS

Nat Johnson - vocals, guitars, piano / **Kevin Gori** - guitars, mandolin, piano / Chris Loftus <r>- bass, guitar / **Roo O' Hare** - viola / **Neil Piper** - drums

Thee Sheffield … / not issued

2008. (cd-s; as NAT JOHNSON) *(SPC 021)* DIRTY ROTTEN SOUL / Mexico / Heart Of Clay [demo] / Judy's First Beats [demo]

Damaged Goods / not issued

Oct 09. (7") *(DAMGOOD 341)* WONDERFUL EMERGENCY. / DON'T WORRY BABY

Oct 09. (cd/lp) *(DAMGOOD 342 CD/LP)* **ROMAN RADIO**
- Agnes / Wonderful emergency / Wasted / Envy / January / Careful / Truth / Dirty rotten soul / This tide will turn / Oh, face! / Watching for life / Interlude / All this.

Mar 10. (7") *(DAMGOOD 347)* WASTED. / Padre Volante

—— **Emily Gunn**; repl. Roo

Mar 11. (mp3-ep) *(DAMGOOD 374)* WHAT THE HEART POURS INTO
- Margot / We stole light / Mick Kelly.

Robb JOHNSON

Born Robb Jenner Johnson, December 25, 1955, in Hounslow, musician and moralist JOHNSON took up performing in the 1970s when his university folk club gave stage time to his band Grubstreet. Loving the limelight and the political soapbox he had mounted with his agitprop act The Ministry Of Humour (Margaret Thatcher's crushing of the miners' strike of 1984-85 had left him somewhat embittered and caustic), Robb founded his own imprint, Irregular Records.

Inspired by the likes of LEON ROSSELSON, BILLY BRAGG and Jacques Brel, the left-wing singer-songwriter has since delivered numerous solo protest albums and several collaborations with his band The Irregulars, Pip Collings or ROSSELSON.

With his inimitable wit and simple satire (in "stop me if you've heard this one before" style), one could pick out at least a half a dozen JOHNSON numbers such as 'Sunday Morning St Denis', 'The Night Cafe', 'Clockwork Music', 'The Bombing Never Stopped', 'Don't Close The Bar', 'At The Siege Of Madrid', 'Miracle Again', 'The London Rye', and 'Martha In The Mirror' (the 10-minute version). A good starting-point for the uninitiated (most of his sets are a worthy *6/*6+) would be any of the albums **GENTLE MEN** (1997) {*8}, **A BEGINNER'S GUIDE** (2005) {*8}, **LOVE AND DEATH AND POLITICS** (2008) {*8}, **MAN WALKS INTO A PUB** (2010) {*7} and the 4-box CD-set **MARGARET THATCHER: MY PART IN HER DOWNFALL** (2009) {*8}. Robb must be thanked for his part in filling in many tracks for the discography and compiling his favourite cuts. *MCS*

Robb Johnson - vocals, acoustic guitar (with others)

UK Irregular — US not issued

Jun 85. (lp) *(IRR 001)* **IN AMONGST THE RAIN**
- Shots in the dark / In amongst the rain / All through the night / As far as the sea / The ministry of humour / The banks of the Rhine / Music from the streets / Nail in the heart / Bad dreams / O Jerusalem / International steel.

—— the Ministry of Humour consisted of **Johnson** plus **Graham Barnes** + **Mark Shilcock**

Dec 85. (c; as The MINISTRY OF HUMOUR) *(IRR 002)* **LEAKING SECRETS**

Dec 86. (c; as The MINISTRY OF HUMOUR) *(IRR 003)* **ALL THE OTHER ONES YOU NEVER EVEN GET TO HEAR ABOUT**

1987. (c) *(IRR 004)* **SONGS FOR THE NEW JERUSALEM**
- Hearts unbroken / 6B go swimming / Souvenirs / The grove hotel / The Hope & Anchor / The landlord's song / Friday night in paradise / The great west road / D I Y / Everlasting flowers / Upstairs-downstairs.

Sep 88. (lp) *(IRR 005)* **SKEWED, SLEWED, STEWED AND AWKWARD**
- Captain Swing / Boxing day / The animals song / Dancing / Rosa's lovely daughters / Touch and go / I close my eyes / Berlin / Gringos / A ferry ride from Liverpool / County hall. *(cd see comps)*

Nov 88. (7") *(IRR 007)* THE HERALD OF FREE ENTERPRISE. /

Jan 89. (7" ep; as ROBB JOHNSON AND THE BARNYARD CHORUS) *(AFA 005)* THE ANIMAL SONG. / The Abattoir / Carla Lane / Train 45

(above issued on AFA)

Jul 90. (lp) *(IRR 009)* **SMALL TOWN WORLD**
- Towers of Basingstoke / Like a brother / True stories / Evergreen / After the soldiers / On the Broadway / Another cold Saturday / Rhythm talking / No more townships / The strangest places. *(cd see comps)*

1991. (7") *(IRR 010)* WASTED YEARS. /

ROBB JOHNSON & PIP COLLINGS

1991. (12") *(IRR 011)* LIVING IN THE RUBBISH. /

1992. (lp) *(IRR 012)* **OVERNIGHT**
- Singing for the moon / Sporting bar / Small revolutions / Wrecked in Slough / Fairy tales in Feltham / Orange class news / Churches and chimneys / Overnight / Winter turns to spring / Like poetry / The big silence / Vic Williams / Ujama / The last time I saw Paris / You don't have to say goodbye.

1993. (c; as The JOHNSON-COLLINGS BAND) *(IRR 013)* **TOURISTS AND CASUALTIES**
- Here comes summer / Rosa's lovely daughters / Tourists and casualties / Rio dolorosa / Rolling on / etc.

Aug 93. (cd/c) *(IRR 014 CD/C)* **HEART'S DESIRE**
- Weathering the storm / Merrie old Englande / Tomorrow will be better / Happy song / After the rain / The end of the day / Gliders for Tim / Eddie outside / Nobody but yours / Pity and mercy / Heart's desire / Sunlight on the harbour / The wall came down / Die Moorsoldaten / The bells of freedom / More than enough.

Jun 94. (c; as The JOHNSON COLLINGS BAND) *(IRR 016)* **1-2-3**
- The best days of your life / Let it go / Ujama / Overnight / The saints keep marching in / etc.

Oct 94. (cd/c) *(IRR 017 CD/C)* **THE LACK OF JOLLY PLOUGHBOY**
- Welcome to the warehouse / Wendy and Michelle / Paper poppies / The house with nobody home / Shame of a nation / Dancing on a Sunday / Uncle Cyril / The mother and the motorway / The turning year / James Dean and Sameena / We rise up / The lack of jolly ploughboy / Blame the snow for falling.

ROBB JOHNSON

1995. (cd-ep; as ROBB JOHNSON AND The GENTLEMEN OF THE TERRACES) *(IRR 020)* SATURDAY AFTERNOON RED ARMY / I Am The Crowd / Down The Town And Over The Moon / Accordeoke Army

1995. (m-cd) *(IRR 021)* LAVENDER BLUES
- Withered and died / And then there's me / Wheel keeps turning / Lavender blues / A la Pigalle / Love takes no prisoners.

Sep 95. (cd; as The ROBB JOHNSON BAND) *(IRR 023)* **INTERESTING TIMES**
- Gates of Heaven / Push it / December on the boulevard / Songbird / My mother's house / The man in the pub / Interesting times / Not yet Uhuru / As strong as the mountains / One step ahead of the flood / Cold in the trenches / Good at heart / Remember this / Babylon to Basingstoke / Turn this train around / The darkness and the light.

—— In 1996, The ROBB JOHNSON BAND backed Graham Larkbey on cassette 'No Surrender'

May 96. (cd/c) *(IRR 025 CD/C)* **THE NIGHT CAFE**
- The juggler / St. Ives end lane / Sheila held umbrellas / The night café / Almond eyes / Magic Sam / Enfin le printemps / Soho all over again / Lullabye / At the heart of everything / The midnight train / The flowers of Amsterdam / Bricks and string.

Sep 96. (cd; as The ROBB JOHNSON ROOTS BAND) *(IRR 026)* **HELL'S KITCHEN**
- Working on a river / U-have-2 dance / Waiting for bluebirds / Cassandra's song / The room beside the sea / Motherland / The butcher's hand / Lottery land / Hell's kitchen / New moon / Permanent free zone / Armistice day / Red, white and moo.

Feb 97. (cd) *(IRR 027)* **OVERNIGHT** [re-recordings from 1991–1993 sets
- Fairy tales in Feltham / I remember Managua / Orange class news / The last time I saw Paris / The day before the war / Vic Williams / Overnight / 17 again tonight / Tourists and casualties / Winter turns to spring / The suicide tour / Rehoused in Hounslow / Acton town / You don't have to say goodbye.

Aug 97. (c) *(IRR 028)* **UGLY TOWN**
- Not a bad week for the people / Nothing at all / Dead man's pennies / The white flowers of Flanders / Permanent free zone / Ugly town / Hancock in Australia / The king of rhythm / Tonight we dance / The morning after.

Oct 97. (cd) *(IRR 029)* **INVISIBLE PEOPLE**
- Me and the working man / What are we waiting for? / Invisible people / Martha in the mirror / The favourite story / In buttercup class we smile / A mystery / Spanish castles / Hancock in Australia / Anarchy in Hackney / Harbourtown / Tonight we dance / The last girl on the beach.

Dec 97. (d-cd; by ROY BAILEY, VERA COOMANS, ROBB JOHNSON, KOEN DE CAUTER AND THE GOLDEN SERENADERS) *(IRR 030)* **GENTLE MEN**
- Grandfathers / A gentleman always wants horses / Three brothers / And then the trumpet sounded / Deeper that dugouts / RSM Schofield is my shepherd / I played for Kitchener / At the mercy of the guns / A garden / Bloody medals / Soldier on / Empty chair // Noni and his golden serenaders / The boy of my dreams / When Harry took me to see Ypres / Sweet dreams / The silence of the salient / Whistle / The music from between the wars / Nobody's enemy / The German exchange / Hindsight / Dead man's pennies / Candles in the rain / Making the gardens grow.

May 98. (cd-r) *(IRR 031)* **LOVE TAKES NO PRISONERS** [wedding gift] mail-o
- Tonight let's have a good time / Babylon to Basingstoke / Rhythm talking / Greenfields / Famine in the land of plenty / Nobody but yours / The best smile of the day / Harbourtown / We hate the new boss!!!! / Red and green / Be reasonable / Love takes no prisoners / A break in the clouds.

Aug 98. (cd; by The ROBB JOHNSON BANDs) *(IRR 032)* **YEAH YEAH YEAH** [recordings 1991–98]
- The towers of Basingstoke / Tonight let's have a good time / Cathy come home / Famine in the land of plenty / Rolling on / Ujama / The saints keep marching in / Daybreak / Estately homes / We hate the Tories / Ugly town / The next revolution / The king of rhythm / And then there's me / Shine the light / The bells of freedom / Never let go.

Jul 99. (cd) *(IRR 036)* **THE BIG WHEEL**
- Au depart / Changing the guard / Oliver Twist / When Saturday came / The windmill blues / When you're seven years old / Icebergs / Barricades / Firebird / Jubilee gardens / A break in the clouds / Be reasonable / The big wheel / Sunflower.

Aug 99. (c) *(IRR 037)* **THE BIG WHEEL**: THE SECOND XI AND ALTERNATIVE VERSIONS
- [the substitute's bench]: Everybody's happy now / Green fields / Hartlepool rain / Summerhouse hill / I am your spy / The bombing never stopped / Promise and thought / The best smile of the day / Let's go / Red and green / From Conwy Castle to the sea // [out-takes and live takes]: The big wheel / Firebird / Oliver Twist / The suicide tour [live] / U have 2 dance / The night café / Lottery land / Working on a river / Overnight [live].

Aug 00. (cd) *(IRR 042)* **MARGARET THATCHER: MY PART IN HER DOWNFALL**
- Singing for the moon / Where the blues are found / I close my eyes / Touch and go / Captain Swing / Upstairs - downstairs / Rosa's lovely daughters / The animal song / 6B go swimming / The Herald of Free Enterprise / Boxing Day / Evergreen / After the soldiers / St. Valentine's day / Corazon / Sunday morning St Denis / This is the UK talking / Not in my name / Red and green / Undefeated.

May 01. (cd; by ROBB JOHNSON with MIRANDA SYKES & SASKIA TOMKINS) *(IRR 043)* **21ST CENTURY BLUES**

- Voir un ami pleurer / I am the wind / Texan prison songs / A rainy afternoon in the Star / The petals of the rose / Summerhouse hill / Sweetheart / Dear Andy / I apologise / The passers-by / Everybody wants to break your heart / The coastroad / At the siege of Madrid / 21st Century blues / Father Christmas down Hounslow High St. *(bonus bit)*

Apr 02. (cd) *(IRR 045)* **THE TRIUMPH OF HOPE OVER EXPERIENCE**
- Passport, tickets and guitar / One Broadstairs morning / Life is football / When the swing began to swing / Soho heart / Happy birthday, General / Supporting Chumbawamba / London on sea / This song is a rose / Hope street, tomorrow afternoon / You and this city / Sunlight and snow. *(hidden track unknown)*

Nov 02. (cd) *(IRR 047)* **MAXIMUM RESPECT – SONGS FOR ANIMALS**
- Boxing Day / The animals song / Rabbits / Buster / Daybreak / Hell's kitchen / Red, white and moo / The family pet / Like giants / Burning / Monkey stories / Maximum respect / Be reasonable / The animals song [7" version].

Sep 03. (cd) *(IRR 048)* **CLOCKWORK MUSIC**
- Breakfast in Chemnitz / The young man with the girlfriend and guitar / Lucky / We all said thank you very much / Over the hills / Bang! / Lost in the woods / My mother taught me how to waltz / Black and white / We all said stop the war / The rainbow's end / Clockwork music.

Dec 03. (d-cd-r) *(none)* **NOT IN MY NAME** [live at the Evening Star, Brighton in September 2003] bootleg
- 51st state of America / Sympathy for the devil / Not in my name / Lost in the woods / Breakfast in Chemnitz / London on sea / Have you got a licence? / The gates of heaven / Justice in Knightsbridge / I'm so bored with the USA / Stop the war / Martha in the harbour / Straight to hell / Sunday morning St. Denis / Stand clear // Passport, tickets and guitar / Changing the guard / The suicide tour / At the siege of Madrid / You and this city / The young man with the girlfriend and guitar / Hope street – We all said stop the war / Maximum respect / She lives in Slough – Punk rock jubilee / UK talking – London's burning / Anarchy in Hackney / Cheers / Winter turns to spring / Not in my name #2 / Undefeated.

Jun 04. (d-cd) *(IRR 054)* **TONY BLAIR: MY PART IN HIS DOWNFALL**
- Not a bad week for the people / Everybody's happy now / Bedtime stories / Bury Trident (before it buries us) / Barricades / I am your spy / The bombing never stopped / The siege of Madrid / The coastroad / Three minutes silence / In November / She lives in Slough / London's burning / Have you got a licence? / We all said stop the war / And in our dreams / Mission accomplished / No statues / Michael and tin town criminals / Legitimate targets / No justice, no peace / The conscript's song / Hands off my friends / The year of jubilee / Punk rock jubilee / Summertime / Stop the war [sample mix] / Stop the war [samba mix] / Mr president.

Oct 04. (cd) *(UNLABELLED 004)* **FRIDAY NIGHT IN BRENTFORD**: Live @ Stripes Bar in July 2003
- True stories / 6B go swimming / Uncle Cyril / Down the town and over the moon / When Saturday came / Stand clear / Life is football / We get there / Two nil down in the second half / Saturday afternoon red army / Hounslow boys / Fairy tales in Feltham.

(above issued on Unlabelled)

Mar 05. (cd) *(IRR 058)* **A BEGINNER'S GUIDE** [live in the studio w/ six new tracks]
- Everything's all right / Small revolution / The beautiful dark / I apologise / Breakfast in Chemnitz / Bang! / When Harry took me to see Ypres / We all said stop the war / Mission accomplished / Raining teddy bears / Christmas day in heaven / Life is football / You and this city / Anarchy in Hackney / Real cool purple shirt / The London Eye / Be reasonable / A Dorset moon.

Oct 05. (cd) *(IRR 059)* **METRO**
- Don't close the bar / The golden boys / Boulevard des hommes / Stand clear! / Greeneland / A desperate man / S45 and lunch thrown in / Name, rank and number / Gypsy music in the underground / Whatever happened to Paris? / Making sense of Manhattan / The London Eye / The fairest city / Picking up the pieces / The last train tonight / Here comes that miracle again.

ROBB JOHNSON & THE IRREGULARS

with **Naomy Browton** - cello / **John Forrester** - bass, vocals / **Roger Watson** - melodeon, harmonica / **Charlie Waygood** - drums

Nov 06. (cd) *(IRR 063)* **SATURDAY NIGHT AT THE FIRE STATION** (live 50th birthday bash)
- Ugly town / Wooden snowmen / Tin town criminals / Real cool purple shirt / Lightbulbs / Passport tickets and guitar / Saturday afternoon red army / Martha in the mirror / You and this city / Not in my name / Uptheworkers / This is the UK talking / Overnight / Anarchy in Hackney.

Jul 07. (cd) *(IRR 066)* **ALL THAT WAY FOR THIS**
- Carrying your smile / Peanuts / No-one wants to look like you / The beautiful dark / The day after Valentine's Day / Almost the homecoming queen / Moronland / The blue sea says yes / Zapatista coffee / Pinkshoes / Sunny afternoon in Ilmenau / On highway 5.

Oct 08. (cd) *(IRR 068)* **LOVE AND DEATH AND POLITICS**
- Spirit of 45 / Saturday night in Albion / Little angels / The bigger the car / Hard money / Soweto / The great west road / The prince and Private Gentle / Postcard from Blackpool / Even Steve McQueen / I am not at war / The tail of the miracle / Two left feet / Cheers.

Nov 09. (cd) *(IRR 076)* **THE GHOST OF LOVE**: A Christmas Song Suite
- Fairytales in Feltham / Rehoused in Hounslow / Jubilee Gardens / Father Christmas down Hounslow High Street / Wooden snowmen / Meanwhile, on planet earth… / Crisis / Poundshop Christmas / Magic pockets? / The ghost of love / Motorcycle diary / The midnight clear.

ROBB JOHNSON

Sep 10. (cd) *(IRR 077)* **MAN WALKS INTO A PUB**
- Man walks into a pub / A true history of cous-cous / Les deux magots / Dark star / A bracelet from Paris / A very small piece of the real world / Charlie / The wrong train / Thomas among the dandelions / Someone else can save the world / Stay free / A place in the country / The justice bus / Pennypot lane.

- (5-7*) compilations, etc.-

Jul 96. (cd) *Rhiannon; (RHYD 5002)* **THIS IS THE UK TALKING**
- Amateur dramatix / Rosa's lovely daughters / I close my eyes / The jolly sailor / The animals song / The Herald of Free Enterprise / Evergreen / Like a brother / Another cold Saturday in hell / Sunday morning St Denis / Uprising / Justice in Knightsbridge / The wasted years / Not in my name / 6B go swimming / Hounslow boys / UK talking / Undefeated.

- essential boxed sets -

Aug 09. (4-cd-box) *Irregular; (IRR 075)* **MARGARET THATCHER: MY PART IN HER DOWNFALL**
- (SKEWED, SLEWED, STEWED AND AWKWARD tracks + extras) // (SMALL TOWN WORLD tracks + extras) // (THIS IS THE UK CALLING tracks) // (MARGARET THATCHER: MY PART IN HER DOWNFALL tracks in diff. order + extras).

John JONES (⟹ OYSTERBAND)

Martyn JOSEPH

There was a time in the early 1990s when singer-songwriter MARTYN JOSEPH (born July 15, 1960, Penarth in Wales) was being touted as the next Mark Knopfler, RALPH McTELL or Paul Weller. Signing to Epic Records, one of his earlier compositions, 'Dolphins Make Me Cry' (from his godly 1980s period), had climbed into the UK Top 40, but sadly he couldn't sustain his success by way of a hit album.

Martyn's formative years nearly produced a fine golfer, as he became the youngest-ever winner of the Glamorganshire Golf Club championship at seventeen. Relinquishing a promising career in the sport (at least as an amateur) to focus on his other love, music, he signed a deal with religious label Eyes And Ears, for whom he released a string of bright but forgettable LPs. It was his self-financed **AN ACHING AND A LONGING** (1989) {*6}, which quickly sold over 25,000 copies and again listed 'Dolphins…', that made the majors sit up and take notice. Covers from this era included Elvis's 'In The Ghetto' and 'Heartbreak Hotel' and Billy Joel's 'Piano Man'.

1992's Sony/Epic-imprint debut **BEING THERE** {*7} should have garnered him some chart action, having followed 'Dolphins…' with two more minor hits, 'Working Mother' and 'Please Sir', two of many collaborations with lyricist Stewart Henderson. It was an ill-advised three years before his second Sony effort, **MARTYN JOSEPH** {*6}, was delivered. Produced by Mick Glossop and augmented by co-composer Tom Robinson on the set's only Top 50 entry, 'Talk About It In The Morning', the album featured formulaic songs of social lament, whether forlorn or protesting.

Always very much on the fringes of folk music, for reasons unknown to many pundits, nearly-man Martyn's subsequent time was spent trying to re-establish himself among the big boys. Grapevine Records (normally associated with twilight acts such as JOAN BAEZ, etc) issued two albums: **FULL COLOUR BLACK AND WHITE** (1997) {*6} – featuring 'The Ballad Of Richard Lewis' (alias 'Dic Penderyn', the martyr of the Merthyr Rising of 1831) – and **TANGLED SOULS** (1998) {*6}.

Coming full circle from 1989, Martyn took his independence to new strengths and founded his own Pipe label in 1999, its first release being **FAR FROM SILENT** {*6}. A subsequent tour supporting the legendary Shirley Bassey should have produced a full follow-up, although a limited-edition EP did surface in 2001. Further moonlighting projects with STEVE KNIGHTLEY and Tom Robinson (on the "Faith, Folk and Anarchy Live" tour) produced renewed credibility, and his long-awaited 2004 set, **WHOEVER IT WAS THAT BROUGHT ME HERE WILL HAVE TO TAKE ME HOME** {*6}, resurrected his career in one fell swoop. There were numerous unofficial mail-order CDs available, and a few drifted into the retail market, such as the soul-searching **DEEP BLUE** (2005) {*6}, highlighted by 'Can't Breathe' and 'Turn Me Tender'.

His passion for the dispossessed and the needy produced the anthemic 'Kindness', one of the best songs on his **VEGAS** (2007) {*7} set, inspired by the homeless on the streets of Toronto rather than the air-conditioned interiors of Las Vegas. (Indeed, the North Americans might have loved JOSEPH's newfound electric sound, with its more edgy atmosphere than his previous introspective recordings.)

Uniquely adapted from their original form, the songs on the back-to-basics **EVOLVED** (2008) {*7} made sure his back catalogue was brought up to date, while fresh tracks from his latest set, **UNDER LEMONADE SKIES** (2010) {*7}, kept his loyal fanbase more than happy. *MCS*

Martyn Joseph - vocals, acoustic guitar / + session people

UK — US
Eyes And Ears — not issued

1983. (lp) *(EER 003)* **I'M ONLY BEGINNING** [ ] [-]
- Lay down / I could not do him justice / Got to get the timing right / In the garden / I am only beginning / Nothing changes / Handle with care / Don't know what the fuss is all about / It doesn't matter anyway / Everything new.

1984. (lp) *(EER 031)* **NOBODY'S FOOL** [ ] [-]
- Giving it up / Nobody's fool / Do it! / As you intend / Song of a proud man / Hungry for heaven / Pick me up again / What can I do? / Peace like a river / Psalm 127 (Unless the Lord). *(cd-iss.1997 on Word+=; MYRCD 1313)- SOLD OUT*

1986. (lp) *(EER 056)* **SOLD OUT** [ ] [-]
- Sold out / The power of your love / Beautiful woman / Jealous love / I've put my life in his hands / Dance out of the shadows / Heaven she said / Look into his eyes / Standing on tiptoe / Time after time. *(cd-iss.+=)- NOBODY'S FOOL*

1987. (lp) *(EER 074)* **BALLADS … IN QUIETER MOMENTS** [ ] [-]
- Handle with care / He'll be there / A father's love / Time after time / Teach me your ways / I could not do him justice / As you intend / Look into his eyes / Ballad for the children of Ireland / What can I do? *(cd-iss. 1997 on Word; MYRCD 1312)*

1987. (lp) *(EER 093)* **TREASURE THE QUESTIONS** [ ] [-]
- Real world / Not far from Jerusalem / Can't forget / Dolphins make me cry / Sunday's coming / 4 the $ / Don't talk about love / Treasure the questions / Broken wings don't always heal / I will follow / Weight of the world.

Alliance — not issued

Oct 89. (cd) *(ALD 007)* **AN ACHING AND A LONGING** [ ] [-]
- Nobody's fool / Contradictions / Treasure the questions / Reminded of heaven / Vincent / Real world / Power of your love / Candle in the wind / Beautiful woman / I will follow / Dolphins make me cry / Sunday's coming / An aching and a longing / No choices.

Epic — Epic

Jun 92. (7") *(658134-7)* DOLPHINS MAKE ME CRY. / Drag You Bleeding [34] [-]
(cd-s+=) *(658134-2)* - Simply no.
(cd-s) *(658134-5)* - ['A'-acoustic guitar version] / In the ghetto / Summer of flowers [live at Warwick University] / ['A'-live at Warwick University].

Jul 92. (cd/c/lp) *(471820-2/-4/-1)* *<EK 53167>* **BEING THERE** [ ] 1993 [ ]
- Being there / Working mother / I will be waiting / I see you / Swansea / Have I gone too far? / Reminded of heaven / Dolphins make me cry / Please sir / Precious / Next time I see you.

Aug 92. (7"/c-s) *(658293-7/-4)* WORKING MOTHER / Contradictions [65] [-]
(cd-s+=) *(658293-2)* - Please sir [live].
(cd-s) *(658293-5)* - ['A'] / Piano man / The great American novel / Being there.

Dec 92. (7") *(658855-7)* PLEASE SIR. / Always [45] [-]
(cd-s+=) *(658855-5)* - Don't talk about love.
(cd-s) *(658855-2)* - ['A'] / [live at Greenbelt 1992]:- Sunday's coming / Heartbreak hotel / An aching and a longing.

May 95. (cd-s) *(661334-5)* TALK ABOUT IT IN THE MORNING / Arizona Dreams / Pardon Me [43] [-]
(cd-s) *(661334-2)* - ['A'] / He Never Said [with TOM ROBINSON] / War Baby [with TOM ROBINSON] / Swansea.

Jul 95. (cd/c) *(480657-2/-4)* *<32624-2>* **MARTYN JOSEPH** [ ] [ ]
- Change your world / Gift to me / Between the raindrops / Talk about it in the morning / Everything in heaven comes apart / Home to you / If I should fall / If heaven's waiting / Condition of my heart / Cardiff Bay / Carried in sunlight.

Grapevine — not issued

May 97. (cd) *(GRACD 222)* **FULL COLOUR BLACK AND WHITE** [ ] [-]
- Going home / Arizona dreams / Treasure the questions / The ballad of Richard Lewis / Everything's news / Hang the world / Danny / Have an angel walk with her / He never said / Do not disturb.

May 98. (cd) *(GRACD 236)* **TANGLED SOULS** [ ] [-]
- Somewhere in America / Strange way / What a day, what a universe / Better than that / In between rounds girl / I don't know why / Love the light in you / My love my life / I feel your pleasure / Sing to my soul / The tail of the world / Tomorrow.

Pipe — Appleseed

Nov 99. (cd) *(PRCD 1)* **FAR FROM SILENT** [ ] [-]
- All in the past / Celebrity / The mayor of Candor lied / Another chance / One of us / People crazy as me / Good man / The good in me is dead / All this time / Liberal backslider. *(re-iss. Feb 05; same)*

Jun 01. (ltd-m-cd) *(PRCD 003)* THE SHIRLEY SESSIONS [rec. Jul 00] [-] mail-o [-]
- Kiss the world beautiful / Undiscovered love / Half of a man / Between you and me / We are men / Step outside / He's mine / Hush mother (do not cry).

—— In 2003, with Tom Robinson and STEVE KNIGHTLEY, Martyn was credited on the 'Faith, Folk And Anarchy' CD (four tracks, 'Wake Me Up', 'Strange Way', 'The Flood' and 'War Baby'; in 2003 he also recorded 'The Bridgerow Sessions' w/ KNIGHTLEY

Feb 04. (cd) *(PRCD 007)* *<APRCD 1078>* **WHOEVER IT WAS THAT BROUGHT ME HERE WILL HAVE TO TAKE ME HOME** [ ] May 04 [ ]
- Love is / Where the angels sleep / Wake me up / Every little sign / This being woman / Strange kind of friend / Walk down the mountain / Just like the man said / Whoever it was that brought me here will have to take me home. *(US+=)*- The great American novel / The good in me is dead.

Mar 04. (cd-s) *(PRCD 008)* THIS BEING WOMAN / Every Little Sign / Wake Me Up [ ] [-]

Nov 04. (cd) *(PRCD 009)* **RUN TO COVER** [-] mail-o [-]
- Chimes of freedom / The mayor of Candor lied / Ghost of Tom Joad / Why should I cry for you? / The great American novel / Thunder road / Call it democracy / One of us / Rhondda Grey / Stuck in a moment / How the web was woven / Pardon me, anthem.

Pipe — True North

Nov 05. (cd) *(PRCD 014)* *<TN 450>* **DEEP BLUE** [ ] Jun 06 [ ]
- Some of us / Can't breathe / How did we end up here / Six sixty six / I would never do anything in this world to hurt you / This fragile world / Yet still this will not be / Proud valley boy / Turn me tender / Can't breathe [acoustic].

Feb 07. (cd; as MARTYN JOSEPH & STEWART HENDERSON) *(PRCD 015)* **BECAUSE WE CAN…** [-] mail-o [-]
- Domestic lamentation / Everything in heaven / School rules / Working mother / Letterhead / Some of us / Single journey / This being woman / Under the clock / Thunder and rainbows / Do aliens …? / Between you and me / And this is what we leave behind / [out-takes].

Apr 07. (cd-ep) *(ASCCD 010)* THE GREAT AMERICAN NOVEL [ ] [-]
- The great American novel / The good in me is dead [new version] / Arizona dreams [new version] / Swansea [new version] / War baby [live from Faith, Folk and Anarchy tour].

(above issued on 'A Startled Chameleon')

Mar 07. (cd) *(PRCD 017)* **MJGB06** [live at the Greenbelt Festival at Cheltenham racecourse 25th August 06] [ ] [-]
- Some of us / Proud valley boy / How did we end up here / Six sixty six / Can't breathe / I will follow / Wake me up / The good in me is dead / Yet still this will not be / Turn me tender / Mr Robertson.

Sep 07. (cd) *(PRCD 018)* **VEGAS** [ ] [-]
- Vegas / Weight of the world / Coming down / I have come to sing / Invisible angel / Kindness / Nobody loves you anymore / The fading of light / Things that we never carried here / Nobody gets everything.

Oct 08. (cd) *(PRCD 019)* **EVOLVED** [reprised songs] [ ] [-]
- Kiss the world beautiful / Sing to my soul / Proud valley boy / Arizona dreams / Dic Penderyn / Strange way / Can't breathe / Weight of the world / Working mother / Have an angel walk with her / Please sir / The good in me is dead / This being woman / Turn me tender / Cardiff Bay.

Oct 10. (cd) *(PRCD 020)* **UNDER LEMONADE SKIES** [ ] [-]
- Always will be / So many lies / You're the moment / Seahorse / There's always maybe / Lonely like America / One step up / No peace / On my way / Brothers in exile.

- (8-10*) compilations –

Mar 01. (d-cd) *Pipe; (PRCD 1)* **THUNDER AND RAINBOWS (THE BEST WE COULD FIND) 1988–2000** [ ] [-]
- Thunder and rainbows / I will follow / Contradictions / An aching and a longing / Working mother / Change your world / I will be waiting / Please sir / Gift to me / Let's talk about it in the morning / Dolphins make me cry / Between the raindrops / Cardiff Bay / Precious / Carried in sunlight // Treasure the questions / Dic Penderyn / Arizona dreams / Love the light in you / Strange way / In between rounds girl / Hang the world / He never said / Have an angel / My love my life / People crazy as me / The good in me is dead / One of us / Do not disturb / Liberal backslider / All this time / This is us / Undiscovered love.

- essential boxed sets –

Feb 05. (3-cd-box) *Pipe; (PRCD 013)* **MARTIN JOSEPH – 3 ALBUM BOXED SET** [ ] [-]
- (AN ACHING AND A LONGING) // (FULL COLOUR BLACK AND WHITE) // (FAR FROM SILENT).

- (5-7*) compilations, others, etc.-

Mar 04. (cd) *Pipe; (PRCD 3)* **DON'T TALK ABOUT LOVE: LIVE '92–'02 Vol.1** [ ] [-]
- Please sir / Cardiff Bay / Working mother / My love my life / Gone too far / Dophins make me cry / Don't talk about love / An aching and a longing / Have an angel walk with her / Let's talk about it in the morning / Hang the world / Dic Penderyn / All this time / This is us.

Mar 04. (cd) *Pipe; (PRCD 4)* **DON'T TALK ABOUT LOVE: LIVE '92–'02 Vol.2** [ ] [-]
- Being there / He never said / Everything in heaven / Kiss the world beautiful / The good in me is dead / Sing to my soul / Another chance / Strange way / Love the

light / Gift to me / Undiscovered love / One of us / Thunder and rainbows / Liberal backslider / Sunday's coming / Swansea.

Nov 09. (cd) *(PRBCD 001)* **OFFICIAL BOOTLEG SERIES VOLUME 1 LIVE CUTS '92–'08** [–] mail-o [–]
- [Greenbelt '92]: Heartbreak hotel / An aching and a longing / [Swansea '93]: Gone too far / Dolphins make me cry / [Paris '95]: Between the raindrops / [Worcester '00]: Love the light in you / [Toronto '05]: Dic Penderyn / [Stoke On Trent '04]: Cardiff Bay / [Burgess Hill '05]: Still this will not be / [Denver '07]: The good in me is dead / [Berkeley '07]: Love is / [Southampton '08]: We are men / Please sir / Proud Valley boy / Change your world / Turn me tender / [Cardiff '01]: Undiscovered love.

JUMPLEADS

Based in Oxford and led by DYLAN aficionado Jon Moore, with singer/fiddler Caroline Ritson, English-concertina master Dave Townsend and bassist Tracy (Henry Tracy), the JUMPLEADS created a raucous hybrid of rogue-folk, blues and reggae.

THE STAG MUST DIE (1982) {*6} – with a blood-spattered sleeve design – received some rave reviews, although by 1983, after a remix version of their best tune, 'False Knight', they went their separate ways. Fusing noisy trad selections with polkas and dance tunes, the set's highlights included a version of 'Tam Lin'. Invited to join up with ex-TIGER MOTH alumni Rod and Danny Stradling in ceilidh punks EDWARD II, Moore found belated success, while Caroline, after a long time in the wilderness, became Caroline Butler and joined The OXFORD WAITS. *MCS*

Caroline Ritson - vocals, fiddle / **Jon Moore** - guitars / **Dave Townsend** - concertina, accordion, keyboards / **(Henry) Tracy** - bass, keyboards (+ occasional drums)

UK Ock — US not issued

Dec 82. (lp) *(OC 001)* **THE STAG MUST DIE** [ ] [–]
- The day the stag must die / Hunt the squirrel / New York trader / False knight on the road / Poor old horse / Tom Caves / The little fighting chance / Greenwood laddie / Blarney pilgrim / Tam Lin.

Rogue — not issued

Feb 83. (7") *(FMSS 103)* FALSE KNIGHT ON THE ROAD. / Poor Old Horse [ ] [–]

—— split soon afterwards; Moore joined EDWARD II AND THE RED HOT POLKAS, Caroline joined The OXFORD WAITS

JUNGR & PARKER

Formed in 1985 by ex-members of the Three Courgettes (a cabaret-style harmony-vocal act in the manner of Flanders and Swann), Barbara Jungr and Michael Parker, with bassist Paul Zetter, issued a string of cassettes from the mid-1980s onwards before the camp Julian Clary exposed them (oo-er!) to regular stints on his 1989-90 TV show Sticky Moments.

From Eastern European stock (her father was a Czech scientist, her mother a German nurse), JUNGR was born May 9, 1954 in Rochdale, Lancashire, and was raised in nearby Stockport, Cheshire, before she uprooted to London in the 1970s.

Without going into Barb's long-running cabaret-jazz solo career, JUNGR & PARKER issued a couple of bona-fide folk-jazz sets. **OFF THE PEG** (1989) {*6} was released on BILLY BRAGG's Utility offshoot, while Harbourtown Records put out **CANADA** (1992) {*6}. Featuring guests CHRISTINE COLLISTER, ROGER WATSON, Ian Shaw and John Moloney, the latter CD, featuring some good original songs, premiered at smoky clubs around the UK and secured a prestigious Edinburgh Festival Fringe spot.

During a creative spell in the 1990s, boho-chick Barb Jungr (as she was now billed) again performed at the Edinburgh Festival, this time as part of the close-harmony show Hell Bent Heaven Bound, alongside HELEN WATSON, COLLISTER and Shaw. Several sophisticated sets later, JUNGR showed she hadn't completely lost her roots by releasing two easy-listening-type Jungr-sings-Dylan sets, 'Every Grain Of Sand' (2004) and 'Man In The Long Black Coat'. For the purposes of a folk discography, we must leave it at that. *MCS*

Barbara Jungr - vocals, harmonica, mandolin, percussion / **Michael Parker** - vocals, guitar, ukulele, banjo, piano, bass / plus session people

UK self-rel. — US not issued

1986. (c) *(none)* **WICKED** [–] mail-o [–]
- Bad things come in threes / Don't sacrifice me / No news is good news / That black cat / In Soho late at night / Too much for me / Just the whisky talking / Perfect pair / The begging game / Over a low flame / You can't win them all / An empty bottle.

1987. (c) *(none)* **BLUE DEVILS** [–] mail-o [–]

1988. (c) *(none)* **DAY OR NIGHT** [–] mail-o [–]

Utility — not issued

Mar 89. (m-lp) *(UTIL 3)* **OFF THE PEG** [ ] [–]
- Launderette song / Don't sacrifice me / The point / We stayed in / Bad things come in threes / You've changed / Just the whisky talking / Too much for me. *(cd-iss. Jun 90; UTIL 3CD)*

—— In 1990, JUNGR & PARKER released an experimental set, 'Off The Bridge' (Leaping Lizards Records).

Harbourtown — not issued

Aug 92. (cd/c) *(HAR CD/C 023)* **CANADA** [ ] [–]
- Canada / Nothing through the letterbox today / One step away from my heart / Nights in a suitcase / 21 years / The chosen one / Walking wounded / It's not there / You can't win 'em all / The end of the line / Whatever you do / Al fresco / That's what friends are for.

—— she also worked with CHRISTINE COLLISTER, MICHAEL PARKER & HELEN WATSON on the showbizzy Hell Bent Heaven Bound II project/LP, 'Money The Final Frontier'; subsequently became Barb Jungr, releasing numerous easy-jazz CDs.

JUNIP (⟹ GONZALEZ, Jose)

JUSTINE

Missed by almost everyone first time around, JUSTINE was in fact a group of five or six members and not a solo act. Formed in London in 1967 by Anglo-American singer-songwriters John McBurnie and Keith Trowsdale, the group's line-up remains sketchy, but it is thought to have consisted of John and Keith, plus extra vocalists Valerie Cope and the American Laurie Styvers or Bethlyn Bates (pick two from three), and drummer Dougie Wright (who may have replaced Chris Gibb).

Their one and only LP for Uni Records, **JUSTINE** (1970) {*6}, was recently given a Sunbeam CD makeover, adding two sides from an earlier single. Sunshine-pop psych-folk taking the MAMAS and The LOVIN' SPOONFUL as its template (with a little DONOVAN thrown in), highlights included melodious medley tracks such as 'Flying…' and the 10-minute 'Mini Splurge…'. The finale, 'Unknown Journey' was a "Barbarella"-styled wig-out. *MCS*

John McBurnie - vocals, guitar / **Keith Trowsdale** - vocals, guitar / **Valerie Cope** - vocals, percussion / **Laurie Styvers** (or) **Bethlyn Bates** - vocals / **Dougie Wright** - drums; repl. Chris Gibb

UK Dot — US not issued

Nov 69. (7") *(DOT 121)* LEAVE ME BE. / Clowns [ ] [–]

Uni — not issued

May 70. (7") *(UNS 528)* SHE BRINGS THE MORNING WITH HER. / Back To Boulder [ ] [–]

Jun 70. (lp) *(UNLS 111)* **JUSTINE** [ ] [–]
- Flying – Love you more than is good for me to – Nostrils / She brings the morning with her / Back to Boulder / Traveller / See saw / Mini splurge – Mr Jones – Is that good, that's nice / Clocks – Hey I used to know you / Unknown journey. *(cd/lp re-iss. Jun 08 on Sunbeam+=; SBR CD/LP 5053)* - Leave me be / Clown.

—— a case of where are they now? – McBurnie joined Jackson Heights and sessioned for Patrick Moraz, etc; Laurie has since passed away

KASHMIR (⟹ BARKER, Les)

Ron KAVANA

Born in the early 1950s in Fenmoy, County Cork – his mother was American – RON KAVANA has been at the centre of Irish/Celtic roots/folk music since his fling in the 1970s with Irish freak-folk outfit LOUDEST WHISPER; he'd previously earned his musical spurs with R&B outfit The Wizards.

KAVANA subsequently played various instruments in numerous name acts, including Panama Red, Chris Farlowe & The Thunderbirds (replacing Albert Lee), Identity Kit/Juice On The Loose (alongside Ed Deane), Alexis Korner's Boogie Band (featuring Charlie Watts, Jack Bruce and Ian Stewart) and pub-rock band Bees Make Honey.

Plucking musicians from the latter band, KAVANA (and sidekick Gary Rickard) finally branched out on his own. His debut LP, **ROLLIN' & COASTIN' (IN SEARCH OF AMERICA)** (1985) {*5}, was a rootsy affair, influenced by Lowell George (as in opening track 'Man Smart, Woman Smarter'), Tex-Mex, cajun-rock, R&B and olde-timey ditties such as 'Underneath The Harlem Moon' and 'Joanna'. The album was released at a time when The POGUES were kings of contemporary Celtic folk, and KAVANA declined a subsequent invitation to join the band through mutual friend and musician TERRY WOODS.

ALIAS RON KAVANA were formed to reach the POGUES' kind of audience, and the resulting album, **THINK LIKE A HERO** (1989) {*7}, won awards everywhere, while the band were named best live act by Folk Roots (fRoots) magazine. The 'Alias' group comprised former Bees Make Honey guitarist Mick Molloy, bassist Richie Robertson, drummer Lee Morgan and fifth member/auxiliary Mickey Weaver. Notable assistance came from ex-Ace man Fran Byrne (on bodhran).

Influences and global inspirations poured in from all angles: 'Gone Shopping' – Tex-Mex/Ry Cooder; 'Soweto Trembles (The Jo'Burg Jig)' - World/folk; 'Midnight On The Water' – country; and the obvious 'This Is The Night (Fair Dues To The Man)' – VAN MORRISON. The set closed with the self-explanatory 'Rap 'n' Reel (Dream Demons Invoked By Christy's DTs)', while two of the songs were co-written with WOODS: 'Every Man Is A King (In The US Of A)' and the Steve Earle-ish 'Four Horsemen'.

After time spent on the LILT (London Irish Live Trust) charity album for peace in Northern Ireland, he released two albums in 1991. There was the solo, self-penned **HOME FIRE** {*7}, featuring TERRY WOODS again on the two closing two tracks, 'Fermoy Regatta - Tom's Tavern' and 'Young Ned Of The Hill', and the second 'ALIAS' collection, **COMING DAYS** {*8}. Many would argue the latter was the better album, and its link-up with former KAVANA colleagues, plus guests Geraint Watkins, Celtic cousins BOILED IN LEAD and Sons Of The Desert, was awe-inspiring to say the least. The Celtic classic 'Irish Ways' was one of KAVANA's best songs ever, followed by the George Thorogood-esque 'Psycho Mary's Voodoo Blues' and the plucky Cajun singalong 'Hand Me Down'. A couple of covers (Smokey Robinson and the Miracles' 'Ain't That Peculiar' and BRUCE COCKBURN's 'If I Had A Rocket Launcher') showed the versatility of the man and his band, ditto the reggaefied, un-PC 'Pennies For Black Babies', the sign-of-the-times 'Freedom Crazy' and the closing rap song 'Walk, Don't Walk'.

GALWAY TO GRACELAND (1995) {*6} ran a musical gamut of sounds and places, from Irish traditional folk to the birthplace of Elvis and beyond (there was even a cover of the King's 'Are You Lonesome Tonight'), but ALIAS RON KAVANA were finding it hard to cross over into the mainstream – there were too many aliases for people to contend with. Another incarnation, The Bucks, released 'Dancin' To The Ceili' (with Ron, Miriam Kavana, TERRY WOODS and Rod Demick), a set that harked back to more traditional ways.

Towards the end of the millennium Ron released two new project sets, the double Alias Acoustic Band's **IRISH SONGS OF REBELLION, RESISTANCE AND RECONCILIATION** (1998) {*5} – basically what it says on the tin – and **ALIEN ALERT** (1999) {*6} (live in California), with yet another backing outfit, The Resident Aliens.

If VAN MORRISON hadn't already been a megastar, there might have been been room for RON KAVANA and his Irish ways, although judging by the support and applause from the latter's American audience, Ron hadn't been totally ignored. His tales of harsher times were also evident on the exhaustive but nevertheless effective four-CD set **IRISH WAYS** (2007) {*6} – everything you ever needed to know about the 'folk' of Ireland and all the country's troubled times from century to century. *MCS*

Ron Kavana - vocals, banjo, mandolin, guitars, etc / with **Gary Rickard** - vocals, guitar + Juice On The Loose: Alan 'Bam' King, Alan Dunn, Frank Mead, Fran Byrne, Charlie Hart, Nick Pentelow

UK Appaloosa | US not issued

Jul 85. (lp) *(AP 042)* **ROLLIN' & COASTIN'** (IN SEARCH OF AMERICA)
- Man smart, woman smarter / Underneath the Harlem moon / Love has no pride / Roll 'em easy / Life's railway to heaven / Coastin' / I want my baby back / Talk to me / Joanna / Troubles, troubles. *(cd-iss. Apr 92 + Aug 04; AP 042-2)*

ALIAS RON KAVANA

Ron with **Mick Molloy** - guitars, mandolin, percussion, vocals (ex-Bees Makes Honey) / **Richie Robertson** - bass, percussion, vocals / **Les Morgan** - drums, percussion

Chiswick | not issued

Oct 89. (lp/c/cd) *(WIK/WIKC/CDWIK 88)* **THINK LIKE A HERO**
- Waxin' the Gaza / Every man is a king (in the US of A) / Gone shopping / Soweto trembles (the Jo'burg jig) / Felice / This is the night (fair dues to the man) / Gold ochra at Killarney point to points *[c+cd-only]* / Midnight on the water / Caoimhneadh roisin - Tre ceathar a hocht / Four horsemen / Reconciliation *[c+cd-only]* / Rap 'n' reel (dream demons invoked by Christy's DTs).

Jan 90. (7") *(NS 129)* THIS IS THE NIGHT (FAIR DUES TO THE MAN). / Gold Ochra At Killarney Point To Points
(12"+=) *(NST 129)* - Fight it.

May 90. (7") *(NS 131)* SOWETO TREMBLES (THE JO'BURG JIG). / Rap 'n' Reel (Dream Demons Invoked By Christy's DTs)
(12") *(NST 131)* - ('A') / Rain / It's miner this, it's miner that / Working in a coalmine / No surrender.

—— In 1990 he recorded the LILT 'For The Children' charity album

—— added **Fran Byrne** - button accordion, percussion (ex-Bees Make Honey, ex-Ace, ex-Juice On The Loose)

Mar 91. (cd/c/lp) *(CDWIKD/WIKC/WIKAD 94)* **COMING DAYS**
- Galtee mor - Irish ways - Jigs: Daniel O'Connell - Saddle the pony - Merrily kiss the quaker - The Kinnegadd slashers - Annie Mulligan's / Thoughts of Abilene / Psycho Mary's voodoo blues / Hand me down / Connemara - Handcuffs / Ain't that peculiar - The foxhunter's reel / Pennies for black babies / Johnny / Cajun ceili / Freedom crazy / If I had a rocket launcher / Walk, don't walk.

—— added **Terry Woods** - multi (ex-SWEENEY'S MEN, ex-WOODS BAND, ex-POGUES) / with also **Phil Gaston**, etc.

Special Delivery | Green Linnet

Jun 91. (lp/c/cd; as RON KAVANA) *(SPD/+C/CD 1043)* *<GLCD 3070>* **HOME FIRE**
- Home fire - Beyond the pale / Johnny go easy / Blind Sheenan / Handcuffs – Gran' sheriff of Ballydaheen / The Kilshannig wager / Lovely cottage - Gold ochra at Killarney point to points / Sands of time lament / The barleycorn - Kerry polka – Wren's polka / Reconciliation / The Cricklade culchee - Down the lane / Blackwaterside / Fermoy regatta – Tom's tavern / Young Ned of the hill.

—— In 1994 Ron, Miriam, Terry and Rod formed ceilidh band The Bucks, recording one set for WEA, 'Dancing To The Ceili'.

Alias | not issued

Oct 95. (cd) *(CDARK 002)* **GALWAY TO GRACELAND**
- Intro - Shamrock city - The Edmonton reel / True to the end / Watch out Willie

(incl. Trip to Durrow - Gravel walk) / Martha (the flower of sweet Strabane) / Kathy Boyd's waltz - Cajun train / Cap-gun kid and the new Lee highway blues (incl. The spindle shanks) / Nora Lee - Galway to Graceland - Are you lonesome tonight / New rising of the moon / St. Patrick's Day in New Orleans / Mexican holiday - Luz / 19th nervous breakdown - The blacksmith"s daughter / Born with the blues / Fine, fine, fine - Staten Island - Chief O'Neill's favourite / Looney tune - Farewell.

Retro not issued

Dec 98. (d-cd; as The ALIAS ACOUSTIC BAND) *(R2CD 4073)* **IRISH SONGS OF REBELLION, RESISTANCE AND RECONCILIATION**

- Easter 1916 - Caoimhneadh roisin / To welcome Paddy home / Boolavogue / The Shan Van Vocht / Erin's lovely Lee / The boys of Barr na sraide / Johnny I hardly knew ya / Brennan on the moor / The wind that shakes the barley / Reconciliation / The grand auld dame Britannia / Glory o to the bold fenian men / The pursuit of farmer Michael Hayes / James Connolly / Roddy McCorley / Dunlavin green / Robert Emmett's last words - Scaffold passage / Cry, cry, cry / Kitty - Taddy O'Neil // Force of argument - Laments of Limerick / The wearing of the green / The patriot game / Skibereen / Home fire - Beyond the pale / The foggy dew / The boys of the County Cork / Follow me up to Carlow / Four green fields / God bless England / Boys of Mullaghbawn / The praties they grow small / Truth and understanding / The mountains of Pomeroy / Sands of time - Kesh jig / The rocks of Bawn / The sea around us / A nation once again - Amhran na bhfiann. *(re-iss. Sep 06 on Primo; 6015)*

RON KAVANA

with The Resident Aliens: **Bob Bradshaw** (rhythm guitar, vocals), **Chad Clouse** (fiddle), **Scoop McGuire** (bass), **Phil Hawkins** (drums)

Proper not issued

Jun 99. (cd; as RON KAVANA) *(PRPCD 10)* **ALIEN ALERT**: LIVE IN CALIFORNIA WITH THE RESIDENT ALIENS

- Waxin' the Gaza / The shan van vocht / Maria de la Rosa / The shores of America / Medley: Ain't that peculiar + The foxhunters / The ghost of winters gone / Scotia / Leaba Caili / Medley: An leigheas, The blue eagle + The reel with a birl / The banks of the Lee / Soweto trembles / Galtee mor / Irish ways / Blackberry blossom / Alien alert - Tura lura lura / UFOs @ SFO / Medley: The power of love + No cause for alarm.

Feb 07. (4-cd-box) *(PRDP 4001)* **IRISH WAYS**: The story of Ireland in song, music and poetry

- PRE-HISTORIC IRELAND TO NORMANS: Songs of our land / Seevocuda / Before history's tale began / The invaders / Arrival of the Celts / St. Patrick / Partial catastrophe / A pagan cult survives / The Wran / The Vikings and Brian Boru / Weep now for poor Roisin / MacMurrough and the Normans / The bards / HENRY VIII TO WILLIAM OF ORANGE: Henry VIII / For all his wives... / A royal and a reasonable fellow / Irish slaves / Elizabeth and the planters / Liza / Follow me up to Carlow / Cromwell, agent of a wrathful God / Young Ned of the hill / Lament for Ireland / Remember the 12th / Derry, the Boyne, Aughrim and the treaty of Limerick / Sean O'Duibhir a'ghleanna / A farewell to Patrick Sarsfield / Both sides of the Boyne // PENAL LAWS TO AGE OF REVOLUTION: Wild geese / Suil a ruin / Penal days / The penal laws / Farewell Granuaille / Deorai / Rambling Irishman / The bardic tradition and the death of Carolan / An entree / A modest proposal / John Barry / American war of independence / At the siege of Valley Forge / French revolution / The Carmagnoles / THE RIGHTS OF MAN AND 1798: The sean bhean bhocht / The rights of man / The summer soldiers / 1798 and the united Irishmen / Dunlavin green / Boolavogue / Forging of the pikes / The rising of the moon / Who fears to speak of '98 / Roddy McCorley / A winter's tale / By memory inspired / Truth and understanding / The union / The Shamrock shore // ACT OF UNION TO GREAT HUNGER: Young Robert Emmet / Robert Emmet's last words - Scaffold passage / Emmet's no more / After '98 / The plains of Waterloo / The whiteboys / Buachaillin ban / Daniel O'Connell / Daniel O'Connell and Erin go bragh / Further catastrophe / O'Connell's dead / The praties - The Lord's prayer / The great hunger / Mad visions / The famine year / Skibereen / EMIGRATION AND THE DIASPORA: Diaspora / The new road / Canada-I-O / The new dominion / Crossing the Niagara / Bound for South Australia / The plains of Emu / Adieu and farewell / On the tide / No Irish need apply / The battle of Bull Run / Muldoon, the solid man // FENIANS TO CIVIL WAR: Fenians, the land league and Parnell / The wife of the bold tenant farmer / The uncrowned king - The pinch o' snuff / Revival and rising / The foggy dew / Easter 1916 / War of independence and civil war / Four green fields / Cry, cry, cry / FREE STATE TO MODERN IRELAND: Free state to the troubles / In the smoke / The travellin' people - Death chant of the Navaho / You northern gaels / Reconciliation / Old Ireland - New Ireland / Lovers and friends / Irish ways.

Primo not issued

Apr 11. (d-cd; as RON KAVANA AND FRIENDS) *(PRMCD 6111)* **40 FAVOURITE FOLK SONGS**

- The minstrel boy / Madam I'm a darlin' (w/ ANNE ARMSTRONG) / One starry night (w/ KATE O'CUALAIN) / No balls at all (TOMMY McCARTHY) / Wind and rain (ANNE ARMSTRONG) / My flower of Magherally (MICK COYNE) / Tree to tree (w/ ANNE ARMSTRONG) / The mountains of Mourne / Wild mountain thyme / Gobsheen gombeens (w/ ANNE ARMSTRONG) / The sloop John B / Lay down your weary tune (w/ ANNE ARMSTRONG) / McShane (w/ MIKE 'MUNGO' O'CONNOR) / The water is wide – O'Donnell Abu (w/ JOHN SIMPSON) / Captain Weatherbourne's courtship (MICK FLYNN) / Muldoon, the solid man (w/ NIAMH PARSONS) / Goodnight Irene / So long, it's been good to ya / Childhood's end / Puttin' on the style (NORMAN KING) // The night visit / The kissing song (w/ ANNE ARMSTRONG) / The brown and yellow ale (MICK FLYNN) / Where the wild roses grow (ANNE ARMSTRONG) / I want to see the bright lights tonight / There was a man (MICK COYNE) / The Galway shawl (w/ ANNE ARMSTRONG) / Reconciliation (w/ NIAMH PARSONS) / The first time ever I saw your face / The curragh of Kildare (MIKE 'MUNGO' O'CONNOR) / Who knows where the time goes / The wedding (TOMMY McCARTHY) / She moved through the fair / My father's a hedger and ditcher – Love will ya marry me? (w/ ANNE ARMSTRONG) / I'll tell me ma (NORMAN KING) / Bold Doherty (w/ ANNE ARMSTRONG) / As I roved out (KATE O'CUALAIN) / The Spanish lady / The old main drag / Auld lang syne (w/ JOHN SIMPSON).

Paul KELLY

Born Paul Maurice Kelly, January 13, 1955, in Adelaide, Australia, KELLY's musical career began in 1974 with a public performance in Hobart of the trad-folklore number 'Streets Of Forbes'. KELLY has led many bands since his inaugural incarnation as Paul Kelly & The Dots (two LPs, **TALK** (1981) {*4} and **MANILA** (1982) {*5}).

Flitting in the meantime from short-term base Melbourne to Sydney, he recorded his debut solo LP, **POST** (1985) {*4}, but this remained unreleased until he found a bona-fide contract with Mushroom Records. With a new outfit in tow, the inaccurately named Coloured Girls (tipping the hat to Lou Reed's 'Walk On The Wild Side'), KELLY hit the big time with double-set **GOSSIP** (1986) {*8}, a record that produced two Australian chart entries, 'Darling It Hurts' and 'Before Too Long'.

He continued to shine in his native land with albums such as **UNDER THE SUN** (1987) {*6} (with the Coloured Girls); **SO MUCH WATER, SO CLOSE TO HOME** (1989) {*5}; **COMEDY** (1991) {*7}; and the B-sides collection **HIDDEN THINGS** (1991) {*6}, the last three with his third outfit, the Messengers. With production work and other activities in the pipeline (a book of poetry, etc.), a second solo album, **WANTED MAN** (1994) {*5}, saw him find his lyrical folk roots once again.

It was still a mystery how KELLY had never established himself in Britain and America like so many other Australian acts, e.g. Nick Cave, but that didn't stop him trying. Further albums flowed from KELLY's pen, while journeyman excursions into other music genres (techno and bluegrass, with Professor Ratbaggy and Uncle Bill respectively) provided him with more directions than you could throw a boomerang at.

Yet another outlet for his undoubted abilities was film music (he had scored 'Everynight ... Everynight' in 1994), the multi-talented singer-songwriter soundtracking a string of Australian films including **SILENT PARTNER** (2001) {*6}, alongside bluegrass banjo strummer GERRY HALE. It includes several numbers written by KELLY alone, the best of which are the Dylanesque opener, 'Be Careful What You Pray For', and the John Denverish 'Teach Me Tonight' (taken from KELLY's Uncle Bill set, 'Smoke').

When he sings, Paul (who scored and co-starred in **ONE NIGHT THE MOON** (2001) {*6}) is Australia's modern-day DYLAN or COHEN, as the soundtrack's moody opening song 'I Don't Know Anything Any More' testifies. But 'One Night ...' was not down to KELLY alone. It also belonged to violinist Mairead Hannan and Aboriginal musician Kev Carmody. With her uplifting folk fiddle, the former gets into the heritage side of things on 'Flinders Theme' and 'The Gathering' (think of Celtic acts OSSIAN and The CHIEFTAINS), while the lilting title track is sung by cast member Kaarin Fairfax and Paul's young daughter, Memphis Kelly. For further details of his soundtrack work, including **LANTANA** (2001) {*6}, look up my book 'Lights, Camera, Soundtracks' (Canongate, 2008).

Described as Australia's equivalent of Springsteen (or even Mark Knopfler), Kelly continued his eclectic post-millennium career continued with **... NOTHING BUT A DREAM** (2001) {*7}, the double **WAYS AND MEANS** (2004) {*7}, the bluegrass **FOGGY HIGHWAY** (2005) {*6} – with the Stormwater Boys – and **STOLEN APPLES** (2007) {*6}. *MCS*

PAUL KELLY AND THE DOTS

Paul Kelly - vocals, guitar / **Chris Langman** - guitars / **Chris Worrall** - guitars / **Paul Gadsby** - bass / **John Lloyd** - drums

Aus/UK SMX US not issued

1979. (7"; as The DOTS) *(SMX-46968)* RECOGNITION. / Aus

—— **Tony Thornton** - drums; repl. Lloyd

—— **Alan Brooker** - bass; repl. Gadsby

Mushroom not issued

1980. (7") *(???)* BILLY BAXTER. / Aus

1981. (7") *(K 7906)* SEEING IS BELIEVING. / Aus

Mar 81. (lp) *(L 37512)* **TALK** Aus
- Promise not to tell / Lowdown / Want you back / Fall guy / Hard knocks / Billy Baxter / Recognition / Cherry / The way love used to be / I hate to watch you loving him / Please send me. *(re-iss. 1990 cd/lp; D/L 19465)*

May 81. (7") *(???)* LOWDOWN. / Aus

—— **Tim Brosnan** + **Michael Holmes** - guitars; repl. Worrall + Langham (the latter still co-contributed a couple of songs)

Apr 82. (7") *(???)* CLEAN THIS HOUSE. / Aus

Jul 82. (7") *(???)* ALIVE AND WELL. / Aus

Aug 82. (lp) *(L 37636)* **MANILA** Aus
- Forbidden street / Clean this house / Alive and well / Skidding hearts / Some guys / Last resort / See you in Paradise / Touchy babe / When the girl's not even English / Lenny (to live is to burn). *(re-iss. 1990 cd/lp; D/L 19466)*

PAUL KELLY

now w/ **Steve Connolly** - guitar / **Michael Barclay** - drums

Apr 85. (7") *(???)* FROM ST KILDA TO KING'S CROSS. / Aus

May 85. (lp/c) *(L/C 38401)* **POST** Aus
- From St Kilda to King's Cross / Incident on South Dowling / Look so fine, feel so low / White train / Luck / Blues for Skip / Adelaide / Satisfy your woman / You can put your shoes under my bed / Standing on the streets of early sorrows / Little decisions. *(cd-iss. 1990; MUSH 32276.2) (cd re-mast. 2006; 32276)*

PAUL KELLY & THE MESSENGERS

—— added **Jon Schofield** - bass / **Peter Bull** - keyboards

Sep 86. (d-lp/d-c; as PAUL KELLY AND THE COLOURED GIRLS) *(L/C 45961/2)* **GOSSIP** Aus
- Last train to heaven / Leaps and bounds / Before the old man died *[remixed for US]* / Down on my speedway / White train / Randwick bells / Before too long / Adelaide *[not on US+cd]* / I won't be torn apart *[not on US]* / Going about my father's business *[not on US]* / Somebody's forgetting somebody (somebody's letting somebody down) / The ballroom *[not on US+cd]* / Tighten up *[remixed for US]* / I've come for your daughter *[not on US+cd]* / So blue *[not on US+cd]* / The execution *[remixed for US]* / Incident on South Dowling / Maralinga (rainy land) *[not on US+cd]* / Darling it hurts / Look so fine, feel so low / Stories of me / Don't harm the messenger / Gossip *[not on US+cd]* / After the show *[not on US+cd]*. *<US-iss. Jul 1987 on A&M lp/cd; SP/CD 5157> (cd-iss. 1993; MUSH 32282.2)*

Dec 87. (lp/c/cd) *(RML/RMC/RMCD 53248)* **UNDER THE SUN** Aus
- Dumb things / Same old walk / Big heart / Don't stand so close to the window / Forty miles to Saturday night / I don't remember a thing *[Aus-only]* / Know your friends / To her door / Under the sun / Untouchable *[track 6 UK+US-only]* / Desdemona / Happy slave / Crosstown / Little decisions *[UK+US-only]* / Bicentennial. *(Aus cd+=)* - Bradman / Pastures of plenty.

A&M A&M

Sep 88. (7") *(AM 459)* DARLING IT HURTS. / Desdemona, Before Too Long
(12"+=) *(AMY 459)* - ('A'version).

Sep 88. (lp/c/cd) *(AMA/AMC/CDA 5207)* *<SP/CD 5157>* **UNDER THE SUN**
- (for track see above Australian version)

Aug 89. (lp/c/cd) *(AMA/AMC/CDA 5266)* **SO MUCH WATER SO CLOSE TO HOME**
- You can't take it with you / Sweet guy / Most wanted man in the world / I had forgotten you / She's a melody (stupid song) / South of Germany / Careless / Moon in the bed / No you / Everything's turning to white / Pigeon - Jundamurra / Cities of Texas.

Mushroom Doctor Dream

Nov 91. (cd) *(32285-2)* *<DDCD-9265>* **COMEDY** Aus
- Don't start me talking / Stories of me / Wintercoat / It's all downhill from here / Leaving her for the last time / Brighter / Your little sister (is a big girl now) / I won't be your dog anymore / Take your time / Sydney from a 727 / Buffalo ballet / I can't believe we were married / From little things big things grow / Blue stranger / Keep it to yourself / (You can put your) Shoes under my bed / Invisible me / Little boy don't lose your balls. *(hidden +=)* - David Gower.

PAUL KELLY

Demon Vanguard

Aug 94. (cd) *(FIENDCD 758)* *<VSD 79479-2>* **WANTED MAN** Sep 94
- Summer rain / God's hotel / She's rare / Just like animals / Love never runs on time / Song from the sixteenth floor / Maybe this time for sure / Ball and chain / You're still picking the same sore / Everybody wants to touch me / We've started a fire / Lately / Nukkanya.

BMG Vanguard

Sep 95. (cd) *(74321 30541-2)* *<VSD 79485>* **DEEPER WATER**
- Blush / Extra mile / I'll forgive but I won't forget / Queen stone / Deeper water / Madeleine's song / Difficult woman / Give in to my love / I've been a fool / Anastasia changes her mind / California / Gathering storm.

Mushroom Vanguard

Jul 96. (cd) *(32279-2)* *<VSD 79493>* **LIVE**: AT THE CONTINENTAL AND THE ESPLANADE Aus
- When I first met your ma / Maralinga / God's hotel / Everybody wants to touch me / Somebody's forgetting somebody (somebody's letting somebody down) / Just like animals / To her door / Pouring petrol on a burning man / Dumb things / Cities of Texas / She's rare / Darling it hurts / Careless / Summer rain.

May 98. (cd) *(33108-2)* *<VSD 79499>* **WORDS AND MUSIC**
- Little kings / I'll be your lover now / Nothing on my mind / Words and music / How to make gravy / Gutless wonder / Tease me / I'd rather be blind / She answers the sun (lazybones) / The beat of your heart / It started with a kiss / Glory be to God / Saturday night and Sunday morning / Charlie Owen's slide guitar / Melting.

EMI not issued

Jun 00. (cd; as PROFESSOR RATBAGGY featuring PAUL KELLY) *(523267-2)* **PROFESSOR RATBAGGY** Aus
- Please myself / White trash / Can't fake it / Moni, make it good / Coma / Love letter / Blowfly / See the bride fly out / Mannish woman / Rise and shine / Oh, death.

Jul 00. (cd; by PAUL KELLY with UNCLE BILL) *(22880)* **SMOKE** Aus
- Our sunshine / You can't take it with you / Until death do them part / I can't believe we were married / I don't remember a thing / Teach me tonight / Sydney from a 747 / Night after night / Whistling bird / Stories of me / Taught by experts / Gathering storm / Shy before you Lord.

—— the three albums below were recorded for films ...

Sep 01. (cd; by PAUL KELLY & GERRY HALE) *(535569-2)* **SILENT PARTNER** (soundtrack) Aus
- Be careful what you pray for / Silver's theme / Is it a he or a she? / You can't take it with you (instrumental) / Silent partner / Teach me tonight / Now's not the time for a hot sea bath / Silver's on the line / Ain't got the constitution / Better prospects / The gatekeeper / Forest funeral - Silver turns to lead / Little boy don't lose your balls / Silent partner (reprise) / Royal road / Ain't got the constitution (reprise) / Would you be my friend?

Sep 01. (cd) *(535873-2)* **LANTANA** (soundtrack) Aus
- Lantana part 1 / Lantana part 2 / For Eleanor / What's happening to us / Through the window / Numb / Shortcut / Let's tangle. *(UK-iss. Aug 02 on Cooking Vinyl+=; COOKCD 238)- (other artists) (d-cd-iss. 2005 +=; 34877-2)* - ONE NIGHT THE MOON

—— next credited PAUL KELLY *, KEV CARMODY ** & MAIREAD HANNAN ***)

Sep 01. (cd) *(535987-2)* **ONE NIGHT THE MOON** (soundtrack) Aus
- I don't know anything anymore (*) / Flinders theme (***) / One night the moon (KAARIN FAIRFAX and MEMPHIS KELLY) / Moon child (*** & DEIRDRE HANNAN) / The gathering (***) / Now listen here - intro (***) / This land is mine (* & KELTON PELL) / The march goes on - The gathering 2 (***) / Spirit of the ancients (**) / What do you know (KAARIN FAIRFAX and KELTON PELL) *** & ** & * / Carcass - The gathering 3 (***) / Night shadows (* & ***) / Black and white (**) / Moment of death (***) / Hunger (***) / Unfinished business (KELTON PELL and KAARIN FAIRFAX) ** & * / Spirit of the ancients (**) / Moody broody (***) / Little bones (KAARIN FAIRFAX) *** & * / Oh breathe on me (RUBY HUNTER) / Moonstruck (**). *(d-cd-iss.+=)- LANTANA*

Cooking Vinyl EMI

Sep 01. (cd) *(COOKCD 228)* *<534938-2>* **...NOTHING BUT A DREAM** Aug 01
- If I could start today again / Change your mind / Midnight rain / I close my eyes and think of you / Somewhere in the city / Just about to break / Love is the law / The pretty place / I wasted time / Would you be my friend? / Smoke under the bridge.

Cooking Vinyl Capitol

Feb 04. (d-cd) *(COOKCD 283)* *<967928-2>* **WAYS AND MEANS**
- Guinnamatta / The oldest story in the book / Heavy thing / Won't you come around? / These are the days / Beautiful feeling / Crying shame / Sure got me / To be good takes a long time / Can't help you now / Nothing but a dream / Little bit o' sugar / Forty-eight angels / Your lovin' is on my mind / You broke a beautiful thing / My way is to you / Curly red / King of fools / Young lovers / Big fine girl / Let's fall again.

Oct 05. (cd; as PAUL KELLY & THE STORMWATER BOYS) *(COOKCD 313)* *<31667-2>* **FOGGY HIGHWAY** May 05
- Stumbling block / Rally round the drum / Ghost town / Song of the old rake / Don't stand so close to the window / Passed over / They thought I was asleep / You're learning (with KASEY CHAMBERS) / Foggy highway / Down to my soul / Cities of Texas / Meet me in the middle of the air // *(w/ free cd+=)* - Little boy don't lose your balls / Rank stranger / Erina Valley breakout / Surely God is a lover.

Capitol Capitol

Jul 07. (cd) *<(500483-2)>* **STOLEN APPLES**
- Feelings of grief / God told me to / Stolen apples taste the sweetest / Sweetest thing / You're 39, you're beautiful and you're mine / The lion and the lamb / Right outta my head / Keep on driving / The ballad of Queenie and Rover / The foggy fields of France / Please leave your lights on.

- (8-10*) compilations -

May 97. (cd) *Mushroom; (93479-2)* **SONGS FROM THE SOUTH: PAUL KELLY'S GREATEST HITS** May 05
- From St Kilda to King's Cross / Leaps and bounds / Before too long / Darling it hurts / Look so fine, feel so low / Dumb things / To her door / Bradman / Everything's turning to white / Sweet guy / Careless / Winter coat / From little things big things grow / When I first met your ma / Pouring petrol on a burning man / Love never runs on time / Song from the sixteenth floor / Deeper water / Give in to my love / How to make gravy. *(UK-iss. Jan 98; MUSH 17CD) (UK re-iss. Jan 04; 33009-5)*

- (5-7*) compilations, others, etc.-

Nov 91. (cd; by PAUL KELLY & THE MESSENGERS) *Mushroom; (32283-2)* **HIDDEN THINGS** Aus
- Reckless / When I first met your ma / Sweet guy waltz / Hard times / Other people's houses / Special treatment / Little decisions / Rally round the drum / Pastures of plenty / Beggar on the street of love / Pouring petrol on a burning man / From St Kilda to King's Cross / Brand new ways / Rock 'n' soul / Yil lull / Bradman / Ghost town / Elly. *(UK-iss. Mar 95; D 30748)*

Feb 95. (d-cd) *Mushroom; (D 16061)* **LIVE, MAY 1992** (live)
- Foggy highway / To her door / Wintercoat / Taught by experts / From little things big things grow / I can't believe we were married / Until death do them part / Same old walk / Don't explain / Stupid song / Brand new ways / Stories of me / Everything turned to white / Dumb things / Just like animals / Keep it to yourself / I won't be your dog anymore / I was hoping you'd say that / Careless.

Nov 08. (cd) *Capitol; <264692-2>* **SONGS FROM THE SOUTH VOLUME 2: PAUL KELLY 98–08**
- Nothing on my mind / I'll be your lover / Love letter / Our sunshine / Gathering storm / Every fucking city / Be careful what you pray for / Love is the law / If I could start today again / The oldest story in the book / Won't you come around / Gunnamatta / Your lovin' is on my mind / Song of the old rake / They thought I was asleep / Everybody loves you baby / Gos told me to / You're 39, you're beautiful and you're mine / Thoughts in the middle of the night / Shane Warne night.

Rick KEMP

On the strength of his lengthy double stretch as bassist for electric folk icons STEELEYE SPAN from 1972 to 1986 and 2000 to today, rootsy RICK KEMP (born Frederick Stanley Kemp, November 15 1941, Little Hanford, Dorset) is one of the busiest players in the music business. He was married to MADDY PRIOR and is the father of rock starlet Rose Kemp.

Having worked with folk guitarist MICHAEL CHAPMAN in the early 1970s (and briefly with King Crimson in 1971), Rick finally got together with him for a one-off LP, 'Original Owners', in 1984. As a member of his ex-wife's MADDY PRIOR BAND, he was credited on a joint single, 'Happy Families', in 1990.

Together with STEELEYE SPAN drummer Nigel Pegrum (with whom, allegedly, he'd worked in the infamous Pork Dukes punk outfit), he set up the Plant Life imprint in the late 1970s, although it was defunct around five years later. Having been in the biz for around three decades, KEMP finally unleashed his solo demons on two Fellside Records sets, **ESCAPE** (1997) {*6} and **SPIES** (1998) {*5}. He also took time to nurture folk-scene newcomers WHAPWEASEL, producing and playing guitar on a couple of sets. Guitarist Spud Sinclair and drummer Charlie Carruthers have played on his solo work, but it's not certain whether they were behind him on his third blues-folk venture, **CODES** (2004) {*5}. *MCS*

Rick Kemp - vocals, bass / + session band

UK Fellside — US not issued

Jan 97. (cd) *(FECD 114)* **ESCAPE**
- What you see is what you get / Brampton to roadhead blues / Over my head / Deep in the darkest night / Nobody put you on the train / Waiting for a miracle / Queen of light / Phoenix / Genocide / Fighting on the same side / Escape / Somewhere along the road.

Jul 98. (cd) *(FECD 133)* **SPIES**
- Boundaries / Long way from paradise / Pressure's off / Hello peace / Back on your own again / Great divide / New baptism / Heart of stone / Judgement day / All in this together / Georgetown skyline.

L8rd8r — not issued

Dec 04. (cd) *(RKCD 001)* **CODES**
- Good day / More than one way / Stepping out / Roots / Chariot / Codes / Pass me by / Lost for words / World / Waiting for tomorrow / Myths.

Keith KENDRICK

Derbyshire-born, around the 1940s, Keith (mistakenly surnamed Hendrick in some sources) was in late-1960s/early-1970s harmony-folk outfit The DRUIDS. Alongside Judi Longden, John Adams, Mick Hennessey and Dave Broughton, they released two sets for Argo in the early 1970s; 'Burnt Offering' was particularly significant, with its 'Wicker Man' sleeve design.
After The DRUIDS fizzled out, concertinist KENDRICK would resurface in early 1980s group Ram's Bottom Dance Band, while also moonlighting with TUP alongside (Jim) BOYES and (Lester) SIMPSON. One hen's tooth of an LP ('The One May Moon') by the Ram's Bottom Dance Band, for Tradition Records, is supposed to exist from 1981.

Keith had a decade-long association with BOYES & SIMPSON's partner BARRY COOPE from 1977 to 1988, and in the 1990s worked with MUCKRAM WAKES, The East Kent Hoppers and The Anchor Men (the latter a duo, completed by Ian Smith, for the cassette 'Nautical But Nice'), but details of these ventures are blurred – ditto Three Sheets To The Wind, a project featuring GEOFF HIGGINBOTTOM and Derek Gifford.

Keith's first solo effort, the cassette-only **ME 'UMBLE LOT** (1994) {*5}, is hard to track down, although Fellside Records illuminated his obscurity by releasing his first CD, **HOME GROUND** (1997) {*6}. Known for her duo work with PAT TURNER, singer LYNNE HERAUD was credited on KENDRICK's inaugural Wild Goose Records release **STARS IN MY CROWN** (2003) {*6}; they had met in 1998 at the Broadstairs Folk Festival. Two further sets followed for Kendrick, the festive **WELL SEASONED** (2003) {*5} and his career pinnacle , **SONGS FROM THE DERBYSHIRE COAST** (2006) {*6}. *MCS*

Keith Kendrick - vocals, guitar, concertina (ex-DRUIDS)

UK Volume One — US not issued

Jun 94. (c) *(VOR 122C)* **ME 'UMBLE LOT**

Fellside — not issued

Apr 97. (cd) *(FE 118CD)* **HOME GROUND**
- The rag and bone man / Some tyrant has stolen my true-love away / The lion's den / Died for love / A shantyman's life / Ey mam why? / Polkas: Fruits and flowers – Three jolly sailor boys / The humble heart / The last time / The life of a man / Jack the jolly tar / The Irish girl / 'Ospitles / Tha' lowks a proper swell lass / Ball o' yarn / They're taking it away / Janitors and jailers.

Wild Goose — not issued

Aug 03. (cd; by KEITH KENDRICK & LYNNE HERAUD) *(WGS 303CD)* **STARS IN MY CROWN**
- The poor and honest soldier / Awake, awake (New Year's carol) / The miller and the lass / Herod / Will there be any stars in my crown? / The happy man / Bird in a cage / Lord Gregory / The builders / A passionate shepherd to his love / The leaves of life (seven virgins) / A sailor likes his bottle-o / One starry night / Love is come again / Love farewell.

Dec 03. (cd) *(WGS 317CD)* **WELL SEASONED** [festive]
- The ploughshare / Nowell, Nowell / Bring 'im on / The Ashbourne wassail / The great Derby footrace / The moon shines bright / Derwent May carol / Whitsuntide carol / The scarecrow The Nutley waltz – Doug's maggot / The grey cock and the lover's ghost / The harvest supper song words / Norfolk – The gasp reel / Beautiful dale / Hark, hark what news?

Jul 06. (cd) *(WGS 337CD)* **SONGS FROM THE DERBYSHIRE COAST**
- Bold Riley / Lowlands of Holland / Once I courted a damsel / Beulah land / Summon up the sun / Turkish quickstep / Sally free and easy / The echoin' horn / Napoleon's dream / The sailor's prayer / A hundred years ago – Essiquibo river – Rolling down the bay to Juliana / Roman reel – Polka Chinoise / The coast of Peru / Awake! arise!

KERFUFFLE

With so much excitement going on over new-girls-on-the-fRoots-block The UNTHANKS, was there room for another Bright Young Folk thing, fresh-faced teenager Hannah James? Yes there was, and plenty for her equally talented and multi-faceted male colleagues Sam Sweeney and his brother Tom.

Formed 2001, not in Scotland whence their name ('a commotion') derives, but in South Yorkshire and the East Midlands, KERFUFFLE were quickly off the mark with the Steafan Hannigan-produced debut set **NOT TO SCALE** (2003) {*6}, a record recalling the halcyon days of the turn of the 1970s and traditional tunes from a few centuries past.

Adding Chris Thornton-Smith to the equation, second set **K2** (2004) {*6} paralleled its predecessor, while tours supporting SHOW OF HANDS and others gave the quartet some extra exposure. They were also finalists in the 2004/5 BBC Radio Two Young Folk Awards.

In between **LINKS** (2006) {*6} and **TO THE GROUND** (2008) {*7}, Chris (originally their sound engineer) made way for Jamie Roberts, while Sam moonlighted with BELLOWHEAD. The festive **LIGHTEN THE DARK** (2009) {*7} was once again produced by Andy Bell, while HANNAH JAMES (now also of The DEMON BARBER Roadshow) and SAM SWEENEY splintered off with their duo outing **CATCHES AND GLEES** (2009) {*7}. *MCS*

Hannah James - vocals, accordion, piano, step dancing / **Sam Sweeney** (b. 1989, Nottingham,

England) - fiddle, djembe, vocals, percussion / **Tom Sweeney** - bass

UK RootBeat — US not issued

Jun 03. (cd) *(RBRCD 01)* **NOT TO SCALE**
- Catharsis – Peterman – Siobhan O'Donnell's / Ahma – Ruchenitsa – Farewell to Chernobyl / If I was a blackbird / Quendale Bay / Mick's knitted triplets – The ash plant – The bonny Isle of Whalsay / Lochaber drive – Breton tune – Poker signature / The brisk young widow – Gravel walk – Victor's return / Lucy's sox – Morrisons / Falmouth packet / Irish toast.

— added **Chris Thornton-Smith** - guitar

Jul 04. (cd) *(RBRCD 03)* **K2**
- Dance little maid – Monster of Polska / The great silkie of Sule Skerry – The old maid of Galway / Speed the plough – The road to Ballymac – Swedish polska / Mrs. Saggs / Holland handerchief / The orphan – The phone call – The milliner's daughter – The salvation / Ca' the ewes / James and Lara's wedding – Highlander's farewell – Crazy dog / O'Neill's lament / Hold back the tide / Sleeping tune – Vingarden.

Apr 06. (cd) *(RBRCD 05)* **LINKS**
- Intro / Bold: The bold grenadier – The pipe on the hob – Siobhan's O'Donnell's / Maggot: Sam's 16th – The hare's maggot – The Cheshire round / Hangover: Hangover quadrille – O'Neill's cavalcade / Searching for lambs: The convergence – Searching for lambs / Light flight / My heart's in New South Wales / Lark in the clear air / Fiddle Castro: Schottisch Van Zaventem – Fiddle Castro's return to Galway / The willow / [live at the Priddy Folk Festival 2005]: Brisk: The brisk young widow – The red-haired boy – Scrap metal / Twisted: The flogging reel – The twisted bridge.

— **Jamie Roberts** - guitar; repl. Chris (next with Andy Letcher on bagpipes)

Jun 08. (cd) *(RBRCD 06)* **TO THE GROUND**
- Katie Shaw / Dr. Letcher's favourite: Mayden Lane – Mount hills / Down by the greenwood side / Rondo: The bean setting – Mohacs – Rondo de Seltrad / Arise, arise / Castleton carol – Goddesses / Betty Corrigall's lament / The trip: Kemp's jig – Hunt the squirrel / The snows they melt the soonest / Two sisters / Bonapart's retreat / The rogue's march.

Aug 09. (cd; as HANNAH JAMES & SAM SWEENEY) *(RBRCD 07)* **CATCHES AND GLEES**
- Gaol song / Ploughboy's dream / You are the one / Dick's maggot, dog leap stairs / Died for love / Flaxley Green dance – The old wife of Coverdale / Wee weaver / Catches and glees – Comical thought / Three ravens / Polska / The young and single sailor.

Nov 09. (cd) *(RBRCD 08)* **LIGHTEN THE DARK: A MIDWINTER ALBUM** [festive]
- Three ships / Cherry tree carol / The truth from above / Bransles / Lullay my liking / Gallery carol / Sussex carol / Nowell, nowell / The holly and the ivy / Gower wassail / The bitter withy.

— with Sam already part of BELLOWHEAD, they split the following year; Hannah also fronted Lady Maisery

Nancy KERR & James FAGAN

Daughter of children's entertainer and folk singer SANDRA KERR and Northumbrian piper Ron Elliott, violinist and singer NANCY KERR burst on to the scene when she collaborated with fellow fiddler ELIZA CARTHY on a few sets between 1993 and 1995.

Mother and daughter subsequently teamed up for 'Neat And Complete' (1996) and 'Scalene' (1998), the latter with Australian bouzouki player JAMES FAGAN, who continued with Nancy on further albums such as **STARRY GAZY PIE** (1997) {*6}, **STEELY WATER** (1999) {*6}, **BETWEEN THE DARK AND LIGHT** (2002) {*7}, **STRANDS OF GOLD** (2006) {*7}, **STATION HOUSE** (2008) {*6} – with Robert Harbron on concertina – and **TWICE REFLECTED SUN** (2010) {*8}. The latter was a complete contrast with their earlier recordings, the pair this time around writing all their own songs; they'd married in 2007. Among Nancy's extracurricular work, she's fiddled for the TIM VAN EYKEN Band, folk-pop act Epona and a handful of children's CDs with her mother Sandra and LEON ROSSELSON. *MCS*

Nancy Kerr (b. 1975) - vocals, fiddle / **James Fagan** (b. 1972, Sydney, Australia) - vocals, bouzouki

UK Fellside — US not issued

Nov 97. (cd) *(FECD 127)* **STARRY GAZY PIE**
- Mrs. Capron's reel – Murray's reel / Jack Orion – Rusty Jack / The turtle dove – Five fortunes / Lang stayed away – Little fishie – All night I lay awake / The Berkshire tragedy / Song of a drinking man's wife / The wrong door – Choom – Wet physician / Miles Weatherhill / The streams of lovely Nancy / Dancing on the gravel – Pam's polka / Seven yellow gypsies / Young Hunting / Branle de Burgogne – Beyond the border / Starry gazy pie.

— the pair completed an album ('SCALENE') with Nancy's mother SANDRA KERR

Sep 99. (cd) *(FECD 145)* **STEELY WATER**
- Canon / Seven long nights / Anderson's coast / Reel du pendu / The lowlands of Holland / The emu egg / Searching for lambs / Nancy Clough's – Jonny sunshine / The wild colonial boy / Songbirds / Proceed to Slough / Gan to the kye – Peacock follow the hen / Sir Richard's song / Lion island – Manxman.

Apr 02. (cd) *(FECD 167)* **BETWEEN THE DARK AND LIGHT**
- Dance to your daddy / The outside track / Tiller song / Meggy's foot – Coates hall / The false young man / The wire bender / The drover's boy / Something for Liam – Ten million gems / Strawberry town / Ping / Kelly's farewell / Elsie Marley – My laddie sits ower late up / Cuckold come out of the army – Xuan de Mieres – Whoomph / Tiburon / Cave of many colours.

Jan 06. (cd) *(FECD 199)* **STRANDS OF GOLD**
- Barbara Allen / April friend / Peter the cabby / Locks and bolts / Lads of Alnwick / Farewell to the gold / Three magpies / Nancy Taylor's / Sons of liberty / Lovely Nancy / Satellite / Thirty foot trailer.

— added **Robert Harbron** (producer, etc.)

Apr 08. (cd; as KERR, FAGAN, HARBRON) *(FECD 211)* **STATION HOUSE**
- Thaxted – Leaving England / Alan Tyne of Harrow – Alvin's / Favourite duet / Break your fall / Farmhands and masters / The tide coming in – The beehive / The smiling bride – Drummond Castle – Holly's jig / Kissing tree lane – I wish / Let the mystery be – Pie in the sky / Request stop (please inform the guard) / Diamantina drover / Spanish fandangle – Sally Sloane's Varsovienna – Ti tree waltz.

— In 2009, the Fagans (with James, of course) released 'Milk And Honey Land'.

Navigator — not issued

Aug 10. (cd) *(NAVIGATOR 041)* **TWICE REFLECTED SUN**
- Queen of waters / Jerilderie / Dolerite skies / I am the fox / The floating mountains / Flower picker's song / Hauling on / Lover's hymn / Sweet peace / Night night / Rammed earth.

KHARTOUM HEROES (⟹ KING CREOSOTE)

KING CREOSOTE

The chosen name of Fife-born Kenny Anderson (born February 2, 1967, St. Andrews), KING CREOSOTE has become synonymous with Scottish indie and nu-folk music. From his home base at the Fence Collective, KC and his sunshine crew have spread their Caledonian gospel via many CD-rs and proper, scheduled classics.

It was in the late 1980s that singer Kenny (guitar and accordion), his wee brother Een Anderson (double bass, banjo and vocals), Eric Baekeroot (banjo, guitar, mandolin), Andy Robinson (drums, vocals), Atholl Fraser (bass), and fiddlers Donna Vincent and Jason Brass rode into town on the horse that was the SKUOBHIE DUBH ORCHESTRA (pr. 'Scooby Doo'), an energetic Celtic-bluegrass outfit who had barking-mad trad purists up in arms with their thrashy, indie-type arrangements. Two albums surfaced between 1992 and 1994, **39 STEPHS** {*6} and **SPIKE'S 23 COLLECTION** {*6}, both on the unlikeliest of labels, Lochshore Records, better known for Hielan'-type pipers and MOR Gaelic singers.

Retaining Een and a few others, but not youngster Kate (later KT) TUNSTALL, Kenny and his cajun folkabillies, as **KHARTOUM HEROES** {*6}, delivered one self-named set for the same outlet. Incidentally, his original ceilidh band regrouped for live shows in 1998-2003.

Described by the man himself as a micro-indie record label based in Fife (Cellardyke, near Anstruther), Kenny's Fence Collective chose a completely original approach by releasing only records by artists who worked for or were connected with the imprint. Apart from Anderson's KING CREOSOTE bluegrass/folk outfit, there was Pip Dylan (formerly Een Anderson, a talented, busker-type singer-songwriter and guitarist whose inspiration comes from commuting back and forth to Spain and France); their old friend James Wright (alias JAMES YORKSTON); The Jose (swanky lounge lizards Alan Coutts, James Gourley and John McCulloch); country/folk trio The Abrahams (Edinburgh students/pilgrims Martin Noble, Rick Lyons and Joanna Foster); Immigrant (Lingus Gordon), On The Fly, Gummi Bako and former Beta Band songwriter Lone Pigeon (Kenny and Een Anderson's brother Gordon).

Finally we get to KING CREOSOTE, Kenny's uber-folk collective, who take delight in the fact that they have the great Ian Rankin (Fife-born crime novelist and creator of the detective John Rebus) as one of their famous fans. One could get lost in the jungle of self-financed CD-r recordings on Fence, from the 'Chalks' EP of 1999 to post-millennium CD-r's **12 O'CLOCK ON THE DOT** (2000) {*6} and **KENNY AND BETH'S MUSAKAL BOAT RIDES** (2004) {*7}, but all have merit and are much sought-after in this particularly modern-day medium.

Concentrating on his impressive off-Fence 'official' CDs, just about everything that's emerged from KC's bunker can be vouched for, including his Fence finale **ROCKET DIY** (2005) {*7}. On various outsider outlets, check out at least 'Things Things Things' and 'Klutz'. **KC RULES OK** (2005)

{*8}, meanwhile, has all the hallmarks of a classic. It's not exactly folk-music per se (bar 'The Vice-Like Gist Of It' and 'My Favourite Girl'), but a singer-songwriter set that sees Kenny reunited with KT TUNSTALL on 'Locked Together', and with Manchester's The Earlies on several others, including the brilliant opener 'Not One Bit Ashamed'.

Signed to a major label, **BOMBSHELL** (2007) {*7} showed that Anderson could live with the big boys, and with that now unmistakable sharp, Scots-brogue vocal, the bearded KC balanced between the lovelorn intensity of 'Home In A Sentence' and the lo-fi sea shanty of 'Admiral'.

Sketching on his iPad where Badly Drawn Boy once outlined and ruled, KING CREOSOTE and Domino Records got together to release **FLICK THE VS** (2009) {*6}, a sprightly but slightly disappointing (if only by comparison) collection of laptop creations such as 'No One Had It Better' and the accordion-friendly folk ditty 'Two Frocks At A Wedding'. Saviour of the day was Radio 2 Single Of The Week 'Coast On By'.

Formed by Kenny Anderson with several others on the indie-folk supergroup trail (a few picked from Canadian outfits), The BURNS UNIT was yet another act to hop on to the neo-folk gravy train. Most were recruited from the previous Cold Seeds collaborative involving Edinburgh's Meursault and Brighton's Animal Magic Tricks. Stirlingshire traditionalist KARINE POLWART sat nicely alongside fellow Scots Emma Pollack, Sushil Dade and Kim Edgar, while Canadian connections and rappers made up the numbers.

Recorded in 2007, **SIDE SHOW** (2010) {*7} was a hotchpotch in which folk ('Since We've Fallen Out'), Eastern rap ('Send Them Kids To War') and Scots indie-pop ('Future Pilot AKC') were the order of the day, or session.

If there was any question of Anderson/KING CREOSOTE's folk merits or credentials, the answer lay in **DIAMOND MINE** (2011) {*7}, an oblique but romantic field (or village shop) recording and mini-set concept shared with the Eno-like Jon Hopkins. There were seven songs with an atmospheric, soundtrack-like touch (seagulls and all) displaying the folk stoicism of KC's lyrical terrain, defiantly Caledonian from Berwick to John O'Groats and Aberdeen to Stranraer. 'John Taylor's Month Away' (awash with ambient seascapes), and 'Running On Fumes' sounded something akin to ALASDAIR ROBERTS sharing an imaginary studio with an off-colour ROBIN WILLIAMSON. *MCS*

SKUOBHIE DUBH ORCHESTRA

Kenny Anderson - guitar, accordion, vocals / **Een Anderson** (Pip Dylan) - double bass, banjo, vocals / **Andy Robinson** - drums, vocals / **Donna Vincent** + **Jason Brass** - fiddle / **Eric Baekeroot** - banjo, guitar, mandolin / **Atholl Fraser** - bass, guitar

UK Lochshore — US not issued

Apr 92. (cd) *(CDLDL 1203)* **39 STEPHS**
- Little wonder / Precious days / Not by me (no not at all) / Faith / Aftertaste / Wildwood forever / Foggy mountain breakdown / Our last needle / Hung on a wire / Oblongs / Eggshell miles / Amsterdamn / Nellie Kane / Snow queen / What's going on.

Jul 94. (cd) *(CDLDL 1210)* **SPIKE'S 23 COLLECTION**
- The seminar / Baby pink / Old Lloyd / Say something / Long pockets, short arms / Graeme hallelujah Graeme Wilson / Swinging on a gate / Please yourself / Unseen / Bloody red / Clown / Fisticuffs / Stupid world of rails / Spike's 23 collection.

—— the **Andersons** now with **Stu Bastimann** - drums (now in Serial P.O.P.) / **Pete MacLeod** - bass (now Uncle Beasly) / **Steve Mackie** - fiddle, vocals + **Kate Tunstall** - vocals (also known as KT TUNSTALL)

KHARTOUM HEROES

Kenny Anderson - guitar, bouzouki, bass, keyboards, banjo, accordion, etc / **Een Anderson** - banjo, bass, mouth-organ, vocals, etc / **Eric Baekeroot** - guitars, mandolin, banjo, etc / **Jason Brass** - fiddle, bass, vocals / **Andy Robinson** - drums / with also Buck Kinnear (keyboards), Dougi McMillan (samples, keyboards) + Olivia (cello)

Lochshore — not issued

Sep 95. (cd) *(CDLDL 1222)* **KHARTOUM HEROES**
- Cat-gut / St Swithin / Mother Hubbard / Space hopper / Charles and die laughing / Interference / Heaven / Bitter honey / Colossal angel / Song for a flower / Leaves out of bounds / Saints within / Moon barking.

KING CREOSOTE

Kenny Anderson - vocals, acoustic guitar, etc. / + guests

Fence — not issued

1999. (cd-ep) *(fnc 1ep)* CHALKS EP
- Monotony / Space / Homeboy / King of the fairies.

2000. (cd-r) *(fnc 12)* **12 O'CLOCK ON THE DOT**
- Something beginning with d... / Teapot / Abacus / Tumble dry / Greasy railroad / All the threes / Margarita red / Hunger / Harper's dough / Hans Waddesh / Just after eleven she left / Goodbye Mrs Hyde.

2000. (cd-r) *(fnc 13)* **STINKS**
- Tongue in groove / Little grown ups / Punchbag / Sulphur breeze / X-reg bartender / For pity's sake / Handful of 78s / Hellen / Short and sweet / Ten posts nine gaps / Heaven colour dyes / Happily never after / Small child ... cries / La dc di dah / Silence no more / All over Caroline / Marie Celeste / Lost again Billy.

2001. (cd-r) *(fnc 14)* **G**
- Your face / Two of a kind / Missionary / Russian sailor shirts / S.E.P. / Once was lost / Now who'd believe it? / A prairie tale / Walk tall / All I ask / Once was broken / Breaking up ...

2001. (cd-r) *(fnc 15)* **RADGE WEEKEND STARTS HERE**
- Laid if I'm lucky / With hindsight blues / No daddy / Handwashed / Creos'medleyote: Kir(kc)aldy - Fun(kc)rap - Fol(kc)ough / High wire / Heaven come down tonight / Life of lows / Far from saving grace / Mantra-rap / What's with this frown? / Were I not so tired Xhosa.

2001. (cd-r) *(fnc 16)* **KING CREOSOTE SAYS "BUY THE BAZOUKI HAIR OIL"**
- Whine glasses / Conscience / Sunny-side up / Moral tenderhooks / Bubble / It's boredom alright / Fine / Sunshine / Crybaby / You want to walk / I'll fly by the seat of my pants / It's all very well Lester Flatt / How brave am I?

Jun 02. (7") *(fnc 1v - Bebop 35)* SO FORLORN. / Mantra Rap / And So For Lorna

Mar 04. (cd) *(fnck&b)* **KENNY AND BETH'S MUSAKAL BOAT RIDES**
- Lonepigeon's wineglass finale / Homeboy / Pulling up creels / Turps / Spokes / Counselling / So forlorn / Harper's dough / Lavender moon / Space / Meantime / Missionary / A Friday night in New York.

Apr 05. (cd) *(fnc 27)* **ROCKET DIY**
- Twin tub twin / Saffy nool / Klutz / Crow's feet / Spooned out on tick / pH 6.4 / Circle my demise / King bubbles in sand / The things, things, things / A month of firsts / Thrills and spills / The someone else.

Names — not issued

Sep 05. (cd) *(IAMNAMES 11CD)* **KC RULES OK**
- Not one bit ashamed / You are, could I? / The vice-like gist of it / Bootprints / Locked together / Jump at the cats / Guess the time / Favourite girl / I'll fly by the seat of my pants / 678 / Marguerita red.

679 — not issued

Sep 07. (cd) *(256 469 814-8)* **BOMBSHELL**
- Leslie / Home is a sentence / You've no clue do you / Cowardly custard / Church as witness / There's none of that / Nooks / Now drop your bombshell / Admiral / Cockle shell / Spystick / At the WAL / And the racket they made.

Domino — Domino

Apr 09. (cd) *(WIGCD 237)* **FLICK THE VS**
- No one had it better / Two frocks at a wedding / Camels swapped for wives / No way she exists / Fell an ox / Coast on by / Nothing rings true / Curtain craft / Rims / Saw circular process. *(bonus by 'Fence Collective'+=)* - Here on my own / Diamantina drover / Admission #9 / I awoke / I believe it's true.

Feb 11. (cd) *(WIGCD 290) <DNO 290>* **KING CREOSOTE'S THRAWN** [compilation]
- Bootprints / You've no clue do you / King bubbles in sand / Missionary / No way she exists / The vice-like gist of it / Twin tub twin / Homeboy / Little heart / My favourite girl / And the racket they made / No one had it better.

Double Six — Double Six

Mar 11. (m-cd; by KING CREOSOTE & JON HOPKINS) *(<DS 038CD>)* **DIAMOND MINE**
- First watch / John Taylor's month away / Bats in the attic / Running on fumes / Bubble / Your own spell / Your young voice.

The BURNS UNIT

Kenny Anderson - vocals acoustic guitar, accordion, keys / **Emma Pollack** - vocals, guitars, piano (ex-Delgados) / **KARINE POLWART** - vocals, acoustic guitar, percussion, shruti box / **Future Pilot AKA** (Sushil Dade) – bass, atmospherics (ex-Soup Dragons, ex-BMX Bandits, ex-Telstar Ponies) / **Kim Edgar** - vocals, guitars, piano, accordion, organ / **Mattie Foulds** (b. Cape Breton, Nova Scotia, Canada) - drums, percussion (ex-Gordie Sampson) / **Michael Johnston** (b. Toronto, Ontario, Canada) - vocals, piano, accordion, synths, percussion (of Skydiggers) / + female **MC Soom T** - rapper

Burns Unit - Proper — not issued

Aug 10. (cd) *(001)* **SIDE SHOW**
- Since we've fallen out / Trouble / Send them kids to war / Future pilot A.K.C. / Blood, ice and ashes / Sorrys / You need me to need this / Majesty of decay / What is life? / Helpless to turn.

Ian KING

Employing a modus operandi akin to that of THE IMAGINED VILLAGE, Yorkshire-born IAN KING researched his folk heritage to root out worthy ballads to update 21st-century-style with his home help of the On-U-Sound crew, namely Adrian Sherwood (production), Skip McDonald (guitar) and

Doug Wimbush. **PANIC GRASS AND FEVER FEW** (2010) {*7} gives the folk-dub treatment to 'Adieu To Old England', 'Four Loom Weaver', 'Black Eyed Susan' et al, and in some respects it works after a few listens. Of course there's no Paul Weller, Benjamin Zephaniah or CHRIS WOODS to lend star vocal assistance, but KING is effective in his transcendental-troubadour way. This just might be real folk-dance music – and nothing like the 'Morris On' of The ALBION BAND. *MCS*

Ian King - vocals, acoustic guitar / + [see above]

UK Fledg'ling — US not issued

Jan 10. (cd) *(FLED 3082)* **PANIC GRASS AND FEVER FEW** ☐ ⊟
- Adieu to old England / Death and the lady / Black eyed Susan / Evil eye / Four loom weaver / By George / Flash company / Ah robin, gentle robin / Take, o take those lips / How should I your true love know? / Isle of France / Old miner / Jovial broom man. *(lp-iss. Nov 10; FLED 3082LP)*

The KIPPER FAMILY

Formed 1978 in Trunch, Norfolk, the KIPPERs were a parody of the a cappella folk collective The COPPER FAMILY, an invention of creators Dick Nudds and Chris Sugden (yokel lads Henry Kipper and son Sid respectively). Complete with primitive-field-recording crackles, quavering harmonies and almost amateurish box-playing, the duo pay tribute to ye olde traditional dirges and ballads, albeit with their own musically corrupt aplomb. Other fictitious kinfolk, including jailbird cousin George Kipper, appeared on various occasions.

Moving from stage to studio, The KIPPER FAMILY finally unleashed their debut LP, **SINCE TIME IMMORAL** (1984) {*8}, featuring hilarious parodies such as 'A Lightweight Dirge' and 'The Unlaid Maid'. Album two, **THE EVER DECREASING CIRCLE** (1985) {*7} travelled the same path.

THE CRAB WARS (1986) {*6} takes PETER BELLAMY's ballad-opera 'The Transports' and pushes the bawdy boundaries to their limits. This double set featured Bellamy himself (as the town crier) alongside ASHLEY HUTCHINGS (the Prologue), JOHN KIRKPATRICK (the Narrator), Shep Woolley (Captain Upspoke), Cathy LeSurf (Belle Bow), MARTIN CARTHY (Admiral Ben Bow), Mick and Sarah Graves (Cromeo and Sheriet), TIM LAYCOCK (the Bosun), PHIL BEER (the Parson), and FAIRPORT CONVENTION, RICHARD DIGANCE, John Smith and Gary Carpenter. A must for anyone who has in fact heard folk's timelords, The COPPER FAMILY.

Sadly, Henry Kipper was retired in 1991, son Sid subsequently offering more pathos and wit on solo sets from **LIKE A RHINESTONE PLOUGHBOY** (1994) {*7} to 2011's as yet unheard **GUTLESS ...** {*?}. *MCS*

Henry Kipper (Dick Nudds) - vocals, tremelodeon / **Sid Kipper** (Chris Sugden) - vocals, accordion, blow-pipes / plus **Annie, Dot, George, Kevin + Len Kipper**

UK Dambuster — US not issued

Nov 84. (lp) *(DAM 005)* **SINCE TIME IMMORAL**: THE KIPPER FAMILY ALBUM ☐ ⊟
- Introduction by Henry and Sid Kipper / Not sixteen till Sunday / The male female highwayman / The unlaid maid / The cricket match / All on the shore (the body) / Hollow ground / Dido, Fido / The whistling monologue / The village P.I.M.P. / Poor old cow / To be a pharmacist / Adieu you pretty Nancy / A lightweight dirge. *(cd-iss. 2001; DAMCD 005)*

—— next set suffix credits The NEW TRUNCH CORONATION BAND

Dec 85. (lp) *(DAM 012)* **THE EVER DECREASING CIRCLE** ☐ ⊟
- Thirty days / Rusty cold farmer / The turning of the year / The Trunch wassail song / Valentine rhyme / The losing of the whale / Easter week / The Southrepps May song / Derby day / Creeping ivy / The wild mounting time / The glorious twelfth / Bald General Coote / Plough the fields and scatter / Harvest away / Summer is a going out / Joan sugarbeet / Remember, remember / Spencer the wild rover / No ale / The poacher's Christmas / Happy new year. *(cd-iss. 2005; DAMCD 012)*

Aug 86. (d-lp) *(DAM 017)* **THE CRAB WARS** ☐ ⊟
- Sid and Henry arrive / Come all you (overture) / The prologue / Come all you / Sid's round / Unspoke's dream / Henry and Sid get some out / I wish I was plural no more / Sid shuts up / Oh! It's hard / Oh! It's hard (reprise) / Jolly boasting weather / Henry finds talking thirsty work / Lost and foundered / Henry doesn't mind if he does / The parson knows / All washed up / Sid discusses / Brave old world // Here is the news / Henry's a bit short / Belle's on her toes / Sealed with a curse / Sid explains himself / Ninety-eight not out / Henry gets what he deserves / Here is the news (II) / The mason's a prune / The leaving of Sheringham / Here is the news (III) / Henry confuses the issue / In with the in-breed / In with the in-breed (reprise) / Sid loses count / Fall down / A narrator's life / Fall down (reprise) / Henry comes clean. *(cd-iss. Dec 97; DAMCD 017)*

Nov 88. (lp) *(DAM 020)* **FRESH YESTERDAY**: THE KIPPER FAMILY LIVE IN TRUNCH (live) ☐ ⊟
- Uncle Tom Cobbley can't come / Big Musgrave / The seven deadly sins / Bored of the dance / Yes sir, yes / The old Irishman / One drunken maiden / My grandfather's cock / The bloke who came home broke from Cromer bingo. *(cd-iss. Dec 97; DAMCD 020)*

—— next set is credited WITH THE REVEREND DEREK BREAM AND FRIENDS

Nov 89. (lp) *(DAM 022)* **ARREST THESE MERRY GENTLEMEN** ☐ ⊟
- Arrest these merry gentlemen / Thanks a lot, God / Northrepps twelfth night song / The awful story of Black Shag / Oh little town of Gimingham / The roots of the blues / Anna Ingram's sister / Ring out wild jingle bells / Awayday / I know what I believe / That was Christmas Eve / The disabled seaman / Underwood's milk / The ivy and the holly / The Trunch A to Z / Christmas collapso / We wish you a merry Xmas. *(cd-iss. Dec 97; DAMCD 022)*

1991. (lp) *(DAM 023)* **IN THE FAMILY WAY** ☐ ⊟
- Walsingham Matilda / Peculiar ale / (Do) The rock of ages / Probably not / We did it sideways / Fowl Jimmy / Jam tomorrow / Yarmouth races / Are you dry? / Cheap day return to Hemsby / The punnet of strawberries / The trousers in between / The bonny spotted cuckoo / We're Norfolk and good / Daisies up. *(cd-iss. Dec 97; DAMCD 023)*

SID KIPPER

now w/out Henry who retired

Leader — not issued

Mar 94. (cd) *(LERCD 2115)* **LIKE A RHINESTONE PLOUGHBOY** ☐ ⊟
- Sid / The old, waily, windy night / Sid / The innocent dodo / Sid / The bodyline collapso / Sid / The bloody wars / Sid / The twenty pound frog / Sid / The stack of domies / Sid / Gobblers in the garden / Sid / All things are quite equal / Sid / The stick of rhubarb / Folk roots '66 / Sid / Jack onion / Sid / The song of the EU / Sid.

Nov 97. (cd; by SID KIPPER with DAVE BURLAND) *(LERCD 2118)* **BOILED IN THE BAG** ☐ ⊟
- Allan Barber / Bobby Dazzler / Hay! do the Morris / The Roughton wriggle song / The Muntons of Moorgate / The bonny heavy plough horse / The shoals of whiting / A Jimmy Kipper muddley / We will rob you / Shepherd of the ups / Death or glory wassail / The Knapton white hare / The prince of whales / Murder at the red barndance / The mild rover / Breasting the waves / Combing the mane / The harvest moan / The wraggle taggle travellers-oh.

Nov 97. (c) *(LER 2119)* **SPINELESS** (live in the Old Goat Inn, St Just-near-Trunch) ⊟ mail-o ⊟
- The case of the cuckoo's nest / The headless horseman of Happisburgh / Crackers for Fanny / Sir Wayne, the green knight / Piering out to sea / The lesson of Len's lorry / The story of Saint Nick of Trunch / The digression of the three gruff billy goats / The Trunch flitch / The voyage of the Golden Behind / Phyllis Ferret's big day / The horrible history of the Harry Celeste / How the turkey got his gobble / The sirens of Scroby Sands / Cleverclogs and the three bears.

Apr 01. (cd) *(LERCD 2120)* **EAST SIDE STORY** ☐ ⊟
- East side story / The belles of St Just / Lord Hardwick / Hard as oak / Wighton walnut song / Times of the rigs / London spurning / Haul the deck / Queensbury rules, OK / A Runton rousaby / Talking postman blues / Knock down, knock down for Jesus / Narborough fair / Where have all the cauliflowers gone? / Polly on the floor / Pretty Penny-oh / The hard times of old Buckenham / The bold low way man / The wide Miss Audrey / The sailor in diss dress / Old King Cod / The old lamb sigh / Haddiscoe maypole song / Down, duvet down / The farmer's crumpet / Weeds of the wood / Way down in the Bayeux Tapestry / East side story.

Dec 02. (cd) *(LERCD 2121)* **COD PIECES** ☐ ⊟
- Big Dick of Whittington / Ship fashion and Bristol shaped / Sleeping Beauty and the beast / Bunfight at the OK chorale / Christmas with Carol / Mutiny on the Bouncy / Derek's third letter to the Truncheons / The romance of Rumpled Stiltskin O'Bugger / Flora and Fauna / Pathetic / The pied blowpiper of Kings Lynn / The ugly sisters / A partly political broadcast for bigots against tolerance / My bootiful mawther.

Jun 03. (cd) *(LERCD 2122)* **CHAINED MELODY**: SID KIPPER performs THE SONGS OF GEORGE KIPPER ☐ ⊟
- The Gimmingham idiot's song / The writes of man / Dirty old man / Grey is the colour / Shut up, little baby / Biker Bill / To be a milkman / Man of convictions / Searching for songs / The sisters of Percy / The sperm bank of life / The drag hunt / Winterton wassup song / The happy clappy chappy / There is no tavern in the town / Rolling drunk / I know a young lady / I love not where I live / The outrageous night / Hate story / Old rhyme / The dumpling song / The false bridegroom / The cruel she / For he's a jolly good felon / Open prison blues / Skipping rhyme / The illiterate's alphabet / Dashed company / This is my land / As with Gladys / Cool yule / Unpleasant and frightful / Deadly Dick's / The Gimmington idiot's song / The weeds of love.

2007. (cd) *(LEK 2125)* **IN SEASON** ☐ ⊟
- New year / Love divining / January / Willing to woo / February / By the cobblers / March / Moo cows poo / April / Bed and bawd / May / Rue-the-day / June / On Wedlock edge / July / The whaleman's complaint / August / The festive harvestall / September / Arrivederci Cromer / October / The three sisters / November / A larling lullaby / December / Turkey in the door / Old year's night / The Winterton wassup song / The spheres spin on / So tearfully round / The end.

May 11. (cd) *(LEK 2126)* **GUTLESS – THE REAL VILLAGE – FREE-RANGE KIPPER WITHOUT GIBLETS** ☐ ⊟
- [tracks in alphabetical order]:- All things dark and dangerous / A-rowing / The banker's daughter / Bats in the belfry / Bear down below / The bold folk singer /

Bushes and Brians / The complete swine / Constant lovers / The dead cert / The doggy few / The fheep fhearing fong / A for sale shanty / Gentleman's relish / The gift to be sinful / Helen Highwater / Like for like / London spurning / Lord Lambkin / The milkmaid's oath / New Roman times / The old Saint George / One the FA Cup / The second innings / Sing cuckoo doodle doo / The song called Mike Harding / Three points on my licence.

Benji KIRKPATRICK

Born in 1976 in Shropshire, Benji is the son of JOHN KIRKPATRICK – arguably the best anglo concertina and button accordionist in England – and hammered-dulcimer player Sue Harris. He affects a tongue-in-cheek dislike for banjos.

Since Benji's formative years as a Bright Young Folk thing, the multi-instrumentalist has taken on numerous side projects outwith his own solo career, from MAGPIE LANE (with Ian Giles) and DR FAUSTUS (alongside Paul Sartin of BELLOWHEAD and BELSHAZZAR'S FEAST, plus Saul Rose of WATERSON: CARTHY), to his own integral contributions to BELLOWHEAD and SETH LAKEMAN's band, not forgetting The Amber Quartet with Ian Giles. Over the past decade or so KIRKPATRICK has released three trad-meets-contemporary-folk albums for different imprints: **DANCE IN THE SHADOW** (1999) {*6}, **HALF A FRUIT PIE** (2004) {*6} – featuring his best tune by far, 'Unclothed Nocturnal Manuscript Crisis' – and **BOOMERANG** (2008) {*7}, which spotlights his interpretation of The BAND's 'The Moon Struck One'. *MCS*

Benji Kirkpatrick - vocals, bouzouki, guitar, mandolin, bodhran / with guests

UK Wild Goose — US not issued

Aug 99. (cd) *(WGS 291CD)* **DANCE IN THE SHADOW**
- Goatherder / Ridgewalkers / The star of Munster / Bubbles in the earth / Without words / Trooper and the maid / The round house jigs / Paddy Cronin's No.2 – Kitty in the lane / The Curragh of Kildare / Up in the air / Stay where you are – The foxhunter's jig – The merry blacksmith / The bold pedlar / The maid in the cherry tree – The new demesne.

Fellside — not issued

Apr 04. (cd) *(FECD 181)* **HALF A FRUIT PIE**
- A bed between friends – Urge to caper / The holland handkerchief / Half a fruit pie – Gusts of up to 60 mph / The gypsy laddie / Manic expression – Folkjive / Toxic haze / The bold princess royal / Return to olympic looney bin – Death of a jay / Green bushes / Unclothed nocturnal manuscript crisis / The ship carpenter / Such a getting upstairs I never did see – Three jolly sheepskins.

EDJ Prod ... — not issued

Oct 07. (cd-ep) *(014)* PEOPLE
- Wallbreaker / People / Drift / Boomerang / I can't make my mind up [live].

Navigator — not issued

Mar 08. (cd) *(NAVIGATOR 2)* **BOOMERANG**
- Wallbreaker / More life / Flyover / The moon struck one / Boomerang / Willow weeps / The river maid / Rocky Brown / People / Drift. *(d-lp-iss. May 08 +=; NAVIGATOR 5LP)* - DR FAUSTUS

(The) KITCHEN CYNICS

Formed 1988 in Aberdeen, Scotland as the brainchild of psychedelic-fixated Alan Davidson, this project was possibly the only Scottish act around at the time to produce totally independently-released limited-edition cassettes as their main format. The wryly named KITCHEN CYNICS (with part-time help from guitarist Jim Wilkie and friends) almost secretly delivered a prolific flow of little-known underground gems over the course of several years.

Clearly a driven man, psych-poet Davidson milked his wayward muse for all it was worth, his quaint psychedelia likely to appeal to fans of Syd Barrett's 'Madcap Laughs' era. By the time the mid-1990s arrived, more and more folk-rock music was creeping into Alan and the band's repertoire, mostly in the shape of several covers.

Without going into heavy psychedelic detail and keeping it strictly for the freak-folk sect, one album in particular that highlights his love of acid-folk was **COMPULSIVE SONGWRITING DISORDER** (2004) {*6}, a Belgian-only CD featuring covers of songs by BRIDGET ST JOHN, LAL WATERSON and the late, great Ivor Cutler. ST JOHN's 'Ask Me No Questions' would also surface on the 2005 release **MASTER OF THE FUZZY FADEOUT** {*6}, alongside a version of the FAIRPORTs' 'Crazy Man Michael'. 'Hoodie Craw' (2005) {*6} found inspiration in American freak-folk cousins TOM RAPP, ESPERS and co, while songs from the pens of Syd Barrett ('Vegetable Man'), STRAWBS and Kathryn Sawers littered the set.

It's hard to say where to start (possibly **PARALLEL DOG DAYS** (2002) {*7} reaches the greatest heights), but if you can fork out some cash and find his back catalogue, good luck. Meanwhile, Alan is inviting web fans to pay for future songs (c. 2007) as he produces a song a day, and a CD-r to boot. *MCS*

Alan Davidson - vocals, guitar / with at times **Jim Wilkie** - guitars

UK Bi-Joopiter — US not issued

1988. (ltd-c) *(none)* **A GIRL EATS THE MOON** — German

Les Enfants Du Paradiddle — not issued

1989. (ltd-c) *(enf 1)* **CEREBRAL SECURITY** — mail-o
- Renee's relationships / Baba in a pussy willow tree / Adam and naïve (what goes on goes on and on) / Down from the loft / Hidden shallows / Stars still shine / Crumbs of discomfort / Tonite let's make love in Gourdon (to Gordon) / She and her shadow / Cerebral security / Letters from Lucian Freud / Phosphorous tenement / The secret drawer Arthur Negus couldn't find.

1989. (ltd-c) *(enf 2)* **BUZZZZZZ** — mail-o
- The same mistake / She smiled / Persian carpet in reverse / Fab technician / In the dark / This winter since you've gone / Last summer / Rainy song / Fungus man – Fill the space / Underneat my duffel-coat.

1989. (ltd-c) *(enf 3)* **LITTLE DEATHS** — mail-o
- Face to face / You don't love me / Little deaths / Double rainbow days / We two boys clinging together / No broken promises / The first cuckold of spring / Lost empire of the senses / I know where Dan Treacy used to stay / My cloudy heart / The saddest man on the bus / She knows, you know.

1990. (ltd-c) *(enf 4)* **SCHMERZ BABIES** — mail-o
- Anyone can take your place / On our ship of fools / Ten months on a settee / Dream merchant / Dream merchant / Waves / Half-wit angel / Unhappily ever after / I don't want to stand up / Scenes from a museum / Shimmering on gold / I still remember your eyes / My planet new / Everything has surely ended / Schmerz baby.

1991. (ltd-c) *(enf 5)* **TRICK CYCLISTS** — mail-o
- Memories of you / Saint sinner / Vodka, sweat and aniseed / When Joe met Joe in heaven / Lips like battleships / Time of sands / Short sharp shock / When I was a tiny / Bittersweet / You don't exist / Black dog beach (the wind and the waves) / A sense of history / The freeze / I'm glad that tie's not mine / Can you hear the frog?

1991. (ltd-c) *(enf 6)* **GHOSTS OF WASPS** — mail-o
- Empty space / Dragonflys / Ghosts of wasps / Our love was built to last (like Simon Dee) / I've been down / Baby honey / Bad to good to worse / Days of drugs and drink and dances / Katy Murphy (she's my kind of girl) / Hornpipe / East of the sun / Lies upon lies / The wind blew through your hair / Iona / Soda equation for Alan Hake.

1992. (ltd-c) *(enf 7)* **SEAGULL GIRLS** — mail-o
- Kisses / Seagull girl / Even the most boring people / Jennifer is there anywhere? / Daddy, look that man is dancing / Just remember this / Blackwaterside / She's so out of touch / Forgive me / Heavenly bodies / She has everything I love / The end of the tunnel / Four little sex-gods / The land between the bedclothes and the bed. *(re-iss. 1994 on Acid Tapes (German); TAB 096)*

1992. (ltd-c) *(enf 8)* **THIS LITTLE HEADACHE** — mail-o
- On the bus / No but I can hear the dog / Significant date / Please don't ask me / Courting blues / You know nothing too / Morse cat / Burning witches / I don't want it / In my wardrobe / One of those things / Fallen hero / This little headache / Skin deep / Raga doll. *(re-iss. 1995 on Acid Tapes (German); TAB 110)*

Roman Cabbage — not issued

1992. (ltd-7"ep) *(GREY 7)* STICKLEBACKS — mail-o
- My cloudy heart / I still remember your eyes / Face to face / Anyone can take your place.

1992. (ltd-lp) *(GREY 11)* **CAN YOUR HEAR THE FROG?** — mail-o
- Soda equation for Alan Hake / Short sharp shock! / I don't want to stand up and be counted / She and her shadow / Kisses / Ten months on a settee / Dragonflys / This winter since you've gone / If this isn't heaven / Can't get through to you / When I paint your picture / Shimmering on gold / Can you hear the frog? / Double rainbow day. *(re-iss. 1995 on Get Happy!! (German); BIG 04)*

1992. (ltd-lp) *(GREY 12)* **TIME OF SANDS** — mail-o
- Even the most boring people / She's so out of touch / Time of sands / Days of drugs and drinks and dances / Memories of you / Iona / Everything has surely ended / Daddy, look that man is dancing / Vodka, sweat and aniseed / Half-wit angel / Black dog beach / I've been down / Katy Murphy (she's my kind of girl) / No broken promises. *(re-iss. 1994 on Get Happy!! (German); BIG 03)*

Hoppel di Hoy — not issued

1993. (7"ep) *(006)* SEAGULL GIRL EP — German
- Westminster chimes / Dance to the music of time / The land between the bedclothes and the bed / Come little memory / This bloody cold / Seagull girl.

Whitey W. Davis — not issued

1993. (ltd-lp) *(SATURN 93-II)* FADED AND TORN — German

1994. (ltd-one-sided-7") *(SATURN 94-III)* SHE WAS EVERYTHING — German

Farce — not issued

1994. (ltd-7") *(Sentinel 019)* SHE AND HER SHADOW. / Fair Tea Maker — German

Magical Jack — not issued

1994. (ltd-7" ep) *(Jack 003)* MIMOSA — German
- Mimosa / Russell Square Gardens and you / What we did on our holidays / Lady under-eaves.

Les Enfants Du Paradiddle — not issued

1994. (ltd-cd-r) *(enf 09)* **COME LITTLE MEMORY** — mail-o
- The quiet ones / Stone circle me / Anyone can take your place / No broken promises / When we laughed / Relax now / Time of sands / Memories of you / Now's the time / Vodka, sweat and aniseed / A pretty tune / This wind must change / You revisionist, you! / Kisses / Fair tea maker / A cold embrace / She's growing old disgracefully / Come little memory / Polly's on the platform / Black dog beach / Days of drugs and drink and dances / Hush little cynics / For Engelen Alfons / Little song by Matthew.

1994. (ltd-c) *(enf 10)* **SECRET ROOMS** — mail-o
- No weather can! / Lopsided abacus / Magnificent dreams / Such a sad thing / All's fair / Instance / Secret rooms / I'm waiting / Possibly / November day / You and your sister / I'm so unaware / Autopsy / Rik's perplexing letter / Here right now / It's your own fault / Expecting letters.

1994. (ltd-c) *(enf 11)* **KISS ME QUICK** — mail-o
- Fair tea maker / She's growing old disgracefully / All winter long / He never really meant it / Heather hillside / Lady under-eaves / Be with me / Come let me dry your eyes / Kerry's got a new tattoo / Prince of hail / Here we are / Painter man / Your geography is bad / Kevin says / Loss of innocence / Farewell, farewell.

1995. (ltd-c) *(enf 12)* **VICE VERSES** — mail-o
- Prisoner twice over / Don't ever go / Mimosa / Russell Square Gardens and you / Westminster chimes / Gallery of despair / Just like you / What we did on our holidays / Beatle on your back / In the garden / Ask me no questions / Come little memory / Polly's on the platform / This bloody cold / The lies she told / Oh Bennachie / Colour wheel / What's good for me / Dance to the music of time.

1996. (ltd-c) *(enf 13)* **MY APOLOGY** — mail-o
- The quiet ones / Happy days in Holburn Rd / When he laughed / It froze me / Burning toast / A sorry state / Bright young song (by a dull old man) / For Engelen Alfons / Give me bliss / She and her shadow '97 / Life by numbers / Special child / Now's the time / Relax, now / My apology / Shadow cat / Whose fool are you? / Don't let me down, now!

1996. (ltd-7") *(enf 14)* PATRON SAINTS. / My Gothic Novel — mail-o

1996. (ltd-cd-r) *(enf 15)* KRISTMAS AT KILAU [festive] — mail-o
- The holly and the ivy / The King Street bomb / Spencer the rover / Songs of spring [live] / Advice from an old cynic [live] / The Torry ferry [live] / Kristmas time at Kilau.

Bliss — not issued

1997. (ltd-c) *(BLISS 045)* **THE QUIET ONES**
- Oh Bennachie / Now's the time / The quiet ones / Happy days in Holburn Rd / When he laughed / Bright young song (by a dull old man) / For Engelen Alfons / Jennifer is there anywhere? / Life by numbers / Burning toast / Special child / She and her shadow '97 / Rocket song / Crinoline people / Relax, now / My apology / Shadow cat.

Best Kept Secret — not issued

2000. (ltd-c) *(LIE 022)* **SWEARING IN SEMAPHORE**
- The place you hid / Aye aye, well well / North of Balmedie, west of the waves / Best kept secret / Grown up in monochrome / Theme for Gwen / A midsummer night? / Mistress Forsyth's jump / At Villa E.107 / Don't split on me / Great discovery / The day that love turned green / Hard to be happy / The rituals / On that hill again / Tracy E's love song.

Les Enfants Du Paradiddle — Secret Eye

2002. (cd-r) *(enf 16)* *<AB-OC-04>* **PARALLEL DOG DAYS** — Jan 03
- The turnside / The place you hid / Iridium / Another little death / Chinese whispers / The king and queen of Belmont Street / At Villa E.1027 (Eileen Gray reflects) / North of Balmedie, west of the waves / Last night's news / Her ceramic inkwell / All grown up in monochrome / Burnt lasagne and a cold, cold heart / If tomorrow comes a-calling / Fossil song / Time to take your time / Carol by candlelight / Life is getting sweeter / Tune for Tom Rapp / Mr. Hofner, Mrs. Conrad and Mr. Vox / Three cheers.

2003. (cd-r) *(enf 17)* **SEASONING** — mail-o
- Miriam's toes No.2 / Permafrost / Iridium [acoustic version] / Keep true / Bag of brains and bones / The thief of Netherley / Revelations / Seasoning / Now Westlin' winds / Hello haggis! / Room-poom pa ra-ra / Miriam's toes No.1 / What's the new Mary Jane / You fascinate me / The day that love turned green / Mistress Forsyth's jump / Who will love you the worst / A midsummer night's...? / Theme for Gwen.

2004. (ltd-cd-r) *(BOT 015)* **COMPULSIVE SONGWRITING DISORDER** — Belg
- The tartan shawl / Great-Uncle Jack's deathbed dance / Ask me no questions / Murph's song / Waiting for your mail / I want you on a mountain top / Pussy on the mat / Snowflakes, oatcakes and earthquakes / The holy creel / Lethargic lover / Stumbling on / Dialogue / In Dunnotar Woods / Unwoozling invalid woman.

(above issued on Audiobot)

Feb 05. (cd-r) *(enf 18)* **MASTER OF THE FUZZY FADEOUT** — mail-o
- Rue Bonaparte / Now's the time (for Nicholas) / Once and future love / Chemist shop girl / Musing / Crazy man Michael / Songs of spring / Matunga hill / Watersprite / Don't ever go / Song about the dances of the bees / Boulevard tourist / The weaver lass / Games for a winter's evening / Ask me no questions [new version] / Weasel bride / Advice from an old cynic (for Philip) / Now's the time [live at Dr Drake's].

2005. (ltd-cd-r) *(none)* FOR WILL EP
- Sparrow scratch board / Where is my wife? / The big parade / Me and St. George / Dinner for three (including the dog).

(above issued on William Schaff label)

2008. (cd-r) *(enf 55)* **A' THE BONNY BUMPS AND BRUISES**
- Maggie Black the cat / Fits and starts / Boyndlie's braes / Scapegoat / Leesome lane / Here comes the bump [Fri 25th Jan version] / Sally in the shadows / Lionel Jeffries, Sunday morning / Bella Donald / The nightingale's emerald / Our trip to blunderland / Jack Longshanks / Silver city (bloody fool) / Clear rinnin' Burnie / 17452 / Petals (for Susan) / Ups and downs / A' the bonny bumps and bruises / Hot crepe plates and lack of attention / Lemon tree – Wounded Knee / Here comes the bump [Thurs 24th Jan version] / Cell farming.

- (5-7*) compilations, others, etc.-

1995. (c) *Bacchanalian Revel; (BR 06)* **EPHEMERA** — German
- She and her shadow / Beetle on your back / Heather hillside / Expecting letters / Jennifer (is there anywhere) / Katie Murphy / Black dog beach / No broken promises / All's fair / Here right now / Diamond man / Underneath my duffel-coat / Kisses / Fair tea maker / Autopsy / Come little memory / She's growing old disgracefully.

KITSYKE WILL

Named after a miner who worked in the lead mines at Greenhow Hill, Pateley Bridge in North Yorkshire (the place of the group's origins in early 1975), KITSYKE WILL comprised Dublin-born multi-instrumentalist Peadar Long, Scotsman Bob Thomas, Tony 'Bunker' Bayliss and Chas Marshall.

Fusing folk with light jazz, Peadar and his colleagues – now composed of Patrick Gundry-White and John Burge – delivered what was to be their only bona-fide LP, **DEVIL'S RIDE**, in 1982 {*6}. Featuring the leader's own compositions and several sourced Celtic-style folk tunes, the set is best remembered for the bawdy 'Gaberdine Angus' and 'The Old Torn Petticoat'. Peadar would resume his career with The NEW VICTORY BAND after KITSYKE WILL split up. *MCS*

Peadar Long (b. Dublin, Ireland) - clarinet, flute, saxophones, whistles, vocals / **Patrick Gundry-White** - French horn, harmonium, vocals; repl. Bob Thomas (b. Peebles, Scotland) / **John Burge** - guitar, bouzouki, banjo, fiddle; repl. Tony 'Bunker' Bayliss (b. Cleveland, North Yorkshire) - guitar, cittern (without Bob + Tony, Chas Marshall also left before any recordings)

UK Highway — US not issued

1982. (lp) *(SHY 7020)* **DEVIL'S RIDE**
- Gaberdine Angus / Marshall's law / Devil's ride / Crown spindle mill / Rhode Island Fred / Coming of the Celts / The northern lass / The gift of God / The old torn petticoat / Onwards and upwards.

—— after their split, Peadar performed with numerous jazz/classical acts (plus The NEW VICTORY BAND) and Bob joined R&B outfit The Solicitors; Bayliss joined Jiggerpipery.

Lisa KNAPP

Born in 1974 and raised by her single mother in Balham, south London, Lisa – who admits to being a distant relative of horror actor Boris Karloff – discovered folk music by way of raiding a friend's parents' record collection. Inspired by SHIRLEY COLLINS, MADDY PRIOR and SANDY DENNY, and wanting to create her own interpretations, she rediscovered her earlier love of the fiddle and employed London-Irish tutor Peter Cooper to teach her advanced techniques.

After singing at a host of festivals and folk clubs in the early 2000s, she was just about to go professional when she was diagnosed with a pituitary adenoma. Recovering, she got married in 2003 to former SIN E musician Gerry Diver, who had invited her to guest on his 'Diversions' album in 2002; they have had a daughter.

Back on track, KNAPP worked with Youth and CHRIS WOOD, while her husband took the controls for her debut set, **WILD AND UNDAUNTED** (2007) {*8}. With a voice so crystal-clear and reminiscent of folk forebears ANNE BRIGGS and JEANNIE ROBERTSON, her subtle, back-to-basics formula worked on a treat on such passionate pictorials as 'Beggar, Beggar', 'Dew Is On The Grass', 'Little Bird' and the title track. What she's been up to since her joint tour in 2009 with fellow folkies JAMES YORKSTON And The Athletes is not clear. *MCS*

Lisa Knapp - vocals, fiddle, hammered dulcimer, banjo (w/ guests)

UK Ear To The Ground — US not issued

Mar 07. (cd) *(001)* **WILD AND UNDAUNTED**
- Blacksmith / There U R / Beggar, beggar / Wild and undaunted / Little bird / Lavender / Bitter withy / Ride along / Dew is on the grass / Six dukes / Salisbury Plain.

Steve KNIGHTLEY (⟹ SHOW OF HANDS)

KORMORAN (⟹ Celtic & World Music Discography)

Sonja KRISTINA

Born April 14, 1949, in Brentwood, Essex, Sonja was better known as the sultry former singer of 1970s classical-prog-rock outfit Curved Air, for which her acting career (she was in the cast of the London production of the musical 'Hair' in 1970) had been put on hold. During a barren spell studio-wise, she took the lead role in the 1978 TV movie 'Curriculee Curricula', a musical of sorts co-written by keyboard wizard Dave Greenslade and also starring singer Chris Farlowe and Scottish comedian Chic Murray. Still married (with two young children) to Police and ex-Curved Air drummer Stewart Copeland, that relationship led her to Police producer Nigel Gray, who worked on her next project.

When the 1980s kicked off, KRISTINA and her band Escape toured the UK. Clinging to the coat-tails of the New Wave scene, she was groomed to be the next Toyah or Hazel O'Connor; Her haircut and sexy gear on the sleeve of her debut solo LP, **SONJA KRISTINA** (1980) {*6}, certainly suggested she'd moved away from the flagging prog scene, although the band featured Curved Air violin virtuoso Darryl Way. Although the album flopped (as did the accompanying 45, 'St Tropez'), it showed signs that KRISTINA was not ready for retirement – check out 'Man He Colour' and the exciting cover of Spirit's 'Mr Skin'. But it would be over a decade before she returned to the studio.

Influenced by the psychedelic folk movement of the late 1960s/early 1970s, SONJA KRISTINA – complete with acoustic guitar and accordion – once again broke free from the shackles of family life and recorded the self-descriptive set **SONGS FROM THE ACID FOLK** (1991) {*7}.

Augmented by her backing band Ty-Lor and Friends (ex-Deaf School, ex-Pink Military guitarist Tim Whittaker, his drumming brother Simon Whittaker, violinist Paul Silas and female cellist Ali McKenzie), the album surprised many critics, especially the people down at fRoots. Naturally there was the odd revamp of Curved Air nuggets such as 'Melinda More Or Less' and 'Back Street Luv' (the latter an out-take on the re-issue only), while a handful of songs were revived from her 1980 debut, but with a folk re-styling – 'Man He Colour', 'Rollercoaster' and the Norma Tager & Paul Travers cut 'Colder Than A Rose'. Of the rest, the best are opener 'Anna', 'Devil May Care' (Pil meets Curved Air), 'Who Was Hunter' and 'Citadel'.

Continuing on the acid-folk theme, **HARMONICS OF LOVE** (1995) {*6} also echoed her time with Curved Air in songs like 'Sounds Of Sea – Heart Of Glass – Marimbas'. Also notable were the Kate Bush-like 'Woman's Heart' (written by Eleanor McEvoy) and 'Dreamers'.

Dismissing her jazz diversion in 2003 ('Cri De Coeur'), she's now part of trance-meets-classical outfit Mask – a handful of new recordings appear on the Market Square re-issue of HARMONICS OF LOVE, alongside an acoustic cover of Motorhead's 'Don't Believe A Word'. *MCS*

Sonja Kristina - vocals, acoustic guitar, accordion / with Escape and feat. Darryl Way (ex-Curved Air)

UK Chopper — US not issued

Apr 80. (7") *(CHOP 101)* ST TROPEZ. / Mr Skin ☐ ⊟

Aug 80. (lp) *(CHOPE 5)* **SONJA KRISTINA** ☐ ⊟
- Street run / Man he colour / Colder than a rose in snow / Breaking out in smiles / Mr Skin / Roller-coaster / Full time woman / The comforter / St Tropez / Fade-away. *(<cd-iss. Jan 07 on Market Square+=; MSMCD 140>)* - Renegade / We're only human / Walk on by.

— next with TY-LOR & FRIENDS

Fruithouse — not issued

May 91. (cd/c/lp) *(FH CD/MC/LP 1)* **SONGS FROM THE ACID FOLK** ☐ ⊟
- Anna / Devil may care / Melinda more or less / Man he colour / This is not a sanctuary / Colder than a rose / If this was love / One to one / Rollercoaster / Buccaneer / Who was hunter / Citadel. *(<cd re-iss. Feb 02 on Market Square+=; MSMCD 109>)* - Free to be me / Back street luv / Penumbra.

HTD — not issued

Apr 95. (cd) *(HTDCD 34)* **HARMONICS OF LOVE** ☐ ⊟
- Tropical birth / Angel / Sounds of sea - Heart of glass – Marimbas / Lullaby - Baby song / Woman's heart / Divine cloud space - Birdsong - Elfin boy / Glastonbury dawn / Blindman / Dreamers / Chant - Voices - Remember yourself. *(<re-iss. Jan 10 on Market Square+=; MSMCD 150>)* - Melinda more or less / Don't believe a word / Threnody / Beloved / Nightfall / Healing senses.

— In 2003, KRISTINA released a jazz set, 'Cri De Coeur', and with Mask (Marvin Ayres) she issued the collaborative trance-meets-classical CD 'Heavy Petal'.

LADY OF THE SUNSHINE (⟹ STONE, Angus & Julia)

Seth LAKEMAN

Born March 26, 1977, at Yelverton in Devon, SETH LAKEMAN's first ventures into music were family affairs, with his siblings Sam and Sean, as part of The LAKEMAN BROTHERS, Seth's specialities being the violin and the tenor guitar. The trio knocked out a debut, 'Three Piece Suite', in 1994. They toured as an expanded quintet which evolved into a full-time concern, EQUATION – the bratpack of Brit-folk – with the brothers, KATHYRN ROBERTS and Sam's soon-to-be-wife CARA DILLON, another English folk star on the rise. With the odd personnel change, EQUATION ran for three celebrated albums during the 1990s, fizzling out in 2001 and going on permanent hiatus.

Seth struck out on his own at this point with his solo debut **THE PUNCH BOWL** (2002) {*6}, a confident collection which showed LAKEMAN's skills outside the family unit, although his brothers continued to appear in his live band and on studio recordings, and Sean was his producer. The album credibly set out his stall as a solo concern, although he did collaborate with STEVE KNIGHTLEY (of SHOW OF HANDS) on his 'Western Approaches' set.

KITTY JAY {*8} (2004), however, was the game-changer, taking him into mainstream territory as never before. A Mercury Music Prize nomination beckoned, as did tours with the likes of Jools Holland, BILLY BRAGG and old friends the LEVELLERS.

Follow-up **FREEDOM FIELDS** (2006) {*7} was no less compelling, and won Album of the Year at the Radio 2 Folk Awards, LAKEMAN's fiddle finding a home among the strident rhythms. Seth's crossover appeal was never in doubt, but he seemed to be picking tips up from the LEVELLERS on **POOR MAN'S HEAVEN** (2008) {*7}, an altogether rockier proposition with a sound that in all fairness worked well, as it hit the Top 10.

He followed that with **HEARTS AND MINDS** (2010) {*6}, which tried to consolidate the folk and rock sides of LAKEMAN's personality, with limited success but winning a brief Top 20 admission. *MR*

Seth Lakeman - vocals, tenor guitar, violin, viola / with **Sean Lakeman** - guitars / **Sam Lakeman** - piano / **Cara Dillon** - vocals, whistle / **Kathryn Roberts** - vocals / **Iain Goodall** - drums, percussion / **Geoff Lakeman** - concertina / **Ben Nicholls** - upright bass

UK: i Scream — US: not issued

2002. (cd) *(ISCD 004)* **THE PUNCH BOWL** [ ] [–]
- Garden of grace / Image of love / April eyes / It's all your world / Send yourself away / Look outside your window / How much / The punch bowl / Scrumpy's set / Ye mariners all. *(re-iss. Jun 06 on Relentless; CDREL 11)*

—— **Benji Kirkpatrick** - bouzouki, vocals (of BELLOWHEAD) repl. CARA DILLON + Geoff

—— **Audrey Mills** - church organ; repl. Sam

May 04. (cd) *(ISCD 006)* **KITTY JAY** [100] [–]
- John Lomas / The bold knight / Fight for favour / Kitty Jay / Farewell my love / Blood upon copper / Henry Clark / The storm / Cape Clear / The ballad of Josie / The streamers. *(re-iss. Oct 06 on Relentless; CDREL 12)*

—— In Sep 04, Seth (and Jenna) collaborated with Steve Knightley (of SHOW OF HANDS) on the album 'Western Approaches'.

—— **Cormac Byrne** - bodhran, percussion, drums; repl. Goodall

—— guest vocalists:- Kathryn, Cara, Steve + John Jones

Mar 06. (cd) *(ISCD 007)* **FREEDOM FIELDS** [ ] [–]
- The charmer / Lady of the sea / Childe the hunter / The white hare / The colliers / King and country / The setting of the sun / Take no rogues / 1643 / The riflemen of war / The band of gold / The final lot. *(w/ ltd. bonus cd+=)* - Lady of the sea (live) / Ye mariners all (live) / Kitty Jay (video) / The white hare (video) / The white hare (animation) / 2004 live tour video.

Relentless — not issued

Jul 06. (cd-s) *(CDREL 28)* LADY OF THE SEA (HEAR HER CALLING) / Captains' Court [52] [–]

Aug 06. (cd) *(CDREL 10)* **FREEDOM FIELDS** [re-promoted] [32] [–]
- Lady of the sea (hear her calling) / Setting of the sun / The white hare / The colliers / King and country / Childe the hunter / Take no rogues / 1643 / The riflemen of war / The charmer / The final lot / The band of gold / Send yourself away.

Oct 06. (7") *(REL 29)* THE WHITE HARE. / Kitty Jay (live at Beautiful Days 2006) [47] [–]
(live cd-ep) *(CDREL 29)* - ('A') / Take no rogues / Send yourself away / Send yourself away (video).

Feb 07. (7") *(CDREL 32)* KING AND COUNTRY. / The Bold Knight [ ] [–]

Oct 07. (cd-ep) *(REL 44)* POOR MAN'S HEAVEN EP [ ] [–]
- Poor man's heaven / Race to be king / How much / Lillywhite girl.

Jun 08. (7") *(REL 53)* THE HURLERS. / Sound Of A Drum [ ] [–]

Jun 08. (cd) *(CDREL 18)* **POOR MAN'S HEAVEN** [8] [–]
- The hurlers / Feather in the storm / Crimson dawn / Blood sky red / Solomon Browne / Cherry red girl / I'll haunt you / Race to be king / Poor man's heaven / Greed and gold / Sound of a drum.

Jul 08. (dl-s) *(-)* CRIMSON DAWN [ ] [–]

Jul 10. (cd) *(CDREL 21)* **HEARTS AND MINDS** [17] [–]
- Hearts and minds / The watchman / Tiny world / Spinning days / See them dance / Stepping over you / Changes / Tender traveller / Hard working man / Preacher's ghost / The circle grows. *(cd+dvd+=; CDRELX 21)* - Ghost of you / High St rose // [DVD tracks].

The LAKEMAN BROTHERS (⟹ EQUATION)

LAU (⟹ Great Celtic-Folk Discography)

Tim LAYCOCK

Born February 20, 1952, at Malmesbury, Wiltshire (later moving with his family to Fontwell Magna in Dorset), LAYCOCK first got into folk music during his time in the early 1970s at the University of East Anglia in Norwich; the Crows were one of the bands he formed with Terry Fisher and others. Like BILL CADDICK, Tim performed with London-centric theatrical act the Magic Lantern, sticking around at least for a Christmas-period series of shows in 1976. The following year, (alongside Charlie Andrews, Ethel Gumbleton, Frank Hilliar, Margaret Knott, David Strawbridge and The New Scorpion Band), he/they released the poetry LP 'Lydlinch Bells', a selection from the dialect poetry of William Barnes.

Working with PETER BOND and BILL CADDICK, two sets were issued in a relatively short space of time, the collaborative 'A Duck On His Head' (in 1980) and the solo **CAPERS AND RHYMES** (1981) {*5}, the latter featuring BOND and CADDICK plus Bill Horne on tenor banjo. **GIANT AT CERNE** (1984) {*5} saw his band line-up change with the enlistment of Rory Allam, Robin Jeffrey, Roddy Skreaping and Will Ward, while the track 'Voices' was adapted from a poem by Thomas Hardy.

Subsequent LAYCOCK projects have included spells with The ALBION BAND, The Melstock Band and Sneak's Noyse, whose Christmas LP, **CHRISTMAS IS NOW DRAWING NEAR** (1986) {*4}, bore all the hallmarks of previous efforts by other folkies from all over the world – nice! Although there has the odd subsequent solo release by LAYCOCK (**FINE COLOURS** (1999) {*5} was his most recent), The NEW SCORPION BAND was his prime project from the late 1990s onwards (Brian Gulland of GRYPHON and MALICORNE was a member). *MCS*

Tim Laycock - vocals, duet concertinas, melodeon, harmonica, percussion

UK: Greenwich Village — US: not issued

Apr 81. (lp) *(GVR 216)* **CAPERS AND RHYMES** [ ] [–]
- The New Year song / La guignolee / The man who broke the bank at Monte Carlo / A trampwoman's tragedy / The light of the moon / Gavioli capers / The outlandish

knight / How Zamal got upsides wi' camel clock / Six dukes went a-hunting / Munster cloak / Morrissey and the Russian sailor / Row on.

Dingles — not issued

Mar 84. (lp) *(DIN 320)* **GIANT AT CERNE**
- Bold Lovell / Valentine's chant / Ten thousand miles away / Nine burning barrels / Leo / Sizewell ABC / Giant at Cerne / Devil among the tailors / Men of Tolpuddle / I love not where I live / Singing the travels / Voices / Dorset militia song / Organist's polka.

Forest Tracks — not issued

1985. (lp) *(???)* **BLACKMORE BY THE STOUR**

—— next with RAY ATTFIELD, JEREMY BARLOW, MICHAEL BRAIN, ROBIN JEFFREY, LUCIE SKEAPING and RODERICK SKEAPING

Saydisc — not issued

Oct 86. (lp; by/as SNEAK'S NOYSE) *(SDL 371)* **CHRISTMAS IS NOW DRAWING NEAR**
- Christmas is now drawing near at hand / We've been awhile a-wandering / The waits / Lully, lulla, thow little Tyne child (Coventry carol) / Good people all, this Christmastime / Sweet was the ... *(cd-iss. Nov 01; CDSDL 371)*

Laycock — not issued

1989. (lp) *(none)* **SHILLINGSTONE MOSS**

Wild Goose — not issued

Nov 99. (cd) *(WGS 296CD)* **FINE COLOURS**
- The horseman / Jack Robinson / The cuckoo / Shrewsbury lasses - Over the hills to glory / Wounded soldier - Sing me to sleep / The peace tree / Florence Wyndham / Billy Johnson's ball - Cadham Wood / Hanley church bells / Robin Hood and the bishop of Hereford / The village club waltz / Stormalong / Comfrey.

Sep 10. (cd) *(WGS 376CD)* **SEA STRANDS**: Folk Songs and Tunes from Dorset
- Bord granadee – Jack's alive / The night of Trafalgar [Boatman's song] / Ricketty Robin – Tipsy Bob / Husbandman and servantman / The turtle dove / Write me down / A glimpse of a green land / The old smith / John Barleycorn / Cider and brandy – A trip to Bagshot / The boat / Death in the nut / The Broadoak wassail / Blackbeard's diamond / Farewell she.

NEW SCORPION BAND

Tim Laycock with **Brian Gulland** - vocals, harmonium, bassoon, whistles, flute, oboe, cor anglais, tuba, percussion (ex-MALICORNE) / **Robin Jeffrey** - vocals, banjo, guitars, percussion, laouto, mandolin, lute / **Sharon Lindo** - vocals, violin, viola, guitar, rebec, trombone, whistle, curtal / **Robert White** - vocals, bagpipes, whistles and flutes, brass, percussion

New Scorpion Band — not issued

1998. (cd) *(NSB 01CD)* **FOLK SONGS AND TUNES FROM THE BRITISH ISLES** — mail-o
- Dogger Bank / Heaven's a bar / May song / New rigged ship - Off she goes / Row on / Hopping down in Kent / Scots set / John Barleycorn / Blow the candles out / Sca Tester's polkas / Wheat / The fox - The fox chase.

2000. (cd) *(GHP 4CD)* **THE PLAINS OF WATERLOO**: SONGS AND MUSIC OF THE NAPOLEON WARS — mail-o
- The route has just come for the blues / The grenadier's march 1776 - The rogue's march / Drink old England dry / Boney crossing the Rhine - Madame Bonaparte / The plains of Waterloo - The blackbird / Jolly Jack Tar - Lord Nelson's hornpipes / Lady Nelson's - Lord Nelson's waltzes / Bold Nelson's praise / The girl I left behind me - The British grenadiers / Waterloo dance / Little Boney / St Helena march / Boney on St Helena.

2002. (cd) *(NSB 02CD)* **THE CARNAL AND THE CRANE** (festive) — mail-o
- All hail to the dayes / The Sussex carol / The truth sent from above / The salutation carol / There was a pig - In dulce jubilo / The Wexford carol / The sans day carol / Gloomy winter - Christmas day in da morning - I saw three ships / The carnal and the crane / Gillan's apples - Christmas eve air and reel / The Christmas goose / The winter's night Schottishe / Shepherds, arise / The Somerset wassail.

2004. (cd) *(002)* **THE DOWNFALL OF PEARS** — mail-o
- Bold Lovell / The hard times of old England / Derwentwater's farewell - Sir John Fenwick's flower amang them all / A smuggler's song / The friar in the well / The downfall of pears / The sad sea waves / Four Scottish tunes: I wish I were where Helen lies - Banks of the Spey ... / I live not where I love / Lord Bateman.

2004. (cd) *(003)* **OUT ON THE OCEAN** — mail-o
- The collier brig - Percy Brown's - Old Joe / High Barbaree - Major Malley's reel / Rollicking Randy dandy o / The Capstan bar / Nelson's victory - The stormy voyage - The three captains / Sally Brown / The race of long ago / Tom Bowling / The wild goose shanty / Ships are sailing - The black-eyed sailor / Blow, boys, blow / All things are quite silent / On board a 98 / Nelson's death / Rodney's glory - Out on the ocean - The sailor's return / The hogseye man / South Australia / The leaving of Liverpool.

—— also released were: 'The Sun From The East' (by Nick Crump) which featured two Hambledon Hopstep Band tracks; the latter outfit also released a LAYCOCK sampler set, 'Harvest Home'. In 2005, LAYCOCK was also part of the Broadside Band (conducted by Jeremy Barlow), who released the children's CD 'Old English Nursery Rhymes'.

2009. (cd) *(none)* **MASTER MARENGH'S MUSIC MACHINE** — mail-o
- Girl with the blue dress - The Jenny Lind polka / The painful plough / Bridgwater fair / When the cock crows it is day - The gander in the pratie hole / Over the hills and far away / It's a rosebud in June / Donkey riding / Shrewsbury lasses - The 4th Dragoons regimental march - St Vincent's hornpipe / The Derby ram / The gentle maiden - The herd on the hill / A wooing song of the yeoman of Kent's sonne / Hey! John Barleycorn / Welsh droving song - The old drove road / Ye tyrants of England / Spanish ladies.

Cate LE BON

One of the growing number of kooky nu-folk artists in today's market, LE BON is rather different in that she's not American, but Welsh (Penboyr-born, Cardiff-based). The fact that she sings in her own language some of the time, and has supported fellow countryman Gruff Rhys (of Super Furry Animals) on his 2008 Mercury-nominated indie-pop project Neon Neon, shows that she has clout and ambition. Rhys once described her double-A-side download single 'No One Can Drag Me Down' and 'Disappear' as "Bobbie Gentry and Nico fighting over a Casio keyboard".

Translated as "to look a gift horse in the mouth", LE BON's next release was the 'Edrych Yn Llygaid Ceffyl Benthyg' 10" EP, recalling the days when the likes of MEIC STEVENS, GORKY'S and Gruff's act flew the flag for Welsh-language indie folks. Dark and haunting without being too morbid in sound, the new set (working title 'Pet Deaths') was almost immediately turned into her debut release proper, **ME OH MY** (2009) {*7}. A promising start, it featured ten tracks over 35 minutes, highlights being 'Shoeing The Bones', 'Eyes So Bright' and 'Digging Song'. *MCS*

Cate Le Bon - vocals, guitar / with Gruff Rhys (of Super Furry Animals)

UK own label — US not issued

2007. (dl-s) *(none)* NO ONE CAN DRAG ME DOWN / DISAPPEAR

Peski — not issued

Jun 08. (10" ep) *(PESKICD 009)* EDRYCH YN LLYGAID CEFFYL BENTHYG
- Hwylio mewn cyfog / Mas mas / Baw waw / Byw heb farw / O bont i bont.

Irony Bored — not issued

Oct 09. (cd/c) *(BORED CD/TP 001)* **ME OH MY** [also known as 'Pet Deaths']
- Me oh my / Sad sad feet / Shoeing the bones / Hollow trees house hounds / It's not the end / Terror of the man / Eyes so bright / Digging song / Born until the end / Out to sea.

LEATHERAT

Formed in Banbury in Oxfordshire by frontman and mandolinist Pete Bailey in 2004, on a mission to bring back the halcyon days of heavy folk (HORSLIPS, JETHRO TULL, etc) and punk-folk or 'polk!' (LEVELLERS, The POGUES, etc), the high-octane LEATHERAT captured a live audience when they gatecrashed the dormant hardcore-folk scene. Also featuring violinist Jono Watts, guitarist Jim Bennion, bassist Jeremy Paul Carroll and drummer Hugh Edwards, in 2006 the power-ridden LEATHERAT unleashed their debut set **TEMPORARY IMMORTALITY** {*6}, a record that also boasted an array of guests including Ric Sanders (of FAIRPORT CONVENTION), Gareth Turner (LITTLE JOHNNY ENGLAND), P J Wright (The Dylan Project) and Dan Plews (of Dansall).

The Ats (as they were affectionately known in the trade) recorded some pulsating original songs on later sets **GARDEN OF EDEN** (2007) {*6} and **SHORT TIME ON EARTH** (2008) {*6}, but the novice would be advised to start with their live DVD 'Reserved For Freaks And Weirdos' (2008) – parental guidance required! *MCS*

Pete Bailey - vocals, mandolin, guitar / **Jono Watts** - violin / **Jim Bennion** - guitar / **Jeremy Paul Carroll** - bass / **Hugh Edwards** - drums

UK High-Score — US not issued

Feb 06. (cd) *(HSPLTD 0001)* **TEMPORARY IMMORTALITY**
- Folk tonight / Stop / Dream garden / The ring / Doing wrong / Couldn't find the craic / Yesterday / Lost / Five tons (to shift before home) / Large one / People's song.

May 07. (cd) *(HSPLTD 0002)* **GARDEN OF EDEN**
- Garden of Eden / Altruistic hedonist / Boyfriend in a coma / I like a smoke / Yours / Lucky escape / Angel of the north / Rocky road to Dublin / Before / Fiddle player.

Nov 08. (cd) *(HSPLTD 0004)* **SHORT TIME ON EARTH**
- Short time on earth / Celebrity / Blood on the fretboard / Walk away / Folkaine / Party time (in Chavbury) / Moments like these / Innocence / Ugly / Heresy / Fight club / Can't stop.

Nov 10. (cd) *(HSPLTD 0006)* **CHOICE BLEND** [a collection of new, live and studio]
- A song about love / The landlord's lament / I like a smoke [live at Mantlefest] / Altruistic hedonist / The rocky road to Dublin / Boyfriend in a coma [live at Cropredy 2010] / Party time (in Chavbury) [live at Cropredy 2010] / Moments like these [live at Cropredy 2010] / Celebrity / The ring / Yours / Dream garden / Heresy / Stop [live at Mantlefest] / Large one [studio/live].

The LEISURE SOCIETY

Nick Hemming (from Burton-on-Trent) served his musical apprenticeship in a number of firms, firstly as a member of She Talk To Angels (a band who counted actor Paddy Considine, film director Shane Meadows and bassist Richard Eaton in their number) and latterly as a member of one-time Creation shoegazing trippers The Telescopes. Hemming also composed the music for two of Meadows' films, 'A Room For Romeo Brass' and 'Dead Man's Shoes'.

Hemming teamed up with multi-instrumentalist Christian Hardy to form The LEISURE SOCIETY in 2006 and stirred up a favourable critical response for their demo – no less a man than Brian Eno cited them as a favourite.

A peculiar, almost camp mix of acoustic instruments and strident, old-fashioned Englishness is at the heart of their sound. They share the same fey swoon as Belle And Sebastian, and the same expansive production.

Their debut proper, **THE SLEEPER** (2009) {*8}, was an immediate critical success and the band toured the UK on the back of it. The jewel at the centre of the album was 'The Last Melting Of The Snow', a song which, Hemming said, was written on new year's eve with a bottle of vodka after a break-up with his girlfriend. The song was further recognised as the diamond it was, receiving an Ivor Novello Award nomination. The bonus set 'A Product Of The Ego Drain' featured a cover of Gary Numan's 'Cars'.

The second album, **INTO THE MURKY WATER** (2011) {*7}, offered a similar experience to its predecessor, but with Hemming and Hardy upping the multi-instrumentalism further (more mandolin! more maracas!) and broadening the horizons a little – there were even shades of The Modern Lovers and Krautrock legends Neu! While they share a wilful and wayward musical sensibility with US compatriots such as Grizzly Bear and FLEET FOXES, they are at heart a most peculiarly British institution. *MR*

Nick Hemming - vocals, mandolin, ukulele, banjo, guitars, etc. (of SHORELINE, of SONS OF NOEL AND ADRIAN) / **Christian Hardy** - keyboards, multi / plus **William Calderbank** - cello (of SHORELINE, of SONS OF NOEL AND ADRIAN) / **Darren Bonehill** - bass / **Sebastian Hankins** - drums, percussion / **Helen Whitaker** - flute, violin (of SONS OF NOEL AND ADRIAN) / **Mike Siddell** - violin (of SONS OF NOEL AND ADRIAN, ex-Hope Of The States) / **Beatrice Sanjust di Teulada** - vocals (of SHORELINE)

UK Willkommen — US not issued

Mar 09. (cd) *(Willkommen 002)* **THE SLEEPER** ☐ ⊟
- A fighting chance / The sleeper / The last of the melting snow / A short weekend begins with longing / We were wasted / Save it for someone who cares / The darkest place I know / Are we happy? / Come to your senses / A matter of time / Love's enormous wings. *(re-iss. Jul 09 on Full Time Hobby; FTH 081CDA) (d-cd/d-lp iss. Oct 09 +=; FTH 081 CDB/LP)* - A PRODUCT OF THE EGO DRAIN (demos and B-sides):- Save it for someone who cares [single version] / A short weekend begins with longing [original demo] / Cars / A passing thought / Pancake day / If God did give me a choice / Bona fide / The wayfarer.

May 09. (7") *(Willkommen 003)* THE LAST OF THE MELTING SNOW. / A Matter Of Time ☐ ⊟

(above was released as a download in Dec 08)

Full Time Hobby — not issued

Sep 09. (7" pink) *(FTH 082S)* SAVE IT FOR SOMEONE WHO CARES. / Bona Fide ☐ ⊟

Apr 11. (7") *(FTH 113S)* THIS PHANTOM LIFE. / Flying ☐ ⊟

May 11. (cd/lp) *(FTH 116 CD/LP)* **INTO THE MURKY WATER** [??] ⊟
- Into the murky water / Dust on the dancefloor / Our hearts burn like damp matches / You could keep me talking / Although we all are lost / This phantom life / The hungry years / I shall forever remain an amateur / Better written off (than written down) / Just like the knife.

SHORELINE

Nick Hemming, Beatrice Sanjust di Teulada, William Calderbank, Jacob Richardson, Tom Cowan, James de Malplaquet + Magnus Williams

Yesternow — not issued

Apr 06. (10" ep) *(YES 001)* FROM EDEN, HOME AND IN BETWEEN ☐ ⊟
- Lightning / Shipwrecked / Sounds like / Kings / A second thought.

Willkommen — not issued

Sep 08. (cd) *(Willkommen 001)* **TIME WELL SPENT** ☐ ⊟
- Daybreak / Jubeltane / Kings / Heather / Like me / Brigidine / Little song / Sea bird / Without fear / Shipwrecked.

Chris LESLIE (⟹ WHIPPERSNAPPER)

LEVELLERS

Taking their name from the English political radicals of the 17th century, LEVELLERS were one of the most successful and consistent bands to emerge from the free festival/crusty scene, building up a loyal grassroots fanbase with their raggle-taggle blend of electric-folk and Celtic-punk.

Formed out of The Fence in Brighton early in 1988 by singer Mark Chadwick (on guitars and banjo) and Jon Sevink (fiddle), they subsequently recruited Alan Miles (also vocals, mandolin and guitar), Jeremy Cunningham (bass and bouzouki) and Charlie Heather (drums). Incidentally, The Fence released one single in May 1987, 'Frozen Water' flipped with 'Exit'.

After Phil Nelson took over as manager the following year, they released a couple of rough and ready EPs for his Hag imprint before the band signed to European label Musidisc, where they began working on a debut album with WATERBOYS producer Phil Tennant.

While **A WEAPON CALLED THE WORD** (1990) {*7} helped introduce their rootsy assaults to a larger audience, the band subsequently broke from their contract and signed to China Records, while Miles was replaced by songwriter/guitarist Simon Friend. Another hectic UK tour followed, and by autumn 1991 the LEVELLERS' popularity was such that the **LEVELLING THE LAND** (1991) {*8} album made the Top 20 with only the support of minor hit single 'One Way'. With a more accessible, anthemic folk-rock approach, the record took the band's defiantly pro-earth, pro-equality philosophy overground and into the mainstream. The track 'Battle Of The Beanfield' commemorated the 1985 conflict between new age travellers and police in a field in Wiltshire.

In spring 1992 the quintet scored their biggest hit to date with the '15 Years' EP, almost making the Top 10, while they chose to end the year with a series of 'Freakshows' combining the likes of fellow agitpoppers CHUMBAWAMBA with established crusty pastimes such as juggling and fire-eating. The following year's album **LEVELLERS** (1993) {*7} missed the No.1 spot by a whisker, spawning a trio of Top 20 singles in 'Belaruse', 'This Garden' and the lovely ballad 'Julie'; the band were now the unlikeliest of fully-fledged pop stars.

They also became embroiled in a war of words with the music press and fellow musicians, not that this affected their popularity; they finally topped the UK charts with **ZEITGEIST** (1995) {*5} as they found themselves surfing the new wave of enthusiasm for British music in general. Concert set **HEADLIGHTS, WHITE LINES, BLACK TAR RIVERS** (1996) {*7} was a better reflection of what made the band tick.

MOUTH TO MOUTH (1997) {*6}, their final release on China, and **HELLO PIG** (2000) {*5}, their first on EastWest records, gave the fans a bit of heart, while even 2002's **GREEN BLADE RISING** {*5}, on Eagle Records, kept the wolf from the door. The band also worked with fellow Brighton act McDERMOTT'S TWO HOURS for a few sets in the early 2000s.

Certainly one of Britain's more conscientious bands, LEVELLERS were part of a sadly dying breed who still believed that music and politics were a feasible combination; Brit-pop had put paid to all that. Despite that, Chadwick and co. (including newcomer Matt Savage) had never lost their spirit or their dexterity, surrendering nothing to their doubters and releasing album number ten, **TRUTH AND LIES** (2005) {*7}. Its opener 'Last Man Alive' was certainly not one for the folk purist. The comeback was complete when **LETTERS FROM THE UNDERGROUND** (2008) {*6} reached the Top 30, and their struggle was now to maintain this momentum. CHADWICK was the first to break loose, on his solo venture **ALL THE PIECES** (2010) {*5}.

Over the years, the LEVELLERS have covered a few songs on B-sides, etc, including 'Germ Free Adolescents' (X-Ray Spex), 'New York Mining Disaster 1941' (the Bee Gees), 'The Devil Went Down To Georgia' (Charlie Daniels Band), 'Plastic Jeezus' (Paul King), 'English Civil War' (The Clash), 'Police On My Back' (The Equals) and 'Lowlands Of Holland' (trad). *MCS*

Mark Chadwick - vocals, guitar, banjo (ex-The Fence) / **Jeremy Cunningham** - bass, bazouki / **Charlie Heather** - drums / **Jon Sevink** - violin (ex-The Fence) / **Alan Miles** - vocals, guitar, mandolin, harmonica

UK Hag — US not issued

May 89. (12" ep) *(HAG 005)* CARRY ME ☐ ⊟
- Carry me / What's in the way / The last days of winter / England my home.

Oct 89. (12" ep) *(HAG 006)* OUTSIDE - INSIDE. / Hard Fight / I Have No Answers / Barrel Of A Gun

Musidisc not issued

Apr 90. (7") *(105 577)* WORLD FREAK SHOW. / Barrel Of A Gun (acoustic)
(12"+=) *(108 936)* - What you know.

Apr 90. (cd/c/lp) *(10557-2/-4/-1)* **A WEAPON CALLED THE WORD**
- World freak show / Carry me / Outside - Inside / Together all the way / Barrel of a gun / Three friends / I have no answers / No change / Blind faith / The ballad of Robbie Jones / England my home / What you know. *<US-iss. 1992 on JRS cd/c; 35823-2/-4> (cd re-iss. Jan 01 on IMS-Universal+=; E 15397-2)* - Social insecurity / Cardboard Box city / Three friends (remix). *(cd re-mast. Oct 10 on On The Fiddle+=; OTFCD 008X)* - Three friends [remix] / [BBC sessions]: England my home / I have no answers / Barrel of the gun / Carry me.

Oct 90. (7") *(106 897)* TOGETHER ALL THE WAY. / Three Friends (Arfa mix short version)
(12"+=) *(106 896)* - Cardboard Box City / Social Insecurity.

—— **Simon Friend** - guitars, vocals; repl. Alan

China Elektra

Sep 91. (7"/c-s) *(WOK/+MC 2008)* ONE WAY. / Hard Fight (acoustic) / The Last Days Of Winter 51
(12"+=/cd-s+=) *(WOK T/CD 2008)* - ('A'-Factory mix) / The Devil went down to Georgia.

Oct 91. (lp/c/cd) *(WOL/+MC/CD 1022)* <61325-1/-4/-2>
LEVELLING THE LAND 14 May 92
- One way / The game / The boatman / Liberty song / Far from home / Sell out / Another man's cause / The road / The riverflow / Battle of the beanfield. *(cd re-iss. Jul 99 +=; 4509 96100-2)* - 15 years. *(<d-cd-iss. Sep 07 on Rhino-WEA+=; 5144 22429-2>)* - Last days of winter / Dance before the storm / Hard fight / The devil went down to Georgia / Plastic Jeezus / The game (live) / World freak show (live) / Dance before the storm (live) / The boatman (live) / Far from home (live) / Sell out (live) / The riverflow (live) / Battle of the beanfield (live) / Jig - Three friends (live) / Liberty song (live) / One way (live) / The devil went down to Georgia (live).

Nov 91. (7"/c-s) *(WOK/+MC 2010)* FAR FROM HOME. / World Freak Show (live) 71
(12"+=/cd-s+=) *(WOK T/CD 2010)* - Outside - Inside (live) / The boatman (live) / Three friends (live).

May 92. (c-ep/10" pic-d-ep/12"ep/cd-ep) *(WOK MC/X/T/CD 2020)*
15 YEARS / Dance Before The Storm. / The Riverflow (live) / Plastic Jeezus 11

Jun 93. (c-s) *(WOKMC 2034)* BELARUSE / Subvert (live at Transcentral) / Belaruse Return 12
(12"+=/cd-s+=) *(WOK T/CD 2034)* - Is this art?

Sep 93. (lp/c/cd) *(WOL/+MC/CD 1034)* <61532-1/-4/-2> **LEVELLERS** 2
- Warning / 100 years of solitude / The likes of you and I / Is this art? / Dirty Davey / This garden / Broken circles / Julie / The player / Belaruse. *(cd re-iss. Jul 99; 4509 95908-2) (<cd re-iss. Aug 97 on Rhino-WEA+=; 5144 22430-2>)* - The lowlands of Holland / English civil war / Subvert (live at Transcentral) / Belaruse return.

Oct 93. (7" pic-d/c-s) *(WOK P/MC 2039)* THIS GARDEN. / Life (acoustic) 12
(12"+=/cd-s+=) *(WOK T/CD 2039)* - ('A'-Marcus Dravs remix) / ('A'-Banco De Gaia remix).

May 94. (7" clear-ep/10" pic-d-ep) *(WOK P/X 2042)* THE JULIE EP 17
- Julie (new version) / English civil war / The lowlands of Holland / 100 years of solitude (live) (*).
(cd-ep) *(WOKCD 2042)* - (*) repl. by Warning (live).

Jul 95. (7" pic-d) *(WOKP 2059)* HOPE ST. / Leave This Town 12
(7" pic-d) *(WOKPX 2059)* - ('A') / Miles away.
(cd-s++=/c-s++=) *(WOK CD/MC 2059)* - Busking on Hope Street.

Aug 95. (lp/c/cd) *(WOL/+MC/CD 1064)* <61887-1/-4/-2> **ZEITGEIST** 1
- Hope St / The fear / Exodus / Maid of the river / Saturday to Sunday / 4 am / Forgotten ground / Fantasy / PC Keen / Just the one / Haven't made it / Leave this town / Men-an-tol. *(cd re-iss. Jul 99; 0630 11597-2) (<cd re-iss. Aug 07 on Rhino-WEA+=; 5144 22431-2>)* - Miles away / Your 'ouse / Drinking for England / Searchlights.

Oct 95. (7" pic-d/cd-s) *(WOK P/MC/CD 2067)* FANTASY. / Sara's Beach / Searchlights (long version) 16

Dec 95. (7" ep/c-ep/cd-ep) *(WOK/+MC/CD 2076)* JUST THE ONE / A Promise. / Your 'Ouse / Drinking For England 12

Jul 96. (7" ep/c-ep/cd-ep) *(WOK/+MC/CD 2082)* EXODUS - LIVE (live) 24
- Exodus / Another man's cause / Leave this town / PC Keen.

Aug 96. (cd/c) *(WOL CDX/MC 1074)* **HEADLIGHTS, WHITE INES, BLACK TAR RIVERS - BEST LIVE** (live) 13
- Sell out / Hope St / 15 years / Exodus / Carry me / The boatman / Three friends / Men-an-tol / The road / One way / England my home / England my home / Battle of the beanfield / Liberty / The riverflow. *(cd re-iss. Jul 99; 0630 15783-2)*

Aug 97. (c-s/cd-s) *(WOK MC/CD 2088)* BEAUTIFUL DAY / Bar Room Jury / All Your Dreams 13
(cd-s) *(WOKCDX 2088)* - ('A') / Germ free adolescence / Price of love / Hang on to your ego.

Aug 97. (lp/c/cd) *(WOL/+MC/CD 1084)* **MOUTH TO MOUTH** 5
- Dog train / Beautiful day / Celebrate / Rain and snow / Far away / CCTV / Chemically free / Elation / Captains courageous / Survivors / Sail away / Too real. *(cd re-iss. Jul 99; 0630 19856-2) (<cd re-iss. Aug 07 on Rhino-WEA+=; 5144 22433-2>)* - Bar room jury / Angels / All your dreams / Windows.

Oct 97. (c-ep/cd-ep) *(WOK MC/CD 2089)* CELEBRATE / Rain And Snow (the white mountain yarn mix) / Sea Of Pain / Survivors 28
(cd-s) *(WOKCDX 2089)* - ('A') / Men-an-tol (live acoustic) / 4 + 20 / Ring of fire.

Dec 97. (12" ep/c-ep/cd-ep) *(WOK/+MC/CD 2090)* DOG TRAIN / Last Days Of Winter. / Carry Me / What's In The Way 24

Mar 98. (12" ep/c-ep/cd-ep) *(WOK/+MC/CD 2091)* TOO REAL (mixes; Steve Osborne / Morcheeba / Indian Rope Man / Lean Fiddler / Morcheeba instrumental / Bliss) 46

Oct 98. (7"/c-s) *(WOK/+MC 2096)* BOZOS. / Don't You Grieve 44
(cd-s) *(WOKCD 2096)* - Plastic factory.
(cd-s) *(WOKCDR 2096)* - ('A') / New York mining disaster 1941 / Supercharger (heavy mental mix).

Jan 99. (c-s) *(WOKMC 2102)* ONE WAY (new version). / Angel 33
(cd-s+=) *(WOKCD 2102)* - Windows.
(cd-s) *(WOKCDX 2102)* - ('A') / England my home / I have no answers.

East West not issued

Aug 00. (c-s) *(EW 218C)* HAPPY BIRTHDAY REVOLUTION / Surprisingly Easy! 57
(cd-s+=) *(EW 218CD)* - Best part of the day.

Sep 00. (cd/c/lp) *(8573 84339-2/-4/-1)* **HELLO PIG** 28
- Happy birthday revolution / Invisible / The weed that killed Elvis / Edge of the world / Do it again tomorrow / Walk lightly / Voices on the wind / Sold England / Modern day tragedy / Dreams / 61 minutes of pleading / Red sun burns / Gold and silver. *(cd re-iss. Aug 07 on Rhino-WEA+=; 5144 22434-2)* - Michael's bar / Hard life / Good old-fashioned hope.

—— In 2001, Jeremy + Charlie (as LEVELLERS) teamed up with McDERMOTT'S TWO HOURS on the collaborative album 'World Turned Upside Down'.

Eagle-Hag Eagle

Sep 02. (7") *(EHAG7 001)* COME ON. / Welcome To Tomorrow 44
(cd-s+=) *(EHAGXA 001)* - Vanished.
(cd-s) *(EHAGXS 001)* - ('A') / Hooligan / Tranquil blue.

Sep 02. (cd) *(EHAGCD 002)* <20000> **GREEN BLADE RISING** Feb 03
- Four winds / Falling from the tree / Pretty target / Come on / Pour / Aspects of spirit / Wild as angels / Believers / A chorus line / Not what we wanted / Wake the world. *(re-cd+=; EHAGLT 002)* - Galahad / Come on (video) / Wild as angels (video).

Jan 03. (7" ep/cd-ep) *(EHAG 7/XS 003)* WILD AS ANGELS EP 34
- Wild as angels / Galahad / Adulterer's blues / Wild as angels (video).
(cd-s) *(EHAGXA 003)* - ('A') / American air do / Burn.

—— In 2003/04, two further sets ('Claws And Wings' and 'Disorder') were issued by McDERMOTT'S TWO HOURS VS. LEVELLERS.

—— added **Matt Savage** - keyboards, vocals

Apr 05. (cd-s) *(EOTFXS 303)* MAKE U HAPPY / Not In My Name 38
(cd-s+=) *(EOTFXA 303)* - ('A') / Prisoner / What you know (live).

May 05. (cd) *(EOTFCD 302)* <20071> **TRUTH AND LIES**
- Last man alive / Make U happy / Confess / For us all / Knot around the world / Steel knife / Wheels / Said and done / Who's the daddy / The damned / Sleeping.

On The Fiddle not issued

Jul 08. (ltd-7") *(OTFS 001)* BEFORE THE END. / TV Suicides

Aug 08. (cd/lp) *(OTF CD/LP 003)* **LETTERS FROM THE UNDERGROUND** 24
- The cholera well / Death loves youth / Eyes wide / Before the end / Burn America, burn / Heart of the country / Behold a pale rider / A life less ordinary / Accidental anarchist / Duty / Fight or flight. *(d-cd-iss+=; OTFCD 003X)* - On the beach (acoustic) / The everyday (acoustic) / TV suicides (acoustic) / Burn America burn (video).

Nov 08. (ltd-7") *(OTFS 002)* BURN AMERICA, BURN. / Fifteen Years (featuring The ELECTRIC SOFT PARADE)

- (8-10*) compilations -

Oct 98. (cd/c) *(052173-2/-4)* **ONE WAY OF LIFE: THE BEST OF THE LEVELLERS** 15
- One way / What a beautiful day / Fifteen years / Shadow on the sun / Hope St. / Belaruse / Celebrate / Too real (12" mix) / Bozos / This garden / Carry me / Fantasy / Julie / Dog train / Far from home / Just the one. *(ltd.d-cd+=)* - Far from home / Just the one / PC Keen / Sell out / Hope Street / 15 years / Men-an-to. *(<cd re-iss. Jun 02 on East West; 3984 25099-2>)*

- (5-7*) compilations and the rest ...-

Jan 92. (7") *Musidisc; (105 557)* WORLD FREAK SHOW (remix). / What You Know
(12"+=/cd-s+=) *(10893 6/2)* - Barrel of a gun / What you know.

Mar 93. (lp/c/cd) *China; (WOL 1035/+MC/CD)* **SEE NOTHING, HEAR NOTHING, DO SOMETHING** (early recordings)
- 15 years / Far from home (45 mix) / Liberty (US mix) / Dance before the storm / The last days of winter / Hard fight / World freak show / Outside inside / The boatman / Three friends / The riverflow / The devil went down to Georgia / Plastic jeezus.

May 01. (cd) *Hag; (HAG 005)* **SPECIAL BREW**
- Barrel of a gun / Capital gain / Hard fight / England my home / Carry me / What's in the way / The last days of winter / England my home / Outside - Inside / Barrel of a gun / Hard fight / I have no answers / Police on my back / Where the hell are we going to live / Travelogue / Green blade rising (live) / What you know (live).

MARK CHADWICK

Stay By — not issued

Sep 10. (cd/lp) *(StayByCD 001)* **ALL THE PIECES**
- Elephant fayre / All the pieces / Havens / Satellite / Seasons / Say you're gonna be my girl / Indians / The great and the dead / Paramount / Empty now / Inevitable / Whispers.

Jackie LEVEN

Long before Kenny Anderson/KING CREOSOTE put the Scottish county of Fife on the musical map, singer-songwriter/guitarist JACKIE LEVEN (born June 18, 1950 in Kirkcaldy) was treading the boards, in 1973-1975 supporting the likes of Man under the assumed name of John St Field. One very rare LP, **CONTROL** (1975) {*6}, was issued only in Spain, but thankfully re-released many years later on CD by Cooking Vinyl.

Subsequently taking the lead in cultish London-based new wave/roots outfit Doll By Doll (alongside Jo Shaw, Robin Spreafico and David McIntosh), LEVEN emerged in punk's wake after signing to Warner Bros offshoot Automatic Records. Their debut album 'Remember' was unleashed to a mixed response early in 1979. Having replaced Robin with Tony Waite, Doll By Doll issued a second album that year, 'Gypsy Blood', Jackie's Celtic-fringe lyrics and echoing vocals sitting rather uneasily beside the band's elaborate but stirring rock sentiments and arrangements.

Signing up with an unlikely new home in pop label Magnet, the quartet delivered two further sets, 'Doll By Doll' (1981) and 'Grand Passion' (1982), the latter finding Jackie employing a new band including co-vocalist Helen Turner and an array of hired-gun rock veterans (David Gilmour, Tim Cross, Mel Collins and Graham Broad). The inclusion of the Jagger-Richards classic 'Under My Thumb' didn't help their cause much, as the group split in 1983.

A solo deal with Charisma Records was a bright new start, but two flop singles again blighted LEVEN's modest musical ambitions. An album was recorded, but shelved when the singer found himself the victim of a street attack in London – strangling injuries caused severe damage to his larynx that stopped him singing and even speaking for a long spell.

Things went from bad to worse as LEVEN fell into a spiral of heroin abuse, although he nevertheless managed to turn things around, curing himself (with help from his wife Carol) and setting up a support network (Core) for fellow drug addicts. During this period in the musical wilderness he managed a few gigs with former Sex Pistols/Rich Kids bassist Glen Matlock as short-lived outfit Concrete Bulletproof Invisible. One 45 for Radioactive Records, 'Big Tears', was a Melody Maker single of the week in March 1988.

The faded rock star finally emerged as a fully-fledged solo artist and signed to roots label Cooking Vinyl. Recorded in Scotland and released there only, the mini-set **SONGS FROM THE ARGYLL CYCLE** (1994) {*6} reintroduced Jackie as a folk-rock artist, leaving behind all traces of his punk days amid lyrical images of windswept Highland scenes.

LEVEN has since released several more sets in a similar vein while working with American poet Robert Bly, plus varied projects with fellow Fifers Richard Jobson and crime writer Ian Rankin. Like KING CREOSOTE, Jackie has also released many independent and limited-edition CD albums, mainly for his fan base. With poet Bly and Mike Scott from The WATERBOYS (and in a Celtic/Caledonian style not too unlike Big Country), the thematic **THE MYSTERY OF LOVE IS GREATER THAN THE MYSTERY OF DEATH** (1994) {*7} conveyed his lyrical mysticism to its full extent.

That was followed by **FORBIDDEN SONGS OF THE DYING WEST** (1995) {*7}, **FAIRY TALES FOR HARD MEN** (1997) {*7}, **NIGHT LILIES** (1998) {*7} (very VAN MORRISON meets Bacharach-David) and **DEFENDING ANCIENT SPRINGS** (2000), featuring Mann-Weill's 'You've Lost That Loving Feeling' as opener. **CREATURES OF LIGHT AND DARKNESS** (2001) {*6} (with David Thomas) and **SHINING BROTHER, SHINING SISTER** (2003) {*7} – also crediting the Pere Ubu guru, plus poets Bly, Rainer Maria Rilke, Ron Sexsmith, ee cummings and Edith Sitwell – were also worthy recordings, while the Ian Rankin-collaboration double set **JACKIE LEVEN SAID** (2005) {*6} was a fun Festival Fringe night out for the pair (and an unsuspecting audience) at the Queen's Hall, Edinburgh the previous August. Also released in 2005, **ELEGY FOR JOHNNY CASH** {*6} was a nice touch, a tribute without a single Cash cover on board.

Subsequently sharing the limelight with his prolific solo release schedule was Jackie's pseudonymous Sir Vincent Lone side project (think DICK GAUGHAN fronting Portishead) for three ambient/acoustic albums, namely **SONGS FOR LONELY AMERICANS** (2006) {*5}, **WHEN THE BRIDEGROOM COMES (SONGS FOR WOMEN)** (2007) {*6} and **TROUBADOUR HEART** (2008) {*5}. The latter two featured covers of songs by the likes of JUDEE SILL ('When The Bridegroom Comes'), JACKSON C FRANK ('Blues Runs The Game'), DONOVAN ('Ballad Of Geraldine') and Dan Britton ('Leonard'), plus BERT JANSCH ('Strolling Down The Highway'), Chris Conway ('Wake Me Up When It's Over') and a short-take on golden nugget 'It's All In The Game'.

Of late JACKIE LEVEN has produced three more albums for Cooking Vinyl: **OH WHAT A BLOW THAT PHANTOM DEALT ME!** (2007) {*6}, **LOVERS AT THE GUN CLUB** (2008) {*6} – featuring his friend Johnny Dowd, an American country singer – and his latest, **GOTHIC ROAD** (2010) {*6}. All deserve more attention, and are recommended to anyone in need of finding an artist outside the mainstream (folk or otherwise) who performs with consistency and fire in his belly. *MCS*

Jackie Leven - vocals, guitar / with various guests

UK Movieplay — US not issued

1975. (lp; as JOHN ST. FIELD) *(none)* **CONTROL** [recorded 1973] — Spain
- Soft lowland tongue / Raerona / Mansion tension / Dog star / Ruins / I'm always a Prinlaws boy / Problem / Dune voices / Sleeping in bracken. *(UK cd-iss. Sep 97 on Cooking Vinyl; COOKCD 131)*

—— followed by a period fronting Doll By Doll

Charisma — not issued

Aug 83. (7") *(JACK 1)* LOVE IS SHINING DOWN ON ME. / Great Spirit Calls

Jul 84. (7") *(JACK 2)* UPTOWN. / Tropic Of Cool
(12"+=) *(JACK 2-12)* - Beautiful train.

Cooking Vinyl — Thirsty Ear

Mar 94. (m-cd) *(COOKCD 065)* **SONGS FROM THE ARGYLL CYCLE** — Scot
- Stranger on the square / Walking in Argyll / Honeymoon hill / Looking for love / Grievin' at the mishnish / Ballad of a simple heart / As we sailed into Skibbereen / Some ancient misty morning / History of rain / Gylen Gylen / Fly / Crazy song. *(UK-iss. Apr 96; COOKCD 101)*

Jul 94. (d-lp/c/cd) *(COOK/+C/CD 064)* **THE MYSTERY OF LOVE IS GREATER THAN THE MYSTERY OF DEATH**
- Clay jug / Shadow in my eyes / Call mother a lonely field / The crazy song / Farm boy / The garden / Snow in Central Park / Looking for love / Heartsick land / Gylen Gylen / I say a little prayer / Bars of Dundee. *(d-lp+=/d-cd-iss. Sep 94 +=; COOKCDS 064)* - THE RIGHT TO REMAIN SILENT (with ROBERT BLY and JAMES HALLAWELL): - Donna Karan / Ballad of a simple heart / Stranger on the square / Horseshoe and jug / Mary Jane's dog / So my soul can sing.

Jan 95. (cd-ep) *(FRY 036)* I SAY A LITTLE PRAYER / Honeymoon Hill / As We Sailed Into Skibbereen / The Bonnie Earl O' Moray

Sep 95. (d-lp/c/cd) *(COOK/+C/CD 090)* **FORBIDDEN SONGS OF THE DYING WEST**
- Young male suicide blessed by invisible woman / Some ancient misty morning / Working alone - A blessing / Leven's lament / Marble city bar / The wanderer / Exultation / Men in prison / Birds leave shadows / Stornoway girl / Silver roof / Lammermuir hills / Come back early or never have come / By the sign of the sheltered star / The scene that haunts my memory / My Lord, what a morning. *(d-lp+=)* - Exultation.

Oct 95. (cd-s) *(32212)* SOME ANCIENT MISTY MORNING / Snow In Central Park / Fall

Apr 97. (d-lp/cd) *(COOK/+CD 115)* **FAIRY TALES FOR HARD MEN**
- Boy trapped in a man / Desolation blues / Extremely violent man / Old West African song / Saint Judas / Poortoun / Fear of women / The walled covers of Ravenscraig / Sad Polish song / Sexual danger / Jim o' Windygates / Mad as the mist and snow / Kirkconnell flow / Listening to crows pray / Sir Patrick Spens ... / Sunflower. *(d-lp+=)* - Torture blues / A story which could be true / Scotland the brave.

Aug 97. (cd-s) *(32302)* UNIVERSAL BLUE / Desolation Blues / Torture Blues

Sep 98. (cd) *(COOKCD 153)* <57076> **NIGHT LILIES** — Sep 99
- Night lilies / Burning the box of / Beautiful things / Empty in Soho Square / Alvis Green / Live or die / Carnival dark / Universal blue / Deep choking wooded death fix / Me and Angela / Ireland for losers / Sick harbour lament.

Cooking Vinyl — Cooking Vinyl

Jan 00. (cd) *(<COOKCD 191>)* **DEFENDING ANCIENT SPRINGS**
- You've lost that loving feeling / Single father / Paris blues / Defending ancient springs / The working man's love song / I saw my love walk into clouds / Hand is pale with holy kisses / Your winter days / The keys to the forest / Morbid sky.

—— next credited Pere Ubu's David Thomas

Aug 01. (cd) *(<COOKCD 213>)* **CREATURES OF LIGHT AND DARKNESS**
- My Spanish dad / Exit wound / The sexual loneliness of Jesus Christ / Hidden world of she / Billy ate my pocket / Rainy day Bergen women / Friendship between men and women / Stopped by woods on a snowy evening / Washing by hand / Wrapped up in blue.

Feb 03. (cd) *(<COOKCD 250>)* **SHINING BROTHER, SHINING SISTER**
- Classic northern diversions / Irresistible romance / Dust elegy / Savannah waltz / My philosophy / Another man in the old arcade / A little voice in space / Heroin dealer blues / Faces / Tied-up house / Bells of grey crystal / 1798.

May 05. (d-cd; as JACKIE LEVEN & IAN RANKIN) *(COOKCD 322)* **JACKIE LEVEN SAID** (live at Queen's Hall, Edinburgh, August 2004)
- Opening remarks - Story part 1 / Jim O Windygates (live) / Story part 2 / My Spanish dad / Story part 3 / Classic northern diversions / Story part 4 // Ian and Jackie humourous conversation (from live show) / Exit wound (from live show) / End Of Live Show: The haunting of John Rebus / Linseed oil / Edinburgh winter blues / I say a little prayer / Stranger on the square / Friendship between men and women / Honeymoon hill / Irresistible romance.

Sep 05. (cd) *(COOKCD 331)* **ELEGY FOR JOHNNY CASH**
- Blue soul dark road / Museum of childhood / Elegy for Johnny Cash / The law of tide / All the rage / No honour in this love / Vibration white finger / King of the barley / And you'll never hear surf music again / In memory of my mother / Gladly go blind / Why log truckers rise earlier than students of zen.

Jun 06. (cd; as SIR VINCENT LONE) *(<COOKCD 365>)* **SONGS FOR LONELY AMERICANS**
- Moscow train / The war crimes of Ariel Sharon / The lights below / Revenge of memory / In search of stone / (I've never known) Peace on earth / Courtship in Scottish factories / Straight outta Caledonia / Balamory death chant.

Feb 07. (cd) *(COOKCD 395)* **OH WHAT A BLOW THAT PHANTOM DEALT ME!**
- Vox humana / One man one guitar / Another man's rain / Kings of infinite space / Childish blues / I've been everywhere / The long hard field / The silver in her crucifix (homage to Judee Sill) / Here come the urban ravens (homage to Kevin Coyne) / The skaters / Mellow my madness.

Oct 07. (cd; as SIR VINCENT LONE) *(<COOKCD 427>)* **WHEN THE BRIDEGROOM COMES (SONGS FOR WOMEN)**
- Graveyard marimba / When the bridegroom comes / Feels like rain but isn't / Coyne of the realm / Breakfast with Johnny Dowd / Ballad of Geraldine / Blues run the game / A little voice in space (live) / Leonard.

Aug 08. (cd) *(COOKCD 464)* **LOVERS AT THE GUN CLUB**
- Lovers at the gun club / Fareham confidential / The innocent railway / The dent in the fender and the wheel of fate / My old home / Head full of war / I've passed away from human love / To whom it may concern / Olivier blues / Woman in a car / Heart in my soul.

Nov 08. (cd; as SIR VINCENT LONE) *(COOKCD 478)* **TROUBADOUR HEART**
- The potato pickers / I'm gonna drift a little further south / His arms are full of broken things / Rove on wraith of Raith / Holy Rachel blues / Strolling down the highway / Florin-Tweed / It's all in the game / An honest woman / Wake me up when it's over.

Apr 10. (cd) *(COOKCD 519)* **GOTHIC ROAD**
- Gothic road / Last of the badmen / John Paul Getty's silver cadillac / Cornelius Whalen / Song for bass guitar and death / New wreath / Absolutely Joan Crawford (with a bit of Tilda Swinton on the side) / My lost blonde / In a shivering blaze / Hotel mini bar / Shadow of a man / Island.

- essential boxed sets -

Mar 01. (4-cd-box) *Cooking Vinyl; (COOKCD 212)* **GREAT SONGS FROM ETERNAL BARS**
- (FAIRY TALES FOR HARDMEN) // (FORBIDDEN SONGS OF THE DYING WEST) // // (CONTROL) // (THE WANDERER).

- (5-7*) compilations, others, etc.-

Feb 08. (cd; as JACKIE BALFOUR) *Cooking Vinyl; (COOKCD 432)* **CHIP PAN FIRE** (plus "best of" live Scottish stories)
- Welcome to Glenrodent / First day at work / Chip pan fire / The dirty bookshop / Foul play not suspected / The train driver mystery / The Livingstone end / Studio soundcheck / Sting's dead / Stupid local boasts / Sex tourist.

Feb 09. (d-cd) *Cooking Vinyl; (COOKCD 483)* **THE HAUNTED YEAR – WINTER: MEN IN PRISON – LIVE AT BERGEN MEN'S PRISON, NORWAY // MUNICH BLUES**

May 09. (d-cd) *Cooking Vinyl; (COOKCD 484)* **THE HAUNTED YEAR – SPRING: MAN BLEEDS IN GLASGOW // GREETINGS FROM MILFORD**

Aug 09. (d-cd) *Cooking Vinyl; (COOKCD 485)* **THE HAUNTED YEAR – SUMMER: BAREFOOT DAYS // DEEP IN THE HEART OF NOWHERE**

Oct 09. (d-cd) *Cooking Vinyl; (COOKCD 486)* **THE HAUNTED YEAR – AUTUMN: GREEK NOTEBOOK // ONLY THE OCEAN CAN SURVIVE**

- fan club releases, etc.-

Sep 97. (cd) *Haunted Valley; (83032)* **FOR PEACE COMES DROPPING SLOW** (live at the 12 Bar, London) f-club
- Jesus bodybuilder blues - Cocaine blues - Cannot keep from crying / Arctic sex (story) / Uist tramping song / Sacred bond (sour grapes) / Call mother a lonely field / Fear of women / Sexual danger / Acid roast beef (story) / Poortoun / Whisky story (story) / Desolation blues / Jackie losing it (story) / Marble City bar / Pale blues eyes / Main travelled roads / Slim slow slider. *(re-iss. Jan 04 on Cooking Vinyl; COOKCD 282)*

Aug 98. (cd) *Haunted Valley; (HV 1)* **SAINT JUDAS: WHEN I WENT OUT TO KILL MYSELF** (live) mail-o
- Leaving blues / The never song / Ruins / Jazz themes from Rosemary's empty cellar / Clandestine / The air in Langholm / Big question / The ballad of Anne Redmond / Sacred bond (sour grapes) / Love dogs / Deep choking wooded death fix.

Dec 98. (cd; as JACKIE LEVEN AND THE CELTIC SOULMEN) *Haunted Valley; (HV 2)* **MAN BLEEDS IN GLASGOW** mail-o
- Intro (story) / Farm boy / Guardian preview (story) / Glenarm - Burning the box of beautiful things / Looking for love / Man bleeds in Glasgow / Golf on the moon (story) / Night lilies / Snow in Central Park / Fear in Bermondsey (story) / Poortoun / Deep choking wooded death fix / Erotic football results (story) / Call mother a lonely field.

1999. (cd) *Haunted Valley; (none)* **GREEK NOTEBOOK** f-club
- Island one – Island thirty three. *[33 parts]*

Aug 99. (cd) *Haunted Valley; (HV 3)* **THE WANDERER** f-club
- Your winter days / Newfoundland blues - Some ancient misty morning - Working alone - Sex tourist / Heartsick land / Stranger on the square (etc) / The keys to the forest / Poortoun (losing my voice) / I can't afford to care anymore (with DOLL BY DOLL) / A blessing / When a man dies. *(bonus +=)* - Donna Karan / So my soul can sing / Mary Jane's dog.

Nov 00. (cd) *Haunted Valley; (none)* **MUNICH BLUES**
- Looking for love / Stranger on the square / Universal blue / Single father / I saw my love walk into the clouds / Paris blues / You've lost that loving feeling.

Nov 01. (cd) *Haunted Valley; (HV 4)* **DEEP IN THE HEART OF NOWHERE** f-club
- Intro – Wobbly grapefruit / Universal blue / Shit in your garden / Regional forms of complaint – New York plugger / Marble city bar / Bethesda chip shop / Single father / Little bird / Working man's love song / Paris blues – Down by the river.

2002. (cd) *Haunted Valley; (none)* **GREETINGS FROM MILFORD** [JACKIE LEVEN + THE STORNOWAY GIRLS] f-club
- She belongs to me / Pale blue eyes / Walking in Argyll / Waiting for my man / Listening to crows pray / Madame George / Who is he and what is he to you? / Paris blues / Main travelled roads.

2003. (cd) *Haunted Valley; (none)* **MEN IN PRISON – LIVE AT BERGEN MEN'S PRISON, NORWAY** f-club
- Men in prison / Opening remarks to prisoners / Extremely violent men / Poortoun / Call a mother a lonely field / The garden / Classic northern diversions / The crazy song.

2003. (cd) *Haunted Valley; (HV 5)* **BAREFOOT DAYS** f-club
- Barefoot days / Billy ate my pocket / Stopped by woods on a snowy evening / How we met Joni Mitchell – Matt Monro and the chip packet – Dirty underpants / Washing by hand / Desolation blues / Scots John and the eyelash / Exit wound / Rain of Kathleen / Nottamun town.

Mar 04. (cd) *Haunted Valley; (HV6)* **ONLY THE OCEAN CAN FORGIVE** f-club
- Little brown box / Woman in a car / Autumn song / Classic northern diversions / Extremely violent man / My philosophy / Sting's dead (story of the sad death of the well-known singer) / Paris blues / Barefoot days.

LIBERTY CAGE (⟹ The MEN THEY COULDN'T HANG)

LICK THE TINS

Named after an old tramp who lived near one of the group, LICK THE TINS was formed in Kilburn, north London in 1985, out of The Almost Brothers (not the Southern-rock tribute band of the same name), by graphic designer Simon Ryan and Ulster-born veterinary trainee Ronan Heenan. The Almost Brothers released four singles in the early 1980s, including 'Don't Pass The Buck' and 'Bums Rush'.

Joining Ryan and Heenan in LICK THE TINS were Alison Marr (also from Northern Ireland) and Aiden McCroary. Through playing their demo to Bob Barnes, they signed a deal with his Sedition Records. The group's debut single, a version of Elvis's hit 'Can't Help Falling In Love', hit the UK Top 50 four months after its October 1985 release, having been promoted on the Channel 4 music show The Tube.

With songs like 'Belle Of Belfast City' (a Celtic-trad classic), their bustling and raucous Pat Collier-produced debut album **BLIND MAN ON A FLYING HORSE** (1987) {*6} found favour with a steady fan base, although things were brought to an abrupt end soon after its release and the introduction of newcomer Martin Hughes (Ryan had departed). Their Celtic-friendly re-bash of Hendrix's 'Hey Joe' can be recommended. *MCS*

Ronan Heenan (b. Northern Ireland) - vocals, guitar (ex-The Almost Brothers) / **Alison Marr** (b. N. Ireland) - vocals, penny whistle / **Aiden McCroary** - bass, keyboards / **Simon Ryan** - drums (ex-The Almost Brothers)

UK Sedition — US not issued

Oct 85. (7") *(EDIT 3308)* CAN'T HELP FALLING IN LOVE. / Bad Dreams [42] [-]
('A'-ext.12"+=) *(EDITL 3308)* - ('A'-instrumental).

Aug 86. (7") *(EDIT 3312)* THE BELLE OF BELFAST CITY. / Calliope House [ ] [-]
('A'-ext.12"+=) *(EDITL 3312)* - ('A'-instrumental).

Apr 87. (7") *(EDIT 3323)* IN THE MIDDLE OF THE NIGHT. / Looks Like You [ ] [-]
(12"+=) *(EDITL 3323)* - Road to California.

May 87. (lp/c) *(SED/ZCSED 9001)* **BLIND MAN ON A FLYING HORSE** [ ] [-]
- Can't help falling in love / In the middle of the night / Light years away / Every little detail / Hey Joe / Get me to the world on time / Ghost story / Lights out / Only a year / Here comes Kali / Road to California / The belle of Belfast City. *(re-iss. Oct 91 on Mooncrest lp/c; CREST/+MC 012) (cd-iss. May 07 on Talking Elephant+=; TECD 114)* - Bad dreams / Looks like you / Calliope house / Can't help falling in love (extended) / In the middle of the night (extended) / Belle of Belfast city (extended).

—— **Martin Hughes** (b. Northern Ireland) - drums; repl. Ryan

—— split later in 1987; where are they now?

- compilations, others, etc.-

1991. (cd-ep) *Mooncrest; (MOON 1011)* CAN'T HELP FALLING IN LOVE / In The Middle Of The Night / Belle Of Belfast City / Can't Help Falling In Love (extended) [ ] [-]

LIFE AND TIMES

Not to be confused with Kansas City's post-millennium alt-rock band of the same name, this LIFE AND TIMES was formed in Luton, Bedfordshire in 1983 and featured Barry Goodman and former Midas member Graeme Meek, the former having a CV that included playing for Mead (with Steve Rackshaw) and Vermin (alongside Gadfan Edwards). Flautist Gregg Lindsay would play for the latter act before joining as the third part of LIFE AND TIMES.

Aided and funded by the Luton Museum and Art Gallery and the Eastern Arts Association, Meek and Goodman researched and released their debut, **STRAWPLAIT AND BONELACE** (1985) {*6}, an LP featuring "Songs of Bedfordshire history, customs, legends etc". Meek also presented the BBC Radio Bedfordshire programme 'Three Counties Folk', while the duo – true folklorists – represented their shire at the English Folk Dance And Song Society National Gathering.

Cutting another slice off the past, **SHROPSHIRE IRON** (1989) {*6} (also known as "Songs of the Industrial Revolution in 18th-Century Shropshire") maintained the duo's interest in local history. The turn of the decade saw Meek and Goodman (plus caller Brian Scowcroft) become involved with moonlight dance/ceilidh offshoot The Time Of Your Life.

LIFE AND TIMES have since completed two further voluminous chapters to boost their flagging discography (Sara Fox/Hack superseding Greg), the small independent Wixamtree imprint releasing CDs **CHARIVARI** (2005) {*5} – more Songs of Bedfordshire – and **WHERE THE WORKING BOATS WENT** (2009) {*5}. *MCS*

Graeme Meek (b. Sep 7 '54, Luton, Bedfordshire) - vocals, acoustic guitar, bass, bouzouki (ex-Midas) / **Barry Goodman** (b. Dec 3 '50, Sutton, Surrey) - vocals, melodeon, English concertina (ex-Mead, ex-Vermin) / plus early member **Gregg Lindsay** - flute

UK Fellside — US not issued

May 85. (lp/c) *(FE 043/+C)* **STRAWPLAIT AND BONELACE** [ ] [-]
- One man's morris / The Markyate highwayman / Brickmaking / The Scots of the Davis gas stove company / Straw plait / Let's go to the grand / Blocker's seaside / The bonelace weaver - Bonelace / Bedfordshire ale / Easter song / Tell old Charlie Irons - Why axe ye.

1989. (lp/c) *(FE 071/+C)* **SHROPSHIRE IRON** [ ] [-]
- The most extraordinary district in the world - Shropshire iron / Abraham Darby / The simple life of a quaker / Success to all these learned men / Lament for Darby / Boys of Bedlam - Bedlam jig / John Wilkinson / A furnaceman's life / A bridge of iron - The bridge of iron / Colebrook dale / The pride of Englishmen - Contemplate good fortune.

—— Greg departed; replaced by temp. Sara Fox/Hack

Wixamtree — not issued

2005. (cd) *(WIX 051)* **CHARIVARI**: Songs of Bedfordshire [ ] [-]
- Dunstable Downs midsummer's day song / The life and times of Henry Claydon, highwayman / Plough Monday song / A working boatie man / Bushels of Brussels - The Felmersham polka / All in the wintertime / Fuller's earth / One man's morris - Ampthill sunrise / The witch of Conger Hill / Charivari - Rough music / Queen Catherine / Newtown jig - Keysoe row / The ghost of Lady de Grey - The macabre.

2009. (cd) *(WIX 052)* **WHERE THE WORKING BOATS WENT** [ ] [-]
- The Duke of Bridgewater / The bold navigators / The Ivel navigation / A working boatie man / Carrying the load / Lock keepers of the waterways / Narrow boats to tow / Push boys push / Roses and castles / A bit of a do / The row between the boaters / Finest of them all / Banbury white horse - Four up / Iced in / Until the cut runs dry / A light at the end of the tunnel / Where the working boats went.

TIME OF YOUR LIFE

Meek + **Goodman** + **Brian Scowcroft** (caller & bass)

—— Barry was repl. by **Debbie Chalmers** (violin), **Steve Poore** (guitar) + **Howard Newton** (drums) - newest members!

Life And Times — not issued

1990s. (cd) *(none)* **A SELECT FEW!** [-] mail-o [-]
- Bushels of Brussels - The Felmersham polka / The rogue's march / Lemmy Brazil's No.1 - Off to California / Against the grain - Apasthree / Waterloo dance.

The LILAC TIME

If there was a modern-day definition of folk-pop, it would be Stephen Duffy's The LILAC TIME. Birmingham-born Duffy (b. May 30, 1960) had been known to pop fans for his short spell as the original frontman for Duran Duran before he opted for a solo career in the early 1980s, to be replaced by Simon Le Bon. As Stephen 'Tin Tin' Duffy he breached the UK pop charts in 1985 with 'Kiss Me' and 'Icing On The Cake', but if he was looking for a certain credibility he found it in spades with The LILAC TIME.

Featuring Duffy himself, his brother Nick (on bouzouki), Michael Giri, Sagat Guirey and Micky Harris, the group named themselves from a line in a NICK DRAKE song and traded in a suitably pastoral, acoustic, 1960s-styled pop sound that was first aired on their independently released debut, **THE LILAC TIME** (1987) {*8}. Phonogram Records (Fontana UK and Mercury US) were impressed enough to sign the band and re-issue it, Duffy amassing further critical plaudits for its use of exotic folk instruments such as accordions, woodwind and percussion – check out 'Black Velvet' and other singles from it.

Poor sales did not improve with follow-up set **PARADISE CIRCUS** (1989) {*7}, astounding the critics, and as the 1980s were coming to a close fans wanted their music with a little more bite. Techno, Madchester and grunge were taking shape.

Despite the production clout of John Leckie, 1990's **AND LOVE FOR ALL** {*7} again failed to kickstart the band's career, resulting in a move to Creation Records. Lost amid the baggy debris and shoegazing feedback, **ASTRONAUTS** (1991) {*6} was another non-starter. It also marked the end of the band's patience, and in 1992 The LILAC TIME officially split.

Duffy kept a fairly low profile, only a guest spot for Saint Etienne indicating that he was still in the music business. Come the mid-1990s, the veteran popster formed the band Duffy along with US indie-strummers Velvet Crush, signing to RCA offshoot Indolent Records and releasing an eponymous, Mitch Easter-produced debut. A soothing antidote to Brit-pop overload, the record was regarded by longtime Duffy observers as one of his finest efforts to date, combining the man's charming way with a lyric and the subtle guitar interplay of the Velvet Crush boys.

Several years of solo work were again temporarily abandoned as Stephen teamed up with his brother Nick again to re-form The LILAC TIME. Staying on Cooking Vinyl (where he'd released his previous solo set), the group took on a SIMON AND GARFUNKEL persona on worthy comeback set **LOOKING FOR A DAY IN THE NIGHT** (1999) {*6}. 2001's **LILAC6** {*6} was no slouch either, another set of bright, summery folk-rock music. Duffy came full circle in 2002 in a collaboration (as The Devils) with old Duran Duran sparring partner Nick Rhodes. An album's worth of songs, 'Dark Circles', displayed varying styles from Krautrock electro-pop to cutesy indie-rock. Lately, credited as Stephen Duffy and The Lilac Time, there have been two further episodes in his folk-pop story, **KEEP GOING** (2003) {*7} and **RUNOUT GROOVE** (2007) {*6}; it seems you can't keep a good man down. The fact that Robbie Williams asked him to be his songwriting partner speaks volumes for one of England's underrated songsmiths. *MCS*

Stephen Duffy - vocals, multi-instruments / **Nick Duffy** - bouzouki / **Sagat Guirey** -guitar / **Micky Harris** - bass / **Michael Giri** - drums, percussion

UK Swordfish — US not issued

Nov 87. (lp/c/cd) *(SWF LP/MC/CD 6)* **THE LILAC TIME** [ ] [-]

- Black velvet / Rockland / Return to yesterday / You've got to love / Love becomes a savage / Together / The road to happiness / Too sooner late than better / And the ship sails on / Trumpets from Montparnasse. *(re-iss. Jun 88 on Fontana; 834 835-2)* *<US-iss. Nov 88 on Mercury; 836 744-1/-4/-2>* *(cd re-mast. May 06 on Fontana+=; 983890-5)* - Black velvet [remix] / Reunion ball / Gone for a Burton / Streetcorner / [BBC sessions]:- The King and Queen of Carioca / Take time / Hargeesha / Return to yesterday / You've got to love.

Feb 88. (7") *(LILAC 1)* RETURN TO YESTERDAY. / Trumpets From Montparnasse
(12"+=) *(12LILAC 1)* - Railway bazaar / Reunion ball.

Fontana Mercury

May 88. (7") *(LILAC 2)* RETURN TO YESTERDAY. / Gone For A Burton
(12"+=)(cd-s+=) *(LILAC 2-12)(LILCD 2)* - Rooftrees / Reunion ball.

Aug 88. (7") *(LILAC 3)* YOU'VE GOT TO LOVE. / Railway Bazaar
(12"+=)(cd-s+=) *(LILAC 3-12)(LILCD 3)* - Trumpets from Montparnasse.

Nov 88. (7") *(LILAC 4)* BLACK VELVET. / Black Dawn
(12"+=) *(LILAC 4-12)* - Tiger tea.
(cd-s++=) *(LILCD 4)* - Street corner.

Jul 89. (7"/c-s) *(LIL AC/MC 5)* AMERICAN EYES. / World In Her Arms
(12"+=) *(LILAC 5-12)* - Crossing the line.
(cd-s++=) *(LILCD 5)* - Shepherd's plaid.

Sep 89. (7") *(LILAC 6)* THE DAYS OF THE WEEK. / The Queen Of The Heartless
(12"+=)(cd-s+=) *(LILAC 6-12)(LILCD 6)* - Spin a cavalu.

Oct 89. (lp/c/cd) *(<838 641-1/-4/-2>)* **PARADISE CIRCUS**
- American eyes / The lost girl in the midnight sun / The beauty in your body / If the stars shine tonight / The days of the week / She still loves you / Paradise Circus / The girl who waves at trains / The last to know / Father mother wife and child / The rollercoaster song / Work for the weekend / Twilight beer hall. *(cd re-iss. May 06 +=; 983736-5)* - The world in her arms / The queen of heartless / [intended instrumental album]:- Ponderosa pine / Night mail – Dirty armour / Shepherd's plaid / Ounce of nails / Spin a cavalu / Australian worm / On Milkwood Road / Night soil / Rubovia / Silver dagger / November / Paradise circus [Old Smithy version].

Nov 89. (7") *(LIL AC/MC 7)* THE GIRL WHO WAVES AT TRAINS. / If The Stars Shine Tonight [acoustic]
(12"+=) *(LILAC 7-12)* - Ounce of nails.
(cd-s++=) *(LILCD 7)* - American eyes [acoustic].

Apr 90. (7") *(LILAC 8)* ALL FOR LOVE AND LOVE FOR ALL. / Bed Of Roses
(12"+=)(cd-s+=) *(LILAC 8-12)(LILCD 8)* - Rubovia / Night mail – Dirty armour.

May 90. (7"/c-s) *(LIL AC/MC 9)* THE LAUNDRY. / Only Passing Through
(12"+=) *(LILAC 9-12)* - Hurricaned rice.
(cd-s++=) *(LILCD 9)* - Oeil biques a bacs.

Jul 90. (7") *(LILAC 10)* IT'LL END IN TEARS. / Julie Written On The Fence
(12"+=)(cd-s+=) *(LILAC 10-12)(LILCD 10)* - Cover.

Sep 90. (cd/c/lp) *(<846 190-2/-4/-1>)* **AND LOVE FOR ALL**
- Fields / Fields (reprise) / All for love and love for all / Let our land be the one / I went to the dance / Wait and see / Honest to god / The laundry / Paper boat / Skabaskibilio / It'll end in tears (I won't cry) / Trinity / And on we go / Fields [acoustic reprise]. *(cd/c w/free m-lp+=)* **RETURN 1 (GREATEST HITS)** *(RETRO 1)* - Black velvet / Return to yesterday / The beauty in your body / Together / The days of the week / American eyes / If the stars shine tonight / The girl who waves at trains. *(cd re-mast. May 06 +=; (983862-5)* - Julie written on the fence / Only passing through / Bed of roses / Cover / [BBC sessions]:- Fields / Paper boat / All for love and love for all / And on we go.

Caff not issued

Sep 90. (7") *(CAFF 12)* MADRESFIELD. / Bird On The Wire

Creation not issued

May 91. (7") *(CRE 104)* DREAMING. / The Darkness Of Her Eyes
(12"+=) *(CRE 104T)* - ['A'-version].
(cd-s++=) *(CRE 104CD)* - The rain falls deepest on the shortest haircut.

Aug 91. (cd/c/lp) *(CRE CD/MC/LP 098)* **ASTRONAUTS**
- In Iverna Gardens / Hats off, here comes the girl / Fortunes / A taste for honey / Grey skies and work things / Finistere / Dreaming / The whisper of your mind / The darkness of her eyes / Sunshine's daughter / North Kensington / Madresfield. *(cd re-mast. Aug 05 on Castle Music+=; CMQCD 1202)* - Holy man jam / She is all colour / Ghetto child / Ear for silent voices / Galaxy / C'est la vie c'est la guerre / Darling who can't wait to taste you.

—— split after above release but re-formed briefly early '92

—— re-formed with **Stephen** + **Nick** + **Michael** + vocalist **Claire Worral**

Cooking Vinyl SpinArt

Apr 99. (cd) *(COOKCD 176)* *<SPART 77>* **LOOKING FOR A DAY IN THE NIGHT** Sep 99
- Salvation song / The nursery walls / A dream that we all share / A day in the night / I won't die for you / Broken cloud / The family coach / Morning sun / All over again / Back in the car park / Mayfly too / Sleepy / The spirit moves. *<US+=>* - Reunion ball / Hard for her / Come down / Holding hands with grace / Ratoon.

Cooking Vinyl Cooking Vinyl

Oct 01. (cd-s) *(FRYCD 110)* THIS MORNING w-drawn

Oct 01. (cd) *(COOKCD 220)* **LILAC6**
- Dance out of the shadows / This morning / Come home everyone / My forest brown / I want to be your man / Jupe longue / Jeans + summer / Wasted / Entourage / Foglights / The last man on the moon / Junes buffalo.

STEPHEN DUFFY AND THE LILAC TIME

—— same line-up

Folk Modern Psychobaby

Jul 03. (cd) *(FOLKCD 001)* *<PBZ 54022>* **KEEP GOING** Apr 04
- Home / Don't feed the rats / Nothing can last / I wasn't scared of flying / Bank holiday Monday / We used to be so / Keep going / So far away / The silence / Oh God / The twelve tones / Already gone / An open book.

Fruitcake not issued

Oct 07. (cd) *(FCCD 103)* **RUNOUT GROOVE**
- Another time / Driving somewhere / A dream of a girl / Desert shore / Dark squadrons / Until I kissed you / Aldermaston / Pruning the vine / Happy go lucky / Parliament Hill fields / No direction / The kite and the sky.

Oct 08. (cd-ep) *(FCCD 107)* HAPPY BIRTHDAY PEACE EP
- A dream of a girl / Aldermaston / The bird call and the sensitive flame / Talkin' pessimism and pain blues / Runout groove.

- (*8) compilations, others, etc.-

Jul 01. (d-cd) *Mercury; (586151-2)* **COMPENDIUM - THE FONTANA TRINITY**
- If the stars shine tonight / Fields / The lost girl in the midnight sun / Love becomes a savage / Trumpets from Montparnasse / Black velvet [single version] / Return to yesterday / The laundry / The girl who waves at trains / Shepherd's plaid / Paper boat / I went to the dance / All for love and love for all / Night mail – Dirty armour / She still loves you / Trinity / American eyes / Wait and see / Honest to God / Spin a cavalu / The road to happiness / It'll end in tears / Fields [acoustic return] // Julie written on the fence / Cover / Hurricaned rice / The world in her arms / Bed of roses / Tiger tea / The rollercoaster song [unreleased version] / Gone for a burton / Rooftrees / The queen of heartless / Only passing through / Crossing the line / Streetcorner / Ounce of nails / You've got to love [Malvern mix] / Paradise circus [unreleased version] / Reunion ball / Rubovia / Black dawn / Night soil [unreleased version] / If the stars shine tonight [acoustic] / Oeil biques a bacs.

LISA o PIU

The brainchild of Swedish-born siren Lisa Isaksson, this quartet (roughly translated as "Lisa And More") also features musicians David Svedmyr, Joel Munther and Anders Engqvist. Lisa was raised in a small town near Stockholm that was known for its stables, where she discovered her mother's acoustic guitar in the loft. From drawing horses to songwriting, it wasn't long before the twentysomething Lisa formed Piu with a group of school friends. She created the artwork for her debut single 'Whisperers, Wavers, Hunters And Sailors', released on Scottish indie Autumn Ferment in the summer of 2008.

The group's first break came through performing in Britain with COMUS frontman Roger Wootton, and Subliminal Sounds Records signed Lisa almost immediately. Taking production from Matthias Gustavsson of Swedish psychedelic rockers Dungen (who'd dipped his toe into psych-folk) and holing up in a small cottage in Sweden's Vastmanland woodlands, LISA o PIU emerged with a bewitching set of fresh freak-folk songs.

Comparisons being made with LINDA PERHACS, VASHTI BUNYAN and BRIDGET ST JOHN, the beautuful **WHEN THIS WAS THE FUTURE** (2009) {*7} showed fragility and warmth in its eight delicate songs. In 'Cinnamon Sea', 'Forest Echo' and 'The Party' her voice whispered like some candle on its last gasp of air. Album number two, **BEHIND THE BEND** (2010) {*6}, a little less than half an hour long, balanced a handful of elfin tunes (including 'Was It The Moon') against one lengthy, prog-esque track, 'Child Of Trees'. *MCS*

Lisa Isaksson - vocals / **David Svedmyr** + **Joel Munther** + **Anders Engqvist** - instruments

UK US
own label not issued

2008. (ltd; cd-ep) *(none)* CANTERING

Autumn Ferment not issued

Jun 08. (ltd-7") *(AFR 001)* WHISPERERS, WAVERS, HUNTERS AND SAILORS. / Equatorial Changes

Subliminal Subliminal

Jul 09. (ltd;cd/lp) *(<SUBCD 29/XMLP-SUB 33>)* **WHEN THIS WAS THE FUTURE**
- Cinnamon sea / Forest echo / Traitor / The party / Two / Equatorial changes / Alvdans vid kolarkojan / And so on.

Mar 10. (ltd;m-cd/m-lp) *(<SUB 70-CD/69-LP>)* **BEHIND THE BEND**
- Was it the moon / Simplicity / Dream of goats / World falling down / Child of trees / Gong for hours (Jupiter's under the moon).

LITTLE JOHNNY ENGLAND

Resurrecting the Brit-folk sound of the early seventies, LITTLE JOHNNY ENGLAND quit London in 1999 as the FAIRPORTs did in their day, performing at the folk icons' Cropredy Festival to promote their self-financed debut **LITTLE JOHNNY ENGLAND** (1999) {*7}. The gig was recorded for an unofficial **LIVE** (2000) {*6} follow-up, featuring songs from their first set (including three by Swiss friend Pete Scrowther) and a cracking version of Little Feat's 'Dixie Chicken'.

Comprising long-time folk-fringe session accordionist/singer Gareth Turner (he released 'Two's Up' with SIMON CARE and played for The ALBION BAND in 1992), guitarist/singer PJ Wright, keyboards star Guy Fletcher (of TICKLED PINK) and Clarion rhythm section Matt Davies and Edd Frost, LITTLE JOHNNY ENGLAND almost immediately established themselves among the new breed of trad-folk outfits. Their 2002 set **MERCS AND CHEROKEES** {*7} garnered respect from the likes of Q magazine.

And then there was nothing for ages as the group took to other projects. PJ Wright, for one, tackled a solo set ('Hedge Of Sound') and helped re-promote Steve Gibbons's "The Dylan Project" recordings from the late 1990s.

Enlisting the fresh help of Hugh Bunker (bass, ex-Fatima Mansions) and Mark Stevens (drums) to replace Davies and Frost respectively, LITTLE JOHNNY ENGLAND were back in full folk-rocking swing with 2009's **TOURNAMENT OF SHADOWS** {*7}. Meanwhile, the resurrected Dylan Project (PJ, Steve, Phil Bond and FAIRPORTers Gerry Conway and Dave Pegg) was hitting the road in 2010. *MCS*

Gareth Turner (b. Jul 14 '71, London) - vocals, melodeons (ex-ALBION BAND, of PHIL BEER band) / **Guy Fletcher** - keyboards (of TICKLED PINK) / **PJ Wright** (b. Leicester) – guitars, vocals (ex-Steve Gibbons Band) / **Matt Davies** - five-string bass (ex-Clarion) / **Edd Frost** - drums (ex-Clarion)

UK LJE — US not issued

Nov 99. (cd) *(LJECD 1)* **LITTLE JOHNNY ENGLAND** ☐ ⊟
- Whisper of the moon / The gas light march / Johnny England / Le boeuf Anglais / Maybe / Joust – Rocky road / Coppers son / Jake's jig – Goldrush – Hayeswood / I was a young man / Solway dawn – Race to the summit / Early to bed. *(re-iss. Jan 02 on Fellside; FECD 165)*

Nov 00. (cd) *(LJECD 2)* **LIVE** (live at Cropredy) ☐ ⊟
- Le boeuf Anglais / Whisper of the moon / The gaslight march / Johnny England / Jake's jig – Gold rush – Hayeswood / Jenny / Le mystere du box Vulgaire / The swine – UHT / Maybe / Joust – Rocky road to Pitsford / I was a young man / Solway dawn – Race to the summit / Dixie chicken.

Fellside — not issued

Feb 02. (cd) *(FECD 166)* **MERCS AND CHEROKEES** ☐ ⊟
- Way things ought to be / Moon at my window / Swine - UHT / 40 years on / My heart's where my home used to be / Street fair / Witherstone / Rabjerg mile / Widdecombe fair / Mutual crumpet - Battle before bedtime - Nail down the rooster / Lost boys.

—— among other things, PJ Wright issued the 'Hedge Of Sound' set in 2006

—— **Hugh Bunker** - bass, vocals (ex-Fatima Mansions); repl. Matt

—— **Mark Stevens** - drums, vocals; repl. Edd

Talking Elephant — not issued

Oct 09. (cd) *(TECD 150)* **TOURNAMENT OF SHADOWS** ☐ ⊟
- Tournament of shadows / Lily of Barbary / Welcome to the sparrow club / Ginger Billy / Cutthroats, crooks and conmen / Kenzie / Jack's polka – Alexa's hornpipe - A reel and Kelly / Garland gay / Random acts of kindness / The falling down man / Steeltown Saturday night / The plains of Waterloo.

- (8-10*) compilations -

May 09. (d-cd) *Talking Elephant; (TECD 142)* **10 YEARS ON ...** [live – studio – rarities] ☐ ⊟
- My heart is where my home used to be / Jenny / Le mystere du box vulgare / Like the moon at my window / Widdecombe fair / Johnny England / Early to bed / Blow the candle out / 40 years on / I was a young man / Rabjerg mile / Maybe - The joust - The rocky road to Pitsford / Mutual crumpet - The battle before bedtime - Nail down the rooster / Whisper of the moon / The swine - UHT / Dixie chicken / Jake's jig - The gold rush - The Heyeswood reel / Way things ought to be / Solway dawn - Race to the summit.

PJ WRIGHT

Hedge Of Sound — not issued

2006. (cd) *(HOSCD 022)* **HEDGE OF SOUND** ☐ ⊟
- Wait for the whistle to blow / Random acts of kindness / Lily of Barbary / Suite: Nether Bagwash / The skin of my teeth / Peter Brown's fancy / Indisputable things / Electric railway / Madeleine / Going up Leicester / Electric railway (cheap day return).

The LOVE HALL TRYST (⟹ HARDING, John Wesley)

Jez LOWE

Born July 14, 1955, at Easlington in County Durham (and from Irish stock), singer-songwriter JEZ LOWE has had more than three decades in the business, stretching as far back as his duo with HOUSE BAND piper/ guitarist Ged Foley, who had also worked with other Celtic-styled trad outfits including BATTLEFIELD BAND.

With similar aspirations in both the contemporary and the Celtic-folk fields, LOWE took heart and inspiration from songs north of the border as well as the west, although his true roots lay mainly with the coalmining communities and towns of the north-east. It would be Fellside Records of Cumbria that took Jez under its wing, releasing many a fine album throughout the 1980s. One highlight of that series was his collaboration (**TWO A ROUE** (1986) {*7}) with top hurdy-gurdy exponent Jake Walton, while among his solo material one could vouch for 'Back In Durham Gaol', 'Nearer To Nettles', 'Galloways' and 'Another Man's Wife'. Not content with soaking up plaudits for his solo work, LOWE conjured up the Bad Pennies (named after his final solo outing in 1988, **BAD PENNY** {*6}), a backing group starring musicians Bev Saunders and Rob Kay.

From 1990's **BRIEFLY ON THE STREET** {*6}, which contained the minor classics 'Davis And Golightly' and 'The Famous Working Man', to his latest set, **WOTCHEOR** (2010) {*7}, – which was inspired by north-country people, and which homaged the 1950s BBC radio show 'Wot Cheor Geordie' – his songs have reflected every aspect of the culture around him. Some of his better-known songs have been interpreted by MARY BLACK, GORDON BOK, etc.

Every one of his solidly-crafted and well-thought-out albums (the Green Linnet efforts **TENTERHOOKS** (1995) {*8} and **THE PARISH NOTICES** (1998) {*8}, with JOHNNY HANDLE, come off particularly well) can be recommended to every lover of folk music. Having just lost out to JULIE FOWLIS for the coveted BBC Radio 2 Folksinger Of The Year Award in 2008, he was one of many folk stars invited to perform on the bicentennial birthday homage that was the [Charles] DARWIN SONG PROJECT album. *MCS*

Jez Lowe - vocals, acoustic guitar (w/ session people)

UK Fellside — US not issued

1980. (lp/c) *(FE 023/+C)* **JEZ LOWE** ☐ ⊟
- Sedgefield fair - Roxburgh Castle / Pit boy / Willy's lyke wake / Dark shores / Johnny Seddon / Beaumont's light horse / Poor old Wedgebury / Fill the tankard / Kildale jig / Head of Wear water / Pretty Saro / Wheel of fortune.

1983. (lp/c) *(FE 034/+C)* **THE OLD DURHAM ROAD** ☐ ⊟
- The old Durham waltz / Hard life / Cursed by the caller / My keel lad / Mary Martindale / Annie Munro / High part of the town / I'll never get home / Foggy banks / Black diamonds / The old Durham road. *(cd-iss. Jun 99 +=; FE 034CD)* - Time for leaving / Poor old Wedgebury / Fill the tankard / Head of Wear water / Pretty Saro / Wheel of fortune.

1985. (lp/c) *(FE 049/+C)* **GALLOWAYS** ☐ ⊟
- Back in Durham gaol / The Galloway lad / Gatineau girls / The boys of Belly Row / Northern echoes / Galloways / Old bones / Shippwesea Bay / The honest working way / Chick Henderson's march. *(cd-iss. Mar 98 on Music Pangaea+=; MP 1006CD)* - Sedgefield fair - Roxburgh Castle / Pit boy / Willy's lyke wake / Dark shores / Johnny Seddon / Beaumont's light horse.

1986. (lp/c; by JEZ LOWE AND JAKE WALTON) *(FE 055/+C)* **TWO A ROUE** ☐ ⊟
- Patrik's song - Dance / Brockie lads / Todd's dance - Monferrina / Trees / Japs and English / Reign of the fair maid / Galician dances / The Bergen / Rothbury races - Morpeth lasses / Gold and silver / The ballad of Johnny Collier. *(cd-iss. Jun 02 on Tantobie+=; TTRCD 101)* - Over seal sands / Appleby gallop / The spinning of the wheel.

1988. (lp/c) *(FE 070/+C)* **BAD PENNY** ☐ ⊟
- Another man's wife / A small coal song / The midnight mail / Dandelion clocks / London Danny / Nella can keep it for treasure / The land of the living / Nearer to nettles / Father Mallory's dance / Yankee boots / A new town incident. *(cd-iss. Feb 96; FE 070CD)*

JEZ LOWE AND THE BAD PENNIES

with **Bev Sanders** - vocals, percussion, whistle / **Rob Kay** - vocals, keyboards, melodeon, recorder, percussion

1990. (lp/c/cd) *(FE 079/+C/CD)* **BRIEFLY ON THE STREET**
- You can't take it with you / The famous working man / One man bound / Old hammer-head / Boonas / The soda man / Davis and Golightly / Jordan: The begging bowl / Wannie wind *[cd-only]* / Alice / Fun without fools - Swiss reel / The new moon's arms. *(cd re-iss. Jun 96; same)*

—— **Billy Surgeoner** - bass, accordion, banjo, keyboards; repl. Rob

Nov 93. (lp/c/cd) *(FE 094/+C/CD)* **BEDE WEEPS**
- A call for the north country / These coal town days / Kid Canute / Just like Moses / She'll always be freedom / Greek lightning / Dover, Delaware / Tear-drop two-step / Too up and too down / The bulldog breed / Last of the widows / Mike Neville said it / Bede weeps.

Green Linnet — not issued

Nov 95. (cd) *(GLCD 1161)* **TENTERHOOKS**
- Song of the century / Sweep horizons clean / The crake in the morning / The guilts / Alibi child / Song of the Indian lass / Workhouse / Aloysius / Dry season land / Bait up / Tenterhooks / Homefires - Felton Lonnen - Here's the tender coming. *(re-iss. Aug 05 on Tantobie; TTRCD 106)*

—— added **Johnny Handle** - guitars (solo folk star and of HIGH LEVEL RANTERS)

Mar 98. (cd) *(GLCD 1192)* **THE PARISH NOTICES**
- Glad rags / Tom-tom / Propping / Sod all / Spitting cousins / Spares or repair / The limping drinker's polka / Go away Joe / Had away gan on / The parish notices / Idle time / If I had another penny. *(re-iss. Aug 03 on Tantobie+=; TTRCD 104)* - Easy town / A lass to want me / Slack water sea.

Tantobie — not issued

Jan 01. (d-cd) *(TTRCD 100)* **LIVE AT THE DAVY LAMP** (live)
- Another man's wife / The soda man / Black diamonds / Galloways / Sweep horizons clean / The guilts / The military road / Just like Moses / High part of the town / The new moon's arms / Tom-tom / Old bones / Kid Canute - Scotty Moore's reel / London Danny / Greek lightning / Weave and worry / Big meeting day / Last of the widows / Back in Durham gaol / These coal town days / (introductions) / You can't take it with you / The Bergen.

—— **Judy Dinning** - keyboards, guitar, vocals; repl. HANDLE who continued solo

Aug 03. (cd) *(TTRCD 102)* **HONESTY BOX**
- Skin too thin / Ballad of Tasker Jack / I saw hands / Armstrong's army / Maddison / Latchkey lover / Mother's day / Fancy goods / Matchboxes / The big fear / Long iron.

—— **Andy May** - pipes; repl. unknown female

Jul 04. (cd) *(TTRCD 105)* **DOOLALLY**
- You and your golden vanity / Donnini doolally / Sugar water Sunday / Regina inside / Vikings / The fan dancer's daughter / Hoi polloi / Calico / Keep them bairns away / A peninent's lent / Gull's eye / Bloodstained.

May 07. (cd; as JEZ LOWE) *(TTRCD 109)*
JACK COMMON'S ANTHEM
- Jack Common's anthem / The sea and the deep blue devil / Taking on men / Black trade / The Miami / Will of the people / Yellow hair / Heaney's finger / Working dirty / A few frontiers / Jack's return.

Sep 08. (cd) *(TTRCD 110)* **NORTHERN ECHOES: LIVE ON THE TYNE** (live)
- A call for the north country / Cursed by the caller / A dream of steam and freedom / The boys of Belly Row / Mary Martindale / Too up and too down / A hard life / The famous working man / All trawl / Davis and Golightly / Bait up / I'll never get home - The old Durham waltz / The sun and the moon and me / Chick Henderson's march / Northern echoes / Fun without fools - Swiss reel / The honest working way. *(w/ free DVD)* - Northern Echoes: A Song For Geordie

Sep 10. (cd) *(TTRCD 111)* **WOTCHEOR**
- Barnstorming / A tonic for the toffs / The lost piper / Weather / Watter's coming Annie / Darling's other daughter / Sport / It's a champion life / The ex-pitman's pot-holing pub quiz team / The Judas bus / All clear / Back to the land girls / Bare knuckle / Cobblers / Hands feet / Sale / Gramophone dancing / Why that's it folks.

- (5-7*) compilations, others, etc.-

Jan 93. (cd) *Fellside; (FECD 089)* **BACK SHIFT**
- Back in Durham gaol / Brockie lads / Galloways / Black diamond / The Bergen / Sedgefield fair / The old Durham road / Chick Henderson's march / Japs and English / Old bones / Cursed be the caller / High part of town / Grey cock / The old Durham waltz / Shippersea Bay / The ballad of Johnny Collier / Honest working way.

Amy MACDONALD

Purists might dispute Amy's credentials as a folk artist (think KT TUNSTALL and Kirsty MacColl), but many musos with an ear for folk will hear more a tinge of the Caledonian/Celtic variety. Influenced early on in her career by Fran Healy of Travis, one thing that's clear is that the young singer-songwriter (born August 25, 1987 in Bishopbriggs, near Glasgow) has an abundance of talent and pop appeal.

After a stuttering start with debut single 'Poison Prince' (based on the tempestuous history of Pete Doherty), MACDONALD hit paydirt with two hook-laden singles, 'Mr Rock And Roll' and 'This Is The Life', two of the better moments on her strum-friendly, chart-topping debut album **THIS IS THE LIFE** (2007) {*7}. Although not a major success in the discerning US, she's become an international star and award-winning celeb all over Europe. In 2008 she became engaged to journeyman footballer Steve Lovell (ex-Portsmouth, Dundee, Aberdeen and Falkirk).

Three years in the making, **A CURIOUS THING** (2010) {*6} took her further away from bona-fide folk and into the realms of pop, going Top Five, although only lead single 'Don't Tell Me That It's Over' managed a semi-respectable chart placing. The album's high spots – 'Spark', 'This Pretty Face', 'Love Love' and 'Your Time Will Come' failed to win favour with digital-download punters.

Over her few years in the business, Amy has covered several pop/rock songs including 'Mr Brightside' (The Killers), 'Born To Run' and 'Dancing In The Dark' (Bruce Springsteen), 'Rock 'n' Roll Star' (Oasis), 'Fairytale Of New York' (The POGUES), 'Caledonia' (DOUGIE MACLEAN) and 'A Town Called Malice' (The Jam). *MCS*

Amy Macdonald - vocals, acoustic guitar, piano, drums / + session people

UK Vertigo — US not issued

May 07. (7"/cd-s) *(172 980-4/-2)* POISON PRINCE. / Rock Bottom [ ] [-]
Jul 07. (7") *(173 919-0)* MR ROCK AND ROLL. / What Is Love [12] [-]
(cd-s) *(174 6519)* - ('A') / A wish for for something more / Let's start a band.
Jul 07. (cd) *(173 212-4)* **THIS IS THE LIFE** [1] [-]
- Mr Rock and roll / This is the life / Poison prince / Youth of today / Run / Let's start a band / Barrowland ballroom / LA / A wish for something more / Footballer's wife. *(bonus +=)* - The road to home.
Oct 07. (7") *(174 645-9)* - LA / Footballer's Wife [live from King Tut's] [48] [-]
(cd-s+=) *(174 927-9)* - Mr Rock and roll [live from King Tut's].
(cd-s) *(174 645-8)* - ('A') / Mr Brightside [live from King Tut's].
Dec 07. (cd-s) *(175 526-4)* THIS IS THE LIFE / This Much Is True [28] [-]
Mar 08. (cd-s) *(176 224-4)* RUN / Rock 'n' Roll Star (acoustic) [75] [-]
May 08. (cd-s) *(176 793-8)* POISON PRINCE / Rock Bottom [ ] [-]

Mercury — Decca

Jul 08. (re-cd) *(178 945-5)* <B0011335-02> THIS IS THE LIFE [20] Aug 08 [92]
- [as previous += free cd]:- This is the life (acoustic) / This much is true / Somebody new / Footballer's wife (live from Glasgow Barrowlands) / Fairytale of New York (live from Glasgow Barrowlands) / Mr Brightside (live from Glasgow Barrowlands) / Mr Rock and roll (live from Glasgow Barrowlands) / Rock bottom / The road home. *(hidden track +=)* - Caledonia.
Mar 10. (cd-s) *(273 418-7)* DON'T TELL ME THAT IT'S OVER / A Town Called Malice [Simon Mayo Radio 2 session] [48] [-]
Mar 10. (cd/lp) *(273 114-0/495-1)* **A CURIOUS THING** [4] [-]
- Don't tell me that it's over / Spark / No robots / Love love / An ordinary life / Give it all up / My only one / This pretty face / Troubled soul / Next big thing / Your time will come / What happiness means to me. *(+ hidden track)* - Dancing in the dark. *(d-cd++=; 273 360-2)* - [live at the Barrowlands 2007]:- Poison prince / Youth of today / LA / Footballer's wife / Mr Rock and roll / Mr Brightside / The road to home / This is the life / Run / Rock 'n' roll star / Let's start a band / Caledonia / Fairytale of New York / Barrowland Ballroom.
May 10. (dl-s) *(-)* SPARK [ ] [-]
Jul 10. (cd-s) *(274 551-3)* THIS PRETTY FACE / Give It All Up [acoustic, W14 session] / Born To Run [live] / ['A'-Tiesto remix] [ ] [-]
Oct 10. (dl-s) *(-)* LOVE LOVE [ ] [-]
Dec 10. (dl-s) *(-)* YOUR TIME WILL COME [ ] [-]

Shane MacGOWAN & The POPES (⟹ The POGUES)

MAD DOGS AND ENGLISHMEN (⟹ The WHISKY PRIESTS)

The MAGICKAL FOLK OF THE FARAWAY TREE

A mysterious and obscure outfit who sing in English, French, Manx and Gaelic, this young-ish quartet/quintet come across as very old-timey, a la C.O.B. (Clive's Original Band), or indeed DR. STRANGELY STRANGE.

Formed in Raheny, Dublin in September 2002 by Shane Cullinane, along with Dave Colohan and his girlfriend Caroline Coffey, they took their wyrd name from an Enid Blyton story and were inspired by Peter Kennedy's book 'Folksongs of Britain and Ireland' (1975). Gavin Prior (from UNITED BIBLE STUDIES and Murmansk) almost immediately joined the team, recording the odd mini-CD-r in Shane's kitchen.

Self-released on their own Deserted Village imprint, **THE MILDEW LEAF** (2004) {*6} and **THE CAT'S MELODEON** (2005) {*6}combined folklore trad pieces with a handful of Celtic-dimension 'Wicker Man'-like compositions. 'Spencer The Rover', 'Sweet Thames Flow Softly' and 'Twa Corbies' were of course sourced, while banjos, acoustic guitars, harmoniums and a small guest list put the finishing touches to the dark timbre of their sombre sound. Finally released in 2010, the double-CD **THE SOUP AND THE SHILLING** {*7} took these embryonic recordings and tagged on some in-the-can sessions from 2006. 'Blackbirds And Thrushes' and 'Locks And Bolts' were probably the best examples. Of course, ALASDAIR ROBERTS had already become top dog of the trad-meets-nu-folk genre. *MCS*

Gavin Prior, Dave Colohan, Shane Cullinane, Caroline Coffey

Ire/UK Deserted Village — US not issued

2004. (ltd-m-cd-r) *(dv 07)* **THE MILDEW LEAF** [-] Ire [-]
- In aimsir bhaint an fheir / Spencer the rover / Le bon marain / The blackthorn tree / Twa corbies / Is iomaidh coisceim fada / Sweet Thames flow softly [*] / Time to go home.
2005. (ltd-m-cd-r) *(dv 20)* **THE CAT'S MELODEON** [-] Ire [-]
- Trelawny / The mermaid / Caol is eadar mi islain / Daybreak / Donal-G / Mrs. Cudmore's air / Here's health to all true lovers.
Nov 09. (ltd-7" brown; shared) *(AFR-SS02)* SEASONAL SEVENS: AUTUMN [ ] [-]
- [Pamela Wyn Shannon: Woolgathering] / The Blackthorn Tree.
(above issued on Autumn Ferment, below split with 'Deadslackstring')
—— added **Sean Og**
Jan 10. (d-cd) *(TRUENOTE 013 – dv37)* **THE SOUP AND THE SHILLING** [compilation//rec. 2006] [ ] [-]
- (THE MILDEW LEAF minus *) + Being here has caused my sorrow / (THE CAT'S MELODEON) // An bhanaltra / Cambourne hill / Trois jeunes tambours / I binged avree / Blackbirds and thrushes / Locks and bolts / She was a rum one / My lodging it is on the cold ground / The summer will come / Going to mass last Sunday / The deluded lover / Up to the rigs / The cat's melodeon / The Haselbury girl.

MAGPIE LANE

Formed in Oxford and named after one of the city's oldest and narrowest streets, MAGPIE LANE was conceived in 1992, initially as a one-off project to record a cassette album of Oxfordshire songs and tunes called **THE OXFORD RAMBLE** (1993) {*6}. Comprising vocalists and musicians Andy

Turner, Ian Giles (of OXFORD WAITS), Tom Bower, Mat Green, Isobel Dams, Peter Acty and Joanne Acty (Chris Leslie was an auxiliary member in the 1990s), the highly respected folk ensemble performed mainly Morris and country dance tunes.

Earning some degree of success, the group decided to continue as an extra-curricular activity, delivering two further themed sets: **SPEED THE PLOUGH** (1994) {*6} – with newcomer Di Whitehead – and the festive **WASSAIL!** (1995) {*6}. Another Anglo-centric recording, **JACK-IN-THE-GREEN** (1998) {*6}, was the curtain call for Peter and Joanne Acty, to be replaced by the multi-talented Benji Kirkpatrick (son of JOHN KIRKPATRICK).

A TASTE OF ALE (2001) {*7} was exactly what it said on the tin, a celebratory exploration (with accompanying book) of the world of the drinking song through the eyes and mouth of folksong author Roy Palmer. Staggering into album five, but without Tom and Di (replaced by Marguerite Hutchinson and Sophie Polhill, soon to be Sophie Thurman), **SIX FOR GOLD** (2003) {*6} maintained their high profile.

Expanding his horizons further, in-demand sessionman extraordinaire BENJI KIRKPATRICK (who had already completed a few solo CDs) joined BELSHAZZAR'S FEAST, BELLOWHEAD and numerous other trad-folk acts. The Magpies' seasonal album **KNOCK AT THE KNOCKER, RING AT THE BELL** (2006) {*6}, with Jon Fletcher of Epona on board, was a stop-gap while they took a sabbatical. They're still going strong, and 2011 will see their recording comeback. *MCS*

Andy Turner - vocals, Anglo concertina, melodeon, percussion (of OYSTER BAND) / **Ian Giles** - vocals, percussion (of OXFORD WAITS, of Mellstock Band) / **Tom Bower** - vocals, wind, percussion / **Mat Green** - fiddle (ex-Woodpecker Band) / **Isobel Dams** - cello, vocals / **Peter Acty** - guitar, vocals / **Joanne Acty** - vocals

UK Beautiful Jo — US not issued

1993. (c) *(BEJO-3)* **THE OXFORD RAMBLE**: Songs and Tunes of Oxfordshire ☐ ⊟
- Magpie Lane / As I walked through the meadows / The first of May / Oxford city / The Oxfordshire damosel / John Barleycorn / Johnny so long – Eynsham poaching song / Old Molly Oxford / The Boar's Head carol / The Oxford scholar / Great Tom is cast / Old Tom of Oxford – Bonny Christ Church bells / Astley's ride / The Oxford ramble / Trunkles / Near Woodstock town (the Oxfordshire tragedy) / Double lead through / Princess Royal / Husbandman and servingman / Banbury hill – As I was going to Banbury / Adderbury medley: Stourton wake – Constant Billy – Cobb's horse / May Day carol. *(cd-iss. Oct 99; BEJOCD-3)*

—— **Di Whitehead** - cello, recorder, vocals; repl. Dams (Green was also temp. rested)

Jun 94. (c) *(BEJO-4)* **SPEED THE PLOUGH**: Songs and tunes of rural England ☐ ⊟
- The carter's health / Regent's fete – Sir Roger de Coverley / Green bushes / The highwayman outwitted / Jockey to the fair / Bonny at morn / Davy, Davy, knick-knack / Poor old horse / Kempshott hunt – Death of the fox / Swaggering boney / The painful plough / Fool's jig / The mistress's health / Girl with the blue dress on – Swiss boy / Bushes and briars / The Reading summer dance / The Beverly maid and the tinker / The turtle dove – Bobbing Joe / The shepherd's song / Shooter's hornpipe / Bill Brown / Streets of Oxford / All jolly fellows – Speed the plough. *(cd-iss. Oct 99; BEJOCD-4)*

Nov 95. (cd) *(BEJOCD-8)* **WASSAIL!**: A Country Christmas ☐ ⊟
- The Gloucestershire wassail / The bottom of the punchbowl – The Christmas baby / The sheep are neath the snow / Saint Stephen / Lullay my liking / The holly and the ivy / The trees are all bare / Frost and snow – Snow on the hills / Down in yon forest / The king / The Christmas holidays, or, Stuff your guts / The Somerset wassail / Hogmanay jig – We wish you a merry New Year / Babes in the wood / Poor frozen-out gardeners / Here we come a-wassailing / Nowell: The bory's hede / King Herod and the cock / The standing stones / Christmas day in the morning – The Sussex carol.

—— Green was temp. rested once again; always on hand, guest Chris Leslie

Jul 98. (cd) *(BEJOCD-22)* **JACK-IN-THE-GREEN**: English songs and tunes ☐ ⊟
- May song / Mother Goose – The priest in his boots – Hopkinson's favourite / In Sheffield park / Thame fair / The flowers of Edinburgh / A rosebud in June / Jack-in-the-green – Jack's alive / The sheepstealer / Quickstep at the battle of Prague – Welch's polka / Northill May song – The cuckoo's nest / The seeds of love / Just as the tide was flowing / The banks of the Lea / Font Whatling's polka – Galloway girth / Two ravens / Mayer's song – The Rochdale coconut dance – Three around three.

—— the Actys were repl. by **Benji Kirkpatrick** - vocals, bouzouki, guitar (re-**Green**)

Feb 01. (cd) *(BEJOCD-32)* **A TASTE OF ALE** ☐ ⊟
- A drop of good beer / The drunkard and the pig / Bryng us in good ale / The mail coach guard / O good ale / Stingo / Of honest malt liquor / Trowl the bowl / So was I / The beautiful landlady / The merry hostess / The beer drinking Briton / Beer boys beer / Hop picking song / The hop ground / Friezland ale / The bad-husband's folly / Drunk last night / John Barleycorn.

—— **Marguerite Hutchinson** - vocals, recorders, flute, whistles; repl. Tom

—— **Sophie Polhill/Thurman** - vocals, cello; repl. Di

Jan 03. (cd) *(BEJOCD-42)* **SIX FOR GOLD** ☐ ⊟
- The jovial cutler / The constant lovers / Round about the maypole – Asiatic / John Reilly / Juniper, gentle and Rosemary / A-begging I will go / O once I was a shepherd boy / Long peggin' awl / Stottycake polka – Ganivelle / Bold William Taylor / Foggy dew / I saw a maid in my father's garden / Stokes Bay / Argeers – Polka d'Auvergne / Lazarus / My old hat that I got on.

—— **Jon Fletcher** - vocals, guitar, mandolin, bouzouki, harmonica; repl. BENJI KIRKPATRICK who went solo and joined BELSHAZZAR'S FEAST, BELLOWHEAD, etc.

Oct 06. (cd) *(BEJOCD-52)* **KNOCK AT THE KNOCKER, RING AT THE BELL**: Carols, Songs and Tunes for the Christmas Season ☐
- Foster (while shepherds watched) / Nowell Nowell / All you who are to mirth inclined / The winter's tale – Christmas polka / The man that lives / The cherry tree carol / November drinking song / Hymn for Christmas day / A virgin unspotted / This is the truth sent from above / Winter – Christmas day in the mornin' / Lo! the eastern sages rise / The nine joys of Mary / Wren boys' song.

MALCOLM'S INTERVIEW (⟹ GOD'S LITTLE MONKEYS)

Laura MARLING

With maturity and soul beyond her tender years, Hampshire born-and-bred MARLING (b. Feb 1, 1990 in Eversley) is part of a wave of young British artists who have embraced their English folk roots but crossed over to find a mainstream audience. Her simple but playful style evokes as much the spirit of BILLY BRAGG as of JONI MITCHELL or NORMA WATERSON.

MARLING was just sixteen when her first few fizzing tunes, posted on MySpace, caught the attention of the listening public. She cut her teeth as a live act as part of what was supposed to be a new west London folk movement (although she lived in Reading), roughing it with the likes of Jamie T and MUMFORD & SONS and as part of NOAH AND THE WHALE. She drifted away from the latter act as her music took centre stage and her relationship with frontman Charlie Fink went sour. The latter's finest hour, 'The First Days Of Spring', was said to have been written in response to the couple's break-up.

MARLING's brittle but heartfelt debut album, **ALAS I CANNOT SWIM** {*7}, arrived in 2008 to considerable acclaim, receiving a deserved Mercury Music Prize Award nomination (she was, ah, 'Elbow'd' out). Top tracks included the BEIRUT-esque 'Crawled Out Of The Sea' and lead singles 'Ghosts' and 'My Manic And I'.

In late 2009 she teamed up with producer Ethan Johns – son of Glyn Johns, nephew of Andy Johns – to expand her bare-bones style into a collection of crisp, bright and thoughtfully arranged songs for **I SPEAK BECAUSE I CAN** (2010) {*8}. Marcus Mumford showed up to lend some backing vocals, but at the heart there was a set of songs, rich with narratives, about everything from celebrations of her relationship with her father – in 'Goodbye England (Covered In Snow)' – to a woman's letters to her husband during the second world war ('What He Wrote'). Once again she received a Mercury nomination, losing out to The XX this time around.

2011 brought more plaudits as she won Best Solo Artist at the NME awards and beat Girls Aloud's Cheryl Cole to Best British Female Artist at the Brits, but the hyperbole was justified. Laura emerged on to the scene with her talent fully formed, with a deep understanding of songcraft. Chances are that her best is yet to come. *MR*

Laura Marling - vocals, guitar, bass, piano / with **Charlie Fink, Tom Hobden** (from NOAH AND THE WHALE) + others

UK Way Out West — US not issued

Aug 07. (ltd-7" ep) *(WOW 003)* THE LONDON TOWN EP ☐ ⊟
- London town / She's changed / Failure / Tap at my window.

Virgin — Astralwerks

Oct 07. (7" ep) *(VS 1956)* MY MANIC AND I ☐ ⊟
- New romantic / Night terror / My Manic and I / Typical.

Jan 08. (7") *(VS 1964)* GHOSTS. / Man Sings About Romance ☐ ⊟
(cd-s) *(VSCDT 1964)* - ['A'] / The needle and the damage done.

Feb 08. (cd/lp) *(CD+/V 3040)* <ASW 34997> **ALAS I CANNOT SWIM** 45 ☐
- Ghosts / Old stone / Tap at my window / Failure / You're no god / Cross your fingers / Crawled out of the sea (interlude) / My Manic and I / Night terror / The captain and the hourglass / Shine / Your only doll (Dora). *(cd-box-iss. as 'SONG BOX'+=; CDVX 3040)* - Alas I cannot swim. *(lp-iss. Aug 08 on F-Minor; 234997) (lp re-iss. Dec 08 +=; V 3040)* - [live DVD tracks].

Jun 08. (7") *(VS 1973)* CROSS YOUR FINGERS. / I'm A Fly ☐ ⊟
(cd-s) *(VSCDT 1973)* - ['A'] / Blackberry stone.

Oct 08. (ltd-7") *(VS 1979)* NIGHT TERROR. / Alpha Shallows ☐ ⊟

Dec 09. (one-sided-7") *(VS 2004)* GOODBYE ENGLAND (COVERED IN SNOW) ☐ ⊟

Mar 10. (cd) *(CDV 3075)* <???> **I SPEAK BECAUSE I CAN** [4] Apr10 [ ]
- Devil's spoke / Made by maid / Rambling man / Blackberry stone / Alpha shallows / Goodbye England (covered in snow) / Hope in the air / What he wrote / Darkness descends / I speak because I can. *(w/dvd+=; CDVX 3075)* - [Laura Marling And Friends: Live From The Royal Festival Hall].

Mar 10. (dl-s) *(-)* DEVIL'S SPOKE [97] [-]

Virgin Third Man

Nov 10. (7") <*TMR 044*> BLUES RUN THE GAME. / The Needle And The Damage Done [-] [ ]

Beverley MARTYN

Although she'd released two collaborative albums ('Stormbringer!' and 'The Road To Ruin') in the late 60s with her then husband JOHN MARTYN, BEVERLEY MARTYN (nee Kutner, born 1947, Coventry) didn't deliver a solo set until the arrival of the new millennium. Her first solo record, the Randy Newman-penned single 'Happy New Year' (which launched Deram Records), was issued in 1966, credited simply to 'Beverley'. Her second, 'Museum', came out a year later.

She made an appearance at the 1967 Monterey Pop Festival, and suggested to Paul Simon the allusion to Donovan in the SIMON & GARFUNKEL song 'Fakin' It'. Earlier she'd been part of English jug band The Levee Breakers, who released one 45, 'Babe I'm Gonna Leave You' / 'Wild About My Loving' for Parlophone in 1965.

Estranged from John after the birth of her second child in 1971, they were divorced at the end of the 1970s. Beverley was posted missing on the musical front for the next two decades, only to reappear, LINDA THOMPSON-like, with **NO FRILLS** (2001) {*5}, a record that was not exactly the bees' knees, although it did contain a sort of rebuke to her former husband John in 'Lady On The Rampage' and the jazzy 'She Is'. *MCS*

Beverley Martyn - vocals, acoustic guitar / with session people

UK Deram US not issued

Aug 66. (7"; as BEVERLEY) *(DM 101)* HAPPY NEW YEAR. / Where The Good Times Are [ ] [-]

Jul 67. (7"; as BEVERLEY) *(DM 137)* MUSEUM. / [Denny Cordell Ensemble track] [ ] [-]

Beverly married JOHN MARTYN and teamed up with him professionally on two sets.

One World Blueprint

Jan 01. (cd) *(OW 112CD)* <*BPCD 4363*> **NO FRILLS** [ ] Feb 01 [ ]
- Dreaming of justice / Potter's blues / Friends or lovers / Security / Primrose path / How strong / She is / Lady on the rampage / Percy / Ancient wisdom / People that hurt.

MARY JANE

Taking their cue from classic folk-rock acts like TREES, MR FOX and FOTHERINGAY, Southampton outfit MARY JANE set out their wyrd musical agenda in November 1993, having formerly had a brief spell as Magic Cat.

Formed by guitarist Paul Alan Taylor and centred around the substantial talents of vocalist Joanne Quinn (plus fiddler Peter Miln, bassist Geoff Newitt and drummer Nick Beresford-Davies), the quintet signed a deal with German-based imprint September Gurls, releasing a fresh arrangement of the trad standard 'She Moved Through The Fair' as their first single in 1995.

With Martin Griffin in for Newitt, **HAZY DAYS** (1996) {*6} evoked a considerable response from the folk fraternity – the band's versions of 'Blackwaterside' and 'My Lagan Love' were particularly welcome.

Joanne, Paul and funky Chooby multi-instrumentalist Peter Jardine were behind the fragile folk of offshoot trio ZANEY JANEY, although only one eponymous Celtic-jazz-psych collection {*6} (1997) was forthcoming.

The ethereal **THE GATES OF SILENT MEMORY** (1999) {*7}, MARY JANE's second set, embraced the folk of old while updating their unpretentious sounds for the new post-millennium generation. Among the songs to get their treatment were 'Boys Of Bedlam', 'Janey Picking Cockles' and 'The Silver Whistle'; also performing on this set were viola player Chris Lilley and harmony vocalist Gail Holliman.

Stuck together as a stop-gap for the group while personnel changes were rife, **TACIT** (2001) {*6} showed that whatever beset them, the band could cope. With a settled line-up of Joanne and Paul, plus violinist Gillie Leach, bassist Steve Bayley and drummer Andrew Pidgeon, **TO THE PRETTIEST ONE** {*7}, released in 2002, was brighter and sharper than its predecessors. The late 2000s saw MARY JANE finding their feet once again (having worked with vocalist Lucy Rutherford of Arlen on stage), although they were almost knocked off them when Gillie was involved in a serious car crash in 2009. New personnel had previously arrived in the shape of Jon Hawkes and Steve Barker, while American Celtic fiddler Serena Smith took Gillie's place.

The long-time-coming **EVE** (2010) {*7} arrived just in time to save the day. Demure and unassuming, like the best Brit-folk-rock acts at their peak, trad ballads such as 'Cruel Sister' (arguably that song's best arrangement ever) and 'Twa Corbies' showed they'd lost nothing of their ethereal touch, and the title track is a must for ALL ABOUT EVE fans. *MCS*

Joanne Quinn - vocals, flute / **Paul Alan Taylor** - guitars, bouzouki / **Peter Miln** - fiddle, mandolin / **Geoff Newitt** - bass / **Nick Beresford-Davies** - drums, percussion

UK September Gurls US not issued

Nov 95. (7"green) *(SGs 16)* SHE MOVED THRO' THE FAIR. / The Snow / Lagan Love [-] German [-]

—— **Martin Griffin** - bass; repl. Newitt

Jan 96. (cd) *(SGCD 10)* **HAZY DAYS** [-] German [-]
- Hazy days / Dreams of the forest / Under the broad-leaved tree / Mary Jane blues / Medley: Jig of slurs – Blarney – Pilgrim / Blackwaterside / In my garden / 1970 / Wilderness song / Glasgerion / Our Lady Babalon / Lagan love. *(UK-iss. Sep 97; same)*

Nov 97. (7"blue) *(SGs 19)* ISLE OF WIGHT. / Polly Pretty Polly / Oxford City [-] German [-]

May 99. (cd/lp) *(SGCD 21)* **THE GATES OF SILENT MEMORY** [-] German [-]
- Waiting for the storm / Boys of bedlam / Isle of Wight / Medley: Half-sick of shadows – Fiddlin' Mary / The silver whistle / A newer day / Flibbertigibbet / The far watchtowers / Twilight song / Janey picking cockles / Oxford city / Brigit's daughter / The gates of silent memory. *(lp w/ 7")*

—— Emily Tooke (percussion) briefly repl. Nick on stage

Acony Bell not issued

Oct 01. (ltd-lp) *(none)* **TACIT** [live sessions] [ ] [-]
- Reaping the rye – Cliffs of Moher / I loved a lass / Lady Margaret / Maid on the shore / La rotta / Polly on the shore / Morrison's / I roved out – Sleepy Maggie / Wayfaring stranger / Night visiting song / Cooley's – Gravel walk / She moved thro' the fair / Blackwaterside. *(cd-iss. Jan 02 on Seventh Wave; 7W 001CD)*

—— **Jo** + **Paul** added **Gillie Leach** - violin / **Steve Bayley** - bass + **Andrew Pidgeon** - drums

Seventh Wave not issued

Jan 02. (cd) *(7W 002CD)* **TO THE PRETTIEST ONE** [ ] [-]
- Deus meus / Leaves are falling / Three maidens / Journey / Bruton town / Helios / No effort required / Fragments / Medley: The morning dew – The lads of Laois / Mahadev / Phaethon / Spiral / Deus meus (reprise) / Return to Milltown.

—— added **Serena Smith** (b. USA) - fiddle, mandolin, vocals (Gillie was involved in a serious car crash in 2009)

—— **Jon Hawkes** - bass + **Steve Barker** - drums; repl. Griffin + Davies

Talking Elephant not issued

Nov 10. (cd) *(TECD 168)* **EVE** [ ] [-]
- Twa corbies / Eve / Cruel sister / Stubborn / Clonakilty / Let the fire begin / The great silkie / So be wise / When I was in my prime / Lovely Joan / Eve [single version].

- (8-10*) compilations -

Jun 11. (cd) *Talking Elephant; (TECD 180)* **BRIGIT'S DAUGHTER** [ ] [-]
- Hazy days / Dreams of the forest / Wilderness song / Lagan love / Time slides by / Lazy summer days / Sad day / A little bridge / Waiting for the storm / Medley: Half sick of shadows – Fiddlin' Mary / The silver whistle / Twilight song / Janey picking cockles / Oxford city / Brigit's daughter / The gates of silent memory / Reaping the rye – Cliffs of Moher / I loved a lass / Lady Margaret / Maid on the shore / Polly on the shore / Leaves are falling / Journey / Helios / Mahadev / Deus meus (reprise) / Return to Milltown / The rain in the summer.

ZANEY JANEY

Jo + **Paul** plus **Peter Jardine** - guitar, vocals (of Chooby)

Sep 96. (7") *(SGs 18)* SAD DAY. / Prelude [-] German [-]

Jun 97.<6>(cd/lp) *(SGCD 14)* **ZANEY JANEY** [-] German [-]
- Janey's jig / Autumn dream / The trip / Time slides by / Lazy summer days / Meadow fayre / Cut your hair / Sad day / Raspberry jam at the beatnik emporium / Blues for the goddess / Circle / A little bridge / Begin / Janey's gig. *(cd+=)* - [hidden track].

The MARY JANES (⟹ CHRISTOPHER, Mic)

Julie MATTHEWS (⟹ Chris WHILE)

MAWKIN / MAWKIN: CAUSLEY

Formed in Chelmsford, Essex in 2002 by teenage brothers David (on guitar) and James Delarre (fiddle), the lads were unfortunately tagged as "folk's boy band", even several years into their career. Festival folkies MAWKIN (which means "scarecrow") were duly completed by bassist/pianist Danny Crump and melodeon-player Alex Goldsmith, their promise and talent already shining through in 2005's medley-friendly mini-set/EP, **EXTENDED PROCRASTINATION** {*6}; check out its punning finale 'Something About Tents – A Tent Deficit Syndrome'. In much the same manner, debut album proper **THE FAIR ESSEX** (2006) {*7} (another pun) displayed influences from JOHNNY CUNNINGHAM to SHOW OF HANDS on tracks like 'Horses Never Smile – The Villagers'.

And then there were five, fifth member being the much-acclaimed solo singer and accordionist Jim Causley (formerly of DEVIL'S INTERVAL). The Devon man's experience and MAWKIN's exuberance saw MAWKIN: CAUSLEY (as they were now billed) build up a strong fan base over the course of two albums for Navigator Records, the mini-set **COLD RUIN** (2008) {*7} and their first full album, **THE AWKWARD RECRUIT** (2009) {*8}. Produced by Stu Hanna (of MEGSON), the latter record took a fresh approach to the murder ballad 'Cutty Wren' and the continental 'The Saucy Sailor'. The group's dexterity and musicianship were abundant on Gallic/Eastern instrumentals 'L'homme Arme' and 'Todos Los Bienes Del Mundo'. *MCS*

MAWKIN

David Delarre - acoustic guitar, mandolin, banjo / **James Delarre** - fiddle / **Danny Crump** - bass, piano / **Alex Goldsmith** - melodeon

UK Good Form — US not issued

Jan 05. (m-cd) *(MKN 001)* **EXTENDED PROCRASTINATION**
- Saint Anne's reel – Lexy Macaskill / Pachete – Salsonette / Le crump – Jump at the sun / Enviken's waltz – The pernod waltz / The Arran boat – Herbert the sherbet / Something about tents – A tent deficit syndrome.

Sep 06. (cd) *(MKN 002)* **THE FAIR ESSEX**
- The magic mawkin – The wonderful discovery of Bob Smee / Leaving Britanny / Something about tents – A tent deficit syndrome / Banks of Dee – The brown velvet waltz / Trip to Berwick – Not a natural dancer / Woods waltz – Le mas noyer / Alexander's hornpipe / French set / Monday morning – Jack Lavender's No.1 – Cleaveland Park / Salsonette (slight return) / The glorious 13th – Unknown / Horses never smile – The villagers.

MAWKIN: CAUSLEY

—— added **Jim Causley** - vocals, accordion (ex-DEVIL'S INTERVAL)

Navigator — not issued

Aug 08. (m-cd) *(NAVIGATOR 14)* **COLD RUIN**
- George's son / Botany Bay / Marriners / Come my lads / Cookie monster / New York trader.

May 09. (cd) *(NAVIGATOR 19)* **THE AWKWARD RECRUIT**
- Jolly broom man / L'homme arme / Drummer boy for Waterloo / Keeper of the game / Cutty Wren / The saucy sailor / Todos los bienes de mundo / The downfall of Charing Cross / Cropper lads / Greenlander / The awkward recruit / I am the song.

—— CAUSLEY would return to solo work later in 2011

Simon MAYOR (& Hilary JAMES)

If you can vaguely remember the 1970s folk/blues/ragtime outfit SPREDTHICK, you will have heard the first offerings of versatile English violinist SIMON MAYOR (born October 5, 1953, Sheffield, Yorkshire) and his singing partner Hilary Jones (b. August 4, 1952, Stoke-on-Trent). From 1973 to 1980, the duo/trio (Phil Fentimen had superseded a string of players) had performed all over the country, but managed to deliver one solitary set, **SPREDTHICK** (1979) {*6}. Composers included JOHN JAMES, PATRICK SKY, George and Ira Gershwin and of course the trio themselves.

Although they occasionally surfaced as bluegrass swing act Slim Panatella & The Mellow Virginians alongside vocalist/mandolinist Andy Baum, it was really down to HILARY JAMES (still as Jones at this time, to comply with Equity rules) and SIMON MAYOR – as they were billed at times – to continue the recording schedule. **CRAVING THE DEW** (1982) {*5} encompassed traditional tunes, songs by Hoagy Carmichael, the Gershwins and MAYOR himself, plus a few jigs-and-reels medleys. The BBC also enlisted Simon's services as songwriter on a number of TV programmes including 'Newsnight', 'Play School', 'Kilroy', 'Listening Corner', etc.

More than just dabbling in classical music as well as TV themes, etc, the multi-talented MAYOR has released more than his fair share of music over the past three decades or so, while Hilary has taken a less prolific approach to her recordings, all of which (it is hoped) are listed in the discography below. (Note: the Hilary James who released 'Flesh And Blood' with her father Bob James in 1995, and a subsequent festive set, was not the Hilary discussed here.)

Out of the many recordings in MAYOR's exhaustive catalogue (from 1990's **THE MANDOLIN ALBUM** {*7} to his solo comeback in 2006, **MUSIC FROM A SMALL ISLAND** {*7}), the hour-long live 2001 collaborative set with Hilary, **DUOS** {*8}, is perhaps the most representative of the true talent and dexterity of the pair. It was also the Daily Telegraph's Folk Record of the Year.

Simon was also part of trad-folk supergroup The WORKING PARTY (alongside Troy Donockley, CHRIS LESLIE, Chris Parkinson and MAARTIN ALLCOCK) for a special **LIVE AT THE MILL** (2006, recorded in 2005) {*6} night at the Mill Arts Centre in Banbury.

On a footnote: legendary folk pianist Beryl Marriott, who had worked with Hilary and Simon, died after a long illness on July 30, 2010. She had been part of the folk scene since the late 1950s, working with her husband Roger and scores of acts including DAVE SWARBRICK, IAN CAMPBELL and MARTIN CARTHY. *MCS*

SPREDTHICK

Hilary James - vocals, acoustic guitar, double bass / **Simon Mayor** - violin / **Phil Fentimen** (b. Aug 10 '54) – double bass, acoustic guitar; repl. Andy McGhee (banjo), who repl. Peter Jagger (guitar), who repl. Andrew Mathewson

UK Actual — UK not issued

1979. (lp) *(ACT 003)* **SPREDTHICK**
- If only I / Separation blues / My Johnny was a shoemaker / Sonatina in C major / If your kisses can't hold the man you love / The real American / Satisfied and tickled too / Rising sun blues / They all laughed / Black and white rag / Home James / The saucy bold robber.

—— Hilary continued to work with MAYOR on his solo sets …

HILARY JONES and SIMON MAYOR

as she was then credited (Equity-tied)

Waterfront — not issued

1982. (lp) *(WF 017)* **CRAVING THE DEW**
- Hong Kong blues / Melancholy / Daley's reel / Meet me where they play the blues / Russian rag / Weeping willow / Nice work if you can get it / Poor girl blues / The old music master / Polly Vaughan / Wild rose of the mountain / Brave wings / Bold Reynard / Medley: The pig's jig – Radstock – Jack's maggot.

Acoustics — not issued

Nov 84. (7") *(ACS 001)* THE CHRISTMAS LULLABY. / Yorkshire Wassail

HILARY JAMES and SIMON MAYOR

Jul 87. (c) *(ACS 002)* **MUSICAL MYSTERY TOUR: GOBBLE! GOBBLE! GOBBLE!** [children's]
- Sketch: Turkeys / The sailor's hornpipe / The parrot song / The house next door / The hen's march / Sketch: More turkeys / It ain't gonna rain no more / Herring's head / Sally Ann Johnson / The fireman's song / I like to eat / Sketch: Still no more turkeys / The fat fat farmer / Clucking in henhouse / Lime rock / The bucking mule / Gobble! Gobble! Gobble! *(cd-iss. Aug 93; ACS 002CD) (cd re-iss. Jul 00; CDACD 036)*

Jul 88. (c) *(ACS ???)* **MUSICAL MYSTERY TOUR 2: UP IN A BIG BALLOON** [children's]
- I love all the fruit / Sketch: Birdwatching / A flock of fat flamingoes / Sketch: The 37-toed hummingbird / Hum hum hum / The slippery slimy trout / Wait for the wagon / Sketch: Mrs Tucker phones / Old Dan Tucker's tune / Pipped at the post / Old Dan Tucker's song / Give me a drum / The farmyard tango – Donkey can-can / Hoots and whistles / Buffalo girls / Sketch: Simon blows up the balloon / Up in a big balloon. *(cd-iss. Jul 00; CDACS 037)*

Jul 89. (c) *(ACS ???)* **MUSICAL MYSTERY TOUR 3: A BIG SURPRISE** [children's]
- If you want to talk to a bee / Simon's doorbell / My bike / Sketch: Simon sits in a cowpat / A big surprise / Sketch: Counting sheep / Sleepy sheep / Chico the bandit / Sketch: Toffees in the grass / Toss the pancake / Sketch: Cycling in woods / Will a willow / Sketch: Talking to scarecrow / The scarecrow song / The trumpet hornpipe

/ Sketch: Digging for treasure / Bobbed in on the tide / King Canute at Cleethorpes / The road to Banbury. *(cd-iss. Jul 00; CDACS 038)*

Nov 90. (cd) *(ACS ???)* **MUSICAL MYSTERY TOUR 4: SNOWMEN AND KINGS AND ALL SORT OF THINGS** [children's]
- The snowman's song / Australian Father Christmas / I saw three ships / When the snow falls softly down / Sketch: Hilary feeds cat / Shipwreck on Hawaii / Sketch: Hilary waters the plants / Crazy lazy Daisy / The Turkish toetapper / Clickety clack / Sketch: The trainspotter / Under the old oak tree / Sketch: Mrs Tucker and the horse / Flop-eared mule / Sketch: Dan gets a present / Old Dan Tucker's last ride / Sketch: Dan loses his teeth / King Wastelot / A magpie sitting on a broken chair. *(cd-iss. Jul 00; CACS 039)*

Jul 91. (cd) *(ACS ???)* **MUSICAL MYSTERY TOUR 5: MIDSUMMER MARKET** [children's]
- Cocos island / Sketch: Simon phones Hilary / This way that way / The spider in the shed / Sketch: Do you wash your clothes? / Granny had a washboard / The grand old Duke of York / Curly tails / Cajun yodel / Harry the hiccupping horse / Greedy goats / Sketch: At the market / Thomas and the strange Stradivari / Midsummer market / Sketch: Going home / Midsummer market (reprise). *(cd-iss.Jul00; CDACS 040)*

SIMON MAYOR

solo work with traditional and classical leanings

Nov 90. (cd) *(CDACS 012)* **THE MANDOLIN ALBUM**
- Jump the gun – Reelin' over the rooftops / Two seagulls call from my birch tree / Maple flames / Solomon / The exchange / When summer comes again / Concerto for mandolin and strings in C / Les nuits d'ete / Tune for a mop fair / Jericho waltz / Wheelin' and dealin' / Three sonatas and 3 partitas / The moss trooper medley. *(c-iss. Aug 95; ACS 012C) (re-iss. Jul 01; same)*

Nov 91. (cd) *(CDACS 014)* **THE SECOND MANDOLIN ALBUM**
- 21 Hungarian dances / The Buttermere waltz / The hoppings / Symphony No.104, 'London' in D [Haydn] / 15 three-part inventions / Pipped at the post / Two days in Tuscany / The great bear / Double concerto for two mandolins and strings in G / The old man of the mountains / Sonatas for keyboard / Water music / Dead Sea dances. *(c-iss. Aug 95; ACS 014C) (cd re-iss. May 97; same)*

Nov 92. (cd) *(CDACS 015)* **WINTER WITH MANDOLINS** [festive]
- I saw three ships / Ballades / All hallows dance / La rejouissance [from Handel's Music for the Royal Fireworks] / Song of the birds / The angel Gabriel / Toss the pancake / German cradle song / Past three o'clock / God rest ye swinging gentlemen / When the birds fly / Mad as a March hare / Hail smiling morn / Biscay carol / Christmas candle. *(c-iss. Aug 95; ACS 015C) (re-iss.Oct06; same)*

—— (Acoustics CDACS 024) is a 1994 CD by Slim Panatella & The Mellow Virginians

Jul 95. (cd/c) *(CDACS 025/+C)* **THE ENGLISH MANDOLIN**
- St Paul's suite / Molly on the shore / Nell Gwyn / Staines Morris / The unfortunate tailor / Lord Marlborough / The second part of Musick's hand-maid / Capriol suite.

—— (Acousics CDACS 027) may be a shelved Mandolin Allstars set

Sep 96. (cd) *(CDACS 028)* **THE MANDOLIN TUTOR** [instructional]

Nov 97. (cd; as The SIMON MAYOR QUINTET) *(CDACS 034)* **MANDOLINQUENTS** [swing/ragtime/classical]
- Slavonic dance No.8 / Dance of the sugar plum fairy / Eine kleine nachtmusik / Plum blossoms in the snow / Beat out that rhythm on a drum / Down by the Sally Gardens / The Boston ballyhoo / Cheek to cheek / Russian rag / Pavanne pour une infante defunte / The Piccolino / He's gone away / Apanhei-te / A nightingale sang in Berkeley Square. *(re-iss. Jul 01; same)*

—— with guests Hilary, Beryl Marriott + Frank Kilkelly

Mar 98. (cd) *(CDACS 035)* **NEW CELTIC MANDOLIN**
- Mrs Murray of Abercarney / Waynesboro / Carolan's frolics / Little Molly-o / Dance of the water boatmen / Huish the cat / Two Breton tunes: Eliz Iza and Derobee de Guingamp / Welsh medley: Farewell to the shore and Ymdaith gwyr dyfnaint / Ye la le lo / Niel Gow's lament for Abercarney / Mount and go / The butterfly / The wasp reel / Teetotaler's fancy / Dark and slender boy.

Jul 01. (cd; as Simon MAYOR and Hilary JAMES) *(CDASC 042)* **DUOS** [live]
- When the summer comes again / Lime rock / Searching for lambs / Arrival of the Queen of Sheba / Way back in something '92 / Down the road I'll go / Two English dance tunes: Chirping of the nightingale – Bold Princess Royal / Bord Reynard / The parrot song / Villanelle / If your kisses can't hold the man you love / The spider in the shed / Czardas / Double crossin' papa / O'er the ocean / Neil Gow's lament for Abercarney / Black and white rag … with plenty of lively anecdotes and audience banter.

Nov 01. (cd) *(CDACS 043)* **MASTERING THE MANDOLIN** [instructional]

Oct 04. (cd; by SIMON MAYOR and HILARY JAMES) *(CDACS 049)* **LULLABIES with MANDOLINS** [children's, etc.]
- Lavender's blue / Pieds en l'air / Fais dodo / All the pretty little horses / Over the hills and far away / Grieg's cradle song / Dance to your daddy / Andante [from Vivaldi's concerto for two mandolins] / Golden slumbers / Schubert's cradle song / Hush-a-bye baby / Raisins and almonds / German cradle song.

Oct 05. (cd; as SIMON MAYOR and HILARY JAMES) *(CDACS 054)* **CHILDREN'S FAVOURITES from Acoustics** [compilation]
- The Turkish toetapper / The snowman's song / A magpie sitting on a broken chair / The spider in the shed / Ostinato / Sketch: Simon's doorbell / My bike / The slippery slimy trout / The road to Banbury / Sleepy sheep / Sketch: Pink flying flamingoes / Give me a drum / Lavender's blue / Sally Ann Johnson / The farmyard tango / Gobble! gobble! gobble! / Mattachins from the Capriole suite / Clickety clack / Fais dodo / King Canute at Cleethorpes play / Hornpiep / Sketch: A nice cup of tea / Granny had a washboard / Sketch: At the market / Midsummer market / Sketch: Time to go home / Midsummer market / Vivaldi's concerto for mandolin – first movt.

Oct 06. (cd) *(CDACS 055)* **MUSIC FROM A SMALL ISLAND**
- Midnight in Manchester / Rosebud in June / The hunt is up – Bold Reynard / Linden sea / The strid / On Beamsley Beacon / Coming down the moor – Ghyll force / The Laird of Drumblair / Such a parcel of rogues / The barren rocks of Aden / Medley: Auld Rob Morris – I'm doon for lack o' Johnny – John Stephen of Chance Inn / The Middlesmoor waltz.

Jun 07. (cd; as SIMON MAYOR and the MANDOLINQUENTS) *(CDACS 056)* **DANCE OF THE COMEDIANS** [live]
- Pizzicato / Apanhei-tei cavaquinho / Song of India / The typewriter / Lullaby of Birdland / Czardas / Loch Lomond / Rigaudon / The sailor / Caravan / Will you come to the bower / Summer / Dance of the comedians. *(bonus +=)*- The Russian / The spider in the shed.

HILARY JAMES

Acoustics not issued

Nov 93. (cd) *(CDACS 016)* **BURNING SUN**
- O'er the ocean / Busy old fool / La marche de Rois / Polly Vaughan / Two sisters / Bay of Biscay / Lascia ch'io pianga / Seeds of love / Lonesome day / Les berceaux / March borrowed from April / Sail away. *(re-iss. Jun 97; same)*

May 97. (cd; by HILARY JAMES with Beryl Marriott) *(CDACS 029)* **LOVE, LUST AND LOSS**: English, Scottish and Irish folksongs
- Salisbury Plain / Snowy-breasted pearl / Johnny O'Braidiesley / Corn rigs / Barbary Allen / Come to the bower / Appleton fair / The dreamless sleep / Thornaby wood / Annan water / Searching for lambs / Bruton town / The water is wide. *(re-iss. Jul 01; same)*

Oct 99. (cd) *(CDACS 041)* **BLUESY**
- Travellin' blues / Hong Kong blues / Brady and Duncan / Poor wayfaring stranger / Fighting the jug / Double crossin' papa / Melancholy blues / Me and my chauffeur / Meet me where they play the blues / Ready for the river / Blues in the night / One black rat / Rising sun blues / Ain't nobody here but us chickens.

Aug 04. (cd; as HILARY JAMES with Simon Mayor) *(CDACS 047)* **LAUGHING WITH THE MOON**
- The dream / The reel thing / The shearing's not for you / Hunt the squirrel – Long odds / Newcastle / Carolan's concerto / Andrew Lammie / Hey! Johnny Cope – The Athol Highlanders / Fireflies / Laughing with the moon / Shenandoah.

—— next set by sisters **Hilary James** + **Janet Giraudo**

Nov 08. (mp3-dl-s) *(CDACS 058)* LAUDAMUS TE

Jun 11. (cd) *(CDACS 059)* **ENGLISH SKETCHES**
- A song and a jig for good measure / The bold fisherman / The two ravens / Beneath the willow tree / Young Benjie / The bell ringing song / Weathers / Winter / Can love be controlled by advice / Spring / Bredon hill / The lady and the prentice / A song for good measure (reprise) / A song for good measure [full version].

The WORKING PARTY

Troy Donockley - uillean pipes and whistles / **Chris Leslie** - fiddle / **Chris Parkinson** - piano accordion and melodeon / **Simon Mayor** - mandolin / **Maartin Allcock** - guitar and bouzar

Working Party not issued

Apr 06. (cd) *(none)* **LIVE AT THE MILL** [live at the Mill Arts Centre, Banbury in September 2005]
- Three sea captains – Kid on the mountain – Lark in the morning / I wandered by a brookside / Lord Inchiquin – Sheagh bheag, sheagh mhor / Rocky road to Dublin – Graf spey – Mason's apron / Star of the County Down – Frieze britches – Drummond Castle / The yellow bird – When you're sick is it tea you want? – the hag with the money / John Gaudie / Spanish clock – Speed the plough – Mountain road – Flogging reel – Star of Munster.

McDERMOTT'S TWO HOURS

Led by Brighton-born author, poet, songwriter and musician Nick Burbridge (who named the band after a two-hour Derry radio appeal by activist and peacemaker Tommy McDermott), McDERMOTT'S TWO HOURS' earliest incarnation was in 1986 as a five-piece, made up by fiddler Tim O'Leary, bassist Martin Pannett, drummer Marcus Laffan and second guitarist Matthew Goorney. A must-see live outfit, the band were a precursor to the LEVELLERS, a raucous and rollicking Celtic pub-rock folk band and one of the many treading on the coat-tails of The POGUES and The MEN THEY COULDN'T HANG.

The independently-issued **THE ENEMY WITHIN** (1989) {*6} found favour among the crusty brigade for a while, but when Burbridge and O'Leary found their calling with the Tommy McDermott Theatre Company, the band was put on hold for almost the whole of the 1990s.

Kickstarting McDERMOTT's TWO HOURS in a post-millennial collaboration with LEVELLERS rhythm musos Jeremy Cunningham and Charlie Heather (fiddler Jon Sevink was added a tad later), songsmith Burbridge and fiddler O'Leary produced a handful of indie-folk CDs, namely **WORLD TURNED UPSIDE DOWN** (2001) {*6}, **CLAWS AND WINGS** (2003) {*6} and **DISORDER** (2004) {*7}.

McDERMOTT'S TWO HOURS duly regrouped once again (without the LEVELLERS this time), and Burbridge, Paley, Goorney and new drummer Dil Davies recorded a privately-released CD, **LIVE AT FERNEHAM HALL** (2005) {*5}. It was a concert set featuring their best tune, 'Dirty Davey', which was also recorded by the LEVELLERS. Adding Phillippe Barnes and Tim Cotterell, **GOODBYE TO THE MADHOUSE** (2007) {*7} marked a sort-of-proper comeback and the band's 21st anniversary too. *MCS*

Nick Burbridge (b. 1954) - vocals, acoustic guitar, bodhran / **Tim O'Leary** - fiddle, whistle, bouzouki, vocals / **Matthew Goorney** - guitar, banjo, harmonica / **Martin Pannett** - bass, vocals / **Marcus Laffan** - drums, percussion

UK Hag — US not issued

Jul 89. (lp) *(HAGLP 2)* **THE ENEMY WITHIN**
- Dirty Davey / Boys of the blackstuff / Prisoner / Refugees / Paddy in Harare / Darkness and sail / Rosa / The fields round Ballyclare / Fox on the run / Paddy on the level. *(cd-iss. Aug 94; HAGCD 2)*

—— disbanded in 1990: Burbridge + O'Leary joined the Tommy McDermott Theatre Company

McDERMOTT'S TWO HOURS Vs LEVELLERS

Burbridge + **O'Leary** reformed with **Jeremy Cunningham** (bass) + **Charlie Heather** (drums, percussion) – both of LEVELLERS

May 01. (cd) *(HAG 006)* **WORLD TURNED UPSIDE DOWN**
- World turned upside down / Another campaign / The wheel / Blue bandana / Harry Brewer / Taking it on / La pasionaria / Laying the Sligo maid.

—— added **Jon Sevink** - extra fiddles (of LEVELLERS)

Apr 03. (cd) *(HAG 008)* **CLAWS AND WINGS**
- Song of a Leveller / North and south / Song of a brother / Postcard / Travelling to Cockaigne / Snapshot / Song of a Quaker's wife / Sto mo chroi / Song of a father / Asylum / Beach scene / Murphy's wake.

—— O'Leary was repl. by **Ben Paley** - fiddle, mandolin, vocals + the returning **Matt Goorney** - bass, banjo, melodica, vocals

Sep 04. (cd) *(HAG 011)* **DISORDER**
- Tod the ranter / Summer song / Black sun / The old man's retreat / Watering the wine / Party to the process / The madness of John Clare / Bloody Sunday / A fable from Aigge / Just a life / The dutiful man as a moth / Johnny and the jubilee.

McDERMOTT'S TWO HOURS

Burbridge, Paley + **Goorney** added **Dil Davies** - drums

private — not issued

Jun 05. (cd) *(none)* **LIVE AT FERNEHAM HALL** (live)
- Fox on the run / Song of a brother / Harry Brewer / Refugees / Johnny and the jubilee / Prisoner / North and south / Laying the Sligo maid / Bloody Sunday / Darkness and sail / Taking it on / Dirty Davey / Rosa / Farewell to Erin.

—— added **Phillippe Barnes** + **Tim Cotterell**

Otf — not issued

Aug 07. (cd) *(002)* **GOODBYE TO THE MADHOUSE**
- Molloy / River / Crusaders / Bone's farewell / Crazy Jane's day out / True story of Eugene McQuaid / Stowaway / All souls' night / Stand by yourself / Lie down and dream of Ireland / Trickster.

Kirsty McGEE

The missing link between MARIANNE FAITHFULL and RACHEL UNTHANK, Manchester-born singer-songwriter/acoustic guitarist KIRSTY McGEE began her solo career (as a teenager she'd been in early-1990s Northampton indie duo Slumber) by winning the Northwest songwriting competition, an event run by the Buskers' Ball team.

Fellside Records discovered the waif-like northern girl, and in 2002 unleashed her debut set, **HONEYSUCKLE** {*6}. Brit-folk specialists Park Records subsequently took her under their wing for two sets, **FROST** (2004) {*8} – augmented by JON SPIERS and Neil MacColl – and **TWO BIRDS** (2005) {*6}.

Disillusioned with the record industry, McGee formed the Hobopop Collective (alongside touring partner Mat Martin), a totally self-sufficient imprint that signed on new acts as well as releasing two of her own CDs, **THE KANSAS SESSIONS** (2008) {*6} and **No.5 [A LIVE ALBUM]** (2009) {*7}. The latter earned a nomination for the annual Independent Music Awards. *MCS*

Kirsty McGee - vocals, acoustic guitar (+ session people)

UK Fellside — US not issued

Aug 02. (cd) *(FECD 170)* **HONEYSUCKLE**
- Rich / Cats' eyes / Take what you need / Golden honeysuckle rose / Skin / The wrong girl / Wild garlic / Tuba player's wife / Bliss / Venice / Never can last / She's got to travel.

Park — not issued

Mar 04. (cd) *(PRKCD 69)* **FROST**
- Plane vapours / Spit and shine / The prisoner / Coffee coloured strings / Spider lullaby / Cloudwatching / Put back the stars / Safe harbour song / Sophie / Summer frost / Kisses / Bitter aloe / St. Mark's place.

Mar 05. (cd-s) *(PRKCD 77)* COFFEE COLOURED STRINGS

May 05. (cd) *(PRKCD 85)* **TWO BIRDS**
- Thankyou / Fresh water / Alchemy / India / Lazy eye blues / One star / Heart / The right way home / Chicory / Brittle / Steady / Static.

Hobopop — not issued

Sep 08. (cd) *(HPCD 004)* **THE KANSAS SESSIONS**
- Bonecrusher / Gunsore / Sandman / Sparks / Alibi blues / No way to treat a friend / Lamb / Killer wasps / Shame / Dust devils / The profit song / Faith.

—— next was credited to KIRSTY McGEE & THE HOBOPOP COLLECTIVE

Oct 09. (cd) *(HPCD 005)* **No.5** [A LIVE ALBUM]
- Omaha / Alibi blues / Last orders / Sandman / Bliss / The last to understand / Stonefruit / Dust devils / Faith. *(+ video)*: Bonecrusher.

MEGSON

Formed London in 2004, married-couple-to-be Stu Hanna and Debbie Hanna-Palmer (formerly Palmer) were another act in the long line of Bright Young Folk things, Hanna-Palmer (a trained soprano with a degree in music) having moved to London from Cleveland, via Middlesbrough, to study classical music.

Keeping traditional folk alive, the duo (named for the then recently deceased family dog) were rewarded with growing turn-outs while performing locally. One interested party in the audience was SETH LAKEMAN, who introduced the couple to his record-producer brother Sean. MEGSON had already released their debut album, **ON THE SIDE** (2005) {*6}, but Sean was at the controls for their second dollop of Northern/Teesside-friendly delights, **SMOKE OF HOME** (2007) {*6}. Debbie and multi-instrumentalist Stu were married soon afterwards.

With the patronage of BBC Radio 2 DJ Bob Harris for their harmony-fuelled AOR-folk, award nominations were soon forthcoming, and the country-tinged **TAKE YOURSELF A WIFE** (2008) {*7} found favour with the folk-pop fraternity. **THE LONGSHOT** (2010) {*7} was another record steeped in tradition, with songs like 'Working Town' documenting the grim-up-north life of pre-post-industrial Britain. *MCS*

Debbie Hanna-Palmer - vocals / **Stu Hanna** - vocals, acoustic guitar, mandolin

UK EDJ — US not issued

May 05. (cd) *(EDJ 011)* **ON THE SIDE**
- Rose on the stem / Grace darling / The loom / Freefall / Maid on the shore / Butternut hill / Sandy Dawe / Oak and ash / Just stay / More than me / Last rose of summer.

Oct 06. (cd-ep) *(EDJ 012)* MEGSON
- Follow it on / Smoke of home / Just as the tide / Just stay [live] / Grace darling.

Jul 07. (cd) *(EDJ 013)* **SMOKE OF HOME**
- Smoke of home / Lambkin / Follow it on / Fell to the breeze / Sammy's ghost / Just as the tide / I lied / Humanlands / Durham gaol / Flood water / Name of the rose / Every night when the sun goes in.

Sep 08. (cd) *(EDJ 015)* **TAKE YOURSELF A WIFE**
- O Mary will you go / Little Joe / Take yourself a wife / The pitman's happy times / Fourpence a day / The Oakey strike evictions / Jane Jamieson's ghost / The new fish market / Sandgate lassie's lament.

Jun 10. (cd) *(EDJ 016)* **THE LONGSHOT**
- Two match lads / The cabman / Working life out / The longshot / The old miner / The handloom weaver and the factory maid / Time to get up / The last man in the factory / Working town / William Brown / California.

The MEMORY BAND

London-based The MEMORY BAND is the brainchild of Stephen Cracknell, ex-Badly Drawn Boy tour bassist, Trunk Records founder and studio session player for soloist and film composer David Holmes. Signed to Tony Morley's Leaf imprint, Cracknell initially surfaced as GORODISCH (after Gorodish [sic], a character in the French novel and 1981 film 'Diva'), his folktronica mini-set **THURN & TAXIS** (2001) {*5} hardly breaking sweat over its 20-"odd" minutes.

The MEMORY BAND was launched as Stephen's other imaginary laptop-folk act in 2003, releasing a couple of EPs ('Calling On' and 'Fanny Adams'), all eight tracks from which featured on parent album **THE MEMORY BAND** (2004) {*7}. If you need reminding, the unforgettable tracks outwith the EPs were 'Madlove And The Bee' and a version of Arthur Russell's 'This Is How We Walk On The Moon'.

The MEMORY BAND duly became an actual band by adding OWL SERVICE singer and musician Nancy Wallace and fiddler Jennymay Logan, with guest spots from ADEM (who appeared on the debut), Simon Lord (of Garden) and Alexis Taylor (of Hot Chip). The first band album was **APRON STRINGS** (2006) {*6}, a decidedly Brit-folk affair embracing the trad of old with new arrangements of 'Blackwaterside' (an instrumental here), 'Green Grows The Laurel', 'I Wish I Wish', some Cracknell compositions, and strange covers of songs by Ronnie Lane ('The Poacher') and Bernie Edwards/Nile Rodgers ('Why', a hit for Carly Simon).

Not content with just one group, Cracknell helped form another, The ACCIDENTAL, with TUNNG's Sam Genders, The Bicycle Thieves' Hannah Caughlin and soulful solo artist Liam Bailey. The four-piece collective released the indie-folk set **THERE WERE WOLVES** (2008) {*7}. With four effective singers (and musicians) taking turns, one should try to hear 'Slice Open The Day', 'Dream For Me' and 'Knock Knock'.

Verging towards folk-blues (on 'A New Skin'), The MEMORY BAND's third album, **OH MY DAYS** (2011) {*6}, also found room for Hannah and Liam, while Jess Roberts and Jenny McCormick were drafted in as extra voices alongside rhythm section Jon Thorne (of Lamb) and Tom Page (of Rocketnumbernine). The most folk-orientated tracks, SANDY DENNY's 'By The Time It Gets Dark' plus 'Run River Run' and 'Ghosts', have a sense of FAIRPORT déjà vu. *MCS*

Stephen Cracknell - vocals, multi

UK Leaf / US not issued

Jun 01. (m-lp/m-cd; as GORODISCH) *(DOCK 22/+CD)* **THURN & TAXIS**
- Setting sail / Moth to a flame / B.O.F. / A time to listen / The strangest feeling / Blues for Pablo money / Homeward.

Hungry Hill / not issued

Jan 03. (7" ep) *(SLOPE 1)* CALLING ON
- Calling on / Once bitten / Out of town / Last orders.

Aug 03. (7" ep) *(SLOPE 2)* FANNY ADAMS
- Fanny Adams / Tomorrow / Catch as catch can / Ploughshares.

Jul 04. (cd) *(TMB 001)* **THE MEMORY BAND**
- Theme for The Memory Band / Once bitten / Catch as catch can / Madlove and the bee / No one else / Tomorrow / Ploughshares / Calling on / Out of town / This is how we walk on the moon / Fanny Adams / Last orders.

— added **Nancy Wallace** - guitar, vocals, harmonium (solo artist, and of OWL SERVICE) / **Jennymay Logan** - fiddle / plus **Simon Lord** (of Garden) + **Adem Ilhan** - bass / **Alexis Taylor** (of Hot Chip)

Peacefrog / Dicristina Stair Builders

Sep 06. (7") *(PFG 084)* WHY. / Come Write Me Down

Oct 06. (cd) *(PFG 085CD)* <STEP 08> **APRON STRINGS**
- Blackwaterside / Come write me down / Brambles / Green grows the laurel / I wish I wish / The light / Want you to know / Deltic soul / Why / Reasons / Evil / The poacher.

May 07. (7") *(PFG 103)* COME WRITE ME DOWN (Four Tet remix). / Green Grows The Laurel (Jon Hopkins mix)

— now with vocalists: **Liam Bailey, Hannah Caughlin, Jess Roberts + Jenny McCormick** plus **Jon Thorne** - bass (of Lamb) + **Tom Page** - drums (of Rocketnumbernine)

Hungry Hill / not issued

Feb 11. (cd) *(TMB 003)* **OH MY DAYS**
- Crow / A new skin / Run river run / Blackberry way / Electric light / Come wander with me / Apples / Some things you just can't hide / Demon days / Ghosts / Love is the law / By the time it gets dark / The snake.

The ACCIDENTAL

Cracknell plus **Sam Genders** - vocals (of TUNNG) / **Hannah Caughlin** - vocals (of Bicycle Thieves) + **Liam Bailey** - vocals / + guests from MEMORY BAND

Static Caravan / not issued

Feb 08. (ltd-7" @33rpm) *(VAN 158)* KNOCK KNOCK... / Brave New World

Full Time Hobby / Thrill Jockey

Apr 08. (7" white) *(FTH 048S)* WOLVES. / Knock Knock (Hot Chip remix)

Apr 08. (cd) *(FTH 049CD)* <Thrill 199> **THERE WERE WOLVES**
- Knock knock / Wolves / I can hear your voice / Jaw of a whale / The closer I am / Slice open the day / Illuminated red / Birthday / Dream for me / The killing floor / Time and space.

The MEN THEY COULDN'T HANG

From 1984 to 1991, London folk-punks The MEN THEY COULDN'T HANG were the poor man's POGUES. Having stepped out of the shadows of busking around the Shepherd's Bush area, it was a similarity that didn't bother Phil "Swill" Odgers, his brother Jon (both from Scotland), Welshman Stefan Cush, Paul Simmonds and Shanne Hasler/Bradley. Coincidentally, the last-named had plied her musical trade with The Nipple Erectors/Nips alongside SHANE MacGOWAN.

The MEN THEY COULDN'T HANG initially got together for an impromptu performance at the Alternative Country Festival in London, and though they never intended to become a professional outfit, their performance was so well received that promoters were queueing up to offer them concert dates. Elvis Costello was so impressed he signed them to his Imp roster.

Although they were initially lumped in with the folk-punk scene, the band's hard-edged, thrash-bash appeal was always more politically motivated, placing them in the lineage of historical protest; they chose to cover Scottish folkie ERIC BOGLE's anti-war anthem, 'The Green Fields Of France', as their debut single. One of their biggest fans was cult Radio One DJ John Peel, whose audience polled the song at No.3 in his 1984 Festive Fifty.

'Ironmasters' (written by Simmonds) was even more frenetic and just as cutting, while their debut album, **NIGHT OF 1000 CANDLES** (1985) {*8}, brought widespread acclaim, featuring as it did some fine re-interpretations of folk ballads as well as their own compositions. A final, Nick Lowe-produced single for Imp later that year, 'Greenback Dollar' (a US hit many moons ago for The KINGSTON TRIO), preceded a major-label deal with MCA.

The resulting album, **HOW GREEN IS MY VALLEY** (1986) {*6}, was a disappointment in comparison, the band's material not translating well to big-budget production values, although 'Ghosts Of Cable Street' and 'Shirts Of Blue' were of political and historical value. Though it made the Top 75, the album failed to achieve the crossover success that their new label were obviously hoping for, and the band duly found themselves dropped.

Picking up where they left off with Magnet Records, they (Shanne replaced by ex-UK Subs bassist Ricky McGuire) eventually released the much-improved **WAITING FOR BONAPARTE** (1988) {*8}, a record that missed the UK Top 40 by a whisker. Featuring songs about the Napoleonic wars ('The Colours' was banned by the BBC) and the second world war ('The Crest'), the Men had lost none of their political bite.

After being subjected to executive pressure for a change of name, the band again parted company with the powers that be. Finding a more sympathetic door at Silvertone Records (home to The Stone Roses), they added new recruit Nicky Muir and issued **SILVERTOWN** (1989) {*7}, a record which found Simmonds at his most lyrically scathing and provided them with their only Top 40 entry of their career. Three singles also fared reasonably well: 'Rain, Steam And Speed', 'A Place In The Sun' and 'A Map Of Morocco'.

Shortly after the release of 1990's **THE DOMINO CLUB** {*5}, the band called it a day. Concert set **ALIVE, ALIVE-O** (1991) {*6} was a document of their final night at London's Town and Country Club and a testament to the on-stage intensity of these musical vagabonds. The LIBERTY CAGE (Simmonds and Phil Odgers, plus Dave Kent and Neil Simmonds) got together in the studio for **SLEEP OF THE JUST** (1994) {*5}, an album that went unnoticed outside the indie-folk world.

Surprisingly (or not, as it turned out), The MEN THEY COULDN'T HANG came back to haunt the scene late in 1996, courtesy of an EP on Demon Records, 'The Eye'. This was tracked by a full-length album, **NEVER BORN TO FOLLOW** (1996) {*6} – featuring the Goffin-King title cut, recorded by the BYRDS as 'Wasn't Born to Follow' – and the **SIX PACK** mini-set (1997) {*5}, although during this spell their profile remained low.

As retirement looked imminent, Phil and Paul tried desperately to recreate something of their past by issuing the **BABY FISHLIPS** CD (2002) {*5}. Only fans recognised its pseudonymous disguise on its original delivery, a few years earlier, as the work of 'Preacher Jethro Brimstone & The Watermelon Kid'. A fresh impetus reunited the Men for comeback set **THE CHERRY RED JUKEBOX** (2003) {*6}, whose title might have misled people to think it was a Greatest Hits album, and not even of their own hits but of the Cherry Red indie label.

Further moonlight shifts with his own act The Swaggerband (which featured Jon and Ricky), and some group demo collections, persuaded Odgers, along with Simmonds, Odgers and the band, to reunite the band in 2004. A live set in 2005, **SMUGGLERS AND BOUNTY HUNTERS** {*6}, convinced them to keep on keeping on.

With the help of folk star and Irregular label boss ROBB JOHNSON, The MEN THEY COULDN'T HANG pitched up again with their umpteenth set, **DEVIL ON THE WIND** {*7} – featuring a classic opening track – in 2009. Celebrations were unconfined at their 25th-anniversary knees-up.

In their time the Men have recorded several covers, including 'Donald Where's Your Troosers?' (a hit for Andy Stewart), 'Rawhide' (Link Wray), 'Man In The Corner Shop' (Paul Weller), 'Gudbuy T' Jane' (Slade) and 'Harvest Moon' (Neil Young). *MCS*

Phil 'Swill' Odgers (b. Scotland) - vocals, acoustic guitar, tin whistle, melodica / **Paul Simmonds** - guitar, vocals, mandolin, keyboards / **Stefan Cush** (b. Wales) - guitar, vocals / **Shanne Hasler/Bradley** - bass (ex-Nipple Erectors) / **Jon Odgers** (b. Scotland) - drums, percussion

UK Imp-Demon — US not issued

Oct 84. (7") *(IMP 003)* THE GREEN FIELDS OF FRANCE. / ('A'- version)
(12"+=) *(IMP 003T)* - Hush little baby.

Jun 85. (7") *(IMP 005)* IRONMASTERS. / Donald Where's Your Troosers?
(12"+=) *(IMP 005T)* - Rawhide.

Demon — not issued

Jul 85. (lp/c) *(FIEND/+CASS 50)* **NIGHT OF 1000 CANDLES** [91]
- The day after / Jack Dandy / A night to remember / Johnny comes home / The green fields of France (no man's land) / Ironmasters / Hush little baby / Walkin, talkin' / Kingdom come / Scarlet ribbons. *(cd-iss.1988; FIENDCD 50) (cd re-iss. Nov 97 on Diablo; DIAB 839)*

Nov 85. (7") *(D 1040)* GREENBACK DOLLAR. / A Night To Remember
(12"+=) *(D 1040T)* - The bells.

MCA — MCA

Jun 86. (7") *(SELL 1)* GOLD RUSH. / Ghosts Of Cable Street
(12"+=) *(SELLT 1)* - Walkin' talkin'.

Oct 86. (7") *(SELL 2)* SHIRT OF BLUE. / Johnny Come Home
(12"+=) *(SELLT 2)* - Whiskey in me giro / Scarlet ribbons.

Oct 86. (lp/c) *(MCF/+C 3337)* **HOW GREEN IS MY VALLEY** [68]
- Gold strike / Gold rush / Ghosts of Cable Street / Dancing on the pier / The bells / Wishing well / Going back to Coventry / Shirt of blue / Rabid underdog / Tiny soldiers / The parade / Parted from you. *(cd-iss. Jan 90; DMCF 1898) (re-iss. Nov 92 cd/c; MCL D/C 19075)*

Mar 87. (7"/12") *(SELL/+T 3)* GHOSTS OF CABLE STREET. / Dream Machine
(c-s+=) *(SELLC 3)* - Liverpool lullaby.

—— **Ricky McGuire** - bass (ex-UK Subs) repl. Shanne, who joined Wreckless Eric in the Chicken Family

Magnet — Warners

Oct 87. (7"/7" pic-d) *(SELL/+P 5)* ISLAND IN THE RAIN. / Country Song
(7" ep+=/12" ep+=) *(SELL E/T 5)* - Silver dagger / Restless highway.

Mar 88. (7") *(SELL 6)* THE COLOURS. / Rory's Grave [61]
(12"+=) *(SELLT 6)* - Big iron.
(cd-s++=) *(CDSELL 6)* - ('A'-full remix).

Apr 88. (lp/c/cd) *(MAGL/MAGC/DMAG 5075)* **WAITING FOR BONAPARTE** [41]
- The crest / Smugglers / Dover lights / Bounty hunter / Island in the rain / The colours / Midnight train / Father's wrong / Life of a small fry / Mary's present. *(cd+=)* - The crest (12"-version). *(c+=)* - Silver dagger / Restless highway / Country song. *(re-iss. May 88 lp/c)(cd; WX 183/+C)(242380-2)*

WEA — not issued

Jun 88. (7"/12") *(YZ 193/+T)* THE CREST. / Time At The Bar
(cd-s+=) *(YZ 193CD)* - Gudbye T' Jane / Ironmasters.

—— added p/t **Nicky Muir** - keyboards, accordion (ex-Fire Next Time)

Silvertone — not issued

Feb 89. (7") *(ORE 4)* RAIN, STEAM AND SPEED. / Shirt Of Blue
(12"+=) *(ORET 4)* - Scarlet ribbons.
(cd-s++=) *(ORECD 4)* - Ironmasters.

Apr 89. (lp/c/cd) *(ORE LP/MC/CD 503)* **SILVERTOWN** [39]
- Rosettes / A place in the sun / Home fires / Diamonds, gold and fur / Company town / Lobotomy gets 'em home / Blackfriars bridge / Rain, steam and speed / Down all the days / Hellfire and damnation / Homefires / El vaquero. *(cd+=)* - A map of Morocco / Rain, steam and speed (12"-mix).

May 89. (7") *(ORE 7)* A PLACE IN THE SUN. / A Map Of Morocco
(12"+=) *(ORET 7)* - Scarlet ribbons.
(cd-s++=) *(ORECD 7)* - The day after (live).

Dec 89. (7" m) *(ORE 14)* A MAP OF MOROCCO. / Rosettes / The Day The Clock Went Back
(12"+=/12"s+=) *(ORE T/X 14)* - Rosettes (live).
(cd-s++=) *(ORECD 14)* - The iron men of rap (with ATTILA THE STOCKBROKER).

Jul 90. (7") *(ORE 19)* GREAT EXPECTATIONS. / Margaret Pie
(cd-s+=) *(ORECD 19)* - The green fields of France.
(12"+=) *(ORET 19)* - (excerpts from forthcoming album below).

Aug 90. (cd/c/lp) *(ORE CD/MC/LP 512)* **THE DOMINO CLUB** [53]
- The lion and the unicorn / Great expectations / The family man / Handy man / Kingdom of the blind / Grave robbing in Gig Harbor / Industrial town / You're the one / Australia / Dog eyes, owl meat, man-chops / Billy Morgan / On the razzle. *(cd re-iss. Mar 94 and May 01; same)*

Oct 90. (10"/cd-s) *(ORE 22 10/CD)* THE LION AND THE UNICORN. / Kingdom Of The Blind

—— disbanded in February '91 after some farewell gigs (and a few one-offs); Muir was later part of the technoids Bedrock

Fun After All — not issued

May 91. (cd/c/lp) *(CD/T+/AFTER 10)* **ALIVE, ALIVE-O** (live)
- The crest / Billy Morgan / You're the one / Home fires / Going back to Coventry / The colours / Ironmasters / Lobotomy gets 'em home / Man in the corner shop / Australia / A night to remember / Scarlet ribbons.

LIBERTY CAGE

Simmonds + **Phil Odgers** / + **Dave Kent** - whistle, harmonica, trumpet, vocals / **Neil Simmonds** - double bass, sax, bass, guitar

Line — not issued

Sep 94. (cd) *(LICD 9.01293)* **SLEEP OF THE JUST**
- Everything's different now / Fires below / Throwing stones at the sea / On her majesty's service / Swimming against the tide / One for the road / Judgement day / You make my mind stand still / Mercy of the guards / Cat and mouse affair / Murder in cell #9 / CDC

Kronk — not issued

Sep 95. (cd-ep) *(KRONK 001)* I'LL KEEP IT WITH MINE / The Rivers Run Dry / Slip Away Gently / Heaven's Prisoners

—— **Paul Howard** - guitar, vocals (ex-Tender Trap) repl. Kent before they split

The MEN THEY COULDN'T HANG

re-formed; added fifth man **Kenny Harris** - drums, percussion (ex-Screaming Blue Messiahs) repl. Jon

Demon — Demon

Oct 96. (cd-ep) *(D 2000)* THE EYE / Harvest Moon / Perry Border / Pieces Of Paradise

Nov 96. (cd) *(<FIENDCD 788>)* **NEVER BORN TO FOLLOW**
- The eye / Glittering prize / Never born to follow / I survived / Contenders / Our day / Gangland / House of cards / Denis Law and Ali MacGraw / To have and to hold / The spell is broken / Jennifer Grey.

—— **Andy Selway** - drums, percussion; repl. Harris

Jul 97. (cd-ep) *(<VEXCD 15>)* SIX PACK
- Nightbird / The wonder of it all / Moving on / Refugee / Come forward / Henry Krinkle: Alone inna ugly town.

ODGERS & SIMMONDS

Swill + **Paul** (originally credited to PREACHER JETHRO BRIMSTONE & THE WATERMELON KID and recorded in 1999)

Twah! — not issued

May 02. (cd) *(TWAH 116)* **BABY FISHLIPS**
- Khamaseem (sword of the crescent moon) / The trigger / Sky and the sun / The light / Rising road / We came through / Young again / Nightlife / A mountain in Navare / Man overboard / Mayday morning / Barrett's privateers / Leaving in the morning.

—— they also self-financed a second set, 'Folk At The Fortress' (2002), available mail-order

The MEN THEY COULDN'T HANG

Swill + **Paul** reunited the group

Twah! not issued

Sep 03. (cd) *(TWAH 125)* **THE CHERRY RED JUKEBOX** ☐ ⊟
- The sunrise / Singing Elvis / Rivertown / Silver gun / The red rocks of Spain / Ride again / The hill / Colwyn Bay / Highwater / (I loved the) Summer of hate / 10 grand.

Snapper not issued

Sep 05. (d-cd) *(SMDCD 553)* **SMUGGLERS AND BOUNTY HUNTERS**(live 30th July, 2004) ☐ ⊟
- The day after / The ghosts of Cable Street / Wishing well / Bounty hunter / Ride again / Shirt of blue / Company town / Dog's eyes, owl-meat, man chop / Australia / Barrett's privateers / The bells / Silver dagger / Singing Elvis / Rosettes / Smugglers / Nightbird / Silver gun / The colours / (I loved the) Summer of hate / Ironmasters / Going back to Coventry / The green fields of France.

—— Simmonds subsequently released a solo set, 'The Rising Road' (2008), a record leaning more to country-rock than folk

Irregular not issued

Jun 09. (cd) *(IRR 069)* **DEVIL ON THE WIND** ☐ ⊟
- Devil on the wind / The ragged shoreline / Beast of Brechfa / Mrs Avery / Reservoir / Overseas / Heartbreak park / Aquamarine / A real rain coming / Hard to find / Lost world.

- (8-10*) compilations -

Apr 98. (cd) *Demon; (<FIENDCD 940>)* **MAJESTIC GRILL: THE BEST OF THE MEN THEY COULDN'T HANG** ☐ ☐
- Ironmasters / The ghosts of Cable Street / Shirt of blue / Scarlet ribbons / The crest / The colours / Islands in the rain / Rosettes / Dogs' eyes, owl meat and man chop / A map of Morocco / Denis Law and Ali MacGraw / Australia / The eye / Our day / Nightbird / The green fields of France (no man's land).

Mar 11. (d-cd) *Vinyl Star; (???)* **FIVE GO MAD ON THE OTHER SIDE** [B-sides and rarities] ☐ ⊟
- The ghosts of Cable Street / Hush little baby / Rory's grave / Pieces of paradise / Dream machine / Gudbuy t' Jane / The iron men of rap (with ATTILA THE STOCKBROKER) / Walkin' talkin' / Harvest moon / Time at the bar // Whiskey with me giro / Perry border / A night to remember / Liverpool lullaby / Rubber bullets / Johnny come home / Big iron / The day the clocks went back / The colours [remix] / Man in the corner shop.

- (5-7*) compilations, others, etc.-

Aug 88. (12" ep) *Strange Fruit; (SFNT 012)* THE EVENING SHOW SESSIONS [15.6.86] ☐ ⊟
- Dancing on the pier / Ghosts of Cable Street / Going back to Coventry / Tiny tin soldiers.

1992. (7" ep/12" ep/cd-ep) *Silvertone; (ORE 019/+T/CD)* GREAT EXPECTATIONS (BIG DREAMS) / The Colours (live). / Ghosts Of Cable Street (live) / Kingdom Of The Blind ☐ ⊟

SWILL AND THE SWAGGERBAND

Phil Odgers plus **Ricky McGuire** , etc.

own label not issued

2004. (cd) *(none)* **THE DAY AFTER** ⊟ mail-o ⊟

—— Swill financed the next album by making available a mail-order seven-track EP, 'Doh, Ray, Me-Me-Me-Me-Me' in May '06

Irregular not issued

May 06. (cd) *(IRR 062)* **ELVIS LIVES HERE** ☐ ⊟
- Deep blue sea / Drag U down / Elvis lives here / In the breeze / Just a dial tone away / Marjory and Johnny / Missing / Shed fire / Drinkers / World of discontent.

Paul METSERS

Born November 27, 1945, in Noordwijk, Holland, Paul grew up in New Zealand from the age of seven. Inspired by American coffeehouse folk music of the 1960s, he picked up a guitar in 1963, although it would be some time before a solo career got under way. Two cassettes (**ORIGINAL SONGS** and **A SONG FOR YOU**) released in New Zealand in the late 1970s are very rare; even Paul may not have copies.

Abandoning his teaching post and arriving in Britain at the turn of the decade, METSERS spent a few years touring folk clubs, sleeping between gigs in his VW camper van. Recorded in Halifax, Yorkshire, his debut LP, **CAUTION TO THE WIND** (1981) {*7}, offered some examples of his songwriting craft, although others on the session (mainly NIC JONES and HELEN WATSON) guided him on sea shanties such as 'Farewell To The Gold' and 'The Seal Children'. JONES would rework the former track for his 'Penguin Eggs' set.

MOMENTUM (1982) {*6} and the earth-friendly **IN THE HURRICANE'S EYE** (1984) {*7} – the latter featuring two of his best cuts, 'Peace Must Come' and 'Riversong' – secured METSERS the respect of his peers and a growing fan base. **PACIFIC PILGRIM** (1986) {*6}, his second for his own Sagem label and another produced by John Gill, featured handpicked musicians ANDREW CRONSHAW (a delight on 'Need For Wings'), ANDY IRVINE (of PLANXTY), lead guitarist Howard Lees (of acoustic jazz duo Hobson & Lees), keyboard player Matt Clifford, steel guitarist Vic Collins and back-up harmonies from WATERFALL (Gilly Darby and Keith Donnelly).

FIFTH QUARTER (1988) {*5} was METSERS' last release thus far. He moved with his family to Cumbria in 1989, taking up carpentry and keeping bees, and performing only on a part-time/semi-pro basis. It appears however that there might be a new release in the pipeline, albeit from the rare-and-unreleased vault. *MCS*

Paul Metsers - vocals, acoustic guitar, Appalachian dulcimer / with session people

UK US
Jolly Roger not issued

1978. (c) *(none)* **ORIGINAL SONGS** ⊟ NZ ⊟
1979. (c) *(none)* **A SONG FOR YOU** ⊟ NZ ⊟

Highway not issued

May 81. (lp) *(SHY 7014)* **CAUTION TO THE WIND** ☐ ⊟
- Writer's song / Lose myself in you / A thousand years today / Ripple away / A song for you at last / The hunt / Farewell to the gold / Sandy's song / Day comes soon / Crossroads / The seal children.

1982. (lp) *(SHY 7021)* **MOMENTUM** ☐ ⊟
- Still trying / Walls / Some day / Where the blame belongs / The Sarsen stone / Dancing shoes / Hard on your heels / Say you will / The blistering air / Play it all again / Crazy tears.

Sagem not issued

1984. (lp) *(SGM 279)* **IN THE HURRICANE'S EYE** ☐ ⊟
- The faces of love / Good intentions / No quarter / Riversong / Nimbus / Peace descends / Peace must come / It's you in the end / The simple life / The brown bird / One more time.

Nov 86. (lp) *(SGM 379)* **PACIFIC PILGRIM** ☐ ⊟
- Aotearoa 3 / How soon – how long / Need for wings / The journey / No crusaders / Winter afternoon / To Pamplona / Warriors of the rainbow / Deep in the night / Slowin' down.

May 88. (lp) *(SGM 479)* **FIFTH QUARTER** ☐ ⊟
- Joel's song / I.O.U. / The fast lane down / The eagle and the islanders / Bring it to me / Wingless angel / Uncle Sam / Rolling home / The pathway of love / Beat the drum.

—— METSERS retired from the studio to work as a joiner and keep bees.

MICE (⟹ ALL ABOUT EVE)

Dick MILES

Born January 31, 1951, at Blackheath, London, traditional singer and concertina player DICK MILES (not to be confused with the American country artist of the 1960s) turned professional in 1976 after many years mastering his musical techniques. A festival favourite from East Anglia to Lancashire, where he performed with the Suffolk Bell and the Horseshoe Band respectively between 1977 and 1984, Dick was thereafter part of The NEW MEXBOROUGH ENGLISH CONCERTINA QUARTET.

Accompanied by his then wife Sue Miles on clarinet (and JEZ LOWE), the collaboration **THE DUNMOW FLITCH** (1981) {*6} put traditional music and his "box of tricks" back on track. The follow-up, **CHEATING THE TIDE** (1984) {*7}, gave sleeve credits to MARTIN CARTHY, Sue Miles, Sam Richards, Tish Stubbs, Jenny Critchley and Stephen Cassidy for this vaudeville-meets-folk recording. **PLAYING FOR TIME** (1988) {*6} covered a host of popular songs, the most creative reworkings being those of Robert Johnson's 'From Four Until Late' and a medley of Lennon-McCartney's 'Yesterday' and 'All My Loving'.

As well as his renowned solo sets, MILES subsequently released two collaborations, one with RICHARD GRAINGER (the cassette 'Home Routes'), and the other a very rare cassette album, 'On Muintavara', with Celtic artists Suifinn, in 1990.

He now lives in Ballydehob, County Cork, and has continued to work occasionally while delivering the odd concertina-biased CD or two. **AROUND THE HARBOUR TOWN** (2004) {*6} might be one's best starting point from recent years. *MCS*

Dick Miles - vocals, English concertina / with **Sue Miles** - clarinet, vocals

UK US
Sweet Folk All not issued

1981. (lp; by DICK & SUE MILES) *(SFA 106)*
THE DUNMOW FLITCH □ ⊟
- The Dunmow flitch / Primrose polka / Bald headed end of the broom / Archie's fancy / Herd on the hill / Isle of Cloy / Shanty boy / Greenwood laddie / Swaffham tinker / Woodland flowers / The cuckoo / Ball of yarn.

Greenwich Village not issued

Nov 84. (lp) *(GVR 227)* **CHEATING THE TIDE** □ ⊟
- Lady Diamond / Washington Post / Rebel soldier / Bill Charlton's fancy / Tommy's lot / Pakefield parson / Poor boy / There's no one with endurance like the man who sells insurance! / Wages of death / Dillpickle rag / The curse of Hoxne Bridge / The cott / The battle of Bosworth field.

Jul 85. (lp; by The NEW MEXBOROUGH ENGLISH CONCERTINA QUARTET) *(PLR 071)* **THE NEW MEXBOROUGH ENGLISH CONCERTINA QUARTET** □ ⊟
- The carabineer / Echoes of the past / Beauties of Scotland / Belphefgor / Mountain breezes / Mexborough memories / Restless waters / A hunting song / The reapers' chorus / Beauties of Ireland / The liberty bell.

(above issued on Plant Life)

May 88. (lp) *(GVR 238)* **PLAYING FOR TIME** □ ⊟
- Sweetheart of the east / Singer not the song / Yesterday – All my loving / On one April morning / Town green – Spring lane / Careless love / From four till late / The soldier's prayer / Eighteen year Jack / Italian gallop – Hamberger polka.

Brewhouse not issued

May 89. (c) *(BH 8812)* **ON MY LITTLE CONCERTINA** □ ⊟
- Sailortown / Plains of Boyle - New century - Madame Bonaparte / Coasts of Peru / Lea rigs / Jack the lad / Flowing tide / Around the harbour town / Crossed lines / Blarney pilgrim - Cook in the kitchen / Tam Lin / The range of the buffalo / Trails to Mexico / Sitting on top of the world / On my little concertina.

—— In 1990, MILES and RICHARD GRAINGER issued the cassette 'Home Routes'.

SUIFINN

Dick Miles - concertina, guitar and vocals / **Colm Murphy** - bodhran (ex-DE DANNAN) / **Nick Urwin** - bouzouki, guitar / **Martin McGrath** - fiddle / **Geraldine Urwin** - fiddle, flute, uillean pipes

O' hEireamhoin not issued

1990. (c) *(URW 491)* **ON MUINTAVARA** □ ⊟
- Kerry reel – Killarney boys of pleasure – Toss the feathers / Bere island / Blarney roses / Dear little isle – Lady Ann Montgomerty – Boy in the gap / Greenwood laddie / Frieze britches – An Phis Fhluich / Julia's polkas / From Bantry Bay / Where's the cat? – Will you come home with me – Ask my father / The green fields of Canada / Jack the lad – The tunnel road to Kenmare / Ahakista Bay / The west wind – Dublin reel – The mountain lark – Jenny's wedding.

DICK MILES

Milestone not issued

Jun 03. (cd) *(2003)* **NAUTICAL AND ...** ⊟ mail-o ⊟
- Do me amma / The sailor's dream / Johnny come down to Hilo / The boys of Killybegs / Lord Franklin / The Dockyard gate / John Phillip Holland / A fair maid walking / Adieu sweet lovely Nancy / Coil away the trawl warp / Cod banging / Tomgraney Castle - Chief O'Neill's favourite - Home ruler / Home to the haven / Gallant frigate Amphritrite / The death of Parker / The high part of the road - Paddy Canney's / The bold fisherman / The blackbird / Bunclody / The Devonshire farmer's daughter / Cape Clear.

Brewhouse not issued

Feb 04. (cd; as DICK MILES AND FRIENDS) *(BHCD 20037)*
AROUND THE HARBOUR TOWN □ ⊟
- Sailortown / Coasts of Peru / Lea rigs / Jack the lad / Around the harbour town / Flowing tide / Lord Bateman / Blarney pilgrim - Cook in the kitchen / Our sheepshearing's done / Plains of Boyle - New century - Madame Bonaparte / Tam Lin / Buffalo skinners / Trails to Mexico / Sitting on top of the world / On my little concertina / I live not where I love / Bogie's bonny belle / Raglan road / Farewell my friends.

unknown not issued

2007. (cd) *(none)* **CONCERTINAS AND ...** ⊟ mail-o ⊟
- Tarves rant / Sally Gardens / Seeds of love / Christmas day in da morning / Belfast hornpipe - Madam Bonaparte / Blarney roses / The frost is all over - Boys of blue hill - Maid behind the bar / The croppy boy / Random jig / April morning / Bishop's favourite - Falmouth assembly / Brigg fair / Hornpipe selection / The old copperplate - The banshee / Greenwood laddie / The fingerpost - Boscastle breakdown / Dark island / The rebel soldier / Valencia - Providence reel / The gold ring / The swallow's tail - The peeler's jacket / Bonny little bunch of rushes / Woodland flowers / St Patrick's day / The congress reel / The banks of Claudy / Lucy Farr's polkas - Bill the weaver / Killarney boys of pleasure - The silver spear.

2010. (cd) *(none)* **WINDY OLD WEATHER** ⊟ mail-o ⊟
- Game of all fours / Recruited collier / Leitrim fancy – Dunphy's hornpipe / Scarborough fair / Rodney's glory / All my loving / Bantry Bay song / Andy's gone with cattle / Handsome cabin boy / Barbara Allen / Boolavogue – Heart to the ladies / John Blunt / Bushes and briars / The pipe on the hob trip to the cottage / Hard times of old England / Meggy's foot / Tommy's lot / Little birdie / Saddle the pony / Wild winds of Wannie – Johnny Cope / Willy of the Winsbury / Windy old weather / Yesterday / Hopping down in Kent.

Pete MOLINARI

Taking a leaf out of the books of folk-blues artists such as PHIL OCHS and WOODY GUTHRIE, and mixing up the musical medicine with a vocal sound similar in many respects to country icons Hank Williams and Roy Orbison, PETE MOLINARI, born at Chatham in Kent in the early 1980s, perfected his American drawl while playing cafes and bars in New York.

On his return from the States Pete was encouraged by Damaged Goods label bigwig and former punkabilly star Billy Childish to put down some songs in Childish's kitchen studio. **WALKING OFF THE MAP** (2006) {*7} was the result of a day in front of a Revox tape machine, invoking the spirits of Greenwich Village and Roy and Johnny at Sun Studios . **A VIRTUAL LANDSLIDE** (2008) {*8} was marked by a lonesome Nashville country-blues effect, and many pundits, including the people at Mojo and Uncut, gave it the thumbs-up all round. *MCS*

Pete Molinari - vocals, acoustic guitar

UK US
Damaged Goods not issued

Jun 06. (cd/lp) *(DAMGOOD 270 CD/LP)* **WALKING OFF THE MAP** □ ⊟
- Indescribably blue / Love lies bleeding / This wondrous day / Tomorrow is a long time / The ghost of Greenwich Village / I just keep it inside / The ballad of Bob Montgomery / What use is the truth to me now / We belong together / The world has gone away and left me / Walking off the map / Alone and foresaken / A lonesome episode / God's rain / It cuts on either side.

Apr 07. (ltd-7") *(Big Bert 001)* A VIRTUAL LANDSLIDE. / There She Still Remains □ ⊟

(above issued on Big Bertha)

Mar 08. (ltd-7" ep) *(DAMGOOD 298)* SWEET LOUISE EP □ ⊟
- Sweet Louise / Indescribably blue / One stolen moment (acoustic).

Apr 08. (cd/lp) *(DAMGOOD 297 CD/LP)* **A VIRTUAL LANDSLIDE** □ ⊟
- It came out of the wilderness / Oh so lonesome for you / Adelaine / One stolen moment / There she still remains / Hallelujah blues / Look what I made out of my head ma / God damn lonesome blues / I don't like the man I am / Sweet Louise / Dear Angelina / Lest we forget.

Jun 08. (ltd-7" ep) *(DAMGOOD 307)* IT CAME OUT OF THE WILDERNESS EP □ ⊟
- It came out of the wilderness / The ghost of Greenwich Village / Ballad on a milk train.

Oct 08. (ltd-7" ep) *(DAMGOOD 316)* ONE STOLEN MOMENT EP □ ⊟
- One stolen moment / Love lies bleeding / The poet's dream.

—— next featured The Jordanaires

Aug 09. (12" ep) *(39041)* TODAY, TOMORROW AND FOREVER EP □ ⊟
- Today, tomorrow and forever / Satisfied mind / Tennessee waltz / Guilty.
(cd-ep+=) *(DAMGOOD 336)* - One stolen moment (acoustic) / Ballad on a milk train (acoustic) / The poet's dream (acoustic).

MONKEY SWALLOWS THE UNIVERSE (⟹ JOHNSON, Nat & The Figureheads)

Jim MORAY

Few folk artists come from Macclesfield, but once heard, JIM MORAY (born August 20, 1981) is one Englishman you're likely never to forget. Love or loathe him, the man has polarised the British folk world. The purists hate his computer/laptop-generated approach to traditional ballads, but others have applauded his courage and tenacity.

Raised in Staffordshire by folkie parents (his father was a morris dancer), Jim and his sister (singer/fiddler JACKIE OATES) grew up listening to folk music, although in his late teens the shy MORAY initially diverted his attentions to playing drums in a punk band and studying classical music at the Birmingham Conservatoire.

His first 'bedroom' recording, I AM JIM MORAY, came after he almost won a BBC Young Folk Award in 2001 (it went to Scottish sisters Give Way). This, and appearances at Glastonbury and the Cambridge Folk Festival, paved the way for a second home-produced release, **SWEET ENGLAND** (2003) {*8}, delivered as part of his degree course and funded by way of his student grant. Released on the Niblick Is A Giraffe imprint, the record featured one self-penned song, 'Longing For Lucy', among radical laptop arrangements of folk nuggets such as 'Lord Bateman', 'Early One Morning' and 'The Seeds Of Love'.

Its youth appeal and its alienation of old stuck-in-the-mud folk fuddy-duddies helped win SWEET ENGLAND a 2004 BBC Radio 2 Folk and

Horizon Newcomer Awards. Spurning the attentions of major record companies, MORAY turned his attention to producing James Raynard's One Little Indian-released debut, 'Strange Histories', and the following year he was back working solo.

The eponymous **JIM MORAY** (2006) {*7}, featuring a Ziggy Stardust/Aladdin Sane-style sleeve, turned from electronic sounds to an orchestrally-backed approach using his multi-instrumental talents. While treading the same trad-meets-indie-folk ground on versions of 'Lord Willoughby', 'Barbara Allen', 'Gilderoy' and the grungy 'Who's The Fool?', MORAY also shines with two of his own pieces, 'My Sweet Rose' and the Korgis-esque 'Magic When You're Near'.

Having contributed to his sister's 'The Violet Hour' set, MORAY now delivered **LOW CULTURE** (2008) {*7}, a world-folk-themed effort that saw him bring in African instrumentation, including the kora (harp-lute) and mbira (thumb piano), plus mandolin and melodeon. Deservedly Mojo's Folk Album of the Year, it again comprised mainly trad ballads side by side with his own compositions, plus two contrasting covers of XTC leader Andy Partridge's 'All You Pretty Girls' and BELLA HARDY's 'Three Black Feathers'.

IN MODERN HISTORY (2010) {*8} was for many pundits a stunning album, eight tracks that complemented his exacting folk beats. Opener 'Bristol Harbour' and retreads of 'The Lowlands Of Holland' and 'Long Lankin' put the genre back into people's hearts and minds, while retaining a purist sense of tradition. One can only guess what might arrive with MORAY's next ambitious instalment. *MCS*

Jim Moray - vocals, multi (& guests & orchestra)

UK own label — US not issued

2001. (cd-ep) *(none)* I AM JIM MORAY
- Lemady / Poverty knock / Fair Sally / As I roved out / The bonny black hare / Come with me.

Niblick Is A Giraffe — not issued

Jun 03. (cd) *(NIBL 003)* **SWEET ENGLAND**
- Early one morning - Young Collins / Lord Bateman / Sweet England / Gypsies / April morning / The seeds of love / The week before Easter / The Suffolk miracle / Two sisters / Longing for Lucy.

May 04. (cd-s) *(NIBL 004)* SPRIG OF THYME / Early One Morning / Fair And Tender Lovers

May 06. (cd) *(NIBL 005)* **JIM MORAY**
- Prelude / Lord Willoughby / Dog and gun / Barbara Allen / Nightvisiting / Fair and tender lovers / My sweet rose / Flow my tears / Gilderoy / Who's the fool? / Magic when you're near. *(re-iss. Sep 08; same)*

Jul 06. (7" purple) *(NIBL 006)* BARBARA ALLEN. / This Is The Sound

Jul 08. (cd) *(NIBL 007)* **LOW CULTURE**
- Leaving Australia / The Rufford Park poachers / Three black feathers / All you pretty girls / Lucy Wan / Across the western ocean / I'll go list for a sailor / Fanny Blair / Henry's downfall / Valentine.

Sep 09. (ltd-cd-s; as JIM MORAY (feat. BUBBZ)) *(NIBL 008)* LUCY WAN / Inside The Wolf

Jun 10. (cd) *(NIBL 010)* **IN MODERN HISTORY**
- Bristol harbour / Jenny of the moor / Hard / William Taylor / Spencer the writer / The lowlands of Holland / Silver dagger / Cold stone / Long Lankin / Home upon the hill.

- (8-10*) compilations –

Apr 10. (cd) *Navigator; (NIBL 009)* **(A BEGINNER'S GUIDE)**
- Early one morning – Young Collins / Barbara Allen / Poverty knock / Leaving Australia / The seeds of love / All you pretty girls / The Rufford Park poachers / Sprig of thyme / Nightvisiting / Lemady / Lord Bateman.

Elaine MORGAN (⟹ ROSE AMONG THORNS)

MORIARTY

A French-based but cosmopolitan outfit – from the US, Switzerland, Vietnam and of course France – this hillbilly folk-blues group formed way back in 1995, though more than a decade elapsed before the release of their inaugural recording, **GEE WHIZ BUT THIS IS A LONESOME TOWN** {*8} (2008).

Comprising musicians Charles Carmignac, Arthur Gillette, Stephan Zimmerli, Thomas Puechavy and "mean girl" singer Rosemary Stanley, MORIARTY took their name from a character in Jack Kerouac's novel 'On The Road', and the album had all the unearthly traits of DYLAN, Johnny Cash and fellow French roots act Les Negresses Vertes (remember them?). With her distinctively cool and earthy vocal style, Rosemary steals the show somewhat on 'Private Lily', 'Jimmy' and the kooky, KIMYA DAWSONesque 'Lovelinesse'. The deluxe CD arrived later with demos, rarities, live stuff, etc, led by a strummy reading of Depeche Mode's 'Enjoy The Silence'. A new recording was expected for some time in 2011. *MCS*

Rosemary Stanley - vocals, multi / **Charles Carmignac** - guitars, percussion / **Arthur Gillette** - guitar, piano / **Stephan Zimmerli** - bass, guitar / **Thomas Puechavy** - percussion

UK Naïve — US not issued

Feb 08. (cd) *(NV 812111)* **GEE WHIZ BUT THIS IS A LONESOME TOWN**
- Jimmy / Lovelinesse / Private Lily / Motel / Animals can't laugh / (...) / Cottonflower / White man's ballad / Tagono-ura / Fireday / Oshkosh bend / Jaywalker (song for Beryl). *(d-cd-iss. Apr 09 +=; NV 816211)* - Enjoy the silence / Hanoi blue [live] / Oshkosh bend [alt.] / Bacon [live] / (...) No.2 / Private Lily [alt.] / The crimson singer [live] / Jimmy [live] / Jimmy [video] / Private Lily [video].

Pete MORTON

A song craftsman for almost a quarter of a century, Leicester-born (July 30, 1964) folk singer PETE MORTON has delivered well over a dozen albums, and unlike most of his peers has taken his wares beyond Britain and across the Atlantic. Inspired by DYLAN, RALPH McTELL and their ilk, this acoustic musician was a punk/new wave fan in his youth, but his vocation was grounded in folk music, MORTON having entertained many streets in Europe as a busker. Relocating to Manchester in the mid-1980s, he signed a deal with Harbourtown Records, becoming a stalwart of the label over the next two decades.

Lyrically astute from the get-go, **FRIVOLOUS LOVE** (1987) {*7} was proof indeed of Pete's musical manifesto. Social-comment songs such as 'The Sloth And The Greed' and 'The Last God Of England' were compelling to the core, while others pursued a less strident but still serious agenda. Containing his best-known and most-covered song, 'Another Train', **ONE BIG JOKE** (1988) {*7} carried the day for many purist folk pundits, while **MAD WORLD BLUES** (1992) {*6} even took on traditionally sourced ballads.

Several of Pete's albums can be listed as first-rate, but only **HUNTING THE HEART** {*8} has captured an award, being declared Mojo magazine's Folk Album of the Year in 2000. His earlier 'Urban Folk' projects with ROGER WILSON and Simon Edwards found him in ye-olde territory, and 1999's **TRESPASS** {*7} was a full-blown trad set, featuring 'John Barleycorn' (not for the first time), 'Dick Turpin' and 'The Cuckoo'.

More recently, **SWARTHMOOR** (2003) {*7} and **FLYING AN UNKNOWN FLAG** (2005) {*7} show him still stoking his passion and keeping his fire alive. Always one to set new boundaries, his ambitious **CASA ABIERTA** (2008) {*7} project found him taking on 'ten songs in different tongues', a challenge that wasn't beyond him – he was a resident of London. Three years down the line, his newest set of original compositions, **ECONOMY** (2011) {*7}, was again a thought-provoking record of our times, dealing mainly with trust, love and money – and man's desire to obtain all three. *MCS*

Pete Morton - vocals, acoustic guitar

UK Harbourtown — US Philo

Jul 87. (lp/c) *(HAR 001/+C)* *<PH 1122/+C>* **FRIVOLOUS LOVE** — 1988
- The sloth and the greed / Mother's day / The last god of England / Time / Tamlyn / A babe of the world / Without thinking love / The backward king / Frivolous love / Rachel / Just like John Barleycorn.

Harbourtown — Green Linnet

Nov 88. (lp/c) *(HAR 004/+C)* *<SIF/CSIF/GLCD 3047>* **ONE BIG JOKE** — 1991
- The prisoner / Simple love / Water from the house of our fathers / The first day / The little boy's room / Another train / Lucy / The old grey moon / One big joke / Girls like you / River of love / Somewhere in love / Live your life. *(cd-iss. Oct 93; HAR 004CD)*

1991. (ltd-c; by PETE MORTON / ROGER WILSON / SIMON EDWARDS) *(HARC 016)* **URBAN FOLK Vol.I**
- Love's trainee (part one) / The fox / Hey Joe / Lord Randall / Absent love / Old Joe Clark - The Louisiana two-step / Delia / Bleak mist / Rambleaway / False bride / Shadow of an absent friend / It takes a lot to laugh, it takes a train to cry.

1992. (lp/c) *(HAR 018/+C)* *<SIF/CSIF/GLCD 3080>* **MAD WORLD BLUES**
- Mad world blues / Songbird / Kurdistan / It is what it is / Down to earth / John Barleycorn / People who go under / Patriotic claptrap / Malnutrition at Standing Rock / Keys to love / Crazy man / Katie. *(cd-iss. Oct 93; HAR 018CD)*

Harbourtown Flying Fish

Apr 95. (cd/c) *(HAR CD/C 029) <FF 70/90 654>* **COURAGE, LOVE AND GRACE** ☐ Mar 97 ☐
- Change / Heartland / On your side / Family tree / Through it all / Learning of a miracle / From Ireland / One truth / Courage, love and grace / Cheating man / Love me in Eden / The lion and the lamb / The harrowing of pride / Eternity.

Mar 97. (ltd-cd; by PETE MORTON / ROGER WILSON / SIMON EDWARDS) *(HARCD 032)* **URBAN FOLK Vol.II: Self Destructive Fools** ☐ ⊟
- (Vol.I tracks) / Running out of lovin' / When you see those flying saucers / Little Musgrave / Goodbye my love / The belly boys / Cuckoo's nest / O'Reilly / Swimming song / None so fair / Love hurts / Derwentwater's farewell / Jack of diamonds.

—— In 1997, JO FREYA & PETE MORTON released their own mail-order CD

Jan 99. (cd) *(HARCD 037)* **TRESPASS** ☐ ⊟
- The cuckoo / Gay goshawk / Sylvia / Banks of the Nile / A farmer's boy / The mower and the dairymaid / Lincolnshire poacher / Little Musgrave / John Barleycorn / Dick Turpin / Banks of the sweet Dundee / The rose in June / Night visiting song.

Dec 00. (cd) *(HARCD 040)* **HUNTING THE HEART** ☐ ⊟
- Drink to me only / Hunting the heart / Twitching net curtains / Forgiveness hill / Constant motion / Madam or sir / Battle of Trafalgar / Maybe nothing's spoken / Deep blue sea / The desert / Thanksgiving.

Dec 03. (cd) *(HARCD 044)* **SWARTHMOOR** ☐ ⊟
- The two brothers / The luckiest man / Simplicity / Goodbye to oil / Listening to my boots / Love stood in my way / Naseby field / The shepherd's song / The government wall / Six billion eccentrics / St George slew the dragon.

Oct 05. (cd) *(HARCD 048)* **FLYING AN UNKNOWN FLAG** ☐ ⊟
- Harvest / The shores of Italy / Great gold sun / Further / The busker's song / In another life / Corruption country / I'm in love with Emily Dickinson / A love that I don't understand / The post office queue / Another train.

Further not issued

Oct 08. (cd) *(002)* **CASA ABIERTA**: TEN SONGS IN DIFFERENT TONGUES - VOLUME ONE ☐ ⊟
- Casa abierta / Ta me 'mo shui / Dilbar / Dat du mein leevsten bust / La corrida / Malaika / Avond / Tren arall / Karwan / Arirang.
(£2 from each sale of this CD went to the Gambian Schools Trust)

Annson not issued

Jan 11. (cd) *(ANSCD 100)* **ECONOMY** ☐ ⊟
- The sock on the line / Bigger than life / Related to me / Disobedience / The café song / India / The nightmare of the sons / Good enough for me / When we sing together / In the days when time was different.

- (8-10*) compilations -

2001. (cd) *Harbourtown; (HARCD 041)* **ANOTHER TRAIN** ☐ ⊟
- Family tree / The first day / Tam Lyn / Water from the houses of our fathers / Without thinking love / The prisoner / The cuckoo / Songbird / The gay goshawk / The battle of Trafalgar / Another train / Constant motion / Drink to me only / Katie.

- (5-7*) compilations, others, etc.-

2006. (ltd-cd) *Further; (001)* **NAPOLEON JUKEBOX** ⊟ tour ⊟
- Family tree / The two brothers / The shepherd's song / Another train / Further / The luckiest man / On your side / The busker's song / Heartland / I'm in love with Emily Dickinson / Without thinking love / Maybe nothing's spoken / Great gold sun / Harvest / Constant motion / St George slew the dragon.

MOVING HEARTS (⟹ Celtic and World Music Discography)

The MRS ACKROYD BAND (⟹ BARKER, Les)

MUCKRAM WAKES

Formed in 1971 in Derbyshire, the folk-dance group initially consisted of Roger Watson, Helen Wainwright and John Tams. The first was a songwriter, having spent much of the second half of the 1960s in a duo alongside Colin Cater.

After Roger married Helen in 1972, the trio produced their worthy debut LP, **A MAP OF DERBYSHIRE** (1973) {*7}, a record that oozed talent from concertinas, melodeons, harmoniums and Tams's fiddle, all carrying the trad aspects really well. Sadly, it was the only show with the WAKES for ALBION BAND-bound Tams, who later became part and parcel of the folk industry – HOME SERVICE, solo projects, etc.

However, the Watsons took on another couple, John and Suzie Adams (John was ex-DRUIDS), and put together a second set, simply entitled **MUCKRAM WAKES** (1976) {*6}. Although credited to ROGER WATSON solo, **THE PICK AND THE MALT SHOVEL** (1974) {*5} was recorded by the WAKES Mk.II line-up, the Garden Gnome Ceilidh Band and old chum Colin Cater.

Pending the third MUCKRAM WAKES set, **WARBLES, JANGLES AND REEDS** (1980) {*5}, the Watsons and the Adamses moonlighted with a third couple, PETE & CHRIS COE (and a number of others), as The NEW VICTORY BAND, releasing **ONE MORE DANCE AND THEN** (1978) {*6}. For a short time in the early 1980s, various comings and goings led to the MUCKRAM WAKES name being carried on by John Adams, KEITH KENDRICK (concertina), Ian Carter and BARRY COOPE (vocals).

ROGER WATSON had already gone solo with 1980's **MIXED TRAFFIC** {*5} and with two more sets in that decade, **CHEQUERED ROOTS** (1988) {*5} and **RADIOLAND** (1988) {*5}, the latter with American banjo player Debbie McClatchy. HELEN WATSON was carving out her own blues, jazz, country and folk solo career, and was half of early-1980s soul duo Loose Lips. Roger became artistic director of Traditional Arts Projects (TAPS) and has been part of two world-folk outfits, Millan and Boka Halat, from the 1990s onwards; look out also for his involvement with The Irregulars, the sidekicks of ROBB JOHNSON. *MCS*

Roger Watson (b. Feb 6, '46, Mansfield, Nottinghamshire) - concertina, tuba, melodeon / **Helen Watson** (b. Helen Wainwright, May 16, '51, Marchington, Staffordshire) - harmonium, piano, whistle / **John Tams** - fiddle, banjo, concertina

UK Trailer US not issued

1973. (lp) *(LER 2085)* **A MAP OF DERBYSHIRE** ☐ ⊟
- Spencer the rover – Winster processional theme / The cruise of the Sun Glory / Cathy Shaw / Poor old horse / Watercress-o / Mrs. Merry's ball – Polka: Winster gallop / Cow i' th' gate / The squire of Tamworth / Fifty years ago / Gilliver / The bone lace weaver – The mallard / Dumper and Pulling-down song.

—— **John Adams** - trombone, melodeon, fiddle, banjo, harmonium (ex-DRUIDS) repl. Tams - a future ALBION BAND and HOME SERVICE member

—— added **Suzie Adams** - drums, percussion

1976. (lp) *(LER 2093)* **MUCKRAM WAKES** ☐ ⊟
- Muckram wakes – The Duchess of Hamilton's rant / Bitter withy - William Taylor / T'owd brahn 'en - Black boy polka / The two sisters - Black boy jig / The farmer's arms / Winster wakes / Derby ram / Twenty pins - Cromford mills / Stockinger – The Meynell pack / Peg of Derby - Hugh Stenson the deserter / Owd Joe Biggin.

Highway not issued

1980. (lp) *(SHY 7009)* **WARBLES, JANGLES AND REEDS** ☐ ⊟
- Little red house in Cardiff – First of August / Miner's prayer / Mary Anne / Palms of victory / L'etoile Bannero (Reynardine) / Malthouse – Gammel Boon / Poor old weaver's daughter / Song of the pit / Sheffield park / I would that the wars were all over / Coming in on a wing and a prayer.

—— In 1981, John Adams, BARRY COOPE and KEITH KENDRICK (ex-DRUIDS) tried in vain to keep MUCKRAM WAKES afloat

NEW VICTORY BAND

MUCKRAM WAKES + new folk **Pete Coe** - melodeon / **Chris Coe** - hammered dulcimer / **Ian Wordsworth** - drums / **Linda Wordsworth** - tap dancing

Topic not issued

1978. (lp) *(12TS 382)* **ONE MORE DANCE AND THEN** ☐ ⊟
- Harper's frolic - Bonny Kate / The mountain belle / You can't take that on the train / Charles Lynch's - Cajun waltz - Banks of the Dee / Pretty little girl from nowhere / Nellie's first rag / Robbie Hobkirk's – Father's / Mrs. Gracie Bowie - The Hogmanay / Mamie May / Moustache - Cornrigs / One more dance and then / Long long trail. *(cd-iss. 2000 on Backshift+=; BASHCD 47)* - The busby / Looking for a partner / It ain't all honey and it ain't all jam / Speed the plough - Rochdale coconut dance - Britannia (Bacup) coconut dance / Ragged but right.

ROGER WATSON

w/ (on first set) **MUCKRAM WAKES, Garden Gnome Ceilidh Band** + **Colin Cater**

Tradition not issued

1974. (lp) *(TSR 017)* **THE PICK AND THE MALT SHOVEL** ☐ ⊟
- May song / Pick and malt shovel / Thomas Hanley / Malt house / Christmas hare / Manager's daughter / Gathering corn / Salvation band / Sudbury fair / Jack Tattersall / Number two stop seam / Hole in our back yard / Turn him up.

—— now with **Dave Walters** - guitar / **Helen Watson** - clarinet and piano / **John Adams** - trombone

Greenwich Village not issued

1980. (lp) *(GVR 210)* **MIXED TRAFFIC** ☐ ⊟
- Bouree / Venezuela / Where, oh where do I live? / A nightingale sang in Berkeley Square / The bold Princess Royal / Song for the Derbyshire colliers / Planxty Irwin / Stow brow / Three jovial miners / The Inniskillen Dragoon / Jeanette and Jeannot – The lullaby of Broadway / Nottingham miners / Shrimps on the stove / Brother, can you spare a dime?

Plant Life not issued

—— next with several session people

1988. (lp) *(PLR 078)* **CHEQUERED ROOTS** ☐ ⊟
- Galloway girth / Swansea town / Ashling / Mona's delight / Bright Phoebus / A Waterloo dance / Home, lads, home / Laura and Lenza / The dalesman's litany / The German bow.

1988. (lp; by ROGER WATSON & DEBBIE McCLATCHY) *(PLR 079)*
RADIOLAND
- Dixie darling / Three jovial miners / Dreary black hills / Hunt the squirrel / Somebody else's troubles / Sally, free and easy / Radioland / Colorado song / Weavers' march – Miss Bennett's jig – The arcadian nuptials / Women of Greenham Common / It's a long way to Mississippi.

—— In 1998, he joined Millan for the album 'Tiger Tracks' for Irregular Records

—— In 2003/4, Roger was with Boka Halat for two sets, 'Tides' and 'The Drummer'.

Wild Goose — not issued

Sep 09. (cd) *(WGS 367CD)* **PAST AND PRESENT**
- Gilliver / Linnen hall – The fantocini / Lovely Joan / Idbury hill – Broken dagger / Peg of Derby / The gobby-o / Rip Van Winkle / Bengal rounds – Old Sir Simon the king / Lowlands / Hunt the squirrel – The first of August / Two brethren / The manager's daughter / Fred Pigeon's polka – Donkey riding / Seafarers.

HELEN WATSON

Columbia — not issued

Oct 87. (7") *(DB 9158)* YOU'RE NOT THE RULE (YOU'RE THE EXCEPTION). / Chrome Soldier
(12"+=) *(12DB 9158)* - Speechless.

Oct 87. (cd/c/lp) *(CD/TC+/SCX 6710)* **BLUE SLIPPER**
- You're not the rule (you're the exception) / Boy's own world / When you love me, I get lazy / The new Rock Island line / Blue slipper / Don't stop now / I'm jealous dear / Sway / Chrome soldier / Don't forget to say your prayers / Rock myself to sleep / Speechless / Soul infection. *(<cd re-mast. Sep 06 on Fledg'ling+=; FLED 3058>)-* Dangerous daybreak (demo) / This must be paradise (demo).

Feb 88. (7") *(DB 9164)* I'M JEALOUS DEAR. / Don't Forget To Say Your Prayers
(12"+=/cd-s+=) *(12DB/CDDB 9164)* - Soul Infection.

May 88. (7") *(DB 9167)* WHEN YOU LOVE ME, I GET LAZY. / Rock Myself To Sleep
(12"+=/cd-s+=) *(12DB/CDCB 9167)* - The new Rock Island line / You're not the rule (you're the exception).

—— (below features Andy Fairweather-Low)

Mar 89. (7") *(DB 9173)* HANGING OUT THE WASHING (IN A SMALL BACK YARD). / Ready To Fly
(12"+=) *(12DB 9173)* - Heaven suits you.
(cd-s++=) *(CDDB 9173)* - ('A'-radio edit).

Mar 89. (cd/c/lp) *(CD/TC+/SCX 6717)* **THE WEATHER INSIDE**
- I wish that love was simple / You're so hard to get hold of / The road that ends in tears / The weather inside / Your face / Hanging out the washing (in a small back yard) / A thrill enough to know / Dangerous daybreak / Now we'll move the river / Ready to fly / Letters of introduction.

RCA — not issued

Mar 92. (cd-s) *(45226)* #100 WATCH / One Blue Suit

Mar 92. (cd/c/lp) *(PD/PK/PL 75193)* **COMPANION GAL**
- There must be some mistake / Someone you want to be with (more than me) / Not a word like love in sight / Companion gal / Break out the birdcage / Billy but beautiful / The devil in you / I won't tell on you / Manners / Then we came to the sea / #100 watch / One blue suit.

—— In 1992 (together with BARB JUNGR, CHRISTINE COLLISTER and MICHAEL PARKER, i.e. Hell Bent Heaven Bound II), she released 'Money The Final Frontier', a cassette-only set of showbizzy songs.

Building — not issued

Mar 96. (cd; as HELEN WATSON BAND) *(BUILD 001CD)*
NOTES ON DESIRE
- Shiver / Isn't that what it's for? / Since I fell for you / Time of your life / Notes on desire (at its height) / Blame it on the sun / Magnificent / From the top / I told you I loved you - now get out / Conversation / On and on / The last thing I need / Jackie you're moody / I want more / Fell for it.

DAPHNE'S FLIGHT

Helen Watson, Christine Collister, Melanie Harrold, Julie Matthews + Chris While

Fledg'ling — not issued

Apr 96. (cd) *(FLED 1005CD)* **DAPHNE'S FLIGHT**
- Over and over / Ain't no sunshine / Another year, another day / The calling / Gone / The letter / Father adieu / Guilty / Shake out your silver / Circle round the sun / Rise above the tide of life.

HELEN WATSON

Fledg'ling — Fledg'ling

Nov 97. (cd) *(<FLED 3013>)* **SOMERSAULT** — Jun 98
- Help you forget / Smoke signals / You'll never go away / Out of left field / Close to making sense / Ground floor flat / Value / Home before you know it / Flag / All weather girls / Kicking in my stall / Wasted on me / Lowish time.

Nov 99. (cd) *(FLED 3024)* **DOFFING**
- Keep what I got / Personally / Mystery train / I want to live and love / Cruisin' / I thank the Lord my prayers / Losing the feeling / Barefootin' / Icy blue heart / Ain't got you / Have mercy / I'm your puppet / That's all it took / I thought about you / Lush life.

Apr 02. (cd) *(FLED 3031)* **LIFESIZE**
- Windfall / Future bone / Magnificent / Arterials / Crying in my dreams / Lifesize / Too bad I'm a millionaire / Fire goes out / Quicksetts / How come your new lover... / Made for love / Joel's.

own label — not issued

Oct 08. (cd) *(none)* **HEADREST**
- My time now / I thought you should know / Eyebrows / Kitchen top / Can't be satisfied / I'll take good care of you / Made me cry / In place of you / Too many tomorrows / Princess / The last thing I need.

—— In 2009, MATTHEWS, WHILE AND WATSON issued the CD 'Bare Bones'.

MUMFORD & SONS

Don't be misled by the name: the Mumford of the group may be the creative daddy, but that's as far as the family ties go. The group Marcus Mumford formed in October 2007 soon struck up a kinship with other West London acts, such as LAURA MARLING, NOAH AND THE WHALE and JOHNNY FLYNN, that saw them declared leaders of the local folk scene. This scene came to relatively little, but spawned several real talents, MUMFORD & SONS being the most commercially successful.

Taking on heavy touring from the get-go in 2008, culminating in an appearance at the Glastonbury Festival, the band released their second EP, 'Love Your Ground', on both sides of the Atlantic. The band's friendly, inclusive onstage manner helped win them fans on a global scale, and by the time **SIGH NO MORE** (2009) {*8} appeared they were making appearances on late-night US TV, mostly thanks to the popularity of 'Little Lion Man', a track of banjo-driven fury that originally appeared on 'Love Your Ground'. The album was an unashamed hoedown, a stramash of instruments and boundless energy that perfectly captured the warm, gregarious feel of their live shows.

They continued to ride the rollercoaster to stardom as 'Little Lion Man' was nominated for two Grammys (it didn't win, but they got to perform at the ceremony and play as part of BOB DYLAN's backing band on 'Maggie's Farm' at the event). They have gone on to enjoy success in Australia and New Zealand with the album, while it sold over a million copies both in the UK and the US – they were the first British band to do that in the States since Coldplay in 2008. It was announced from the stage at Glastonbury 2011 that a follow-up was being recorded in Nashville, scheduled for release this year. *MR*

Marcus Mumford - vocals, guitar, drums / **Winston Marshall** - banjo, dobro, vocals / **Ben Lovett** - keyboards, organ, vocals / **Ted Dwane** - double bass, vocals

UK Chess Club — US not issued

Jul 08. (ltd; 10" ep) *(CC 006)* LEND ME YOUR EYES
- Roll away your stone / White blank page / Liar / Awake my soul.

Nov 08. (ltd; 10" ep) *(CC 009)* LOVE YOUR GROUND
- Little lion man / Feel the tide / Hold on to what you believe / The banjolin song.

Apr 09. (ltd; one-sided-10") *(CC 015)* THE CAVE AND THE OPEN SEA
- The Cave / But My Heart Told My Head (Winter Winds).

Island — V2

Sep 09. (ltd-7") *(2720975)* LITTLE LION MAN. / To Darkness — 24 — 61

Oct 09. (cd/lp) *(2722538)* *<VVR 728595>* **SIGH NO MORE** — 3 — Feb 10 — 16
- Sigh no more / The cave / Winter winds / Roll away your stone / White blank page / I gave you all / Little lion man / Timshel / Thistle and weeds / Awake my soul / Dust bowl dance / After the storm. *<lp-iss. on Glassnote; GLS-0109-01>*

Dec 09. (7" cream) *(2728222)* WINTER WINDS. / Hold On To What You Believe — 44

Mar 10. (7") *(2733942)* THE CAVE. / Untitled — 31

Jun 10. (7" dark green) *(2742411)* ROLL AWAY YOUR STONE. / White Blank Page (live at Shepherd's Bush Empire)

Nov 10. (dl-s) *(-)* WHITE BLANK PAGE

MUNDY (⟹ Celtic Connections)

MUZSIKAS (⟹ Celtic and World Music Discography)

Le MYSTERE DES VOIX BULGARES (⟹ Celtic and World Music Discography)

N

NEW SCORPION BAND (⟹ LAYCOCK, Tim)

NEW VICTORY BAND (⟹ MUCKRAM WAKES)

Lea NICHOLSON

One of many low-key trad-folk artists who could easily be missed amid the vast choice available to pick from in the early 1970s (DAVE EVANS, PAUL DOWNES, DAVE CARTWRIGHT, et al), singer and concertina specialist LEA NICHOLSON (born c. 1944 in Lancashire) was nevertheless known to peers such as STEELEYE SPAN, BOB PEGG and ROBIN DRANSFIELD, who all guested on his Bill Leader-produced debut LP **HORSEMUSIC** (1971) {*6}. One track appeared on a late-1960s various-artists compilation for Topic Records, 'Deep Lancashire'.

With fresh arrangements by Lea of several traditional tunes and ballads, it was the oddities, such as J.S. Bach's 'Allegro From The Trio Sonata In C...' and the Bonzo Dog Doo-Dah Band cover 'I'm The Urban Spaceman', that stood out in an off-kilter kind of way.

Nat Joseph took Lea to his bulging Transatlantic roster for **GOD BLESS THE UNEMPLOYED** (1972) {*5}, a collaboration with guitarist Stan Ellison (a guest on his previous LP), with RICK KEMP (bass) and Ian Whiteman (keyboards) helping them out. Both partners took on their fair of songwriting this time around, only to have their version of ANNE BRIGGS's 'Living By The Water' outshine a few of their own, such as 'Lazy Afternoon' (a minor hit in France) and 'Song For A Dead Mole'.

Lea's part-classical comeback set for STEFAN GROSSMAN, **THE CONCERTINA RECORD** (1980) {*4}, featuring Mike Oldfield, was just what it said on the tin. He'd already completed a great deal of session work for the likes of Oldfield, JOHN RENBOURN, STEVE ASHLEY, ROBIN DRANSFIELD, Russ Ballard and the BBC Philharmonic Orchestra. Other musical employment occupied NICHOLSON and his trusty concertina until he retired in 1992. *MCS*

Lea Nicholson - vocals, concertina / + session + guests

UK Trailer — US not issued

Apr 71. (lp) *(LER 3010)* **HORSEMUSIC**
- Here we come a-wassailing / Glory of the north / Greenland bound / Lea Rigs variations / I live not where I love / I'm the urban spaceman / Allegro from the trio sonata in C for two manuals and pedal / Along the Rossendale / The coast of Peru / The false knight on the road / Kopya / All through the beer.

Transatlantic — not issued

Jun 72. (lp) *(TRA 254)* **GOD BLESS THE UNEMPLOYED**
- Lazy afternoon / Mr. Finch / Boogaloo / Hitch-hike song / Pipe on the hob – Boring with the gimlet / A mistake no doubt / God bless the unemployed / Just because / Song for a dead mole / Jule's birthday / Just another song / Sootyfoot / Living by the water / The dark islander.

Jul 72. (7") *(BIG 504)* GOD BLESS THE UNEMPLOYED. / Piece Of Cake

Virgin — not issued

Jun 76. (7") *(VS 149)* LAZY AFTERNOON. / Sorry About The Phone Stephanie

(next single credited Lea Nicholson and The Rawtenstall Concertina Band)

Nov 76. (7") *(VS 164)* THE DAMBUSTER MARCH. / Southampton

Kicking Mule — Kicking Mule

Aug 80. (lp) *(SNKF 165)* *<KM 11>* **THE CONCERTINA RECORD**
- The Liberty bell / Kopya / Glenn Miller medley: Moonlight serenade – Chattanooga choo choo – In the mood / Lea Rigs / Lasst uns erfreuen / The Dambuster march / Courtly masqueing Ayres / Fourth Brandenburg concerto: Allegro – Andante – Presto. *(cd-iss. 1999 on Jamring; JRINGCD 001)*

—— Lea went into session work and self-released a cassette, 'THE CONCERTINA TAPES' (1993)

Ken NICOL

Born May 27, 1951, in Preston, Lancashire, singer-songwriter and guitarist KEN NICOL will be known mostly to followers of The ALBION BAND (he was a member between 1997 and September 2001) and STEELEYE SPAN (from December 2002 until his departure in June 2010). Just before leaving the latter, Ken had recorded a joint effort, 'Copper, Russet And Gold' (2010) alongside former ALBION/STEELEYE legend ASHLEY HUTCHINGS.

However, NICOL's folk life can be traced way back to the early 1970s, when he lived in London and played the London circuit. His first recorded dabblings were as Nicol & Marsh (with his brother-in-law Peter), a bluesy soft-rock combination that recorded four sets between 1974 and 1978, the earlier ones as (or with) Easy Street, alongside pre-Landscape drummer Richard James Burgess.

The fourth set, **NICOL & MARSH** {*5} (1978), which featured a cover of Lennon-McCartney's 'I'll Be Back', was recorded in Hollywood with help from seasoned session players such as Craig Doerge, Leland Sklar, Victor Feldman, Bill Payne, Tony Berg, David Kemper, Tom Hensley and producer Randy Bishop. Returning from LA after several years, NICOL settled back into life as a recording artist, although his cassette-only releases from the turn of the 1990s were rarely seen in shops.

Without going into too much intricate detail about his time with the aforesaid giants of folk (and chameleon comedian/musician Phil Cool), one must recommend his "official" album projects **THIRTEEN REASONS** (2005) {*6} and **INITIAL VARIATIONS** (2008) {*6}. Ken has also been a Christmas guest star with The HOUGHTON WEAVERS. *MCS*

NICOL AND MARSH'S EASY STREET

Ken Nicol - vocals, acoustic guitar / **Peter Marsh** - vocals, acoustic guitar / + guest/sessions, etc.

UK Epic — US not issued

Mar 74. (7") *(S EPC 2046)* I'VE BEEN PRAYING. / When You Put Me Down

Jun 74. (7") *(S EPC 2395)* MIDNIGHT CAT. / Poor And Lonely Ones

Oct 74. (7") *(S EPC 2733)* SINKING DOWN. / Day By Day

Jan 75. (lp) *(EPC 80468)* **NICOL AND MARSH'S EASY STREET**
- Midnight cat / My quietness / Have I done the right thing / I wish that I could see you now / Poor and lonely ones / Bernie's / I've been praying / Day by day / Peaceful easy feeling / Sinking down / Roses and Rose.

—— added **Richard James Burgess** - drums, percussion (he later joined Landscape)

Polydor — Capricorn

1976. (lp; as EASY STREET) *(2383 415)* *<CP 0174>* **EASY STREET** — French
- Feels like heaven / Lazy dog shandy / Things I've done before / Illogical love / Shadows on the wall / I've been lovin' you / Blame the love / Part of me / Easy street / Wait for summer / What have we become.

1977. (lp; as EASY STREET) *(2383 444)* **UNDER THE GLASS** — French
- Flying / How can you take it so hard / Rely on you / What does the world know / Is this real / Look for the sun / Only a fool / Strange change / I see you / Night of the 11th.

NICOL & MARSH

Polydor — not issued

Oct 78. (7") *(2059 061)* HURT BY LOVE. / Lady Of Windermere

Nov 78. (lp) *(POLD 5012)* **NICOL & MARSH**
- Streets of the angels / Holdin' on to you / Hurt by love / Back out of love again / As the years roll 'round / Save the station / Lady of Windermere / I'll be back / For what seems crazy now / Anthem of the time.

Jan 79. (7") *(2059 083)* STREETS OF THE ANGELS. / Back Out Of Love Again

—— NICOL would subsequently back comedian Phil Cool

KEN NICOL

Ess'ntial Productions not issued

1989. (c) *(none)* **HOLLYWOOD THIS, HOLLYWOOD THAT** [-] mail-o [-]
1989. (c) *(none)* **KEN NICOL** [-] mail-o [-]
(cd-iss.2007 on MVS; MVS-CD 014)
1989. (c) *(none)* **LITTLE CHILDREN'S BLUES** [-] mail-o [-]
(cd-iss.2007 on MVS; MVS-CD 017)
1990. (c) *(none)* **TIDINGS** [festive] [-] mail-o [-]
(cd-iss.2007 on MVS; MVS-CD 015)
1991. (c) *(none)* **ACROSS THE SPECTRUM** [-] mail-o [-]
Jun 94. (cd/c) *(EP 0074 CD/C)* **LIVING IN A SPANISH TOWN** [ ] [-]
- Midnight cowboy / Last night in Paris / Should've known better / Credit card blues / Living in a Spanish town / Last chances / I'd rather be with you / Down on the island / One more night / This time it's me / Jigs and reels / Back out of love / Same old lang syne.
1995. (cd-s; as KEN NICOL & JOHN ST RYAN) *(none)*
LAST NIGHT IN PARIS [ ] [-]
1995. (cd) *(none)* **TWO FRETS FROM THE BLUES** [-] mail-o [-]
- Two frets from the blues / Black cat blues / I feel good / Key to the highway / Georgia / No better love / Sitting on top of the world / Fast blues / Steamroller blues / Sometimes you just can't win.
1995. (c; w/ CHRIS WHILE) *(none)* **SHADOWS ON THE WALL** [ ] [-]
(cd-iss. 2006; ???)
1998. (cd) *(none)* **CLEAN FEET – NO SHOES** [-] mail-o [-]
- Last of the great whales / Those travelling days / The sun is god / Just a little closeness / Early bird rag / Shiver mi timbers / Sweet surrender / Mary of Dungloe / How could I forget about you / Fisherman's priest / You washed my feet and you stole my shoes / The level plain.

MVS not issued

Nov 01. (cd) *(MVS-CD 004)* **THE BRIDGE** [-] mail-o [-]
- Nowhere fast (on the road) / The bridge / If ever I return this way / All he wants to do is fishing / Dangerous / The road beneath my wheels / 'Til the English summer's done / Rags to riches / For love and money / Oh Mavis / The land of the free / Wailing at the summer wall.
Nov 05. (cd) *(MVS-CD 013)* **THIRTEEN REASONS** [ ] [-]
- Southern skies / In the wake of forward motion / For what seems crazy now / The angels' share / Insobriety / / Song for a sailor / The liquid petroleum gas song / When I get home / The water is wide / Ten reasons / On holiday in Stornoway / Give me time / That could've been me.
2007. (cd+dvd) *(none)* **LIVE IN FLORENCE** [five nights live at the Teatro del Sale] [-] mail-o [-]
- Midsummer night dream / Dangerous / The bridge / Rags to riches / Two frets from the blues / Ken's hornpipes / Steamroller blues / The water is wide / etc.
Nov 08. (cd) *(MVS-CD 018)* **INITIAL VARIATIONS** [ ] [-]
- C.M. / F.Y. / L.H. / P.C. / A.K. / E.P. / B.H. / P.W. / R.B. / P.A.

— In 2010, NICOL teamed up with ASHLEY HUTCHINGS on 'Copper, Russet And Gold'

Linde NIJLAND (⇒ YGDRASSIL)

NOAH AND THE WHALE

Their name inspired partly by Noah Baumbach's film 'The Squid And The Whale', the Charlie Fink-led Twickenham quintet/sextet were touted by the British music press in 2007/08 as part of a West London nu-folk scene which also included MUMFORD & SONS, Pull Tiger Tail, LAURA MARLING, EMMY THE GREAT and JOHNNY FLYNN. This was no momentous movement, just a bunch of like-minded individuals, but aside from some musical sensibilities they also sometimes shared personnel, MARLING and EMMY both providing a female vocal foil for Fink.

Their debut album, **PEACEFUL THE WORLD LAYS ME DOWN** (2008) {*6}, appeared to modest acclaim, drawing on some trad English folk influences and using recorders, ukulele, and whistles, but crossing over to appeal to an indie/ NME audience. Around the release of the album, drummer Doug Fink left to pursue a career in medicine, while solo- bound MARLING and Charlie Fink's relationship went south. There was no significance in the B-side cover of The Smiths' 'Girlfriend in a Coma'.

The couple's split signalled a step-change for the band, who dropped some of their more folksy traits and instrumentation in favour of a more straight-ahead rock-band line-up, which in retrospect suited Fink's songs better. Their second long player, **THE FIRST DAYS OF SPRING** (2009) {*8}, was an ambitious, expansive collection, addressing in part Fink and MARLING's break up. There is a glacial, stark quality to the recordings, focusing on Fink's melancholy musings of a man rubbing his eyes in bewilderment in the aftermath of a break-up. Fink also wrote and directed a film to accompany the album, which enjoyed screenings at art-house cinemas around the UK.

Swiftly becoming a regular fixture on the UK festival circuit, they appeared at Leeds and Reading, and with repeated visits to Glastonbury the band's stature grew in the UK and (slowly) abroad. They took a further right turn away from their folk roots and towards full-blown AOR with their third album, **LAST NIGHT ON EARTH** (2011) {*7}. Having worked through Fink's introspections on their second set, the band got happy with a record filled with unashamedly cheery Tom Petty-isms ('Waiting For My Chance To Come' is an unsubtle lift of 'Won't Back Down') and even moments of Lou Reed at his most chipper (think 'Coney Island Baby' rather than `Heroin'). Although an enjoyable album nonetheless, it did illustrate how far the band had travelled away from their folk roots and into the mainstream. *MR*

Charlie Fink - vocals, guitar, harmonica, ukulele / **Tom Hobden** - fiddle / **Matt Urby** - harmonium, bass / **Doug Fink** - drums / **Laura Marling** - backing vocals

UK Young And Lost Club — US not issued

Sep 07. (7") *(yalc 0018)* FIVE YEARS TIME. / Yocasta [ ] [-]
Jan 08. (7") *(yalc 0021)* TWO BODIES ONE HEART. / Rocks And Daggers [ ] [-]

Mercury — Cherry Tree

May 08. (7") *(1765450)* SHAPE OF MY HEART. / Death By Numbers [ ] [-]
(7"yellow) *(1765455)* - ['A'] / Beating.
(cd-s) *(1765449)* - ['A'] / Jealous kind of love [Engine Room session] / Jocasta [Huw Stephens session].
Jul 08. (7" blue) *(1774968)* FIVE YEARS TIME. / Red Alert [7] [-]
(7") *(1774969)* - ['A'] / I Have Nothing.
(cd-s) *(1774960)* - ['A'] / If I die tonight / Girlfriend in a coma.
Aug 08. (cd) *(1768177)* *<B0011652-02>* **PEACEFUL THE WORLD LAYS ME DOWN** [5] Sep 08 [ ]
- Two atoms in a molecule / Jocasta / Shape of my heart / Do what you do / Give a little love / Second lover / Five years time / Rocks and daggers / Peaceful the world lays me down / Mary / Hold my hand as I'm lowered.

— now without Doug; LAURA MARLING was already piecing together a solo act

Oct 08. (re-7"/cd-s) *(same)* SHAPE OF MY HEART [94] [-]
Aug 09. (ltd-7") *(06025 2710501-7)* BLUE SKIES. / [Yacht remix] [95] [-]
Sep 09. (cd) *(2710496)* *<B0013454-02>* **THE FIRST DAYS OF SPRING** [16] Oct 09 [ ]
- The first days of spring / Our window / I have nothing / My broken heart / Instrumental I / Love of an orchestra / Instrumental II / Stranger / Blue skies / Slow glass / My door is always open.
Jan 11. (dl-s) *(-)* L.I.F.E.G.O.E.S.O.N. [19] [-]
Mar 11. (cd) *(2760096)* *<B0015434-02>* **LAST NIGHT ON EARTH** [8] [ ]
- Life is life / Tonight's the kind of night / L.I.F.E.G.O.E.S.O.N. / Wild thing / Give it all back / Just me before we met / Paradise stars / Waiting for my chance to come / The line / Old joy.

Ruth NOTMAN

In the tradition of The UNTHANKS and Scottish singers KATE RUSBY and KARINE POLWART, the Nottingham-born (c. 1988) vocalist joined a new generation of bright young stars setting the Brit-folk scene alight. A finalist in BBC2's highly desirable Young Folk award in 2007, NOTMAN (with stalwart sidekick Saul Rose of FAUSTUS) also promoted several of her best songs at festivals up and down the country.

Her debut set, **THREADS** (2007) {*7}, featured some atmospheric cello by Hannah Edmonds, while ROGER WILSON (of WOOD, WILSON & CARTHY) helped out on others; pick of the bunch were 'Farewell Farewell' and DOUGIE MACLEAN's 'Caledonia'.

Highlighted by another FAIRPORT favourite, 'Si Tu Dois Partir' (written by DYLAN as 'If You Gotta Go'), and trad staples 'The Cruel Sister' and 'The Hedger And Ditcher', **THE LIFE OF LILLY** (2009) {*7} was rated by many, including KATE RUSBY, as a contender for album of the year. *MCS*

Ruth Notman - vocals, acoustic guitar, piano (+ session people)

UK Mrs Casey's — US not issued

Nov 07. (cd) *(MCRCD 7003)* **THREADS** [ ] [-]
- Billy don't you weep for me / Caledonia / Dark eyed sailor / Heather down the moor / Over the hill / Fause fause / Limbo / Lonely day dies / Farewell farewell / Still I love him / Roaming. *(bonus+=)* - What's going on?
Jun 09. (dl-s) *(-)* SI TU DOIS PARTIR [ ] [-]
Sep 09. (cd) *(MCRCD 9002)* **THE LIFE OF LILLY** [ ] [-]
- The hedger and ditcher / The squire of Tamworth / Holding on / The cruel sister / Si tu dois partir / The life of Lilly / Lark in the clear air / Johnny be fair / The bonny boy / Waters of Tyne / Here's to belief / Hold back the tide.

NYAH FEARTIES

Formed in 1986 in Lugton, Ayrshire by brothers Davie and Stephen Wiseman ('Feartie' was the adopted surname of all principal band members, on the same principle as The 'Ramones'), they began their musical career as street buskers in London, falling in with fellow folk-punk rebels The POGUES, whom they later supported.

The latter band's drummer, Andrew Ranken, later contributed vocals to NYAH FEARTIES' debut album **A TASTY HEIDFU'** (1987) {*6}, wherein the brothers laid down their patented soundclash of screaming, bastardised acoustic-thrash, folk/rockabilly and brain-clanking percussion. To promote the album the band appeared on 1980s youth TV showcase The Tube, scaring the Sassenachs with their manic Caledonian meltdown and ensuring themselves a permanent place on the alternative scene's outer limits.

Boasting a psychedelic orange/tartan sleeve, the 'Good, Bad And Alkies' EP of 1988 marked the group's return to their homeland and featured a live version of crowd favourite 'Drunken Uncle'. 1989's 'Graveside / Graham Side', meanwhile, was a home-produced, cassette-only affair recorded for the European market, where NYAH FEARTIES' crazed Celtic-folk appeal was greatly appreciated, although they also managed to get on the bill of many a folk hoedown in Wales and Ireland.

The NYAHs' long-awaited second album, **DESPERATION O' A DYIN' CULTURE** {*5}, arrived in 1990, recorded partly at the Trashcan Sinatras' Shabby Road studio in Kilmarnock and featuring a version of live favourite 'Gamblin' Bar Room Blues', a traditional drinking song once sung by Alex Harvey. With the addition of Allan Henry, Francis Lopez and Michael Woods, the group changed their name to The Collaborators, releasing an eponymous (initially Dutch-only) cassette in anticipation of a European tour.

The name change proved temporary, and the good old NYAH FEARTIES badge was back in place for 1992's 'Red Kola' EP. Although they were always more popular in Europe than in Scotland, it's hard to say what European fans might have made of the dialect title of the 1994 cassette 'A Keech In A Poke'. The band's final album, **GRANPA' CRAW** (1995) {*5}, was initially released by French label Danceteria, the original sleeve featuring a painting of Kirkcaldy darts hero Jocky Wilson, while the Scottish version featured samples of Kilmarnock FC's crowd in full song. Following NYAH FEARTIES' demise, Davie Wiseman and Michael Woods continued on the folk-crossover path with the wonderfully named Dub Skelper. *MCS*

Davie Wiseman - bass, vocals / **Stephen Wiseman** - banjo, percussion / plus **Donald Cuthbertson** - percussion

UK L.Y.T. — US not issued

Mar 87. (lp) *(DOLLP 001)* **A TASTY HEIDFU'**
- Red roller / Glen Ashdale falls / Theme fae in the barn / Lugton calling / Rantin' Robbie / Bludgeon man / Where the wind blows cold / Apathy / Hallelujah.

DDT — not issued

Jan 88. (12"ep) *(DISP 14T)* GOOD, BAD AND ALKIES
- Raisin' Bible John / Recobite Grace / Theme fae in the barn / Drunken uncle (live).

—— the NYAH FEARTIES moonlighted with Anna Palm, who released two albums for One Little Indian, 'Arriving And Caught Up' (1990) and 'Anna Palm' (1992).

L.Y.T. — not issued

1989. (c) *(none)* **GRAVESIDE / GRAHAM SIDE** — Europe
- Barassie / Lightnin' bolt / Pagan man / Barnweil boys / Lullaby / etc Brockwellmuir Broadcast

1990. (lp) *(BBR 001)* **DESPERATION O' A DYIN' CULTURE**
- Trashcans / Puddocks in the mist / The railway beast waltz / Release / Life's endless grind / Flight o' the country boys / Hills o' new Galloway / Vexation / Lugton junction / Sair erse / Baith sides o' the bed / Desperate jig / Gamblin' bar room blues. *(w/ free 7" ep)* - BARRASIE. / Motorway / Puddocks in the mist.

—— added **Allan Henry** - bass / plus **Francis Lopez** - guitar / **Michael Woods** - fiddle, penny whistle

1991. (c; as The COLLABORATORS) *(none)* THE COLLABORATORS

1992. (c-ep) *(none)* RED KOLA
- Red kola / Living room rock 'n' roll / Rantin' sonsie and free / Kirk ha' jig.

1994. (c) *(none)* **A KEECH IN A POKE**

Danceteria — not issued

Feb 95. (cd) *(NYAH 942)* **GRANPA' CRAW**
- Jolly walkers / Bullworker jig / Slash and burn / Safe as houses - Dub housing / Granpa' Craw / Good times / MOR / Lightning bolt / Away away - All the boys in Ayrshire / Wendy doon the banking / Campbeltown loch / Restless.

—— split in the summer of 1995; Davie and Michael formed Dub Skelper (eponymous set in '98)

- (5-7*) compilations, etc.-

1994. (cd) *Jivaroc; (none)* **SKUD** — French

OAK (⟹ The OLD SWAN BAND)

Jackie OATES

With a slight air of Celtic folk music apparent in her work, fiddler and singer JACKIE OATES (born 1983 in Congleton, Cheshire) had already captivated the hearts and minds of the nu-Brit-folk fraternity when she was an integral part of RACHEL UNTHANK & THE WINTERSET. The album she featured on, 'Cruel Sister', was the Mojo Folk Album of the Year (2005).

Gaining further experience from playing on her brother JIM MORAY's albums 'Sweet England' (2002) and 'Jim Moray' (2006), the 2003 BBC Radio 2 Young Folk Awards finalist was ready to find her own way with her album **JACKIE OATES** (2006) {*6}. Recorded a year earlier in Exeter with SHOW OF HANDS stalwart PHIL BEER at the controls and in session, her collection of mostly sourced ballads (check out 'Cruel Ship Carpenter' and 'Streams Of Lovely Nancy') was complemented by musicians BELINDA O'HOOLEY, Matt Norman, Emma Blake, Martin Keates, Ed Rennie and Jonathan Shoreland.

Taking guidance and production once again from BEER, and with a number of star musicians in session including brother MORAY, O'HOOLEY, JIM CAUSLEY, TIM VAN EYKEN and Steve Turner, Jackie excelled on the many traditional ballads on her second set, **THE VIOLET HOUR** (2008) {*8}. Highly regarded from the start, her performances of songs like 'Young Donald', 'Billy Reilly' and 'Our Trip To Croyden' were compared with SANDY DENNY, JUNE TABOR and SHIRLEY COLLINS by many pundits.

Signed to One Little Indian Records (home to Icelandic pixie Bjork), album number three, **HYPERBOREANS** (2009) {*8}, carried her rising reputation ever higher. Described as her coming-of-age album, the big ballads on show here were 'The Pleasant Month Of May', 'Young Leonard' and 'Past Caring', the last a moving reworking of a poem by Australian poet Henry Lawson. Produced and played on by her brother Jim, the record's Bjork connection came out in her reading of the Sugarcubes' 'Birthday', while ALASDAIR ROBERTS provided vocals on 'The Butcher's Boy' and guitar on 'The Isle Of France', and contributed the title song to the mix. Dave Wood wrote finale track 'May The Kindness', while Saul Rose (melodeon) and James Dumbleton (guitar) also played their part.

Lately, OATES has won further nominations and awards, and has performed on the main stage at folk festivals as a guest singer with the much-acclaimed ensemble The IMAGINED VILLAGE. *MCS*

Jackie Oates - vocals, violin, viola, shruti box / with session people

		UK	US
		Hands On Music	not issued
Sep 06.	(cd) *(HMCD 25)* **JACKIE OATES** - Banks of green willow / Cruel ship carpenter / Streams of lovely Nancy / Mormond braes / I wish it was last September – Ickbod / Lord abore and Mary Flynn / Flower of Northumberland / Lavenders blue – Mazurka / Staffordshire maid / Mistletoe bough / Rambleaway / Broken town / 14th November.	☐	⊟
		Chudleigh Roots	not issued
Apr 08.	(cd) *(CR 002)* **THE VIOLET HOUR** - Lark in the morning / The bonny labouring boy / Billy Reilly / Hampton lullaby / Tobias the grinder – Our trip to Croyden / Richie's lady / Young Donald / Rob Roy / Crockery ware / Summer's end / Goodbye to Beesands and to magic / My ship's lost its rigging / Wishfulness waltz / 3/8 bourrees [live].	☐	⊟
		One Little Indian	not issued
Sep 09.	(cd) *(TPLP 1034CD)* **HYPERBOREANS** - The miller and his three sons / Hyperboreans / Locks and bolts / The pleasant month of May / Past caring / The Sheffield grinder – Mavis / Young Leonard / Birthday / Isle of France / Butcher's boy / May the kindness.	☐	⊟
Oct 09.	(ltd-7") *(1045 TP7)* BIRTHDAY. / Past Caring	☐	⊟
Mar 10.	(dl-s) *(-)* (NOW WE PART) / ISLE OF FRANCE	☐	⊟

—— in 2010, Jackie featured on a single ('Selection of Marches') w/ ALASDAIR ROBERTS

Agnes OBEL

Whether simply performing instrumentals on her piano or singing like a nightingale, Agnes Caroline Thaarup Obel (born October 28, 1980 in Copenhagen, Denmark) was clearly inspired by classical music. Having learned the works of Bartok and Chopin from an early age, but equally at home with Swedish jazz giant Jan Johansson, singer-songwriter and bit-actress Agnes formed her own local band, Sohio, and followed a learning curve to become a fully-fledged folk star in the anything-goes genre.

Subsequently signing to the PIAS label, her album **PHILHARMONICS** (2010) {*8} almost immediately won the hearts and pockets of the Danes, hitting the top of their charts. Other Continental countries followed suit, and eventually the feat will be repeated in Britain, if it hasn't already happened by the time you read this. One of the sepulchral and sedate songs on the set was the massive Danish hit 'Riverside', while the quirky 'Brother Sparrow' and the cinematic 'Wallflower' and 'Avenue' were picture postcards of rainy days on the set of a Swedish film. Agnes had meanwhile removed to Berlin.

One thing that's clear is that if 1980s indie/neo-classical pianist and singer Virginia Astley had wanted to be a folk artist, she'd have sounded like OBEL, who has also produced a handful of cover versions, including John Cale's 'I Keep A Close Watch', Elliott Smith's 'Between The Bars' and the trad 'Katie Cruel'. *MCS*

Agnes Obel - vocals, piano

		UK	US
		PIAS	not issued
Jun 10.	(10"/cd-s) *(PIASR 202 T/CDS)* RIVERSIDE. / Close Watch / Sons And Daughters	☐	⊟
Oct 10.	(cd/lp) *(PIASR 195 CD/LP)* **PHILHARMONICS** - Falling, catching / Riverside / Brother sparrow / Just so / Beast / Louretta / Avenue / Philharmonics / Close watch / Wallflower / Over the hill / On powdered ground. *(deluxe d-cd-iss. May 11 +=; PIASR 195CDX)* - Riverside [instrumental] / Just so [instrumental] / Over the hill / Just so / Smoke and mirrors.	☐	⊟

ODGERS & SIMMONDS (⟹ The MEN THEY COULDN'T HANG)

O'HOOLEY & TIDOW

Once a regular among the Mercury Prize nominations, Leeds-born Belinda O'HOOLEY, formerly of RACHEL UNTHANK & THE WINTERSET, combined forces with fellow singer-songwriter Heidi Tidow, who'd worked with CHUMBAWAMBA, for **SILENT JUNE** (2010) {*7}.

A bold cocktail of neo-classical folk, the JO FREYA/No Masters-produced album boasted the talents of JACKIE OATES on fiddle, alongside the textured strings of UISCEDWR's Cormac Byrne and Anna Esslemont, in a set that appeared in Mojo magazine's Top 10 Folk Albums of the Year. Lyrically and musically, the songs were formed on a yearning, sombre template, the best being 'All Stand In Line', trad staple 'Spancil Hill' and 'Que Sera'. The last-named was not the Doris Day hit, but a murder ballad of sorts, inspired by the execution of first world war heroine Nurse Edith Cavell.

O'HOOLEY's brief solo career got under way when she won the TV soundalike contest 'Stars In Their Eyes', impersonating Annie Lennox. Her musical family tree originated in County Sligo, where her uncle, the multi-instrumentalist Tony Howley, performs regularly, while her Celtic cousins TOMMY FLEMING and Colm O'Donnell are/were leading members of DE DANAAN and The Border Collie Band respectively.

Her only solo set, **MUSIC IS MY SILENCE** {*7} (2005), showed her love of both traditional and contemporary songs, tracks like 'All That Remains' and 'Moon Over Water' helping her win plaudits from her peers. It might have been even better had it included versions of 'Blackbird' and

'Whitethorne', two of her compositions for RACHEL UNTHANK & THE WINTERSET's album THE BAIRNS.

Recently the duo have returned to work with CHUMBAWAMBA on the agitpop group's seventeenth album, 'ABCDEFG' (2010). *MCS*

Belinda O'Hooley (b. Jul '71, Leeds) – vocals, piano / **Heidi Tidow** (b. Sep '80, Huddersfield, England) - vocals / plus session people

UK No Masters — US not issued

Feb 10. (cd) *(NMCD 32)* **SILENT JUNE** ☐ ⊟
- Flight of the petrel / All stand in line / Shelter me / Banjololo / Spancil hill / Too old to dream / Hidden from the sun / Que sera / Beautiful danger / One more Christmas / Cold and stiff.

BELINDA O'HOOLEY

Boulevard Village — not issued

Sep 05. (cd) *(RR 001)* **MUSIC IS MY SILENCE** ☐ ⊟
- All that remains / Blanket of night / Moon over water / Izuko, no more / Lover / Music is my silence / Different light / Afterglow / Monalea / With her.

OIGE (⟹ DILLON, Cara)

OLA (⟹ BELL, Helen)

The OLD SWAN BAND

Great oaks from little acorns grow, or in this case, just one tiny oak in the shape of the great OLD SWAN BAND. Folk band OAK, formed in 1970 in Kingston upon Thames, London, were a one-album quartet comprising frontman Tony Engle, fiddler PETA WEBB (soon to be a solo artist) and the husband-and-wife team of Rod and Danny Stradling. Released on Topic Records, **WELCOME TO OUR FAIR** (1971) {*5} was typical trad material for the time, not exactly brilliant but worth a wee sum on eBay today.

From the ashes of the Cotswold Liberation Front (not exactly a troublesome group), The OLD SWAN BAND arose in 1974, the Stradlings joined almost immediately by Martin Brinsford (mouth organ and melodeon), Ron Field (autoharp and banjo) and just-turned-teenage sisters Fi and Jo Fraser (vocals and various string and wind instruments).

Drawing inspiration from Walter Bulwer, SCAN TESTER and The COPPER FAMILY as much as English country-dance morris masters The ALBION BAND, the sextet's musical manifesto was firmly in place on their self-descriptive debut LP, **NO REELS** (1977) {*6}. Marking the addition of Mel Dean, and verging on Celtic-folk but with few or no Irish-Scottish jigs and reels (only English "polkas" and "dances"), 1979's **OLD SWAN BRAND** {*7} was respected for the band's traditional dexterity and sense of musical identity.

Shifting labels from Free Reed to Dingles (the latter more associated with FIDDLER'S DRAM), Field and Dean made way for multi-instrumentalist Paul Burgess and pianist Richard Valentine. The 1981 album **GAMESTERS, PICKPOCKETS AND HARLOTS** {*6} was the last before the Stradlings were on their way – Rod would find employment with The English Country Blues Band, TIGER MOTH (with IAN A. ANDERSON) and EDWARD II AND THE RED HOT POLKAS.

Newcomers such as fiddler Flos Headford and trombonist Johnny Adams joined Paul, Martin, Fi and Jo for an eponymous one-off EP released in 1983; Jo had already joined BLOWZABELLA before changing her professional name to Jo Freya. Martin Brinsford became an integral part of BRASS MONKEY. Taking friend Heather Horsley along from their Token Women outfit, Fi and Jo rounded up the usual suspects for the comeback set **SWAN UPMANSHIP** (2004) {*6}. *MCS*

OAK

Tony Engle - vocals, anglo concertina, fiddle, bones / **Rod Stradling** - vocals, melodeons / **Danny Stradling** - vocals, tambourine / **Peta Webb** - vocals, fiddle

UK Topic — US not issued

Oct 71. (lp) *(12TS 212)* **WELCOME TO OUR FAIR** ☐ ⊟
- Thousands or more / New rigged ship – Rig-a-jig-jig / The lakes of cool flynn / The Nutley waltz – The faithful sailor boy / Roving the county Tyrone / The scarlet and the blue / Shepherds arise / Scan's polkas / Australia / Cupid's garden / False, false / Our good ship lies in the harbour / The bunch of thyme / The perfect cure – The sweets of May.

—— split in '72; PETA WEBB went solo, while the Stradlings formed …

The OLD SWAN BAND

Rod Stradling - melodeon / **Danny Stradling** - tambourine, triangle drum / **Martin Brinsford** (b. Aug 17 '44, Gloucester, England) – mouth organ, melodeon, skulls / **Fi Fraser** (b. Fiona Mildred Newmarch Fraser, Jul 31, '59, Barnet, Hertfordshire) – fiddle, banjo-mandolin, clarinet, vocals / **Jo Fraser** (b. Dec 4 '60, St Albans, Hertfordshire) – whistles, recorder, vocals / **Ron Field** - autoharp, banjo

Free Reed — not issued

1977. (lp) *(FRR 011)* **NO REELS** ☐ ⊟
- Walter Bulwer's polkas Nos. 2 & 1 / The Dannish waltz – The Indian polka – Rigs of Marlow / Belle Isles march – Lass of Richmond Hill – Once I loved a maiden fair / Not for Joe – Oscar Wood's polka – Heel and toe polka / The Sherborne waltz – Lovely Nancy / Bonnets so blue – Starry night for a randy uncle's jig / George Privett's polka – Percy Brown's polka / The Manchester hornpipe – The Cliffe hornpipe / The Blakeney breakdown – William Kimber's Schottische-hornpipe / The Winster gallop – The four-hand reel – The dark girl dressed in blue / Dan Leno's boat / Woodland flowers – Oscar Wood's jig / Lucy Campbell – Nip the bunny – Mr Rew's polka / Up the sides and down the middle – The new-rigged ship / Bonny breast knots / The curly-headed ploughboy – The quaker – Three around three. *(cd re-mast. Apr 08 +=; FRRR 5)* - Huntsman's chorus – Buttered peas / The man in the moon – Varsoviarna / Perfect cure – Bugle call jig.

—— added **Mel Dean** - Anglo concertina, bass trombone

1979. (lp) *(FRR 028)* **OLD SWAN BRAND** ☐ ⊟
- The matelot – Michael Turner's jig No.3 – Captain Lemo's quick march / The king of the gypsies / Can't stop polka – The Evesham stick dance / Jack Tar on shore / Stoney's waltz – Neriah Benfield's waltz – Jack Robinson / April morning / The British man of war – The Redower polka – Scan's stepdance No.2 – The crabfish stepdance / The bunch of violets / Symondsbury mummers' tune – Dr Casey's fin book – My love, my love / Fare thee well dearest Nancy / Trip to the forest – The triumph – The Bourton six / Speed the plough. *(cd re-mast. Jun 08; FRRR 14)*

—— **Paul Burgess** - fiddle, piano, crumhorn, cornet, mandolin-banjo; repl. Field

—— **Richard Valentine** - piano; repl. Dean

Dingles — not issued

1981. (lp; as OLD SWAN BAND) *(DIN 322)* **GAMESTERS, PICKPOCKETS AND HARLOTS** ☐ ⊟
- The woodcutter's jig – The Swedish dance / Stephen Baldwin's schottisches Nos.1 and 2 – The Kennet jig / Story: The fire brigade / The vine tree / Little Polly – Double figure eight / The Worcestershire hornpipe – Morning star / Old Heddon of Fawley – The marriage vow / Give us some treacle and bread – Mrs. Claxton's polka / Story: The cricket match / The Gloucestershire hornpipe – Polly put the kettle on / The quickstep – Trip to the forest / Over the hills to glory – Bobbing around / The sloe.

—— in 1982 the Stradlings took on other projects; Rod moved on to The English Country Blues Band and offshoot TIGER MOTH.

—— new post-millennium line-up consisted of: **Fi, Jo (Freya), Martin + Paul** plus **Flos Headford** - fiddle / **Johnny Adams** - trombone

Waterfront — not issued

1983. (12" ep) *(WFEP 003)* THE OLD SWAN BAND ☐ ⊟
- The rose polka – J.B. Milne's polka / Trois jolis mineurs / Staffordshire hornpipe – Mad Moll of the Cheshire hunts / Factory girl / Sonny's mazurka – Waterloo dance.

—— Fi + Jo took off to join BLOWZABELLA; returned later …

—— when Martin joined BRASS MONKEY with MARTIN CARTHY; he was repl. (briefly) by **Neil Gledhill** - bass saxophone / (and right into new album) + **Heather Horsley** - keyboards

Wild Goose — not issued

Aug 04. (cd) *(WGS 320CD)* **SWAN UPMANSHIP** ☐ ⊟
- The green-clad hills – Jimmy Garson's march / Jack Robinson – William Irwin's No.3 – The Tipputs / Steamboat hornpipe – Gloucester hornpipe / False start / General Ward – The day room / Winster gallop – Four-hand reel – Dark girl dressed in blue / Church street – Redwing – St. Mary's / Flowers of Edinburgh – Soldier's joy – Morpeth rant / Wenlock edge – Summer waltz / Flowers of Edinburgh / Schottis fran Havero – Another fine mess / George Green's college hornpipe / Basquet of oysters and Sally Sloanes / Freedom of Ireland – Kitchen girl / Beatrice Hill's three-hand reel / Ger the rigger – Mickey chewing bubble gum.

- (8-10*) compilations -

Jul 95. (cd) *Free Reed; (FRCD 31)* **STILL SWANNING … AFTER ALL THESE YEARS!** ☐ ⊟
- Walter Bulwer's polkas Nos.2 & 1 / Bonnets so blue – Starry night for a randy uncle's jig / Not for Joe – Oscar Wood's polka – Heel and toe polka / The man in the moon – Fire burning bright – Varsoviarna / The Dannish waltz – The Indian polka – Rigs of Marlow / Dan Leno's boat / The Sherborne waltz – Lovely Nancy / The curly-headed ploughboy – The quaker – Three around three / The rose polka – J.B. Milne's polka / The matelot – Michael Turner's jig No.3 – Captain Lemo's march / Can't stop polka – The Evesham stick dance / Symondsbury mummer's tune – Dr. Casey's fin book – My love, my love / Speed the plough / Staffordshire hornpipe – Mad Moll of the Cheshire hunts / Woodcutter's jig – Swedish dance / Little Polly – Double figure eight / Old Heddon of Fawley – The marriage vow / Gloucester hornpipe – Polly put the kettle on / Give us some treacle and bread – Mrs. Claxton's polka / Worcestershire hornpipe – Morning star / The vine tree / The sloe.

- (5-7*) OAK compilation –

2003. (d-cd) *Musical Traditions; (MTCD 327-8)*
COUNTRY SONGS AND MUSIC □ ⊟
- Thousands or more / Bob Cann's barndance – Hilligo filligo / Roving round the county Tyrone (PETA solo) / The rose of Allendale / Australia (ROD) / The bluebell polka / The bonny hawthorn / False, false (DANNY) / Cupid's garden (TONY & PETA) / a) The Nutley waltz, b) Your faithful sailor boy (DANNY w/ chorus) / The caning girl (TONY) / The scarlet and the blue / The lovely banks of Lea (PETA) / The lass of Newcastle town / Maggie (DANNY) / a) The bunch of thyme (PETE, DANNY & ROD), b) The perfect cure – The sweets of May // Shepherds arise / Steamboat hornpipe – Speed the plough / The lakes of cold flynn (TONY) / Genevieve / Pretty Nancy of Yarmouth / New rigged ship – Rig-a-jig-jig / The rambling royal (ROD) / Our good ship in the harbour / Our ship is ready (PETA) / Scan's polka Nos.1 & 2 / Maggie May / The Broomfield wager / See me dance the polka – Oh Joe the boat is going over / The old rustic bridge (DANNY) / Young Ellender / My old man – Tipperary – Troubles – Daisy – Dicky bird – Hour.

The OMEGA 3 (⟹ ROARING JELLY)

OPHIUCHUS

Formed in 1986 in Castle Combe, Wiltshire, the loose collective of crusty folk-rockers OPHIUCHUS released the vinyl-only set **PRONOUNCED OFFEE-ICK CUSS** (1989) {*7} – recorded live at the Moles Club in Bath the year before – and a Pete Haycock-produced 45, 'Serpent And The Bearded King'.

A succession of personnel adjustments more than likely blighted the band's chances of breaking through, but twin brothers Jon and Simon Cousins (both from Stonehenge Festival garage band Random Gender) held them together for at least a year. Simon was to join Merseyside musos The Onset alongside Mike Badger of The La's fame.

Melodeon player Pete Causer, bassist Xavier Tutein (the replacement for Simon Cousins), and drummer Ed Grimshaw (who was followed by Simon 'Bud' Millais and then Myke Vince), but not RED JASPER-bound sax-player Pat d'Arcy, all claimed their places in the Mk.I line-up, but by the turn of the decade the rural rockers had broken up again. The live album (released by Geoff Davis at Probe Plus) earned favourable reviews, best tracks being 'Dreaming Of James Joyce And Virginia Woolf', 'Some Say The Devil Is Dead' and 'Serpent And The Bearded King'.

For Mk.II Jon enlisted the services of former Random Gender sound engineer Glenn Wardle plus new boys Dave Woodward (guitar), Andy Hargreaves (bass) and Steve Garvey (drums). Support dates with label-mates Half Man Half Biscuit gave the group status among the indie elite, but the shelving of their EP 'Lost Tribe Of England' and its accompanying promotional film left them reeling.

Mk.III was quickly put together in spring 1991, Jon's recruitment drive bringing in drummer George Laidlaw, Pat d'Arcy (again), cittern player Gary Price (ex-WHISKY PRIESTS) and bassist Paul 'Wil' Wilson. But even a change of name to Wicca Man did little or nothing to help their fortunes, leaving LEVELLERS to fly the crusty flag.

Spurred on by an internet fan page, a scrubbed-up OPHIUCHUS (Jon, Simon, Myke, Pete, Pat, Xavier, Glenn, Mike Slater and ex-Random Gender accordionist Richard Hughes) performed a reunion gig in June 2010, helping to mark the 40th anniversary of the Glastonbury Festival. *MCS*

Jon Cousins - vocals, guitar, tin whistle / **Pat d'Arcy** - saxophone / **Pete Causer** - melodeon, flute, bodhran / **Xavier Tutein** - bass; repl. Simon Cousins who joined The Onset / **Myke Vince** - drums; repl. Simon 'Bud' Millais, who repl. Ed Grimshaw, who joined The Fontaines (and later Warm Jets)

UK Ophiuchvs — US not issued

Sep 87. (7") *(OPH 001)* SERPENT AND THE BEARDED KING. / Song For Pym □ ⊟
(re-dist. Jul 88; same)

—— now without d'Arcy to RED JASPER (repl. by Si Cousins + Mike Badger)

Probe Plus — not issued

Jun 89. (lp) *(PROBE 23)* **PRONOUNCED OFFEE-ICK CUSS** (live September 1988) □ ⊟
- Mayfire circles / Memories of an Atlantic beach / Silver and grey / Dreaming of James Joyce and Virginia Woolf / Serpent and the bearded king / Some say the devil is dead / Like a child / The lost tribe of England / Jacks in the green / The Dorset four hand reel - Not for Joe - Song for Pym / The cajun stomp.

—— split after release of above - re-formed late '89/90 **Jon Cousins** + **Glenn Wardle** (sound engineer) (ex-Random Gender) + **Dave Woodward** - guitar / **Andy Hargreaves** - bass / **Steve Carvey** - drums (ex-Pagan Fringe)

—— **George Laidlaw** - drums; repl. Carvey + Wardle

—— (split late 1990 - re-formed spring 1991: **Jon, George, Pat D'Arcy** + **Gary Price** - cittern (ex-WHISKY PRIESTS) + **Paul 'Wil' Wilson** - bass; all became Wicca Man

ORIENTAL SUNSHINE

Could this be the best band ever to come out of Norway? Probably not, but they did have their 15 minutes of fame, although only around Bergen. "Relaxing raga-psychedelic-mantra-folk sung in English" would more or less describe the music of the trio ORIENTAL SUNSHINE, whose principal members were singers Nina Johansen and Rune Walle and sitar player and flautist Satnam Singh.

Although it lasted only about half an hour, their one and only Norwegian LP, **DEDICATED TO THE BIRD WE LOVE** (1970) {*8}, certainly lived up to the hype surrounding it, and even better when the magnificent re-issue imprint Sunbeam gave it a spin some 36 years later – it had lost none of its shine. One thing was clear: virtuoso Satnam was the star here, but singer Nina (think of Grace Slick fronting The INCREDIBLE STRING BAND) took the honours on 'Across Your Life' (a classic), 'Mother Nature', 'My Way To Be Hurt' and 'Let It Be My Birth'. The near-six-minute 'Can Anybody Tell?' was the pick of the others.

And then nothing. What happened to such a great outfit? Are there any other recordings? These are questions you'll be asking after you hear the garden of delights on show on this album. *MCS*

Nina Johansen - vocals, acoustic guitar / **Rune Walle** - vocals, acoustic guitar / **Satnam Singh** - sitar, flute / plus **Helge Grosli** - keyboards / **Sture Janson** - bass / **Espen Rud** - drums, percussion

UK Philips — US not issued

1969. (7") *(PF 353 339)* MOTHER NATURE. / Visions ⊟ Norway ⊟
1970. (7") *(6084 003)* ACROSS YOUR LIFE. / Unless ⊟ Norway ⊟
1970. (lp) *(6317 002)* **DEDICATED TO THE BIRD WE LOVE** ⊟ Norway ⊟
- Across your life / Mother nature / Look at me / Unless / Land of wisdom / Let it be my birth / Can anybody tell / Visions / My way to be hurt / Where you went (tum kahan gaye) / I'm going. *(cd/lp re-iss. Apr 06 on Sunbeam; SBR CD/LP 5013)*

—— split in 1971 – where are they now?

Beth ORTON

Born Elizabeth Caroline Orton, December 14, 1970, at East Dereham in Norfolk, the unassuming BETH ORTON has become the reluctant heroine at the pinnacle of the folktronica genre.

For a time a Buddhist nun after her single mother, a political activist, died in 1989, she was brought up in the London district of Dalston from the age of fourteen. Her father had left the family home when Beth was eleven, and died soon after.

Her meeting at a party with technoid legend William Orbit (soon to be her boyfriend) led to work with his Strange Cargo project. Her vocal contributions to the track 'Water From A Vine Leaf' preceded their collaborative cover of JOHN MARTYN's 'Don't Wanna Know About Evil' (working initially under the name of Spill) and the opener of the Japan-only CD release **SUPERPINKYMANDY** (1993) {*5} (named after a doll of her childhood), which contained an early version of the ORTON/Orbit gem 'She Cries Your Name'.

Coming to the ears of in-vogue electronica boffins The Chemical Brothers (and later Red Snapper's Ted Barnes and Ali Friend), her downbeat, poignant vocals were used on the duo's groundbreaking 1995 album 'Exit Planet Dust' (on tracks 'Alive Alone' and 'One Too Many Mornings'), and she worked on the Strange Cargo set 'Hinterland' the same year.

Almost immediately, the solo Beth found herself on the books of Heavenly Records. Her debut single, 'I Wish I Never Saw The Sunshine', was a revamp of a Ronettes hit from the 1960s; follow-up 'She Cries Your Name' didn't chart this time around. Parent debut album **TRAILER PARK** (1996) {*9} was issued shortly afterwards.

An affecting blend of fragile folk and subtle, lo-fi trip-hop rhythms, it won praise from such diverse camps as fRoots magazine and Mixmag, and was nominated for a 1997 Mercury Music Prize. Beth's singles 'Touch Me With Your Love', 'Someone's Daughter' and the re-released 'She Cries Your Name' (a song plumbing the melancholy depths of her NICK DRAKE/SANDY DENNYesque muse) scored successively higher chart placings. The lanky ORTON (she's six feet tall) ended the year on a high note, collaborating with her long-time hero TERRY CALLIER on the Top 40 EP 'Best Bit'.

The princess of bedsitter music served up a second helping of rich, thought-provoking tunes in the shape of 1999's **CENTRAL RESERVATION** {*8}, featuring guest appearances by Ben Watt, Ben Harper, Dave Roback and Dr. John. It deservedly made the Top 20, and Beth also made some headway in the States, where she had befriended Beck. Songs such as 'Stolen Car', the title track (both Top 40 hits) and 'Stars All Seem To Weep' were "emotionally and lyrically attuned like paintings set on the deepest canvas taking every colour imaginable from palettes of silver" – as one pundit put it.

DAYBREAKER (2002) {*6} paired ORTON's girl-next-door lilt with yet more A-list guest artists. Ryan Adams appeared on 'Concrete Sky' and harmonised with Emmylou Harris on 'God Song', while the Chemical Brothers returned to electro-fi the title track; the swooning production came courtesy of Everything But The Girl's mainman Ben Watt. There was a sense that the girlish folkie was finally outgrowing her growing pains, and while critics were divided on its sombre merits, the record made the UK Top 10, the biggest chart success of her career.

Album number four (not counting that false start in Japan), **COMFORT OF STRANGERS** (2006) {*7}, with its end-of-the-rainbow sleeve art, was an altogether brighter-sounding record. Produced by the ubiquitous Jim O'Rourke, it found ORTON finally taking on the singer-songwriter mantle she'd been avoiding throughout her career. While its UK Top 30 chart placing was perhaps a little disappointing, the album was her first entry in the US Top 100.

ORTON has been taking a motherhood sabbatical with her baby daughter, although 2011 hopefully will see her back in business. She's taken the stage a few times in recent years, notably with a gig at the 2009 Mojo party at the Slaughtered Lamb in Clerkenwell, London. *MCS*

Beth Orton - vocals, acoustic guitar (ex-Spill) + **William Orbit** - electronics

UK not issued — US Toshiba

1993. (cd) *(TOC 7984)* **SUPERPINKYMANDY** [–] Japan [–]
- Don't wanna know about evil / Faith will carry / Yesterday's gone / She cries your name / When you wake / Roll the dice / City blue / The prisoner / Where do you go / Release me.

—— now with **Ted Barnes** - guitar (of Junctions) / **Ali Friend** - double bass (of Red Snapper) / **Will Blanchard** - drums (of Sandals) / guest David Boulter <r>- harmonium / + string section

Heavenly — Dedicated

Jul 96. (7" one-sided) *(HVN 56)* I WISH I NEVER SAW THE SUNSHINE [ ] [–]

Sep 96. (10" ep/cd-ep) *(HVN 60 10/CD)* SHE CRIES YOUR NAME / Tangent. / Safety / It's Not The Spotlight [ ] [–]

Oct 96. (cd/c/lp) *(HVNLP 17 CD/MC/LP)* <44007> **TRAILER PARK** [68] [ ]
- She cries your name / Tangent / Don't need a reason / Live as you dream / Sugar boy / Touch me with your love / Whenever / How far / Someone's daughter / I wish I never saw the sunshine / Galaxy of emptiness. *(d-cd iss. Sep 05 on Heavenly+=; 82876 71870-2)* - CENTRAL RESERVATION *(re-mast. Mar 09 as d-cd "Legacy Edition" on Sony+=; 88697 42442-2)* - Safety / It's not the spotlight / Galaxy of emptiness / Pedestal / Touch me with your love (instrumental) / It's this I am, I find / Bullet / Best bit (early version) / Best bit / Skimming stone / Dolphins / Lean on me / I love how you love me.

Jan 97. (10" ep/cd-ep) *(HVN 64 10/CD)* TOUCH ME WITH YOUR LOVE. / Pedestal / Galaxy Of Emptiness [60] [–]

Mar 97. (c-ep/10" ep/cd-ep) *(HVN 65 CS/10/CD)* SOMEONE'S DAUGHTER. / I Wish I Never Saw The Sunshine / It's This I Am, I Find [49] [–]

Jun 97. (c-s) *(HVN 68CS)* SHE CRIES YOUR NAME (1997 version) / It's Not The Spotlight [40] [–]
(10"+=/cd-s+=) *(HVN 68-10/CD)* - Bullet / Best bit.

Heavenly — Heavenly

Dec 97. (c-ep; BETH ORTON featuring TERRY CALLIER) *(<HVN 72CS>)* **BEST BIT EP** - Best bit / Skimming stone / Dolphins. [36] [ ]
(12" ep+=/cd-ep+=) *(<HVN 72 12/CD>)* - Lean on me.

—— next with guitarist **Ben Harper**

Mar 99. (c-s) *(HVN 89CS)* STOLEN CAR / Precious Memory [34] [–]
(cd-s+=) *(HVN 89CD)* - I love how you love me.
(cd-s) *(HVN 89CD2)* - ('A') / Stars all seem to weep (shed version) / Touch me with your love (live).

Mar 99. (d-lp/c/cd) *(HVNLP 22/+MC/CD)* <19038> **CENTRAL RESERVATION** [17] [ ]
- Stolen car / Sweet decline / Couldn't cause me harm / So much more / Pass in time / Central reservation / Stars all seem to weep / Love like laughter / Blood red river / Devil song / Feel to believe / Central reservation. *(d-cd iss.+=)* - TRAILER PARK

Sep 99. (cd-s) *(HVN 92CD1)* CENTRAL RESERVATION (+ mixes: Spiritual Life - Ibadan remix + William Orbit remix) [37] [–]
(cd-s) *(HVN 92CD2)* - ('A'-Deep dish modern red rock mixes; remix edit / remix / 2000 dub).
(12") *(HVN 92-12)* - ('A'-Spiritual Life - Ibadan remix) / ('A'-Deep dish modern red rock 2000 dub).

Jul 02. (cd-ep) *(HVN 115CD)* CONCRETE SKY EP [ ] [–]
- Concrete sky / Ali's waltz / Bobby Gentry / Carmella (Four Tet remix).

Jul 02. (lp/cd) *(HVNLP 37/+CD)* <39918> **DAYBREAKER** [8] [ ]
- Paris train / Concrete sky / Mount Washington / Anywhere / Daybreaker / Carmella / God song / This one's gonna bruise / Ted's waltz / Thinking about tomorrow. *(ltd-cd-iss. Oct 02; HVNLP 37CDX)*

Nov 02. (cd-s) *(HVN 125CDS)* ANYWHERE / Beautiful World / Anywhere (Two Lone Swordsmen remix) / Anywhere (video) [55] [–]

Nov 02. (d-12") *<ASW 77821>* ANYWHERE (remixes) [–] [ ]
- Anywhere (mixes; Two Lone Swordsmen / instrumental / Adrian Sherwood / instrumental) / Carmella (Four Tet remix) / Daybreaker / Daybreaker (instrumental).

Mar 03. (cd-s) *(HVN 129CD)* THINKING ABOUT TOMORROW / Daybreaker (Roots Manuva mix) / Daybreaker (Four Tet mix) [57] [–]

Sep 03. (cd) *<5 92266-2>* **THE OTHER SIDE OF DAYBREAK** (remixes) [–] [ ]
- O-o-h child (alt. take) / Thinking about tomorrow (Ipg dub) / Ali's waltz / Daybreaker (Four Tet remix) / Bobby Gentry / Carmella (Four Tet remix) / Beautiful world / Concrete sky (acoustic) / Daybreaker (Roots Manuva remix) / Anywhere (Two Lone Swordsmen remix). *(bonus video +=)* - Concrete sky.

EMI — Astralwerks

Jan 06. (7") *(EM 681)* CONCEIVED. / Rectify #2 [44] [–]
(cd-s) *(CDEM 681)* - ('A'-Michael Brauer mix) / Endless day.

Feb 06. (cd) *(353400-2)* <49847> **COMFORT OF STRANGERS** [24] [92]
- Worms / Countenance / Heartlandtruckstop / Rectify / Comfort of strangers / Shadow of a doubt / Conceived / Absinthe / A place aside / Safe in your arms / Shopping trolley / Feral / Heart of soul / Pieces of sky. *(ltd-cd w/cd+=; 353401-2)* - What we begin / On my way home / Comfort of strangers (alt. take #9) / Did somebody make a fool of you / Northern sky.

Jun 06. (cd-s/7") *(CD+/EM 694)* SHOPPING TROLLEY / Comfort Of Strangers [87] [–]
(cd-s+=) *(CDEMS 694)* - Pieces of sky [early version].

- (8-10*) compilations -

Sep 03. (d-cd) *Heavenly; (HVNLP 45CD)* <56163> **PASS IN TIME - THE DEFINITIVE COLLECTION** [45] Oct 03 [ ]
- She cries your name / Someone's daughter / Touch me with your love / Sugar boy / Galaxy of emptiness / I wish I never saw the sunshine / Best bit / The same day / Stolen car / Sweetest decline / Pass in time / Central reservation / Concrete sky / Thinking about tomorrow / Central reservation (Ibaden remix) / Where do I begin (with The CHEMICAL BROTHERS) / Stars all seem to weep / Safety / Pedestal / Dolphins (with TERRY CALLIER) / It's not the spotlight / Don't wanna know 'bout evil / Where do you go / Water from a vine leaf (with WILLIAM ORBIT).

The OWL SERVICE

Formed in the summer of 2006 and taking their name from a 1967 novel by Alan Garner, the collective The OWL SERVICE was the brainchild of Blackwaterside resident Steven Collins, aided by vocalists Nancy Wallace, Jo Lepine and Diana Collier and percussionist Dominic Cooper.

Not unlike late-1960s/early-1970s folk icons MELLOW CANDLE, TREES and FAIRPORT CONVENTION, Collins' wyrd-acid compositions mixed effectively alongside trad pieces on two self-released CD-rs. Properly issued in 2008, but actually released a year previously, **A GARLAND OF SONG** {*8} recreated in spades these halcyon days of old. Sourced and beautifully rearranged staple Child ballads such as 'No.49 (Or The Rolling Of The Stones)', 'No.219 (Or The Gardener Child)', 'Katie Cruel', 'The North Country Maid', 'Turpin Hero', etc, were stitched together with cinematic-sounding gems 'Hoodening', 'The Dorset Hanging Song' and the title track.

To resemble MELLOW CANDLE even further, that group's former singer Alison O'Donnell was roped in to perform on the EP 'The Fabric Of Folk'. The simultaneously released 'The Bitter Night' EP was highlighted by the PENTANGLE nugget 'A Lyke Wake Dirge', sung by Rebsie Fairholm. There was plenty of trad-folk fare to shake your hat at on the follow-ups, the wintry mini-set **THE BURN COMES DOWN** (2010) {*7} and **THE VIEW FROM A HILL** (2010) {*8}.

To coincide with her OWL SERVICE and MEMORY BAND exploits, NANCY WALLACE issued a string of EPs and an album. The 2005 covers EP 'Young Hearts' featured folk reinterpretations of disco tunes from Candi Staton, Elton John, Chic and Barry White, while the full set **OLD STORIES** (2009) {*8} was reminiscent of SHIRLEY COLLINS and ANNE BRIGGS. *MCS*

Steven Collins - vocals, multi-instruments / **Jo Lepine** - vocals / **Diana Collier** - vocals / **Nancy Wallace** - vocals, multi (of The MEMORY BAND) / **Dominic Cooper** - percussion, vocals

UK Hobby-Horse — US not issued

2006. (ltd-cd-r) *(OAK 001)* WAKE THE VAULTED ECHO
- Wake the vaulted echo / The two magicians / - Interlude I - / Fine horseman / - Interlude II - / By the setting of the sun.

2006. (ltd-3" cd-ep) *(OAK 002CD)* CINE (THE DIRECTOR'S CUT)
- Psychomania / Daniel - Take me to your lover / Marianne / Searching for Rowan - Cave chase. *(re-iss. 2007 on Static Caravan; VAN 140)*

2007. (ltd-cd) *(OAK 005CD)* **A GARLAND OF SONG**
- A garland of song (folk revival) / Child ballad No.49 (or the rolling of the stones) / Hoodening / The north country maid / Katie cruel / The lammas / Oxford City (or the jealous lover) / Turpin hero / The Dorset hanging oak / Apple tree man / Child ballad No.219 (or the gardener child) / Corn dollies / Flanders shore. *(re-iss. Jun 08 on Southern; 28149-2)*

Sep 08. (ltd; 7" ep/cd-ep) *(OAK 008LC/+CD)* THE BITTER NIGHT EP
- A lyke wake dirge (with REBSIE FAIRHOLM) / The stone bequest / The church grim / Fine horseman. // *(bonus+=)* - Untitled / Untitled.

—— next with **Alison O'Donnell** - vocals, autoharp, bodhran (ex-MELLOW CANDLE)

Static Caravan — not issued

Sep 08. (ltd-cd-ep) *(VAN 142)* THE FABRIC OF FOLK
- The wooden coat / William and Earl Richard's daughter / Flodden field / Scarlet threads and silver needles / The fabric of life. *(12" ep iss. Aug 10 on Midwich; WYND 003)*

Rif Mountain — not issued

Apr 10. (m-cd) *(RM-003)* **THE BURN COMES DOWN**
- January snows / Drive the cold winter away / When a man's in love / Fire and wine / Bitter withy / Cold and raw / January snows / The snow it melts the soonest / Winter (a dirge).

Jun 10. (cd) *(RM-004)* **THE VIEW FROM A HILL**
- Polly on the shore / The banks of the Nile / Ladies, don't go a-thieving / I was a young man / Sorry the day I was married / Willie O'Winsbury / In Thorneymoor woods (part 1) / The bold poachers / In Thorneymoor woods (part 2) / The lover's ghost / The ladies go dancing at Whitsun / Willie O'Winsbury (reprise) / The loyal lover / Within sound / Cruel mother.

May 11. (cd) *(RM-016)* **GARLAND SESSIONS**

- (5-7*) compilations, etc.-

2008. (ltd-cd) *Midwich; (WYND 005CD)* **THE PETRIFYING WELL** [collected early recordings] — mail-o

NANCY WALLACE

Hungry Hill — not issued

Dec 05. (cd-ep) *(SLOPE 003)* YOUNG HEARTS EP
- Young hearts run free / Are you ready for love? / At last I'm free / You're the first, the last, my everything.

Midwich — not issued

Jan 09. (m-cd) *(WYND 001CD)* **OLD STORIES**
- Sleeping sickness / Many years / I live not where I love / The woods / Waiting / The true lovers' farewell / Joy to the world / The way you lie / The drowned lover.

Feb 09. (cd-ep) *(WYND 002CD)* LIVE IN LONDON, JAN 27th 2009 [live at the Electroacoustic Club]
- Flora / Sleeping sickness / Many years / Young hearts run free.

Rif Mountain — not issued

May 10. (ltd-cd-r) *(RM-007)* UNTITLED [shared w/ Jason Steel] — free
- Through the morning, through the night / [JS track] / Everything's finer [live in Broadstairs] / [JS live in Broadstairs track].

own label — not issued

Jan 11. (ltd-cd-r) *(none)* N W E P
- Walking into walls / Through the morning, through the night / Ploughman lads / Jack Hall.

The OXFORD WAITS

1970s medievalists The AMAZING BLONDEL were never like this – and more's the pity, some might say. Formed in Oxford by 16th/17th-century period-costume singers and musicians Tim Healey, Ian Giles, Edward Fitzgibbon and former JUMPLEADS singer Caroline Butler (Ritson, at that time), the quartet retained a sense of humour in their revival of a folk and country-dance music that was popular until its apparent decline in 1712.

Instruments such as the shawm and the lute took centre stage with the fiddle for evenings of splendid musical re-enactments, which quickly developed into days in the studio. Their inaugural recorded outing (shared with The MELLSTOCK BAND) was **HEY FOR CHRISTMAS** (2000) {*6}.

From bawdy street ballads to John Playford dances and Henry Purcell rounds, the classical/folk quartet offered up an hour of inspirational broadsides on their second excursion, **SWITTER SWATTER** (2004) {*7}. Track titles such as 'Sir Walter Enjoying His Damsel' and 'The Ranting Whore's Resolution' just about say it all.

Straight out of ye olde minstrel handbook of yore, The OXFORD WAITS (with the added attraction of younger musician Sophie Matthews on pipes) gathered their hey-nonny-nonnys for a third batch of jolly banter and song. **LOVE'S HOLYDAY** (2009) {*6} carried the festive folk tradition on from their earlier efforts, and many will recognise 'There Were Three Ravens', 'Drive The Cold Winter Away' and their like. *MCS*

Tim Healey - vocals, shawm / **Caroline Butler** - vocals (ex-JUMPLEADS) / **Ian Giles** - multi, vocals / **Edward Fitzgibbon** - multi, vocals

UK Beautiful Jo — US not issued

Dec 00. (cd; as The OXFORD WAITS with The MELLSTOCK BAND) *(BEJOCD-31)* **HEY FOR CHRISTMAS** [festive]
- The Christmas goose / Remember the poor / Hey for Christmas / The mistletoe bough / Herald angels / Christmas hymn / The Christmas holiday, or stuff your guts / Joseph was an old man / Arise and hail / The moon shines bright / The beggars' delight / Christmas with friends at home / News from the river of Thames / Blanket fair / Christmas in 1859 / The wish / The holly and the ivy.

2002. (cd-ep) *(BEJOCD-35)* OXFORD WAITS [live EP]

Jan 04. (cd; as OXFORD WAITS) *(BEJOCD-44)* **SWITTER SWATTER**
- Portsmouth – Newcastle / Sir Walter enjoying his damsel / The beggar's chorus / Stanes morris / The ranting whore's resolution / Remember o thou man / Oxford waits / The lusty young blacksmith – Mal Peatly / The poore man pays for all / Alman / Cavy Lilyman – Sawney and jockey / Pillycock / Mayden lane / The doleful dance and song of death / Belle qui tiens ma vie – Parson upon Dorothy – Hunting song / Had she not care enough / Put in all – Childgrove / Joan's ale is new / Stingo – Bobbing Joe / Good morrow 'tis St Valentine's day / The maiden's complaint / Argeers, or the wedding night / Christchurch bells / Duke of York's march – The garter / The comical dreamer / Gather ye rosebuds / A rebus upon Mr Anthony Hall / Whether men do laugh or weep / A new rigadoon.

—— added **Sophie Matthews** - vocals, pipes

May 09. (cd) *(BEJOCD-54)* **LOVE'S HOLYDAY** [part festive]
- Come bring with a noise / Drive the cold winter away / Love is a bauble / Cuckoo / The loving couple / Love's holyday / Come follow your leader follow / The swimming lady / Hunsdon House / The Lancashire cuckold / There were three ravens / Watkin's ale – Grimstock / Death by custard / Tomorrow the fox – Trenchmore / The West Country delight / Ham House / Thinkst thou then / The infallible doctor – The gun / Fine knacks for ladies / The great bells of Oesney / Good morrow Gossip Joan / My Robin is to the greenwood gone – The Earl of Essex measure / Since I first saw your face / The hunting of the coney – Room for cuckolds / Christmas's lamentation / Love for love: Danc'd in the play / Old Christmas return'd.

OYSTERBAND

Breakers of folk-genre boundaries to rank with RICHARD THOMPSON, The CHIEFTAINS and The MEN THEY COULDN'T HANG, The OYSTER BAND (as they were known in their 1980s heyday) might never have happened but for the perseverance of diehard group musicians and singers such as Welshman John Jones, Midlander Alan Prosser, and Scotsman Ian Telfer (of New Celeste) leading the way.

However, the roots of this punk-fuelled trad-folk outfit can be traced back to 1976 and Canterbury's unfairly lambasted novelty one-hit wonders FIDDLER'S DRAM, a group famous or notorious for their Christmas 1979 Top 3 hit 'Day Trip To Bangor (Didn't We Have A Lovely Time)' – Prosser, Telfer and Jones were apparently among their number. Once led by fiddler extraordinaire Dave Arbus (formerly of 'Jig-A-Jig' hitmakers East Of Eden), the ensemble was really the inheritance of singer Cathy Lesurf, bouzouki player Chris Taylor, John Taylor, Will Ward and the said Oyster players.

Breakaway act the OYSTER CEILIDH BAND attempted to combine the energy and invention of the pop/rock scene with the spirit and instrumentation of traditional folk, and one LP, **JACK'S ALIVE** (1980) {*4} was released, while Cathy and company decided to carry on with the flagging FIDDLER'S DRAM. By the time she left to join folk veterans The ALBION BAND, The OYSTER BAND were in full swing, though without Ward and bassist CHRIS WOOD, who had made way for London-born multi-instrumentalist Ian Kearey.

Following a series of fair-to-middling independent LP releases, the band (with drummer Russell Lax replacing Taylor) signed with hip roots label Cooking Vinyl, releasing their first proper album, **STEP OUTSIDE** {*7}, in 1986. Featuring traditional cuts ('Hal-An-Tow' among them) alongside mainly Jones-Telfer originals suach as 'Another Quiet Night In England' and 'Liberty Hall', the CLIVE GREGSON-produced quintet received a much-needed commercial boost from favourable reviews. A cover of David Bowie's hit 'Ashes To Ashes' was a CD out-take.

The following year they were pitched in with BILLY BRAGG and LEON ROSSELSON on a one-off collaboration, 'The Ballad Of A Spycatcher', a single that defined their intentions and confirmed their earlier promise.

With a vocal style at times not too far removed from that of RUNRIG's Donnie Munro, John Jones was the heart of the band, while Telfer, Prosser and company were heading towards the future musical realignment of Celtic-folk and folk music in general. Very much in tune with the times, **WIDE BLUE YONDER** (1987) {*7} was a prime example of how far they could stretch the boundaries between trad and roots genres. Songs that appealed to a new generation of Celtic-crusties were 'Generals Are Born Again', 'Oxford Girl', and versions of Nick Lowe's 'Rose Of England' and BILLY BRAGG's 'Between The Wars'.

With Ray "Chopper" Cooper on board (Kearey had teamed up with Gerald Langley of the Blue Aeroplanes), **RIDE** (1989) {*6} was one rollicking rollercoaster of an album. The OYSTER BAND were taking folk-rock in new directions, and not all of them worked. They could be commended for the boisterous hoedown of 'Polish Plain' (but not the reggae-fuelled 'My Dog Knows Where The Bones Are Hid'), and for taking on the trad cut 'New York Girls', but things went awry on attempts at PF Sloan's 'The Sins Of A Family' and New Order's 'Love Vigilantes'. Their B-side cover of Sam Cooke's 'A Change Is Gonna Come' might have been a preferable inclusion.

A better measure of the group in the late 1980s was the part-live set **LITTLE ROCK TO LEIPZIG** (1990) {*7}, a record combining golden Oysters originals next to reinterpretations of PHIL OCHS's 'Gonna Do What I Have To Do', Sonny Curtis's 'I Fought The Law' and an a cappella take on Kay Sutcliffe's 'Coal Not Dole'. By the end of a busy year, the group had teamed up with JUNE TABOR (and not for the last time) on the celebrated collaborative album 'Freedom And Rain'.

Changing their name slightly to OYSTERBAND, Jones, Prosser, Telfer, Chopper and new percussionist Lee Partis delivered **DESERTERS** (1992) {*7}, an album that was more subtly introspective (check out 'Diamond For A Dime' and 'Elena's Shoes') and commercial, with PETE SEEGER's 'The Bells Of Rhymney' closing the set. **HOLY BANDITS** (1993) {*7} kept their momentum high: only 'Rambling Irishman' was sourced, while they kept up to the mark on the fiddle-friendly 'When I'm Up I Can't Get Down' and the Celtic-flavoured 'The Road To Santiago' and 'Gone West'.

Demonstrating the vitriol and vitality of a Celticised Clash and the POGUES (the latter happened to be struggling at this point), **THE SHOUTING END OF LIFE** (1995) {*7} was described as "the thinking man's folk-punk". Jones, Prosser and Telfer were never more politically assertive than on 'Jam Tomorrow', 'We'll Be There' and the LEON ROSSELSON cover 'The World Turned Upside Down'; another highlight was their uplifting rendition of BRUCE COCKBURN's 'Don't Slit Your Wrists For Me'. **DEEP DARK OCEAN** (1997) {*5} was a little disappointing in comparison, their edge a little blunted on songs such as REV HAMMER's 'Drunkard's Waltz'.

With Celtic/ceilidh/folk more in vogue than ever (although English-based, the OYSTERBAND had been a catalyst), the quintet continued to strive amidst the many newcomers and bandwagon-jumpers. **HERE I STAND** (1999) {*6}, recorded in various people's homes, was another step up the ladder to the folk-rock hall of fame, and **RISE ABOVE** (2002) {*6} continued to set the bar high.

The trad collaboration **THE BIG SESSION – VOLUME 1** (2004) {*6} featured many a duet with the likes of STEVE KNIGHTLEY, ELIZA CARTHY and others, while competent solo sets from just about every member followed on from what is at the time of writing their most recent album, **MEET YOU THERE** (2007) {*6}.

Over the years the OYSTERs have also covered 'Valentine's Day Is Over' (BILLY BRAGG), 'All Tomorrow's Parties' (The Velvet Underground), 'Night Comes In' (RICHARD THOMPSON) and 'Lullaby Of London' (the POGUES). *MCS*

FIDDLER'S DRAM

Cathy Lesurf - vocals, bodhran / **Chris Taylor** - bouzouki, harmonica, Appalachian dulcimer, tenor banjo / **Alan Prosser** - guitar, fiddle, bones / **John Taylor** - chorus / **Will Ward** - bassoon, crumhorn; repl. Dave Arbus (ex-East Of Eden) / plus **Ian Telfer** - fiddle, viola (of New Celeste) / **John Jones** - chorus, melodeon

UK Dingle's — US not issued

Nov 78. (lp) *(DIN 304)* **TO SEE THE PLAY** –
- Jack in London city / Song of victory - Song of the blackbird / Day trip to Bangor / The flash lad / Ythanside / Keyhole in the door / Youankis - Skraperez - Guerz ar gechantez / Wa'ney Island cockfight / The two brothers / Peel the tatties - The pig in the kitchen - The barony jig / False knight on the road / Nottingham goose fair.

—— **Telfer** moved up to repl. John Taylor (while Jones was still in tow)

Nov 79. (7") *(SID 211)* DAY TRIP TO BANGOR (DIDN'T WE HAVE A LOVELY TIME). / (version) 3 –

Feb 80. (lp/c) *(DID/+C 711)* **FIDDLER'S DRAM** –
- Thirteen pence a day / Darley's jig / The flash lad / Fedora / The farmer's cursed wife / Sloe gin / Mamma's ill / Johnny John / Beercart lane / The bad girl / Whiskey / Stick morris / Day trip to Bangor.

Mar 80. (7") *(SID 221)* BEERCART LANE. / Ythanside –

Jul 81. (7") *(SID 225)* BLACK HOLE. / Agony –

Dec 81. (7") *(SID 231)* LITTLE RAY OF SUNSHINE. / Sweet Chiming Bells –

(The) OYSTER BAND

John Jones (b. Oct 19 '49, Aberystwyth, Wales) - vocals, melodeon, piano / **Cathy Lesurf** - vocals, caller / **Alan Prosser** (b. Apr 17 '51, Wolverhampton, England) - guitars, fiddle, vocals / **Ian Telfer** (b. May 28 '48, Falkirk, Scotland) - fiddle, viola, concertina, sax / **Chris Taylor** - bouzouki, mandola, guitars, jews-harp / **Will Ward** - bassoon, recorders, crumhorn, synthesizers / **Chris Wood** - bass, percussion, vocals

Dingle's — not issued

Nov 80. (lp; as OYSTER CEILIDH BAND) *(DIN 309)* **JACK'S ALIVE** –
- The Blean hoodening song - The city Branle / Hunting the hare - The clog / Schottische d'Auvergne - Belle rosine / Oyster river hornpipe - Herne Bay dance - The curly-headed ploughboy / Marche du fin du bal - The committee jig / The lakes of cool flynn / The rambling sailor / Brandy / The Shaalds of Foula / The lawyer / News of the victory - The one-horned sheep / Limbo / Boscastle breakdown.

—— **Ian Kearey** (b. Oct 14 '54, London) - bass, guitars, banjo, autoharp; repl. Ward + WOOD (now solo) (Lesurf remained as a guest only; she was to join The ALBION BAND)

Pukka — not issued

Mar 82. (lp) *(YOP 01)* **THE ENGLISH ROCK 'N' ROLL - THE EARLY YEARS 1800–1850** –
- The Prentice boy / Rufford Park - Bobbing Joe / Sons of freedom / A Longport hymn / Annan water / Abroad as I was walking / Bold Wolfe / Old Molly Oxford / Slippin' and slidin' / The dockyard gate / Holligrave - Wayfaring stranger.

Jun 83. (lp) *(YOP 04)* **LIE BACK AND THINK OF ENGLAND** –
- Waiting on glory / Gallop hey / The furze field / My young man / La valse du cochon noir - Port Arthur stomp / The green bed / Fanny Blair / Stonecutter boy / The sheepstealer / William Hall / Think of England / Michael Turner's waltz.

Dec 84. (lp) *(YOP 06)* **20 GOLDEN TIE-SLACKENERS** –
- Kentish cricketers - Galopede / The Belfast almanac - Folkestone for the day / Three jolly sheepskins - Speed the plough / Mrs. Forster's - The first of May / Dumbarton Castle - 'Twas within a mile / Not the fiery clockface / P's / Jack's alive - The Clare jig / Go and enlist / Spaghetti Junction – Dixie's - Stack Ryan's / The Redowa polka / La Morisque. *(cd-iss. Dec 03 on Running Man+=; RMCD 4)* - Hunting the hare - The clog / News of the victory - The one-horned sheep.

—— now without Taylor (demoted to guest); he joined GAS MARK 5

Mar 85. (lp) *(YOP 07)* **LIBERTY HALL** –
- Arise, arise / Bonnie Susie Cleland / The breaking of our Lord's birthday / Liberty hall / Euston station / Cropper lads / Steal for joy / Banstead downs (Geordie) / St Peter's tea gardens / Six grey men / Drink again (drowning ballad No.142).

—— added **Russell Lax** - drums

Cooking Vinyl — Varrick

Oct 86. (7") *(FRY 001)* HAL-AN-TOW. / Ashes To Ashes –

Oct 86. (lp/c) *(COOK/+C 001)* <VR-034> **STEP OUTSIDE** 1987
- Hal-an-tow / Flatlands / Another quiet night in England / Ashes to ashes *[c-only]* / Molly Bond / Bully in the alley / The day that the ship goes down / Gaol song / The old dance / Bold Riley. *(cd-iss. Jan 88 +=; COOKCD 001)* - Ashes to ashes. *(re-iss. Jun 90 lp/c/cd+=; BAKE/+C/CD 001)* - Liberty hall. <*cd-iss. Oct 90; CDVR-034*>

Cooking Vinyl — Polydor

Aug 87. (lp/c) *(COOK/+C 006)* <*422 837 387-1*> **WIDE BLUE YONDER**
- 1. The generals are born again / 2. Pigsty Billy / 3. The Oxford girl / 4. Following in father's footsteps / 5. The lost and found / 6. Coal creek mine / 7. Rose of England / 8. A careless life / 9. The early days of a better nation / 10. The lakes of cool flynn / 11. Between the wars. *(cd-iss. Apr 88 diff. track order; COOKCD 006 /* <*422 837 387-2*> - [tracks 1, 9, 2, 3, 7] / Hal-an-tow / Flatlands / [track 5] / Another quiet night in England / [tracks 6, 11, 10, 4].

Oct 87. (7") *(CHEF 001)* ROSE OF ENGLAND. / (B-side by EDWARD II AND THE RED HOT POLKAS) –

—— In Oct '87 The OYSTER BAND teamed up with LEON ROSSELSON and BILLY BRAGG for the single 'Ballad Of A Spycatcher'.

—— **Ray 'Chopper' Cooper** (b. Sep 22 '54, Romford, Essex) - bass, cello, vocals; repl. Kearey, who had teamed up with Gerald Langley of the Blue Aeroplanes

Jan 89. (7") *(FRY 006)* THE LOST AND FOUND. / A Change Is Gonna Come –
(12"+=) *(FRY 006T)* - McLeod's reel / The generals are born again (intro) / Between the wars.

Apr 89. (7") *(FRY 009)* NEW YORK GIRLS. / My Dog (Knows Where The Bones Are Hid) –
(12"+=) *(FRY 006T)* - Galopede.

Apr 89. (lp/c) *(COOK/+C 020)* <*422 838 400-1/-4*> **RIDE**
- Too late now / Polish plain / Heaven to Calcutta / Tincans / This year, next year / New York girls / Gamblers (we do not do that anymore) / Take me down / Cheekbone city / Love vigilantes.

Apr 89. (cd) *(COOKCD 020)* <422 838 400-2> RIDE
- New York girls / Gamblers (we do not do that anymore) / Polish plain / Too late now / Tincans / Heaven to Calcutta / This year, next year / My dog (knows where the bones are hid) / The sins of a family / Take me down / Cheekbone city / Love vigilantes.

Oct 89. (7") *(FRY 012)* LOVE VIGILANTES. / Polish Plain
(10"+=/cd-s+=) *(FRY 012 X/CD)* - I fought the law / Between the wars.

Cooking Vinyl — Rykodisc

Apr 90. (lp/c/cd) *(COOK/+C/CD 032)* <RCD 50098> **LITTLE ROCK TO LEIPZIG** (live)
- Jail song two / The Oxford girl / Gonna do what I have to do / Too late now / Galopede / Red barn stomp / I fought the law / Coal not dole / New York girls / Johnny Mickey Barry's - Salmon tails down the water.

—— In Sep '90 The OYSTER BAND teamed up with JUNE TABOR on a collaborative album, 'FREEDOM AND RAIN'.

OYSTERBAND

—— **Jones, Prosser, Telfer + Chopper** added **Lee Partis** - drums, bodhran, percussion

Mar 92. (cd) *(COOKCD 041)* <RCD 10237> **DESERTERS**
- All that way for this / The deserter / Angels of the river / We could leave right now / Elena's shoes / Granite years / Diamond for a dime / Never left / Ship sets sail / Fiddle or a gun / Bells of Rhymney.

Aug 93. (cd) *(COOKCD 058)* <RCD 10288> **HOLY BANDITS**
- When I'm up I can't get down / The road to Santiago / I look for you / Gone west / We shall come home / Cry cry / Here's to you / Moving on / Rambling Irishman / A fire is burning / Blood wedding.

Oct 93. (c-ep/cd-ep) *(FRY C/CD 024)* GONE WEST / After London / Star Of The County Down / Curragh Of Kildare

Feb 94. (cd-ep) <RCD5 1034> CRY CRY / After London / Star Of The County Down / Curragh Of Kildare

Oct 94. (cd-s) *(FRYCD 037)* OXFORD GIRL / 20th Of April / Hal-An-Tow

Oct 94. (cd/c) *(COOK CD/C 078)* **TRAWLER** (re-recordings)
- Hal-an-tow / Another quiet night in England (1994) / We could leave right now / Blood wedding / Oxford girl / Granite years / Rambling Irishman / Love vigilantes / Polish plain / 20th of April / The lost and found / One green hill / Coal not dole / Bells of Rhymney. *(some cd copies+=)* - Another quiet night in England / Oxford girl / Love vigilantes / Hal-an-tow / We could leave right now. (d-cd-iss.+=) - DEEP DARK OCEAN

Cooking Vinyl — Cooking Vinyl

Sep 95. (cd/c) *(<COOK CD/C 091>)* **THE SHOUTING END OF LIFE** — Oct 95
- We'll be there / Blood-red roses / Jam tomorrow / By northern lights / The shouting end of life / Long dark street / Our lady of the bottle / Everywhere I go / Put out the lights / Voices / Lovers in a dangerous time *[US-only]* / Don't slit your wrists for me / The world turned upside down.

Mar 96. (cd) *(RUNNINGMANCD 1)* **ALIVE AND SHOUTING** (live in Denmark and Sweden) — tour
- (introduction) / The shouting end of life / We'll be there / The world turned upside down / When I'm up I can't get down / Everywhere I go / One green hill / 20th of April / By northern light / We shall come home / Put out the lights / Don't slit your wrists for me / Blood wedding / Another quiet night in England / We could leave right now.

(above issued on Running Man)

Aug 97. (cd-ep) *(FRYCD 067)* SAIL ON BY / Be My Luck / One Green Hill (Chumbawamba mix) / Jam Tomorrow (Chumbawamba mix)

Aug 97. (cd) *(<COOKCD 128>)* **DEEP DARK OCEAN**
- Sail on by / Little brother / Only when you call / Native son / Not like Jordan / North star / Milford haven / The story / Be my luck / No reason to cry / Drunkard's waltz. *(hidden +=)* - Native son [in Welsh]. *(d-cd-iss. 2000 +=; COOKCD 128X)* - TRAWLER

Running Man — not issued

Jun 98. (cd) *(RMCD 2)* **ALIVE AND ACOUSTIC** (live)
- Sail on by / Voices / Be my luck / The Oxford girl / Native son / This year, next year / Reels: McMahon's - The sailor's bonnet / I look for you / Blood-red roses / The story / Moving on / Milford haven / Molly Bond / A fire is burning / Polkas: Scartaglen - Johnny Leary's - The humours of Ballydesmond / All that way for this / I once loved a lass / The old triangle.

May 99. (cd) *(RUNMANCD 101)* <OMM 2023> **HERE I STAND** (recorded in various private homes) — Aug 99
- On the edge / This is the voice / In your eyes / Street of dreams / Ways of holding on / A time of her own / After rain / I know it's mine / Someone you might have been / Kantele / She's moved on / And as for you / Cello drop / Jump through the fire / This town / A last glass. *(re-iss. Oct 02; same)*

Oct 99. (cd-ep) *(RUNMANEP 101)* THIS IS THE VOICE
- This is the voice / On the edge / The false knight on the road / Funny time of life.

2000. (cd-ep) *(RUNMANEP 102)* WAYS OF HOLDING ON (WAITING FOR THE SUN)
- Ways of holding on (waiting for the sun) / On the edge / Ways of holding on / Someone you might have been.

Plane — Omnium

Sep 02. (cd) *(88874)* <OMM 2032> **RISE ABOVE** — Apr 03
- The soul's electric / Uncommercial song / If you can't be good / Everybody's leaving home / My mouth / Shouting about Jerusalem / Blackwaterside / Rise above / Wayfaring / Bright morning star.

Running Man — not issued

Dec 03. (cd-ep) *(RUNMANEP 03)* 25
- Noah and the raven / Boy in the window / Factory girl / Up on the bridge / Road to nowhere / The government gets in / Climb back to heaven.

Westpark — True North

Aug 04. (cd) *(87105)* <TND 356> **THE BIG SESSION - VOLUME 1** (live) — Canada
- John Barleycorn / Whitehaven / Lowlands / Country life / Fuse / Ten thousand miles - Hungarian march / The new Jerusalem / When that helicopter comes / The house carpenter / The cuckoo's next / We shall come home / Love will tear us apart / Factory girl / Country life ('I like to rise') / The Cornish farewell shanty.

Apr 07. (cd) *(87141)* **MEET YOU THERE**
- Over the water / Here comes the flood / Where the world divides / Walking down the road with you / Bury me standing / Everything must go / Control / The boy's still running / Someone somewhere / Just one life / Dancing as fast as I can.

Oct 07. (cd-s) *(87149)* HERE COMES THE FLOOD

- (8-10*) compilations -

Jun 98. (d-cd) *Snapper; (SMDCD 148)* **PEARLS FROM THE OYSTERS**
- Between the wars / The early days of a better nation / Rose of England / Another quiet night in England / The lost and found / Love vigilantes / The lakes of cool flynn / Bold Riley / Polish plain / Flatlands / Molly Bond / A careless life / Coal not dole / Tincans / Take me down // New York girls / Cheekbone city / The generals are born again / Galopede / Heaven to Calcutta / Bully in the alley / This year, next year / Gonna do what I have to do / Too late now / Gaol song / Coal creek mine / Gamblers / Johnny Mickey's Barry's - Salmon tails down the water / Star of the County Down / The Curragh of Kildare. *(re-iss. Oct 03; same)*

Aug 00. (d-cd) *Cooking Vinyl; (COOKCD 196)* <6483-2> **GRANITE YEARS** (Best of ... 1986 to 1997) — Nov 00
- When I'm up I can't get down / The road to Santiago / Native son / By northern light / We could leave right now / Rambling Irishman / Be my luck / The shouting end of life / We'll be there / Mississippi summer / The deserter / Love vigilantes / We shall come home / Hal-an-tow / Molly Bond // Granite years / Everywhere I go / One green hill / Another quiet night in England (1994) / Put out the lights / Voices / Here's to you / Blood wedding / Milford haven / Jam tomorrow / The sailor's bonnet / 20th of April / All that way for this / The Oxford girl / Coal not dole - Bells of Rhymney.

May 09. (cd) *Running Man; (RMCD 5)* **THE OXFORD GIRL AND OTHER STORIES** (re-acoustic)
- The early days of a better nation / When I'm up I can't get down / By northern light / Blood-red roses / The soul's electric / The Oxford girl / Little brother / What wondrous love is this? / Angels of the river / After rain / Shouting about Jerusalem / The lakes of cool flynn / The false knight on the road / Put out the lights.

- (5-7*) compilations, etc.-

Feb 04. (cd) *Running Man; (RMCD 3)* **BEFORE THE FLOOD**: oyster origins 1
- The Prentice boy / Six grey men / The breaking of our Lord's birthday / Stonecutter boy / Old Molly Oxford / Liberty hall / Rufford park - Bobbing Joe / The sheepstealer / Think of England / The dockyard gate / Steal of joy / Gallop hey / The lakes of cool flynn / A Longport hymn / Limbo / Michael Turner's waltz.

ALAN PROSSER

Rafting Dog — not issued

Feb 97. (cd) *(RD 01)* **HALL PLACE**
- Sheepscar Beck / That melancholy way / Harry Edward / The leaves of life / Two crows / Cromwell I / Something has got to change / Cromwell II / He feels no pain / Elham valley / Cold winter's night / By Lagan streams / Think of you / Money and love / Raise me up / Empire building.

Jun 03. (cd) *(RD 02)* **MAKERFIELD**
- Canmore / NER 1003 / Tanyardside / The move / Air of distinction / River of steel / Seymour place / Makerfield / William and Claire / East Tytherley / Cavendish road / A rainy day where you are / The day is ending.

JOHN JONES

with session people: Seth Lakeman, Benji Kirkpatrick, Ian Kearey, Rowan Godel, Sophie Walsh, Francois deVille, Alan Prosser, Dil Davies

Westpark — not issued

Jul 09. (cd) *(87179)* **RISING ROAD**
Searching for lambs / One morning in the spring / Henry Martin / Fire Marengo / One night as I lay on my bed / Boy in the window / Newlyn town.

RAY COOPER

Westpark — not issued

May 10. (cd) *(87188)* **TALES OF LOVE, WAR AND DEATH BY HANGING**
- The puritan / The dark days are over / Border widow's lament / McPherson's rant / I kiss the night – Jamtland bridal march / The grey goose wing / In your sweet arms / The highwayman / My compass points to north / Ye Jacobites by name – Sir Archibald MacDonald of Keppoch.

P

The PACK (⟹ HARDY, Bella)

PANTALEIMON

Sparse, oblique and a bit of a curiosity in the ever-expanding and evolving world of freak-folk, PANTALEIMON (pronounced "pan-ta-lay-mon") was the brainchild of Andria Degens, wife of CURRENT 93 mainman David Tibet; the name is drawn from that of a daemon in author Philip Pullman's 'Northern Lights' trilogy. Of Dutch and Irish ancestry, English-born globetrotter Andria first attracted attention with her dulcimer, bouzouki and voice when she guested in the early 1990s for indie acts Wire (live only), Dirty Three and the aforementioned experimental project CURRENT 93. Nurse With Wound, Band Of Susans and Hobotalk have since requested her presence in the studio.

Released originally by her husband in 1999, **TREES HOLD TIME** {*7} perched precariously on the periphery of folk music, bookended by lengthy instrumentals 'Bowing And Parting' and the 14-minute 'Thomas's House In Quiet Contemplation'. In some aspects a precursor to IN GOWAN RING and a host of other ethereal freak-folkies, its highlight is the vocally wondrous 'Sitting On The Mountain Of Suan Mok'.

More or less a mini-CD, with a half-hour running time (and therefore not an EP), **CHANGE MY WORLD** (2003) {*6} came across like something akin to a humourless female Ivor Cutler. Guests John Contreras (cello), Josef Budenholzer and Ryan Lowe were her backing band at the Bloomsbury Theatre (April 2001) in London on three live performances from her debut.

Not exactly prolific in the mid-2000s, in 2007 PANTALEIMON did however produce two delicate ambi-folk releases, the EP 'Cloudburst' (featuring lyrical psych-acid finale 'Numinosum') and their second full set, **MERCY OCEANS** (2007) {*7}. Vocally expansive and quite beautiful in places, the best places were 'Under The Water', 'We Love' and 'The Sun Came Out'. Degens was joined on this occasion by Keith Wood (guitars), ex-Belle And Sebastian member Isobel Campbell (cello, piano, glockenspiel and backing vocals) and Baby Dee (harp).

PANTALEIMON's most recent delivery, the download-only **LIVE IN BARCELONA** (2009) {*6}, featuring JAMES BLACKSHAW on guitars, hasn't exactly kept her profile high. Word-of-mouth seems enough to appease her internet fan base. *MCS*

Andria Degens (b. 1969, Caterham, Surrey) - bouzouki, dulcimer, vocals, percussion

UK: Durtro — US: not issued

Nov 99. (ltd-cd) *(durtro 047cd)* **TREES HOLD TIME** — –
- Bowing and parting / Insignificant dance / Trees hold time / Wasps changing gear as they make their way uphill / Sitting on the mountain of Suan Mok / Crater full of goldfish / Thomas's house in quiet contemplation. *(ltd-lp - + clear-lp -iss. Jun 00 on Streamline, Germany; 1018) (ltd signed edition iss. Dec 05 on Durtro/Jnana+=; Durtro Jnana 1968)* - Change my world / Change my world (instrumental).

Pan Durtro — not issued

2003. (m-cd) *(PanDurtro 005)* **CHANGE MY WORLD** (live *) — –
- Change my world / Change my world (instrumental) / Bowing and parting (*) / Trees hold time (*) / Nature's child sitting on the mountain of Suan Mok (*).

not issued — Blue Sanct

Dec 06. (one-sided-7"clear) *<INRI 082>* UNDER THE WATER — –

Durtro/Jnana — Durtro/Jnana

Feb 07. (cd-ep) *(Durtro Jnana 003)* CLOUDBURST — –
- Cloudburst / Crystalline rain / Ascension of the sun / Numinosum. *(ltd-edition 2006 incl. book 'Peeling Oranges Into Flowers')*

Nov 07. (cd) *(<Durtro Jnana 007>)* **MERCY OCEANS**
- Under the water / We love / The sun came out / High star / All the birds / Born into you / At dawn / Raw heart / I am / Storm and thunder.

Jun 08. (cd) *(<Durtro Jnana 008>)* HEART OF THE SUN (MERCY OCEANS remixed and realised by other artists) — Jul 08

Jun 08. (cd-r-ep) *(abaton 029)* TALL TREES — –
- The warming / Dance of the honey bees / Sing night swallow / Tall trees.

(above issued on Abaton Book Company)

Jan 09. (m-dl) *(1123)* **LIVE IN BARCELONA** (at the Apolo in Barcelona on November 23, 2008) – –
- Amamos / El sol sali / Corazon crudo / Canto de la golondrina nocturna / Arboles altos / En el amanecer / Soy.

Alun PARRY

Liverpudlian folk singer-songwriter/guitarist ALUN PARRY has brought a breath of fresh air to the genre. A champion of Merseyside's busking fraternity from the early 1990s, his storytelling, social commentary and thought-provoking lyrical repertoire have grown in stature since he first entered his local studio.

CORRIDORS OF STONE (2006) {*7} received a fair bit of airplay; highlights include the poignant modern-day love songs 'You Are My Addiction' and 'Because You're Beautiful'. A boyhood hero of Alun's, WOODY GUTHRIE (Alun runs Liverpool's Woody Guthrie Folk Club), gets the homage treatment on 'Woody's Song'. Another favourite cause is AFC Liverpool – not the Anfield bunch, but a football co-operative of which Alun is chairman.

With a band that comprised bassist Rob Harper (ex-Mighty Wah!) and drummer Thomas Western, PARRY completed another release, the mini-set **LIVERPOOL 800: TRUE LOVE OF MINE** (2007) {*6}.

Protest-folk singer ROBB JOHNSON, never short of up-and-coming talent on his Irregular Records imprint, signed Alun up for his third CD, **WE CAN MAKE THE WORLD STOP** (2009) {*7}. It's hard to predict how PARRY will fare among the Bright Young Things of folk's fickle elite, but the site of the Working Class Music Festival, of which he is the organiser, describes him best: "[He sounds as] if John Lennon were a folk singer and Tony Benn wrote his lyrics". *MCS*

Alun Parry - vocals, acoustic guitar / + session people

UK: ParrySongs — US: not issued

Nov 06. (cd) *(none)* **CORRIDORS OF STONE** — –
- You are my addiction / Corridors of stone / Because you're beautiful / Woody's song / Life of crime / Make a man / Today's just yesterday / Thursday night drinking song / I want Rosa to stay / The ship song.

Aug 07. (m-cd; as The ALUN PARRY BAND) *(none)* **LIVERPOOL 800: TRUE LOVE OF MINE** — –
- True love of mine / Under Neptune's hand / Liverpool love song / Red and blue / My granddad was a docker / Coming home / You are my addiction [sample].

Irregular — not issued

Aug 09. (cd) *(IRR 070)* **WE CAN MAKE THE WORLD STOP** — –
- We can make the world stop / Run Patsy run / The Limerick soviet / Together / Princess Deborah / Waiting for the lovers / John Lennon said / Hello barren desert / Any change at all / Chasing yourself / Take the mother's name / All hail to the market.

PEGGY SUE

Far from the ghost-group of 1950s rock 'n' roll icon Buddy Holly, Brighton's PEGGY SUE are a fiery folk duo of youngsters Rosa 'Rex' Slade and Katy 'Klaw' Young. From basement rehearsals in 2006 to supporting MUMFORD & SONS in 2009 (via a couple of limited-edition EPs, 'The Body Parts' and 'The First Aid'), the girls signed a favourable deal with the folks at Wichita Records (Too Pure had issued a one-off, 'Lazarus').

Like contemporary rivals ALESSI'S ARK and FIRST AID KIT, their debut album, **FOSSILS AND OTHER PHANTOMS** (2010) {*6}, twisted the folk ethos of yesteryear into a cool, torch-like folk-noir. 'Long Division Blues', the alt-country single 'Watchman' and a revamp of the well-sourced 'Green GrowThe Rushes' were passages of positive pop pleasure. *MCS*

Rosa Rex/Slade - vocals, guitar / **Katy Klaw/Young** - vocals, guitar / with session band/ musicians

UK Broken Sound — US not issued

Aug 08. (ltd-2x7" ep; as PEGGY SUE AND THE PICTURES) *(BSMVIN 001)* THE BODY PARTS EP
- Spare parts / Pupils blink / Gettysburg / Escargot.

Dec 08. (ltd-2x7" ep; as PEGGY SUE AND LES TRIPLETTES) *(BSMVIN 002)* THE FIRST AID EP
- First aid – Once we were strangers / Clockwork / Eisenstein / The sea, the sea.

Too Pure — not issued

Feb 09. (ltd-7" white) *(PURE 242S)* LAZARUS. / Alice In The Kitchen

Wichita — Yep Roc

Jul 09. (cd-ep) *<YEP 2205>* LOVER GONE
- Lover gone / Milk and blood / Revision / The conservationist.

Mar 10. (7") *(WEBB 244S)* WATCHMAN. / Trouble

Apr 10. (cd) *(WEBB 245CD) <YEP 2206>* **FOSSILS AND OTHER PHANTOMS** — Jun 10
- Long division blues / Yo mama / I read it in the paper / Green grow the rushes / Watchman / She called / Careless talk costs lives / The remainder / Matilda / February snow / Fossils / The shape we made.

Apr 10. (7" shared) *(WEBB 248STEN)* [First Aid Kit track]. / I READ IT IN THE PAPER

Brian PETERS

A long-standing exponent (nay, ambassador) of the English squeezebox, melodeon and Anglo concertina, traditional singer BRIAN PETERS kicked off his illustrious folk career as a guitarist, having performed in clubs in and around the Greater Manchester area. He played residencies at the city's Unicorn Folk Club from his inaugural gig in September 1981.

Born December 15, 1954, in Stockport, Cheshire, he was 30 years old when he picked up the melodeon and its musical cousins. His one-off debut for Fellside Records, **PERSISTENCE OF MEMORY** (1986) {*6}, marked an ambitious departure for the one-time troubadour. **FOOLS OF FORTUNE** (1989) {*7}, on Harbourtown Records, consisted of mainly traditionally-sourced material, although played in a contemporary manner, and it won the prestigious fRoots Album of the Year award.

THE SEEDS OF TIME (1992) {*7} continued at the same pace, augmented by friends Gordon Tyrrall, Peadar Long and George Faux on material from the pens of LEON ROSSELSON, Jim Woodland and Brian himself. Hs own session shifts included work with MIKE HARDING, HUGHIE JONES (of The SPINNERS) and old-timey outfit The Lost Nation Band, a duo that was completed by flautist/guitarist Gordon Tyrrall (who had replaced SARA GREY and ROGER WILSON).

Since 1994, Brian's own independent label Pugwash has delivered eight above-par CDs, from the eclectic folk pot-pourri of **SQUEEZING OUT SPARKS** {*6} (1994) to the boozy murder-balladeering of **GRITSTONE SERENADE** (2010) {*6} – this man is never one to shirk the challenge of a good dirge. Two sets with Tyrrall, **CLEAR THE ROAD** (1996) {*6} and **THE MOVING MOON** (2001) {*6}, bucked the trend of stereotypical English folk music. PETERS has also moonlighted with hillbilly acts The Rocky Mountain Playboys and rootsy electric outfit The Blazing Chevrolets. *MCS*

Brian Peters - vocals, squeezebox, concertina, melodeon, acoustic guitar

UK Fellside — US not issued

1986. (lp) *(FE 051)* **PERSISTENCE OF MEMORY**
- Miners' lockout / Ninian south / Bloddaur drain / Merch Megan / Lankin / Bring the sea to Manchester / No dough blues / The demon lover / Cunning cobbler / Jenny Bell / Herd on the hill / Farewell to the brine.

Harbourtown — not issued

Aug 89. (lp/c) *(HAR/+C 005)* **FOOLS OF FORTUNE**
- Lost fourteen hundred / Schottis Fran Norrbotten / Oldham white hare / A Swedish dance - Sherwood Forest / La belle halimande / John Barbour / The northern lass / Dallas rag / Last God of England / Shelter from the storm / Doed a ddel - Ap siencyn - Mopsi don / Sir Patrick Spens / Unquiet grave.

May 92. (cd/c) *(HAR CD/C 021)* **THE SEEDS OF TIME**
- The Manchester jig - Welcome home - The Pippingo reel / History lesson / Living in the past that never was / Cropper lads / Kitty Fisher - My lad's ower bonny - Coffee and tea / The lowlands of Holland / The box in the attic - Northern nanny - The low flier / A servant of the company / Lovely Joan / The oyster girl - The lad with the trousers on - Mad Moll / False foudrage / Old Haile hornpipe / Padlocks / The ruins by the shore / The dark island - The Arran boat.

Pugwash — not issued

Apr 94. (cd) *(PUGCD 001)* **SQUEEZING OUT SPARKS**
- Kershaw's – Sportsman's - Norwegian hornpipe / Downfall of the Ginn - Lads and lasses / John Hardy / Miss Dillon's waltz - Pandean air / Full of joy / Three coney walk - The rattler - Chester races / The blossom and the rain / Bricks in my pillow / Ton y botel - Le saut du chien / Daddy's polka - Viva el west side / Scarborough fair / Nanny-o - Chester Castle / Lancaster lasses - Tekely - Portuguese dance / Back in the USSR / The waltzing fool / A starry night in Shetland - Fritz Schick's waltz.

1996. (cd) *(PUGCD 002)* **SHARPER THAN THE THORN**
- Lay the bent to the bonny broom / The banks of sweet primroses / Jockey to the fair - Spotted borders - The insomniac / Sheepcrook and black dog / Y pren ar y bryn / Henry Martin / First chill of autumn - Peg Hugleston's hornpipe - Northern frisk / Cold stringy pie / The dragoon's ride / Old man / Whitehaven volunteers - The green ship - Come let us dance and sing / Kemp Owyne / The tapestry - The mill race / Stand up.

Dec 96. (cd; by BRIAN PETERS AND GORDON TYRRALL) *(HARCD 031)* **CLEAR THE ROAD**
- Skipton ram / Daniel Wright's hornpipe - The pearl wedding - The old grey cat / Just as the tide was flowing / Where do I fit in? / Throw the wood, laddie - The catching of fleas - Buxton races / Roads to ruin / The musical priest - The green fields of America / Farewell my dearest dear / The trip to the toilet - The random jig - Fair Jenny / The ship in distress / Blow the winds i-o / Almost satisfied / Colm O'Donnell's - The humours of Lissadel - The hunter's purse / Bonny George Campbell / Cleaning windows / Swansea town.

(above issued on Harbourtown)

1998. (cd) *(PUGCD 003)* **THE BEAST IN THE BOX**
- Mr James Knowles - The snake pass hornpipe / Mayday - Miss Twentyman's delight - Down with the French / New railroad / The spiral staircase - The squall - Royal burlesque hornpipe / Johannespolka / Adieu sweet lovely Nancy / Nantwich fair - The white petticoat - The recruiting officer / The charming fair - What you will / Hojby Schottische - Mat Eden's Schottische / October song / Double the cape - Rusty gully / Studentenmarch / Jack's alive - Old Fluz - Duke William's hornpipe / Working on a pushboat / The crystal wedding - The heart aches for home / The four seasons - The silly season.

2001. (cd; by BRIAN PETERS & GORDON TYRRALL) *(GAHCD 03)* **THE MOVING MOON**
- High Barbary / The Santa Fe trail / The price of a pig – Troy's wedding - The Sound of Sleat / Long a-growing / The hang of it all / The moving moon / The green willow tree / Earth / Iron legs - What you will - Manage / The miser / Crockery ware / The wild rover / Trip to the Pantheon - Bell in flag - The surrender of Callais / It's not dark yet / The Kirkgate hornpipe - Come ashore / Jolly tar with your trousers on / The last time.

(above issued on Gaho)

2002. (cd) *(PUGCD 004)* **LINES**
- The rambling blade / The sidewinder - The magic tomato - Captain Cook's jig / The gypsy laddie / Polly on the shore / Prince of Cabourg's hornpipe – Brown's hornpipe / Cefn coed polka - The first of August - Caepantywyll / Sir William Gower / Hind horn / Double jeopardy – Hatters' delight / Betsy Bell - Rattle and roll - Scornful Nancy / Jack the jolly tar / Young Hunting / The bouncing bomb - Dark peak polka - Up in the night / The garden off the green / The Derby ram.

2004. (cd) *(PUGCD 005)* **DIFFERENT TONGUES**
- Jolly roving tar / All around my hat / Nottingham Castle - The spa / The outlandish knight / Bold Lovell / Mr Moore's hornpipe - The red otter / The bonny bunch of roses-o / Pretty Nancy of Yarmouth / Sailor's delight – Cobbler's hornpipe / Her bright smile haunts me still / The gallant poacher / Two sisters / Pretty Maggie - Marquis of Huntley's reel - The dead cow / Waltzing's for dreamers / The water's edge.

2005. (cd) *(PUGCD 006)* **ANGLOPHILIA**
- Kissing stones - The spud-spattered piper - Go away Miss Ashton / Farewell Manchester / Chips and fish / The northern lass / Polkas: Nymph - Babes in the wood - The black cat piddled in the white cat's eye / Turks' march - Tom Fowler's hornpipe / Things we said today / Winter minuets / The entertainer / Jigs: The peasant - The celebrated quadrille - Matthew Briggs / Adieu my lovely Nancy / Morris tunes: Old Mother Oxford - Young Collins - Trunkles / The tankard of ale / Dallas rag / Accordion / Vive la bagatelle - Bachelors of every nation - Double lead through / Sweet sorrow.

May 08. (cd) *(PUGCD 007)* **SONGS OF TRIAL AND TRIUMPH**
- The banks of green willow / Green broom / The demon lover / Lucy / Sir Aldingar / Six nights drunk / Georgie / The farmer's curst wife / All alone and lonely / The Golden Vanity / Lord Randall / False foudrage / Sailor's song / Three ravens.

Nov 10. (cd) *(PUGCD 008)* **GRITSTONE SERENADE**
- Turpin hero / Paddy resource – The red ribbon – Hopkinson's favourite / Ten thousand miles / Yorkstone flags – The pokerwork polka / The bold Princess Royal / The Devil's courtship / Jackson's united hornpipes, Nos. 1 & 2 / The brake of Briars / The twenty-sixth of forever / Prospect, Providence / The cotton lords of Preston / Frank and easy – The English paspy – Hodgson Square / The banks of Airdrie / The white joke – The black joke / Good companion.

The PICTISH TRAIL (⟹ FLYNN, Johnny)

PILLOWFISH (⟹ BELL, Helen)

PLEXUS

Formed in 1976 by singer-songwriters Andy Speechley (vocals and guitar) and Nicky Wright (keyboards, etc), PLEXUS were on the go for only a few years and are probably one of the most obscure and underwritten English folk outfits of all time. Their debut LP **PLEXUS** (1977) {*4} featured traditional songs as well as a version of 'Mr Bojangles'.

And then they were joined by Paul Sax on fiddle, guest acoustic bassist Phil Murray and, more importantly, MARTIN ALLCOCK (fretless bass and guitar) – a future player with Celtic act The BULLY WEE BAND, folk icons FAIRPORT CONVENTION and rock outfit JETHRO TULL – on second set **LIFE UP THE CREEK** (1979) {*5}. Maybe that's why it sells on eBay for over £60. *MCS*

Andy Speechley - vocals, acoustic guitar / **Nicky Wright** - keyboards, mandolin, acoustic guitar, vocals

		UK Look	US not issued
1977.	(lp) *(LK/LP 6175)* **PLEXUS**	☐	⊟

- Merrie England / Barbara Allen / Wild world / The rock machine / Lavinia Forsyth Jones / Wish I had a troubadour / The song of the ents / The man of the earth / Mr Bojangles / John o' dreams.

—— added **Paul Sax** - fiddle, percussion, vocals + guests

		Hill and Dale	not issued
1979.	(lp) *(HD 004)* **LIFE UP THE CREEK**	☐	⊟

- Desperado / Whose garden was this / LA freeway / Jessie come home / Last thing on my mind / Davy / The reels / Knock on the door / Dill pickle rag / Clockwork man / The hornpipes.

—— where are they now?

The POGUES

Contrary to popular belief and unlettered pub pundits, The POGUES are not from Ireland, but from King's Cross in north London. The Celtic connection comes from Tipperary-raised Shane MacGowan, their English-born frontman, whose parents were indeed from Ireland. Of course, some of the other personnel had roots in the country – bassist/singer Cait O'Riordan's father was Irish, while later additions Philip Chevron (from The Radiators From Space) and Terry Woods (from SWEENEY'S MEN and STEELEYE SPAN) had full Irish passports. From their formation in the autumn of 1982 through their manifold bust-ups over the course of nearly 30 years, Shane and The POGUES have been at the pinnacle of folk-rock music, Celtic or otherwise.

Alongside female punk artist Shanne Hasler/Bradley (later co-founder of The MEN THEY COULDN'T HANG), MacGowan had earlier (1978-80) been part of the punkabilly outfit The Nipple Erectors. This motley crew released a solitary single, 'King Of The Bop', before shortening their name to The Nips and enlisting future POGUES guitarist James Fearnley.

A few follow-up singles appeared, and even an album, recommended to diehard POGUES fiends only, was released.

POGUE MAHONE (Gaelic for "kiss my arse"), as they were briefly named, were subsequently formed by MacGowan, Fearnley and (a little later) O'Riordan, plus former Millwall Chainsaws alumni Spider Stacy (on tin whistle) and Jem Finer (banjo). The sextet was completed by drummer Andrew Ranken, who joined in 1983 with Cait. By the spring of 1984 they had formed their own group-titled imprint, issuing the classic debut single 'Dark Streets Of London' not long afterwards. The B-side was a reading of ERIC BOGLE's 'And The Band Played Waltzing Matilda'.

Demonstrating all the Celtic melancholy, romance and gritted-teeth stoicism that marked the best of the band's work, the ballad unfairly but predictably received an official BBC radio ban (apparently after the Beeb managed to translate the band's rather rude name). A month later they secured a deal with Stiff Records, changing their name to The POGUES when they supported punk pal Joe Strummer's band The Clash.

Their Stan Brennan-produced debut album, **RED ROSES FOR ME** (1984) {*8}, dented the UK Top 100 as they earned growing support from live audiences the length and breadth of the country. Whether interpreting trad Irish folk songs ('Waxies' Dargle', 'Greenland Whale Fisheries', 'Poor Paddy' and Dominic Behan's 'The Auld Triangle') or reeling off bawdy but brilliant MacGowan originals, The POGUES were apt to turn from high-spirited revelry ('Streams Of Whiskey') to menacing threat ('Boys From The County Hell') in the time it took to neck a pint of Guinness. Which, in Shane's case, was not very long at all.

April 1985 saw the release of perhaps their finest single (and first Top 20 hit), the misty-eyed, Elvis Costello-co-produced 'A Pair Of Brown Eyes'. Costello also oversaw the accompanying album, **RUM, SODOMY AND THE LASH** (1985) {*9}, a debauched, bruisingly beautiful classic that elevated The POGUES (who had added guitarist/co-producer Phil Chevron) to the position of modern-day folk heroes. MacGowan's gift for conjuring up a feeling of time and place was never more vivid than on the likes of 'A Pair Of Brown Eyes', the rousing 'Sally MacLennane', EWAN MacCOLL's 'Dirty Old Town' and the cursing malice of 'The Sickbed Of Cuchulainn', while O'Riordan put in a spinetingling performance as a Scottish laird on the traditional 'I'm A Man You Don't Meet Every Day'.

On May 16, 1986, Cait O'Riordan married Costello, and when she left the band that November (after writing their Top 50 hit 'Haunted' for the Alex Cox film 'Sid and Nancy'), a vital component of The POGUES' chemistry went with her. Around the same time, the group played 'The McMahon Gang' in Cox's cowpunk movie 'Straight To Hell', combining soundtrack duties and on-set thespian abilities with ex-Clash frontman Strummer. The veteran punk would subsequently deputise for the absent MacGowan on an early-1988 US tour.

This period also saw The POGUES peak at No.3 in the album charts with **IF I SHOULD FALL FROM GRACE WITH GOD** (1988) {*8}, an album which spawned an unlikely near-chart-topping Christmas 1987 hit in 'Fairytale Of New York'. A faux-drunken duet with Kirsty MacColl (daughter of Ewan), the ballad was certainly more subversive than the usual Yuletide fodder, and for a brief period The POGUES were bona-fide pop stars. Their rampant collaboration with The DUBLINERS on 'Irish Rover' earlier that year had already breached the Top 10.

Expanding to an untenable eight-piece ensemble when they enlisted Darryl Hunt and Terry Woods, the band were untouchable live. MacGowan's errant, tin-tray-wielding genius was the stuff of legend, particularly for many who witnessed their blood 'n' guts gigs at places like the Glasgow Barrowlands. Channelling Eastern and Mediterranean-type folk respectively on 'Turkish Song Of The Damned' and 'Fiesta' (another massive party hit), the album was also graced by Chevron's emigration ballad 'Thousands Are Sailing' and the highly charged, Woods-penned piece 'Birmingham Six'.

Inevitably, MacGowan's hard-drinking ways were beginning to affect his writing, and **PEACE AND LOVE** (1989) {*6} signalled a slow slide into mediocrity; the swing/jazz opener, 'Gridlock', was ambitious and ill-advised. Taking inspiration from their home city, rather than just Dublin, Ireland and the like, tracks such as 'White City', 'Misty Morning, Albert Bridge' and 'London, You're A Lady' found the cracks showing through, although 'Gartloney Rats' brought back their Celtic wit and banter.

1990's **HELL'S DITCH** {*5} carried on in much the same rawkish vein, although this was to be MacGowan's final album under the banner of The POGUES, his failing health incompatible with the demands of a successful major-label band. Tracks like 'Sunny Side Of The Street' were stop-me-if-you've-heard-this-one-before material, while others such as the set's saviour, 'Summer In Siam' were abandoning the folk formula that had made them great in the first place.

While the gap-toothed frontman eventually got a solo career together, The POGUES bravely soldiered on with a surprisingly impressive hit single, 'Tuesday Morning', the opening salvo from their 1993 UK Top 20 album **WAITING FOR HERB** {*5}. Two years on, a nostalgically titled follow-up set, **POGUE MAHONE** (1995) {*6}, failed to rekindle their former glory, while a solo MacGOWAN continued to dominate the limelight. Alongside original contributions, mainly from Finer (Hunt and Ranken also penned a few), their rootsy appeal was intact on two covers: Ronnie Lane's 'How Come' and BOB DYLAN's 'When The Ship Comes In'. In 1999 some of the POGUES (Stacy, Hunt and Ranken) got together as The Wisemen, while Finer has emerged with the band Longplayer.

Following his messy departure from The POGUES, the Irish Keith Richards (though even Richards's mythical debauchery would struggle to match MacGOWAN's self-destructiveness for sheer dogged determination) threatened to form his own outfit, The Popes. Sceptics who doubted that the man could even form an opinion were at least partly silenced by his Christmas 1992 duet with fellow maverick Nick Cave on a brilliantly skewed cover of Louis Armstrong's 'Wonderful World'.

A few years on and much press rumination later, The Popes' debut single,

'The Church Of The Holy Spook', finally put an end to the speculation, demonstrating that MacGOWAN's muse was as darkly fertile as ever. Released on the ZTT imprint (once the home of Frankie Goes To Hollywood), the song's up-tempo thrash recalled the unholy spirit of the POGUES classic 'Sickbed Of Cuchulainn', but it only scraped into the UK Top 75.

Follow-up single 'That Woman's Got Me Drinking' (excuses, excuses) reached the Top 40, while Hollywood heartthrob (and fellow Keith Richards impersonator) Johnny Depp played guitar on the group's debut Top Of The Pops appearance. The accompanying album, **THE SNAKE** (1994), was the best album the POGUES never recorded, finding MacGOWAN back at his cursing, doomed romantic best. Alongside the obligatory traditional songs ('The Rising Of The Moon' and 'Nancy Whiskey'), the record featured an amusingly appropriate cover of GERRY RAFFERTY's 'Her Father Didn't Like Me Anyway', while a revamped 'Haunted' was a duet with Sinead O'Connor that reached the Top 30 when released as a single in the spring of 1995.

CLANNAD's Maire Brennan also hooked up with MacGOWAN for 'You're The One', underlining the depth of respect afforded the wayward genius even among his more conventional peers. The live appearances that followed the record's release might not have matched the ferocious abandon of the POGUES in full flow, but they came damn near it, while MacGOWAN followed in Sid Vicious's unsteady footsteps (his love of the Sex Pistols was revealed to the nation in a barely coherent interview on Jo Whiley's Channel 4 TV show) by recording a version of 'My Way' in gloriously two-fingered style. 1997 saw the release of a disappointing follow-up set, **THE CROCK OF GOLD** {*5}, a record that was at times easier on the ear but hardly threatened to set the pulse racing.

Surely only SHANE MacGOWAN could perform at two St Patrick's Day shows on the same day on opposite sides of the Atlantic, and due to a quirk of fate, that was exactly what he did. The cream of both performances was collected on **ACROSS THE BROAD ATLANTIC: LIVE ON PADDY'S DAY** (2002) {*7}. As expected, the atmosphere is raucous, the banter paints the air blue and the set list is primed for maximum whiskey-soaked celebration. Since 2001 The POGUES, with Shane on his best behaviour, have reunited every Christmas (echoing the perennial hit 'Fairytale Of New York' with the sadly missed Kirsty), and on other celebratory days, for global concerts. *MCS & BG*

Shane MacGowan (b. Dec 25, '57, Kent) - vocals, guitar (ex-Nipple Erectors)/ **James Fearnley** (b. Oct 10, '54, Manchester) - accordion (ex-Nipple Erectors) / **Spider Stacy** (b. Peter Richard Stacy, Dec 14, '58, Eastbourne) - tin whistle / **Jem Finer** (b. Jeremy Max Finer, Jul 29, '55, Stoke-on-Trent, England) - banjo, guitar / **Cait O'Riordan** (b. Jan 4, '65, Nigeria) - bass, vocals / **Andrew Ranken** (b. Nov 13, '53, Ladbroke Grove, London) - drums

UK Pogue Mahone — US not issued

May 84. (ltd-7"; as POGUE MAHONE) *(PM 1)* DARK STREETS OF LONDON. / And The Band Played Waltzing Matilda [ ] [–]

Stiff — not issued

Jun 84. (7") *(BUY 207)* DARK STREETS OF LONDON. / And The Band Played Waltzing Matilda [ ] [–]

Sep 84. (lp) *(SEEZ 55)* **RED ROSES FOR ME** [89] [–]
- Transmetropolitan / The battle of Brisbane / The auld triangle / Waxies' dargle / Boys from the County Hell / Sea shanty / Dark streets of London / Streams of whiskey / Poor daddy / Dingle regatta / Greenland whale fisheries / Down in the ground where the dead men go / Kitty. *(cd-iss. May 87; CDSEEZ 55) <US on Enigma c+=/cd+=; 4XT/D2 73225>* - Whiskey you're the devil / Muirshin Durkin / Repeal of the licensing laws. *(re-iss. Jan 89 on WEA lp/c; WX 240/+C) (cd re-iss. Jan 89; 244494-2) (<cd re-mast.Dec04 on WSM+=; 5046 75958-2>)* - The leaving of Liverpool / Muirshin Durkin / Repeal of the licensing laws / And the band played Waltzing Matilda / Whiskey you're the devil / The wild rover.

Oct 84. (7") *(BUY 212)* BOYS FROM THE COUNTY HELL. / Repeal Of The Licensing Laws [ ] [–]
(d-7"+=) *(BUY 212 - 207)* - (see debut 45).

Mar 85. (7"/7" pic-d) *(BUY/DBUY 220)* A PAIR OF BROWN EYES. / Whiskey You're The Devil [72] [–]
(12"+=) *(BUYIT 22)* - Muirshin Durkin.

—— added p/t **Phil Chevron** (b. Jun '57, Dublin, Ireland) - guitar, producer (ex-Radiators From Space)

Jun 85. (7", 7" green/7" shaped-pic-d) *(BUY/PBUY 224)* SALLY MacLENNANE. / Wild Rover (acoustic) [51] [–]
(12"+=) *(BUYIT 224)* - The leaving of Liverpool (acoustic).
(c-s++=) *(BUYC 224)* - Wild cats of Kilkenny.

Aug 85. (lp/c/cd) *(SEEZ/CSEEZ/CDSEEZ 58)* **RUM, SODOMY AND THE LASH** [13] [–]
- The sickbed of Cuchulainn / The old main drag / Wild cats of Kilkenny / I'm a man you don't meet every day / A pair of brown eyes / Sally MacLennane / Dirty old town / Jesse James / Navigator / Billy's bones / The gentleman soldier / The band played Waltzing Matilda. *(c+=/cd+=)* - A pistol *for Paddy Garcia. (re-iss. Jan 89 on WE' lp/c; WX 241/+C) (cd-iss. Jan 89; 244495-2) (<cd re-mast. Dec 04 on WSM+=; 5046 75959-2>)* - A pistol for Paddy Garcia / London girl / A rainy night in Soho / The body of an American / Planxty Noel Hill / The parting glass.

Aug 85. (7"/7" pic-d) *(BUY/PBUY 229)* DIRTY OLD TOWN. / A Pistol For Paddy Garcia [62] [–]
(12"+=) *(BUYIT 229)* - The parting glass.

Feb 86. (7"ep/12"ep/c-ep/7" pic-ep) *(BUY/BUYIT/BUYC/PBUY 243)* POGUETRY IN MOTION [29] [–]
- London girl / A rainy night in Soho / The body of an American / Planxty Noel Hill.

Aug 86. (7") *(MCA 1084)* HAUNTED. / Junk Theme [42] [–]
(12"+=) *(MCAT 1084)* - Hot dogs with everything.

—— (above single from the movie 'Sid & Nancy' on MCA)

—— **Darryl Hunt** (b. May '50, Bournemouth, England) - bass (ex-Pride O' The Cross) repl. Cait

Mar 87. (7"; by The POGUES & The DUBLINERS) *(BUY 258)* THE IRISH ROVER. / The Rare Ould Mountain Dew [8] [–]
(12"+=) *(BUYIT 258)* - The Dubliner's fancy.

—— added **Terry Woods** (b. Dec '47, Dublin) - banjo (ex-STEELEYE SPAN, The WOODS BAND, ex-SWEENEY'S MEN)

Hell-Stiff — Enigma

Jun 87. (cd/c/lp) *(C/Z/+DIABLO 1) <D2/4XJE 73308>* **STRAIGHT TO HELL** [soundtrack w/ Various Artists] [ ] Nov 87 [ ]
- The good, the bad and the ugly / Rake at the gates of Hell / If I should fall from grace with God / Rabinga / Danny boy / (other artists). *(cd re-iss. Aug 91 on Repertoire; REP 4224-WY) (<cd re-iss. Jun 04 as STRAIGHT TO HELL - RETURNS on Big Beat+=; CDWIKD 239>)* - Long cool day in Hell / Bolero del perro listo (also known as Bolero) / Night on Bald Mountain / Harmonicas / Big question mark / L'amoria / Obsession / Quiet day in Blanco town / Taranta del fuente / (+ other artists).

Pogue Mahone-EMI — Island

Nov 87. (7"; The POGUES with KIRSTY MacCOLL) *(NY 7)* FAIRYTALE OF NEW YORK. / The Battle March Medley [2] [–]
(12"+=)(cd-s+=) *(NY 12)(CDNY 1)* - Shanne Bradley.

Jan 88. (cd/c/lp) *(CD/TC+/NYR 1) <90872-2>* **IF I SHOULD FALL FROM GRACE WITH GOD** [3] [88]
- If I should fall from grace with God / Turkish song of the damned / Bottle of smoke / Fairytale of New York (with KIRSTY MacCOLL) / Metropolis / Thousands are sailing / Fiesta / Medley:- The recruiting sergeant - The rocky road to Dublin - Galway races / Streets of sorrow - Birmingham six / Lullaby of London / Sit down by the fire / The broad majestic Shannon / Worms. *(cd+=)* - South Australia / The battle march medley. *(re-iss. Jan 89 on WEA lp/c; WX 243/+C) (cd-iss. Jan 89; 244494-2) <(cd re-mast. Dec 04 on WSM+=; 5046 75960-2>)* - The battle march medley / The Irish rover / Mountain dew / Shanne Bradley / Sketches of Spain / South Australia.

Feb 88. (7") *(FG 1)* IF I SHOULD FALL FROM GRACE WITH GOD. / Sally MacLennane (live) [58] [–]
(12" red-ep)(cd-ep+=) - ST PATRICK'S NIGHT *(SGG 1-12) (CDFG 1)* - A pair of brown eyes (live) / Dirty old town (live).

Jul 88. (7") *(FG 2)* FIESTA. / Sketches Of Spain [24] [–]
(12"+=)(cd-s+=) *(FG 2-12)(CDFG 2)* - South Australia.

WEA — Island

Dec 88. (7") *(YZ 355)* YEAH, YEAH, YEAH, YEAH, YEAH. / The Limerick Rake [43] [–]
(12"+=/cd-s+=) *(YZ 355 T/CD)* - Honky tonk woman / ('A'-long).

Jun 89. (7"/c-s) *(YZ 407/+C)* MISTY MORNING, ALBERT BRIDGE. / Cotton Fields [41] [–]
(12"+=) *(YZ 407T)* - Young Ned of the hill (dub version).
(3"cd-s++=) *(YZ 407CD)* - Train of love.

Jul 89. (lp/c)(cd) *(WX 247/+C)(246086-2) <91225-2>* **PEACE AND LOVE** [5] [ ]
- Gridlock / White City / Young Ned of the hill / Misty morning, Albert Bridge / Cotton fields / Blue heaven / Down all the days / USA / Lorelei / Gartloney rats / Boat train / Tombstone / Night train to Lorca / London you're a lady. *(<cd re-mast. Dec 04 on WSM+=; 5046 75961-2>)* - Star of the County Down / The Limerick rake / Train of love / Every man is a king (in the US of A) / Yeah, yeah, yeah, yeah, yeah / Honky tonk women.

Aug 89. (7") *(YZ 409)* WHITE CITY. / Every Man Is A King (In The US Of A) [ ] [–]
(12"+=) *(YZ 409TX)* - Maggie May (live).
(c-s+=/cd-s+=) *(YZ 409 C/CD)* - The star of the County Down.

May 90. (7"/c-s; as The POGUES & The DUBLINERS) *(YZ 500/+C)* JACK'S HEROES. / Whiskey In The Jar [63] [–]
(12"+=/cd-s+=) *(YZ 500 T/CD)* - ('B'-extended).

(above theme song used by Ireland in the football World Cup)

Aug 90. (7") *(YZ 519)* SUMMER IN SIAM. / The Bastard Landlord [64] [–]
(12"+=/cd-s+=) *(YZ 519 T/CD)* - Hell's ditch (instrumental) / The Irish rover (with The DUBLINERS).

Sep 90. (cd)(lp/c) *(9031 72554-2)(WX 366/+C) <422 846999-2/-4/-1>* **HELL'S DITCH** [21] [ ]
- The sunny side of the street / Sayonara / The ghost of a smile / Hell's ditch / Lorca's novena / Summer in Siam / Rain street / Rainbow man / The wake of the Medusa / House of the gods / Five green queens and Jean / Maidrin Rua / Six to go. *(<cd re-mast. Dec 04 on WSM+=; 5046 75962-2>)* - Whiskey in the jar / The bastard landlord / Infinity / Curse of love / Squid out of water / Jack's heroes / A rainy night in Soho (remix).

Nov 90. (cd-ep) *<422-846 723-2>* YEAH, YEAH, YEAH, YEAH, YEAH (long version) / Honky Tonk Woman / Jack's Heroes / Whiskey In The Jar (long version) [–] [ ]

Apr 91. (7") *(YZ 548)* SAYONARA. / Curse Of Love [ ] [-]
(12"+=/cd-s+=) *(YZ 548 T/CD)* - Infinity.
Sep 91. (7") *(YZ 603)* A RAINY NIGHT IN SOHO (remix). / Squid Out Of Water [67] [-]
(12"+=) *(YZ 603)* - Infinity.
(cd-s+=) *(YZ 603CD)* - POGUETRY IN MOTION *(ep)*.
Nov 91. (7") *(YZ 628)* FAIRYTALE OF NEW YORK. / Fiesta [36] [-]
(12"+=/cd-s+=) *(YZ 628 T/CD)* - A pair of brown eyes / The sickbed of Cuchulainn (live) / Maggie May (live).

—— (Sep 91) MacGowan left when his health deteriorated (ex-Clash singer/guitarist JOE STRUMMER deputised for him on tour)

—— p/t Joe Strummer (ex-Clash) was deposed by Spider Stacy, who took over on vocals

May 92. (7"/c-s) *(YZ 673/+C)* HONKY TONK WOMEN. / Curse Of Love [56] [-]
(12"+=) *(YZ 673T)* - Infinity.
(cd-s+=) *(YZ 673CD)* - The parting glass.

—— added eighth member & producer **Michael Brook** - infinite guitar

WEA Chameleon

Aug 93. (7"/c-s) *(YZ 758/+C)* TUESDAY MORNING. / First Day Of Forever [18] [-]
(cd-s+=) *(YZ 758CD)* - Turkish song of the damned (live).
(YZ 758CDX) - ('A') / London calling (live with JOE STRUMMER) / I fought the law (live with JOE STRUMMER).
Sep 93. (cd/c/lp) *(4509 93463-2/-4/-1) <61598>* **WAITING FOR HERB** [20] Oct 98 [ ]
- Tuesday morning / Smell of petroleum / Haunting / Once upon a time / Sitting on top of the world / Drunken boat / Big city / Girl from the Wadi Hammamat / Modern world / Pachinko / My baby's gone / Small hours. *(<cd re-mast. Dec 04 on WSM+=; 5046 75963-2>)* - First day of forever / Train kept rolling on / Paris St Germain.
Jan 94. (7"/c-s) *(YZ 771/+C)* ONCE UPON A TIME. / Train Kept Rolling On [66] [-]
(12"+=/cd-s+=) *(YZ 771 T/CD)* - Tuesday morning / Paris St Germain.

—— Fearnley + Woods departed; apparently due to the brief Xmas comeback of MacGowan

—— **Spider, Jem, Darryl + Ranken** added **Jamie Clarke** - banjo / **James McNally** - accordion, uilleann pipes / **David Coulter** - mandolin, tambourine

Sep 95. (7"green/c-s) *(WEA 011 X/C)* HOW COME. / Eyes Of An Angel [ ] [-]
(cd-s+=) *(WX 011CD)* - Tuesday morning (live) / Big city (live).
Oct 95. (cd/c/lp) *(0630 11210-2/-4/-1)* **POGUE MAHONE** [ ] [-]
- How come / Living in a world without her / When the ship comes in / Anniversary / Amadie / Love you till the end / Bright lights / Oretown / Pont Mirabeau / Tosspint / Four o'clock in the morning / Where that love's been gone / The sun and the moon. *(<cd re-mast. Dec 04 on WSM+=; 5046 75964-2>)* - Eyes of an angel / Love you till the end.

—— The POGUES split in 1996

—— note:- The POGUES (and the track 'Just One Of Those Things') also appeared on the flip side of Kirsty MacColl's Cole Porter tribute single 'Miss Otis Regrets'.

- (8-10*) compilations -

Sep 91. (cd)(lp/c) *WEA; (9031 75405-2)(WX 430/+C)* **THE BEST OF THE POGUES** [11] [-]
- Fairytale of New York (with KIRSTY MacCOLL) / Sally MacLennane (live) / Dirty old town / The Irish rover (with The DUBLINERS) / A pair of brown eyes (live) / Streams of whiskey / A rainy night in Soho (remix) / Fiesta / Rain street / Misty morning, Albert Bridge / White City / Thousands are sailing / The broad majestic Shannon / The body of an American.
Nov 91. (cd/c) *Island; <314-510610-2/-4>* **ESSENTIAL POGUES** [-] [ ]
- The sunny side of the street / If I should fall from grace with God / Lorelei / Thousands are sailing / White City / Fairytale of New York / Fiesta / Rain street / Turkish song of the damned / Summer in Siam / Misty morning, Albert Bridge / Blue heaven / Honky tonk women / Yeah, yeah, yeah, yeah, yeah (long version).
Mar 01. (cd/c) *Warners ESP; (<8573 87459-2/-4>)* **THE VERY BEST OF ...** [18] Jun 01 [ ]
- Dirty old town / The Irish rover (with The DUBLINERS) / Sally MacLennane / Fiesta / A pair of brown eyes / Fairytale of New York / The body of an American / Streams of whiskey / The sickbed of Cuchulainn / If I should fall from grace with God / Misty morning, Albert Bridge / Rain street / White City / A rainy night in Soho / London girl / Boys from the County Hell / The sunnyside of the street / Summer in Siam / Hell's ditch / The old main drag / The band played Waltzing Matilda.
Mar 05. (d-cd) *Warners; (2564 62254-2)* **THE ULTIMATE COLLECTION** [15] [ ]
- THE ULTIMATE POGUES: Rainy night in Soho / Sally MacLennane / The Irish rover / Dirty old town / Fairytale of New York (feat. KIRSTY MacCOLL) / Streams of whiskey / If I should fall from grace with God / Fiesta / Body of an American / Misty morning Albert Bridge / Repeal of the licensing laws / Boys from the County Hell / Sunny side of the street / A pair of brown eyes / Summer in Siam / The sickbed of Cuchulainn / London girl / Tuesday morning / White city / Hell's ditch / Young Ned of the hill / Thousands are sailing // LIVE AT BRIXTON ACADEMY: Streams of whiskey / If I should fall from grace with God / Boys from the County Hell / The broad majestic Shannon / Young Ned of the hill / The Turkish song of the damned / Rainy night in Soho / Tuesday morning / Rain street / A pair of brown eyes / Repeal of the licensing laws / Old main drag / Thousands are sailing / The body of an American / Lullaby of London / Dirty old town / Bottle of smoke / The sick bed of Cuchulainn / Sally MacLennane / Fairytale of New York / Fiesta / The Irish rover.

- essential boxed sets -

Jan 06. (3xcd-box) *WEA; (111700-2)* **TRILOGY** [ ] [-]
- (IF I SHOULD FALL FROM GRACE WITH GOD) // (RUM, SODOMY AND THE LASH) // (PEACE AND LOVE).
Aug 07. (3-cd-box) *Rhino-WEA; (514 423777-2)* **THE WORKS - A 3 CD RETROSPECTIVE** [ ] [-]
- Boys from the County Hell / Dark streets of London / Streams of whiskey / Transmetropolitan / Greenland whale fisheries / Repeal of the licensing laws / A pair of brown eyes / Sally MacLennane / Dirty old town / The sickbed of Cuchulainn / London girl / The body of an American / If I should fall from grace with God / Turkish song of the damned / Metropolis / Thousands are sailing / Fiesta / The Irish rover / Lullaby of London // Fairytale of New York / A rainy night in Soho / White City / Misty morning, Albert Bridge / Every man is a king / Yeah, yeah, yeah, yeah, yeah / Young Ned of the hill / Gridlock / Sunny side of the street / Hell's ditch / Summer in Siam / Rain street / Whiskey in the jar / Tuesday morning / Drunken boat / Paris St Germain / When the ship comes in / Pont Mirabeau / Love you till the end // (LIVE AT BRIXTON ACADEMY tracks).
Jun 08. (5-cd-box) *Rhino-WEA; (514 428134-2)* **JUST LOOK THEM STRAIGHT IN THE EYE AND SAY... POGUE MAHONE!!: THE POGUES BOX SET** [ ] [-]
- The Kerry polka / The rocky road to Dublin / Boys from the County Hell / NW3 / The Donegal express - The hen and the cock are in Carrickmacross / Do you believe in magic? / Hot asphalt / Danny boy (BBC session) / Maggie May / Haunted / The travelling people / Eve of destruction / My baby's gone (demo) / North Sea holes / Garbo (also known as In and out) / The last of McGee / Afro-Cuban be-bop (alt. mix by JOE STRUMMER & THE ASTRO-PHYSICIANS) / Young Ned of the hill (dub version) / Pinned down – I'm alone in the wilderness / When the ship comes in (demo) / Waxies' dargle (live in Sweden) // Repeal of the licensing laws (demo) / Dark streets of London (demo) / Greenland whale fisheries (demo) / Streams of whiskey (BBC session) / The auld triangle (BBC session) / Poor Paddy on the railway (BBC session) / Sea shanty (demo) / Transmetropolitan (demo) / Kitty (demo) / Boys from the County Hell (BBC session) / Connemara, let's go (also known as Down in the ground where the dead men go) (demo) / Billy's bones (BBC session) / The old main drag (BBC session) / Sally MacLennane (BBC session) / The town that never sleeps / Something wild / Driving through the city / Rainy night in Soho ('oboe version') / Fairytale of New York (extract 1st demo) / Fairytale of New York (extract 2nd demo) / Fairytale of New York (extract 3rd demo) / Navigator // The aria / The good, the bad and the ugly / Haunted (demo) / Love theme from Sid And Nancy / Junk theme / Glued up and speeding / Paris / A needle for Paddy Garcia / JB 57 / Bowery snax - Spiked / Hot dogs with everything / Rince del emplacada / The rake at the gates of Hell (BBC session) / Turkish song of the damned (BBC session) / If I should fall from grace with God (BBC session) / Battle march (demo) / Lullaby of London (demo) / Shanne Bradley (demo) / Streets of sorrow (demo) / Thousands are sailing (extract) / The Balinalee / Nicaragua libre / Japan (live in Tokyo) // (live at the Barrowlands, Glasgow, 17/19 December, 1987):- Sally MacLennane / A pair of brown eyes / Kitty / Maggie May / Dirty old town / The sickbed of Cuchulainn / Fiesta (single remix) / If I should fall from grace with God (remix) / Johnny come lately (STEVE EARLE) / Boat train (demo) / Night train to Lorca (demo) / The mistlethrush / Got a lot of livin' to do / Victoria / Murder (version 1) / Lust for vomit / The wake of the Medusa (demo) / The black dog's ditch / Aisling / Murder (version 2) / Yeah yeah yeah yeah yeah (remix) / Maidrin Rua / Johnny come lately (live) // Johnny was (SEXY BONGO) / Miss Otis regrets - Just one of those things (The POGUES & KIRSTY MacCOLL) / All the tears that I cried (KIRSTY MacCOLL) / The one and only (KIRSTY MacCOLL) / Afro-Cuban be-bop (JOE STRUMMER AND THE ASTRO-PHYSICIANS) / Turkish song of the damned (live featuring JOE STRUMMER) / London calling (live featuring JOE STRUMMER) / I fought the law (live featuring JOE STRUMMER) / The girl from Wadi-Hammamat (demo) / Moving to Moldova (demo) / Call my name / The sun and the moon (demo) / Living in a world without her (demo) / Who said romance is dead? (demo) / Sound of the city night (demo) / Four o'clock in the morning (demo) / (live at Brixton Academy, London 21/22 December, 2001):- The star of the County Down / White City / Medley: The recruiting sergeant - The rocky road to Dublin - The Galway races / The parting glass - Lord Santry's fairest daughter.

- (5-7*) compilations, others, etc.-

Jun 92. (cd)(lp/c) *WEA; (9031 77341-2)(WX 471/+C)* **THE REST OF THE BEST** (compilation out-takes) [ ] [-]
- If I should fall from grace with God / The sickbed of Cuchulainn / The old main drag / Boys from the County Hell / Young Ned of the hill / Dark streets of London / The auld triangle / Repeal of the licensing laws / Yeah, yeah, yeah, yeah, yeah / London girl / Honky tonk women / Summer in Siam / Turkish song of the damned / Lullaby of London / The sunny side of the street / Hell's ditch.
Jan 02. (cd) *Castle; (CMRCD 388)* **STREAMS OF WHISKEY** (live in Leysin, Switzerland 1991) [ ] [-]
- Streams of whiskey / If I should fall from grace with God / Boys from the County Hell / Young Ned of the hill / Rain street / Sayonara / Battle of Brisbane / The body of an American / Summer in Siam / Thousands are sailing / The sunnyside of the street / Dirty old town / The sickbed of Cuchulainn / Yeah, yeah, yeah, yeah, yeah / Fiesta / Sally MacLennane.
Sep 05. (cd) *W.S.M.; (510 110404-2)* **DIRTY OLD TOWN: THE PLATINUM COLLECTION** [ ] [-]
- Streams of whiskey / A pair of brown eyes / Dirty old town / Sally MacLennane / Dingle regatta / Turkish song of the damned / Metropolis / Thousands are sailing / A rainy night in Soho / Misty morning, Albert Bridge / I'm a man you don't meet

every day / Gridlock / Young Ned of the hill / Tuesday morning / Paris St Germain / Drunken boat / Love you till the end.

Dec 05. (7"; with KIRSTY MacCOLL) *Warners; (WEA 400CD)*
FAIRYTALE OF NEW YORK. / The Battle March Medley [3] [–]
(cd-s) *(WEA 400CD)* - ('A') / ('A'-instrumental).
(cd-s) *(WEA 400DVD)* - ('A') / ('A'-video) / ('A'-Top Of The Pops performance 1987).

Dec 06. (re-) *(same)* FAIRYTALE OF NEW YORK [6] [–]
Dec 07. (re-) *(same)* FAIRYTALE OF NEW YORK [6] [–]
Dec 08. (re-) *(same) FAIRYTALE OF NEW YORK* [13] [–]

SHANE MacGOWAN & THE POPES

Shane MacGowan - vocals / **Paul McGuinness** - guitar / **Bernie France** - bass / **Danny Pope** - drums / **Tom McManamon** - banjo

ZTT Warners

Sep 94. (7"/c-s/cd-s) *(ZANG 57/+C/CD)* THE CHURCH OF THE HOLY SPOOK. / Rake At The Gates Of Hell [74] [–]
(cd-s+=) *(ZANG 57CDX)* - King of the bop / Nancy Whiskey.

Oct 94. (c-s) *(ZANG 56C)* THAT WOMAN'S GOT ME DRINKING / Her Father Didn't Like Me Anyway [34] [–]
(12"+=/cd-s+=) *(ZANG 56 T/CD)* - Roddy McCorley / Minstrel boy.

Oct 94. (cd/c/lp) *(4509 98104-2/-4/-1)* <45821> **THE SNAKE** [37] Jan 95 [ ]
- The church of the holy spook / That woman's got me drinking / The song with no name / Aisling / I'll be your handbag / Her father didn't like me anyway / A Mexican funeral in Paris / The snake with the eyes of Garnet / Donegal express / Victoria / The rising of the moon / Bring down the lamp. *(re-iss. Jun 95 cd/c; 0630 10402-2/-4)* - Haunted (with SINEAD O'CONNOR) / You're the one (with MAIRE BRENNAN) / Cracklin' Rosie / Bring down the lamp. *(cd re-iss. Nov 98; MACG 004CD)*

Dec 94. (c-s) *(ZANG 60C)* THE SONG WITH NO NAME / Nancy Whiskey
(12"+=/cd-s+=) *(ZANG 60 T/CD)* - Cracklin' Rosie. [ ] [–]

Apr 95. (c-s; SHANE MacGOWAN & SINEAD O'CONNOR) *(ZANG 65C)* HAUNTED / The Song With No Name [30] [–]
(cd-s+=) *(ZANG 65CD)* - Bring down the lamp / Cracklin' Rosie.

Jun 95. (c-s; SHANE MacGOWAN & MAIRE BRENNAN) *(ZANG 68C)* YOU'RE THE ONE / Aisling [ ] [–]
(cd-s) *(ZANG 68CD)* - Victoria.

Apr 96. (c-s; SHANE MacGOWAN) *(ZANG 79C)* MY WAY / The Song With No Name [29] [–]
(cd-s+=) *(ZANG 79CD)* - Aisling / My way (your way).

—— **Lucky Dowling** - bass; repl. Bernie

—— added **Kieran Kiely** - accordions, whistles, vocals + **John Myers** - fiddle, whistle, guitar

Oct 97. (cd-s) *(MACG 001CD)* LONESOME HIGHWAY / A Man Called Horse / Joey's In America [ ] [–]

Oct 97. (cd/c) *(MACG 002 CD/C)* **THE CROCK OF GOLD** [59] [–]
- Paddy rolling stone / Rock 'n' roll Paddy / Paddy public enemy No.1 / Back in County Hell / Lonesome highway / Come to the bower / Ceilidh cowboy / More pricks than kicks / Truck drivin' man / Joey's in America / B & I ferry / Mother mo chroi / Spanish lady / St John of God's / Skipping rhymes / Maclennan / Wanderin' star.

Mar 98. (cd-s) *(MACG 003CD)* ROCK 'N' ROLL PADDY / She Moves Through The Fair [ ] [–]

Jan 02. (cd) *(ZTT 178CD)* <18036> **THE RARE OUL' STUFF** [ ] Feb 02 [ ]
- You're the one / The song with no name / Nancy Whiskey / Roddy McCorley / Rock 'n' roll Paddy / Christmas lullaby / Danny boy / Minstrel boy / Rake at the gates of Hell / Victoria / Donegal express / Ceilidh cowboy / Paddy rolling stone / Paddy public enemy No.1 / Back in the county hell / The snakes with eyes of garnet / Cracklin' Rosie / Aisling / Spanish lady / Come to the bower / St. John of God's.

Eagle Red Ink

Feb 02. (cd; as SHANE MacGOWAN'S POPES) *(EAGCD 192)* <57068> **ACROSS THE BROAD ATLANTIC: LIVE ON PADDY'S DAY - NEW YORK - DUBLIN** (live) [ ] [ ]
- If I should fall from grace with God / Rock 'n' roll Paddy / Nancy Whiskey / A rainy night in Soho / Poor Paddy works on the railway / The broad majestic Shannon / Popes instrumental:- My Ballyvourney love - The limpin' general - Bag of chips / Dirty old town / Mother Mo Chroi / Body of an American / Granuaille / More pricks than kicks / Aisling / A pair of brown eyes / Streams of whiskey / Lonesome highway / Angel of death / Sickbed of Cuchulainn / The Irish rover / Fairytale of New York.

—— footnote: MacGOWAN and the POGUES reunite every so often for special gigs/tours, etc. - but as yet, no more recordings.

Karine POLWART

For a decade or so, Scots singer-songwriter, guitarist and bouzouki player KARINE POLWART (born December 23, 1970, Banknock in Stirlingshire) has been at the core of Celtic and contemporary traditional music as a solo artist, an original member of MALINKY 1998-2004 (you must hear her emotionally charged 'The Dreadful End Of Marianna For Sorcery' from 'Last Leaves'), a member of MacALIAS (with GILL BOWMAN in 2000) and also of The BATTLEFIELD BAND (in 2001). Karine's university career was crowned with a First and a Master's in philosophy.

FAULTLINES (2003) {*7} confirmed her potential, an award-winning album that showcased her country-esque overtones, with light Celtic touches, sung in her distinctive but intimate Scots brogue. The rawkish and rootsy 'Four Strong Walls' sounds particularly Corrs-like, without the cheesy sauce, while Appalachian inspirations show up in 'What Are You Waiting For?', and the darker 'Azalea Flower' is quite alternative for an artist of her pedigree.

Of her many outside projects, her most high-profile (at least in folk circles) was her songwriting and backing vocals on Idlewild frontman RODDY WOOMBLE's solo folk-reincarnation album 'My Secret Is My Silence' (2006).

Once again lyrically attuned to modern-day woes and aspirations, solo album number two, **SCRIBBLED IN CHALK** (2006) {*8}, maintained her personal approach, never flinching from hardcore subject matter such as sex trafficking ('Maybe There's A Road') and the Holocaust ('Baleerie Baloo'). However, it was inevitable that POLWART should be drawn back into traditional fare on **FAIREST FLOO'ER** (2007) {*6}, a record to please the purist, although stark and dark murder ballads rose to the surface with 'The Death Of Queen Jane' and 'The Wife Of Usher's Well'.

If one song could catapult Karine up there with the greats, it would be the banjo-friendly 'Sorry', one of several highlights from fourth album **THIS EARTHLY SPELL** (2008) {*8}. Along with 'The Good Years', written with Scotland's national poet or 'Makar' Edwin Morgan (who passed away in 2010) in the course of one of her moonlighting projects, Radio 2's The Radio Ballads, and 'Sorrowlessfield', written with her brother Steven Polwart, it took the listener beyond the pigeonholes of the critics, some of whom have filed her as a country act. Her contributions to Shrewsbury Festival act the DARWIN SONG PROJECT in 2009, and her work with KING CREOSOTE's/ Kenny Anderson's genre-crossing BURNS UNIT the year after, ought to put paid to ill-advised generalisations (she has also recorded with LAU) while we await a fifth chapter in her wondrous solo career. *MCS*

Karine Polwart - vocals, acoustic guitar, bouzouki / + band

UK Neon — US not issued

Dec 03. (cd) *(NEONCD 005)* **FAULTLINES** [ ] [–]
- Only one way / Faultlines / Four strong walls / The sun's comin' over the hill / Resolution road / Waterlily / What are you waiting for? / Skater of the surface / Harder to walk these days than run - Harder to walk jig / The light on the shore / Azalea flower.

Oct 05. (ltd-cd-ep) *(KARINE 01)* THE PULLING THROUGH EP [ ] [–]
- Holy Moses / [live at the Cambridge Folk Festival]: Only one way / Daisy / [live at the Darvel Festival]: Waterlily / The light on the shore.

Shoeshine — not issued

Apr 06. (cd) *(SPIT 028)* **SCRIBBLED IN CHALK** [ ] [–]
- Hole in the heart / I'm gonna do it all / Daisy / Maybe there's a road / Where the smoke blows / Holy Moses / Don't know why / Take its own time / I've seen it all / Baleerie baloo / Terminal star / Follow the heron.

Apr 06. (cd-s) *(SPIT 029)* I'M GONNA DO IT ALL / John C. Clarke (The Gasman Song) [ ] [–]

Jul 06. (cd-s) *(SPIT 030)* DAISY / Where The Smoke Blows [bothy acoustic mix] / Terminal Star [bothy acoustic mix] [ ] [–]

Hegri Music - Proper — not issued

Dec 07. (cd) *(Hegri 03 – 52597032)* **FAIREST FLOO'ER** [ ] [–]
- Dowie dens of Yarrow / Thou hast left me ever Jamie / Mirk, mirk is the midnight hour / Birks of Invermay / Will ye go tae Flanders? / The learig / The death of Queen Jane / The wife of Usher's Well / Can't weld a body.

Mar 08. (cd) *(Hegri 04 – 52597042)* **THIS EARTHLY SPELL** [ ] [–]
- The good years / Sorry / Better things / Rivers run / Painted it white / Firethief / Behind our eyes / The news / Sorrowlessfield / Tongue that cannot lie.

—— In 2010, she was credited on 'Evergreen' EP with/vs. LAU

—— In 2010, her work with The BURNS UNIT saw light on the 'Side Show' set

The POOZIES (⟹ Celtic Connections)

Emily PORTMAN (⟹ The DEVIL'S INTERVAL)

POOKA

Initially described as a cross between JONI MITCHELL and Kristin Hersh of Throwing Muses, Nottingham's POOKA (named for an Irish goblin) were certainly out of time in their embryonic, London-based days, given the contemporary musical climate of grunge and shoegazing. The duo comprised harmony-fuelled singer/songwriters Sharon Lewis and Natasha Jones.

Songs like 'City Slick' and 'Graham Robert Wood' (both subsequently singles) drew attention to their Elektra/WEA-released debut, **POOKA** (1993) {*6}. It was produced by the multi-talented John Coxon, and other highlights were 'Breeze', 'Bluebell' and the bodhran-driven 'Rolling Stone'.

Rough Trade Records signed the girls in 1995, but it was Island subsidiary Trade 2 that gave them their second chance with **SPINNING** (1997) {*7}. Capitalising on their unconventional vocal manner and some exacting instrumentation, the album sold well; excellent indie singles 'Sweet Butterfly', 'The Insect', 'Mean Girl' and 'Lubrication' were all included.

The direction they were taking was hinted at on a self-financed classical/goth-type CD-r, **FOOLS GIVE BIRTH TO ANGELS** (2001) {*?}, which had very limited distribution. Darker and more sinister, POOKA's third album, **SHIFT** (2001) {*6}, turned them sharply away from the folk-rock market and into Bjork-meets-Nicolette trip-hop territory, though their trademark ethereal harmonies were still intact. Apart from Lewis's collaboration with ROSE POLENZANI on the 'Kings And Queens' EP in 2007, and a low-key solo effort in 2005, 'The Hour Lilies', there has since little to write home about. *MCS*

Sharon Lewis (b. 1971) - vocals, acoustic guitar, keyboards / **Natasha "Tash" Jones** (b. 1971) - vocals, acoustic guitar / with **John Coxon** - multi, producer

UK WEA / US Elektra

Sep 93. (cd/c) *(4509 93515-2/-4)* <61624-2/-4> **POOKA** ☐ ☐
- City sick / Bluebell / The car / Graham Robert Wood / Breeze / Nothing in particular / Dream / Boomerang / Demon / Rolling stone / Between my knees / Sleepwalking.

Oct 93. (7" ep/c-ep/cd-ep) *(YZ 774/+C/CD)* CITY SICK ☐ ⊟
- City sick / Moon lover / The pebble / Falling.

Mar 94. (12" ep/c-ep/cd-ep) *(YZ 810 T/C/CD)* GRAHAM ROBERT WOOD ☐ ⊟
- Graham Robert Wood / Blue star / Stuart Strange / Sex on.

—— the duo now with **Steve Lamb** - bass / **Rob Ellis** - drums (ex-PJ Harvey)

Rough Trade Singles Club / not issued

Jul 95. (7") *(45REV 38)* SWEET BUTTERFLY. / Love Song ☐ ⊟

Rough Trade / not issued

Jun 96. (7") *(R 407-7)* THE INSECT. / The Sun ☐ ⊟

—— **Joe Leach** - programming, keyboards; repl. Ellis

Trade 2 - Island / not issued

Jun 97. (7") *(TRDS 009)* MEAN GIRL. / Cherry Orchard ☐ ⊟
(cd-s+=) *(TRDCD 009)* - Cool heart / Swan song.

Aug 97. (7") *(TRDS 010)* LUBRICATION. / Rocking Chair ☐ ⊟
(cd-s+=) *(TRDCD 010)* - All I want (is a life) / One in a million.

Sep 97. (cd) *(TRDCD 1003)* **SPINNING** ☐ ⊟
- Mean girl / Higher / God sir / Shine / Lubrication / Rubber arms / Sweet butterfly / She is a rainbow / The insect / Spinning / This river / Ocean.

Nov 99. (cd-ep) *(PIC 1)* MONDAY MOURNING EP ☐ ⊟
- The rocking chair / One day we will see / You were enough / More than I love myself / Spirit boy.

(above issued on Telescopic, below was self-released)

2001. (ltd-cd) *(none)* **FOOLS GIVE BIRTH TO ANGELS** ⊟ ⊟

Oct 01. (cd) *(RTRADECD 012)* **SHIFT** ☐ ⊟
- What you need / One in a million / Yellow fever / Joy / Constant / Music is the light / Ovum / Face / Empty / Exit.

—— in 2007, SHARON LEWIS & ROSE POLENZANI released an EP, 'Kings And Queens'

PRESSGANG

Not to be confused with an American punk act of the mid-90s, Reading's festival-friendly PRESSGANG (led by Damian Clarke since 1986) were a different kettle of fish. Declaring "We want to play louder than Deep Purple", Damian, George Whitfield (who replaced original member Gabriel King), bassist Sprog and drummer Jonathan Kirby were noted as the noisiest folkers in the land.

ROGUES! (1989) {*6} captured the firebrand alt-folk of The POGUES or The OYSTERBAND and their kind on English trad songs such as 'The Outlandish Knight', 'Bonny Ship The Diamond' and 'The Raggle Taggle Gypsies'. With a near-total clear-out of personnel leaving only Damian and George in place (see discography below), **BURNING BOATS** (1994) {*6} saw them come safely ashore time and time again.

Further line-up changes (funky bassist Cliff Eastabrook was a notable addition in 1995) left the group in something of a quandary, but **FIRE** (1996) {*7} and **MAPPA MUNDI** (1997) {*6} garnered several good reviews. The latter contained a near-unrecognisable 'Lyke Wake Dirge', and the former did the same for 'Hard Times'. Without captivating large audiences, PRESSGANG continued into the new millennium, their last studio effort being **DANCING IN OUR DREAMS** (2000) {*5}; Clarke took off on solo projects. *MCS*

Damian Clarke - vocals, guitar, hurdy-gurdy, hammered dulcimer / **George Whitfield** - vocals, accordion, whistles; repl. Gabriel King (keyboards) / **Jonathan Kirby** - drums / **Sprog** - bass

UK Voxpop / US not issued

1988. (7") *(VOX 021)* WATCH THE WALL. / New South Wales ☐ ⊟

May 89. (lp; //B-side 45rpm) *(VOX 022)* **ROGUES!** ☐ ⊟
- The outlandish knight / The tailor / John White / Spanish ladies / Nancy / Bonny ship the Diamond // The raggle taggle gypsies.

—— **Ian Munt** - bass; repl. Sprog

Apr 90. (12" ep) *(VOX 023)* WHIP JAMBOREE. / Donkey / The Weaver / Watch The Wall ☐ ⊟

—— **Steve** - bass (ex-Jo Jo Namoza) repl. Munt

—— **Steve Cruikshank** - drums (ex-Dub Warriors, ex-RDF) repl. Jon

—— **Damian** + **George** continued with **Neil Carter** (drums) + **Johnny Forrester** (vocals, bass) + **Imogen Gunner** (fiddle)

—— **Tony Lyons** - drums, percussion; repl. Neil

Cat / not issued

Apr 94. (c/cd) *(Puss 002/+CD)* **BURNING BOATS** ☐ ⊟
- Joseph Ward / Brandy of the damned / She walks in beauty / Riddle song / Storyteller / Child miner / Devil's away / Bodmin Moor / Adam catch / Shule gra - Snow that melts the soonest / Head, heart and the hand / You're all I see / Jessie Brodie / Rosin.

—— **Cliff Eastabrook** - bass, vocals; repl. Johnny + Imogen

Twah! / not issued

Jan 96. (cd/c) *(efa 61101-2/-4)* **FIRE** ☐ ⊟
- Cutty Wren / Sherrif's ride / Flanders / Hard times / Bad bread / Stain / John Knowx / Sussex medley / Take a jump / Rebel soldier / Merrily merrily.

—— **Miranda Sykes** - vocals, double bass; repl. Cliff

1997. (cd) *(efa 61109-2)* **MAPPA MUNDI** ⊟ German ⊟
- The sylkie / Forty summers / Flowers of the forest / Death of the last crusader / Lyke wake dirge / Trip to the glen / Lock the gates / River song / Chainsaw reel / Walking in the wild / Rocks and stones / Locksley Hall.

—— **Maclaine Colston** - vocals, hammered dulcimer; repl. Tony

Vox Pop / not issued

1999. (cd) *(VOX 024)* **MOVERS AND SHAKERS** (live) ⊟ mail-o ⊟
- Pace-eggin' / Forty summers / Trip to the glen / Away the Borders set / Death of the last crusader / The sylkie / The Cutty Wren / Flanders / The brandy of the damned / Joseph Ward / Devil's away.

May 00. (cd) *(VOX 025)* **DANCING IN OUR DREAMS** ⊟ mail-o ⊟
- Dancing in our dreams / Three brothers from Spain / The gallop / And all of that / Widcombe flight / Lords of misrule / Death and the lady / High Germany / Lying for tomorrow / Parlour dance / Green gravel / Give us the vote / Family quarrel / Blow the candle out / Vicar of Bray.

—— the original line-up (original to the mid-1990s, anyway) re-formed in 2006

—— Damian Clarke has since released a solo CD

The PROCLAIMERS

Scotland's own modern-day Everly Brothers, singing twins Craig and Charlie Reid (lifelong Hibernian football supporters both) have become folk-rock celebrities since their pop career began a quarter of a century ago. Not just heroes in their homeland, the bespectacled siblings have stretched their appeal across the seas to Australia and indeed America, where their tag of one-hit-wonders doesn't seem to be an albatross around their neck.

Born in Leith, Edinburgh, they ended up in Auchtermuchty, Fife (via Cornwall), but the Scottish capital became their permanent locale again in 1986. It's not always pointed out, but Craig and Charlie played in punk bands The Hippie Hasslers and Reasons For Emotion before forming The PROCLAIMERS. With the help of fan/manager Kenny McDonald (who had sent a demo to The Housemartins c/o Chrysalis Records), they found themselves supporting The Housemartins on tour, while a bemusing but stunning appearance on Channel 4's music show The Tube helped gain them exposure for their forthcoming Top 50 debut album **THIS IS THE STORY** (1987) {*7}.

At first without a hit (lead-off track 'Throw The "R" Away' had failed) to support it, the record was a showcase for their boy-next door, uber-geek appeal and heavily accented Scots voices on the likes of 'The Joyful Kilmarnock Blues', minor hit-to-be 'Make My Heart Fly' and a cover of George Jones's '(I'm Gonna) Burn Your Playhouse Down'. The set might never have got off the ground if not for their classic GERRY RAFFERTY-produced 'band version' of 'Letter From America' (a song about emigration, the Highland Clearances and the de-industrialisation of Scotland in the

1980s), which hit the UK Top 3 in December 1987. The twins were proud activist members of the Scottish National Party (SNP).

The following year The PROCLAIMERS went electric, recruiting a full band comprising guitarist Jerry Donahue, bassist Phil Cranham, drummer Paul Robinson and (on keyboards and production) Pete Wingfield for their country-tinged Top 10 second set **SUNSHINE ON LEITH** (1988) {*8}. Bombastic, emotional and rousing, the set was enhanced and led by stomp-along classic 'I'm Gonna Be (500 Miles)', while the equally stirring 'I'm On My Way' and the title track entered the charts in minor placings. The token cover this time around was Steve Earle's 'My Old Friend The Blues'.

While the twins took an extended sabbatical to record their new album and help with the campaign to save their beloved and beleaguered Hibernian FC (who were on the verge of being taken over by Wallace Mercer, chairman of Edinburgh rivals Hearts), a stop-gap EP, 'King Of The Road' (led by the titular Roger Miller cover) reached the Top 10.

Shocking even the brothers themselves, and boosted by airplay and its inclusion in the 1993 movie 'Benny And Joon', 'I'm Gonna Be (500 Miles)' took the States by storm, eventually reaching Top 3. The parent album went double platinum.

The long-awaited third set, the Top 10 entry **HIT THE HIGHWAY** {*5}, eventually emerged in 1994, a more contemporary country outing with equally traditional, gospel-flavoured lyrics to match on songs like 'Let's Get Married', 'What Makes You Cry' and Otis Redding's 'These Arms Of Mine'. Another cover was a revamp of The Consolers' 'I Want To Be A Christian'.

After another long hiatus the twins emerged, Blue Nile-like, in 2001 with their first LP in seven years, the delightful and appropriately titled **PERSEVERE** {*5}. Not much had changed since the whimsical 'I'm Gonna Be', with The PROCLAIMERS remaining true to their original style and accents. If 'There's A Touch' was one of the less serious offerings on the set, 'Scotland's Story' was a politicised 'Letter From America'.

Still the harmonious heart and soul of Caledonia, but finding it hard to regain lost momentum after those wilderness years, the twins' credibility was given a massive injection with their critically acclaimed fifth album, **BORN INNOCENT** (2003) {*7}. While there was that token cover again, this time Allen Reynolds's 'Five O'Clock World', you could shake your hat at the bawdy rock 'n' roller 'Role Model', the Cajun-pumping 'Dear Deidre' and the foot-tapping opening title track. **RESTLESS SOUL** (2005) {*5} was another above-par album, though it contained good songs rather than great. Recorded in London, it seemed to be stuck in a timewarp of sorts, although the Reids' genuinely infectious appeal shone through on 'When Love Struck You Down' and 'I'm Gone'.

Just when things looked to be tailing away again, up popped the comedian Peter Kay, a huge fan, to save the day not just for The PROCLAIMERS but the BBC's 2007 Comic Relief appeal. Kay (alias Brian Potter of 'Phoenix Nights' infamy) and Matt Lucas (Andy Pipkin of 'Little Britain') joined Craig and Charlie on a revamped 'I'm Gonna Be (500 Miles)' that hit No.1. Back on track with Universal Records and A&R/producer John Williams (from their debut days), The PROCLAIMERS entered the Top 20 album charts again with **LIFE WITH YOU** (2007) {*6} – check out their version of Wreckless Eric's '(I'd Go The) Whole Wide World'.

It seemed that the public had taken the songwriting twins back into their hearts when **NOTES AND RHYMES** (2009) {*6} also reached the Top 30, highlighted by one of their greatest ballads in yonks, 'Love Can Move Mountains', and covers of DAMIEN DEMPSEY's 'Sing All Our Cares Away' and Moe Bandy's 'It Was Always So Easy (To Find An Unhappy Woman)'. If not exactly one of Scotland's trendiest bands, The PROCLAIMERS remain one of her best-loved. *MCS*

Craig Reid (b. Mar 5 '62, Leith, Edinburgh) - vocals, tambourine, bongos, maraccas / **Charlie Reid** (b. Mar 5 '62) - acoustic guitar, 12-string bass, vocals / plus sessioners

UK Chrysalis — US Chrysalis

Apr 87. (lp/c/cd) *(<CHR/ZCHR/CCD 1602>)* **THIS IS THE STORY** [43] [ ]
- Throw the 'R' away / Over and done with / Misty blue / The part that really matters / (I'm gonna) Burn your playhouse down / Letter from America (acoustic) / Sky takes the soul / It broke my heart / The first attack / Make my heart fly / Beautiful truth / The joyful Kilmarnock blues. *(cd+=)* - Letter from America (band version). *(cd re-iss. Mar 93; same) (d-cd-iss.+=)* - SUNSHINE ON LEITH

May 87. (7") *(CHS 3144)* THROW THE 'R' AWAY. / A Train Went Past The Window [ ] [–]
(12"+=) *(CHS12 3144)* - Long gone lonesome (live) / I can't be myself (live).

Oct 87. (7") *(CHS 3178)* LETTER FROM AMERICA (band version). / Letter From America (acoustic version) [3] [–]
(12"+=) *(CHS12 3178)* - I'm lucky / Just because / Twenty flight rock.

Feb 88. (7") *(CLAIM 1)* MAKE MY HEART FLY. / Wish I Could Say [63] [–]
(12"+=) *(CLAIMX 1)* - (I'm gonna) Burn your playhouse down (live) / Throw the 'R' away.
(cd-s+=) *(CDCLAIM 1)* - Letter from America (band version).

Aug 88. (7") *(CLAIM 2)* I'M GONNA BE (500 MILES). / Better Days [11] [–]
(12"+=) *(CLAIMX 2)* - Teardrops.
(cd-s++=) *(CDCLAIM 2)* - I can't be myself.

Sep 88. (lp/c/cd) *(<CHR/ZCHR/CCD 1668>)* **SUNSHINE ON LEITH** [6] [ ]
- I'm gonna be (500 miles) / Cap in hand / Then I met you / My old friend the blues / Sean / Sunshine on Leith / Come on nature / I'm on my way / What do you do / It's Saturday night / Teardrops / Oh Jean. *(cd re-iss. Mar 94; CD25CR 18) (d-cd-iss. Sep 03 +=; 592143-2)* - THIS IS THE STORY [ ] [–]

Oct 88. (7") *(CLAIM 3)* SUNSHINE ON LEITH. / Leaving Home [41] [–]
(12"+=/cd-s+=) *(CLAIMX/CDCLAIM 3)* - The first attack / Letter from America (live).

Feb 89. (7") *(CLAIM 4)* I'M ON MY WAY. / Over And Done With [43] [–]
(12"+=/cd-s+=) *(CLAIMX/CDCLAIM 4)* - Throw the 'R' away / Cap in hand.

Nov 90. (7" ep/c-ep/12" ep/cd-ep) *(CLAIM/TCCLAIM/CLAIMX/CDCLAIM 5)* KING OF THE ROAD EP [9] [–]
- King of the road / Long black veil / Lulu selling tea / Not ever.

May 93. (c-s) *<24846>* I'M GONNA BE (500 MILES) / Better Days [–] [3]
(above taken from movie 'Benny and Joon' on Capitol)

Aug 93. (c-s) *<24847>* I'M ON MY WAY / King Of The Road [–] [ ]
(cd-s+=) *<F2-58017>* - Letter from America (band version).

Sep 93. (re-cd) *(<CCD 1668>)* **SUNSHINE ON LEITH** [ ] Jul 93 [31]

Feb 94. (c-s/7") *(TC+/CLAIM 6) <58127>* LET'S GET MARRIED. / I'm Gonna Be (500 Miles) [21] [ ]
(cd-s+=) *(CDCLAIM 6)* - Gentle on my mind / Waiting for a train.
(cd-s) *(CDCLAIMS 6)* - ('A') / Invitation to the blues / Letter from America / ('A'-acoustic).

Mar 94. (cd/c/lp) *(<CD/TC+/CHR 6066>)* **HIT THE HIGHWAY** [8] [ ]
- Let's get married / The more I believe / What makes you cry / Follow the money / These arms of mine / Shout shout / The light / Hit the highway / A long long long time ago / I want to be a Christian / Your childhood / Don't turn out like your mother.

Apr 94. (c-s/7") *(TC+/CLAIM 7)* WHAT MAKES YOU CRY. / Guess Who Won't Beg [38] [–]
(cd-s+=) *(CDCLAIM 7)* - Shout shout (acoustic) / Follow the monkey (acoustic).
(cd-s) *(CDCLAIMS 7)* - ('A') / Bobby / King of the road / ('A'-acoustic).

Oct 94. (c-s/7") *(TC+/CLAIM 8)* THESE ARMS OF MINE. / Sunshine On Leith [51] [–]
(cd-s+=) *(CDCLAIM 8)* - The Joyful Kilmarnock blues / What makes you cry.
(cd-s) *(CDCLAIMS 8)* - ('A') / I'm on my way / Let's get married / I'm gonna be (500 miles).

Persevere — Nettwerk

May 01. (cd-s) *(PERSRECCD 02B) <33124-2>* THERE'S A TOUCH / A Land Fit For Zeros / They Really Do [ ] [ ]

May 01. (cd) *(PERSRECCD 004) <30193-2>* **PERSEVERE** [61] [ ]
- There's a touch / Sweet little girls / A land fit for zeros / How many times / One too many / That's when he told her / Scotland's story / When you're in love / She arouses me so / Everybody's a victim / Don't give it to me / Heaven right now / Slowburner / Act of remembrance.

Sep 03. (cd) *(PERSRECCD 09) <30831-2>* **BORN INNOCENT** [70] Nov 03 [ ]
- Born innocent / Should have been loved / Blood on your hands / Unguarded moments / Hate my love / Redeemed / You meant it then / Five o'clock world / He's just like me / Role model / No witness / Dear Deidre / There's no doubt.

Persevere — Persevere

Aug 05. (cd) *(<PERSRECCD 10>)* **RESTLESS SOUL** [74] Sep 05 [ ]
- When love struck you down / Restless soul / Turning away / I'm gone / That's better now / Everyday I try / He just can't / Bound for your love / What I saw in you / The one who loves you now / She's brighter / DIY / Now and then / One more down.

—— (below featured Brian Potter (Peter Kay) of 'Phoenix Nights' and Andy Pipkin (Matt Lucas) of 'Little Britain' - all proceeds to Comic Relief)

Mar 07. (dvd-s) *(none)* I'M GONNA BE (500 MILES) / (original version) / (CD-ROM video) [1] [–]

W14 — Universal

Aug 07. (cd-s) *(1742097)* LIFE WITH YOU / Disgrace / A Woman's Place (acoustic) [58] [–]

Sep 07. (cd) *(<174087-2>)* **LIFE WITH YOU** [13] [ ]
- Life with you / In recognition / New religion / S-O-R-R-Y / No one left to blame / Here it comes again / Blood lying on snow / Harness pain / The long haul / The lover's face / Whole wide world / Calendar on the wall / If there's a God. *(ltd-cd+=; 174087-0)* - (live Glasgow Hogmanay 2003):- Born innocent / Hate my love / Let's get married / You meant it then / Should have been loved / There's a touch / Joyful Kilmarnock blues / acoustic:- Blood lying on the snow / The calendar on the wall / A woman's place.

Oct 07. (cd-s) *(1747739)* WHOLE WIDE WORLD (Steve Evans remix) / She Wanted Romance / A Woman's Place [ ] [–]

Feb 08. (cd-s) *(1757126)* NEW RELIGION / IN RECOGNITION [ ] [–]

Mar 09. (dl-s) *(-)* "17" [ ] [–]

Jun 09. (dl-s) *(-)* LOVE CAN MOVE MOUNTAINS [ ] [–]

Jun 09. (cd) *(<2706547>)* **NOTES AND RHYMES** [30] [ ]
- Notes and rhymes / Love can move mountains / Three more days / Just looks now / Sing all our cares away / It was always so easy to find an unhappy woman / Like

a flame / I know / Shadows fall / Free market / Wages of sin / On Causewayside / I know (reprise). *(ltd-d-cd+=; 2706950)* - (acoustic): - Love can move mountains / Three more days / Sing all our cares away / It was always so easy to find an unhappy woman / (live at Edinburgh Castle):- I'm on my way / Letter from America / Scotland's story / Sky takes the soul / Life with you / Whole wide world.

- (8-10*) compilations (+ associated) -

May 02. (cd) *EMI; (<5 38682-2>)* **THE BEST OF...** [30] Jun 02 [ ]
- Letter from America (acoustic) / There's a touch / Let's get married / I'm gonna be (500 miles) / The doodle song / I'm on my way / King of the road / Ghost of love / Throw the 'R' away / What makes you cry? / Sunshine on Leith / When you're in love / Cap in hand / I want to be a Christian / Act of remembrance / Lady luck / Make my heart fly / The light / The joyful Kilmarnock blues / Oh Jean.

Mar 07. (dl-s) *(same)* I'M GONNA BE [26] [–]

Apr 07. (re-cd) *Chrysalis; (3912382)* **THE BEST OF ...** [5] [–]
- (as previous +) / I'm gonna be (500 miles) [Comic Relief version].

- (5-7*) compilations, etc.-

Sep 03. (cd) *EMI Gold; (<592159-2>)* **FINEST** [ ] May 04 [ ]
- I'm gonna be (500 miles) / Better days / Sunshine on Leith / Leaving home / Then I met you / A train went past the window / Twenty flight rock / Make my heart fly / (I'm gonna) Burn your playhouse down / Misty blue / Long black veil / Not ever / These arms of mine / Shout shout.

Sep 00. (3-cd-box) *EMI; (528370-2)* **THIS IS THE STORY / SUNSHINE ON LEITH / HIT THE HIGHWAY** [ ] [–]

Alan PROSSER (⟹ OYSTERBAND)

PUMAJAW

This Perthshire-based folk outfit were formed by Edinburgh-born and Banff-raised avant-indie solo artist Pinkie Maclure and former shoegazer and Loop guitarist John Wills, genre-busters of sorts who had formerly disguised themselves as both Fingerfood and Lumen, who issued 'This Day And Age' in 2003. They met when Wills produced Maclure's 1995 solo set 'Favourite'.

Pinkie's discography is mainly electronic-indie and stretches back to a 12" collaboration ('Bite The Hand That Feeds You') with David Harrow in 1985. 'This Dirty Life' (credited to Pinkie Maclure And The Puritans, with a sleeve depicting her naked on a cross) followed in 1990. Ten years on, Wills was behind her on her third album proper, 'From Memorial Crossing' (2000).

A couple more Maclure/Wills electro-folk collaborations were delivered between 2002 and 2005 (one for Fife outlet The Fence Collective), while PUMAJAW evolved via the release of **BECOMING PUMAJAW** (2006) {*7}.

It seemed natural that Britain should regain its mantle of purveyor of eerie freak-folk, having had it pinched by our American cousins (IN GOWAN RING, FAUN FABLES, JOANNA NEWSOM, etc) who were fond of ye olde PENTANGLE, FAIRPORT and FOREST. Picking up bodhran, lyre and concertina, Wills was a fine musical foil for Maclure's deep but penetrating Salem Witch-like voice. It's hard to pick the best among their originals ('Buttons' and 'The Red Petticoat' have their spooky appeal), but the set is worth buying for trad cuts 'Rosemary Lane' and 'The Holly King' and the Jacques Brel number 'La Chanson Des Vieux Amants'.

CURIOSITY BOX (2008) {*8} took the freak-folk genre to new heights, featuring self-penned compositions alongside ethereal Scottish traditional numbers including 'The Burning Of Auchindoun', 'Lang, Lang a' Growing' and 'Lamkin'), assisted by Pinkie's Scottish neo-folk cousins JAMES YORKSTON and ALASDAIR ROBERTS. Maclure had meanwhile laid down roots in Balloch, Edinburgh, Paris and London. *MCS*

Pinkie Maclure (b. Eileen Jane Manson Maclure, Jan 19, '61, Edinburgh) - vocals, concertina, autoharp, accordion, bells / **John Wills** (b. London) - guitar loops, drums, synths, mandolin, dulcimer

UK / US
Tongue Master / not issued

Sep 02. (ltd-7"; as PINKIE MACLURE AND MR WILLS) *(TONG 004)* CAMOUFLAGE. / In Time [ ] [–]

Fence / not issued

2004. (m-cd-r; as PINKIE MACLURE AND JOHN WILLS) *(PFC 01)* A SMALL PIECE OF AFTERWARDS [ ] [–]
- Star anise / Slowly, slowly, the water flows / The long way round / Miniature / How the canary cries / Lay down your arms.

Trefingle / not issued

Apr 05. (cd; as PINKIE MACLURE AND JOHN WILLS) *(TreCD 101)* **CAT'S CRADLE** [ ] [–]
- The bending wood / Slowly, slowly, the water flows / Cat's cradle / Good luck look upon you / Fine flowers in the valley / I take the long way round / Over and over and over / Lay down your arms.

Jul 06. (cd; as PUMAJAW, also known as PINKIE MACLURE AND JOHN WILLS) *(TreCD 102)* **BECOMING PUMAJAW** [ ] [–]
- Buttons / Rosemary lane / The ivy and roses / No lamentin' / The red petticoat / Weather potions / Downstream / La chanson des vieux amants / The holly king / Outside it blows.

Fire / not issued

Aug 08. (7") *(BLAZEX 160)* JACKY DAW. / Horseshoe Nail [ ] [–]

Sep 08. (cd) *(FIRECD 115)* **CURIOSITY BOX** [ ] [–]
- Visiting hour pt.1 / Visiting hour pt.2 / Mother and the two trees / Spangler / The burning of Auchindoun / The auld rigmarole / Buds / Lang, lang-a-growin' / Horseshoe nail / Lamkin.

May 09. (cd-r) *(FIRECD 130)* **FAVOURITES** [–] Europe [–]
- Sorcery / The swings / Weird light / The bending wood / Frozen in sleep / Buttons / We spin / Stranded / Downstream / Memorial crossing / I take the long way round / Sweet kind of suffering / Harbour song / Outside it blows.

PYEWACKETT

Folk music was stretched to its limits when Croydon's PYEWACKETT were about in the first half of the 1980s. Formed in 1975 by melody-driven veterans Rosie Cross (also the singer), Ian Blake, Mark Emerson, Laurie Harper and Bill Martin, their music drew on John Playford's 'The English Dancing Master' (pub. 1651) and American swing and jazz of the pre-second world war era. The name 'Pyewackett' originated in the impish mind of the self-proclaimed 'Witchfinder General' (Matthew Hopkins) on his hunt for Essex witches in the 17th century, as the name of one of his victims' supposed devilish familiars.

Morris dance music was part of their early manifesto, introduced by caller and scholar Michael Barraclough, who had been their bear-suit-wearing mascot Morris-man early on. Engineered by Bill Leader and produced by Dave Foister, **PYEWACKETT** (1981) {*6} declared their playful/Playford intentions from the get-go, with three songs in particular showing their diversity: 'Tomorrow The Fox Will Come To Town' (set to Playford tune 'Trenchmore'), the supernatural seduction of 'Reynardine' and the 1940s Guy Lombardo nugget 'We Just Couldn't Say Goodbye'.

THE MAN IN THE MOON DRINKS CLARET (1982) {*7}, produced by zither player ANDREW CRONSHAW, was a record of global aspirations, drawing on songs from Britain, Europe and the Americas. PLANXTY cut 'The Well Below The Valley' is recognisable, although refined in a cappella mode, while 'The Merry-Go-Round Broke Down' is the Looney Tunes cartoons theme tune. Before he left for hard rockers Magnum in 1984, drummer Mickey Barker had been deputising for the departing Harper.

With only one vocal from Rosie (on the Rodgers and Hart opener 'Ten Cents A Dance'), their third album, **7 TO MIDNIGHT** (1985) {*5} disappointed a little by the standards they'd set.

Subsequent tours of the Middle East, North Africa and Europe saw the quintet expand their horizons somewhat, but with outside commitments taking precedence (the BBC Radio schools project 'The Song Tree' was quite popular), PYEWACKETT released only one more LP, **THIS CRAZY PARADISE** (1987) {*5}.

After their split, Bill Martin was the only member to achieve much success – he was partly responsible for the novelty No.1 'Star Trekkin'' with The Firm. Cross returned to her Humberside roots as a folk music development worker, and Emerson toured as back-up to JUNE TABOR. *MCS*

Rosie Cross (b. Oct 6 '54, Leeds, Yorkshire) - vocals, bassoon, hammer dulcimer, tambourine / **Ian Blake** (b. Dec 9 '55, Finchley, London) - clarinet, saxophone, recorder, keyboards, bass / **Mark Emerson** (b. Aug 15 '58, Ruislip, Middlesex) - violin, viola, keyboards, vocals / **Laurie Harper** (b. Nov 22 '53, Lambeth, London) - mandola, violin, bass, vocals / **Bill Martin** (b. May 3 '55, Woolwich, London) - piano, synths, guitar, accordion, vocals

UK / US
Dingle's / not issued

Dec 80. (7"; as DES DORCHESTER & HIS DANCE ORCHESTRA) *(DIV 114)* THE LAMBETH WALK. / Poor Little Angeline [ ] [–]

1981. (lp) *(DIN 312)* **PYEWACKETT** ☐ ⊟
- Halfe Hannikin / Harry the tailor / Weary cutters / Bonny hawthorn / Two sisters / Peppers black / Tomorrow the fox will come to town / Kettle drum / Goddesses / Parson's farewell / Hey then, up we go / Jack a lent / Reynardine / We just couldn't say goodbye / Aunty Hessy's white horse.

—— added new drummer **Mickey Barker**; less Laurie, who left

Familiar not issued

Sep 83. (lp) *(FAM 43)* **THE MAN IN THE MOON DRINKS CLARET** ☐ ⊟
- Amoroso / Hey we to the other world / Bedlam city / Grays Inn maske / Tam Lin / The merry-go-round broke down / Ce mois de mai / The B de B - Borborygmi - The bear dances / The well below the valley / The grey cock / Dan and the wombat. *(cd-iss. Jan 95 on Music And Words; MWCD 4007)*

—— Barker left to join hard-rock act Magnum

1985. (lp) *(FAM 47)* **7 TO MIDNIGHT** ☐ ⊟
- Ten cents a dance / Moll Pately / Portsmouth / Rufty Tufty / The limousine / Woodicock – An old man is a bed full of bones / Bransle du chien / Cuckolds all in a row / Mount hills / Winter's night schottische / Nonesuch.

—— added sess. drummer **Ralph Salmins** (b. Jun 4 '64, Farnborough, Kent)

Jan 87. (lp/c/cd) *(FAM 59/+C/CD)* **THIS CRAZY PARADISE** ☐ ⊟
- For Saheli / Christmas day in the morning / Love me or leave me / Homes for heroes / Ek se ou windhoek toe nou / Resting place / Illusions / Fever.

—— the group split in 1989; Martin subsequently worked on the UK No.1 hit, `Star Trekkin'' for The Firm; Ian Blake moved to Canberra, Australia, and went solo, releasing a handful of children's albums with Mike Jackson

Q

The QUEENSBERRY RULES

For the past decade and a bit, The QUEENSBERRY RULES (Gary Wilcox, his brother Duncan Wilcox and Phil Hulse) were on the fringes of folk's inner circle, needing just the right break and/or song to catapult them into the company of the big boys.

Initially as Mad Dogs And Englishmen (from 1994 to 1996), the trio from Stoke-on-Trent issued three singles before adopting the football-related title of Bonetti (from 1997 to 2000). They featured on a Various Artists compilation for Oxford/London imprint Snakebite City.

By early 2001 they were known by their new name (drawn from boxing this time), and The QUEENSBERRY RULES were an acoustic-roots act for two albums, **LOOKING BEYOND THE PHYSICAL** (2002) {*5} and **SIX GUN HEROES** (2003) {*6} (the latter was aired on North American radio), but things didn't really get going folk-wise until they supported JEZ LOWE, SHOW OF HANDS and WHILE & MATTHEWS.

With their star in the ascendant, the albums **HERITAGE AND HISTORY** (2004) {*6} and **THE BLACK DOG AND OTHER STORIES** (2006) {*7}, their first for Fellside Records, gave them a contemporary working-class voice that only ROBB JOHNSON, BILLY BRAGG and LEON ROSSELSON could outclass at that time.

Strong harmonies and hook-laden rhythms were prominent on **LANDLOCKED** (2008) {*7} and **TAKE YOUR OWN ROADS** (2009) {*7}, two sets that walked a tightrope between tradition and creativity. Limited to just 500 copies, the seven-track, half-hour mini-CD that was **SIX TOWNS** (2010) {*5} apparently stretched them to breaking point, while HULSE had released a fine solo set, **UNPREDICTED STORM** {*6}, in 2008. An indefinite hiatus ensued – as Gary has put it himself – when the trio went back to their day jobs. *MCS*

Gary Wilcox - vocals, percussion / **Phil Hulse** - vocals, guitars / **Duncan Wilcox** - double bass, mandolin, vocals

UK: Acoustic Squeeze — US: not issued

Jun 02. (ltd-cd) *(ASCD 001)* **LOOK BEYOND THE PHYSICAL** ☐ ⊟
- The ballad of Johnny Blue / Win, lose or draw / When this was all fields / Problem shared / Preserves song / The man who walked into the sea / Woody Guthrie's hands / Single bedrooms / Arcane magician / Moving to California / You don't need heroes you just need friends. *(re-iss. Oct 05; same)*

Aug 03. (ltd-cd) *(ASCD 002)* **SIX GUN HEROES** ☐ ⊟
- GOSH / Swings and roundabouts / Chip on my shoulder / Good fortune / Songs for the background / Girl at Hanover airport / Soldier father working man / Monophobia / Long day in the field / Take the blame / Editorial / Blame it on the bigamy. *(re-iss. Oct 05; same)*

Jun 04. (cd) *(ASCD 003)* **HERITAGE AND HISTORY** ☐ ⊟
- Heritage and history / Mapman / Jam jar wakes / Writing on the front line / Both sides the Tweed / Conspiracy / The swagger makers – Bottom knocker / A song about life / You can't please everyone / Birmingham song / Flowers.

Fellside — not issued

Jul 06. (cd) *(FECD 201)* **THE BLACK DOG AND OTHER STORIES ...** ☐ ⊟
- Sinking town / The black dog / Perkin Warbeck / The herring girl / New Columbus / The miles around / Rounding the Horn – Foragers' tune / Can't comprehend / Architects of the fall / A mother's love / The unluckiest man / Follow your direction.

Jan 08. (cd) *(FECD 210)* **LANDLOCKED** ☐ ⊟
- I still believe in England / Molly Leigh / Dol-li-a / The Minnie pit disaster / Goldrush / Pushing the boat out / Landlocked / High Germany / Have a go hero / Little Saturday / Farewell. *(bonus +=)* - Preservers song.

Oct 09. (cd) *(FECD 227)* **TAKE YOUR OWN ROADS** ☐ ⊟
- Top dog / Dark peak moor / Tracks / Away, away / When you come home again / The milehouse – Breakfast at Tebay / Canal song / No pardon / Sauntering Ned / When the last one is gone / Your own roads / Plant a tree.

Acoustic Squeeze — not issued

Nov 10. (ltd; m-cd) *(ASCD 004)* **SIX TOWNS**: A celebration of the federation of Stoke-on-Trent 1910–2010 ☐ ⊟
- Sons of a hundred years / Upon / Mr Tawney's classes / Plucky little Tunstall / Mother town / Forgotten town / When the Beatles came to Hanley.

—— the band have since announced their split after 17 years in the business

PHIL HULSE

Fellside — not issued

Oct 08. (cd) *(FECD 217)* **UNPREDICTED STORM** ☐ ⊟
- Not in my name / The place that brought us up / The rural heart / Lovers in a nanny state / At my side / Matchday / Bad blood, dead soil, old ghost / The chained oak / A thousand times before / Mary Read / Badge of the Bevin boys / Peace in Manifold Valley.

RAGGED HEROES (⟹ CLAYTON, Vikki)

RATTLE ON THE STOVEPIPE (⟹ COOPER, Pete)

Eddi READER

Ever since fronting skiffle-pop chartbusters FAIRGROUND ATTRACTION in the late 1980s, Scottish singer and musician EDDI READER (born Sadenia Reader, August 29, 1959, Anderston, Glasgow) has been at the forefront of traditionally-based pop-folk music.

Growing up on the Arden housing estate in Glasgow and then in Irvine, Ayrshire, 'Edna' (her parents' pet name for her) honed her acoustic guitar-playing skills by busking in Glasgow's Sauchiehall Street, a good apprenticeship indeed for her time spent trying to breach the London music scene in the early 1980s. To obtain her ticket to London she even performed in a circus troupe.

From 1982 to 1985 Eddi's career was showing signs of improvement. A brief spell as backing singer with Disc O'Dell's "Y" Records outfit Disconnection (Pigbag guitarist James Johnstone and Hi-Tension bassist Leroy Williams) yielded her first appearance on a record, the single 'Bali Hai', while subsequent session work for Gang Of Four, Eurythmics, Alison Moyet, the Associates and The WATERBOYS gave her the impetus to start her own band.

Abandoning a very sorry chapter with EMI-signed synth-pop act Outbar Squeak in 1986 (on two singles, 'When The Bad Men Come (Hoki-bo Sado-bo)' and 'Away From The Heart'), Eddi answered the call from English-born songwriter Mark E. Nevin, and after literally busking around city centres, FAIRGROUND ATTRACTION were officially formed with the addition of bass and guitarron player Simon Edwards (from Red Box) and drummer Roy Dodds (ex-Working Week).

Snapped up by RCA, the quartet's debut 45 'Perfect' raced to the top of the charts, paving the way for its Top 3 parent album **THE FIRST OF A MILLION KISSES** (1988) {*7}. An endearingly charming cajun-folk-jazz-C&W shuffle (or skiffle), the album was carried by READER's honey-coated Scots voice, which dominated the rootsy pop songs of the set, none better than subsequent hits 'Find My Love', 'A Smile In A Whisper' and 'Clare'.

Despite winning a couple of Brit Awards the following year, FAIRGROUND ATTRACTION's tenure was all too brief as their rollercoaster ride came to an abrupt end at the turn of the decade. READER had had her first child with her French-Algerian partner Milou Louines, and although rehearsals resumed, they were abandoned by Nevin after arguments arose. The album **AY FOND KISS** (1990) {*5} was duly pieced together out of B-sides, live tracks, etc, but it was little consolation to their growing legion of fans, especially in Japan.

While Nevin joined ex-Smiths icon Morrissey in 1991 and later worked with Sweetmouth, READER branched off into an acting career, winning a major role as singer/accordionist Jolene Jowett in the acclaimed BBC TV country-and-western comedy-drama 'Your Cheatin' Heart'. With Dodds staying on as drummer, READER subsequently hooked up with guitarists Neill MacColl (brother of Kirsty) and Dominic Miller, and alongside double-bassist Phil Steriopulos they became Eddi Reader And The Patron Saints Of Imperfection. Under this guise she recorded **MIRMAMA** (1992) {*7}, a well-received set that also featured contributions from Jools Holland on piano.

Shifting labels to Warner Bros subsidiary Blanco Y Negro, the singer found herself high in the charts once more (Top 5) with the solo album **EDDI READER** (1994) {*7}, a record that won her Best Female Artist at the Brit Awards. Having made up with Nevin, who supplied a handful of songs (one, 'Dear John', was donated by Kirsty MacColl), the majority of the material was written by or with BOO HEWERDINE, including minor hits 'Patience Of Angels' and 'Joke (I'm Laughing)'.

HEWERDINE shared the writing credits again on 1996's **CANDYFLOSS AND MEDICINE** {*6}, a Top 30 effort with a gentle musical ebb and hypnotic lyrical flow. It also featured a hit cover of 'Town Without Pity' (once a smash for Gene Pitney) and READER's arrangement of the Robert Burns ballad 'I Loved A Lass' (as 'I Loved A Lad'). Ironically but hardly surprisingly, the flame-haired singer's commercial pickings became progressively leaner as her records became more refined. **ANGELS AND ELECTRICITY** (1998) {*6} was another late-night lullaby, featured Ron Sexsmith's 'On A Whim', Nevin's 'Kiteflyer's Hill' and a sterling version of HEWERDINE's Bible-days chestnut 'Bell, Book And Candle', one of several contributions from Boo.

On her first set for Rough Trade Records, **SIMPLE SOUL** (2001) {*6}, Eddi was now musically maturing into middle age as tastefully and as temptingly as a fine red wine, while hints of ethnic instrumentation and flourishes of Americana (mainly from a JACKSON C. FRANK cover, 'Blues Run The Game') enriched its reassuringly acoustic bouquet. 2001 also saw the release of **DRIFTWOOD** {*6}, a Japanese import featuring a choice selection of her latter-day solo material and a handful of live tracks (notably another Sexsmith song, 'Wasting Time'). In May 2002 Eddi delivered a fantastic rendition of 'Green Grow The Rashes O' at the open-air Burns Festival at Culzean Castle.

It was then inevitable that Eddi would turn her hand to a whole album of Burns settings. **THE SONGS OF ROBERT BURNS** (2003) {*7} was premiered at her Celtic Connections appearance earlier that year, where, alongside retainers HEWERDINE and Dodds, there was room for a Caledonian crew of PHIL CUNNINGHAM, JOHN McCUSKER, COLIN REID, KATE RUSBY, Ian Carr, John Douglas and Ewen Vernal.

Mixing traditional material with the odd Boo contribution, **PEACETIME** (2006) {*6} kept her profile reasonably high, while writers John Douglas, Sandy Wright, Declan O'Rourke and Boo were helping out again on 2009's **LOVE IS THE WAY** {*6}. Her mash-up arrangement of Fleetwood Mac's 'Never Going Back' with a rarely heard Brian Wilson song, `Sweet Mountain Of Love', is worth checking out.

EDDI READER solo has also performed several B-side covers including 'My Old Friend The Blues' (Steve Earle), 'What You Do' (SI KAHN), 'Spirit' (The WATERBOYS), 'Wonderboy' (The Kinks) and 'Earlies', by the Trash Can Sinatras – her brother Francis Reader's band. *MCS*

FAIRGROUND ATTRACTION

Eddi Reader - vocals / **Marc E. Nevin** - guitars (ex-Jane Aire & The Belvederes) / **Simon Edwards** - guitarron/ bass (ex-Red Box) / **Roy Dodds** - drums, percussion (ex-Weekend, ex-Working Week, ex-Vic Godard)

		UK RCA		US RCA
Mar 88.	(7") *(PB 41845)* <8789> PERFECT. / Mythology	1	Nov 88	80
	(12"+=/cd-s+=) *(PT/PD 41846)* - Falling backwards / Mystery train.			
May 88.	(lp/c/cd) *(PL/PK/PD 71696)* <8596> **THE FIRST OF A MILLION KISSES**	2	Jan 89	
	- A smile in a whisper / Perfect / Moon on the rain / Find my love / Fairground attraction / The wind knows my name / Clare / Comedy waltz / The moon is mine / Station street / Whispers / Allelujah. *(cd+=)* - Falling backwards / Mythology. *(cd re-iss. May 93; 74321 13439-2) (d-cd-iss. Apr 95 +=; 74321 25959-2)* - AY FOND KISS			
Jul 88.	(7") *(PB 42079)* FIND MY LOVE. / Watching The Party	7		–
	(12"+=/cd-s+=) *(PT/PD 42080)* - You send me / Ay fond kiss.			
Nov 88.	(7") *(PB 42249)* A SMILE IN A WHISPER. / Winter Rose	75		–
	(12"+=/cd-s+=) *(PT/PD 42250)* - Walkin' after midnight / Trying times.			
Jan 89.	(7") *(PB 42607)* CLARE. / Games Of Love	49		–
	(12"+=/cd-s+=) *(PT/PD 42608)* - Do you want to know a secret? / Jock O' Hazeldean.			

May 90. (7"/c-s) *(PB 43654)* WALKIN' AFTER MIDNIGHT. / Comedy Waltz [live] [ ] [-]
(12"+=/cd-s+=) *(PT/PD 43654)* - Clare [live].

Jun 90. (cd/c/lp) *(PD/PK/PL 74596)* **AY FOND KISS** [rare + demos, etc.] [55] [-]
- Jock O' Hazeldean / The game of love / Walkin' after midnight / You send me / Trying times / Mystery train / Winter rose / Do you want to know a secret? / Allelujah [live] / Cajun band / Watching the party / Ay fond kiss. *(cd re-iss. Apr 94; 74321 19371-2) (d-cd-iss.+=)* - THE FIRST OF A MILLION KISSES

—— Fairground had already disbanded early 1990; READER went solo, as did Nevin (who also joined Morrissey and subsequently formed Sweetmouth); Edwards joined BILLY BRAGG & THE BLOKES

- (5-7*) compilations, others, etc.-

Feb 93. (7"/c-s) *R.C.A.; (74321 13491-7/-4)* PERFECT. / Captured [featuring BRIAN KENNEDY] [ ] [-]
(cd-s+=) *(74321 13491-2)* - Walkin' after midnight / You send me.

Sep 94. (cd) *RCA; (74321 23251-2)* **THE COLLECTION** [ ] [-]
- Perfect / Do you want to know a secret? / A smile in a whisper / Walkin' after midnight / Find my love / You send me / The moon is mine / Moon on the rain / Winter rose / The wind knows my name / Comedy waltz [live] / Allelujah / Ay fond kiss / Clare [live] / Watching the party / Fairground attraction.

Apr 96. (cd) *RCA Camden; (74321 37541-2)* **THE VERY BEST OF FAIRGROUND ATTRACTION featuring Eddi Reader** [ ] [-]
- Perfect / Find my love / Fairground attraction / A smile in a whisper / Clare / Walkin' after midnight / Do you want to know a secret? / Allelujah / The moon is mine / Watching the party / Winter rose / The wind knows my name / Jock o' Hazeldean / Comedy waltz / You send me / Ay fond kiss. *(re-iss. Feb 97; 74321 44675-2/-4)*

Sep 03. (cd) *RCA; (82876 55088-2)* **KAWASAKI: Live In Japan 02.07.89** [ ] [-]
- Winter rose – Allelujah / The waltz continues / The moon is mine – Get happy / Don't be a stranger / Dangerous / I know why the willows weep / Home to the heartache / Fear is the enemy of love / Find my love / Broken by a breeze / Whispers / Goodbye to songtown / Fairground attraction / Clare / Perfect / Moon on the rain.

Sep 04. (cd) *RCA; (82876 63721-2)* **THE VERY BEST OF FAIRGROUND ATTRACTION** [ ] [-]
- Perfect / Find my love / Moon on the rain / Clare / The wind knows my name / The moon is mine / Allelujah / The waltz continues / Whispers / Winter rose / Walkin' after midnight / Jock o' Hazeldean / A smile in a whisper / Broken by a breeze / Falling backwards / Dangerous / Fairground attraction / Don't be a stranger / You send me / Home to the heartache / Ay fond kiss.

- essential boxed sets -

Dec 02. (3-cd-box) *R.C.A.; (74321 98321-2)* **FIRST OF A MILLION KISSES // AY FOND KISS // (EDDI READER: MIRMAMA).**

- budget releases, etc.-

May 96. (cd-s) *Old Gold; (1262 36379-2)* PERFECT / Find My Love [ ] [-]

Nov 00. (cd) *Armoury; (ARMCD 010)* **PERFECT** [ ] [-]
- Do you want to know a secret? / Find my love / Station street / Perfect / Ay fond kiss / Clare / Comedy waltz / Walkin' after midnight / The moon is mine / A smile in a whisper / Allelujah / The wind knows my name / Whispers / Fairground attraction / Moon on the rain / The game of love.

EDDI READER

Eddi Reader - vocals, acoustic guitar, concertina, ukulele, harmonica piano (with various personnel and session players)

RCA — not issued

Nov 91. (12"ep) *(PT 45114)* ALL OR NOTHING EP [ ] [-]
- All or nothing / Sunday morning / Ole buttermilk sky / Broken vows.
(cd-ep) *(PD 45132)* - (first and last track) / The blacksmith / The girl with the weight of the world in her hands.

Feb 92. (7"/c-s) *(PB/PK 45017)* WHAT YOU DO WITH WHAT YOU'VE GOT. / I Wish You Were My Boyfriend [ ] [-]
(cd-s+=) *(PD 45018)* - Broken vows / Ole buttermilk sky (take 2).

Mar 92. (cd/c/lp; as EDDI READER WITH THE PATRON SAINTS OF IMPERFECTION) *(PD/PK/PL 75156)* **MIRMAMA** [34] [-]
- What you do with what you've got / Honeychild / All or nothing / Hello in there / Dolphins / The blacksmith / That's fair / Cinderella's downfall / Pay no mind / The swimming song / My old friend the blues. *(cd re-iss. Sep 94; 74321 15865-2) <US cd-iss. Jul 97 on Compass+=; 7 4242-2>* - Broken vows / The girl with the weight of the world in her hands.

Haven — not issued

Mar 93. (cd-ep; by EDDI READER, CLIVE GREGSON & BOO HEWERDINE) *(HAVENT 3CD)* WONDERFUL LIE EP [ ] [-]
- Wonderful lie / Last night I dreamt somebody loved me / Who's your jailer now.

Blanco Y Negro — Reprise

May 94. (7"/c-s) *(NEG 68/+C)* PATIENCE OF ANGELS. / Red Face Big Sky [33] [-]
(cd-s+=) *(NEG 68CD)* - Shirt and comb.

Jun 94. (cd/c) *(4509 96177-2/-4) <45713-2>* **EDDI READER** [4] Sep 04 [ ]
- The right place / Patience of angels / Dear John / Scarecrow / East of us / Joke (I'm laughing) / The exception / Red face big sky / Howling in Ojai / When I watch you sleeping / Wonderful lie / Siren. *(cd re-iss. Dec 96 as 'HUSH'; same)*

Aug 94. (7"/c-s) *(NEG 72/+C)* JOKE (I'M LAUGHING). / Saturday Night [42] [-]
(cd-s+=) *(NEG 72CD)* - Wonderboy.
(cd-s) *(NEG 72CDX)* - ('A') / Three crosses / Go and sit upon the grass.

Oct 94. (7"/c-s) *(NEG 75/+C)* DEAR JOHN. / Battersea Moon [48] [-]
(cd-s+=) *(NEG 75CD)* - When I watch you sleeping / What you do with what you've got / That's fair.

Sep 95. (c-s) *(NEG 82C)* NOBODY LIVES WITHOUT LOVE / Wonderful Lie [ ] [-]
(cd-s+=) *(NEG 82CD)* - Red face big sky.

Jun 96. (c-s) *(NEG 90C)* TOWN WITHOUT PITY / Leave The Light On [ ] [-]
(cd-s+=) *(NEG 90CD1)* - Wonderboy / Shall I be mother.
(cd-s) *(NEG 90CD2)* - ('A') / Sex lives boy / If you gotta minute.

Jul 96. (cd/c) *(0630 15129-2/-4)* **CANDYFLOSS AND MEDICINE** [24] [-]
- Glasgow star / Town without pity / Medicine / Rebel angel / Semi precious / Lazy heart / I loved a lad / Butterfly jar / Candyfloss / Darkhouse.

Aug 96. (c-s) *(NEG 95C)* MEDICINE / Sugar On The Pill [ ] [-]
(cd-s+=) *(NEG 95CD1)* - Earlies / Nameless.
(cd-s) *(NEG 95CD2)* - ('A') / Green grow the rushes / John Anderson my Joe / Who knows where the time goes.

Jul 97. (cd) *<7599 46370-2>* **CANDYFLOSS AND MEDICINE** [-] [ ]
- Glasgow star / Candyfloss / Rebel angel / Sugar on the pill / Semi precious / Medicine / If you got a minute, baby / Lazy heart / Shall I be mother / Butterfly jar / I loved a lad / Darkhouse.

Blanco Y Negro — Compass

May 98. (cd/c) *(6398 422816-2/-4) <7 4265-2>* **ANGELS AND ELECTRICITY** [49] Mar 99 [ ]
- Kiteflyer's hill / Prayer wheel / Postcard / Wings on my heels / On a whim / Hummingbird / Barcelona window / Bell, book and candle / California / Follow my tears / Psychic reader / Please don't ask me to dance / Clear.

Rough Trade — Compass

Jan 01. (cd) *(RTRADECD 011) <7 4302-2>* **SIMPLE SOUL** [ ] [ ]
- Wolves / The wanting kind / Lucky penny / Simple soul / Adam / Footsteps fall / Blues run the game / I felt a soul move through me / Prodigal daughter / Eden / The girl who fell in love with the moon.

Feb 01. (cd) *(ERCD 001)* **LIVE** (live 1st February, 2001) [-] tour [-]
- Wolves / Candyfloss / Simple soul / Please don't ask me to dance / Adam / Hummingbird / Lucky penny / Clare / Patience of angels / The girl who fell in love with the moon.

Oct 01. (cd) *(ERCD 002)* **DRIFTWOOD** [-] tour [-]
- Old soul / Sarasota / Meantime / Curragh of Kildare / Good girl / Wasting time / Paper wings / Holiday / Small soul sailing / New pretender / Forgive the boy / Everything. *(a version of this set was issued in Japan 2002)*

(above two issued on her own self-titled imprint)

May 03. (cd) *(RTRADECD 097) <7 4368-2>* **SINGS THE SONGS OF ROBERT BURNS** [ ] Feb 04 [ ]
- Jamie come try me / My love is like a red red rose / Willie Stewart - Molly Rankin / Ae fond kiss / Brose and butter / Ye Jacobites / Wild mountainside / Charlie is my darling / John Anderson my Jo / Winter it is past / Auld lang syne. *(re-iss. Jan 09 +=; same)* - Green grow the rashes o / Comin' through the rye - Dram behind the curtain / Ye banks and braes o' bonnie Doon / Ay waulkin-o / Dainty Davie / Leezie Lindsay / Of a' the airts.

Dec 06. (cd) *(RTRADECD 233)* **PEACETIME** [ ] [-]
- Baron's heir + Sadenia's air / Muddy water / Mary and the soldier / Aye waulkin-o / Prisons / The shepherd's song / Ye banks and braes o' bonnie Doon / Should I pray? / The Afton / Leezie Lindsay / Safe as houses / Galileo (someone like you) / Peacetime. *(bonus choice +=)* - The Calton weaver (or) Nancy Whisky.

Apr 09. (cd) *(RTRADCDX 454)* **LOVE IS THE WAY** [ ] [-]
- Dragonflies / Silent bells / New York City / Dandelion / Love is the way / Sweet mountain of love / Never going back again (Queen of Scots) / Over it now / Fallen twice / It's magic / Roses (new version) / My shining star / I won't stand in your way.

RED COVEN SKY (⟹ REV HAMMER)

RED JASPER

Eclectic in their Celtic-esque prog-folk-rock style, Welsh act RED JASPER (led by Davey Dodds) first burst on to the music scene with metal-cum-folk LP **ENGLAND'S GREEN AND PLEASANT LAND?** (1987) {*5}. Think of Marillion or Van Der Graaf, backed by the musicians of STEELEYE SPAN circa 1974, and you might get the picture.

With the addition of former OPHIUCHUS bassist/sax playerist Pat d'Arcy and new drummer Dave Clifford (he replaced Mark Ollard) alongside originals Robin Harrison (on an Octivider guitar), bassist Tony Heath and tin-whistler Dodds, the quintet was complete for second set **STING IN THE TALE** (1990) {*6}. This album had Gothic appeal, while the folk-rockers that shone through were 'Guy Fawkes', 'Secret Society' and the near-acappella live staple 'Magpie'. The last was a highlight of the prematurely-released concert set **ACTION REPLAY** (1992) {*6}, a hit-or-miss affair with new recruits Jonathan Thornton (bass) and Lloyd George (keyboards) superseding Heath and d'Arcy.

RED JASPER really came of age with **A MIDSUMMER NIGHT'S DREAM** (1993) {*8}, a record bracketed by two versions of the infectious 'Sonnet', while 'Treasure Hunt' and the two-part, 13-minute 'Dreamscape' stole the show. **THE WINTER'S TALE** (1994) {*7} continued the onslaught of their preceding Shakespearean-themed career high, its partly festive-styled jigs and jaunts ('The Shamen's Song' and 'Bread And Circuses') sharing space between the third parts of 'Dreamscape' and 'Sonnet', the former disguised as 'The Night Visitor'.

RED JASPER signed off with **ANAGRAMARY** (1997) {*7}, a record that abandoned their melodious jigs much as the STRAWBS had done in the mid-1970s. The fact that Dodds was a vocal ringer for DAVE COUSINS, Peter Gabriel or even Fish led them to this neo-prog swansong. Tracks such as 'In The Name Of The Empire', 'Babylon Rising' and finale 'Waterfalls (Rhaeadreau)' make it quite sad that there was nothing more to come from this criminally underrated outfit. *MCS*

Davey Dodds - vocals, mandolins, tin whistle / **Robin Harrison** - guitars, Octivider guitar / **Tony Heath** - bass, guitars, keyboards / **Mark Ollard** - drums, etc.

UK Vixen — US not issued

Sep 87. (m-lp) *(VIX 101)* **ENGLAND'S GREEN AND PLEASANT LAND?**
- Drinking song / Come and buy / Nuclear power / Song for summer / Company director / Go for it.

—— **Dave Clifford** - drums, percussion; repl. Ollard

—— added **Pat d'Arcy** - saxophone, bass, vocals (ex-OPHIUCHUS)

HTD — not issued

Dec 90. (cd/lp) *(HTD CD/LP 3)* **STING IN THE TALE**
- Faceless people / Guy Fawkes / TV screen / Second coming / Old Jack / Company director / Secret society / Magpie / I can hew.

—— **Jonathan Thornton** - bass; repl. Heath

—— **Lloyd George** - keyboards; repl. d'Arcy

Nov 92. (cd) *(HTDDWCD 9)* **ACTION REPLAY** [live]
- Hostage to fortune / Go for it / Come and buy / World turned upside down / Contented man / England's green and pleasant land / Old Jack / Crawling into work / Land fit for heroes / Second coming / The shamen's song / Soldier's vision / The magpie / The king of the fairies / Cool to be crazy.

Si-Music — not issued

Nov 93. (cd) *(SIMPly 35)* **A MIDSUMMER NIGHT'S DREAM**
- Sonnet I / Virtual reality / Berkana / Dreamscape (parts I & II) / Jean's tune / Invitation to a dance / Treasure hunt / Sonnet II.

Nov 94. (cd) *(SIMPly 55)* **THE WINTER'S TALE**
- Overture / Introduction / The shamen's song / The night visitor (Dreamscape part III) / The scent of something (what every new day yearns for most) / Ship on the sea (Jean's song) / Bread and circuses / Shepherds' revels / Dark room / Sonnet III.

Cymbeline — not issued

1997. (cd) *(5082-2)* **ANAGRAMARY**
- Perfect symmetry / Babylon rising / In her eyes / In the name of the empire / Flag / Island of mighty / People of the hills / Through the dawn / Waterfalls (Rhaeadreau).

—— disbanded after above set

Jon REDFERN

Born 1985 in Brighton, of Chinese and British parentage, JON REDFERN has quickly established himself as one of folk music's most promising new acts. With an uncanny penchant for sounding like a cross between Travis, Elbow and NICK DRAKE, the acoustic singer-songwriter has released two full sets, **MAY BE SOME TIME** (2007) {*7} and **WHAT ELSE BUT LOVE?** (2009) {*8}.

Many may recall his time in youthful Borders/Celtic folkies TARRAS (alongside fellow musicians Joss Clapp, Ben Murray, Emma Hancock and Rob Armstrong), who released two sets for Topic/Rounder, 'Rising' (1999) and 'Walking Down Mainstreet' (2002), the latter without Emma and Robb. Jon's solo career was indeed a marked change of direction.

REDFERN's debut solo set retained all the elements of his musical past (example: 'I'm Still Young'), but his second album touched on recent inspirations such as Pink Floyd (on 'Spark In The Sky') and Guy Garvey/Elbow ('Part Of You' and 'Troubadour'). His folk-rock traits were tinged with JOHN MARTYNesque jazz on 'Future Lies', and BECKY UNTHANK duetted with him on the finale, 'Don't Worry'. *MCS*

Jon Redfern - vocals, acoustic guitar, multi (+ session people)

UK Reveal — US not issued

Jan 07. (cd/lp) *(REVEAL 13 CD/LP)* **MAY BE SOME TIME**
- I'm still young / Am I a fool / Lost / All this time I / Demons I / Demons II / Can't take the heat / All this time II / Give away your heart I / Give away your heart II / I love the sun / Somewhere. *(lp w/ bonus cd+=)* - Down the line / Can't take the heat [band version] / Home at last / Departure / Spencer the rover.

Jun 07. (ltd-12") *(REVEAL 24)* GIVE YOUR HEART AWAY II. / I Love The Sun [Brooks remix]
(w/ free 3"cd-s+=) *(same)* - [same two tracks].

Nov 07. (m-cd) *(REVEAL 38CD)* **ACOUSTIC**
- I love the sun / Part of you / Lost / Glad / Harmonics / Give away your heart I / Give away your heart II / Troubadour.

Aug 08. (cd/lp) *(REVEAL 47 CD/LP)* **WHAT ELSE BUT LOVE?**
- Spark in the sky / Part of you / Future lies / Play of fear / Troubadour / Forever bound / Temporary / Rowing away / Don't worry (feat. BECKY UNTHANK).

REDGUM

Along with predecessors The BUSHWACKERS, Adelaide's REDGUM have been Australia's biggest and best political folk-rock act since their inception in 1975. Basically a quartet featuring singer-songwriter John Schumann, guitarist and vocalist Michael Atkinson, flautist and singer Verity Truman and violinist Chris Timms, plus the odd recruit now and then, the band were students at Flinders University, which was a training ground for their acerbic wit and political insight.

IF YOU DON'T FIGHT YOU LOSE (1978) {*8} – title lifted from a line in the blues song 'Killing Floor' – found REDGUM setting out their stall nicely, highlighting as it did the flute-friendly satirical ditty 'Beaumont Rag', the heroic 'Poor Ned' and the plucky white-settlement theme 'H.M.A.S. Australia'. Almost immediately signing to Epic Records, Schumann and co. (with additional back-up from Dave Flett and Tom Stehlik) delivered the equally observational and thought-provoking **VIRGIN GROUND** (1980) {*7}. Their sound on 'Ted', 'Stewie', 'Long Run' and the title track lay somewhere between STRAWBS and ERIC BOGLE.

Taking 'Waltzing Matilda' as its template (the Australian national song, not BOGLE's 'And The Band Played …), the single '100 Years On' was one of the best songs on REDGUM's third album, **BROWN RICE AND KEROSENE** (1981) {*7}, while 'Caught In The Act' and 'Where Ya Gonna Run To?' had all the hallmarks of genuine classics. It would be their last set with Timms, who was replaced by full-time member Hugh McDonald.

REDGUM were by now a massive live outfit in their homeland, and chart-toppers with 'I Was Only 19' (an anti-Vietnam War ballad). The TREVOR LUCAS-produced concert set **CAUGHT IN THE ACT** (1983) {*7} was a well-timed stopgap pending 1984's **FRONTLINE** {*6}. However, the band suffered a little when SCHUMANN departed in 1985, McDonald taking over the lead role on what turned out to be their swansong set, **MIDNIGHT SUN** (1986) {*5}.

In 1987, REDGUM got into a sticky situation when their condom-promoting single 'Roll It On Robbie' single was given short shrift by the church and conservatives. In 1990, with several further personnel changes hampering them creatively, the group decided to call it a day.

SCHUMANN was already carving out a fruitful solo career, although many wondered where he'd got to after his resounding success **ETCHED IN BLUE** (1987) {*7}. **LOOBY LOO** (1989) was an album for children, while **TRUE BELIEVERS** (1993) {*6} brought him back to AOR-land. With politics and song always key to his life, John stood for the Australian Democrats in 1998's federal elections, very nearly winning the seat of Mayo from the Foreign Minister. He opted out of electoral politics in favour of family commitments in 2001, but continued to campaign against social injustices.

Maintaining an affiliation with his former REDGUM associates Hugh McDonald and Michael Atkinson, SCHUMANN formed the loose ensemble The VAGABOND CREW. Taking inspiration from the works of Australian poet Henry Lawson, they released the album **LAWSON** (2005) {*6}.

Australian hip-hop band The Herd revived 'I Was Only 19' in 2005 with a hit cover version, approved by the composer, and with the theme of Australians at war still relevant, SCHUMANN and the VAGABOND CREW released a second set, **BEHIND THE LINES** (2008) {*6}, though without the participation of Atkinson. *MCS*

John Schumann (b. 1953) - vocals, acoustic guitar / **Verity Truman** - vocals, tin whistle, saxophone / **Michael Atkinson** - vocals, guitar, mandolin / **Chris Timms** - violin, vocals / + other brief members over the years

Aus/UK Larrikin — US not issued

1978. (lp) *(LRF 037)* **IF YOU DON'T FIGHT YOU LOSE** [–] Aus [–]
- One more boring Thursday night in Adelaide / Carrington cabaret / Critique in G / Beaumont rag / Peter the cabby / H.M.A.S. Australia / Raggin' / So goodbye / Poor Ned / Killing floor / Letter to BJ / Servin' USA *(re-iss. 1981 on Epic; ELPS 4184)* *(UK-iss. Jul 85 on CBS lp/c; CBS/+40 26527)*

—— added **Dave Flett** - bass + **Tom Stehlik** - drums

Epic — not issued

Nov 80. (lp/c) *(ELPS/EPC 4137)* **VIRGIN GROUND** [–] Aus [–]
- Virgin ground / Maria / Stewie / Domination quickstep / The money's no good / Nuclear cop / Women in change / Ted / It doesn't matter to me / Long run.

Jan 81. (7") *(ES 543)* THE LONG RUN. / Little Hampton's Calling Me [–] Aus [–]

Nov 81. (7") *(???)* 100 YEARS ON. / Nuclear Cop [–] Aus [–]

Nov 81. (lp) *(ELPS 4257)* **BROWN RICE AND KEROSENE** [–] Aus [–]
- 100 years on / Lear jets over Kulgera / Caught in the act / Yarralumla wine / Where ya gonna run to / Brown rice and kerosene / Federal two-ring circus / Your OS trip / The last frontier / Parramatta gaol 1843. *(cd-iss. 1990; 469396-2)*

—— **Hugh McDonald** - violin, vocals; repl. Timms

Sep 82. (12"ep) *(EX 12020)* CUT TO THE QUICK [–] Aus [–]
- Working girl / Fabulon / The Diamantina drover / Where ya gonna run to.

Mar 83. (7") *(ES 844)* I WAS ONLY 19 (A WALK IN THE GREEN LIGHT). / Yarralumla Wine [–] Aus [–]
(UK-iss.1985; A 6418)

Jun 83. (7"m) *(ES 864)* CAUGHT IN THE ACT. / Stewie / Lear Jets Over Kulgera [–] Aus [–]

Jun 83. (lp) *(ELPS 4371)* **CAUGHT IN THE ACT** [live] [–] Aus [–]
- Beaumont rag / The last frontier / Brown rice and kerosene / Nuclear cop / I was only nineteen / Caught in the act / Stewie / Lear jets over Kulgera / Fabulon / The Diamantina drover / Where ya gonna run to / It doesn't matter to me / Long run / Poor Ned / Raggin'. *(cd-iss. 1988 +=; 462552-2)* - Caught In The Act EP

Aug 83. (7") *(???)* LONG RUN. / Fabulon [–] Aus [–]

Feb 84. (7") *(ES 953)* I'VE BEEN TO BALI TOO. / Still Life [–] Aus [–]

Apr 84. (7") *(ES 965)* FRIDAY NIGHT. / The Last Frontier [–] Aus [–]

—— **Brian Czempinski** - drums; repl. Gifford, who had repl. Russell Coleman

—— **Michael Spicer** - keyboards + **Stephen Cooney** - didgeridoo, bass, mandolin, banjo; repl. Flett

Jul 84. (7") *(ES 986)* A.S.I.O. / Hira [–] Aus [–]

Aug 84. (lp) *(ELPS 4428)* **FRONTLINE** [–] Aus [–]
- I've been to Bali too / A.S.I.O. / Friday night / Spirit of the land / Gladstone pier / Spark of the heart / Still life / Working girls / Beyond reason / Hira.

1985. (7") *(???)* JUST ANOTHER MOMENT ON YOUR OWN. / Kerang (Moon Over Water) [–] Aus [–]

1985. (7") *(ES 1045)* THE DROVER'S DOG. / It Doesn't Matter To Me [–] Aus [–]

Oct 85. (7") *(A 6645)* I'VE BEEN TO BALI TOO / The Diamantina Drover [ ] [–]

—— (1985) McDonald (now lead vocals); SCHUMANN left for a solo career

—— **Ray Rafael** - drums; repl. Czempinski

—— **Peter Bolke** - bass; repl. Cooney

Nov 86. (7") *(???)* RUNNING WITH THE HURRICANE. / Street To Die [–] Aus [–]

Nov 86. (lp) *(ELPS 4570)* **MIDNIGHT SUN** [–] Aus [–]
- Talk / When your luck ran out / Running with the hurricane / Empty page / Midnight sun / Too many dollars / Another country / In their hands / Blood upon the rain / La partida (The parting). *(cd-iss. 1987; EPCD 450348)*

—— **Darryn Deland Darryn** - bass, vocals; repl. Atkinson

May 87. (7") *(650793-7)* ROLL IT ON ROBBIE. / Empty Page [–] Aus [–]

Mar 88. (7" ep) *(???)* 4 PLAY VOL 19 [–] Aus [–]

—— the group disbanded in 1990; McDonald went solo, starting with 1994's 'The Lawson Album'; he then teamed up with JOHN SCHUMANN in The VAGABOND CREW

- (8-10*) compilations –

Nov 04. (cd) *Columbia; (5190092000)* **AGAINST THE GRAIN: THE REDGUM ANTHOLOGY 1976-1984** [–] Aus [–]
- Poor Ned / Killing floor / Servin' USA / Maria / Ted / Long run / Brown rice and kerosene / Yarralumla wine / The last frontier / Where ya gonna run to / Fabulon / The Diamantina drover / I was only 19 (a walk in the light green) / I've been to Bali too / A.S.I.O. / Spirit of the land / Gladstone pier / Still life / Just another moment on your own.

May 11. (d-cd) *Epic; (???)* **THE ESSENTIAL** [–] Aus [–]
- Poor Ned / Servin' USA / Killing floor / Beaumont rag / One more boring night in Adelaide / Carrington cabaret / H.M.A.S. Australia / Maria / Ted / It doesn't matter to me / Virgin ground / Domination quickstep / Stewie / Nuclear cop / Long run / 100 years on / Brown rice and kerosene / Lear jets over Kulgera / The last frontier [live] // Where ya gonna run to? / Caught in the act / Yarralumla wine / The federal two-ring circus / Working girls / Fabulon / The Diamantina drover / I was only 19 (a walk in the light green) / I've been to Bali too / A.S.I.O. / Friday night / Spirit of the land / Gladstone pier / Still life / Just another moment on your own / The drover's dog / Running with the hurricane / When your luck ran out / Blood upon the rain.

- (5-7*) compilations, etc.

Nov 84. (lp) *Epic; (ELPS 4512)* **EVERYTHING'S LEGAL, ANYTHING GOES** [–] Aus [–]
- Just another moment on your own / I've been to Bali too / The Diamantina drover / Gladstone pier / I was only 19 / The long run / It doesn't matter to me / Killing floor / A.S.I.O. / Where ya gonna run to / Poor Ned / The drover's dog.

1987. (lp) *J&B; (???)* **THE VERY BEST OF REDGUM** [–] Aus [–]

JOHN SCHUMANN

Schumann with session people/guests

CBS — not issued

Nov 87. (lp/cd) *(460271-1/-2)* **ETCHED IN BLUE** [–] Aus [–]
- Borrowed ground / Thunder across the reef / Holy Mary / Coming home / Safe behind the wire / He's got the money / Yuppy days / After the party / For the children / Borrowed ground reprise… 1788-1988. *(cd re-iss. Apr 09; same)*

Jan 89. (lp) *(463255-1)* **JOHN SCHUMANN goes LOOBY LOO**: a collection of songs for little kids [–] Aus [–]
- She'll be coming around the mountain / I had a cat / The alley-alley-oo / This old man / Do your ears hang low? / Little rabbit in the wood / I hear thunder / The fox / Michael Finnigin / Mum does't like us playing the drums around here / Working on the railway / Mr Frog / Dr. Knickerbocker / One man went to mow a meadow / Worms / Looby-Loo / Six little ducks / For the children / Mr Quangle-wangle-quee.

Feb 93. (cd) *(473818-2)* **TRUE BELIEVERS** [–] Aus [–]
- If I close my eyes / Leigh Creek road / Fallen angel / Eyes on fire / Working class man / Roll on the day / Clancy of the overflow / If the war goes on / Hyde Park calling (King William road, scene 1) / Plympton high / Eyes on fire (acoustic) / If I close my eyes (reprise). *(cd-reiss.2009)*

JOHN SCHUMANN & THE VAGABOND CREW

Schumann with **Hugh McDonald** + **Michael Atkinson** (ex-REDGUM) + others

ABC-Universal — not issued

Oct 05. (cd) *(GUM 3694)* **LAWSON** [–] Aus [–]
- To an old mate / Knocking around / The glass on the bar / Second class wait here / Faces in the street / The bush girl / Taking his chance / Scots of the Riverina / To Hannah / A prouder man than you / The low lighthouse / The shame of going back / To Jim. *(re-iss. Oct 07 on Warners+= DVD; 5144 22772-2)*

—— without Atkinson; solid band incl. **Dave Folley** - drums, percussion / **Kat Kraus** - vocals / **Mark Kraus** - audio

Sep 08. (cd) *(1778130)* **BEHIND THE LINES** [–] Aus [–]
- Boy on the run / And the band played Waltzing Matilda / Scots of the Riverina / No man's land (Green fields of France) / To an old mate / Ted / Mothers, daughters, wives / Khe Sahn [long tan version] / My country / I was only 19 (a walk in the light green) / Rachel / Wings of an eagle / Safe behind the wire / When the war is over / I'll be gone / Waltzing Matilda.

- (5-7*) compilations, etc.-

Mar 03. (cd) *Sony; (5109202000)* **PORTRAIT: THE VERY BEST OF JOHN SCHUMANN** [–] Aus [–]
- I was only 19 / Borrowed ground / Holy Mary / Thunder across the reef / Safe behind the wire / For the children / If I close my eyes / Leigh Creek road / Clancy of the overflow / Eyes on fire / Roll on the day / If the war goes on / One true game / Borrowed ground reprise … 1788-1988.

Oct 07. (cd) *Warners; (5144 22771-2)* **GELIGNITE JACK: THE JOHN SCHUMANN COLLECTION** [–] Aus [–]

Fionn REGAN

A bluesy singer-songwriter with a penchant for rootsy finger-picking folk (draw a line through WOODY GUTHRIE, NICK DRAKE and DAMIEN RICE), FIONN REGAN was taught guitar, piano and violin by his musician father. Born in the early 1980s in the coastal town of Bray, County Wicklow, Ireland, he relocated to Brighton to go busking.

A series of singles and EPs (his first, 'Slow Wall' under the pseudonym of Bilbo) was issued in the first half of the 2000s, their bohemian appeal and media praise leading to a contract with Robin Guthrie's Bella Union imprint (Lost Highway in the US). Recorded in a barn, **THE END OF HISTORY** (2006) {*8}was highlighted by 'Put A Penny In The Slot', the missing link between PAUL SIMON and a host of anti-folk artists (MOLDY PEACHES, anyone?). 'Be Good Or Be Gone', 'Noah (Ghost In A Sheet)' and the quirky 'The Underwood Typewriter' were other gems on this Mercury Award-nominated album, while the epic finale medley of 'Bunker Or Basement'/'Campaign Button' (hidden track) echoed all his musical heroes and progenitors.

Released four years later, **THE SHADOW OF AN EMPIRE** {*6} (2010) suffered from the loss of a little career momentum, but there were a handful of strum-friendly items on hand, such 'Catacombs', The Libertines-like 'Coat Hook' and 'Protection Racket'. As to whether Fionn's slight change of direction was a gain for rootsy rock 'n' roll (check out 'Genocide Matinee', which echoes 'Subterranean Homesick Blues' and 'Folsom Prison Blues') or a loss to folk music in general, the jury is out pending his next outing. *MCS*

Fionn Regan - vocals, guitars, harmonica

UK Donkey Boy / US not issued

Oct 00. (cd-s; as BILBO) *(CDDB 2023)* SLOW WALL / Rocking Horse Town / Hello L [–] Irish [–]

Anvil / not issued

Jul 02. (7") *(anv 08)* LITTLE MISS DRUNK. / Black Water Child [ ] [–]

Jan 03. (cd-ep) *(anv 09)* RESERVOIR EP [ ] [–]
- Reservoir / Red lane / Noah (ghost in a sheet) / After the fall.

Mar 04. (cd-ep) *(anv 10)* HOTEL ROOM EP [ ] [–]
- Hotel room / Change the locks / Hunter's map / Abacus / Old folks.

2005. (cd-ep) *(3)* CAMPAIGN BUTTON EP [–] Irish [–]
- Campaign button / Medicine chest / The ballad of thetoad eaters / Ice cap lullaby.

Bella Union / Lost Highway

Aug 06. (cd/10" d-lp) *(BELLACD 119)* <*B0009135-02/-01*> **THE END OF HISTORY** [ ] Jul 07 [ ]
- Be good or be gone / The Underwood typewriter / Hunter's map / Hey rabbit / Black water child / Put a penny in the slot / The cowshed / Snowy Atlas mountains / Noah (ghost in a sheet) / The end of history / Abacus / Bunker or basement. *(cd-iss.+=; BELLACD 119X)* - Campaign button [hidden track].

Feb 07. (7") *(BELLAV 133)* BE GOOD OR BE GONE [live]. / Ice Cap Lullaby [ ] [–]

Sep 07. (cd-s) *(BELLACD 155)* BE GOOD OR BE GONE / Getting better / Be Good Or Be Gone [video] [ ] [–]

Heavenly / not issued

Nov 09. (7") *(HVN 195)* PROTECTION RACKET. / Genocide Matinee [acoustic] [ ] [–]

Feb 10. (cd) *(HVNLP 75CD)* **THE SHADOW OF AN EMPIRE** [ ] [–]
- Protection racket / Catacombs / Coat hook / Genocide matinee / Violent demeanour / Lines written in winter / House detective / Little Nancy / Lord help my poor soul / The shadow of an empire. *(lp-iss. Feb11 on Diverse; ???)*

Apr 10. (7") *(HVN 198)* CATACOMBS. / Violent Demeanour [acoustic] [ ] [–]

REV HAMMER

REV HAMMER is the musical identity of Stephen Ryan, whose sound is gritty, blood-and- guts folk-rock, akin to a fusion of Gallon Drunk, his hero Johnny Cash and CHRISTY MOORE. A friend of indie stars such as LEVELLERS, Justin Sullivan (of New Model Army) and punk-poet Joolz, Ryan was raised by Irish parents in Buntingford, Hertfordshire.

After working as a busker for almost two years, his association with Justin and Joolz kicked off in 1986 when they (along with bassist Brett Selby) formed travelling folk club RED COVEN SKY. He had surfaced earlier on record as half of Hammer & Sickle, and also under the alias of Crowman & Rokk Artthrobbe (Justin and Robb Heaton made up the latter trio).

Recorded in winter in a cowshed in deepest Essex with new best buddies the LEVELLERS, **INDUSTRIAL SOUND AND MAGIC** (1991) {*7} was gathered together from his time spent on the road, playing Glastonbury and beyond. Cooking Vinyl Records gave it further promotion the following year and released the Justin Sullivan-produced follow-up, **THE BISHOP OF BUFFALO** (1994) {*6}. Stepan Pasicznyk of The UKRAINIANS and members of New Model Army were on the guest list.

The ambitious folk-opera concept album **FREEBORN JOHN** (1997) {*8} was the story of John Lilburne, leader of 17th-century radicals the Levellers and a big influence on the group of that name. MADDY PRIOR, EDDI READER, Rory McLeod, Justin Sullivan and Robb Heaton all played a part in bringing British history's greatest protesters to life in theatre, song and poetry. Try the Delta blues cut 'The Whipping Song', the bluebeat 'Elizabeth's Great Gallop', 'Return To London' and the neo-Celtic 'Burford Stomp'.

Taking time off to help bring up his children, REV HAMMER went back to work (augmented by sound engineer Phil Johnstone) with **SPITTING FEATHERS** {*6} (2004), a marked departure from the roots and folk of his 1990s music. His career high was recreated for the stage as **FREEBORN JOHN LIVE** (2007) {*7} and given the DVD treatment, featuring a panoply of well-known names to provide the necessary oomph. **DOWN THE ALLEY** (2010) {*6} reached out once more to his acoustic followers. *MCS*

Stephen Ryan (b. 1965, Kent) - vocals, guitars / with various back-up

UK Hag / US not issued

Nov 91. (lp) *(HAGLP 3)* **INDUSTRIAL SOUND AND MAGIC** [ ] [–]
- Down by the river o' / True blue / Punchdrunk / Ole Welsh soul / California bound / Raise that lion / Johnny Reggae / Caledonia rain / Shuttin' the ole dirt town / Jimmy Flanagan.

Cooking Vinyl / not issued

Jun 92. (re; cd/c) *(COOK CD/C 046)* **INDUSTRIAL SOUNDS AND MAGIC** [ ] [–]

Feb 94. (lp/cd) *(COOK/+CD 063)* **THE BISHOP OF BUFFALO** [ ] [–]
- The lamb / Tranquility of solitude / Etain / Ellan Vannin / Circular blues / Like the son of a goat (worse and worse) / Every step of the way / Drunkard's waltz / Shanty / The chase.

—— In 1995, REV HAMMER contributed several songs from above to the 'RED SKY COVEN: Volumes 1 & 2' double-CD compilation on Woolpack, featuring Joolz and Justin Sullivan (New Model Army); an updated 'Volume 3' was issued in 1999; same line-up

1996. (cd) *(REVCD 1)* **THE GREEN FOOL RECORDINGS** [–] mail-o [–]
- Ghosts of Walachin / Stealing / Paling of the moon / Connersville girl / Child of the wind / Old bell country / Swansfeather / The mutineer / The green fool / Black coal hole.

(above issued on Velvel)

Apr 97. (lp) *(COOK 111)* **FREEBORN JOHN: THE STORY OF JOHN LILBURNE - THE LEADER OF THE LEVELLERS** [ ] [–]
- Overture / Pillory scene - Commons of England / The whipping song / The battle of Brentford / Elizabeth's great gallop / Return to London / England's new chains / Speech 1 / Bonny Besses / Burford stomp / Speech 2 / Exile / Return from exile / Seventeen years of sorrow / Lilburne's death song / Valediction. *(cd-iss. Mar 98; COOKCD 111)*

Attack Attack / not issued

Jul 04. (cd) *(ATK 2308-2)* **SPITTING FEATHERS** [ ] [–]
- Put it on red / Dementia pugilistica / Cold wind / Ferninand / Happy birthday revolution / When I come through for you / Mary, Mary / Little boy blue / Sweetest heart / Wedding ground / Rosie / Pour your whisky on my road.

RED SKY COVEN

Brett Selby, Joolz, Justin Sullivan + Rev Hammer

2009. (cd) *(ATK 2315-2)* **5** [live in UK and Germany 2004] [ ] [–]
- Intro / Tecumsen Valley / Bread 'n' ducks / Dementia pugilistica / Punchdrunk / [JOOLZ tracks] / JUSTIN SULLIVAN tracks] / Ensemble: Louie Louie.

REV HAMMER

with numerous musicians including **Levellers**

Freeborn John / not issued

Mar 07. (cd+dvd) *(FBJCD 001)* **FREEBORN JOHN LIVE** [–] mail-o [–]
- [same tracks as studio set above].

Apr 10. (cd) *(none)* **DOWN THE ALLEY** [–] mail-o [–]
- The great eradicator / Down in the alley / Alabaster / No one or nothing / Righteous / Springtime in England / Jack o' green / Just like Trevelyan / Every woman's pain / Rocks / Mimi Mae.

Damien RICE

On a par with folk royalty such as DAVID GRAY, NICK DRAKE or even James Blunt, Irishman DAMIEN RICE (b. December 7, 1973 in Celbridge, County Kildare) has built a reputation around his well-crafted ballads and his folk ethos.

Damien (under the name of Dodi Ma) formed his first band, indie-rock outfit Juniper, in the early 1990s, with Paul Noonan, David Geraghty, Brian Crosby and Dominic Philips. A tour of Ireland and a debut EP, 'Manna' (1995) led to a deal with Polygram . However, after a pair of promising singles ('Weatherman' and 'Single Of The Fortnight'), artistic and contractual disagreements eventually split the band.

RICE moved to Tuscany before travelling across other parts of Europe, busking as he went, before returning to Ireland in 1999. He had written a handful of songs, which he sent off to producer and film composer David Arnold (his cousin), who has scored the last five James Bond films. Arnold encouraged Damien to record an album and donated money so that he could set up his own studio, whence he released 'The Blower's Daughter', his first hit in Ireland.

With the help of vocalist LISA HANNIGAN, drummer Tomo/Tom Osander, bassist Shane Fitzsimmons and cellist Vyvienne Long, RICE released his debut album, **O** {*8}, in 2003. Hushed vocals, windswept pianos and floating melodies were all present on what was perhaps the most gentle acoustic-folk release of the year. Just missing out on the top spot in Ireland, it was issued in Britain and the US a year later, where it reached No.8 and No.114 respectively. Boasting three hit singles including 'The Blower's Daughter' and `Volcano', the show was stolen by the moody bedsit crooner 'Cannonball', which charted twice.

With anticipation and hype for his follow-up in full flow, RICE brought LISA HANNIGAN to fame by giving her a co-billing on a stop-gap Top 30 single `Unplayed Piano'.

Second album, **9** {*5} (2006), was initially a massive transatlantic chart success, although to many critics, including the NME (which branded it "IKEA rock"), it was a flop. Led by the melancholy Top 30 track '9 Crimes', the pace of the record never quite moved out of first gear; witness the formulaic 'The Animals Were Gone' and 'Dogs'.

LISA HANNIGAN (now a solo star in her own right) was not asked to return to the set-up in March 2007, and RICE has since taken a somewhat lower profile. 2011 found him working with French actress/singer Melanie Laurent on her forthcoming 'En T'Attendant' album. *MCS*

Damien Rice - vocals, multi / + session band

UK: Damien Rice Music — US: not issued

Sep 01. (cd-s) *(drm 001cd)* THE BLOWER'S DAUGHTER / The Professor + La fille danse / Moody Mooday - The Blower's Daughter (original demo) [–] Irish [–]

May 02. (cd-s) *(drm 003cd)* CANNONBALL / Lonelily (original demo) / Woman Like A Man (live unplugged) / Cannonball (instrumental) [–] Irish [–]

Oct 02. (cd-s) *(drm 004cd)* VOLCANO / Delicate (live acoustic) / Volcano (instrumental) / (hidden demo + CD-ROM track) [–] Irish [–]
(UK-iss. Feb 04; dr 04cd1/2)

UK: 14th Floor — US: Vector

Mar 03. (cd-ep) *(dr 01)* WOMAN LIKE A MAN EP [ ] [–]
- Woman like a man / Delicate / Lonelily / The professor.

Jul 03. (cd) *(505046-64788-5-6) <48507>* **O** [8] Jun 03 [ ]
- Delicate / Volcano / The blower's daughter / Cannonball / Older chests / Amie / Cheers darlin' / Cold water / I remember / Eskimo. *(hidden tracks+=)* - Prague / Silent night. *(orig. Ire Feb 02; drm 02cd) (cd re-iss. Jun 04 w/dvd+=; 2564 61495-2)* - Cannonball (live) / The blower's daughter (live) / Volcano (live).

Oct 03. (cd-s) *(dr 03cd1) <69532>* CANNONBALL / Moody Mooday / ('A'-video) [32] Dec 03 [ ]

Jul 04. (cd-s) *(dr 03cd2)* CANNONBALL (live) / Amie (live) / The Blower's Daughter (live) [19] [–]
(dvd-s) *(dr 03dvd)* - ('A'-radio) / ('A'-remix) / (dialogue).

Aug 04. (m-cd) *(5046 75006-2) <48830>* **B-SIDES** (compilation) [ ] Aug 04 [ ]
- The professor + la fille danse (live at Cornucopia) / Lonelily (demo) / Woman like a man (live unplugged) / Moody Mooday / Delicate (live in Dublin) / Volcano (instrumental) / Volcano (1997 demo). *(UK+=)* - Cannonball (radio remix). *<re-iss. Jan 05 on WEA+=; 675006>*

UK: 14th Floor — US: WEA

Dec 04. (7" white/cd-s) *(dr 06 v/cd2) <676515>* THE BLOWER'S DAUGHTER. / Silent Night [27] Jan 05 [ ]
(cd-s) *(dr 06cd1) <676515>* - ('A') / The Professor + la fille danse (live at Cornucopia) / Moody Mooday (remix).

Apr 05. (7" toffee) *(dr 07v) <677788>* VOLCANO. / Lonely Soldier (live) [29] Jul 05 [ ]
(cd-s+=) *(dr 07cd2)* - ('A'-live from Shortlist awards) / ('A'-video).
(cd-s) *(dr 07cd1)* - ('A') / The blower's daughter.

Jul 05. (7"/cd-s; as DAMIEN RICE & LISA HANNIGAN) *(dr 08 v/cd)* UNPLAYED PIANO (Chris Lord-Alge mix) / (instrumental) [24] [–]

Nov 06. (cd) *(64042-2) <43249-2>* **9** [4] [22]
- 9 crimes / The animals were gone / Elephant / Rootless tree /Dogs / Coconut skins / Me, my yoke and I / Grey room / Accidental babies / Sleep don't weep.

Nov 06. (7" clear/cd-s) *(dr 09 v/cd)* 9 CRIMES. / The Rat Within The Grain [29] [–]

Nov 06. (7"pic-d) *<7-15557>* 9 CRIMES. / 9 Crimes (original demo) [–] [ ]

Feb 07. (7"white) *(dr 10v)* ROOTLESS TREE. / 9 Crimes (live on KCRW)
(cd-s) *(dr 10cd)* - ('A'-edit) / ('A'-piano version live KCRW). [50] [–]

Sep 07. (cd-s) *(dr 11cd)* DOGS (remix) / Childish (live at Wisseloord Studios) [88] [–]
(7") *(dr 11v1)* - ('A') / Elephant (live at Wisseloord Studios).
(7") *(dr 11v2)* - ('A') / Accidental babies (live at Wisseloord).

Oct 07. (m-cd) *<349244-2>* **LIVE AT FINGERPRINTS: WARTS AND ALL** [live at the store in Long Beach, California in November 2006] [–] [ ]
- Cannonball / Coconut skins / (intro...) / Grey rooms / Volcano / (intro...) / Rootless tree / I remember.

Nov 07. (m-cd) *(505144-2)* **LIVE FROM THE UNION CHAPEL** [live promo from 2003] [58] [–]
- Delicate / The blower's daughter / Volcano / Then go / Baby sister / Be my husband / Amie / Silent night.

—— In March 2007, RICE let go his musical accomplice HANNIGAN

ROARING JACK (⟹ HULETT, Alistair)

ROARING JELLY

Derby's funniest (and probably its only) alternative comic-folk act, ROARING JELLY, was founded in 1970 by former Nottingham/Trent Polytechnic furniture design students Clive Harvey and Derek Pearce; the first-named had previously performed alongside Rowland 'Miggi' Middleton in folk duo The Few.

Taking their name from an Irish jig, ukulele strummer Clive and multi-instrumentalist Derek won local talent contests and played folk festivals in the first half of the 1970s, adding Mick Hennessy (an exile from The DRUIDS) to enhance their sound and vision around 1975/76.

Sounding like an unholy fusion of retro-rock 'n' rollers Sha Na Na and avant-folkers The HOLY MODAL ROUNDERS, **ROARING JELLY'S GOLDEN GRATES** (1977) {*7} had some rib-tickling moments, and some that seem bizarre and dated now. Produced by JOHN TAMS and Neil Wayne, it led to their first TV appearance for BBC Midlands and a subsequent "Christmas Trifle" special in 1979/80.

With the festive scene never far from their thoughts ('Family Christmas' had opened their debut set), airplay from Radio 2's Terry Wogan for novelty 45 'Christmas In Australia' gave the trio a boost in 1980. **IN THE ROAR** (1981) {*6} was a surprise release from Topic Records. If one could pick only one track, it would have to be 'Valerie Wilkins'.

Why ROARING JELLY never returned to the studio is a mystery, especially after a rousing appearance (including a four-minute standing ovation) at 1983's Cambridge Folk Festival. Chris Tarrant, Stuart Hall and MIKE HARDING were all enamoured of their comic-musical routines. Sadly, the group split in 1985, Clive subsequently deciding to take on a more serious vocation as a member of R. CAJUN & THE ZYDECO BROTHERS.

ROARING JELLY issued a compilation, **HERE'S SOME WE MADE EARLER** (2004) {*6}, available from Clive at his solo gigs, prompting Clive and Derek to reunite as The OMEGA 3 with Graeme Taylor, releasing (**ESSENTIAL BATTY ACIDS** {*6} in 2007. Former ROARING JELLY member Hennessy was said to be not amused - or was that part of the joke? *MCS*

Clive Harvey (b. Nov 27 '45, Watford, Hertfordshire) - vocals, ukulele, guitar, harmonica / **Derek Pearce** (b. Sep 11 '48, Birmingham, Warwickshire) - vocals, multi / **Mick Hennessy** (b. Derby, Derbyshire) - vocals, bass (ex-DRUIDS)

UK: Free Reed — US: not issued

Feb 77. (lp) *(FRR 013)* **ROARING JELLY'S GOLDEN GRATES** [ ] [–]
- Family Christmas / (Tucked up in a flowerbed with my) Rose / Mansfield royal visit / Trev and the Rock and Roll Rockets / Mazawattee tea-break / Home-to-tea-girl / Last night on the back porch / Monster movie nightmare blues / Riff-raff / What a silly place to kiss a girl / For the sake of days gone by / You and me and a wind-up gramophone. *(cd-iss. Jun 08 +=; FRRR 17)- (Michael Hebbert): The Rampin' Cat LP tracks*

UK: Spot — US: not issued

Nov 80. (7" m) *(SPOT 4)* CHRISTMAS IN AUSTRALIA. / Poor Little Turkey [live] / Family Christmas [live] [ ] [–]

next featured guests including **Graeme Taylor** - guitar

UK: Topic — US: not issued

Jun 81. (lp) *(12TS 420)* **IN THE ROAR** [ ] [–]
- Beethoven's bluebeat / Bucketful of mud / Maybe it's just as well / Irretrievable breakdown / Cajun gumbo / Valerie Wilkins / Maracas in Caracas (Edmundo's song) / Dirty little stop-out / Thundercloud / The ides of March / Not for the soul / Christmas in Australia / Bed bug.

—— after their split in 1985, Harvey formed the Beverley Brothers with Ian Carter; later he joined R. CAJUN & THE ZYDECO BROTHERS and another trio, the Back Seat Jivers.

The OMEGA 3

Harvey + **Pearce** plus **Graeme Taylor**

		A.D.A.	not issued
Oct 07	(cd) *(ADA 111CD)* **ESSENTIAL BATTY ACIDS**	– mail-o	–

- It's only Thursday (the clothes peg song) / Second song (we don't look as stupid as we are) / Baby baby / Bournemouth / Peeing in the swimming pool (Harvey's Water Music) / Money won't make me happy / Scrambled eggs / 1 in 7 / Banjovi / My dog has fleas / The menopause calypso (naturally, naturally) / Big opening number / Christmas in Australia 07 [mad wombat dance mix] / Massive rug sale.

Alan ROBERTS

Born December 18, 1946, in Scotland, ALAN ROBERTS was the father of folk guitarist ALASDAIR ROBERTS. Though Alan doesn't have much of a discography, he is unique in the fact that he figures in all three books of The Great Folk Discography, from Volume I, "Early Pioneers and Legends" (under the ALEX CAMPBELL entry, for the 1979 'CRM' project set with DOUGIE MACLEAN) to Volume III, "Celtic and World Music" (in the MACLEAN section again, for their collaborative 1979 LP 'Caledonia' and a session credit on his 'Snaigow' album).

With his wife, the German booking agent and promoter Annegret, Alan continued to work in folk music in the 1980s and onwards, discovering the likes of SILLY WIZARD, The TANNAHILL WEAVERS and NIC JONES. Sadly, just as his son Alasdair's career was beginning to bloom, he passed away on August 13, 2001. *MCS*

Alasdair ROBERTS

Unless you've been keeping up to date with post-millennium nu-folk artists, you may have missed the work of the genre's brightest and most unassuming star, ALASDAIR ROBERTS - and more's the pity. From aspiring indie troubadour to the 2000s' most endearing voice of folk (both traditional and contemporary), Callander's favourite export has been tipped by many pundits to become the next big thing. It's only a matter of time.

Born August 8, 1977 in Swabia, Germany, but raised in the village of Kilmahog near Callander in Stirlingshire, Scotland by his German mother Annegret (a booking agent and promoter) and his father and main influence, 1970s folk guitarist ALAN ROBERTS, he was only a teenager when he followed in his father's footsteps, having been inspired by his friend and colleague, folk guitar hero NIC JONES.

Ali's initial venture into music was as a member of APPENDIX OUT (alongside Dave Elcock and Kenny McBride), an alt/indie act formed in Glasgow in the summer of 1994. PALACE leader and label chief WILL OLDHAM released their first single, 'Ice Age', in 1996. Later the group of acoustic no-fi folkies enlisted the help of cellist Louise D and percussionist Eva Peck, the latter bringing undoctored rhythm to the combo's folky weepcore.

With the APPENDIX OUT line-up almost finalised, they contributed material to the Up Records compilation CD '4x4', while the split single 'Well-Lit Tonight' was much sought after in some quarters. This immediately caught the attention of labels eagerly planning to take folk/country screaming into the the 21st century, but astonishingly it was US imprint Drag City who signed the band in 1997, adding them to a list of brilliant new-generation songsmiths. This prompted the release of the outfit's debut set **THE RYE BEARS A POISON** (1997) {*6}, a groundbreaking achievement for an ostensibly minor band in 1997. With its calming guitars, emotional vocals and splendid tranquillity, reminiscent of NICK DRAKE's 'Pink Moon' era, it was most definitely a Sunday-morning record.

ROBERTS added guitarist and percussionist Gareth Eggie, and Eva Peck on flute and keyboards, to the cauldron of country karma, both making their debuts on the band's second and most realised work, **DAYLIGHT SAVING** (1999) {*7}. Sticking with the WILL OLDHAM-vs-Smog formula, the set was unique in its own right, with the opener 'Foundling' leading the way into a record that should have blasted Belle And Sebastian out of the water.

The troupe's style was very much from the heart of Americana, but they should still have been an asset to a new Scottish music to rival the Postcard Records era. Their softly-sung harmonies, mandolin breaks and acoustic set-ups were very much rooted in traditional folk (they even covered ANNE BRIGGS's 'Lowlands'), giving them the opportunity to shine where other bands would only sparkle. 'Lieder Fur Kaspar Hauser' (a 7" EP) was the group's next release, late in 1999. It featured the tracks 'Ein Grauerstar In Der Kavallerie' and the sombre instrumental 'An Der Nachtimmel Gewohnt'.

A perfect marriage of acoustic and electric lo-fi folk, the Ryan Murphy-produced **THE NIGHT IS ADVANCING** (2001) {*7} continued to move the American desert gently towards the Highlands on tracks such as 'Year Waxing, Year Waning', 'A Path To Our Beds' and the closing 'Organise A March'.

Released almost simultaneously, ROBERTS's own traditionally-sourced solo venture **THE CROOK OF MY ARM** (2001) {*7}, recorded as ALASDAIR ROBERTS for Secretly Canadian Records over a single day in Glasgow (subsequently his home city), found him in contemplative mood on the likes of 'Lord Gregory', 'As I Came In By Huntly Town', 'The Magpie's Nest' and 'The False Bride'.

Ali regrouped APPENDIX OUT in 2002 for their fantastic and folksy five-track covers EP 'A Warm And Yeasty Corner', which included a rendition of The INCREDIBLE STRING BAND's 'A Very Cellular Song' and EWAN MacCOLL's 'The First Time Ever I Saw Your Face'. 'Sally Free And Easy' and 'Josephine' were also given the APPENDIX OUT spin, with hushed flutes, pianos and a whole host of acoustic instruments adding to the sparse effect.

His second solo set (but still featuring Appendix Out members), **FAREWELL SORROW** (2003) {*8}, reaped rewards on a critical level for the beauty of pastorals like 'Join Our Lusty Chorus' and 'Slowly Growing Old', while the opening title track and 'Carousing' harked back to early STEELEYE SPAN and the FAIRPORTs.

Bringing together a wide range of established neo-traditionalists (including old collaborator WILL OLDHAM, ex-Belle And Sebastian star Isobel Campbell, ex-BATTLEFIELD BAND fiddler JOHN McCUSKER, Gareth Eggie, et al), **NO EARTHLY MAN** (2005) {*7} was Alasdair's stab at a fully traditional Brit-folk album, comprised mostly of long murder ballads (mainly from the Child collection). Ghostly melodramas such as 'Lord Ronald', 'The Cruel Mother' (once a favourite of SHIRLEY COLLINS, LIZZIE HIGGINS and SILLY WIZARD) and 'The Two Brothers' (formerly the property of BELLE STEWART) get the ROBERTS lo-fi-folk treatment.

Commonly known as 'Polly Vaughan', 'Molly Bawn' dates from the 17th Century and was recorded by Packie Manus Byrne, while a number of the ballads are history lessons in themselves. Most purists will recognise 'Sweet William' (collected by Cecil Sharp) and the best of the set, 'A Lyke Wake Dirge', in this version as far removed from The YOUNG TRADITION or PENTANGLE as you could get. Whether this album resurrects tradition and folklore in folk, or is simply another vocal exercise for ROBERTS, other historians and critics are invited to decide.

A Caledonian hybrid of Scottish folklore ballad and off-kilter lo-fi, **SPOILS** (2009) {*7}
was delivered in the unmistakable squeaky Scots accent that one had come to expect. Supported by several musicians including Tom Crossley, Alex Neilson, Niko-Matti Ahti, Gordon Ferries, Emily McLaren, David McGuinness and Alison McGillivray, ROBERTS lyrically harked back to days of Norse sea raids, religious fishermen and "ships made of fingernails". 'Unyoked Oxen Turn', 'You Muses Assist' and 'The Book Of Doves' (with a mention of "the plains of Slamannan") press the right buttons, although the tunes carry the weight of ye-olde-traditional too far. But let Alasdair take you back to wherever you want. All you need is imagination and complete darkness to complete the effect.

Containing only one short original composition (the instrumental 'Kilmahog Saturday Afternoon'), the otherwise traditionally-sourced **TOO LONG IN THIS CONDITION** (2010) {*7} raises Brit-Celtic ghosts with a tinge of tactful humour. Readings of 'Long Lankin', 'The Golden Vanity', 'Barbara Allen' and 'The Lover's Ghost' sound as though they had arisen from the graves of Bonnie Prince Charlie, Robert Burns and a kindred host of Caledonian kings. *MCS*

APPENDIX OUT

Ali Roberts - vocals, guitar / **Dave Elcock** + **Kenny McBride** - bass, violin, keyboards

UK Palace — US Palace

Dec 96. (ltd-7") *(<PR 10>)* ICE AGE. / Pissed With You — Jan 96

—— **Eva Peck** - drums, vocals / **Louise D** - cello

Creeping Bent — not issued

Sep 97. (7") *(bent 027)* WELL-LIT TONIGHT. / (other track by The Leopards)

Drag City — Drag City

Oct 97. (lp/cd) *(<DC 126/+CD>)* **THE RYE BEARS A POISON**
- Our sea / Brazil / East Coast wedding / Many-legged boatmen / Frozen blight / Wild I lived in Flanders / Seagulls, belts / Lassie, lie near me / The harp key / Autumn.

Jun 98. (7") *(bent 034)* LASSIE, LIE NEAR ME. / (other track by Policecat)

(above issued on Creeping Bent, below on Liquefaction/Bad Jazz)

Jul 98. (7" ep) *<Bebop 3>* SECOND PERTHSHIRE HOUSE SONG / Round Reel Of Eight / Twelve Of Them / Hay Bale Blues. / (others by Songs: Ohia)
(UK-iss. 2000 on Bad Jazz; same)

Jan 99. (7" ep) *(milk 001)* WILD LIVING / Boyhood. / (other three by the MONGERS)

(above issued on Galvani)

—— **Roberts** recruited **Tom Crossley** - drums (of International Airport) / **Gareth Eggie** - guitar, percussion / **Dave Elcock** + **Annabel Wright**

Jul 99. (lp/cd) *(<DC 152/+CD>)* **DAYLIGHT SAVING** — Apr 99
- Foundling / The grey havens / Tangled hair / The scything / Little owl / Row upstream / Merchant city / Exile / Arcane lore. *(lp re-iss. Aug 00; same)*

Nov 99. (7") *<WEST 007>* LIEDER FUR KASPAR HAUSER
- Ein grauerstar in der kavallerie / An den nachtimmel gewohnt.

(above on Western Vinyl)

—— added **Mark Harvey** (of Den Alma; with Gareth)

Mar 01. (cd/lp) *(<DC 189 CD/LP>)* **THE NIGHT IS ADVANCING** — Apr 01
- A path to our beds / The seven widows (the sprigs of night) / The groves of Lebanon / Golden tablets of the sun / Year waxing, year waning / Fortified jackdaw grove / The night is advancing / Cyclone's vernal retreat / (Bringing the yearlings) Home / Hexen in the anticyclone / Campfire's burning (round) / Organise a march.

not issued — Temporary Residence

2001. (cd-ep) *<none>* TRAVELS IN CONSTANTS VOLUME 13
- Daylight saving, Gibson Street (part one) / Speech / Ritual ingestion of a yellow rhizome / Invocation of the corn mother / Daylight saving, Gibson Street (part two).

Shingle Street — not issued

Apr 02. (cd-ep) *(Shing 001)* A WARM AND YEASTY CORNER
- Window over the bay / Sally free and easy / The first time ever I saw your face / Josephine / A very cellular song (coda).

ALASDAIR ROBERTS

In 2000, (Jason) Molina & ROBERTS released double-A single 'Ten Thousand Miles' + 'The Green Mossy Banks Of The Lea' *(SC 16)*

Secretly Canadian — Secretly Canadian

Apr 01. (cd/lp) *(<SC 48 CD/LP>)* **THE CROOK OF MY ARM**
- Lord Gregory / As I came in by Huntly town / Bonnie lass among the heather / The magpie's nest / Ploughboy lads / Lowlands / Master Kilby / Standing in yon flowery garden / Ye banks and braes o' bonny Doon / The false bride / The month of January / The wife of Usher's well.

Rough Trade — Drag City

Apr 03. (cd/lp) *(RTRADE 094) <DC 240 CD/LP>* **FAREWELL SORROW**
- Farewell sorrow / Join our lusty chorus / Carousing / I fell in love / I went hunting / Down where the willow wands weep / When a man's in love he feels no cold / Come, my darling Polly / The whole house is singing / I walked abroad in an evil hour / I am a young man / Slowly growing old.

Drag City — Drag City

Mar 05. (cd/lp) *(<DC 283 CD/LP>)* **NO EARTHLY MAN**
- Lord Ronald / Molly Bawn / The cruel mother / On the banks of red roses / The two brothers / Admiral Cole / Sweet William / A lyke wake dirge.

Jan 07. (cd/lp) *(<DC 326 CD/LP>)* **THE AMBER GATHERERS**
- Riddle me this / Where twines the path / Waxwing / I had a kiss of the king's hand / Cruel war / Let me lie and bleed awhile / Firewater / River Rhine / I have a charm / Old men of the shells / Calfless cow.

May 09. (cd/lp) *(<DC 392 CD/LP>)* **SPOILS**
- The flyting of grief and joy (eternal return) / You muses assist / So bored was I (dark triad) / Unyoked oxen turn / The book of doves / Ned Ludd's rant (for a world rebarbarised) / Hazel forks / Under no enchantment (but my own).

Oct 09. (12" ep/cd-ep) *(<DC 394/+CD>)* THE WYRD MEME
- The hallucinator and the king of the silver ship of time / The yarn unraveller / The royal road at the world's end / Coral and tar.

Jun 10. (ltd-7" ep; by ALASDAIR ROBERTS & JACKIE OATES) *<RMV 403>*
A SELECTIONS OF MARCHES, QUICKSTEPS, LAMENTS, STRATHSPEYS, REELS AND COUNTRY DANCES
- The bloody fields of Flanders - The red haired boy / Mrs MacDonald of Dunacht - Cunnla larach do Thaicaideran / Hard is my fate traveller's joy / Hyperboreans.

(above issued on Room 40)

Jun 10. (cd/lp) *(<DC 421 CD/LP>)* **TOO LONG IN THIS CONDITION**
- The daemon lover / Young Emily / Long Lankin / The two sisters / Little Sir Hugh / Kilmahog Saturday afternoon / The Golden Vanity / The burning of Auchindoun / The lover's ghost / What put the blood on your right shoulder, son? / Barbara Allen.

AMALGAMATED SONS OF REST

Alasdair Roberts + **Jason Molina** + **Will Oldham**

not issued — Galaxia

Sep 02. (m-cd,m-lp) *<GLX 16>* **AMALGAMATED SONS OF REST**
- Maa bonny lad / My Donal / The gypsy he-witch / The last house / Major march / Jennie Blackbird's blues. *(hidden +=)* - I will be good.

Kathryn ROBERTS (⟹ EQUATION)

David ROTHERAY (⟹ HOMESPUN)

RUBUS (⟹ The DEVIL'S INTERVAL)

RUBY BLUE

Formed in Edinburgh in 1986 by gorgeous, Massachusetts-born drama student Rebecca Pidgeon (raised from five years old in Edinburgh) and Roger Fife. Completing the quartet with Anthony Coote and Erika Spotswood (later Woods), the group released their debut album, **GLANCES ASKANCES** (1987) {*6}, on Dave Kitson's Red Flame imprint.

A fresh, spontaneous combination of pop, folk and jazz, the record showcased Pidgeon's high, purist-folk vocals (shades of ANNE BRIGGS and SANDY DENNY), which brought a traditional feel to the proceedings. With radio support from the likes of DJs Andy Kershaw and Nicky Campbell, the band soon became the subject of major-label interest and signed to Fontana at the turn of the decade. By this point they'd bolstered their sound with drums, while attracting attention for support slots for the likes of JOHN MARTYN, VAN MORRISON and MARTIN STEPHENSON.

Yet despite all the media attention, the band's big-league set **DOWN FROM ABOVE** (1990) {*4} failed to spawn a hit single, although tracks such as 'Epitaph' (about the 1989 Marchioness pleasure boat disaster on the Thames, with lyrics by Rebecca's husband, David Mamet) were thought-provoking. Erika and Roger were survivors of the tragedy, in which 51 lives were lost.

Rebecca's final recording with the band came at the end of the year in the shape of the 'Can It Be' single (she was fast becoming a film star, having appeared opposite Anthony Hopkins in 1988's 'The Dawning'). Also included on the CD single was a glacial folk cover of CYRIL TAWNEY's 'Sally Free And Easy' and 'The Raven', the latter a haunting track co-written, like 'Epitaph', with her playwright husband. Rebecca subsequently released a number of solo sets, but her only excursion into Celtic-folk was the traditionally-rich 'Four Marys' (1998), which featured Scottish musician JOHNNY CUNNINGHAM and uillean piper Jerry O'Sullivan.

Post-Pidgeon, the band carried on with Erika as vocalist, re-signing to Red Flame and releasing a couple more albums, **PARADISE** (1992) {*3} and **ALMOST NAKED** (1993) {*3}, before finally splitting. *MCS*

Rebecca Pidgeon (b. Oct 10 '65, Cambridge, Massachusetts) - vocals / **Roger Fife** (b. 1963) - guitar, bass / with **Anthony Coote** - bass / **Erika Spotswood** (later Erika Woods) - backing vocals / plus drummer **Chris Buck**

UK Red Flame — US not issued

Jun 87. (7") *(RF7-53)* GIVE US OUR FLAG BACK. / The Quiet Mind

Sep 87. (lp) *(RF-53)* **GLANCES ASKANCES**
- Give us our flag back / The quiet mind / Just relax / So unlike me / Walking home / The meaning of life / Wintry day / Sitting in the cafe / Bless you. *(cd-iss. Jan 91; RFCD 2)*

Sep 87. (7"/12") *(RF 7/12-56)* SO UNLIKE ME. / Life And Times Of The 20th Century

Mar 88. (7") *(RF7-57)* BECAUSE. / The Ruby Blue
(12"+=) *(RF12-57)* - The ruby blue (extended).

Nov 88. (7") *(RF7-59)* BLOOMSBURY BLUE. / Save Me
(12"+=) *(RF12-59)* - Childs song.

Feb 89. (7") *(RF7-62)* STAND TOGETHER. / Easy -
(12"+=) *(RF12-62)* - Too many suitcases.

Fontana — not issued

Apr 90. (7") *(RB 1)* THE QUIET MIND (FOR JOE). / POSITIVE LOVE SONG -
(12"+=)(cd-s+=) *(RB 1-12)(RBCD 1)* - Say goodbye (live).

Apr 90. (cd/c/lp) *(842568-2/-4/-1)* **DOWN FROM ABOVE** -
- Primitive man / The quiet mind / Take your money / Can it be / Away from here / Pavan / Stand together / Betty's last letter / Bloomsbury blue / Midnight road / Not alone / Song of the mermaid / Something's gone wrong / Epitaph.

Jun 90. (7") *(RB 2)* PRIMITIVE MAN. / The Traveller -
(12"+=)(cd-s+=) *(RF 2-12)(RFCD 2)* - ('A' extended) / Betty's last letter.

Nov 90. (7") *(RB 3)* CAN IT BE. / Something's Gone Wrong (Chiltern radio session) -
(cd-s+=) *(RBCD 3)* - Sally free and easy / The raven.

now without Coote and without Rebecca Pidgeon, who married and later went solo, releasing three jazz-orientated albums for Chesky, 'The Raven' (1994), 'The New York Girls' Club' (1996) and 'Four Marys' (1998); she became a film star.

—— **Erika** now lead vocals + with new drummer **Karlos Edwards**

Red Flame — not issued

Jun 91. (7") *(RF7-63)* I FEEL GOOD NOW. / Get Your Life Back -
(12"+=) *(RF12-63)* - Am I turning into you?
(cd-s+=) *(RFCD-63)* - Too far / Smile slow.

Jan 92. (c; fan club) *(TAPE 2)* **PARADISE** - -
- Bless you / Strength of mind / Paradise / Elvis / Should know better / I feel good now / Beyond us / Too far / High 'n' low.

Mar 93. (cd) *(RFCD 54)* **ALMOST NAKED** -
- Recreate your kiss / New way / High for a while / Goddess / You'll find out / I still love you / Done my thinking / Strength of mind / Magnificent truth / Almost naked.

Jun 93. (cd-ep) *(RFSCD 64)* DONE MY THINKING / Magnificent Truth / Almost Naked -

—— split for the final time after above

- (5-7*) compilations, etc.-

Jan 92. (cd) *Red Flame; (RFCD 5)* **BROKEN WATER** -
- Easy / Stand together / Away from here / Life and times of the 20th century / Somebody say something / Because / Shining snow / Save me / Childs song / The ruby blue / Too many suitcases / Bloomsbury blue / Betty / Stuart.

Kate RUSBY

Born December 1, 1973, in Sheffield, Yorkshire, Kate is one of the rare breed of folk artist to have had a Mercury Prize nomination. Growing up as part of a talented musical family from Barnsley, it's no wonder that this English folk singer and multi-instrumentalist has made some of the best folk music since Sinead O'Connor's earlier releases.

At the age of 12, RUSBY had formed a band with her older sister Emma, playing fiddle and guitar and stretching her vocal talents to maximum effect. She launched her career at the Holmfirth Festival when she was only 15, making friends with rising folk star and fellow Barnsley girl KATHRYN ROBERTS.

The two began recording together (including time spent with INTUITION), releasing much of their material on **KATE RUSBY & KATHRYN ROBERTS** (1995) {*7}, an album which was issued to much acclaim and was named as the fRoots Album of the Year. ROBERTS's vocals had a more mature sound than her sidekick RUSBY's, which were at this stage thrillingly raw and in development. RUSBY's debut solo set, the underrated **HOURGLASS** (1997) {*6}, saw her taking an independent stance when the album grew extremely popular on both sides of the Atlantic. She had already guested on the BATTLEFIELD BAND's 'Across The Borders' set (1997) and The POOZIES' 'Come Raise Your Head' (1997) and 'Infinite Blue', (1998), marking her out as a singer in demand.

SLEEPLESS (1999) {*7} was RUSBY's second solo album. Demonstrating a more mature tone, the Mercury Prize-nomination set included covers of IRIS DeMENT's 'Our Town' and trad numbers 'I Wonder What Is Keeping My Love True This Night', 'The Unquiet Grave' and 'The Fairest Of All Yarrow'.

With another session cast list featuring Ian Carr, DANNY THOMPSON, ANDY CUTTING, EDDI READER, Ewen Vernal, Tim O'Brien, Michael McGoldrick, Malcolm Stitt, John Jones and her producer and husband JOHN McCUSKER (of BATTLEFIELD BAND), **LITTLE LIGHTS** (2001) {*6} was as bright as the title suggested, although traditional fare was slightly overshadowed by her RICHARD THOMPSON recital 'Withered And Died'. **10** (2002) {*5} was a stopgap collection, largely comprising re-mastered recordings and live cuts.

Twinning some of the best of her previously recorded songs with new material by McCUSKER, the **HEARTLANDS** (2003) {*6} soundtrack was a wee gem that sparkled quite independently of the film that gave rise to it.

The pair were already the golden couple of folk, individually and collectively trailing a history of acclaim and awards, and this set made it easy to see why: "The album itself is both vibrant and soothing, and a beguiling demonstration that less is more", was how one critic put it. Almost simultaneously, and with more or less the same musicians, **UNDERNEATH THE STARS** (2003) {*6} found her picking out her best trad songs, including her personal favourite 'The Blind Harper'.

Kate's fear of flying provided the title of her next set, **THE GIRL WHO COULDN'T FLY** (2005) {*7}. Although not present among the session list of usual suspects (which included RODDY WOOMBLE, KRIS DREVER and KELLIE WHILE), ex-Blur star Graham Coxon put in a contribution by way of the sleeve artwork. The record also featured a cover of the 1952 pop-ballad nugget 'You Belong To Me'.

Having since parted company with McCUSKER domestically, **AWKWARD ANNIE** (2007) {*6} was her first self-produced effort. 'Bitter Boy' was the pick of her own compositions, while the trad 'John Barbury' (also known as 'Fause Foodrage', Child ballad 89) made the set a worthwhile buy. An interesting bonus track was her reading of The Kinks' 'The Village Green Preservation Society', which became the theme to the TV sitcom 'Jam And Jerusalem'.

A standby of every folk artist around the world, festive albums are not everyone's cup of tea, but **SWEET BELLS** (2008) {*7} was a beautifully free-flowing set, giving Yorkshire carols pride of place. At the suggestion of Jennifer Saunders, co-star and co-writer of 'Jam And Jerusalem', Kate took on the task of writing her next solo work, **MAKE THE LIGHT** (2010) {*7}, alone. Co-produced with her brother Joe Rusby, and highlighting another array of talented musicians that included her new husband Damien O'Kane (their daughter was born in 2009), the album displayed an eclectic approach, from the Celtic-tinged 'The Wishing Wife' to alt-country dirge 'Lately'. *MCS*

Kate Rusby - vocals, piano, acoustic guitar (ex-INTUITION) / with session people incl. Ian Carr, John McCusker and Michael McGoldrick

UK Pure — US Compass

May 95. (cd/c; by KATE RUSBY & KATHRYN ROBERTS) *(PRCD/PRMC 01)* **KATE RUSBY & KATHRYN ROBERTS** -
- Recruited collier / Ned on the hill / Lorry ride / The queen and the soldier / Courting is a pleasure / Constant lovers / Dark-eyed sailor / Hunting the hare / Plains of Waterloo / Exile. *<US cd-iss. Jan 99 on Compass; COM 4270>*

Mar 97. (cd) *(PRCD 02)* **HOURGLASS** -
- Sir Eglamore / As I roved out / Jolly ploughboys / Annan waters / Stananivy - Jack and Jill / A rose in April / Radio sweethearts / I am stretched on your grave / Old man time / Drowned lovers / Bold Riley. *<US-iss. Aug 98 on Compass; COM 4255>*

Nov 98. (cd-s) *(PRCD 04)* COWSONG / Botany Bay / The Wild Goose (live) -

May 99. (cd) *(PRCD 06) <COM 4277>* **SLEEPLESS** Aug 99
- Cobbler's daughter / I wonder what is keeping my true love / The fairest of all Yarrow / Unquiet grave / Sho heen / Sweet bride / All God's angels / The wild goose / The duke and the tinker / Our town / Sleepless sailor / Cowsong.

Jun 01. (cd) *(PRCD 07) <COM 4310>* **LITTLE LIGHTS** 75
- Playing of ball / I courted a sailor / Withered and died / Merry green broom / Let the cold wind blow / Canaan's land / Some tyrant / William and Davy / Who will sing me lullabies? / Matt Hyland / My young man.

Oct 02. (cd) *(PRCD 10) <COM 4350>* **10** (collection of re-mastered ***, live ** and new versions *) Jan 03
- The recruited collier (*) / I wish / Over you now / The sleepless sailor (*) / The fairest of all Yarrow (*) / I wonder what is keeping my true love (*) / Sweet bride (***) / The maid of Llanwellyn (*) / The wild goose (*) / Sir Eglamore (**) / Night visiting song (***) / Cowsong (***) / Botany Bay (*) / Drowned lovers (**) / Bold Riley (***).

May 03. (cd) *(PRCD 11)* **HEARTLANDS** (soundtrack by KATE RUSBY ** & JOHN McCUSKER *) -
- Colin's farewell (*) / Sweet bride (**) / Weeping crisps (*) / The fairest of all Yarrow (**) / I wonder what is keeping my true love (**/*) / Leafy moped (*) / William and Davy - instrumental (**) / Drowned lovers (**/*) / The wild goose (**/*) / Beer garden (*) / I saw that Sandra (*) / Let the cold wind blow (**) / Yodelling song (TIM O'BRIEN) / The brownies (*) / Over you now (**) / Round the next corner (* & TIM O'BRIEN) / The sleepless sailor (**).

Aug 03. (cd) *(PRCD 12) <COM 4370>* **UNDERNEATH THE STARS** Jan 04
- The good man / The daughter of Megan / Let me be / Cruel / The blind harper / The white cockade / Young James / Falling / Bring me a boat / Polly / Sweet William's ghost / Underneath the stars.

Nov 05. (cd) *(PRCD 17) <COM 4420>* **THE GIRL WHO COULDN'T FLY**

- Game of all fours / The lark / No names / Mary Blaize / A ballad / You belong to me / Elfin knight / Bonnie house of Airlie / Moon shadow / Wandering soul / Fare thee well. *(bonus +=)* - Little Jack Frost.

In summer '06 Kate was co-credited on Ronan Keating's UK Top 10 hit 'All Over Again'.

Pure Pure

Sep 07. (cd) (*<PRCD 23>*) **AWKWARD ANNIE**
- Awkward Annie / Bitter boy / John Barbury / High on a hill / Farewell / Planets / The old man / Andrew Lammie / Streams of Nancy / Daughter of heaven / Blooming heather / The village green preservation society.

May 08. (cd-s) *(PRCD 27)* WHO KNOWS WHERE THE TIME GOES? / Elfin Knight ('Jam And Jerusalem' wedding version) □ ⊟

Dec 08. (cd) *(PRCD 28)* **SWEET BELLS** (festive) □ ⊟
- Here we come a-wassailing / Sweet bells / Poor old horse / Hark the herald / Holly and the ivy / Hark hark / Candlemas eve / Hail chime on / Serving girl's holiday / Awake arise / Miners dream.

Nov 10. (cd) *(PRCD 32)* **MAKE THE LIGHT** □ ⊟
- The wishing wife / The mocking bird / Let them fly / Only hope / Lately / Shout to the devil / Green fields / Fair weather friend / Walk the road / Not me / Four stars.

Mick RYAN

With whoever he collaborates alongside, and there's been more than a few, underrated folk singer MICK RYAN (born 18th May 1953, Swindon, Wiltshire) has been performing nigh-on four decades. Although many folk fans outside his locale might've missed him first time around when he was part of 70s outfit Mrs Casey's Choice and its splinter duo MICK RYAN & JON BURGE (**FAIR WAS THE CITY** (1978) {*5}), he's certainly come of age in recent times having teamed up with multi-in"strum"entalist PETE HARRIS, a veteran of roots outfits The New St. George, the Bursledon Village Band (from Hampshire), The Bob Pearce Blues Band and his own Pete Harris Blues Band.

Folk Roots raved about the CROWS, a traditional 80s act that initially housed the aforemention Harris, plus Silas alumni James Patterson and Ralph Jordan on their well-received eponymous LP, **CROWS** (1980) {*6}; covers included were from RICHARD THOMPSON ('Withered And Died'), SANDY DENNY ('Long, Long Time') and DYLAN ('Just Like A Woman').

Ryan would subsequently recruit Steven Faux for the long-time-coming **NO BONES OR GREASE** (1987) {*6}. It would be around this time that Ryan would kickstart another folk-based quartet, FIELDWORK; **SHARPEN THE SICKLE** (1986) {*6} is probably the one to look out for as the rest just might be a tad hard to track down.

The combination of MICK RYAN & PETE HARRIS got underway in 1993, although their well-crafted songs (traditionally-sourced/Mick compositions arranged by Pete) couldn't find their way past the limited-edition cassette format; their debut CD, **THE WIDOW'S PROMISE** (1998) {*6}, was in fact a collection of two tapes from the mid-90s. But then Wild Goose Records came a-calling toward the end the millennium.

HARD SEASON (1999) {*7} recalled the halcyon days of BOB FOX, TONY ROSE and NIC JONES, none more so derivative (and that's not a put down) as set highlights 'The Leaves Of Life' and 'Night Visiting Song'. **THE LONG ROAD** (2002) {*6} extended their journey, managing airplay as far afield as Australia and America for such gems like 'The Wrong Side Of The World' and 'Song For John'. Fiddler Paul Burgess (of The OLD SWAN BAND) and oboe-player Paul Sartin (from DR. FAUSTUS and BELSHAZZAR'S FEAST) were also on the guest list (alongside associate TIM VAN EYKEN on melodeon) for 2004's **SOMETHING TO SHOW** {*6}. Another formulaic piece, it showcased two outsider ballads from Ian Palmer ('The Queen Of The May') and Graham Moore ('The Last Of England').

The latter songsmith was also responsible for 'A Tolpuddle Man', a part of the pair's Irish-tinged follow-up, **THE ISLAND OF APPLES** (2007) {*6}; the title track stems from the prophetic return of King Arthur from his Glastonbury burial ground; the anthemic finale 'The Song Goes On' pays homage to the late, great CYRIL TAWNEY.

Mick's prolific work as part of the said duo and his FIELDWORK project sets **THE VOYAGE** (1998) {*6} and **TANKS FOR THE MEMORY** (2003) {*6} were put to one side for his most ambitious set to date, **THE NAVVY'S WIFE** (2008) {*7}. A tribute to the itinerant ways of wifes of canal and railway workers, the record featured a host of folk elite, namely JACKIE OATES, ROGER WATSON, Paul Downes, and other vocalists Judy Dunlop and Heather Bradford; the similarly-thematic **THE PAUPER'S PATH to Hope** (2011) {*6} was also a delight.

If variety be the spice of life, Mick has it in bundles, and one can't fault his dexterity and unlimited passion for bringing traditional folk music from beyond its eternal sell-by-date. This was apparent on two further collaborative works. Not totally foresaking his dual role with Harris (just taking a wee break), his decision to work with a new sidekick PAUL DOWNES (on vocals and instruments) was another master-stroke. So far they pair have combined for two albums, **GRAND CONVERSATION** (2008) {*6} and **AWAY IN THE WEST** (2010) {*6}, the latter - with guests Paul Hutchinson on accordion and JACKIE OATES on fiddle - the first to include the absorbing 'The Pauper's Path' track. *MCS*

MICK RYAN & JON BURGE

Mick Ryan - vocals / **Jon Burge** - guitar, etc.

UK Trailer US not issued

1978. (lp) *(LTRA 506)* **FAIR WAS THE CITY** □ ⊟
- Lucy Wan / Football match / January / Young girl cut down in her prime / Brown Robin's confession / Rufford Park poachers / Monday morning / English lord / Green beds / Cruel ship's carpenter / Widow of Westmoreland's daughter / Banks of the roses.

CROWS

Mick Ryan + Jon Burge + Silas: James Patterson + Ralph Jordan

Dingle's not issued

1980. (lp) *(DIN 317)* **CROWS** □ ⊟
- Two magicians / Moreton Bay / Withered and died / Northfields / Devil and the farmer's wife / Long, long time / Coast of Peru / Just like a woman / Bold Wolfe / Lonesome sea / Take them away.

now down to **Ryan + Steven Faux** (Patterson Jordan Dipper released an eponymous CD for Wild Goose in 2000)

Dragon not issued

1987. (lp) *(DRGN 861)* **NO BONES OR GREASE** □ ⊟

FIELDWORK

aka **Mick Ryan** + three other members

Mek not issued

Oct 86. (lp) *(MEK 003)* **SHARPEN THE SICKLE** □ ⊟
- Sharpen the sickle / Song of the lower classes / Sunna na / Major road ahead / East Ohio / Unemployment / Dark-haired Liza - Do it again Ikey - I saw diamonds / Nail it down.

self-rel. not issued

1988. (7"ep) *(SUN 002)* THE BALLAD OF CRANE TINKERMAN □ ⊟
- The ballad of Crane Tinkerman / The great silkie / Do you see my face / Fishing.

1991. (cd) *(none)* **FROM HUMDRUM TO TONGUE DRUM** □ ⊟
- Acid rain / Springhill / Sharpen the sickle / The go'ole captain / Horses brawl / Fishing / Do you see my face / Unemployment / The captain cried / Abrasha's lament / The great silkie / Zhankoye / The fisherman sleeps / Lament for a sailor.

MICK RYAN & PETE HARRIS

with **Pete Harris** - vocals, multi / + session people

Wild Goose not issued

1993. (c) *(WGS 261MC)* **DRINK UP THE SUN** □ ⊟
- Adieu, adieu / Poor couple / Rambling boys of pleasure / Prison farm blues / Night of the hunter / John Barleycorn / Channels / The bird in the bush / The false bride / Blues / Bonny light horseman.

1995. (c; by MICK RYAN) *(none)* **A DAY'S WORK** □ ⊟

1996. (c) *(none)* **ANOTHER TIME ANOTHER PLACE** □ ⊟

1996. (c; as CANTORIS) *(WGS 282MC)* **HOWLING AT THE MOON** □ ⊟
- Bold Nelson's praise / Children of the mine / The bells of Rhymney / Love is life / The prince of peacve / Gather and stand / The wagon of the Lord / The hangman / Prison bars / Bright shining morning.

Terra Nova not issued

Apr 98. (cd) *(TERRCD 011)* **THE WIDOW'S PROMISE** [compilation of two cassettes] □ ⊟
- The widow's promise / Bonny hight horseman / The old couple / Poor old horse / The man I killed / Channels / Hash house blues / Rambleaway / Salisbury Plain / Love is life / Adieu adieu.

Wild Goose not issued

Aug 99. (cd) *(WGS 295CD)* **HARD SEASON** □ ⊟
- I won't take that lying down / Spencer the rover / Long hard season / The lass of Islington / The drunkard's lament / Leaves of life / Night visiting song / The recruited collier / The foggy dew / Fair was the city / Just as the tide was flowing / The plains of Waterloo / Willy Worrell / The leaving time / Come and be a soldier.

Jan 02. (cd) *(WGS 305CD)* **THE LONG ROAD** □ ⊟
- The road to Dorchester / The black horse / Poppies / The journey / Time to remember the poor / The bonnie Irish maid / Strange fruit / Holmes and Watson / The two sisters / Song for John / Voices from the past / The crafty maid's policy / Desperate Dan / The wrong side of the world.

Jun 04. (cd) *(WGS 318CD)* **SOMETHING TO SHOW**
- The ballad seller / The queen of the May / Sons of the land / Farewell my dearest dear / Jack went a-sailing / The grey hawk / King Kaley / Work, work, when it's gonna stop? / Something to show / Faithless Sally Brown / The last of England / Two brethren / The prince of peace / The eighteenth of June.

Jan 07. (cd) *(WGS 339CD)* **THE ISLAND OF APPLES**
- The labourer's cause / The land / There was a man / Cupid's garden / Life / The island of apples / Tom Baine's bones / The boy remembers his father / The banks of the Bahn / Here comes Mick / When we take 'em over - Sailing west / A Tolpuddle man / The song goes on.

FIELDWORK

Dec 98. (cd) *(WGS 290CD)* **THE VOYAGE**
- Voices from the city / The leaving time / Behind me / The emigrant / When we take them over / Sailing west / How deeps the sea / Green island / Lying down / Reprisals / Prisoners of the past / The sea / The soldier's song (part 1) / Fever on board / The bargain / Farewell my child / The soldier's song (part 2) / Home / Safe harbour / Keep you in peace / The promised land.

Aug 03. (cd) *(WGS 307CD)* **TANKS FOR THE MEMORY**
- The Dorset four hand reel - The huntsman's chorus / Dorset (rap!) / Tyneham / The tank / Defending the island / Whose is this land? / Life / Farewell / Partings do come / The leaving time / Promises, promises / Peace at last / Promises, promises (reprise) / Shadows / Listen / Country gardens / Time / Listen / The land / The grace / Tyneham (reprise) / What does it mean to be English?

MICK RYAN

next with **Paul Downes** - guitars, banjo, bass, mandolin

Jun 08. (cd; by MICK RYAN & PAUL DOWNES) *(WGS 355CD)*
GRAND CONVERSATION
- Grand conversation / Reprisals / The bell ringing / Sleep of death / The light / Young men all / Put them down / The lark above the downs / Banks of the Bann / Land of Cockayne / The foe / The lazy man / Green island / Thomas Brassey.

—— with contributions from **Jackie Oates, Roger Watson, Heather Bradford, Paul Downes + Judy Dunlop**

Dec 08. (d-cd) *(WGS 360CD)* **THE NAVVY'S WIFE: A Musical Drama by Mick Ryan**
- (Act 1):- Men from Limerick / The women's song / My Paddy / Don't forget / Mammy's poem / Farewell my son / My Paddy (part 2) / The right thing / Don't forget (part 2) / I miss him / The railway age (poem) / Brassey / The navvy's wife / Women not their wives / They all hate / The eyes have it / Farewell / Dangerous enough (poem) / So many ways to die // (Act 2):- Poppies / The journey / What brought Paddy over (poem) / We get all sorts / Here comes Mick / Just like you / Something to show / The journey (part 2) / Wasn't he the lucky one? / Aren't we the lucky ones? / The land around you.

—— plus **Jackie Oates** - five-string viola / **Paul Hutchinson** - accordion

Sep 10. (cd; by MICK RYAN & PAUL DOWNES) *(WGS 375CD)*
AWAY IN THE WEST
- The pauper's path / The bells rang / Summer is a-coming in / Jack in luck / Greenland / South Armagh / The people must be amused / Love is life / Vinland / No evil / Upon a field / Fire against the cold / How wide's the ocean / The institute.

—— next feat. **Paul Downes, Roy Clinging, Heather Bradford, Judy Dunlop, Maggie Boyle + Phoebe Kirrage**

May 11. (cd) *(WGS 379CD)* **THE PAUPER'S PATH to Hope**
- The workhouse / Let us in / This is the workhouse - You can't have that / Time / Locks and bolts / Turn that mill / Fire against the cold / Long ago and far away / Free at last / Who? / My child / The workhouse child (part one) - Work! work! when it's gonna stop? / Industry, usefullness, virtue / In their eyes / The vagrant's song / The union (part one) / Do you remember? / A jolly good job / That's my story / Down among the dead men / The union (part two) / The workhouse child (part two) / Is that you? / No one saw me / Where shall I go? / My home / The path to hope / The pauper's path.

S

Ric SANDERS

Not many artists have embraced both the folk and the jazz genres. In Britain PENTANGLE fused them together, while on the other side of the pond trad-jazz finger-picker DUCK BAKER had drifted out and in. Virtuoso violinist RIC SANDERS (born Richard Sanders, December 8, 1952 in Birmingham), however, detached his jazz-rock callings from his folk-rock pursuits, and his discography here concentrates mainly on his latter excursions.

For most of the 1970s Ric's time was spent in jazz-orientated outfits - Stomu Yamash'ta's Red Buddha Theatre, Johnny Patrick, Michael Garrick and Soft Machine - his only diversions being with trad-folk act The ALBION BAND on their 1978 set 'Rise Up Like The Sun', plus numerous sessions for folkies including ANDREW CRONSHAW, GORDON GILTRAP and Mick Stevens.

Having released a collaborative jazz-fusion LP, 'First Steps' for Chrysalis in 1980 alongside John Etheridge (Jonathan Davie, Dave Bristow and Micky Barker were also on board), SANDERS finally found a steady home from 1985 onwards with folk legends FAIRPORT CONVENTION, starting with the album 'Gladys' Leap', and he's still with them as of 2011's 'Festival Bell'. In the meantime, Ric has guested with a great many artists, from MARTIN SIMPSON, JUNE TABOR, ALL ABOUT EVE and The Mission to ROY HARPER and RAINBOW CHASERS. In 1989 he released a second joint effort, 'One To One', this time with GORDON GILTRAP.

For our purposes his solo work, which comes across as improv chamber-folk (quite hard to pigeonhole), comprises two albums, **WHENEVER** (1984) {*6} and **NEITHER TIME OR DISTANCE** (1992) {*6}, standouts being 'Calm Waters' from the first and 'Gymnopedie For An Angel' from the second. Note that the RIC SANDERS GROUP on 2002's 'In Lincoln Cathedral' was essentially a jazz combo, featuring guitarist Vo Fletcher and percussionist Michael Gregory; Rick Wakeman guests. *MCS*

Ric Sanders - fiddle / + session players

UK Waterfront — US not issued

Jun 84. (lp/c) *(WF 021/+C)* **WHENEVER** ☐ ⊟
- Dancing spiral / Freedom calypso / Rainshine / Calm waters / Ain't she sweet / Clows top / Improvisation / Cherokee archer / Improvisation on 'Constant Billy' / Whenever. *(cd-iss. Aug 89 on Nico Polo; NP 001CD)*

In 1985, Ric joined up with FAIRPORT CONVENTION and performed on many sets; in 1989, he teamed up with GORDON GILTRAP on the collaboration 'One To One'.

Woodworm — not issued

Feb 92. (cd/c) *(WRCD/WRC 017)* **NEITHER TIME OR DISTANCE** ☐ ⊟
- Remembrance day / Gymnopedie for an angel / Three jigs for Jamie / The selfish giant suite / The little owl / Black Bryony / Domino / Blue roses I-IV / The unbroken promise / Hopes and dreams.

(below releases are of jazz persuasion - tracks not listed therefore)

Heliopause — not issued

Nov 02. (d-cd; as RIC SANDERS GROUP) *(HPVP 101CD)* **IN LINCOLN CATHEDRAL** [live] ☐ ⊟

Oct 03. (cd; as RIC SANDERS GROUP) *(HPVP 102CD)* **PARABLE: MUSIC FOR THE ANJALI DANCE COMPANY** [score] ☐ ⊟

- (5-7*) compilations, others, etc.-

Sep 08. (cd) *Talking Elephant; (TECD 129)* **STILL WATERS** [instrumental ballads 1980–2008] ☐ ⊟
- A lifetime's love / Portmeirion (2001) / The rose hip / Gymnopedie for an angel / Summer in December / Calm waters / Black Bryony / A year and a day / Your heart and mine / Even in sadness / Some special place / Remembrance day / Following on / Improvisation on 'Constant Billy' / Portmeirion / Calm waters.

The SAW DOCTORS

The celebratory sound of The SAW DOCTORS could be described as a hybrid of The POGUES' drunken punk and traditional Irish Celtic-roots rock (folk 'n'roll?), with a working-class ethos thrown in for good measure. Throughout the years in which the band have been active, they almost outsold U2 at one time and were on their way to becoming the second most successful band in Ireland.

Formed in 1986 in Tuam, Galway by Irish punk-reggae veteran Leo Moran and former Blaze X man Davy Carton (they had performed together in an embryonic SAW DOCTORS since the late 1970s), the line-up at this stage also boasted John Burke, Tony Lambert and Pearse Doherty; an early member, Mary O'Connor, emigrated to London.

They set off on their road to stardom when The WATERBOYS' lead singer MIKE SCOTT invited the small local band to be the support act on his UK tour. This happened around the release of The SAW DOCTORS' debut single, 'N17' (produced by SCOTT), which was quite successful when imported into Britain. After a subsequent tour supporting Hothouse Flowers was over, a second single, 'I Useta Love Her' (a rip-roaring track about the perils of Catholic love), generated so much hype that it went straight to No.1 in Ireland and stayed there for a further nine weeks, becoming the biggest-selling record of all time in Ireland.

The band subsequently re-issued their debut single (which also reached No.1), one of more than a dozen great numbers on their humorous and delightful full-length set **IF THIS IS ROCK AND ROLL, I WANT MY OLD JOB BACK** (1991) {*7}. Check out 'That's What She Said Last Night' and 'Sing A Powerful Song'. Following the release of **ALL THE WAY FROM TUAM** (1992) {*6}, 'A Small Bit Of Love' became the group's first British hit, reaching the Top 30. Live favourites from the album included 'Green And Red Of Mayo', 'Wake Up Sleeping' and 'Exhilarating Sadness'.

And then something quite unique took place: Lambert literally hit the jackpot when, in April 1993, his ticket came up for a £1 million win on the Irish lottery. It was said he was living in a converted bus at the time, but he moved to a proper house in County Galway on leaving the band.

Understandably, The SAW DOCTORS took time out to recuperate and regroup, one of their songs, 'To Win Just Once' (written before Tony's big win), surfacing in 1996 on the back of Ireland's appearance in the Uefa European Football Championship. Early in 1996, the group (with Derek Murray on board as replacement; Anto Thistletwaite was a brief member) finally issued their third long-player, **SAME OUL' TOWN** {*6}, a record that advanced their UK credibility when it reached the Top 10. The following year, **SING A POWERFUL SONG** {*6} (a collection of earlier material) was released to the usual fanfare, followed in 1998 by 'She Says', an EP of songs written for the BBC Northern Ireland TV sitcom 'Give My Head Peace'.

The SAW DOCTORS finally achieved some recognition in the US when the single 'Never Mind The Strangers' received some airplay there. The track had been co-written by a recent recruit, drummer Padraig Stevens, who had left the group at the time of the single's release. The popularity of the song was largely credited to the TV commercial for Harp lager that it accompanied in the US.

The fourth album proper, **SONGS FROM SUN STREET** (1998) {*6}, sold well enough to hit the UK Top 30, the two founding members (plus mainstay Doherty) adding to the fresh line-up, which included John Donnelly and Murray. Three years later they returned with comeback set **VILLAINS?** {*5}, which cracked the UK Top 60 in 2001. Post-millennium, the band played on regardless of critical disapproval, live sets and DVDS coming thick and fast. Just to prove the doubters wrong, a compilation album, **TO WIN JUST ONCE - THE BEST OF THE SAW DOCTORS** (2009) {*7}, went platinum almost immediately, prompting the band to regroup for the 40th-anniversary Glastonbury Festival in 2010.

THE FURTHER ADVENTURES OF... (2010) {*5}, their first studio outing since 2005's **THE CURE** {*4}, kept Messrs Carton, Moran, Thistlethwaite (on bass and sax), Eimhin Craddock (drums) and Kevin Duffy (on keyboards) ticking over nicely. *MCS*

Davy Carton - vocals, guitars / **Leo Moran** - vocals, guitars, organ, etc / **John "Turps" Burke** - mandolin, organ, guitars, vocals / **Tony Lambert** - accordion, organ / **Pearse Doherty** - bass, vocals, piano, flute / guest **John Donnelly** - drums, tambourine

UK Solid — US WEA

Dec 90. (cd-s) *(ROK 731)* I USETA LOVE HER. / Captain Joe Fiddle's / I Used To Love Her [by BLAZE X] [-] Irish [-]

Jun 91. (cd/c/lp) *(ROCD/ROCC/ROCK 7)* **IF THIS IS ROCK AND ROLL, I WANT MY OLD JOB BACK** [69] [-]
- I useta love her / Only one girl / Why do I always want you / It won't be tonight / Irish post / Sing a powerful song / Freedom fighters [live] / That's what she said last night / Red Cortina / Presentation boarder / Don't let me down / £25 / What a day / N17 / I hope you meet again. *(re-iss.Dec93 cd/c; ROC DG/CG 7) (re-iss. Dec 94 on Shamtown cd/c; SAWDOC 001 CD/MC)*

Jul 91. (7"/c-s) *(ROK/+C 747)* N17. / N17 [live inc. Paddy's Poem] [-] Irish [-]
(cd-s+=) *(ROKCD 747)* - At least pretend.

Nov 91. (7"/c-s) *(ROK/+C 751)* THAT'S WHAT SHE SAID LAST NIGHT. / Hay Wrap - The West's Awake [ ] [-]
(cd-s+=) *(ROKCD 751)* - The trip to Tipp.

WEA — not issued

Oct 92. (cd/c/lp) *(4509 91146-2/-4/-1)* **ALL THE WAY FROM TUAM** [33] [-]
- Green and red of Mayo / You got me on the run / Pied piper / My heart is livin' in the sixties still / Hay wrap / Wake up sleeping / Midnight express / Broke my heart / Exhilarating sadness / All the way from Tuam / F.C.A. / Music I love / Yvonne / Never mind the strangers. *(re-iss. Dec 93 on Solid cd/c; ROC D/C 11) (re-iss. Dec 94 on Shamtown cd/c; SAWDOC 002 CD/MC)*

Feb 93. (7"/c-s) *(YZ 731/+C)* WAKE UP SLEEPING. / Joe Wall Broke My Heart [ ] [-]
(cd-s+=) *(YZ 731CD)* - Thank God it's a Tuesday / I hope you melt again.
(cd-s) *(YZ 731CDX)* - ['A'] / Why do I always want you [live] / What a day [live] / N17 [live].

—— **Anto Thistlethwaite** - saxophone, bass (ex-WATERBOYS) repl. Burke

—— now without Thistlethwaite (solo + back to WATERBOYS); fifth member on below album **Derek Murray** - keyboards, accordion, guitar, mandolin, banjo; Lambert left when he won the Irish lottery.

Shamtown — Paradigm

Oct 94. (c-ep/cd-ep) *(SAW 001 MC/CD)* SMALL BIT OF LOVE / Michael D. Rocking In The Dail / I'd Love To Kiss The Bangles / Where's The Party [live] [24] [-]

Jan 96. (c-ep/cd-ep) *(SAW 002 MC/CD)* WORLD OF GOOD EP [15] [-]
- World of good / Bless me father / Letter from Louise / Tuam beat.

Feb 96. (cd/c) *(SAWDOC 004 CD/C)* **SAME OUL' TOWN** [6] [-]
- All the one / Same oul' town / To win just once / Everyday / World of good / Back to Tuam / Mercy gates / Macnas parade / Share the darkness / I want you more / All over now / Clare Island.

Jul 96. (c-ep/cd-ep) *(SAW 004 MC/CD)* TO WIN JUST ONCE / Sound Sham / Winter's Just A Dream / Green And Red Of Mayo [live] [14] [-]
(cd-ep) *(SAW 004CDX)* - ['A'] / Teenage kicks [live] / I useta love her [live] / Clare Island [live].

Nov 97. (c-s) *(SAW 006MC)* SIMPLE THINGS / I Wish That She Was Mine [56] [-]
(cd-s+=) *(SAW 006CD)* - Joyce country ceili band / Fishy fishy.

Sep 98. (cd-ep) *(SAW 007CD)* SHE SAYS / School Of Beauty / Days / Bushwhackin [-] Ire [-]

Oct 98. (cd/c/lp) *(SAWDOC 006 CD/MC/LP)* <42>
SONGS FROM SUN STREET [24] Nov 98 [ ]
- Good news / Sugar town / Galway and Mayo / Carry me away / Heading for the sunshine / Catriona tell lies / Blah, blah, blah / D'ya wanna hear my guitar? / Joyce country ceili band / High Nellie / Best of friends / Will it ever stop raining? / Tommy K. / Away with the fairies / I'll be on my way.

Dec 98. (cd-s) *(SAW 008CD)* SUGARTOWN / I'll Be On My Way / Catriona Tell Lies [-] Irish [-]

—— now just trio of **Moran, Carton + Doherty**

Shamtown — Shamtown

Oct 01. (cd/c) *(<SAWDOC 008 CD/MC>)* **VILLAINS?** [58] Feb 02 [ ]
- Villains / This is me / Still afraid of the dark / Happy days / Bound to the peace / Darkwind / Always gives me more / I know I've got your love / Chips / DNA / Still the only one.

May 02. (cd-s) *(SAW 012CD)* THIS IS ME / Lost Child / The Prodigal Son / ['A'-Cd-Rom] [31] [-]
(cd-s) *(SAW 012CDX)* - ['A'] / Midnight express [live] / Galway and Mayo [live].

Mar 04. (cd) *(SAWDOC 010CD)* **LIVE IN GALWAY** [live in Ireland, July 2003] [ ] [-]
- Intro / N17 / To win just once / Red Cortina / What a day / Bless me father / Share the darkness / Green and red of Mayo / I'll be on my way / Same oul' town / Joyce country ceili band / Exhilarating sadness / Clare Island / Why do I always want you / That's what she said last night / I useta love her / Hay wrap.

Oct 05. (cd) *(SAWDOC 013CD)* **THE CURE** [ ] [-]
- Out for a smoke / Last summer in New York / Addicted / Stars over Cloughanover / If only / Wisdom of youth / Vulnerable / Me without you / Going home / Your guitar / Funny world / I'll say goodnight.

Oct 05. (7"/cd-s) *(SHAM 001/SAW 014CD)* STARS OVER CLOUGHANOVER / Your Guitar [69] [-]

—— new line-up: **Moran, Carton** plus **Kevin Duffy** - keyboards, vocals / **Anthony Thistlethwaite** - bass, mandolin, vocals / **Eimhin Craddock** - drums

Aug 09. (cd) *(80800)* **LIVE AT THE MELODY TENT** [live 14th August 2008] [ ] [-]
- Intro / Macnas parade / Will it ever stop raining? / Out for a smoke / Never mind the strangers / Green and red of Mayo / Galway and Mayo including maroon and white / This is me / I'll be on my way / That's what she said last night / Clare Island / N17 / Chips / Hay wrap.

(above issued on Cambridge Records)

2009. (cd-s) *(SAW 018CD)* SHE LOVES ME / Some Hope / Lucky Boy / About You Now [video] [-] Irish [-]

2010. (cd-ep) *(SAW 019CD)* TAKIN' THE TRAIN EP [-] Irish [-]
- Takin' the train / Be yourself / Hazard / Last call.

2010. (cd-s) *(SAW 020CD)* FRIDAY TOWN [-] Irish [-]

Sep 10. (cd) *(SAWDOC 017CD)* **THE FURTHER ADVENTURES OF...** [58] [-]
- Takin' the train / Friday town / Someone loves you / Hazard / Indian summer / Well byes / Be yourself / Last call / As the light fades / Songs and stars / Goodbye again.

2010. (cd-s) *(SAW 022CD)* WELL BYES [-] Irish [-]

- (8-10*) compilations -

Dec 09. (cd) *Shamtown; (SAWDOC 16CD)* **TO WIN JUST ONCE: THE BEST OF THE SAW DOCTORS** [ ] [-]
- About you now / N17 [live] / Last summer in New York / She loves me - she loves me not / Green and red of Mayo / To win just once / That's what she said last night / Small bit of love / I useta lover / Clare Island / Joyce country ceili band / Exhilarating sadness / Why do I always want you / What a day / Stars over Cloughanover / Sing a powerful song / World of good / Same oul' town / Red Cortina / It won't be tonight / Hay wrap / Never mind the strangers.

- (5-7*) compilations, others, etc.-

Nov 97. (cd/c) *Shamtown; (SAWDOC 005 CD/MC)*
SING A POWERFUL SONG [ ] [-]
- Green and red of Mayo / It won't be tonight / Wake up sleeping / Macnas parade / What a day / Hay wrap / N17 / Exhilarating sadness / Red Cortina / Clare island / To win just once / Share the darkness / Same oul' town / Never mind the strangers / Why do I always want you / Sing a powerful song / I useta love her.

Jul 03. (cd) *Shamtown; (SAWDOC 009CD)* **PLAY IT AGAIN SHAM!** [-] Irish [-]
- World of good / I'd love to kiss The Bangles / Michael D. rocking in the Dail / Bless me father / Joe Wall broke my heart / Me heart is livin' in the sixties still / Howya Julia / Apples, sweets or chocolates / Broke my heart / Crock of gold / We're the Popsuckers / Small ball / Winter's just a dream / She says / Small bit of love / Bushwhackin' / Sound sham / School of beauty / Letter from Louise / Where's the party?

Dec 07. (cd) *Shamtown; (mp3)* **THAT TAKES THE BISCUIT!** [fancy versions of old favourites] [-] [-]
- Fortunately / She's got it [Spiddal recording] / Some hope / An cailin sin / The winter is long / Bebo / Villains [Giles Packham mix] / Good news [live 2002] / Will it ever stop raining? [live 2002] / Chips [live 2002] / California sun / Maroon and white / You're in love with someone else / Forty years in Tuam / I think it might be you / Dreamgirl / Yaygour guitaygar / Ways of the world / Merry Christmas Tuam / She's got it [Nashville recording] / Somewhere far away / The hash my father smoked / (reprise).

John SCHUMANN (⟹ REDGUM)

Mike SCOTT (⟹ The WATERBOYS)

SEBO ENSEMBLE (⟹ Celtic And World Music Discography)

The SHANTY CREW

Giving the game away in their name (though Seasick Steve was never press-ganged into joining), this flexible and fluctuating folk outfit from all over England kept the sea shanty tradition alive from their formation in 1976. Revivalists, but also catalysts in their day, STAN ROGERS and GORDON BOK were inspirational in their treatments of ye olde sailor/shanty song, but The SHANTY CREW (principally Chris Roche, Gerry Milne, Steve Belsay, Dave Diamond and Dominic Magog) carried it to the landlubber.

LET THE WIND BLOW FREE (1984) {*6} was typical shanty banter, full of 'Haul Away' songs and cheery 'splice up yer life' staples, but what stole the show was their reading of 'Rolling Down To Old Maui'. Without Milne and Diamond, but with the added attraction of Francophone Tony Goodenough (he had also featured on the debut), there was a French flavour to the long-awaited follow-up, **STAND TO YER GROUND** (1990) {*5}. Stalwart captain Roche was said to have amassed a private collection of sea-shanty folk material second to none, much of it surfacing on the group's final set to date, **SEA SHANTIES AND SAILOR SONGS** (1996) {*5}. *MCS*

Chris Roche - vocals / **Gerry Milne** - vocals / **Steve Belsay** - vocals / **Dave Diamond** - vocals / **Tony Goodenough** - vocals / **Dominic Magog** - vocals; instruments played: fiddle, bodhran + concertina

UK Coach House — US not issued

Nov 84. (lp/c) *(ESSAR 014/+C)* **LET THE WIND BLOW FREE** □ ⊟
- Royal artillery man / Haul away for Rosie-o / Mobile bay / Flash frigate / Hog eye / Twenty-fourth of February / Lahoula t'chalez / Roll the woodpile down / Haul 'er away / Rolling down to old Maui / Shake her Johnny / Fire maringo / Is the big fella gone / Cheerly man / Six feet of mud / Haul on the bowline / Coal black rose / Eddystone light / Emma Emma let me be / Mingulay boat song.

—— **Phil Money** + **Phil Jarrett** - vocals; repl. Milne + Diamond

1990. (lp/c) *(none)* **STAND TO YER GROUND** □ ⊟
- Rise 'er up / Hob y derri dando / Anglesey / A la Rochelle / Heave away boys / Blow ye winds / Sailor fireman / Brother Noah / Slav o / Pump shanty / Seraphina / C'est l'aviron / Shiny o / High Barbary / Shantyman / Essequibo river / Lime scurvy / Sailorman's port in a storm / Hilo somebody / Stand to yer ground / The mate.

Brewhouse — not issued

Dec 96. (cd/c) *(BHCD/BHC 9601)* **SEA SHANTIES AND SAILOR SONGS: Classics From the Great Days of Sail 1840–1890** □ ⊟
- Prologue: The Lee force brace / Old Moke pickin' on the banjo / Can't ye hilo / Where am I to go m' Johnnies / One more day / Rolling coal / Randy Dandy o / Ranzo Ray / Yankee John stormalong / Frankie's trade / Bring 'em down / Do let me 'lone Susan / General Taylor / The gals o' Dublin town / Paddy Doyle's boots / Bully in the alley / Heave away, boys, heave away / Johnny Bowker / Common sailors / Spanish ladies / I'm bound away / Shallow brown / Fire down below / John Kanaka / Cheerly man / Hi-o come roll me over / The East Indiaman / Paddy lay back / Epilogue: D'ye mind.

SHORELINE (⟹ The LEISURE SOCIETY)

SHOW OF HANDS

Formed in the early 1980s, initially as a part-time concern, by Steve Knightley and multi-instrumentalist Phil Beer (the latter had already released collaborative work with PAUL DOWNES), SHOW OF HANDS had a difficult time breaking through from their hometown of

Exeter in Devon. (NB: this band is not to be confused with a short-lived American acoustic trio of the same name, who played in the People's Republic of China in the late 1980s to promote an eponymous set.)

Phil's history featured many credits for the Arizona Smoke Revue, The ALBION BAND, etc, while Steve's CV was a little blank by comparison. A handful of SHOW OF HANDS cassettes were met with a decent response from those who heard them, but it was really the intercultural **ALIANZA** set of 1992 (featuring an array of fine Chilean musicians) that set them off on the right path.

SHOW OF HANDS were back in contention in 1994, and studio sets such as that year's **BEAT ABOUT THE BUSH** {*6} and 1995's **LIE OF THE LAND** {*8} were the beginnings of something special. Augmented by seasoned session players and prize guests, the debut credited Pete Zorn, Matt Clifford, Stefean Hannigan and RALPH McTELL among many others, while the accomplished second set, tight-knit and Celtic-like, featured Clifford (again), Sarah Allen and piper Nick Scott.

Not counting a number of concert albums, the prolific duo continued to release acoustic roots sets including **DARK FIELDS** (1997) {*7} - featuring DYLAN's 'Farewell Angelina' and a live recording of 'High Germany' with KATE RUSBY, CHRIS WOOD and ANDY CUTTING - and the unaugmented collection **FOLK MUSIC** (1998) {*6}.

Unconventional but with an air of defiance, **COVERS** (2000) {*6} was exactly what it said on the tin. It was also in part an escape from the confines of folk material, mingling songs by DYLAN, RALPH McTELL, MICHAEL CHAPMAN, John Richards, NIC JONES and 'trad' with an eclectic selection of rock tunes. Billy Joel ('The Downeaster Alexa'), The Kinks ('Waterloo Sunset'), Peter Gabriel ('Don't Give Up'), Radiohead ('Fake Plastic Trees'), Jethro Tull ('Wond'ring Aloud'), Tom Robinson ('Ringing it Up Duncannon') and Little Feat ('Willin'') supplied the non-folk numbers.

COLD FRONTIER (2001) {*6}, the live **COLD CUTS** (2002) {*6}, **THE PATH** (2003) {*6} and **COUNTRY LIFE** (2003) {*6} also had their fair share of folk staples from the likes of STAN ROGERS, CYRIL TAWNEY, SYDNEY CARTER, McTELL and LEONARD COHEN as well as songs by Cyndi Lauper, Free, and Kelly Joe Phelps.

Accompanied by Matt Clifford (also a song provider), Miranda Sykes and guest SETH LAKEMAN, the production of Simon Emmerson and Simon Massey (of AFRO CELT SOUND SYSTEM) helped pump a new ambient-versus-trad approach into **WITNESS** (2006) {*7}. Studio set number 10, **ARROGANCE IGNORANCE AND GREED** (2009) {*6} was equally well regarded, again featuring songs by DYLAN and Gabriel.

COVERS 2 (2010) {*6} was the first to credit Sykes (also on the sleeve), songs this time around stemming from RICHARD SHINDELL, Bruce Springsteen, Stereophonics, Don Henley, Steve Earle, Mark Knopfler, Peter Gabriel ('Secret World'), Tom Robinson ('2-4-6-8 Motorway'), Boz Scaggs, REV. GARY DAVIS, Roscarrock and Bob Marley.

Not content with just their duo, both BEER and KNIGHTLEY have released numerous solo sets with a high degree of critical success. BEER's include **HARD HATS** (1994) {*7} and **RHYTHM METHODIST** (2005) {*7}, and KNIGHTLEY's include **TRACK OF WORDS** (2000) {*7}, **WESTERN APPROACHES** (2004) {*6} (crediting SETH LAKEMAN and Jenna), **CRUEL RIVER** (2007) {*7} and **LIVE IN SOMERSET** (2011) {*6}. *MCS*

Steve Knightley (b. 1954) - vocals, acoustic guitar, cuatro, mandocello / **Phil Beer** (b. May 12 '53, Exminster, Devon) - vocals, acoustic guitars, fiddle/viola, mandolin, melodeon (ex-ALBION BAND, ex-JOHNNY COPPIN) / and numerous session players

UK own label — US not issued

1987. (ltd-c) *(none)* SHOW OF HANDS ⊟ ⊟
1990. (ltd-c) *(none)* TALL SHIPS ⊟ ⊟
1991. (ltd-c) *(none)* OUT FOR THE COUNT ⊟ ⊟

ALIANZA

Beer + **Knightley** plus **Sergio Avila, Mauricio Venegas, Vladimir Vega** + **Dave Townsend** (Chilean instruments)

Road Goes On Forever — not issued

Nov 92. (cd/c) *(RGF CD/MC 012)* **ALIANZA** □ ⊟
- Morna / Tobin's favourite / Ojos azules / Ay paloma / Man of war / Nuca llacta / Surtierra / Buttered peas - Carnival / Shallow brown - Elegva / Tall ships / Idbury hill - Carnavolito / List for a sailor / Santiago.

SHOW OF HANDS

see last SOH line-up

Isis — not issued

Mar 94. (cd/c) *(CDIS/MCIS 05)* **BEAT ABOUT THE BUSH** □ ⊟
- Beat about the bush / The class of '73 / Armadas / Nine hundred miles - Poor wayfaring stranger / Shadows in the dark / The Galway farmer / White tribes / Day has come / The hook of love / Cars / The blue cockade / Mr. May's - Gloucester hornpipe / The oak. *(cd re-iss. 1999 on Hands On Music; HMCD 08) (cd re-iss. Sep 03 on Twah!; TWAH 105)*

Apr 94. (c) *(MCIS 06)* **LIVE** (recorded June 8, 1992 at the Bull Hotel, Bridport) □ ⊟
- Silver dagger / The blind fiddler / Don't it feel good / I still wait / Exile / Yankee clipper / Man of war / Bonnie light horseman / I'll put a stake through his heart / Low down in the Broome / Six o'clock waltz / Sit you down / Wolf at the door / Caught in the rain / Santiago / It's all your fault. *(cd-iss. Mar 95; CDIS 06) (cd re-iss. 1999 on Hands On Music; HMCD 07)*

Oct 95. (cd/c) *(CDIS/MCIS 09)* **LIE OF THE LAND** □ ⊟
- The hunter / Unlock me / The well / The keeper / Captains / Weary / Ratcliffe highway / Safe as houses / The man in green / The preacher / M Ferguson / Exile. *(cd re-iss. 1998 on Hands On Music; HMCD 02) (cd re-iss. Sep 03 on Twah!; TWAH 110)*

Hands On Music — not issued

Aug 96. (cd) *(HMCD 01)* **LIVE AT THE ROYAL ALBERT HALL** (24 MARCH 1996) □ ⊟
- Columbus (didn't find America) / Day has come / The preacher / Cutthroats, crooks and conmen / The blue cockade / The soldier's joy / Exile / The man in green / The dove / The well / The hunter / Captains / The blind fiddler / Santiago / Galway farmer / Time after time. *(re-iss. Aug 98; HMCD 04)*

Aug 97. (cd) *(HMCD 03)* **DARK FIELDS** □ ⊟
- Cousin Jack / Longdog / The shout / Wessex medley: Carrick roads - Plum pudding - The rocky road to Chudleigh / Dark fields / The train / Flora / Crazy boy / The warlike lads of Russia / Farewell Angelina / The Bristol slaver / High Germany - Molly Oxford (live). *(bonus +=)* - The train (reprise).

Dec 98. (ltd-cd) *(???)* **FOLK MUSIC** □ ⊟
- John Riley / Broomfield hill / All things are quite silent / Lonesome stockade blues / Mary from Dungloe / Down in yon forest / Je ne sais quoi - Le boeuf Anglais / Digging down / Matt Hyland / The train - Blackwaterside.

May 00. (cd) *(HMCD 12)* **COVERS** □ ⊟
- Wond'ring aloud / Ripping it up Duncannon / Willin' / No song to sing / Corrina Corrina / The setting / The Downeaster Alexa / Fake plastic trees / Is your love in vain / Courting is a pleasure / Roaring water bay / Don't give up / Waterloo sunset.

Sep 01. (cd) *(HMCD 13)* **COLD FRONTIER**
- Cold frontier / Are we alright / Come by / Northwest passage / Widecombe fair / Things I learnt this year / You're mine / Windchanges / Don't look now / Sally free and easy / Yeovil town / Cold heart of England / The street of Forbes / The flood.

Jul 02. (cd) *(HMCD 17)* **COLD CUTS** (live on tour November 2001)
- Faith in you / Crow on the cradle / First they take Manhattan / Track of words / Crazy boy / Lonesome stockade blues / The battle of Somme / The keeper / Time after time / Sally free and easy / The rose in the thorn / My brother Jake / The setting - Mary from Dungloe / Tall ships / The train - Sit you down.

Apr 03. (cd) *(HMCD 18)* **THE PATH (An Instrumental Journey Around The West Country)**
- Foreland Point / Braunton Burrows / Buck's Mills / Port Isaac / Carbis Bay / Land's End / Lamorna Cove / Pendennis Castle / Charlestown / Rame Head / Hallsands / Paignton / The Exe Estuary / Lyme Regis / Golden Cap / The Foreland (reprise).

Oct 03. (cd) *(HMCD 19)* **COUNTRY LIFE**
- Country life / Hard shoulder / Suntrap / Smile she said / Reynardine / Seven days / Tommy / Be lucky / Drake / I promise you / Adieu, sweet lovely Nancy / Red diesel / Don't be a stranger.

—— next featured guest Miranda Sykes (double bass)

Mar 05. (d-cd) *(HMCD 22)* **AS YOU WERE** (live on tour late 2004)
- Longdog / You're mine / Willin' / Mary from Dungloe - The setting / The oak / The blue cockade / Crazy boy / Crow on the cradle / I promise you / Maybe / Be lucky // The blind fiddler - Galway farmer / Captains / Corrina, Corrina / Smile she said / Crooked man / Are we alright / Cousin Jack / The train - Santiago - The soldier's joy / Widecombe fair / Country life / Don't be a stranger.

May 06. (cd) *(HMCD 23)* **WITNESS**
- Witness / Roots / The dive / The Falmouth packet - Haul away Joe / Undertow / If I needed someone / Innocents song / Union Street (last poet) / The bet / Ink devil / Scratch / All I'd ever lost.

Oct 09. (cd) *(HMCD 29)* **ARROGANCE, IGNORANCE AND GREED**
- Lowlands / Evolution / The man I was / The Napoli / Senor (tales of Yankee power) / IED - science or nature / The vale / Arrogance, ignorance and greed / Secret world / The worried well / The keys of Canterbury / Drift.

—— added **Miranda Sykes** - double bass, vocals

Nov 10. (cd) *(HMCD 32)* **COVERS 2**
- You stay here / Youngstown / Dakota / Boys of summer / The devil's right hand / Tunnel of love / Secret world / 2-4-6-8 motorway / King of El Paso / Cocaine blues / First and last / No woman, no cry / AIG 2 [the 'lite' version].

- (8-10*) compilations -

Nov 07. (d-cd) *Hands On Music; (HMCD 28)* **ROOTS: THE BEST OF SHOW OF HANDS**
- Roots / Are we alright / Exile / Country life / Widecombe fair / The Falmouth packet - Haul away Joe / Santiago / Armadas / The blue cockade (live) / Crow on the cradle (live) / The preacher / Cousin Jack / Cold frontier / Hard shoulder / Captains / The Galway farmer (live) // Columbus (didn't find America) / You're mine / The blind fiddler / The setting - Mary from Dungloe / The Bristol slaver / Port Isaac / The train / Blackwaterside / Be lucky / Longdog / The keeper / The Downeaster Alexa / The oak / Innocents' song - Gwithian / Tall ships.

- (5-7*) compilations, others, etc.-

Mar 95. (cd) *Isis; (CDIS 08)* **BACKLOG 1987–1991**
- Ah so! / The tramp stamp - Chasing the jack / Solo / Limbo / Lovers, never friends / The leaving blues / Walking in the rain / The last picture show / Homes for heroes / See my baby again / First they take Manhattan / Friends / The pleasure of the town - The Seneca two step / The dominion of the sword / Tall ships.

Sep 04. (d-cd) *Track; (TRKMP 0002)* **SHOW OF HANDS**
- Medley: Man of war - The well - The oak - Breakfast for Altan / Exile / The blind fiddler / Armadas / Cars / Columbus (didn't find Columbus) / Cutthroats, crooks and conmen / Crow on the cradle / The preacher / Longdog / Cousin Jack / The train - Blackwaterside.

- budget compilations, etc.-

May 01. (cd) *Delta; (CD 47054)* **NO SONG TO SING: THE COLLECTION**
- John Riley / Willin' / Broomfield hill / The setting - Mary from Dungloe / Lonesome stockade blues / Wond'ring aloud / Seven yellow gypsies / My death / Down in yon forest / Roaring water bay / Fake plastic trees / Courting is a pleasure / No song to sing / Blackwaterside.

PHIL BEER

first recordings ('Dance Without Music') were with solo artist Paul Downes
Beer also feat. on Downes's 'Life Ain't Worth Living' (1973) and 'Live In Concept' (1980)

Avida — not issued

Aug 80. (7") *(AVS 101)* DANCE WITH ME. / Fairweather Friend

Greenwich Village — not issued

May 81. (lp) *(GVR 206)* **MANDOLIN**
- Dan Tucker / Morning sky / Banks of the Bann / Three pretty maidens / Good King Arthur's days / Green rag / Up to the rigs / Buddy can you spare a dime / etc.

In 1982, Beer (alongside Bill Zorn, Paul Downes and Gene Vogel) released their Arizona Smoke Revue set, 'A Thundering On The Horizon'.

HTD — not issued

Aug 94. (cd) *(HTDCD 24)* **HARD HATS**
- Fireman's song / The blind fiddler / Chance / This year / This far / Hard hats / Blinded by love / She could laugh / More / Think it over / Fireman's song (acoustic). *(cd re-iss. Nov 00 as 'HARD WORKS' on HTD+=; HTDCD 117) (cd re-iss. Sep 01 as 'HARD WORKS' on Blueprint+=; BPCD 027) (cd re-iss. Oct 08 as 'HARD WORKS' on Talking Elephant+=; TECD 132)* - THE WORKS

Old Court — not issued

Feb 96. (cd/c) *(OCO CD/C 1)* **THE WORKS**
- General Ward - Tobins - The starling / Swannee River / Staten Island - Soldier's joy / Haste to the wedding - Mohawk / The cap sizun / Thomas' morris - Chasing the jack / Michael Turner's waltz / Gypsy moth / Jig - Banish misfortune / Lost in space - Altan - Teetotalers / Flash company / Jenny on the shore - The bull / Rocky road to Mylor. *(cd re-iss. Sep 98 on HTD; HTDCD 85) (cd re-iss. Nov 00/Sep 01/Oct 08 +=)* - HARD HATS

—— In 1999, Beer, ASHLEY HUTCHINGS, CHRIS WHILE and others collaborated on the soundtrack to TV series 'Ridgeriders'.

Hands On Music — not issued

May 05. (cd) *(HMCD 21)* **RHYTHM METHODIST**
- Old Riley / All my loves laughter / Gloucester hornpipe - Off to California / Fire in the hole / Alex Patterson's return / Holy brook / Varso vianna / Our lady of the well / Lizzie's set / Telling me lies / Acadian driftwood / Mampy moose - Brilliant pebbles - Philip Brunels / Vive l'amour - Masters of this hall / Limbo / Abroad for pleasure / Flowers of the forest - When this bloody war is over. *(re-iss. Apr 08 on Talking Elephant; TECD 121)*

STEVE KNIGHTLEY

Hands On Music — not issued

Oct 00. (cd) *(HMCD 10)* **TRACK OF WORDS**
- Ahh! (Running away) / You're mine / Rush of blood / Castaway / Track of words / Faith in you / The cold heart of England / Don't look now / Face in the frame / It wasn't you / Caught in the rain / Pain away / Broken. *(re-iss. May 09 as 'TRACK OF WORDS - RETRACED'+=; ???)* - Rock you to sleep.

Sep 04. (cd; by STEVE KNIGHTLEY, SETH LAKEMAN & JENNA) *(HMCD 20)* **WESTERN APPROACHES**
- Jigsaw / Surfer's storm / Crooked man / Captain's court / Image of love / Track of words / The keeper / Sand in your shoes / Ye mariners all / The ballad of Josie / If I fall / Dawn wave.

Jun 07. (cd) *(HMCD 27)* **CRUEL RIVER**
- Raining again / Poppy day / All quiet on the western front / Tall ship story / She's gone / Cruel river / The rocks / Tout va bien? / Transported / Caragana wind / Crooked man '07 / Romeo and Juliet.

May 11. (cd) *(HMCD 33)* **LIVE IN SOMERSET** [live at a 19th-century former church]
- All things are quite silent / John Harrison's hands / Hook of love / Transported / The Oakham poachers / Stop copying me / Exile / Reynardine / The Galway farmer / The girl from the north country / Coming home / Banks and braes / Downbound train - Country life / Cousin Jack / Now you know.

Lester SIMPSON (⟹ COOPE BOYES & SIMPSON)

SKUOBHIE DUBH ORCHESTRA (⟹ KING CREOSOTE)

SKYCLAD

Famous for being quite possibly the only thrash-folk exponents in the metal sphere, SKYCLAD have had a succession of female violinists (Fritha Jenkins was the first) among their ranks, not exactly a common sight in the world of exploding amps and all-men-play-on-10 bravado. Their name is from a pagan/Wiccan term for ritual nudity, when pagans dance as one with the sky – Morris dancing with no clothes on.

Founded in Newcastle by ex-Sabbat frontman Martin Walkyier, the original line-up was rounded off in 1991 by ex-Pariah/ex-Satan alumni Steve Ramsey (guitar) and Graeme English (bass), plus drummer Keith Baxter. Signed to Noise International, the group introduced their unashamedly pagan agenda with their 1991 debut set, **THE WAYWARD SONS OF MOTHER EARTH** {*6}. With Dave Pugh (on guitar and banjo) and Fritha on board, their follow-up, **A BURNT OFFERING FOR THE BONE IDOL** (1992) {*7} found their direction ascending into the realms of folk-metal, played at thrash pace.

Interest in the band was initially fairly intense, although subsequent albums such as **JONAH'S ARK** (1993) {*6} and **PRINCE OF THE POVERTY LINE** (1994) {*6} moved ever further towards a Celtic-folk-rock sound (imagine Thin Lizzy on stage with HORSLIPS), alienating many fans who had originally been enthralled by their early, pioneering efforts. Cath Howell had now superseded Fritha on violin, but not for long, as Georgina Biddle was in place for **THE SILENT WHALES OF LUNAR SEA** (1995) {*7}.

In the mid-1990s, with personnel leaving and entering as though through a revolving door, SKYCLAD switched to the Massacre label, ironically getting even more pastoral on **IRRATIONAL ANTHEMS** (1996) {*6}, **OUI AVANT-GARDE A CHANCE** (1996) {*6} (featuring covers of New Model Army's 'Master Race' and Dexy's 'Come On Eileen') and **THE ANSWER MACHINE?** (1997) {*7}.

VINTAGE WHINE (1999) {*6} and **FOLKEMON** (2000) {*7} were significant for the fact they were the last with Walkyier, who was replaced on vocals by guitarist and producer Kevin Ridley, who had joined in 1998. Ramsey and English wrote the bulk of the material, and there was a bonus cover of Ten Pole Tudor's 'Swords Of A Thousand Men'. Drummer Aaron Walton subsequently replaced Jay Graham.

Not as prolific in this century as in their halcyon 1990s period, SKYCLAD have still managed to produce another handful of folk-ish metal albums: the acoustic-LEVELLERS-style **NO DAYLIGHT ... NOR HEELTAPS** (2003) {*6}, **A SEMBLANCE OF NORMALITY** (2004) {*6}, and thirteenth (unlucky for some?) album **IN THE ... ALL TOGETHER.** The latter set (2009) {*6} was stripped down to the bare bones and recorded live in the studio. *MCS*

Martin Walkyier - vocals (ex-Sabbat) / **Steve Ramsey** - guitar (ex-Satan, ex-Pariah) / **Graeme English** - bass (ex-Satan, ex-Pariah) / **Keith Baxter** - drums

UK Noise — US Noise

May 91. (cd/c/lp) *(N 0163-2/-4/-1)* <4839> **THE WAYWARD SONS OF MOTHER EARTH**
- The sky beneath my feet / Trance dance (a dreamtime walkabout) / A minute's piece / The Widdershins jig / Our dying island / Intro: Pagan man / The cradle will fall / Skyclad / Moongleam and meadowsweet / Terminus. *(cd re-iss. Aug 01; same)*

—— added **Dave Pugh** - guitars, banjo, vocals + **Fritha Jenkins** - violin, keyboards

Apr 92. (cd/c/lp) *(N 0186-2/-4/-1)* **A BURNT OFFERING FOR THE BONE IDOL**
- War and disorder / A broken promised land / Spinning Jenny / Salt on the earth (another man's poison) / Karmageddon (the suffering silence) / Ring stone round (*) / Men of Straul / R'vannith / The declaration of indifference / Alone in death's shadow. *(cd+= *) (cd re-iss. Nov 96; same)*

Nov 92. (m-cd) *(N 0194-2)* TRACKS FROM THE WILDERNESS
- Emerald / A room next door / When all else fails / The declaration of indifference (live) / Spinning Jenny (live) / Skyclad (live). *(re-iss. Nov 96; same)*

May 93. (cd/c/lp) *(N 0209-2/-4/-1)* **JONAH'S ARK**
- Thinking allowed? / Cry of the land / Schadenfreude / A near life experience / The wickedest man in the world / Earth mother, the sun and the furious host / The ilk of human blindness / Tunnel visionaries / A word to the wise / Bewilderbeast / It wasn't meant to end this way. *(cd re-iss. Nov 96; same)*

Jun 93. (cd-ep) *(N 0209-3)* THINKING ALLOWED? / The Cradle Will Fall (live) / The Widdershins Gig (live)

—— **Cath Howell** - violin; repl. Jenkins

Mar 94. (cd/c/lp) *(N 0239-2/-4/-1)* **PRINCE OF THE POVERTY LINE**
- Civil war dance / Cardboard city / Sins of emission / Land of the rising slum / The one piece puzzle / A bellyful of emptiness / A dog in the manger / Gammadion seed / Womb of the worm / The truth famine. *(cd re-iss. Nov 96 & Aug 01 +=; same)* - Brothers beneath the skin.

Apr 94. (7" m) *(N 0239-5)* BROTHERS BENEATH THE SKIN. / The Widdershins Jig / The Cradle Will Fall

—— **Georgina Biddle** - fiddle, keyboards; repl. Howell

Apr 95. (cd/lp) *(N 0228-2/-4)* **THE SILENT WHALES OF LUNAR SEA**
- Still spinning shrapnel / Just what nobody wanted / Art-Nazi / Jeopardy / Brimstone ballet / A stranger in the garden / Another fine mess / Turncoat rebellion / Halo of flies / Desperanto (a song for Europe?) / The present imperfect. *(on some versions +=)* - Dance of the dandy hound. *(cd re-iss. Aug 01; same)*

—— **Dave Ray** - guitar + **Jed Dawkins** - drums; repl. Pugh + Baxter

Massacre — Century Media

Jan 96. (cd/lp/pic-lp) *(MASS CD/LP/PD 084)* <7853> **IRRATIONAL ANTHEMS**
- Inequality street / The wrong song / Snake charming / Penny dreadful / The sinful ensemble / My mother in darkness / The spiral starecase / No deposit, no return / Sabre dance / I dubious / Science never sleeps / History lessens / Quantity time.

—— **Paul Smith** - drums; repl. Dawkins + Ray

Nov 96. (cd) *(MASSCD 104)* <7854> **OUI AVANT-GARDE A CHANCE** — Aug 97
- If I die laughing, it'll be an act of God / Great blow for a day job / Constance eternal / Postcard from planet earth / Jumping my shadow / Bombjour! / History lessens (the final examination) / A badtime story / Come on Eileen / Master race / Bombed out (instru-mental) / Penny dreadful (full shilling mix).

—— **Mitch Oldham** - drums; repl. Paul

—— added **Nick Acons** - guitar, violin + **John Leonard** - flute, mandolin, etc

Sep 97. (cd) *(MASSCD 128)* **THE ANSWER MACHINE?**
- A clown of thorns / Building a ruin / Worn out sole to heel / Single phial / Helium / The thread of evermore / Eirenarch / Troublesometimes / Isle of Jura / Fainting by numbers / My naked I / Catherine at the wheel / Dead angels on ice. *(w/ free acoustic cd-ep+=)* - OUTRAGEOUS FOURTUNES: Land of the rising slum / Sins of emission / Alone in death's shadow / Spinning Jenny.

—— **Kevin Ridley** - guitar; repl. Acons + Leonard

—— **Jay Graham** - drums; repl. Mitch

Mar 99. (cd/lp) *(MASS CD/LP 178)* **VINTAGE WHINE**
- Kiss my sweet brass (instrumental) / Vintage whine / On with their heads! / The silver cloud's dark lining / A well beside the river / No strings attached / Bury me / Cancer of the heart / Little Miss Take / Something to cling to / By George (instrumental).

May 99. (ltd-cd-pic-ep) *(MASSSH 203)* CLASSIX SHAPE
- Vintage whine / Inequality street / Constance eternal / Building a ruin / Sins of emission (unplugged).

Nuclear Blast — Nuclear Blast

Nov 00. (cd) *(NB 502-2)* <6502> **FOLKEMON** — Jan 01
- The great brain robbery / Think back and lie of England / Polkageist! / Crux of the message / The disenchanted forest / The antibody politic / When God logs off / You lost my memory / Deja-vu ain't what it used to be / Any old irony? *(bonus +=)* - Swords of a thousand men.

—— **Aaron Walton** - drums; repl. Jay

—— guitarist and producer **Kevin Ridley** - vocals; repl. Walkyier

Demolition — not issued

Jun 03. (cd) *(DEMCD 115)* **NO DAYLIGHTS ... NOR HEELTAPS** (acoustic re-recordings)
- Penny dreadful / Inequality street / Spinning Jenny / The cry of the land / Another fine mess / Sins of emission / The Widdershins jig / History lessens / Land of the rising slum / Single phial. *(bonus cd-ep+=)* - No deposit, no return / A great blow for a day job / No strings attached / Building a ruin / Loco-commotion.

Sep 03. (cd-s) *(DEM 119)* SWORDS OF A THOUSAND MEN (featuring Ten Pole Tudor) / Swords Of A Thousand Men / The Widdershins Jig (2001 mix)

Jun 04. (cd) *(DEMCD 142)* **A SEMBLANCE OF NORMALITY**
- Intro (pipes solo) / Do they mean us / A good day to bury bad news / Anotherdrinkingsong / A survival campaign / The song of no-involvement / The parliament of fools / Ten little kingdoms / Like... a ballad for the disenchanted / Lightening the load / NTRWB / Hybrid blues / Outro (the dissolution of parliament).

2006. (cd-ep) *(none)* JIG-A-JIG — gigs
- Jig-a-jig / Mr Malaprope & Co. / They think it's all over (well it is now?) / The Roman wall blues.

Scarlet — not issued

May 09. (cd) *(17668-2)* **IN THE ... ALL TOGETHER**
- Words upon the street / Still small beer / A well-travelled man / Black summer rain / Babakoto / Hit list / Superculture / Which is why / Modern minds / In the ... all together.

- (8-10*) compilations -

Nov 96. (cd) *Noise; (N 0275-2)* **OLD ROPE**
- The Widdershins jig / Skyclad / Spinning Jenny (live) / Alone in death's shadow / Thinking allowed? / The wickedest man in the world / Earth mother, the sun and the furious host / Cardboard city / Land of the rising slum / The one-piece puzzle / Just what nobody wanted / Brothers beneath the skin / The present imperfect / The cradle will fall / The declaration of indifference (live) / Ring stone round / Men of straw.

- essential boxed sets -

Nov 04. (3-cd-box) *Massacre; (MASSBX 467)* **PLATINUM EDITION**
- (THE ANSWER MACHINE?) // (VINTAGE WHINE) // (HISTORY LESSENS).

- (5-7*) compilations, others, etc.-

Sep 01. (cd) *Demolition; (DEMCD 112)* **ANOTHER FINE MESS** (live at the Dynamo // acoustic EP)
- Intro / Another fine mess / Cardboard city / Art-Nazi / The wickedest man in the world / The one piece puzzle / Still spinning shrapnel / Just what nobody wanted // (*):- Sins of emission / Land of the rising sun / Alone in death's shadow / Spinning Jenny. *(re-iss. Aug 02 as 'LIVE AT THE DYNAMO' on Burning Airlines+= w/out *; PILOT 139)* - The Widdershins jig / The declaration of indifference / The cradle will fall / Spinning Jenny.

Mar 02. (cd) *Massacre; (MASSCD 296)* **HISTORY LESSENS**
- Penny dreadful (full shilling mix) / The silver cloud's dark lining / Isle of Jura / No deposit, no return / Brimstone ballet / Constance eternal / Building a ruin / Emerald / I dubious / Jumping my shadow / A bellyful of emptiness / Kiss my sweet brass / Bury me / Single phial / By George.

Judy SMALL

One of several Australian protest-folk artists to emerge in the 1980s (such as PAUL KELLY, KEV CARMODY and arguably ERIC BOGLE), Judy was born in 1953 in Coffs Harbour and relocated to Sydney when she turned eighteen. Best known for her songwriting talent (examples include 'Mothers, Daughters, Wives' and 'Charlesworth Bay'), Judy's thought-provoking compositions have been interpreted by many traditionally-styled folk artists, including BOGLE, The McCALMANS, The CORRIES, PRISCILLA HERDMAN, CHARLIE KING and RONNIE GILBERT.

Working as a civil servant by day and performing at night at local coffeehouses and clubs, SMALL's career took an upswing when she played the Vancouver Folk Festival in 1982 at BOGLE's invitation. It was the inspiration and the push she needed, and since then she's been one of her country's greatest musical exports. She was honoured with a tribute concert of her songs at the Maleny Folk Festival in Queensland in 1993, and her work has won numerous awards.

On the recording front, albums that have achieved above-average critical acclaim (not including compilations) include her Redwood sets of the 1980s, namely **LADIES AND GEMS** (1984) {*7}, **ONE VOICE IN THE CROWD** (1985) {*7}, **HOME FRONT** (1988) {*7} and **SNAPSHOT** (1990) {*7}. With Kavisha Mazzella and Bronwyn Calcutt, Judy has released one set as The Three Sheilas, and she also contributed to the gay and lesbian album 'Out And Proud'. *MCS*

Judy Small - vocals, acoustic guitar / with session people

Aus/UK Plaza — US not issued

1982. (lp) *(PZ 005-220)* **A NATURAL SELECTION** — Aus
- To be a woman / I don't know you any more / Mothers, daughters, wives / Festival of light / Backyard abortion waltz / Girls in our town / For the women who write (Carole's song) / Family maiden aunt / Mary Parker's lament / Lest we.

1984. (lp) *(???)* **LADIES AND GEMS** — Aus
- Alison and me / The White Bay paper seller / Bridget Evans / Mothers, daughters, wives / The manly ferry song / Just another crazy on the street / They promise you diamonds / Speaking hands, hearing eyes / Much too much trouble / A song for the roly-poly people / Mary Parker's lament / Turn right, go straight / From the lambing to the wool.

Redwood — not issued

1985. (lp) *(RR 8503)* **ONE VOICE IN THE CROWD**
- One voice in the crowd / Walls and windows / The IPD / If I ever sing a love song / A heroine of mine / Women of our time / The futures exchange / Just another death in New York York City / Alice Martin / Family maiden aunt / Thirty years a princess / Our best friend / Never turning back.

Jan 88. (lp) *(RR 8808)* **HOME FRONT**
- Home front / Ivy says (she has no time left) / Golden arches / The sky of the southern cross / When the party's over / Song for Jacqueline / Silo / You don't speak for me / Planning for the future / Annie / How many times.

1990. (lp) *(RR 9003)* **SNAPSHOT**
- The revolution's here / Ella Whelan / No tears for the widow / Starstruck / Pearl / Montreal, December '89 / Charlesworth Bay / Evil angels / The advertising game / Never rock 'n' rollers. *(cd-iss. 1993 on 'Crafty Maid'; CMM 005CD)*

Sep 93. (12" ep) *(RR 3100)* MOTHERS, DAUGHTERS, WIVES

Crafty Maid — not issued

Jul 94. (cd) *(CMMCD 008)* **SECOND WIND**
- Daughters of the second ... / Sacred ground / I thought I'd be much older / No news / Life begins at forty / Albion revisited / A man among men / Final cut / Apart from that / Lunch in a modern world / Reflections / Woman in the wings / Until...

Jul 96. (cd/c) *(CMM CD/C 009)* **GLOBAL VILLAGE**
- We know it's gonna rain / Marlborough sounds / Living in the fast lane / Love is a fearsome thing / The portrait of Margot Berard / What was her name? / Music in the movement / Leila's dance / No love lost / When Cecilia sings / Global village / La vie en pose (the French song) / Song about a writer.

In 1997 she was one of three singers on the album 'Three Sheilas'.

Jul 99. (cd) *(CMM 011)* **LET THE RAINBOW SHINE** — Aus
- Love in parallel / Country gaytime blues / A man among men / Influenced by queers / An ordinary love / Lesbian chic / From this day forward / No tears for the widow / Friday night / I can be a lesbian / Everything possible / Let the rainbow shine.

Jun 03. (cd) *(CMM 012)* **MOSAIC** — Aus
- Stolen gems / Joseph Nkolo is singing / Mosaic (the house that I grew up in) / Our best friend / There's life in the old girl yet / Song of my father / Days like these / Fifty something / Wanted woman / Nobody knew she was there / Never lose hope.

Aug 07. (d-cd) *(CMM 013)* **LIVE AT THE ARTERY**
[live 1st/2nd December 2006] — Aus
- Stolen gems / When Cecilia sings / Fifty something / Mary Parker's lament / (intro to...) / Montreal, December '89 / Charlesworth Bay / (intro to...) / Never rock 'n' rollers / Song for Jacqueline / Global village / (intro to...) / The IPD / (intro to...) / The widow in waiting / How many times / You don't speak for me // Joseph Nkolo is singing / (intro to...) / Walls and windows / (intro to...) / Song of my father / There's life in the old girl yet / The White Bay paper seller / From the lambing to the wool / Love is a fearsome thing / La vie en pose / (intro to...) Everything possible / Anchor and sail / (intro to...) / Mothers, daughters, wives / Under control.

- (8-10*) compilations -

Jul 99. (cd) *Crafty Maid; (CMM 010)* **NEVER TURNING BACK: A RETROSPECTIVE**
- Sacred ground / Sky of the southern cross / How many times / Advertising game / Montreal, December '89 / Until / Alice Martin / Starstruck / Charlesworth Bay / The White Bay paper seller / Never rock'n'rollers / Ivy says / Daughters of the second wave / Life begins at forty / Just another crazy on the street / No news / Women of our time / Just another death in New York City / Never turning back.

- (5-7*) compilations, others, etc.-

Mar 92. (cd/c) *Greentrax; (CD/C TRAX 050)* **THE BEST OF JUDY SMALL: WORD OF MOUTH**
- Alison and me / How many times / Mothers, daughters, wives / The manly ferry song / Walls and windows / Much too much trouble / Golden arches / Speaking hands, hearing eyes / One voice in the crowd / Song for Jacqueline / Alice Martin / Mary Parker's lament / Family maiden aunt / You don't speak for me / Women of our time / The futures exchange.

Jun 94. (cd/c) *Crafty Maid; (CMM CD/C 007)* **THE BEST OF THE 80s**
- Walls and windows / Song for Jacqueline / Ordinary people / Mother, daughters, wives / If I ever sing a love song / The manly ferry song (for Cora) / From the lambing to the wool / The IPD / Heroine of mine / Golden arches / Speaking hands, hearing eyes / One voice in the crowd / Family maiden aunt / Annie / Mary Parker's lament / Song for the roly-poly people / You don't speak for me / The futures exchange.

The Amazing Mr. SMITH

Comedy played a big part in folk music in the 1970s, and The AMAZING MR. SMITH (born Derek Smith, April 1, 1948 in Croydon, Surrey) and his self-dubbed "Laughs, Inventions and Music" one-man show was a good example. From his folky days in the late 1960s and early 1970s with Wild Oats, to sticking his head in a birdcage while performing on stage, MR. SMITH (as he was initially billed) was folk music's outsider act, always on the fringes but never far away from the action. He appeared on TV shows 'Game For A Laugh' and its spin-off, 'Prove It', featuring future 'Who Wants To Be A Millionaire' host Chris Tarrant.

Described as "Monty Python's answer to John Williams", Derek performs on an array of inventive instrumentation including the cardboard-tube double bass, musical shoelaces, tutu xylophone (for 'The Nutcracker Suite') and the condom harp (for 'The Blue Danube'), while his three-minute rendition of 'Riverdance' is truly breathtaking. Two of his earliest LPs, **TWO VERY SIMILAR VIEWS OF MR SMITH** (1979) {*6} and **NORMAL SERVICE WILL BE RESUMED AS SOON AS POSSIBLE** (1983) {*6}, should be of particular interest to collectors and anyone interested in having a giggle. It must be said that his live set from 2000, **LAUGHS, INVENTIONS AND MUSIC,** is much better on DVD, where the full effect of his maniacal performance is appreciated by one and all, with the exception of hard-nose classical music fans. *MCS*

Derek Smith - vocals, acoustic guitar, harmonica, etc.

UK Sweet Folk and Country — US not issued

1979. (lp; as MR. SMITH) *(SFA 105)* **TWO VERY SIMILAR VIEWS OF MR. SMITH**
- March from a little suite / Society ladies / Barbara Allen / With her head tucked underneath her arm / Buddy can you spare a dime / A g-nu / She had to go and lose it at the Astor / The star of County Down / The owl and the pussycat / Mock Morris / If you were the only girl in the world / Liberty bell / Halfway down the stairs.

1983. (lp) *(SFA 125)* **NORMAL SERVICE WILL BE RESUMED AS SOON AS POSSIBLE**
- Oh,, I do like to be beside the seaside - Washington Post / The policeman's song / The teddy bears' picnic - Me and my teddy bear / Air on a G string / March militaire No.3 / The elephant / Excerpts from the Nutcracker Suite / When my little Pomeranian met your little Pekinese / Clair de lune / Gold and silver waltz / Also sprach Zarathustra / I wanna be like you / When I take my sugar to tea - Goodbye.

HTD — not issued

1993. (c) *(HTDMC 16)* **IN THE MOOD FOR SHEEP**
- Superman / Cortina / Vat 69 / Humpty Dumpty - Pop goes the weasel / The Cutty Wren / I feel pretty / Classical gas / We'll gather lilacs in the spring again / Jumping bean / We're a couple of swells / Clog dance / In the mood for sheep / Crossroads - Poirot / Right said Fred / Listen with mother / The seeds of love / Coronation Scot - Chatanooga choo-choo - Pasadena / Spanish omelette / The dambusters' march / As time goes by / The laugh.

own label — not issued

1999. (cd) *(none)* **NO MESSING ABOUT (JUST GUITAR)** — mail-o
- St Emilion / The hidden well / Haiku / Georgia on my mind / Gentleman Jim / Semper fidelis / The star of County Down / Pictures at an exhibition / Farewell to Stromness / Buddy can you spare a dime / Barbara Allen / Any umbrellas / It's a rosebud in June - Brigg fair / Eleven-bar blues / Chanson de Matin / The end of the line.

2000. (c/cd) *(none)* **LAUGHS, INVENTIONS AND MUSIC**
[live clips from various shows]

2006. (cd) *(none)* **SERIOUS STUFF** — mail-o
- Out of the mist / The happy tune / Miss Melanie / Lullaby / I'm beginning to see the light / Van rouge / The cutty wren / Number 20 / The liberty bell / Agatha Christie's Poirot / Late arrival / Boarsbarrow / Largo (ex. New World Symphony) / Nimrod (ex. Enigma Variations) / Partial derivative / Island song / God only knows / Tubular condoms.

2011. (d-cd; as MR. SMITH) *(none)* **OLD STANDARDS AND NEW CLASSICS** mail-o
- Try a little tenderness / Ev'ry time we say goodbye / Ain't misbehavin' / It was a very good year / A nightingale sang in Berkeley Square / Tenderly / These foolish things / It's alright with me / When I fall in love / You do something to me / Star dust / I can't give you anything but love / Cry me a river / Til there was you / The Irishish tune / Stormy weather / Gold and silver waltz / Ol' man river / As time goes by / Buddy, can you spare a dime / Can't help lovin' dat man / The twelfth of never // Eleanor Rigby / Songbird / Tears in heaven / Raining in my heart / It had better be tonight / Happy tune / Babooshka / In my life / If you leave me now / Lately / And I love her / Clare de lune / Desperado / Gentleman Jim / Walk on by / On Broadway / Coronation Street / B.O.S. / Michelle / Classical gas + Angi.

TV SMITH [folk part]

Better known for his punk pursuits with The Adverts, one-time 'Bored Teenager' TV (Tim) SMITH found his acoustic voice on his Cooking Vinyl set **MARCH OF THE GIANTS** (1992) {*7}. Years of burning the midnight oil with Gaye Advert and the crew had taken its toll on the mighty SMITH, but his modern-day take on folk-tinged rock was as observational, confrontational and anthemic as in the 1970s. 'Can't Pay Won't Pay', 'Haves And Have-Nots', 'Useless' and 'Empty Wallet' might have sounded a little different had they been written in the punk era or the new-wave 1980s, but they are as poignant as old Adverts favourites like 'No Time To Be 21' and 'Safety In Numbers'. For something a little more recent, you could do worse than buy his latest set, 'Coming In To Land' (2011). Punk or folk – what does it matter? *MCS*

TV Smith - vocals, acoustic guitar (with session people)

UK Cooking Vinyl — US not issued

Jul 92. (cd/c/lp) *(COOK CD/C/LP 047)* **MARCH OF THE GIANTS**
- Lion and the lamb / March of the giants / Can't pay won't pay / Atlantic tunnel / Haves and have-nots / Straight and narrow / Free world / Ship in a bottle / Empty wallet / Useless / Runaway train driver / Borderline. *(cd re-iss. Mar 94; same)*

Smith continued with his acoustic-punk career...

SMOKE FAIRIES

British folk-rock was going through a bit of a renaissance when this Chichester-based duo of singer-songwriters, Jessica Davies and Katherine Blamire, burst on to the scene in 2007. Friends from school (where they had sung in the choir), their influences were grounded in 1970s Americana and Brit-folk giants such as FAIRPORT CONVENTION and PENTANGLE - their enthusiasm for the genre had been heightened when they worked as car park attendants at the Sidmouth Folk Festival.

Returning to London from a year out in Vancouver, Canada, the SMOKE FAIRIES secured a support slot on a Bryan Ferry tour, a chance to promote their self-financed debut set **STRANGE THE THINGS** (2007) {*6}. Described as "dark, lustful blues-folk" by Mojo magazine, SMOKE FAIRIES went from strength to strength and earned another prestigious billing with The HANDSOME FAMILY. With Jack White as patron (and producer, and session guitarist and drummer), the duo's first real break came with the Third Man release of their limited-edition 'Gastown' single. Surfacing from rural Cornwall via New Orleans, SMOKE FAIRIES (now on an offshoot of the V2 imprint) finally delivered that difficult second set, **THROUGH LOW LIGHT AND TREES** (2010) {*8}. A trip to the States to support LAURA MARLING, and a guest appearance on Richard Hawley's EP 'False Lights From The Land', helped boost their CV.

Of the album itself, comparisons have been made with KATE & ANNA McGARRIGLE, and their sublime hippie-folk harmonies and intertwining blues guitar playing on ethereal beauties like 'Summer Fades', 'Devil In My Mind' (very TREES), 'Hotel Room' and 'Storm Song' were all compelling cuts with cult appeal. Later in the year, Mojo invited them to cover 'Ohio' for a NEIL YOUNG/ 'Harvest' 40th-anniversary compilation CD. *MCS*

Jessica Davies - vocals, guitar / **Katherine Blamire** - vocals, guitar / (+ session people)

UK Concentrated — US not issued

Aug 07. (cd) *(CP 002CD)* **STRANGE THE THINGS**
- Dinner plate / Smoke filled room / Always in the back / Catching leaves / Wedding gown / Cold wind / Strange the things / Good day to be alive / I'll move on / You can't / Running alongside a train. *(+ hidden track)*

Music For Heroes — not issued

Aug 08. (ltd-7") *(HEROES 801)* LIVING WITH GHOSTS. / Troubles

Jul 09. (ltd-7") *(HEROES 901)* FROZEN HEART. / He's Moving On
(w/cd-ep) - ['A'] / Fences / Morning light / We had lost our minds / ['B'].

Oct 09. (ltd-7") *(HEROES 902)* SUNSHINE. / When You Grow Old
(w/cd-s) - [same tracks].

not issued — Third Man

Dec 09. (ltd-7", 8"colrd) *<TMR 021>* GASTOWN. / River Song

not issued — 453 Music

Apr 10. (colrd-lp) *<453-001>* **GHOSTS** [singles compilation]
- Sunshine / When you grow old / Living with ghosts / Troubles / Frozen heart / Fences / Morning light / We had lost our minds / He's moving on.

Cooperative - V2 — not issued

Sep 10. (cd/lp) *(SF 001 CD/LP)* **THROUGH LOW LIGHT AND TREES**
- Summer fades / Devil in my mind / Hotel room / Dragon / Erie Lackawanna / Strange moon rising / Morning blues / Storm song / Blue skies fall / Feeling is turning blue / After the rain.

Sep 10. (ltd-7") *(SF 002S)* HOTEL ROOM. / Human Concerns

Sep 10. (ltd-cd-ep) *(SF 003CD)* SONGS FROM AN AFTERNOON SESSION
- Hotel room / Devil in my mind / Living with ghosts / Storm song / Strange moon rising.

Jan 11. (ltd-7") *(SF 004S)* STRANGE MOON RISING. / Requiem
(ltd-7"white) *(SF 005S)* - ['A'] / Alabama.

SONGS OF GREEN PHEASANT

Like a one-man SIMON & GARFUNKEL or Crosby, Stills and Nash, Duncan Sumpner is the man behind the acoustic ambient-folk act SONGS OF GREEN PHEASANT. Straight outta Oughtibridge in Sheffield, Kayak (as he was then calling himself) produced a double-tracked demo tape in 2002 of recordings that Fat Cat Records found too good to turn down.

SONGS OF GREEN PHEASANT (2005) {*8} was lo-fi-folk functioning at its own pastoral pace, probably on a par with American counterpart DEVENDRA BANHART. Not quite running into freak-folk territory, harmony-fuelled tracks like 'Hey, Hey, Wilderness', 'I Am Daylights', 'Nightfall (For Boris P)' and 'Truth But Not Fact' were vignettes against a backdrop of lilting Flying Saucer Attack-esque electronics/acoustics.

Not quite an album, although comprising several decent-length songs, the mini odds-and-sods set **AERIAL DAYS** (2006) {*6}, featuring a cover of The Beatles' 'Dear Prudence', was basically a psychedelic companion-piece to Duncan's debut. 'Wintered' and 'Pink By White' make it a worthwhile purchase on their own.

With seven tracks to show again, although three broke eight minutes, **GYLLYNG STREET** (2007) {*6} introduced a fresh, ethereal element to the mix, while a rhythm section of Oliver Bird (bass) and Jonathan Gill (drums) fleshed out the sound. One can't really file this long-player under folk: the trumpet of Clive Scott on 'Alex Drifting Alone' and Julie Cole's vocal contribution on follow-on cut 'Fires P.G.R.' let loose the indie soul from Green Pheasant's deep inner psyche. *MCS*

Duncan Sumpner (b. 1974) - vocals, guitars, synths

UK Fat Cat — US Fat Cat

Sep 05. (cd) *(<FATCD 40>)* **SONGS OF GREEN PHEASANT**
- I am daylights / Nightfall (for Boris P) / The burning man / Knulp / The wraith of loving / Until... / Hey, hey, wilderness / Truth but not fact / Soldiers kill their sisters / From here to somewhere else. *<US lp-iss. 2006 on Ruined Potential; FTK 06>*

Nov 06. (m-cd) *(<FATCD 58>)* **AERIAL DAYS**
- Pink by white / Remembering and forgetting / Wolves among snowmen / Stars from birds / Dear Prudence / Wintered / Brody jacket.

Jul 07. (cd) *(FATCD 61)* **GYLLYNG STREET**
- Boats / King Friday / The ballad of Century Paul / West Coast profiling / Alex drifting alone / Fires P.G.R. / A sketch for Maenporth.

SONS OF NOEL AND ADRIAN

Formed in Brighton as a 12-piece folk-noir collective by members of Hope Of The States, The Miserable Rich, The LEISURE SOCIETY and SHORELINE, this ensemble were Britain's answer to FLEET FOXES, BON IVER and ESPERS.

Under the umbrella of the burgeoning Willkommen team (who had produced a surprise Ivor Novello Award nomination for The LEISURE SOCIETY), the experimental group were led by SHORELINE's Jacob

Richardson and Tom Cowan, The LEISURE SOCIETY's Nick Hemming and Hope Of The States's Mike Siddell. The freak-folk element was clear on tracks such as 'Damien, Lessons From What's Poor', one of a handful of gems on their debut set, **SONS OF NOEL AND ADRIAN** (2008) {*8}. A haunting listen, featuring songs such as the eerie 'Indigo' and 'The Wreck Is Not A Boat', it was recorded live at the Chicken Shed, Hemyock in Devon in 2007. *MCS*

Jacob Richardson - vocals, guitar (of SHORELINE) / **Tom Cowan** - guitar (of SHORELINE) / **Nick Hemming** - vocals (of The LEISURE SOCIETY, of SHORELINE) / **Mike Siddell** - violin, etc (ex-Hope Of The States, of The Miserable Rich, of The LEISURE SOCIETY) / other musicians: **William Calderbank** (of The LEISURE SOCIETY, of SHORELINE, of The Miserable Rich), **Helen Whitaker** (of The LEISURE SOCIETY), **Daniel Green, Marcus Hamblett, Jo White, Cathy Cardin, Alistair Strachan + Rowan Coupland** (all from the Willkommen Collective)

UK Shelsmusic — US Shelsmusic

Jun 08. (cd) *(SHELS 009)* **SONS OF NOEL AND ADRIAN**
- Indigo / Hernow / Damien, lessons from what's poor / Cave / Ragwort / Divorce / Violent violet / The wreck is not a boat / Inside Olympia.

Apr 09. (ltd; cd-ep) <???> THE WRECK IS NOT A BOAT / Go Jo Jee / Ruby Red (Isan's) / Elsa's House

One Inch Badge — not issued

Apr 11. (ltd-7"ep) *(OIB 015)* RIVERS EP
- Black side of the river / Big, bad, bold / Leaving Mary's hand.

SPIERS & BODEN

The 2000s have produced many talented folk musicians, but none more dedicated than the workaholic duo of (John) SPIERS and (Jon) BODEN. Alongside an industrious career on other people's records - from their inaugural session appearances with The Ratcatchers on post-millennium sets by ELIZA CARTHY, to their many moonlighting shifts with the BELLOWHEAD collective - SPIERS on melodeon and BODEN on fiddle have produced a string of redefining traditional folk albums.

Playing mostly traditional material including hornpipes and usual-suspect Child ballads, they have reeled off four albums for Fellside Records, their technique and musicianship apparent on all from **THROUGH AND THROUGH** (2001) {*7} and 2003's **BELLOW** {*8} to 2005's **TUNES** {*6} and **SONGS** {*6}, the last-named set featuring both vocalists on concertinas and Boden on guitar.

Spurred on by some rave reviews from fRoots and BBC Radio 2, their debut Navigator Records release, **VAGABOND** (2008) {*8}, was another choice collection of English songs and sea shanties; 'Captain's Ward' would become a festival favourite of the Glastonbury set.

Meanwhile, JON BODEN was putting on his own show with two acoustic-folk albums, **THE PAINTED LADY** (2006) {*7} - a darker, more intense crossover recording (check out 'Blue Dress') - and **SONGS FROM THE FLOODPLAIN** (2009) {*6}, an apocalyptic concept album that re-imagines England in the future.

Since August 2010, Jon has been providing his internet fans with a song a day on his own webpage, and as of July 2011 he's keeping it up. Do the math ... *MCS*

John Spiers - vocals, melodeon, concertina, squeezeboxes / **Jon Boden** - vocals, fiddle, guitar, etc.

UK Fellside — US not issued

Oct 01. (cd; as; JOHN SPIERS & JON BODEN) *(FECD 161)* **THROUGH AND THROUGH**
- Rambling sailor / The Rochdale coconut dance / Earl Richard / The Quaker - Brighton camp / Oswestry wake - Morgan rattler / Golden glove / Red kites / Boston harbour / The three-two set / The Shropshire rounds - Rusty gully - The three-footed chestnut / Adieu sweet lovely Nancy / Three around three / Down the moor / The gooseberry bush - Laudanum bunches / Banks of green willow.

In 2002, Ian Giles, SPIERS, and BODEN (with Graham Metcalfe on vocals) released ltd-edition tourist centre CD 'Sea Shanties'; BODEN, JOEY OLIVER, SPIERS & GILES later delivered 'Old Irish Jigs And Reels' (2007)

as part of the Ratcatchers, they backed ELIZA CARTHY on 'Anglicana' (2002); another collaboration, 'Rough Music', was issued in 2005.

next with **Benji Kirkpatrick** - bouzouki, guitars

May 03. (cd) *(FECD 175)* **BELLOW**
- Prickle eye bush / Sloe gin set: a) Frozen gin, b) Vinegar reel, c) The sloe / Courting too slow / Dawn chorus / The outlandish knight / Jiggery pokerwork - Haul away - Seven stars / Go and leave me / Jack Robinson - Argiers - Old Tom of Oxford / Copshawholme fair / Princess Royal - Cuckoo's nest / Brown Adam / Ginger up lustily - Old woman tossed up in a blanket.

Jun 05. (cd) *(FECD 192)* **TUNES**
- Sportsman's hornpipe / Monkey-cokey / Cokey hornpipe - Mexican tent jig - Monkey hornpipe / The old Lancashire hornpipe - The third beekeeper / Dee-light / Banks of the Dee - The cuckoo - Queen's delight / Flapjacks and firesticks - The minor rigged ship / Stoney steps hornpipe / Cuckoo's nest / Cheshire waltz / Rampant / Union / Dearest Dickie / Blow the winds / Holly's reel - Blow the winds high-o - The pork pie polka / The Shropshire miner / Trunkles.

Oct 05. (cd) *(FECD 194)* **SONGS** (rec. October 02)
- Bold Sir Rylas (child 18) / Old Maui / Horn fair / Child morris / Innocent when you dream / Cruel knife / Derry gaol / On Christmas day / Doleful dance of death / Bill Brown / Lucy Wan.

Navigator — not issued

Aug 08. (cd/lp) *(NAVIGATOR 12 CD/LP)* **VAGABOND**
- Tom Padget / The birth of Robin Hood / Three tunes / Captain Ward / Beggar boy / Mary Anne / Speed the plough - The princess royal / Rambling Robin / Gentlewoman / The rain it rains / Vignette.

Jul 11. (cd) *(NAVIGATOR 46)* **THE WORKS** [re-recordings with guests]
- Tom Padget / Horn fair / Gooseberry bush - Laudanum bunches / The birth of Robin Hood / The Cheshire waltz / Brown Adam / Rochdale coconut dance / Old Maui / Haul away / Bold Sir Rylas / Prickle-eye bush.

JON BODEN

Soundpost — not issued

May 06. (cd) *(5001)* **PAINTED LADY**
- Get a little something / Blue dress / Josephine / Pocketful of mud / Drunken princess / Lemany / Win some lose some Sally / True love / Ophelia / Broken things / Painted lady / Drinking the night away.

Navigator — not issued

Mar 09. (cd) *(NAVIGATOR 21)* **SONGS FROM THE FLOODPLAIN**
- We do what we can / Going down to the wasteland / Days gone by / Penny for the preacher / Dancing to the factory / Beating the bounds / The pilgrim's way / April queen / When the walls come tumbling down / Don't wake me up 'til tomorrow / Under the breath / Has been cavalry.

SPREDTHICK (⟹ MAYOR, Simon)

STARLESS AND BIBLE BLACK

Taking their name from Dylan Thomas's radio play 'Under Milk Wood', this nu-Brit-folk quintet were from Manchester, though their singer-songwriter Helene Gautier was French-born. Finding a home at Chicago's Locust Records, Gautier and musicians Peter Philipson (guitars, banjo and co-songwriter), Raz Ullah (electronics), Paul Blakesley (double bass) and Brian Edwards (drums) received critical acclaim for their eponymous debut **STARLESS AND BIBLE BLACK** (2006) {*8}.

Floating on a tide of tranquillity with a rustic and rural charm, almost every song on the set ('B.B', 'Hermione', et al) recalls 1969-era FAIRPORT CONVENTION, Gautier's ethereal vocals lying somewhere between SANDY DENNY and French pop chanteuse Francoiz Breut. Often credited to Wild Billy Childish, traditional song 'The Bitter Cup' injects a bit of fire into the set, while opener 'Everyday And Everynight' has an acoustic JONI MITCHELL flavour.

A one-off single for Static Caravan Records, 'Up With The Orcadian Tide', was something of a stopgap as the group found theit feet as festival favourites. Support slots to ESPERS, ALASDAIR ROBERTS and VETIVER bolstered their CV.

Recorded in the mountainous Bryn Derwyn wilds of Snowdonia in Wales, **SHAPE OF THE SHAPE** (2009) {*6} broke free from folky shackles (banjos and dulcimers were booted into touch). It was a confident chanson-pop affair with a gothic Topanga Canyon country-blues backdrop, most typically on 'Country Heir' and 'Hanging On The Vine'. The nine-minute psych-drones of 'Les Furies' certainly put paid to any folk foibles of the past; a little Led Zeppelinesque in texture, it finally breaks sweat into a crescendo half-way through. The group should learn lessons from this 'difficult second album'. *MCS*

Helene Gautier (b. France) - vocals / **Peter Philipson** - guitars, banjo, dulcimer / **Raz Ullah** - electronics, guitar / plus **Paul Blakesley** - double bass, vocals / **Brian Edwards** - drums

UK Locust — US Locust

Oct 06. (cd/lp) *(<L 85 CD/LP>)* **STARLESS AND BIBLE BLACK** — Jul 07
- Everyday and everynight / Time is for leaving / Sirene / Tredog / The Birley tree / Hermione / B.B. / Allsight / Untitled cantiga / The bitter cup / 016-013.

Static Caravan — not issued

Jun 07. (ltd-7") *(VAN 132-7)* UP WITH THE ORCADIAN TIDE. / All In A Day

Oct 09. (cd) *(VAN 192CD)* **SHAPE OF THE SHAPE**
- Say Sonny say / Your majesty man / Hanging on the vine / Radio blues / Les furies / Country heir / Popty ping / Year of dalmations. *(lp-iss. Nov 09 on Locust; LOCUST 118LP)*

Angus & Julia STONE

Brother-sister folk duos are rare, and even rarer is the fact that the STONE siblings (Angus and Julia) are from sun-kissed Newport in north Sydney, Australia. Growing up in a musical family (their father had been in a covers group, Backbeat), the young singer-songwriters learned their trade while following their academic pursuits. Initially billed as a package but performing separately on stage, they decided to combine their obvious talents.

2006 was a turning point for the duo as a couple of EPs ('Chocolates And Cigarettes' and 'Heart Full Of Wine') were released to an enthusiastic response. Fran Healy of Travis had already taken them under his wing, and they recorded the latter EP at his London home. Julia provided backing vocals on Travis's 2007 set 'The Boy With No Name'.

With a voice not too dissimilar to the kooky flutterings of JOANNA NEWSOM, Julia's fairytale-folk contributions to the duo's debut album, **A BOOK LIKE THIS** (2008) {*7}, were spot-on for today's market - 'Here We Go Again', 'Soldier' and the title track certainly had the edge. That's not to say that Angus wasn't up to the job; his acoustic guitar and fRootsy vocals on 'Just A Boy' and 'The Beast' fitted in perfectly on a set best described as two for the price of one.

Three years in the making, **DOWN THE WAY** (2010) {*7} was the pair's coming-of-age album, not exactly a folk record per se but a hybrid of chamber pop and Americana. The Australians bought this in droves, plying it with several awards along the way; check out star turns 'Big Jet Plane' (also recorded on Angus's offshoot LADY OF THE SUNSHINE's **SMOKING GUN** {*6} set in 2009), 'The Devil's Tears' and 'Hold On'. *MCS*

Angus Stone - vocals, acoustic guitar, trombone / **Julia Stone** - vocals, acoustic guitar, keyboards, trumpet

UK Independiente — US Capitol

Oct 06. (12" ep) *(ISOM 113T)* CHOCOLATES AND CIGARETTES
- Private lawns / Mango tree / All of me / Paper aeroplane / Babylon / Chocolates and cigarettes.

—— added **Mitch Connelly** - percussion / **Clay McDonald** - bass

Mar 07. (m-lp/d-cd-ep) *(ISOM 66 LP/DCD)* **HEART FULL OF WINE**
- What you wanted / Fooled myself / Heart full of wine / I'm yours / Sadder than you / Wooden chair. *(d-cd-ep+=)* - CHOCOLATES AND CIGARETTES

2007. (7") *(ISOM 120S)* PRIVATE LAWNS. / Malakai

EMI — not issued

2008. (cd-ep) *(CDRP 869)* HOLLYWOOD — Austra
- Hollywood / All the colours / Johnny and June / Lonely hands.

Flock — not issued

Mar 08. (cd) *(FLOCKCD 1)* **A BOOK LIKE THIS**
- The beast / Here we go again / Wasted / Just a boy / Bella / Hollywood / A book like this / Silver coin / Stranger / Soldier / Jewels and gold / Another day / Horse and cart. *(w/ dvd tracks)*

May 10. (cd) *(FLOCKCD 8)* **DOWN THE WAY**
- Hold on / Black crow / For you / Big jet plane / Santa Monica dream / Yellow brick road / And the boys / On the road / Walk it off / Hush / Draw your swords / I'm not yours / The devil's tears.

- (5-7*) compilations, etc.-

May 11. (cd) *EMI; (094743-2)* **MEMORIES OF AN OLD FRIEND**
- Private lawns / Babylon / Paper aeroplane / Take you away / My Malakai / Lonely hands / Little bird / Chocolate and cigarettes / Old friend / Choking / Mango tree [US version] / Heart full of wine / All of me.

LADY OF THE SUNSHINE

Angus with **Govinda Doyle**

Flock — not issued

Apr 09. (cd) *(FLOCKCD 2)* **SMOKING GUN**
- Silver revolver / Home sweet home / White rose parade / Jack nimble / Big jet plane / Smoking gun / Daisychain / The wolf / Anna / King's black magic / Dead man's train / Lady of the sunshine.

STRANGE FOLK

With a name now more associated with a genre and a various-artists compilation, STRANGE FOLK were strange folk indeed. Eccentrically weird or weirdly eccentric, two-man-band Mike Willoughby and Mike Gavin toured the English toilet festival scene in a camper van between 1987 and 1988, releasing one solitary LP for Fellside Records before they split.

"UNHAND ME, YOU BEARDED LOON!" {*5} was a manic blend of skiffle, protest folk and a bit of poetical licence - think TONIGHT AT NOON, GONE TO EARTH or McDERMOTT'S TWO HOURS. Willoughby stayed on Fellside's books and sessioned for PETE MORTON on his mid-1990s set 'Courage, Love And Grace'. *MCS*

Mike Willoughby - vocals, acoustic guitar / **Mike Gavin** - percussion, vocals

UK Fellside — US not issued

1988. (lp/c) *(FE 069/+CD)* **"UNHAND ME, YOU BEARDED LOON!"**
- The jolly hangman / Shoot the hippy / The badger and the bird / Meg Murphy's sons / Midnight in Preston / Pottingshed polka / Polka piquee / Rats of the 40 / Bitts Park polka / Frozen ponds / The Langdale gang / The Upland geese / Benbecula hornpipe / Fields of the glen / The Whitewater dash / Face the day / The Wynass jig.

SUIFINN (⟹ MILES, Dick)

SWAN ARCADE

Formed in 1970 in Bradford, Yorkshire, SWAN ARCADE had two rolls of the dice when Dave Brady (who had lost an arm in a motorcycle accident at 17), his future wife Heather Johnston and Jim Boyes had two periods of musical activity, one in the 1970s, the other in the 1980s. Taking their name from a demolished landmark local shopping centre, SWAN ARCADE were bold enough to try their hand at close-harmony a cappella, previously the preserve of folk contemporaries The YOUNG TRADITION and The WATERSONS.

The **SWAN ARCADE** (1973) {*5} album that found its way on to Bill Leader's Trailer label was a mixture of trad pieces of varying quality that went down quite well with the purist brigade. Unfortunately, it also saw the almost immediate departure of Bridlington-born Boyes, who relocated to Sheffield. The YOUNG TRADITION connection ran true to form when the Bradys enlisted the help of former YOUNG TRADITION member Royston Wood (and later Brian Miller), to fulfil concert and BBC Radio One/John Peel Show commitments. Boyes was back in tow from 1974 onwards.

Released early in 1977, **MATCHLESS** {*7} was certainly a degree more adventurous as the trio, with numerous session people, provided some interesting musical backing to a few choice cover versions of songs by RICHARD THOMPSON ('The Great Valerio'), Janis Joplin ('Mercedes Benz') and Tommy Armstrong ('Trimdon Grange Explosion'). The set was a fixture in the Belgian folk charts for almost three years.

However, the group disbanded, later finding work on an album by COUNTRY JOE & THE FISH luminary Barry Melton ('We Are Like The Ocean') and FAIRPORT-addled sessions with RICHARD & LINDA THOMPSON, ASHLEY HUTCHINGS and The ALBION BAND. Jim formed Jiggery Polkary.

It took some persuasion to prise the Bradys away from the hotel they ran in the Lake District, but the three were once again in circulation for comeback set **TOGETHER FOREVER** (1985) {*6}, a record pieced together from varied sources including 'For The Sake Of Days Gone By' (from the daddy of country music, Jimmie Rodgers), 'Georgie On A Spree' (RICHARD THOMPSON), 'Dives And Lazarus' (from ex-member Royston Wood), 'Paperback Writer' (the Beatles), 'Goodnight Loving Trail' (BRUCE 'UTAH' PHILIPS), 'Together Forever' (RAB NOAKES), 'Lola' (the Kinks) and 'Keep The Faith' (Barry Melton). 'Mighty Rocky Road' was heard from Helen Schneyer at a folk festival in Inverness in 1973, likewise 'Go From My Window' from Jon Rennard.

SWAN ARCADE's second set for Fellside Records, **DIVING FOR PEARLS** (1986) {*5}, repeated the prescription, albeit with a guest list to die for that included MADDY PRIOR, MICHAEL CHAPMAN and Rick Kemp. Covers this time came from: JOHN TAMS ('Raise Your Banner'), Sting ('Black Seam'), TOMMY MAKEM ('Four Green Fields'), Elvis Costello ('Brilliant Mistake' and, with Clive Langer, 'Shipbuilding'). A line from the last-named song supplied the set's title.

The advent of a new folk supergroup, BLUE MURDER (a la The WATERSONS and MARTIN CARTHY), led to SWAN ARCADE paddling along a little less frequently. A cassette-only release, **NOTHING BLUE** (1988) {*5}, featuring a take of CYRIL TAWNEY's 'The Grey Funnel Line', was a tad too low-key for some. Showcasing RAB NOAKES, DAVE BURLAND and Dixie Kidd, the trio bade farewell with their swansong set **FULL CIRCLE** (1990) {*5}, a blatant attempt to get back to their traditional-only roots.

The Bradys split and BOYES completed one solo set, **OUT OF THE BLUE** (1993) {*5}; he later helped form COOPE BOYES & SIMPSON, who were soon to be part of BLUE MURDER. Sadly, Dave Brady died, aged 62, on May 29, 2006. *MCS*

Dave Brady (b. Dave Christopher Bradley, Aug 12 '43) - vocals, (later) concertina / **Heather Brady** (b. Heather Johnston) - vocals / **Jim Boyes** (b. Nov 14 '45, Bridlington, Yorkshire) - vocals, (later acoustic guitar)

UK Trailer — US not issued

1973. (lp) *(LER 2032)* **SWAN ARCADE**
- Bright shining morning / Anti-Gallacian privateer / Battle of Sowerby bridge / Admiral Benbow / Roll, Alabama, roll / Last Valentine's day / Lord Willoughby / Hunt is up / Peat bog soldiers / All the good times.

—— Boyes had already left; Royston Wood (ex-YOUNG TRADITION) and then Brian Miller took over until **Boyes** returned in the mid-1970s

Stoof — not issued

Jan 77. (lp) *(MU 7428)* **MATCHLESS**
- Babylon / The Great Valerio / Foster's mill / Further along / The rainbow / Van Diemen's land / Lowlands of Holland / Mercedes Benz / Little maiden / Baron of Brackley / Down in the valley to pray / Trimdon Grange explosion.

—— the band split in 1978, but the originals regrouped in 1983

Fellside — not issued

May 85. (lp) *(FE 037)* **TOGETHER FOREVER**
- For the sake of days gone by / Georgie on a spree / Dives and Lazarus / Paperback writer / Goodnight loving trail / Mighty rocky road / Go from my window / Together forever / Lola / Boomers story / Keep the faith. *(cd-iss. Oct 01 as 'ROUND AGAIN'+=; FECD 160)* - DIVING FOR PEARLS

Jul 86. (lp) *(FE 054)* **DIVING FOR PEARLS**
- Raise your banner / Black seam / Donibristle mine disaster / Four green fields / Dwelling in Beulahland / Hounds of the Meynall / Shipbuilding / Weary whaling grounds / Brilliant mistake / Peat dog soldiers / Children's crusade / Only remembered. *(cd-iss+=)* - TOGETHER FOREVER

Sygnet — not issued

Jul 88. (c) *(SY 01)* **NOTHING BLUE**
- Babylon / Children's crusade / Bitter fruit / Roll, Alabama, roll / Little maiden / The bright shining morning / Foster's mill / Rolling home / Palms of victory / The rainbow / The grey funnel line / Last Valentine's day / Further along / The battle of Sowerby Bridge / Mercedes Benz.

1990. (c/cd) *(SY/+CD 02)* **FULL CIRCLE**
- The verdant banks of Skreen / A sailor's life / Shule agra / William Taylor / The banks of the roses / The old triangle / Sliav gallion braes / Four loom weaver / The doffin mistress / Lowlands away / Blood red roses / Wild mountain thyme.

—— SWAN ARCADE teamed up with the WATERSONS (Boyes went solo and helped form COOPE BOYES & SIMPSON)

—— Dave and Heather subsequently split up

Laurel SWIFT (⟹ The GLOWORMS)

SWILL & THE SWAGGERBAND (⟹ The MEN THEY COULDN'T HANG)

T

Heidi TALBOT

Born 1980 in Kill, County Kildare, HEIDI TALBOT was formerly better known for her work from 2002 with CHERISH THE LADIES, a US-based, all-female Celtic-folk ensemble, She had relocated to New York in 1999 after a brief spell in Irish trad quintet The Whole Shabang. Without losing too much of her Celtic connection (she later married Edinburgh-based musician JOHN McCUSKER), Heidi self-financed an eponymous debut, recorded mainly to get her re-established back in Britain.

Funded by Compass Records in Nashville (released on Navigator in the UK), **DISTANT FUTURE** (2004) {*7} was the singer's first album proper, the record a mixture of trad tunes and others recorded with multi-instrumentalist Dirk Powell, fiddler Rayna Gellert and concertinist John Williams, all under the control of producer John Doyle.

Musical and domestic commitments, among other things, caused TALBOT to forsake CHERISH THE LADIES late in 2007. A solo launch the following January at the prestigious Celtic Connections festival in Glasgow won her a new audience for her second album, **IN LOVE AND LIGHT** (2008) {*7}, and work with McCUSKER, KRIS DREVER and RODDY WOOMBLE, plus EDDI READER, BOO HEWERDINE and Radiohead's Philip Selway, helped push her profile even higher.

With McCUSKER on hand to recruit a crew of musical friends (HEWERDINE, DREVER, READER, Ian Carr, MICHAEL McGOLDRICK, ANDY CUTTING and KARINE POLWART), third set **THE LAST STAR** (2010) {*7} was impressive from the get-go. From the narrative opener 'Willie Taylor' to the SANDY DENNY cover 'At The End Of The Day' (not forgetting 'Tell Me Truly' and 'Hang Me' in between), her emotive singing kept at least a foothold on the past, without sinking into it like so many of her peers. *MCS*

Heidi Talbot - vocals / with session people

		UK own label	US not issued
2002.	(cd) *(none)* **HEIDI TALBOT**	☐	⊟
	- Summerfly / Scorn not his simplicity / Invisible / I know you by heart / The only love I knew (Roisin's song) / Promise me / Hard times / Stop / Raglan road / Patience of angels / Slumber my darling.		
		Navigator	Compass
Feb 04.	(cd) *<7 4373-2>* **DISTANT FUTURE**	⊟	☐
	- In silence I go / Jealousy / Muddy water / I dream of you / Geography / High Germany / Said to me sweetly / Distant future / MacCrimmon's lament / Summer's gone / Your favourite star.		
Aug 08.	(cd) *(NAVIGATOR 6CD) <7 4469-2>* **IN LOVE AND LIGHT**	☐	Mar 08 ☐
	- If you stay / Cathedrals / Invisible / Bedlam boys / Time / Glenlogie / Music tree / Parting song / The blackest crow / Everything / Whispering grass / When they ring the golden bells.		
Sep 10.	(cd) *(NAVIGATOR 43CD) <7 4545-2>* **THE LAST STAR**	☐	☐
	- Willie Taylor / Tell me truly / Hang me / The shepherd lad / The last star / Sally Brown / Bantry girls / Bleecker street / Start it all over again / Cherokee rose / At the end of the day.		

The TALLEST MAN ON EARTH

It may be unavoidable to use the words 'Bob' and 'Dylan' when describing Sweden's The TALLEST MAN ON EARTH's oeuvre, given his bare acoustic rattle and nasal delivery, but Kristian Matsson (b. April 30, 1983) should take such comparisons as a compliment. Despite his unwieldy (and clearly untrue) stage name, the singer-songwriter has, over a relatively short career, collated a creditable cache of songs, ballads and tall tales.

His material is American folklore through the prism of a Scandinavian upbringing. A self-titled EP in 2006 hinted at his skills, but the richness of storytelling and imagery in his debut album **SHALLOW GRAVE** (2008) {*7} was considerable, creating a vivid picture of the man alone with a gnarly guitar, conjuring up scene after scene.

The most accurate analysis of Matsson's work, however, came in a press review of his second album, **THE WILD HUNT** (2010) {*8}, which said that Matsson interpreted DYLAN as Dylan interpreted WOODY GUTHRIE. And it's true: the early 20th century of Woody's great American land was reshaped and reconsidered for DYLAN's 1960s output, which was in turn transposed to the lush green loneliness of the Swedish countryside by Matsson.

The album itself is as spare as its predecessor, but benefits from more confident playing, deft lyricism - more about emotion than narrative, but no less engaging for that - and the addition of splashes of piano and banjo to the spidery acoustic. His one-that-got-away single 'King Of Spain' was given a deserved reboot courtesy of BBC2's 'Later ... With Jools Holland' music programme.

Demonstrating his way with titles again, an EP called 'Sometimes The Blues Is Just A Passing Bird' arrived in 2010 as Matsson continued on a singular journey that, so far, has proved most surprisingly fruitful. *MR*

Kristian Matsson - vocals, acoustic guitar, banjo, piano

		UK Gravitation	US Mexican Summer
Nov 06.	(cd-ep) *(gra 025)* THE TALLEST MAN ON EARTH	⊟ Sweden	⊟
	- It will follow the rain / Walk the line / Steal tomorrow / Over the hills / Into the stream. *(<UK/US-iss. Sep 10 on Dead Oceans; DOCSPEC 004CD>)*		
Mar 08.	(cd)<lp> *(gra 028) <MEX 006>* **SHALLOW GRAVE**	⊟	Dec 08 ☐
	- I won't be found / Pistol dreams / Honey won't you let me in / Shallow grave / Where do my bluebird fly / The gardener / The blizzard's never seen the desert sands / The sparrow and the medicine / Into the stream / This wind. *<US w/ 7" ep+=>* - It will follow the rain / Walk the line / Steal tomorrow / Over the hills. *(<UK/US cd-iss. Sep 10 on Dead Oceans; DOCSPEC 005CD>)*		
		Dead Oceans	Dead Oceans
Mar 10.	(cd-s) *<DOC 039>* KING OF SPAIN / Graceland / Where I Thought I Met The Angels	⊟	☐
Apr 10.	(lp/cd) *(<DOC 040/+CD>)* **THE WILD HUNT**	☐	☐
	- The wild hunt / Burden of tomorrow / Troubles will be gone / You're going back / The drying of the lawns / King of Spain / Love is all / Thousand ways / A lion's heart / Kids on the run.		
Nov 10.	(12"ep/cd-ep) *(<DOC 048/+CD>)* SOMETIMES THE BLUES IS JUST A PASSING BIRD	☐	☐
	- Little river / The dreamer / Like the wheel / Tangle in this trampled wheat / Thrown right at me.		

John TAMS (⟹ HOME SERVICE)

The TANSADS

Formed in 1990 in Wigan, Lancashire by the Kettle brothers, John, Andrew and Bob, along with Janet Anderton, Ed Jones (a CND employee), Dominic Lowe (on brass), Shrub, Bug and Cudo, The TANSADS dealt in salt-of-the-earth, honest-to-goodness, heart-on-the-sleeve folky indie/rock. Named after a brand of pram, apparently, the band are real-ale northern spiritual cousins to Brighton's LEVELLERS.

The self-financed **SHANDYLAND** (1991) {*7} got the band's career off to a frothy start, attracting the attention of LEVELLERS/WATERBOYS producer Phil Tennant, who also worked on the band's follow-up for Musidisc, **UP THE SHIRKERS** (1993) {*6}. Initially released on Probe Plus, the interplay of singers John and Janet was the key to their debut, and tracks such as 'Feed Me', 'Spirit Move' and 'Big Wednesday' were already regular singalongs, The second set contained no less than four attempts at the indie singles charts: 'Brian Kant', 'Up The Revolution', 'The English Rover' and 'Camelot'.

Following the replacement of founding members Dominic and Bug (Shrub was already grounded) by Guy Keegan and Lee Goulding, a slightly modified TANSADS signed to the reactivated folk-roots label Transatlantic. A third set, **FLOCK** (1994) {*7}, was a more relaxed affair, taking aim at the usual lyrical targets (religion, business suits, etc). The album's harmony-happy rave-ups were leavened by a couple of fine, string-enhanced ballads, 'She's Not Gone' and 'Sunlight In The Morning', both powerfully carried by Anderton.

Not quite the success it deserved to be, the album was followed by a live set, **DRAG DOWN THE MOON** (1995) {*7}, a record capturing the band in their element and in Wigan. 1998's **REASON TO BE** {*6} was The TANSADS' swansong before the inevitable split.

While never quite managing to fire the average music fan's imagination in the same way as the LEVELLERS, for example, The TANSADS were an institution for their diehard fans. After their demise, journalist and Lancaster University graduate Jones ended up writing a book about his experiences, entitled 'This Is Pop: The Life And Times Of A Failed Rock Star', telling the story of the nearly men who used to be supported by the Verve, Pulp and Cast. *MCS*

Andrew Kettle - vocals / **Janet Anderton** - vocals / **John Kettle** - guitars, banjo / **Bob Kettle** - mandolin, guitar, harmonica / **Ed Jones** (b. 1964, Geneva, Switzerland) - bass, vocals / **Dominic Lowe** - accordion, trumpet / **Shrub** - keyboards / **Bug** (b. Chris Atherton) - drums / **Cudo** - percussion

UK: Probe Plus - Wayward / US: not issued

1991. (lp) *(PROBEWAY 31)* **SHANDYLAND**
- Cobbly back yard / Wood in th' hole / Right on / Big Wednesday / Feed me / Horses / Shandyland / Juvenile / No more / London's burning / Spirit move / Big bad devil. *(cd-iss. Nov 95 on Essential; ESMCD 351)*

—— now without Shrub

UK: Musidisc / US: not issued

Nov 92. (7") *(10937-7)* BRIAN KANT (YEAH-YEAH-YOOH). / Zig Zag
(cd-s+=) *(10937-2)* - Fear of falling / Set you free.

Jan 93. (cd-ep) *(11005-2)* UP THE REVOLUTION [radio edit] / Up The Revolution [LP version] / John John / Sun Golden Sun

Feb 93. (cd/c/lp) *(10985-2/-4/-1)* **UP THE SHIRKERS**
- Eye of the average / Camelot / Brian Kant / Zig zag / Music down / Waste of space / Chip pan ocean / The English rover / John John / Reason to be / Up the revolution / Turn on, tune up, drop out, be late. *(cd re-iss. Nov 95 on Essential; ESMCD 352)*

Jul 93. (cd-ep) *(11033-2)* THE ENGLISH ROVER / Feed Me / Four Leaf Clover / The Girlfriend Of The Free

Oct 93. (cd-s) *(11099-2)* CAMELOT / Gelignite / Satisfied

—— **Lee Goulding** - keyboards; repl. Lowe + Cudo

—— **Guy Keegan** - drums (ex-Railway Children) repl. Bug

May 94. (cd-s) *(???)* IRON MAN / A Band On The Rainbow / I Don't Know

Aug 94. (cd/c) *(11212-2/-4)* **FLOCK**
- A band on the rainbow / Fear of falling / She's not gone / God on a string / Iron man / Waiting for the big one / Dance / Sunlight in the morning / G man / Ship of fools / I know I can (but I won't) / Heading for the heart / Separate fools. *(re-iss. Oct 94 and Apr 96 on Transatlantic cd/c; TRA CD/MC 101)*

—— **Phillip Knight** - drums; repl. Keegan

—— **Robbie Ryan** - bass, vocals; repl. Jones

UK: Transatlantic / US: not issued

Sep 94. (c-s) *(TRAM 1001)* A BAND ON THE RAINBOW / Thursday's Child
(cd-s+=) *(TRAX 1001)* - The English rover (live) / Cobby back yard (live).

Oct 95. (cd/c) *(TRA CD/MC 118)* **DRAG DOWN THE MOON** (live)
- Iron man / Where have all the flowers gone / Up the revolution / She's not gone / A band on the rainbow / John John / Turn on tune in drop out be late / Spirit move / Sunlight in the morning / Reason to be / The English rover / Waiting for the big one / G man / Fear of falling / Eye of the average / I know I can, but I won't / Drag down the moon.

Apr 96. (cd-s) *(TRAX 1006)* I KNOW I CAN, BUT I WON'T / Drag Down The Moon / And Oh ...

—— the band were now **Janet Anderton, John Kettle, Robbie Ryan** plus **Tim Howard** - guitar + **Andy Jones** - drums

UK: Wayward / US: not issued

Mar 98. (cd) *(none)* **REASON TO BE** — mail-o
- Roll away your stone / Higher ground / All the mad men / Hello / Reason to be / Sad song / Jealousy / Middle of the night / Julian / Miss the bus / Burning bridge / Drunken serenade.

—— after their split, John Kettle went into production work

- (5-7*) compilations, others, etc.-

2010. (cd) *Voice Of Reason; (VOR 001)* **ROUGH AND READY - THE EARLY TAPES** — mail-o
- Fear of falling / Father's day / Say it with flowers / Big Wednesday / 25 years / Sun golden sun / Fit to drop / I close my eyes / Pendle hill / Parachute song / Untitled / Nursery rhyme for '89 / Set you free / Too many spots / I can see you all / Diamonds in the rain / Shandyland / Big sunrise / Jealousy / I know I can / Juvenile / Ocean heart.

TANTEEKA (⟹ FREYA, Jo)

TARLETON'S JIG

Formed 1978 out of City Waites and Common Ground, TARLETON'S JIG and their fluid, revolving-door set-up produced only three albums in their time together. The group's classically-trained players (led by Jim/James Bisgood, with Jeremy West, David Miller, Keith Thompson, Martin Pope and Sharon Lindo) performed a mediaeval chamber music that harvested a range of sounds from 16th-, 17th- and 18th-century England to the far east.

Performing on crumhorns, lutes, bagpipes, theorbo, baroque violin and other exotic instruments, the group played mainly for stately homes, royalty and the odd battle re-enactment. Sourcing music from battlefields and soldiers' camps, from street corners and taverns, their debut LP **FOR KING AND PARLIAMENT** (1986) {*6} was not your typical "folk" record. A line could possibly be drawn through AMAZING BLONDEL and GRYPHON, but only at a push.

Further personnel changes (see discography) blurred the band's identity, but it was clear that their purpose was not for team and players, just the music itself. Jonathan Morgan was a member before he left late in 1989, and his contributions could be heard on their second album, **A FIT OF MIRTH FOR A GROAT** (1989) {*6}.

By the time Martin Pope decided it was time to depart, and the ensemble (with, at various times, Lindo, Nicholas Perry, and Keith McGowan) released **ELIZABETHAN STREET SONGS** (1991) {*5}, the formula was probably a little outworn. Subtitled "From the alehouse to the whore-house - jigs, ballads & bawdy songs", the record lived up to its description. Most of the band still perform live at functions and in period-costume television dramas. *MCS*

Jim/James Bisgood (b. Mar 3 '59, Isleworth, Middlesex) - vocals, multi / **Jeremy West** (b. Nov 29 '53, Sussex) - instruments / **Keith Thompson** (b. Aug 7 '51, Whitstable, Kent) - multi, vocals / **David Miller** (b. Apr 13 '53, Glamorgan, Wales) - lutes, chitarrone, guitars / **Martin Pope** (b. Jun 22 '55, Kuala Lumpur, Malaysia) - multi / added **Sharon Lindo** (b. Dec 11 '59, Romford, Essex) - violins, multi, vocals

UK: Nuns Meadows / US: not issued

Nov 86. (lp) *(NMP 1521)* **FOR KING AND PARLIAMENT**
- Prince Rupert's march / French report / Vive le roy / Battle of Worcester / Gather your rosebuds / Half hannikin / We be soldiers three / Cuckolds all in a row / Sir Thomas Fairfax: his march / Psalm CXVII / Scots march / Drive the cold winter away / Lord of Carnavan's jegg / When cannons are roaring / Clean contrary way / King / Millfield / Rump song.

—— added **Jonathan Morgan** - multi

Apr 89. (c) *(NMP 1522)* **A FIT OF MIRTH FOR A GROAT**
- Selenger's round / The dragon of Wantley / Tombeau de Mezangeau / The Turnbridge doctors of physics / Over the hills and far away / Joan's plackett is torn / Childgrove / The Hyde Park frolic / Parsons farewell / Courtiers, courtiers / Toccata apreggiata / Mr George Tolitt's division upon a ground / Cheshire round / The west country jig.

—— now without Martin Pope

—— new line-up: **Bisgood, Thompson, Lindo + Keith McGowan** - multi

1991. (c) *(???)* **ELIZABETHAN STREET SONGS: From The Alehouse to the Whore-house - Jigs, Ballads & Bawdy Songs**
- Kemp's jegg / The Stanes morris / Bransle - Horses bransle / The baffled knight / Packington's pound / The three ravens / Bransle de Bretaigne - Nonsuch / Cuckolds all a-row / Bobbing Joan - Goddesses / We be soldiers three / Never let the creultie dishonour bewtie - The picking of sticks - Selenger's round / All in a misty morning / Bara Faustas' dream / Mall Peatley - Half hannikin / The Carman's whistle / Give me my yellow hose again / The grog galliard / The owl. *(cd-iss. Sep 08 on Globe Editions; GE 002)*

—— the revamped/re-issued CD (due to contractual constrictions) only allowed four out of six members to appear - from (**James Bisgood, Nicholas Perry, Adrian Woodward, Richard Thomas, David Miller + William Lyons**)

Bram TAYLOR

Generally overlooked by pundits outside the folk fraternity, balladeering singer Bramwell Taylor (born August 6, 1951, at Leigh, Lancashire) was initially inspired by the likes of HARVEY ANDREWS, VIN GARBUTT and The SPINNERS. His parents were singers and musicians with the Salvation Army.

1975 was a transitional period for Bram. His voice was now to be heard on BBC Radio Manchester's children's radio programme Chatterbox, and a cassette album, **THE HAYMAKERS** {*6} (a marketing tool to help him get gigs), was recorded at his friend Dave Howard's studio in 1982. Bram's crystal-clear voice was put to one side when his part in comedy band Inclognito (alongside banjo/ukulele players Dave Dutton and Eric White) took precedence from 1979 to 1985, although it's unclear whether there were any releases. Jackie Finney replaced Eric until the band split in 1989.

The merits of the cassette led to TAYLOR's first LP for Fellside Records, **BIDE A WHILE** (1985) {*6}, featuring contributions from Fiona Simpson (harmonies), Dave Howard (mandola, mandolin, bass), Paul Witty (fiddle), Gwynne Basnett (treble recorder) and Paul Adams (percussion), plus a brass section. Using a more contemporary template, Bram won many plaudits for his award-winning follow-up, **DREAMS AND SONGS TO SING** (1987) {*7}, a record that was as much new-country as folk.

Fellside Records (run by Paul and Linda Adams) have kept faith with Bram over the years, releasing several albums with an MOR-folk appeal. Possibly his best selections (including songs by EWAN MacCOLL, BRIAN McNEILL, etc) are featured on **FURTHER HORIZONS** (1993) {*7}, while **FRAGILE PEACE** (2001) {*6} and his most recent, **SONG SINGER** (2007) {*6}, found a market not just in Britain but as far afield as Holland, Switzerland and Canada.

Taylor has visited New York, and it remains a haunting memory that, five days before the 9/11 atrocities, he was at the top of one of the Twin Towers. *MCS*

Bram Taylor - vocals, acoustic guitar, duet concertina (with sessioners)

UK Freestyle / US not issued

1982. (lp) *(none)* **THE HAYMAKERS** — gigs
- Young Collins / Searching for lambs / The haymakers / Brookland bells / Rise up Jock / Rare auld times / The reaper / Ned of the hill / I just can't wait / Edward / Fairy tale lullaby / Farewell shanty / Young Collins (reprise).

In 1979-85, Bram, Dave Dutton and Eric White formed comedy troupe Inclognito

Fellside / not issued

May 85. (lp) *(FE 041)* **BIDE A WHILE**
- The valley of Strathmore / Mind hussy what you do / Fields of Athenry / Sally Wheatley / I'll lay you down / Brookland roads / On board the Kangaroo / The miner's wife's lament / Red is the rose / Mary from Dungloe / The little husband / Bide a while.

Feb 87. (lp) *(FE 057)* **DREAMS & SONGS TO SING**
- Lady of beauty / Cry wild bird / How can I keep from singing / Annan water / April morning / Dancing at Whitsun / The ferrybank piper / The sally gardens / Wheel the perambulator / Together at heart / Hard times / Wheel of fortune.

Jan 90. (lp/c) *(FE 075/+C)* **TAYLOR MADE**
- Time and trouble / Too far from she / Withered and died / Man in the moon / Asikatali / The Earl of March's daughter / Lessons of time / Bonny blue eyed Nancy / The broom o' the Cowdenknowes / The flowers of Lancashire / Albert's party flowers / From a distance.

Oct 93. (cd/c) *(FE 092 CD/C)* **FURTHER HORIZONS**
- Hills of the west / The snows of France and Holland / The killing time / Bonnie Bessie Logan / Blaina boys 1930 / The gypsy / Schooldays over / Let her go down / The blue hills of Tyrone / Maybe I'll forget you / Whisper your name / Jock o' Hazeldean / The green and the blue / Somewhere along the road / The girl I left behind me - Brighton camp.

Sep 97. (cd) *(FECD 120)* **PICK OF THE GRINDER**
- River run / Gin' I were a baron's heir / Feed the children / Language of the land / A thousand years / Harbour in the storm / High Germany / The low road / Why walk when you can fly / Banks of the Bann / Never be the sun / William Taylor / Katie / Picker and a grinner.

Jun 01. (cd) *(FECD 159)* **FRAGILE PEACE**
- Fragile peace / Home away from home / When my morning comes around / The troubles of Erin / Stone by stone / Lover's heart / Sailors all / Loch Tay boat song / Thorn upon the rose / I lay you down love / Fields of gold / Jubilee / On the seas and far away / April morning.

Mar 04. (cd) *(FECD 183)* **THE NIGHT IS YOUNG**
- Bogie's bonnie belle / Song for Bowdoin / Struck it right this time / If I should leave you / Wisdom guide me / The holy ground / Isle of hope / Ay waulkin' o / Robin D / Come all you fair and tender ladies / Annan water / Next time around / Banks of green willow / Marking time / The night is young.

Sep 07. (cd) *(FECD 206)* **SONG SINGER**
- Geordie will dance the jig tonight / Across the blue mountains / Green among the gold / The shape of my father / Harbour lights / Sing me a song Mr Bloom / Come all you weary factory girls / Hillcrest mine / The rose of Allendale / If you can walk you can dance / King cotton / The two brothers / See that rainbow shine / Bridget Donaghue / Writing home.

- (8-10*) compilations -

Feb 00. (cd) *Fellside; (FECD 148)* **SINGING! THE BRAM TAYLOR COLLECTION**
- How can I keep from singing / Dancing at Whitsun / The valley of Strathmore / Red is the rose / Fields of Athenry / The broom o' the Cowdenknowes / Albert's pretty flowers / The sally gardens / Lady of beauty / Together at heart / Lessons of time / The flowers of Lancashire / On board the Kangaroo / Withered and died / Bonnie blue eyed Nancy / Man in the moon / Wheel of fortune / The miner's wife's lament / Bide a while.

THIS IS THE KIT

THIS IS THE KIT is the musical project of Kate Stables, who sings her own pretty folk numbers and plays banjo and guitar. In 2005 she worked with ex-Moonflowers multi-instrumentalist Jesse D. Vernon in chamber-pop outfit Morning Star.

Later based in France, Kate also sidelined for WHALEBONE POLLY with Virpi Kettu and solo artist Rachael Dadd. Their collaborative album, RECORDING WITH THE WINDOW OPEN, was released (only in Japan) around the same time as THIS IS THE KIT's inaugural set, WHERE IT LIVES (2006).

A series of limited-edition singles preceded her debut album proper, **KRULLE BOL** (2008) {*7}. Produced by John Parish (one-time collaborator of PJ Harvey), it was basically the first set, refashioned for British ears. With banjo in hand, singer Kate impresses with delicate songs such as 'Our Socks Forever More' ('One Of These Socks' re-titled), 'Creeping Up Our Shins', 'Birchwood Beaker' and the classy 'Two Wooden Spoons' - lo-fi neo-folk at its most magical - and extends her range with JONI MITCHELL/JANIS IAN-like numbers 'With Her Wheels Again', 'Tangled Walker' and 'Moths'. The intimate combination of banjo and voice is in the ascendancy, and the title track is another rootsy cracker that leaves the listener looking forward what was next on the horizon.

The answer was the ethereal **WRIGGLE OUT THE RESTLESS** (2010) {*7}, which featured guests Jim Barr (of Portishead) on bass, Rozi Plain (on guitar, banjo and clarinet) and Francois Marry (like Rozi, part of the Fence Collective) on organ, trumpet and piano. By all accounts it has all the hallmarks of another great set; check out 'Waterproof' and 'Sometimes The Sea'. *MCS*

Kate Stables - vocals, banjo, acoustic guitar / **Jesse D. Vernon** - guitar, violin, piano, drums, vocals (of Morning Star, ex-Moonflowers)

UK disco-ordination / US not issued

2006. (cd-ep) *(???)* LAST OF THE SECRET FISH EATERS
- (instrumental four-track pieces).

Sunday Best / not issued

Jul 06. (7") *(sbests 37)* TWO WOODEN SPOONS. / Come A Cropper

Angel's Egg / Angel's Egg

Jul 06. (cd) *<DDCA-5037>* **WHERE IT LIVES** — Japan
- With her wheels again / We need our knees / Two wooden spoons / Creeping up our shins / Come a cropper / Do more dancing / Greasy goose / Wednesday / One of these socks / Up to my ears / Fighting talk (by GREG ASHBY) / She does.

May 07. (cd-ep) *(AEMCS 046D)* THIS IS THE KIT
- With her wheels again / Greasy goose / Krulle bol / We need our knees / Tangled walker.

Microbe / not issued

May 08. (cd) *(MIC.CD.023)* **KRULLE BOL**
- Our socks forever more / Creeping up our shins / Shared out / Birchwood beaker / With her wheels again / Two wooden spoons / We need our knees / Moths / Krulle bol / Greasy goose / Tangled walker / She does.

Dreamboat / not issued

Oct 10. (cd) *(DRMBT 020)* **WRIGGLE OUT THE RESTLESS**
- Sometimes the sea / Easy pickings / See here / Waterproof / Spinny / Trick you / The turnip / White ash cut / Earquake / Sleeping bag / Moon.

WHALEBONE POLLY

Kate Stables - vocals, banjo, guitar, melodica, toy piano / **Rachael Dadd** - vocals, guitar, clarinet, melodica / **Virpu Kettu** - vocals, violin, accordion, shaker not issued Angel's Egg

Oct 06. (cd) <DDCA-5043> **RECORDING WITH THE WINDOW OPEN** (taken from two demos of the same name) [–] Japan [–]
- Sweetest in the land / Do more dancing / Blessed by this devil / She does / Boa / Harold and Maud / Don't forget to chew / No sleep in the meadow / Pigeons / Our socks for evermore / A map.

—— Rachael Dadd has since released 'SUMMER/AUTUMN RECORDINGS' (Sep '06) and 'THE WORLD OUTSIDE IS IN A CUPBOARD' (Feb '08)

Mick THOMAS (⟹ WEDDINGS PARTIES ANYTHING)

Danny THOMPSON

Initially more at home with the jazz fraternity, double-bassist DANNY THOMPSON has become famous for top-flight session work rather than for his solo exploits. But who could forget that he was the rhythm - alongside drummer Terry Cox - that held together the great folk-jazz supergroup, PENTANGLE?

Born April 4, 1939, in Teignmouth, Devon, Danny cut his teeth with Alexis Korner's Blues Incorporated before finding psych-pop fame with Piccadilly Line (soon to be Edwards Hand). From 1967 to 1972 (and between 1982 and 1984) THOMPSON forged a great partnership with Cox, JACQUI McSHEE, BERT JANSCH and JOHN RENBOURN on several PENTANGLE sets. A sidekick and drinking buddy of JOHN MARTYN, up to the late 1970s at least, he also shared studio space with RICHARD THOMPSON (no relation), NICK DRAKE, DONOVAN, TIM BUCKLEY, DAVEY GRAHAM, JULIE FELIX, MARIANNE FAITHFULL, DORRIS HENDERSON, HEDY WEST, Rod Stewart and Cliff Richard (on Cliff's 'Congratulations' Eurovision entry). Contemporary pop stars such as Kate Bush, David Sylvian and Talk Talk employed his services in the 1980s.

Danny's long-awaited debut set, **WHATEVER** (1987) {*7}, brought together co-writers Bernie Holland (guitar) and Tony Roberts (sax, flute, clarinet, reeds) in what was perhaps an extension of his jazz days, although there was space for two trad-folk pieces, 'Lovely Joan' and 'Swedish Dance'. On the fringes of flamenco folk and worldbeat, THOMPSON's next musical excursion was a collaboration with Spanish gypsy band Ketama and Malian kora player Toumani Diabate for the album **SONGHAI** (1988).

His second solo set, **WHATEVER NEXT** (1989) {*5}, followed a similar pattern to its predecessor, but not exactly with the same results. **ELEMENTAL** (1990) {*5} and 'Songhai 2' were not particularly folk music, while his collaborative set with RICHARD THOMPSON, 'Industry' (1997), drifted as close to the folk-music margins as possible without losing his hard-earned jazz brownie points. *MCS*

Danny Thompson - double bass, guitar, mandolin, etc. (w/ session people)

UK Hannibal — US Hannibal

Jul 87. (lp/c/cd) *(<HNBL/HNBC/HNCD 1326>)* **WHATEVER** [ ] 1991 [ ]
- Idle Monday / Till Minne av Jan / Yucateca / Lovely Joan / Swedish dance / Lament for Alex / Crusader / Minor escapade. *<cd re-iss. 1999; 8810-2>*

Dec 88. (lp/c/cd; by KETAMA / TOUMANI DIABATE / DANNY THOMPSON) *(HNBL/HNBC/HNCD 1323)* **SONGHAI** [ ] [–]
- Jarabi / Mani mani kuru / Caramelo / A Toumani / Vente pa' Madrid / Africa / A mi Tia Marina / Ne ne kiotaa.

Antilles — not issued

Apr 89. (lp/c/cd) *(AN/+C/CD 8743)* **WHATEVER NEXT** [ ] [–]
- Dargai / Hopdance (invitation to dance) / Beanpole / Wildfinger / A full English basket / Sandansko oro (Bulgarian dance) / Take it off the top / Major escapade. *(re-iss. May 91 on Island cd)(lp/c; IMCD 117)(ILPM/ICM 2055) (cd re-iss. Mar 03 on La Cooka Ratcha-Voiceprint; LCVP 152CD)*

Sep 90. (lp/c/cd) *(AN/+C/CD 8753)* **ELEMENTAL** [ ] [–]
- Beirut / Fair Isle friends / Musing Mingus / Searchin' / Women at war / Freedom - Prayer - Dance - Thanksgiving. *(re-iss. May 91 on Island cd)(lp/c; IMCD 118)(ILPM/ICM 2057) (cd re-iss. Mar 03 on La Cooka Ratcha-Voiceprint; LCVP 153CD)*

with DANNY THOMPSON (as guest), Ketama, Toumani Diabate & Jose Soto released 'Songhai 2' (Aug 94) for Hannibal records CD; *HNCD 1383)*

Resurgent — not issued

Apr 97. (cd; by PETER KNIGHT & DANNY THOMPSON) *(RES 108CD)* **PETER KNIGHT & DANNY THOMPSON** [ ] [–]
- Number one / Number two.

Also in 1997, Danny collaborated with RICHARD THOMPSON on the set 'Industry'.

- (8-10*) compilations -

Feb 95. (cd) *Whatever; (<WHAT 001CD>)* **WHATEVER'S BEST** [ ] Nov 98 [ ]
- Sandansko oro / Searchin' / Freedom - Prayer - Dance - Thanksgiving / Hopdance / Women at war / Fair Isle friends / Beanpole / Musing Mingus / Dargai. *(d-cd-iss. Oct 03 on Voiceprint+=; VP 241024CD)* -(DANNY & PETER set)

- (5-7*) compilations, others, etc. (jazz)-

Dec 99. (cd) *Resurgent; (RES 4376)* **DANNY THOMPSON TRIO LIVE 1967** (live) [ ] [–]
- Celia / 3rd floor Richard / Naima / All blues / In your own sweet way / Anthropology.

2009. (cd; by DANNY THOMPSON, ALLAN HOLDSWORTH, JOHN STEVENS) *Art Of Life; (1038)* **PROPENSITY** (recorded 1978) [ ] [–]
- Jools toon / It could have been mono.

THREE DAFT MONKEYS (⟹ forthcoming Celtic & World Folk Discography)

Holly THROSBY

The daughter of Australia's ABC Classic FM radio presenter Margaret Throsby, folk-pop singer-songwriter HOLLY THROSBY was born December 28, 1978 in Sydney.

Encouraged by her extended family (her grandmother was a classical cellist, her uncle - David Throsby - a cultural economist) and after earning a BA at university, Holly took to the road.

Recorded under the wing of producer Tony Dupe at his Saddleback Mountain cottage studio, **ON NIGHT** {*7} was finally issued by indie label Spunk Records in 2004, complete with barking dogs, bird calls and nature itself in the background.

A heavy touring schedule followed soon afterwards, and support slots to North American folkies DEVENDRA BANHART, BONNIE 'PRINCE' BILLY, JOANNA NEWSOM, M. WARD and Bill Callahan did her CV no harm. With Dupe at the controls once again (and with some hand-picked session players), **UNDER THE TOWN** (2006) {*7} was promoted in the US on an extensive tour with David Pajo.

THROSBY's wispy voice is clearly her endearing selling point, and it was given a fresh slant on her Nashville-recorded third set, **A LOUD CALL** (2008) {*8}, featuring Mark Nevers and the Lambchop/Silver Jews contingent plus WILL 'Bonnie "Prince" Billy' OLDHAM (on 'Would You'). UK/Irish tours with countryman PAUL KELLY took her profile even higher. A LOUD CALL was her first record to go Top 40 in her home country, and the fragile, unassuming, lo-fi folk ballads that come off best are 'Warm Jets', 'To Begin With' and 'On The Wharf'.

Although not generally a covers artist, she's recorded three so far: Crowded House's 'Not The Girl You Think You Are' (for the Tim/Neil Finn tribute set 'She Will Have Her Way'), 'Mistress' (Red House Painters) and 'Berlin Chair' (You Am I).

2011 just might be Holly's year, whether with her fourth solo item, **TEAM** {*7}, or her 'Seeker Lover Keeper' album project with Sarah Blasko and Sally Seltmann. *MCS*

Holly Throsby - vocals, acoustic guitar, piano (+ session people)

Aus/UK Spunk-EMI — US not issued

Nov 04. (cd) *(URA 137)* **ON NIGHT** [–] Austra [–]
- We're good people but why don't we show it? / Up with the birds / Things between people / Waiting all night for you to come home / Damn that new body / Some nights are long / The morning / Don't be howling / Some days are long / As the night dies. *(UK-iss. Jan 06 on Woo Me!; 003)*

Jan 05. (cd-s) *(URA 143)* THINGS BETWEEN PEOPLE / Dark / Things Between People [–] Austra [–]

Jul 06. (cd) *(URA 180)* **UNDER THE TOWN** [–] Austra [–]
- Under the town / Making a fire / If we go easy / On longing / I worry very well / Come visit / Swing on / Shoulders and bends / What becomes of us / Only a rake. *(UK-iss. Jan 07 on Woo Me!; 006)*

Jul 07. (cd-ep) *(URA 222)* ONE OF YOU FOR ME [–] Austra [–]
- One of you for me / By this river / Three questions / A widow's song (demo) / If we go easy (live) / Things between people (live).

Jul 08. (cd) *(URA 244)* **A LOUD CALL** [–] Austra [–]
- Warm jets / A heart divided / Now I love someone / The time it takes / On the wharf / Would you? / One of you for me / We carry / And then we're gone / A widow's song / To begin with. *(<UK/US-iss. May 09/Jul 09 on Woo Me!; 007>)*

In 2010, Holly issued a children's album entitled 'See'.

Feb 11. (cd) *(???)* **TEAM** [–] Austra [–]
- What I thought of you / It's only need / Here is my co-pilot / Hi, you reckless darling / It's funny / To see you out / Come back to see me / Waiting for me / We are glowing / When? *(UK-iss. Jun 11 on Woo Me!)*

the THROSBY, (Sarah) Blasko and (Sally) Seltmann supergroup collaboration set/project 'Seeker Lover Keeper' was also released in Jun 11

TICKAWINDA

Formed in 1974 by guitarist Dave Birchwood and flame-haired singer Kath Richmond, TICKAWINDA (their name is Lancashire slang/dialect for "knock/tick a window") performed as a trio in their formative years, the line-up being completed by Dave's rock-climbing friend and mandolinist Jim Schofield.

For a few years they performed at folk clubs in and around the Oldham, Ashton-under-Lyne and Stalybridge areas, the last providing a Friday-night residency at the Rose & Crown pub. With harmony singer Alison Tullock on board from early 1977, the dynamics of the group changed dramatically, leading to support slots with Australia's The BUSHWACKERS at Manchester's Free Trade Hall and JAKE THACKRAY at the Poynton Folk Centre. The latter venue was where they won the North West heat of the 'Search For The Stars Of The 80s' talent competition in 1979.

With rave reviews, an appearance at the Cambridge Folk Festival and an invitation to lay down tracks with good friend CLIVE GREGSON (then of power-pop band Any Trouble), everything looked promising for the quartet. **ROSEMARY LANE** (1979) {*6} was cut live in the studio for Pennine Records with Oldham engineer Paul Adshead, the title track coming from the pen of BERT JANSCH. The rest of the set was mostly traditional songs, many of which had previously graced recordings by such luminaries as PENTANGLE, STEELEYE SPAN and FAIRPORT CONVENTION. It looked as though a breakthrough was inevitable (thanks to momentous gigs, radio sessions and a chance to shine at the BBC), but the group disbanded after this LP.

The album had cult appeal, however, and because of the GREGSON connection it rose in the Rare Record Price Guide to over £400, prompting a CD re-issue on Kissing Spell in 2001. Rehearsals got under way with a view to a reunion, at least to celebrate the album's forthcoming 25th anniversary in 2004. Sadly it was not to be, as Kath was taken ill, and she died in July 2005. *MCS*

Kath Richmond - vocals / **Dave Birchwood** - vocals, guitar / **Jim Schofield** - acoustic guitar, mandolin, vocals / **Alison Tullock** - harmony vocals / plus **Clive Gregson** - acoustic guitar, bass, piano (of Any Trouble)

UK Pennine — US not issued

Nov 79. (lp) *(PSS 153)* **ROSEMARY LANE** [ ] [–]
- John Barleycorn / Coalhole / She moves through the fair / Old Pendel / Young man / Cold and raw / The blackleg miner / Rosemary lane / A lyke wake dirge / The Galtree farmer / The weary cutters / Go your way / And the band played Waltzing Matilda. *(cd-iss. Jul 01 on Kissing Spell; KSCD 916)*

—— disbanded after above; Schofield subsequently formed a folk club and pub

TICKLED PINK (⟹ CARE, Simon)

Tanita TIKARAM

If fellow German-born singer NICO had been on uppers rather than downers, she would have sounded like sultry singer-songwriter TANITA TIKARAM. For that matter, if LEONARD COHEN had been a woman he would have sounded like TIKARAM – no offence intended.

Born August 12, 1969 in Munster, Germany, to an Indian-Fijian father and a Bornean-Malayan mother, Tanita moved to Basingstoke, England as a teenager. A budding starlet, she was soon making a name for herself on London's small-venue circuit, and through agent Paul Charles she signed to WEA/Warner Bros.

Featuring veterans Peter van Hooke and Rod Argent working in both production and writing capacities, TIKARAM's promising debut set **ANCIENT HEART** {*8} was released in summer 1988. Previewed by the uncharacteristically upbeat fireside waltz of Top 10 single 'Good Tradition', the album revealed the smoulderingly exotic TIKARAM to be a moody, sensual and intense pop-folkie in a kind of latter-day COHEN/Joan Armatrading style. The brooding follow-up single, 'Twist In My Sobriety', arguably remains her finest moment, its relatively lowly Top 30 chart placing hardly reflecting the quality of a song that's since been the subject of countless covers.

Though her voice was sufficently husky to lend her songs an air of rootsiness, subsequent albums **THE SWEET KEEPER** (1990) {*5} and **EVERYBODY'S ANGEL** (1991) {*6} veered ever closer to coffeehouse safety, the last-named set failing to match the sales of her previous efforts. Jennifer Warnes sang with her on two tracks.

Despite a fairly rigorous touring schedule, 1992's **ELEVEN KINDS OF LONELINESS** {*4} saw her critical stock and popular appeal drop away further, and TIKARAM has since been marginalised to cult status. Augmented once again by Jennifer Warnes, **LOVERS IN THE CITY** (1995) {*6} continued her trend toward orchestral arrangements, scraping a Top 75 placing but hardly reclaiming her lost commercial standing.

Her first record for Mother Records, **THE CAPPUCCINO SONGS** (1998) {*6}, won several good reviews for a change, although they were tempered by her choice of coffee-table cover, an upbeat reading of Abba's 'The Day Before You Came' - Annie Lennox she was not. Several years in the making, and released on French label Naïve, **SENTIMENTAL** (2005) {*5} was torch jazz, boosted by two collaborations with Nick Lowe. A return to her folk roots might be recommended. *MCS*

Tanita Tikaram - vocals, acoustic guitar (with session people)

UK WEA — US Reprise

Aug 88. (7"/7"s/7"g-f) *(YZ 196/+L/G)* GOOD TRADITION. / Valentine Heart [10] [–]
(12"+=) *(YZ 196T)* - Poor cow (demo).
(cd-s++=) *(YZ 196CD)* - Cathedral song.

Sep 88. (lp/c)(cd) *(WX 210/+C)(K2 43877-2)* <1-/4-/2-25839>
ANCIENT HEART [3] [59]
- Good tradition / Cathedral song / Sighing innocents / I love you / World outside your window / For all these years / Twist in my sobriety / Poor cow / He likes the sun / Valentine heart / Preyed upon. *(cd re-iss. Feb 95; 2292 43877-2) (d-cd-iss. Aug 08 +=; 2564 69459-5)* - EVERYBODY'S ANGEL

Oct 88. (7") *(YZ 321)* TWIST IN MY SOBRIETY. / Friends [22] [–]
(ext.12"+=) *(YZ 321T)* - For all these years.
(10"++=/cd-s++=) *(YZ 321 TE/CD)* - The kill in your heart.

Jan 89. (7") *(YZ 331)* CATHEDRAL SONG. / Sighing Innocents [48] [–]
(12"+=) *(YZ 331T)* - Fireflies in the kitchen (live) / Let's make everybody smile today (live).
(7"box+=/cd-s+=) *(YZ 331 B/CD)* - Let's make everybody smile today (live) / Over you all (live).

Mar 89. (7") *(YZ 363)* WORLD OUTSIDE YOUR WINDOW (remix). / For All These Years (instrumental) [58] [–]
(ext.12"+=) *(YZ 363T)* - Good tradition (live).
(cd-s++=) *(YZ 363CD)* - ('A'-extended).
(box-cd-s++=) *(YZ 363CDX)* - He likes the sun (live).

Jan 90. (7"/7"g-f) *(YZ 443/+G)* WE ALMOST GOT IT TOGETHER. / LOVE STORY [52] [–]
(12"+=/cd-s+=) *(YZ 443 T/CD)* - Over you all.

Feb 90. (cd)(lp/c) *(9031 70800-2)(WX 330/+C)* <2-/1-/4-26091>
THE SWEET KEEPER [3] [ ]
- Once and not speak / Thursday's child / It all came back today / We almost got it together / Consider the rain / Sunset's arrived / Little sister leaving town / I owe it all to you / Love story / Harm in your hands.

Mar 90. (7"/c-s) *(YZ 459/+MC)* LITTLE SISTER LEAVING TOWN. / I LOVE THE HEAVEN'S SOLO (acoustic) [ ] [–]
(12"+=/cd-s+=) *(YZ 459 T/CD)* - Hot pork sandwiches (acoustic).
(cd-s+=) *(YZ 459CDP)* - Hot pork sandwiches (acoustic) / Twist in my sobriety (acoustic).

Jun 90. (7"/c-s) *(YZ 481/+C)* THURSDAY'S CHILD. / Once And Not Speak [ ] [–]
(12"+=/cd-s+=) *(YZ 481 T/CD)* - Cathedral song (live).

East West — Reprise

Jan 91. (7"/c-s) *(YZ 558/+C)* ONLY THE ONES WE LOVE. / Me In Mind [69] [–]
(12"+=) *(YZ 558T)* - Mud in any water.
(cd-s+=) *(YZ 558CD)* - Cathedral song.

Feb 91. (cd)(lp/c) *(9031 73341-2)(WX 401/+C)* <2-/4-/1-26486>
EVERYBODY'S ANGEL [19] [ ]
- Only the ones we love / Deliver me / This story in me / To wish this / Mud in any water / Sunface / Never known / This stranger / Swear by me / Hot pork sandwiches / Me in mind / Sometime with me / I love the Heaven's solo / I'm going home. *(d-cd-iss.+=)* - ANCIENT HEART

Mar 91. (7"/c-s) *(YZ 569/+C)* I LOVE THE HEAVEN'S SOLO. / Only In Name [ ] [–]
(12"+=/cd-s+=) *(YZ 569 T/CD)* - To wish this / I'm going home.

Feb 92. (7"/c-s) *(YZ 644/+C)* YOU MAKE THE WHOLE WORLD CRY. / Rock Me 'Til I Stop / Me, You And Lucifer [ ] [–]
(cd-s) *(YZ 644CD)* - (1st two tracks) / This stranger (alt.version).
(cd-s) *(YZ 644CDX)* - (1st and 3rd tracks) / This stranger (alt.version).

Mar 92. (cd/c/lp) *(9031 76427-2/-4/-1)* <2-/4-/1-26835>
ELEVEN KINDS OF LONELINESS [ ] Jun 92 [ ]
- You make the whole world cry / Elephant / trouble / I grant you / Heal you / To drink the rainbow / Out on the town / Hot stones / Men and women / Any reason / Love don't need no tyranny / The way that I want you.

Jan 95. (c-s/cd-s) *(YZ 879 C/CD)* I MIGHT BE CRYING / Five Feet Away [64] [–]
(cd-s+=) *(YZ 879CDX)* - Not waving but drowning.

Feb 95. (cd/c) *(4509 98804-2/-4) <2-/4-45883>* **LOVERS IN THE CITY** [75] [ ]
- I might be crying / Bloodlines / Feeding the witches / Happy taxi / My love tonight / Lovers in the city / Yodelling song / Wonderful shadow / Women who cheat on the world / Leaving the party.

Mar 95. (c-s) *(YZ 922C)* WONDERFUL SHADOW / Good Tradition [ ] [–]
(cd-s+=) *(YZ 922CD1)* - Have you lost your way?
(cd-s) *(YZ 922CD2)* - ('A') / ('A'-reconstruction) / Out on the town.

Jul 95. (cd-s) *(YZ 968CD)* THE YODELLING SONG / To Drink The Rainbow / Bloodlines [ ] [–]

Jun 96. (cd/c) *(<0630 15106-2/-4>)* **THE BEST OF TANITA TIKARAM** (compilation) [ ] [ ]
- Twist in my sobriety / Cathedral song / World outside your window / Good tradition / Love don't need no tyranny / Little sister leaving town / Only the ones we love / You make the whole world cry / Trouble / Wonderful shadow / Men and women / I might be crying / Happy taxi / My love tonight / Lovers in the city / And I think of you - e penso a te / Twist in my sobriety (Tikaramp radio).

Sep 96. (7") *(EW 064C)* TWIST IN MY SOBRIETY. / Friends [ ] [–]
('A'-ext.12"+=) *(EW 064T)* - For all these years.
(cd-s++=) *(EW 064CD1)* - The kill in your heart.
(cd-s) *(EW 064CD2)* - ('A'-mixes; Tikaramp radio / Phil Kelsey vocal / Extende bumps fluidity mix / Tikaramp vocal / SFX Sobriety).

Mother — not issued

May 98. (cd-s) *(MUMCD 102)* STOP LISTENING / The Cappuccino Song / Feeling Is Gone / ('A'-director's cut) [67] [–]
(cd-s) *(MUMXD 102)* - ('A') / Twist in my sobriety (new version) / Good tradition (new version).

Aug 98. (cd-s) *(MUMCD 105)* I DON'T WANNA LOSE AT LOVE / ('A'-Love loss ADF remix) / In Your Time [73] [–]
(cd-s+=) *(MUMXD 105)* - ('A') / ('A'-XT Talvin Singh mix) / Only one boy in the crowd.

Sep 98. (cd/c) *(MUM CD/C 9801)* **THE CAPPUCCINO SONGS** [69] [–]
- Stop listening / Light up my world / Amore si / Back in your arms / The cappuccino song / I don't wanna lose at love / The day before you came / If I ever / I like this / I knew you. *(cd bonus track+=)* - I don't wanna lose at love (mix).

Naive-V2 — not issued

Jun 05. (cd) *(VVR 103217-2)* **SENTIMENTAL** [ ] [–]
- Something new / Play me again / My love / Don't shake me up / Everyday is new / Love is just a word / Don't let the cold / Forever / Got to give you up / Heart in winter.

Martha TILSTON

Many artists would envy the fact that Martha - born June 7, 1976 in Bristol – is practically folk royalty, having had English folk singer STEVE TILSTON for her dad and fellow folk singer MAGGIE BOYLE as her stepmother, but her strict independence has been a commendable aspect of her steady rise to fame.

Kicking off her career in Brighton at the turn of the millennium, Martha and her duo Mouse (with guitarist Nick Marshall) delivered two self-released albums, while touring as support to DAMIEN RICE helped her gain experience on the circuit. A look into her discography will see her output balanced between CDs and MP3s/downloads, which is an example of her willingness to compromise with the modern world.

Politics plays a big part in her life and her music. 'Artificial' explores the weirdness of life in an office; 'The Saddest Game' reports on child soldiering in Africa; 'Corporations' speaks for itself.

Concentrating on the "official" releases, mainly for her own Squiggly imprint, **BIMBLING** (2005) {*7} and **OF MILKMAIDS AND ARCHITECTS** (2006) {*8} are by far her best, her hushed happy/sad material possessing strength and fragility in equal measure (think BUFFY SAINTE-MARIE), as can be heard in prime examples 'Firefly', 'Tribal Kidz', 'Winter Flowers' and 'Good World'. With further listens every track seems to unearth something fresh, and it's a pity her music hasn't found a global audience. Time will tell. *MCS*

Martha Tilston - vocals, acoustic guitar (with session people)
—— debut with **Nick Marshall** - guitar

UK own label — US not issued

2001. (cd; as MOUSE) *(none)* **MOUSE-TALES** [–] self [–]
- Big green / Tiniest kiss / By the lake / Breathe again / February / Only to land / Love has come to get me / All I ever wanted / Helicopter trees / Candy boy / Zennor hill / How long will you stick around / Bring him home.

pondlife — not issued

2003. (mp3) *(none)* **ROLLING** [–] gigs [–]
- Rolling / Sublime / Night rambling / Golden / Glastonbury hum / Symmetry / Blackbird / Lilly of the west / Wave machine / Bonny boy.

Squiggly — not issued

Feb 05. (cd) *(SQRCD 01)* **BIMBLING** [ ] [–]
- Space / Red / Firefly / Seagull / Brighton song / Tribal kidz / Mary and the prince / Monkey boy / Over to Ireland / Cycles / The numbness / Sprig of thyme / Fire wood.

2006. (mp3; MARTHA TILSTON & THE WOODS) *(none)* **ROPESWING** [–] net [–]
- Frizzby / Artificial / Falcon / A surfer courted me / Kinvarna / Corporations / Up in the tower / Simple / Cobwebs.

(above also available to download for 1p from pondlife)

Oct 06. (cd) *(SQRCD 03)* **OF MILKMAIDS AND ARCHITECTS** [ ] [–]
- Winter flowers / Artificial / Polly Vaughan / Music of the moon / Milkmaid / The architect / Good world / Songs that make Sophie fizz / Silver dagger / The tulip effect / Scientist. *(hidden +=)* - I wish I wish.

Jan 07. (m-cd) *(none)* **TILL I REACH THE SEA** [ ] [–]
- Artificial / Red / Firefly / Falcon / The architect / Night rambling / Symphonies and vans.

Apr 10. (cd) *(none)* **LUCY AND THE WOLVES** [ ] [–]
- The cape / Rockpools / Lucy / Who turns / Wild swimming / 350 bells / My chair / Seabirds / Searching for lambs / Old tom cat / Wave machine.

May 10. (cd-ep) *(none)* FOUR SONGS FROM LUCY [–] [–]
- The cape / Who turns / Searching for lambs / Wild swimming.

TIME OF YOUR LIFE (⟹ LIFE AND TIMES)

TO HELL WITH BURGUNDY

Tony Wilson's Factory Records were never at the front of the queue to sign folk acts, but with the the help of A&R man Mike Pickering (ex-Quando Quango), TO HELL WITH BURGUNDY were on the label's roster for a few years. Taking their name from a line in Czech composer Rudolf Friml's 1925 operetta 'The Vagabond King', TO HELL WITH BURGUNDY were formed in Manchester in October 1987 by drama students and accomplished musicians and singers Karl Walsh, Joanne Hensman and Kevin Metchear.

In March 1988 the Hensman-written track 'Mother Of The Sea' was served up with music by other artists on an EP issued on a friend's independent label, From Chorley. It was later one of the highlights (along with singles 'Go' and 'Who Wants To Change The World?') of their arty-folk set **EARTHBOUND** (1989) {*6}.

Subsequent tours supporting Barclay James Harvest, Graham Parker, CLANNAD and Bob Geldof improved their CV without extending their potential to be folk music's next big thing; the Factory association must have created some confusion about the band's identity and direction. Despite their folksy pop harmonies and the several decent songs in their repertoire, further sets such as **ONLY THE WORLD** (1992) {*5}, **3** (1994) {*4} and **THE MARVEL OF THE AGE** (1998) {*5} - released on their own Stig Europe imprint - did little in the way of sales. John Lees of Barclay James Harvest invited them to play as support act again in March 2001, but it was thought best to call it a day thereafter. *MCS*

Kevin Metchear - vocals, acoustic guitar / **Karl Walsh** - vocals, acoustic guitar / **Joanne Hensman** - vocals, percussion

UK From Chorley — US not issued

Mar 88. (7" ep; shared) *(FCR 2)* GROOVY GOINGS ON EP [ ] [–]
- (RED JOE MOON track) / Mother of the sea / (PASSION PLAY track).

Factory — not issued

May 89. (lp/c)(cd) *(FACT 217/+C)(FACD 217)* **EARTHBOUND** [ ] [–]
- Who wants to change the world? / Somewhere, anywhere / On a ship / The razor of truth ('slice up yer life' mix) / Falling / Go / Mother of the sea / Earthbound / Dangerously loose / For whom the bell tolls.

Jun 89. (cd-s) *(FACD 218)* WHO WANTS TO CHANGE THE WORLD? / Money / Mother Of The Sea [ ] [–]

Really Original — not issued

Nov 90. (12" ep) *(ROR 12001)* GO (new version with string quartet) / The Flight. / Beaches / Yesterday's News [ ] [–]

Stig Europe — not issued

Feb 92. (cd/c) *(STIG CD/C 05)* **ONLY THE WORLD** [ ] [–]
- 1:8 million / I can't understand you / Going under / Only the world / Heart / Telephone song / Bell song / Grain of sand / Money / Beaches.

Jul 94. (cd-ep) *(STIGCD 06)* THE KING AND I / Cormorant Wave / Only The World (acoustic version) / Where Is Your Love [ ] [–]

Aug 94. (cd/c) *(STIG CD/C 07)* **3** [ ] [–]
- The king and I / Honest man / Cormorant wave / If I was God / Under the sun / Gentle / Bring flowers / Waiting for rain / I could be that man / The lady of the lake / Encore.

Apr 98. (cd/c) *(STIG CD/C 08)* **THE MARVEL OF THE AGE** [ ] [–]
- The hard way / Big wheel / Beautiful / One song / Angel / Goodbye moon /

Maureen / Sad Lazarus / She sings all the time / Ordinary life / Rag and bone / Photographs.

—— they split in 2001; Walsh formed indie-rock band The Visitors

TOKEN WOMEN (⟹ FREYA, Jo)

Kazuki TOMOKAWA (⟹ Celtic-folk/World-music Discography)

TREMBLING BELLS

If you could imagine SHIRLEY COLLINS fronting The INCREDIBLE STRING BAND, Glasgow's TREMBLING BELLS would be folk's fantasy league team. The fact that former ISB member MIKE HERON combined with the quartet on the 2010 Christmas promo single 'Feast Of Stephen' (flipped with a group collaboration with BONNIE 'PRINCE' BILLY) gives the notion more substance.

Prior to the formation of TREMBLING BELLS (Lavinia Blackwall on vocals, Alex Neilson on vocals and drums, with Ben Reynolds and Simon Shaw), Alex's recording history began with avant-indie collaboratives. There was a mini-CD-r, 'Helvetica Is The Perfume Of The City' (2004), with Ben Reynolds, Isobel Campbell, Phil Todd and Andy Jarvis, and the LPs 'Belsayer Time' (2006), with Alistair Galbraith and Richard Youngs, and 'Graveside Doles' (2006), with Greg Kelley. Neilson also received credits on Matt Valentine's 'Untitled' LP (2006), BONNIE 'PRINCE' BILLY's 'Is It The Sea?' (2008) and the free-jazz improv 'Passport To Satori' (2009), with Greg Kelley. Experimentalists Motor Ghost (featuring Neilson and Reynolds) issued a limited-edition LP, 'A Gold Chain Round Her Breast', in 2007.

Alex's free-jazz/noise outfit Directing Hand (featuring a revolving-door cast of group musos including Reynolds), released several limited-edition mini-CD-rs, etc, including the neo-folk set 'Bells For Augustin Lesage' (2005). BLACK FLOWERS (Alex and Lavinia's other project, with Michael Hastings) preceded TREMBLING BELLS by a matter of months with their one-off project/set **I GREW FROM A STONE TO A STATUE** (2009) {*6}, featuring the TREES staple 'Polly On The Shore', shared with guest ALASDAIR ROBERTS.

With folk music becoming a force to be reckoned with in the US (FLEET FOXES, ESPERS, et al), it was time for fresh-faced young Brit-folkies to take some plaudits, and rock luminaries Paul Weller and Joe Boyd almost immediately endorsed TREMBLING BELLS' debut set for Honest Jon's Records, **CARBETH** (2009) {*7}. It was rather DENNYesque in nature (as on 'Willows Of Carbeth'), but Caledonian/COLLINS cues like 'I Listed All Of The Velvet Lessons', 'I Took To You (Like Christ To Wood)' and 'Garland Of Stars' harked back to the halcyon days of the late 1960s and early 1970s.

ABANDONED LOVE (2010) {*6} was another to bring back the old magic of yore, with Lavinia's near-operatic range and Alex's ISB-like minstrelsy twisting and turning between mediaeval and baroque freak-folk. Check out 'All Good Men Come Last', 'Man Is A Garden Born' (ah, the crumhorn!) and 'September Is The Month Of Death'.

Enlisting BLACK FLOWERS associate Michael Hastings, **THE CONSTANT PAGEANT** (2011) {*6} was born. Steeped in tradition and seething with fuzz, acid and full-on arrangements, Lavinia's high-pitched, Grace Slick-like swoons struggle to surface above the rhapsodic glam crescendos. But with patience and diligence (which are needed to appreciate all great rock bands), 'Where Do I Go From You?', 'Just As The Rainbow' and 'Colour Of Night' are tracks that should shake the shackles from your heart. *MCS*

Lavinia Blackwall - vocals / **Alex Neilson** (b. Yorkshire) - vocals, drums / plus **Ben Reynolds** (drone soloist/of Motor Ghost, of Ashtray Navigations) + **Simon Shaw** - bass, vocals

UK Honest Jon's — US Honest Jon's

Apr 09. (cd/lp) *(<HJR CD/LP 43>)* **CARBETH**
- I listed all the velvet lessons / I took to you (like Christ to wood) / When I was young / The end is the beginning born knowing / Summer's waning / Willows of Carbeth / Your head is the house of your tongue / Garlands of stars / Seven years a teardrop.

Apr 10. (cd/lp) *(<HJR CD/LP 47>)* **ABANDONED LOVE** — May 10
- Adieu, England / Man is a garden born / Baby, lay your burden down / Did you sing together? / September is the month of death / Love made an outlaw of my heart / Ravenna / All good men come last / Darling / You are on the bottom (and the bottle's on my mind).

—— **Michael Hastings** - guitar, vocals, repl. Reynolds

Mar 11. (cd/lp) *(<HJR CD/LP 55>)* **THE CONSTANT PAGEANT** — Apr 11
- Just as the rainbow / All my favourite mistakes / Colour of night / Cold heart of mine / Where do I go from you? / Otley rock oracle / Goathland / To see you again / Torn between loves / New year's eve's the loneliest night of the year.

BLACK FLOWERS

Lavinia + **Alex** +**Michael** with guest **Alasdair Roberts**

Bo Weavil — not issued

Feb 09. (m-cd) *(weavil 34cd)* **I GREW FROM A STONE TO A STATUE** — -
- Calvary cross / Hot crosses / Polly on the shore / And the words fell like malting blossom / Sweet rivers of redeeming.

TRIAKEL (⟹ Celtic-folk/World-music Discography)

The TRIO BULGARKA (⟹ Celtic and World Music Discography)

TUNDRA

Sadly overlooked in the first Great Folk Discography volume (their mid-1970s appearances on various-artists LPs were not taken into account), TUNDRA were forerunners of the comic-folk scene that thrived between London and Kent (and beyond) from the early 1970s.

Formed by Doug Hudson while studying for (and attaining) a degree in French and Russian at Bradford Technical College, the group comprised Doug, his wife-to-be Sue Carroll (vocals), Peter Learmouth (mandolin, banjo and guitar) and Mick Peters (bass, etc). Learmouth would later be part of DR COSGILL'S DELIGHT.

In 1978, and now down to Doug and his wife Sue (now teachers and singers by profession), the duo released **A KENTISH GARLAND** {*7}, a spirited trad album that was promoted by the couple on a US tour and on local television and radio. Songs from Doug's Kent-to-Greenwich (London) locale were the inspiration for two subsequent LPs, **THE KENTISH SONGSTER** (1980) {*6} and **SONGS FROM GREENWICH** (1982) {*6}, the latter featuring the musicianship of a young Alan Prosser of The OYSTER BAND.

The couple split in 1984, and Doug at first carried the TUNDRA name on before embarking on a solo career that developed an even more humorous side of his musical persona, while Sue subsequently formed country outfit Small Town Romance.

Without delving too much into Doug's comical genius, he was one of the first comic-folk acts to tour Hong Kong, Australasia and the Middle East, while his own 'Hudson's Half Hour' found airtime on the BBC. He played the Comedy Store venue in London with his stand-up routine (including the character of a nude radio interviewer).

Of his post-TUNDRA albums, his work with Ian Cutler and others in the 1990s and 2000s with HOT RATS is essential listening for anyone with a pulse. Titles such as **SHREDDED WIT** (1989) and **EXCUSE ME, I'M LOOKING FOR LUXEMBOURG** (1992) should give you an inkling of their contents. Doug now lives in the Broadstairs area with second wife Nicole. *MCS*

Doug Hudson (b. Feb 4, '51, Thornton Heath, South Norwood) - vocals, guitar / **Peter Learmouth** - mandolin, banjo, guitar, vocals; repl. Nigel Martin (on cornet and trumpet) / **Mick Peters** - bass, harmonica, vocals; repl. drummer Peter Carr

—— (1972) added **Sue Carroll** (b. Jan 25, '52, Farnham, Surrey) - vocals

UK Eron Enterprises — US not issued

1973. (lp; by various artists) *(ERON 002)* **FOLK IN SANDWICH** — -
- Medway flows softly / [tracks by Keith Pearson / Mariners / Holly Gwinn-Graham / Stephanie & Leonie Clarke / Paul Wilson] / Chips with everything / [tracks by Mariners / Holly Gwinn-Graham (2) / Keith Pearson / Paul Wilson / Stephanie & Leonie Clarke] / Battle of Edgehill.

—— split after Doug and Sue got married (retained group name); Learmouth formed Dr Cosgill's Delight, which evolved into BLOWZABELLA

—— next as MINGLED; with **Phil Burkin** - vocals, banjo, dulcimer, spoons / **Kay Burkin - vocals** (both of VULCAN'S HAMMER)

1975. (lp; by various artists) *(ERON 004)* **GOOD FOLK OF KENT** — -
- (MINGLED tracks):- 3. All me fancy / 8. Holmfirth anthem / 13. New York gals / 16. Admiral Benbow / 17. The Dreadnought / 19. Weary whaling ground.

1976. (lp; by various artists) *(ERON 006)* **TRAVELLING FOLK** — -
- [Skinner's Rats tracks] / Bold fisherman / Battle of Balaclava / [Mariners tracks] / Stephanie Clarke tracks] / [Keith Pearson & Treacle Line tracks] / [Merruwyn tracks].

—— now down to **Doug** + **Sue**

Sweet Folk And Country — not issued

1978. (lp) *(SFA 078)* **A KENTISH GARLAND**
- The jovial man of Kent / Hopping down in Kent / The lady of Rochester Castle / Captain Ward and the rainbow / Jezreels / The petition of the pigs / Come on the fleet / John Appleby / The pear tree / Tarry trousers / The Chathamites / Medway flows softly.

Greenwich Village — not issued

1980. (lp) *(GVR 208)* **THE KENTISH SONGSTER**
- Jolly Jack of Dover / Herne Bay dance / The Dutchman / Sweet orange pippin / The yeoman of Kent / The cells / The Lullingstone hunt / The pretty maids of Greenwich / The Kentish frolic / The hops / The old man and his wife / The hop supper.

1982. (lp) *(GVR 218)* **SONGS FROM GREENWICH**
- Greenwich park / The pretty maids of Greenwich / The rambling sailor / The rebellion of Wat Tyler / Admiral Benbow / The Greenwich lovers / Garland / Homeward bound / Blackheath burglar / The lady of Greenwich / So handy / Jack at Greenwich / Shallow brown.

DOUG HUDSON

solo (part-song and "part-comedy intro/routine")

Sweet Folk And Country — not issued

1984. (c) *(SFA 123)* **TUNDRA LIVE** [live at the Medway Theatre]
- Barrett's privateers / "Mercenary tales" / The jovial broom man / "Hertz van Rental and the Dutch fleet" / The Dutch in the Medway / "Adverts" / The battle of Balaclava / "I must, I must, I must" / Last Valentine's day / "The truth about Admiral Benbow" / Admiral Benbow / "The flasher" / Grey funnel line / "Life on the road" / The folksinger's lament / Show me your yo-yo.

Doug Hudson — not issued

1987. (c) *(DH 001)* **DOUG HUDSON 1987 AND ALL THE REST OF IT**
- Will Adams / Scream at the umpire / Election fever / My name is Ronald Reagan (I think) / Fel-lat-eeo / Always wear a cover / Hayfever / The Katherine Bowes-Lyon rag / The twelve drinks of Christmas.

One Off — not issued

1989. (lp) *(ONE OFF 001)* **SHREDDED WIT**
- Health food / Smoking song / Noah's ark / Serbo Croat / Booker prize / Where to sit on a plane / Latin football / Mozart.

1992. (lp) *(ONE OFF 004)* **EXCUSE ME, I'M LOOKING FOR LUXEMBOURG**
- CNN News / Gabriel Yacoub / Zambia Airways / Aussies and Kiwis / World Cup qualifier / Twelve drinks of Christmas / Scouting for boys / Teaching practice.

HOT RATS

Doug Hudson - vocals, guitar / **Ian Cutler** - fiddle (ex-BULLY WEE BAND, of Feast Of Fiddles) / plus at various times **Tony Rico** - sax / **Mick Peters**

1993. (c) *(ONE OFF 005)* **THE HOT RATS with DOUG HUDSON**
- Kid on the mountain / Carrickfergus / The rakes of Kildare - Tenpenny bit / Nine points of roguery - The teetotaller / Whiskey in the jar / The merry blacksmith - The scholar / The fields of Athenry / Seven inch reel - Foggy mountain breakdown - Sweets of May.

1997. (cd) *(ONE OFF 006)* **HOT RATS LIVE** [live at the Prince of Wales pub in Strood]
- Andy Renwick's ferret / Banks of Newfoundland / Nine points of roguery - The teetotaller / Billy / Cooley's reel - Maid behind the bar / White walls, white rum / Drunken priest - Ash plant / Mira dreams of England / Rocky road to Dublin - Foxhunters' jigs - Kid on the mountain / Carrickfergus / Killarney boys of fun / The pigeon on the gate / Farewell to Ireland - Mason's apron.

1999. (cd) *(ONE OFF 008)* **LIKE FLIES**
- Macedon expresz variation / Lark in the morning - Rakish Paddy / Mercedes in the drive / Orange blossom special / Duna rol fuja szel (A cold wind blows over the Danube) / Music for a found harmonium / Die moorsoldaten (Peat bog soldiers) / Smeceno horo / Like flies / Bonny Kate - The teetotaller / Moscow nights / Dashing white sergeant.

2000. (cd; by DOUG HUDSON) *(ONE OFF 009)* **HAPPY NOW?**
- White walls, white rum / Dead man blues / Like flies / Cameraman / (I don't care if they all think she's) Marilyn / Mira dreams of England / Mercedes in the drive / Billy / Happy now?

2003. (cd) *(ONE OFF 011)* **HOT RATS THREE**
- Jig of slurs / Santy Anna / Monti Czardas / Step it out Mary / Last night's fun - Hardimann the fiddler / Katusha / Bulgaro / January man - Paddy Ryan's dream / Salmon tails up the water - Flowers of Edinburgh / Rehradice - A walk in Brevnov.

2009. (cd) *(ONE OFF 012)* **TOUR DE FRANCE** [live in France]
- Cooley's reel / Song of the plains / Americans / Merrily kissed the Quaker / Sany Anna / Orange blossom special / Dark eyes / Arabesque - Hava nagila / Step it out Mary / Jig of slurs / Farewell to Ireland / Katyusha.

TUNNG

The core duo of London-dweller Mike Lindsay and Derbyshire lad Sam Genders brought TUNNG to the world with an untidy but enjoyable debut, **THIS IS TUNNG: MOTHER'S DAUGHTER AND OTHER SONGS** (2005) {*7}, a wilfully skewed collection where English folk met electronic dabbling. The result was a little style-over-substance, but distracting enough. Perhaps correctly, they earned the tag 'folktronica'.

After creating their debut with the help of sundry friends and relatives, the pair recruited a five-member team to put flesh on the bones of their songs, only for Genders to decide to take a back seat on the performance front and leave Lindsay to lead the group live. Genders remained the main songwriter, however, though they recorded Bloc Party's 'The Pioneers' for a single. The resulting album, **COMMENTS OF THE INNER CHORUS** (2006) {*7}, felt marginally more of a group effort, but no less scattergun in its approach. The band's penchant for odd instruments (such as seashells) was an attempt to lift them beyond expected folk norms, but there was still a pair of songwriters at the heart of it all in Genders and Lindsay.

On their third album, the contrast between Genders's limpid lyricism and Lindsay's everything-and-the-kitchen-sink production gave the band a fuller sound than ever before, vocalist Becky Jacobs's bird-like tones making an even greater impression. **GOOD ARROWS** (2007) {*7} was a more coherent and compelling album than those it followed.

A collaboration and tour with Malian Tuareg desert-rock outfit Tinariwen added more colours and textures to a sound already overloaded with disparate elements. Something had to give - and it did. Jacobs moved closer to centre-stage as Genders decided to step out of the band altogether (in favour of The ACCIDENTAL), and their sound evolved from sweet and odd to simply sweet. Long-time band friend Ben Bickerton arrived to bolster the lyrics in the absence of Genders, and they outgrew the folktronica label with **... AND THEN WE SAW LAND** (2010) {*7}, becoming almost what they had resisted being at the start - a genuine, quality British psych-folk outfit in the original 1960s mould. *MR*

Mike Lindsay - vocals, guitar, sound effects / **Sam Genders** - vocals, guitar

UK: Static Caravan — US: Ace Fu

Jun 04. (ltd-7") *(VAN 72)* A TALE FROM BLACK. / Pool Beneath The Pond

Aug 04. (ltd-7" clear@33rpm) *(VAN 73)* MAYPOLE SONG (THE). / Surprize Me

Jan 05. (cd/lp) *(VAN 88/+V)* <ace 036> **THIS IS ... TUNNG: MOTHER'S DAUGHTER AND OTHER SONGS** — Feb 06
- Mother's daughter / People folk / Out the window with the window / Beautiful and light / Tales from black / Song of the sea / Kinky vans / Fair Doreen / Code breaker / Surprise me 44.

2005. (ltd-7" split) *(VAN 94 + DIF7 28)* PEOPLE FOLK (The Rushey Green Morris mix). / (other by Dollboy)

(above shared on Different Drummer) (below iss. on Nowhere Fast)

Nov 05. (ltd-7" @33rpm) *(SLOW 03)* MAGPIE BITES. / The Bonny Black Hare — Nether

Jan 06. (ltd-7" etched) *(VAN 99V)* THE PIONEERS
(cd-s+=) *(VAN 99)* - Tale from black / Pool beneath the pond / Fair Doreen (video).

—— added **Becky Jacobs** - vocals / **Ashley Bates** - vocals / **Phil Winter** - multi / **Martin Smith** - multi

Full Time Hobby — Thrill Jockey

Apr 06. (ltd-7") *(FTH 020S)* WOODCAT. / Woodcat (Viva Voce remix)

May 06. (cd/lp) *(FTH 019 CD/LP)* <Thrill 181> **COMMENTS OF THE INNER CHORUS**
- Hanged / Woodcat / The wind up bird / Red and green / Stories / Jenny again / Man in the box / Jay down / It's because ... we've got hair / Sweet William / Engine room. *(ltd-cd+=; FTH 019CDX)* - Band stand / Bodies.

Sep 06. (ltd-7") *(FTH 025S)* JENNY AGAIN. / Jenny Again (The Earlies remix)

Nov 06. (ltd-7") *(FTH 030S)* IT'S BECAUSE ... WE'VE GOT HAIR. / It's Because ... We've Got Hair (Department Of Eagles remix)

Aug 07. (7") *(FTH 041S)* BRICKS (Dntel remix). / Bricks (Daedalus remix)

Aug 07. (cd/lp) *(FTH 040 CD/LP)* <Thrill 190> **GOOD ARROWS**
- Take / Bricks / Hands / Bullets / Soup / Spoons / King / Arms / Secrets / String / Cans. *(ltd-cd+=; FTH 040CDX)* - Wood / Clump.

Sep 07. (7") *(FTH 042S)* BULLETS (Max Tundra remix). / Bullets (edit)

Feb 09. (ltd-7" gold) *(needno 005)* ROBIN. / [other version by Soy Un Caballo]

(above issued on Need No Water)

—— Sam left to join w/ Stephen Cracknell (of MEMORY BAND) to form The ACCIDENTAL

Feb 10. (ltd-7") *(FTH 089S)* HUSTLE. / The Source

Mar 10. (cd/lp) *(FTH 088 CDA/LP)* <Thrill 242> **...AND THEN WE SAW LAND**
- Hustle / It breaks / Don't look down or back / The roadside / October / Sashimi / With whiskey / By dusk they were in the city / These winds / Santiago / Weekend away.

May 10. (7") *(FTH 091S)* SASHIMI. / Hustle [Surehand remix]

Aug 10. (cd-r) *(FTH 099D)* DON'T LOOK DOWN OR BACK / Weekend (In The Cabin)

KT TUNSTALL

Folk music is a broad church when it can include artists like KT TUNSTALL, a rootsy pop singer-songwriter who has from time to time given the public the odd folk song, but whose music is a pot-pourri of everything from blues and country to rock.

Born Kate Victoria Tunstall, June 23, 1975, Edinburgh, to a Chinese-Scottish mother and Irish father, she was adopted and grew up among the Sloane Ranger students and bracing climate of St Andrews, Fife. She learned to sing from an Ella Fitzgerald tape and began writing songs and playing guitar in her mid-teens.

A year's scholarship to a private American prep school was the cue for her to form her first band, The Happy Campers, and take her first stab at busking. Back in the UK, she studied theatre and music at London's Royal Holloway College before heading home to Fife, where she hooked up with the nascent Fence Collective, starting a band with Pip Dylan and touring with the Skuobhie Dubh Orchestra. A stint in Edinburgh saw her promoting her own Acoustic Extravaganza nights (a forerunner of the still-going-strong Acoustic Edinburgh) before a 2002 move to London and a publishing contract.

In 2004 she joined worldbeat electronica ensemble Oi Va Voi, providing vocals on tracks (including 'Refugee') on their album 'Laughter Through Tears'. Despite the disappointment of a scuppered Columbia deal, her perseverence eventually paid off with the recording of a Steve Osborne-produced debut album for Relentless Records (also home to bluesy-eyed girl Joss Stone).

EYE TO THE TELESCOPE (2005) {*7} announced TUNSTALL as a no-frills singer with a yen for cathartic, Celtic-anthemic choruses. A string of singles edged her ever closer to household-name status, with 'Suddenly I See' and the swooning 'Other Side Of The World' knocking on the Top 10. But it is as an albums artist that she has made her name, attracting a Mercury nomination, selling a million and seeing off the competition (outselling even Madonna) with a deft flick of her beloved loop pedal.

Jools Holland's 'Later With ...' was the first TV show to beam her foot-stomping charisma into British living-rooms, followed by celebrated spots on BBC4's DYLAN tribute (performing 'Simple Twist Of Fate') and a Hogmanay shindig in Edinburgh's Princes Street Gardens. Subsequently nominated for three Brit awards, she won Best British Female Solo Artist.

A CD/DVD combination, the odds-and-ends **ACOUSTIC EXTRAVAGANZA** (2006) {*5}, featuring a rendition of Beck's 'Golden Age', marked time while she worked on a proper follow-up, the Top 10 **DRASTIC FANTASTIC** (2007) {*6}. Dressed like a glam-rocker on the sleeve (imagine Suzi Quatro in white), TUNSTALL had lost the folky punch of her debut as her producers got their way on the sound and image, e.g. on singles 'Hold On', 'If Only' and 'Saving My Face'.

Putting electro-beats into the mix, **TIGER SUIT** (2010) {*7} found TUNSTALL re-inventing herself once again with lead single '(Still A) Weirdo' - quirky, kooky and potential fodder for 'X-Factor' contestants. Folk music it was not.

Her B-side cover versions, etc, include 'Get Ur Freak On' (Missy Elliott), 'Fake Plastic Trees' (Radiohead), 'Walk Like An Egyptian' (The Bangles) and 'The Prayer' (Bloc Party). *BG & MCS*

KT Tunstall - vocals, acoustic guitar, piano, flute, drums / + session people

UK Outcaste — US not issued

Mar 04. (ltd-7") *(OUT 56)* THROW ME A ROPE. / Black And White [ ] [–]

Relentless — EMI

Oct 04. (2x7" ep/cd-ep) *(REL/+CD 12)* FALSE ALARM EP [ ] [–]
- False alarm / Heal over / Miniature disasters / Throw me a rope.

Jan 05. (cd/lp) *(CD/LP REL 06)* **EYE TO THE TELESCOPE** [3] [–]
- Other side of the world / Another place to fall / Under the weather / Black horse and the cherry tree / Miniature disasters / Silent sea / Universe and U / False alarm / Suddenly I see / Stoppin' the love / Heal over / Through the dark. *(ltd-cd+=; CDRELX 06)* - Black horse and the cherry tree (live).

Feb 05. (7") *(REL 14)* BLACK HORSE AND THE CHERRY TREE. / Barbie [28] [–]
(cd-s) *(RELCD 14)* - ('A') / One day (live).

May 05. (7" burgundy) *(REL 18)* OTHER SIDE OF THE WORLD. / Morning Stars [13] [–]
(cd-s) *(RELCD 18)* - ('A') / Boo hoo.
(dvd-s) *(RELDVD 18)* - ('A'-video) / Black horse and the cherry tree (video) / Throw me a rope.

Sep 05. (7") *(REL 21)* SUDDENLY I SEE. / Moment Of Madness (live) [12] [–]
(cd-s) *(RELCD 21)* - ('A') / Girl and the ghost.
(dvd-s) (RELDVD 21) - ('A') / Miniature disasters (live at Glastonbury) / Get ur freak on (BBC Radio 1 live lounge).

Dec 05. (7") *(REL 23)* UNDER THE WEATHER. / Little Favours [39] [–]
(cd-s) *(RELCD 23)* - ('A') / Tangled up in blue (BBC4 live)

Feb 06. (cd) *<50729>* **EYE TO THE TELESCOPE** [–] [33]

Feb 06. (-) *<radio>* BLACK HORSE AND THE CHERRY TREE [–] [20]

Mar 06. (7") *(REL 24)* ANOTHER PLACE TO FALL. / Universe And U (acoustic extravaganza version) [52] [–]
(cd-s) *(RELCD 24)* - ('A') / Fake plastic trees (Radio 1 live).

May 06. (-) *<radio>* SUDDENLY I SEE [–] [21]

Sep 06. (cd w/dvd) *(CDREL 08) <76142>* **ACOUSTIC EXTRAVAGANZA** [32] [–]
- Ashes / Girl and the ghost / One day / Golden age / Boo hoo / Gone to the dogs / Change / Miniature disasters / Universe and U / Throw me a rope. // (Five go to Skye) / Gone to the dogs / Throw me a rope / The wee bastard pedal.

Aug 07. (7") *(REL 40)* HOLD ON. / Suddenly I See (live) [21] Jul 07 [ ]
(cd-s) *(RELCD 40)* - ('A') / Journey.
(dvd-s) *(RELDVD 40)* - ('A'-video) / ('A'-Behind the scenes) / Hopeless (live acoustic).

Sep 07. (cd/lp) *(CD/LP REL 15) <95618>* **DRASTIC FANTASTIC** [3] [9]
- Little favours / If only / White bird / Funnyman / Hold on / Hopeless / I don't want you now / Saving my face / Beauty of uncertainty / Someday soon / Paper aeroplane.

Sep 07. (d-cd) *(509036-2)* **EYE TO THE TELESCOPE / ACOUSTIC EXTRAVAGANZA** (w/ bonus material) [38] [–]

Nov 07. (7") *(REL 46)* SAVING MY FACE. / Ain't Nobody [50] [–]
(cd-s+dl-s) *(RELCD 46)* - ('A') / Mothgirl.

Nov 07. (m-cd) *<07724>* **SOUNDS OF THE SEASON: THE KT TUNSTALL HOLIDAY COLLECTION** [–] [92]
- 2000 miles / Christmas (baby please come home) / Mele kalikimaka (Christmas in Hawaii) / Sleigh ride / Fairytale of New York / Lonely this Christmas.

Mar 08. (7") *(REL 48)* IF ONLY. / The Prayer (Radio 1 live version) [45] [–]
(cd-s/dl-s) *(CDREL 48)* - ('A') / Walk Like An Egyptian (live in Liverpool).

Aug 10. (dl-s) <-> FADE LIKE A SHADOW [–] [ ]

Sep 10. (dl-s) *(-)* (STILL A) WEIRDO [39] [–]

Sep 10. (cd) *()* **TIGER SUIT** [5] Oct 10 [43]
- Uummannaq song / Glamour puss / Push that knot away / Difficulty / Fade like a shadow / Lost / Golden frames / Come on, get in / (Still a) Weirdo / Madame Trudeaux / The entertainer.

Frank TURNER

Punky singer-songwriter FRANK TURNER has filled the void left by anti-folk celebrity BILLY BRAGG, who has curtailed his recording schedule somewhat since the millennium. Born Francis E. Turner, December 28, 1981 in Manama, Bahrain, he was raised in Meonstoke (a village in Hampshire) by his relatively well-off parents and went to Eton College at the same time as Prince William.

Railing against society from within, Frank spent time as lead singer in a couple of London's new breed of post-hardcore outfits, Kneejerk and Anglo-Aussies Million Dead. The latter were a popular quartet with several singles and a couple of albums under their belt, 'A Song To Ruin' (2003) and 'Harmony No Harmony' (2005). Frank's mother Jane (a headmistress and the daughter of a bishop) guested on the latter set.

After opening his socially subversive solo career with the six-song EP 'Campfire Punkrock' in 2006 (not forgetting the odd split single), TURNER and his indie-rock backers Dive Dive (formerly The Unbelievable Truth) toured in support of his much-touted debut set **SLEEP IS FOR THE WEEK** (2007) {*6}. Folk-rock singles 'The Real Damage' and 'Vital Signs' were radio-playlisted at the time.

With Ben Lloyd from Dive Dive at the controls, and a tour supporting Andy Yorke (brother of Radiohead's Thom), Biffy Clyro and yourcodenameis: milo, things looked bright as TURNER's second set, **LOVE IRE AND SONG** (2008) {*8}, cracked the UK Top 75 and led him on to the roster of tasty American punk imprint Epitaph. A bout of gastro-enteritis, however, led to gig cancellations at the end of the year, his growing fan base missing out on modern-day classics such as 'Reasons Not To Be An Idiot', 'Photosynthesis' and the charity single 'Long Live The Queen'. His cover versions include The Lemonheads' 'Outdoor Type', the old country standard 'You Are My Sunshine', Springsteen's 'Thunder Road' and Abba's 'Dancing Queen'.

Produced by Nailbomb leader Alex Newport, **POETRY OF THE DEED** (2009) {*8} was Frank's first Top 40 entry in Britain, an anthemic semi-classic for the country's disillusioned and politically-minded youth awaiting a new Oasis, LEVELLERS or Stiff Little Fingers. His punk background came to the fore on 'Live Fast Die Old' (hardly a folk song); others included 'Dan's Song', 'The Road' and 'Richard Divine'.

Throwing a cat into the audience (at the 02 Academy in Oxfordshire on June 23, 2011) might not have been a great idea to promote his UK Top 20 fourth album, **ENGLAND KEEP MY BONES** {*8}, but it certainly kicked up a stir among animal protection groups. On the album, ballady tracks were laced with all the familiar traits of folk's new kid on the block. One song, 'Peggy Sang The Blues' was a dedication to the memory of his grandmother, while two of the most infectious songs ('If Ever I Stray' and 'Wessex Boys') were co-written by loyal band member Nigel Powell. *MCS*

Frank Turner - vocals, guitar / + band/sessions

UK: Xtra Mile — US: Welcome Home

Jan 06. (7" red) *(XMR 714)* [REUBEN track]. / The Real Damage [ ] [-]

May 06. (cd-ep) *(XMREP 115)* CAMPFIRE PUNKROCK [ ] [-]
- Nashville Tennessee / Thatcher fu*ked the kids / This town ain't big enough for the one of me / Casanova lament / I really don't care what you did in your gap year. *(German 10" ep-colrd iss. 2008 on Good Friends+=; GFR 004)* - The ballad of me and my friends.

Aug 06. (12" ep; some yellow) *(XMREP 116)* <HOME 005>
split w/ JONAH MATRANGA [ ] [ ]
- [JONAH MATRANGA tracks) / Outdoor type / You are my sunshine.

Dec 06. (dl-s) *(-)* VITAL SIGNS / Heartless Bastard Motherfucker [demo] [ ] [-]

Jan 07. (cd) *(XMR 004CD)* **SLEEP IS FOR THE WEEK** [ ] [-]
- The real damage / Vital signs / Romantic fatigue / A decent cup of tea / Father's day / Worse things happen at sea / My kingdom for a horse / Back in the day / Once we were anarchists / Wisdom teeth / The ladies of London town / Must try harder / The ballad of me and my friends.

May 07. (cd-ep) *(XMREP 118)* THE REAL DAMAGE [ ] [-]
- The real damage / Sea legs / Back to sleep / Sunshine state / Heartless bastard motherfu*ker.

UK: Xtra Mile — US: Epitaph

Mar 08. (dl-d) *(-)* PHOTOSYNTHESIS [ ] [-]

Mar 08. (cd/lp) *(XMR 011 CD/LP)* <87037-2/-1>
LOVE IRE AND SONG [72] Jul 08 [ ]
- I knew Prufrock before he got famous / Reasons not to be an idiot / Photosynthesis / Substitute / Better half / Love ire and song / Imperfect tense / To take you home / Long live the queen / A love worth keeping / St Christopher is coming home / Jet lag.

Jun 08. (dl-s) *(-)* REASONS NOT TO BE AN IDIOT [ ] [-]

Oct 08. (7"shared) *(XMR 748)* LONG LIVE THE QUEEN. / [Crazy Arm track] [65] [-]

Jan 09. (ltd-7" shared) *<SH 124-7>* [Austin Lucas track]. / Thunder Road [-] [ ]

(above issued on Suburban Home records)

Sep 09. (cd/lp; red,white) *(XMR 022 CD/LP)* <87039-2/-1>
POETRY OF THE DEED [36] [ ]
- Live fast die old / Try this at home / Dan's song / Poetry of the deed / Isabell / The fastest way back home / Sons of liberty / The road / Faithful son / Richard Divine / Sunday nights / Our lady of the campfires / Journey to the Magi.

Sep 09. (dl-ep) *(-)* THE ROAD / Mr Richards [solo acoustic] / Poetry Of The Deed [solo acoustic] / The Road [video] [62] [-]

Oct 09. (7" colrd; shared) *<SH 155-7>* [Tim Barry track]. / Try This At Home [acoustic] [-] [ ]

(above issued on Suburban Home Records)

Aug 10. (ltd-7" shared) *(XMR 754)* TRY THIS AT HOME. / [tracks by The Retrospective Soundtrack Players and Isaac Graham] [ ] [-]

Oct 10. (dl-s) *(-)* **I STILL BELIEVE** [ ] [-]

Dec 10. (cd-ep) *(XMREP 127)* <87137-2> ROCK AND ROLL [ ] [ ]
- I still believe / Pass it along / Rock and roll / Romance / To absent friends / The next round.

Dec 10. (ltd-green-lp; as FRANK TURNER & JON SNODGRASS)
(XMR 035LP) **BUDDIES** [ ] [-]
- Buddies / Styx: The man, the band / The ballad of Steve / Susannah / Old fast songs / Shut the chicken / New Orleansy / Big rock in Little Rock / Mo'squitoz / Remember that time when we wrote this record?

Apr 11. (dl-s) *(-)* PEGGY SANG THE BLUES [ ] [-]

Jun 11. (cd/lp) *(XMR 043 CD/LP)* <87163-2> **ENGLAND KEEP MY BONES** [12] [ ]
- Eulogy / Peggy sang the blues / I still believe / Rivers / I am disappeared / English curse / One foot before the other / If ever I stray / Wessex boy / Nights become day / Redemption / Glory hallelujah. *(bonus +=; XMR 043CDB)* - Song for Eva Mae / Wanderlust / Balthazar, impresario.

- (8-10*) compilations -

Dec 08. (cd) *Xtra Mile; (XMR 016CD)* **THE FIRST THREE YEARS** [72] [-]
- (CAMPFIRE PUNKROCK tracks) / The outdoor type / You are my sunshine / Sea legs / Back to sleep / Sunshine state / Heartless bastard motherfucker / Pay to cum / Fix me / Hold your tongue / Front crawl / Jet lag (rock) / Photosynthesis / Worse things happen at sea / Imperfect tense / District sleeps along tonight / Smiling at strangers on trains / Dancing queen.

Pat TURNER (⟹ HERAUD, Lynne &...)

Cath & Phil TYLER

Formed in Newcastle upon Tyne by American singer and musician Cath Oss (ex-CORDELIA'S DAD and ex-NORTHAMPTON HARMONY) and her Brit-folk husband Phil Tyler, a couple united by their love of Appalachia and its ambience. The latter artist had self-released one CD-r in 2002 entitled 'Banjo', a traditional/old-timey recording taped at Brancepeth Castle in County Durham. Here Phil also proved he could write a decent song, even though plucked from some cyber-hillbilly ghost town.

Both albums so far, **DUMB SUPPER** (2008) {*7} and **THE HIND WHEELS OF BAD LUCK** (2010) {*6} were firmly rooted in and by tradition, going further back in time than even STEELEYE SPAN in their halcyon days. Cath - the link between Maybelle Carter and The HANDSOME FAMILY's Rennie Sparks - has an almost monotone delivery/drone on the likes of 'Wether's Skin' (a gem with links to 'The Well Below The Valley'), 'Fisherman's Girl', '1000 Years' and the a cappella 'Queen Sally' (all from the debut), but Phil was more than capable of stealing some limelight on the second set with the medley 'Golden Ace' - 'Courting Is A Pleasure'. *MCS*

Cath Tyler - vocals, guitar (ex-CORDELIA'S DAD) / **Phil Tyler** - acoustic guitar, banjo, vocals

UK: No-Fi — US: not issued

Feb 08. (cd) *(NEU 008)* **DUMB SUPPER** [ ] [-]
- Wether's skin / Queen Sally / Fisherman's girl / Farewell my friends / Death of Queen Jane / Yellowhammer / Devil song / 1000 years / False true love / Dewdrop / Morning / Slumber boats (baby's boats) / Wild stormy deep.

Apr 10. (cd) *(NEU 018)* **THE HIND WHEELS OF BAD LUCK** [ ] [-]
- Dearest dear / Imaginary trouble / Our captain cried / Whip poor Will / Three maidens / Golden ace - Courting is a pleasure / Lady Gay / Hi-spy / The wind that shakes the barley / Castle by the sea / Long time travelling.

U

The UKRAINIANS

Formed in Leeds, initially for a series of John Peel sessions, as a lighthearted moonlighting side project for The Wedding Present's Peter Solowka (whose Ukrainian father handed down to him the tradition of playing the mandolin and balalaika). Their first release was 'Ukrainski Vistupi V Johna Peela' in the spring of 1989. A few years later, after he parted company with The Wedding Present, Solowka put the group on a more official basis with like-minded traditionalist associates Len Liggins (vocals/violin) and accordionist Roman Remeynes.

Signed to independent roots label Cooking Vinyl, the group unveiled a self-titled EP (led by NME Single of the Week 'Oi Divchino') in autumn 1991, and later the same year an album, **THE UKRAINIANS** {*6}. 1991 was also the year Ukraine became an independent nation from the old Soviet Union.

Turning their impressively authentic Eastern European folk style to The Smiths on the 'Pisni Iz The Smiths' EP, Liggins sounded too close to Morrissey for comfort on the likes of 'Batyar' (i.e. 'Bigmouth Strikes Again') and 'Koroleva Ne Pomerla' (The Queen Is Dead). With the addition of Stepan Pasicznyk and Paul 'Dino' Briggs (to replace Roman), The UKRAINIANS released a follow-up set, **VORONY** (1993) {*7}, applying their dolorous charm to a reading of The Velvet Underground's 'Venus In Furs' (under the guise of 'Chekannya').

1994's **KULTURA** {*8} was a rockier affair (courtesy of new members Michael L.B. West and former guest Dave Lee), combining breakneck stompalongs like 'Europa' with more easy-going fare in the vein of the countrified 'Horilka'.

Almost four years passed before the band inflicted the self-explanatory 'Prince' EP on an unsuspecting public, Solowka and his friends lending a measure of threadbare austerity to the lavish creations of The Artist Formerly Known As.

On the long-awaited **RESPUBLIKA** (2002) {*7}, the folk revisionists set their sights on The Sex Pistols, cranking out rather ridiculous versions of 'Anarchy In The UK' and 'Pretty Vacant'. Nevertheless, these detracted only slightly from what was otherwise, for its more reverent treatment of Eastern European traditional music, the most accomplished album of their career.

Several years on, following the **LIVE IN CZEREMCHR** (2008) {*6} set, their next studio album, **DIASPORA** (2009) {*6}, was worth the wait. From Brahms's 'Hungarian Dance' ('Uhorskiy Tanets') to a cover of Marc Bolan's 'Children Of The Revolution', one still can't help noticing the resemblance of the 'Legendary' Len Liggins's voice to Morrissey's. The band (Solowka, Liggins, West, Woody, Jim Howe, Steve Tymruk and Paul Weatherhead) are currently (2011) celebrating their official 20th anniversary by playing as many British Ukrainian clubs as they can. *MCS*

The 'Legendary' Len Liggins (b. London, England) - vocals, violin (ex-Sinister Cleaners) / **Peter Solowka** - guitars, mandolin, vocals (ex-Wedding Present) / **Roman Remeynes** - accordion, vocals

UK Cooking Vinyl — US Omnium

Sep 91. (12") *(FRY 019T)* THE UKRAINIANS
- Oi divchino / Kolyadka / Zavtra / Sertsem I Dusheyu.

Sep 91. (cd/c) *(COOK CD/C 044)* *<OMM 2002 CD/C>* **THE UKRAINIANS**
- Oi Divchino [Hey, girl] / Hopak / Ti moyi radoshchi [You are my happiness] / Zavtra [Tomorrow] / Slava Kobzarya [Kobzar's gloey] / Dity plachut [Children are crying] / Cherez richku, cherez hai [Across the river, through the wood] / Pereyidu [I will cross] / Tebe zhdu [Waiting for you] / Son [Dream].

—— added **Stepan 'Ludwig' Pasiczynk** - accordion, vocals

Cooking Vinyl — Cooking Vinyl

Jan 93. (cd-ep) *(FRYCD 023)* *<CKV 5023>* PISNI IZ THE SMITHS
- Batyar (Bigmouth strikes again) / Koroleva ne Pomerla (The Queen is dead) / M'yaso - Ubivstvo (Meat is murder) / Spivaye solovey (What difference does it make?).

—— **Paul 'Dino' Briggs** - bass; repl. Roman

Cooking Vinyl — Green Linnet

Feb 93. (cd/c) *(COOK CD/C 054)* *<GLCD 4015>* **VORONY** — 1994
- Vorony / Koroleva ne Pomerla (The Queen is dead) / Chi skriptsi hrayu / Sche raz / Nadia pishla / Doroha / Rospryahaite / Durak / Sertsem i dusheyu / Dvi lebidky / De ye moya mila? / Teper mi hovorymo / Chekannya (Venus in furs).

—— added **Michael L.B. West** - mandolin, duda, piano + **Dave Lee** - drums (guest on last set)

Cooking Vinyl — Cooking Vinyl

Sep 94. (cd) *(<COOKCD 070>)* **KULTURA**
- Polityka / UkrainAmerica / Kievskiy express / Smert / Horilka / Slava / Europa / Kinets / Tycha voda / Zillya zelenenke / Ya / Tsyhanochka / Dyakuyu i dobranich.

—— added **Allan Martin** - bass

Apr 96. (cd-ep) *(LC 7180)* RADIOACTIVITY (radio edit) / Radioactivity (German mix) / Radioactivity (orthodox mix) / Revelation — -

—— **Woody** - drums, percussion; repl. Lee

Aug 98. (cd-ep) *(FRYCD 071)* PRINCE EP — -
- Nothing compares 2 U / Sign o' the times / Purple rain (Slavs in the temple mix) / Nothing compares 2 U (U got the uke mix).

—— **Paul Weatherhead** - mandolin, spoilka, theremin; repl. Briggs

Zirka — Omnium

Sep 02. (cd-ep) *(ZRKCDS 2)* ANARCHY IN THE UK / God Save The Queen / Pretty Vacant / Anarchy In The UK (acoustic) — -

Feb 03. (cd) *(ZRKCD 3)* *<OMM 2028CD>* **RESPUBLIKA** — Oct 02
- Ty zh mene pidmanula (You deceived me) / Anarchy in the UK / Chervona rozha troyaka (Three red roses) / Horila sosna (The pine tree was burning) / Arkan (The lasso) / Oi vydno selo (You can see a village) / Srebrncia / Stoyit yavir nad vodoyu (The maple tree stood at the water's edge) / Oi na hori (On the hill) / Pretty vacant / Reve ta stohne dnipr shyrokyy (The broad river Dnieper roars and moans) / Nalyvaimo brattya (Let's fill our drinking cups, brothers) / O Ukraino (Oh Ukraine).

—— **Jim Howe** - bass; repl. Allan

Mar 08. (cd) *(037CD 13)* **LIVE IN CZEREMCHA** (live) — -
- Nalyvaimo brattya / Polityka / Oi na hori / Anarkhiya (Anarchy in the UK) / Chervona rozha troyaka / Zavtra / Smert / Ti moyi radoshchi / Cherez richku cherez hai / Vorony / Ty zh mene pidmanula / Chekannya (Venus in furs) / Arkan / Horila sosna / Teper my hovorymo / UkrainAmerica / Oi vydno selo / O Ukraino / Verkhovyno.

—— **Steve Tymruk** - accordion; repl. Stepan who formed Here Be Dragons

Jan 09. (dl-s) *(none)* HUNGARIAN DANCE / Diaspora (third wave mix) / Children Of The Revolution (strange orchestras mix) / Refugees (live) — -

Feb 09. (cd) *(038CD 14)* *<OMM 2046CD>* **DIASPORA** — Mar 09
- Diaspora / Emigranty / Panovy molodtsi / Vykhid [Exodus] / Sobache zhyttya / Skilky revolutsiy / Olenka / Newilnyk waltz / Marusya bohuslavka / Medestra / Nevelychki khvyli / Dodumu / Dity revolutsiyi / Souveniry [Souvenirs] / Uhorskiy tanets [Hungarian dance].

- (5-7*) compilations, etc. -

Feb 01. (cd) *Zirka; (<ZRKCD 1>)* **DRINK TO MY HORSE! (LIVE!) (1989-1994)**
- Oi Divchino / Cherez richku cherez hai / Davni chasy / Teper my hovorymo / Yikhav kozak za dunai / Ti moyi radoshchi / Zavtra / Sertsem I dusheyu / Hopak / Na skriptsi hrayu / Koroleva ne pomerla (The Queen is dead) / Chekannya (Venus in furs) / Kievskiy express / Tykha voda / Batyar (Bigmouth strikes again) / Europa / Rospryahaite / Tsyhanochka / Davni chasy / Verkhovyno.

Jul 02. (cd) *Cooking Vinyl; (GUMBOCD 028)* **# 1 INTERNATIONAL UKRAINIAN GROUP** (early 1990s material) — -
- Zavtra / Slava kobzarya / Chi znayesh ty? / Shche raz / Nadia pishla / Doroha / Rospryahaite / Dvi lebidky / De ye moya mila? / Pereyidu / Tebe zhdu / Son.

Apr 04. (cd) *Zirka; (ZRKCD 4) / Omnium; <OMM 2035CD>* **ISTORIYA: The Best Of The Ukrainians** — Feb 04
- Telstar / Ty zh mene pidmanula / Polityka / Oi Divchino / Chlib / Slava / Dity plachut / Batyar / Ukrainamerica / Hopak / Vorony / Ti moyi radoshchi / Anarkhiya / Durak / Chekannya / Smert / Koroleva ne pomerla / Cherez richku cherez hai / Europa / Nalyvaimo brattya (Let's fill our drinking cups, brothers).

UNITED BIBLE STUDIES

A loose experimental improv outfit from Dublin, the UNITED BIBLE STUDIES collective could claim to be the weirdest sounding freak-folk band in the genre's history - possibly the link between LOUDEST WHISPER, DR STRANGELY STRANGE, IN GOWAN RING and the Wicker Man.

Founded in the winter of 2001 by David Colohan and James Rider, but never settling for a consistent line-up (Gavin Prior, Aine O'Dwyer, Bryan O'Connel, Ivan Pawle, Michael Tanner and Richard Moult were all part of the set-up around the mid-2000s), UNITED BIBLE STUDIES have performed their edgy Irish trad-to-future folk to bewildered audiences around the globe. Without going into too much detail about their limited-edition CD-r sets, or assess something that might be just plain unobtainable, you might try the 2006 concept release **THE SHORE THAT FEARS THE SEA** {*7} or 2009's **THE JONAH** {*7} - which features a freak-folk guest list to die for (Alison O'Donnell of MELLOW CANDLE, Richard Moult of Current 93, Ivan Pawle of Scented Candle and SHARRON KRAUS) - and see how you get on. Best of Irish to you. *MCS*

David Colohan - vocals, multi / **James Rider** - guitar, piano / **Gavin Prior** - vocals, guitar, percussion / **Aine O'Dwyer** - harp / **Bryan O'Connel** - percussion, drums

UK Deserted Village — US not issued

2003. (ltd-cd-r) *(???)* **STATIONS OF THE SUN, TRANSITS OF THE MOON** — Irish
- Glitter on ice / Holly and frost / Backwards across the burren / Venus aloft, I spy'd a single crow / Ice forms on Obelesk / Shanaglish cemetery / More tongues to catch the snowfall / Herne lays down his bow / Every time we find a dead Viking. *(UK-iss. 2006 on Barl Fire; BF 012)*

Foxglove — not issued

Jun 04. (ltd-cd-r) *(foxglove 033)* THE LUNAR OBSERVATORY — Irish
- Stag horn mountains (Cernunnos rising) / Sea of rains / The gibbous stones / Dark lowland plains / Prosper Henry / The lunar observatory / Old moon in the new moon's arms.

Slow Loris — not issued

Sep 04. (ltd-3" cd-r) *(slo 07)* HUNTLY TOWN — Irish
- An cailin Gaelach / With ravens on our wrists / The roving ploughboy-o / Ghostwritten / Bogie's bonnie bell / Pillar of cloud.

Deserted Village — 23 Productions

2005. (ltd-cd-r) *(dv 22)* **AIRS OF SUN AND STONE** — Irish
- Airs of sun and stone. *<US cd-r iss.2008 on Deep Water; dw 014>*

2005. (ltd-cd-r) *<23CD 0402>* **THE SOLAR OBSERVATORY**
- Kroton mammaii / The solar observatory.

2006. (cd) *(dv 23)* **THE SHORE THAT FEARS THE SEA** — Irish
- Rivers rotting in the earth / Hellical rising / Columba's song / Watching the rain reshape Galway / Crofts of Copeland / Tributaries of the Styx under Dublin / The one true God lies to himself while the one true Goddess sings / The shore that fears the sea / Captain William Coey.

Rusted Rail — not issued

2006. (ltd-cd-r) *(none)* THE NORTHERN LIGHTS AND NORTHERN DARK — Irish
- Bubble of earth / Pictures of Katia / Note of hope / Hedge school drop out / Elbow of dawn / Spoon of Haar.

Ruralfaune — not issued

2007. (ltd-cd-r) *(rur 029)* **BLACK COLCANNON** — French
- A manly shanty / Who will put me in my grave? / Caoneadh cill chais - She moved through the Belfast child / Candles for Albert / Medley: Tributaries of the Styx under Dublin - Christ is nailed to many crosses - The shore that fears the sea.

Humbug — not issued

Dec 08. (ltd-clear-lp) *(055)* **THE ARBOREAL OBSERVATORY** — Nor
- Scealp solais / The arboreal observatory / For Alice Coltrane / Guthanna sa dorchadas / The black lighthouse.

—— added numerous guests: **Alison O'Donnell, David Colohan, Caroline Coffey, Ivan Pawle, Paul Condon, Richard Moult, Sharron Kraus, Richard Skelton, Sean Og, Shane Cullinane + Scott McLaughlin**

Camera Obscura — not issued

Mar 09. (cd) *(CAM 084CD)* **THE JONAH**
- The swallowing / The Jonah / To the newly risen mountains / A for Andromeda / Veil song / The Lowlands of Holland / Skelly's fireplace / The mildew leaf / Mirror in Cherwell / Death in the Arctic.

Perhaps Transparent — not issued

2010. (ltd-cd-r) *(none)* **A SHATNER OBSERVATORY** — Irish
- Part I / Part II.

—— the band now consisted of **Aine, Alison, Gavin, Ivan, Paul + Diarmuid MacDiarmada**

Deserted Village — not issued

2010. (free-dl) *(dv 39)* **THE KITCHEN SESSIONS [new versions]**

2011. (ltd-m-lp; by UNITED BIBLE STUDIES & JOZEF VAN WISSEM) *(dv 40)* **DOWNLAND**
- Downland / Seven tears / Trade boys for prostitutes sell girls for wine / Come holy ghost / Altars of brick (the day is coming) / I rith na hOiche / The seas have lifted up their voice.

- others, etc.-

2006. (ltd-cd-r) *Paha Porvari; (prec 008)* **LIVE AT THE WAREHOUSE** [live] — French
- Untitled x 6.

The UNTHANKS

With an ear for Northern-based folk and the heritage that comes with it, singer and cellist RACHEL UNTHANK (of Ryton, Newcastle) formed The Winterset with her younger sister Becky (vocals), 'Stars In Their Eyes' winner Belinda O'Hooley (on piano) and Jackie Oates (sister of JIM MORAY, on viola and vocals). The sisters were brought in a traditional-folk-loving family, more likely to play music by the singing STEWART clan (Sheila, Belle, etc.) than their neo-folk counterparts.

Guided by producer/guitarist Adrian McNally (with sound engineer Oliver Knight) and not forsaking Rachel's wispy Geordie accent, the group's debut set, **CRUEL SISTER** (2005) {*7}, was released to critical appraisal and strong live promotion. Mojo's Folk Album Of The Year was the toast of many a forlorn post-SANDY DENNY/Judie Tzuke fan, its best songs being the jazzy, piano-led opener 'On A Monday Morning' (CYRIL TAWNEY), DAVE GOULDER's 'January Man', NICK DRAKE's 'River Man', MATT McGINN's 'Troubled Waters' and Alex Glasgow's doleful 'Twenty Long Weeks'. With many traditional songs ('Fair Rosamund', 'The Fair Flower Of Northumberland' and 'Rap Her To Bank') included, they were more than competent to rearrange storytelling folklore like 'Cruel Sister' (all eight-plus minutes of it) and the Keelers/Jim Mageean favourite, 'John Dead'.

Just as the girls were finding their feet (the sisters were also useful clog-dancers), one of them, JACKIE OATES, decided to branch out on her own. Her replacement, Anglo-Irish fiddler Niopha Keegan, was in place for their second set, **THE BAIRNS** (2007) {*7}. Sometimes accompanied at times by an full orchestra, an eclectic array of outside sources was employed by way of JOHNNY HANDLE's 'Felton Lonnin', BELLE STEWART's 'Blue Bleezing Blind Drunk', Robert Wyatt's 'Sea Song', OWEN HAND's 'My Donald' and WILL OLDHAM/Bonnie 'Prince' Billy's short and sweet 'A Minor Place'.

The multi-talented O'Hooley presented two of her own compositions, 'Blackbird' and 'Whitethorn', which stood tall alongside trad numbers like 'I Wish' and Ma Bonny Lad', Richard Scott's 'Can't Stop It Raining' and Terry Conway's 'Fareweel Regality'. A winner of numerous folk awards, the set was also nominated for the Mercury Music Prize the following year.

A slight adjustment to their name was a chancy decision to make, but as The UNTHANKS, Rachel and Becky were hardly straying too far from their tried and tested formula. Rounded off by a bigger band sound (including Niopha, plus Adrian McNally and Chris Price), **HERE'S THE TENDER COMING** (2009) {*7} was another treasure, featuring half trad and half cover songs. Of the former, the beautiful 'Annachie Gordon' and the equally lengthy title track came off best, while the richness of the covers was typified by ANNE BRIGGS's 'Living By The Water', LAL WATERSON's 'As First She Starts', LIZZIE HIGGINS's 'The Testimony Of Patience Kershaw' and EWAN MacCOLL's 'Nobody Knew She Was There'.

Taking a diverse range of ballads and songs from unusual sources (their brassy take on King Crimson's 'Starless' sticks out a mile), **LAST** (2011) {*8} brought the girls joyously up to date despite the use of Northern-based sourced material. 'Gan To The Kye' and 'The Gallowgate Lad' were complemented by Alex Glasgow's 'Close The Coalhouse Door', Tom Waits's 'No One Knows I'm Gone' and JON REDFERN's 'Give Away Your Heart' (Becky had featured on Jon's 2008 album 'What Else But Love?'). Recent recruit McNally contributed the title track. *MCS*

RACHEL UNTHANK & THE WINTERSET

Rachel Unthank (b. 1978) - vocals, cello / **Becky Unthank** (b. 1985) - vocals / **Belinda O'Hooley** - piano / **Jackie Oates** - five-string viola, vocals

UK Rabble Rouser — US Cortex

May 05. (cd) *(RR 005) <392>* **CRUEL SISTER** — 2008
- On a Monday morning / January man / Fair Rosamund / Cruel sister / Rap her to bank / Raven girl / Twenty long weeks / The fair flower of Northumberland / The Greatham calling-on song / River man / Bonny at morn / John dead / Troubled waters. *(re-iss. Oct 06; same)*

—— **Niopha Keegan** (b. 1977) - fiddle, vocals; repl. Oates who went solo and joined TIM VAN EYKEN

EMI Universal

Aug 07. (cd) *(50999 5 04380 2 0)* *<80158>* **THE BAIRNS**
- Felton Lonnin / Lull I / Blue bleezing blind drunk / I wish / Blue's gaen oot o' the fashion: The wedding o' Blythe - When the tide come / Lull II: My lad's a canny lad / Blackbird / Lull III: A minor place / Sea song / Whitethorn / Lull IV: Can't stop it raining / My Donald / Ma bonny lad / Fareweel regality / Newcastle lullaby.

The UNTHANKS

Rachel + Becky with **Niopha** plus **Adrian McNally** - piano / **Chris Price** - guitar

EMI Rough Trade

Sep 09. (cd) *(687122-2)* *<RTRADECD 548>* **HERE'S THE TENDER COMING** Mar 10
- Because he was a bonny lad / Sad February / Annachie Gordon / Lucky Gilchrist / The testimony of Patience Kershaw / Living by the water / Where've yer bin Dick? / Nobody knew she was there / Flowers of the town / Not much luck in our house / As first she starts / Here's the tender coming. *(UK+=)* - Betsy Bell.

Mar 11. (cd) *(095594-2)* *<RTRADECD 617>* **LAST** Apr 11
- Gan to the kye / The Gallowgate lad / Queen of hearts / Last / Give away your heart / No one knows I'm gone / My laddie sits ower late up / Cannie Hobbie Elliott / Starless / Close the coalhouse door / Last (reprise).

VAGABOND CREW (⇒ REDGUM)

Tim VAN EYKEN

Singer and accordionist TIM VAN EYKEN (born March 7, 1978 in Bristol, England) was raised in Somerset, although his family line is drawn from Belgian ancestry; his great-grandparents settled in Wells after the First World War.

Influenced by the tutelage of mentor ANDY CUTTING, himself a leading light in the revival of the accordion, Tim (a BBC Young Folk Award winner in 1998) led the way in bringing to life the dance tunes of Sweden, the British Isles and beyond, which were much in evidence on two of his earliest sets, **NEW BOOTS** (1998) {*6} and **ONE SUNDAY AFTERNOON** (2001) {*6}, the latter a collaboration with concertina player Robert Harbron.

Side by side with moonlight shifts in DR FAUSTUS (along with BENJI KIRKPATRICK and Paul Sartin) and WATERSON: CARTHY (as replacement for Saul Rose), he maintained a solo career throughout. **STIFFS LOVERS HOLYMEN THIEVES** (2006) {*7} featured an array of traditional songs and guest spots from fiddler NANCY KERR and LAL WATERSON's guitarist Oliver Knight. British folk music was definitely on a high when Adrian Sutton's music for the stage play 'War Horse' - with VAN EYKEN as 'Songman' and some ballads by JOHN TAMS - was released in 2008. *MCS*

Tim Van Eyken - vocals, accordion, melodeon, guitar

UK Appledore / US not issued

Dec 98. (cd) *(AMU 01CD)* **NEW BOOTS**
- The Heyseyside reel - The Morpeth rant / Rounding the horn / The Liverpool hornpipe - Delahunty's hornpipe - Mona's delight / Twa corbies / Spirit of the dance / The keys of sorrow / The Washington hornpipe - Old Tom of Oxford - The rose of Lisieux / Ouvrez le porte - Michael Turner's waltz / The wild woman of Bawdsey - General Wolfe / Rosline Castle - Breaking digits / Wim Claeys' Schottische.

Beautiful Jo / not issued

Jun 01. (cd; by TIM VAN EYKEN & ROBERT HARBRON) *(BEJOCD 34)* **ONE SUNDAY AFTERNOON**
- Sussex waltz / Frenchmen in the moon / Ye mariners / Old Swedish: Det stod en jungfru - Unknown / New Swedish: Paul & Jenny's wedding tune - Polska after Jonas Ollson / The handsome dark lover / Poynton / Set la cardeuse / Farmer Slough: Once a farmer - Proceed to Slough / Bold Riley.

—— Van Eyken took time off solo work to join DR FAUSTUS (see below) and WATERSON: CARTHY ('Fishes And Fine Yellow Sand' in 2004 and 'Holy Heathens And The Old Green Man' in 2006).

Topic / Topic

Jun 06. (cd) *(<TSCD 565>)* **STIFFS LOVERS HOLYMEN THIEVES**
- Barleycorn / Australia / The pearl wedding - Nancy Taylor's / Fisherman / Gypsy maid / Fair Ellen of Ratcliffe / Young Alvin / Worcester city / Babes in the wood / Bonny breast knot - Barseback polka / Twelve joys of Mary.

—— after he left WATERSON: CARTHY in May 2007, Tim was part of the National Theatre production project/CD WAR HORSE, (orchestral music by Adrian Sutton and songs by JOHN TAMS), released in Sep 2008.

Foy VANCE

Born in Bangor, County Down, Foy spent his early days in Oklahoma, Alabama and New Orleans with his family before going back to his home town; he now lives in London.

With a sound that embraces harmony-fuelled folk, rootsy blues and heart-twisting soul, the singer-songwriter from Northern Ireland is the missing link between VAN MORRISON, RICHIE HAVENS and Stevie Wonder. **HOPE** (2007) {*7}, his only full-length set so far (though something should be released later in 2011), is a record that oozes hope itself, his heartfelt themes coming across most strongly on 'Treading Water', 'First Of July' and 'I Was Made'.

Vance, whose fan base includes Pete Townshend and Bonnie Raitt, recorded the album in a hired cottage in Northern Ireland's Mourne mountains, his only accompaniment provided by London-born pianist and composer Jules Maxwell. *MCS*

Foy Vance - vocals, guitar, organ (with session people)

UK Freshwater / US not issued

Aug 05. (cd-ep) *(1)* LIVE SESSIONS AND THE BIRTH OF THE TOILET TOUR (live)
- Indiscriminate act of kindness / Intro to Billie Jean / Billie Jean [live] / Bailie's blood [live] / Sweethearts footage: Journey / Toilet song (itchy feet).

Jun 06. (cd-ep) *(2)* WATERMELON ORANGES
- Home / Stoke my fire / Homebird / Don't please yourself / Sometimes.

Dec 06. (cd-s) *(3)* GABRIEL AND THE VAGABOND. / Indiscriminate Act Of Kindness

Rubyworks / Wurdamouth

Jun 07. (dl-s) *(-)* BE WITH ME

Jul 07. (cd) *(RWXCD 59)* *<05>* **HOPE**
- Be with me / Shed a little light / Doesn't take a whole day / Fifteen / I was made / Treading water / Gabriel and the vagabond / First of July / Elshaneed / Indiscriminate act of kindness / Hope, peace and love / If only you could see yourself like I see you / Dry wells / Pull me through / Two shades of hope.

next with the Ulster Orchestra

Wurdamouth / not issued

Nov 09. (cd-ep) *(none)* LIVE AT THE WATERFRONT, BELFAST [live]
- Gabriel and the vagabond / If only you could see yourself like I see you / Doesn't take a whole day / Be with me / Indiscriminate act of kindness.

James VARDA

Born in the 1960s in Twickenham, London, Varda's story began in the 1980s when he performed frequently at the Clapham Folk Club. It was there that he was discovered by the great ROY HARPER, who invited him on his tour, and into his studio to record his dark and introspective debut album, **HUNGER** (1988) {*7}. Boosted by contributions from Roy's son NICK HARPER, the singer-songwriter received rave reviews, but after resounding spots at the Cambridge and Reading Festivals in 1989 and 1990 respectively (and playing to the inmates of Wormwood Scrubs prison), VARDA retired to take up teaching in Suffolk.

He re-emerged in 2004 with his long-awaited second set, **IN THE VALLEY** (2004) {*6}, a tender record that was described as "consummately unassuming, and achingly affecting", which just about sums it up. *MCS*

James Varda - vocals, acoustic guitar (with guests on first set only)

UK MurMur / US not issued

May 88. (lp) *(MUR 1001)* **HUNGER**
- Just a beginning / From the Bellevue hotel / Sunday before the war / I can't stand it / Strange weather / This train is lost / Crawl in the pen / Trust the rain / In my house / Black on black. *(cd-iss. Jul 07 on Small Things; SMALLTR 0701)*

Small Things / not issued

Jan 04. (cd) *(SMALLTR 0301)* **IN THE VALLEY**
- Down here / That's the time / Small things / Message to playwright / I'm the one / The things that matter most / Something fell / In the valley / Inside the volcano / If this book.

VARTTINA (⇒ Celtic-folk/World-music Discography)

VOICE OF THE SEVEN WOODS

On a mission to retrieve the acoustic echoes of 1960s folk-guitar heroes ROBBIE BASHO, JOHN FAHEY and SANDY BULL, VOICE OF THE SEVEN WOODS is the brainchild of Bolton-born, Manchester-raised folktronica merchant Rick Tomlinson. As Richard Tomlinson, he and Naomi Hart were credited on a Dave Tyack set in 2001.

Although Tomlinson intended VOICE to be only a short-term project when it began in 2003, the guitarist, sitarist, oud-player, pianist and singer has (with drummer Chris Walmsley) issued numerous rare singles and EPs. A long-time stalwart of the Twisted Nerve label, Tomlinson - now with third member Pete Hedley - finally reached a proper album-buying audience with **VOICE OF THE SEVEN WOODS** (2007) {*7}.

Diverse in all aspects of psychedelia, folk and Eastern world music, the set was redolent of The Bevis Frond and Can (on 'Second Transition' and 'Return From Byzantium'), NICK DRAKE (on 'Silver Morning Branches' and 'Dusk Cloud') and DAVEY GRAHAM (on 'The Smoking Furnace'). From the opening 'Sand And Flames' (interpolating the climatic 'Sayat Nova'), the musical emphasis lies heavily on Eastern guitar rhythms, and one can't help thinking of John Lydon's Pil or DEVENDRA BANHART on hearing the hypnotic highlight, 'The Fire In My Head'.

Tomlinson, Walmsley and new boy Rory Gibson (on bass) were up for another psychedelic bash on the acid-orientated, Cluster/Amon Duul II-like **VOICE OF THE SEVEN THUNDERS** (2010) {*8}, a modern-day masterpiece that erupts from the speakers. It's not exactly folk music as such (apart from 'Disappearances' and the instrumental 'Dry Leaves'), but you can expand your mind and hair-do wigging out to reverb delights such as 'Set Fire To The Forest' 'The Burning Mountain' and 'Kommune'. *MCS*

Rick Tomlinson - guitar, sitar, vocals, piano, percussion, oud / + guest **Chris Walmsley** - drums, percussion, piano

UK Twisted Nerve — US B-Music

May 03. (7" split) *(???)* SVARKA (Rick Tomlinson with Chris Walmsley)

Jan 06. (7" ep) *(TN 064)* AN HOUR BEFORE DAWN
- An hour before dawn / Spiral / Sky of grey / Beginning.

Aug 06. (7") *(TN 072)* THE FIREFLY DUSK. / Winter's Temper

2006. (7" split) *(???)* GONE ON THE WAY TO KNOW. / (other by Hush Arbors)

(above issued on Great Pop Supplement) (below on other labels)

2007. (ltd;cd-ep) *(none)* THE JOURNEY
- Solitary breathing / Departure / The journey / Breaking moonlight / 3 am, home / 6. *(re-iss. Jun 08 on Swedish Kning Disk cd-ep/12" ep; KD 048CD)*

2007. (ltd-3" cd-r) *(singular 032)* THE WITHERING OF THE BOUGHS

(above issued on First Person)

2007. (ltd;cd-ep) *(BRR 21a)* THE FAR GOLDEN PEAK PART ONE

(above release on Blackest Rainbow)

—— now a trio with **Pete Hedley** - bass, violin

Aug 07. (cd/lp) *(TN 077 CD/LP)* <800107> **VOICE OF THE SEVEN WOODS**
- Sand and flames / Sayat nova / The fire in my head / Silver morning branches / Second transition / Valley of the rocks / Underwater journey / Return from Byzantium / The smoking furnace / Dusk cloud. <US+=> - The holy harbour / Sailing to Byzantium.

Oct 07. (10") *(TN 079)* THE HOLY HARBOUR. / Sailing To Byzantium

VOICE OF THE SEVEN THUNDERS

Rick + Chris plus **Rory Gibson** - bass

Tchantinler — Holy Mountain

Dec 09. (ltd-7") *(TCHANT 002)* THE BURNING MOUNTAIN. / Dry Leaves[alt. version]

Feb 10. (lp/cd) *(TCHANT 001/+CD)* <HOLY 1968> **VOICE OF THE SEVEN THUNDERS** — Mar 10
- Open lighted doorway / Kommune / Out of the smoke / Third transition / The burning mountain / Dry leaves / Dalalven / Cylinders / Set fire to the forest / Disappearances.

apart from Twisted Nerve releases, this discography is extremely selective

The WAIFS

Australia has been the stamping ground of many a rootsy folk outfit over the years, and The WAIFS, from Albany, Melbourne, are one of its more recent successes. They were formed in the mid-1990s by singing sisters Vicki and Donna Simpson when they abandoned their duo Colours and enlisted the help of co-songwriter and guitarist Josh Cunningham.

While DYLAN was a major influence on the trio (they covered his 'Don't Think Twice, It's Alright'), country legend Willie Nelson was equally idolised (his 'Circles' was later recorded on their 2005 live double **A BRIEF HISTORY...** {*7}).

As they extended their territory to North America and Britain for numerous folk festivals, earlier Aussie-only albums such as **THE WAIFS** (1996) {*7}, **SHELTER ME** (1998) {*7}, **SINK OR SWIM** (2000) {*7} and **UP ALL NIGHT** (2003) {*5} began to emerge on import, and the demand was high enough for US re-issues of all their work.

The lush voice of young Donna was the highlight of the sound, and dreamy songs like 'Circles', 'Crazy Train', 'Billy Jones' and Cunningham's 'Take It In' and 'Gillian' were gems on their effective, country-esque debut. From pop to jazz via other genres, their music was a patchwork of styles, but folk-rock was their base. Check out 'London Still', 'Fisherman's Daughter' and 'Rescue' from this period.

Four years in the making, The WAIFS' fifth studio album, **SUNDIRTWATER** (2007), {*7}, found them likened to PETER, PAUL & MARY, with tight harmonies their forte. **TEMPTATION** (2011) {*6} struck a chord mainly in their homeland and in North America, although they had toured in Britain alongside FRANK TURNER. Donna lives in Minneapolis with her son, Vicki in Utah with her husband and Josh in California with his wife. The last-named launched his solo album 'Into Tomorrow' in Australia in 2010. *MCS*

Donna Simpson - vocals, acoustic guitar / **Vicki Thorn/Simpson** - vocals, harmonica, acoustic guitar / **Josh Cunningham** - guitars, mandola, ukulele, vocals

UK/Aus Jarrah — US Compass

May 96. (cd) *(WAIFSCD 001)* **THE WAIFS** — own
- Take it in / Gillian / Circles / Sunflower man / Intimate / Jealousy / Crazy train / Billy Jones / Brain damage / I believe / Company / Waif song / Shiny apple. *(UK-iss. Feb 04; same) <US-iss. 2004 on Compass; COM 4379-2>*

Mar 98. (cd) *(WAIFSCD 002)* **SHELTER ME** — own
- Heart lies / People who think they can / Shelter me / Lest we forget / Smith St / Time to part / Sound the alarm / Stuck / The river / Spotlight / Attention / Billy Jones [jazz version]. *(UK-iss.Feb04; same) <US-iss. 2004 on Compass; COM 4380-2>*

—— added **David Ross Macdonald** - drums, percussion

2000. (cd) *(WAIFSCD 003)* **SINK OR SWIM** — own
- The waitress / Lies / Danger / Without you / The haircut / Love serenade / Taken / Service fee / A brief history... / Where I die / Sink or swim. *(UK-iss. Feb 04 on ATO; 21506)*

—— added **Ben Franz** - bass; double bass, Dobro

Jun 02. (cd-ep) *(WAIFSCD 004)* LONDON STILL — Austra
- London still / Crazy train / Lies / Here if you want / Jealousy.

Jul 03. (cd) *(WAIFSCD 005)* *<COM 4360-2>* **UP ALL NIGHT**
- Fisherman's daughter / Nothing new / London still / Lighthouse / Flesh and blood / Highway one / Since I've been around / Fourth floor / Rescue / Three down / Sweetness / Up all night. *<d-cd+= in Canada; 23339-4009-2LTD>* - Sunflower man / Crazy train [live] / Lies / Here if you want / Jealousy [unreleased version] / Shelter me.

Nov 03. (cd-ep) *(WAIFSCD 006)* LIGHTHOUSE / Heartbreakin' / Gillian / Don't Think Twice, It's Alright — Austra

Mar 04. (cd-s) *(WAIFSCD 007)* BRIDAL TRAIN / Strings Of Steel / Sweetness [live] — Austra

Jan 05. (d-cd) *(WAIFSCD 008)* **A BRIEF HISTORY... [live]**
- Lighthouse / London still / Take it in / Love serenade / The waitress / Fisherman's daughter / Papa / Crazy train / Brain damage / Don't think twice, it's alright / Lies / Haircut / The river / Gillian / A brief history / Bridal train [studio] // Willow tree / (intro to...) / When I die / Sunflower man / Flesh and blood / Highway one / (intro to...) / Bridal train / Since I've been around / Here if you want / Billy Jones / Company / Spotlight / Shelter me / Shiny apple / Crazy - Circles.

Aug 07. (cd-s) *(WAIFSCD 009)* SUNDIRTWATER / Mess Around / Trouble At My Door — Austra

Sep 07. (cd) *(WAIFSCD 010)* *<974472>* **SUNDIRTWATER**
- Pony / Sundirtwater / Vermillion / How many miles / Without you / Sad sailor song / Get me some / Eternity / Sweetest dream / Goodbye / Stay / Love let me down / Feeling sentimental.

Mar 09. (cd) *(WAIFSCD 011)* *<974513>* **LIVE FROM THE UNION OF SOUL** [live]
- How many miles / London Still [acoustic] / Sundirtwater / Downroads / When I die [bluegrass version] / Rescue / Stay [acoustic] / Take it in / From little things [feat. JOHN BUTLER] / I remember you [feat. CLARE BOWDITCH] / Feeling sentimental / Sweetest dream / Eternity / Pony. *(bonus +=)* - London still [acoustic] / When I die / Stay [acoustic] / From little things / I remember you.

Mar 11. (cd) *(WAIFSCD 012)* *<4552-2>* **TEMPTATION**
- I learn the hard way / Buffalo / Just like me / Beautiful night / Moses and the lamb / Falling / Somedays / Drifting dreaming / Day dreamer / Temptation / Goodbye darlin'.

Nancy WALLACE (⟹ The OWL SERVICE)

The WATERBOYS

When The WATERBOYS surfaced from their London hideaway in 1983, not even mercurial leader Mike Scott perhaps knew in what direction he'd take them, but the fact that they subsequently veered away from the U2/VAN MORRISON-type alt-rock of their first album was down to Scott and his ever-evolving supporting cast.

Edinburgh-born college punk Scott had previously fronted New Wave outfit Another Pretty Face, a turn-of-the-1980s singles outfit that featured, among others, Ayrshire school friends John Caldwell and Jim Geddes. Another embryonic incarnation of The WATERBOYS had a brief career as Funhouse.

Taking their name from a lyric from the song 'The Bed' on Lou Reed's sleaze-noir masterpiece LP 'Berlin', Edinburgh-born Scott (vocals, guitar and piano), English multi-instrumentalist Anthony Thistlethwaite and Welsh keyboards player Karl Wallinger were all aboard when the trio secured a deal with the Irish-run Ensign label. A self-financed debut single in spring 1983, entitled 'A Girl Called Johnny' (a tribute to punk priestess Patti Smith), received a fair amount of airplay and deserved better success.

Debut album **THE WATERBOYS** (1983) {*7} followed later that summer, an esoteric set of avant-rock 'big music' that drew comparisons with TIM BUCKLEY's more ambitious meanderings and introduced Scott as a promising singing/songwriting seer. Opener 'December', the Psychedelic Furs-like 'I Will Not Follow', the Tom Verlainesque 'The Girl In The Swing' and 'A Girl Called Johnny' stole the show.

Embellished with additional instrumentation such as horns and violin (trumpeter Roddy Lorimer was now a recruit), **A PAGAN PLACE** (1984) {*6} was a confident follow-up, Scott venturing ever further out on his spiritual journey with the likes of 'The Big Music' and 'Church Not Made With Hands'. Their VAN MORRISON/Celtic-rock sound was beginning to take shape with 'The Thrill Is Gone' and the title track finale.

A burgeoning live reputation and gushing critical praise saw The WATERBOYS' third set **THIS IS THE SEA** (1985) {*8} break into the UK Top 40, its epic centrepiece 'The Whole Of The Moon' becoming the group's first Top 30 single. Melodious and multi-layered, the glorious set was praised by critics and newfound fans alike, who swooned over gems such as 'Don't Bang The Drum', 'Old England', 'The Pan Within' and the closing title piece.

Despite this overdue success, Wallinger subsequently departed to form his own outfit, The World Party.

Relocating to Galway in Ireland for an extended sabbatical at the behest of new fiddler, Steve Wickham from IN TUA NUA, who had played on the previous set, Scott and Thistlethwaite increasingly infused their music with traditional Irish folk influences.

It was an earthier WATERBOYS, then, who eventually emerged in late 1988 with the acclaimed **FISHERMAN'S BLUES** {*8}, Scott seemingly having at last found his true musical calling. From the strident Celtic clarion call of the title track to the soulful cover of Van Morrison's 'Sweet Thing', the record sounded as if the group had been playing this music for centuries, especially on trad song 'When Will We Be Married?' and Wickham's short contribution, 'Dunford's Fancy'. The transitional record almost made the UK Top 10, established The WATERBOYS as a major-league act and remains their biggest seller. Check out also 'And A Bang On The Ear' and 'The Stolen Child'.

Falkirk-born flautist Colin Blakey (ex-WE FREE KINGS), with Irish folks Sharon Shannon (on accordion) and Noel Bridgeman (drums, replacing J.D. Doherty), stayed on for **ROOM TO ROAM** (1990) {*7}, which continued in the same Celtic-folk vein, much to the annoyance of their original 'big music' fan base. While The POGUES would have loved to tackle 'The Raggle Taggle Gypsy' in their own inimitable style, here Mike Scott gives it the Andy Stewart treatment. It is overshadowed by the soulful 'Something That Is Gone' and the lilting 'A Man Is In Love'.

Bang on cue, Ensign/Chrysalis re-promoted 'The Whole Of The Moon' to catch both sets of fans, the result being Top 3 status, while the track was played to death by radio all over again. By this point, however, the original WATERBOYS line-up had splintered, following a final UK tour on which the group drew criticism for their return to an all-out rock sound. Thistlethwaite formed the Blue Stars, while Scott eventually moved to New York and gathered together a new group of musicians.

Now signed to Geffen Records, he recorded **DREAM HARDER** (1993) {*5}, the sixth WATERBOYS album but a Scott solo set (with session players) in all but name. Exploring many familiar themes, the cosmic-Celtic album spawned two Top 30 singles in 'The Return Of Pan' and 'Glastonbury Song', and boasted a brief contribution (on 'Spiritual City') from Scottish comedy legend BILLY CONNOLLY. Despite critical lambasting, it wasn't as bad as many pundits made out - it was just out of place.

MIKE SCOTT returned to Scotland and adopted a style reminiscent of AL STEWART, delivering two solo albums, **BRING 'EM ALL IN** (1995) {*6} and **STILL BURNING** (1997) {*7}. The latter, a return to his 'big music' days, was not necessarily folk-rock flavour of the era.

The WATERBOYS, out of action for almost seven years, returned with **A ROCK IN THE WEARY LAND** (2000) {*6}. Fusing psychedelia, folk-rock and pop, the album was a lacklustre attempt to break back into the mainstream, but it did have its moments. Scott toyed with the current trend of rock 'n' roll nihilism on opening track 'Let It Happen', and the finale, 'Crown', was quietly poignant.

It's easy to see why Scott still carries on despite critical disapproval from some of the press. He at least enjoys what he does, as do his dedicated fan base, who will never forget what the man and his group have achieved. An odds-and-ends collection of out-takes and unreleased material from the band's early days, **TOO CLOSE TO HEAVEN** (2001) {*6}, was a fascinating document of Mike Scott's progress from punk Beat Poet to fledgling folk mystic.

Named after a theatre run by Scotland's Findhorn Foundation spiritual centre (which remains very much a place of inspiration for Scott), **UNIVERSAL HALL** (2003) {*5} was markedly different from its predecessor. Heavily laden with spiritual and religious concerns, though not in any dogmatic way, the record was close in spirit, if not exactly in feel, to VAN MORRISON's latter-day quasi-religious searching.

The next few years saw the WATERBOYS tour all over Britain, and a live document, **KARMA TO BURN** (2005) {*6}, was Scott and co.'s first official concert set. Two covers were included, Rodney Crowell's 'A Song For Life' and the Felice and Boudleaux Bryant oldie 'Come Live With Me'.

Other covers to be found on various compilations include 'Cathy' (Nikki Sudden), 'Lost Highway' (Hank Williams), 'Death Is Not The End' (BOB DYLAN), 'Wayward Wind' (Lebawsky-Newman), 'Because The Night' (Patti Smith & Bruce Springsteen), 'Purple Rain' (Prince) and 'All Things Must Pass' (George Harrison).

Re-enlisting old chums such as Thistlethwaite, Lorimer, Wickham and Julian Cope associate Thighpaulsandra, Scott re-ignited The WATERBOYS for one last stab at the full Celtic 'big music' rock 'n' folk sound with **BOOK OF LIGHTNING** (2007) {*6}. It's not the place to start if you're looking for a great WATERBOYS set, but it had its moments, including 'Crash Of Angel's Wings', the Beatles-esque 'Nobody's Baby Anymore' and 'Everybody Takes A Tumble'. *MCS*

Mike Scott (b. Dec 14 '58, Edinburgh, Scotland) - vocals, guitar, piano / **Anthony Thistlethwaite** (b. Aug 8 '55, Leicester, England) - saxophone (ex-Robyn Hitchcock) / **Karl Wallinger** (b. Oct 19 '57, Prestatyn, Wales) - keyboards, bass

UK Chicken Jazz — US not issued

May 83. (7") *(CJ 1)* A GIRL CALLED JOHNNY. / The Late Train To Heaven [ ] [-]
(12") *(CJT 1)* - ('A') / Ready for the monkey house / Somebody might wave back / Out of control (APF; John Peel session).

Ensign — Chrysalis

Jul 83. (lp/c) *(ENC L/C 1)* **THE WATERBOYS** [ ] [-]
- December / A girl called Johnny / The three day man / Gala / I will not follow / It should have been you / The girl in the swing / Savage Earth heart. *(re-iss. Aug 86 on Chrysalis-Ensign lp/c; CHEN/ZCHEN 1) (cd-iss. Feb 87; CCD 1541) <US cd-iss. 1987; 21541> (cd re-mast. Mar 02 on Chrysalis+=; 537703-2)* - Where are you now when I need you? [new track 5] / Something fantastic / Ready for the monkey house / Another kind of circus / A boy in black leather / December (original eight-track mix) / Jack of diamonds.

Sep 83. (7") *(ENY 506)* DECEMBER. / Where Are You Now When I Need You? [ ] [-]
(12") *(12ENY 506)* - ('A') / Red army blues / The three day man (Peter Powell session).

—— added **Kevin Wilkinson** - drums / **Roddy Lorimer** (b. Glasgow, Scotland) - trumpet / **Tim Blanthorn** - violin

Apr 84. (7") *(ENY 508)* THE BIG MUSIC. / The Earth Only Endures [ ] [-]
(12"+=) *(12ENY 508)* - Bury my heart.

May 84. (lp/c) *(ENC L/C 3)* **A PAGAN PLACE** [100] [-]
- Church not made with hands / All the things she gave me / The thrill is gone / Rags / Somebody might wave back / The big music / Red army blues / A pagan place. *(re-iss. Aug 86 on Chrysalis-Ensign lp/c; CHEN/ZCHEN 2) (cd-iss. Feb 87 & Jul 94; CCD 1542) <US cd-iss.1987; 21542> (cd re-mast. Mar 02 on Chrysalis+=; 537704-2)* - Some of my best friends are trains [new track 5] / The late train to heaven (Rockfield mix) / Love that kills (instrumental) / The madness is here again / Cathy / Down through the dark streets.

—— **Mike** + **Karl** recruited new people for tour/set **Terry Mann** - bass / **Charlie Whitten** - drums / **Steve Wickham** (b. Dublin, Ireland) - violin / **Delahaye** - organ / + **Roddy Lorimer**

Sep 85. (lp/c) *(ENC L/C 5)* **THIS IS THE SEA** [37] [-]
- Don't bang the drum / The whole of the moon / Spirit / The Pan within / Medicine bow / Old England / Be my enemy / Trumpets / This is the sea. *(re-iss. Aug 86 on Chrysalis-Ensign lp/c; CHEN/ZCHEN 3) (cd-iss. Feb 87; CCD CCD 1543) <US cd-iss. 1987; 21543> (lp re-iss. Aug 00 on Simply Vinyl; SVLP 234) (d-cd-iss. 2002 on EMI+=; 543140-2)* - FISHERMAN'S BLUES *(d-cd re-mast. Mar 04 on EMI+=; 591451-2)* - Beverly Penn / Sleek white schooner / Medicine bow (extended) / Medicine Jack / High far soon / Even the trees are dancing / Towers open fire / This is the sea (live) / Then you hold me / Spirit (extended) / Miracle / I am not here / Sweet thing / The waves.

Oct 85. (7") *(ENY 502)* THE WHOLE OF THE MOON. / Medicine Bow [26] [-]
(ext.12"+=) *(12ENY 520)* - Spirit (extended) / The girl in the swing (live).

—— now down to **Scott** + **Thistlethwaite**); Karl formed World Party

—— added band **Steve Wickham** - violin (ex-IN TUA NUA) / **JD Doherty** - drums / **Colin Blakey** - flute (ex-WE FREE KINGS) / **Sharon Shannon** (b. Ireland) - accordion

—— **Noel Bridgeman** (b. Dublin, Ireland) - drums; repl. Doherty

Oct 88. (lp/c/cd) *(CHEN/ZCHEN 5)(CCD 1589) <41589>*
FISHERMAN'S BLUES [13] Nov 88 [76]
- Fisherman's blues / We will not be lovers / Strange boat / World party / Sweet thing / Jimmy Hickey's waltz *[not on lp]* / And a bang on the ear / Has anybody here seen Hank? / When we will be married? / When ye go away / Dunford's fancy *[not on lp]* / The stolen child / This land is your land *[not on lp]*. *<US cd+=>* - The lost highway. *(lp re-iss. Sep 00 on Simply Vinyl; SVLP 245) (d-cd-iss.+=)* - THIS IS THE SEA *(d-cd re-mast. May 06 on EMI+=; 357673-2)* - Carolan's welcome / Killing my heart / You in the sky / When will we be married? / Nobody 'cept you / Fisherman's blues / Girl of the north country / Lonesome and a long way from home / If I can't have you / Rattle my bones and shiver my soul / Let me feel holy again / Meet me at the station / The good ship Sirius / Soon as I get home (Roscoe's corner).

Dec 88. (7"/12"/cd-s) *(ENY/+X/CD 621)* FISHERMAN'S BLUES. / The Lost Highway [32] [-]

Jun 89. (7"/c-s/12"/cd-s) *(ENY/+MC/X/CD 624)* AND A BANG ON THE EAR. / The Raggle Taggle Gypsy [51] [-]

—— added **Kev Blevins** - drums; repl. sessioners

Sep 90. (cd)(c/lp) *(CCD 1768)(Z+/CHEN 16) <21768>*
ROOM TO ROAM [5] [ ]
- In search of a rose / Songs from the end of the world / A man is in love - Calliope House / Bigger picture / Natural bridge blues / Something that is gone / The star and the sea / A life of Sundays / Islandman / The raggle taggle gypsy / How long

will I love you? / Upon the wind and waves / Spring comes to Spiddal / The trip to Broadford / Further up further in / Room to roam. *(cd+=)* - The kings of Kerry. *(d-cd re-mast. Aug 08 on EMI++=; 228409-2)* - In search of a rose (full band) / My Morag (the exile's dream) / A man is in love (alt. take) / The wyndy wyndy road / Three ships / Sunny sailor boy / Sponsored pedal pusher's blues / The wayward wind / Danny Murphy - Florence / The raggle taggle gypsy (live) / Custer's blues (live) / Twa recruitin' sergeants (live) / A reel and a stomp in the kitchen / Down by the sally gardens / A strathspey in the rain at dawn - The Sound of Sleat / A song for the life / The kings of Kerry (outdoor).

—— disbanded (Thistlethwaite formed the Blue Stars)

—— **Mike Scott** re-formed the group with **Chris Bruce** - guitars / **Scott Thunes** - bass / **Carla Azar** - drums / **Bashiri Johnson** - percussion / **Ljubisa 'Lubi' Ristic** - sitar / **George Stathos** - Greek clarinet / **James Campagnola** - sax

Geffen Geffen

May 93. (7"/c-s) *(GFS/+C 42)* THE RETURN OF PAN. / Karma [24] [–]
(12"+=/cd-s+=) *(GFS T/CD 42)* - Mister Powers / ('A'-demo).

May 93. (cd/c/lp) *(<GED/GEC/GEF 24476>)* **DREAM HARDER** [5] [ ]
- The new life / Glastonbury song / Preparing to fly / The return of Pan / Corn circles / Suffer / Winter winter / Love and death / Spiritual city / Wonders of Lewis / The return of Jimi Hendrix / Good news. *(cd re-iss. Jul 96; GFLD 19318)*

Jul 93. (7"/c-s) *(GFS/+C 49)* GLASTONBURY SONG. / Chalice Hill [29] [–]
(12"+=/cd-s+=) *(GFS T/CD 49)* - Burlington Bertie - Accrington Stanley / Corn circle symphony (extended).

—— Scott split the band after above

MIKE SCOTT

mostly solo (vocals + instruments) with some guests (+ later session people)

Chrysalis Chrysalis

Sep 95. (c-s/7") *(TC+/CHS 5025)* *<58503>* BRING 'EM ALL IN. / City Full Of Ghosts (Dublin) [56] Nov95 [ ]
(cd-s+=) *(CDCHS 5025)* - Mother Cluny / Beatles reunion blues.

Sep 95. (cd/c/lp) *(<CD/TC+/CHR 6108>)* **BRING 'EM ALL IN** [23] [ ]
- Bring 'em all in / Iona song / Edinburgh Castle / What do you want me to do? / I know she's in the building / City full of ghosts (Dublin) / Wonderful disguise / Sensitive children / Learning to love him / She is so beautiful / Wonderful disguise (reprise) / Long way to the light / Building the city of light.

Nov 95. (7") *(CHS 5026)* BUILDING THE CITY OF LIGHT. / Where Do You Want The Boombox, Buddy [60] [–]
(cd-s+=) *(CDCHSS 5026)* - Goin' back to Glasters (live) / The whole of the moon (live).
(cd-s) *(CDCHS 5026)* - ('A') / Two great waves / My beautiful guide / Building the city of light (Universal Hall demo).

Sep 97. (c-s) *(TCCHS 5064)* LOVE ANYWAY / King Of Stars [50] [–]
(cd-s) *(CDCHS 5064)* - ('A') / King electric (including Moonage Daydream) / Blues is my business.
(cd-s) *(CDCHSS 5064)* - ('A') / Big lover / Careful with the Mellotron, Eugene / Since I found my school.

Oct 97. (cd/c) *(<CD/TC CHR 6122>)* **STILL BURNING** [34] [ ]
- Questions / My dark side / Open / Love anyway / Rare, precious and gone / Dark man of my dreams / King electric *[US-only]* / Personal / One of many rescuers *[US-only]* / Strawberry man / Man on the mountain *[US-only]* / Sunrising / Everlasting arms / Since I found my school *[US-only]*.

Feb 98. (cd-ep) *(CDCHSS 5073)* RARE, PRECIOUS AND GONE / Kiss The Wind / When Will We Be Married? (live) / Love Anyway (demo) [74] [–]
(cd-ep) *(CDCHS 5073)* - ('A') / All things she gave me (live) / She is so beautiful (live) / Nectar (7 days).

note: the white-bearded Mike Scott who issued 'Shed Songs' and 'Massacre Songs' in the mid-2000s is nothing to do with the Waterboys singer.

The WATERBOYS

Scott + **Thistlethwaite** (electric slide mandolin) re-formed the band with **Livingston Brown** + **Mark Smith** - bass / **Jeremy Stacey** - drums / others on session

RCA RCA

Sep 00. (cd/c) *(<74321 78305-2/-4>)* **A ROCK IN THE WEARY LAND** [47] Nov 00 [ ]
- Let it happen / My love is my rock in the weary land / It's all gone / Is she conscious? / We are Jonah / Malediction / Dumbing down the world / His word is not his bond / Night falls on London / The charlatan's lament / The wind in the wires / Crown. *(d-cd-iss. Sep 07 on Sony-BMG+=; 8869 715203-2)* - TOO CLOSE TO HEAVEN

Oct 00. (7") *(74321 79417-7)* MY LOVE IS MY ROCK IN THE WEARY LAND. / Your Baby Ain't Your Baby Anymore (with the Half Mast Flag Country & Western Band) [ ] [–]
(cd-s) *(74321 79417-2)* - ('A') / Lucky day - Bad advice / Time space and the bride's bed.
(cd-s) *(74321 79418-2)* - ('A' side) / Trouble down yonder / Send him down to Waco.

Feb 01. (m-cd) *(74321 83649-2)* **IS SHE CONSCIOUS?** [ ] [–]
- Is she conscious? (album version) / Sad procession / Faeries' prisoner / Is she conscious? / Savage earth heart / My Lord what a morning / Is she conscious (video).

Apr 01. (7") *(74321 84870-7)* WE ARE JONAH. / Time, Space And The Bride's Bed [ ] [–]
(cd-s) *(74321 84870-2)* - ('A') / Lucky day - Bad advice / Dumbing down the world (live at Glastonbury 2000).
(cd-s) *(74321 84871-2)* - ('A') / Martin descent / Send him down to Waco.

—— **Scott** brought back **Wickham** - fiddle / plus **Richard Naiff** - flute, piano

Puck Minty Fresh

Jun 03. (cd) *(PUCK 1)* *<MF 70053>* **UNIVERSAL HALL** [74] May 03 [ ]
- This light is for the world / The Christ in you / Silent fellowship / Every breath is yours / Peace of Iona / Ain't no words for the things I'm feeling / Seek the light / I've lived here before / Always dancing, never getting tired / The dance at the crossroads / E.B.O.L. / Universal Hall.

Sep 05. (cd) *(PUCK 4)* **KARMA TO BURN** (live) [ ] [–]
- Long way to the light / Peace of Iona / Glastonbury song / Medicine bow / The Pan within / Open / The return of Jimi Hendrix / My dark side / A song for the life / Bring 'em all in / The whole of the moon / Fisherman's blues / Come live with me.

—— **Scott** recruited **Leo Abrahams** - guitar

W14 - Universal Decca

Mar 07. (7") *(1725644)* EVERYBODY TAKES A TUMBLE. / Ain't Doin' Too Bad [ ] [–]
(cd-s) *(1725643)* - ('A') / Killing my heart / All things must pass.

Apr 07. (cd) *(1721305)* *<965570-2>* **BOOK OF LIGHTNING** [51] [ ]
- The crash of angel wings / Love will shoot you down / Nobody's baby anymore / Strange arrangement / She tried to hold me / It's gonna rain / Sustain / You in the sky / Everybody takes a tumble / The man with the wind at his heels.

- (8-10*) compilations, etc.-

Mar 91. (7"/c-s) *Ensign; (ENY/+MC 642) / Alex; <1516>* THE WHOLE OF THE MOON. / A Golden Age [3] Jul 91 [ ]
(12"+=/cd-s+=) *(ENY X/CD 642)* - Higher in time / High far soon / Soon as I get home.

Apr 91. (cd)(c/lp) *Ensign; (CCD 1845)(Z+/CHEN 19) / Chrysalis; <21845>* **THE BEST OF THE WATERBOYS (1981-1990)** [2] [ ]
- A girl called Johnny / The big music / All the things she gave me / The whole of the moon / Spirit / Don't bang the drum / Fisherman's blues / Killing my heart / Strange boat / And a bang on the ear / Old England / A man is in love. *(cd re-iss. Aug 00; same) (<cd re-iss. Mar 03 as THE ESSENTIAL WATERBOYS on EMI; 582226-2>)*

May 91. (7"/c-s) *Ensign; (ENY/+MC 645) / Alex; <1581>* FISHERMAN'S BLUES. / Lost Highway [75] Jun 91 [ ]
(12"+=/cd-s+=) *(ENY X/CD 645)* - Medicine bow (live).

Sep 98. (cd/c) *Chrysalis; (496505-2/-4)* **THE WHOLE OF THE MOON: the music of Mike Scott and The Waterboys** [ ] [–]
- The whole of the moon / Glastonbury song / Medicine bow / Fisherman's blues / A girl called Johnny / The Pan within / She is so beautiful / Rare, precious and gone / Strange boat / Red army blues / This is the sea / Higher in time / The return of Pan / What do you want me to do / When ye go away / Love anyway.

- essential boxed sets -

Sep 00. (3xcd-box) *EMI; (528661-2)* **A PAGAN PLACE / THIS IS THE SEA / FISHERMAN'S BLUES** [ ] [–]

Oct 06. (3xcd-box) *EMI; (378346-2)* **THE PLATINUM COLLECTION** [ ] [–]
- (THIS IS THE SEA) // (FISHERMAN'S BLUES) // (ROOM TO ROAM).

- (5-7*) compilations, others, etc.-

Oct 94. (cd/c) *Ensign; (CD/TC CHEN 35)* **THE SECRET LIFE OF THE WATERBOYS 81–85** [ ] [ ]
- Medicine bow / That was the river / A pagan place / Billy Sparks / Savage earth heart / Don't bang the drum / The ways of men / Rags (second amendment) / The earth only endures / Somebody might wave back / Going to Paris / The three day man / Bury my heart / Out of control / Love that kills. *(cd re-iss. Sep 97; same)*

Aug 98. (d-cd/t-lp) *Burning Airlines; (<PILOT 40/+LP>)* **THE LIVE ADVENTURES OF THE WATERBOYS** (live from bootlegs) [ ] [ ]
- Death is not the end / The earth only endures / Medicine bow / Fisherman's blues / This is the sea / Meet me at the station / We will not be lovers / The wayward wind / A girl called Johnny / Purple rain / Be my enemy / Old England / The thrill is gone - And the healing has begun / The Pan within (including 'Because the night') / The whole of the moon / Spirit / Savage earth heart / Saints and angels. *(t-lp+=)- Medicine Jack.*

Sep 01. (cd) *Arista; (74321 88152-2)* **TOO CLOSE TO HEAVEN** (rarities from mid-86 to early-01) [ ] [–]
- On my way to heaven / Higher in time / The ladder / Too close to heaven / Good man gone / Blues for your baby / Custer's blues / A home in the meadow / Tenderfootin' / Lonesome old wind. *(d-cd-iss.+=)* - A ROCK IN THE WEARY LAND

Jul 02. (cd) *Razor & Tie; <82880-2>* **FISHERMAN'S BLUES, PART 2** [–] [ ]
- (TOO CLOSE TO HEAVEN tracks) / Higher in time / Ain't leaving, I'm gone / Lonesome and a long way from home / The good ship Sirius / Too close to heaven (live).

May 11. (cd) *EMI; (<0984102>)* **IN A SPECIAL PLACE: the piano demos for This Is The Sea** [ ] [ ]
- Don't bang the drum / Be my enemy / All the bright horses / Custer's blues / Beverly Penn / The day I ran out of people / The Pan within / Winter in the blood / The woman in me / Looking for Dickon / Paris in the rain / Talk about wings / The whole of the moon / Old England / Trumpets [headstrong remix 2011].

WATERFALL

Formed 1974 at Warwick University by musicians Keith Donnelly (from the north) and Martyn Oram (from the south), who combined forces to play mainly covers at the university's folk club. Repertoire featured songs by JONATHAN KELLY, AL STEWART and GERRY RAFFERTY.

1977 was a turning point for WATERFALL as, after six months or so traversing the toilet circuit as country-rock trio Van de Hogg's Elderflower Remedy (with future Wonder Stuff player Martin Bell), the duo laid down tracks at Woodbine Studios in Leamington Spa for their debut LP, **THE FLIGHT OF THE DAY** (1977) {*6}. Containing mainly Donnelly originals plus two by Oram and a traditionally-sourced instrumental medley, the record was best served by 'To A Blindman' and 'Princess Star'.

The addition of vocalist Gilly Darbey in 1978 was another step in the group's evolution. The JOHNNY COPPIN-produced **THREE BIRDS** (1979) {*5} and the Phillip Goodhand-Tait-produced **BENEATH THE STARS** (1981) {*5} were the trio's only other sets (now collectable at around £30 each). Somewhere in between these releases were tours supporting The Hollies, Gilbert O'Sullivan and RICHARD DIGANCE, while overseas they were invited on tours by HARVEY ANDREWS, DAVE BURLAND, WALLY WHYTON and the McCALMANS. A string of television appearances in 1981 culminated with a half-hour 'In Concert' BBC1 broadcast and a Pebble Mill At One spot.

By February 1982 the group had split. Keith and Gilly became Little Aeroplane, and Oram ventured upon a solo career, releasing several albums (see discography below), a few with German singer-songwriter Walter F Diet and another with the group Maybug. In 2003, Keith and Martyn played several 25th-anniversary WATERFALL reunions. *MCS*

Keith Donnelly (b. South Shields) - vocals, acoustic guitar / **Martyn Oram** (b. Plymouth) - violin, acoustic guitar, vocals

UK Bob — US not issued

Dec 77. (ltd-lp) *(FRR 001)* **THE FLIGHT OF THE DAY** ☐ ⊟
- To a blindman / Anniversary song / For you / Sylvia / And for you / Rainbow lady / Lonely / Little man / Instrumental medley (Lament for her leaving - Sunday is my wedding day - Rakish Paddy - The mountain road) / Princess star. *(cd-iss. Nov 97 on English Garden; ENG 1019CD)*

—— added **Gilly Darbey** - vocals

Avada — not issued

Aug 79. (lp) *(AVA 104)* **THREE BIRDS** ☐ ⊟
- But I love you / Woodland glade / Three birds / Smiler / Thanks / The stranger / Friends / Swansong.

Gun Dog — not issued

1981. (lp) *(GUN 003LP)* **BENEATH THE STARS** ☐ ⊟
- Wally the whale / The foyboatman / Beneath the stars above / Silver like the moon / City / Blowin' kisses / If you could love me too / Mon coeur est la / The answer / The old lady's song / Before forever.

—— acoustic balladeer Oram went solo, releasing several self-financed sets:- 'Flying South' (1982 German lp), 'Together' (1986 cassette by Oram & Diet), 'The Men Who Dream' (1988 lp), 'Pawns In The Game' (1991 cd by Martyn Oram & Walter F Diet), 'Our Roadie's In Turkey' (1993 cd by the Oram & Diet band), 'Golfstream' (1999 cd as Maybug), 'A Flying Dream' (2000 cd compilation), 'A Drop In The Ocean' (2003 cd), 'The Bridge Of Broken Dreams' (2006 cd); Keith and Gilly continued until the 1990s.

Helen WATSON (⟹ MUCKRAM WAKES)

Roger WATSON (⟹ MUCKRAM WAKES)

WAZ! (⟹ ALLCOCK, Maartin)

WE FREE KINGS

Formed in Edinburgh in the mid-1980s by lyricist and singer Joe Kingman and guitarist Seb Holbrook, WE FREE KINGS were the raggle-taggle gypsy punks of indie-folk, with not a hint of Christmas or The WATERBOYS (apart from being their support act) in sight - that would come later.

Also comprising Pam Dobson (melodeon), Geoff Pagan (fiddle), Kenny Welsh (drums), Philippa Bull (cello) and Falkirk-born Colin Blakey (multi) from Green Telescopes, this seven-piece ensemble had more than a penchant for Lou Reed and The Velvet Underground, whom they covered, or ripped apart, on several occasions. In 1986, WE FREE KINGS unleashed their Clash-meets-POGUES debut single 'Death Of The Wild Colonial Boy' - Geoff was to proclaim in a press interview that "The Clash's debut was a folk album". Political, but optimistic with a capital O, WE FREE KINGS inked a wee deal with Fast Forward outlet DDT, releasing a couple of gutsy 45s ('Oceans' and 'T-Shirt') and the celebrated LP **HELL ON EARTH AND ROSY CROSS** (1988) {*6}.

A rockier swansong EP, 'Howl And Other Songs', was issued to a mixed reception in 1991, Blakey having already teamed up with MIKE SCOTT of the band's patrons The WATERBOYS. New to the group were Greg Drysdale (drums), Mark Ritchie (guitar) and Simon (bass). Blakey and most of the team later surfaced with his more traditional/Celtic-type outfit The CLAN, although only a cassette album, **THE ROKE** (1990) {*5}, made it into the shops. *MCS*

Joe Kingman - vocals, guitar / **Seb Holbrook** - guitar, vocals / **Colin Blakey** (b. Falkirk, Scotland) - flute, guitar, mandolin, vocals (ex-Green Telescopes) / **Geoff Pagan** - fiddle / **Pam Dobson** - melodeon / **Phil(ippa) Bull** - cello / **Kenny Welsh** - drums

UK Howl — US not issued

Jul 86. (7") *(WOOF 1)* DEATH OF THE WILD COLONIAL BOY. / Love Is In The Air ☐ ⊟

DDT — not issued

Mar 87. (7") *(DISP 007)* OCEANS. / Wipe-Out Gang ☐ ⊟
(12"+=) *(DISP 007T)* - Death of the wild colonial boy / Love is in the air.

Jan 88. (12"/cd-s) *(DISP 009T/+P)* T-SHIRT. / Still Standing ☐ ⊟

Jan 88. (lp/c) *(DISP LP/PC 010)* **HELL ON EARTH AND ROSY CROSS** ☐ ⊟
- Motorcycle rain / Stupidity street / Long train / Scarecrow / Flowers / Jesus wept / Still standing / Rosy cross / Brilliant / Old coal train / Wipe-out gang / Gold.

—— Blakey left to join The WATERBOYS; he and Dobson were repl. by **Mark Ritchie** - guitar / **Simon** - bass / **Greg Drysdale** (b. Grangemouth) - drums (ex-One Over The Eight)

Avalanche — not issued

Mar 91. (12"ep) *(AGA P008T)* HOWL AND OTHER SONGS ☐ ⊟
- Howl / She said / Firewood / Be so cruel.

—— after they split, most reconvened in Celtic-folk act ...

The CLAN

Blakey with also **Philippa Bull** - cello / **Dave Robb** - bouzouki / **Geoff Pagan** - violin / **Rob Welsh** - digeridoo / **Robbie The Pict** - guitar / **Lucy Johnstone** - voice, guitar, percussion / **Kenny Welsh** - bodhran, etc / **Steve Bradley** - harmonica / **Wendy Blakey** - drums / **Mark Ritchie** - mandolin, guitar / **Seb Holbrook** + **Kirsten Webster** - percussion / **Julian Goodacre** - Scottish smallpipe / **Marshall Stormonth** - voices / **Rob Blakey** - clarinet / **Billy Smith** + **Pete Livingstone** - violin / **Joe Kingman** - mandolin / **Shona McMillan** - violin

Temple — not issued

1990. (c; as The CLAN featuring COLIN BLAKEY) *(CTP 038)* **THE ROKE** ☐ ⊟
- Spiddel / The battle of Sherrifmuir / Comati (the Pictish national anthem) / Pandaemonium / Two Muneiras / Achmelvich Bay / Scarlet / The roke, the row and the wee pickle tow / Deoch slainte nan gillean / Keel row / Whelans / Ye Jacobites by name / The hermit.

Jane WEAVER

Born 1972 in Liverpool, but now living in Manchester, singer-songwriter/guitarist JANE WEAVER has been around longer than people might think, having been part of Brit-pop outfit Kill Laura (releasing five singles between 1993 and 1996) and neo-folktronica act Misty Dixon (for a one-off set, 'Iced To Mode', 2003).

Setting up home with Mancunian producer, DJ mixer and solo artist Andy Votel (Andrew Shallcross, her husband), Jane's solo career slowly kicked into gear after a handful of singles on Rob Gretton's Manchester Records imprint. Indie-pop act Doves featured on her 'Everyone Knows Everyone Else' late in 1998.

Augmented by Votel, Dave Tyack, Sam Yates, Naomi Hart, Rick Tomlinson (of VOICE OF THE SEVEN WOODS) and Elbow stars Craig Potter and Richard Jupp, the **LIKE AN ASPEN LEAF** (2002) {*7} mini-set was her introduction to freak-folk. From tracks like the PJ Harveyesque 'A Bird Stole The Gold' to others in a more VASHTI BUNYAN/BETH ORTON vein ('Ridiculous', 'Why Don't You Smile' and the title track), it was a fine start for the kooky star.

With funding from Twisted Nerve Records (i.e. Votel and Badly Drawn Boy), WEAVER formed the Bird label in 2002, releasing a number of vintage psych-folk artists such as BONNIE DOBSON, CATE LE BON, Brigitte Fontaine and Susan Christie, plus three albums of her own: **SEVEN DAY**

SMILE (2006) {*6}, **CHERLOKALATE** (2007) {*6} and **THE FALLEN BY WATCH BIRD** (2010) {*7}. Best described by her publicist as "a new conceptual pop project featuring seven chapters of cosmic aquatic folklore", Jane's twee folktronica metamorphosed between the Brainticket-like 'A Circle And A Star', the modern-day-hillbilly beat of 'Whispers Of Winter' (complete with fuzz guitar) and the Morricone-meets-JONI MITCHELL gem 'My Soul Was Lost...'. Psych-folk was back for good. *MCS*

Jane Weaver - vocals, acoustic guitar (w/ session players)

		UK	US
		Manchester	not issued
Nov 97.	(cd-s) *(MANC 6)* WE ARE MODERN / Fast Song / Slow Song	☐	⊟
May 98.	(cd-s) *(MANC 7)* SCREAM AND SHOUT / Ride Song / Dynamite	☐	⊟
Oct 98.	(cd-s) *(MANC 8)* CUPBOARD LOVE / Oh I'm In A Mink / Gutter Girl	☐	⊟
Dec 98.	(cd-s) *(MANC 9)* JANE WEAVER v DOVES v ANDY VOTEL: Everyone Knows Everyone Else	☐	⊟

- Seven day smile (DOVES & JANE WEAVER) / Gutter girl (ANDY VOTEL & JANE WEAVER).

(cd-s+=) *(MANC CD 9)* - You're not the person that I used to know.

		Pleasure	not issued
Oct 00.	(7") *(XXX002)* STARGLOW. / (Andy Votel remix)	☐	⊟

In 2001 she was credited (and co-wrote) with Andy Votel on the single 'Girl On A Go-Ped (remix)'.

		Bright Star	not issued
May 02.	(m-cd) *(BSR 16)* **LIKE AN ASPEN LEAF**	☐	⊟

- Like an aspen leaf / A bird stole the gold / Bow and arrow, ball of string / The heart that buckled you / Ridiculous / Flowers bloom again / Why don't you smile.

		Bird	B-Music
Mar 06.	(ltd-7"; as JANE WEAVER and The Meadows) *(1EGG)* IS EVERYONE HAPPY? / Dragging Heels. / You're A Riot	☐	⊟
Apr 06.	(cd) *(2EGGS)* **SEVEN DAY SMILE**	☐	⊟

- Slow song / Seven day smile / Weathered / Starglow / The sink / You're a riot / Once you'd given me up / In summer / You're not the only person that I used to know / Gutter girl.

Mar 07.	(cd) *(3EGGS)* <BMS 009> **CHERLOKALATE**	☐	2008 ☐

- It's only pastures / Bits and pieces / O to be in this land / Shoulder seasons / Like an aspen leaf / The pain / Is everyone happy? / It's not over yet / Oh you lucky ones / Outro. <US+=>- *I already coped / You're so good to be around.*

Jun 10.	(cd/lp) *(10EGGS CD/LP)* <BMS 022> **THE FALLEN BY WATCH BIRD**	☐	May 10 ☐

- Europium alluminate / A circle and a star / The fallen by watch bird / Turning in circles / Hud a Llefrith / Whispers of winter / Noctilumina / My soul was lost, my soul was lost, and no one saved me / Silver chord.

The WEBB SISTERS

At first groomed to be the next The Corrs or Fleetwood Mac, Kent-based The WEBB SISTERS (harmony singers and multi-instrumentalists Charley and Hattie) had elements of folk-pop in their well-produced AOR sound. Their father had played with the Dave Travis Band, and their mother was a tennis coach.

The American crossover sound was probably due to their work with Nashville producer Johnny Pierce, who in 2004 polished up a CD for them to sell at gigs on the Los Angeles circuit, while the girls themselves stayed in an artists' commune in Venice Beach, California. On their return to England, The WEBB SISTERS almost immediately signed a deal with Mercury, and although there was a big push to get radio airtime for their singles 'I Still Hear It' and 'Still The Only One', parent album **DAYLIGHT CROSSING** (2006) {*5} was met with a mixed response.

Undeterred, the sisters raised their heads high again when they were invited to perform on a comeback concert alongside the great LEONARD COHEN. They took one of his songs, 'If It Be Your Will', for the decidedly folkier, Peter Asher-produced follow-up set **SAVAGES** (2011) {*6}. It was still commercial, but their natural multi-instrumental abilities were put to good use on dreamboat-folk songs such as 'Baroque Thoughts', 'Words That Mobilise', 'Blue And You' and 'The Goodnight Song' (very 'With Or Without You'). Other tracks were reminiscent of Kate Bush. *MCS*

Charley Webb (b. 1979) - vocals, acoustic guitar, piano, sax, clarinet, drums / **Hattie Webb** (b. 1981) - vocals, harp, piano / with four-piece band

		UK	US
		not issued	self-rel.
2004.	(ltd-cd) <none> A PIECE OF MIND	⊟	US tour ⊟
		Mercury	not issued
Jul 06.	(cd-s) *(9841484)* I STILL HEAR IT / Dead Old Leaves / Do It All Over Again	☐	⊟
Jul 06.	(cd) *(1700974)* **DAYLIGHT CROSSING**	☐	⊟

- Blue / I still hear it / Still the only one / Torches / Please / Turn the lights on / Tomorrow now / Ferris wheel / Boomerang / Momentary / My way to you / Everything changes.

Oct 06.	(cd-ep) *(9843959)* STILL THE ONLY ONE / My Way To You (acoustic) / Last Night	☐	⊟
Nov 08.	(cd-ep) *(none)* COMES IN TWOS	⊟	tour ⊟
		Proper	not issued
May 11.	(cd) *(PRPCD 079)* **SAVAGES**	☐	⊟

- Baroque thoughts / Calling this a life / Words that mobilise / Savages / Dark sky / Burn / Amelie's smile / If it be your will / In your father's eyes / Blue and you / 1000 stars / The goodnight song.

WEDDINGS, PARTIES, ANYTHING

Bush bands and folk music had previously collided in larger-than-life 1970s Australian outfits The BUSHWACKERS and REDGUM, and although formed (in Melbourne) in 1983, WEDDINGS, PARTIES, ANYTHING were an extension of those acts, served up with a Clash-versus-anything mentality. The fact that leader Mick Thomas took their name from a line in The Clash's take on reggae gem 'Revolution Rock' was proof enough of their intentions.

Formed by Thomas and fellow guitarist David Steel, WEDDINGS ... enlisted the help of Mark Wallace (piano accordion), ex-Saints girl Janine Hall (bass) and David Adams (drums), the latter soon superseded by Marcus Schintler.

Going from independent EPs on Suffering Tram Records to albums on the mighty Warners in the space of a couple of years' touring, they unleashed their thought-provoking, politics-soaked set **SCORN OF THE WOMEN** (1987) {*7}. The title track itself takes a feminine perspective, as do 'Ladies Lounge', 'Woman Of Ireland', 'She Works' and the R&B-esque 'The Infanticide of Marie Farrar'. The emotionally and politically charged opener, 'Hungry Years', was their first single in Australia.

Completed without Janine (her replacement being Peter Lawler), **ROARING DAYS** (1988) {*7} was equally raucous and riveting, highlighted by 'Industrial Town', 'Gun', 'Sisters Of Mercy' and two covers by PAUL KELLY ('Laughing Boy', a sorrowful tribute to Brendan Behan) and Tex Morton ('Sergeant Small'). 'Morton (Song For Tex)' was the band's own homage to their Country & Western hero. It would prove to be Steel's swansong as Pete Clark (and then Richard Burgman) took over his guitar duties.

THE BIG DON'T ARGUE (1989) {*6} kicked off with the The MEN THEY COULDN'T HANG-like trad number 'Streets Of Forbes', but many pundits would agree that it was pub singalongs 'Knockbacks In Halifax' and 'A Tale They Won't Believe' (very POGUES) that nailed their colours to the mast. With extensive touring taking up precious time, there was little to show on the recording front other than the covers EP/mini-set **THE WEDDINGS PLAY SPORTS (AND FALCONS)** (1990) {*5}, with six covers of material by lesser-known Australian exports The Sports and The Falcons. Only Mark Wallace seemed to be busy studio-wise, on his solo set 'Squeezebox Wally' for Au Go Go Records.

Working with Patricia Young as second vocalist, on songs including 'Step In, Step Out' on their comeback concept set **DIFFICULT LOVES** (1992) {*8}, was another page-turner in the book of WPA. It's clear that producer Alan Thorne gave the band a commercial, folk-pop effect on the opener, 'Father's Day' (about Saturday visits for an estranged divorcee), and the equally emotive 'The Four Corners Of The Earth'.

Although not licensed to Cooking Vinyl in the UK this time around, **KING TIDE** (1994) {*7} saw principal songwriter Mick Thomas let the rest of the group, as a whole and individually, get in their twopennorth. Former patron BILLY BRAGG sang on the duet 'Island Of Humour'.

Left to pick up the pieces after nearly every other member took off (Lawler would release 'King Rooster' in 1998), Mick and Mark regrouped with former WPA session people Jen Anderson (mandolin and violin), Michael Barclay (drums), Paul Thomas (steel guitar) and Stephen O'Prey (bass), but the independently-delivered mini-set **DONKEY SERENADE** (1995) {*4} was a poor reflection on the band. It comprised an odds-and-ends reprise of best-left-live recordings and country-boy covers of 'Rosy And Grey' (by Canada's Lowest Of The Low), 'Wide Open Road' (The Triffids) and DYLAN's 'If You Gotta Go'.

RIVER'ESQUE (1996) {*7} put them back in favour, and Thomas's trademark voice and the virtuoso violin playing of Jen Anderson seemed to gel on this occasion, from opener 'Houses' and 'A Decent Cup Of Coffee' to 'For A Short Time' and 'Luckiest Man'. The critical success of the set led to a deserved re-promotion the following year, with the 'Garage Sale' bonus CD including further covers 'Reason To Believe' (TIM HARDIN), 'From The Heart' (Gene Clark) and 'Sweet Thames Flow Softly' (EWAN MacCOLL).

As a Christmas farewell to their Australian fans, WPA signed off with the concert double-set **"...THEY WERE BETTER LIVE"** (1999) {*7}, a splendid collection that opened with a STAN ROGERS sea shanty, 'Barrett's Privateers'. A fitting epitaph for a band who had given so much to folk music and who had deserved more attention from outside Australia.

The prospect of Mick hanging up his boots was highly unlikely, though, as almost immediately he took up a solo career as well as forming MICK THOMAS & THE SURE THING. From the turn of the millennium (and still going strong), the band spread themselves thick on several WPA-like albums, and three that stood out were **DEAD CERT CERTAINTY** (1999) {*6} (comprising trad, covers and Thomas originals), **DUST ON MY SHOES** (2001) {*8} (with Michael Barclay and Mark Wallace in tow), and the double set **THE HORSE'S PRAYER** (2003) {*7}. **SPIN! SPIN! SPIN!** (2009) {*6} is the outfit's most recent album. *MCS*

Mick Thomas (b. Geelong, Australia) - vocals, guitar, bass / **David Steel** - guitar, vocals / **Mark Wallace** - piano accordion / **Janine Hall** - bass (ex-Saints) / **Marcus Schintler** - drums; repl. David Adams

Aus/UK Suffering Tram — US not issued

1985. (ltd-7"ep) *(ST 001)* WEDDINGS, PARTIES, ANYTHING [–] Austra [–]
- Industrial town / Nothing left to say / A summons in the morning / Roaring days.

1986. (ltd-7") *(ST 003)* SERGEANT SMALL (live). / Go! Move! Shift! (live) [–] Austra [–]

WEA — not issued

1987. (7") *(7-258196)* HUNGRY YEARS. / The Swans Return [–] Austra [–]

1987. (7") *(7-258307)* SHOTGUN WEDDING. / Australia Goodnight / The Bells Of Rhymney [–] Austra [–]

1987. (lp/cd) *(254705.1/.2)* **SCORN OF THE WOMEN** [–] Austra [–]
- Hungry years / Ladies lounge / Lost boys / The infanticide of Marie Farrar / She works / Scorn of the women / Away, away / The river is wide / Up for air / By tomorrow / Woman of Ireland / Shotgun wedding.

1987. (7") *(7-258351)* AWAY, AWAY. / Bourgeois Blues [–] Austra [–]

—— now without Janine who was repl. by **Peter Lawler**

1988. (12" ep) *(0-257793)* GOAT DANCING ON THE TABLES [–] Austra [–]
- Laughing boy / Tough time (in the old town tonight) / Goat dance at Falafel Beach / Sergeant Small (live).

1988. (7") *(7-25952)* TILTING AT WINDMILLS. / Misfits [–] Austra [–]

1988. (lp/cd) *(255430.1/.2)* **ROARING DAYS** [–] Austra [–]
- Industrial town / Under the clocks / Gun / Brunswick / Tilting at windmills / Sergeant Small / Sisters of mercy / Roaring days / Say the word / Missing in action / Laughing boy / Big river / A summons in the morning / Morton (song for Tex). *(UK-iss. Nov 89 on Cooking Vinyl lp/c/cd; COOK/+C/CD 026)*

1988. (7") *(7-258059)* SAY THE WORD. / Bright Lights Tonight [–] Austra [–]

—— **Richard Burgman** - guitar; repl. Paul Clark who repl. Steel who left to go solo ('The Edge Of The World')

1989. (7") *(7-171102)* DARLIN' PLEASE. / Ticket In Tatts [–] Austra [–]

1989. (lp/cd) *(256796.1/.2)* **THE BIG DON'T ARGUE** [–] Austra [–]
- Streets of Forbes / The ballad of Peggy and Col / Knockbacks in Halifax / Never again (Albion Tuesday night) / A tale they won't believe / Hug my back / The wind and the rain / Darlin' please / Ticket in Tatts / Rossarden / Manana, manana.

1989. (7") *(7-257354)* THE WIND AND THE RAIN. / Marie Provost [–] Austra [–]

1989. (7") *(7-257447)* STREETS OF FORBES. / Missing In Action (re-recorded) [–] Austra [–]

Utility — not issued

Jun 90. (m-lp/m-cd) *(UTIL/UTICD 004)* **NO SHOW WITHOUT PUNCH** (compilation) [ ] [–]
- Hungry years / The infanticide of Marie Farrar / She works / Goat dancing at Falafel beach / Away, away / Tough time / Scorn of the women.

Virgin — not issued

1990. (7") *(VOZ 089)* RECKLESS. / The Great North West [–] Austra [–]

1990. (m-lp/m-cd) *(VOZ EP/+CD 001)* **THE WEDDINGS PLAY SPORTS (AND FALCONS)** [–] Austra [–]
- Reckless / Strangers on a train / So young / Last house on the left / Stop the baby talking / Softly softly.

—— added **Patricia Young** - vocals

rooArt-WEA — rooArt-WEA

1991. (cd-s) *(9031 77297-2)* FATHER'S DAY / Fortitude Valley / Alone And Forsaken / Ship In The Harbour / The Hungry Years - narration [–] Austra [–]

1992. (cd) *(4509-90092-2)* **DIFFICULT LOVES** [–] Can [ ]
- Father's day / Taylor Square / Difficult loves / Old Ronny / Telephone in her car / Nothin' but time / Alone amongst savages / Rambling girl / Step in, step out / The four corners of the earth / For your ears only / Do not go gently... *(UK-iss. Sep 93 on Cooking Vinyl cd/c; COOK CD/C 059)*

1992. (cd-s) *(4509 90177-2)* STEP IN, STEP OUT / Shores Of Americay / Wrapped Up And Blue / Over In The West [–] Austra [–]

1993. (cd-s) *(4509 93378-2)* MONDAY'S EXPERTS / Things Will Be Different / One Perfect Day / The Taming Of The Shrew / Theatre Of Rascals [–] Austra [–]

1993. (cd-s) *(4509 94078-2)* THE RAIN IN MY HEART / Chewin' On Her Fingernails / Everybody Moves / All Over Bar The Shouting / Everywhere I Go [–] Austra [–]

1994. (cd-s) *(4509 96707-2)* ISLAND OF HUMOUR / Bring 'Em Home / Bring 'Em Home (outro) [–] Austra [–]

May 94. (cd/c) *(<4509 93773-2/-4>)* **KING TIDE** [ ] Can [ ]
- Monday's experts (with BILLY BRAGG) / Live it everyday / Money cuts you out / The rain in my heart / It wasn't easy / Keep talking to me / Island of humour / Easy money / In my lifetime / Always leave something behind / If you were a cloud / The year she spent in England / Stalactites.

Jun 94. (c-s) *(YZ 821C)* MONDAY EXPERT / Theatre Of Rascals [ ] [–]
(cd-s+=) *(YZ 812CD)* - Things will be different / One perfect day.

—— **Michael Thomas** + **Mark Wallace** recruited former WPA session people **Jen Anderson** - mandolin, violin (ex-Black Sorrows) / **Michael Barclay** - drums (ex-PAUL KELLY's band) / **Paul Thomas** - guitar, steel guitar / **Stephen O'Prey** - bass

WPA-Oz — not issued

1995. (m-cd/m-c) *(WPA 02)* **DONKEY SERENADE** [–] Austra [–]
- Where the highway meets the cane / In a city, girl / Grey skies (over Collingwood) / Rosy and grey / Wide open road / Nothing left to say / A long time between drinks / If you gotta go / In your memory. *(w/ secret bonus track)*

Mushroom — not issued

1996. (cd-s) *(D 1450)* LUCKIEST MAN / Lights Of Devonport / Reason To Believe / Sweet Thames Flow Softly [–] Austra [–]

Nov 96. (cd) *(TVD 93467)* **RIVER'ESQUE** [–] Austra [–]
- Houses / Don't need much / A decent cup of coffee / The ghosts of Walhalla / For a short time / The sound of a train / Lifestyles of the rich and famous / In your room / Lights of Devonport / The afternoon sun / Luckiest man / Five shows a day / Walkerville. *(re-iss. Oct 97 += cd; MUSH 33032.2)* - GARAGE SALE:- Rolling on home / When your travelling days are done / Reason to believe / Don't need much (acoustic) / Cheap brandy and foundation / Garage sale / Sweet Thames flow softly / September's gone / From the heart.

1997. (cd-ep) *(D 1544)* DON'T NEED MUCH (remix) / House Of Ghosts (live acoustic) / Sergeant Small (live 1930s acoustic version by TEX MORTON) / Away Away (live acoustic) [–] Austra [–]

1998. (cd-s) *(MUSH 01800.2)* ANTHEM / Traffic Goes By [–] Austra [–]

May 99. (d-cd) *(MUSH 33223.2)* **"...THEY WERE BETTER LIVE": LIVE AT THE CENTRAL CLUB CHRISTMAS 1998** [–] Austra [–]
- Barrett's privateers / Away away / Ticket in Tatts / Monday's experts / Industrial town / Laughing boy (with PAUL KELLY) / Sisters of mercy / Hungry years / Tilting at windmills / Rambling girl / Under the clocks / Manana manana / A decent cup of coffee / Father's day / Rain in my heart / For a short time (with TIDDAS) / Wide open road / Knockbacks in Halifax / Grey skies over Collingwood / Luckiest man / Step in step out / Rosy and grey (with DONNA SIMPSON of the WAIFS) / Jolly old Christmas time (with PETE LAWLER) / Scorn of the women / Ladies lounge / Roaring days / Streets of Forbes / Sergeant Small / Women of Ireland / A tale they won't believe / No no never / Leave her Johnny.

—— disbanded Christmas 1998; most took on solo projects; Mick Thomas wrote the score for 'Five Bells' (1997) and featured (alongside Paul Thomas and Pete Lawler) on the original cast recording of 'Over In The West' (1997).

- (8-10*) compilations, etc.-

Aug 98. (d-cd) *Mushroom; (MUSH 33152.2)* **TROPHY NIGHT: THE BEST OF WEDDINGS PARTIES ANYTHING** [–] Austra [–]
- Away away / Woman of Ireland / Hungry years / Scorn of the women / Industrial town / Under the clocks / Roaring days / Sergeant Small / Ticket in Tatts / A tale they won't believe / Knockbacks in Halifax / Step in step out / Father's day / Rain in my heart / Monday's experts / Wide open road / For a short time / Anthem / Traffic goes by // BENCHED:- Been coming here for years (demo) / City of light (demo) / If you gotta go (demo) / Swans return / Tough time / All over the bar shouting / Everywhere I go / Nothing left to say / One perfect day.

MICK THOMAS and the SURE THING

Mick Thomas + **Darren Hanlon** + others

Croxton — not issued

Nov 98. (cd; as MICK THOMAS) *(001)* **UNDER STARTER'S ORDERS** (Live at the Continental) [–] Austra [–]
- Shanks' pony / The auctioneer song / The year she spent in England / 57 years / Step in step out / Simone, Michelle, Emma, Justine, Maria... / Half way up the hill / New Moon cafe / Father's day / Talking talking lion blues / Scorn of the women / The cap me granda' wore.

Nov 99. (cd) *(004)* **DEAD SET CERTAINTY: 12 Songs That Wouldn't Go Away** [–] Austra [–]
- Comb and cutter / Dead letter office / Island of dreams / When you go / Brandy... you're a fine girl / American sailors - Ship in my harbour / Jim Jones at Botany Bay / Big geographical / Sunday too far away / Billy boy / Morton Bay (with NICK BARKER).

—— added **Michael Barclay** - drums + several guests

2001. (cd) *(007)* **DUST ON MY SHOES** [–] Austra [–]
- The lonely goth / I could spot you anywhere / You remind me / Baked a cake / Lawrence Durrell / Song for the seven seas / As far as the eye can see / Planxty John Meillon / Tom Wills / Wayward wind / Hard currency / No picnic. *(UK-iss. May 02 on Twah!; TWAH 122)*

2002. (cd) *(009)* **LIVE DUST** (live) [–] Austra [–]
- I could spot you anywhere / You remind me / Lawrence Durrell / Five shows a day / The lonely goth / When you go / Song for the seven seas / Under the clocks / Tom Wills / American sailors - Ship in the harbour / Fortitude valley / For a short time.

Mar 03. (d-cd) *(014)* **THE HORSE'S PRAYER** [–] Austra [–]
- Shanks' pony / Half a dog / In the perfect world / Life's too short / The cap me granda' wore / Something to fight for / From the heart / The northern lights of Aberdeen / The auctioneer song / Anywhere but here / Simone, Michelle, Emma, Justine, Maria... / Miles to go // Our sunshine / For a few less candles (better days) / Close, but no cigar / Made of stone / Dancing man / Disrepair / Ewan and the gold / Wind up man / Someone else's suit / 57 years / A tired old hat.

Nov 03. (m-cd) *(018)* **SOMETHING TO FIGHT FOR** [–] Austra [–]
- Something to fight for / For a few less candles / Make you feel my love (with MIA DYSON) / Dominion road / Worked out good / No.1 doctor's rocks / All of my yesterdays / Been coming here for years / Titania's place / Something to fight for *[film clip]*.

In 2004, Thomas supplied the music to the 'The Tank' stage play

Liberation — not issued

Aug 04. (cd; as MICK THOMAS) *(BLU 072.2)* **ANYTHINGS, SURE THINGS, OTHER THINGS** (acoustic series) [–] Austra [–]
- Father's day / Houses / Away away / Step in step out / The lonely goth / The rain in my heart / Hard currency / For a short time / Tilting at windmills / Our sunshine / Monday's experts / Hungry years / Man crazy / A tale they won't believe / I'll remember.

Thomas also released tour bootleg 'Other Things, Sure Things, Extra Things' (2005)

Oct 06. (cd) *(BLU 082.2)* **PADDOCK BUDDY** [–] Austra [–]
- Tommy didn't want to / Lust in translation (with ANGIE HART) / Maltby by-pass / Coat of paint / Making a list / Forgot she was beautiful / (Let's talk about) Me / Tired little shop / Last holiday with the family / Back of the storm / Half way up the hill. // *(w/ free live at Queenscliff Festival 2006)* - PADDOCK BOMB:- Lust in translation / You remind me / Maltby by-pass / Your racist friend / Our sunshine / A coat of paint / Tired little shop / The cap me granda' wore / From the heart / Tommy didn't want to.

May 09. (cd) *(0400407)* **SPIN! SPIN! SPIN!** [–] Austra [–]
- Selling the cool car for you / Can I sleep on your floor? / As you lay sleeping / Spin! spin! spin! / Driving rain (highway song) / Stop meeting like this / Streets of Forbes / No-one compares like you / At their record launch / Eddie Merckx / Last train to Marseilles / Big geographical / She works / House of ghosts / Cave clan / Walking talking gout blues / Explaining the off-side rule to you / The red pirate of Borocay / Seeya Leigh / Garage sale / All right okay / In the perfect world.

Valve — not issued

Jul 10. (cd; as MICK THOMAS and MICHAEL BARCLAY) *(VALVE 2287)* **HEAD FULL OF ROAD-KILL: LIVE IN GERMANY** [–] German [–]
- Forgot she was beautiful / The lonely goth / Can I sleep on your floor? / Stop meeting like this / Away away / Selling the cool car for you / You remind me / Driving rain / As you lay sleeping / At their record launch / Our sunshine / Tommy didn't want you / For a short time / A tale they won't believe / The rain in my heart.

Benjamin WETHERILL

Never been freaked out by freak-folk? Then the sound of Leeds-born acoustic singer-songwriter BENJAMIN WETHERILL should do the trick. Characterised by dulcet, warbling vocals (recorded in a palace and accompanied at times by bird noises), the production of Jeremy Barnes (of A HAWK AND A HACKSAW) and the backing of the Hun Hangar Ensemble, featuring viola player Heather Trost, **LAURA** (2008) {*8} is reminiscent of the late Clifford T. Ward, HARVEY ANDREWS, Colin Blunstone and Peter Sarstedt.

In 'Kissing Under Poplars' you might recognize a few lines from the FUREYS' 'When You Were Sweet Sixteen', while 'Shallow Brown' and 'Black Waterside' are unmistakeably crafted from traditional sources but very ESPERS in formula. The gorgeous 'So Dark The Night' and 'Oh Sorrow' could be what might happen after swallowing Tiny Tim. You have been warned. *MCS*

Benjamin Wetherill - vocals, acoustic guitar / + session people

UK self-rel. — US not issued

2005. (7") *(none)* ORANGE AND SILVER. / John Barleycorn [–]

Apollolaan — Ba Da Bing! - Red Deer Club

May 08. (ltd-cd-r) *(apan 002)* BENJAMIN WETHERILL [–] [–]
- Beside the bonny hawthorn / War branle / Come ye heavy states.

Jun 08. (cd) <BING 058 - RDC 014> **LAURA** [–] [ ]
- For all the headlines / Ada / So dark the night / Folds in the curtain / Kissing under poplars / A willowing / Shallow brown / Black waterside / How lonely the moon / Oh sorrow.

WHALEBONE POLLY (⟹ THIS IS THE KIT)

WHAPWEASEL

It's refreshing in this day and age to find a English country dance band, or indeed a trad-folk outfit, who write their own material, and positively unusual to find such an outfit that doesn't source anything but their own ideas and initiatives.

WHAPWEASEL (the name is taken from a little stream that flows through Hexham in Northumberland) were formed in 1996 by melodeon players Brian Bell and Robin Jowett, who recruited other players to boost their live shows. Settling with guitarist Dave Ainsley, drummer Bob Wilson and cittern player Mike Coleman (Bell took over bass and multi-tasking duties), the quintet delivered a self-released debut set, **SKIRL NAKED** (1998) {*6}.

STEELEYE SPAN's electric guitarist Rick Kemp was on hand to produce their second and third efforts, **BURN** (2000) {*6} and **RELENTLESS** (2003) {*7}, by which time Kemp himself had replaced Ainsley (with Brian's daughter Heather Bell on keys), while a sax section ('The Toots', i.e. Stuart Finden and Fiona Littlewood) was added. This ska element added another dimension to the WHAPWEASEL sound, a sound that won them the Best Dance Band category at the Radio 2 Folk Awards in 2005. Robin then made way for fiddler Tom Fairburn, whom they met at the Sidmouth Festival.

PACK OF JOKERS (2005) {*6} and **COLOUR** (2008) complemented their increasing activity on the live circuit, while former ALBION BAND alumni Simon Care and Saul Rose (on melodeons) were enlisted to replace Fairburn and Kemp. With the addition of Joe Fowler (trombone) and replacement drummer John Hirst, the octet can be expected to regain momentum with a sixth "songs" album, due for release later in 2011. *MCS*

Brian Bell - bass, multi / **Robin Jowett** - melodeon / **Dave Ainsley** - guitar / **Mike Coleman** - cittern / **Bob Wilson** - drums

UK Whapweasel — US not issued

1998. (cd) *(CDWW 03)* **SKIRL NAKED** [ ] [–]
- Frost on the gatepost / Barnbrack / El sombrero grande / Ride the applecart / Burt's tankard - Black Sally / Foul weather call - The three Andersons / Witch Hazel / Waltzing at Chollerford - French connection / Pyewacket / Vinegar Tom / Rusty bucket / Turn of the drum / Lucy's waltz. *(re-prom. May 04; same)*

—— added **Stuart Finden** + **Fiona Littlewood** - saxes

2000. (cd) *(CDWW 04)* **BURN** [ ] [–]
- Last banana / Badger's moon - Cat among the pigeons / Kemp's hornpipe / Polka Chinoise / All in good time - Ghosts / Captain Crunch / Thomas's jig / The bloody snood / One for Eddie / Owl on the bonnet / One such / Sheep in the hatchback. *(re-prom. May 04; same)*

—— added producer **RICK KEMP** - guitar (ex-STEELEYE SPAN) repl. Ainsley

—— added **Heather Bell** - keyboards (now an eight-piece)

2003. (cd) *(CDWW 05)* **RELENTLESS** [ ] [–]
- Relentless / Badunga / Bus to Bombay / The HT polka / The tinted quiff / Stonk / The final last banana - The sleeve in the cheese / Sunset sunrise - Raiders' road / The Italian bell muffler - Peter's polka / Jessica's welcome / Beard madam / The ship. *(re-prom. May 04; same)*

—— **Tom Fairburn** - fiddle; repl. Robin

Jun 05. (cd) *(CDWW 0006)* **PACK OF JOKERS** [ ] [–]
- Hanging off the edge / Pack of jokers / Polka dynamo - Charismatron / Pedalo / Toot's suite / Make the sign / JWJ / To the trees / Weasels of Ming / Rocking horse / Destination Venus.

Jun 08. (cd) *(CDWW 0007)* **COLOUR** [ ] [–]
- Colour / Aren't crisps brilliant? / Brighton / Votre tour pour la moustache / One way ticket / Mayday / Los gatos: Sarah's sunshine jig / No money for vodka / Sunday morning / Our bus / Freetrade.

—— **Simon Care** + **Saul Rose** - melodeons (former ex-ALBION BAND) repl. Fairburn + Kemp / added **Joe Fowler** - trombone

—— **John Hirst** - drums; repl. Wilson

a new album is expected later in 2011

Dave WHETSTONE

A seasoned session man, English folk accordionist DAVE WHETSTONE will probably be best known to fans of The ALBION BAND (whom he played for in the 1980s), The COCK & BULL BAND (until 1981) and as songwriter with the late-1980s incarnation of FAIRPORT CONVENTION.

More recently, Dave was part of the WAZ! trio alongside fellow folk veterans MAARTIN ALLCOCK and Pete Zorn, although after only one eponymous set in 1998 he was superseded by STEVE TILSTON. It's indeed a shame that WHETSTONE has only managed to secure a deal for one traditional album, but the sleeve credits on **THE RESOLUTION** (1996) {*6} include MAARTIN ALLCOCK, Dave Lockwood, SIMON NICOL and Pete Zorn. Check it out for 'The Black Swan', 'Rocky And The Gopher' and 'Hare In The Long Grass'. *MCS*

Dave Whetstone - vocals, accordion / + backing band (see biog)

UK Monkey's Knib — US not issued

Nov 96. (cd) *(MKRCD 410)* **THE RESOLUTION** ☐ ⊟
- Rocky and the gopher / Bonavista 1 & 2 / The resolution / Emilia's angels - Jolly jolly demons / The black swan / Hotfoot 2 / Henry's moat / Fish pie polka - Timberline / Sherborne rose / Fingers in the jam / Sweet ginger / Candlemas moon / Cummerbund - Heads up / Hare in the long grass / Rachel's delight.

Chris WHILE and Julie MATTHEWS

For almost 20 years both CHRIS WHILE and her ALBION BAND replacement (in 1993) JULIE MATTHEWS have performed as a duo and as part of various collectives including DAPHNE'S FLIGHT (along with HELEN WATSON, CHRISTINE COLLISTER and MELANIE HARROLD).

CHRIS WHILE was born Christine Mills in 1956 in Barrow-in-Furness, Cumbria, and she retains her married name although divorced in 1991 from singing partner Joe While. As a folk singer-songwriter she has released a string of contemporary solo sets, and her most memorable songs can be found on **IN THE BIG ROOM** (1997) {*6} and **ROSELLA RED** (2007) {*7}. It was when Chris was recording the latter that she was invited to take the SANDY DENNY part in FAIRPORT CONVENTION's Cropredy Festival recreation of their classic 'Liege And Lief' album in front of an estimated 30,000 fans. Chris and her daughter Kellie While have also from time to time worked as a duo.

JULIE MATTHEWS (born April 2, 1963, Sheffield), has been just as prolific, if not more so. From her duo/project sets with Pat Shaw - including **LIES AND ALIBIS** (1993) {*6} - and Yorkshire collective INTUITION (alongside Pat, KATE RUSBY, KATHRYN ROBERTS, and Kathleen & Rosalie DEIGHTON), to her solo albums **SUCH IS LIFE** (1996) {*6} and **SLOW** (2004) {*6}, and as a writer with the FAIRPORTs, Julie's musical career has uncannily paralleled Chris's.

It's no wonder then, that WHILE and MATTHEWS have teamed up on several well-received rootsy-folk albums, from **PIECEWORK** (1998) {*6} and **HIGHER POTENTIAL** (1999) {*6} to the double concert set **STAGES** (2000) {*8} and their latest offerings, **TOGETHER ALONE** (2008) {*7} and **HITTING THE GROUND RUNNING** (2010) {*7}.

During a productive era for WHILE and MATTHEWS, the pair still managed to combine in 2003 with former ALBION alumni MAARTIN ALLCOCK, Pete Zorn and Neil Marshall for the eponymous **BLUE TAPESTRY** {*6} live set. Have they ever had a day off? *MCS*

CHRIS WHILE

Chris While - vocals, acoustic guitar (with session people)

UK own label — US not issued

1991. (c) *(none)* **STILL ON FIRE** ☐ ⊟
- Safe place (still on fire) / Living apart / 100 miles / Sneakin' / Someone to love me / Lonely morning blues / Another year another day / Empty hearts / Living with strangers. *(cd-iss.1993 on Blue Moon+=; BMMCD 03)* - BY REQUEST

1992. (c) *(none)* **BY REQUEST** ☐ ⊟
- Memories of you / The weakness in me / Blue songs on a red guitar / Some people's lives / Highwayman / Loving Hannah / Rock 'n' roll slave / Van Diemen's land / The letter. *(cd-iss.+=)- STILL ON FIRE*

Water On The Wall — not issued

Nov 93. (cd/c) *(WOW 015 CD/C)* **LOOK AT ME NOW** ☐ ⊟
- Look at me now / How will I know / Poor sad fool / I can't stay / Edge of the knife / The moon looks gold / Only one man / No matter how / 100 miles / Friendship song / He haunts me / It's been too long. *(cd re-iss. Aug 94 on Fat Cat; FAT 003CD)*

In '95 WHILE was credited w/ Ken Nicol on album 'Shadows On The Wall'.

Fledg'ling — not issued

Mar 97. (cd) *(FLED 3009)* **IN THE BIG ROOM** ☐ ⊟
- River song / Living apart / Too good for me / Broken things / Sister moon / Half a lifetime / You and your heart / Susan / Loving hand / Every word we speak (sounds like goodbye) / Give me wings / Walk beside you. *(re-iss. Sep 99 on Fat Cat; FATCD 005)*

JULIE MATTHEWS

Fat Cat — not issued

Jun 93. (cd/c; as PAT SHAW and JULIE MATTHEWS) *(FAT CD/C 001)* **LIES AND ALIBIS** ☐ ⊟
- Down in the tall grass / Ball, anchor and chain / All the way / Storm damage / Road to Eden / Go north / Turn of the dice / Turning point / Till all the people (of the world are free) / The thorn upon the rose / Sound of time / Bridge of hope.

—— next feat. **Julie Matthews, Kathleen & Rosalie Deighton, Kathryn Roberts, Kate Rusby + Pat Shaw**

Sep 93. (cd/c; by INTUITION) *(FAT CD/C 002)* **INTUITION** ☐ ⊟
- Bonnie light horseman / I am the one / Sally gardens / Leather britches - Miller's reel / Blue old Saturday night / Baby can I hold you / The moon and St Christopher / The willow / Road to Eden / Barbara Allen / Bonnie Kate - Jenny's chickens / Gulf Coast highway / Polly Parker / Letters home to England.

Road Goes On Forever — not issued

Mar 96. (cd) *(RGFCD 030)* **SUCH IS LIFE** ☐ ⊟
- Such is life / The devil in me / Love me or not / Blue songs on a red guitar / Colours of love / Love can build bridges / Nothing you can't be / Girl gone wrong / Love is an abandoned car / Jewel in the crown / Shot through the heart / The light in you / Train / Crashing to your knees.

—— both Chris and Julie joined HELEN WATSON in DAPHNE'S FLIGHT

CHRIS WHILE AND JULIE MATTHEWS

Blue Moon — not issued

1996. (cd-ep) *(BMMCD 01)* BLUE MOON ON THE RISE ☐ ⊟
- Blue moon on the rise / Sleep on it / Young man cut down in his prime / Union station / Love me or not.

Fat Cat — not issued

1998. (cd-ep) *(FAT 004)* THE BALLADS ☐ ⊟
- Separate lives / Thorn upon the rose / I'm restless / Going home.

1998. (cd) *(FATCD 006)* **PIECEWORK** ☐ ⊟
- Class reunion / Starting all over again / This is your instant karma / Hard to be the way / Piecework / Factory floor / Seven years of rust / From this wood / White water running / Winter shines / Even the desert bears a seed.

Nov 99. (cd) *(FATCD 007)* **HIGHER POTENTIAL** ☐ ⊟
- Everything turns / Tyre tracks in the snow / The light in my mother's eye / Angels walk among us / The leaving / It's a wonderful life / Love has gone to war / When love asks / Two shades deeper than blue / The weight of loving you / The heart may be right / Racing to millennium / Diggin' holes.

Nov 00. (d-cd) *(FATCD 008)* **STAGES** (live) ☐ ⊟
- Girl gone wrong / Class reunion / 100 miles / Even the desert bears a seed / Piecework / Winter shines / Seven years of rust / Love has gone to war / The devil in me / Hard to be the way / The weight of loving you / Starting all over again / From this wood / I can't stay / Shot through the heart / The fool on the hill // The leaving / The jewel in the crown / Blue songs on a red guitar / Angels walk among us / Diggin' holes / The light in my mother's eye / The thorn upon the rose / Lonely morning blues / Find my way back home / Tyre tracks in the snow / The heart maybe right / White water running / Only one man / I only want to be with you / Circle round the sun / Separate lives.

Oct 01. (cd; as JULIE MATTHEWS / CHRIS WHILE) *(FATCD 009)* **QUEST** ☐ ⊟
- Quest / Walk the line / Money money yeah! yeah! yeah! / Shadow of my former self / When I come down again / Blind faith / Ten thousand miles away / Doris was a spy / Find my way back home / Distant as the poles / Freedom song / Quest reprise.

Nov 01. (cd-s) *(FAT 010)* SHADOW OF MY FORMER SELF / Class Reunion / Lean On Me ☐ ⊟

—— Towards the end of 2001, WHILE & MATTHEWS teamed up with Chris Leslie and David Hughes to form Christmas offshoot St Agnes Fountain, releasing 'Acoustic Carols For Christmas'; subsequent releases include 'Comfort And Joy' (2002), 'The Show' (2002), 'Three Ships' (2004), 'The White Christmas Album' (2006) and 'Soul Cake' (2008).

—— next credited **CHRIS WHILE, JULIE MATTHEWS, MAARTIN ALLCOCK, PETE ZORN + NEIL MARSHALL**

Mar 03. (cd; by BLUE TAPESTRY) *(FATCD 011)* **BLUE TAPESTRY** (live) ☐ ⊟
- I feel the earth move / Free man in Paris / It's too late / Natural woman / Beautiful / You turn me on I'm a radio / Little green / So far away / California / In France they kiss on Main Street / It's gonna take some time / Coyote / Will you love me tomorrow / Case of you / Tapestry / Raised on robbery / Where you lead.

Jan 04. (cd; as WHILE and MATTHEWS) *(FATCD 012)* **PERFECT MISTAKE** ☐ ⊟
- Make each moment count / Westward / Perfect mistake / Follow your heart / Pass it on / When you think it's all over it's just begun / Dancing with the angels / Shattered / Now that love has gone / Road fever / Broken wheel / Generation game.

Oct 04. (cd; by JULIE MATTHEWS) *(FATCD 015)* **SLOW** ☐ ⊟
- Faithless heart / All things / Where is my angel / Slow / Home in my heart / Hands against the wall / One step to the side / The unspoken word / The better me / Run to me / Dylan's lullaby.

May 06. (cd) *(FATCD 016)* **HERE AND NOW** ☐ ⊟

- On my way / The here and now / Breathe / Flourish / Cover our eyes / Steady breathing / All around the world / Feel good list / Innocent new year / So long old pal.

Aug 07. (cd) *(FATCD 019)* **STAGE 2: LIVE AT THE FIREHOUSE, GERMANY** (live)
- Quest / On my way / Shadow of my former self / Walk the line / Westward / Now that love has gone / Steady breathing / Feel good list / Perfect mistake / Distant as the poles / Blind faith / All around the world / Minstrel's lullaby.

Sep 07. (cd; by CHRIS WHILE) *(FATCD 020)* **ROSELLA RED**
- Falling ashes / You didn't think it through did you? / Pennyweight hill / Safe in your arms / Dark blue eyes / When I watch you sleep / Think I'll let it ride / The promises / Walking in my shoes / Both sides now.

Sep 08. (cd) *(FATCD 021)* **TOGETHER ALONE**
- Together alone / Welcome to your life / Take these bones / Healed / A simple twist of fate / Little man Jake / Blue old Saturday night / Single act of kindness / Old Morocco / Shame / The sum of what I am / What goes around.

May 09. (cd; as MATTHEWS, WHILE AND WATSON) *(RTV 001)* **BARE BONES**
- Can't stand up alone / You gotta move / Why walk when you can fly / Didn't leave nobody but the baby / For the longest time / By the mark / Ain't got you / Way down deep / Orphan girl / Gone at last / Hard times come again no more / Devoted to you / On children.

(above issued on RTV)

Sep 10. (cd) *(FATCD 022)* **HITTING THE GROUND RUNNING**
- Carved in stone / The coldest winds do blow / Rock of gelt / We're not over yet / The darkside wood / Somewhere I walk alone / Hitting the ground running / Four walls / Bridge over time / Ghost of you / Where the year has gone.

- (8-10*) compilations -

Oct 06. (cd) *Fat Cat; (FATCD 017)* **THE BEST OF WHILE & MATTHEWS**
- The light in my mother's eye / Westward / Shadow of my former self / Walk the line / Generation game / Distant as the poles / Even the desert bears a seed / Piecework / Seven years of rust / Steady breathing / Perfect mistake / On my way / Thorn upon the rose / Starting all over / Class reunion.

CHRIS & KELLIE WHILE

Chris and her daughter

Jul 04. (cd) *(FATCD 014)* **CHRIS & KELLIE WHILE**
- Broken things / Give me wings / Talk to me Mendocino / Van Diemen's land / In my room / Power of two / Memories of you / One of these days / Safe place / Empty hearts / 100 miles.

Jun 07. (cd) *(FATCD 018)* **TOO FEW SONGS**
- The words we never use / Greenfields / 36 miles away from the sea / Love is an abandoned car / Mississippi / Persuasion / Don't let me come home a stranger / Play it all again / Neptune / Baking bread / Let it be so.

WHIPPERSNAPPER

Formed in Northampton in 1983/84, WHIPPERSNAPPER were a folk supergroup of sorts, led by the frenetic fiddle work of former FAIRPORT CONVENTION stalwart DAVE SWARBRICK alongside fellow mandolinist, fiddler and singer Chris Leslie (also a violin-maker) and former DANDO SHAFT players Kevin Dempsey and Martin Jenkins.

Steeped in traditional ballad covers but also writing original material, WHIPPERSNAPPER recorded three studio albums and one live album as a quartet before Swarbrick continued his solo career late in 1989. Issued on their self-financed WPS label, **PROMISES** (1985) {*7}, **TSUBO** (1987) {*6} and **FORTUNE** (1990) {*5}, with the concert set **THESE FOOLISH STRINGS** (1988) {*6}, spanned their career up to his departure. As a trio, with guests Rob Armstrong and David Oddy, they recorded **STORIES** (1991) {*5}.

While Jenkins found work with his own family group The STORY, DEMPSEY and LESLIE took on solo ventures. LESLIE had already worked with DEMPSEY on DEMPSEY's second solo LP, the 1989-recorded **ALWAYS WITH YOU** (1994) {*5}. DEMPSEY's first was **THE CRY OF LOVE** (1988) {*5}.

CHRIS LESLIE's first solo album, **THE GIFT** (1994) {*6}, featured Beryl Marriott, and his second, **THE FLOW** (1997) {*7}, was recorded with a stellar cast of MAARTIN ALLCOCK, Anne-Marie Doyle, Margaret Knight, SIMON MAYOR, RIC SANDERS and MARTIN SIMPSON.

In 1997 Chris was invited into the fold of FAIRPORT CONVENTION as singer and multi-instrumentalist, and has remained there ever since. His third solo album, **DANCING DAYS** (2003) {*6}, was subtitled 'A Celebration of Music from the Morris in the Glorious Company of Gerry Conway, ASHLEY HUTCHINGS, SIMON NICOL, DAVE PEGG, RIC SANDERS, Mat Green & Mikey Radford'.

More recently, Dempsey has been credited on new boy Jonathan Day's 'Carved In Bone' (2010) album, alongside CHRIS WHILE, Joe Broughton and Paloma Trigas.

Sadly, Martin Jenkins died in Sofia, Bulgaria, on May 17, 2011. *MCS*

Dave Swarbrick (b. Apr 5, '41, London) - fiddle, mandolin, vocals (ex-FAIRPORT CONVENTION, etc) / **Chris Leslie** (b. Dec 15, '56, Banbury, Oxfordshire) - fiddle, mandolin, vocals (ex-Hookey Band) / **Martin Jenkins** (b. Jul 17, '46, London) - mandocello, mandolin, flute, vocals (ex-DANDO SHAFT) / **Kevin Dempsey** (b. May 29, '50, Coventry, Midlands) - guitar, vocals (ex-DANDO SHAFT, ex-HEDGEHOG PIE, ex-BERT JANCH, ex-Pzazz, ex-Blue Aquarius)

UK WPS — US Varrick

Mar 85. (lp) *(WPS 001)* *<VC-027>* **PROMISES** — 1990
- Whenever / Banks of sweet primroses / An sean bhean bhocht - The gipsy's rest - Atholl Highlanders' farewell to Loch Katrine / John Gaudie - John broke the prison door / One way donkey ride / Hard times of Old England / Downtown rodeo / Carolanning: Mrs Bermingham - Mrs Maxwell - John Jameson / Loving Hannah / Lizzie Wan. *(cd-iss. 1990s; WPSCD 001)*

May 87. (lp/cd) *(WPS/+CD 002)* *<VC-030>* **TSUBO** — 1990
- Farewell my lovely Nancy / The pride of Kildare / Rouge and red shoes / I wandered by a brookside / The seven keys / Romanitza / Deneze-sous-doue (on the wall) / Frank Dempsey's lament and joy / My little fiddle / There's a fiddle.

Nov 88. (lp/c) *(WPS/+C 003)* **THESE FOOLISH STRINGS** (live 1984–88)
- Foolish / The fiddle duet (Mason's apron etc) / A week before Easter / Coming back to stay / The hen's march - The four poster bed / John Gaudie / The banks of the Bann / Lizzie Wann / Rosie - Canon in D.

Jan 90. (lp) *(WPS 004)* **FORTUNE**
- Pedlar's pack / Love's embers / The lark in the clear air - Sailing into Walpole's marsh - Lynden lea / No more / The seeds of love / John here - Jab hurt / The reel of Tulloch - The high road to Linton / The maid from Coolmore.

—— now without solo SWARBRICK

1991. (cd) *(WPS 005)* **STORIES**
- Heartbeat of London town / Coleman's / William Taylor / Walking out / Living on dreams / She moved through the fair / The lake / Wounds of word play / Mill Bay.

—— disbanded and both LESLIE and DEMPSEY went solo; Jenkins formed The STORY

KEVIN DEMPSEY

Plane — not issued

1988. (lp) *(88627)* **THE CRY OF LOVE** — Dutch
- Who do you think you are / Hey lady / It's all over now / Your love / All for you / Come on Gigi / Miso soup / Family / Nuevo nido. *(UK cd-iss. Apr 98 on WPS; WPSCD 006)*

1988. (7") *(88629)* COME ON GIGI. / Nuevo Nido — Dutch

Spindrift — not issued

Nov 94. (cd) *(SPINCD 136)* **ALWAYS WITH YOU** [recorded with CHRIS LESLIE in 1989]

—— In 2001, KEVIN DEMPSEY and Joe Broughton released 'Every Other World'; in 2009/2010 he teamed with with Rosie Carson on 'The Salty Diamond' and 'Between The Distance'.

CHRIS LESLIE

Beautiful Jo — not issued

Jun 94. (cd) *(BEJOCD 5)* **THE GIFT**
- Tenpence coloured / Shaker music / Samuel's shoes - Imogen's reel / Sir John Fenwick's - John's fairy dance / No sleep for the wicked / The red-haired man's wife / 18th-century English dances / Gow rediscovered / I wandered by a brookside / Linda's tune / Of all the ways a wind can blow / Cape Breton set / She once loved me / The buffoon - Black joke / Highland medley.

Aug 97. (cd) *(BEJOCD 20)* **THE FLOW**
- Ballydesmond - Scartaglen / Eliz Iza - Derobee de guincamp / Aignish / The witch of the glen / Believe me if all those endearing young charms / Lime rock / The old blackbird / The flow / Niel Gow's lament for Abercairney / Paddy Ryan's dream - Inimitable reel - Macroom lassies / Kishnul's gallery / Tune for the land of snows.

Talking Elephant — not issued

Nov 03. (cd) *(TECD 058)* **DANCING DAYS**
- Flowers of Edinborough - Old Tom of Oxford / Laudnum bunches - Orange in bloom - Banks of the Dee / Bower processional / Princess Royal - Speed the plough / Old Marlborough / The dancer / Joekey to the fair - Double jig / Lumps of plum pudding - Bean setting - Bobbing a Joe / Sweet Jenny Jones - Brighton camp - Beaux of London City / Stourton wake / Haste to the wedding - Bluebells of Scotland - Shepherds away / Bumpus o' Stretton / Janet Blunt poem / Morning star - Getting upstairs - Wheatley processional / A secret.

The WHISKY PRIESTS

Formed in Durham in 1985 by teenage twins Gary and Glenn Miller (with mandolin player Bill Bulmer), these northern-accented ruffians trod hot on the heels of punk-folk forebears The POGUES and The MEN THEY COULDN'T HANG.

With performances akin to a nightmarish Alexander Brothers gig on acid, singer/guitarist Gary and self-taught accordionist Glenn were often described as the Joe Strummer and Mick Jones of folk music. With their DIY-punk ethos intact, and with a little boost from an appearance on Channel 4 music show 'The Tube', the extended quintet (having added rhythm section Sticks and Michael Stephenson) released their first record, the single, 'The Colliery', in 1987.

Forming their own label, Whippet Records, the cloth-capped precursors to the DROPKICK MURPHYS unleashed a string of EPs and cassettes and a full set, **NEE GUD LUCK** (1989) {*8}, all the while operating a revolving-door personnel policy. Bulmer's stalwart replacement Mick Tyas (bass) stayed on, but newcomers Steve Green (drums) and Pete French (Northumberland pipes and fiddle) were surplus to requirements when Kevin Wilson, Piers Burgoyne and fiddler Simon Chantler came on board for the sextet's long-awaited return, **TIMELESS STREET** (1992) {*7}. The concert set **BLOODY WELL LIVE!** (1993) {*7} demonstrated that as stage performers The WHISKY PRIESTS were the ones to watch, whatever the line-up - which had, unsurprisingly, changed again.

THE POWER AND THE GLORY (1994) {*7}, **BLEEDING SKETCHES** (1995) {*6} (with contemporary poet Keith Armstrong), **LIFE'S TAPESTRY** (1996) {*7} and **THINK POSITIVE!** (1998) {*6} all created a stir among their loyal fan base. That fan base now included followers all over Europe (the band survived a violent gang attack in Slovenia), but years on the road had taken their toll. The Whiskys signed off with another concert set, **"HERE COME THE RANTING LADS" - LIVE!** (1999) {*6}, though the twins returned for a one-off collaboration with the MAD DOGS AND ENGLISHMEN project on **GOING DOWN WITH ALICE** (2001) {*6}, alongside former Blyth Power mainman Joseph Porter. GARY MILLER has since delivered two website-only CDs. *MCS*

Gary Miller - vocals, acoustic guitar / **Glenn Miller** - accordion, vocals / **Bill Bulmer** - mandolin, bouzouki, harmonica, jew's harp, vocals / added **Sticks** - drums + **Michael Stephenson**

UK Teesbeat / US not issued

1987. (7" m) *(TB 8)* THE COLLIERY. / Keep Your Feet Still Geordie Hinny / The Clog Dancer

Whippet / Big Easy

Jul 88. (12" ep) *(WPT 1)* NO CHANCE
- No chance / The coal-digger's grave / The hard men / Wise man / The bonnie pit laddie.

1989. (12" ep) *(WPT 2)* GRANDFATHA'S FATHA
- Grandfatha's fatha / Instrumental medley: The Hexhamshire lass - Dance to yer daddie - The Keel row - Kafoozalum - Weshin' day / Georgie Black / The row between the cages / The ghost of Geordie Jones / Byker hill - Elsie Marley.

—— **Mick Tyas** - bass, vocals / **Steve Green** - drums / **Pete French** - Northumberland pipes, fiddle; repl. Stephenson + Sticks (Gary Price was also a member around this time before he joined OPHIUCHUS)

1989. (c-ep) *(WPT 3)* HALCYON DAYS
- Halcyon days / Bill Hartnell / Adam Buckham / Grandfatha's fatha / Geordie Black / The clog dancer.

1989. (lp) *(WPT 4)* **NEE GUD LUCK**
- The colliery / Shut doon the waggon works / The rising of the north / Streets paved with gold / Jenny Grey / The coal-digger's grave / Dol-li-a / Halcyon days / Death of the shipyards / The Oakey strike evictions / Pressgang medley: Captain Bover - Here's the tender comin' - Proudlock's hornpipe - Harvest home / The Durham lock-out / Spring-heeled jacks / Collier's rant / The Durham light infantry. *(cd-iss. Mar 94 +=; WPT 11CD)* - Bill Hartnell / Adam Buckham / Grandfatha's fatha / Geordie Black / The clog dancer.

Nov 91. (cd) *(WPTCD 5)* **THE FIRST FEW DROPS: Early EPs, Singles and Demos 1987/88**
- (NO CHANCE EP tracks) / Shut doon the waggon works (demo) / (GRANDFATHA'S FATHA EP tracks). *(cd-iss. Mar 94 +=; WPTCD 10)* - The colliery / Keep your feet still Geordie hinny / The clog dancer / Jenny Grey (demo) / Collier's rant (demo) / The rising of the north (demo).

—— **Kevin Wilson** - mandolin, bouzouki, vocals; repl. Bulmer

—— **Piers Burgoyne** - drums; repl. Green

—— **Simon Chantler** - fiddle; repl. French

1992. (cd) *(WPTCD 6)* **TIMELESS STREET**
- Susan's song / Old man forgotten / Easington / Goblins / Jim Jones / Perfect time / Aal faal doon / Bonnie Gateshead lass / Poor Johnny Coal / The raven / Pride / William's tale. *(cd-iss. Mar 94+=; WPTCD 12)* - The hills of Alva - The lads of North Tyne / Rio Grande / The recruited collier / The waggoner.

—— **Paul Carless** (guest on previous set) - mandolin, harmonica; repl. Wilson

—— **Mike McGrother** - fiddle; repl. Chantler

—— **Tony McNally** - drums; repl. Burgoyne

May 93. (cd/c) *(WPT CD/C 7)* **BLOODY WELL LIVE!** (live)
- The row between the cages / Halcyon days - Old man forgotten / Bonnie Gateshead lass / Jenny Grey / See the whippet run / Instrumental medley No.2: The border widow's lament - Nee gud luck - The Helseyside reel / The raven / Easington / No chance *[re-CD-only *]* / The rising of the north / Land of the dinosaur / Perfect time / Dol-li-a / William's tale - Aal faal doon *[re-CD-only *]* / The Durham light infantry *[re-CD-only *]* / Goblins / General Taylor *[re-CD-only *]* / Shut doon the waggon works / Farewell Johnny miner / The colliery / The hard men. *(d-cd iss. Apr 01 += *; WPTCD 20)* - The coal-digger's grave / Isn't it grand boys.

—— **Nick Buck** - drums, percussion; repl. McNally + McGrother

Apr 94. (cd/c) *(WPT CD/C 8)* *<85208>* **THE POWER AND THE GLORY**
- The man who would be king / When the wind blows, Billy boy / Manimal farm / Land of the dinosaur / Shot at dawn / Three rivers / Lead them to their graves / Rime of the not-so-ancient mariner / Brandon, Browney and Boyne / See the whippet run / Epitaph and lament for the setting sons / Digging for victory.

Sep 94. (cd-ep) *(WPTCD 9)* WHEN THE WIND BLOWS, BILLY BOY
- When the wind blows, Billy boy / No chance (live) / William's tale (live) / Aal faal doon (live) / Isn't it grand boys (live).

—— added **Keith Armstrong** - poetry / now without Carless

Oct 95. (cd) *(WPTCD 13)* **BLEEDING SKETCHES**
- Everybody's got love bites but me / Hexham tans / Widows of Hartley / Success road / Peterlee / Mother, waiting / My father worked on ships / Granda Craghill / 'Spring': Pit pony / Ballad of the little Count / The jinglin' Geordie / Durham / Turn it upside down / Angels playing football.

—— The **Millers** recruited **Thomas Fisk** - guitar, mandolin, euphonium / **Mick Howell** - bass / **Paul Stipetic** - drums

Sep 96. (cd/c) *(WPT 14 CD/C)* **LIFE'S TAPESTRY**
- Ranting lads / This village / Favourite sons / Legacy of the Lionheart / Which side of bedlam? / He's still my son / Workhorse / Silver for the bairn / Farewell jobling! / Forever in our hearts / Sweet magpie / Quiet angel / When I'm born again - I am redeemed.

—— The **Millers** recruited **Hugh Bradley** - mandolin, guitar, flute, whistle, vocals / **Andy Tong** - bass, vocals / **Cozy Dixon** - drums

Jun 98. (cd) *(WPT 15CD)* **THINK POSITIVE!**
- A better man than you / Side by side / My ship / Alice in Wonderland / Song for Ewan / The man who sold his town / Going to the mine / What I could have been / Car boot sale / Wherever you go / Brothers in arms again / Positive steps / Leave her Johnny, leave her.

Sep 99. (cd) *(WPT 18CD)* **"HERE COME THE RANTING LADS" - LIVE!**
- Ranting lads / Widows of Hartley / Everybody's got love bites but me ... / This village / Alice in wonderland / Success express / Side by side / Song for Ewan / A better man than you / Workhouse / Blackleg mining man / When the wind blows, Billy boy / Grandfatha's fatha / The Oakey strike evictions / Mother waiting / Car boot sale.

—— split around 2002 and 2004; the twins formed...

MAD DOGS AND ENGLISHMEN

Gary + Glenn / + Joseph Porter - vocals, acoustic guitar, percussion (ex-Blyth Power)

Whippet - Downward Spiral / not issued

Jan 01. (cd) *(WPTCD 19 - DR 009CD)* **GOING DOWN WITH ALICE** web
- A rich seam / House of war / Kate Murr / Soldier on the mantelpiece / Canard's grace / Cynthia's revels / Seven hills / Land, sea and sky / It's your time to leave / Full circle.

GARY MILLER

first with German **Ralf Weihrauch** - accordion

2005. (cd; by GARY MILLER & RALF WEIHRAUCH) *(WPTCD 21)* **STAND FAST, STAND STEADY** web
- Pitman Tom / The Sandgate lass's lament / Bellingham boat - Lambskinnet / Lament / The colliery / Stand fast, stand steady / The golden eagle - The wonder hornpipe / Easington / Dol-li-a / Where the violets grow / Keep your feet still Geordie hinny / Bookend.

2010. (cd) *(WPTCD 22)* **REFLECTIONS ON WAR** web
- Twa Scots soldiers / Bold as brass / Sister of mercy / Somewhere at the front, somewhere / Grandpa mill / Battleships / A hospital ship at Tobruk / Yellow bird / Soldiers of the Lord / One soldier's thoughts.

Kathryn WILLIAMS

For a short space of time in the early 2000s, things looked upwardly mobile for the versatile Brit-folk singer-singwriter KATHRYN WILLIAMS (born 1974 in Liverpool). Her second album, 'Little Black Numbers', had notched up a Mercury nomination on her CV, while a subsequent deal with EastWest/Atlantic Records and manager Alan McGee was promising to bring her bedsitter voice to a wider audience. It's one of life's mysteries that the former Newcastle art college student didn't quite fulfil expectations, but it wasn't for the want of trying. Maybe the melancholic BETH ORTON and NICK DRAKE approach was too much for fickle post-millennium folkies waiting for something even fresher.

Going back to 1999, it was her debut, **DOG LEAP STAIRS** {*7} - reportedly recorded for a mere £80 - that caused critics to sit up and take notice. Recalling Joni, NICO, and even Dusty, the session cellists gave the album an intimate, brooding appeal on such brittle performances as 'Leazes Park' and 'Lydia'. 'Night Came' and 'No-One To Blame' also stood out.

Also initially issued on the independent Caw label, **LITTLE BLACK NUMBERS** (2000) {*8} produced some of her most emotional pieces, including 'Jasmine Hoop', 'Stood', 'Fell Down Fast' and 'We Came Down From Trees'. The heavy orchestration was tempered by the light touch of cellist Laura Reid, double bassist Jonny Bridgwood, classical guitar maestro David Scott and percussionist Alex Tustin.

With basically the same backing players, third album **OLD LOW LIGHT** (2002) {*7} once again sent critics into raptures, but yet again only managed to bubble outside the elusive UK Top 50. Confusingly, it opened with the track 'Little Black Numbers', a jazzy-folk cut that recalled post-hippie days of the 1960s/70s (think Burt Bacharach), but it's the smoochy 'Beatles', 'Daydream And Saunter' and 'On For You' that steal the show.

A sleeve depicting furniture wrapped in covers was a clue to the contents of the ill-advised **RELATIONS** (2004) {*6}, which completed her commercial undoing when she was unceremoniously dropped by EastWest. It's an album of contrasts, with a wide range from post-grunge (Nirvana's 'All Apologies' and Pavement's 'Spit On A Stranger') to obscure/avant-garde (Ivor Cutler's 'Beautiful Cosmos' and Ralph Rainger's 'A Guy What Takes His Time'), and it's her versions of LEONARD COHEN's 'Hallelujah' and Jackson Browne's 'These Days' (once the property of NICO) that suit her style best. Other artists covered were Python Lee Jackson ('In A Broken Dream'), NEIL YOUNG ('Birds'), Big Star ('Thirteen'), The BYRDS ('The Ballad Of Easy Rider'), The Velvet Underground ('Candy Says'), TIM HARDIN ('How Can We Hang On To A Dream'), The Bee Gees ('I Started A Joke') and Lee Hazlewood ('Easy And Me').

Subsequent independent sets **OVER FLY OVER** (2005) {*5} and **LEAVE TO REMAIN** (2006) {*6} were overshadowed by her collaboration with former Bible singer-songwriter Neill MacColl (brother of Kirsty, son of EWAN MacCOLL) on the one-off **TWO** (2008) {*6}, which features their cover of Tom Waits's 'Innocent When You Dream'.

An upward move to One Little Indian secured a better chance for her seventh album, **THE QUICKENING** (2010) {*7}, a return to her smoky folk roots that was recorded in a matter of days. Check out '50 White Lines', 'Winter Is Sharp' and the piano-laden 'Black Oil'.

It was still a long way from her bright start of a decade before, when she provided backing for JOHN MARTYN on his 'Glasgow Walker' set and appeared in front of a 2000-plus crowd at an 'English Originals' NICK DRAKE tribute night in 1999. *MCS*

Kathryn Williams - vocals, acoustic guitar / with session people, etc.

UK Caw — US not issued

Aug 99. (cd) *(CAW 001)* **DOG LEAP STAIRS**
- Leazes park / Night came / What am I doing here? / No-one to blame / Something like that / Lydia / Handy / Dog without wings / Fade / Madmen and maniacs [live]. *(lp-iss. 1999 on Snowstorm w/ 7"+=; STORM 009LP)* - Kiss The Forehead. / Cradle *(re-iss. May 04; same)*

Oct 99. (cd-ep) *(CAW 002)* THE FADE EP
- Fade / Kiss the forehead / Madmen and maniacs [studio] / Cradle.

Jun 00. (cd) *(CAW 003)* **LITTLE BLACK NUMBERS**
- We dug a hole / Soul to feet / Stood / Jasmine hoop / Fell down fast / Flicker / Intermission / Tell the truth as if it were lies / Morning song / Toocan / Each star we see / We came down from the trees.

Oct 00. (cd-s) *(CAW 004)* SOUL TO FEET / Flicker / Some Kind Of Wonderful

East West — not issued

Sep 01. (re-cd) *(8573-89924-2)* LITTLE BLACK NUMBERS [70]

Nov 01. (cd-s) *(EW 240CD)* JASMINE HOOP / Foreign Skies / Jasmine Hoop [album version]

Sep 02. (cd) *(0927-47552-2)* **OLD LOW LIGHT** [56]
- Little black numbers / White, blue and red / Mirrorball / Devices / Daydream and saunter / Beatles / Wolf / Tradition / Swimmer / On for you / No one takes you home / 3am phonecall.

In Dec'02, 'Moshi Moshi' issued a collaboration cd-s between Pedro Vs. Kathryn Williams

May 04. (cd) *(5046 7 21665 5)* **RELATIONS** [covers]
- In a broken dream / Birds / Thirteen / Hallelujah / The ballad of Easy Rider / A guy what takes his time / Candy says / How can we hang on to a dream / I started a joke / Easy and me / Spit on a stranger / All apologies / Beautiful cosmos / These days.

Caw — Sidecho

Jul 04. (7") *(CAW 02V)* IN A BROKEN DREAM. / Set Me Free

May 05. (cd) *(CAW 007)* **OVER FLY OVER**
- Three / Indifference #1 / Breath / Old low light #2 / Just like a birthday / Shop window / Beachy Head / Escaping / City streets / Untilt the dark / Baby blues / Full colour.

Jun 05. (7") *(CAW 08V)* SHOP WINDOW. / Breath [live]

Oct 05. (7") *(CAW 010V)* BEACHY HEAD. / People Ain't No Good

Oct 06. (cd) *(CAW 011)* <20> **LEAVE TO REMAIN** — Aug 07
- Blue onto you / Let it happen / Sustain pedal / Stevie / Sandy L / When / Glass bottomed boat / Hollow / Opened / Room in my head. *(re-iss. Aug 08 on Pastel+=; 2026)* - [untitled track].

—— next with singer/songwriter Neill MacColl (son of EWAN MacCOLL)

Mar 08. (cd; by KATHRYN WILLIAMS and NEILL MacCOLL) *(CAW 013)* **TWO**
- 6am corner / Innocent when you dream / Come with me / Before it goes / Blue fields / Frame / Grey goes / Weather forever / Shoulders / Armchair / Rolling down / All / Holes in your life.

One Little Indian — not issued

Feb 10. (cd) *(TPLP 1046CD)* **THE QUICKENING**
- 50 white lines / Just a feeling / Winter is sharp / Wanting waiting / Black oil / Just leave / Smoke / Cream of the crop / There are keys / Noble guesses / Little lesson / Up north.

—— next set by **Kathryn Williams + Anna Spencer** (of Delicate Vomit)

Sep 10. (cd; as The CRAYONETTES) *(TPLP 1079CD)* **PLAYING OUT: songs for children and robots**
- Robots in the rain / Disco teeth / Rainy day / Hopscotch / Emergency / Sweet on the floor / Let's dance on moon / Spooky way home / How hot is a toad? / Pirates on the bus / Illegal.

Brian WILLOUGHBY

Born September 20, 1949 at Glenarm in County Antrim, Northern Ireland, guitarist and singer BRIAN WILLOUGHBY will be known to fans of the STRAWBS, having played with the folk-rock/prog-pop outfit on and off from 1979 onwards. The group's leader, DAVE COUSINS, also collaborated with Brian on a couple of folk albums, 'Old School Songs' (1979) and 'The Bridge' (1994).

While his tenure with the STRAWBS is well documented in the Great Folk Discography Volume I, things that may have been overlooked include his session duties with 'Tom Tom Turnaround' hitmakers NEW WORLD in the mid-1970s and his stints as back-up for Roger Whittaker and Joe Brown. In 1978 he helped form the short-lived No Sweat.

Having played on tour with folk-pop star MARY HOPKIN in the 1970s (through her husband and producer Tony Visconti), it was no surprise when she returned the compliment some 25 years on as a special guest on his long-awaited debut album, **BLACK AND WHITE** (1998) {*6}.

Although not credited on the sleeve, as she was on subsequent sets, American country-blues singer Cathryn Craig was the power behind that record. In between commitments to the STRAWBS/Acoustic STRAWBS, the Craig-Willoughby duo completed further singer-songwriter/folk-based albums **I WILL** (2002) {*6} and **CALLING ALL ANGELS** (2009) {*6}. Brian featured on her 'Pigg River Symphony' (2001) album and delivered a second solo set, **FINGERS CROSSED** (2004) {*6}. *MCS*

Brian Willoughby - vocals, guitars (all feat. **Cathryn Craig** - vocals)

UK Pyo — US Pyo

Sep 98. (cd) *(<PYOCD 001>)* **BLACK AND WHITE** — May 99
- In this room / Alice's song / Black and white / Totally in your hands / The fire / Hard luck cafe / Love belongs right here / He lies / More than you loved me / Willow / Then someone says your name / The feel of letting go.

Goldrush not issued

Apr 02. (cd; as CATHRYN CRAIG AND BRIAN WILLOUGHBY) *(GOLDCD 009)* **I WILL**
- All the way to Denver / That ol' guitar / Snake / Goodbye old friend / Mysterious ways / Mr Jefferson / There will come a day / Rod Stewart / Amazing grace / Amazing grace (reprise) / I will / Wedding vows (forevermore) / What a wonderful world.

Road Goes On Forever not issued

Oct 04. (cd) *(RGF/BWCD 055)* **FINGERS CROSSED**
- Cry no more / Honeylick / These nights, these dreams and you / Spanish fly / The Bonas track / Wedding vows / Sweet insanity / George's tune / Cailin Dall / Ramblin' road - Pride of America / JJ's blues / Goodbye old friend / Acklen avenue / Broken hearts in Nashville / She lies / The harmonic suite: Alice's song - Origine del la source - Fingers crossed / She rang my bell.

Cabritunes not issued

Feb 09. (cd; as CRAIG & WILLOUGHBY) *(CAB 002)* **CALLING ALL ANGELS**
- Alice's song / Two hearts one love / Calling all angels / The rejected lover / Accanoe / Genevieve / Genevieve in flight / Rumours of rain / These dreams / Glenarm / The green glens of Antrim.

Roger WILSON

Born July 22, 1961, in Leicester, ROGER WILSON worked his way as a busker through a graphic design course at Wolverhampton Polytechnic. He hasn't been the most prolific of solo artists, but his numerous collaborations more than make up for that.

A singer-songwriter, guitarist and fiddler for more than 30 years, Roger's debut solo set (his most recent is 2007's **YOU LOOK FAMILIAR** {*5}) was the much-lauded **THE PALM OF YOUR HAND** {*7} (1988). Featuring Karen Tweed (accordion), Jan Jodelko (drums) and Pete Townsend (double bass), the record, released on the Harbourtown label, was a fine blend of traditional and contemporary songs.

Before forming the Urban Folk trio (with PETE MORTON and Simon Edwards) for two volumes in the first half of the 1990s, journeyman WILSON toured all over the world and found time to play in three folk outfits: The Lost Nation Band (with SARA GREY and BRIAN PETERS), Scam (in the late 1980s), and Celtic-folkies The HOUSE BAND (for three albums in the mid-1990s). More recently, he's toured with The Little Back Room Dance Band and The Bezzas, in the latter alongside Anglo-Swedish fiddler Emma Reid.

STARK NAKED (1994) {*6} was his second solo album, but it was really his celebrated collaboration with CHRIS WOOD and MARTIN CARTHY on 'Wood Wilson Carthy' (1998) that brought him the critical respect he deserved. A couple of years later he was singing and acting in the National Theatre production of 'The Mysteries'. If there's one track of Roger's to fire you up, it's his rendition of the great Jimi Hendrix number 'Hey Joe'. *MCS*

Roger Wilson - vocals, acoustic guitar, fiddle

UK Harbourtown US not issued

May 88. (lp) *(HAR 002)* **THE PALM OF YOUR HAND**
- John Henry / John Hilt's - Richmond - The peg in the hole / Mother's day / Ramble away / The unlikely trip - The gumble waltz / Jack Frazer and Lucy Brown / Don't you go / The cotton reel - The trip to Windsor - McKerron's / Sleepy eyed John / The great Titanic / My laddie sits ower late up.

1991. (ltd-c; by PETE MORTON / ROGER WILSON / SIMON EDWARDS) *(HARC 016)* **URBAN FOLK Vol. I**

Whiff not issued

Apr 94. (cd/c) *(WH 001 CD/C)* **STARK NAKED**
- Barbara / Fair and tender lovers / Payday / Sick of the working life / The banks of red roses / When this hour is gone / Where my feet are going I don't know / Pride and prejudice / Nottamun town / The northern lass / Delia / The luckiest man.

—— In the mid-1990s Roger joined Celtic-folk outfit The HOUSE BAND

Harbourtown not issued

Mar 97. (ltd-cd; by PETE MORTON / ROGER WILSON / SIMON EDWARDS) *(HARCD 032)* **URBAN FOLK Vol. II: Self Destructive Fools**
- (all tracks - plus Vol. I - see Pete MORTON)

—— In Nov 98 (Chris) WOOD, (Roger) WILSON and (Martin) CARTHY released an eponymous set (see Wood's discography)

Whiff not issued

Sep 07. (cd) *(WH 002CD)* **YOU LOOK FAMILIAR** mail-o
- Wellies / Little dog / Bad hair day / Holy blue / Little Miss Muse / Rockface wall / My planet / Birthday song / The man in the moon / Bob's building a boat.

The WITCHES OF ELSWICK

Their name playfully adapted from the John Updike novel 'The Witches of Eastwick' in honour of their origin in Elswick, Tyne and Wear, where they all shared digs while studying at Newcastle University, the "four buxom lasses" (as they put it themselves) formed their a cappella folk quartet in 2001. Comprising Fay Hield, Byrony Griffith, Gillian Tolfrey and Becky Stockwell, The WITCHES OF ELSWICK sourced much of their material from olden times, a notable exception being 'I Once Lived In Service', by the late, great PETER BELLAMY (formerly of the sadly missed singing group The YOUNG TRADITION). Traditional ballads such as 'Two Sisters', 'Lord Randall' and 'Daddy Fox' came thick and fast on the group's fiery debut, **OUT OF BED** (2003) {*6}, and a second helping came along with **HELL'S BELLES** (2005) {*6} - imagine SILLY SISTERS multiplied by two and minus the instruments.

Lately the "drinking buddies" have been taking a bit of a sabbatical, although they have been part of the similar septet WitchNotes alongside GRACE NOTES. Time out was very necessary for FAY HIELD, who with her partner JON BODEN (of BELLOWHEAD) had two children between 2006 and 2009. Multi-instrumentalist Boden was present alongside Sam Sweeney and others on her debut trad set for Topic Records, **LOOKING GLASS** (2010) {*7}. In the meantime, Byrony (on vocals and violin) had carved out a sideline with brother Ben Griffith (on drums) for fresh-folk act The DEMON BARBERS. *MCS*

Fay Hield (b. Keighley, West Yorkshire) - vocals / **Bryony Griffith** (b. Huddersfield, West Yorkshire) - vocals / **Becky Stockwell** (b. Broadstairs, Kent) - vocals / **Gillian Tolfrey** (b. Jarrow, Tyne and Wear) - vocals

UK Fellside US not issued

Aug 03. (cd) *(FECD 180)* **OUT OF BED**
- Daddy fox / Sovai / Lord Randall / Two sisters / The blue cockade / I once lived in service / The scarecrow / Bring us a barrel / Bonny at morn / Maids at eighteen / The tree in the wood / Soldier, soldier / Honey for the bee.

Selwyn not issued

Jul 05. (cd) *(SYNMCD 006)* **HELL'S BELLES**
- Jan Knuckey / Soldiers three / Our captain calls / The saucy sailor / Old Molly Metcalfe / Must I be bound / The ballad of the butcher and the bookbinder's wife / John of Hazelgreen / A shepherd of the downs / The squire's daughter / Billy boy / Lullay, lullay / The parting glass.

—— with other commitments (WitchNotes, a collaboration with Grace Notes, and Bryony's involvement with The DEMON BARBERS), the group took a sabbatical

FAY HIELD

Topic Topic

Sep 10. (cd) *(<TSCD 573>)* **LOOKING GLASS**
- The huntsman / Mad family / Two brothers / The looking glass / Little yellow roses / The banks of the Nile / Kemp Owen / Sheepcrook and black dog / Grey goose and gander / The shepherd's daughter / King Henry.

Jah WOBBLE [folk part]

Perhaps surprisingly, dub bass player JAH WOBBLE (born 1958 in Stepney, London) had brief flirtations with Celtic-roots and traditional folk music in 1998 and 2003 respectively. WOBBLE had a past in punk, having been an integral part of Public Image Ltd with old friend and former Sex Pistol John Lydon/Johnny Rotten. His contributions to the albums 'Public Image' and the excellent 'Metal Box' were a little neglected at the time, probably due to Lydon's full-frontal vocal attacks. One lasting memory of the bassist's memorable TV appearances was undoubtedly his gap-toothed grin on 'Top Of The Pops' while plucking along to their Top 20 hit 'Death Disco'. Jah's sudden departure in 1980 was due to Lydon's annoyance at his use of PiL rhythm tracks on his awful punk/dub debut 'The Legend Lives On'.

Flying out to Germany, he cut the 'Full Circle' album with Can members Holger Czukay and Jaki Liebezeit, while in 1983 he was the moving spirit behind another collaboration, 'Snake Charmer' (this time with Czukay and The Edge of U2). In the mid-1980s, WOBBLE was forced to endure the trials of a real job when he worked for London Underground.

Sporadic releases helped pay the bills, although it wasn't until 1991's comeback set 'Rising Above Bedlam' (which introduced vocalist Natacha Atlas of Transglobal Underground) that WOBBLE became a full-time musician once more. With his ever-expanding Invaders Of The Heart, he even hit the Top 40 with the beautiful 'Visions Of You' single, featuring vocals by Sinead O'Connor. Numerous latter-day avant-dub works could be cited, but they're not on the present agenda.

The 2003 set **ENGLISH ROOTS MUSIC** {*6}, credited to his ensemble Jah Wobble & The Invaders Of The Heart, marked a sharp departure from his exacting but ambitious outings of yore. Augmented by a group that included the SANDY DENNYesque Liz Carter and (from past ventures) piper maestro Jean-Pierre Rasle, this curveball of a record hosted some wayward arrangements of trad tunes 'Banks Of The Sweet Primrose', 'Unquiet Grave', 'Sovay', etc alongside Chris Cookson and Jah's compositions, including 'They Came With A Swagger', and EWAN MacCOLL's perennial (here almost unrecognisable) 'Cannily Cannily'.

Concert piece **JAH WOBBLE & THE ENGLISH ROOTS BAND** (2006) {*6} complemented the aforementioned set, 'Blacksmith's Song' and 'Byker Hill' sitting awkwardly next to avant-WOBBLE tracks like 'Visions Of You', but the chance was missed to reprise an earlier sourced tune, 'Will The Circle Be Unbroken'.

Several years earlier, **THE CELTIC POETS** (1997) {*7} had been WOBBLE's diversion into world music, setting Irish poems (two written by SHANE MacGOWAN and read by DUBLINERS icon RONNIE DREW) to jazz-dub. Atmospheric, esoteric and romantic, this set mislaid none of Jah's ethnic eclecticism and pulsing bass lines, but augmented his Middle Eastern themes by fusing them with the British multi-cultural cause. *MCS*

(selected discography - folk)

30 Hertz — 30 Hertz

Jun 97. (cd; as JAH WOBBLE'S INVADERS OF THE HEART) *(<30hzcd 1>)* **THE CELTIC POETS** — Nov 98
- The dunes / The man I knew / Market Rasen / London rain / Star of the east / Third heaven / Bagpipe music / Saturn / Gone in the wind / Thames.

Nov 03. (cd; as JAH WOBBLE'S INVADERS OF THE HEART) *(<30hzcd 21>)* **ENGLISH ROOTS MUSIC**
- Cannily cannily / Banks of the sweet primrose / Unquiet grave / Blacksmith / Blacksmith (dub) / Strange duet / They came with a swagger / Press ganged / Sovay / Bykerhill / Trance of the willow / Cannily cannily (reprise).

Nov 06. (cd) *(30hzcd 28)* **JAH WOBBLE & THE ENGLISH ROOTS BAND**
- One day / No, no, no / Ploughboy's dream / Visions of you / Blacksmith's song / Rocky road to Dublin / And there was the sea / Byker hill / My love's in Germany / Full stead.

WOLFSTONE (⟹ Celtic-folk/World-music Discography)

Chris WOOD

Not to be confused with the ex-TRAFFIC flautist of the same name, or with the jazz bass player who sidelined with Medeski & Martin, this CHRIS WOOD is one of folk music's best known fiddlers and songwriters of recent times. His repertoire of instruments includes guitar, viola and voice.

Born August 25, 1959, in Whitstable, Kent, Chris's first love was the music of Handel and Bach. Early in his career he joined the Royal Shakespeare Company as a musician and composed music for the National Theatre. His French-Canadian influences on some recordings stem from his time in Canada, where he studied Quebecois traditional music. One of his earliest albums was the shelved 1989 cassette-only 'Ever Simpler' (for Harbourtown), while almost a decade earlier he played bass with The OYSTER CEILIDH BAND on 'Jack's Alive' (1980).

Setting up his own RUF label, his career really got under way on a handful of jointly-credited sets with melodeon maestro ANDY CUTTING, who has featured on more than a hundred folk (and other) recordings.

Traditionally-sourced from all over the world, **LISA** (1992) {*6}, **LUSIGNAC** (1995) {*7} and **KNOCK JOHN** (1999) {*7} were probably the duo's best-loved studio albums, concert set **LIVE AT SIDMOUTH** (1995) {*7} also coming in for praise. CUTTING would go on to join Tanteeka alongside Alice Kinloch (ex-BARELY WORKS) and JO FREYA (of BLOWZABELLA). Their 'A New Tradition' was issued in 1997.

Further collaborations with ROGER WILSON and the great MARTIN CARTHY resulted in the **WOOD WILSON CARTHY** (1998) {*7} set, a Brit-folk trad record (highlights 'Lord Bateman' and 'Scarborough Fair') apart from a few WILSON-penned exceptions and Tucker Zimmerman's 'The Taoist Tale'.

WOOD's French-Canadian experience led to another joint effort, **CROSSING** (1999), with violinist Jean-Francois Vrod. Chris and CUTTING meanwhile were also part of the Two Duos Quartet (alongside Karen Tweed & Ian Carr), who released the album 'Half As Happy As We' (1999). The ENGLISH ACOUSTIC COLLECTIVE (Chris plus fellow music tutors Robert Harbron and Miranda Rutter) issued a one-off set of the same name in 2005, having formed several years previously.

Finally, with that simple but unmistakable silk-smooth voice, WOOD unleashed his first solo CD, the stunning **THE LARK DESCENDING** (2005) {*8}. Dark, desolate and spiritual, the record revolves around two songs incorporating the lyrics of Hugh Lupton, 'Bleary Winter' and the 10-minute 'One In A Million' revealing WOOD's new artistic maturity. The renditions of 'Lord Bateman' (again) and 'John Barleycorn' (TRAFFIC had recorded this with 'their' Chris Wood 34 years before) were not the usual run-of-the-mill trad fare.

Squeezed in between his contributions to The IMAGINED VILLAGE and DARWIN SONG PROJECT folk collectives, **TRESPASSER** (2008) {*7} was another album to feature storyteller Lupton ('England In Ribbons', all 13 minutes of it), while SYDNEY CARTER's 'John Ball' and Cotswold poet Frank Mansell's 'The Cottager's Reply' were rearranged into modern-day protest songs.

Following on from its two award-winning predecessors, **HANDMADE LIFE** (2010) {*7} was Chris's first with a proper backing band (Barney Morse Brown on subtle cello, Robert Jarvis on trombone and Andy Gangadeen on drums), pursuing themes of extreme nationalism, government corruption and profiteering. The dark 'No Honey Tongued Sonnet' (with its nursery-rhyme opening line "All the king's horses..."), 'Turtle Soup' and 'The Grand Correction' were played and sung with the artist's inimitable aplomb. CHRIS WOOD is, as the Irish Times so rightly pointed out, "the renaissance man of English folk". *MCS*

CHRIS WOOD & ANDY CUTTING

Chris Wood - vocals, fiddle, viola, acoustic guitar / **Andy Cutting** - melodeon

UK RUF — US not issued

1992. (c) *(RUFC 01)* **CHRIS WOOD / ANDY CUTTING**
- Reels: Reels a Philippe Bruneau / Reels: La contredanse - Jules Verret's / Reel: Unknown / Song: The history man - Roseville fair / Thing: Anglo-American polka / Reels: Unknown - La voyager / Waltzes: In continental mood - Flatworld / Reels: Unknown - Hommage a nos racines / Marches: Bouchard quadrille - Marche Duverner / Thing: Mrs Saggs. *(cd-iss. Aug 03; same)*

1992. (cd) *(RUFCD 02)* **LISA**
- Coroare / Quadrille des Laurentide - Unknown / Valcartier set first part - Second balance / When I first came to Caledonia / When Cloe - Ville de Quebec / Unknown reel - La grand jigue simple / Galope de la malbaie - Homage a Edmond Parizeau / The silver swan / Out come the freaks / Valse efter tor lohne - Retour de Montaignac - Waltz Harry Lane / The first of May - The last of June / Reel a pointe-au-pic / Polka Chinoise. *(re-iss. Apr 99; same)*

1995. (cd; as WOOD & CUTTING) *(RUFCD 03)* **LIVE AT SIDMOUTH** [live]
- Set La cardeuse / Le bout du monde - L'autre bout de monde - Adders / When I first came to Caledonia / Quadrille des Laurentide - Unknown / Waltz clog / The lazy farmer / Brandy / Hares on the mountain - Elizabeth Clare / Une autre fois - Le canal en Octobre / Potpourri of reels / Valse des jouets / Newly weds - La voyager 13. J'ai vu le loup. *(re-iss. Apr 99; same)*

1995. (cd) *(RUFCD 04)* **LUSIGNAC**
- La boite a frissons - Lusignac / The old queen - La choca / The man of double deed / Le reel du Queteux / Hares on the mountain - Elizabeth Clare / Le gabier de terre-neuve / Waffelwaltzen - Siberian stomp / Following the old oss / Florinda - Organdi / Back at Lusignac. *(re-iss. Mar 00 & Jan 05; same)*

—— CUTTING would join Tanteeka, alongside Alice Kinloch (ex-BARELY WORKS) and JO FREYA (of BLOWZABELLA); one set: 'A New Tradition' was issued for Osmosys in 1997

WOOD WILSON CARTHY

Chris with guitarists **ROGER WILSON & MARTIN CARTHY**

Nov 98. (cd) *(RUFCD 05)* **WOOD WILSON CARTHY**
- Three jovial Welshmen / Ultrasound / Turtle dove / You must unload / Scarborough fair / Glorishears / Two sisters / The Taoist tale / Billy boy / Young Collins / Lord Bateman / Indian tea.

CHRIS WOOD & JEAN FRANCOIS VROD

Sep 99. (cd) *(RUFCD 06)* **CROSSING**
- Mazurkas / Goodwin - Marchoise - When the land is white with snow / Seeds of love / Kettledrum - Glory of the west / Al's march - Astor's - Bourees / Through lonesome woods - Bouree longue - Bogue d'or / Marsh waltz - Les Marquayres / Tout en m'y promenant / Pace egging - Ribatz ribatz.

CHRIS WOOD & ANDY CUTTING

Sep 99. (cd) *(RUFCD 08)* **KNOCK JOHN**
- Bonny breast knot - Bonny Kate / Mrs Casey - Knock knock who? - The Bishop of Chester's / Down the wagon way - Sweet Jayne - The North Downs way / Miss Lindsay Barker - Spencer the rover / Attingham waltz / Country gardens - The rambling comber / While gamekeepers lie sleeping - Charlie's march / Paddy Carey's - The spirit of the dance.

ENGLISH ACOUSTIC COLLECTIVE

Chris Wood, Robert Harbron + Miranda Rutter

Jan 05. (cd) *(RUFCD 09)* **GHOSTS**
- Copernicus / Bleary winter / Train tune - Tomcat / Swap your love / St George's day - Cuckoo's nest / The colour of amber / Bonnets of blue - Kennington jig / Hare's maggot - Isaac's maggot / Variation on bacapipes - Greensleeves / Mari Lwyd / Ruskin mill waltz.

CHRIS WOOD

RUF RUF

Jun 05. (cd) *(<RUFCD 10>)* **THE LARK DESCENDING**
- Hard / Albion / Bleary winter / Lord Bateman / One in a million / Our captain calls all hands / John Barleycorn / Walk this world.

Feb 08. (cd) *(RUFCD 11)* **TRESPASSER**
- Summerfield avenue / The cottager's reply / John Ball / England in ribbons / Mad John / Riches of the bold / The lady of York / Come down Jehovah.

Mar 10. (cd) *(RUFCD 12)* **HANDMADE LIFE**
- No honey tongued sonnet / Two widows / Spitfires / My darling's downsized / Asparagus / Hollow point / Caesar / Johnny East / Turtle soup / The grand correction.

- (8-10*) compilations -

Jun 09. (cd) *Navigator; (NAVIGATOR 29)* **ALBION: AN ANTHOLOGY**
- The shouter / I feel a smile coming on / The colour of amber / Albion / Down the wagon way / Summerfield avenue / Lusignac / One in a million / Hares on the mountain / The farmer // Cold haily rainy night / The land: When the land is white with snow / Mad John / The Mari Llwyd / Valtz efter tor lohne / The Taoist tale / John Ball / Copernicus / The history man / Pace egging - Ribatz / Walk this world with music.

ANDY CUTTING

Lane not issued

Aug 10. (cd) *(-)* **ANDY CUTTING** web
- Uphill way / Cuckoo's nest - Old Molly Oxford / CEG / Atherfield / Charlie - Come back! / Edges - Thin waltz / Still hearing you - The resplendent jig / Granton fish bowl / Covered in people / Potato - Theatre / Old light / The abbess.

WOODENBOX WITH A FISTFUL OF FIVERS

Formed in Edinburgh in 2009 by singer/songwriter and guitarist Ali Downer (alias WOODENBOX) with his spaghetti western-referencing Fistful Of Fivers (musicians Nick Dudman, Fraser McKirdy, Jordan Croan, Phil Caldwell and Sam Evans), this band were like a cross between experimentalists The Phantom Band, MUMFORD & SONS and FLEET FOXES – with brass. Following performances at Rockness, Belladrum and the Grassroots stage at Glastonbury, the sextet were signed up by Electric Honey, the indie label of Glasgow's Stow College, and released **HOME AND THE WILD HUNT** {*7} to wide acclaim in the spring of 2010.

Drawing on influences including soulful folk legends The BAND (as though enhanced by Van Morrison's horn section), WOODENBOX and the Fivers carry that weight on scintillating numbers such as 'Heart Attack', the single 'Draw A Line', 'Hang The Noose' and 'Besides The Point'. But why does every fresh-faced Scots act have to sound like Paulo Nutini? *MCS*

Ali Downer - vocals, acoustic guitar, harmonica / **Nick Dudman** - drums, vocals / **Fraser McKirdy** - bass, organ, vocals / **Jordan Croan** - electric guitar, vocals / **Phil Caldwell** - trumpet / **Sam Evans** - sax

UK Electric Honey US not issued

Mar 10. (dl-s) *(-)* DRAW A LINE

Apr 10. (cd) *(EH 1001)* **HOME AND THE WILD HUNT**
- Intro / Life from above / Twisted mile / Fistful of fivers / Draw a line / Immigrant (don't think nothing's not wrong) / Letting go / Besides the point / Nothing to nobody / Hang the noose / Heart attack / My mule.

Roddy WOOMBLE

For several years now the frontman of Scottish indie-rock band Idlewild has been moonlighting as an acoustic-folk star. Born August 13, 1976, in Irvine, Ayrshire, Roddy's formative years were spent in France and the US, and his return to Scotland (Edinburgh, to be precise) led to a friendship with Idlewild buddies Colin Newton and Rod Jones. Formed in 1995, the band have released seven albums, from 1998's 'Captain' to 2009's 'Post Electric Blues', the most successful - 'The Remote Part' (2002) - hitting the UK Top 3.

His love of folk music was presumably always present, but what may have spurred him on to become a fully-fledged folk singer was the occasion when he presented KARINE POLWART with the Horizon Award at the BBC Folk Awards in 2005. He guested on KATE RUSBY's set 'The Girl Who Couldn't Fly' around the same time.

With Idlewild guitarist and co-writer Rod Jones playing unplugged, WOOMBLE unleashed his softer side with **MY SECRET IS MY SILENCE** (2006) {*7}, featuring folk guests RUSBY (returning the favour), JOHN McCUSKER (also on production), singer POLWART, Donald Shaw, ANDY CUTTING, DAVE BURLAND, Ian Carr, David Gow, MICHAEL McGOLDRICK and WOOMBLE's wife Ailidh Lennon, of Sons And Daughters.

Kicking off with the ironically titled ballad 'I Came In From The Mountain', the album (with Roddy sporting a woolly hat and a beard on the sleeve) caused a degree of shock among the rock fraternity, although critically it earned much approval. 'If I Could Name Any Name' and 'Waverley Steps' come off best.

Two years on, and now living on Mull with his family, WOOMBLE teamed up with KRIS DREVER and JOHN McCUSKER for the collaborative set 'Before The Ruin' (2008). The following year Idlewild featured three soft-folk songs on 'Post Electric Blues', namely '(The Night Will) Bring You Back To Life', 'Take Me Back To The Islands' and 'Take Me Back In Time'.

His long-awaited second solo set, **THE IMPOSSIBLE SONG AND OTHER SONGS** {*7} (2011) was another swooning acoustic record of a dozen songs, with a band that comprised multi-instrumentalist Sorren Maclean, bassist Gavin Fox, drummer Gregor Donaldson, guest Rob Hall (on sax) and backing singer Jill O'Sullivan. Check out 'Living As You Always Have' and 'Between The Old Moon'. *MCS*

Roddy Woomble - vocals / with **Rod Jones** - acoustic guitar

UK Pure US 7-10 Music

Jul 06. (cd) *(PURE 021)* *<0011>* **MY SECRET IS MY SILENCE** Jul 07
- I came in from the mountain / As still as I watch your grave / Every line of a long moment / My secret is my silence / Act IV / From the drifter to the drake / If I could name any name / Whiskeyface / Waverley steps / Under my breath / Play me something.

—— In 2007 Roddy returned to Idlewild duties on the set 'Make Another World'.

—— In 2008 he collaborated with KRIS DREVER and JOHN McCUSKER on 'Before The Ruin'.

—— In 2009 a little Celtic-folk crept into Idlewild's set 'Post Electric Blues'

EMI not issued

Mar 11. (cd) *(5099909735026)* **THE IMPOSSIBLE SONG AND OTHER SONGS**
- A new day has begun / Make something out of what it's worth / Work like you can / Tangled wire / Roll along / Hour after hour / Leaving without gold / New frontier / Old town / Living as you always have / Gather the day / Between the old moon.

Greenvoe not issued

Mar 11. (ltd-7") *(GV 002)* ROLL ALONG. / [album version]

The WORKING PARTY (⟹ MAYOR, Simon)

YGDRASSIL

Definitely not to be confused with 1980s Norwegian act Yggdrassil, harmony folk duo YGDRASSIL (note the spelling variation) were formed in the Netherlands in 1992 by singer-songwriters Linde Nijland and Annemarieke Coenders.

Singing in beautiful light voices over a contemporary lo-fi folk backing, the duo drew their inspiration from the American and British revivals of the late 1960s and early 1970s, the closest comparisons being SANDY DENNY and TREES, both of whom YGDRASSIL covered on their 2005 set **EASY SUNRISE** {*7} (the former's 'The North Star Grassman And The Ravens' and the latter's 'The Garden Of Jane Delawney'). Other tracks included NEIL YOUNG's 'Motorcycle Mama' and trad cuts 'Cruel Sister' and 'Nazad'.

There were also many covers on their self-named debut **YGDRASSIL** (1995) {*6} - 'Femme Fatale' (The Velvet Underground), 'A Man Needs A Maid' (NEIL YOUNG), '4 + 20' (Stephen Stills), 'Winter Lady' (LEONARD COHEN) and 'Troy' (Sinead O'Connor).

NICE DAYS UNDER DARKEST SKIES (2002) {*6} included their readings of DYLAN's 'It Takes A Lot To Laugh...' and the trad 'Once I Had A Sweetheart', while LINDE NIJLAND's 2007 effort **WINTERLIEDEREN** {*6} covered 'Follow The Heron' by KARINE POLWART. Four years earlier, Linde had released a SANDY DENNY tribute set.

Working alongside multi-instrumentalist Bert Ridderbos (who performed with YGDRASSIL in their latter days), NIJLAND took a two-year hike to the Himalayan kingdom of Bhutan, where they recorded material for a musical road-movie documentary. *MCS*

Linde Nijland - vocals, acoustic guitar / **Annemarieke Coenders** - vocals, acoustic guitar / + guests

UK VIA — US not issued

1995. (cd) *(9950302)* **YGDRASSIL** [–] Dutch [–]
- Once upon a time / The sea / Midnight forest / Fragile faces / Water / Valeri / Femme fatale / A man needs a maid / Little princess / Broken / 4 + 20 / Strange melody / Winter lady / Troy / Renewal (part 1): Intro - (part 2): Within. *(re-iss. Aug 04 on Pink; PRCD 200312)*

1995. (cd-s) *(9950303)* WATER. / Little Princess [–] Dutch [–]

1997. (cd) *(995045-2)* **PIECES** [–] Dutch [–]
- Pieces / A darkening season / Grey birds / Brown / In a cave / I met a friend today / Blanket / The trumpet player / Last supper / Old rotten longing / Learning anthropology / Liminal / Man of snow / Encounter.

Real Harm - Pink — not issued

Apr 00. (cd) *(PRCD 200004)* **WE VISIT MANY PLACES** [–] Dutch [–]
- The storyteller / In this graceless source / Big whales of oceans deep / Fish / The pillow gets wept upon / She's like a ghost to me / I knew he loved me / Love we won't break / Oh such an evening / This waiting, waiting / We visit many places / The bay of waiting whales / Once I lay asleep / Drunk heart / Never mind the fog / Traveller.

Apr 02. (cd-s) *(PRCS 200213)* ONE MORNING IN THE SPRINGTIME / HOME IS A BUILDING [–] Dutch [–]

Apr 02. (cd) *(PRCD 200202)* **NICE DAYS UNDER DARKEST SKIES** [–] Dutch [–]
- Lover's wings / Snowwhite / Here, right here and I'm looking at the sun / One morning in the springtime / The sailor boy / There are nice days under darkest skies / This here is my mountain / Months gone, passed / The slain man's door / It takes a lot to laugh, it takes a train to cry / Dark the meadows to the north / Once I had a sweetheart / Home is a building / In the middle of a fortress. *(UK-iss. Jun 04; same)*

Rounder — not issued

2005. (cd) *(RRECD 12)* **EASY SUNRISE** [–] Dutch [–]
- The garden of Jane Delawney / For there's a perfect lover / Cruel sister / In a lonesome town / Down in yon green garden / Plenty green fields / This heat / All by a river / Motorcycle mama / The blue sky / Easy sunrise / You know why / Nazad / The north star grassman and the ravens.

2005. (cd-s) *(none)* THE GARDEN OF JANE DELAWNEY [–] Dutch [–]

—— In 2006, American folkie Si Kahn credited YGDRASSIL on his set 'Thanksgiving'

LINDE NIJLAND

VIA — not issued

1998. (cd) *(995054-2)* **VISMAN** [–] Dutch [–]
- Ergens gloei je nog na / Branding / Als je komt / Zee / Gras / Ergens vind ik vast / Bodemvoeten / Visman / Schemertijd / Blauw / Regenvogels / Brandhout / In dit land / Uit.

Real Harm - Pink — not issued

2003. (cd) *(PRCD 200320)* **LINDE NIJLAND sings SANDY DENNY** [–] Dutch [–]
- The sea / Matty Groves / Nottamun town / What is true / Winter winds / Banks of the Nile / This train / Sweet Rosemary / Autopsy / No end / Who knows where the time goes? *(UK-iss. Feb 07 on Rounder Europe; RRECD 16)*

—— next with **Henk Scholte** - vocals + **Bert Ridderbos** - multi

Noordfolk — not issued

Nov 07. (cd; by LINDE NIJLAND, HENK SCHOLTE & BERT RIDDERBOS) *(CD001)* **WINTERLIEDEREN** [festive] [–] Dutch [–]
- The snows they melt the soonest / Drij rozen / Kannel liedje / Haardriederij op scheuvels te Winneweer / Follow the heron / The road to Dundee / Jan mosterd / Deunen en dreumen / Cold, cold world / In de winter / End of the year / Fivelgoer kerstlied / In the winter of my longing.

David Music — not issued

Mar 11. (cd+dvd; by LINDE NIJLAND & BERT RIDDERBOS) *(none)* **A MUSICAL JOURNEY: ON THE ROAD TO BHUTAN** [ ] [–]
- Road to Bhutan / Zaspo janko / Ajde kato / Iranian tune / Improvisation in Qazvin / Waltzing for dreamers / The snow they melt the soonest / Dimming of the day / Chumola dingso / Farewell, farewell / In a lonesome town / Traveller / [DVD tracks].

James YORKSTON

Born in Kingsbarns, Fife in 1971, JAMES YORKSTON began performing at the tender age of eight when he made his own musical entertainment with a friend named Mike. Eclectically influenced by the songwriting talents of artists such as ANNE BRIGGS, DICK GAUGHAN and The Bhundu Boys, James moved to Edinburgh with his girlfriend when they were both 17. He became a vital part of the city's thriving folk music scene, supporting the likes of BERT JANSCH and JOHN MARTYN (MARTYN would later invite him on a 30-date support tour) and playing bass with noisekins Huckleberry.

YORKSTON eventually left the group ("I was going deaf" he says) to pursue his own adventures, and a demo tape was passed through industry hands until it landed on the desk of Radio One DJ John Peel. Peel played tracks from the tape live on air, which led to Bad Jazz issuing the single 'Moving Up Country, Roaring The Gospel' (split with Scottish cult hero Lone Pigeon) to critical acclaim in 2001.

Folky and very hushed, YORKSTON had a lot in common with fellow Scots APPENDIX OUT (ALASDAIR ROBERTS), and his backing band (Faisal Rahman, Reuben Taylor, Doogie Paul, Sun-Li and Holly Taylor) represented the WILL OLDHAM/PALACE factor. A proper signing with indie label Domino led to the seminal 'The Lang Toun' single in 2002 with his band The Athletes, complete with a complementary remix by none other than Kieran Hebden of Four Tet.

'St Patrick' was issued months later as a warm-up for his debut set **MOVING UP COUNTRY** (2002) {*7}, a placid and very emotive introduction. Along with the singles there were a few surprises that defied the notion that YORKSTON was just another Scottish folk singer. The record also featured Fence Collective alumni Lone Pigeon and co-producer KING CREOSOTE/Kenny Anderson.

Tours supporting Lambchop, The Divine Comedy and Gemma Hayes were rounded off with his second album. Produced by Hebden, **JUST BEYOND THE RIVER** (2004) {*7} was another critical success for the group, the fragility and tenderness of the likes of 'Heron', 'Hermitage' and the excellent 'Hotel' offset by trad ballads 'Edward' and 'The Snow It Melts The Soonest'.

Credited to JAMES YORKSTON solo, **THE YEAR OF THE LEOPARD** (2006) {*7} was his warmest offering to date, 'Steady As She Goes' and 'Summer Song' being probably the best songs. **WHEN THE HAAR ROLLS IN** (2008) {*7} was more rooted in tradition, featuring the LAL WATERSON number 'Midnight Feast'. Teaming up with Sheffield collective The BIG EYES FAMILY PLAYERS, **FOLK SONGS** (2009) {*6} was an interesting addition to YORKSTON's CV - this time around he gets to grips with an entire set of sourced material, from 'Hills Of Greenmoor' to 'Little Musgrave' and 'Low Down In The Broom'. *MCS*

JAMES YORKSTON AND THE ATHLETES

James Yorkston - vocals, acoustic guitar, banjo, harmonica (ex-Huckleberry) / **Doogie Paul** - double bass, bouzouki, banjo, vocals / **Faisal Rahman** - lap steel, percussion, harmonium, banjo, vocals / **Reuben Taylor** - accordion, concertina, piano / plus **Sun-Li** - violin / **Holly Taylor** - mandolin, pipes, whistles

UK Bad Jazz — US not issued

Jan 01. (7") *(BEBOP 21)* MOVING UP COUNTRY, ROARING THE GOSPEL. / Are You Coming Home Tonight?

Jan 02. (7") *(BEBOP 33)* ST PATRICK. / (other by LONE PIGEON)

—— **Wendy Chan** - small pipes, violin, vocals; repl. Sun-Li

Domino — Domino

Apr 02. (10") *(RUG 136T)* THE LANG TOUN. / The Lang Toun (Four Tet remix)

May 02. (10") *(RUG 141T)* ST PATRICK. / St Patrick (Vitus mix)
(cd-s+=) *(RUG 141CD)* - Catching eyes / Blue Madonnas.

Jun 02. (cd/lp) *(WIG CD/LP 107)* **MOVING UP COUNTRY**
- In your hands / St Patrick / Sweet Jesus / Tender to the blues / Moving up country, roaring the gospel / Cheating the game / I spy dogs / 6:30 is just way too early / The patience song / I know my love.

Sep 02. (10"/cd-s) *(RUG 145 T/CD)* TENDER TO THE BLUES. / 6:30 (Reuben's string mix) / A Man With My Skills / Hares On The Mountain; Old Maid

Jan 03. (10" ep/cd-ep) *(RUG 149 T/CD)* SWEET JESUS EP
- Sweet Jesus / La magnifica / Blue bleezin' blind drunk (live) / You want to talk.

Nov 03. (cd-ep) *(RUG 168CD)* SOMEPLACE SIMPLE
- Someplace simple / Scarecrow / Rosemary lane / False true love / In Dessexshire as it befel.
(12" ep+=) *(RUG 168T)* - Spittoon.

Sep 04. (cd/lp) *(WIG CD/LP 142)* <37> **JUST BEYOND THE RIVER** — Nov 04
- Heron / Shipwreckers / Surf song / Hermitage / Hotel / This time tomorrow / We flew blind / Banjo #1 / Edward / Banjo #2 / The snow it melts the soonest. *(cd w/bonus cd+=)* - Lowlands away - Don't leave home / Fearsome fairytale lover - Safe havers / Under the moon - Higher Germanie.

Feb 05. (7") *(RUG 193V)* SHIPWRECKERS (remix). / The Route To The Harmonium
(cd-s) *(RUG 193CD)* - ('A') / Heron (demo) / The A of the oboe.

Jun 05. (7") *(RUG 201)* SURF SONG. / Song To The Siren

Oct 05. (m-cd) <HPR 128> **HOOPOE**
- Seven streams / The sea song / Sir Patrick Spens / I awoke / Bleed the crops / Home to the heron.

(above on Hollywood Party)

2006. (cd) *(beryk 1)* **LIVE AT LE POISSON MOUILLE** (live)
- Heron / Moving up country, roaring the gospel / This time tomorrow / Hotel / Cheating the game / Surf song / Someplace simple / Banjo #1 / 6:30 is just way too early / A Friday night in New York / Tender to the blues / I know my love.

(above was self-released - below on Picket Fence)

2007. (m-cd) *(C12CDR)* LANG CAT, CROOKED CAT, SPIDER CAT (instrumentals)
- Pepparmynste / The a of the oboe / The route to the harmonium / Beyond the just river / A lang cat / Banjono.3 / Yorkston Athletic.

JAMES YORKSTON

Sep 06. (7") *(RUG 239)* STEADY AS SHE GOES. / Steady As She Goes (Dolphin Boy remix)

Sep 06. (cd/2x10" lp) *(WIG CD/LP 183)* <123> THE YEAR OF THE LEOPARD — Jan 07
- Summer song / Steady as she goes / The year of the leopard / 5 am / Woozy with cider / I awoke / The Brussels rambler / Orgiva song / Don't let me down / Us late travellers. *(cd w/bonus cd+=)* - acoustic:- 5 am / Organ song / Steady as she goes / Thar she blows / Us late travellers / The year of the leopard.

Mar 07. (7") *(RUG 252)* WOOZY WITH CIDER. / Sunday Jacket

Apr 07. (cd/lp) *(WIG CD/LP 157)* **ROARING THE GOSPEL** (compilation of B-sides)
- A man with my skills / Someplace simple / Blue Madonnas / Seven streams / The hills and the heath / Song to the siren / Moving up country, roaring the gospel / Blue bleezin' blind drunk / Sleep is the jewel / Are you coming home tonight? / The lang toun / La magnifica.

Sep 08. (cd/2x10"lp) *(WIG CD/LP 221)* **WHEN THE HAAR ROLLS IN**
- B'jig / Tortoise regrets hare / Temptation / When the haar rolls in / Queen of Spain / Midnight feast / Would you have me born with wooden eyes / Summer's not the same without you / The capture of the horse / Sail on. *(ltd cd-box+=; WIGCD 221X)* - CD2 covers:- The lang toun (ROZI PLAIN) / In your hands (PICTISH TRAIL & HMS GINAFORE) / St Patrick (DAVID THOMAS BROUGHTON) / Are you coming home tonight? (SUZY MANGION) / Us late travellers (CHARLOTTE GREIG) / Shipwreckers (ADRIAN CROWLEY) / Sweet Jesus (NANCY ELIZABETH) / Tender to the blues (CATHAL COUGHLAN) / Summer song (UNPOC) / Tortoise regrets hare (KING CREOSOTE) / Banjo 2 (JOHN SMITH) / Would you have me born with wooden eyes (ARCHIE BRONSON OUTFIT) / Banjo #1 (DOOGIE PAUL AND THE ATHLETES) / Steady as she goes (VIKING MOSES) / Sail on (JAMES YORKSTON) / Heron (JOHN HOPKINS). // CD3 remixes:- I know my love (JAMES YORKSTON) / Summer song (DOLPHIN BOY) / Woozy with cider (KING BISCUIT TIME) / The river just beyond (ON THE FLY) / The capture of the horse (JAMES YORKSTON) / Orgiva song (ON THE FLY) / The Brussels rambler (REUBEN TAYLOR) / Would you have me born with wooden eyes (CHICKEN FEED) / When the haar rolls in (KING CREOSOTE) / Tortoise regrets hare (DOWN THE TINY STEPS) / The lang toun (FOUR TET) / St Patrick (JAMES YORKSTON).

Aug 09. (cd/lp; as JAMES YORKSTON & THE BIG EYES FAMILY PLAYERS) *(WIG CD/LP 236)* **FOLK SONGS**
- Hills of Greenmoor / Just as the tide was flowing / Martinmas time / Mary Connaught and James O'Donnell / Thorneymoor woods / I went to visit the roses / Pandeirada de entrimo / Little Musgrave / Rufford Park poachers / Sovay / Low down in the broom.

ZANEY JANEY (⟹ MARY JANE)

Pete ZORN

Younger brother of Bill Zorn (a member of the new KINGSTON TRIO), American multi-instrumentalist PETE ZORN (born May 29, 1950, in Somerset, Pennsylvania) has had a chequered career in folk music since his arrival in London in the early 1970s.

He signed up to CBS with husband and wife Gary and Paula Fishbaugh, and their one-off LP **FISHBAUGH FISHBAUGH & ZORN** {*6} (1972) was a record lying somewhere between FRASER & DeBOLT and Joy Of Cooking.

Though relegated to the scenery somewhat, Pete was behind brother-in-law Paul Phillips and his one-hit-wonder Driver 67 on 'Car 67', a surprise UK Top 10 in early 1979. The pair subsequently formed Tax Loss, who released the album 'Hey Mister Record Man').

In 1980/81, Pete was a session man for bluegrass outfit Arizona Smoke Review (a quartet led by brother Bill and PAUL DOWNES), and over the years he has established himself as an integral part of SHOW OF HANDS, the PHIL BEER BAND, the RICHARD THOMPSON band, WAZ! and now (in 2009-2011) STEELEYE SPAN. *MCS*

FISHBAUGH, FISHBAUGH & ZORN

		UK CBS		US not issued
Mar 72.	(7") *(CBS 7905)* LOVE COMES AROUND. / Hint Of A Freeze	☐		⊟
1972.	(lp) *(S 64783)* **FISHBAUGH, FISHBAUGH AND ZORN**	⊟	Dutch	⊟

- Love comes around / Hint of a freeze / I owe her my life / This time around / Door into tomorrow / Leave me alone (let me rock'n'roll) / Rock and roll / Spaced on happy / Children are wandering / Red (became the colour of spring) / Sorrows from your dreams / That sweet sweet music / So deep.

Aug 72.	(7") *(CBS 8163)* EVERYBODY GET OUT OF BED. / Spaced On Happy	☐		⊟
Jan 73.	(7") *(CBS 1331)* NEW YORK. / The Whole World Ought To Rock 'n' Roll	☐		⊟
Jul 73.	(7") *(CBS 1685)* SWEET SWEET MUSIC. / Honey	☐		⊟

ZUMZEAUX

Featuring the double fiddle attack of Dutch-Texan Neti Vaandrager and Anglophile Chris Haigh (alongside Irishman Bernard O'Neill on double bass and Londoner Ashley Drees on cittern), Balkan-type folk act ZUMZEAUX had their brief moment in folk history.

Haigh was probably the better known of the two fiddlers, having played with prog-rockers Speedy Bears and jazz-rockers Inner Ear at a time when punk rock was kicking up a storm, later playing sessions for Alison Moyet, The Quireboys and Michael Ball.

Blending cajun, swing and a pot-pourri of folk, ZUMZEAUX embarked on an "impossibly eclectic" musical journey, taking a Best Busking prize in the Ever Ready BBC Radio talent competition in 1988. A day's session at CBS's Rooftop Studio was overseen by producer ANDREW CRONSHAW, resulting in the independently-released set **WOLF AT YOUR DOOR** (1989) {*6}.

A split soon afterwards led to Vaandrager forming The Companions Of The Rosy Hours (she also split an album, 'Little Red Wagon', with Bart Ramsey in 1999). O'Neill joined the George Bernard Shaw trio. Haigh became a noted session fiddler after a spell in Tziganarama and a solo album, 'Off The Wall', working with the likes of Rolf Harris, James Galway, JENNY BEECHING and Steps. *MCS*

Neti Vaandrager (b. Aug 21 '57, Rotterdam) - fiddle, vocals / **Chris Haigh** (b. Aug 17 '57, Huddersfield) - fiddle, mandolin, vocals / **Bernard O'Neill** (b. Sep 4 '61, Dublin) - double bass, vocals / **Ashley Drees** (b. May 25 '56, Paddington, London, England) - cittern

		UK Pug	US not issued
Aug 89.	(lp) *(PUG 1)* **WOLF AT YOUR DOOR**	☐	⊟

—— split soon afterwards; most members went on to bigger and better things

Section 2
North America

Doris ABRAHAMS

A somewhat overlooked figure on the Greenwich Village scene in the 1960s who was inspired by PETE SEEGER, DAVE VAN RONK and DYLAN), New York-born DORIS ABRAHAMS glided gently into the 1970s as a folkie Laurel Canyon-type solo artist. In the early 1970s MARIA MULDAUR and Ellie Greenberg (billed as The Sleazettes) were her vocal backing group, and they performed together at the Philadelphia Folk Festival in 1972. Doris succumbed to peer pressure with the release of the MOR/country-blues pot-pourri that was her only LP, **LABOR OF LOVE** (1976) {*6}.

She was supported on the occasional concert by Greenberg, fiddler Larry Packer, guitarist Allen Friedman and bassist Fred Holman, but only the first two made it on to a packed session list that also contained in-house songsmith Pat Alger and ARTIE TRAUM. JESSE COLIN YOUNG's 'Sunlight', Mickey Newbury's 'Are My Thoughts With You' and Cole Porter's 'Let's Do It' gave the record its laidback-to-ragtime diversity. Whatever happened to Doris? *MCS*

Doris Abrahams - vocals / (with session people)

US Philo / UK not issued

1976. (lp) *<PH 1034>* **LABOR OF LOVE**
- Dance the night away / Hurricane in my heart / See saw / I'll be your old lady / Sunlight / Last unicorn / Are my thoughts with you / Ridin' / Let's do it / It's about time. *<cd-iss. 2009 on Big Pink (Korea); 40>*

—— totally retired from the music business

Ed ALKALAY

Blending folk, country, blues and just about everything under the roots umbrella, singer-songwriter ED ALKALAY (born 1966 in Mountainside, New Jersey) was raised in New York City and studied English literature and philosophy.

From covers bands to playing solo resident turns at the famous Fast Folk Café (run by the Fast Folk magazine), his poignant songs such as 'I Never Rode A Freight Train' first came to light on the 'New Faces In NYC' various-artists set. Almost immediately, Ed's debut album **DIAMOND CHAIN** (1996) {*6} began to circulate from friends and fans to parts of the media and radio, winning him critical acclaim.

With a fresh batch of songs ready to perform, Ed moved to Washington D.C. and performed either solo, alongside Jack Gregori, or in his roots-rock act Liquid Poodle. 2001 was a transitional year for Ed as he won a string of lyric and songwriting contests, mainly for 'A Two-Faced Lady And A Two-Timin' Man', 'Texas' and the title track from his long-awaited second set **TURNING DORIAN GRAY** (2001) {*6}. Comprising self-penned narratives except for trad tune 'Rovin' Gambler', his unclassifiable sound was a plus point for the critics, but the album went unnoticed in the fickle world of the major-label record industry.

Currently living with his family in the White Mountain district of northern New Hampshire, in 2009 ALKALAY delivered his third album **I HATE YOU** {*6}, a record combining wit and humour ('That Girl's Gonna Make A Woman Out Of Me'), the blues ('One More Time'), post-grunge ('To Fit Me') and his C&W gem 'Texas'. *MCS*

Ed Alkalay - vocals, acoustic guitar, banjo (+ session people)

US private / UK not issued

Jan 96. (cd) *<none>* **DIAMOND CHAIN**
- Straight walkin' man / I never rode a freight train / Sarah's troubled mind / Diamond chain / One more tune / The fountain and the rain / Understandably confused / Sampson / Takin' chances / The cuckoo / Central Park / Backdoor man / Breezes / It / Gonna be a long time.

Orchard / not issued

Nov 01. (cd) *<801687>* **TURNING DORIAN GRAY**
- One last minute / A better version of me / Turning Dorian Gray / Marie / With the Devil in my band / A hundred years from now / A quiet ticking / Rovin' gambler / The deal's gone down / The blind man / A two- faced lady and a two-timin' man / A dozen roses.

—— Ed subsequently joined roots act Liquid Poodle

Ed Alkalay / not issued

Jan 09. (cd) *<none>* **I HATE YOU**
- Another man's crown / You / I hate you / Lumberjack / Surrounded by alone / Night bound train / Grumble / Texas / Bob Jones / One more time / That girl's gonna make a woman out of me / Speed / To fit me.

Lesser Gonzalez ALVAREZ

Known primarily for his artwork rather than his indie-folk music (his visuals have graced exhibits in Sao Paulo, Brazil), Lesser's horizontal acoustics began to take shape when he discovered a musical kinship with John Lennon, Syd Barrett and DONOVAN. He cut his teeth in the short-lived Cache Cache and The Tall Grass, although no recordings were issued.

Based in Baltimore, Maryland due to academic pursuits at the local Institute of Art, LESSER GONZALEZ ALVAREZ was actually born (1983) in Havana, Cuba, his music finally finding an outlet at the small Washington D.C. label Carpark. 2008's flighty folk debut **WHY IS BEAR BILLOWING?** {*8} and one track in particular, 'Pinecone Eyes', recall indie star Mark Kozelek (of Red House Painters), while 'A Twist In The Sky' and 'A Magic' have a DONOVAN hallmark stamped all over them. The most interesting tracks, however, are his whimsical musical reading of Edward Lear's poem 'The Owl And The Pussycat', the Barrett-friendly 'All With Golden Locks' and the Bolanesque 'The Letter B'. We await a second instalment from a man no lesser than most of today's rising stars. Do we have to start a fan club? *MCS*

Lesser Gonzalez Alvarez - vocals, acoustic guitar

US Carpark / UK Carpark

Sep 08. (cd) *<(CAK 44)>* **WHY IS BEAR BILLOWING?**
- A magic / All with golden locks / Pinecone eyes / A twist in the sky / Narwhal horn / Little island / Love for longer / The letter B / Build a tiny hill / The owl and the pussycat / Mostly a friend.

AMPS FOR CHRIST

How mindblowing could things could get if you lived in a mid-terraced house between two parties of extreme noise terrorists and a hippie Celtic/traditional music fan? The answer is the AMPS FOR CHRIST project - think FUGS and The INCREDIBLE STRING BAND in performance with drone-king John Cage.

Formed in the mid-1990s in Claremont, California by former Man Is A Bastard frontman Henry Barnes and a loose group including Enid Snarb, Joel Connell, Tara Tiki Tavi and others, AFC were the epitome of experimental waveforms with global world-folk music as their catalyst. It's impossible to describe Barnes's uber-alternative approach to his distinctive soundscapes, and many purist fans of the genre might be up in arms at the suggestion that the AMPS were even folk music. However, albums such as debut **THE PLAINS OF ALLUVIAL** (1995) {*4} and **THORNY PATH** (1997) {*4} stretched the concept beyond the realms of strangeness; screeching electronic bagpipe sounds might not be everybody's cup of tea.

Ditto **THE BEGGARS GARDEN** (1997) {*5}, with the exception of 'Too Different', several short takes and the eight-minute Eastern ditty 'Egg Mountain'. Shrimper Records was also behind the double-disc **ELECTROSPHERE** (1999) {*6}. It was scary at first, but on closer inspection the sourced 'Blackwaterside' gets a rare successful AMPS FOR CHRIST arrangement.

Branching out somewhat without leaving their maniacal roots, **THE OAK IN THE ASHES** (2001) {*7} dispelled all apprehensions. The most uplifting of their efforts were two pieces of 'Scotland The Brave', the finger-pickingly Kentucky-fried 'Serbia' and the Mike Oldfieldesque 'She Saw'. The truckstop-friendly nine-minute closing excursion 'Prepared Hammond For Five Hands' takes the concept once again far beyond purist boundaries.

Now signed to 5 Rue Christine, Barnes's room for improvement and improvisation expanded into two listenable sets, **THE PEOPLE AT LARGE** (2004) {*7} – a protest album – and **EVERY ELEVEN SECONDS** (2006) {*6}, the latter featuring a few re-adaptations of earlier tracks including 'Cock O' The North' and 'Scotland The Brave'. And then, zero. Had the Devil finally found all the best tunes? *MCS*

Henry Barnes - vocals, instruments (incl. electric sitar)

US Shrimper / UK Shrimper

1995. (ltd-c) <*SHR 82*> **THE PLAINS OF ALLUVIAL** ☐ ⊟
- Bandwell land / Healing feeling / Enid's jig / River land / The hills of Marshall / Nick's Café Trevi / Bonnie Charlie / Moderna / Canyon of Palmer / Enid's march / Samhrad Samhrad / Sitron / Amazing grace / Oscillin / Logarhythem / Pulse Hammond / Prepared Hammond I / Comfort zone / Harmonic distortion in D minor / Prepared Hammond II / Olive / Chromium molybdinium.

Apr 97. (ltd; lp/cd) <*(VMFM 35/+CD)*> **THORNY PATH** ☐ Jun 97 ☐
- Cock of the worth / A very mode-ular song / Whistletron / Native soil / Inja / Country core / Patriots / National war / Folkcore / Millennium / Global warming / Prepared Teac / Prepared Conn in D minor / Heathkit / Pain of the fire / Carrickfergus / Lynn Ann's flower / Raspberry box / Eleven twelfths / Hamtar / Old Paint / Wolffskill Falls / Time is the coupler.

(above issued on Vermiform, below on Westside Audio)

1997. (d-7" ep) <*ws 15*> SECRET OF THE ALMOST STRAIGHT LINE ☐ ⊟
- March to winter / Pure Hammond / The sweet sunny west / 1-2 stomp / The southern mountains of California / Raga for midnight.

—— added **Joel Connell** - drums, percussion, tabla / **Enid Snarb** - electronics

Aug 97. (cd; as AMPS FOR CHRIST AND TWO AMBIGUOUS FIGURES) <*(SHR 87)*> **THE BEGGARS GARDEN** ☐ Jun 97 ☐
- 6sn7 pipes / Not of the world / Tungsten aire / Too different / McFarlands' lute / Still dreaming / Three part intention / Packing house march / Sink or swim / Esau's mandolin / Nick's Café Trevi / Healing feeling / Enid's jig / Canyon of Palmer / Thatcher Hall blues / The lamb of God / Laverne dream / Egg mountain / Spider on statue of Buddha / Grove House revisited / Indigo rain / Banwell land revisited / Electron wind 1 / Electron wind 2 / Electric moderna / Three guitars / Bakelite thump / Enid's march / Prepared Hammonds / Montana storm / Juicer in F major / Reverse arpeggios in C / Tubes driven to cut off / The glass man.

1998. (ltd-cd) <*none*> **SONGS FROM MT. ION** ⊟ ⊟
- Live at Twin Palms I ('Wyoming') / Live at Twin Palms II / Bouzouki mountain / Interruptor with pipes / Broad Center live I / Broad Center live II / Edward (trad. Child #13) / Thug III / Live on KSPC / Japeth's fire dream / Live at the Spanish Kitchen studio / The tumbler room song / Broad Center live III / Broad Center IV ('Son of man') / Broad Center live V ('Modulatory') / Ancient Tokarians.

(above issued on Total Annihilation)

—— added **Tara Tavi** - vocals

Feb 99. (cd) <*(VMFM 51)*> **CIRCUITS** ☐ ☐
- Sweet William and Lady Margret / Cities of refuge / Janitor of lunacy / The grey funnel line / Colors / The blacksmith / Edward / Wishful thinking / Memorial immemorial / Eyes that shine / Detrimental anesthesia / The wife of Usher's Well / Over the hills of Marshall / Echo location / Chinese fascination with westerns / Moon dog / Esau's blessing / The cruel sister / Snap dragons.

(above issued on Vermiform)

Oct 99. (d-cd) <*(SHR 109)*> **ELECTROSPHERE** ☐ ☐
- Forward pipes / Blackwaterside / Hammond HC / Eucalyptus prayer / Butterfly / Coppertar / Edward / Cold as stone / Single E-133 / Peaceful / King of nothing / Isle of Man / Dirrish / The lakes of Pontchartrain / Reversed pipes / Lament for Omri (Ka) / Clean pipes / Haydn in D / Fugue in D minor I // Hiz AFC oscillator thru AM / 1809 / Morning time / Love is teasin' / Omkanda / Fugue in D minor II / Snap dragons / Tryin' to escape / Warehouse blues / Bouzouki for river / Y2k march / Shrimp noise / The fig tree / Prepared Conn II / Ebp low pipes / Interruptor beat song / Double E-133 / 10,000 miles / This isn't a rebel song / Son of man.

—— added guest **Charlie White** - voice/poetry

Oct 01. (cd) <*(SHR 127CD)*> **THE OAK IN THE ASHES** ☐ Oct 02 ☐
- She's with me / Give - Leave / Scotland the brave - Ditches / Fractured / Cricket / Nese 1 / Little angel / My blood has a name / Serbia / She saw / Thodse thing / Painter / Tongue is a verb / Mission accomplished / Cherry tree carol / Mother's night / Nese 2 / Scotland the brave - Cheeks / Bishop / The race / As I walked out / String theory / Prepared Hammond for five hands.

Empty Chairs / not issued

2001. (7"ep; shared) *(ETCH 4)* **w/ 1-EYED CYCLOPS** ⊟ Italy ⊟
- [1-Eyed Cyclops side] // Oh Amerigo / Bouzouki - Noise in F#.

Helicopter - Kill Frank Lentini / not issued

Sep 03. (cd-ep; shared) <*H23 - KFLR 09*> **w/ BASTARD NOISE** ☐ ⊟
- Devine intervention / 78911 891112 / Imitation / The bus ride / Bonnie Greenwoodside // [Bastard Noise side].

5 Rue Christine / 5 Rue Christine

Feb 04. (cd) <*(GER 032CD)*> **THE PEOPLE AT LARGE** ☐ ☐
- Tsaress / Use use use / Old palm tree / Prince Charlie Stuart / Freddie the mockingbird / Banjo hymn / AFC tower song / Tarsit / Bug / Midianite prelude / Old lang syne - Tube / Branches / Evening / Gold on Mars / Claremont raga / Been to the rock? / Enid's rant / The Morlough shore / Flower and leaves / Memorial immemorial (revisited) / Tethered ball / Old lang syne - Transistor / Firecube.

Jun 06. (cd) <*(GER 068CD)*> **EVERY ELEVEN SECONDS** ☐ ☐
- Augmented - Demented / Cock o' the north / Out of the moon (slight return) / Thompson Hunter / Violated / El corazon de San Vicente / I hate this dumpster / Shiploaf / Scotland the brave / Proof man / The crossing / Chorus / Sweet dove / W I B / Monkeys gone wild.

—— Barnes was last heard on Whitman's LP, 'White Sunrise' (2008), on Folktale

ANIMAL COLLECTIVE [folk part]

Evolving from a noise-driven alt-rock outfit in the early 2000s and into a psychedelic freak-folk affair, Baltimore-based ANIMAL COLLECTIVE (David Portner, alias Avey Tare; Noah Lennox, alias Panda Bear; Josh Dibb, alias Deakin; and Brian Weitz, alias Geologist) have taken the Olivia Tremor Control-meets-Flaming Lips method to new extremes.

Their journey from the experimental 'Spirit They're Gone, Spirit They've Vanished' (2000) and others of this era such as 'Here Comes The Indian' (2003) was in no way related to folk (well, maybe at a push), but ANIMAL COLLECTIVE's time at English indie imprint Fat Cat produced the odd folk insemination.

SUNG TONGS (2004) {*7} was as close as the quirky quartet got to sounding like The Beach Boys, The HOLY MODAL ROUNDERS and The INCREDIBLE STRING BAND. From the excellent short take of 'Who Could Win A Rabbit' to 'Mouth Wooded Her' and 'Good Lovin' Outside' (but forget the 12-minute Floydean 'Visiting Friends'), the album is mind-blowing to the nth degree. Awash with autoharps and the voice of VASHTI BUNYAN, ANIMAL COLLECTIVE unleashed the EP 'Prospect Hummer' in 2005, a record that offered up four primal folk numbers from the brilliant 'It's You' to the whimsical 'I Remember Learning How To Drive'.

For the group's subsequent releases, from 2005's 'Feels' (featuring the XTC-like 'Grass' and 'The Purple Bottle') to the US Top 20 brilliance of 2009's 'Merriweather Post Pavilion' (via 2007's 'Strawberry Jam'), ANIMAL COLLECTIVE dipped their feet into the big musical jungle, a million miles away from the ethos of folk.

PANDA BEAR might well have bought the voices of the Beach Boys if they'd been for sale, but his take on experimental acid folk (think FLEET FOXES or Spiritualized) was rather out-there. While his US 2011 set **TOMBOY** {*7} tinkered only minimally with folk music and hit the US Top 30 ('You Can Count On Me' is a modern-day classic), his 2004 mini-effort for Paw Tracks, **YOUNG PRAYER** {*6}, was a touch ambiguous, with nothing identifiable among its nine untitled tracks. **PERSON PITCH** (2007) {*7} was indie industrial on a grandiose scale. *MCS*

- part-discography only -

Avey Tare (b. David Michael Portner, Apr 24 '79) - vocals, guitar, piano, synths, percussion / **Panda Bear** (b. Noah Lennox, Jul 17 '78) - vocals, piano, drums, guitar, samplers / **Deakin** (b. Josh Dibb) - guitar, vocals / **Geologist** (b. Brian Ross Weitz, Mar 26 '79) - electronics, samplers

US Fat Cat / UK Fat Cat

Jun 04. (cd/d-lp) <*(FAT-SP 08/+LP)*> **SUNG TONGS** ☐ May 04 ☐
- Leaf house / Who could win a rabbit / The softest voice / Winters love / Kids on holiday / Sweet road / Visiting friends / College / We tigers / Mouth wooed her / Good lovin' outside / Whaddit I done.

—— next featured **Vashti Bunyan** - vocals

May 05. (cd-ep; as AC) *(FAT-SP 09)* PROSPECT HUMMER ⊟ ☐
- It's you / Prospect hummer / Baleen sample / I remember learning how to dive.
the group reverted to their original avant-pop agenda

PANDA BEAR

aka **Noah Lennox** - vocals and instrumentation [only 2004–2007 really folk]

his first release was an eponymous experimental-rock CD on Soccer Star in 1999

		Paw Tracks	Paw Tracks
Sep 04.	(m-cd) <*(PAW 2CD)*> **YOUNG PRAYER**		
	- [untitled tracks 1-9].		
2005.	(cd-s/7") <*UUAR 006/+EP*> I'M NOT. / Comfy In Nautica		-
(above issued on U United Acoustic Recordings)			
Jan 07.	(cd-ep) <*(PAW 13CD)*> CARROTS / KKKKK		
Feb 07.	(12") *(12FAT 059)* BRO'S. / Bro's [terrestrial tones mix]	-	
(above issued on Fat Cat)			
Mar 07.	(cd/d-lp) <*(PAW 14 CD/LP)*> **PERSON PITCH**		
	- Comfy in Nautica / Take pills / Bro's / I'm not / Good girl - Carrots / Search for delicious / Ponytail.		
Jul 07.	(ltd-7") <*PAW 17*> TAKE PILLS. / Bonfire Of The Vanities		-
Jul 10.	(ltd-7") <*PAW 33*> TOMBOY. / Slow Motion		-
(above issued on Domino, below issued on Fat Cat)			
Oct 10.	(ltd-7") <*DNO 952*> *(RUG 375SI)* YOU CAN COUNT ON ME. / Alsatian Dog		
Dec 10.	(ltd-7") *(7FAT 94)* LAST NIGHT AT THE JETTY. / Drone	-	
Apr 11.	(cd/clear-lp) <(PAW 36 CD/LP)> **TOMBOY**	29	62
	- You can't count on me / Tomboy / Slow motion / Surfers hymn / Last night at the jetty / Drone / Alsatian darn / Scheherazade / Friendship bracelet / Afterburner / Benfica.		

APOTHECARY HYMNS

APOTHECARY HYMNS was the brainchild of singer-songwriter and multi-instrumentalist Alex Stimmel, a former bass player with country-inflected alt-rockers The Court And Spark whose day job was teaching dysfunctional and autistic children from the Bushwick, Brooklyn area.

With a distinct Syd Barrett/ Spirit/ ESPERS psych-folk feel, the act recreated west-coast America at the turn of the 1970s on their one and only album, **TROWEL AND ERA** (2005) {*7}. One of the tracks, 'The Human Abstract', took poetry by William Blake for its lyrics, while others such as 'The Marigold', 'Abandoned Factories' and '(A Sailor Song)' were blissful in their electric underground-folk fuzz. They kept a low profile for a while thereafter, expanded into a full-blown live trio from June 2007, adding bassist Rob Fellman and drummer Aaron Nixon. *MCS*

Alex Stimmel - vocals, multi

		US Jugendstil	UK not issued
Sep 04.	(ltd-7") <*JSI-77*> HALF OF WHAT IS SEEN. / The Marigold		-
		Locust	not issued
Apr 05.	(cd/lime-lp) <*L 69*> **TROWEL AND ERA**		-
	- Abandoned factories / The father / The marigold / The human abstract / Watching the bay / (A sailor song) / The conclusion, in which nothing is concluded / All true love is happiness / In the icy beds. *(UK-iss. Dec 08; same as US)*		

—— added **Rob Fellman** - bass / **Aaron Nixon** - drums

Scott APPEL

Many solo artists have copied or cloned the sound of the late, great British folk icon NICK DRAKE, but very few have been endorsed by DRAKE's parents Rodney and Molly, who gave SCOTT APPEL access to their son's private recordings.

Born March 3, 1954 in Brooklyn, New York, but raised in northern New Jersey, singer and guitarist APPEL, whose early influences included BERT JANSCH and DAVEY GRAHAM, left Boston's Berklee School of Music in the early 1970s, finding part-time night work performing anywhere he could (in a Led Zeppelin tribute act, among other things) and teaching guitar by day.

With technical expertise that stretched to playing blacktop bottleneck guitar, APPEL issued his Celtic-folk/swing debut **GLASSFINGER** (1985) {*6} for California-based label Kicking Mule. With tracks like 'Haste To The Wedding', GORDON LIGHTFOOT's 'If You Could Read My Mind' and the sombre 'Meshes Of The Afternoon' (inspired by a cult Maya Deren film) on offer, the LP received decent reviews. It awaits a CD release.

After listening to NICK DRAKE's import collection 'Fruit Tree', the bearded Scott took it on himself to replicate the late singer's odd tunings and stylings. **NINE OF SWORDS** {*7} was released in 1989, a truly inspirational set breathing life into Drake's legacy while painting his own funereal landscapes. Exhuming DRAKE's old attic recordings such as 'Bird Flew By', 'Blossom', 'Our Season', 'Place To Be', 'Parasite' and the collaborative mix-and-match 'Far Leys', APPEL champions and celebrates the tortured genius's life. Apart from a traditional working of 'Spencer The Rover' and Phil Colclough's 'Song For Ireland', the rest of the LP was down to APPEL himself (with guest session musicians Chris McNally, Brian Cantazaro, Bill Greenberg, Tim Solook and Don Sternecker). Melancholy and moody but uplifting and joyous, the talented guitarist shone in his own right with 'Blur', 'Nearby', ''Silent Snow', 'Thanatopsis' and the title track.

APPEL later recorded two songs, 'From The Morning' and 'Hazey Jane') on the NICK DRAKE tribute set 'Brittle Days' (1992), issued on Imaginary Records. His third and best set, **PARHELION** (1998) {*8} covered three DRAKE tracks, 'Brittle Days', 'Hazey Jane' and 'Road' alongside Steve Miller's 'Love's Riddle', FAIRPORT CONVENTION's 'Walk Awhile' and Moby Grape's '8.05', the listener was brought back to the present day with Scott's own masterpieces 'Let All The Clocks Stop', 'Winter Light' and 'Just Lately'.

Tragically, on March 11, 2003, only days after his 49th birthday, SCOTT T. APPEL succumbed to the heart disease that had blighted and curtailed his sparse but outstanding musical career. *MCS*

Scott Appel - vocals, guitars / with session people

		US Kicking Mule	UK not issued
1985.	(lp/c) <*KM/+C 180*> **GLASSFINGER**		-
	- Intro / Slipped away / Beauty in tears - Killakee House - Haste to the wedding / At dusk - Bridge / Queer street - Bridge / Talk is circular / If you could read my mind / Just lately / Glassfinger / Meshes of the afternoon / Sun - Bridge / Rent party / When face gets very pale / Leaving.		
Aug 89.	(lp/c/cd) <*KM/+C/CD 343*> **NINE OF SWORDS**		-
	- Bird flew by / Somnus / Blur / Nearly - Far leys / Blossom / Our season / Nine of swords / Place to be / Thanatopsis / Parasite / Spencer the rover / Silent snow / Song for Ireland. *<cd re-iss. Oct 95 on Schoolkids; SKR 1521>*		
		One Man Clapping	not issued
Aug 98.	(cd; as SCOTT APPEL 3) <*OMC 0015*> **PARHELION**		-
	- Let all the clocks stop / Brittle days (parts I, II and III) / Just lately / Hazey Jane / Hideaway - Sunwise turn / Stills / Road / Winterlight / From the morning / Meshes of the afternoon / Love's riddle / Walk awhile / Secret snow / 8:05.		

—— after bouts of ill-health, APPEL died in March 2003

ARBOREA

Named after an old town in Sardinia, but formed in Maine in 2005 by Buck Curran and his singer wife Shanti, ARBOREA were psych-folk's answer to The HANDSOME FAMILY – spooky, but without the stage-prop animals or the geek guise.

Taking their inspiration from old-time woodspeople trying to escape from the Great Depression, their shimmering harmonies and ethereal vocals gained exposure with the release of a mini-set, **WAYFARING SUMMER** (2006) {*7}. Titles such as 'River And Rapids', 'Alligator' and 'Shagg Pond Revival' showed clearly where they were coming from.

On the back of some interesting gigs abroad (the Green Man Festival in Wales and the Tanned Tin Festival in Spain), their second set, **ARBOREA** (2008) {*7}, sold out by word of mouth in its first couple of months on release. Augmented by cellist Helena Espvall (of ESPERS), it no doubt struck a chord with her freak-folk family of fans. Shanti's cool drawl and Buck's Cooderesque finger-pickin' were prominent on the likes of 'Black Mountain Road', 'Seadrift' and 'Red Bird', while Buck sings 'Dark Horse' and plays an instrumental, 'Leaves Among The Ruins'. **HOUSE OF STICKS** (2009) {*7} was a delightful compilation of their rare-as-hen's-teeth singles.

Released by Oregon-based label Strange Attractors Audio House, **RED PLANET** (2011) {*6} carried on ARBOREA's spine-chilling backwoods-to-basics formula with Helena still on board. Their dustbowl take on trad tune 'Black Is The Colour' sets the template for their avant-folk style, and there's a cover of TIM BUCKLEY's 'Phantasmagoria In Two' *MCS*

Shanti Curran - vocals, banjo, banjammer, harmonium, ukulele, fiddle, hammered dulcimer / **Buck Curran** - vocals, guitars (+ slide), fiddle

		US Summer Street	UK not issued
Nov 06.	(ltd; m-cd) <*001*> **WAYFARING SUMMER**		-
	- Wayfaring summer / River and rapids / Wake up, little sparrow / Alligator / Shagg pond revival / On to the shore / Beirut / Rain / Dance, sing, fight / Coda.		

Fire Museum not issued

Apr 08. (ltd; cd) *<FM 17>* **ARBOREA**
- Forewarned / Red bird / Ides of March / Seadrift / Black mountain road / Dark horse / Leaves among the ruins / Dark is the night (in the wind) / Swan / Echo of hooves / Plains of Macedonia.

Borne-Acuarela not issued

Feb 09. (cd) *(002)* **HOUSE OF STICKS** [collection] Spain
- River and rapids / Beirut / Alligator / Dance, sing, fight / Look down fair moon / House of sticks / On to the shore / In the tall grass.

Strange Attractors Audio House not issued

May 11. (cd/lp) *<SAAH 067 CD/LP>* **RED PLANET**
- The fossil sea / Black is the colour / Phantasmagoria in two / Spain / Careless love / Red planet / Wolves / Song for Obol / Arms and horses / A little time. *(hidden +=)- Torchbearer.*

ARROWWOOD

On the basis of only one and a half albums, ARROWWOOD - basically a vehicle for pastel-folk whisperer Chelsea Robb and multi-instrumentalist Pythagamus of NOVEMTHREE - are worthy entries in the world of wyrd-folk, escaped from the faerie-filled forests of Washington and the Little Somebody label.

Backed by Lindsay Hoffman, Jaimie Truva and Josh Lovejoy on an array of instruments, their debut, **HEMLOCK AND SPINDLE FLOWER** (2006) {*6}, should scare the life out of purist folk punters with its 'Wicker Man'/ LARKIN GRIMM soundscapes on 'Blackbird' 'In Ruin' and 'The Mourners' Song'. The shared mini-set **ARROWWOOD / NOVEMTHREE** (2007) {*6} is equally hard to obtain, although thankfully there was more than a limited edition of 99 copies. The track 'Funeral Lullaby' just about describes what's in store - you have been warned. *MCS*

Chelsea Robb - vocals, bouzouki, zither, harp, keyboards, percussion, etc / with **Pythagumus** - multi-instruments / + other guests

US Little Somebody UK not issued

Jan 06. (ltd-cd-r) *<LSR 1>* **HEMLOCK AND SPINDLE FLOWER**
- In ruin / Treasure ghost / From the branch of a hemlock tree / Blackbird / Buried / I was born in the forest / Moths / All things rise / Sub umbra alarum / Mount Tabor dream maze / Ringsel / Mountain water / Clumsy dance. *<also on Circumstantial; CIR 05>*

Dec 07. (ltd-d-m-cd-r) *<LSR 8>* **ARROWWOOD // Novemthree**
- Hawthorne wheel / Funeral lullaby / Bells in an old forest / With my heart in my head like one eye / Rising hill / Hockwold / Winged sirens / Mountain water reprise // [NOVEMTHREE cd tracks].

B

Noa BABAYOF

Born in Israel (probably in the mid-1980s), singer-songwriter NOA BABAYOF took inspiration from such 1960s greats as BAEZ, MITCHELL and BUNYAN. A graduate of the Rimon School of Jazz and Contemporary Music, English-speaking Noa was discovered in Philadelphia by ESPERS leader Greg Weeks. Her fragile, ethereal delivery in the JUDY COLLINS/ Hope Sandoval style, with lush string arrangements, first came to light on her debut set, **FROM A WINDOW TO A WALL** (2007) {*7}. Greg's own Language Of Stone label issued it internationally the following year.

With a guest list that included Weeks, FERN KNIGHT's Margaret Wienk (on cello), session player Jesse Sparhawk (on harp and mandolin) and Katt Hernandez (on violin), the album's strengths lie in the melancholy touches on 'A Song For Me', 'At Your Death' and 'This Year's Parade'. Short and sweet, her a cappella 'Them That Are Writing These Songs' is the finale. A second batch should hopefully be along soon. *MCS*

Noa Babayof - vocals, acoustic guitar / with session guests

US Anova — UK not issued

Nov 07. (cd) *(004)* **FROM A WINDOW TO A WALL** [–] Israel [–]
- Prelude / A song for me / Indian queen / Marching band / Loving you / One song / At your death / Cotton strings / Midtown fair / This year's parade / Before sleep / Them that are writing these songs. *<US/UK-iss. Jun/Jul 08 on Language Of Stone; LOS-008)>*

Kathleen BAIRD / TRAVELING BELL (⟹ SPIRES THAT IN THE SUNSET RISE)

Meg BAIRD (⟹ ESPERS)

Duck BAKER

Born Richard Royal Baker IV, July 30, 1949 in Washington, D.C, BAKER acquired the nickname of Duck while growing up in Florida and Richmond. Although he treads deeply in jazz, ragtime, gospel and blues, the finger-picking guitarist also took inspiration from his Celtic ancestry and from traditional-folk music sourced from the Appalachian mountains.

His move to San Francisco in the early 1970s saw Duck get his first break on STEFAN GROSSMAN's Kicking Mule label. Albums from that era were **THERE'S SOMETHING FOR EVERYONE IN AMERICA** (1976) {*5}, **WHEN YOU WORE A TULIP** (1977) {*5}, **THE KING OF BONGO BONG** (1977) {*6}, **THE ART OF FINGERSTYLE JAZZ GUITAR** (1979) {*7} and his "Irish, Scottish English fiddle tunes for The Finger-picking Guitarist", **THE KID ON THE MOUNTAIN** (1980) {*7}. For several years between 1978 and 1987 he toured and lived in Europe, although his flow of work had subsided somewhat; there was a German-only release, **UNDER YOUR HEART** (1985) {*6}.

Inspired as much by Scott Joplin, Count Basie and The Ink Spots (he toured with the latter two acts during this period) as by LEO KOTTKE and GROSSMAN, Duck wove his magnetic and transcendental finger-picking technique in and out of a potpourri of exacting albums with Eugene Chadbourne and John Zorn in New York City and Henry Kaiser and Bruce Ackley in San Francisco.

The early 1990s delivered a number of collaborations, one self-penned set crediting JOHN RENBOURN on **A THOUSAND WORDS** (1992) {*6}, featuring renditions of Charles Mingus's 'Mr. Jellyroll Soul', Pat Kirtley's 'B. Rod's Rag' and DAVEY GRAHAM's 'Lashta's Room'. With bluegrass touring partner Molly Andrews he recorded **AMERICAN TRADITIONAL** (1993) {*6} and **THE MOVING BUSINESS** (1994) {*5}.

Still going strong in all traditional departments, Duck's most revered albums are probably 1993's **OPENING THE EYES OF LOVE** {*7}, a mixture of jazz, classical and Celtic styles (featuring DAVEY GRAHAM's 'Forty Ton Parachute' and a couple from Thelonious Monk), and 2000's Irish/Celtic album **MY HEART BELONGS TO JENNY** {*6}. Duck's most recent folk-orientated set was **The ROOTS AND BRANCHES of AMERICAN MUSIC** (2009) {*6}. *MCS*

Duck Baker - acoustic guitar, (some) vocals

US Sonet - Kicking Mule — UK Sonet - Kicking Mule

Apr 76. (lp) *<(SNKF 116)>* **THERE'S SOMETHING FOR EVERYONE IN AMERICA** [ ] [ ]
- The Jackson stomp / Mission Street blues / Allegheny County / Matty Powell / Zebra blues / The Wolverines / Melancholy baby *[cd track 8]* / Take me out to the ball game - America *[cd 15]* / Temperance reel *[cd 16]* / The pineapple rag *[cd 11]* / Hick's farewell *[cd 17]* / Doctor Jazz *[cd 14]* / The old folks' polka *[cd 12]* / There'll be a happy meeting *[cd 13]* / The wreck of Old 97 *[cd 10]*. *<cd-iss. Jun 08 on Stefan Grossman's Guitar Workshop+=; SGGW 140>* - Rapid transit blues *[cd 7]* / *[CD-ROM track]*.

Feb 77. (lp) *<(SNKF 123)>* **WHEN YOU WORE A TULIP** [ ] [ ]
- You took advantage of me / Grace Street / Was / Liza (all the clouds'll roll away) / Boys from Blue Hill / (Back home again in) Indiana / Rapid transit blues / Two cats with new shoes / Angeline the baker / Plymouth rock / Honeysuckle rose / Cousin / Lazy river / Drunken wagoner / When you wore a tulip / Thou swell.

Nov 77. (lp) *<(SNKF 137)>* **THE KING OF BONGO BONG** [ ] Jan78 [ ]
- New righteous blues / Crazy rhythm / I found a new baby / No love / There'll be some changes made / See you in my dreams / I ain't got nobody / Mama's getting younger / Papa's getting older each day / Immaculate conception rag / River blues / A chicken ain't nothin' but a bird / King of the Bongo Bong / Business as usual. *<re-iss. 1980s on Kicking Mule; KM 144> <cd-iss. Nov 10 on Stefan Grossman's Guitar Workshop; SGGW 141)>*

Jul 79. (lp) *<(SNKF 154)>* **THE ART OF FINGERSTYLE JAZZ GUITAR** [ ] Sep 79 [ ]
- Tintiyana *[cd track 2]* / Summertime *[cd 5]* / White with foam *[cd 7]* / Take the 'A' train / Yes, yes *[cd 8]* / Sweet and lovely *[cd 9]* / Medley: Wishes - Plain as the winter *[cd 11]* / Stompin' at the Savoy *[cd 1]* / Southern cross *[cd 3]* / Everything that rises must converge *[cd 6]* / Good intentions *[cd 12]* / In a sentimental mood *[cd 17]* / You're a lady *[cd 10]*. (*cd-iss. Jul 91 & Mar 00 on Shanachie+=;* SHAN 98005CD)- Always *[13]* / Turnaround *[14]* / Immaculate conception rag *[15]* / Black monk *[16]* / The stroll *[18]* / The clown *[19]*.

1980. (lp) *<(SNKF 167)>* **KID ON THE MOUNTAIN** [ ] Nov 80 [ ]
- Medley: The Wicklow hornpipe - Proudlock's hornpipe / Blind Mary / The Blarney pilgrim / Duke of Fife's welcome to Deeside / Sir Sidney Smith's march / Bantry bay / Morgan Magan / Kid on the mountain / Medley: Fanteladda - Boys of Ballisodare / Rights of man / Elsie Marley / Sheebeg an Sheemor / Lament for Limerick. *<(cd-iss. Jun 99 +=; KMCD 3913)>* - The march of the King of Laois / Medley: The south wind - The blackbird / No love / Mardi Gras dance.

not issued — Edition Collage

1985. (lp) *(10-1751)* **UNDER YOUR HEART** [–] German [–]
- Holding pattern / Keep it under your heart / Putney Bridge / Crawl, don't walk / Flowers of Belfast / Advent / Waltz with a smile / Contra Costa dance / Not the first time / Waltz on Sunday.

— also iss. on the label, You Can't Take The Country Out Of The Boy.

Fisher... — not issued

1988. (book+cd) *<???>* **THE SALUTATION** (festive) [–] [–]
- O come, o come Emmanuel / Angelus ad virginum (The blessed virgin's lullaby) / The bagpiper's carol - The snow lay on the ground / The Wexford carol / The Salutation - In Bethlehem / While shepherds watched their flocks - Furry day carol - Il est / Rorate / Trettondedagsmarschen / Let all earthly flesh keep silent / I saw three ships - Good Christian men rejoice / What is this fragrance? / Es ist ein ros' entsprungen / A virgin most pure - The holly and the ivy / The boys' carol - Patapan - Noel nouvelet / The virgin gives birth. *<cd-iss. 2006 on Day Job; none>*

— In 1990 (with LEO KOTTKE), BAKER released their soundtrack to the film 'Paul Bunyan'

not issued — Acoustic Music

Nov 92. (cd; by DUCK BAKER and JOHN RENBOURN) *(319-1021-2)* **A THOUSAND WORDS** [–] [ ]

- Waltz on Sunday / Old world / A thousand words / Friday / What the wind went whispering / Europa / Mr. Jellyroll soul / B. Rod's rag / The Magus / The blood of the lamb / Lashta's room / The Tao of swing / Little boy / God save us from angels.

May 93. (cd) *(SHAN 97025CD)* **OPENING THE EYES OF LOVE**
- Pharaoh's army / Forget me not / Seven point one / Opening the eyes of love / Keep it under your heart / Forty ton parachute / 'Round about midnight / The dirtman cometh / Contra Costa dance / The Dodder bank / Holding pattern / Come to papa / Miss Meadows / Light blue / Letter to Davey.

(above issued on Shanachie; both below on Day Job)

Jul 93. (cd; by DUCK BAKER & MOLLY ANDREWS) *(DBMA 1CD)* **AMERICAN TRADITIONAL**
- Muddy water / Yellow billed magpie / I've endured / Right or wrong / Promised land / Mother's advice / Hurry home or I'll be gone / Brown-eyed handsome man / A pretty fair miss / Robinson County - Peacock rag / Moonshiner / Nobody knows but me / Sea of Galilee / Ducks on the pond / Planxty Irwin - The lark in the morning / Snow dove.

Oct 94. (cd; by DUCK BAKER & MOLLY ANDREWS) *(DBMA 2CD)* **THE MOVING BUSINESS**
- The you and me that used to be / Sittin' on top of the world / I'm not turning backward / Blackberry blossom - June apple / Nottamun town / High on a mountain - Poll ha'penny / The march of the King of Laois / That twenty-five cents that you paid / Carryin' that load / Deep river / Leavin' home / Nighttime in Nevada / Where the morning glories grow / Bad girl / Searching for lambs / River blues / Train of life.

Apr 95. (cd) *(319-1065-2)* **THE CLEAR BLUE SKY**
- Night shift / The cure / Cross keys / Harvest / Baja Maria / The rakes of Waterloo / TGV / The clear blue sky / Crawl, don't walk / Soureba / The bachelor's waltz / The road to Richmond / Amnesia in Trastevere.

Jul 96. (cd) *<(AVAN 040)>* **SPINNING SONG: DUCK BAKER PLAYS THE MUSIC OF HERBIE NICHOLS** [jazz] — Jan 97

(above issued on Avant records)

—— In 1997, BAKER again teamed up with STEFAN GROSSMAN, this time for the Northern Skies, Southern Blues CD.

1998. (cd) *(319-1130-2)* **MS RIGHT**
- Snapshots / St James infirmary / Advent / Ms Right / He who waits / Digger and Ed / Waltz with Mary's smile / Squaring the triangle / First frost / Susanna / Putney Bridge / The flowers of Belfast.

not issued — Day Job

1999. (cd; by KIERAN FAHY and DUCK BAKER) *<none>* **THE FAIRY QUEEN** — mail-o
- The fairy queen / Paddy now won't you be easy - The exile / The fairy lament / The drunken sailor / Come under my dimity - The humours of whiskey / Child of my heart / Ramble over Stennis - Galway Bay / Miss Forbes's farewell - Poll halfpenny / The joy of my life - The banks of Lough Gowna / Bridget Cruise - Planxty Sweeny / The Blarney pilgrim - Market girls / The Wexford carol.

2000. (cd) *<none>* **MY HEART BELONGS TO JENNY** — mail-o
- My heart belongs to Jenny / Pretty girl milking a cow / Banish misfortune / Polly put the kettle on / John O'Dwyer of the glen - The plains of Boyle / The joy of my life - The banks of Lough Gowna / Little beggar man - Sandy river belle / Little brown jug - Market girls / Oliver Goldsmith's lament / Charles O'Connor / Huggerth the puss / The blackbird and the thrush / Swedish jig / Temperance reel - The green fields of America / The bonnie bunch of roses / Catholic Bill's jig - Planxty Sweeney.

2001. (cd; by DUCK BAKER & JAMIE FINDLAY) *<none>* **OUT OF THE PAST: Classic Jazz Guitar Duets** — mail-o

Aug 06. (cd) *<none>* **DO YOU KNOW WHAT IT MEANS TO MISS NEW ORLEANS?** [swing/jazz] — mail-o

Apr 09. (cd; by DUCK BAKER, MAGGIE BOYLE, BEN PALEY) *(DCD 106)* **THE EXPATRIATE GAME: Traditional Irish and American Music** [recorded 2005]
- Little beggar man - Monaghan twig / Miss Forbes's farewell - Poll ha'penny / The banks of Claudy / The blackbird / A youth inclined to ramble / The golden keyboard - Sandy river belle - Grub spring / Rye whiskey / Kitty lie over / Sea O'Dwyer of the glen - Come under my dimity - The humours of whiskey / Bonny Portmore / Temperance reel - June apple / The fairy queen / Over the waterfall - Robinson County.

not issued — Les Cousins

Sep 09. (cd) *(LC 10)* **The ROOTS AND BRANCHES of AMERICAN MUSIC**
- Sergeant Early's dream - Chief O'Neill's favorite / Souareba / Maple Leaf rag / Midnight on the water - Peacock rag / Don't be ashamed of your age / Buddy Bolden's blues / Somewhere around a throne / Say it simple / Blue monk / Whistling Rufus / A thousand words / Berkeley hambone blues / The Duke of Fife's welcome to Deeside / Swing low, sweet chariot / Wink the other eye - Buffalo gals / Mother Ann's song.

—— next featured **Duck** alongside **Alex Ward & Joe Williamson**

Sep 09. (cd; as DUCK BAKER TRIO) *(LC 11)* **THE WALTZ LESSON** [jazz]

Mighty Quinn — not issued

Oct 09. (cd) *<1117>* **EVERYTHING THAT RISES MUST CONVERGE: Free Jazz Guitar Solos** [jazz]

Sam BAKER

Born in Itasca, a small prairie town in southwest Texas, singer-songwriter SAM BAKER is a modern-day folk and country-blues artist, something akin to roots greats JOHN PRINE, James McMurtry and even TOWNES VAN ZANDT. The fact that he's here at all is testament to his tenacity; he almost died in a Peruvian terrorist bomb blast in 1986 (on his way by rail to Machu Picchu) that took part of his hearing away and caused serious injuries to his left arm, leaving his hand almost disabled. With a voice that rasps and croaks its way into the listener's heart, Sam's literate narratives have endeared him to a loyal fan base.

From 2004's **MERCY** {*7} to 2009's **COTTON** {*6}, with **PRETTY WORLD** (2007) {*6} in between, BAKER demonstrates his autobiographical storytelling prowess in his unique vocal fashion, hushed and unassuming but so far, unfortunately, not to a wider audience. Check out the irony-fuelled 'Baseball' and 'Waves', both from his debut. *MCS*

Sam Baker - vocals, acoustic guitar

US self-rel. — UK not issued

2004. (cd) *<none>* **MERCY**
- Waves / Truale / Baseball / Thursday / Change / Pony / Kitchen / Iron / Prelude / Steel / Angels / Mercy. *<re-iss. Aug 07 on Blue Lime Stone; BLSR 04PW>*

Blue Lime Stone — not issued

Aug 07. (cd) *<BLSR 07PW>* **PRETTY WORLD**
- Juarez (a song to himself) / Orphan / Slots / Pretty world / Odessa / Sweetly undone / Psychic / Boxes / Prelude / Broken fingers / Days / Recessional.

Music Road — Music Road

Aug 09. (cd) *<(MRRCD 104)>* **COTTON**
- Dixie / Cotton / Moon / Mennonite / Signs / Palestine II / Who's gonna be your man / Say the right words / Angel hair / Not another Mary / Palestine I / Bridal chest / Snow.

The BALANCING ACT

Not to be confused with a neo-soul act of the same name, The BALANCING ACT described here comprised main songwriter Jeff Davis with William Aron, Steve Wagner and Robert Blackmon. Formed in Los Angeles, California in 1984, they were hardly typical for a 1980s LA band, trying as they did to combine the authenticity of traditional roots music with the spontaneity of rock's avant-garde.

After an obscure debut EP in 1986, The BALANCING ACT laid down tracks with noted producer and former Plimsouls leader Peter Case, the results surfacing as **NEW CAMPFIRE SONGS** {*7}, issued on IRS subsidiary Primitive Man. Featuring a cover of Captain Beefheart's 'Zig Zag Wanderer', the mini-set's quirky jangle-pop sound was quite unlike anything else around at the time.

Two further sets, **THREE SQUARES AND A ROOF** (1987) {*8} and **CURTAINS** (1988) {*7}, developed their style without ever threatening the mainstream. The latter was produced by Andy Gill (of Gang Of Four) and featured a cover of Funkadelic's 'Can You Get To That'.

A particularly bad spell for the band led to a split as session man Aron teamed up with singer Simon Glickman (alongside Miles Lally on bass and Perry Ostrin on drums) in power-pop outfit Spanish Kitchen around 1993. After one self-financed single, this outfit became Mystery Pop and released a self-titled CD in 2002. *MCS*

Jeff Davis - vocals, guitar / **Willie Aron** - guitar, vocals / **Steve Wagner** - bass, vocals / **Robert Blackmon** - drums, vocals

US IRS — UK Illegal

May 86. (m-lp/m-c) *<IRS/+C 39097>* **NEW CAMPFIRE SONGS**
- Wonderful world tonight / Who got the pearls / A TV Guide in the Olduvai gorge / A girl, her sister, and a train / The neighborhood phrenologist / Zig zag wanderer. *<originally issued on Type A>*

Nov 87. (lp/c/cd) *<IRS/+C/D 42082>* *(ILP 023)* **THREE SQUARES AND A ROOF** — Jul 88
- Three cards / This is where it all begins / Kicking clouds across the sky / Whiskered wife / Adventure / Ballad of Art Snyder / Red umbrella / Governor of Pedro / Waiting for the mail / Searching for this thing / We're not lost. *<US cd+=>* - NEW CAMPFIRE SONGS

Nov 88. (lp/cd) *<IRS/+D 42237>* **CURTAINS**
- Generator / She doesn't work here / Lost in the mail / Red pants and romance / Dangerous roof / Can you get to that / Understanding furniture / Sleep on the trusty floor / Fishing in your eye / Between two oceans / Learning how to cheat.

Jun 89. (7") *(EIRS 116)* CAN YOU GET TO THAT. /
(12"+=) *(EIRST 116)* -

—— disbanded after above

Devendra BANHART

While many have dipped a toe in the freak-folk pond, few have evoked its unhinged magic like DEVENDRA BANHART. His singular style has evolved from lone singer/songwriter to peddler of sun-kissed psychedelia.

Born May 30, 1981 in Houston, Texas and spending his formative years between Los Angeles, San Francisco and Caracas, Venezuela, the art-school drop-out took to busking at 14, honing his skills as a solo performer. He decamped to Paris in early 2000, cosying up to the US indie-rock cognoscenti and finding the likes of Beck, Sonic Youth and Swans leader Michael Gira among his growing coterie of admirers.

While his homespun, home-made acoustica CD-r debut **THE CHARLES C. LEARY** (2002) {*5} made little impression beyond his clique, Gira was impressed enough to release a collection of BANHART's early highlights on his Young God label as **OH ME OH MY...** (2002) {*7}. It took him until his second album proper, 2004's **REJOICING IN THE HANDS** {*8}, to make an record that shows his skill at deft, scuttling phrasing and off-kilter melodies. Songs like 'This Is The Way' and the fantastically titled 'This Beard Is For Siobhan' are simple and playful.

He followed this in quick succession with **NINO ROJO** (2004) {*9}. The weary cover of Ella Jenkins's 'Wake Up, Little Sparrow' was breathtaking, and 'Little Yellow Spider' (heard by millions on a TV commercial for the Orange mobile phone network) succinctly illustrated how his music was becoming the perfect blend of the beautiful and the absurd. BANHART became the figurehead of the burgeoning freak-folk movement in the US (although "movement" is too big a word for a bunch of people hanging out jamming), which included kindred spirits VETIVER and JOANNA NEWSOM.

CRIPPLE CROW (2005) {*7} was a sprawling, bawling, often dawdling collection that, depending on format, contained between 22 and 30 songs. BANHART's lack of self-editing was counteracted by some great songs, including several in Spanish, tipping the nod to his Venezuelan heritage. The album cover was reminiscent of sleeves like 'Sgt. Pepper's', The INCREDIBLE STRING BAND's 'The Hangman's Beautiful Daughter' and anything by TYRANNOSAURUS REX, and summed up the celebratory, inclusive nature of Devendra's music at the time.

After several albums of spare, stripped-down, almost entirely acoustic music, BANHART decamped for his old stamping ground of Topanga, California with his band the Spiritual Bonerz, which included Joanna's brother Pete Newsom, to record **SMOKEY ROLLS DOWN THUNDER CANYON** (2007) {*7}. With the spirit if not the musical sensibility of Laurel Canyon in his heart, Devendra seemed keen to play with his own conventions as he drew in various collaborators including members of The Strokes, The Black Crowes and, impressively, a pair of true folk legends in LINDA PERHACS and VASHTI BUNYAN. The result was disappointingly scattergun and unfocused, throwing flashes of reggae, funk, samba and soul into an already crowded melting-pot to negligible effect.

Growing up, BANHART has grown less effective with age. His sixth album (and first for new label Reprise) further illustrated his ability to grate along, constantly throwing genres into the mix. **WHAT WILL WE BE** (2009) {*5} is a limp collection that sounds frightfully clichéd, considering how idiosyncratic his output had been less than five years earlier; the pseudo-soul groove of 'Baby' was just pedestrian. A Grammy nomination for Best Packaging damned the record with the faint praise that it just about deserved.

BANHART has been relatively quiet since, signing to NEIL YOUNG's management team. Contributing to the 'Red Hot And Blue' series of AIDS awareness compilation albums, and co-soundtracking (with Beck) the Todd Solondz film 'Life During Wartime', are among his few appearances above the parapet since 2009. *MR*

Devendra Banhart - vocals, guitar, piano, harmonium, ukulele / with session people

US not issued — UK Hinah

Aug 02. (cd-r) *(010)* **THE CHARLES C. LEARY** French
- Bish-bash falls / Soothe my soul, mend my mind / Sarah sings / Mmplushumblehorse / Michigan State / Rainwater pigfarmers / Aymama-aymama / The Charles C. Leary / Whistling / The thumbs touch too much / Todo los dolores / Catastrophie / Me and Andy singing El Rio / The fish are scratched up flies / Artsandcrafts [live at 40th St W.] / The animal map / Cads casa que crece / Ride away like Roy Orbison / Red lagoon whistling / Noah / Cosmos and Damien / Aperpareplane [early recording] / I played organ while Colter played guitar / Joe Cain.

Young God — Young God

Oct 02. (cd) *<(YG 20CD)>* **OH ME OH MY... THE WAY THE DAY GOES BY THE SUN IS SETTING DOGS ARE DREAMING LOVESONGS OF THE CHRISTMAS SPIRIT**
- Tick eats the olives... / Roots... / The Charles C. Leary / Nice people... / Animals... / Cosmos and demos / Michigan State / Lend me your teeth / Hey Miss Cane / Soon is good / Tell me something / The red lagoon / A gentle soul / Happy happy oh / Pumpkin seeds / The thumbs... / Legless love... / Marigold / Make it easier / Ones / Little monkey / The spirit is near. *<lp-iss. 2003 on Mod Lang; ML 011>*

May 03. (m-cd) *(YG 23)* **THE BLACK BABIES** (UK)
- Bluebird / Surgery I stole / Cosmos and demos / Onward the Indian / Lagoon / The Charles C. Leary / Long song / Old Thunderbird.

Young God — XL Recordings

May 04. (cd) *<YG 24>* (XLCD 180) **REJOICING IN THE HANDS**
- This is the way / A sight to behold / The body breaks / Poughkeepsie / Dogs they make up the dark / Will is my friend / This beard is for Siobhan / See saw / Tit smoking in the temple of artisan mimicry / Rejoicing in the hands / Fall / Todo los dolores / When the sun shone on Vetiver / There was sun / Insect eyes / Autumn's child.

May 04. (ltd-d7"ep) *(XLS 184)* HERE ARE FOUR SONGS FROM REJOICING IN THE HANDS
- The body breaks / This beard is for Siobhan / Insect eyes / Rejoicing in the hands.

Jul 04. (7"/cd-s) *(XLS 194/+CD)* A SIGHT TO BEHOLD. / Be Kind

Sep 04. (7") *(XLS 200)* LITTLE YELLOW SPIDER. / Will Is My Friend (live in St Giles-in-the-fields church, London)
(cd-s) *(XLS 200CD)* - ('A') / Sunrise - A long time ago / Autumn's child - A long time ago.

Sep 04. (cd) *<YG 25>* *(XLCD 185)* **NINO ROJO**
- Wake up, little sparrow / Ay mama / We all know / Little yellow spider / A ribbon / At the hop / My ships / Noah / Sister / Water may walk / Horseheadedfleshwizard / An island / Be kind / Owl eyes / The good red road / Electric heart. *<d-lp iss. Feb 05 +=; YG26>* - REJOICING IN THE HANDS

Nov 04. (7") *(XLS 206)* AT THE HOP. / At The Hop (live)
(cd-s) *(XLS 206CD)* - ('A') / Pardon my heart (live at the Royal Raymond Brake, North Carolina) / Roots (live at the Great American Music Hall, San Francisco).

Troubleman Unlimited — not issued

May 05. (lp; shared w/ JANA HUNTER) *<TMU 153>* **JANA HUNTER / DEVENDRA BANHART**
- (tracks by JANA HUNTER) / At the hop / In golden empress hands / We all know / The good red road / Little monkey - Step in the name of love.

5 Rue Christine — not issued

2005. (7") *<GER 038>* XIU XIU AND DEVENDRA BANHART
- The body breaks (XIU XIU) / Support our troops oh!

XL Recordings — XL Recordings

Sep 05. (7") *(XLS 217)* I FEEL JUST LIKE A CHILD. / Ice Rat — 68
(cd-s) *(XLS 217CD)* - ('A') / Stewed bark of an old tree / Shame.

Sep 05. (cd) *<(XLCD 192)>* **CRIPPLE CROW** — 69
- Now that I know / Santa Maria de Feira / Heard somebody say / Long haired child / Lazy butterfly / Quedate luna / Queen bee / I feel just like a child / Some people ride the wave / The Beatles / Dragonflys / Cripple crow / Inaniel / Hey mama wolf / How's about tellin' a story / Chinese children / Sawkill river / I love that man / Luna de Margarita / Korean dogwood / Little boys / Canela. *(d-lp iss. 2006 +=; XLLP 192)* - There's always something happening / La ley / Chicken / Stewed bark of an old oak tree / La pastorcita perdida / Lickety split / Ice rat / White reggae troll.

Nov 05. (ltd-7") *(XLS 222)* HEARD SOMEBODY SAY. / La Pastorcita Perdida
(cd-s) *(XLS 222CD)* - ('A') / Lickety split / Chicken.

Jun 06. (ltd-12" one-sided) *(DEV 1T)* WHITE REGGAE TROLL

Sep 07. (cd) *<(XLCD 283)>* **SMOKEY ROLLS DOWN THUNDER CANYON**
- Cristobal / So long old bean / Samba vexillographica / Seahorse / Bad girl / Seaside / Shabop shalom / Tonada yanomaminista / Rosa / Saved / Lover / Carmensita / The other women / Freely / I remember / My dearest friend.

Warners — Warners

Oct 09. (cd/lp) *<(520960-2/520962-1)>* **WHAT WILL WE BE**
- Can't help but smiling / Angelika / Baby / Goin' back / First song for B / Last song for B / Chin chin and muck muck / 16th and Valencia Roxy Music / Rats / Maria Lionza / Brindo / Meet me at lookout point / Walilamdzi / Foolin'. *(lp+=)* - Welcome to the island / Pray for the other person's happiness.

MEGAPUSS

Devendra Banhart + Greg Rogove - percussion (ex-Priestbird)

Vapor — Vapor

Oct 08. (cd/lp) <514102> **SURFING** Nov 08
- Crop circle jerk '94 / Duck people duck man / To the love within / Adam and Steve

/ Theme from Hollywood / Surfing / Lavender blimp / Mister meat (hot rejection) / Hamman / A gun on his hip and a rose on his chest / Chicken titz / Sayulita / Older lives / Another mother.

Kevin BARKER (⟹ CURRITUCK CO.)

The BE GOOD TANYAS

A melting honeypot hybrid of old-timey folk, country and bluegrass, The BE GOOD TANYAS were put together by singer and mandolinist Samantha Parton and Jolie Holland, fiddler and singer. Parton bolstered the all-girl Vancouver outfit with her friends from tree-planting camp (it's a Canadian thing), Frazey Ford and Winnipeg native Trish Klein (on banjo), who had struck up a musical kinship during their time at Selkirk Music School in Nelson, British Columbia.

Almost immediately the Canadian buskers stepped up from coffee-shop venues to the big Lilith Fair touring festival, but in the midst of recording their rootsy debut set **BLUE HORSE** (2000) {*7}, JOLIE HOLLAND upped sticks and left.

Rejuvenating a handful of traditional tunes ('The Coo Coo Bird', 'Lakes Of Pontchartrain', 'Rain And Snow' and Stephen Foster's minstrel song 'Oh, Susanna'), they also echoed Appalachia with Ford and Parton originals (the best were 'Only In The Past' and 'Dogsong' (also known as 'Sleep Dog Lullaby'). Parton and Holland even had the courage to insert a few bookending lines from Syd Barrett's Pink Floyd-era ditty 'Jugband Blues' on opening track 'The Littlest Birds', and the only cover proper was of fellow Canadian GEOFF BERNER's 'Light Enough To Travel'.

Picked up by the Nettwerk label, the remaining trio worked on the similar **CHINATOWN** (2003) {*7}, this time covering TOWNES VAN ZANDT ('Waiting Around To Die') and Peter Rowan ('Midnight Moonlight'). Folk sources were represented by trad/DYLAN standards 'House Of The Rising Sun' and 'In My Time Of Dying', plus 'Reuben' and 'I Wish My Baby Was Born'. Avant-jazz artist Olu Dara performs on Parton's JONI MITCHELLesque 'Dogsong 2'.

HELLO LOVE (2006) {*6} was almost formulaic, the girls' back-porch cool and kitchen-table tales once again overshadowed by some effective readings from the pens of NEIL YOUNG ('For The Turnstiles'), SEAN HAYES ('A Thousand Tiny Pieces') and MISSISSIPPI JOHN HURT ('Nobody Cares For Me'). An ill-advised rendition of Prince's 'When Doves Cry' was a step too far.

With The BE GOOD TANYAS temporarily on hold (Trish had been moonlighting with alt-country project Po' Girl), it was down to vocalist FRAZEY FORD, with Trish in tow, to keep the neo-trad flag flying.

OBADIAH (2010) {*7} was FORD's attempt to draw music from other genres into her manifesto - one can hear acoustic R&B a la NEIL YOUNG throughout. Pick of the bunch were 'Lay Down With You', 'Gospel Song', 'Goin' Over' and a shimmering take on DYLAN's 'One More Cup Of Coffee'. *MCS*

Samantha Parton - vocals, guitar, mandolin / **Frazey Ford** - vocals, guitar / **Jolie Holland** (b. Sep 11 '75, Houston, Texas) - fiddle, vocals / **Trish Klein** - guitar, banjo, vocals (of Po' Girl)

US/Can self-rel. — UK not issued

Nov 00. (cd) *<bgt 9605>* **BLUE HORSE** □ ⊟
- The littlest birds / Broken telephone / Rain and snow / Lakes of Pontchartrain / Only in the past / The coo coo bird / Dogsong (also known as Sleep dog lullaby) / Momsong / Don't you fall / Up against the wall / Oh, Susanna / Light enough to travel. *<(US/UK-iss. Sep 01/Feb 02 on Nettwerk; 30245-2)>*

Nettwerk — Nettwerk

Jan 03. (cd-s) *(33156-2)* THE LITTLEST BIRDS [video version] / Rain And Snow [live] / Momsong [live] □ ⊟
(cd-s) *(33166-2)* - ['A'-album version] / Light enough to travel [live] / Only in the past [live].

—— now a trio when JOLIE HOLLAND went solo

Nettwerk — EMI

Feb 03. (cd) *<30304-2> (581463-2)* **CHINATOWN** □ □
- It's not happening / Waiting around to die / Junkie song / Ship out on the sea / Dogsong 2 / Rowdy blues / Reuben / House of the rising sun / In spite of all the damage / Lonesome blues / In my time of dying / I wish my baby was born / Horses / Midnight moonlight.

Nettwerk — Nettwerk

Oct 06. (cd) *<30416-2> (30631-2)* **HELLO LOVE** □ □
- Human thing / For the turnstiles / Thousand tiny pieces / Ootischenia / Little blues / Scattered leaves / Hello love / Nobody cares for me / Out of the wilderness / Song for R / What are they doing in heaven today / Crow waltz / When doves cry. *(UK+=)* - Back, back train / Birds.

FRAZEY FORD

Nettwerk — Nettwerk

Jul 10. (cd) *<(30896-2)>* **OBADIAH** □ □
- Firecracker / Lay down with you / Bird of paradise / If you gonna go / Blue streak mama / Lost together / I like you better / Hey little mama / Gospel song / Goin' over / Half in / One more cup of coffee / Mimi song.

BEIRUT

Combining gypsy folk music with lo-fi spaghetti-western-meets-psychedelia, BEIRUT was the brainchild of Albuquerque, New Mexico-born multi-instrumentalist Zach Condon. From the age of 16, the high-school drop-out travelled extensively in Europe (mainly the Balkans), learning about many cultures and musical instruments in the process. Meeting up with likeminded A HAWK AND A HACKSAW members Jeremy Barnes (ex-Neutral Milk Hotel) and Heather Trost, Condon set about perfecting his debut album.

Thanks to Barnes's efforts, **GULAG ORKESTAR** (2006) {*7} found an outlet in New Jersey-based indie imprint Ba Da Bing, while youngster Zach moved to Brooklyn, New York. Like an old-timey 78 one might find in grandfather's attic, the music spins out like a mariachi desert band at sunset in some romantic black-and-white film from the 1950s. With exotic and picturesque titles such as 'Bratislava', 'Rhineland', 'Brandenburg', 'Prenzlauerberg' and 'Mount Wroclai', the listener is transported to unknown lands. There is the occasional non-folk Bontempi plod ('After The Curtain' and 'Scenic World'), but the melodious set was one large step for a 19 year-old.

In an unexpected minor breakthrough, **THE FLYING CLUB CUP** {*8} (2007) bubbled under the US Top 100 for a week or so, its gypsy-meets-Tex-Mex songs appealing to a new generation of world-music folk buffs: Condon's merry-go-round tunes had strength, passion and spirit. Owen Pallett of Final Fantasy collaborated on the track 'Cliquot'.

The double-EP/mini-album **MARCH OF THE ZAPOTEC/HOLLAND** (2009) {*7} was an unusual artefact, shared as it was with his Realpeople project (alias The Jimenez Band, a 19-piece brass band from Oaxaca, Mexico). The BEIRUT disc finds Zach turning folk-electro a la 1980s New Order or The Associates. *MCS*

Zach Condon (b. 1986) - vocals, ukulele, piano, accordion, mandolin, trumpet / with **Jeremy Barnes** - percussion, accordion (of A HAWK AND A HACKSAW, ex-NEUTRAL MILK HOTEL) / **Heather Trost** - violins / plus **Perrin Cloutier** - cello / **Hari Ziznewski** - clarinet

US Ba Da Bing! — UK 4ad

May 06. (lp/cd) *<BING 048/+CD> (CADD 2619/+CD)*
GULAG ORKESTAR □ Nov 06 □
- The gulag orkestar / Prenzlauerberg / Brandenburg / Postcards from Italy / Mount Wroclai (idle days) / Rhineland (heartland) / Scenic world / Bratislava / The bunker / The canals of our city / After the curtain. *(w/ bonus +=)* - LON GISLAND

Dec 06. (cd-ep) *<BING 052>* LON GISLAND □ ⊟
- Elephant gun / My family's role in the world revolution / Scenic world / The Long Island sound (*) / Carousels. *<one-sided-12" on Choquette w/out *; OUE 01>*

Jul 07. (7") *(AD 2729)* ELEPHANT GUN. / Transatlantique / Le Moribond - My Family's Role In The World Revolution ⊟ □

Oct 07. (lp/cd) *<BING 055/+CD> (CAD 2732/+CD)*
THE FLYING CLUB CUP □ □
- A call to arms / Nantes / A Sunday smile / Guyamas sonora / La banlieue / Cliquot / The penalty / Forks and knives (la fete) / In the mausoleum / Un dernier verre (pour la route) / Cherbourg / St Apollonia / The flying club cup.

Pompeii — not issued

Feb 09. (d-12" ep/d-m-cd; shared w/ REALPEOPLE) *<92124-2/-1>*
MARCH OF THE ZAPOTEC // HOLLAND [87] ⊟
- El Zocalo / La Llorona / My wife / The Akara / On a bayonet / The shrew / REALPEOPLE: My night with the prostitute from Marseille / My wife, lost in the wild / Venice / The concubine / No dice.

Geoff BERNER

Taking Jewish culture and klezmer beyond their musical horizons, Canadian singer-songwriter and accomplished accordionist GEOFF BERNER (born November 26, 1971 in Vancouver) concocts a blend of old-timey folk music, jazz and punk (the last genre was the vocation of his first band, Terror Of Tiny Town). Like some refugee from a war-torn eastern European country

– and very reminiscent of Belgian cabaret star Jacques Brel - Geoff is witty and political. He was active in the Green Party of British Columbia between 1988 and 2001, standing in four elections.

His debut mini-set, **LIGHT ENOUGH TO TRAVEL** (2000) {*5}, attracted attention through The BE GOOD TANYAS recording the title track. After discovering Norwegian combo the Kaizers Orchestra and releasing his first full set, **WE SHALL NOT FLAG OR FAIL, WE SHALL GO ON TO THE END** (2003) {*7}, featuring 'We All Gotta Be A Prostitute Sometimes', BERNER's career was on the rise.

Following an inspirational field trip to study klezmer music in Romania, he released the first of his klezmer-themed trilogy, **WHISKEY RABBI** (2005) {*6}, which, like its follow-up concept set **THE WEDDING DANCE OF THE WIDOW BRIDE** (2007) {*7}, credited violinist Diona Davies (of Po' Girl) and percussionist Wayne Adams (of Zolty Cracker). One track in particular, the lyrically risque 'Weep, Bride, Weep', is typical BERNER – as was the third volume, **KLEZMER MONGRELS** (2008) {*6}.

BERNER regularly covers the songs of his friends Cramaig de Forest (who plays the ukulele) and songwriter Kris Demeanor, and he guested on fellow Canadian Carolyn Mark's set 'Just Married: An Album Of Duets'. In February 2008 he released (online) his self-proclaimed 'Official Theme Song for the 2010 Vancouver/Whistler Winter Olympics: The Dead Children Were Worth It', a slight on the Games' German sponsors Volkswagen.

His sixth set, **VICTORY PARTY** (2011) {*6}, took folk into new realms of techno with the Public Image Ltd-like 'Oh My Golem' and 'I Kind Of Hate Songs With Ambiguous Lyrics' - think The Fall meets Tymon Dogg. *MCS*

Geoff Berner - vocals, accordion

US Sudden Death — UK not issued

2000. (m-cd) *<SD 34>* **LIGHT ENOUGH TO TRAVEL** — Canada
- Light enough to travel / I.Y.M. / Public relations / Suburban family of spies / My dad's a lawyer / A blimp made of human skin. *<re-iss. Feb 07; same>*

Black Hen — not issued

Feb 03. (cd) *<???>* **WE SHALL NOT FLAG OR FAIL, WE SHALL GO ON TO THE END** — Canada
- Volcano god / Clown and bard / We all gotta be a prostitute sometimes / Maginot line / In the year 2020 / Porn queen girlfriend / A settling of accounts / Beautiful in my eyes / The way that girl drinks beer / Iron grey. *<re-iss. 2009 on 9 PM+=; 82428-2>* - LIGHT ENOUGH TO TRAVEL ep tracks.

—— next two credited with **Diona Davies** (violin) and **Wayne Adams** (percussion)

not issued — Checkpoint Charlie...

Dec 05. (cd) *(CCAP 041)* **WHISKEY RABBI** — Norway
- Whiskey rabbi / Lucky god damn Jew / Song written in a Romanian hospital / Drunk all day / Unlistenable song / The true enemy / And promises to break before I sleep / The traveller's curse / The violins - Al kamanjaat / Volcano god.

Feb 07. (cd) *(CCAP 050)* **THE WEDDING DANCE OF THE WIDOW BRIDE** — Norway
- Good luck now / Weep, bride, weep / Widow bride / Queen Victoria / The fiddler is a good woman / Traitor bride / Can't stay dry / Song to reconcile / Would it kill you? / Weep, bride, weep [instrumental].

9 PM — not issued

Oct 08. (cd) *<91563-2>* **KLEZMER MONGRELS** — Canada
- Shut in / Luck in exile / The whiskey / Half German girlfriend / King of the gangsters / No tobacco / Play, gypsy, play / Authentic klezmer wedding band / One shoe / High ground / Fukher.

Mint — not issued

Mar 11. (cd/lp) *<MRD/MRL-132>* **VICTORY PARTY**
- The victory party / Laughing Jackie the wimp / Wealthy poet / Mayn rue platz [My resting place] / I kind of hate songs with ambiguous lyrics / Daloy polizei / Jail / Rabbit Berner finally reveals his true religious agenda / Oh my golem / Cherry blossoms.

Cindy Lee BERRYHILL

American singer-songwriter CINDY LEE BERRYHILL (born June 12, 1968 in Silverlake, Los Angeles) may or may not be classed as a modern-day folk artist, but she was certainly part of the loose group of musicians living in New York in the late 1980s who first called their kind of music anti-folk.

After pursuing theatre studies in LA, Cindy Lee fell in with the local punk scene and formed her first band, The Stoopids (a few recordings exist on cassette). Becoming disillusioned with her musical environment, she suffered a nervous breakdown, and it was the second half of the decade before she fully recuperated. The stalwart feminist and liberal finally made it on to vinyl on a various-artists compilation, 'The Radio Tokyo Tapes, Vol. 3', with her sardonic, CHRISTINE LAVIN-like song 'Damn, Wish I Was A Man'. It also featured on her debut Rhino Records solo set, **WHO'S GONNA SAVE THE WORLD?** (1987) {*7}, which was released on UK folkie imprint New Routes a year later.

BERRYHILL's Lenny Kaye-produced follow-up, **NAKED MOVIE STAR** (1989) {*6}, found her dabbling with jazz styles but failing to convince record buyers. One track that stands head and shoulders above the rest is 'What's Wrong With Me?', but the 13-minute 'Yipee' goes beyond its Patti Smith-like avant-poetry. At the turn of the decade, she lost all her personal effects when they were stolen on her way to her new home in San Diego.

A few years later, Cindy Lee's career was reactivated following interest from the Earth Music stable. Her long-awaited third set, **GARAGE ORCHESTRA** (1994) {*8}, was named after her backing band. There was more than a nod to the Beach Boys (as on her Brian Wilson homage 'Song For Brian'), and a swerving away from folk music. Try to hear the longest track, 'UFO Suite'.

BERRYHILL suffered further misfortune when her boyfriend was injured in a serious motorcycle accident. Nursing him through his ordeal, the resilient Cindy found time to cut a fourth album, **STRAIGHT OUTTA MARYSVILLE** (1996) {*6}, released on British independent Demon Records. A bit of a let-down in comparison, it still contained one her best tunes, 'Unwritten Love Song' and a cover of DONOVAN's 'Season Of The Witch'. The intimate live concert set **LIVING ROOM 16** (1999) {*7} contained at least four new tracks (from the autobiographical 'Family Tree' to the fragile 'This Way Up'), alongside past gems including 'Gary Handeman' from her fine third long-player.

2007 saw her make a comeback with **BELOVED STRANGER** {*7}, which showed she had lost none of her caustic and sardonic wit (as on 'Make Way For The Handicapped'), while there were fractured pop explorations in 'Unexpected Passages' and the anti-Bush sentiments of 'When Did Jesus Become A Republican'. In-session veterans from her New Wave salad days included John Doe (X), Peter Case (The Plimsouls) and Dave Alvin (The Blasters). *MCS*

Cindy Lee Berryhill - vocals, guitars, harmonica (w/ sessions from various personnel)

US Rhino — UK New Routes

Oct 87. (lp) *<RNLP 70834> (RUE 001)* **WHO'S GONNA SAVE THE WORLD?** — Jun 88
- She had everything / Damn, I wish I was a man / Steve on H / Looking through portholes / Whatever works / Who's gonna save the world? / Spe-C-I-Al ingredient / Ceallaigh green / Ballad of a garage band / This administration / Heat.

Rhino — Awareness

Apr 89. (lp/c/cd) *<R1/R4/R2 70845> (AWL/AWT/AWCD 1016)* **NAKED MOVIE STAR** — Jul 89
- Me, Steve, Kirk and Keith / Old trombone routine / Supernatural fact / Indirectly yours / Trump / 12 dollar motel / Turn off the century / What's wrong with me / Yipee / Baby (should I have the baby?).

Sep 89. (7") *(AWP 001)* ME, STEVE, KIRK AND KEITH. / Baby (Should I Have The Baby?)
(12"+=) *(AWPX 001)* - 12 dollar motel.

—— her subsequent sets were non-folk

Earth Music — Unique Gravity

Sep 94. (cd) *<008> (UGCD 5502)* **GARAGE ORCHESTRA** — Jul 95
- Father of the seventh son / I wonder why / Radio astronomy / Gary Handeman / Song for Brian / UFO suite / I want stuff / Every someone tonight / The scariest thing in the world / Etude for ph. machine. *(re-iss. Apr 98; same)*

Earth Music — Demon

Mar 96. (cd) *<84503> (FIENDCD 782)* **STRAIGHT OUTTA MARYSVILLE** — Apr 96
- High jump / Unknown master painter / Diane / Season of the witch / Riddle riddle / Jane and John / The virtues of being apricot / Unwritten love song / Just like me / Talkin' with a mineral / I'm a tumbleweed / Caravan / Elvis of Marysville / California.

Griffith Park — Griffith Park

Mar 99. (cd) *<(GPR 001)>* **LIVING ROOM 16** (live January 17 1998)
- Diane / She had everything / Family tree / Damn, I wish I was a man / This way up / UFO suite / Witness / I wonder why / Look at that grin / Gary Handeman / Every someone tonight.

Populuxe — Populuxe

Sep 07. (cd) *<(112-2)>* **BELOVED STRANGER** — Jan 08
- Unexpected packages / When did Jesus become a Republican? / Forty cent raise / Make way for the handicapped / Beloved stranger / Cry me a Jordan / Feel like I owe somebody somethin' / Where are they now / Bars, booze and boysclubs / Hugs and kisses / Plenty enough.

The BIG HUGE

Naming a band after a classic folk-rock album by The INCREDIBLE STRING BAND might seem audacious, but The BIG HUGE triumphantly wore their hearts and influences on their sleeves.

Formed in 2003 by Baltimore-based singer-songwriter Drew Nelson (from ambient indies Sonna) and musical accomplice Michael Lambright (plus Tarantel drummer Tim Redd and Chris Freeland on initial sessions), the outfit completed two records for release in 2004/5, then disappeared unceremoniously. The first of these, **CROWN YOUR HEAD WITH FLOWERS, CROWN YOUR HEART WITH JOY** {*8} (2004), garnered rave reviews from those in the know for Drew's wavering, transcendental Caledonian confessionals, on a par with WILL OLDHAM and Neutral Milk Hotel. 'Atop A Secret Mountain', 'Harbor To A Hill', 'Autumnal Hymn' and a couple of traditional songs ('Willie Of Winsbury' and 'Bonnie Boy') are woven with grace, the dulcimers and banjos blending neatly alongside the group's neo-Brit-folk stance.

Only half an album (in fact a mini-CD) but no less effective for that, **A WOVEN PAGE OF SILVER LIGHT** {*6} (2005) was recorded by Michah Blue Smaldone at Cerberus Shoal's house in Portland, Maine. Psychedelic, in terms of getting high from fresh air on top of the Appalachians, the record proved to be a worthy follow-up. Nelson and his accordionist buddy Lambright gel gently and gracefully, and although three cuts are quite short, the longest track (four and a half minutes), 'The Ballad Of North Haywood', is epic in proportion. Hopefully there will be more from Drew and his BIG HUGE clan one day soon. *MCS*

Drew Nelson - vocals, guitar, dulcimer, percussion (ex-Sonna) / **Michael Lambright** - glockenspiel, ukulele, accordion, percussion / plus **Tim Redd** - drums, percussion / **Chris Freeland**

US: Secret Eye — UK: not issued

Sep 04. (cd) *<AB-OC-12>* **CROWN YOUR HEAD WITH FLOWERS, CROWN YOUR HEART WITH JOY** [ ] [–]
- Lows at the highland games / Harbor to a hill / Sweetest lily / Slumbering lioness / Autumnal hymn / Bonnie boy / A lofty hill, a shady nook / Dogwood and sky / Atop a secret mountain / Willie of Winsbury / A fond farewell.

Nov 05. (m-cd) *<AB-OC-21>* **A WOVEN PAGE OF SILVER LIGHT** [ ] [–]
- Will I follow you to sea / Wrapped in the cloths of heaven / A cricket's call come one and all / The ballad of North Haywood / A subtle tune / Weep not wandering willow / North country.

BIG LOST RAINBOW

BIG LOST RAINBOW (Ridley Pearson, Otis Head, Adam Berenson, Robin Pfoutz, J.P. Bailhe and Tony Morse) got together in 1971 after rehearsals at their school in Pomfret, Connecticut, where it was reported the drummerless band once played to a crowd of 10,000.

Like all true psych-folk hippies of their generation, BIG LOST RAINBOW moved around a lot, touching base with Los Angeles, Cape Cod, Maryland and elsewhere while they performed the occasional gig and delivered the odd demo cassette. With demand growing from their expanding circle of friends and fans, the cassette was turned into a vinyl LP. **BIG LOST RAINBOW** (1973) {*7}, mostly written by leader Pearson, was riddled with baroque CSN/JAMES TAYLOR harmonies. Some were gentle and gorgeous, like ('Oh! Idaho' and 'Lady Love'); some fragile and sentimental, such as 'Slow Rider'. The finale, 'Lady Of Music', lasts just over 13 minutes.

Taking up residence in New England, the band couldn't find backers for their easy-going concept, and although they played support tours around the country, they decided to call it a day in 1975. Pearson would subsequently become a bestselling crime author (latest as of 2010 is 'In Harm's Way'), and he reconnected with his BIG LOST RAINBOW pals in a brief 1992 reunion at his Idaho home. One song from the reunion, 'Allegiance Of Apathy', was tagged on to the CD re-issue of their long-lost album. *MCS*

Ridley Pearson - vocals, guitar, piano, sax / **Otis Head** - guitar, piano, vocals / **Adam Berenson** - piano / **Robin Pfoutz** - cello / **J.P./Jacques Bailhe** - bass / **Tony Morse** - flute

US: test press — UK: not issued

1973. (ltd-lp) *<CO 6364>* **BIG LOST RAINBOW** [ ] [–]
- Sail / I go alone / Lady love / Brothers of the future / Ocean / Oh! Idaho / It's over now / Morning sunshine / Lady of music. *<cd+=/lp-iss. Aug 99 on 'Gear Fab'; GF-118>* - Slow rider / Patricia Jane Moon / Allegiance of apathy [from 1992 reunion].

—— the band split in 1975

BIRCH BOOK (⟹ IN GOWAN RING)

Andrew BIRD [solo, folk-only]

Once a member of modern swing-rock outfits The Squirrel Nut Zippers and Andrew Bird's Bowl Of Fire, the croaky singer-songwriter, violinist and whistler flits in and out of folk, mostly in the old-timey traditional style.

Born Andrew Wegman Bird, July 11, 1973, in Chicago, he surfaced as a solo artist on 1996's back-porch album **MUSIC OF HAIR** (recorded 1992) {*6}. Three Bowl Of Fire sets appeared on Rykodisc - 'Thrills', 'Oh! The Grandeur' and 'The Swimming Hour' - before the chamber-folk EP 'The Ballad Of The Red Shoes' brought him back into the folk fold.

Signed to Righteous Babe (home to ANI DiFRANCO, etc) and calling on retainer Kevin O'Donnell (his drummer in Bowl Of Fire) and singer Nora O'Connor (of The Blacks), **WEATHER SYSTEMS** (2003) {*8} displayed dark and bright subject matter, with weeping and waltzing pizzicato violins complementing BIRD's booming voice on songs like 'Lull' and his take on The HANDSOME FAMILY's 'Don't Be Scared'. Sticking with Kevin and Nora for support, the same could be said of his follow-up **ANDREW BIRD AND THE MYSTERIOUS PRODUCTION OF EGGS** (2005) {*8}, another slice of alternative rock with a hint of folk, ambitious and mesmerising on gems like 'Sovay', The Naming Of Things' and 'Banking On A Myth'.

A switch to Fat Possum resulted in BIRD's US Top 100 breakthrough with 2007's **ARMCHAIR APOCRYPHA** {*8}, another structurally sound expression of where the man was at. Drummer and electric pianist Martin Dosh was on hand, and bassist Chris Morrissey turned up on five tracks. Of the dozen cuts 'Armchairs', 'Fiery Crash' and a revamp of 'I', from 'Weather Systems' (as 'Imotosis'), come off best.

NOBLE BEAST (2009) {*7} cast off his indie-folk shackles and broke into the US Top 20, the classic 'Oh No', 'Fitz And The Dizzyspells' and 'Anoanimal' finding a new audience among the wanton alt-rock brigade. His folk and swing fans could look to the schizoid six minutes of 'Masterswarm'. *MCS*

Andrew Bird - vocals, violin (+ session people)

US: Andrew Bird — UK: not issued

1996. (cd) *<001>* **MUSIC OF HAIR** [rec. 1992] [ ] [–]
- Nuthinduan waltz / Ambivalence waltz / Oh so insistent / Rhodeaoh / Two sisters / St Francis reel / Ratitat - Peter's wolf - Oblivious reel / The greenhorn - Exile of Erin - Glasgow reel / Pathetique / Song of foot / Minor Beatrice / Oh so sad.

—— between 1996 and 2001, Andrew Bird's Bowl Of Fire released three swing-pop sets

Grimsey — not issued

Jun 01. (cd-ep) *<none>* THE BALLAD OF THE RED SHOES [–] mp3 [–]
- Theme 1 (waltz) / Something sinister / Chorus of the swan / Theme 1 (restated) / Dance of death / The door / Swedish folk tune.

Righteous Babe — Fargo

Jun 03. (cd) *<RBR 032-D>* (FA 20426) **WEATHER SYSTEMS** [ ] Feb 04 [ ]
- First song / I / Lull / Action-adventure / (untitled) / Savoy *[UK-only]* / Skin / Weather systems / Don't be scared / (untitled) / [12-minute video]. *<orig. iss. Apr 03 on Grimsey; 025>*

Feb 05. (cd-ep) *<FA EP04>* SOVAY [ ] [–]
- Sovay / First song [live] / Why? [live] / Action-adventure [live] / Sovay [live with My Morning Jacket].

Feb 05. (cd) *<RBR 043-D> (FA 20527)* **ANDREW BIRD AND THE MYSTERIOUS PRODUCTION OF EGGS** [ ] [ ]
- Bird symbol 1 / Sovay / A nervous tic motion of the head to the left / Fake palindromes / Measuring cups / Banking on a myth / Masterfade / Opposite day / Skin is, my / The naming of things / MX missiles / Bird symbol 2 / Tables and chairs / The happy birthday song. *<US lp-iss. on Grimsey; 032>*

Fat Possum — Fargo

Mar 07. (cd/lp) *<FP 1058-2/-1> (FA 0090)* **ARMCHAIR APOCRYPHA** [76] Apr 07 [ ]
- Fiery crash / Imitosis / Plasticities / Heretics / Armchairs / Darkmatter / Simple X / The supine / Cataracts / Scythian empires / Spare-ohs / Yawny at the apocalypse.

Fat Possum — Bella Union

Jan 09. (cd/d-lp) *<FP 1124-2/-1> (BELLACD 190)* **NOBLE BEAST** [12] Feb 09 [ ]
- Oh no / Masterswarm / Fitz and the dizzyspells / Effigy / Tenuousness / Nomenclature / Ouo / Not a robot, but a ghost / Unfolding fans / Anoanimal / Natural disaster / The privateers / Souverian / Oh ho! *<(deluxe d-cd-iss.+=; FP 1124-9>(BELLACD 190X)* - USELESS CREATURES

May 09. (cd-ep) *(BELLACD 200)* FITZ AND THE DIZZYSPELLS [–] [ ]
- Fitz and the Dizzyspells / Section 8 city / Ten-you-us / See the enemy / The nightshade gets in it.

Oct 09. (7") *<FP 1200-7>* ANOANIMAL. / See The Enemy [ ] [–]

Oct 10. (cd/lp) <*FP 1219-2/-1*> (mp3) **USELESS CREATURES**
- Master sigh / You woke me up! / Nyatiti / The barn tapes / Carrion suite / Spinney / Dissent / Hot math / Sigh master.

- special releases -

2002. (cd) Grimsey; <*none*> **FINGERLINGS** [live in 2001]
- Action-adventure / Keep your lamp trimmed and burning / Gotholympians / Richmond woman / Sweetbreads / Why? / Headsoak / How indiscreet / T'N'T.

2004. (cd) Grimsey; <*none*> **FINGERLINGS 2** [live]
- First song / Skin is, my / Masterfade / Banking on a myth / MX missiles / Spanish for monsters / Sovay / Way out west / Depression pasillo / Happy day.

2006. (cd) Grimsey; <*none*> **FINGERLINGS 3** [live]
- Grinnin' / Darkmatter / The water jet cilice / Measuring cups / The happy birthday song / A nervous tic motion of the head to the left / Scythian empire / Dear Dirty / Tin foil / Ethiobirds.

2010. (cd) Wegawam; <*none*> **FINGERLINGS 4: GEZELLIGHEID, CHICAGO** [live in 2009] mail-o
- Dance of death / Master sigh / Make hay / You woke me up! / Danse carribe / The barn tapes / The sifters / Carrion suite / Meet me here at dawn / Oh Baltimore / Section 8 city.

Sir Richard BISHOP

A self-appointed knight of no particular realm, Phoenix, Arizona-based improv guitar maestro SIR RICHARD BISHOP (born August 19, 1960, Saginaw, Michigan) is probably better known to fans of experimental outfit the Sun City Girls. In fact, his first official solo album, **SALVADOR KALI** (1998) {*6} - delivered on JOHN FAHEY's Revenant imprint - drew on those roots and sources.

It was experimental, but on a worldly avant-folk template - FAHEY, Reinhardt and Shankar were particular influences, presumably - and it would be six long years before the Locust label released a follow-up, **IMPROVIKA** (2004) {*7}, a free-flowing finger-picking set with a title that more than suggested what was within. The Eastern flavours of 'Rudra's Feast' and 'Gnostic Gem' displayed his dexterity to the max.

ELEKTRONIKA DEMONIKA (2006) {*5} was vinyl-only - later given free with his 'God Damn Religion' DVD/film in 2008 - and **FINGERING THE DEVIL** (2006) {*7} was BISHOP's next proper port of call. Drawn from London label Southern Lord's 'Latitude' series (think John Peel sessions), the concept was recorded unrehearsed in July 2005. The Turkish-tinged 'Anatolia', the desert-bowl boldness of 'Dream Of The Lotus Eaters' and the gypsy jazz of 'Romany Trail' were impressive examples of his to-die-for talent.

Conjuring up moments of frenetic acoustic finger-picking, **WHILE MY GUITAR VIOLENTLY BLEEDS** (2007) {*7} - a playful reference to a George Harrison/Beatles song - weaves his Eastern-style folk explorations into three freak-out instrumentals kicking off with 'Zurvan'. In the manner of PETER WALKER in his 1960s 'Rainy Day Raga' period, or early Pink Floyd and Tangerine Dream, the 11-minute drone of 'Smashana' can be safely filed under feedback-folk, while his guitar does indeed bleed - to death. A test of musical survival and endurance, the 25 minutes of finale 'Mahavidya' (imagine ROBBIE BASHO on a Popol Vuh soundtrack) is arguably daunting, but the skill and technique of Sir Richard wins the day.

Moving stables from Locust to Drag City, he released **POLYTHEISTIC FRAGMENTS** (2007) {*7}, comprised of shorter tracks with the exception of the minimalistic 10-minute 'Saraswati'. If world-fusion music - beset with flamenco tango, Brazilian samba and Appalachian folk - is your bag, Richard's free-flowing, electrifying improvisations will put your pulse in overdrive. From deep in a Louisiana back porch, 'Hecate's Dream' and 'Tennessee Porch Swing' explore a cinematic Ry Cooder avenue with their dreamy cactus soundscapes, while the 12-string wonderment of 'Free Masonic Guitar' is quite breathtaking. The weirdness of short composition 'Cemetery Gates' and the Dick Dale/bluegrass-surf cut 'Canned Goods And Firearms' bring a little light relief to an almost decadently elegant set. The album closes with the luscious 'Ecstasies In The Open Air', a horizontally laidback piece that recalls the likes of Gary Moore in 'Parisienne Walkways' mood.

Turning his idolatry to revered Middle Eastern guitarist Omar Khorshid, **THE FREAK OF ARABY** (2009) {*7} took on a handful of Arabian-sourced music ('Sidi Mansour' a reverb delight). Of a few more from that particular neighbourhood, Mohamed Abdel Wahab's 'Enta Omri' sticks out as another highlight of BISHOP's entry into Egyptian raga. *MCS*

Richard Bishop - vocals, guitars (+ some guests)

US Revenant / UK Revenant

Apr 98. (cd) <*(Rev 102)*> **SALVADOR KALI** May 98
- Burning caravan / Rasheed / Cadaques / Pedro's last ride / Al-Darazi / Hadley / Rose room / Kamakhya / Morella.

Locust / not issued

Sep 04. (cd) <*LOCUST 61*> **IMPROVIKA**
- Provenance unknown / Gnostic gem / Rudra's feast / Cryptonymus / Jaisalmer / Mystic minor 23 / Tripurasundari / Rose secretions / Skull of Sidon. *(ltd-UK lp-iss. 2005 on Bo'Weavil; Weavil 04)*

Jun 06. (ltd-lp) <*LOCUST 80*> **ELEKTRONIKA DEMONIKA** mail-o
- Untitled / Untitled / Untitled / Untitled.

Latitudes / No-Fi

Jun 06. (cd) <*GMT 0:07*> **FINGERING THE DEVIL**
- Abydos / Dream of the lotus eater / Romany trail / Anatolia / Fingering the devil / Spanish bastard / Gypsum / Black eyed blue / Howrah station. *<ltd-clear-lp iss. Feb 07; GMT 0:07 LP>*

Jun 06. (7") *(NARC 001)* PLAYS SUN CITY GIRLS
- Space prophet dogon / Esoterica of Abyssinia.

Locust / not issued

Jun 07. (cd/ltd-lp) <*LOCUST 90*> **WHILE MY GUITAR VIOLENTLY BLEEDS**
- Zurvan / Smashana / Mahavidya.

Drag City / Drag City

Sep 07. (cd/lp) <*(DC 349 CD/LP)*> **POLYTHEISTIC FRAGMENTS**
- Cross my palm with silver / Hecate's dream / Elysium number five / Rub' Al Khali / Free masonic guitar / Cemetery games / Quiescent return / Saraswati / Tennessee porch swing / Canned goods and firearms / Ecstasies in the open air.

Feb 08. (12") <*SUNN 90.5*> [track by Earth]. / NARASIMHA
(above issued on Southern Lord)

May 09. (cd/lp) <*(DC 398 CD/LP)*> **THE FREAK OF ARABY**
- Taqasim for Omar / Enta Omri / Barbary / Solenzara / The pillars of Baalbek / Kaddak el Mayass / Essaouira / Ka'an Azzaman / Sidi Mansour / Blood-stained sands.

Rachel BISSEX

Born December 27, 1956 in Boston, Massachusetts and raised in nearby Newton, Rachel began her musical career as a young teenager when her mother bought her a $35 acoustic guitar. Self-taught from JOAN BAEZ and PETER, PAUL & MARY songbooks, she took her fine arts degree from Johnson State College to Burlington, Vermont, where she stayed for a while with her father and brother.

Taking folk music as well as jazz as her template (she was a big fan of JONI MITCHELL), she opened up a coffee-house folk venue in Burlington and founded the local jazz festival. The 1980s turned into the 1990s, and although Rachel was working hard playing the circuit (she opened for Joan Armatrading, SHAWN COLVIN and Ray Charles), she had to her name only one, self-financed set, **LIGHT IN DARK PLACES** {*5} (1991).

That was put right when Alcazar delivered the first of two CDs. **DON'T LOOK DOWN** (1995) {*7} was definitive, featuring covers of Jackson Browne's 'Colors Of The Sun', Carol Abair's 'Whistle Me Dixie', JONI MITCHELL's 'The Last Time I Saw Richard', and LEONARD COHEN's 'A Singer Must Die' alongside her own little gem 'Dancing With My Mother'. **I USED TO BE NICE** (1998) {*6} continued in the same the easy folk style, and it looked as though BISSEX's career was on the up.

Two further album releases, **BETWEEN THE BROKEN LINES** (2001) {*6} and **IN WHITE LIGHT** (2004) {*6} - the former containing another gem, 'Drive All Night' - came perhaps a little late in the day. She began a film acting career in 2004's 'Nothing Like Dreaming' and directed her husband Stephen Goldberg's play 'Sun Spot: The Crime Of The Need To Be Right'.

Sadly, she died of complications of breast cancer on February 20, 2005 after two painful years of illness. To show their appreciation, her folk-fraternity friends, family and fan club put together a various-artists tribute album, 'Remember Rachel', that summer. *MCS*

Rachel Bissex - vocals, acoustic guitar

US own label / UK not issued

1991. (cd) <*none*> **LIGHT IN DARK PLACES**
- Shadow / Paint brush / Letter to Martin / How I feel / Edge / At twenty-nine / Without a sound / Old child / Never go back / Daddy / Christine / Great mother / Climb inside / November 9 1989.

Alcazar / not issued

Nov 95. (cd/c) <*121*> **DON'T LOOK DOWN**
- Don't look down / Wildflowers / Eve of construction / Colors of the sun / Oh Jackson / Beauty in the dark / Whistle me Dixie / Toward the ocean / The last time I saw Richard / Leave it open / A singer must die / Anchor / Dancing with my mother.

Feb 98. (cd) *<132>* **I USED TO BE NICE**
- In the middle / For Florence / In the magazines / Royal blues / Passion / What's right / December moon / Angel / Witness / The ballad of Eunice and Pearl / There's a river / Cold November wood. *(bonus +=)- Untitled.*

One Take — not issued

Oct 01. (cd) *<none>* **BETWEEN THE BROKEN LINES**
- Starting over / Flying / Hurricane desire / Hey Marianne / Sean Connery looks / Gravity's gone / More than you / Down / Drive all night / One another / For Andy / Busy man / Oh Jackson.

Jun 04. (cd) *<none>* **IN WHITE LIGHT**
- In white light / Here now / Just like that / Last blast of winter / Waitin' on the rain / Welcome to the game / A little wild / Into my arms / Standing in the dark / No more songs / Never go back / Dancing with my mother.

sadly, Rachel died in 2005

- essential tribute album -

Jul 05. (cd) Rachel Bissex; *<none>* **REMEMBERING RACHEL: SONGS OF RACHEL BISSEX**
- For Florence (ELLEN BUKSTEL, KATE McDONNELL & SIOBHAN QUINN) / Last blast of winter (SLOAN WAINWRIGHT) / Starting over (GROOVELILY, RACHEL GARLIN & STEPHANIE CORBY) / Never go back (GREG GREENWAY, KIM & REGGIE HARRIS) / One another (LUCIE BLUE TREMBLAY) / In the middle (DIANE ZEIGLER) / Drive all night (RONNY COX w/ ERIC SCHWARTZ) / Waitin' on the rain (AMY CAROL WEBB) / Welcome to the game (TRACY GRAMMER & JIM HENRY) / Flying (DAVID LAMOTTE, EMMA GOLDBERG & DANIEL BISSEX) / Royal blues (HOLY FIGUEROA & ANNIE WENZ) / Here now (TRET FURE) / Hey Marianne (The KENNEDYS) / Oh Jackson (RUTHIE FOSTER) / For Andy (FREEBO & PHOTOGLO) / Just like that (DAR WILLIAMS & PATTY LARKIN) / Angel (ANNIE GALLUP) / Gravity's gone (DREAMSICLES & NEW HICKS) / Into my arms (KRISTIN DeWITT) / In white light (JENNIFER KIMBALL & CATIE CURTIS) / Flame warm (STEPHEN GOLDBERG) / VPR interview / Dancing with my mother (RACHEL BISSEX).

BLACK FOREST/BLACK SEA (⟹ The IDITAROD)

BLACKGIRLS

Not actually black girls, but a modern folk trio of pale-faced ladies dressed in black from Raleigh, North Carolina, this group comprised Eugenia Lee (vocals and guitar), Dana Kletter (vocals and piano) and violinist Hollis Brown, recruited in 1985.

After a few low-key single releases, they went into the studio with veteran British producer Joe Boyd, a legend who had worked with FAIRPORT CONVENTION, NICK DRAKE, NICO, etc, and was now head of Hannibal Records. Licensed to their local independent, Mammoth, they surfaced from the TGS studios in Chapel Hill, North Carolina with their debut album, **PROCEDURE** (1989) {*6}.

Sharing the quirky punk energy and girly angst of Brit-indie act The Raincoats and femme-folkies The ROCHES, or even a Celtic-folk ALL ABOUT EVE or Kate Bush, the album marked them out as defiantly different. Kletter and Lee divided the songwriting (with the exception of the collectively jazzed-up title track), and the set excels through strong vocals and instrumentation, nowhere better than on Kletter's schizoid 'Too Many', the mournful 'The Thing Is' and the lilting 'Translator', and Lee's pixieish 'Moonflower' and 'Bathtub'.

Two years later, the BLACKGIRLS (and Boyd) returned with a second helping of quirky/sadcore folk-pop, **HAPPY** (1991) {*5}. Without the existence of the similar INDIGO GIRLS, and the slight disappointment of this album, the trio might have climbed higher. Where tracks such as Lee's 'Fat' or Kletter's 'Thunder' could have fitted into the grunge-fixated world of the early 1990s is anyone's guess, but with the trio splitting in 1992 it didn't matter.

Disillusioned with folk music, the classically-trained DANA KLETTER turned her talents to grunge, augmenting Courtney Love and Hole on choice cuts ('Doll Parts' and 'Credit In The Straight World') from their breakthrough 'Live Through This' set. Continuing on the alt-rock theme, Dana and her band, Dish (with the help of Love), signed with Interscope, issuing 'Boneyard Beach' in 1995, following on from their 1994 debut, the independently-released EP 'Mabel Sagittarius'. Together with ex-Dish multi-instrumentalist Sara Bell, Dana later formed Dear Enemy, although this formation lapsed when she decided to team up with her twin sister, Karen Kletter, who sang backing vocals for the BLACKGIRLS.

As DANA & KAREN KLETTER, and with Joe Boyd once again in tow, the harmonious duo (whose Hungarian-born mother was an Auschwitz survivor) completed an album in 1998, **DEAR ENEMY** {*7}. Introspective, and understandably deep and thought-provoking, tracks such as 'Flight Into Egypt' and 'Father Song' overshadowed lighter items 'We Died In August' and the traditional Yiddish lullaby 'Raisins And Almonds'. *MCS*

Eugenia Lee - vocals, guitar, mandolin / **Dana Kletter** (b. 1960, Baltimore, Maryland) - vocals, piano, guitar / **Hollis Brown** - violin, vocals

US — UK
Palindrome — not issued

1986. (7") *<none>* BROKEN LEG. / Procedure

(above was available only in the palindromically titled various-artists box set 'Evil I Do Not To Nod I Live')

Tom Tom — not issued

1987. (12" ep) *<SO 17930>* SPEECHLESS
- Queen Anne / Speechless / Devil's garden / Insects / Stupid metaphor.

Mammoth — Hannibal

Nov 89. (lp/c/cd) *<MR 0017-1/-4/-2> (HNBL/HNBC/HNCD 1348)* **PROCEDURE**
- Too many / Moonflower / Window - Door / Biting / The thing is / Loser / Translator / Procedure / A visit to the behaviorist / Bathtub / One lie / Hope / Friends.

May 91. (cd/c/lp) *<MR 0024-2/-4/-1> (HNCD/HNBC/HNBL 1365)* **HAPPY** — Sep 91
- Happy / In the room / Cathedral / Car / Charleston / Talk / Letter / Fat / Thunder / The I love you song / Tell you everything / Smart man / Mother.

split after above release

DANA & KAREN KLETTER

with her identical twin Karen

Hannibal — Hannibal

Apr 98. (cd) *<(HBCD 1420)>* **DEAR ENEMY**
- We died in August / Meteor mom / Father song / Directions / Your mother wants to know / Sister song / Flight into Egypt / Maria Marie / Beach song / Raisins and almonds / Anna O / Blue glass.

BLACK HAPPY DAY (⟹ STONE BREATH)

Kath BLOOM

Born in New Haven, Connecticut (daughter of oboe player Robert Bloom) and based in nearby Litchfield, singer-songwriter KATH BLOOM's musical career began with appearances on Bruce Neumann's early-1970s recordings. Progressing, she recorded several LPs with avant/improv guitarist Loren MazzaCane. The first, **GIFTS** (1978, for Daggett) {*5}, credited her only on the side-long title track. His other LPs, 'Unaccompanied Acoustic Guitar Improvisations Volume I' and further volumes II-VIII, featured either her voice or her cover artwork. This partnership ended in 1984 after their **MOONLIGHT** {*6} set, while she subsequently concentrated on bringing up her family as a single mother.

Film director Richard Linklater, who had been a fan from early in the 1990s, used her song 'Come Here' in his 1995 movie 'Before Sunrise', and revamps of some old tracks and some new songs appeared on her part-compilation solo debut **COME HERE: THE FLORIDA YEARS** (1999) {*7}.

Another decade passed by before three fresh BLOOM sets materialised. **TERROR** (2008) {*6} and **THIN THIN LINE** (2010) {*6} were released either side of a double-CD tribute set, 'Loving Takes This Course'. Currently, Kath works at training horses and moonlights with the Love At Work project alongside husband Stan Bronski and long-time collaborator Tom Hanford. *MCS*

Kath Bloom - vocals, acoustic guitar / with **Loren Mazzacane (Connors)** - vocals, acoustic guitar

US — UK
Daggett — not issued

1978. (ltd-lp; by LOREN MAZZACANE) *<DTT-01>* **GIFTS**
- Acoustic guitar / Gifts [with KATH BLOOM].

from 1979–1980, Bloom guested on, and provided cover art for, Loren Mazzacane's 'Unaccompanied Acoustic Guitar Improvisations' LPs.

In 1980 they also issued the very limited 'A Dwight Chapel Concert'.

—— next also credited **Tom Hanford** - vocals, acoustic guitar

1981. (ltd-lp; as HANFORD, BLOOM AND MAZZACANE) *<dtt 10>* **HANFORD, BLOOM AND MAZZACANE**
- Been listening all day long / Down this road / Goin' home / Fall again / Held my baby last night / Religion / Some happy day / Let me hold you for a while / Baby let it come down on me / Come to me now / Some these days / Biggest light of all.

In Sep '81, Kath and her acoustic guitar feat. on Loren Mazzacane's EP 'Listen To The Blues'.

1982. (ltd-lp; LOREN MAZZACANE & KATH BLOOM) <*dtt-12*>
ROUND HIS SHOULDERS GONNA BE A RAINBOW
- Graveyard / It's so hard / I've been listening all day long / Fall again / Swing low sweet chariot / Floating bridge / Religion is something within you / Come on in my kitchen / Moses / Swing low sweet chariot / Broken dream / Man it's a long long lonesome road / Give me Jesus / What a joke.

1982. (ltd-7" ep; LOREN MAZZACANE & KATH BLOOM) <*dtt 13*>
PUSHIN' UP DAISIES
- Little tree / Swing low sweet chariot / Loren's blues / Lay my burden down / Kath's blues.

Ambiguous not issued

1982. (ltd-lp; by LOREN MAZZACANE & KATH BLOOM)
<*AMB-002*> **SING THE CHILDREN OVER**
- Last fair deal / The breeze - My baby cries / Nobody's fault but mine / All my trials here / It's so hard to come home / I've been working on the railroad / Moses / In the garden / Light from the lighthouse / There was a boy / Lullaby / I was wondering. <*re-iss. Jul 01 on Secretly Canadian; SC 1002*> <*d-cd-iss. Nov 08 on Chapter;* <*cstyle:*>*063*> - (SAND IN MY SHOE tracks) / I just have to tell you *(live at Gerde's Folk City, NYC, 1981 with TOM HANFORD)* / Pretty little flowers *(live at Gerde's Folk City, NYC, 1981 with TOM HANFORD)* / Little tree.

St. Joan not issued

1983. (ltd-lp; by KATH BLOOM & LOREN MAZZACANE) <*St.J.1*>
SAND IN MY SHOE
- We're on our way / Window / Give it slow / Baby now / You make my dreams come true / My stupid little heart / I'm as good as I want to be / Sand in my shoe / When you smile / This river / Same streets / Seems like I'm always waiting for you / Since I met you. <*d-cd-iss.+=*> - SING THE CHILDREN OVER

Feb 84. (ltd-lp; KATH BLOOM / LOREN CONNORS) <*St.J.2*>
RESTLESS FAITHFUL DESPERATE
- Tall grass / Hold on / When I see you / You give me something / How we live / When your dreams come true / How it rains / Look at me / Just don't tell me that it's good / How it rains / Wait for my love / The key / Out in the woods / Then I come home.

Dec 84. (ltd-lp; KATH BLOOM & LOREN CONNORS) <*St.J.3*>
MOONLIGHT
- To love a man / Come here / Can you find me? / Puccini / Turn on your head lights / End of the night / What if I found out (instrumental) / You cleared up the sky / Breath in my ear / Bicycle / Blues song / What if I found out / Love makes it all worthwhile.

—— in 1993 and 1996 respectively she issued two very limited CD-rs, **LOVE EXPLOSION** and **IT'S JUST A DREAM**

1999. (cd-r) <*none*> **COME HERE: THE FLORIDA YEARS**
[part compilation]
- Come here / Tired / Fall again / Let's go walking / Open road / Equal / Work at love / Sand in my shoes / What is really beautiful / Love this earth / Little flower / A homeless dream / It's gonna pay / Calling your name. <*re-iss. 2005 on Japanese label Power Shovel Audio; PSA-002*>

Chapter Music not issued

Jan 05. (cd) <*CH 51*> **FINALLY** [compilation]
- Come here / It's just a dream / Forget about him / A homeless dream / Who you are / You and I keep falling / Can't rise to your feet / What is really beautiful / Fall again / Sand in my shoe / We crossed over / I wanna love / In your school / Finally.

May 08. (cd) <*CH 61*> **TERROR**
- Everything looks different at night / Love me / Midnight moon / Close to something / Just can't handle it / Something to tell you / Your house was burning / Didn't do this to you / Terror / Moon through a dusty window / Open road / Baby it's now / You walk beside me / Bye bye baby / Most beautiful day.

Caldo Verde not issued

Feb 10. (cd) <*CDCV 010*> **THIN THIN LINE**
- Thin thin line / Dangerous days / Heart so sadly / Like this / Such a tease / Back there / Is this called living? / Long ago / Another point of view / Let's get living / Freddie / I'm thinking of love / Who'll shoot the horse? / Not through with this yet.

- (5-7*) compilations -

Mar 00. (cd; KATH BLOOM / LOREN MAZZACANE CONNORS)
Megalon; <*(MEG 07CD)*> **1981–1984**
- Biggest light of all / Moses / Swing low, sweet chariot / I was wondering / My stupid little heart / When I feel you coming / Come here my sweetest one / How it rains / Without you / Love makes it worthwhile / Bicycle song / Puccini / What if we were together / A homeless dream.

Hugh BLUMENFELD

Born October 11, 1958, in Brooklyn, New York but now living in Coventry, Connecticut, singer-songwriter and guitarist HUGH BLUMENFELD first came to light in Greenwich Village in the 1980s as editor and contributor with the Fast Folk Musical Magazine and the vinyl records that came with it. His songs 'Hillside' and the audience-participation tongue-twister 'The Phenomenology Sing-Along' were particularly awe-inspiring.

A winner of the Kerrville New Folk Competition and a guest on CHRISTINE LAVIN's festive 'On A Winter's Night' collection, he was the first artist to sign for the then newly founded 1-800-Prime imprint. In 1994 they re-issued on CD two of his earlier recordings, **BAREHANDED** (1991) {*5} and his debut **THE STRONG IN SPIRIT** (1988) {*7}. His simple, intimate songs such as 'Sailing To The New World', 'Rising Moon', 'Brothers' and 'Song Of Florence' became signature tunes, and he covered Andrea Gaines's 'Snow Grain Stone' on the remixed second set.

Produced by David Seitz and augmented by fellow folk singers LUCY KAPLANSKY and Judith Zweiman, third album **MOZART'S MONEY** (1996) {*7} brought BLUMENFELD some plaudits from fans of STEVE GOODMAN, while there was a homage to Kurt Cobain by way of 'Mr Rain'. 1998's **ROCKET SCIENCE** {*5} was disappointing in comparison, although his cover of ANDREW CALHOUN's 'No Secret Castle' was a highlight.

In the past decade, Hugh has delivered only the occasional album: the European-only collaboration **BIG RED** (2000) {*5}, alongside Doris Ackermann and Shane Shanahan; a basement-tapes odds-and-ends curiosity, and a concept comeback set, **DAD** (2011) {*6}. *MCS*

Hugh Blumenfeld - vocals, guitar (with session people)

US Grace Avenue UK not issued

1988. (ltd-lp) <*none*> **THE STRONG IN SPIRIT**
- Brothers / Leather and lace / Let me fall in love before the spring comes / All the wood of Lebanon / Sailing to the new world / The strong in spirit / Rising moon / Soweto / I knew a boy / Song of Florence / Get the word. <*cd-iss. Dec 94 on 1-800-Prime PCD 06*>

1991. (ltd-c) <*none*> **BAREHANDED**
- Bring stones / Thread city / America redux / Carrie (intro) / Carrie / Camel filters / Quiet of the night / Watertowers / Jerusalem / Wedding song / Snow grain stone / Road and the rose / Hugh's 30th birthday party. <*remixed cd-iss. Sep 94 on 1-800-Prime; PCD 01*>

1-800-Prime not issued

Feb 96. (cd) <*PCD 21*> **MOZART'S MONEY**
- Mozart's money / Raphael / Waiting for the good humor man / This mountain / Talking island / Mr Rain / Main street sky / What if you do nothing - Winter suite / Sweet October / Sparrowhawk / Blizzard / Friends of a traveler / Visit. *(hidden track +=)* - When Hiroshima comes to Disneyland.

Jul 98. (cd) <*PCD 43*> **ROCKET SCIENCE**
- Shoot the moon / The snail / Saxton's river / Wormwood hill / Hands and feet / Is this enough / Longhaired radical socialist Jew (the gospel song) / Zhang jingsheng / Mighty quiet [instrumental] / Why am I awake / No secret castle / I only sing about love.

(next credited 'with Doris Ackermann and Shane Shanahan')

not issued Brambus

Apr 00. (cd) *(BRAM 30)* **BIG RED** Euro
- Big red / King of Chicago / Bring stones / Brothers / Shoot the moon / Did you hear the rain / Where's Marlene / Snow grain stone / The raven / Paul Cezanne / Raphael / Just say the word / Loony @ the Muni. <*(US/UK-iss. Apr 08/Sep 09; same)*>

not issued Jukebox Hydrogen

2004. (cd) *(none)* **MR JEKYLL & DR HYDE** [basement tapes, bootlegs and live performances]
- Shadow government / George the third / Hole in the sky / When Hiroshima comes to Disneyland / Long-haired radical socialist Jew / Lacrimae Laramie (song for Matthew Shepard) / How long / Talking hypothetical American pastime blues (the baseball song) / John Wayne (was a thespian) / Southern baptist / Bill's dick / Tinkie winkie / This mountain [FND debut live performance] / Quiet of the night / America redux.

Waterbug Waterbug

Jan 11. (cd) <*(WBG 91)*> **DAD** Dec 10
- Welcome to the world / NICU @ nite (the Preemie song) / Cradle song / Rock you / Sail on little sailor / I knew a boy / Daddy I'm awake / Cry little guy / Wonder wonder why / Daddy's got you now / Sad hard dream / Visitation / Sleep Sarah sleep / Till the morning / You gotta have coffee / My little boy's moon.

BON IVER

Among all the mournful acoustic strummers to have come out of America's backwaters, few people's money would have been on BON IVER to hit the big time.

How Justin Vernon's debut came together is now the stuff of indie-folk legend. Reeling from the break-ups of his band DeYarmond Edison and his relationship with his girlfriend, plus a bout of glandular fever, the singer-songwriter relocated from his home in Raleigh, North Carolina, hiding himself away in his father's hunting cabin in northwestern Wisconsin. There, during three months alone, chopping wood every morning, he found inspiration and wrote and recorded the bulk of the tracks that would appear on his debut set.

FOR EMMA, FOREVER AGO (2008) {*9} was nothing short of

breathtaking. Stark, beguiling and filled with layer upon layer of vocal harmonies underpinned by austere guitar and percussion, this is as intimate and compelling as folk records should sound. The album received universally great reviews and was a fixture in end-of-year polls and critics' best-of lists on both sides of the Atlantic. In a novel twist, it caught the attention of several TV producers, and songs from the album ended up soundtracking US TV series such as 'Grey's Anatomy', 'One Tree Hill' and 'Chuck'. The album also came to the attention of US rap star Kanye West, not known for his indie-folk leanings, who recruited Vernon to work on his album 'My Beautiful Dark Twisted Fantasy'. Vernon contributed to the tracks 'Monster' and 'Lost In The World'.

Vernon then shocked everyone and did the unthinkable by bettering his debut. His self-titled second set, **BON IVER** (2011) {*9}, was recorded in a re-modelled veterinary clinic and adjacent swimming pool in Fall Creek, Wisconsin, converted into a studio by Vernon and his brother. The recordings sat Vernon firmly at the centre of the process, but he augmented them with seasoned session players like pedal steel guitarist Greg Leisz, bass saxophonist Colin Stetson and string arranger Rob Moose. The heart of the songs was Vernon's evocative, stirring whine and growl, and musically, while more expansive and exploratory, he never lost the rural, earthy feel of the material. Each song, Vernon claimed, was based on thoughts of a particular place.

The album was a massive initial success both critically (again, acclaim was near-universal) and commercially, selling over 100,000 copies in its first week of release in the US alone and debuting at No.2, kept off the top spot only by soul diva Jill Scott. *MCS*

Justin Vernon - vocals, guitars, etc. (+ a few session people)

US / UK
self-rel. / not issued

Feb 06. (cd; with DeYARMOND EDISON) <*none*> **SILENT SIGNS** [–] [–]
- Lift / Silent signs / Heroin(e) / Love long gone / First impression / Bones / Heart for hire / Dead anchor / Ragstock / Dash / We / Time to know.

Jagjaguwar / 4 ad

Feb 08. (lp/cd) <*JAG 115/4115*> (*CAD 2809/+CD*) **FOR EMMA, FOREVER AGO** [64] May 08 [42]
- Flume / Lump sum / Skinny love / The wolves (acts I and II) / Blindsided / Creature fear / Team / For Emma / Re: stacks.

Sep 08. (7") (*AD 2817*) FOR EMMA. / Wisconsin [–] [ ]

Jagjaguwar / Jagjaguwar

Jan 09. (12" ep/cd-ep) <(*JAG 134/+CD*)> BLOOD BANK [16] [37]
- Blood bank / Beach baby / Babys / Woods.

Apr 10. (ltd-7" shared) <*JAG 170*> COME TALK TO ME. / (other track by PETER GABRIEL) [ ] [–]

Jun 11. (cd) <(*JAG 135*)> **BON IVER** [2] [4]
- Perth / Minnesota, WI / Holocene / Towers / Michicant / Hinnom, TX / Wash / Calgary / Lisbon, OH / Beth - Rest.

A.A. BONDY

American singer-songwriters don't come much cooler or more horizontally laid-back than Birmingham, Alabama-born Auguste Arthur Bondy (also known as Scott Bondy). Reminiscent of Ryan Adams, BRIGHT EYES and Jackson Browne, A.A. BONDY has the qualifications to be the next big thing in rootsy folk music.

After three sets with post-grungesters Verbena (one of which was produced by Dave Grohl), BONDY split the band to write solo songs in his Catskills retreat. Solo debut **AMERICAN HEARTS** (2007) {*6}, the product of a couple of years spent perfecting his trademark drawl, paved the way for his second set, **WHEN THE DEVIL'S LOOSE** (2009) {*7}. Accompanied by only Macey Taylor (bass) and Paul Buchignani (drums), A.A.'s freewheeling late-night narratives struck a chord on 'I Can See The Pines Are Dancing', 'False River', 'A Slow Parade' and the title track. *MCS*

A.A. Bondy - vocals, guitars (with session band/players)

US / UK
Superphonic / not issued

Aug 07. (cd) <*SUPR-2167*> **AMERICAN HEARTS** [ ] [–]
- How will you meet your end / There's a reason / Black rain, black rain / Rapture (sweet rapture) / American hearts / No man shall / World without end / Lovers' waltz / Vice rag / Killed myself when I was young / Witness blues / Of the sea.

Fat Possum / Fat Possum

Apr 08. (re; cd) <(*FP 1112-2*)> AMERICAN HEARTS [ ] [ ]
<*lp-iss. Jul 09; FP 1112-1*>

Sep 09. (cd/lp) <(*FP 1198-2/-1*)> **WHEN THE DEVIL'S LOOSE** [ ] Oct 09 [ ]
- Mightiest of guns / A slow parade / When the devil's loose / To the morning / Oh the vampyre / I can see the pines are dancing / False river / On the moon / The mercy wheel / The coal hits the fire.

BORN HELLER (⟹ FOSTER, Josephine)

BOWERBIRDS

One of many alt-indie refugees to jump ship into the ever-expanding fraternity of neo-folk acts, the Raleigh, North Carolina-based BOWERBIRDS took their cue from the likes of DEVENDRA BANHART and IRON & WINE. Formed in 2006 from the ashes of indie-rockers Ticonderoga, frontman and guitarist Phil Moore and his visual-arts girlfriend Beth Salmon/Tacular (on self-taught accordion, etc) surfaced from a cabin in the woods with enough recordings for an EP, 'Danger At Sea'.

To flesh out and expand the potential of their clappy-happy songs, the duo enlisted the services of producer and multi-instrumentalist Mark Paulson for debut set **HYMNS FOR A DARK HORSE** (2007) {*7}. Now signed to Dead Oceans Records, they pushed the record out again in 2008, boosted with two tagged-on tracks. Within their second set, **UPPER AIR** (2009) {*7}, nestled some amiable and quirky tunes in 'Teeth', 'Silver Clouds' and 'Northern Lights'. *MCS*

Phil Moore - vocals, guitar / **Beth Tacular** (b. Beth Salmon) - accordion, bass drum, vocals

US / UK
self-rel. / not issued

2006. (m-cd) <*none*> DANGER AT SEA [–] [–]
- My oldest memory / The Ticonderoga / In our talons / Bur oak / La denigracion / Knives, snakes and mesquite.

—— added **Mark Paulson** - multi

Burly Time / not issued

Jul 07. (cd) <*001*> **HYMNS FOR A DARK HORSE** [ ] [–]
- Hooves / In our talons / Human hands / Dark horse / Burr oak / My oldest memory / The marbled godwit / Slow down / The Ticonderoga / Olive hearts.

Dead Oceans / Dead Oceans

Jun 08. (re; cd/lp) <(*DOC 017 cd/lp*)> **HYMNS FOR A DARK HORSE** [ ] Aug 08 [ ]
- [original tracks] (*+=*) - La denigracion / Matchstick maker.

Jul 09. (cd/lp) <(*DOC 018 cd/lp*)> **UPPER AIR** [ ] [ ]
- House of diamonds / Teeth / Silver clouds / Beneath your tree / Ghost life / Northern lights / Chimes / Bright future / Crooked lust / This day.

BRIGHT EYES [folk part]

Contrary to popular belief, although Conor Oberst has been described as a modern-day BOB DYLAN, his BRIGHT EYES collective is not folk music – more like roots or alt-country, maybe; indie-rock, definitely. From his formative solo works in the 1990s and his time on the Saddle Creek label with Commander Venus, Park Ave and Desaparecidos, he has had the air of a man going places higher than the limited indie/alt scene. He now combines his BRIGHT EYES work with solo records that have taken America and the world by storm.

One album, **I'M WIDE AWAKE, IT'S MORNING** (2005) {*6} (there was a shared mini-set in 2004, **ONE JUG OF WINE, TWO VESSELS** {*5}), is regarded by many as his breakthrough, a US Top 20 record simultaneously released alongside his equally fruitful indie electric/electro 'Digital Ash In A Digital Urn' set. **I'M WIDE AWAKE ...** indeed takes leaves out of DYLAN's and PAUL SIMON's books, but precious songs such as 'We Are Nowhere And It's Now' (featuring country star Emmylou Harris) owe as much to Robert Pollard of Guided By Voices. A better picture is given in two other Discography books, Rock and Indie. *MCS*

- (selected folk discography) -

Conor Oberst - vocals, guitars, etc / **Mike Mogis** + **Mike Sweeney**

US / UK
Crank!: A Record Company / Saddle Creek

Apr 04. (shared m-cd; BRIGHT EYES // NEVA DINOVA) <*crc 40*> (*SCE 60-2*) **ONE JUG OF WINE, TWO VESSELS** [ ] [ ]
- [ND track] / Black comedy / [ND track] / I'll be your friend / [ND track] / Spring cleaning. <*re-iss. 2010 on Saddle Creek prefix +=; LBJ-145*> - [ND track] / Happy accident / [ND track] / I know you.

—— **Jason Boesel** - drums; repl. Sweeney

Jan 05. (lp/cd) <(*SCE 72 V/CD*)> **I'M WIDE AWAKE, IT'S MORNING** [10] [23]

- At the bottom of everything / We are nowhere and it's now / Old soul song (for the new world order) / Lua / Train under water / First day of my life / Another travelin' song / Land locked blues / Poison oak / Road to joy.

Chuck BRODSKY

With more than a nod to the DYLAN of 'Subterranean Homesick Blues', rootsy folk singer-songwriter CHUCK BRODSKY (born May 20, 1960, Philadelphia) is known for his barbed and witty social narrative and his jocular songs about his favourite subject, baseball. As 'Florida Today' put it, "If Mark Twain were reincarnated as a musician, his name might be Chuck Brodsky".

From his debut set for Waterbug Records, **A FINGERPAINTER'S MURALS** (1995) {*7} - featuring his classic 'Lefty' and 'Acre By Acre' stories, plus 'We Are Each Other's Angels' (covered by Kathy Mattea) and 'Blow 'Em Away' (covered by DAVID WILCOX) - to his most recent, the self-released **SUBTOTAL ECLIPSE** (2011) {*6}, Chuck has explored the territory of his North Carolina neighbourhood and beyond with inimitable aplomb.

A child prodigy who played piano and guitar early, he followed his studies at Penn State University with a musical apprenticeship of hitchhiking to open-mic nights in San Francisco coffee-houses and busking all over northern Europe. He played the Kerriville Folk Festival in 1992.

Taking up residence with fellow artist ANNIE GALLUP in North Carolina, he released three albums for Red House Records: **LETTERS IN THE DIRT** (1996) {*6}, **RADIO** (1998) {*6} (featuring GALLUP's song 'Circle') and **LAST OF THE OLD TIME** (2000) {*7}), all easy-going folk-country records full of sardonic wit and fanciful lyrics.

Of his post-millennium sets, the compilation **THE BASEBALL BALLADS** (2002) {*6} has been his most revered, the sport's fans loving every moment of his incisive creations, such as 'The Ballad Of Eddie Klepp' (about the first white man to play in the Negro leagues of the 1940s), 'Letters In The Dirt' (a homage to Richie Allen) and his nod to hero Steve Carlton in 'Lefty'. Other BRODSKY releases of the past decade include **COLOR CAME ONE DAY** (2004) {*6}, **TULIPS FOR LUNCH** (2006) {*6} and the essential North Carolina-Georgia-Ireland concert double album **TWO SETS** (2008) {*7}. *MCS*

Chuck Brodsky - vocals, acoustic guitar (+ session people)

US Waterbug — UK not issued

Jan 95. (cd) <*WBG 11*> **A FINGERPAINTER'S MURALS**
- Lefty / The ballad of me and Jones / Acre by acre / Maria's lament / Home away from home again / Happy little world / Unbridled reins / Blow 'em away / The ghost of Mrs Addison / Red skies and red waters / We are each other's angels / Fighting.

Red House — Red House

Aug 96. (cd) <*(RHRCD 87)*> **LETTERS IN THE DIRT** — Oct 96
- The ballad of Eddie Klepp / She's gone / Bill and Annie / No more Mr Nice Guy / Letters in the dirt / Talk to my lawyer / Sweet little Lou / Until you can forgive / Missing each other's cues / Long story short / The hands of Victor Jara / The goodbye kid.

Aug 98. (cd) <*(RHRCD 119)*> **RADIO** — Sep 98
- La migra viene / Moe Berg: the song / Bad whiskey / Our gods / Creepsville / Radio / On Christmas I got nothing / Blow 'em away / Hockey fight song / The come heres and the been heres / Circle.

Aug 00. (cd) <*(RHRCD 141)*> **LAST OF THE OLD TIME**
- Take it out back / The boys in the back room / Gone to heaven / He came to our town / In the country / Third dead cat / Restless kid / Bonehead Merkle / How beautiful she looks / Schmoozing / 40 years.

Chuck Brodsky — not issued

Jun 04. (cd) <*030*> **COLOR CAME ONE DAY**
- The 9:30 pint / The ballad of Stan Rogers and Leo Kennedy / Seven miles upwind / G-Ddamned blessed road / Miracle in the hills / Trees falling / Claire and Johnny / The room over the bar / Forest Hills sub / The goat man / Dangerous times / Al's ashes & me.

Apr 06. (cd) <*(8022)*> **TULIPS FOR LUNCH**
- Curse of the billy goat / Old song handed down / A toast to the woman in the holler / The great Santa snowball debacle of 1968 / The point / Death row all-stars / The unreliable taxi / Mary the elephant / The man who blew kisses / In the beginning / Liar liar, pants on fire / Two left feet / The ballad of DB Cooper.

Waterbug — Waterbug

Jul 08. (d-cd) <*(WBG 84)*> **TWO SETS** (live)
- He came to our town / Bill and Annie / (intro) / Doc Ellis's no-no / (intro) / Radio / A toast to the woman in the holler / (intro) / Dangerous times / Lili's braids / Old song handed down / The point / (intro) / The man who blew kisses / (intro) / The 9:30 pint / Armitage Shanks // Take it out back / Irate letter / The come heres and the been heres / Trees falling / (intro) / La migra viene / (intro) / Letters in the dirt / Talk to my lawyer / (Parent pressure) / Two left feet / (intro) / We are each other's angels / Our gods / The boys in the back room / (intro) / On Christmas I got nothing / The goodbye kid / Blow 'em away.

Chuckbrodsky.com — not issued

Jun 11. (cd) <*none*> **SUBTOTAL ECLIPSE**
- Out of time and place / Roberto / The world as you once knew / It that guy / Same dress twice / The bellyache heard 'round the world / The phenom / William Henry Paddle / Lili's braids / Gerta / People up here / I tried fitting in.

- (5-7*) compilations, etc.-

May 02. (cd) Chuckbrodsky.com; <*020*> **THE BASEBALL BALLADS**
- The ballad of Eddie Klepp / Gone to Heaven / Lefty / Dock Ellis's no-no / Letters in the dirt / Bonehead Merkle / 7th inning stretch (take me out to the ball game) / Moe Berg: the song / The unnatural shooting of Eddie Waitkus / Whitey and Harry.

Jonatha BROOKE (⟹ The STORY)

Tom BROSSEAU

Born Thomas Anderson Brosseau, November 3, 1976 in Grand Forks, North Dakota, the Los Angeles-based singer-songwriter's earliest influences were DYLAN, WOODY GUTHRIE, LEADBELLY, country star Marty Robbins and his bluegrass-playing grandmother. Starting out on his own in 2001, Tom was soon performing alongside San Diego musician Gregory Page, who recorded his initial indie-folk efforts **NORTH DAKOTA, '02** (2004) and **LATE NIGHT AT LARGO** (2004), the latter a live set taped at his local club in Largo, LA.

Loveless Records subsequently took compassion, issuing his debut album proper, **WHAT I MEAN TO SAY IS GOODBYE** (2005) {*7}, a record that harked back to the glory days of the 1960s, recalling DYLAN and a host of troubadours from the Elektra and Reprise stables. With his LES SHELLEYS duo partner Angela Correa on board as guest singer, plus LA session alumni Jon Brion (on second guitar), Benmont Tench (keyboards), Pete Thomas (drums) and Sara Watkins (violin), BROSSEAU was at his most impressive on 'West Of Town', 'Wandering', a cover of Hank Williams's 'That's When Your Heartaches Begin' and a laid-back arrangement of trad standard 'In My Time Of Dyin'' (DYLAN, Zeppelin and the others can rest easy).

2006 brought forth two back-catalogue CDs, Loveless's **TOM BROSSEAU** {*5} set and the Fat Cat retrospective (recorded 2001-2004) **EMPTY HOUSES ARE LONELY** {*6}. His fragile and quavering falsetto on the miserabilist 'Heart Of Mine' and 'How To Grow A Woman From The Ground' is worth hearing.

GRAND FORKS {*6} and **CAVALIER** {*7} bookended the following year, two alt-folk sets with more than a nod to NEIL YOUNG and the late, great PHIL OCHS. Retaining his literate bent and idiosyncratic eye for poignancy and detail, Tom continued his run of bittersweet albums with **POSTHUMOUS SUCCESS** (2009) {*6}, while his duo with Correa finally got around to releasing the self-titled trad-covers set **LES SHELLEYS** (2010) {*6} - very poetical indeed. *MCS*

Tom Brosseau - vocals, guitars, harmonica, banjo, violin / (+ session guests)

US own label — UK not issued

2002. (cd) <*none*> **NORTH DAKOTA, '02**
- Portrait of George Washington (John Doe version) / Heart of mine / Will Henry / Luke / Drayton, ND / Grafton, ND / The horses will not ride, the gospel won't be spoken / Old piano blues / Fare thee well thee wed / Fit to be tied.

2004. (cd) <*none*> **LATE NIGHT AT LARGO** (live)
- Still building / Maryanne / Kick Matilda out of bed / Lonesome valley / How to grow a woman from the ground / Portrait of George Washington / Broken ukulele / Real life video game (do what you want) / Fragile mind / Young and free / Don't get around much anymore.

Loveless — Fat Cat

Jun 05. (cd) <*LOV 021*> **WHAT I MEAN TO SAY IS GOODBYE**
- West of town / Jane and Lou / Tonight I'm careful with you / Wandering / Wear and tear / Grafton / Unfamiliar places / That's when your heartaches begin / St Joe St / In my time of dyin' / My little babe / Quiet drink.

Mar 06. (cd) *(FATCD 41)* **EMPTY HOUSES ARE LONELY** (rec. 2001–2004)
- Fragile mind / Empty houses are lonely / Hurt to try / Mary Anne / Dark garage / Heart of mine / The broken ukulele / How to grow a woman from the ground / Lonesome valley / Bars.

Apr 06. (cd) <*LOV 022*> **TOM BROSSEAU** (rec. 2003)
- No reason / I have been a prisoner, O Lord / The young and the free / Broken hearted love / Rose / Josephine / Never had much luck / Yodeling for you / The apple girl / I tuned my guitar to the hum of the train / *[bonus tracks +=]* I live with other

people in mind [session] / Ballad of a wandering farmhand [session] / My bonnie brae [session] / Used to own a rowing boat / The young and the free [live].

Jan 07. (cd) <*LOV 024*> **GRAND FORKS**
- I fly wherever I go / Fork in the road / There's more than one way to dance / Blue part of the windshield / Down on skid row / Here comes the water now / Plaid lined jacket / Dark and shiny gun / 97 flood.

Fat Cat Fat Cat

Oct 07. (cd) <*(FATCD 62)*> **CAVALIER**
- Amory / Brass ring blues / Committed to memory / My heart belongs to the sea / Brand new safe / My Peggy dear / I want to make this moment last / Instructions to meet the devil / I'm travelling the river on the Dakota Queen / Kiss my lips.

Jun 09. (cd) <*(FATCD 81)*> **POSTHUMOUS SUCCESS**
- My favorite color blue / Been true / Big time / Boot hill / You don't know my friends / Love to new heights / Youth decay / Give me a drumroll / Miss Lucy / Axe and stump / Chandler, AZ / Wishbone medallion / My favorite color blue.

LES SHELLEYS

Tom Brosseau - vocals, acoustic guitars / **Angela Correa** - vocals, acoustic guitar

Fat Cat Fat Cat

Nov 10. (cd) <*(FATCD 96)*> **LES SHELLEYS**
- The world is waiting for the sunrise / The late John Garfield blues / Green door / Cocktails for two / The band played on / Rum and Coca Cola / Billy / The lonesome death of Hattie Carroll / Oh babe ain't no lie / Pastures of plenty / Deep purple / Wheel of fortune.

Greg BROWN

Born July 2, 1949 in Hacklebarney, Iowa, crossover country-folk singer-songwriter GREG BROWN was the first of the many artists who embraced rootsy Americana to feel it from the heart. The enigmatic acoustic guitarist had come of age musically in the early 1970s after winning talent competitions and playing a residency at Gerde's Folk City, NYC, but he returned to his roots in Iowa after a miserable time working in Los Angeles as a ghostwriter for Platters manager Buck Ram.

His recording debut was in fact a collaborative effort with musical sparring partner Dick Pinney, the record itself (the live-in-concert **HACKLEBARNEY** (1974) {*4}) testament indeed to his rustic charm. Before Greg and manager Bob Feldman ever got his own Red House Records off the ground (although the label did later re-issue his early-1980s LPs), two studio sets emerged from out of nowhere - the underrated **44 & 66** (1980) {*6} and his regional breakthrough **THE IOWA WALTZ** (1981) {*6}. His live **ONE NIGHT** (1983) {*7}, recorded before a capacity theatre audience in October 1982, left no doubt that Greg was a mighty promising storyteller on the verge of bigger and better things.

IN THE DARK WITH YOU {*6} finally opened his Red House Records account in 1985, a reflective and at times humorous set that sold well enough thanks to exposure on Garrison Keillor's old-timey radio show 'A Prairie Home Companion'. The concept of setting the poems of William Blake must have been daunting, but on BROWN's **SONGS OF INNOCENCE AND EXPERIENCE** (1986) {*6} it worked for the most part, the effect lilting and timeless.

ONE MORE KISS GOODNIGHT (1988) {*7}, the Mark Knopfleresque **ONE BIG TOWN** (1989) {*7} (which premiered the future SHAWN COLVIN hit 'One Cool Remove'), **DOWN IN THERE** (1990) {*6} and the steely **DREAM CAFE** (1992) {*6} continued BROWN's surge upwards, while he and BILL MORRISSEY earned a Grammy nomination for their 'Friend Of Mine' collaboration in 1993.

There was a children's album, **BATHTUB BLUES** {*5}, in 1993, and another concert set, **THE LIVE ONE** (1995) {*7}, (featuring VAN MORRISON's 'Moondance' and RICHARD THOMPSON's '1952 Vincent Black Lightning)', but Greg's course was set in a political direction on **THE POET GAME** (1994) {*6}, **FURTHER IN** (1996) {*8} and **SLANT 6 MIND** (1997) {*7}. The charity-fundraiser set 'Solid Heart' rounded the decade off nicely.

There were ups and downs for Greg in his domestic life, but things settled a little when he wed country star Iris DeMent in 2002. He had three daughters from his previous marriages, one of whom, PIETA BROWN, has become a star in her own right. In the post-millennium years, although he was prolific on a number of labels, it was Red House that stood by him on **COVENANT** (2000) {*7}, **MILK OF THE MOON** (2002) {*7} and **THE EVENING CALL** (2006) {*5}. Between the latter two came the double live retrospective **IN THE HILLS OF CALIFORNIA: LIVE FROM THE KATE WOLF FESTIVAL 1997-2003** (2004) {*6}, featuring covers of WOLF's 'Tequila And Me', Smokey Robinson's 'You Really Got A Hold On Me', Robert Johnson's 'Kind Hearted Woman Blues' and Lennon-McCartney's 'Don't Let Me Down'.

The bluesy **YELLOW DOG** {*6} benefit concert album was recorded in 2005 and released in 2007, and **FREAK FLAG** (2011) {*6} reunited him with Memphis producer/guitarist Bo Ramsey. The latter project was jeopardised when the studio was struck by lightning, wiping some of the tapes; among the tracks that survived was his cover of his wife Iris's 'Let The Mystery Be'. *MCS*

Greg Brown - vocals, guitars (w/ session people)

US UK
Mountain Railroad not issued

1974. (lp; by GREG BROWN / DICK PINNEY) <*MR 52774*>
HACKLEBARNEY [live in Rockford, Illinois]
- My pa, he came home as quiet as the evening / Hacklebarney / On New Year's day / Bad roads in spring / The last shepherd / Tornado / Dickens *[DP-only]* / Dancing round and round / Even Ozzie and Harriet get the blues *[DP-only]* / Walk me 'round your garden *[DP-only]* / Driftin' *[w/ DP]* / How black the fields.

Brown Street not issued

1980. (lp) <*none*> **44 & 66**
- 44 & 66 / Don't you think too much / Bozo's in love again / Twenty or so / Ring around the moon / Downtown / People hide their love / Lullaby at the edge of town / Early / Beatniks gonna rise again / Comin' into you (*). <*re-iss. 1984 on Red House- = *; RHR 02*> <*(cd-iss. Mar 92/Oct 96 += *; RHRCD 02)*>

1981. (lp) <*none*> **THE IOWA WALTZ**
- The Iowa waltz / Mississippi serenade / Counting feedcaps / Grand junction / Out in the country / Walking the beans / My home in the sky / King corn / Daughters / Four wet pigs / The train carrying Jimmie Rodgers home. <*re-iss.1984 on Red House; RHR 01*> <*(cd-iss. Mar 92/Oct 96; RHRCD 01)*>

Coffeehouse Extempore not issued

1983. (lp) **ONE NIGHT...** (live October 8-9, 1982)
- Dream on / Canned goods / Every street in town / Flat stuff / Downtown / Heart of my country *[* cd-only]* / Butane lighter blues *[* cd-only]* / Banjo moon *[* cd-only]* / Waiting / Ships *[* cd-only]* / You don't really get me, babe / On records the sound just fades away / Love is a chain / Ella Mae / All the little places around the town *[* cd-only]* / Never shine sun. <*(cd-iss. May 99 on Red House+= *; RHRCD 128)*>

Red House not issued

1985. (lp) <*RHR 08*> **IN THE DARK WITH YOU**
- Who woulda thunk it? / In the dark with you / Help me make it through this funky day / I slept all night by my lover / Where do the wild geese go? / Good morning coffee / All the money's gone / Letters from home / Who do you think you're fooling? <*(cd-iss. Mar 92/Oct 96 +=; RHRCD 08)*> - People with bad luck / In the water.

1986. (lp) <*RHR 14*> **SONGS OF INNOCENCE AND EXPERIENCE**
- Introduction / The lamb / Infant joy / The chimney sweeper / The ecchoing green / Night / On another's sorrow / The tyger / The angel / The garden of love / Infant sorrow / Holy Thursday / Ah! Sun-flower / The little vagabond / A poison tree / London. <*(cd-iss. Mar 92/Oct 96; RHRCD 14)*>

Oct 88. (lp) <*RHR 23*> **ONE MORE GOODNIGHT KISS**
- One more goodnight kiss / Say a little prayer / Mississippi moon / Cheapest kind / Canned goods / I can't get used to it / Rooty toot toot for the moon / Walking down to Casey's / Speed trap boogie / Our little town / Wash my eyes. <*(cd-iss. Mar 92/Oct 96; RHRCD 23)*>

Oct 89. (lp) <*RHR 28*> **ONE BIG TOWN**
- The way they get themselves up / The monkey / One cool remove / Back home again / Just live / One big town / Lotsa kindsa money / Things go on / America will eat you / Tell me it's gonna be alright. <*(cd-iss. Mar 92/Oct 96; RHRCD 28)*>

Oct 90. (lp) <*RHR 35*> **DOWN IN THERE**
- If I had known / Hillbilly girl / A little place in the country / Worrisome years / Hacklebarney tune / Poor backslider / Fooled me once / Band of gold / All day rain / You are a flower. <*(cd-iss. Mar 92/Oct 96; RHRCD 35)*>

Red House Sky Ranch

May 92. (cd) <*RHRCD 47*> *(SR 87837-2)* **DREAM CAFE** Jul 93
- Just by myself / Sleeper / I don't know that guy / So hard / You can watch me / Dream café / You drive me crazy / Spring wind / Nice when it rains / Laughing river / No place away / I don't want to be the one.

—— In Apr '93, BILL MORRISSEY & GREG BROWN issued the album 'Friend Of Mine'.

Sep 93. (cd) <*RHRCD 42*> **BATHTUB BLUES**
- I see the moon (intro) / Late night radio / Bathtub blues / Payday / So long, you old tooth / Green leaf / Young Robin / Down at the sea hotel / Shake sugaree / Flabbergabbie / I remember when / Four wet pigs / Monsters and giants / Two little boys / You might as well go to sleep / I see the moon. *(UK-iss. Oct 96; same as US)*

Red House Red House

Nov 94. (cd) <*(RHRCD 68)*> **THE POET GAME** May 95
- Brand new '64 Dodge / Boomtown / The poet game / Ballingall hotel / One wrong turn / Jesus and Elvis / Sadness / Lately / Lord, I have made you a place in my heart / My new book / Driftless / Here in the going, going, gone.

Oct 95. (cd) <*(RHRCD 78)*> **THE LIVE ONE** (live June 1994) Dec 95
- Just by myself / Billy from the hills / Boomtown / Spring wind / Laughing river / You drive me crazy / Canned goods / I don't want to have a nice day / Brand new '64 Dodge / 1952 Vincent Black Lightning / One more goodnight kiss / Moondance.

Sep 96. (cd) <*(RHRCD 88)*> **FURTHER IN** Oct 96
- Small dark movie / Think about you / Two little feet / Hey baby hey / China / Where is Maria / If you don't get it at home / You can always come to me / Someday when we're both alone / Not high / Further in / If I ever do see you again. *(re-iss. Apr 97 on Sky Ranch; SR 842580-2)*

Oct 97. (cd) <*(RHRCD 98)*> **SLANT 6 MIND** Nov 97
- Whatever it was / Loneliness house / Mose Allison played here / Spring and all / Vivid / Dusty woods / Billy from the hills / Speaking in tongues / Enough / Hurt so nice / Wild like a sonny boy / Down at the mill / Why don't you just come home.

—— In 1999, BROWN (and others) were behind a special limited-edition CD, SOLID HEART, for The In-Harmony Benefit Concert.

Aug 00. (cd) <*(RHRCD 148)*> **COVENANT**
- 'Cept you and me babe / Rexroth's daughter / Real good friend / Blues go walking / Waiting on you / Living in a prayer / Dream city / Lullaby / Blue car / Walkin' daddy / Pretty one more time. *(bonus +=)* - (untitled).

Trailer-Rubric Trailer-Rubric

Aug 00. (cd) <*(TRUB 33)*> **OVER AND UNDER** Oct 02
- River will take you / Mattie Price / Summer evening / Why do you even say that? / Shit out of luck / Beyond the sunset / Fairfield / Almost out of gas / Betty Ann / 857-5413 / Your town now / Dear wrinkled face / Inabell sale / Like a dog.

—— In 2001, GREG BROWN (with CHARLIE PARR and JEFF WHITE & THE FRONT PORCH) released the DOWN IN THE VALLEY: BARN AID BENEFIT CONCERT charity CD.

Mar 02. (cd) <*(RHRCD 168)*> **MILK OF THE MOON**
- Lull it by / A little excited / Let me be your gigolo / Smell of coffee / Milk of the moon / Mud / Ashamed of our love / Steady love / The moon is nearly full / Telling stories / Never so far / Oh you.

(above issued on his usual record label, Red House)

—— In Aug '03, GREG BROWN, Pete Heitzman, Garnet Rogers and Karen Savoca issued the concert set, 'Live At The Black Sheep' (on Alcove); GREG sings lead on 'Last Fair Deal', 'Milk Of The Moon', 'Little Satchel', 'Summer Lightning' and 'Goodnight, Irene'.

Jan 04. (cd) <*(TRUB 35)*> **HONEY IN THE LION'S HEAD** May 04
- Railroad Bill / I believe I'll go back home / Who killed Cock Robin / Old Smokey / The foggy dew / Down in the valley / Ain't no one like you / Green grows the laurel / I don't want your millions mister / I never will marry / Samson / Jacob's ladder.

Red House Red House

Sep 04. (d-cd) <*(RHRCD 180)*> **IN THE HILLS OF CALIFORNIA: LIVE FROM THE KATE WOLF MUSIC FESTIVAL 1997–2003**
- For all / Wash my eyes / Never so far / The way my baby calls my name / Spring and all / Slow food / Inabell sale / Tequila and me / China / Introduction to... / Kate's guitar / Say a little prayer / You really got a hold on me / I want my country back / I shall not be moved / Two little feet // Introduction to... / Lord I have a place in my heart / The poet game / Think about you / Where is Maria / Lullaby / Almost out of gas / Livin' in a prayer / Introduction to... / Mose Allison played here / Rexroth's daughter / Vivid / Kind hearted woman blues / Just be myself / Your town now / Don't let me down.

Aug 06. (cd) <*(RHRCD 198)*> **THE EVENING CALL**
- Joy tears / Evening call / Cold + dark + wet / Bucket / Mighty sweet watermelon / Treat each other right / Eugene / Coneville Slough / Kokomo / Pound it on down / Skinny days / Whippoorwill.

Earthworks Earthworks

Aug 07. (cd) <*(EWA-CD001)*> **YELLOW DOG** (live August 26, 2005) Oct 07
- Intro / Cold + wet + dark / Dream café / Better days / Conesville Slough / Oily boys / All of those things / Canned goods / "Pitchin' in..." / Laughing river / Please don't talk about me when I'm gone. *(bonus +=)* - Untitled.

YepRoc YepRoc

May 11. (cd/lp) <*B0004909-2*> *(???)* **FREAK FLAG**
- Someday house / Where are you going when you're gone / Rain and snow / Freak flag / Lovinest one / I don't know anybody in this town / Flat stuff / Mercy mercy mercy / Let the mystery be / Remember the sun / Tenderhearted child.

- (8-10*) compilations -

Sep 03. (cd+dvd) Red House; <*(RHRCD 171)*> **IF I HAD KNOWN: ESSENTIAL RECORDINGS, 1980–1996**
- If I had known / Worrisome years / Laughing river / Canned goods / Who woulda thunk it / The train carrying Jimmie Rodgers home / Ella Mae (live) / Our little town / Good morning coffee / Downtown / You drive me crazy / Spring wind / The poet game / Where is Maria / Boomtown / Two little feet / Driftless. // (DVD documentary: Hacklebarney Tunes - The Songs Of Greg Brown).

Jul 09. (d-cd) Red House; <*(RHRCD 218)*> **DREAM CITY: ESSENTIAL RECORDINGS VOL.2, 1997–2006** Aug 09
- Dream city / Rexroth's daughter / Evening call / Vivid / Whatever it was / Your town now / Lull it by / Joy tears / Samson / Summer evening / Blue car / Living in a prayer / Mattie Price / Kokomo / Never so far / Why don't you just go home // Lull it by (alt. take) / Verona road / Gallery / Christmas song (live).

- essential tribute sets -

Sep 02. (cd) Red House; <*(RHRCD 145)*> **GOING DRIFTLESS: An Artists' Tribute to GREG BROWN**
- Lately (LUCINDA WILLIAMS) / The poet game (ANI DiFRANCO) / The train carrying Jimmie Rodgers home (IRIS DeMENT) / Where is Maria? (FERRON) / Sleeper (ELIZA GILKYSON) / Ella Mae (CONSTIE BROWN, PIETA BROWN and ZOE BROWN) / Summer evening (GILLIAN WELCH) / Small dark movie (LUCY KAPLANSKY) / Spring and all (MARY CHAPIN CARPENTER) / Say a little prayer (SHAWN COLVIN) / Early (VICTORIA WILLIAMS) / Two little feet (KAREN SAVOCA) / Hey baby hey (ROBIN LEE BERRY) / Wash my eyes (LEANDRA PEAK).

Pieta BROWN

Being the daughter of Grammy-nominated folk-blues singer-songwriter GREG BROWN might be daunting for some, but PIETA BROWN (born 1974 in Iowa) has quickly established herself among her peers and rootsy contemporaries. With four albums under her belt since the millennium, she has been compared to singers such as Margo Timmins (of the Cowboy Junkies) and LUCINDA WILLIAMS.

It's a long way from her formative days living with her divorcee mother in Birmingham, Alabama, at times estranged from her father Greg. But Pieta overcame her difficulties, moving back to Iowa City as a young teenager and graduating from university with a degree in linguistics. She was well into her twenties before she thought seriously about writing songs and tracking her famous father in music.

Produced by Bo Ramsey (Greg and the aforementioned Lucinda had worked with him), Pieta finally delivered her debut set, **PIETA BROWN** (2002) {*6}, an admirable start for the introspective newbie singer-songwriter. Her style brings a little country-blues to the table ('Bury Me' is a good example), but one can also hear a touch of jazz and of course folk in her cool and mellow voice. Check out 'Fly Right', 'Without You' and 'Tell Me How'.

Album number two, **IN THE COOL** (2005) {*6}, was just as relaxed as her previous effort - imagine Rickie Lee Jones covering DYLAN - but this was gritty roots, smoothed down somewhat by Bo's production and the harmonies of the great IRIS DeMENT. Her second set for One Little Indian, **REMEMBER THE SUN** (2007) {*7}, took her into back-porch country-blues territory, succeeding best on 'Rollin' Down The Track' and her homage 'In My Mind I Was Talkin' To Loretta [Lynn]'.

Joining her father on Red House Records brought her back to her roots again, producer Don Was coaxing her into that distinctive vocal drawl on the earthy, stripped-down mini-set **SHIMMER** (2009) {*6}. Her first full set for three years, **ONE AND ALL** (2010) {*6}, brought her once again under the wing of Bo Ramsey, who guided the sultry Pieta on gems like 'Calling All Angels', 'Flowers In The Kingdom' and 'It Wasn't That'. *MCS*

Pieta Brown - vocals, acoustic guitar (w/ session people)

US Rubric UK Rubric

Jun 02. (cd) <*(TRUB 47)*> **PIETA BROWN** Sep 02
- Lullaby / Blind dog yell / Without you / Even when / Tell me how / Fly right / Out in a field / On the edge / Bury me / Down to Memphis / Don't turn away / Pass you by / Can't take it away.

Valley Entertainment One Little Indian

Sep 05. (cd) <*15199*> *(TPLP 704CD)* **IN THE COOL**
- #807 / Fourth of July / In the cool / This old dress / Ring of gold / Tears won't do any good / Precious game / Still around / How many times / Lonesome songs / I don't want to come down / Far away.

One Little Indian One Little Indian

Jun 07. (cd) <*(TPLP 782CD)*> **REMEMBER THE SUN**
- Innocent blue / Rollin' down the track / Sonic boom / West Monroe / In my mind I was talkin' to Loretta / Song for a friend / Not scared / Are you free? / Hey run / Worlds within worlds / Remember the sun.

Red House Red House

Nov 09. (m-cd) <*(RHRCD 227)*> **SHIMMER** Dec 09
- I know a girl / Lovin' you still / Hey Joey / Over you / El guero / Diamonds in the sky / You're my lover now.

Apr 10. (cd) <*(RHRCD 229)*> **ONE AND ALL**
- Wishes falling through the rain / Other way around / Out of the blue / Prayer of roses / Calling all angels / El guero / Faller / Flowers in the kingdom / Shake / Grass upon the hills / Never did belong / It wasn't that.

Richard BUCKNER

Chisel-chinned, husky-voiced and a country boy at heart, maverick singer-songwriter RICHARD BUCKNER (born 1967 in San Francisco) had his roots grounded firmly in Nashville and Lubbock on his C&W-tinged debut set **BLOOMED** (1995) {*6}. With some of its leaves borrowed from the books of all-American dustbowl types Butch Hancock, Joe Ely and Jimmie Dale Gilmore, this set can safely be filed under Californian canyon country music. The same goes for the cassette-only live follow-up, **UNRELEASED** (1995) {*5}, while his first effort for MCA, **DEVOTION AND DOUBT** (1997) {*6} - recorded during a distressing divorce - takes in his cross-country/Son Volt diversions.

Not particularly redneck-friendly, or at ease with the faded folk fraternity, BUCKNER would take his style beyond alt-country and into the realms of post-grunge roots music on his fragile but poignantly upbeat **SINCE** (1998) {*7}. Edgar Lee Masters's 'Spoon River Anthology' (a series of poems dating back to 1914-1915) came under the spotlight in Richard's unique and ambitious blues-folk concept **THE HILL** (2000) {*6}. Channeling his emotions into deep tales of despair and heartache, Richard released all his demons in what was basically one 34-minute track with 18 segues. It might have been better suited to a soundtrack, but it was commendable for an artist of BUCKNER's stature to take on such an enterprise.

No longer augmented by Calexico buddies Joey Burns and John Convertino, he played all the instruments bar second wife Penny Jo Buckner's drums on **IMPASSE** (2002) {*6}, a record that brought him back to earth. BUCKNER's grizzly tones could best be compared to the ghost of Kurt Cobain thinking he had found his pals in the Meat Puppets, and he almost completely abandoned his Opry-styled croon in favour of becoming a newfound alt-country folkie. Tracks like 'A Year Ahead... And A Light', 'Born Into Giving It Up' and 'Hoping Wishers Never Lose' were a bit of a shock for many pundits.

It seemed as though a heavy heart and dark despair were never far away from his introspective lyrics, and his split from his second wife sparked a new batch of brooding ballads on **DENTS AND SHELLS** (2004) {*6}. Helping him out on this occasion were alt-rock friends from the Butthole Surfers (King Coffey) and the Meat Puppets (Andrew DuPlantis), while the pedal steel made its long-awaited reappearance courtesy of Mike Hardwick and Gary Newcomb. Check out 'A Chance Counsel', 'Her' and 'As The Waves Will Always Roll' for immediate effect and empathy.

Produced by J.D. Foster (who enlisted some Guided By Voices guys plus Steve Goulding and Rob Burger), **MEADOW** (2006) {*7} focused on the positive poetry, his songwriting now revisiting the optimism shown on his early works. 'Lucky', 'Kingdom' and finale 'The Tether And The Tie' suggested there was indeed hope for this master of miserabilist moping - Morrissey, eat your heart out. *MCS*

Richard Buckner - vocals, acoustic guitar (+ session players)

US not issued — UK Glitterhouse

Mar 95. (cd) *(GRCD 340)* **BLOOMED** ⊟ German ⊟
- Blue and yonder / Rainsquall / 22 / Mud / Six years / This is where / Gauzy dress in the sun / Daisychain / Desire / Up north / Surprise, AZ / Cradle to the grave. *(UK-iss. Mar 00 & Mar 06; same) <(US/UK-iss. Feb 98/Apr 02 on Slow River+=; SRRCD 44)>* - The last ride / Settled down / The worst way / Emma / Hutchinson.

Chelsea — not issued

1995. (ltd-c) *<none>* **UNRELEASED** [live] ⊟ ⊟
- House of rotten timber / Sister / Hutchinson / The worst way / Tracy truly / Hard ground / Gauzy dress in the sun / Lil wallet picture / Jewelbomb / Song of 27.

self-rel. — not issued

May 96. (cd) *<none>* **RICHARD BUCKNER** [live at the Black Eyed Pig, SF] ⊟ tour ⊟
- On traveling / Boys, the night will bury you / Ed's song / A goodbye rye / Home / Song of 27 / Roll / Pull / Figure / Jewelbomb / Lil wallet picture. *<(re-iss. Jan 03 on Overcoat; OC 03CD)> (re-iss.+=)* - IMPASSE-ETTE EP

MCA — not issued

Mar 97. (cd) *<MCAD-11564>* **DEVOTION AND DOUBT** □ ⊟
- Pull / Lil wallet picture / Ed's song / Home / A goodbye rye / Fater / Kate Rose / 4am / Roll / Polly waltz / Figure / On traveling / Song of 27. *(UK-iss. Mar 03 on Universal; AAMCAD 11564)*

Aug 98. (cd) *<MCAD-11780>* **SINCE** □ ⊟
- Believer / Faithful shooter / Ariel Ramirez / Jewelbomb / The ocean cliff clearing / Gone w/ souvenir / Slept / Pico / Coursed / Lucky buzz / 10-day room / Brief and boundess / Hand @ the Hem / Boys, the night will bury you / Once. *(UK-iss. Sep 00 on Universal; AAMCAD 11780)*

Overcoat — Overcoat

Oct 00. (cd) *<(OC 08CD)>* **THE HILL** [spoken word] □ □
- Mrs Merritt - Tom Merritt - Elmer Karr - Ollie McGee - Fletcher McGee - Julia Miller - Willard Fluke - Elizabeth Childers - A.D. Blood - Oscar Hummel - Mellie Clark - Johnnie Sayre - Dora Williams - Reuben Pantier - Emily Sparks - Amanda Barker - The hill - William and Emily.

Sep 02. (cd-ep) *<(OC 16CD)>* **IMPASSE-ETTE** □ □
- Born into giving it up / Strumble-ette / Loaded at the wrong door [acoustic] / Remainder / It's still '56 / Born into giving it up [acoustic]. *(UK-iss. Nov 05 on Fargo+=; FA 0073)* - RICHARD BUCKNER

Overcoat — Fargo

Oct 02. (cd) *<OC 14CD> (FA 20200)* **IMPASSE** □ Nov 02 □
- Grace-I'd-said-I'd-known / Born into giving it up / Hoping wishers never lose / Loaded at the wrong door / A year ahead... and a light / Put on what you wanna / A shift / ...And the clouds've lied / Stumble down / Count me in on this one / Dusty from the talk / Were you tried and not as tough / Impasse / I know what I knew / Stutterstep.

Merge — Fargo

Oct 04. (cd) *<MRG 249> (FA 20405)* **DENTS AND SHELLS** □ □
- A chance counsel / Firsts / Invitation / Straight / Her / Charmers / Fuse / Rafters / Picture day / As the waves always roll.

Oct 05. (cd; by RICHARD BUCKNER & JON LANGFORD) (FA 0065) **SIR DARK INVADER VS. THE FANGFORD** ⊟ promo ⊟
- Rolling of the eyes / Nothing to show / Sweet anybody / From attic to basement / Torn apart / Stayed / The Inca princess / No tears tonight / Do you wanna go somewhere?

Sep 06. (cd) *<MRG 279>* **MEADOW** □ ⊟
- Town / Canyon / Lucky / Mile / Before / Window / Kingdom / Numbered / Spell / The tether and the tie.

Aug 11. (cd/lp) *<MRG 339>* **OUR BLOOD** □ ⊟
- Traitor / Escape / Thief / Collusion / Ponder / Witness / Confession / Hindsight / Gang.

Basia BULAT

The dreamy blonde Canadian folk singer and multi-instrumentalist BASIA BULAT (born in Toronto in 1984) is confident with the hammered dulcimer, autoharp, ukulele or virtually anything that comes to hand. She was raised in Etobicoke, Ontario before moving to the nearby city of London, and began her career in 2004 after attaining her English degree at the University of Western Ontario.

Her sugar-coated indie-folk music was almost immediately heard on a self-financed debut EP, its release in 2005 leading to a contract with Rough Trade (in Canada, Hayden's Hardwood Records). Produced by Howard Bilerman, **OH, MY DARLING** (2007) {*7} won critical acclaim around the world, songs such as 'I Was A Daughter', 'Snakes And Ladders' and 'Little One' ensuring her a nomination for a Polaris Music Prize the following year. She also recorded Sam Cooke's 'Touch The Hem Of His Garment' for a UK single around this time.

Nearly three years in the making (Basia had been visiting the Yukon) and still with Bilerman at the controls, **HEART OF MY OWN** (2010) {*6} was as autumnal, fragile and twee as ever, her quavery voice lying somewhere between TRACY CHAPMAN and fellow Canadian BUFFY SAINTE-MARIE. Of the dozen tracks, you could start with 'Run', 'Sparrow', 'If It Rains' and 'Gold Rush'. *MCS*

Basia Bulat - vocals, guitar, autoharp, hammered dulcimer, ukulele, piano / + sessioners

Can self-rel. — UK not issued

Nov 05. (cd-ep) *<none>* BASIA BULAT ⊟ Canada ⊟

Hardwood — Rough Trade

Jun 07. (cd) *<006> (RTRADCD 368)* **OH, MY DARLING** □ Apr 07 □
- Before I knew / I was a daughter / Little waltz / December / Snakes and ladders / Oh, my darling / In the night / Little one / Why can't it be mine / The pilgriming vine / La-da-da / Birds of paradise / A secret. *<US-iss. Feb 08 on Rough Trade; RTRADCD 431>*

Feb 08. (7") *(RTRADS 453)* TOUCH THE HEM OF HIS GARMENT. / Before I Knew ⊟ □

Secret City — Rough Trade

Jan 10. (cd/lp) *<SCR 013 CD/LP> (RTRAD CD/LP 468)* **HEART OF MY OWN** □ □
- Go on / Run / Sugar and spice / Gold rush / Heart of my own / Sparrow / If only you / I'm forgetting everyone / The shore / Once more, for the dollhouse / Walk you down / If it rains. *(bonus +=)* - Hush.

The BUNDLES (⟹ The MOLDY PEACHES)

Jane BYAELA

A child prodigy from as young as six, when she was taught violin by her classically-trained mother (by the age of eleven she had conquered the classical guitar too), New York-born singer/songwriter and multi-instrumentalist JANE BYAELA took the resurgent Greenwich Village scene by storm on her arrival in the 1980s from the Fast Folk fraternity.

Influenced by folk idols TRACY CHAPMAN, BUFFY SAINTE-MARIE and SUZANNE VEGA, Jane's studious and meticulously crafted confessional lyrics and melancholy sounds lay somewhere between folk, jazz and blues. The toast of New York's radio programmers, her efforts quickly spread to Boston and beyond when her debut album **ON THE EDGE** (1986) {*7} created a stir; check out 'Child Of The Sun', 'Secrets Are Burning' and 'Jimi's Song'.

What happened in the eight years between that and 1994's **BURNING SILVER** {*6} is unclear, but her time away from the recording studio was soon put to one side. Effectively produced by David Seitz, her original compositions (thirteen in all) were very JONI MITCHELL in structure and texture (e.g. the title track, 'King Of Empty Shadows', 'The Winter Song' and a few others), but, like her previous album, it was a slow-burner. It's a pity that she chose not to release any further records. Where is she now? *MCS*

Jane Byaela - vocals, acoustic guitar, violin, viola, etc.

US Spark / UK Sawdust

1986. (white-lp) <*JB 903*> (SDLP 4.00437) **ON THE EDGE** German –
- Child of the sun / On the edge / Child keeper / Mr dream maker / Longer than time / Business of love / Riddles of blue / Running in the rain / Secrets are burning / Jimi's song / After the storm / Angel of dreams / Drifter of the wind [instrumental] / Road of autumn. *(UK cd-iss. 1990; SDCD 9.00437)*

1-800-Prime / not issued

Jul 94. (cd) <*PCD 007*> **BURNING SILVER** –
- Shattered light / Doin' time / My two cats / Burning silver / King of empty shadows / Like a child's smile / The breaking / Liars learn to fly / You don't frighten / Slave dreamer / Sunny day / The winter song / Melting snow. <*re-iss. Sep 03; same*>

—— Jane retired from the recorded-music industry

Andrew CALHOUN

Inspired by a wide spectrum of folk singers from JOHN PRINE and LEONARD COHEN to EWAN MacCOLL and MARTIN CARTHY, ANDREW CALHOUN (born November 30, 1957 in New Haven, Connecticut) has been playing acoustic guitar and writing songs from the age of twelve - his mother would take in wayward hippie students, who would teach the young man a few chords and techniques to help him play his newly acquired guitar. Settled in Chicago at this point, he later moved to Evanston, Illinois with his singer/songwriter wife KAT EGGLESTON. They have since divorced.

A sensitive and unassuming performer, CALHOUN joined the Flying Fish label (after his debut, **WATER STREET** (1983) {*6}), where he released two LPs, **THE GATES OF LOVE** (1984) {*6} and **WALK ME TO THE WAR** (1987) {*6}. In 1992 he set up his own label, Waterbug, which has now delivered over a hundred titles by artists from CHUCK BRODSKY to DAR WILLIAMS and SLOAN WAINWRIGHT. The ninety-ninth was CALHOUN's latest work, **GRAPEVINE** (2011) {*6}.

CALHOUN is blessed with a rich and poetic voice, and his most interesting albums include **HOPE** (1993) {*7} (featuring the humorous 'You Better Get A Lawyer' and the Appalachian-meets-a-cappella 'Balls'), **TELFER'S COWS: FOLK BALLADS FROM SCOTLAND** (2004) {*6} and **BOUND TO GO** (2008) {*6}, the last a traditionally-sourced set with backing from musicians Campground. *MCS*

Andrew Calhoun - vocals, acoustic guitar (+ session people)

US Hogeye — UK not issued

1983. (lp) *<002>* **WATER STREET** ☐ ⊟
- Lie of a poet / Moses / John's wife / The bull / The living and the breathing wind / The snake / Water street / I have not lost it all / Gabriel / God told me I could come.

Flying Fish — Flying Fish

1984. (lp/c) *<(FF/+90 341)>* **THE GATES OF LOVE** ☐ Mar 89 ☐
- The gates of love / Roads in disrepair / Gavotte rondeau / Never enough / Vancouver / Ice grows on the water / Sam / Seat in the mezzanine / Atmospheres / Ain't no one.

1987. (lp/c) *<(FF/+90 398)>* **WALK ME TO THE WAR** ☐ 1988 ☐
- Battling tops / Walk me to the war / Trumpet / Jack and Jill / Etude in D / Deliver me / Smile for your daddy / Spit from the sky / Bow and arrow / The eagle / You bother me / Rye, New Hampshire.

Waterbug — not issued

Aug 93. (cd) *<WBG 0002>* **HOPE** ☐ ⊟
- Getaway / I love you all the time / Glad old man / The swimmer / Veteran / You better get a lawyer / Balls / Scrapbook / Long legged lover / She's like the autumn / If / Survivor / Recall.

Oct 96. (cd) *<WBG 0025>* **PHOENIX ENVY** ☐ ⊟
- Time / Tunnel vision / Sparrow / Folksingers are boring / No secret castle / Here comes that lady again / Never enough / It's not you that I'm leaving / Journey / Trenches / Lonesome / Freedom road / Paul Scott rap / The model / At the bar / Sheila / Narnia song / O my son / While Jesus was waiting to die / Jack and Jill / When my time comes.

Sep 99. (cd) *<WBG 0049>* **WHERE BLUE MEETS BLUE** ☐ ⊟
- The king / Buffalo / Roads in disrepair / Peach song / Portrait of a girl and her parents / Where blue meets blue / Vancouver / River song / Cows and the highway / Wild birds / Baby-o / Garage / Hello in there / The golden gate bridge / Politics / Reflections / Sea of snow / Flowers on the weekend / You will know God.

Jun 02. (cd) *<WBG 0053>* **TIGER TATTOO** ☐ ⊟
- Joy / Catching on fire / Miss Hill / Goin' down to see John Prine / Fred's brother / Day in and day out / Tom Brown / Tiger tattoo / I'm a rover / The scyther / Shadow song / When I have arms again / I shall not look away / Everyone sang.

Feb 04. (cd) *<WBG 0054>* **TELFER'S COWS: FOLK BALLADS FROM SCOTLAND** ☐ ⊟
- King Orfeo / The two sisters / The battle of Harlaw / Eppie Morrie / Jeannie O'Bethelnie / Hughie Grime / Kinmont Willie / Telfer's cows / Clark Colven / A shake in the basket / The beggarman / The unquiet grave.

Sep 04. (cd) *<WBG 0057>* **SHADOW OF A WING** ☐ ⊟
- Meditation song / Window / Sammy / The promise / Two roads / Witches / Daughter of a drunk / A hoosier in Paris / Smokin' and drinkin' / Folklore / Inside out / Single roses / Fluttering wings / Broken feeder / Raining / I love your letters / Farewell butterfly / Hualapai mountain.

Oct 05. (cd) *<WBG 0067>* **STARING AT THE SUN: SONGS 1973–1981** ☐ ⊟
- The living and the breathing wind / Walk me to the war / Circle of killers / History / Kiss that goblet! / I have run and I have crawled / Atmospheres / Broken boundaries / A seat in the mezzanine / God told me I could come / From time to time / Moses / John's wife / Eugene / Walking through sand / Deliver me.

May 08. (cd; as ANDREW CALHOUN & CAMPGROUND) *<WBG 0083>* **BOUND TO GO** ☐ ⊟
- Blow your trumpet Gabriel / Roll Jordan roll / Turkle dove / Come and go with me / Bound to go / O'er the crossing / Run to Jesus / Run brother run / Molly Cottontail / Go to sleep, my baby / Old man's song / Jaybird and sparrow / Sheep and goat / Them ol' black gnats / Milly Biggers / Sandy land / Anchor line / Rough and rolling sea / Four and twenty elders / Hammering judgment / Wake up Jacob / Way up on the mountain / Ol' Egyp' / Calvary / Run Mary run / Sun don't set in the morning / Uncle Billy / Ol' Elder Brown / No more cane on the brazos / Lost John / Back home in Georgia / Hear the trumpet sound / Open the window Noah / Michael haul the boat ashore / Tree of life.

Jun 11. (cd) *<WBG 0099>* **GRAPEVINE** ☐ ⊟
- I gave my love a cherry / The fox / Gartan mother's lullaby / The little beggarman / O Susanna / Noah's dove / O Mary don't you weep / Hanging out the linen clothes / We'll rant and we'll roar / Sperm whale fishery / Shenandoah / Fifteen years on the Erie canal / I ride an old paint / John Henry / Casey Jones / Johnny has gone for a soldier / The foggy dew / Buskers / How can I keep from singing?

Craig CARDIFF

Canadian singer/songwriter CRAIG CARDIFF (born July 9, 1976 in Waterloo, Ontario) has been around on the fringes for a good decade and a half, although many folk buffs will have missed the unique albums that he distributes himself through his own label (many of them live). The pick of his studio sets are his debut album proper, **JUDY GARLAND! (YOU'RE NEVER HOME...)** (1996) {*7}, **GREAT AMERICAN WHITE TRASH NOVEL** (1997) {*7}, **HAPPY** (2001) {*6} and **GOODNIGHT (GO HOME)** (2007) {*7}.

Coming across as a modern-day JOHN MARTYN, Craig is also known for the occasional collaboration with Rose Cousins and Les Cooper, and for numerous pop/rock cover versions. His concert album **FISTFUL OF FLOWERS** (2005) {*6} takes on 'When You Were Mine' (Prince), 'Why' (Annie Lennox), 'Luka' (SUZANNE VEGA), '1979' (Smashing Pumpkins) interpolated with 'Time After Time' (Cyndi Lauper), 'Dreams' (Fleetwood Mac), 'The One I Love' (R.E.M.), 'God's Comic' (Elvis Costello), 'River' (JONI MITCHELL), 'Glory Bound' (MARTIN SEXTON) and 'Mercy Street' (Peter Gabriel).

Accompanied at times by his sisters on harmony vocals, CARDIFF has also toured supporting Toad The Wet Sprocket frontman Glen Phillips, and he performs for a younger audience at summer camps, mainly YMCA Pinecrest. He now lives in Arnprior, Ontario. *MCS*

Craig Cardiff - vocals, acoustic guitar, harmonica, piano

US unknown — UK not issued

1996. (cd) *<none>* **STUCK UP IN OUTERSPACE** ⊟ Canada ⊟
- [info not available]

Craig Cardiff — not issued

1996. (cd) *<CC 001>* **JUDY GARLAND! (YOU'RE NEVER HOME...)** ⊟ Canada ⊟
- Circus / Radio #9 / Never home / Judy Garland / Grandma / Your road / Oxygen tent / If your name ain't Hank (you're a nobody) / Open window / Lion and the dragon / Pushed. *<re-iss. Aug 06; same>*

1997. (cd) *<CC 002>* **GREAT AMERICAN WHITE TRASH NOVEL** ⊟ Canada ⊟
- Stabilize / Bellyful / Year of funerals / Great American white trash novel / Here there be tigers / Fisherking / Bullpen / Dancing like Pierre / Everybody / Memphis/ TN. *<re-iss. Sep 06; same>*

2000. (cd) *<CC 003>* **LIVE FROM THE BOEHMER BOX COMPANY** Canada
- Dumbest / Driving / Driving / February / Accident car / Nelson's answering machine.

2001. (cd) *<CC 004>* **HAPPY** Canada
- Albion hotel / Everything / Dance me outside (Brantford) / Jokes / Happiest / That band / Props to the peeps / Time after time. *<re-iss. Aug 06; same>*

2003. (cd; with ROSE COUSINS) *<CC 005>* **GINGERS ON BARRINGTON ST** [live] Canada
- Radio home / Miles to go / Barney and Miriam / Four feet on the ground / Soda / Heart for the taking / That band / Doggone lonely / Story about Chicopee / Circus / Brandon from Ithica / Always goes. *<re-iss. Aug 06; same>*

2003. (cd-ep) *<CC 006>* SODA Canada
- Soda / Year of funerals [bathmix] / Stabilize [bathmix] / Everything [bathmix] / Brandon from Ithica. *<re-iss. Aug 06; same>*

2005. (cd) *<CC 007>* **FISTFUL OF FLOWERS** [live covers] Canada
- When you were mine / Why / Luka / 1979 / Joel's fleece pants / Dreams / One I love / God's comic / River / Glory bound / Mercy street. *<re-iss. Aug 06; same>*

2005. (cd; by CRAIG CARDIFF + LES COOPER) *<CC 008>* **BOMBSHELTER LIVING ROOM** [live] Canada
- Bread / Emm + May / County road Christmas time / Lost [LES COOPER track] / No rules [LES COOPER track] / Slowdive [LES COOPER track] / Bird down / Trouble on the floor / Africville / Sudbury / Saskatchewan / Homecoming / Foolish boy [LES COOPER track]. *<re-iss. Aug 06; same>*

Jan 07. (m-cd) *<CC 009>* **AUBERGE BLACKSHEEP** Canada
- Dig in / Smallest wingless / Revival day / Montreal / Peterborough / Dearest, when you called.

Oct 07. (cd) *<CC 010 - NR! 10>* **GOODNIGHT (GO HOME)** Canada
- Revival day / Maybe you should drive / Heaven / Dirty old town / When people go / Dig in / Smallest wingless / Kingston / Bird down / Dance me outside / Dearest, when you called / Rowantree / God said no.

(above also licensed to Neato!)

2008. (cd) *<CC 011>* **EASTER EGGS** [live] Canada
- Radio #9 / Africville intro / Africville / Judy Garland / Albion hotel / God said no / Grandma / Sandusky (Dirty old town) / County road intro / County road Christmas time / Year of funerals / Wingless intro / Smallest wingless / I will follow you into the dark (Death Cab For Cutie) / That band intro / Fisherking / Dance me outside / Hogtown / Circus intro / Dumbest / Stabilize / Maybe you should drive.

2009. (cd) *<CC 012>* **KISSING SONGS (MISTLETOE)** Canada
- End of the world / Human / Safe free / Mondays / Barney and Miriam little deaths / Sallyanne jacket / Circus / County road Christmas time / Ballad of love and hate / Carsleepers / Stabilize [live].

Oct 10. (free-cd) *<CC 013>* SONGS FOR LUCY [live at the Black Sheep in Wakefield, Quebec] net
- (on groups) / Safe here / On fake European boyfriends / Italian boys / (on weddings) / Dirty old town / (on long distance relationships) / Radio 9 / Cologne (Ben Folds) / (on getting your drugs back) / The very last night of the end of the world / Dance me outside / (on sharing) / Circus / Porchlight / Gate / (on seniors making out) / (on the importance of underwear) / Winter.

Jan 11. (cd) *<CC 014>* **MOTHERS AND DAUGHTERS** Canada
- Black boys on mopeds / Miss Ohio / Making pies / True colors / River / Luka / Mystery / I miss you / Time after time / The arrivals gate / Untouchable face.

Dave CARTER & Tracy GRAMMER

A modern-day country-folk combination formed in Portland, Oregon, singer/ songwriter DAVE CARTER (born August 13, 1952 in Oxnard, California but raised in Oklahoma and Texas) and the equally gifted fiddler TRACY GRAMMER (born April 8, 1968 in Homestead, Florida) released three albums before his tragic death from a heart attack on July 19, 2002.

Easy-going, reflective and sentimental, the three albums **WHEN I GO** (1998) {*7}, **TANGLEWOOD TREE** (2000) {*7} and **DRUM HAT BUDDHA** (2001) {*7} were laced with picturesque old-timey tunes, their interplay underpinning their delicate arrangements. They also covered PETE SEEGER's 'The Emperor Is Naked Today-O'.

Greatly affected by the untimely death of Dave, TRACY GRAMMER finally re-booted her own solo career with 2005's **FLOWER OF AVALON** {*6}, a set of nine CARTER compositions plus the traditional 'Laughlin Boy'. The mini-set **THE VERDANT MILE** (2005) {*6} was released around the same period, featuring Kieran Kane's 'This Dirty Little Town', Goffin & King's 'Wasn't Born To Follow', Neil Diamond's 'Solitary Man', Emory Gordy's 'When I Reach The Place I'm Goin'' and the traditional 'Old Paint'.

BOOK OF SPARROWS (2008) contained another two CARTER songs ('Lord Of The Buffalo' and 'Gypsy Rose') plus a handful of choice readings from relative unknowns such as Tom Russell ('Blue Wing'), Kate Power ('Travis John') and DAVID FRANCEY ('The Waking Hour'). Bigger artists were covered by way of SIMON & GARFUNKEL's 'April Come She Will' and Jackson Browne's 'In The Shape Of A Heart'.

Since CARTER's death GRAMMER has also been behind two albums of material recorded by the duo but previously unreleased: **SEVEN IS THE NUMBER** (2006) {*6} - with nine songs re-recorded from CARTER's hard-to-get solo debut **SNAKE HANDLIN' MAN** (1995) {*6} - and the festive set **AMERICAN NOEL** (2008) {*5}. *MCS*

DAVE CARTER

Red River / not issued

1995. (cd) *<none>* **SNAKE HANDLIN' MAN**
- Cowboy singer / Snake-handlin' man / Red (elegy) / The promised land / Hey Tonya / The river where she sleeps / Long black road into Tulsa town / Texas underground / Workin' for Jesus / Gun-metal eyes / Sarah turn 'round.

DAVE CARTER & TRACY GRAMMER

Dave Carter - vocals, acoustic guitar, banjo, organ, trumpet / **Tracy Grammer** - vocals, fiddle/violin, mandolin, acoustic guitar

US Red River / UK not issued

Oct 98. (cd) *<RR 1>* **WHEN I GO**
- When I go / Don't tread on me / Annie's lover / Grand prairie TX homesick blues / Kate and the ghost of lost love / The river, where she sleeps / Lancelot / Frank to Valentino / Little Liza Jane / Elvis Presley. *<(re-iss. 2002/Aug 04 on Signature; SIG 1272)>*

Signature / not issued

Mar 00. (cd) *<SIG 1257>* **TANGLEWOOD TREE**
- Happytown (all right with me) / Tanglewood tree / The mountain / Farewell to Saint Dolores / Hey conductor / Crocodile man / Walkin' away from Caroline / Farewell to Fiddler's Rim / Cat-eye Willie claims his lover / Cowboy singer / Farewell to Bitterroot Valley. *(UK-iss. Aug 04; same as US)*

Jun 01. (cd) *<SIG 1266>* **DRUM HAT BUDDHA**
- Ordinary town / Tillman Co. / Disappearing man / The power and glory / 236-6132 / 41 thunderer / Gentle arms of Eden / I go like the raven / Highway 80 (she's a mighty good road) / Love, the magician / Merlin's lament / Gentle soldier of my soul. *(UK-iss. Aug 04; same as US)*

—— sadly, Carter died in July 2002; Tracy eventually went on with her solo career

TRACY GRAMMER

Tracy Grammer / not issued

Feb 05. (m-cd) **THE VERDANT MILE**
- The verdant mile / This dirty little town / Wasn't born to follow / Solitary man / When I reach the place I'm going / Jackson's tune - Trickster tale - St. Anne's reel / Old paint. *<re-iss. May 08; same>*

Signature / Signature

Apr 05. (cd) *<(SIG 1292)>* **FLOWER OF AVALON** May 05
- Shadows of Evangeline / Gypsy rose / Laughlin boy / Hard to make it / Hey ho / Mother, I climbed / Preston miller / Winter when he goes / Phantom doll / Any way I do.

Tracy Grammer / not issued

Jan 08. (m-cd) *<71106>* **BOOK OF SPARROWS**
- Blue wing / Travis John / The waking hour / Lord of the buffalo / Gypsy rose (aka Gypsy down) / April come she will / In the shape of a heart.

- duo releases after CARTER's death -

Oct 06. (cd) Tracy Grammer; *<060719>* **SEVEN IS THE NUMBER** [final re-recorded studio recordings]
- Seven is the number / Snake-handlin' man / Red (elegy) / The promised land / Hey Tonya / Texas underground / Gas station girl / Long, black road into Tulsa town / Workin' for Jesus / Gun-metal eyes / Sarah turn 'round.

Nov 08. (cd) Signature; *<(SIG 2011)>* **AMERICAN NOEL**
- Go tell the fox / Bring a torch, Jeanette Isabella / Lo, how a rose e'er blooming / Footsteps of the faithful / The ditching carol / Giddyup said Santa Claus / The Coventry carol / American noel.

CASTANETS

Neo-folk and freak-folk come in many shapes and forms, none more weird and wildly wonderful than the alt-country-inflected CASTANETS, the brainchild of San Diego native Raymond Raposa with revolving-door associates from bands as diverse as Rocket From The Crypt, Pinback and Tristeza. Bearded singer/songwriter Raposa, whose band sounds something like Lambchop without the gruff bite of Kurt Wagner, dropped out of school at the age of 15, stepped on a Greyhound bus and hit the road.

A series of CD-rs preceded his initial delivery for the Asthmatic Kitty imprint, **CATHEDRAL** (2004) {*7}. Hatched in a cabin in California, its weird Americana and apocalyptic vision is akin to that of some deranged spiritual hobo. Check out 'Your Feet On The Floor...' and 'You Are The Blood'.

FIRST LIGHT'S FREEZE (2005) {*7} followed the former set's example, an intense and brooding affair that was followed by a long bout of depression and a mugging outside his home in Bedford-Stuyvesant, Brooklyn. The off-kilter **IN THE VINES** (2007) {*6} showed a fragile beauty that was both haunting and subdued. Around this bleak period, he covered The Knife's 'Like A Pen' and Viking Moses's 'One Arm Around The Sinner'.

CITY OF REFUGE (2008) {*7} was just as desolate and searching as its predecessors (Raposa recorded it alone in a motel room in the Nevada desert), but it was nevertheless compelling avant-alt-country, as was his 2009 follow-up, **TEXAS ROSE, THE THAW AND THE BEASTS** {*6}. *MCS*

Raymond Raposa - vocals, guitars, etc / + interchangeable band

US Asthmatic Kitty / UK Asthmatic Kitty

Oct 04. (cd,lp) *<AKR 011>* **CATHEDRAL** □ ⊟
- Cathedral 2 (your feet on the floor sounding like rain) / Just to break free from a hundred families / Industry and snow / You are the blood / No light to be found (fare thee faith, the path is yours) / Three days, four nights / As you do / Cathedral 3 (make us new) / The smallest bones / We are the wreckage / Cathedral 4 (the unbreaking branch and song). *(UK-iss. Oct 07; same as US)*

2005. (ltd-12" grey; shared) *<AS 002>* CASTANETS // I HEART LUNG □ ⊟
- You ain't goin' nowhere / Nothing was delivered //[I Heart Lung tracks x3].

Oct 05. (cd,lp) *<AKR 016>* **FIRST LIGHT'S FREEZE** □ ⊟
- (The waves are rolling beneath your skin) / Into the night / A song is not the song of the world / Good friend, yr hunger / (We drew uncertain breath) / Bells aloud / First light's freeze / Evidence (a mask of horizon, distortion of form) / No voice was raised / (Migration concentric) / All that I know to have changed in you / Dancing with someone (privilege of everything) / Reflecting in the angles. *(UK-iss. Oct 07; same as US)*

2006. (ltd-7"; shared from box) *<INSBOX-4>* LUCKY. / [Wooden Wand track] □ ⊟
(above issued on In-Sound)

Apr 07. (ltd-10" ep; shared) *<AKR 402>* UNUSUAL ANIMALS VOL.2 □ ⊟
- Black water / [Dirty Projectors track].

Aug 07. (ltd-cd-ep; shared) *<AKR 032>* SHAPES AND SIZES // CASTANETS ⊟ tour ⊟
- [Shapes And Sizes tracks x 3] // Like a pen / Blood (for James Brown and Alice Coltrane) / One arm around the sinner / Vine prelude.

Oct 07. (cd, lp) *<(AKR 033)>* **IN THE VINES** □ □
- Rain will come / This is the early game / Westbound, blue / Strong animal / Sway / The fields crack / Three months paid / The night is when you can not see / Sounded like a train, wasn't a train / And the swimming.

Jan 08. (ltd-7") *<AKR 034>* STRONG ANIMAL [rafter remix]. / Golden □ ⊟

Oct 08. (cd,lp) *<(AKR 041)>* **CITY OF REFUGE** □ Nov 08 □
- Celestial shore / High plain 1 / The destroyer / Prettiest chain / Refuge 1 / The quiet / Glory B / High plain 3 / I'll fly away / The hum / Savage / Shadow valley / High plain 2 / Refuge 2 / After the fall.

Nov 08. (lp; as CASTANETS vs. ERO) *<AKR 042>* **DUB REFUGE** □ ⊟
- Celestial dub / High plain dub 1 / The dubstroyer / Dub vulture chain / Dub refuge 1 / The quiet dub / Glory dub / High plain dub 3 / I'll dub away / Hum dub / Dub savage / Dubby baby / High dub chaos 2 / City of dubfuge / After dub fall.

Sep 09. (cd/lp) *<(AKR 066)>* **TEXAS ROSE, THE THAW AND THE BEASTS** □ Oct 09 □
- Rose / On beginning / My heart / Worn from the fight (with fireworks) / No trouble / Thaw and the beasts / We kept our kitchen clean and our dreaming quiet / Down the line, love / Lucky old moon / Ignorance is blues / Dance, dance.

Nick CASTRO

Born Nicolas Javier Castro (c. 1980) in Hollywood, Los Angeles, CASTRO is part of the post-millennium freak-folk revival scene. He studied piano under jazz giant Daniel Jackson and subsequently avant-gardeist Igor Korneitchouk while working as a sound engineer in Hollywood's Amoeba Music shop. With an ear for the weird and wonderful, the frontman and multi-instrumentalist cast his shadow further afield, leading and performing with San Diego garage outfit Children Of Gauhd.

Taking his cue from a wide spectrum of acid-folk inspirations including NICK DRAKE, CLIVE PALMER and BREAD, LOVE AND DREAMS, his psychedelic solo debut, **A SPY IN THE HOUSE OF GOD** (2004) {*8}, found favour with the freak-folk faithful. Weaving a cosmic tapestry of sound like a fusion of JOHN RENBOURN, ESPERS and SIX ORGANS OF ADMITTANCE, tracks such as 'Dear Stranger', 'The Jack Of All Seasons' and 'Winter's Chill' jumped from the speakers with ease and grace. Unusual instrumentation, from ouds to teapots, was employed on 'If Your Soul Could Sing' and the Kaleidoscopeish 'The Opposite Of It'.

Having previously appeared at Chicago's Million Tongues festival (performing along with JOSEPHINE FOSTER, SIMON FINN, Michael Yonkers and LSD-March), CASTRO was ready to start a full-time band, The Poison Tree. Made up of moonlighting ESPERS musicians Helena Espvall, Otto Hauser, Chris Smith and Adam Hershberger, plus MEG BAIRD and JOSEPHINE FOSTER, their album **FURTHER FROM GRACE** (2005) {*6} was released on the Strange Attractors imprint.

A gothic-psych approach was in evidence on the opener, 'Sun Song', and CASTRO took the acoustic spotlight with Helena on the next track, 'To This Earth'. Not far removed musically from ESPERS' trippy debut of a year before (listen to 'Unborn Child' or the Middle Eastern 'Music For Mijwiz'), this album was not as effective as his solo effort, although it was still a pivotal move in his career.

Mostly written, arranged and produced by NICK CASTRO, and now accompanied by The Young Elders, **COME INTO OUR HOUSE** (2006) {*7} was structured around mediaeval and minstrel-like psych-folk, lying somewhere between ESPERS and IN GOWAN RING (the latter's B'eirth played in the backing group). The Young Elders ensemble included vocalist Wendy Watson (who sang lead on their reading of JEAN RITCHIE's 'One I Love'), Ryan Kirkpatrick, drummer-percussionists Brian Dyson and Chris Guttmacher and others, taking new-school folkies back to the olden days of DRAKE, JANSCH and 'Greensleeves' (check out 'Picolina'). With closing improv-folk soundscapes 'Lay Down Your Arms' and 'Promises Unbroken' each clocking in at over 13 minutes ('Voices From The Mountains' reaches nine), CASTRO and the group exceeded the boundaries of even HERON and WILLIAMSON.

CASTRO has since been on sabbatical, only a limited-edition 10" EP, 'A Day Without Disaster' (released on Italian label A Silent Place), breaking the silence. *MCS*

Nick Castro - vocals, guitars, harmonium, keyboards, percussion

US Records Of Gauhd / UK not issued

Sep 04. (cd/lp) *<RoG CD/LP 4>* **A SPY IN THE HOUSE OF GOD** □ ⊟
- Jack of all seasons / No sweeter thing / Ukelin suite / Winter's chill / Flight of the mourning dove / Zoey / If your soul could sing / This was that and then / Dear stranger / The opposite of it / Ordinary life.

—— added **Otto Hauser** - percussion, dumbek, trap kit / **Adam Hershberger** - flugelhorn / **Helena Spevall** - flute, cello, percussion / **Chris Smith** - bass / + guests **Josephine Foster + Meg Baird**

Strange Attractors Audio House / Strange Attractors Audio House

Jun 05. (cd; as NICK CASTRO & THE POISON TREE) *<(SAAH 030)>* **FURTHER FROM GRACE** □ □
- Sun song / To this earth / Unborn child / Won't you sing to me / Waltz for a little bird / Guilford / Music for Mijwiz / Deep deep sea / Walk like a whisper. *<lp-iss. on Eclipse; ECL-047>*

—— now with **Wendy Watson** - vocals, harmonium, percussion / **Ryan Kirkpatrick** - vocals, contraband, fuzz bass, gong / **B'Eirth** - vocals, whistle, harmonica / **Tom Wunder** - mountain drum, Moroccan tabla / **Chris Guttmacher** - percussion / **Brian Dyson** - percussion / **Julia Cunningham** - Celtic harp / **Martin Salisbury** - trombone / **John Contreras** - cello / **Joolie Wood** - tenor recorder

Jun 06. (cd; as NICK CASTRO & THE YOUNG ELDERS) *<(SAAH 042)>* **COME INTO OUR HOUSE** □ Jul 06 □
- Winding tree / Sleeping in a dream / Picolina / One I love / Altar / Voices from the mountain / Standing on the standing stone / Lay down your arms / Promises unbroken. *<re-iss. Dec 06 10"/12" d-lp on Daffodelic w/7" ep+=; D 0000601>* - Beggar's tongue / Dance with death / It's all a dream.

—— now w/ **Watson, Kirkpatrick, Christof Certik** (of Winter Flowers) + guest Jeb Lipson

A Silent Place / A Silent Place

May 07. (ltd; 10" ep; some gold) *<(ASP 25)>* A DAY WITHOUT DISASTER □ Dec 07 □
- Lock and key / Great divide / Yadmur / Sirens / The voyager.

The CAVE SINGERS

Risen from the ashes of various Seattle, Washington indie outfits, jangly folk-rock trio The CAVE SINGERS arrived in early 2007. Frontman Pete Quirk (from Hint Hint), guitarist Derek Fudesco (from Pretty Girls Make

Graves) and drummer and guitarist Marty Lund (ex-Cobra High) had the perfect pedigree for today's fickle indie-folk market.

Augmented by another Pretty Girls member, Andrea Zollo (on washboard and some vocals) and producer Colin Stewart, the band's first album for Matador, **INVITATION SONGS** (2007) {*8}, was praised for its WOODY GUTHRIE-meets-Smashing Pumpkins moments on tracks like 'Royal Lawns', 'Oh Christine', 'Called' and 'Elephant Clouds'). Yes, back-porch music was alive and kicking.

Once again with Stewart at the controls, and joined by Black Mountain/ LIGHTNING DUST connection Amber and Ashley Webber, **WELCOME JOY** (2009) {*7} was another broody attempt to fuse country-folk with something rollicking and jam-friendly. But, featuring only ten songs at around three minutes each ('Shrine' was the exception), the album fell short of its potential. Quirk's voice resembled that of 'Rumours'-era Lindsey Buckingham on 'At The Cut', 'I Don't Mind' and 'Township'.

Filling out their sound with electric instruments (violins, etc.) under producer Randall Dunn, **NO WITCH** (2011) {*7} was their first set for Jagjaguwar (home to BON IVER). Opening with 'Gifts And The Rafts' (very Penguin Café Orchestra), wigging out on 'Black Leaf' (think Rolling Stones) and getting back to BYRDS-like basics on 'Distant Sures', The CAVE SINGERS showed they had more than one string to their creative bow. *MCS*

Pete Quirk - vocals, melodica, harmonica / **Derek Fudesco** - acoustic guitar, bass / **Marty Lund** - drums, guitar

		US Matador	UK Matador
Aug 07.	(ltd-7") *<OLE 784-7>* SEEDS OF NIGHT. / After The First Baptism		-
Sep 07.	(cd/lp) *<(OLE 771-2/-1)>* **INVITATION SONGS** - Seeds of night / Helen / Dancing on our graves / Cold eye / Royal lawns / Elephant clouds / New monuments / Oh Christine / Bricks of our home / Called.		Feb 08
Aug 09.	(cd/lp) *<(OLE 842-2/-1)>* **WELCOME JOY** - Summer light / Leap / At the cut / Shrine / Hen of the woods / Beach house / VV / I don't mind / Townships / Bramble.		
		Jagjaguwar	Jagjaguwar
Feb 11.	(cd/lp) *<(JAG 176/+LP)>* **NO WITCH** - Gifts and the raft / Swim club / Black leaf / Falls / Outer realms / Haller lake / All land crabs and divinity ghosts / Clever creatures / Haystacks / Distant sures / Faze wave / No prosecution if we bail.		

Tracy CHAPMAN

Inspired by the likes of Joan Armatrading, Phoebe Snow and ODETTA, although more politically centred, singer-songwriter TRACY CHAPMAN (born March 20, 1964 in Cleveland, Ohio) was relatively young when she won the hearts of Britain and America in the late 1980s.

A budding guitarist and vocalist from childhood, her break came while attending Medford University (Tufts), where she met Brian Koppelman, son of industry bigwig Charles. Through this valuable contact Tracy secured a manager, Elliot Roberts, and a deal with Elektra. Debut album **TRACY CHAPMAN** (1988) {*9} followed in the spring of 1988.

Critically acclaimed upon release, its sparse and grainy yet soulful and cathartic nu-folk sketched vivid portraits of everyday suffering, shot through with the desire for individual freedom and the redemptive power of love. Although the record's initial release was fairly low-key, CHAPMAN landed a support slot with 10,000 MANIACS and the rave reviews continued. So far, so good, but what really got her career moving was a show-stopping performance (replacing headliner Stevie Wonder) at the Nelson Mandela 70th birthday concert in London, an event beamed around the world by satellite. Sales of her debut went into overdrive, the album eventually topping both the UK and US charts, while 'Fast Car' raced up the singles chart, as did 'Talkin' Bout A Revolution' and 'Baby Can I Hold You'.

It may be a cliché, but CHAPMAN had become an international superstar almost literally overnight, her success especially surprising given that she was a young black woman singing about issues many people would rather ignore.

She subsequently undertook a high-profile Amnesty International tour and released a strong follow-up set, **CROSSROADS** (1989) {*6}, with 'Freedom Now', dedicated to South African icon Mandela, giving her another UK No.1. Some felt the album had been a little hastily recorded, and the record failed to scale the commercial heights of its predecessor. While CHAPMAN was an articulate, observant voice for the dispossessed, she was also a singer who shied away from the showbiz limelight. Introspective and challenging, the best songs here were 'Be Careful Of My Heart' and 'All That You Have Is Your Soul'.

It would be another three years before the release of **MATTERS OF THE HEART** (1992) {*5}, a competent effort which nevertheless brought criticisms of water-treading. 'Bang Bang Bang' (about the disenfranchised) and 'Woman's Work' (about feminism) were the lights in a dark tunnel.

Although CHAPMAN's profile had diminished considerably by the mid-1990s, a fourth set, **NEW BEGINNING** (1995) {*6}, made the US Top 5, while 'Give Me One Reason' became her highest-charting US single to date. Her socio-political stance was never stronger than on the likes of 'The Rape Of The World' (all seven minutes of it), 'Heaven's Here On Earth' and the title track.

The new millennium brought Tracy's first album for five years, **TELLING STORIES** (2000) {*6}, a US Top 40 set and a return to basics under the guidance of co-producer David Kershenbaum. Always majestic and impressionistic on the lyrical front, she still struggled to break new musical ground, though songs like 'Less Than Strangers', 'Paper And Ink' and the title track were exceptions.

With the John Parish-produced **LET IT RAIN** (2002) {*6}, CHAPMAN continued in her own quietly effective way, playing to her own committed band of fans and ceding little if any ground to contemporary trends of whatever genre. Her voice trembling on expressive and lyrical gems like 'In The Dark', 'Say Hallelujah' and the title track, the set still achieved Top 30 status in the US.

WHERE YOU LIVE (2005) {*7} teamed her up with Tchad Blake, the feted American producer noted for his distinctive, compressed sound (Pearl Jam, Peter Gabriel, Tom Waits, etc. had all enlisted his services). Working with CHAPMAN, he took a more naturalistic approach, allowing the singer's quiet art to do the talking, and directed her into the Top 50 in both the US and the UK. Each track had a slow-burn effect (check out 'Talk To You', 'Never Yours' and America'), but no singles were released.

Never prolific, she released her eighth album in twenty years, **OUR BRIGHT FUTURE** (2008) {*6}, to no great sales. However, co-produced by Larry Klein (best known for his work with JONI MITCHELL) and augmented by Dean Parks on guitar and Steve Gadd on drums, it did feature a few understated gems such as 'Save Us All', 'Something To See' and the title track. Tracy's 'peace, love and understanding' manifesto was clearly still intact and heartfelt. *MCS*

Tracy Chapman - vocals, acoustic guitar / with her band/session people

		US Elektra	UK Elektra
Apr 88.	(cd)(lp/c) *<(K 960774-2)>* (EKT 44/+C) **TRACY CHAPMAN** - Talkin' bout a revolution / Fast car / Across the lines / Behind the wall / Baby can I hold you / Mountains o' things / She's got her ticket / Why? / For my lover / If not now... / For you. *(d-cd-iss.+=)- CROSSROADS*	1	1
May 88.	(7") *<69412>* *(EKR 73)* FAST CAR. / For You (12"+=) *(EKR 73T)* - Behind the wall.	6	5
Aug 88.	(7"/12") *(EKR 78/+T)* TALKIN' 'BOUT A REVOLUTION. / If Not Now... (cd-s+=) *(EKR 78CD)* - She's got her ticket.	-	
Sep 88.	(7") *<69383>* TALKIN' 'BOUT A REVOLUTION. / Behind The Wall	75	-
Oct 88.	(7") *<69356>* BABY CAN I HOLD YOU. / If Not Now...	48	-
Nov 88.	(7") *(EKR 82)* BABY CAN I HOLD YOU. / Across The Lines (12"+=/cd-s+=) *(EKR 82 T/CD)* - Mountain o' things.	-	
Sep 89.	(7"/c-s) *<69273>* *(EKR 95/+C)* CROSSROADS. / Born To Fight (12"+=) *(EKR 95T)* - Fast car. (cd-s+=) *(EKR 95CD)* - Mountain o' things (live).	90	61
Oct 89.	(cd)(lp/c) *<(K 960888-2)>* *(EKT 61/+C)* **CROSSROADS** - Crossroads / Bridges / Freedom now / Material world / Be careful of my heart / Subcity / Born to fight / A hundred years / This time / All that you have is your soul. *(d-cd-iss. Aug 08 +=; 8122 79908-9)- TRACY CHAPMAN*	9	1
Feb 90.	(7") *(EKR 107)* ALL THAT YOU HAVE IS YOUR SOUL. / Subcity (12"+=) *(EKR 107T)* - Freedom now.	-	
Feb 90.	(c-s) *<5423>* ALL THAT YOU HAVE IS YOUR SOUL. / Material World (12") *<5424>* - ('A') / ('A'-extended).		-
Apr 92.	(7"/c-s) *(EKR 144/+C)* BANG BANG BANG. / Woman's Work (12"+=/cd-s+=) *(EKR 144 T/CD)* - House of the rising sun.	-	
May 92.	(cd)(lp/c) *<(7559 61215-2)>* *(EKT 98/+C)* **MATTERS OF THE HEART** - Bang bang bang / So / I used to be a sailor / The love that you had / Woman's	53	19

work / If these are the things / Short supply / Dreaming on a world / Open arms / Matters of the heart.

Jul 92. (7"/c-s) *(EKR 152/+C)* DREAMING ON A WORLD. / Woman's Work [-] [ ]
(cd-s+=) *(EKR 152CD)* - ('A'-ext.) / House of the rising sun.

Nov 95. (cd/c) *<7559 61850-2/-4>* **NEW BEGINNING** [4] [ ]
- Heaven's here on earth / New beginning / Smoke and ashes / Cold feet / At this point in my life / The promise / The rape of the world / Tell it like it is / Give me one reason / Remember the Tinman / I'm ready. *<bonus +=>* - Save a space for me.

Mar 96. (c-s) *<64346>* GIVE ME ONE REASON / The Rape Of The World [3] [-]

May 96. (cd-s) *(EKR 222CD)* GIVE ME ONE REASON / The Rape Of The World / House Of The Rising Sun [-] [ ]

Mar 97. (c-s) *(E 3969C)* GIVE ME ONE REASON / Fast Car [-] [ ]
(cd-s+=) *(E 3969CD)* - Talkin' bout a revolution.

Feb 00. (cd/c) *<(7559 62478-2/-4)>* **TELLING STORIES** [33] [ ]
- Telling stories / Less than strangers / Speak the word / It's ok / Wedding song / Unsung psalm / Nothing yet / Paper and ink / Devotion / The only one / First try. *<(d-cd-iss. May 00 +=; 7559 62541-2)>* - live:- Fast car [UK-only] / Talkin' 'bout a revolution [UK-only] / Three little birds / House of the rising sun / Mountains o' things / Behind the wall / Baby can I hold you.

Oct 02. (cd-s) *(E 7335CD)* YOU'RE THE ONE / I Am Yours [-] [ ]

Oct 02. (cd) *<(7559 62836-2)>* **LET IT RAIN** [25] [36]
- Let it rain / Another sun / You're the one / In the dark / Almost / Hard wired / Say hallelujah / Broken / Happy / Goodbye / Over in love / I am yours. *<(d-cd-iss. Mar 03 +=; 7559 62861-2)>* - live:- You're the one / Give me one reason / Talkin' bout a revolution / I am yours / Get up stand up.

Sep 05. (cd) *<(7567 83803-2)>* **WHERE YOU LIVE** [49] [43]
- Change / Talk to you / 3,000 miles / Going back / Don't dwell / Never yours / America / Love's proof / Before Easter / Taken / Be and be not afraid.

Oct 08. (dl-s) <-> SING FOR YOU [ ] [ ]

Nov 08. (cd) *<514061> (7567 89821-2)* **OUR BRIGHT FUTURE** [57] [75]
- Sing for you / I did it all / Save us all / Our bright future / For a dream / Thinking of you / A theory / Conditional / Something to see (no war) / First person on earth / Spring.

- (8-10*) compilation -

Oct 01. (cd/c) Elektra; *<(7559 62700-2/-4)>* **COLLECTION** [ ] Sep 01 [3]
- Fast car / Subcity / Baby can I hold you / The promise / I'm ready / Crossroads / Bang bang bang / Telling stories / Smoke and ashes / Speak the word / Wedding song / Open arms / Give me one reason / Talkin' 'bout a revolution / She's got her ticket / All that you have is your soul.

Vic CHESNUTT

Born James Victor Chesnutt, November 12, 1964 in Jacksonville, Florida, Vic had been using a wheelchair since 1983 after a car crash left him paraplegic. The Athens, Georgia-based CHESNUTT developed a distinctive singing/songwriting style so popular among fellow musicians that Columbia released a tribute album, 'Sweet Relief - Gravity Of The Situation: The Songs Of Vic Chesnutt' (1996). Among the contributors were such luminaries as Madonna, Smashing Pumpkins, Hootie And The Blowfish and R.E.M. The last-named connection had already been pivotal in Vic's career, Michael Stipe having produced his first two albums, **LITTLE** (1989) {*6} and **WEST OF ROME** (1991) {*7}.

Whether it's twangy, pre-Lambchop country, gothic urban-folk or anything that's rock 'n' roll, Vic has a characteristic style all his own. His craggiest narratives are his debut's 'Isadora Duncan', 'Speed Racer', 'Soft Picasso' and 'Grupetto', while he namechecks a heroine in 'Lucinda Williams' on his second set. 'Miss Mary', 'Florida' and 'Steve Willoughby' were also songs of personal dedication.

Critics focused on the bitterness and vivid despair of the lyrics, and CHESNUTT trawled the depths of his psyche for 1993's **DRUNK** {*8}. His laid-back approach to his craft was clear on 'Sleeping Man', 'When I Ran Off And Left Her' and 'Dodge'. A characteristically semi-detached, ironic delivery leavened the weight of CHESNUTT's burden, while by this point he'd also begun to flesh out the rootsy, acoustic spareness of his sound, adhering to a more disciplined approach to song structure.

IS THE ACTOR HAPPY? (1995) {*7} found Vic indulging his eccentricity in a concept affair based on the notion of playing live. **ABOUT TO CHOKE** (1996) {*7} was one of his most accessible albums to date, and the beauty of 'New Town', 'Giant Sands' (Howe Gelb comes under the spotlight this time) and 'See You Around' are fine examples of his newfound depth and maturity.

While 1996 found his peers paying their dues to his alcohol-sodden muse on the 'Sweet Relief ...' tribute album, CHESNUTT hooked up with local band Widespread Panic for an album, 'Nine High A Pallet', released on the recently revamped Capricorn Records under the group name of Brute. A second set, 'Co-Balt' was delivered in 2002.

The rise of the alt-country scene certainly did CHESNUTT little harm. **THE SALESMAN AND BERNADETTE** (1998) {*7} had him working with Nashville revivalists Lambchop and the elder stateswoman of country-rock, Emmylou Harris. Weaving a multi-instrumental tapestry featuring clarinet, euphonium and trumpet, supplied by Lambchop, the record offered up a string of positively zestful efforts (lyrics aside, of course), such as 'Until The Led', alongside the trademark lugubriousness. 'Bernadette And Her Crowd' and 'Woodrow Wilson' show his unassuming fragility at its best.

With Jack Logan associates Nikki and Kelly Keneipp in the credits, **MERRIMENT** (2000) {*7} was a slight diversion from the norm, weird in a Robert Wyatt or Kurt Wagner sort of way. The title track, 'Sunny Pasture' and 'You May Not Be Interested' can be recommended.

Working out a deal with rootsy stable New West, CHESNUTT released some of his best work on **SILVER LAKE** (2003) {*8} - backed by a big-band studio ensemble - and **GHETTO BELLS** (2005), the latter augmented by Van Dyke Parks (on keyboards and accordion) and jazz guitarist Bill Frisell. Cover versions were few and far between for Vic (one that comes to mind is HOYT AXTON's 'Snowblind Friend'), but 2007's **NORTH STAR DESERTER** {*7} unfolded Nina Simone's 'Fodder On Her Wings'. Neutral Milk Hotel's Jeff Mangum helped out on 'Glossolalia' as part of a star guest list featuring Guy Picciotto of Fugazi, Bruce Cawdron of Godspeed You! Black Emperor and Frankie Sparrow's Nadia Moss and Chad Jones. The album was, after all, released on Constellation Records, a nexus for the alt-folk crew.

As emotive and lyrically eccentric as ever, **DARK DEVELOPMENTS** (2008) {*7} kept the fans happy, its Southern quirkiness and raw appeal (some of it supplied by members of neo-psych group Elf Power) coming across on the NEIL YOUNGish 'Phil The Fiddler' and `Little Fucker'. Whether anybody stirred outside his large circle of fans when two sets (the Silver Mount Zion Memorial Orchestra workout **AT THE CUT** {*7} and the minimalist **SKITTER ON TAKE-OFF** {*6}, featuring Jonathan Richman) were released almost simultaneously in autumn 2009 is anybody's guess, but they were in any case overshadowed by Chesnutt's death, from an overdose of muscle relaxants, on Christmas Day. His legacy should live on in these dozen or so albums. While his unique dexterity and talent are underrated in some quarters, to others of a more discerning nature he's simply a god. *MCS*

Vic Chesnutt - vocals, acoustic guitar

US Texas Hotel / UK Texas Hotel

Mar 89. (lp) *<TXH 020>* **LITTLE** [ ] [-]
- Isadora Duncan / Danny Carlisle / Grupetto / Bakersfield / Mr Riley / Rabbitt box / Speed racer / Soft Picasso / Independence day / Stevie Smith. *(UK cd-iss. Feb 95 & Jul 96; TXH 020-2) <(cd re-mast. Jun 04 on New West+=; NWCD 6053)>* - Bernadette / Vernon / Acting so bad / Miss Mary / Elberton fair.

Nov 91. (cd) *<TXH 021-2>* **WEST OF ROME** [ ] [-]
- Latent - blatant / Bug / Withering / Sponge / Where were you / Lucinda Williams / Florida / Stupid preoccupations / Panic pure / Miss Mary / Steve Willoughby / West of Rome / Big huge valley / Soggy tongues / Little fugue. *(UK-iss. Jul 94 & Jul 96; same) <(cd re-mast. Jun 04 on New West+=; NWCD 6054)>* - Nathan / Where's the clock? / Latent - blatant / Flying / Intro / Dying young / Confusion / Shippin' out.

Nov 93. (cd/lp) *<(TXH 022-2/-1)>* **DRUNK** [ ] Mar 94 [ ]
- Sleeping man / Bourgeois and biblical / One of many / Supernatural / When I ran off and left her / Dodge / Gluefoot / Drunk / Naughty fatalist / Super Tuesday / Sleeping man (Syd version) / Kick my ass. *(re-iss. Jul 96; same) <(cd re-mast. Jun 04 on New West+=; NWCD 6055)>* - Cutty Sark / Lillian Gish / Arthur Murray / Bad boy town / Great buffet / (intro) / Aunt Avis / (intro) / Gravity of the situation / (intro) / I dreamed I saw St Augustine / (intro) / Naw.

—— now backed by his wife Tina, plus the Scared Skiffle Band, Alex McManus + Jimmy Davidson and various session people

Apr 95. (cd) *<(TXH 023-2)>* **IS THE ACTOR HAPPY?** [ ] [ ]
- Gravity of the situation / Sad Peter Pan / Strange language / (interlude) / Onion soup / Doubting woman / Wrong piano / Free of hope / Betty lonely / (interlude) / Thumbtack / Thailand / Guilty by association. *(re-iss. Jul 96; same) <(cd re-mast. Jun 04 on New West+=; NWCD 6056)>* - Assist / What surrounds me / Duck in a tree (live) / Parameters (live) / Thailand / Fun party - Shoestring store.

—— In 1995, Vic teamed up with Widespread Panic to form the Southern-jam offshoot collaboration Brute (album 'Nine High A Pallet')

Capricorn / PLR

Nov 96. (cd) *<5 37556> (PLR 005-2)* **ABOUT TO CHOKE** [ ] [ ]
- Myrtle / New town / Ladle / Tarragon / Swelters / (It's no secret) Satisfaction / Little vacation / Degenerate / Hot seat / Giant sands / Threads / See you around.

Nov 98. (cd/lp) *<5 38239> (PLR CD/LP 011)* **THE SALESMAN**

AND BERNADETTE Sep 98
- Duty free / Bernadette and her crowd / Replenished / Maiden / Until the led / Scratch, scratch, scratch / Mysterious tunnel / Arthur Murray / Prick / Woodrow Wilson / Parade / Blanket over the head / Square room / Old hotel.

—— next with **Kelly & Nikki Keneipp**

Backburner Backburner

May 00. (cd; as VIC CHESNUTT AND MR AND MRS KENEIPP) <*(BB 008CD)*> **MERRIMENT** Aug 00
- Merriment / Fissle / Feather / Sunny pasture / Haiku / Mighty monkey / DNA / Deeper currents / Merriment (reprise) / You may not be interested.

SpinArt SpinArt

Apr 01. (cd) <*(SPART 092CD)*> **LEFT TO HIS OWN DEVICES** [recent demos, outtakes] Jun 01
- Deadline / Very friendly lighthouse / Fish / Twelve Johnnies / Wounded prince / We should be so brave / Cash / In amongst the millions / Hermitage / Caper / Thought you were my friend / My last act / Distortion / Squeak / Look at me.

—— In 2002, Chesnutt recorded again with Brute (second set, 'Co-Balt')

New West New West

Mar 03. (cd) <*(NWCD 6044)*> **SILVER LAKE**
- I'm through / Stay inside / Band camp / Girl's say / 2nd floor / Styrofoam / Zippy Morocco / Sultan, so mighty / Wren's nest / Fra-la-la / In my way, yes. *<lp-iss. 2007 on Sonic Rendezvous; 012>*

Mar 05. (cd) <*(NWCD 6071)*> **GHETTO BELLS**
- Virginia / Little Caesar / What do you mean? / Got to me / Ignorant people / Forthright / To be with you / Vesuvius / Rambunctious cloud / The garden / Gnats.

Constellation not issued

Sep 07. (cd/lp) <*10046-2/-1*> **NORTH STAR DESERTER** –
- Warm / Glossolalia / Everything I say / Wallace Stevens / You are never alone / Fodder on her wings / Splendid / Rustic city fathers / Over / Debriefing / Marathon / Rattle.

Oct 08. (cd/lp; as VIC CHESNUTT, ELF POWER & The AMORPHOUS STRUMS) <*(OTR 31)*> **DARK DEVELOPMENTS**
- Mystery / Little fucker / And how / Teddy bear / We are mean / Stop the horse / Bilocating dog / The mad passion of the stoic / Phil the fiddler.

(above was a non-folk release on Orange Twin)

Sep 09. (cd/lp) <*10060-2/-1*> **AT THE CUT** –
- Coward / When the bottom fell out / Chinaberry tree / Chain / We hovered with short wings / Philip Guston / Concord country jubilee / Flirted with you all my life / It is what it is / Granny.

Vapor Vapor

Oct 09. (cd/lp) <*(2/1 521680)*> **SKITTER ON TAKE-OFF**
- Feast in the time of plague / Unpacking my suitcase / Dimples / Rips in the fabric / Society Sue / My new life / Dick Cheney / Worst friend / Sewing machine.

—— sadly, Vic died on December 25, 2009

The CHILDREN'S HOUR (⟹ FOSTER, Josephine)

CHRIS AND THOMAS

Although they formed up as a duo in Los Angeles in 2003, the roots of the cosmopolitan Memphis-born Chris Anderson and German Thomas Hein were in Liverpool, where they attended the local university. They subsequently toured the UK, not as a music act but as a travelling cookery/café show. Finally settling in LA, the talented harmony singers and multi-instrumentalists (Dobro, banjo, piano, etc.), played to folk audiences around California, gaining a reputation that led to their songs being picked up by KCRW radio station.

LAND OF SEA (2006) {*7}, the product of those early times, saw them being compared with SIMON & GARFUNKEL, Crosby & Nash and the more recent, SAMAMIDON. Tracks such as 'Isn't That So', 'You're The One That I Want' and 'Don't Hang Your Heart' fitted nicely into the contemporary Americana-folk mould, while the radio-friendly 'Take These Thoughts', the GORDON LIGHTFOOTesque 'Broken Chair' and the alt-folk-tinged 'Riversong' were nothing if not distinctive. An EP, 'Vista Street Sessions', featured half of the album's songs.

In 2007 CHRIS AND THOMAS provided a song, 'Horse In The Sky', for the soundtrack of the film 'Georgia Rule', which starred Jane Fonda and Lindsay Lohan. *MCS*

Chris Anderson (b. Memphis) - vocals, acoustic guitar, banjo / **Thomas Hein** (b. Germany) - vocals, acoustic guitar, banjo / with **Hal Cragin** - upright bass / **Don Heffington** - drums, percussion / **Josh Grange** - pedal steel / **Oli Kraus** - cello

UK Boar US Boar

Jun 06. (cd) *(BOAR 02)* **LAND OF SEA** –
- Land of sea / Broken chair / Bettin' on the moon / You're the one I want / Isn't that so / Don't hang your heart / Take these thoughts / Riversong / Time to find out / In my time / Dreaming of relief. *<re-iss. Aug 07 on Defend; DFN 80021>*

Jul 06. (cd-ep) *(BOAR 03)* VISTA STREET SESSIONS –
- Time to find out / Take these thoughts / Land of sea / Bettin' on the moon / Don't hang your heart / Show me the way.

Susan CHRISTIE

Unfortunately overlooked in the first volume of the Great Folk Discography, Philadelphia-born SUSAN CHRISTIE (sister of 1960s US teen pop idol Lou Christie), is probably best known for her kazoo-infused one-hit-wonder novelty 'I Love Onions' of 1966, a vaudeville ditty that might have been better suited to some French songbird like Francois Hardy or Brigitte Bardot.

But that's not why Susan has an entry here: her later recordings are now of interest to a new breed of psych-folkies including Manchester-based electro-DJ Andy Votel. Buying one of the few available copies of her shelved late-1960s recordings (there were only between three and six demos), he created a SUSAN CHRISTIE revival of sorts when he released the tapes on his Twisted Nerve label as **PAINT A LADY** (2006) {*7}.

Reminiscent of MELANIE, SANDY DENNY and MARIANNE FAITHFULL, the trippy half-hour appears to have been written by someone with the surname of Soden and arranged and conducted by Michael Hill. The rare Chante-label 45 'No One Can Hear You Cry' (flipped with 'When Love Comes') seems to be have been a pop addendum to the other half-dozen quality tracks, from 'Rainy Day' and 'For The Love Of A Soldier' to Stan Jones's '(Ghost) Riders In The Sky' and the nine-minute epic 'Yesterday, Where's My Mind?'. In the manner of the VASHTI BUNYAN and ALISON O'DONNELL (ex-MELLOW CANDLE) comebacks, interest increased when Susan was invited by Brit-folk revivalist JANE WEAVER (Votel's other half) to appear on her 2010 project/set 'The Fallen By Watchbird'. *MCS*

Susan Christie - vocals, acoustic guitar (+ session people)

US Columbia UK CBS

May 66. (7") <*4-43595*> *(202261)* I LOVE ONIONS. / Take Me As You Find Me 63 Jun 66

Chante not issued

1968. (7") <*202*> NO ONE CAN HEAR YOU CRY. / When Love Comes –

—— an album from 1970 was shelved

- post-era releases -

not issued Finders Keepers

Sep 06. (cd/lp) *(FKR CD/LP 007)* **PAINT A LADY** –
- Rainy day / Paint a lady / For the love of a soldier / Ghost riders in the sky / Yesterday, where's my mind? / Echo in my mind / When love comes / No one can hear you cry.

2006. (ltd-7") <*FKR45-001*> PAINT A LADY. / Ghost Riders In The Sky –

Frank CHRISTIAN

Born in 1952 in New York City, singer-songwriter FRANK CHRISTIAN is best known for his work with, and his songs written for, his Texan contemporary NANCI GRIFFITH. 'Three Flights Up' was a particular favourite with Nanci, who covered it on her 1993 set 'Other Voices, Other Rooms', and she guested (with The BAND's Garth Hudson) on Frank's long-awaited second album, **FROM MY HANDS** (1995) {*8}.

The latter record opened with 'Three Flights Up', which first appeared on record in 1988 on the Fast Folk magazine's various-artists 'Sixth Anniversary Issue' compilation. Frank's own career goes back to the 1970s, when his guitar lessons from jazz player Roosevelt Span (starting in 1966) looked like bearing fruit.

Finally released by a small independent, CHRISTIAN's debut, **SOMEBODY'S GOT TO DO IT** (1982) {*8} - featuring his signature tune 'Where Were You Last Night?' – was a fusion of bluesy urban folk and jazzy, neo-classical moments, variously reminiscent of DYLAN, STEVE GILLETTE or TIM HARDIN. A decade later the re-arranged CD re-issue/version **WHERE WERE YOU LAST NIGHT?** (1992) gave folks another chance to catch up on his masterful works, from 'Song For Autumn' and 'Nancy Reynard' to 'Rondo: Rumor For A Roscian Romance' and 'Musician's Lament'.

MISTER SO AND SO (1996) {*7} was a different kettle of fish, consisting of half a dozen originals and eight cover versions. There were two folk covers: 'Did She Mention My Name' (GORDON LIGHTFOOT) and 'No Regrets' (TOM RUSH); four blues: Mance Lipscomb's 'Sugar Babe', Willie Brown's 'Mississippi Blues', Blind Willie McTell's 'Statesboro Blues' and the trad 'Make Me A Pallet On The Floor', plus Jacques Brel's 'Amsterdam' and the 1928 Donaldson- Kahn Broadway standard 'Makin' Whoopee'.

Sadly, Frank decided to hang up his guitar and take a long sabbatical, but examples of his session work can be found on albums by JOHN GORKA, CHRISTINE LAVIN, SUZANNE VEGA, DAVE VAN RONK and even brash-poppers The Smithereens. *MCS*

Frank Christian - vocals, acoustic guitar (+ a few guests)

US Great Divide — UK not issued

1982. (lp) *<GDSR 1764>* **SOMEBODY'S GOT TO DO IT**
- Musician's lament / Nancy Reynard / All night long / Drops from the faucet / Love burlesque / Introduction to Where were you last night? / Where were you last night? / Song for autumn / Big-time Bob / Rondo: Rumor for a Roscian romance / Memphis blade.

—— in 1985 Frank was part of the one-off The Song Project LP alongside LUCY KAPLANSKY, Tom Intondi and Martha Hogen

Gazell — not issued

1992. (cd) *<GPCD 2009>* **WHERE WERE YOU LAST NIGHT?** (re-issue of last LP)
- All night long / Song for autumn / Introduction to... / Where were you last night? / Big-time Bob / Memphis blade / Drops from the faucet / Love burlesque / Rondo: Rumor for a Roscian romance / Nancy Reynard / Musician's lament. *(UK-iss. Jan 00; same as US)*

Palmetto — Palmetto

Nov 95. (cd) *<(PM 2011)>* **FROM MY HANDS**
- Three flights up / From my hands / Look at the stars / Snow angel / Lock and key / Two wheels in the rain / Brother can you spare a dime? / Night time / Separate solitude / Apologies / Turning of the screw.

Sep 96. (cd) *<PM 2021>* **MISTER SO AND SO**
- Gary's blues / Smile and show some skin / Did she mention my name? / Make me a pallet on the floor / No regrets / Mississippi blues / Can't you believe me / Champagne on the roof / Makin' whoopee / Port of Amsterdam / Statesboro blues / Time takes a twist / Banquo's holiday / Sugar babe.

—— Frank retired from solo work but subsequently sessioned for NANCI GRIFFITH - as always.

Slaid CLEAVES (⟹ forthcoming Great Country-Rock Discography)

Diane CLUCK

Everyone knows that the anti-folk movement expands the folk genre further afield than ever, but pigeonholing DIANE CLUCK into intuitive folk, neo-folk, or even freak-folk lands us with another couple of file-unders to look into. A multi-instrumentalist singer and songwriter who was raised in an Amish community in Pennsylvania, she has worked with fellow genre-busters JEFFREY LEWIS, HERMAN DUNE, COCOROSIE and TOBY GOODSHANK.

Of her dark and introspective solo releases since her self-titled CD-r of 2000, **OH VANILLE / OVA NIL** (2003) {*7} can be recommended above all, complete with her own artwork on the sleeves. Pick-and-mixing a bit of Joni, a bit of Kate (Bush) and a bit of JOANNE NEWSOM, tracks like 'Hold Together (Let Go If You Will)', 'Easy To Be Around' and 'Wild Deer At Dawn' give off an air of rehearsals in a backwoods cabin.

MACY'S DAY BIRD (2001) {*6} - which also took in mini-CD **BLACK WITH GREEN LEAVES** (2002) {*5} on its re-release - and **COUNTLESS TIMES** (2005) {*6}, her final release thus far, were somewhat on the experimental fringe of folk. *MCS*

Diane Cluck - vocals, acoustic guitar, piano

US own label — UK not issued

2000. (cd-r) *<none>* **DIANE CLUCK**
- Ink and needles / Fourscore lightnings / Monte Carlo / Ambulance / PSU Vs. Louisiana tech (67 to 7, 9/9/00) / Touch deprivation / You are like Elvis / Auction.

2001. (ltd-cd-r; by DIANE CLUCK and JEFFREY LEWIS) *<none>* AFNY COLLABORATIONS
- The river / Travel light / Finish line. *<cd re-iss. 2002 on Olive Juice+=; OJD 0082>- (tracks by KIMYA DAWSON & JEFF LEWIS).*

2001. (cd) *<none>* **MACY'S DAY BIRD**
- Untitled / Save me / God made it rain / Heat from every corner / Hover not / Macy's day bird / Untitled / A beast in a barn / Yatzee dice / I like you as soon as I saw you / Battlefield nurse / Impatient sun / Untitled. *<(d-cd-iss. Jul 07 on Important+=; IMPREC 078>)- BLACK WITH GREEN LEAVES*

2002. (m-cd) *<none>* **BLACK WITH GREEN LEAVES**
- Crash through the half-light / Casting about / Pathway to Eden / I'm yr here-I-am / Focus on their eyes / The party tonight.

2003. (cd-r) *<none>* **OH VANILLE / OVA NIL**
- All I bring you is love / Half a million miles from home / Telepathic desert / Easy to be around / The turnaround road / Sandy Ree / Bones and born again / Petite roses / Held together (let go if you will) / Yr million sweetnesses / Wild deer at dawn. <(cd re-iss. Mar 05 on Important; IMPREC 049)> *(lp-iss. Nov 10 on 3 Syllables+=)* - EZ demo / Gedifra.

Voodoo-Eros — not issued

Nov 05. (cd) *<002>* **COUNTLESS TIMES**
- How long? / Mundane and its mystery / Sylvania / A phoenix and doves / Love me if ye do / Just as I should be / United. The way you were / Wasn't I glad! / Mystery over mind / My teacher died-Countless times / My teacher died.

- (5-7*) compilations, others, etc.-

Jul 06. (cd) Very Friendly; *(VF 035CD)* **MONARCANA** (home recordings 2001–2004)
- Snake / Beatless wonder / Real good time / Countless times / Countless times / Lucifer / Ribbon-cutting ceremony / Diamonds / Gardenovena / Leave me alone / My virtue's gone (hooray hooray) / Reverly / Dilapidalliance / Reveller / Untitled / Modern day / Parlor trick / Untitled / Pray headaches away / Honed. Hemmed in. / Nothing but God / Untitled / If you see sunlight.

Aug 07. (7") *Twisted Nerve; (TN 071)* SELECTIONS FROM OH VANILLE / OVA NIL
- Easy to be around / Petite roses / Sandy Ree / Yr million sweetnesses.

COCOROSIE

Such an unlikely confection of indie folk-blues, opera and torch-like trip-hop may never be heard again. This is a new brand of freak-folk, weirder than JOANNA NEWSOM and FAUN FABLES and at times comparable with Bjork, Portishead and, astonishingly, Billie Holiday.

COCOROSIE was formed by sisters Bianca and Sierra Casady, whose unusual upbringing was probably the foundation of their ethereal, eclectic sound.

When Bianca was three and Sierra was five, their parents divorced. While they lived with their farmer father on Native American reservations in the summer, the rest of the time was spent with their musician and artist mother, of Native American and Syrian ancestry, who lived in Hawaii, New Mexico and Arizona, among other places. She gave them their nicknames of Coco (Bianca) and Rosie. Sierra moved to New York City in 1998, aged 18, and two years later headed to Paris to pursue her dream of being an opera star. She regained contact with Bianca only when the latter left Brooklyn in 2003 to join her sister in a tiny apartment in Montmartre.

The reunited sisters emerged from their bathroom rehearsals with the essence of their first album, **LA MAISON DE MON REVE** (2004) {*7}, which was snapped up by the Touch And Go label, and when they returned to New York, where they were noted for their punky Parisian chic, it was to play support to the likes of DEVENDRA BANHART, The Gena Rowlands Band and Battles. With its soundscape of chirping birds, crickets and plinky-plonk pianos, the album fell into the category of unhinged, like a warped old Billie Holiday 78. The cool, sweet and sour combination of 'By Your Side', 'Terrible Angels' and 'Good Friday' unearthed a treasure of nu-folk sounds.

Augmented by BANHART, Antony & The Johnsons (on 'Beautiful Boyz') and a pot-pourri of exotic noise collages, **NOAH'S ARK** (2005) {*6} continued their organic assault, but now more reminiscent of Shirley Temple than Billie Holiday on unadulterated material like 'K-Hole', 'South 2nd' and 'Honey Or Tar'. **THE ADVENTURES OF GHOSTHORSE AND STILLBORN** (2007) {*7} pushed the mischief beyond their usual childlike lullabies and fractured faerie foibles, and their Native American ancestry came to the fore by way of the trip-hop 'Rainbowarriors' and 'Promise'. The Bjork-like 'Houses' was written by BANHART. The sisters later covered The Beach Boys' 'Surfer Girl'.

A switch to the Sub Pop label resulted in **GREY OCEANS** (2010) {*6}, an operatic hark-back to the mid-1990s sounds of Portishead rather than anything indebted to freak-folk. Titbits of the genre were scattered throughout the record, but if you take their kooky, NEWSOM-meets-FABLES eclectic equation away from 'Trinity's Crying', 'Smokey Taboo' and 'The Moon Asked The Crow', there's nothing to align the girls to anything remotely folk. Let the debate begin. *MCS*

Sierra Casady (b. 1979, Iowa) - vocals, guitar, harp, flute / **Bianca Casady** (b. 1981, Hawaii) - vocals, percussion

US Touch And Go — UK Touch And Go

Mar 04. (pink-lp/cd) *<(TG 253/+CD)>* **LA MAISON DE MON REVE** — Sep 04
- Terrible angels / By your side / Jesus loves me / Good Friday / Not for sale / Tahiti rain song / Candy land / Butterscotch / West side / Madonna / Haitian love songs / Lyla.

Sep 04. (cd-ep) *<TG 264CD>* BY YOUR SIDE / Terrible Angels / Beautiful Boyz — promo

Sep 05. (lp/cd) *<(TG 281/+CD)>* **NOAH'S ARK**
- K-hole / Beautiful boyz / South 2nd / Bear hides and buffalo / Tekno love song / The sea is calm / Noah's ark / Milk / Armageddon / Brazilian sun / Bisounours / Honey or tar.

Apr 07. (lp/cd) *<TG 306/+CD> (TG 314CD)* **THE ADVENTURES OF GHOSTHORSE AND STILLBORN**
- Rainbowarriors / Promise / Bloody twins / Japan / Sunshine / Black poppies / Werewolf / Animals / Houses / Raphael / Girl and the geese / Miracle. *(UK hidden +=)* - Childhood.

Jul 08. (ltd-7" pic-d) *<TG 333>* GOD HAS A VOICE, SHE SPEAKS THROUGH ME. / Untitled

self-rel. — not issued

Jun 09. (cd-ep) *<none>* COCONUTS, PLENTY OF JUNK FOOD — tour
- Happy eyez / Coconuts / Milkman / Joseph city / Spirit lake.

Sub Pop — P.I.A.S.

Apr 10. (7") *<SP 884>* (942.A193.140) LEMONADE. / Surfer Girl

May 10. (lp/cd) *<SP 880/+CD>* (942.A191.022/010) **GREY OCEANS**
- Trinity's crying / Smokey taboo / Hopscotch / Undertaker / Grey oceans / R.I.P. burn face / The moon asked the crow / Lemonade / Gallows / Fairy paradise / Here I come.

Ora COGAN

Born November 7, 1982 in Salt Spring Island, Canada, torchy folksinger ORA COGAN blends a unique mélange of delicate finger-picking, old-timey Appalachian folk and Americana soundscapes - think THIS IS THE KIT, ODETTA or a soulful VASHTI BUNYAN. Raised in a family of musicians (her parents' house had a recording studio), young Ora was writing songs from the age of twelve, taking her inspiration from the musos and travellers who would drop by to use the studio equipment.

Three albums into her career, COGAN can apply her voice to her own compositions and to genre classics such as 'Motherless Child', a live-in-Edmonton additional track on her debut mini-album **TATTER** (2007) {*6}. Listen out for The BE GOOD TANYAS girls Frazey Ford and Trish Klein.

A little freaky on the folk side, **HARBOURING** (2008) {*7} achieved a greater audience from being issued on the small independent Borne. 2010 found Ora on album three, the Jesse Taylor-co-produced **THE QUARRY** {*7}, initially released as an LP-only set and containing formulaic covers, the trad cut 'Down To The River' and Sam Cooke's 'Troubled Mind', plus two instrumentals, 'Lily' and 'Nite Prison'. *MCS*

Ora Cogan - vocals, guitar, violin, dulcimer, etc. / (+ session people)

Can/US Ora Cogan — UK not issued

Apr 07. (m-cd) *<00207>* **TATTER** — own
- Worry / Old black swan / Sparkling ground / My sweetie went away / Hospital / Take me home / Picket line / Daisy / Thirst / Black coat / Road in the dark [live] / Motherless child [live].

Borne — not issued

Oct 08. (cd) **HARBOURING** — Canada
- Prairies / Vatican City / The way / You're not free / True heart / My belle / Destroyer / Archer / Cabin fever / The light / Riverside / You're gonna leave me.

Isolated Now Waves — not issued

Feb 10. (cd/ltd-lp) *<INW 220>* **THE QUARRY** — Canada
- Daughter / Troubled mind / Shine / Blood debt / The quarry / In the dark / Down to the river / Nite prison / Glass tower / Mean as a sun / Gather / Lily.

Lui COLLINS

If Carly Simon's career had continued along the lines of its folkie beginnings in the SIMON SISTERS, she might have sounded like spiritual-folk singer-songwriter LUI COLLINS (born Louise Collins, 1950 in Barre, Vermont). Later a resident of New England, COLLINS found her musical vocation in the early 1970s, singing JOAN BAEZ and JONI MITCHELL songs in coffee-houses to get her through her sociology and music studies at Storrs University in Connecticut.

Her first album, **MADE IN NEW ENGLAND** (1978) {*6}, seemed to strike a chord in the folk fraternity with her contemporary ballads of the places and people around her. After her marriage to stonemason Rod Zandler she produced her second set, **BAPTISM OF FIRE** (1981) {*6}, another fine collection of patchwork, session-friendly songs with a handful of cover versions, namely Paul Lauzon's 'Bring Your Mind Back Home', JACK HARDY's 'The Tinker's Coin', STAN ROGERS's 'Second Effort' and GREG BROWN's 'Rooty Toot Toot For The Moon'.

Released in 1985 with former SILLY WIZARD musician JOHNNY CUNNINGHAM producing and playing, **THERE'S A LIGHT** {*6} was another delightful example of her new age/folk craft. Covers included BOB FRANKE's 'For Real', Rev. John Leland's 'Ecstasy', Martha P. Hogan's 'All You Can Do' and Jane Yolen's 'The Ballad Of The White Seal Maid'.

After several family-life years out of the limelight, Lui took time to deliver her fourth album, **MOONDANCER** (1993) {*6}, an introspective collection subtitled 'The Journey Of The Child Within' and including Jane Yolen's 'Mermaid's Lullaby'. The fact that her subsequent album projects would be child-friendly (with the exception of 1997's **STONE BY STONE** {*6}) was a mark of her endearing and caring nature. Her latest album, **CLOSER** (2006), for the Waterbug label, has no fewer than 22 tracks, including a cover of CHERYL WHEELER's 'His Hometown'. *MCS*

Lui Collins - vocals, acoustic guitar, piano (+ session people)

US Fretless — UK not issued

1978. (lp) *<FR 134>* **MADE IN NEW ENGLAND**
- The mushy one / Wake up time / Distance / Love is losin' hold / The silkie / Jealous lover / The endless mile / You are the songbird / I'll know the time / Everything's fine right now / Almost (eiderdown quilt) / Born and bred / Vermont is afire in the autumn. *<re-iss.1981 on Philo; PH 1081> <cd-iss. Feb 89 on Green Linnet; GLCD 1056)>*

Philo — not issued

1981. (lp/c) *<PH 1077>* **BAPTISM OF FIRE**
- Baptism of fire / Passion / Bring your mind back home / The tinker's coin / Who do you love / Hold the last note out / Wildflower song / January thaw / Sweet goodbye / Second effort / Awaiting the snow / I'm looking for a song / Rooty toot toot for the moon. *<cd-iss. Feb 89 on Green Linnet; GLCD 1060>*

1985. (lp/c) *<(SIF/CSIF 1061)>* **THERE'S A LIGHT**
- Dance me 'round / All you can do / The ballad of the white seal maid / Leaf in the winter / There's a light / For real / Midwinter night / Thye enfolding / Ecstasy / Lullabye. *<cd-iss. Feb 89 on Green Linnet; GLCD 1061>*

Molly Gamblin — Molly Gamblin

1993. (cd) *<CD 1001>* **MOONDANCER: THE JOURNEY OF THE CHILD WITHIN**
- Moon dancer / Hibernation / Invocation / Move to the now / The holy instant / Triceps / Blessed / Mermaid's lullaby / God bless the children / Holy child / Flicker of light / Moon dancer.

Jan 95. (cd) *<(CD 1002)>* **NORTH OF MARS**
- Peace on earth / Storyteller / Bearline / Red creek rising / Ms A. Hulas / Joyful noise / Sedna / Two stones, one river - Reflection / Waltzing with bears / Maggie's reel - Raven song / Two pterodactyls / Poppa bear's hum.

Jan 97. (cd) *<CD 1003>* **STONE BY STONE**
- Maisha ni safi / Friendship waltz / Gold upon the trees / Surrender / Step into the water / Blessing / Guinevere and the fire / Stone by stone / Midnight / Pretty bird / The vision / Lovers' fire.

—— next w/ **Dana Robinson** - vocals, guitar, mandolin, fiddle, banjo

1998. (cd; by LUI COLLINS & DANA ROBINSON) *<CD 1004>* **PAIRED DOWN**
- Loose the ties / The trade / Saudade / Jackstraw - Bear left / The jewel / Burrow down / Rarest rose / One last stop / Little Sadie.

1999. (cd; by LUI COLLINS & DANA ROBINSON) *<CD 1005>* **PAIRED DOWN VOL.2**
- Things to do / Ernie Carpenter's grandpappy's favorite - The horny ewe / Hoosac tunnel / Chautauqua day / Podunk rogue / Ballad tree / Song of the waters / Licorice / Won't miss you darlin'.

—— Collins took up the banjo

Oct 00. (cd) *<(CD 1006)>* **LEAVING FORT KNOX** (live)
- Things to do / Loose the ties / Saudade / Rarest rose / Leaving Fort Knox / Spark - Wings / The dark silkie / Green light / Song of the waters / Mystery play / Won't miss you darlin' / Swimming to the other side.

Waterbug — not issued

Apr 06. (cd) *<WBG 69>* **CLOSER**
- Spring! / Red red robin / The creek / Susquehanna / Making pies / Precipice / Step into the water / Astilbe / Blood red the stain / Journey's end / Someone to come home to / Holiday / Gone but not forgotten / Glance in a mirror / Where? / Bells of May Street / Shiny white-toed hightops / All the pretty birds / His hometown / I wrest my joy / Blessed / Hanging up the snowshoes.

Shawn COLVIN

Contemporary American folk music has such a homogeneous identity that its hard to separate the wood from the trees, but Grammy-award winner SHAWN COLVIN stands out from the forest as one of the leading exponents of her genre.

Born Shanna Colvin, January 10, 1956 in Vermillion, South Dakota, her formative years were spent travelling around the country, staying in Texas, New York City (at the Fast Folk cooperative in the Village) and London, Ontario; she has since returned to her childhood home of Carbondale, Illinois.

Inspired by JONI MITCHELL from as far back as her schooldays, COLVIN met up with future producer and co-writer John Leventhal, and her first real job in the business was as a backing vocalist for SUZANNE VEGA. The latter returned the compliment by doing the same on Shawn's debut set, **STEADY ON** (1989) {*8}. Although the record only bubbled outside the US Top 100, it won COLVIN her first Grammy, for Best Contemporary Folk Album. Seductive and almost provocative, its best moments are on 'Ricochet In Time', 'Diamond In The Rough' and the title track.

Grammy-nominated again, Shawn's second set, **FAT CITY** (1992) {*7} - this time with producer Larry Klein and numerous worthy session players - was another stab at the rootsy, radio-friendly AOR market. Her formulaic girl-with-guitar approach seemed to be paying off when **COVER GIRL** (1994) {*4} entered the Top 50. Led by a minor UK hit cover of The Police's 'Every Little Thing (He) Does Is Magic', her interpretative muse was in full flow through Tom Waits's '(Looking For) The Heart Of Saturday Night', GREG BROWN's 'One Cool Remove' (another UK hit), Willis Alan Ramsey's 'Satin Sheets', JUDEE SILL's 'There's A Rugged Road', Roly Salley's 'Killing The Blues', Tom Littlefield's 'Window To The World', Steve Earle's 'Someday', Robbie Robertson's 'Twilight', Jim Webb's 'If These Walls Could Speak', Talking Heads' 'This Must Be The Place (Naïve Melody)' and DYLAN's 'You're Gonna Make Me Lonesome When You Go'. On reflection, this was indeed a surprise Grammy nomination in the folk category, though, going back to basics, COLVIN was featured with VICTORIA WILLIAMS on JULIE MILLER's 1995 album, 'He Walks Through Walls'.

Her follow-up, **A FEW SMALL REPAIRS** (1996) {*8}, was undeniably her best album so far, though her musical collaborator Leventhal shared the plaudits. She was overcoming a messy divorce from her partner - it seems some stars need a few heartaches along the way before they can hit their creative peak. With the delightful 'Sunny Came Home' (a Top 10 single) and the darker 'Get Out Of This House' on board, the album ran a gamut of emotional demons and lyrical resolutions. It's hard to see why she chose to follow it up with a seasonal/festive set of trad and old-timey songs in **HOLIDAY SONGS AND LULLABIES** (1998) {*5} - not particularly career-enhancing.

WHOLE NEW YOU (2001) {*7} brought Shawn back into circulation, but just missed out on the Top 100, and it took another five years for her new label, Nonesuch, to let go **THESE FOUR WALLS** (2006) {*6}. A three-night residency at San Francisco's Yoshi's jazz club in 2008 inspired the now 50-something COLVIN to release **LIVE** (2009) {*6}, virtually a collection of her finest songs. To judge by her release pattern, her next studio outing must be due as this book goes to press in 2011. *MCS*

Shawn Colvin - vocals, acoustic guitar, keyboards / with numerous session people

US: Columbia — UK: CBS

Oct 89. (cd/c/lp) *<FC/FCT 45209> (466142-2/-4/-1)* **STEADY ON** [ ] Mar 90 [ ]
- Steady on / Diamond in the rough / Shotgun down the avalanche / Stranded / Another long one / Cry like an angel / Something to believe in / The story / Ricochet in time / The dead of the night. *(cd re-iss. Aug 93 on Columbia; 474564-2) <(cd re-iss. Aug 95 & Oct 01; same)> (UK cd re-iss. Sep 00 on Columbia+=; 499873-2)* - FAT CITY

May 90. (7"/c-s) *(655558-0/-4)* STEADY ON. / ('A'-live) [–] [ ]
(12"+=) *(655558-8)* - Something to believe in.
(cd-s++=) *(655558-2)* - ('A'-lp version).

Columbia — Columbia

Oct 92. (cd/c) *<CK/CT 47122> (467961-2/-4)* **FAT CITY** [ ] Apr 93 [ ]
- Polaroids / Tennessee / Tenderness on the block / Round of blues / Monopoly / Onion in the sky / Climb on (a back that's strong) / Set the prairie on fire / Object of my affection / Kill the messenger / I don't know why. *<(cd re-iss. Jul 98; same)> (cd re-iss.+=)- STEADY ON*

Nov 93. (7"/c-s) *(659827-7/-4)* I DON'T KNOW WHY. / Cry Like An Angel (live) [–] [62]
(cd-s+=) *(659827-2)* - Polaroids (live).

Feb 94. (7"/c-s) *(659428-7/-4)* ROUND OF BLUES. / Steady On [–] [73]
(cd-s+=) *(659428-2)* - Cry like an angel / ('A'-version).

Aug 94. (c-s) *(660774-4)* EVERY LITTLE THING (HE) DOES IS MAGIC / ('A'-live) [–] [65]
(cd-s+=) *(660774-2)* - Fearless heart (live) / Knowing what I know (live).

Aug 94. (cd/c) *<57875> (477240-2/-4)* **COVER GIRL** [48] Sep 94 [67]
- Every little thing (he) does is magic / (Looking for) The heart of Saturday night (live) / One cool remove / Satin sheets (live) / There's a rugged road / Killing the blues (live) / Window to the world / Someday / Twilight (live) / If these walls could speak / This must be the place (naive melody) / You're gonna make me lonesome when you go (live). *(cd re-iss. Feb 98 & Jul 03 +=; same)* - Ol' 55.

Jan 95. (c-s; SHAWN COLVIN with MARY CHAPIN CARPENTER) *(661134-4)* ONE COOL REMOVE / Every Little Thing (He) Does Is Magic [–] [40]
(cd-s) *(661134-2)* - ('A') / Knowing what I know (live) / (Looking for) The heart of Saturday night (live) / Polaroids (live).
(cd-s) *(661134-5)* - ('A') / Someday (live with MARY CHAPIN CARPENTER) / Another long one.

Jul 95. (c-s) *(662272-4)* I DON'T KNOW WHY / Main Theme From Clockwork Mice [–] [52]
(cd-s+=) *(662272-2)* - You're gonna make me lonesome when you go (live) / Object of my affection (live).
(cd-s) *(662272-5)* - ('A') / Window to the world (live) / Diamond in the rough (live) / Shotgun down the avalanche (live with MARY CHAPIN CARPENTER).

Oct 96. (cd/c) *<67119> (484327-2/-4)* **A FEW SMALL REPAIRS** [39] [ ]
- Sunny came home / Get out of this house / The facts about Jimmy / You and the Mona Lisa / Trouble / I want it back / If I were brave / Wichita skyline / 84,000 different delusions / Suicide alley / What I get paid for *[UK-only]* / New thing now / Nothin' on me.

Mar 97. (c-s) *(663852-4)* GET OUT OF THIS HOUSE / I Want It Back (live) [–] [70]
(cd-s+=) *(663852-2)* - If I were brave (live) / Round of blues (live).
(cd-s) *(663852-5)* - ('A') / Wichita skyline / Polaroids.

Jul 97. (cd-s) *<38K 78528>* SUNNY CAME HOME / What I Get Paid For [7] [–]

May 98. (c-s) *(664802-4)* SUNNY CAME HOME / You And The Mona Lisa (live) [–] [29]
(cd-s+=) *(664802-2)* - Get out of this house (live) / The facts about Jimmy (live).
(cd-s) *(664802-5)* - ('A') / Tennessee (live) / Ricochet in time (live) / Shotgun down the avalanche (live).

Oct 98. (cd-s) *(665705-2)* NOTHIN' ON ME / (remix) / Shotgun down the avalanche (live) / Tennesse (live) / Ricochet in time (live).

Dec 98. (cd/c) *<69550-2/-4>* **HOLIDAY SONGS AND LULLABIES** (festive) [ ] [–]
- In the bleak midwinter / Christmas time is here / Now the day is over / Rocking / Windy nights / All through the night / Love came down at Christmas / Silent night / All the pretty li'l horses / Little road to Bethlehem / Seal lullaby / Evening is a little boy - The night will never stay / The Christ child's lullaby / Close your eyes.

Mar 01. (cd) *<69889> (494938-2)* **WHOLE NEW YOU** [ ] [ ]
- A matter of minutes / Whole new you / Nothing like you / Anywhere you go / Bonefields / Another plane went down / Bound to you / Roger Wilco / Mr. Levon / One small year / I'll say I'm sorry now. *(re-iss. Dec 02; same as US)*

Jun 01. (cd-s) *(671399-2)* WHOLE NEW YOU / Another Plane Went Down / Sunny Came Home (live) [–] [ ]

Nonesuch — Nonesuch

Sep 06. (cd-s) *<79979-2>* FILL ME UP / Wild Country [ ] [–]

Sep 06. (cd) *<(7559 79937-2)>* **THESE FOUR WALLS** [ ] [ ]
- Fill me up / These four walls / Tuff kid / Summer dress / Cinnamon road / Venetian blue / The bird / I'm gone / Let it slide / Even here we are / So good to see you / That don't worry me now / Words.

Nov 06. (cd-s) *<79990-2>* LET IT SLIDE / I'm Gone [ ] [–]

Jun 09. (cd) *<(7559 79966-2)>* **LIVE** [live mid-'08] [ ] [ ]
- Polaroids / A matter of minutes / Shotgun down the avalanche / Twilight / Trouble / Tennessee / Nothing like you / Sunny came home / Fill me up / Wichita skyline / I'm gone / Ricochet in time / Diamond in the rough / Crazy / Naive melody (this must be the place).

- (8-10*) compilations -

Oct 95. (cd) Plump; *<(PLUCD 002)>* **LIVE '88** [live March 1988 in Somerville, Massachusetts] [ ] Mar 96 [ ]
- Diamond in the rough / Shotgun down the avalanche / I don't know why / Cry like an angel / Ricochet in time / Another long one / Stranded / Something to believe in / Don't you think I feel it too / Kathy's song / Knowing what I know now.

Nov 04. (cd) Columbia; *(519299-2)* **POLAROIDS: A Greatest Hits Collection** [–] [ ]
- Steady on / Diamond in the rough / Shotgun down the avalanche / Round of blues / Polaroids / I don't know why / Every little thing (he) does is magic / This must be the place (naive melody) / Sunny came home / You and the Mona Lisa / Get out of this house / The facts about Jimmy / Whole new you / A matter of minutes. *(bonus +=)* - I'll be back.

- (5-7*) compilations, others, etc.-

Aug 07. (cd) Sony; *(684990-2)* **SUNNY CAME HOME** [–] [ ]
- Sunny came home / Shotgun down the avalanche / Nothin' on me / I don't know

why / Steady on / Diamond in the rough / Tenderness on the block / Bound to you / One cool remove / You're gonna make me lonesome when you go.

Aug 10. (cd) Camden-BMG; *(88697 69576-2)* **THE BEST OF SHAWN COLVIN**
- Never saw blue like that / In the bleak midwinter / Little road to Bethlehem / Sunny came home / When the rainbow comes / Every little thing (he) does is magic / One cool remove / If these walls could speak / Get out of this house / Steady on / Wichita skyline / You and the Mona Lisa / A matter of minutes / Now the day is over / Polaroids.

CORDELIA'S DAD

American folk was again in the ascendency as the beginning of the 1990s, and CORDELIA'S DAD were part of a growing contingent of college bands who combined Celtic and Appalachian folk tunes with an alternative, electric grunge-rock feel.

Formed in Northampton, Massachusetts in 1987, Amherst College undergraduates Tim Eriksen (vocals and bass), Tom King (guitar) and Peter Irvine (drums) were all the rage in their heyday, which dawned with a fine, traditionally-sourced set of songs on their debut album, **CORDELIA'S DAD** (1990) {*7}. Taking us through a selection of ye-olde material ('Banks Of The Lee', 'Her Bright Smile Still Haunts Me' and 'Lowlands Of Holland' work great, but 'Loch Lomond' and 'Scarborough Fair' don't), the trio come across as Stiff Little Fingers or RUNRIG trying to be Dinosaur Jr. King's 'My Frozen Hedgehog' was the only original composition.

Produced by Dave Schramm, 1992's **HOW CAN I SLEEP?** {*8} was another step up the ladder, and it broke from the FAIRPORT/Brit-folk formula, songs such as opener 'Idumea' (wigged-out folk), 'San Francisco', 'Texas Rangers' and the banjo-infused 'Little Margaret' stepping out of their at times claustrophobic genre confines.

Cath Oss superseded King during the recording of mini-set **THE JOY FUN GARDEN** (2004) {*7}, and the group continued in the trad spirit with another adventurous record, the live-in-the-studio album **COMET** (1995) {*7}. Oss shared vocals on the likes of 'Katy Cruel', the a cappella 'Seven Long Years' and a few others. 'Sugar Baby' is a nine-minute banjo instrumental.

The bona-fide concert set **ROAD KILL** (1996) {*6} was their electric swansong, and the outfit took an acoustic, stripped-down approach to subsequent releases such as **SPINE** (1998) {*7} (with new acquisition Laura Risk on fiddle) and **WHAT IT IS** (2002) {*7}, with Eriksen now almost the sole songwriter.

Without dismissing Eriksen and Oss's NORTHAMPTON HARMONY project set (Oss would perform in England with CATH & PHIL TYLER), Eriksen himself had already become something of an old-timey/neo-traditional solo act, releasing three sets: **TIM ERIKSEN** (2001) {*5}, **EVERY SOUND BELOW** (2004) {*7} and **SOUL OF THE JANUARY HILLS** (2010) {*6}. Look out also for his contributions ('Am I Born To Die?', 'The Cuckoo' and 'I Wish My Baby Was Born') on the excellent soundtrack to the 2003 film 'Cold Mountain'. *MCS*

Tim Eriksen - vocals, bass, banjo / **Tom King** - guitar / **Peter Irvine** - drums, bodhran, vocals

US Omnium — UK not issued

Feb 90. (cd) *<OMM 2009D>* **CORDELIA'S DAD**
- Will the circle be unbroken? / Rolling down to old Maui / Loch Lomond / Poor man's labor / Banks of the Lee / My frozen hedgehog / Scarborough fair / Her bright smile haunts me still / The baby song / Lowlands of Holland / Johnny has gone for a soldier / My pretty little pink / When sorrows encompass me 'round. *(UK-iss. Mar 94; OKCD 33011)*

1992. (cd) *<OMM 2010D>* **HOW CAN I SLEEP?**
- Idumea / Narragansett Bay / Farewell to old Bedford / Imaginary trouble / San Francisco / Swiss nanny / Texas Rangers / Delia / Sweet William / Little Margaret / Shallow brown / Harvest home. *(UK-iss. Mar 94 on Okra; OKCD 33019)*

Okra — not issued

1992. (7"clear-ep) *<OKEP 002>* FOUR SONGS: ACOUSTIC EP
- Sweet William / Last chance / Johnny oh Johnny / Rogers' gray mare.

not issued — Return To Sender

Mar 94. (m-cd) *(RTS 3CD)* **THE JOY FUN GARDEN**
- George Collins / Drowsy sleeper / Johnny oh Johnny / Dark hills / Rambling beauty / As I travel / The Montrealer / The dying Californian / Idumea [live].

—— **Cath Oss** - dulcimer, accordion, vocals; repl. King

Omnium — Normal

Apr 95. (cd) *<OMM 2011D> (NORMAL 179CD)* **COMET** (live in the studio)
- May blooming field / Katy cruel / Old Virginia / Gypsy Davy / Booth shot Lincoln - Hangman's reel / Seven long years / The sun and the moon / George Collins / The dying Californian / The frozen girl / Sugar baby / Jersey City. *(UK bonus +=)* - Three snake leaves / Hush.

Scenesof — Scenesof

Nov 95. (7") *<SCOF 1002>* THREE SNAKE LEAVES. / Hush

Apr 96. (ltd-cd) *<(SCOFCD 1004)>* **ROAD KILL** (live and on the wireless)
- Brother Judson / Rapture bird / Young woman / Idumea / Bright smile / Circle / Pink / Recess / Johnny / Stranger / Edward.

—— In 1997 Eriksen sidelined with his girlfriend, Mirjana Lausevic, on her Zabe i Babe CD, 'Drumovi' (a collaboration w/ Ansambl Teodosijevski).

not issued — Ferric Mordant

1998. (7"; as Io) *(???)* SOMETHING OUT THERE. / Leave Your Light Out

—— added **Laura Risk** - fiddle

Appleseed — Appleseed

May 98. (cd) *<(APRCD 1023)>* **SPINE**
- Granite mills / Imaginary trouble / Knife / Wake up / Clyde Davenport tunes: Jenny in the cotton patch - Sally in the garden - Callahan / Spencer rifle / Montcalm and Wolfe / In the cars on the Long Island railroad / Louis Boudreault tunes: Le reel a neuf - Le reel a Philibert / Three babes / Abe's retreat / Pilgrim / Return again.

Risk departed as the trio became part-time; re-formed in 2002

Kimchee — not issued

Jul 02. (cd) *<KC 16>* **WHAT IT IS**
- Camille's not afraid of the barn / Upswing / Inhaler / Eyelovemusic / Five way flashlight / Little speckled egg / Despair / Hammer / Rock me (to sleep) / Brother Judson / Dark and rolling eye / Leave your light on / Song of the heads / Brethren sing.

Dark Beloved Cloud — not issued

Apr 03. (cd-s) *<DBC 242>* JANE / Promise / Closing Year

TIM ERIKSEN

Appleseed — Appleseed

May 01. (cd) *<(APRCD 1053)>* **TIM ERIKSEN** — Jun 01
- Farewell to old Bedford / Boston / I wish the wars were all over / Lass of Glenshee / Mobile serenade polka - Shep Jones hornpipe / Garden hymn / Hick's farewell / Dress it in blue / Hope / Village churchyard / Last chance / Brown girl / Leave your light on / I love music.

May 04. (cd) *<(APRCD 1080)>* **EVERY SOUND BELOW** — Jul 04
- The stars their match / The southern girl's reply / The Cumberland the Merrimac / The soldier's return / Careless love / A tiny crown / Occom's carol (o sight of anguish) / Friendship / John Colby's hymn / Bassett creek / Red rosy bush / Two sisters / Omie wise / Every sound below.

May 10. (cd) *<(APRCD 1120)>* **SOUL OF THE JANUARY HILLS**
- As I travel / Queen Jane / Son of God / The gallows tree / Drowsy sleeper / John Randolph / Two babes / Lass of Glenshee / Amazing grace / A soldier traveling from the north / Hope / I wish the wars were all over / Wrestling Jacob / Better days coming.

NORTHAMPTON HARMONY

Tim Eriksen, Cath Oss, Kelly House + Jeff Colby - vocals only

Hazmat — not issued

Dec 03. (cd) *<HAZ 047D>* **THE HOOKES' REGULAR SING** [recorded 1996]
- Lisbon / Christian warfare / Despair / Devotion / Fisher / Sacred mount / Gethsemane / Walpole / Millbrook / New Concord / In evil long / Spring / Washington's dirge / Psalm 119 / No.8 / All is well / Montgomery / Consecration / Lisbon (again) / David's lamentation / Green street.

—— Oss would subsequently help form the duo CATH & PHIL TYLER

Jim COUZA

Regarded by his peers as the best hammered-dulcimer player, JIM COUZA (born April 27, 1945 in New Bedford, Massachusetts) became a stalwart favourite with knowledgeable English audiences after he moved to Britain in the early 1980s. He had met the likes of Ray Fisher (of The FISHER FAMILY) and folklorist and collector Howard Glasser in the late 1960s, but the following decade was rather nondescript for him. **ANGELS HOVERIN' ROUND** (1972, released 1982) {*5} was his first low-key effort, an album of which very few copies appear to exist. It may have been by one of his embryonic folk/bluegrass groups.

Big in stature and a mighty presence on stage, COUZA released a second set, **BRIGHTEST AND BEST** (1982) {*6} - featuring PAUL DOWNES and PHIL BEER - and went on a tour of British folk clubs, while **THE ENCHANTED VALLEY: MUSIC FOR THE HAMMERED DULCIMER** (1983) {*6} was released on IAN A. ANDERSON's Saydisc imprint. Collaborating with Celtic harpist Eileen Monger, he recorded **JUBILEE**

(1989) {*6}, which features contributions from hammered-dulcimer prodigy MacLaine Colston, Brian Golbey (guitar and fiddle), Pete Stanley (banjo) and Dave Hatfield (double bass). His virtuoso status was such that he was invited by rock-pop celebrities Bjork and Peter Gabriel to perform on their albums.

With Pete Stanley and Dave Hatfield, COUZA released one set, **APPALACHIAN BEACH PARTY** {*5}, under the name of The D'Uberville Ramblers, in 1993. Sadly, Jim died on August 2, 2009. *MCS*

Jim Couza - vocals, hammered dulcimer, acoustic guitar

US Folktrax — UK not issued

1982. (lp) <*FTX-909*> **ANGELS HOVERIN' ROUND** (rec. 1972)

US Greenwich Village — UK Greenwich Village

1982. (lp) <*GVR-211*> **BRIGHTEST AND BEST**
- French Canadian medley / Lao Pan / Brightest and best / Sweet Georgia Brown / Captain Kydd / Irish medley / Soldiers' joke / Prelude No.1 / The seasons of peace / Pennsylvania medley / Rumanian tune / Goodbye pork pie hat.

1983. (lp) <*(GVR-212)*> **FRIENDS AND NEIGHBOURS** May 84
- Chariots / Windhover / Call me the whale / Water lily / Madame Bonapart / The Abyssinian desert monkey rag / Pumpkin creek / The barnyard dance / Golden slippers / Ballad of Lewis Mills / Christine / Wexford carol - Mason's apron / Friends and neighbours.

not issued — Saydisc

Aug 83. (lp/c; by EILEEN MONGER & JIM COUZA) *(SDL/CSDL 335)* **THE ENCHANTED VALLEY: MUSIC FOR THE HAMMERED DULCIMER**
- Jenny Lind polka - Johnny get your hair cut / Intrada - Minuet / The Londonderry air - The maid at the spinning wheel / Nola, a silhouette for piano / The high-cauled cap - polka / As I roved out - Miss Hamilton - Christine's waltz - Gentle maiden / The bells of St. Mary's / The Devil's dream / The enchanted valley / La belle Katherine - Fischer's hornpipe - Swinging on a gate / Norwegian wood (this bird has flown) / Flowers of England - The snowflake / Los ejes de mi carretta / Starry night to ramble - The perfect cure - Peel the parrot / Take five. *(cd-iss. Dec 93 as 'MUSIC FOR THE HAMMERED DULCIMER'; CDSDL 335)*

not issued — Folksound

Jun 89. (lp/c/cd) *(FSLP/FSMC/FSCD 6)* **JUBILEE**
- Jubilee / Mississippi jubilee - Year of jubilo / You've joined our heart / My old man / Bach invention No.13 / Gallo de Cielo / Cranes over Hiroshima / Jesu joy of man's desiring / Alabama jubilee / Puncheon floor - Oklahoma rooster / St Paul's song / Poor wayfaring stranger / There were roses / If you don't love your neighbour / Jubilee (reprise).

1991. (cd) *(FSCD 14)* **OUT OF THE SHADOWLAND**
- Canon in D / Song of the whale / Falls of Richmond / Hard love / Kitchen girl / I'll tickle Nancy / Christmas concerto No.8 / Forever / Green Willis / Out of the shadowland / Concerto No.1 in D maj. / Jonah and the whale / Wish I could fall in love / William Tell overture / St. Francis's prayer / Seek ye first. *(re-iss. Jun 97; same)*

Oct 92. (d-cd) *(FSCD 16)* **WELCOME TO THE FAIR** (live at mediaeval fairs)
- (THE TUNES): Pumpkin creek / Greensleeves / Chariots of fire / Londonderry air / Now o now / Beginning of the world - Black nag / Danse reel / Blessed be the maid Marie - Parson's farewell / Golden slippers / 1st prelude in C / Irish medley / Jesu joy of man's desiring / Invention #13 in A min / Sweet Georgia Brown / Canon in D // (THE SONGS): Seasons of peace / Wee wee tot - Soldier's joy / The frog and the mouse / Simple gifts - Lord of the dance / Bunch of thyme / I care not for the ladies / The leaves of life / Ghost riders in the sky / William Tell overture / How great thou art / Amazing Grace / The Albion Oyster Co advert / Good fish chowder / Hang on the bell Nellie / Poor wayfaring stranger.

—— next with **Dave Hatfield + Gordon Campbell**

not issued — Dragon

Jan 93. (cd; as JIM COUZA with The D'UBERVILLE RAMBLERS) *(DRGNCD 922)* **APPALACHIAN BEACH PARTY**
- Sally Ann / Little rabbit / Blackberry blossom / Ways of the world / Sugar in the gourd / Redwing / Cotton eyed Joe / Golden slippers / Ebeneezer / Darkest hour / Cherokee shuffle / Cuffy / Jordan / Richmond cotillion / Rock the cradle Joe / Arkansas traveller / Planxty Jack Daniels / Whiskey before breakfast / You ain't talkin' to me / Battle hymn of the Republic / Waitin' for the federals / Sail away ladies / Katie Boyd's waltz.

—— Couza went into semi-retirement from music, making occasional reappearances; he died in August 2009

Samantha CRAIN

Born August 15, 1986 in Shawnee, Oklahoma, singer/songwriter and multi-musician SAMANTHA CRAIN is one of the new breed of kooky contemporary folk stars that has emerged in recent times. Taking her cue from her father's record collection (as in DYLAN and the Grateful Dead), newbie JOANNA NEWSOM and wigged-out fellow Okies The Flaming Lips, she found her vocation through her English Literature course at Oklahoma Baptist University and an off-campus songwriting semester at Martha's Vineyard.

Her busy performance schedule attracted the attention of Ramseur Records, who gave her a home to develop and create her unique songwriting talent. The 2007 EP 'The Confiscation' was her first proper effort, a five-chapter musical novella augmented by The Midnight Shivers (Jacob Edwards, Stephen Sebastian and Andrew Tanz).

SONGS IN THE NIGHT (2009) {*7} was definitely of the alt-folk variety, and the songs that came out best were 'Boston', 'Get The Fever Out' and the title track. Released a year later, **YOU (UNDERSTOOD)** (2010) {*8} displayed a pop sensibility that might unfold her musical canvas to the right people. The whole album can be recommended, but 'Blueprints', 'We Are The Same' and the rocking 'Two-Sidedness' stand out. *MCS*

Samantha Crain - vocals, acoustic guitar, harmonica / with The Midnight Shivers

US Ramseur — UK Ramseur

Aug 07. (cd-ep) <*(2722-2)*> THE CONFISCATION: A MUSICAL NOVELLA OF SAMANTHA CRAIN — Jul 08
- Chapter I: The river / Chapter II: Beloved, we have expired / Chapter III: Traipsing through the aisles / Chapter IV: In smithereens, the search for affinity / Chapter V: The last stanchion goes belly up.

Apr 09. (cd) <*(2727-2)*> **SONGS IN THE NIGHT**
- Rising sun / Songs in the night / Long division / Get the fever out / Bananafish revolution / Scissor tales / Devils in Boston / Bullfight (change your mind) / Calm down / You never know / The dam song.

Jun 10. (cd) <*(2737-2)*> **YOU (UNDERSTOOD)**
- Lions / Blueprints / Equinox / We are the same / Religious wind / Holdin' that wheel / Up on the table / Santa Fe / Wichitalright / Two-sidedness / Toothpicks.

Paul CURRERI

If the name of folk-blues artist PAUL CURRERI (born January 28, 1976 in Seattle, Washington) comes up, it's usually in the context of his musical alliance with his wife and fellow singer/songwriter DEVON SPROULE, whom he married in May 2005. That the couple, now based in Charlottesville, Virginia, often perform on the same bill (check out their one collaborative set, **VALENTINE'S DUETS** (2007) {*6}), and that Paul has serenaded her in album form with **SONGS FOR DEVON SPROULE** (2003) {*6}, testify to their Sonny-meets-Cher affinity.

Raised in Richmond, Virginia, CURRERI graduated from the Rhode Island School of Design, turning down work at MTV to perform some of his many songs (said to more than a few hundred) on a touring support slot with blues artist Kelly Joe Phelps. With demos in hand (referred to as "the red one" and "the blue one"), the Brooklyn-based City Salvage label gave him his first recording deal.

FROM LONG GONES TO HAWKMOTH (2002) {*7} was a worthy start to any campaign, and songs such as 'Bees', 'Senseless As A Cuckoo' and 'Hawkmoth' were performed in a delicate, finger-picking, folk/country-blues manner. The same goes for **THE SPIRIT OF THE STAIRCASE** (2004) {*6} and the live concert set **ARE YOU GOING TO PAUL CURRERI** (2006) {*6}. On the latter album he was backed by local rhythm section Randall Pharr and Spencer Lathrop.

Taking an unconventional Smog-meets-Tom Waits approach, **THE VELVET RUT** (2007) {*8} pitched itself between experimental and traditional folk-blues, never more distinctly than on the fuzz-friendly growler 'Mantra'. The alt-country formula was defined by the lengthy finale, 'Freestylin' Crost The Pond'. CURRERI had now come of age.

He covered Mississippi Fred McDowell's 'Louise' on SONGS FOR ..., and his own material on **CALIFORNIA** (2009) {*7} was complemented by two outsider tracks by MICHAEL HURLEY ('Wildegeeses') and his Tin Angel labelmate Brady Earnhart ('Stephen Crane'). CURRERI was at his cool and laid-back best on 'Here Comes Another Morning', 'I Can Hear The Future Calling' and the acoustic-Zeppelinesque title track. The good thing is, he's just getting going. *MCS*

Paul Curreri - vocals, guitars

US City Salvage — UK not issued

Apr 02. (cd) <*paulcurreri 1*> **FROM LONG GONES TO HAWKMOTH**
- Miles run the daffodil down / Senseless as a cuckoo / Blame love / Bees / On hopeless love / Southfried backyard train / Another for Allen and Sally / Maria / Beautiful gun and a locketful of honey / God moves on the city / Hawkmoth.

May 03. (cd) *<paulcurreri 2>* **SONGS FOR DEVON SPROULE** ☐ ⊟
- Greenville / Letting us be / Night jet trails / If your work is shouting / Tomorrow we'll wake again / Come near to me / The last year of the red breast / Louise / Fishbowl / It's a little room (and I need a little room) / Beneath a crozet trestle bridge / Long gone again / Tomorrow night. *<(re-iss. May 08 on Tin Angel; TAR 006)>*

Dec 04. (cd) *<paulcurreri 3>* **THE SPIRIT OF THE STAIRCASE** ☐ ⊟
- Beauty fades / Drag some revelating / On the fiddle / March kitchen and what was said / Memory makes all this / Middledrift's lament / Something comes / The party at the house / Spirit of the staircase / Charlie bear / You will look at me.

Apr 06. (cd) *<paulcurreri 4>* **ARE YOU GOING TO PAUL CURRERI** [live] ☐ ⊟
- Introduction / Senseless as a cuckoo / The island drag / Azalea / The heavy deal / Maria / Come back baby / Hawkmoth / The party at the house / Bees / Greenville / If your work is shouting / Overboard / On hopeless love.

Apr 07. (cd) *<paulcurreri 5>* **THE VELVET RUT** ☐ ⊟
- Mantra / The velvet rut / A song on robbing / The wasp / The ugly angel / Keep your master's voice in your mouth / Fat killer at dawn / Intermission for beer / Loretta / Don't drink / Where you got ain't what you're from / Why I turned my light off / Freestylin' crost the pond. *<(re-iss. Jul 07 on Tin Angel; TAR 002)> <re-iss. Jan 09 on Kindred Rhythm; 1143>*

Dec 07. (cd; as CURRERI & SPROULE) *<none>* **VALENTINE'S DUETS** ⊟ net ⊟
- I've been a long time leaving / If you don't want me / I'm on fire / Little glass of wine / Two sleepy people / Havana moon / Don't hurry for heaven / Female impersonator / You belong to me / Crazy as a loon.

(above was available only as an mp3 download)

Tin Angel - Hi-Ya | Tin Angel - Hi-Ya

Oct 09. (cd) *<(TAR 012)>* **CALIFORNIA** ☐ Nov 09 ☐
- Now I can go on / Once upon a rooftop / Stephen Crane / Here comes another morning / Tight pack me sugar / California / Off the street, onto the road / The line / When what you do don't do it anymore / I can hear the future calling / Wildegeeses / I can't return / Down by the water.

Catie CURTIS

'Cool, countrified folk' best describes the music of Boston-based singer-songwriter CATIE CURTIS (b. May 22, 1965 in Saco, Maine), a throwback to Rickie Lee Jones and a cross between Patty Griffin and Sheryl Crow – in a folk way.

A leading voice for women's rights and same-sex partnerships, Catie is married to Liz Marshall and lives with their two daughters in Newton, Massachusetts. **CATIE CURTIS** (1997) {*6} won Best Album at the Gay And Lesbian American Music Awards. This polished, well-crafted record featured session players such as Roy Bittan and Lee Sklar on favourite tracks including 'Soulfully', 'I Don't Cry Anymore' and 'Memphis'.

That wasn't her first album; it's necessary to go back to 1989 for the demo cassette 'Dandelion', and to 1991 for her first official CD release, **FROM YEARS TO HOURS** {*7}, which moved her up the league in terms of songwriting ability. Thought-provoking gems like 'Hole In The Bucket', 'Exception To The Rule' and 'Grandmother's Name' stood out from the pack, and there was a nice reading of The WATERBOYS' 'Fisherman's Blues'. Her major-label debut (for EMI-Guardian) was **TRUTH FROM LIES** (1996) {*6}, and it was at this point that her sexual politics came to prominence.

Inevitably, the roots of her fringe folk-rock sound were just the ticket for Rykodisc, which subsequently re-issued some of her back catalogue as well as two fresh albums, **A CRASH COURSE IN ROSES** (1999) {*7} and **MY SHIRT LOOKS GOOD ON YOU** (2001) {*6}. The latter found her working alongside fellow-songwriters Mary Gauthier ('Sugar Cane'), her band players Jimmy Ryan (ex-Blood Oranges), Andrew Mazzone and Morphine's Billy Conway (on 'Run', etc) and the late Morphine frontman Mark Sandman ('Patience'). Sandman's 'The Night' appeared on her next set. Duke Levine completed the band line-up.

A brief sojourn on the re-activated Vanguard label brought forth her seventh album, **DREAMING IN ROMANCE LANGUAGES** (2004) {*5}, which was a shade derivative and probably not her best achievement.

Her work for Compass Records saw a marked improvement in her observational and lyrical approach, and her first set for the label, **LONG NIGHT MOON** (2006) {*7}, contained 'People Look Around', which won her and her co-author MARK ERELLI the Grand Prize in the International Songwriting Competition. They wrote one other song together, 'Passing Through'. **SWEET LIFE** (2008) {*7} continued the upward trend. Fred Wilhelm was now her chosen co-writer, and there was an inspired cover of Death Cab For Cutie's 'Soul Meets Body'.

Something of a thrown-together project, **HELLO STRANGER** (2009) {*5} revamped some of Catie's early material alongside covers of RICHARD THOMPSON's 'Walking On A Wire', CAT STEVENS's 'Tuesday's Dead', JOHN MARTYN's 'Don't Want To Know (No Evil)', Dallas Taylor's 'I Wish I Knew How It Would Feel To Be Free' and the A.P. Carter title track. Catie has just delivered a new album, **STRETCH LIMOUSINE ON FIRE** (2011). *MCS*

Catie Curtis - vocals, acoustic guitar (+ session players)

US Mongoose | UK not issued

1989. (demo-c) *<MGS 101>* DANDELION ☐ self ⊟

1991. (cd) *<MGS 102CD>* **FROM YEARS TO HOURS** ☐ ⊟
- Mine fields / On the phone with my sister / Hole in the bucket / Wallpaper dreams / Fisherman's blues / Night so still / Same dream / Exception to the rule / Strange as it seems / Got me wondering / Grandmother's name / Oops I'm sorry. *<re-iss. Sep 03 as FROM YEARS TO HOURS ... the early recordings on Sam The Pug; 002>*

EMI-Guardian | not issued

Jan 96. (cd/c) *<35435-2/-4>* **TRUTH FROM LIES** ☐ ⊟
- You can always be gone / Troubled mind / Radical / Dad's yard / Silhouette / Everybody was dancing / Slave to my belly / The party's over / Crocodile tears / The wolf / Just getting by / Cry fire. *<(re-iss. Jan 00 on Rykodisc; RCD 10601)>*

Oct 97. (cd) *<57209-2>* **CATIE CURTIS** ☐ ⊟
- Soulfully / I don't cry anymore / River winding / Falling silent in the dark / Heroes / Forgiveness / I still want to / Memphis / The truth is / Do unto others / Larry / Come to me. *<(re-iss. Jan 00 on Rykodisc; RCD 10602)>*

Rykodisc | Rykodisc

Aug 99. (cd) *<(RCD 10478)>* **A CRASH COURSE IN ROSES** ☐ ☐
- Gave me love / World don't owe me / 100 miles / Fail away / Wise to the ways / What's the matter / I'll cover you / Burn your own house down / Roses / Look at you now / Stay up all night / Magnolia street / Start again.

Aug 01. (cd) *<RCD 10613>* **MY SHIRT LOOKS GOOD ON YOU** ☐ ⊟
- Run / Kiss that counted / Jane / Patience / Love takes the best of you / Bicycle named Heaven / My shirt looks good on you / Don't lay down / Elizabeth / Now / Walk along the highway / Sugar cane / Hush / The big reprise.

Apr 02. (cd-s) *<RCD 51060>* WHAT'S THE MATTER ☐ ⊟

Vanguard | Vanguard

Mar 04. (cd) *<(VCD 79757)>* **DREAMING IN ROMANCE LANGUAGES** ☐ ☐
- Saint Lucy / Deliver me / Hold on / The night / It's the way you are / The trouble you bring / Cross over to me // Life goes on / Red light / Doctor / Dark weather.

Compass | Compass

Aug 06. (cd) *<(COM-4436-2)>* **LONG NIGHT MOON** ☐ Sep 06 ☐
- Find you now / Strange / Water and stone / It's a wonder / Rope swings and avalanches / People look around / Innocent / Passing through / Hey California / New flowers / Hard time with goodbyes / Long night moon.

Sep 08. (cd) *<(COM-4491-2)>* **SWEET LIFE** ☐ ☐
- Sweet life / Are you ready to fly? / Everything waiting to grow / For now / Happy / What you can't believe / Lovely / Sing / Soul meets body / Fools / The princess and the mermaid / Over.

Aug 09. (cd) *<(COM-4517-2)>* **HELLO STRANGER** ☐ Oct 09 ☐
- 100 miles / Walking on a wire / Hello stranger (duet with MARY GAUTHIER) / Tuesday's dead / Be sixteen with me / Don't want to know (no evil) / Dad's yard / I wish I knew how it would feel to be free / Passing through / Deliver me / Saint Lucy.

Aug 11. (cd) *<(COM-4563-2)>* **STRETCH LIMOUSINE ON FIRE** ☐ ☐
- Let it last / Shadowbird / Highway del sol / Stretch limousine of fire / River wide / Another day on earth / After hours / I do / Wedding band / Seeds and tears.

CURRITUCK CO.

Although named after a county in North Carolina's Outer Banks, CURRITUCK CO. was actually formed in and around Washington D.C. as the solo project of singer-songwriter Kevin Barker (of indie-pop act Aden). A one-man band (with a few assistants), his finger-picking technique embraced avant-FAHEY folk, country and indie-pop on a selection of instruments including acoustic guitar, banjo and melodica.

With the added talents of bassist Eddie Carlson and producer/session player Mark Greenberg of the Coctails, **UNPACKING MY LIBRARY** (2002) {*7} was a more than adequate introduction to Barker/CURRITUCK's warm, gentle and wayward folk. Among the 17 tracks [subsequently edited for a UK release], bookended by 'Introduction' and the whimsical 'Outroduction', you might want to try 'Your Sway', 'Let It Rain' and 'Where Is My Friend?'.

GHOST MAN ON FIRST (2003) {*7} veered away from the pop angle and took a progressive-folk stance, with name-dropping numbers such as 'Requiem For John Fahey' and 'Dedication: Fred Neil' and a couple of nine-minute ragas. BERT JANSCH's 'Silly Woman' was equally striking. The double set **GHOST MAN ON SECOND** (2005) {*6} followed the unruly formula, only with longer, stretched-out jams - 'Space Cruisin' takes 50 minutes, running over to the second disc. A retread of 'Where Is My Friend?' was tagged on to the end.

CURRITUCK's swansong, **SLEEPWALKS IN THE GARDEN OF THE DEAD ROOM** (2006) {*5}, morphed neo-folk with psychedelic old-timey arrangements, Barker's definitive moments coming in the transcendental 10-minute garden of delight that is 'Wisdom Of The Weeks'. Kevin would find solace in another indie-folk venture, VETIVER, for whom he played bass from 2006.

Just when Kevin seemed to have settled for band domesticity, he distilled all his Jerry Garcia-like tones and California dreaming into a solo set, **YOU AND ME** (2010) {*6}, with VETIVER drummer Otto Hauser on board. Check out 'I Will Fly' and 'Bless You On Your Way'. *MCS*

Kevin Barker - vocals, acoustic guitar, banjo, melodica (ex-Aden)

US Teenbeat — UK Teenbeat

Apr 02. (cd) <*(TEENBEAT 336)*> **UNPACKING MY LIBRARY** ☐ Jul 02 ☐
- Introduction / Hang your coat / Antichrist / The collision / Where is my friend? / Nightmares are the sounds / Your sway / Texas / Henry / Let it rain / Staynor family breakdown / Concrete / Lie beside me / Paris / Now you're leaving / Old Song / Outroduction.

not issued — Trust Me

Apr 03. (cd) *(TMR 017)* **UNPACKING MY LIBRARY** (edited) [–] ☐
- Concrete / Hang your coat / Antichrist / The collision / Henry / Let it rain / Where is my friend? / Lie beside me / Paris / Now you're leaving / Old song.

not issued — Lexicon Devil

Oct 03. (cd) *(lexdev 010)* **GHOST MAN ON FIRST** [–] Austra [–]
- A raga called Nina / Requiem for John Fahey / A raga called Pat Cohn / Dedication: Fred Neil / Silly woman / The tropics of Cancer / The march of the people who do not know you / I truly understand. *(UK-iss. Sep 06 on Track & Field; heat 39)*

not issued — Troubleman Unlimited

Apr 05. (d-cd) *(TMU 145)* **GHOST MAN ON SECOND** [–] ☐
- (IN TWO TOWARDS): Embark / The ark / My home / Don't the road look rough and rocky / Space cruisin' // (IN TURN RETURNS): Space cruisin' boogie (remix) / Don't the C look wide and deep / Disembark / Where is my friend?

Track & Field — Track & Field

Jan 06. (cd) <*(heat 31)*> **SLEEPWALKS IN THE GARDEN OF THE DEAD ROOM** ☐ Mar 05 ☐
- Paid for grace / I went outside today / 8 pm on a Friday / Sleepwalking I / Run away from the sun / One too many comforts / Wisdom of the weeks / Sleepwalking II.

KEVIN BARKER

Gnomonsong — Gnomonsong

Jan 10. (cd/lp) <*(GONG 14/+LP)*> **YOU AND ME** ☐ ☐
- Little picture of you / You and me / Mountain and bear / Amber / Walking along / My lady / I will fly / Bless you on your way. *(bonus tracks +=)* - Tiny tattered tale / Ten toes to sister sky / Jerry Jeff on the radio.

The DECEMBERISTS

Named for the 1825 Russian political ructions that gave Tolstoy the title for an unfinished novel, this quintet from Portland, Oregon are founded on the musings of bespectacled frontman Colin Meloy, the quintessence of a 21st-century musical magpie. Scholarly in their approach and literary in their intentions, The DECEMBERISTS create an expansive sound that shares an ambition and musical sensibility with globe-bestriding indie Canadians Arcade Fire, but their heritage has more to do with FAIRPORT CONVENTION than with any new-wave New Yorkers.

The band formed in 2000, springing up from the fertile oasis that is Portland's art and music scene. One of the first musical ventures of Meloy, Chris Funk, Nate Query and Ezra Holbrook was the scoring of a silent movie. They scraped together enough cash for a debut EP, '5 Songs' (2001), and sold it at live shows around their local area and pockets of the west coast. Their early sound was nearer to alt-country than to any folksy aspirations they might have had.

Meloy's fondness for the melodramatic has led him down a path of tales of pirates, sea shanties, murder ballads and black humour - part Dickens, part Poe, part Twain - which set the band apart from pretty much everyone else around at the time.

The group ended up in cahoots with Portland's own underground cult label, Kill Rock Stars, for their debut album, **CASTAWAYS AND CUTOUTS** (2002) {*7}. It was by all accounts a spirited affair; one reviewer called it "a collection of dark bedtime stories". It also showcased Meloy's growing songwriting prowess.

They followed this with **HER MAJESTY** (2003) {*6}, which was solid but very much more of the same, while **PICARESQUE** (2005) {*7} showed greater scope and bite - the stomp and swagger of 'Sixteen Military Wives' saw the band rocking and swaying as never before, while 'This Sporting Life' was like a US Belle And Sebastian, bittersweet and swoony, showing Meloy's writing fully formed.

THE CRANE WIFE (2006) {*9}, recorded with the line-up of Meloy, Query, Funk, John Moen (who superseded Rachel Blumberg) and Jenny Conlee, remains their crowning achievement. Receiving critical praise from all corners, it projected the band out of indie obscurity, helped no doubt by their shift from KRS to major label Capitol. The centrepieces, the 10-minute-plus song suites 'The Island' and 'The Crane Wife', were almost prog, such was their scale. The black heart of the album, however, is arguably one of their darkest, finest songs, 'The Shankill Butchers', about a bloody Loyalist paramilitary gang who terrorised 1970s Belfast.

The band indulged in a series of concerts with full orchestra in 2007, including a date at the Hollywood Bowl, indicating that this was no band of indie underachievers any more. This wild ambition manifested itself in the joyously overblown **THE HAZARDS OF LOVE** (2009) {*8}, which trumped its predecessor in scale but divided critics over its execution. Inspired initially by the ANNE BRIGGS EP of the same name, it turned into a full-blown folk opera, running the gamut from sinister rock songs like the infanticide-fuelled 'The Rake's Song' to the harpsichord-driven tumult of 'The Wanting Comes In Waves'. A much-underrated gem.

Follow-up **THE KING IS DEAD** (2011) {*7} was not a sideswipe at Elvis Presley or a veiled Smiths tribute, but simply The DECEMBERISTS drawing on some more mainstream influences (Springsteen, R.E.M.); they even enlisted Peter Buck to provide some licks. It was still a substantial success, hitting the top of the US charts in its first week of release and also reaching the UK Top 30. 'Don't Carry It All' is probably the best song RICHARD THOMPSON never wrote. *MR*

Colin Meloy - vocals, guitars / **Chris Funk** - multi / **Nate Query** - double bass / **Ezra Holbrook** - drums, percussion, vocals

US own label / UK not issued

2001. (cd-ep) *<none>* 5 SONGS [–] [–]
- Oceanside / Shiny / My mother was a Chinese trapeze artist / Angel, won't you call me? / I don't mind. *<re-iss. Mar 03 on Hush+=; HUSH 40>* - Apology song.

Hush / not issued

May 02. (cd) *<HUSH 36>* **CASTAWAYS AND CUTOUTS** [ ] [–]
- Leslie Anne Levine / Here I dreamt I was an architect / July, July! / A cautionary tale / Odalisque / Cocoon / Grace cathedral hill / The legionnaire's lament / Clementine / California one - Youth and beauty brigade. *<re-iss. May 03 on Kill Rock Stars; KRS 397CD)> <lp-iss. 2005 on Jealous Butcher; JB-052>*

—— **Jesse Emerson** - double bass; repl. Query
—— **Rachel Blumberg** - percussion, organ; repl. Holbrook
—— added **Jenny Conlee** - keyboards, accordion

Kill Rock Stars / Kill Rock Stars

Sep 03. (cd) *<(KRS 375)>* **HER MAJESTY** [ ] [ ]
- Shanty for the Arethusa / Billy Liar / Los Angeles, I'm yours / The gymnast, high above the ground / The bachelor and the bride / Song for Myla Goldberg / The soldiering life / Red right ankle / The chimbley sweep *[not on all copies]* / I was meant for the stage / As I rise. *<lp-iss. Sep 03 on Jealous Butcher; JB-046>*

Mar 04. (cd-ep) *<HSH 38>* **THE TAIN** [ ] [–]
- The tain (part I-V). *<re-iss. 2005 on Kill Rock Stars; KRS 372> <re-iss. 2005 on Jealous Butcher+=; JB-047>* - 5 SONGS

(above originally released on Acuarela Discos in Spain)

Sep 04. (cd-s) *<KRS 419>* BILLY LIAR / Los Angeles, I'm Yours / Everything I Try To Do, Nothing Seems To Turn Out Right / Sunshine [ ] [–]

Nov 04. (7") *(RTRADS 271)* SIXTEEN MILITARY WIVES. / From My Own True Love (demo) [–] [ ]
(cd-s) *<RTRADSCD 271>* - ('A') / The kingdom of Spain / ('A'-video).

—— **Nate Query** - double bass; returned to repl. Emerson

Kill Rock Stars / Rough Trade

Mar 05. (cd) *<KRS 425> (RTRADCD 256)* **PICARESQUE** [ ] Aug 05 [ ]
- The infanta / We both go down together / Eli, the barrow boy / The sporting life / The bagman's gambit / From my own true love (lost at sea) / Sixteen military wives / The engine driver / On the bus mall / The mariner's revenge song / Of angels and angles. *<d-lp iss. Sep 05 +=; KRS 425LP> <+ on Jealous Butcher; JB-053>* - PICARESQUETIES:- Bandit queen (with dialogue and tap dancing) / Bridges and balloons / Constantinople / Kingdom of Spain (version Prescott) / Bandit queen (version Prescott).

—— **John Moen** - drums, melodica, vocals; repl. Blumberg

Capitol / Rough Trade

Oct 06. (cd/lp) *<53984-2/-1> (RTRADCD 456)* **THE CRANE WIFE** [35] [ ]
- The crane wife (part 3) / The island: Come and see - The landlord's daughter - You'll not feel the drowning / Yankee bayonet (I will be home then) (duet with LAURA VEIRS) / O Valencia! / The perfect crime #2 / When the war came / Shankill butchers / Summersong / The crane wife (parts 1 & 2) / Sons and daughters.

Feb 07. (7") *(RTRADS 386)* O VALENCIA! / Culling Of The Fold *[not After The Bombs]* [–] [ ]

Sep 07. (12"ep) *<0946 3 98178 1 8>* THE PERFECT CRIME #2 [ ] [–]
- (remixes): A Touch Of Class Robs The Bank / Diplo's Doing Time / Junior Boys / #2.5.1.

Oct 08. <12"red>(7") *<JB-074> (RTRADS 472)* VALERIE PLAME. / O New England [ ] [ ]

Nov 08. <12"green>(7") *<JB-075> (RTRADS 473)* DAYS OF ELAINE. / Days Of Elaine [long] / I'm Sticking With You [ ] [ ]

Dec 08. <12"blue>(7") *<JB-076> (RTRADS 474)* RECORD YEAR FOR RAINFALL. / Raincoat Song [ ] [ ]

(above three in a limited series on Jealous Butcher - Rough Trade UK - records entitled ALWAYS THE BRIDESMAID: VOLUME I–III)

Mar 09. (cd/d-lp) *<509992 14710-20/-18> (RTRADCD 556)* **THE HAZARDS OF LOVE** [14] [50]
- Prelude / The hazards of love 1 (The prettiest whistles won't wrestle the thistles undone) / A bower scene / Won't want for love (Margaret in the Taiga) / The hazards of love 2 (wager all) / The queen's approach / Isn't it a lovely night? / The wanting comes in waves - Repaid / An interlude / The rake's song / The abduction of Margaret / The queen's rebuke - The crossing / Annan water / Margaret in captivity / The hazards of love 3 (revenge!) / The wanting comes in waves (reprise) / The hazards of love 4 (the drowned).

Apr 09. (ltd-7") *<50999 2 14710-7>* THE RAKE'S SONG. / East India Lanes [ ] [–]

Dec 10. (7") *<50999 6 42726-7> (RTRADS 608)* JANUARY HYMN. / Row Jimmy [ ] [ ]

Jan 11. (cd/lp) *<50999 9 47547-2/42727-1> (RTRAD CD/LP 656)*
THE KING IS DEAD [1] [24]
- Don't carry it all / Calamity song / Rise to me / Rox in the box / January hymn / Down by the water / All arise! / June hymn / This is why we fight / Dear Avery.

Kris DELMHORST

Born and raised in Brooklyn, New York (b. December 22, 1970), the much-acclaimed singer/songwriter and multi-instrumentalist KRIS DELMHORST has been in and around the Boston country-folk scene since her arrival there in 1996. A campaigner and fundraiser for several organisations against domestic violence, her cool, whispering tones have been aired on a handful of contemporary-Americana solo albums. Many folk music buffs will associate her with her husband and fellow folk artist JEFFREY FOUCAULT; alongside PETER MULVEY, the couple released a widely praised set in 2003, credited eponymously to 'Redbird'.

Of her own solo outings, from 1998's **APPETITE** {*6} to fifth album **SHOTGUN SINGER** (2008) {*7}, 2001's **FIVE STORIES** {*7} may have given her most satisfaction - even a brooding new arrangement of old-timey number 'Cluck Old Hen' was a delight. With The Vinyl Avenue String Band (Sean Staples and Ry Cavanaugh) she made a couple of records, including the 'Oddlot' EP in 1999 and the full-length 'Respond' set a few years later.

Having played fiddle on Carl Cacho's 'Spark' album in 2002, Kris's first set for Signature Records, **SONGS FOR A HURRICANE** (2003) {*7}, was delivered in her understated but inimitable emotional-rock fashion; check her rocking out on 'Hurricane'. **STRANGE CONVERSATION** (2006) {*6} was a slight diversion, setting the work of some worthy wordsmiths (Byron, e.e. cummings, Edna St Vincent Millay, etc) to music. Byron's 'So, We'll Go No More A-Roving' becomes jazzy and gets somewhat lost in translation, while DELMHORST's own composition 'Water Water' comes across like Bonnie Raitt meeting the Tom Waits band - just brilliant. *MCS*

Kris Delmhorst - vocals, guitars, cello, keyboards, etc / with session band(s)

US Big Bean — UK not issued

Sep 98. (cd) *<BB 1D>* **APPETITE** [ ] [-]
- Sleeping dogs / Weatherman / Arm's length / Gravity / World gives you wings / North Dakota / Sink or swim / Moscow song / Red herring / Open road / Summer breeze. *<re-iss. Mar 03; same>*

—— in 1999 she was part of the Vinyl Avenue String Band (see biog)

Nov 01. (cd) *<BB 3D>* **FIVE STORIES** [ ] [-]
- Cluck old hen / Damn love song / Broken white line / Little wings / Just what I meant / Yellow brick road / Garden rose / Mean old wind / Honeyed out / Gave it away / Lullaby 101. *(w/ bonus untitled track) <re-iss. on Signature; SIG 500-2> (UK-iss. Jan 04 on Acoustic Roots; AR 005)*

Signature — Acoustic Roots

Aug 03. (cd) *<SIG 1279> (AR 007)* **SONGS FOR A HURRICANE** [ ] Feb 04 [ ]
- Waiting under the waves / East of the mountains / You're no train / Bobby Lee / Weathervane / Juice + June / Hummingbird / Come home / Too late / Wasted word / Short work / Mingalay.

—— early in 2003, the eponymous 'REDBIRD' set was issued (by DELMHORST, husband JEFFREY FOUCAULT + PETER MULVEY)

Jun 06. (cd) *<(SIG 1299)>* **STRANGE CONVERSATION** [ ] Jul 06 [ ]
- Galuppi Baldassare / So, we'll go no more a-roving / Light of the light / Since you went away / Strange conversation / The drop and the dream / Invisible choir / Pretty how town / Tavern / Water, water / Sea fever / Everything is music.

Apr 08. (cd) *<(SIG 2012)>* **SHOTGUN SINGER** [ ] May 08 [ ]
- Blue Adeline / Heavens told the sun / To the wire / Midnight ringer / If not for love / Riverwide / 1000 reasons / Birds of Belfast / Oleander / Kiss it away / Freediver / Brand new sound.

Big Bean — not issued

Nov 08. (dl-ep) *<none>* HORSES SWIMMING [-] [-]
- Love and everything / Anybody's heaven / Sliptime / Early everlasting / Strangers / Made of time.

Iris DeMENT (⟹ forthcoming Great Country-rock Discography)

Krista DETOR

Surely it's only a matter of time before some industry big-wig takes the plunge and signs this rootsy folk singer-songwriter? Although very SUZANNE VEGA, Lisa Germano or even JANE SIBERRY, sullen but warm Indiana-based piano player KRISTA DETOR (born January 14, 1969 in Burbank, California) has established herself among the genre's most promising acts while keeping a foothold in its traditions of material and instrumentation. In 2009 she was invited (alongside fellow American MARK ERELLI) to take part in the all-star British folk ensemble DARWIN SONG PROJECT.

Among her post-millennium solo work, in which she is accompanied by partner, producer and co-writer David Weber, **A DREAM IN A CORNFIELD** (2003) {*6} got her off the mark, while **MUDSHOW** (2005) {*7} brought her to wider audiences through a heavy concert schedule. Over the years she has played support for VEGA, Armatrading, WAINWRIGHT III, and many more.

With more than a nod to country (played at a cool, bluesy jazz pace), **COVER THEIR EYES** (2007) {*8} won deserved praise around the world; some tracks, such as 'Pretty Horses Run', the lilting 'The World Is Water' and 'Lay Him Down', her duet finale with CARRIE NEWCOMER, soundtrack the 2000s as well as anything from old-timey halcyon days.

Leaving aside the Darwin project and the obligatory folk-festive effort from 2008, **THE SILVER WOOD: WINTERSONGS** {*5}, DETOR's ambitious concept album **CHOCOLATE PAPER SUITES** (2010) {*8} found her turning her back on all previous patterns and formulas. Split into five emotion-fuelled chapters (inspired by Lorca, Dylan Thomas and Charles Darwin), every track here fits into place, with contributions from a host of star session players including 'Darwin' associates KARINE POLWART, CHRIS WOOD, MARK ERELLI, RACHAEL McSHANE and Emily Smith, plus Colin Linden, Dena Al Saffar, Malcolm Dalglish, Moira Smiley and Sara Caswell. Watch this space. *MCS*

Krista Detor - vocals, piano / with session people

US self-rel. — UK not issued

Jan 03. (cd) *<none>* **A DREAM IN A CORNFIELD** [ ] [-]
- I don't think so / Artless / Blue sky / Fishing / Something missing / Penny on the road / Bus to Indiana / Under his skin / Calling Robert / Salome / On the water.

Aug 05. (cd) *<none>* **MUDSHOW** [ ] [-]
- Mudshow / Abigayle's song / Buffalo Bill / Dancing in a minefield / The ghosts of Peach Street / She will not say / Steal me a car / I'm still here / Tell me a story / A red bowl / The Hampton sisters (glory). *<(re+UK-iss. Jun 06 on Corazong+=; 255 087)>* - Gaslight / All I need is a driver.

Corazong — Corazong

Sep 07. (cd) *<(255 102)>* **COVER THEIR EYES** [ ] [ ]
- Pretty horses run / Marlene in a movie / The world is water / Go ahead and wait / Robert Johnson has left Mississippi / Cover their eyes / Anemic moon / Dinner with Chantel / Icarus / Waterline / How will I know / Lay him down.

2008. (cd-s; by JP DEN TEX & KRISTA DETOR) *<255 507>*
FOR YOU / Gaslight / [track by JP Den Tex] [ ] [-]

Tightrope — Tightrope

Nov 08. (cd) *<1007>* **THE SILVER WOOD: WINTERSONGS** [festive] [ ] [ ]
- Christmas in London / Hot buttered rum / Awake the voice / The first Christmas star / My love's eyes / The water round / A traveler in winter / Sheriff Santa from Montana / One too many Christmases / All of the laughter / Sing to me of Dover / More than I dare say.

—— in 2009, she was part of DARWIN SONG PROJECT (see Brit-folk section)

Mar 10. (cd) *<(110)>* **CHOCOLATE PAPER SUITES** [ ] [ ]
- Oranges fall like rain: Rich man's life / Lorca in Barcelona / Recklessness and rust / Night light: Dazzling / All to do with the moon / Teeter-totter on a star / Madness of love: Innuendo / Middle of a breakdown / Deliver me / By any other name: A hundred years more / So goes the night / Small things / Darwin's songhouse: From Miss Emma Brawley / Clock of the world / Emma's lullabye.

DEVONSQUARE

DEVONSQUARE, from Portland, Maine, can be traced back to the late 1960s, when tenor singer Herb Ludwig and his pals Jeff Rice and Steve Romanoff (from Schooner Fare) formed their tight-knit harmony folk group. Abandoning their infectious KINGSTON TRIO-like arrangements, Ludwig set about recruiting new talent in the shape of Alana MacDonald (a classically-trained violinist) and Tom Dean.

By the late 1970s, and more so the early 1980s, the drastically transformed DEVONSQUARE self-financed two AOR/pop-orientated sets, **(DEVON)2** (1984) {*5} and **NIGHT SAIL** (1985) {*5}. The latter featured two covers, 'Velvet Elvis' (by Rex Fowler of AZTEC TWO-STEP) and 'I Don't Know Why' (SHAWN COLVIN).

Described as the Fleetwood Mac of folk-pop or the poor man's CSN (the author's own assessment), they signed to Atlantic for their next two sets. **WALKING ON ICE** (1987) {*6}, contained some decent songs, such as 'Black Africa'. **BYE BYE ROUTE 66** (1991) {*7} won awards, but not a chart placing.

Inspired by Jack Kerouac and his Beat Generation, their fifth album, **INDUSTRIAL TWILIGHT** (1996) {*6}, found a release on German record label SPV, but it was all a little late in the day for a band that showed promise but little solid direction. *MCS*

Herb Ludwig - vocals, guitars (ex-Schooner Fare) / **Alana MacDonald** - vocals, violin / **Tom Dean** - vocals, acoustic guitar / + session musicians

US Blind Date — UK not issued

1984. (lp) <*WRA1-133*> **(DEVON)2**
- Donner pass / Blue on the water / Cold love / Face in the mirror / Because I never held you / The winner / HTTL *[not on cd]* / Radio romance / Alibis / The road not taken. <*cd-iss. Apr 05 on Devonsquare+=; none*> - NIGHT SAIL

1985. (lp) <*WRA1-186*> **NIGHT SAIL**
- Night sail / Velvet Elvis / Is it over / Take my love away / I don't know why / Joan of Arc / Hollywood / Can't take your Saturday nights / Here we go again. <*cd-iss.+=*> - (DEVON)2

Atlantic — Atlantic

Nov 87. (lp/c/cd) <*(7 81843-1/-4/-2)*> **WALKING ON ICE** — Feb 88
- Walking on ice / Black Africa / Caffe Lena / World without walls / Chinalight / Straightaway / The sandman / Las Vegas brides / Elevator man / Just like paradise.

Nov 91. (cd/c) <*7 82343-2/-4*> **BYE BYE ROUTE 66**
- The clowns lead the band / If you could see me now / Message of love / Raining down on Bleecker Street / Diamond days / Looking for lovers' lane / Bye bye route 66 / Straighaway / Far side of love / Move on.

Mar 92. (c-s) <*87564-4*> IF YOU COULD SEE ME NOW

— re-united for a one-off set below...

not issued — SPV

1996. (cd) *(SPV 2912)* **INDUSTRIAL TWILIGHT** — German
- Adream at the wheel / I had a dream / Bum and the angel / Industrial twilight / Brave new world / Mystery road / Nickel on a dime / Tin man / Who man / I'm scared / Acirema / Industrial twilight / Grenade / World in a drop of blood / Newport lawns.

— Ludwig released his own set, 'Your Own Backyard' in 1996.

Brian DEWAN

A comical manic theatre preacher with an 88-string electric zither, Brooklyn-based furniture designer and avant-folk artist BRIAN DEWAN (born Lexington, MA) is quite unique in his field, or indeed his front room. Like a modern-day OSCAR BRAND or ED McCURDY with ANDREW CRONSHAW as sidekick, he could give Neil Hannon of The Divine Comedy a run for his money in the vocal stakes, but macabre comedy is his forte. Check out his second oddity, **THE OPERATING THEATER** (2001) {*7}, and the tracks 'Where They Belong', 'The Human Heart' and 'Cadavers'.

But it was a little different several years back when his debut album, **TELLS THE STORY** (1993) {*8}, hit town. Numbers like 'The Cowboy Outlaw' and 'Drinking Bird' (also called 'The Cuckoo'), 'Obedience School' (from his self-titled EP) and the Joe Satriani-like opener '99 Cops' are more than ample examples of his besuited 'gangsta folk' sardonic wit.

Taking something from his experiences of working on the children's TV show 'Sesame Street', the idiosyncratic DEWAN rescued from obscurity numerous examples of weird old Americana on his third set, **WORDS OF WISDOM** (2007) {*7}. You might recognise 'The Big Rock Candy Mountains', but as for 'Carve That Possum' and 'Horse Named Bill', maybe the RSPCA should have been called.

In 2005, he and his cousin Leon brought his techno fans some diversion as **DEWANATRON** {*4}. 2009's wayward **RINGING AT THE SPEED OF PRAYER** {*1}, featuring the Liverpool Cathedral Bell Ringers, was a strange combination of campanology, prayer and background street sounds. Better was his earlier work with They Might Be Giants and the off-Broadway ensemble the Blue Man Group on his 'Humanitarium' series. *MCS*

Brian Dewan - vocals, electric zither, organ, accordion

US Hello Recording Club — UK not issued

Mar 93. (cd-ep) <*HEL-33*> BRIAN DEWAN
- My eye / Wastepaper basket fire / Tobacco's but an Indian weed / Obedience school.

Bar/None — not issued

Nov 93. (cd/c) <*AHAON 033-2/-4*> **TELLS THE STORY**
- 99 cops / Obedience school / The cowboy outlaw / The record / The letter / The day the day stood still / Wastepaper-basket fire / The creatures / My eye / Cut your hair / Breezes are blowing / Drinking bird / Feel the brain.

Instinct — not issued

Mar 01. (cd) <*72084 1 0553-2*> **THE OPERATING THEATER** [rec. 1998]
- Where they belong / The human heart / The kids / Solomon Grundy / Loathsome idols / Rumpelstiltskin / Cadavers / The trial / Flexible flyer / Sick day / Fruitless labors / First day of school.

— next set with his cousin **Leon Dewan**

Dewanatron — not issued

Dec 05. (cd; as DEWANATRON) <*none*> **SEMI AUTOMATIC**
- Amphibious assault / Pollenatrix / Disco Kelvinator / Pedestrians / Force feed / Conveyor / Eternal feast.

Eschatone — not issued

Nov 07. (cd) **WORDS OF WISDOM**
- Words of wisdom / The kettle valley line / The civil war / Horse named Bill / Tobacco's but an Indian weed / The Devil made Texas / Only a brakeman / There was an old woman / The mirimachi fire / The big rock candy mountains / Girls of Ohio / Blue-haired boy / Carve that possum / The mountaineer's wedding / Abalone / I cannot sing the old songs.

— next credited to Brian Dewan with the Liverpool Cathedral Bell Ringers

Innova — not issued

Feb 09. (cd) <*725*> **RINGING AT THE SPEED OF PRAYER**
- Split staircase, for alpine bells / Rock of ages / Ringing at the speed of prayer, for bell ringers / Ages and ages, for musical stones.

DeYARMOND EDISON (⟹ BON IVER)

Alela DIANE

With a distinctive voice not unlike those of fellow freak-folkies JOANNA NEWSOM and LARKIN GRIMM, although not as squeaky or kooky, Portland, Oregon-based singer/songwriter ALELA DIANE (born Alela Diane Menig, April 20, 1983 in Nevada City, California) has slowly but surely edged her way into the hearts and minds of music buffs on both sides of the Atlantic.

Not forgetting early stints with the Black Bear band, ALELA (as she was then known) self-financed two half-hour CD-rs, **FOREST PARADE** (2003) {*6} and **THE PIRATE'S GOSPEL** (2004) {*7}. The latter - which featured family members plus MARIEE SIOUX - was repackaged and largely revamped for general release in 2006, roping in a wider audience for hillbilly-folk songs like 'Tired Feet', 'The Rifle', 'Pieces Of String', 'Oh! My Mama' and 'Clickity Clack'.

Chosen through a newspaper ad by executive producers Eddie Bezalel and Hugo Nicolson (along with musicians LEO ABRAHAMS, Joey Waronker, Gus Seyffert, Josh Klinghoffer and Woody Jackson) to front indie-folk covers act HEADLESS HEROES on their one-off project **THE SILENCE OF LOVE** (2008) {*7}, it was clear that DIANE had more than one ribbon to her bow. The covers were: 'True Love Will Find You In The End' (Daniel Johnston), 'Just One Time' (The Misunderstood), 'Here Before' (VASHTI BUNYAN), 'Just Like Honey' (The Jesus And Mary Chain), 'To You' (I Am Kloot), 'Blues Run The Game' (JACKSON C. FRANK), 'Hey, Who Really Cares?' (LINDA PERHACS), 'Nobody's Baby Now' (Nick Cave), 'The North Wind Blew South' (Philamore Lincoln) and The GENTLE SOUL's 'See My Love'.

Cutting back to basics on her second solo set proper, **TO BE STILL** (2009) {*6}, she took on old-timey country-folk on her own terms, twangy slides and guitars echoing her shiny vocal tones. The timeless 'Age Old Blue', 'The Ocean' and 'Lady Divine' were three of the most effective songs on board. Augmented by a fuller west coast, Laurel Canyon-like sound and some hired help, including guitarist and co-songwriter (on four tunes) Tom Bevitori, **ALELA DIANE & WILD DIVINE** (2011) {*6} marked a change of direction for this Californian country girl. *MCS*

Alela Diane - vocals, guitars

US self-rel. — UK not issued

2003. (cd-r; as ALELA) <*none*> **FOREST PARADE**
- Brown dirt / Red tin roof / Her garden / Unraveling / The snow / In your voice / You / Blue swallows / The axe / Clothesline / I'm sorry / Strong daughter / For tonight.

2004. (cd-r; as ALELA) <*none*> **THE PIRATE'S GOSPEL**
- The rifle / Foreign tongue / The pirate's gospel / Pink roses / My tired feet / Gypsy eyes / Pieces of string / Mother's love / Somethin's gone awry / Heavy walls / Laundromat lady / Clickity clack / Pigeon song / Oh! my mama / Sister self.

Holocene — Names

Oct 06. (re; cd/lp) <04> *(NAMES 26CD)* **THE PIRATE'S GOSPEL** — Apr 07
- Tired feet / The rifle / The pirate's gospel / Foreign tongue / Can you blame the sky? / Something's gone awry / Pieces of string / Clickity clack / Sister self / Pigeon

song / Oh! my mama. *(lp-iss. 2008 on Fargo [France] +=; FR 21140)* - Heavy walls / Gypsy eyes.

Dec 06. (ltd-10" ep) *(NAMES 25)* SONGS WHISTLED THROUGH WHITE TEETH [-] [ ]
- Dry grass and shadows / My brambles / Tatted lace / Lady divine / Slow your dancing / Up north.

Rough Trade / Names

Feb 09. (cd/d-lp) *<RT 488-2/-1> (NAMES 33CD)* **TO BE STILL** [ ] [ ]
- Dry grass and shadows / White as diamonds / Age old blue / To be still / Take us back / The alder trees / My brambles / The ocean / Every path / Tatted lace / Lady divine.

not issued / Family

Oct 09. (ltd-10" m-lp; by ALELA DIANE featuring ALINA HARDIN) *(FAM 001)* **ALELA & ALINA** [-] [ ]
- Amidst the movement / Bowling green / Crying wolf / Matty Groves / I have returned / Rake.

Rough Trade / Rough Trade

Apr 11. (cd/lp) *<11945> (RTRAD CD/LP 616)* **ALELA DIANE & WILD DIVINE** [ ] [ ]
- To begin / Elijah / Long way down / Suzanne / The wind / Of many colors / Desire / Heartless highway / White horse / Rising greatness.

HEADLESS HEROES

Alela Diane - vocals / plus musicians **Leo Abrahams, Joey Waronker, Gus Seyffert, Josh Klinghoffer** + **Woody Jackson**

Headless Heroes / Names

Nov 08. (7") *(NAMES 31)* THE NORTH WIND BLEW SOUTH. / Just Like Honey [Pocketknife's dripping mix] [-] [ ]

May 09. (cd/d-lp) *<HRS-0016/0017> (NAMES 30CD)* **THE SILENCE OF LOVE** [covers] [ ] Nov 08 [ ]
- True love will find you in the end / Just one time / Here before / Just like honey / To you / Blues run the game / Hey, who really cares? / Nobody's baby now / The north wind blew south / See my love.

Nov 09. (ltd-12" clear-ep) *(NAMES 39)* HEADLESS HEROES [the remixes] [-] [ ]
- Blues run the game [Tunng remix] / Here before [James Yuill remix] / Hey, who really cares? [Jon Hopkins remix] / True love will find you in the end [The Earlies remix].

Ani DiFRANCO

Part of a resurgent late-1980s arty urban-folk scene in her home state, feminist singer-songwriter ANI DiFRANCO (b. Angela Marie DiFranco, September 23, 1970 in Buffalo, New York) has become a true punk-folk artist against the grain of the corporate music industry.

Having learned to sing and play guitar at an early age, DiFRANCO began performing professionally after a move to New York City. As fiercely independent and enterprising as she was talented, the kooky stylist set up her own Righteous Babe imprint for the release of her debut album, **ANI DiFRANCO** {*7}. Issued (US-only) in 1990, the album had originally been on sale at live shows before demand outstripped supply and called for a larger operation. Featuring the cream of the apparently massive catalogue of songs she'd built up through her teens, the record's intimate acoustic confessionals ('Lost Woman Song' among them) went down a storm with both militant lesbians and straight-down-the-line folk-rock fans. Openly bisexual, the tattooed, pierced and shaven-headed DiFRANCO steadily built up a diehard following of kindred spirits through a punishing tour schedule.

1991's **NOT SO SOFT** {*6} was another bare-bones acoustic affair dealing in heartfelt sexual politics, although it wasn't until the release of the instrumentally richer **IMPERFECTLY** (1992) {*7} and **PUDDLE DIVE** (1993) {*6} that Ani began to draw attention from major labels. Standing by her DIY ethos, she released her best-known album up to that time, **OUT OF RANGE** (1994) {*7}. Again embellishing her rhythmic acoustic guitar playing with eclectic instrumental textures, the record set the scene for her breakthrough opus, **NOT A PRETTY GIRL** (1995) {*8}. Heavy-duty subject matter was always in Ani's musical manifesto, and here 'Tiptoe' (about abortion), 'Crime For Crime' (capital punishment) and 'The Million You Never Made' (dealing with her major-label angst) disappointed no one.

With girl power very much on the agenda in the mid-1990s, DiFRANCO finally gained recognition as one of America's foremost female commentators alongside the likes of SUZANNE VEGA, Liz Phair, Heather Nova, etc. The one-woman powerhouse also finally clinched a UK deal with Cooking Vinyl Records, while 1996's acclaimed **DILATE** (1996) {*7} gave DiFRANCO her first Top 100 chart placing. Following on from 1997's equally well-received double concert set, **LIVING IN CLIP** {*8}, she scored her biggest success to date with the near-Top 20 (US) album **LITTLE PLASTIC CASTLES** (1998) {*7}.

1999 proved a busy year for DiFRANCO as she released the solo set **UP UP UP UP UP UP** {*5} and a second collaboration effort with UTAH PHILLIPS, entitled **FELLOW WORKERS** {*6}; their first, a few years before, was 'Past Didn't Go Anywhere'. While these collaborations were an alt-folk history of the beleaguered American working class, Ani was back on familiar (if unerringly downbeat and mercilessly self-critical) ground with **TO THE TEETH** {*6}, her third album of 1999.

Yet however much the singer seemed to exorcise her demons through music, it seemed there were more waiting in the wings. **REVELLING/ RECKONING** (2001) {*7} found DiFRANCO's self-confessional and apocalyptic worldview as uncompromising as ever, proving that integrity, at least, was not a quality she lacked. **SO MUCH SHOUTING, SO MUCH LAUGHTER** (2002) {*6}, a double set like its 1997 predecessor, documented the singer's live career in the first two years of the new decade. Split roughly into two thematic segments, the first disc rounded up longtime concert favourites while the second homed in on her more gender-centred pieces. Judging by the enthusiasm of the various crowds, the fact that DiFRANCO's studio albums have become increasingly uneven hardly matters given the passion she still puts into each and every performance.

While **EVOLVE** (2003) {*5} didn't exactly lack that passion, and definitely benefited from more adventurous arrangements, she again stretched herself just a little too thin in places, diluting the intended impact. That said, the epic 10-minute 'Serpentine' almost succeeded in its lofty ambitions, an agit-folk tour-de-force that distilled recurring themes in her writing. **EDUCATED GUESS** (2004) {*6} and the Joe Henry-co-produced **KNUCKLE DOWN** (2005) {*6} continued the trend of hitting the Top 50 without a major label behind her. **CARNEGIE HALL** (2006) {*6} featured live recordings from 2002 and virtually bootlegged the bootleggers.

Only **REPRIEVE** (2006) {*6} and her 18th studio set, **RED LETTER YEAR** (2008) {*7} - inspired respectively by her pregnancy and the birth of her baby daughter with partner and producer Mike Napolitano - have surfaced during recent times, but it's clear she still has lots more to offer. *MCS*

Ani DiFranco - vocals, acoustic guitar, bass, piano

US Righteous Babe / UK Haven

Sep 90. (cd) *<RBR 001CD>* **ANI DiFRANCO** [ ] [-]
- Both hands / Talk to me now / The slant / Work your way out / Dog coffee / Lost woman song / Pale purple / Rush hour / Fire door / The story / Every angle / Out of habit / Letting the telephone ring. *(UK-iss. Jul 95; same) (re-iss. Jun 97 on Cooking Vinyl; COOKCD 112) <(re-iss. Mar 02; same)>*

Aug 91. (cd) *<RBR 002CD>* **NOT SO SOFT** [ ] [-]
- Anticipate / Rockabye / She says / Make me stay / On every corner / Small world / Not so soft / Roll with it / Itch / Gratitude / The whole night / The next big thing / Brief bus stop / Looking for the holes. *(UK-iss. Sep 97 on Cooking Vinyl; COOKCD 133) <(re-iss. Mar 02; same)>*

Jul 92. (cd) *<RBR 003CD>* **IMPERFECTLY** [ ] [-]
- What if no one's watching / Fixing her hair / In or out / Every state line / Circle of light / If it isn't her / Good, bad, ugly / I'm no heroine / Coming up / Make them apologize / The waiting song / Served faithfully / Imperfectly. *(UK-iss. Jul 95 & Mar 02; same)*

Jul 93. (cd/c) *<RBR 004 CD/C> (HAVEN CD/MC 002)* **PUDDLE DIVE** [ ] [ ]
- Names and dates and times / Anyday / 4th of July / Willing to fight / Egos like hairdos / Back around / Blood in the boardroom / Born a lion / My IQ / Used to you / Pick yer nose / God's country. *(re-iss. Jan 95 & Mar 02; same)*

Jul 94. (cd/c) *<RBR 006CD> (HAVEN CD/MC 3)* **OUT OF RANGE** [ ] Jan 95 [ ]
- Buildings and bridges / Out of range (acoustic) / Letter to a john / Hell yeah / How have you been / Overlap / Face up and sing / Falling is like this / Out of range (electric) / You had time / If he tries anything / Diner. *<(cd re-iss. Mar 02; same)>*

Righteous Babe / Righteous Babe

Jul 95. (cd) *<(RBR 007CD)>* **NOT A PRETTY GIRL** [ ] Nov 95 [ ]
- Worthy / Tiptoe / Cradle and all / Shy / Sorry I am / Light of some kind / Not a pretty girl / The million you never made / Hour follows hour / 32 flavors / Asking too much / This bouquet / Crime for crime. *(bonus +=)* - 32 flavors (live). *(UK-iss. Jan 97 on Cooking Vinyl; COOKCD 113) <(re-iss. Mar 02; same)>*

Righteous Babe / Cooking Vinyl

May 96. (cd) *<RBR 008CD> (COOKCD 103)* **DILATE** [87] Jul 96 [ ]
- Untouchable face / Outta me, onto you / Superhero / Dilate / Amazing grace / Napoleon / Shameless / Done wrong / Going down / Adam and Eve / Joyful girl. *<(re-iss. Mar 02; same)>*

—— In 1996, UTAH PHILLIPS & ANI DiFRANCO released 'The Past Didn't Go Anywhere'

Dec 96. (cd-ep) *<RBR 010CD> (COOKCD 119)* MORE JOY, LESS SHAME [ ] [ ]

- Joyful girl (danger and uncertainty mix) / Joyful girl (peace and love mix) / Joyful girl (peace and love extended mix) / Joyful girl (live with The Buffalo Philharmonic) / Shameless (bathtub mix) / Both hands (live in Austin, Texas). *<(re-iss. Mar 02; same)>*

Jan 97. (cd-s) *(FRYCD 049)* OUTTA ME, ONTO YOU / Shy [–] [ ]

Apr 97. (d-cd) *<RBR 011CD> (COOKCD 122)* **LIVING IN CLIP** (live) [59] Jun 97 [ ]
- Whatever / Wherever / Gravel / Willing to fight / Shy / Joyful girl / Hide and seek / Napoleon / I'm no heroine / Amazing grace / Anticipate / Tiptoe / Sorry I am / The slant - The diner / 32 flavors / Out of range // Untouchable face / Shameless / Distracted / Adam and Eve / Fire door / Both hands / Out of habit / Every state line / Not so soft / Travel tips / Wrong with me / In or out / We're all gonna blow / Letter to a john / Overlap. *<(re-iss. Mar 02; same)>*

Feb 98. (cd) *<RBR 012CD> (COOKCD 140)* **LITTLE PLASTIC CASTLE** [22] [ ]
- Little plastic castle / Fuel / Gravel / As is / Two little girls / Deep dish / Loom / Pixie / Swan dive / Glass house / Independence day / Pulse.

Jan 99. (cd) *<RBR 013CD> (COOKCD 173)* **UP UP UP UP UP UP** [29] [ ]
- Tis of thee / Virtue / Come away from it / Jukebox / Angel food / Angry anymore / Everest / Up up up up up up / Know now then / Trickle down / Hat shaped hat. *<(re-iss. Sep99 & Mar 02; same)>*

Mar 99. (cd-s) *(FRYCD 079)* NOT ANGRY ANYMORE / (mixes; album / extended) [–] [ ]

May 99. (cd; by ANI DIFRANCO & UTAH PHILLIPS) *<(RBR 015CD)>* **FELLOW WORKERS** [ ] Sep 99 [ ]
- Joe Hill (instrumental) / Stupid's song / The most dangerous woman / Stupid's pledge / Direct action / Pie in the sky / Shoot or stab them / Lawrence / Bread and roses / Why come? / Unless you are free / I will not obey / The long memory / The silence that is me / Joe Hill / The saw-playing musician / Dump the bosses / The internationale.

(above was also issued in the UK on Righteous Babe)

Nov 99. (cd) *<RBR 017CD> (COOKCD 190)* **TO THE TEETH** [76] [ ]
- To the teeth / Soft shoulder / Wish I may / Freakshow / Going once / Hello Birmingham / Back back back / Swing / Carry you around / Cloud blood / The arrivals gate / Providence / I know this bar. *<(re-iss. Mar 02; same)>*

Righteous Babe Righteous Babe

Jul 00. (cd-ep) *<RBRCD 20> (74873 17020-2)* SWING SET [ ] [ ]
- Swing (radio set) / Swing (album version) / To the teeth (shoot-out remix) / Do re me (live) / When I'm gone / Hurricane.

Apr 01. (d-cd) *<(RBRCD 024)>* **REVELLING/RECKONING** [50] [ ]
- Ain't that the way / OK / Garden of simple / Tamburitza lingua / Marrow / Heartbreak even / Harvest / Kazoointoit / Whatall is nice / What how when where (why who) / Fierce flawless / Rock paper scissors / Beautiful night // Your next bold move / This box contains ... / Reckoning / So what / Prison prism / Imagine that / Flood waters / Grey / Subdivision / Old old song / Sick of me / Don't nobody know / School night / That was my love / Revelling / In here.

Sep 02. (d-cd) *<(RBRCD 029)>* **SO MUCH SHOUTING, SO MUCH LAUGHTER** (live) [32] [ ]
- Swan dive / Letter to a john - Tamburitza lingua / Grey / Cradle and all / Whatall is nice / What how when where (why who) / To the teeth / Revelling / Napoleon / Shrug / Welcome to: // Comes a time / Ain't that the way / Dilate / Gratitude / Rock paper scissors / 32 flavors / Loom - Pulse / Not a pretty girl / Self evident / Reckoning / My IQ / Jukebox / You had time.

Mar 03. (cd) *<(RBRCD 030)>* **EVOLVE** [30] [ ]
- Promised land / In the way / Icarus / Slide / O my my / Evolve / Shrug / Phase / Here for now / Second intermission / Serpentine / Welcome to:

Jan 04. (cd) *<(RBR 034)>* **EDUCATED GUESS** [37] [ ]
- Platforms / Swim / Educated guess / Origami / Bliss like this / The true story of what was / Bodily / You each time / Animal / Grand Canyon / Company / Rain check / Akimbo / Bubble.

Jan 05. (cd) *<(RBR 042)>* **KNUCKLE DOWN** [49] [ ]
- Knuckle down / Studying stones / Manhole / Sunday morning / Modulation / Seeing eye dog / Lag time / Parameters / Callous / Paradigm / Minerva / Recoil.

Aug 06. (cd) *<(RBR 052)>* **REPRIEVE** [46] [ ]
- Hypnotized / Subconscious / In the margins / Nicotine / Decree / 78% H20 / Millennium theater / Half-assed / Reprieve / A spade / Unrequited / Shroud / Reprise.

Sep 08. (cd) *<(RBR 063)>* **RED LETTER YEAR** [55] [ ]
- Red letter year / Alla this / Present - Infant / Smiling underneath / Way tight / Emancipated minor / Good luck / The atom / Round a pole / Landing gear / Star matter / Red letter year (reprise).

- (8-10*) compilations -

Sep 07. (d-cd) Righteous Babe; *<(RBR 055)>* **CANON** [89] [ ]
- Fire door / God's country / You had time / Buildings and bridges / Coming up / Cradle and all / Shy / 32 flavors / Dilate / Distracted / Gravel / Untouchable face / Joyful girl / Little plastic castle / Fuel / As is / Napoleon (new version) / Shameless (new version) // Hello Birmingham / This box contains / Grey / Prison prism / Marrow / Here for now / Subdivision / Rain check / Swim / Paradigm / Manhole / Studying stones / Hypnotized / 78% H2O / Millennium theater / Your next bold move (new version) / Both hands (new version) / Overlap (new version).

- (5-7*) compilations, others, etc.-

Jul 94. (cd) Righteous Babe; *<(RBR 005CD)>* **LIKE I SAID: SONGS 1990–91** [ ] [ ]
- Anticipate / Rockabye / Not so soft / Roll with it / Work your way out / Fire door / Gratitude / The whole night / Both hands / She says / Rush hour / Out of habit / Lost woman song / Talk to me now / The slant. *<(re-iss. Mar 02; same)>*

Dec 94. (cd) Tradition & Moderne; *(T&M 105)* **WOMEN IN (E)MOTION FESTIVAL** (live in Bremen, Germany, March 7, 1994) [ ] [–]
- Buildings and bridges / Letter to a john / Face up and sing / Out of range / Not so soft / Lullaby / Asking too much / Sorry I am / In or out / If he tries anything / Blood in the boardroom. *<US-iss. Jun 98 on Imprint; 28376>*

Jun 04. (cd) Righteous Babe; *<RBR 036>* **ATLANTA 10.9.03** (live) [–] on-line [–]
- Shy / Your next bold move / Two little girls / Evolve / Subdivision / Here for now / Phase / Swim / Everest / Gravel / Bubble / Second intermission / Animal / Grand Canyon / Names and dates and times.

(above and below releases were part of her 'official bootleg' series)

(also available: 'SACRAMENTO 10.25.03', 'PORTLAND 4.7.04', 'BOSTON 11.16.03', 'CHICAGO 1.17.04', 'MADISON 1.25.04', 'ROME 11.15.04', 'BOSTON 11.10.06', 'HAMBURG 10.18.07')

Apr 06. (cd) Righteous Babe; *<RBR 051>* **CARNEGIE HALL 4.6.02** (live) [ ] [–]
- God's country / Subdivision / Angry anymore / Educated guess / Not so soft / Two little girls / Story / Gratitude / Detroit Annie, hitchhiking / In the way / 2nd intermission / Names and dates and times / Serpentine / Self evident / Out of range.

Alix DOBKIN

A controversial figure even by today's liberal standards, lesbian activist folk singer/songwriter ALIX DOBKIN (born August 16, 1940 in New York City) was raised in Philadelphia and Kansas City. Graduating with a Bachelor of Fine Arts degree, Alix was part of the Greenwich Village scene in the 1960s, where she performed in various coffee-houses. One of them, the Gaslight Club, was run by her husband Sam Hood; they divorced in the late 1960s, a few years after the birth of their daughter Adrian.

In 1970 or thereabouts she came out as a lesbian. Nothing new in the world of entertainment, but the difference was that she sang about it on her earliest, pioneering LPs, **LAVENDER JANE LOVES WOMEN** (1975) {*7} and **LIVING WITH LESBIANS** (1976) {*6}.

There was humour and wit in her pro-feminist agenda, and even her few choice covers (the Dusty Springfield hit 'I Only Want To Be With You' and DYLAN's 'Just Like A Woman') were light-hearted in intention. She was free of contracts, issuing all her material on her own Women's Wax Works imprint. Two DOBKIN songs that have become classics are 'A Woman's Love' and the singalong 'View From Gay Head', fragments of which David Letterman used to air on his TV show.

XX ALIX (1980) {*6} and **THESE WOMEN NEVER BEEN BETTER** (1986) {*6} introduced a bit of Jewish lesbian humour; her own identity was gracious and at the same time strict, as a matriarchal figurehead should be. This was also evident on her live album **YAHOO AUSTRALIA!** (1990) {*6}, recorded in Sydney, which featured the traditional Yiddish song 'Ot Azoy Neyt A Shnayder', Mary O'Sullivan's 'Women Of Ireland' and Talking Heads' 'The Girls Want To Be With The Girls'. She retired from the music business to devote herself to family life as mother and grandmother. *MCS*

Alix Dobkin - vocals, acoustic guitar / + others

US Women's Wax Works — UK not issued

1975. (lp) *<A001>* **LAVENDER JANE LOVES WOMEN** [ ] [–]
- The woman in your life is you / Caledonia county / (yells) / Eppie Morrie / Jovano / I only want to be with you / The little house / Her precious love / Fantasy girl / Quartet / Jo's B-day song / Charlie / Beware, young ladies / Talking lesbian / A woman's love / View from Gay Head / (hug-ee-boo). *<cd-iss. Feb 98; same> <cd re-iss. Jul 01 as LIVING WITH LAVENDER JANE +=; none>* - LIVING WITH LESBIANS

1976. (lp) *<A002>* **LIVING WITH LESBIANS** [ ] [–]
- Living with lesbians / Over the banks / Chewing gum / Legnala / Hearts and struggles / Good old Dora / Amazon ABC / Mary B / Toughen up! / Thoughts for Penny / The lesbian power authority. *<cd-iss.+=>* - LAVENDER JANE LOVES WOMEN

1980. (lp) *<WWWA003>* **XX ALIX** [ ] [–]
- Woman to woman / Gwyn's tune / O.K.O.Y? / Theme from 'Getting Ready' / Just like a woman / Living with contradictions / Separation '78 / A mother knows / Denny's tune / Living in the country.

—— next credited **Carol McDonald** + **Witch** on the sleeve

1985. (12" ep) *<WWW 004>* NEVER BEEN BETTER [ ] [–]
- The woman in your life / Some boys / Boy-girl rap.

—— added another friend: **Lucie Blue Tremblay**

1986. (lp/c; as ALIX DOBKIN AND FRIENDS) *<WWWA05/+C>* **THESE WOMEN NEVER BEEN BETTER** [ ] [–]

- Never been better / Pitfalls of true love / Some boys / Boy-girl rap / The woman in your life / Big girls / Crazy dance / Dortn, dortn / I hate men - 100 easy ways to lose a man / Best friends / These women.

1990. (cd/c) *<A006>* **YAHOO AUSTRALIA!: ALIX LIVE FROM SYDNEY** [live]
- Yahoo Australia / Shameless hussies / Lesbian code / Intimacy / The women of Ireland / Women singing in Zimbabwe / Crushes / Ot azoy neyt a shnayder [This is how the tailor sews] / Hedda on TV / The girls want to be with the girls / New ground.

- (8-10*) compilations -

Jun 94. (cd/c) Women's Wax Slippers; *<A007>* **LOVE AND POLITICS: A 30 Year Saga**
- Shinin' thru / The woman in your life / A woman's life / View from Gay Head / Over the banks / Mary B / Amazon ABC / My lesbian wars / If it wasn't for the woman / Just like a woman / Denny's tune / Theme from 'Getting Ready' / Never been better / Some boys / These women / Yahoo Australia / Crushes / Intimacy / Lesbian code.

Orion Rigel DOMMISSE

Another strange one from the land of freak-folk, pixie-punks and haunting hippies, Providence-based singer-songwriter ORION RIGEL DOMMISSE (born December 9, 1983 in Virginia) was only on the fringes of these genre-busting categories. In a similar vein to JOANNA NEWSOM, RIO EN MEDIO and EX REVERIE, her multi-instrumental talents and nightingale-like singing were clearly earmarked for GREG WEEKS's Drag City offshoot label Language Of Stone. The ESPERS man would also guest on her debut album.

"WHAT I WANT FROM YOU IS SWEET" (2007) {*7} sat on a precipice between chamber-folk and neo-classical, an at times unnerving balance that comes good on gothic-like funereal cuts such as 'Fake Yer Death', 'Drink Yourself (To Death)' 'Ashes From Your Burning Wood' and 'Suicide Kiss (Because Dead)'. Just when you thought it might be safe to venture back into the haunted house, Orion was back from the dead again with **CHICKENS** (2011) {*6}. On first listen this sounds quite bright (MARY HOPKIN, at a push), but only in comparison with her first eerie effort. *MCS*

Orion Rigel Dommisse - vocals, piano, harmonium, cello, synths / with guests

US: Language Of Stone — UK: Language Of Stone

Sep 07. (cd) *<(LOS-001)>* **"WHAT I WANT FROM YOU IS SWEET"**
- Fake yer death / Alice and Sarah / Simon sent for me / A faceless death / Capricorn / Ashes from your burning wood / Suicide kiss (because dead) / A giver / Little neighbor / Drink yourself (to death).

US: self-rel. — UK: not issued

May 11. (cd/mp3) *<none>* **CHICKENS** — mail-o
- Squirrels / Chickens / Swamp / Richard / Gun / Skinwalkers / Windshield / Cord.

Linda DRAPER

Whether you call her part of the growing legion of anti-folk artists or just plain, honest-to-goodness indie-folk, New Yorker LINDA DRAPER has been compared with the likes of SUZANNE VEGA, JONI MITCHELL and Aimee Mann. Having had a musical upbringing, she was a child prodigy at least from the age of 14, when she took up her mother's acoustic guitar (her father was a classical guitarist who played Carnegie Recital Hall in 1976). Singer/songwriter DRAPER launched her recording career with the occasional self-financed mp3 album, namely **RICOCHET** (2001) {*6}, **SNOW WHITE TRASH GIRL** (2002) {*6} and **PATCHWORK** (2003) {*7}, all produced by indie stalwart Kramer.

ONE TWO THREE FOUR (2005) {*7} was her first effort for the Planting Seeds label, while invitations to perform supporting REGINA SPEKTOR, KIMYA DAWSON, JEFFREY LEWIS, Lucy Wainwright Roche and others came thick and fast.

MAJOR MATT MASON USA co-produced her fifth album, **KEEPSAKE** (2007) {*7}, which was highlighted by the single 'Traces Of' and Rick Nelson's 'How Long'. Having already covered PHIL OCHS's 'Flower Lady' and ODETTA's 'Sail Away Ladies' on recent compilations, The Rolling Stones' 'Mother's Little Helper' was a welcome addition to her 2009 set, **BRIDGE AND TUNNEL** {*7}. Produced by multi-instrumentalist Brad Albetta, its best songs were 'Limbo', 'Pushing Up The Day' and 'I Will'. *MCS*

Linda Draper - vocals, acoustic guitar

US: own label — UK: not issued

Apr 01. (mp3) <-> **RICOCHET**
- As the story goes / Watch your step / Airplane / Tuesday / La lalala la / Take your turn / Dollhouse town / Gather apart / Get it to go / Lullabye / Richochet. *<cd re-iss. 2006 on Planting Seeds; PSRCD 039>*

Jan 02. (mp3) <-> **SNOW WHITE TRASH GIRL**
- Thin ice / Snow white trash girl / Retrograde / Dear anonymous / Full moon / Hey Dante / A little raven / The one / The priest who looked like Elvis / Indifferent / Disconnected. *<cd re-iss. 2006 on Planting Seeds; PSRCD 040>*

Jan 03. (mp3) <-> **PATCHWORK**
- Seven black crows / Colorblind / The sleeping giant / Here I am / A little bit goes / Patchwork / A name to remember / Merry Christmas / Flower lady / My boomerang baby / It's not all about love. *<cd re-iss. 2006 on Planting Seeds; PSRCD 041>*

US: Planting Seeds — UK: Planting Seeds

Jan 05. (cd) *<(PSRCD 033)>* **ONE TWO THREE FOUR** — Mar 05
- Super zero / Big blue sky / Baby inchworm / The broken muzzle / Needlessly / Jezebel / Parasite / Seven black crows / Lifeboat / The sleeping giant / Candle opera / One two three four.

Aug 05. (cd-ep) *<PSRCD 034>* NEEDLESSLY
- Needlessly [Pinkie mix] / Super zero / Candle opera / The broken muzzle [Punkie mix] / It's not all about love / A little bit goes.

Nov 06. (cd-ep) *<PSRCD 047>* TRACES OF
- Traces of / Big blue sky [alt.] / Flower lady [alt.] / The lottery song [w/ Brian Wurschum].

Apr 07. (cd) *<(PSRCD 048)>* **KEEPSAKE**
- Shine / Keepsake / Cell phone / Too late / Traces of / Kissing ground / Sunburned / Among every stone that has been cast / Full moon / How long.

Apr 09. (cd) *<PSRCD 059>* **BRIDGE AND TUNNEL**
- Limbo / Sharks and royalty / I will / Time will tell / Pushing up the day / Close enough / Broken eggshell / Bridge and tunnel / Mother's little helper / Last one standing.

- (5-7*) compilations, etc.-

Nov 10. (cd) Planting Seeds; *<(PSRCD 068)>* **NO FRILLS** [best of 2001–03]
- As the story goes / Airplane / La lalala la / Dear anonymous / The one / The priest who looked like Elvis / Colorblind / The sleeping giant / A little bit goes / Here I am.

DROPKICK MURPHYS (⟹ Great Celtic-folk Discography)

Liz DURRETT

Born in Athens, Georgia in 1978, a niece of the late VIC CHESNUTT, singer and songwriter LIZ DURRETT has been filed under indie-folk since her debut album **HUSK** (2005) {*6}. The album was recorded between 1993 and 1996, when she was just a bright young teenager, and produced by CHESNUTT.

With husky vocal cords only a whisper away from those of Judie Tzuke, SUZANNE VEGA or NICK DRAKE, Liz's equally intimate follow-up, **THE MEZZANINE** (2006) {*7}, was issued on the Warm label and was also produced by her uncle. For 2008's melodious **OUTSIDE OUR GATES** {*7}, DURRETT and her great new songs such as 'Wake To Believe', 'We Build Bridges' and 'The Sea A Dream' were produced by Archers Of Loaf leader Eric Bachmann, who also added orchestral and choral arrangements. Hopefully there's more to come. *MCS*

Liz Durrett - vocals, guitar / + session people

US: Warm — UK: Warm

Feb 05. (cd) *<(WRM 113CD)>* **HUSK**
- Vine / Husk / Ablaze / Lull / Captive / BC / Slip / Net / You there.

Jan 06. (cd) *<(WRM 115CD)>* **THE MEZZANINE**
- Knives at the wall / All the spokes / Cup on the counter / The mezzanine / Creepyaskudzu / Marlene / Silent partner / Shivering assembly / Little ascendent / No apology / In the throes.

Sep 08. (cd) *<(WRM 120CD)>* **OUTSIDE OUR GATES**
- Wake to believe / Wild as them / In the eaves / We build bridges / Lost hiker / All of them all / Note for a girl / You live alone / Always signs / Not running / The sea a dream.

Antje DUVEKOT

ANTJE DUVEKOT (born in Heidelberg, Germany in 1976) is among a raft of rising acoustic-folk stars, a new breed awaiting their deserved breakthrough into the big time. Raised by her divorcee mother in Wilmington, Delaware from the age of 13 (she now lives in Somerville, Massachusetts), Antje has delivered a handful of relaxing sets, winning many awards along the way.

Her first two records proper, **LITTLE PEPPERMINTS** (2002) {*6} and **BOYS, FLOWERS, MILES** (2005) {*6}, were followed by her first studio effort for Black Wolf, **BIG DREAM BOULEVARD** (2006) {*7}, aided by Seamus Egan of Celtic-type American-Irish outfit Solas, who would later record some of her compositions. ELLIS PAUL was her touring partner at the time.

With RICHARD SHINDELL taking over at the controls, **THE NEAR DEMISE OF THE HIGHWIRE DANCER** (2009) {*7} was a deliberate attempt to find a bigger audience, and there was room for a MARK ERELLI collaboration on 'Vertigo' - think ANAIS MITCHELL or ANI DiFRANCO. Also of note is the 'Winterbloom: Winter Traditions' (2009) set alongside fellow folk fringe stars ANNE HEATON, MEG HUTCHINSON and Natalie Zukerman.

DUVEKOT is currently working on her third studio album, for Kickstarter, and a downloadable live set was issued by CD Baby in March 2011. *MCS*

Antje Duvekot - vocals, acoustic guitar / with session people

US Megaphon — UK not issued

Dec 02. (cd) <*none*> **LITTLE PEPPERMINTS**
- Streets of Soho / (talk #1) / Sirens / Merry-go-round / Long way / (talk #2) / Noah's Titanic / (intro #1) / Anna / Milk and trash / (intro #2) / Black Annis / Diana's song.

Apr 05. (cd) <*none*> **BOYS, FLOWERS, MILES**
- Dublin boys / Judas / (talk) / Dandelion / (talk) / Anabelle / Pearls / (talk) / Erin / (talk) / Landladysong / Sex bandaid / (talk) / Go now / (talk) / Reasonland / Opium / (talk ... continuous) / [track by Lizanne Knott].

Black Wolf — not issued

Apr 06. (cd) <*BW 006*> **BIG DREAM BOULEVARD**
- Dandelion / Go now / Diamond on your hand / Jerusalem / Sex bandaid / Helpless kiss / Judas / Peals / South / Anna / Hold on.

Apr 09. (cd) <*BW 008*> **THE NEAR DEMISE OF THE HIGH WIRE DANCER**
- Vertigo / Ragdoll princes and junkyard queens / Long way / Lighthouse / Dublin boys / The bridge / Scream / Reasonland / Coney Island / Merry-go-round / Augen, ohren und herz.

—— In 2009, with MEG HUTCHINSON, Anne Heaton and Natalie Zukerman, she was part of the collaborative set 'Winterbloom: Winter Traditions'.

- (5-7*) compilations, others, etc.-

Jun 08. (cd) Black Wolf; *(5822)* **SNAPSHOTS** [live from first two sets with "intros"]
- Dublin boys / Dandelion / "Annabelle intro" / Annabelle / Pearls / Merry-go-round [prev. unreleased] / "Garbage" / Landlord song / Ode to music [prev. unreleased] / "Ellis Paul" / Milk and trash / Streets of Soho / Sirens / Diana's song / "Postcards" / "Pig song" / Soma [prev. unreleased].

Cliff EBERHARDT

Folk music takes many shapes and forms. CLIFF EBERHARDT's music springs from the blues of MISSISSIPPI JOHN HURT, Muddy Waters and Bonnie Raitt and the folk ethos of JAMES TAYLOR, Jackson Browne and BRUCE SPRINGSTEEN, along with the melodic sophistication of the Gershwins and Cole Porter.

Born and raised in Bryn Mawr, Pennsylvania (b. January 7, 1954), Cliff performed in coffee-houses as an acoustic duo with his brother Geoff, and by the age of twenty-one he found a voice in Carbondale, Illinois before relocating to a post-new-wave New York, where he was soon putting in long hours as a taxi driver.

While the 1980s were spent formulating his easy-going blend of folksinger blues at the Speakeasy, The Bitter End and Folk City, the 1990s saw him getting off the ground on the recording front. Having worked with numerous folkies on tour (he could call VEGA, GORKA, KAPLINSKY, LAVIN, FORBERT, MASSENGILL and COLVIN acquaintances), Cliff also managed a few collaborations with MELANIE and RICHIE HAVENS.

The latter performed with EBERHARDT on the title track of his Windham Hill-released debut set **THE LONG ROAD** (1990) {*8}. Highlighted by opening salvo 'My Father's Shoes' and several other small-town romantic songs such as 'Your Face' and 'Goodnight', the record revealed a man who'd had a few of life's hard knocks.

Three years in the making for Shanachie, **NOW YOU ARE MY HOME** (1993) {*7} paralleled his first, although it was derivative in his formulaic rasping delivery, with the exception of the Smokey Robinson cover version 'You Really Got A Hold On Me'. Produced by Peter Gallway (who contributed the 'Leap Of Faith' track), 1995's **MONA LISA CAFÉ** {*6} featured his version of Dire Straits' 'Romeo And Juliet' and a duet co-written with DAVID WILCOX, 'Voodoo Morning'.

Moving to Red House Records (the new house of the blues), he released **12 SONGS OF GOOD AND EVIL** (1997) {*7}, a set of rootsy Americana on lines drawn through folk, gospel and of course the blues. The SPRINGSTEEN/John Waite comparisons were beginning to shine through on songs like 'Carnival Girl' and the anti-drugs song 'Joey's Arms').

BORDERS (1999) {*6} and **SCHOOL FOR LOVE** (2002) {*6} continued his surge towards greatness, the latter aided by Seth Farber and his wife Liz Queler, who had guided him through dark times after a near-fatal car accident that left Cliff with crippling back injuries. His mother also went through a period of ill-health during the same time.

Back on life's conveyor belt, EBERHARDT returned in 2007 and 2009 with **THE HIGH ABOVE AND THE DOWN BELOW** {*7} and **500 MILES: THE BLUE ROCK SESSIONS** {*6}, the latter accompanied by the likes of Billy Crockett, Mike Hardwick, Glenn Fukunaga, Joel Guzman, Colin Brooks and Chris Maresh. *MCS*

Cliff Eberhardt - vocals, guitars, dobro (w/ session people)

US Windham Hill — UK Windham Hill

Aug 90. (cd/c) <*(WD 1092/+C)*> **THE LONG ROAD** □ Jun 91 □
- My father's shoes / The long road / Your face / Right now / Always want to feel like this / That kind of love / (Just want to) Walk down the street with you / Voyeur / White lightning / I am the storm / Nowhere to go / Goodnight.

Shanachie — Shanachie

Nov 93. (cd/c) <*(SHCD/SHMC 8008)*> **NOW YOU ARE MY HOME** □ Dec 93 □
- Ever since I lost your love / You really got a hold on me / Now you are my home / Not alone in this world / Everytime I see your face / I'm not quite over you / Baton Rouge / Now that you are mine / Motel room dreams / I thought that you should know / One or two things / Make me believe.

Aug 95. (cd/c) <*(SHCD/SHMC 8017)*> **MONA LISA CAFÉ** □ Oct 95 □
- Life is hard / Mona Lisa waits / Voodoo morning / Romeo and Juliet / Brave little grey / Leap of faith / Caretaker / Everything is almost gone / Why do lovers (have to say goodbye) / Trouble for life / She loved he / Is it wrong to feel so good (at this time in my life).

Red House — Red House

Aug 97. (cd) <*(RHRCD 105)*> **12 SONGS OF GOOD AND EVIL** □ Oct 97 □
- The devil in me / Carnival girl / Good example / Joey's arms / Valerie / This old world / Someone like you / Little things for you / Thieves and kings / The best of you / Memphis / Ladder of gold.

Mar 99. (cd) <*(RHRCD 129)*> **BORDERS** □ □
- Why is the road so long / Fix your blues / The long goodbye / The land of the free / The wrong side of the line / Lines / Anna Lee / Isn't that the way things are / Your face / Everybody knows / Unrequited / Why is the road so long.

Aug 02. (cd) <*(RHRCD 159)*> **SCHOOL FOR LOVE** □ □
- Sugartown / Blessings / Love slips away / Memories of you / School for love / Every time you break my heart / My sweet Liza / Merry-go-sorry / Will you ever love again / Whenever I sing the blues / Where did you go to school (to learn to be so cruel) / Never fall in love / Clementine.

Apr 07. (cd) <*(RHRCD 199)*> **THE HIGH ABOVE AND THE DOWN BELOW** □ May 07 □
- The high above and the down below / Missing you / It's home everywhere I go / The next big thing / The right words / After the rain falls / Assembly line / Dug your own grave / Let this whole thing burn / New is what's come over you / I'm all right / Goodbye again.

Sep 09. (cd) <*RHRCD 221*> **500 MILES: THE BLUE ROCK SESSIONS** □ ⊟
- 500 miles / Have a little heart / I want to take you home / Lonelyville / I love money / Break a train / Easy street / Little town / When the leaves begin to fall / You won't come back to me / Back of my mind / The long road.

—— EBERHARDT's latest release is a joint effort, 'All Wood And Doors', with James Lee Stanley

Kat EGGLESTON

Born in Los Angeles (February 17, 1958), but raised from the age of three on Vashon Island off the coast of Washington State, alto singer-songwriter KAT EGGLESTON (a 1983 acting graduate of the Interplayers Ensemble of Spokane) has been part of the folk scene since her first self-financed recordings in 1989. The accomplished acoustic guitarist had previously turned out with Fool Moon, Four Women At Play and DAVID BROMBERG.

Tracks from that album, **FIRST WARM WIND** {*6}, were subsequently promoted at the Kerriville and Columbia River festivals. The best were 'China', 'Rose Tattoo' and 'Dark Side Of The Moon'. Her second set, **SECOND NATURE** (1994) {*7}, took her to the Waterbug label with a bare-bones presentation, also including tracks from her husband ANDREW CALHOUN ('Day In And Night Out') and Jano Brindisi ('On My TV'), and two trad cuts, 'I Live Not Where I Love' and 'Banks of Sweet Dundee'.

OUTSIDE EDEN (1997) {*6} was her last solo album for some time. Perhaps songs like 'Shit' and 'Powerless' depicted her feelings at the time, but it was a strong set that stretched her songwriting ability in leaps and bounds. She covered Woody GUTHRIE's 'Pastures Of Plenty', and Jano's 'Again, Again!' was another contemporary folk highlight.

Kat had contributed to her now ex-husband CALHOUN's sets in the past, and her two co-credited records alongside KATE MACLEOD ('Drawn From The Well' 2002 and `Lost And Found' 2011) were worthy of better success. EGGLESTON has issued a fifth solo set, the independently-released, award-winning **SPEAK** (2009) {*7}. *MCS*

Kat Eggleston - vocals, acoustic guitar / + session people

US Kat Eggleston — UK not issued

1989. (cd/c) <*kecd/kecs 100*> **FIRST WARM WIND** □ ⊟
- China / Rose tattoo / Cherry tree / Empty glass / Dark side of the moon / Equinox / Autumn / True story / Your window / First warm wind. <*cd re-iss. Feb 99 on Waterbug; WBG 0041*>

Jul 94. (cd/c) <*kecd/kecs 101*> **SECOND NATURE** □ ⊟
- Home / Trouble / Paper boats / Fury / My father's garden / I live not where I love /

Trick or treat / On my TV / Darling wake up / Banks of sweet Dundee / The stranger / Day in and night out. *<cd re-iss. Nov 95 on Waterbug; WBG 0005>*

Waterbug — not issued

Dec 97. (cd) *<WBG 0028>* **OUTSIDE EDEN**
- Go to the water / No laughing matter / Brian / Dreaming in color / Outside Eden / Powerless / Mirror, mirror / Flower of Northumberland / Shit / Pastures of plenty - Kitchen girl / Meeting Stucky at the gas station / Again, again! *<re-iss. Jun 00; same>*

—— in 2002, she collaborated with KATE MACLEOD on the album 'Drawn From The Well'

Redwing — not issued

Jun 05. (cd) *<RWCD 5414>* **THE ONLY WORD**
- Show / Measure for measure / Mercy / Impact / Rain / Careless / Hansel and Gretel / Both our houses / Lily Langtree / I will set my good ship in order / Hindsight / One more step / The only word - Clumsy lover.

own label — not issued

Aug 09. (cd) *<none>* **SPEAK** — mail-o
- 49 rooms / Road to ruin / Everybody knows / Home / Birken tree / Sanctuary - History man / Outside Eden / Trespass / Careless / Some kind of wondering / Your window / One.

—— in 2011, she again collaborated with MACLEOD on the set 'Lost And Found'

ELYSE

A promising starlet of the hippie times, Canadian-born Elyse Weinberg was the toast of Toronto for a time in the late 1960s, although she made Los Angeles her home to record her one and only long-player, **ELYSE** (1968) {*7}. Helped along by Mama Cass Elliott and released on Bill Cosby's soon-to-be-defunct record label Tetragrammaton, the record drew comparisons with MELANIE, Laura Nyro and a squeakier Janis Joplin. Morbid themes were explored in 'Mortuary Bound' (composed, like 'Iron Works', by the spoons player who is credited simply as 'Maureen'), 'If Death Don't Overtake Me' and 'Last Ditch Protocol'. BERT JANSCH's 'Deed I Do' was also covered, and Colin Walcott plays sitar and tabla.

Sadly, although NEIL YOUNG played guitar on the re-issue CD out-take 'Houses' (covered by B'Eirth's BIRCH BOOK in 2010), two subsequent sets ('Grease Paint Smile' and 'Wildfire', the latter for Asylum) went unreleased.

For reasons unknown, ELYSE changed her name to Cori Bishop and settled in Santa Fe, New Mexico. If there are recordings by her post-millenium outfit Baby Cori & The Buds - a writers' group she formed after Andrew Rieger of Elf Power bought the rights to re-release her long-lost classic debut - they are not known to this Discography. *MCS*

Elyse Weinberg - vocals, acoustic guitars / with session people

US Tetragrammaton — UK not issued

1968. (lp) *<T-117>* **ELYSE**
- 1. Band of thieves / 2. Deed I do / 3. Iron works / 4. Spirit of the letter / 5. Here in my heart (underneath the spreading chestnut tree) / 6. Last ditch protocol / 7. Sweet pounding rhythm / 8. Meet me at the station / 9. Simpleminded harlequin / 10. Painted raven / 11. Mortuary bound / 12. If death don't overtake me. *<cd-iss. May 01/Sep 07 on Orange Twin+=; OTR 001)> <lp re-iss. Nov 05 on Abraxus/Isota+=; SODY 032>* - [tracks 6 & 1 swapped] / Houses / What you call it.

—— albums two and three were shelved

Mark ERELLI

Coming across like some roots/Americana version of Nick Lowe or Dave Edmunds, country-blues folk singer-songwriter MARK ERELLI (born in Reading, Massachusetts in 1974) took a degree in evolutionary biology at the University of Massachusetts before winning a contract with Signature Records and taking top prize at the Kerriville New Folk Contest.

The late 1990s were good times for young Mark; still in his mid-20s, he was widely praised for some fine tracks ('Do It Everyday', 'Northern Star' and 'Thought I Heard You Knocking') on his eponymous debut, **MARK ERELLI** (1999) {*6}. Two years on, **COMPASS AND COMPANIONS** (2001) {*7} - twice a Boston Music Awards nomination- also hit the right notes critically, while tours supporting roots artists Dave Alvin, John Hiatt, GILLIAN WELCH, and others boosted his CV no end.

THE MEMORIAL HALL RECORDINGS (2002) {*6} combined his own originals (bookends 'Call You Home' and 'Goodbye) with traditional Massachusetts material such as 'The Drinking Gourd', 'Blue-Eyed Boston Boy' and the Civil War commemorative 'Dear Magnolia'. There was also room for the eight-minute 'Ichabod' (a setting of a poem by John Greenleaf Whittier) and BILL MORRISSEY's 'Summer Night'.

With a nod to the hootenanny country-folk days of yore, **HILLBILLY PILGRIM** (2004) {*5} and **HOPE AND OTHER CASUALTIES** (2006) {*6} - the latter featuring Ron Sexsmith's 'God Loves Everyone' - were aimed at the Stetson-on-the-backporch listener. 'Snowed In' was the soulful/BEN HARPER-esque exception.

DELIVERED (2008) {*7} turned up the amps on the SPRINGSTEEN-like 'Baltimore', but it was the lyrics of the political 'Hope Dies Last' and 'Shadowlands' that put ERELLI's star in the ascendant, at least critically.

After contributing to the one-off traditional Brit-folk DARWIN SONG PROJECT alongside another couple of North Americans, Mark was back in the land of the free, and the esteemed company of fellow roots-player JEFFREY FOUCAULT, for the **SEVEN CURSES** (2010) {*6} collaboration. *MCS*

Mark Erelli - vocals, acoustic guitar, multi (+ session people)

US Signature — UK Signature

Apr 99. (cd) *<SIG 1249>* **MARK ERELLI**
- Do it everyday / One too many midnights / Thought I heard you knocking / River road / I always return / Hollow man / Nothing ventured, nothing gained / Midnight train / Only wondering where you are / Northern star.

Feb 01. (cd) *<SIG 1263>* **COMPASS AND COMPANION**
- Ghost / Compass and companion / Why should I cry / Miracle man / My love / Little sister / Free ride / Before I knew your name / Take my ashes to the river / All behind me now / Almost home. *(UK-iss. Aug 04; same as US)*

Mar 02. (cd) *<SIG 1271>* **THE MEMORIAL HALL RECORDINGS**
- Call you home / Every goodbye / What's changed / Fine time of year / The drinking gourd / Blue-eyed Boston boy / Guitar interlude / Dear Magnolia / Summer night / Devil's train / Ichabod / Little torch / Theresa / Goodbye. *(UK-iss. Aug 04; same as US)*

Jan 04. (cd) *<(SIG 1281)>* **HILLBILLY PILGRIM** — Aug 04
- Brand new baby / Troubadour blues / A bend in the river / Pretend / The farewell ball / Let's make a family / Troubles (those lonesome kind) / My best was just not good enough (for you) / Fool No.1 / Ain't no time of the year to be alone / Pilgrim highway.

Mar 06. (cd) *<(SIG 1296)>* **HOPE AND OTHER CASUALTIES** — Jul 06
- Herr and now / Imaginary wars / Snowed in / The only way / Evening's curtain / Seeds of peace / Undone / Seasons pass / Hartfordtown 1944 / Passing through / God loves everyone.

Sep 08. (cd) *<(SIG 2014)>* **DELIVERED** — Oct 08
- Hope dies last / Baltimore / Shadowland / Volunteers / Five beer moon / Not alone / Delivered / Man of the family / Once / Unraveled / Abraham.

—— In 2009 Mark was part of all-star Brit-folk ensemble DARWIN SONG PROJECT

Continental Song City — Continental Song City

Apr 10. (cd; by MARK ERELLI / JEFFREY FOUCAULT) *<(CSCCD 1060)>* **SEVEN CURSES**
- Philadelphia lawyer / Johnny 99 / Tom Merritt / Billy Gray / Louise / Pretty Polly / Sonoras death row / Ellis unit 1 / Cole Durhew / The first Mrs. Jones / Powderfinger / Wyoming wind.

Tim ERIKSEN (⟹ CORDELIA'S DAD)

ESPERS

Arguably the greatest and most influential neo-folk act to emerge from the US in the post-millennium era, Philadelphia's ESPERS (singer/songwriter and multi-instrumentalist Greg Weeks, singer Meg Baird and guitarist Brooke Sietinsons) have expanded 1960s-styled baroque-folk into blissful pastoral chamber-pop - imagine SANDY DENNY fronting early MAGNA CARTA or PENTANGLE.

Debut album **ESPERS** (2004) {*9} is as creepy as it is dreamy, airy and light, their cosmic manifesto shining through on 'Flowery Moontide', 'Riding', 'Voices', 'Hearts And Daggers' and 'Meadow', while 'Travel Mountains' stretches the weirdness into COMUS territory while conjuring up the odd spell. It's as good as that.

Marking time until their follow-up, mini-set **THE WEED TREE** (2005) {*6} brought three new members into the fold, namely Otto Hauser (percussion), Chris Smith (bass) and Helena Espvall (cello). With a running time of 35 minutes it was hardly an EP, as many review blogs called it, but fitting in only one new song ('Dead King') alongside six covers probably constituted some sort of demotion as the second album proper was nearing completion. Trad was represented by 'Rosemary Lane' (once the property of BERT JANSCH) and 'Black Is The Color', and the modern covers were The

Durutti Column's 'Tomorrow', Blue Oyster Cult's 'Flaming Telepaths' (all 10 minutes of it), NICO's 'Afraid' and MICHAEL HURLEY's 'Blue Mountain'.

ESPERS II (2006) {*8}, on their new label Drag City, found Weeks and Baird developing a complicated interplay on dreamlike voices and instrumentation, the repeated 'Dead King' overshadowed by the heavenly funereal opener 'Dead Queen', a beauty that breaks out into RICHARD THOMPSON-like fuzz guitar licks. 'Widow's Weed' is another message from the eerie hippie fortress of folk-rock; don't bother trying to get in without the key, as it'll blow your mind. Other wondrous post-apocalyptic dirges to try are 'Cruel Storm' (Baird rises like a phoenix), 'Children Of Stone' and 'Mansfield And Cyclops'.

Meg, Greg, Helena, Brooke, and Otto returned for another stab at recreating Brit-folk in their own inimitable freak-folk style with **ESPERS III** (2009) {*8}. The songs are a little shorter and more numerous, and the mood switches from melancholy to mindwarp at the turn of a chord change. Songs to die for this time are 'Caroline' (like The Velvet Underground with JACQUI McSHEE at the helm), 'I Can't See Clear', 'The Road Of Golden Dust', 'The Pearl' and the mediaeval musings of 'Meridian'.

When GREG WEEKS wasn't running his ESPERS collective, he was being employed as a prolific producer, seasoned session man and solo star in his own right, although the freak-folk side was hardly to the fore on his string of albums and mini-sets; his obvious inspirations are dead heroes TIM BUCKLEY and NICK DRAKE. **FIRE IN THE ARMS OF THE SUN** (1999) {*7}, mini-set **BLEECKER STATION** (2000) {*6}, **AWAKE LIKE SLEEP** (2001) {*7} (featuring Jackson Browne's 'These Days'), **BLOOD IS TROUBLE** (2005) {*6} and **THE HIVE** (2008) {*6} were all equally desirable acquisitions for his growing fan base.

BAIRD, ESPVALL and SHARRON KRAUS, meanwhile, delivered the trad-biased **LEAVES FROM OFF THE TREE** (2006) {*6}, a splendid effort for folk purists with a few spare dollars. 'Bruton Town', 'Barbry Ellen' and 'False Sir John' were coffee-house delights in full flight. MEG BAIRD's solo set, **DEAR COMPANION** (2007) {*8}, confirmed her classicist folk leanings with a handful of trad covers, including the title track, alongside modern material from The New Riders Of The Purple Sage ('All I Ever Wanted'), Jimmy Webb ('Do What You Gotta Do') and CHRIS THOMPSON ('River Song'). *MCS*

Greg Weeks - vocals, guitars, dulcimer, keyboards, autoharp, bass, violin, recorder, chimes / **Meg Baird** - vocals, guitars, dulcimer / **Brooke Sietinsons** - acoustic guitars, finger cymbals, chimes, harmonica

US Locust / UK Locust

Jan 04. (cd) <(LOCUST 44)> **ESPERS** — Apr 04
- Flowery noontide / Meadow / Riding / Voices / Hearts and daggers / Byss and abyss / Daughter / Travel mountains. *<ltd orig. rel. 2003 on Time-Lag; TIME-LAG 015> (re-iss. Aug 05 on Wichita; WEBB 084CD)*

—— added **Otto Hauser** - percussion / **Chris Smith** - bass / **Helena Espvall** - cello

Oct 05. (m-cd/m-lp) <(LOCUST 73 CD/LP)> **THE WEED TREE**
- Rosemary lane / Tomorrow / Black is the color / Afraid / Blue mountain / Flaming telepaths / Dead king.

not issued / Wichita

Jul 05. (7") *(WEBB 083S)* RIDING. / Under The Waterfall

—— now without Chris Smith

Drag City / Drag City

May 06. (cd/lp) <(DC 310 CD/LP)> **ESPERS II** — Jul 06
- Dead queen / Widow's weed / Cruel storm / Children of stone / Mansfield and Cyclops / Dead king / Moon occults the sun.

Drag City / Drag City

Oct 09. (cd/lp) <(DC 416 CD/LP)> **ESPERS III**
- I can't see clear / The road of golden dust / Caroline / The pearl / That which darkly thrives / Sightings / Meridian / Another mood song / Colony / Trollslanda.

—— Helena Espvall has since released two experimental sets, 'Nimis and Arx' (2006) and 'Overloaded Ark' (2009), the latter a collaboration for Drag City with Masaki Batoh. She also guested with ARBOREA on their 2011 album 'Red Planet'.

GREG WEEKS

vocals, guitars, Moog, keyboards / with **Jesse Sparhawk** - multi

Ba Da Bing! / Ba Da Bing!

Feb 99. (cd) <(BING 018)> **FIRE IN THE ARMS OF THE SUN** — Mar 99
- Tin angel of death / Starless / Joan of Arc / Shady skies and lullabies / The flesh of terrain / Tracey Bowen's double life / The pale shade / Leaves and limerance / New silver finger II / Molly Bloom / Cutting blue / Trading touch / Harvester of sighs / Straw days.

—— now with **Meg Baird** - vocals

2000. (m-cd) <KEY 04> **BLEECKER STATION**
- Front to back / When galaxies collide / Deeper waters / Heart murmur / Distance / One in ten / Down a dark corridor / Duress.

(above issued on Keyhole)

Oct 01. (cd) <BING 027> **AWAKE LIKE SLEEP**
- These days / Made / One true song / East 5th Street / Past four corners / I will fall to meet her / Ash rising / Sleep right / Sun way off.

Jan 03. (cd-ep) <(BING 029)> SLIGHTLY WEST — Mar 03
- One summer night / Unsettled (by the sun) / Slightly west / Devils / Settle down.

(above issued on Acuarela - Red100 / below on Keyhole)

Mar 04. (cd-ep) <hinah 006> TRAIN IN VEIN: BLEECKER-ERA OUTTAKES
- Self-elimination diet / Why are we so weak? / No sleep / Sewn to a dying age / Downcast / West river road.

Jan 05. (cd) <(BING 044)> **BLOOD IS TROUBLE**
- Day for night / Dusted / Violence lake / Eyes arise / These hands / Don't you open up (your eyes) / Interchange / Skelp Level Rd / Aftermath / Cold light of quiet / Wet set / Run silent / Country at night / Nearer thine eyes.

Wichita / Wichita

Oct 08. (cd) <(WEBB 181)> **THE HIVE**
- You won't be the same ever again / The lamb's path / Lay low / Borderline / Burn the margins / The hive / Funhouse / Not meant for light / The wait / Donovan / Division.

The VALERIE PROJECT

Greg Weeks, Brooke Sietinsons, Helena Espvall-Santoleri, Margaret Wienk (vocals, cello, harmonium), **Jesse Sparhawk** (electric bass), **Jim Ayre** (percussion, bells; of FERN KNIGHT), **Jessica Weeks** (of the Grass), **Tara Burke** - vocals (of Fursaxa), **Charles Cohen + Mary Lattimore**

Drag City / Twisted Nerve

Nov 07. (cd/d-lp) <DC 352 CD/LP> *(TN 080 CD/LP)* **THE VALERIE PROJECT** (rescore)
- Prelude / Introduction / Torchlight / Grandmother / A letter / Tree of life / The sermon / Eagle's theme / Dungeon / Fire mountain / The feast / Dove, pearl, priest / Vampires / Eagle's theme (reprise) / The crypt / Elsa / Machine room / Bookshelf serenade / Flower girl / Blood sacrifice / The crypt (reprise) / A second letter / Hedvica / Burned at the stake / Den of iniquity / An end to enchantment / A final letter / Death and rebirth / Reunion / Crib.

MEG BAIRD - HELENA ESPVALL - SHARRON KRAUS

not issued / Bo' Weavil

Oct 06. (cd) *(Weavil 16CD)* **LEAVES FROM OFF THE TREE**
- Bruton town / Barbry Ellen / Fortune my foe / Willie of Winsbury / The nightingale / John Hardy / The Derry dems of Arrow / Now westlin' winds / False Sir John.

MEG BAIRD

Drag City / Wichita

May 07. (cd/lp) <DC 340 CD/LP> *(WEBB 145 CD/LP)* **DEAR COMPANION** — Jun 07
- Dear companion / River song / The cruelty of Barbry Ellen / Do what you gotta do / Riverhouse in Tinicum / The waltz of the tennis players / Maiden in the moor lay / Sweet William and fair Ellen / All I ever wanted / Willie o' Winsbury / Dear companion.

EX REVERIE

The project of bohemian-folk singer/songwriter and multi-instrumentalist Gillian Chadwick, with her husband David, EX REVERIE was an unusual breed of star act, something akin to a woodcutting glam-rocker from mediaeval times. Chadwick, raised in an Appalachian shack overlooking the Blue Ridge Mountains of Virginia, had formerly played with Pennsylvanian outfits including psychedelic rockers Golden Ball (who had two sets for Honeymoon Records in 2005/07, 'The Luxury Of Pause' and 'The Antique Barking Swirls Of Dawn'). She also sang and played with Jessica Weeks in Woodwose around the time of EX REVERIE's debut EP, 'Phronesis'.

Emerging from the woods with a band of musos from ESPERS, FERN KNIGHT and The VALERIE PROJECT (mainly Greg Weeks, his wife Jessica, Margie Wienk and a few others), she released **THE DOOR INTO SUMMER** (2008) {*8}. This album was a light beaming from the shadows of the deepest well, something akin to The Velvet Underground fronted by the Bangles. 'Dawn Comes For Us All' is probably the eeriest record ever to come out of the acid-folk movement - even the hand-clapping makes you think of the film 'The Wicker Man' as though re-scored by Tony Iommi of Black Sabbath. Yet it was still folk music.

The JEFFERSON AIRPLANE/FAIRPORT-like 'Days Away' is another track that jangles its way into one's brain, only to blow it skyward with fuzzed-up guitar aneurysms. Ditto 'Second Son', but not the sedate 'The Years' or the strum-friendly 'Wooden Sword'. But EX REVERIE's crowning glory is undoubtedly the nine-minute 'Cedar', a dark but heart-pulling number that could summon the dead without need of a ouija board; you have been warned. You will become addicted. Please give us more, Gillian. *MCS*

Gillian Chadwick - vocals, guitars, dulcimer, piano, synths / **David Chadwick** - bass

US self-rel. — UK not issued

Jul 05. (ltd-cd-r) <*none*> PHRONESIS [–] [–]
- Perennial / Orange flame / Thumbtacks.

—— with added guests **Greg Weeks** - organ, recorder, backing vocals (solo and of ESPERS) / **Margie Wienk** - cello (of ESPERS, of FERN KNIGHT) / **Jessica Weeks** - flute (of The VALERIE PROJECT) / **Julius Masri** - drum kit, pandeiro, shakers / plus **Katt Hernandez** + **Gretchen Lohse** - violins

Language Of Stone — Language Of Stone

Jan 08. (cd) <*(LOS-004)*> **THE DOOR INTO SUMMER** [ ] Feb 08 [ ]
- Second son / The crowning / Dawn comes for us all / The years / Days away / Cedar / Clouds? or smoke? / Wooden sword / Cedar, pt.2.

—— in 2007, Gillian collaborated with SHARRON KRAUS on the RUSALNAIA set

FAUN FABLES

From beneath the undergrowth of a bleak forest, somewhere in a land close to nothing and as far away as possible from any 'folks', comes FAUN FABLES, the mind-blowing brainchild of Spokane, Washington's Dawn McCarthy. Dawn the Faun, who inaugurated the project in Oakland, California around 1997, has a penchant for everything arty, pagan and ethereal. On a par with the late, great NICO, Dagmar Krause and freak-folk contemporaries like JOANNA NEWSOM, JOSEPHINE FOSTER and MARISSA NADLER, she has reached new heights (or indeed depths; delete as appropriate) in experimental/indie-folk.

Recorded after her extremely low-key cd-r debut FAUN'S FABLES in 1998 and likewise self-released a year later, the eerie **EARLY SONG** {*5} established the howling banshee as the protagonist or catalyst of a new world of nocturnal noise. Described as "near and dear to her heart", the set suffered from dull arrangements, especially in her brooding readings of traditional material such as 'Old Village Churchyard', 'Only A Miner', and two live numbers, 'Honey Babe Blues' and 'O Death' - blues/folk purists beware. The yodelling 'Ode To Rejection' comes closest to anything that can be described as folk, Appalachian or otherwise. In parallel with her next set, the record was belatedly issued in 2004 (with bonus cuts) on Drag City.

With multi-instrumentalist Nils Frykdahl (of Sleepytime Gorilla Museum) on board, **MOTHER TWILIGHT** (2001) {*7} marked a musical upturn, although this wasn't to say Dawn had walked out on her wigged-out transcendental meditations. One difference was her newfound and creative use of serpentine melody, especially on opening tracks 'Begin' and 'Sleepwalker'. With a running time of 62 minutes, the wheat ('Traveller Returning', 'Lightning Rods' and 'Girl That Said Goodbye') could at least be distinguished from the chaff ('Train', 'Washington State', 'Beautiful Blade'). 'Moth', like some out-take from 'The Wicker Man', is the hypnotic flyer here, her best track thus far.

Filled with the same passion and mysticism, **FAMILY ALBUM** (2004) {*8} was worthy of the return fare, Dawn's pseudo-operatic songs exorcising ghostly demons of some other world. 'Eyes Of A Bird' (featuring her sister, Sheila McCarthy, on drums) is particularly intense and hypnotic, while Nils gets in his twopennorth by way of the Uriah Heep/Judas Priestish (sic) 'Lucy Belle', 'Rising Din' and the duet 'Still Here'. But it's the wee faerie herself who steals the limelight; she's altogether enchanting and indeed folky on gems like 'Joshua', 'Old And Light', 'Fear March' and the pixie-yodel number 'Mouse Song'. There are a few more spaced-out oddities here, none more so than 'Nop Of Time', written and sung by seven-year old Cassie Rorie. We also have an English reading of the 1960s Polish song 'Karuzela Madonnami' ('Carousel With Madonnas'), a Bjork-ish cover of Brigitte Fontaine's 'Eternal' and the uplifting congregational trad item 'Higher'.

Written, developed and premiered on stage in 2002, the soundtrack of **THE TRANSIT RIDER** {*8} was released in 2006. 'Birth' opens the set with an eerie ghost-train backdrop, while the lush 'Transit Theme' (think Dead Can Dance in cabaret) has a wobbly, almost carousel feel. From mediaeval times Dawn uproots a biblical reading of 'House Carpenter' (formerly performed by BAEZ, PENTANGLE, MR FOX, etc.), contrasted by the Swans-like dual vocals of Nils on 'In Speed'. From a 1963 poem by Polish songwriter Zygmunt Conieczny, the eight-minute 'Taki Pejzaz' ('Such A Landscape') is the most gothic, ambitious and dramatic number in the FAUN FABLES repertoire bar none. Nils is afforded three contributions - the acidic ballad of 'Roadkill', the Kurt Weillesque 'Fire And Castration' and the Erik Satie-meets-Tom Waits 'The Corwith Brothers' - but it's Dawn's delicious rendition of The Singing Nun/SOEUR SOURIRE's 'I'd Like To Be' that closes out a great show.

After an invitation to sing on Bonnie 'Prince' Billy's 'The Letting Go' in 2006, DAWN McCARTHY and Billy (Will Oldham) released the demo recordings as **WAI NOTES** (2007) {*5}. Probably for diehard fans only, the rough-edged 10-track CD (complete with hiss) nevertheless includes two beauties, 'God Is Love' and 'The Signifying Wolf'.

With only four tracks and running only 17 minutes, A TABLE FORGOTTEN (2008) {*6} (McCarthy and Frykdahl, with Meredith Yayanos on violin and producer Matt Waldron of Nurse With Wound on percussion) packs quite a punch. Hopefully these gems will reappear on a future album. But for now, fans should be content with another intoxicating and earthy full set, **LIGHT OF A VASTER DARK** (2010) {*8}, a record that sweeps from old-timey minstrelesque movements to pastoral psychedelic atmospherics, performed by Dawn, Nils, Meredith and recent recruits Kirana Peyton (multi), Cornelius Boots (wind) and Mark Stikman (harmonica). Check out 'Violet', the title track and 'Hibernation Tales'. *MCS*

Dawn McCarthy (b. Oct 30 '71) - vocals, guitars, percussion, autoharp, gamelan

US self-rel. / UK not issued

1998. (c) <*none*> FAUN'S FABLES [–] [–]
- This bliss / Only a miner / Apple trees / Ode to rejection /. Lullaby for conscious / Schmeetz / In the old village courtyard.

1999. (cd-r) <*none*> **EARLY SONG** [–] [–]
- Muse / Lullaby for consciousness / Ode to rejection / The crumb / Only a miner / Old village churchyard / Apple trees / Sometimes I pray / Bliss. *<(re-iss. Aug 04 on Drag City; DC 273CD)>* - Muse / The crumb / Old village churchyard / Apple trees / Only a miner / Sometimes I pray / Honey baby blues / Lullaby for consciousness / O death / Ode to rejection / Bliss.

—— added **Nils Frykdahl** - guitars, flute, vocals, percussion, autoharp (of Sleepytime Gorilla Museum, ex-Idiot Flesh)

Earthlight / not issued

2001. (cd) <*none*> **MOTHER TWILIGHT** [ ] [–]
- Begin / Sleepwalker / Shadowsound / Hela / Traveller returning / Train / Beautiful blade / Mother twilight / Lightning rods / Moth / Girl that said goodbye / Washington State / Catch me / Live old. *<(re-iss. Aug 04 on Drag City; DC 274CD)>*

Drag City / Drag City

Feb 04. (cd) *<(DC 262CD)>* **FAMILY ALBUM** [ ] Apr 04 [ ]
- Eyes of a bird / Poem 2 / A mother and a piano / Lucy Belle / Joshua / Nop of time / Still here / Preview / Higher / Carousel with Madonnas / Rising din / Fear March / Eternal / Mouse song / Old and light.

Mar 06. (cd) *<(DC 314CD)>* **THE TRANSIT RIDER** [ ] May 06 [ ]
- Birth / Transit theme / House carpenter / In speed / Taki pejzaz (Such a landscape) / Roadkill / Earth's kiss / Fire and castration / The questioning / I no longer wish to / The Corwith brothers / Dream on a train / I'd like to be.

—— added **Meredith Yayanos** - vocals, violin, theremin / **Kirana Peyton** - vocals, harmonium, bass, percussion

Jul 08. (cd-ep) *<(DC 370CD)>* A TABLE FORGOTTEN [ ] [ ]
- With words and cake / Pictures / A table forgotten / Winter sleep.

—— added **Cornelius Boots** - clarinet, flute / **Mark Stikman** - harmonica

Nov 10. (cd) *<(DC 371CD)>* **LIGHT OF A VASTER DARK** [ ] [ ]
- Darkness (intro) / Light of a vaster dark / Housekeeper / On the open plains / Violet / Interlude 1 / Hollow in the home / Interlude 2 / Parade / Hear the grinder creak / Interlude 3 / Sweeping spell / O Mary / Bells for Ura / Hibernation tales / Light (outro).

DAWN McCARTHY & BONNY BILLY

Bonnie Billy is of course **Will Oldham**

Sea Note / Sea Note

Dec 07. (cd) *<(SN 14)>* **WAI NOTES** [ ] [ ]
- Then the letting go / Strange form of love / Lay and love / God is love / The signifying wolf / The seedling / I called you back / Wai / Cursed sleep / God's small sleep.

Stephen FEARING

For well over 20 years Canadian singer-songwriter STEPHEN FEARING (born in Vancouver in 1963, raised in Dublin, Ireland) has been mixing his own blend of acoustic and electric folk music. Returning to Vancouver in the early 1980s, Stephen released a couple of cassettes, billed as by the Fearing-Hunter-Wake Band, before he plucked up the courage for a solo career. Mixing traditional with contemporary in his own creative compositions, he made his vinyl debut with **OUT TO SEA** (1988) {*7}, featuring tracks by Michael Johnson ('Cain's Blood') and Donny Hathaway ('Tryin' Times'). The closing track, 'Beguiling Eyes', incorporates JONI MITCHELL's 'Both Sides Now' into the mix.

Showcasing a style not too dissimilar in parts to those of JOHN MARTYN, his old friend RICHARD THOMPSON or a soulful Justin Currie, **BLUE LINE** (1990) {*6} was another great example of his talented strumming and strong voice. Check out 'The Bells Of Morning'.

With contributions from THOMPSON, Sarah McLachlan and producer Steve Berlin (of Los Lobos), **THE ASSASSIN'S APPRENTICE** (1995) {*5} was FEARING's stab at semi-major-label (Cooking Vinyl) stardom, but a slight disappointment to his fans. 'Martin's' was dedicated to a certain Mr CARTHY, and there was a cover of Hank Williams's '(I Heard That) Lonesome Whistle'.

INDUSTRIAL LULLABY (1998) {*6}, the live **SO MANY MILES** (2000) {*7} and **THAT'S HOW I WALK** (2003) {*6} continued his steady progress in the business, although it would be his eighth set, **YELLOWJACKET** (2006) {*7}, that gave the rootsy folk-rocker his best chance of success. Never one to be pigeonholed, FEARING was also behind the country-blues project Blackie & The Rodeo Kings (alongside Colin Linden and Tom Wilson), who have made several albums for True North between 1996 and 2008. *MCS*

Stephen Fearing - vocals, guitar / with various people

US / UK
own label / not issued

1986. (c) *<none>* **STEPHEN FEARING** (THE YELLOW TAPE)

Aural Tradition / not issued

1988. (lp) *<none>* **OUT TO SEA**
- Out to sea / Dublin Bay / Carsten / Welfare Wednesday / Cain's blood / August 6th and 9th / Tryin' times / The James medley / Beguiling eyes. *<cd-iss. 1991 & May 08 on True North; TNMD 80> (UK cd-iss. Dec 97 on Black Crow; CROCD 222)*

True North / New Routes

Apr 90. (cd/c/lp) *<TNMD 76>* (RUE CD/MC/LP 3) **BLUE LINE**
- The bells of morning / Our father and the big wheel of fortune / Sarah's song / Race of fractions / Little child eyes / Blind horses / Blue line / Born in a story / Turn out the lights / Jesse meets his future wife Zee Mimms. *(re-iss. Nov 97; same as US/Canada)*

CRS / Cooking Vinyl

Apr 95. (cd) <9002> *(CSCCD 1001)* **THE ASSASSIN'S APPRENTICE** Aug 95
- The assassin's apprentice / Give it up / The longest road / Expectations / The station / Lark and duke / Down the wire / Echoes / (I heard that) Lonesome whistle / The brillance you need / The life / Martin's. *<(re-iss. May 08 on 'True North')>*

Red House / Red House

Aug 98. (cd) *<(RHRCD 120)>* **INDUSTRIAL LULLABY**
- The upside down / Anything you want / Industrial lullaby / Home / Coryanna / Long suffering waltz / Blind indifference / Dog on a chain / Man o' war / So many miles away / All the king's horses / Robert's Waterloo / When the world was a well. *(re-iss. Jan 07 on True North; TND 151)*

Sep 00. (cd) *<(RHRCD 149)>* **SO MANY MILES** (live in April 2000 at the Tranzac Club, Toronto)
- Blind indifference / Toronto-Vancouver / The longest road / Wailing wall / Expectations / Dog on a chain - James medley / So many miles away / Anything you want / When my baby calls my name / Glory train / The bells of morning / Know your audience / The lark - Robert's Waterloo / Tryin' times / Thrasher. *(re-iss. Apr 07 on True North; TND 215)*

Philo / Philo

Jan 03. (cd) *<(CDPH 1221)>* **THAT'S HOW I WALK** Feb 03
- Like the way that you said / The finest kind / Town called Jesus / Showbiz / On the great divide / Me and Mr Blue / Rave on captain / When my baby calls my name / That's how I walk / Glory train / Wailing wall / Black silk gown / Meghan Haydon's / The parting glass.

True North / True North

Apr 06. (cd) *<(TND 410)>* **YELLOWJACKET**
- Yellowjacket / The man who married music / One flat tire / Love only knows / Like every other morning / When my work is done / Whoville / This guitar / Johnny's lament / Ball 'n' chain / Goodnight moon.

- (8-10*) compilations -

May 09. (cd) True North; *<(TND 527)>* **THE MAN WHO MARRIED MUSIC: THE BEST OF STEPHEN FEARING**
- Home / Yellowjacket / The finest kind / Beguiling eyes / The bells of morning / Turn out the lights / Expectations / That's how I walk / The longest road / Welfare Wednesday / Anything you want / Dog on a chain - James medley / The man who married music / The big east west / No dress rehearsal.

FEATHERS

With an extended family of over a dozen hippie campers on the front sleeve of the self-titled **FEATHERS** (2005) {*7} album, it was clear they'd taken a leaf from the book of The INCREDIBLE STRING BAND's 'The Hangman's Beautiful Daughter'.

In fact, there were only three core members (Asa Irons, Kyle Thomas and Ruth Garbus), with five auxiliaries in the supporting cast.

From Battleboro in East Vermont, this acid-folk ensemble was a brew-up of Eastern-styled psychedelia, Marc Bolan's TYRANNOSAURUS REX and an experimental DONOVAN. They released a handful of CD-rs on their own Feathers Family label before the eponymous limited-edition vinyl album was issued on CD by Andy Cabic (of VETIVER) and DEVENDRA BANHART's Gnomonsong label in 2006.

Titles such as 'Old Black Hat With A Dandelion Flower' and 'Silverleaves In The Air Of Starseedlings' immediately draw the listener into the world of JOANNA NEWSOM and JOSEPHINE FOSTER, while 'Van Rat' stretches the freak side of folk a little too far and sounds like 10cc at the wrong speed. While Kyle and Ruth subsequently founded Sub Pop outfit Happy Birthday, Asa went on to play guitar (J Mascis was on drums) in stoner-rock outfit Witch. *MCS*

Asa Irons - guitar, vocals / **Kyle Thomas** (b. New Orleans) - bass, vocals / **Ruth Garbus** - drums, vocals / plus **Greg Petrovado, Kurt Weisman, Jordan Morris, Meara O'Reilly, Shayna Kipping**

US / UK
Feathers Family / not issued

2004. (cd-r) *<FF-01>* GNOMEOZOIC LIVE [live]
- Old black hat with a dandelion flower / Past the moon / Ibex horn.

2005. (ltd-lp) *<FF-03>* **FEATHERS**
- Old black hat with a dandelion flower / To each his own / Past the moon / Ulna / Van rat / Silverleaves in the air of starseedlings / Ibex horn / Come around. *<cd-iss. Apr 06 on Gnomonsong; GONG 02>*

2005. (cd-r) *<FF-04>* TOUR PAINT
- Wandering with you / Grandmother constellation fade away into the earth / Angel in the sky / Abacus.

2006. (cd-r) *<FF-05>* **SOMETHING'S WRONG WITH FEATHERS**
- Waterdust / Feathers / Tiny lights / Space alien blues / Raindrops / Howndawg / Turacoverdin / We are in danger now / Be prepared to defend your title at three o'clock tomorrow.

—— Asa continued with Witch, Ruth and Kyle with Sub Pop glam act Happy Birthday

ASA IRONS & SWAAN MILLER

Spirit Of Orr / not issued

2003. (ltd-lp) *<r9>* **ASA IRONS / SWAAN MILLER**
- Abacus / Frost line blues / To Ellis Pass / A fourfold offering *[track 6 cd]* / Only the chosen *[track 8 cd]* / The wounded grouse *[track 4 cd]* / Whitwill *[track 5 cd]* / A bardrock pattern *[track 7 cd]* / Silent on the wind. *<cd-iss. Apr 07 on Important; IMPREC 143>*

The FELICE BROTHERS

When the three FELICE BROTHERS (Ian, Simone and James) headed down from Palenville in the Catskill mountains north of New York City in 2006, there was more than a resemblance to the 'Basement Tapes' style of BOB DYLAN & THE BAND in their sound, although rootsy Americana and alt-country were certainly more apparent than DYLAN's earlier folk-rock inclinations.

With Christmas Clapton filling in on bass, the quartet went from subway-station busking to chicken-coop rehearsals and recording for their debut set, **THROUGH THESE REINS AND GONE** (2006) {*6}. The limited-edition **IANTOWN** {*5} had surfaced a year earlier, although apparently featuring only Ian.

The FELICE BROTHERS really got under way when the V2 label released most of their 2006 set under the title of **TONIGHT AT THE ARIZONA** (2007) {*7}, a record shot through with such whimsical flights of fancy as 'The Ballad Of Lou The Welterweight' (a story passed on by their grandfather) and 'Rockefeller Druglaw Blues' (the best song DYLAN never wrote).

Issued on Team Love Records, **THE FELICE BROTHERS** (2008) {*7} and **YONDER IS THE CLOCK** (2009) {*7} continued in their vein of suburbanised homesick blues, but it was the final outing for drummer Simone, who took his talents to The Duke And The King. Recruiting fiddler Greg Farley and new drummer Dave Turbeville, The FELICE BROTHERS signed to Fat Possum and released the ambient, alt-country **CELEBRATION, FLORIDA** (2011) {*7}. *MCS*

Ian Felice - vocals, guitar / **James Felice** - accordion, vocals / **Simone Felice** - drums, vocals / **Christmas Clapton** - bass, vocals

US Felice Brothers — UK not issued

2005. (ltd-cd) *<none>* **IANTOWN** — own
- You're all around / Devil as a child / The long road ahead / In the arms of Buffalo Bill / Her eyes dart 'round / Rosie, I'm wrong / Steal a memory / Trouble been hard / Roll on Arte / In my life.

Nov 06. (cd) *<none>* **THROUGH THESE REINS AND GONE** — own
- Trailer song / Ballad of Lou the welterweight / Hey hey revolver / Your belly in my arms / Got what I need / Soldier's song / Valentine's song / Roll on Arte / Christmas song / Mercy / Song to die to / Going going gone.

not issued — V2

Jun 07. (cd) *(VVR 1048732)* **TONIGHT AT THE ARIZONA**
- Roll on Arte / Ballad of Lou the welterweight / Hey hey revolver / Your belly in my arms / Lady day / T for Texas / Rockefeller druglaw blues / Mercy / Christmas song / Going going gone / Take this hammer [live]. *(lp-iss. Jun 07 on Loose; VJLP 171) (re-iss. 2009 on Loose+=; VJCD 171)* - Nowhere New York / The country is gone / Got what I need.

Nov 07. (7") *(VJS 12)* ROLL ON ARTE. / Radio Song

Team Love — Loose

Mar 08. (cd) *<TL-27> (VJCD 177)* **THE FELICE BROTHERS**
- Little Ann / Greatest show on earth / Frankie's gun! / Goddamn you, Jim / Wonderful life / Don't walk the scarecrow / Take this breed / Saint Stephen's end / Love me tenderly / Ruby Mae / Murder by mistletoe / Whiskey in my whiskey / Helen Fry / Radio song / Tip your way. *<d-lp iss. Apr 08 on Coppertree; CTR 005>*

Team Love — Team Love

Apr 09. (cd/d-lp) *<(TL-39)>* **YONDER IS THE CLOCK**
- The big surprise / Penn station / Buried in ice / Chicken wire / Ambulance man / Sailor song / Katie dear / Run chicken run / All when we were young / Boy from Lawrence County / Memphis flu / Cooperstown / Rise and shine.

now w/out Simone, who formed The Duke And The King: one set, 'Nothing Gold Can Stay'.

—— added **Greg Farley** - fiddle + **Dave Turbeville** - drums

Fat Possum — Loose

May 11. (cd/lp) *<FP 1246-2/-1> (???)* **CELEBRATION, FLORIDA** — 89
- Fire at the pageant / Container ship / Honda Civic / Oliver Stone / Ponzi / Back in the dancehalls / Dallas / Cus's Catskill gym / Refrain / Best I ever had / River Jordan.

- (5-7*) specials, others, etc.-

Nov 07. (ltd-cd) New York Pro; *<none>* **THE ADVENTURES OF THE FELICE BROTHERS VOL.1**
- Frankie's gun! / Trouble been hard / Ruby Mae / Radio song / Helen Fry (she's a master of disguise) / Walk a while / Whiskey in my whiskey / Doris Day / Oxycontin / Where'd you get the liquor / The Devil is real / Glory glory / San Antonio burning.

Mar 10. (ltd-cd) New York Pro; *<none>* **MIX TAPE**
- Forever green / Ahab / White limo / Let me come home / The captain's wife / Indian massacre / Old song / Marie / Marlboro man.

FERN KNIGHT

Formed in Providence, Rhode Island in 1999, FERN KNIGHT was the brainchild of singer and multi-instrumentalist Margaret Wienk, as an offshoot or breakaway from playing cello and double bass with ALEC K. REDFEARN & THE EYESORES. Guitarist Mike Corcoran sat in on early FERN KNIGHT recordings.

On a mission to recreate everything Brit-folk, Margaret and friends surfaced from a few years in the studio with **SEVEN YEARS OF SEVERED LIMBS** (2003) {*7}. Featuring guest spots from accordionist ALEC K. REDFEARN (on 'Kingdom' and 'Chelyabinsk') and drummer Joel Thibodeau (on 'She Who Was So Precious To You' and 'Dog Named Summer'), the album was in similar freak-folk vein to sets by FAUN FABLES, ESPERS and The IDITAROD. Brooding, rustic and bittersweet, there are a handful of introspective gems that stand out from the pack, mainly 'Wolf II', 'If I Could Write A Book About You' and longer pieces such as 'Boxing Day' and folk-shoegazer 'Mover Ghost - Mark The Days Off On Your Wall'.

Now accompanied by a host of modern-day freak-folkies (Redfearn again, Otto Hauser, Jesse Sparhawk, ORION RIGEL DOMMISSE, GREG WEEKS, MEG BAIRD and Chris Saraullo), poetic vocalist Wienk surged upwards and onwards on the second set, **MUSIC FOR WITCHES AND ALCHEMISTS** (2006) {*8}. Disregarding the obvious PENTANGLE and SALLYANGIE comparisons, most of the songs span neo-Celtic and prog-folk. Examples include 'Song For Ireland', 'W. Memphis', 'Shingle River' and 'Murder Of Crows'. GREG WEEKS delivers a Fripp-like acid lead guitar on such eerie cuts as 'Awake, Angel Snake' and 'Lullaby', while Saraullo's sombre bowed saw is effective on the folk mantra 'Marble Grey'. Bringing in a French cafe-bar feel, 'Summer Of Throg' is brooding and rustic, its exotically melancholy mood complementing Wienk's sweet singing.

The effervescent Wienk was also involved with various projects involving IN GOWAN RING, solo sets by GREG WEEKS, ESPERS, Alec K. Redfearn, CURRITUCK CO, MOUNTAIN HOME, ORION RIGEL DOMMISSE, Bonnie 'Prince' Billy, The VALERIE PROJECT, EX REVERIE and SILVER SUMMIT.

To install a sense of sonic cohesion for her third set, Wienk re-established FERN KNIGHT as a quartet, recruiting boyfriend Jim Ayre (on electric guitar, drums and percussion), James Wolf (violin) and Jesse Sparhawk (harp and electric bass). The self-titled **FERN KNIGHT** (2008) {*6} album sounds as though it had stepped out of the early 1970s, but it brings acid-prog-folk tentatively into the 21st century. The touches of GREG WEEKS are also evident throughout (it was recorded in his studio), and Wienk is as vocally seductive as Meg Baird (also of ESPERS).

Much of the set drifts along at a prudent, pastoral pace, the best example being 'Silver Fox', while traditional funereal echoes come and go in various vintage forms. The set begins to come into its own on 'Hawk Mountain' and 'Synges Chair', but it's the 12-minute, three-part 'Magpie Suite' that steals the show. Featuring WEEKS (alongside Gillian Chadwick and Dommisse on the 'Prelude' segment), the suite creates a wintry, chamber-music feel, although other shadings might be discovered too.

Now credited as Margaret Ayre, having married Jim, her fourth album, **CASTINGS** (2010) {*7}, was another conceptual 1970s-styled recording, this time taking the power of the tarot cards and their cryptic imagery as its musical landscape. Not unlike Ayre's own 'The Poisoner', it excels on King Crimson's prog-rock number 'Epitaph', but it was down to the eerie 'From Zero To Infinity', 'The Eye Of The Queen', 'Cave Of Swords' and 'Crumbling Stairs' to steal the show. *MCS*

Margie Wienk (b. Wisconsin, US) - vocals, acoustic guitar, piano, cello, upright bass, Fender Rhodes, drums, percussion / **Mike Corcoran** - guitars, vocals, violin, lap steel / with guests **Alec K. Redfearn** - accordion + **Joel Thibodeau** - drums

US Normal — UK Normal

May 03. (cd) *<(N 246CD)>* **SEVEN YEARS OF SEVERED LIMBS**
- She who was so precious to you / If I could write a book about you / Wolf I / Theme / Kingdom / Wolf II / Chelyabinsk / Boxing day / Mover ghost - Mark the days off on your wall / Sunday afternoons / Dog named Summer.

self-rel. — not issued

Nov 05. (ltd;cd-ep) *<none>* BLITHEWOLD EP
- Theme from 'The Bird With The Crystal Plumage' / Give me your hand / The summer day reflection song / Eulogy to Lenny Bruce / Pearl's dream / 'Plume Di Cristallo' reprise.

—— **Wienk** + **Redfearn** now with **Otto Hauser** - percussion, drums (ex-NICK CASTRO) / **Jesse Sparhawk** - harp / **Orion Rigel Dommisse** - synth and harmonium / **Greg Weeks** - vocals and acid leads (of ESPERS) / **Meg Baird** - vocals / **Chris Saraullo** - bowed saw

VHF — VHF

Nov 06. (cd) *<(#101)>* **MUSIC FOR WITCHES AND ALCHEMISTS**
- Song for Ireland / Awake, angel snake / W. Memphis / Murder of crows / Lintworme, pt.1 / Marble grey / Shingle river / The dirty south / Summer of Throg / What the crows left behind / Lullaby. *<lp-iss. May 08 on Eclipse; ECL-057>*

—— **Wienk** + **Sparhawk** now with **Jim Ayre** - Flying V electric guitar, drums, percussion / **James Wolf** - violin

May 08. (cd) *<#110>* **FERN KNIGHT**
- Bemused / Silver fox / Sundew / Loch Na Fooeq / Hawk mountain / Synges chair / Magpie suite: Prelude - Part II - Part III.

Nov 10. (cd) *<#122>* **CASTINGS**
- From zero to infinity / The poisoner / Pentacles / Long dark century / Cave of swords / Cups + wands / The eye of the queen / Epitaph / Crumbling stairs.

FERRON

"Foggy-night funky folk" might best describe Canadian singer-songwriter FERRON's emotive and picturesque soundscapes. A sketchy line of reference could be drawn through folk-star peers TRET FURE, CRIS WILLIAMSON, PHRANC and INDIGO GIRLS.

Born Debby Foisy (June 1, 1952 in Vancouver), the eldest of seven children, FERRON left home at 15, finding work as a waitress, cab driver, coffee-packer and so on before she finally found her vocation. Taking her cue from personal anguish and the day-to-day struggles around her, she rehearsed and recorded a couple of albums in her basement, **FERRON** (1977) {*5} and **BACKED UP** (1978) {*5}. They aren't much like her later efforts, but they found her a fan in Gayle Scott, who took her under her managerial for her tour de force long-players **TESTIMONY** (1981) {*8} and **SHADOWS ON A DIME** (1984) {*9}.

Although critical acclaim had come by way of a great Rolling Stone album review, FERRON took a much-needed sabbatical courtesy of a Canadian Arts Council grant, which helped support her through a time-out in the middle-to-late 1980s. Reconnected to her spiritual roots, and with a new, polished voice, **PHANTOM CENTER** (1991) {*8} celebrated her comeback in earnest. In marked contrast, **RESTING WITH THE QUESTION** (1992) {*6} was a new-age/ambient instrumental set, out of character with her previous repertoire but effective nonetheless.

Recorded live at the Great American Music Hall in 1992, **NOT A STILL LIFE** (1994) {*7} showed why FERRON had become such a star to in-the-know Canadians, while **DRIVER** (1994) - with a kd lang-like, leather-jacketed FERRON on the sleeve - was narratively smoother and more romanticised than her back catalogue.

STILL RIOT (1996) {*6}, which was revamped in 2009 (she was given to retreading her own golden oldies from time to time), and **TURNING INTO BEAUTIFUL** (2005) {*6} sandwiched a pleasing 1999 pop covers set **INSIDE OUT: THE IMA SESSIONS** {*6}. Her covers had been hits for Linda Ronstadt ('Different Drum'), The Four Tops ('Walk Away Renee'), The Carpenters ('Close To You'), Skeeter Davis ('The End Of The World'), Jackie DeShannon ('Needles And Pins'), The Drifters ('Save The Last Dance For Me'), The Beatles ('I Feel Fine'), Gene Pitney ('A Town Without Pity'), Jimmy Ruffin ('What Becomes Of The Broken Hearted'), The Toys ('A Lover's Concerto'), The Temptations ('My Girl'), The Turtles ('Happy Together'), The Beach Boys ('Don't Worry Baby') and Van Morrison ('Crazy Love').

The re-recordings comprising **BOULDER** (2008) {*5} were a FERRON tribute set of sorts, compiled by her violinist and producer Bitch. *MCS*

Ferron - vocals, acoustic guitar / + session people

US Lucy — UK not issued

1977. (ltd-lp) *<LR-001>* **FERRON**
- O baby / Slender wet branches / Who loses / Dead men and lovers / Rollspin / Under the weather / Fly on my nose / Just the wind / Luckie / Bourbon street vision / I am hungry (how are you) / Borderlines / Freedom / In retrospect.

1978. (ltd-lp) *<LR-002>* **BACKED UP**
- Boom boom / The kid song / Dear Marly / Willow tree / White wing mercy / Light of my light / Soggy dream / I come to your window / Call me friend / Misty mountain / Testimony.

1981. (ltd-lp) *<LR-003>* **TESTIMONY**
- Almost kissed / Rosalee / Our purpose here / Who loses / Testimony / Bellybowl / Satin blouse / O baby / Misty mountain / Ain't life a brook. *<cd/c-iss. May 07 on Cherrywood Station; CW 003>*

1984. (ltd-lp) *<LR-004>* **SHADOWS ON A DIME**
- [Dreaming Back]: Knot 53 / Snowin' in Brooklyn / As soon as I find my shoes I'm gone / Proud crowd - Pride cried / I never was to Africa / [The Return]: Shadows on a dime / Circle round / The return / It won't take long. *<cd/c-iss. 1993 on Cherrywood Station; CW 004>*

Chameleon — not issued

Jul 91. (cd/c) *<D2/D4 74830>* **PHANTOM CENTER**
- Stand up [*] / The cart / Harmless love / Indian dreams / Sunken city / White wing mercy / Heart of destruction / My, my / Phantom center / Higher wisdom. *<(re-iss. Sep95/ Jan96 on EarthBeat w/[*] revised with INDIGO GIRLS; 9 42576-2)>*

Cherrywood Station — not issued

1992. (cd) *<CW 006>* **RESTING WITH THE QUESTION** [instrumental]
- Anything we want / High head Sept. '90 / Beacon / Forgiveness / In your eyes / Old haunts / Cave at Montana de Oro / Just leave / Resting with the question / No matter what happens / Anything we want.

Jul 94. (cd/c) *<CW 007>* **NOT A STILL LIFE: LIVE AT THE GREAT AMERICAN MUSIC HALL** [live in 1992]
- (introduction) / Light of my life / Shadows on a dime / Our purpose here / I am hungry / Ain't life a brook / I know a game / Call me friend / Snowin' in Brooklyn / I never was to Africa / Higher wisdom / Dear Marly / The cart / Shady gate / Harmless love / Testimony / The wind's all a whisper. *<cd re-iss. May 07 on Ferron>*

EarthBeat — not issued

Sep 94. (cd) *<EB 42564CD>* **DRIVER**
- Breakpoint / Girl on a road / Call me / Cactus / Love loves me / Borderlines / Sunshine's lament (prologue) / Sunshine / Sunshine's lament (epilogue) / Independence day / A name for it / Maya.

Warners — not issued

Aug 96. (cd/c) *<9 46292-2/-4>* **STILL RIOT**
- 1. The chosen ones / 2. Alice says yes / 3. Venus as appearances / 4. Still riot / 5. Primitive future / 6. (intro to...) / 7. Takes a little time / 8. Ain't life a brook / 9. I am hungry / 10. Dazzle the beast / 11. Signals and messages / 12. Easy with love. *<cd re-iss. Jun 09 on Ferron>* - [tracks 8, 2, 1, 10, 12, 9, 5, 11, 4, 7, 6, 3].

Cherrywood Station — not issued

May 99. (cd) *<CW 010>* **INSIDE OUT: THE IMA SESSIONS**
- Different drum / Walk away Renee / (They long to be) Close to you / Needles and pins / The end of the world / Save the last dance for me / I feel fine / A town without pity / What becomes of the broken hearted / A lover's concerto / My girl / Happy together / Don't worry baby / Crazy love / So happy together.

May 05. (cd) *<CW 1>* **TURNING INTO BEAUTIFUL**
- More than that / Souvenir / In the mean time / Never your own / Nothing now / Already gone / Goat path / Witness to the years / Turning into beautiful.

—— added **Bitch** - violin (she picked out the re-recordings below)

Short Story — Short Story

Jun 08. (cd) *<(2)>* **BOULDER** [re-hashed]
- Souvenir / Never your own / Already gone / Girl on a road / The cart / It won't take long / Shadows on a dime / Our purpose here / Highway / Misty mountain / Shady gate / In the meantime.

- (8-10*) compilations -

Aug 02. (d-cd) Cherrywood Station; *<100>* **IMPRESSIONISTIC**
- The chosen ones / Girl on a road / Stand up / Ain't life a brook / Misty mountain / Alice says yes / Call me / Shady gate / Independence day / Shadows on a dime / Our purpose here / I am hungry / I never was to Africa / Higher widsom // Who loses / Venus as appearances / My, my / Phantom center / Proud crowd - Pride cried / Almost kissed / Sunshine / Sunken city / Snowin' in Brooklyn / Cactus / Maya / Testimony / Harmless love / Still riot.

Sally FINGERETT

Formerly the lead singer with middle-to-late 1970s bluegrass outfit the Buffalo Gals (with Bill Monroe and John Hartford), the Columbus, Ohio-based pianist, singer-songwriter and humorist SALLY FINGERETT will be best known for her moonlighting stints with FOUR BITCHIN' BABES.

Born December 25, 1955 in Chicago, Illinois, Sally released her first album, **ENCLOSED** {*6}, in 1983, but apart from her song 'Home Is Where The Heart Is' being covered by a resurgent PETER, PAUL & MARY, little was heard from her until the turn of the decade, when she met, married and collaborated with producer Dan Green. He was the man behind the FOUR BITCHIN' BABES' material and four of her subsequent solo albums, from **UNRAVELED** (1991) {*7} to **A WOMAN'S GOTTA DO HER THING** (2004) {*7}. The latter was a collection of her best work, among which songs from **GHOST TOWN GIRL** (1993) {*6} and the AOR-friendly **MY GOOD COMPANY** (1998) {*6} would probably have best suited Carly Simon, or another folk-pop refugee, Linda Ronstadt.

Divorced and remarried (to Michael Stan), a temporary illness of her vocal nerves led her to make more of her comic talents, and she created her one-woman show 'It's A Crazy World ... But Where Else Would We Live? - The Musical Musings Of A Mental Yentl'. *MCS*

Sally Fingerett - vocals, piano, acoustic guitar (w/ session people)

US Amerra — UK not issued

1983. (lp) *<197 7797>* **ENCLOSED**
- Ladies lunch / She's got your love / Here in the midwest / Here's to the women / My famous bed / Ask any mermaid / Rock-a-line, Caroline / The red man / Play for them / Wildberries. *<cd-iss. Jan 91 on Amerisound; AMR-2-977-797>* *<cd/c re-iss. Feb 05 on Rounder Select; 7797>*

Dec 91. (cd) *<AMR-2-977-798>* **UNRAVELED**
- Let a dream be coming on / Smilin' boy / The return / The wheel / Home is where the heart is / Sweetness / Graceful man / He loved her so, the ballad of Harry and Esther / Whatever we did / Let 'em go. *<cd/c re-iss. Feb 05 on Rounder Select; 7798>*

since 1990 she has been part of FOUR BITCHIN' BABES, releasing many sets

Aug 93. (cd) *<AMR-2-977-799>* **GHOST TOWN GIRL**
- True love / Ghost town girl / Mama Ghetto Rose / Don't look back / She won't be walking / Save me a seat / Ho Chin / The lullaby thief / When I wake up from this night / Windows / The fight song. *<cd/c re-iss. Feb 05 on Rounder Select; 7799>*

Shanachie Shanachie

Aug 98. (cd) <(*SHANCD 8033*)> **MY GOOD COMPANY** Sep 98
- Silent silent / My good company / Pink lemonade / Ten pound bass / This town's alright / Little girl please wait / Lorinda Lea / My friend Elaine / Home / I danced with a man / Boy on wheels / Thirsty woman / Private plenty.

Jan 04. (cd) <(SHANCD 8040)> **A WOMAN'S GOTTA DO HER THING: A Collection**
- A woman's gotta do her thing / Save me a seat / Take me out to eat / Lorinda Lea / (live chatty intro) / It's been said / Little girl please wait / When I wake up from this night / My friend Elaine / Harry and Esther / Wild berries / Whatever we did / Boy on wheels / Home is where the heart is / The return / I wanna be an engineer.

Sally was still an integral member of The FOUR BITCHIN' BABES

FIRE ON FIRE

With folk music on the upsurge and just about everyone jumping on the bandwagon, it was no shock when members of jamming post-rock/indie stalwarts Cerberus Shoal took their place among the fixated FLEET FOXES wannabes. First releasing a well-received self-titled EP for Young God (lead track 'Hangman'), FIRE ON FIRE (Chriss Sutherland, Tom Kovacevic, Colleen Kinsella, Caleb Mulkerin and Micah Blue Smaldone) finally served up **THE ORCHARD** {*7}, recorded in 2006 but not released, and then only in a limited CD edition, in 2008.

A collection of modified field-type recordings in the spirit of old-timey Appalachian traditionals, the record was steeped and deep-rooted in some kind of time loop, opener 'Sirocco' and the eight-minute finale 'Haystack' probably coming off best. *MCS*

Chriss Sutherland - vocals, upright bass, acoustic guitar, percussion / **Tom Kovacevic** - vocals, oud, ney, percussion / **Colleen Kinsella** - vocals, harmonium, accordion, acoustic guitar / **Caleb Mulkerin** - acoustic guitar, banjo, vocals / **Micah Blue Smaldone** - upright bass, banjo, vocals

US Young God — UK not issued

Nov 07. (ltd-cd-ep) <*YGX 01*> FIRE ON FIRE –
- Hangman / Liberty unknown / My lady coffin / Amnesia / Three or more.

Dec 08. (ltd-cd) <*YG 38*> **THE ORCHARD** –
- Sirocco / Heavy D / Assanine race / The orchard / Flordinese / Hartford blues / Toknight / Squeeze box / Fight song / Grin / Tsunami / Haystack. *<re-prom. Apr 09; same>*

FLEET FOXES

If The Beach Boys (or Yes) had turned their hands to CROSBY, STILLS & NASH or SIMON & GARFUNKEL-styled folk, they might have sounded like FLEET FOXES, a harmony-fuelled folk-rock group of Seattle-based singers and musicians who have released two platinum-selling albums.

Led since 2006 by singer/songwriter Robin Pecknold with his friends Skyler Skjelset, Casey Wescott, Bryn Lumsden and Nicholas Peterson, they signed a major deal with Sub Pop in the US and Robin Guthrie's Bella Union in the UK, issuing the excellent 'Sun Giant' EP in 2008. 'Mykonos' was later released as a single, flipped with 'False Knight On The Road' (Child ballad No.3, famously recorded by STEELEYE SPAN).

Touching on time spent in the Blue Ridge Mountains, quite possibly listening to their fathers' prog-rock LPs, **FLEET FOXES** (2008) {*9} was ambitious and anthemic in its lush choral arrangements, but without the self-indulgence of their proggy peers. From the old-timey-intro opener 'Sun It Rises' through 'Oliver James', the spiritual singalong 'Your Protector' (a tearjerker) to the repetitive but not derivative 'White Winter Hymnal', the Foxes raid a chicken-coop of past masters for inspiration.

With former rhythm section Bryn and Nicholas replaced by Christian Wargo and Joshua Tillman (also known as J. TILLMAN), plus sixth member Morgan Henderson, **HELPLESSNESS BLUES** (2011) {*7} finally gave their fans something new to shout about. Although it was formulaic, stand-out tracks such as 'Montezuma', 'Bedouin Dress', 'Grown Ocean' and the title track meant FLEET FOXES had secured their place in folk music's hall of fame. *MCS*

Robin Pecknold (b. Mar 30 '86) - vocals, guitar / **Skyler Skjelset** - lead guitar / **Casey Wescott** - keyboards, vocals (ex-Crystal Skulls) / **Bryn Lumsden** - bass / **Nicholas Peterson** - drums, vocals

US self-rel. — UK not issued

2006. (ltd-cd-r) <*none*> Demo EP – –
- She got dressed / In the hot, hot rays / Anyone who's anyone / Textbook love / So long to the headstrong / Icicle tusk.

Sub Pop — Bella Union

Feb 08. (cd-ep) <*SPCD 781*> *(BELLACD 165)* SUN GIANT May 08
- Sun giant / Drops in the river / English house / Mykonos / Innocent son.

Jun 08. (cd/lp) <*SPCD 777*> *(BELLA CD/V 167)* **FLEET FOXES** 36 3
- Sun it rises / White winter hymnal / Ragged wood / Tiger mountain peasant song / Quiet house / He doesn't know why / Heard them stirring / Your protector / Meadowlarks / Blue ridge mountains / Oliver James. *<(lp w/free 12" ep+=; SP 781)>* - SUN GIANT EP

Jul 08. (ltd-7") *(BELLAV 177)* WHITE WINTER HYMNAL. / Isles – 77

—— **Christian Wargo** - bass, guitar, vocals (ex-Scientific, ex-Crystal Skulls) repl. Lumsden

—— **Joshua Tillman** - drums, vocals (solo artist: J. TILLMAN) repl. Peterson

May 09. (7") <*SP 838*> *(BELLAV 191)* MYKONOS. / False Knight On The Road Feb 99 53

Jun 09. (7") *(BELLAV 203)* YOUR PROTECTOR. / Silver Dagger –

—— added **Morgan Henderson** - bass (ex-Blood Brothers, of Past Lives)

May 11. (cd/d-lp) <*SPCD/SPLP 888*> *(BELLA CD/V 283)* **HELPLESSNESS BLUES** 4 2
- Montezuma / Bedouin dress / Sim sala bim / Battery Kinzie / The plains - Bitter dancer / Helplessness blues / The cascades / Lorelai / Someone you'd admire / The shrine - An argument / Blue spotted tail / Grown ocean.

The FOLKLORDS

Overlooked in Volume I, Canadians The FOLKLORDS comprised Toronto singers Tom Martin [also known as Tom Waschkowski] on bass and his girlfriend Martha Johnson on autoharp, plus guitarist Paul Seip and drummer Craig Boswell. They are among psych-folk's forgotten and collectable ones from the late 1960s.

Could they sing? Not very well, judging by their album **RELEASE THE SUNSHINE** (1969) {*6}, a record wrongly described by modern-day reviewers as something akin to the early, Signe Anderson-fronted JEFFERSON AIRPLANE. Produced by Jack Boswell and Bill Bessey, the original vinyl (complete with rare 45 'Forty Second River' b/w 'Unspoken Love') can cost a princely sum on eBay. *MCS*

Tom Martin (b. Tom Waschkowski) - vocals, bass / **Martha Johnson** - vocals, autoharp

US/Can Cob — UK not issued

1968. (7") <*M.S. 105*> FORTY SECOND RIVER. / Unspoken Love – Canada –

—— added **Paul Seip** - guitar, vocals / plus **Craig Boswell** - drums

Allied — not issued

1969. (7") <*6358*> JENNIFER LEE. / Pardon Me Jesus – Canada –

1969. (lp) <*11*> **RELEASE THE SUNSHINE** – Canada –
- Jennifer Lee / Don't hide your love from me / Child / Unspoken love / Windows / Forty second river / Pardon me Judas / Thank you for your kindness / We'll love like before / Suzanne Marie / Don't look back / The slave. *<cd-iss. 2005 on Pacemaker; PACE 047> <US cd/lp w/7"-iss. Jun 08 on Lion+=; LION-CD/-LP 104>* - Forty second river [alt.] / Unspoken love [alt.].

—— disappeared from the music scene

Steve FORBERT

Playing cool contemporary folk music with a tinge of country, singer/songwriter STEVE FORBERT (b. December 13, 1954 in Meridian, Mississippi) was hailed as the new DYLAN when his first album appeared in 1978. From playing in rock bands to busking in New York's Grand Central Station, then on to the bright lights of the Manhattan circuit, the former truck driver turned guitarist and harmonica-blower had come a long way in a short time.

The debut in question, **ALIVE ON ARRIVAL** {*7}, was in sharp contrast to the new-wave music of the day, but tracks like his signature tune 'Thinkin'', the autobiographical 'Grand Central Station, March 18, 1977' and 'Goin' Back To Laurel' appealed to a slightly older generation stuck in the 1960s.

The Nemperor label (affiliated with CBS at the time) was rewarded with a major hit single, 'Romeo's Tune', and a Top 20 second album, **JACKRABBIT SLIM** (1979) {*7}, which updated his storytelling by way of 'January 23-30, 1978' and 'Say Goodbye To Little Jo'.

But his folk appeal was fading as fast as his star, and his sideslip into soft-rock began with **LITTLE STEVIE ORBIT** (1980) {*6}, while Nashville beckoned after his pop set **STEVE FORBERT** (1982) {*4}, a disappointment to his fans and to the critics who tore into his cover of JACKIE DeSHANNON's 'When You Walk In The Room'.

Contractual disagreements and his label's refusal to release his fifth album ensued, but Geffen took him on in 1988. By this time a new producer had been found in Garry Tallent, from the E Street Band, but **STREETS OF THIS TOWN** {*6} was no Springsteen classic. The flop single 'Running On Love' was typical 1980s pop-rock fodder. The same goes for another long-awaited set, **THE AMERICAN IN ME** (1992) {*5}.

Tallent was also behind FORBERT's 1995's **MISSION OF THE CROSSROAD PALMS** {*5} set, although his best days looked to be behind him, while the DYLAN tag was revived with 'Lay Down Your Weary Tune Again', a country-flavoured folk ballad with a touch of wit. With Brad Jones bringing in alt-country-rock band Wilco for **ROCKING HORSE HEAD** (1996) {*4}, Steve's voice was beginning to sound like a weaker Rod Stewart or Tom Petty rather than a rootsy rocker.

Post-millennium he positioned himself a little closer to his old style, and albums such as **EVERGREEN BOY** (2000) {*6}, **JUST LIKE THERE'S NOTHIN' TO IT** (2004) {*6}, **STRANGE NAMES AND NEW SENSATIONS** (2007) {*5} and **THE PLACE AND THE TIME** (2009) {*6} were acceptable recordings. A few live collections, and a Jimmie Rodgers C&W tribute, **ANY OLD TIME** (2002) {*5}, were slight diversions. *MCS*

Steve Forbert - vocals, guitar / (+ session people)

US Nemperor — UK Epic

Nov 78. (lp/c) *<JZ 35538> (EPC/40 83308)* **ALIVE ON ARRIVAL** [82] May 79 [56]
- Goin' down to Laurel / Steve Forbert's midsummer night's toast / Thinkin' / What kinda guy? / It isn't gonna be that way / Big city cat / Grand Central Station, March 18, 1977 / Tonight I feel so far away from home / Settle down / You cannot win if you do not play. *(re-iss. Nov 81 lp/c; EPC/40 32053) <cd-iss. Dec 99 & Mar 08 on Sony 724437>*

Apr 79. (7") *(EPC 7275)* GOIN' DOWN TO LAUREL. / Steve Forbert's Moon River [–] [ ]

Jul 79. (7"m) *(EPC 7491)* THINKIN'. / You Cannot Win If You Do Not Play / Midsummer Night's Toast [–] [ ]

Oct 79. (lp/c) *<JZ 36191> (EPC/40 83879)* **JACKRABBIT SLIM** [20] Nov 79 [54]
- Romeo's tune / The sweet love that you give (sure goes a long, long way) / I'm in love with you / Say goodbye to little Jo / Wait / Make it all so real / Baby / Complications / Sadly sorta like a soap opera / January 23-30, 1978. *(w/ free 1-sided 7"; OIL 1)* - The Oil Song. *<cd re-iss. Sep 96 on Sony-BMG; 485107-2> (cd re-iss. Apr 08 on Sony; 726757-2)*

Oct 79. (7") *<7525>* ROMEO'S TUNE. / Make It All So Real [11] [–]

Oct 79. (7") *(EPC 7945)* ROMEO'S TUNE. / Sadly Sorta Like A Soap Opera *(re-iss. Apr 81; EPCA 1106)* [–] [ ]

Jan 80. (7") *(EPC 8124)* THE SWEET LOVE THAT YOU GIVE (SURE GOES A LONG, LONG WAY). / Make It All So Real [–] [ ]

Mar 80. (7") *<7529> (EPC 8342)* SAY GOODBYE TO LITTLE JO. / You're Darn Right [85] [ ]

Sep 80. (7") *(EPC 8995)* GET WELL SOON. / A Visitor [–] [ ]

Oct 80. (lp/c) *<JZ 36595> (EPC/40 84501)* **LITTLE STEVIE ORBIT** [70] Nov 80 [ ]
- Get well soon / Cellophane city / Song for Carmelita / Laughter Lou (who needs you?) / Song for Katrina / One more glass of beer / Lucky / Rain / I'm an automobile / Schoolgirl / If you've gotta ask you'll never know / Lonely girl / A visitor.

Nov 80. (7") *(EPC 8983)* LONELY GIRL. / Rain [–] [ ]

Jun 82. (7") *(EPCA 2464)* WHEN YOU WALK IN THE ROOM. / I Don't Know [–] [ ]

Jul 82. (lp/c) *<ARZ 37434> (EPC/40 85297)* **STEVE FORBERT** [ ] Aug 82 [ ]
- He's gotta live up to his shoes / Ya ya (next to me) / When you in the room / Listen to me / Oh so close (and yet so far away) / You're darn right / Prisoner of stardom / On the beach / Lost / It takes a whole lotta help (to make it on your own) / Beautiful Diana.

Geffen — Geffen

Apr 88. (lp/c)(cd) *<1-/M5G-/2-24194> (WX 167/C)(924194-2)* **STREETS OF THIS TOWN** [ ] Jun 88 [ ]
- Running on love / Don't tell me (I know) / I blinked once / Mexico / As we live and breathe / On the streets of this town / Hope, faith and love / Perfect stranger / Wait a little longer / Search your heart. *(re-iss. Apr 91 cd/c; GEF D/C 24194) (re-iss. Feb 94 cd/c; GFL D/C 24459)*

Sep 88. (7") *<27846> (GEF 45)* RUNNING ON LOVE. / Mexico [ ] [ ]
(12"+=) (GEF 45T) - The only normal people.

Jan 92. (cd/c) *<(GEF D/C 24459)>* **THE AMERICAN IN ME** [ ] [ ]
- Born too late / If you're waiting on me / Responsibility / When the sun shines / The American in me / Baby don't / Change in the weather / You cannot win if you do not play / Rock while I can rock / New working day. *(re-iss. Jun 97; GED/GEC 24459)*

Feb 92. (cd-s) *(GFSTD 22)* BORN TOO LATE / The American In Me / Mexico / Rock While I Can Rock (live acoustic) [–] [ ]

Giant-Warners — R.C.A.

Mar 95. (cd/c) *<WB 24611> (74321 25990-2/-4)* **MISSION OF THE CROSSROAD PALMS** [ ] Apr 95 [ ]
- It sure was better back then / It is what it is (and that's all) / Is it any wonder / Lay down your weary tune again / So good to feel good again / Oh, to be back with you / Real, live love / The trouble with angels / How can you change the world? / Don't talk to me / The last rays of sunlight / Thirteen blood red rosebuds.

Sep 96. (cd/c) *<2/4 24663>* **ROCKING HORSE HEAD** [ ] [–]
- If I want you now / My time ain't long / Shaky ground / Dear Lord / Moon man (I'm waiting on you) / Don't stop / Some will rake the coals / I know what I know / Good planets are hard to find / Big new world / Open house / Dream dream.

not issued — UlfTone

Oct 99. (cd) *(UTCD 006)* **BE HERE AGAIN - LIVE SOLO 1998** (live) [–] [ ]
- What kinda guy / Real, live love / Some will rake the coals / Good planets are hard to find / Stardust / Goin' down to Laurel / Don't talk to me / Honey don't / So good to feel good again / It was sure better back then / Everyone's got to have a dream / Midsummer night's toast / Jamaica farewell / Complications / Responsibility / My time ain't long / Rock while I can rock / Sea of love / Thinkin' / Good night Irene / Romeo's tune / Moon man (I'm waiting on you).

Koch — Koch

Jan 00. (cd) *<(KOCCD 8054)>* **EVERGREEN BOY** [ ] Aug 05 [ ]
- Something's got a hold on me / She's living in a dream world / Strange / Evergreen boy / Rose Marie / Now you come back / Your own hero / Late winter song / Breaking through / It doesn't matter much / Listen to the mockingbird / Trusting old soul.

Apr 01. (cd; as STEVE FORBERT and the Rough Squirrels) *<(KOCCD 8227)>* **LIVE AT THE BOTTOM LINE** (live 8th July 2000) [ ] [ ]
- Real live love / Goin' down to Laurel / Good planets (are hard to find) / Strange / The American in me / Now you come back / Evergreen boy / Rose Marie / It sure was better back then / So good to feel good again / Oh, to be back with you / Something's got a hold on me / She's living in a dream world / Complications / The sweet love that you give (sure goes a long, long way) / Romeo's tune / Nadine - You cannot win (if you do not play).

Oct 02. (cd) *<KOCCD 8400>* **ANY OLD TIME: Songs Of Jimmie Rodgers** [ ] [–]
- Waiting on a train / My blue-eyed Jane / Why should I be lonely? / Any old time / Ben Dewberry's final run / Miss the Mississippi and you / Standin' on a corner (blue yodel No.9) / Gambling bar-room blues / Desert blues / Train whistle blues / My rough and rowdy ways / My Carolina sunshine girl.

May 04. (cd) *<(KOCCD 9354)>* **JUST LIKE THERE'S NOTHIN' TO IT** [ ] Jun 04 [ ]
- What it is is a dream / Wild as the wind / The change song / The world is full of people / Autumn this year / I just work here / There's everybody else (and then there's you) / Oh, yesterday / I married a girl / The pretend song / I'm in love / About a dream.

Rolling Tide — not issued

2005. (cd) *<none>* **GOOD SOUL FOOD: LIVE AT THE ARK ANN ARBOR, MICHIGAN / JUNE 3, 2004 featuring Mark Stuart** [ ] [–]
- It's been a long time / Real, live love / Rock while I can rock / She's living in a dream world / I just work here / There's everybody else (and then there's you) / Any old time / Autumn this year / It sure was better back then / Starstruck / Wild as the wind (a tribute to Rick Danko) / Honky tonk women / Good planets are hard to find / About a dream / The change song / Lonesome Cowboy Bill's song / Steve Forbert's midsummer night's toast / Goodnight - Goodnight Irene / Romeo's tune / What it is is a dream.

429 — Hypertension

Jun 07. (cd) *<1765> (7257)* **STRANGE NAMES AND NEW SENSATIONS** [ ] Dec 07 [ ]
- Middle age / Strange names (North New Jersey's got 'em) / Simply Spalding Gray / Man, I miss that girl / You're meant for me / I will sing your praise / Something special / My seaside brown-eyed girl / The Baghdad dream / Thirty more years / Around the bend / Romeo's tune.

429 — Freeworld

Mar 09. (cd) *<17731> (5003)* **THE PLACE AND THE TIME** [ ] [ ]
- Blackbird tune / Sing it again, my friend / Stolen identity / Write me a raincheck / Who'll watch the sunset? / Simply must move on / The beast of Ballyhoo (rock show) / Building me a fire / Labor day '08 / The coo coo bird / Hang on again till the sun shines (NYC) / Blue, clear sky.

- (8-10*) compilations -

Apr 93. (cd) Columbia-Legacy; *<ZK 53170>* **THE BEST OF STEVE FORBERT: WHAT KINDA GUY?** [ ] [–]
- What kinda guy? / Romeo's tune / Ya ya (next to me) / Cellophane city / Song for Katrina / Sweet love that you give (sure goes a long, long way) / I'm in love with you / Complications / You cannot win if you do not play / Thinkin' / Goin' down to Laurel / January 23-30, 1978 / Get well soon / Schoolgirl / Samson and Delilah's beauty shop / The oil song / Listen to me / Steve Forbert's midsummer night's toast / It isn't gonna be that way.

- (5-7*) compilations, others, etc.-

Feb 96. (cd) King Biscuit Flower Hour; *<KBFH 141CD>* **IN CONCERT** (live August 14th, 1982 at My Father's Place, Roslyn, NY) [ ] [–]
- Ya ya (next to me) / He's gotta live up to his shoes / Too much monkey business / Goin' down to Laurel / Steve Forbert's midsummer night's toast / It isn't gonna be that way / It takes a whole lotta help (to make it on your own) / Complications / Song for Katrina / Cellophane city / Schoolgirl / Every time that you (walk in the room) / Say goodbye to little Jo / Romeo's tune / The sweet love that you give (sure

goes a long, long way) / I'm an automobile / You gotta go / Love is all around / You cannot win if you do not play.

Nov 97. (cd; as STEVE FORBERT and the Rough Squirrels) Paladin; *<924692>* Demon; *(FIENDCD 936)* **HERE'S YOUR PIZZA** (live in Florida 1987) □ Sep 97 □
- Stop breakin' down blues / What kinda guy? - Rockin' robin / One after 909 / Years ago / Everybody does it in Hawaii / You're darn right / Runaway train of love / All because of you / Song for Katrina / Honky tonker / Samson and Delilah's beauty shop / You cannot win (if you do not play) - Polk salad Annie / Tribute to Ritchie Valens: His was the sound - La bamba / Sweet pea / Backin' up boys / You cannot win 'em all.

Mar 01. (cd) Madacy; *<(M2N 1259)>* **YOUNG GUITAR DAYS** □ Jul 01 □
- It's been a long time / House of cards / Song for the south / Steve Forbert's moon river / Lonesome Cowboy Bill's song / In the jailhouse now, No.1 / Ho, Camille / Witch blues / Poor boy / Planet Earth song / Smoky windows / One short year gone by / Get that vagabond reeling / Leaving blues / I will be there (when your train comes to the station) / I don't know / The weekend / No use running from the blues / Suspicion / Thirty thousand men.

Apr 02. (cd) Disky; *(SI 79219)* **SCHOOLGIRL** (live concert of King Biscuit Flower Hour recordings) ⊟ □
- The sweet love that you give (sure goes a long, long way) / Ya ya (next to me) / Complications / He's gotta live up to his shoes / Romeo's tune / I'm an automobile / Song for Katrina / Steve Forbert's midsummer night's toast / Too much monkey business / It takes a whole lotta help (to make it on your own) / You gotta go / Say goodbye to little Jo / Schoolgirl / You cannot win if you do not play.

Aug 02. (cd) Valley; *<15163>* Southbound; *(SR 251)* **MORE YOUNG GUITAR DAYS** (odds and ends from 1975 to 1982) □ Aug 03 □
- Listen to me (slow version) / Everybody needs a real good friend / Smoky windows (piano version) / Witch blues (alt. take) / You gotta go / No use running from the blues / The oil song (original) / Down by the sally gardens (live) / Young guitar days (demo) / Romeo's tune (live) / Grand Central station (live) / Oh, Camille (live) / Get that vagabond feeling (country version) / It's wrong / Comedy heights.

Oct 03. (cd) Universal; *<(AAB000 12690-2)>* **ROCK WHILE I CAN ROCK: THE GEFFEN YEARS** □ □
- (STREETS OF THIS TOWN tracks) / The only normal people / (THE AMERICAN IN ME tracks).

The FOREMEN

Long before the 2003 film 'A Mighty Wind' and its gentle satire on the protest-folk era, the genre had its own political satirists in The FOREMEN, disguised as suit-and-tie comic folkies on a quest to update the likes of The KINGSTON TRIO, The LIMELITERS and The BROTHERS FOUR.

This 1990s harmony-folk group was led by humorous singer-songwriter Rob Zimmerman on banjo, with fellow southern California musicians and singers Doug Whitney, Andy Corwin and Kenny Rhodes plus several session players. They took the Michael (as in Moore) out of anyone in power, and even the Oliver North case got the FOREMEN treatment in 'Ollie Ollie Off Scot Free' on their major-label debut **FOLK HEROES** (1995) {*7}; see other tracks for further details. What happened to them after **WHAT'S NEXT?** (1996) {*6} is unclear. *MCS*

Rob Zimmerman - vocals, banjo, guitars / **Doug Whitney** - acoustic guitar, trumpet, vocals / **Andy Corwin** - acoustic bass, vocals / **Kenny Rhodes** - bass, vocals

US Reprise / UK not issued

Sep 95. (cd) *<45993-2>* **FOLK HEROES** □ ⊟
- No shoes / Ain't no liberal / Hell froze over today / Don't pity me / Ollie Ollie off scot free / Building for the future / Peace is out / Do the Clinton / Send 'em back / My conservative girlfriend / Russian Limbaugh / Firing the surgeon general / Every man for himself.

Jun 96. (cd) *<46246-2>* **WHAT'S LEFT?** □ ⊟
- Scorched Earth Day / San Diego / What did you do on election day? / California couldn't pay our education / My school prayer / Three strikes and you're out / Uncle Sam's lament / Who needs art? / Black / Hidden agenda / Privateers of the public airwaves / Dear parking offender / Chicago (love song to a Democrat).

- (5-7*) compilations -

Sep 06. (cd) Metaphor; *<none>* **THE BEST OF THE FOREMEN** □ ⊟
- I been singin' / Bug bites [spoken] / Song of many deaths / Workin' on an MBA / Building for the future / A-whalin' / Peace is out / Lazin' in the shade / California couldn't pay our education / Godzilla has a mid-life crisis / Hell froze over today / No shoes / Do the Clinton / Don't pity me / Ain't no liberal / Michael / Lenny Hudbutter intro / Jeeter / Shh - it happens / My home town / The greatest Los Angeles disaster of them all / Firing the surgeon general / The water is wide.

Josephine FOSTER

Born April 19, 1974 in Colorado, singer/songwriter and ukulele player JOSEPHINE FOSTER has been one of the mainstays of neo-psych-folk, although her scope has been varied by her excursions into children's and off-kilter, old-timey folk on the mini-CD-rs **THERE ARE EYES ABOVE** (2000) and **LITTLE LIFE** (2001).

Relocating to Chicago, FOSTER and Andy Bar (an art school graduate from Cleveland) formed The CHILDREN'S HOUR (named for verses by the 19th-century American poet Longfellow), releasing a one-off set, **SOS JFK** (2003) {*7}. A collection of lullabies and ballads ('Adoption Day' was a favourite), it introduced Jo's wistful and tuneful voice to a wider market. Fans of JOANNA NEWSOM, Cat Power or folk legend SHIRLEY COLLINS might well have been pleased.

The **BORN HELLER** (2004) {*7} project with jazz musician Jason Ajemian (on double bass, guitar and vocals) was her next release, another autumnal, avant-garde set featuring FOSTER's sleepy transfiguration of the territory of Tiny Tim or VASHTI BUNYAN. Listen to 'I Want To', 'The Left Garden' and 'Pansies, Will You Ever Grow?'.

Credited to Josephine Foster And The Supposed (with the rhythm section of Brian Goodman, also on lead guitar, and Rusty Peterson), **ALL THE LEAVES ARE GONE** (2004) {*7} captured the essence of 1960s West Coast psych-folk and transported it four decades onwards. 'Well-Heeled Man' is a primeval slide into Grace Slick territory, while the fuzz-guitared 'The Most Loved One' is The Velvet Underground incarnate, and the title track itself might induce some heavy pot-smoking or pill-popping if the listener hasn't done that already. Sadly, the set wears off a little too soon.

Her esoteric solo set **HAZEL EYES, I WILL LEAD YOU** (2005) {*6} was an antiquated, organic, old-timey affair that seemed rather back-porch and rocking-chair beside the garage-folk of her preceding classic. So did **THIS COMING GLADNESS,** (2008) {*7}, but it fared better critically. The weird and bewildering **A WOLF IN SHEEP'S CLOTHING** (2006) {*6} ventures into the world of German Lieder, setting texts (sung in German) adapted from poets including Goethe to music drawn from Brahms, Schumann, and Schubert. Goodman's acid guitar licks save the day.

GRAPHIC AS A STAR (2010) {*6} returned Josephine to safer pastures, although her fixation on the 19th century, this time focused on the poems of Emily Dickinson, left the 26 short fireside-folk tracks a little wanting. On too many occasions promising songs are left abandoned, but the exceptions (such as 'In Falling Timbers Buried', 'Tell As A Marksman' and 'I Could Bring You Jewels') create some kind of funereal singalong fete for dysfunctional DYLANites.

The idiosyncratic Foster took us to hotter climes with her world-music, BAEZ-like set **ANDA JALEO** (2010) {*7}, sung in Spanish and credited to Josephine Foster & The Victor Herrero Band. She's everything but staid. *MCS*

Josephine Foster - vocals, ukulele, acoustic guitar, banjo, harp, etc

US self-rel. / UK not issued

2000. (m-cd-r) *<none>* **THERE ARE EYES ABOVE** ⊟ ⊟
- 100 songs I sing / Emily told me / Teeter totter / Little life / I am a guest in here / Robber song / Hey Matthew / These are eyes above / Codcake / Yippee I'm leaving / Two not one.

2001. (m-cd-r) *<none>* **LITTLE LIFE** ⊟ ⊟
- Shay shay / Stones in my heavy bag / Charles in the park / Francie's song / Run Maroona / Three day days / Tom Peck, neighbor friend / Birdo / Warsong / Hell's bells are ringing / Little life. *<re-iss. Aug 98 on My Kung Fu; 35>*

The CHILDREN'S HOUR

Josephine Foster with **Andy Bar** - guitar

Minty Fresh / Rough Trade

2002. (cd-ep) *<mf 47>* THE CHILDREN'S HOUR □ ⊟
- Wyoming / The lumberjack song / Mary / Going home.

May 03. (cd) *<mf 50>* (RTRADECD 104) **SOS JFK** □ Sep 03 □
- Little boy / Mary / Wyoming / Kindness of strangers / Anna / The lumberjack song / Adoption day / Nearby room / Lost love / Special king / SOS JFK / The Chinese song / Going home.

—— split...

BORN HELLER

Josephine - vocals, ukulele, guitar / **Jason Ajemian** - vocals, double bass, guitar

Locust Locust

Apr 04. (cd) <*(LOCUST 51CD)*> **BORN HELLER**
- I want to / No more lamps in the morning / Mountain song / Good times / I am a guest in here / Lulu fellows / First kiss / The left garden / Pansies, will you ever grow? / Lullaby No.5 / Big sky No.4. <*lp-iss. 2007 on Bo' Weavil; ???*>

JOSEPHINE FOSTER

Josephine - vocals, classical guitar, tambourine / with **Brian Goodman** - vocals, guitar, bass / **Rusty Peterson** - drums

Locust Locust

Oct 04. (cd; as JOSEPHINE FOSTER AND THE SUPPOSED) <*(LOCUST 62CD)*> **ALL THE LEAVES ARE GONE**
- Well-heeled men / The most loved one / All the leaves are gone / Nana / Deathknell / Silly song / Jailbird (hero of the sorrow) / Worried and sorry / Who will feel bitter at the days end? / John Ave. seen from the gray train / Don't wait, Mary Jane / (You are worth) A million dollars.

—— In late 2004/early '05, she self-released a mini 'LIVE' set (recorded at the Andy Warhol Theater) and an EP, 'A DIADEM'.

Apr 05. (cd) <*(LOCUST 68CD)*> **HAZEL EYES, I WILL LEAD YOU** Sep 05
- The siren's admonition / Hazel eyes, I will lead you / By the shape of your pearls / Stones throw from heaven / Where there are trees / The golden wooden tone / There are eyes above / Celebrant's song / Good news / Trees lay by / The pruner's pair / Crackerjack fool / The way is sweetly mown / Hominy grits.

—— In Oct 2005, Australian label Art School Dropout issued the 7" EP 'Joey Will Come If You Invite Her' *(ASD 011)*.

Apr 06. (cd) <*(LOCUST 79CD)*> **A WOLF IN SHEEP'S CLOTHING** May 06
- An die musik / Der konig in Thule / Verschwiegene liebe / Die schwestern / Wehmut / Auf einer burg / Nahe des geliebten.

—— In 2007 she self-released three sets, 'WHAT IS IT THAT EVER WAS?', 'LIVE IN CAMBRIDGE' (mini) and 'UNTITLED' (with The Cherry Blossoms).

Bo' Weavil Bo' Weavil

Jul 08. (cd/lp) <*(WEAVIL 31 CD/LP)*> **THIS COMING GLADNESS**
- The garden of earthly delights / The lap of your lust / Lullaby to all / I love you and the springtime blues / All I wanted was the moon / Waltz of green / Sim nao / Second sight / A thimbleful of milk / Indelible rainbows.

Fire Fire

Jan 10. (cd/lp) <*(FIRE CD/LP 136)*> **GRAPHIC AS A STAR** Nov 09
- Trust in the unexpected / How happy is the little stone / She sweeps with many-colored brooms / Ah, Teneriffe! / Who is the east? / They called me to the window / This is the land the sunset washes / Like mighty footlights / Exultation is the going / In falling timbers buried / With thee in the desert / I see thee better in the dark / Your thoughts don't have words every day / My life had stood a loaded gun / Eden is that old-fashioned house / Beauty crowds me till I die / I could bring you jewels / Wild nights - wild nights! / Only a shrine, but mine / Tho' my destiny be fustian / What shall I do - it whimpers so / Heart! We will forget him / Strong draughts of their refreshing minds / Tell as a marksman / The spider holds a silver ball / Whoever disenchants / Touch lightly nature's sweet guitar.

Oct 10. (cd/lp; by JOSEPHINE FOSTER & THE VICTOR HERRERO BAND) <*(FIRE CD/LP 150)*> **ANDA JALEO** Sep 10
- Los cuatro muleros / Los pelegrinitos / Lalas Morillas de Jaen / Anda Jaleo / Las tres hojas / Los mozos de Monlean / Sevillanas del Siglo XVIII / Los reyes de la Baraja / El café de Chinitas / Zorongo / Nana de Sevilla.

Jeffrey FOUCAULT

Born into a musical family in Janesville, Wisconsin in January 1976, singer and songwriter JEFFREY FOUCAULT is one of the leading lights of the folk/country crossover scene. Many will know of his equally talented spouse, KRIS DELMHORST; they had a daughter, Hazel, in June 2008.

Armed with a good knowledge of songs by DYLAN (particularly 'Highway 61 Revisited'), TOWNES VAN ZANDT, Springsteen and JOHN PRINE, Jeffrey followed his musical vocation after taking a history degree at Madison University, and a songwriting hibernation in the San Bernardino mountains gave him the inspiration to get into a recording studio.

The self-financed and self-produced **MILES FROM THE LIGHTNING** (2001) {*6} was a mighty fine debut, although it was slightly overshadowed by his part in the supergroup album (and later touring) project **REDBIRD** (2003) {*7}, alongside DELMHORST, PETER MULVEY and co-producer David Goodrich. Interesting covers included GREG BROWN's 'Ships', DYLAN's 'Buckets Of Rain', R.E.M.'s 'You Are The Everything', Willie Nelson's 'I Gotta Get Drunk' and Tom Waits's 'Hold On'. Several years on, REDBIRD delivered **LIVE AT THE CAFÉ CARPE...** (2011) {*6}, recorded at local gigs a few years before. Effective covers this time around featured songs by MISSISSIPPI JOHN HURT, Merle Haggard, NEIL YOUNG, Duke Ellington and The Faces.

STRIPPING CANE (2004) {*7} (featuring John Fogerty's 'Lodi'), **GHOST REPEATER** (2006) {*6} and the JOHN PRINE tribute **SHOOT THE MOON RIGHT BETWEEN THE EYES** (2009) {*6} were the epitome of cool, never losing that rootsy, sharp-edged dustbowl-country appeal while keeping his lyrics focused on subjects introspective and close to his heart. His one-off 2010 collaboration with MARK ERELLI, 'Seven Curses', shared the same qualities. Taking a slight detour into bona-fide country, his fifth solo album, **HORSE LATITUDES** (2011) {*6}, was another sombre and moody bout of melancholy Americana. *MCS*

Jeffrey Foucault - vocals, acoustic guitar, banjo

US own label UK not issued

Jul 01. (cd) <*none*> **MILES FROM THE LIGHTNING** –
- Ballad of Cooper junction (a journeyman's lament) / Dove and the waterline / Walking at dusk (the liberty bell) / Thistledown tears / Californ-i-a / Highway and the moon / Battle hymn (of the college dropout farmhand) / Crossing Mississippi / Secretariat / Sunrise in the rearview / Street light halos / Buckshot moon / I'm alright / Miles from the lightning (a song for Townes Van Zandt). <*(re+UK-iss. Jun 04/Feb 03 on Acoustic Roots; AR 003)*>

—— next feat. KRIS DELMHORST, PETER MULVEY and David Goodrich

Nov 03. (cd; by REDBIRD) <*none*> **REDBIRD** –
- Ships / Moonglow / Patience / Buckets of rain / The whole world round / Ithaca / Lovely as the day is long / Moonshiner / Redbird waltz / Lullaby 101 / I gotta get drunk / Lighthouse light / You are the everything / Down by the sally gardens / Redbird / Drunk lullaby / Hold on. <*(re-iss. Feb 05 on Signature Sounds; SIG 1291)*>

Signature Sounds Signature Sounds

Aug 04. (cd) <*(SIG 1286)*> **STRIPPING CANE** Sep 04
- Cross of flowers / Mayfly / Doubletree / Stripping cane / The bluest blade / Pearl handled pistol / Northbound 35 / 4 & 20 blues / Don't look for me / Tropic of Cancer / Lodi / Every new leaf over.

May 06. (cd) <*(SIG 1298)*> **GHOST REPEATER**
- Ghost repeater / Americans in corduroys / I dream an old lover / One for sorrow / Train to Jackson / One part love / Wild waste and welter / City flower / Tall grass on old Virginny / Mesa, Arizona / Appeline.

Feb 09. (cd) <*(SIG 2018)*> **SHOOT THE MOON RIGHT BETWEEN THE EYES: JEFFREY FOUCAULT SINGS THE SONGS OF JOHN PRINE** Mar 09
- The late John Garfield blues / Billy the bum / He was in heaven before he died / Unwed fathers / Hello in there / One red rose / Speed of the sound of loneliness / Far from me / Daddy's little pumpkin / Mexican home / Storm windows / That's the way that the world goes 'round / Clocks and spoons.

—— In 2010, FOUCAULT and MARK ERELLI released the collaborative 'Seven Curses' set.

Dec 10. (cd) <*none*> **COLD SATELLITE** – web –
- Deserter's information center / Cold satellite / Nothing I wouldn't do (except stay) / Voices talking / Geese fly by / Twice I left her / Standing ovation / Call off the dogs / Late season (reprise) / There I go / Appeline / In our own country.

(above issued on BlueBlade)

Jan 11. (cd; as REDBIRD) <*(SIG 2033)*> **LIVE AT THE CAFÉ CARPE: FORT ATKINSON, WISCONSIN, DECEMBER 2008 & 2009** [live]
- I'm beginning to see the light / Strangers / What made Milwaukee famous (has made a loser out of me) / Come all ye fair and tender ladies / For the turnstiles / Ships / Snowed in / Let the mermaids flirt with me / Silver wings / Ooh la la / Phonebooth of love / Stewart's coat / Sad, sad, sad / 4 & 20 blues.

May 11. (cd) <*(SIG 2037)*> **HORSE LATITUDES**
- Horse latitudes / Pretty girl in a small town / Starlight and static / Heart to the husk / Last night I dreamed of television / Goners most / Everybody's famous / Idaho / Passerines / Tea and tobacco.

FOUR BITCHIN' BABES

Formed in 1990 by MEGON McDONOUGH, CHRISTINE LAVIN, SALLY FINGERETT and PATTY LARKIN, the folk-revue quartet released their live debut **BUY ME BRING ME TAKE ME: DON'T MESS MY HAIR!!! - LIFE ACCORDING TO...** {*7} in 1991. The first in a series of such frivolities, it was followed by **...VOL.2** (1993) {*5}, which introduced pianist Julie Gold (composer of the standard 'From A Distance', featured on this album) in place of LARKIN.

Debi Smith, satirical singer/songwriter Camille West and singer Suzzy Roche (of The ROCHES) have also played their parts in subsequent FOUR BITCHIN' BABES albums, but the essential ingredients are still sole-original

Sally and their cosmopolitan country-folk approach. Of several later sets for Shanachie, **GABBY ROAD** (1997) {*6}, **BEYOND BITCHIN'** (2000) {*6} and **SOME ASSEMBLY REQUIRED** (2002) {*6} are all worthwhile. *MCS*

Megon McDonough - vocals, acoustic guitar / **Christine Lavin** - vocals, acoustic guitar / **Patty Larkin** - vocals, acoustic guitar / **Sally Fingerett** - vocals, acoustic guitar / + session people/band

US Philo — UK Philo

Sep 91. (cd/c) *<(CD-/C-PH 1140)>* **BUY ME BRING ME TAKE ME: DON'T MESS MY HAIR!!! - LIFE ACCORDING TO FOUR BITCHIN' BABES** [live at the Birchmere in Alexandria, Virginia on August 14/15, 1990] ☐ Nov 91 ☐
- (Dick Cerri introduction) / Prisoners of their hairdos / Wake up and dream / Not bad for a broad / Ladies lunch / Good thing he can't read my mind / (Megon on 'co-dependency' and Wuthering Heights) / Painless love / Dave's holiday / Home is where the heart is / (Christine reads mailing list cards) / (Sally explains game show) / She moved through the fair / (Megon draws the next audience suggestion) / Junk food / (Sally draws the next audience suggestion) / Sensitive new age guys / But still he loved her so (the ballad of Henry and Esther) / I'm fine / (Meg channels Patty) / Every little thing / These boots are made for walkin'.

—— **Julie Gold** - vocals, piano; repl. LARKIN who continued solo

Mar 93. (cd/c) *<(CD-/C-PH 1150)>* **BUY ME BRING ME TAKE ME: DON'T MESS MY HAIR - LIFE ACCORDING TO FOUR BITCHIN' BABES Volume 2** ☐ May 93 ☐
- Oh great spirit / Bald headed men / Save me a seat (homeward bound) / From a distance / Sealed with a kiss / Butter / Graceful man / Try love / Take me out to eat / As close to flying / (Fun to be) Perfect / The choice / Good night, New York. *(+ hidden excerpt)*

—— **Debi Smith** - vocals, multi; repl. Gold

Shanachie — Shanachie

Oct 95. (cd) *<(SHAN 8018)>* **FAX IT! CHARGE IT! DON'T ASK ME WHAT'S FOR DINNER!** ☐ ☐
- My mother's hands / Stars / TV talk / Great big bug / Shadow / Microwave life / She won't be walkin' / Energy vampires / Dreams of deep water / Muzak / Cover / What was I thinking? / A lullaby.

—— **Camille West** - vocals, guitar; repl. CHRISTINE LAVIN who continued solo

Oct 97. (cd) *<(SHANCD 8028)>* **GABBY ROAD** [live at Birchmere] ☐ Nov 97 ☐
- (stage intro, Four Bitchin' Babes) / Dyslexic / My father / Cyberspace / When I wake up from this night / The nervous wreck of Edna Fitzgerald / Intertwined / (game show explanation) / (Sally draws - Megon plays) / Zensong / (Debi draws - Sally plays) / Breakfast dishes / (Sally draws - Debi plays) / Chevy Impala / Crazy / Wild berries / (Camille takes a poll) / L.A.F.F. (Ladies Against Fanny Floss) / These boots are made for the tap dancing wild thing / Lullaby.

May 00. (cd) *<(SHANCD 8035)>* **BEYOND BITCHIN': MORE LIFE ACCORDING TO FOUR BITCHIN' BABES** ☐ ☐
- Little stars / Lovely mistake / The body is a car / Toe to toe with the HMO / My kinda man / This town's all right / Beautiful fool / Viagra in the waters / Italy and France / I don't wanna know / If I were brave / Hold on to my love.

—— **Suzzy Roche** - vocals, acoustic guitar (of The ROCHES) repl. McDonough

Sep 02. (cd) *<(SHANCD 8039)>* **SOME ASSEMBLY REQUIRED** ☐ ☐
- Changing / Don't mess with me (I'm somebody's mother) / Bob Dylan's poetry / New age swing / I'll be the one / The doctor / These ruby shoes / I don't think I'm gonna like it / Spear carrier: a life in the theater / True love's gonna come along / He believed in me / Nobody beats my Bob.

—— as The FOUR BITCHIN' BABES: **Sally** + **Debi** recruited **Deirdre Flint** + **Nancy Moran**

Hen & Haw — not issued

Apr 06. (cd) *<none>* **HORMONAL IMBALANCE! A Mood Swinging Musical Revue** ☐ ⊟
- Oh no / Walk the walk / Cheerleader / Hot flash / Honestly! / Pass it on / The boob fairy / One easy day / Just ask your doctor / Unconditional love / Taxidermal therapy / Faces on my wall / Viagra in the waters / (the Babes suspect foul play) / Someone's inner diva invades our CD!!

Sep 09. (cd) *<none>* **DIVA NATION** ☐ ⊟
- Babesland / Elastic waistbands / Chocolate / American woman / The introvert song / A happy song / These are the things / Arm candy / New shoes - New tools / (No such thing as) Girls like that / Metric is coming / Long lonesome road / Viva la diva / Babesland [fun version].

David FRANCEY

Born in Kilmarnock, Ayrshire in 1954, Scottish-Canadian immigrant and folk singer/songwriter DAVID FRANCEY has, remarkably, maintained his sharp Scots accent as well as his Scots wit despite having lived in and around Toronto since he moved there with his family at the age of 12.

After years of day jobs and night-time performances (with spots at many festivals), David finally delivered his rootsy folk debut set, **TORN SCREEN DOOR** (1999) {*6}, a record that reflected his Caledonian-Canadian working-class roots in tracks like 'Hard Steel Mill', 'Gypsy Boys' and 'Working Poor'.

FAR END OF SUMMER (2001) {*7} and **SKATING RINK** (2003) {*7} both won Juno Awards in the 'Best Roots and Traditional Album' category, while his country collaboration **THE WAKING HOUR** (2004) {*6}, alongside the genre's next-big-things Kieran Kane, Kevin Welch and Fats Kaplin, also came close. The latter set was as political as usual, taking on the powers that be with ballads such as 'Fourth Of July' (addressing post-9/11 America) and 'Wishing Well' (about the execution of US-born terrorist Timothy McVeigh).

RIGHT OF PASSAGE (2007) {*7}, **SEAWAY** (2009) {*6} (with Mike Ford of MOXY FRUVOUS) and the countrified **LATE EDITION** (2011) {*6} have all maintained his high profile north of the Great Lakes, but David, who now lives in Elphin, Ontario with his wife Beth Girdler and their three children, surely deserves more reward and recognition in his homeland. *MCS*

David Francey - vocals, acoustic guitar / (+ a few session people)

Can/US Laker — UK not issued

1999. (cd) *<1001>* **TORN SCREEN DOOR** ⊟ Canada ⊟
- Borderline / Hard steel mill / Sorrows of the sailor / Blue water / Saints and sinners / Sumach streech / Wind in the wires / Gypsy boys / Red-winged blackbird / Working poor / St Johns train / Gypsy boys reprise / Torn screen door / Long way home.

2001. (cd) *<1002>* **FAR END OF SUMMER** ⊟ Canada ⊟
- Paper boy / Mill towns / Banks of the seaway / Hammers / Brakeman's daughter / Flowers of Saskatchewan / Saturday night / Highway / A thousand miles / Lucky man / Highwire / February morning drive / Green fields / Things they do / Far end of summer.

Jan 03. (cd) *<1003>* **SKATING RINK** ⊟ Canada ⊟
- Skating rink / Broken glass / Exit / Come rain or come shine / Midway / Belgrade train / Streets of Calgary / Evening news / Grim cathedral / Annie's house / Valley's edge / Nearly midnight / A winter song.

Nov 04. (cd) *<1004>* **THE WAKING HOUR** ⊟ Canada ⊟
- The waking hour / Highway 95 / Ankle tattoo / Morning train / Wishing well / Ashtabula / Tonight in my dreams / Over you / Fourth of July / Wanna be loved / Badlands / Sunday morning / Gone. *<US-iss. Feb 05 on Red House; RHRCD 182>*

Jan 06. (cd) *<1005>* **THE FIRST SET: LIVE FROM FOLK ALLEY** [live] ⊟ Canada ⊟
- (intro by Jim Blum) / (intro to...) / Paper boy / (intro to...) / The waking hour / (intro to...) / Ashtabula / (intro to...) / Broken glass / (intro to...) / Tonight in my dreams / (intro to...) Fourth of July / (intro to...) / Torn screen door / (intro to...) / Morning train / (intro to...) / Lucky man.

Nov 06. (cd) *<1006>* **CAROLS FOR A CHRISTMAS EVE** [festive] ⊟ Canada ⊟
- Good Christian men rejoice / O come all ye faithful / Good King Wenceslas / Hark the herald angels sing / Silent night / God rest ye merry gentlemen / Angels we have heard on high / The first noel / I saw three ships / O little town of Bethlehem / We three kings / The holly and the ivy / Away in a manger / Joy to the world.

Nov 07. (cd) *<1007>* **RIGHT OF PASSAGE** ⊟ Canada ⊟
- Leaving Edmonton / Ballad of Bowser MacRae / Kansas / A conversation / Waves / Ferry to Cortez / New Jerusalem / The gate / Stone town / Promised land / Their wedding day / Under the Portland weather / All lights burning bright.

Dec 09. (cd; by DAVID FRANCEY and MIKE FORD) *<1008>* **SEAWAY** ⊟ Canada ⊟
- Banks of the seaway / Eastern gap / The chief engineer / The seaway / The unloading / Climbing up to the Soo / Dustless road to the happy land / The parting / There's no rush / Canal / The ballad of Bowser Macrae / When you're the skip / Ashtabula / 21st century Great Lake navigators / The bottom of the Great Lakes / All lights burning bright.

Out — not issued

May 11. (cd) *<AUD 737413014>* **LATE EDITION** ⊟ Canada ⊟
- Yesterday's news / Pretty jackals / Solitary wave / When I'm not thinking about you / Wonder / Blue heart of Texas / Just the same / Borderlands / High wall / I live in fear / Long brown hair / Grateful.

Ruthann FRIEDMAN

Sounding rather like JONI MITCHELL or Carole King before the Laurel Canyon ladies got into their big yellow taxis and tapestries, singer/songwriter RUTHANN FRIEDMAN was a folky bohemian of the middle-to-late 1960s who incidentally wrote 'Windy' for bubblegum-pop hitmakers The Association in 1967. Her own long-lost version (on her CD compilation **HURRIED LIFE**) was just brilliant, while her take on Tandyn Almer's 'Little Girl Lost And Found' (one of her few covers) was a favourite at the time.

Born in the Bronx, New York City on July 6, 1944, Ruthann was in The Garden Club around the same time, with Tom Shipley (of BREWER & SHIPLEY), and in Petrus alongside Peter Kaukonen (of Black Kangaroo, and brother to Hot Tuna's Jorma Kaukonen) before she opted for an all too brief solo career with **CONSTANT COMPANION** (1970) {*6}, her only official LP release, for Reprise.

Formerly she had kept company with West Coast luminaries Van Dyke Parks, Janis Joplin and David Crosby among others, and those halcyon hippie days were trips she would write about on that album; check out 'Piper's Call', 'Ringing Bell' and 'Look Up To The Sun'. Ruthann disappeared from the music scene, marrying Jeffrey Carlisle in the late 1970s, and after more than 30 years she is still with him and has two daughters, Sandy and Lisabeth. Her rediscovery was down to DEVENDRA BANHART and Nat Russell, who brought her recordings to the attention of Water Records. *MCS*

Ruthann Friedman - vocals, acoustic guitar

US Reprise / UK not issued

1970. (lp) <*RS 6363*> **CONSTANT COMPANION**
- Topsy-turvy moon / Piper's call / Fairy prince rainbow man / Too late to be mourning / Ringing bells / Looking back over your shoulder / People / Morning becomes you / Peaceable kingdom / No time / Danny / Look up to the sun. <*(cd-iss. Mar 06 on Water+=; WATER 167)*> - Carry on (glittering dancer).

—— she continued to write until 1971, and thereafter designed and marketed the "Easy Writer" portable travelling stationery kit

- (5-7*) compilations, others, etc.-

Oct 06. (cd) Water; <*(WATER 185)*> **HURRIED LIFE: LOST RECORDINGS 1965–1971**
- Hurried life / That's all right / To treat a friend / Sky is moving south / Looking glass / Silver bird / Between the lines / I'm askin' / Windy / Typical Sunday / Southern comfortable / Alone at last / Boy took a ticket / Method madness / Little girl lost and found.

FRONTIER RUCKUS

Formed in East Lansing, Michigan, FRONTIER RUCKUS are an outfit balancing between alt-country, bluegrass and neo-folk. Led by the tremulous-voiced singer/songwriter and multi-instrumentalist Matthew Milla, with a line-up variously including David Winston Jones, Zachory Nichols, Eli Eisman, Ryan "Smalls" Etzcorn and Anna Burch, the Ruckus played banjo, brass and broadsheets - imagine NEIL YOUNG backed by The BAND.

Off the mark in 2007 with a fine six-song EP/mini-set, 'I Am The Water You Are Pumping', the young band found their way on to the roster of Ann Arbor-based label Quite Scientific for debut album **THE ORION SONGBOOK** (2008) {*8}. Named Best Folk Group by the Real Detroit Weekly and winners of Best Alt-Country Album by Hear/Say, their sound caused conflict and disarray among critics uncertain of the thin lines they were crossing. 'Dark Autumn Hour', 'The Back-Lot World' and 'Bethlehem' (all demonstrating great lyrical finesse) were worthy of the price on their own, the band's back-porch approach paying off in spades. The vinyl version included an extra 12" EP, 'Way Upstate And The Crippled Summer, Pt.1'.

North Carolina imprint Ramseur took over for their second set, **DEADMALLS AND NIGHTFALLS** (2010) {*7}, which was recorded without Burch (Eisman had left before the first album). Spearheaded by 'Nerves Of The Nightmind', and a little more countrified than before, the new album still left fans in awe of their post-millennial Americana. *MCS*

Matthew Milla - vocals, guitar, pedal steel, harmonica, piano, organ / **David Winston Jones** - banjo, elbow, vocals / **Zachory Nichols** - trumpet, musical saw, melodica / **Eli Eisman** - bass / **Ryan "Smalls" Etzcorn** - drum kit, percussion / **Anna Burch** - vocals, harmonium, piano

US Frontier Ruckus / UK not issued

Jan 07. (cd-ep) <*none*> I AM THE WATER YOU ARE PUMPING
- The blood / Dark autumn hour / The back-lot world / Rosemont / June is our mother's name / Adirondack Amish holler.

—— now without Eisman

Quite Scientific / Quite Scientific

Nov 08. (cd/d-lp) <*(QSR-010)*> **THE ORION SONGBOOK**
- Animals need animals / The latter days / What you are / Dark autumn hour / Mount Marcy / The blood / Bethlehem / Foggy lilac windows / Orion town 2 / The back-lot world / Rosemont / Orion town 3 / Adirondack Amish holler / The deep-yard dream. <*d-lp+=*> - WAY UPSTATE AND THE CRIPPLED SUMMER, PT.1:- One-story-carport-houses / The great laketown / Ann Arbortown / Mohawk, New York / Driving home, Christmas eve / Abigail.

—— on tour **Brian Barnes** - bass, vocals; repl. Burch + John Krohn

Ramseur / Ramseur

Jul 10. (cd) <*(RR 3728)*> **DEADMALLS AND NIGHTFALLS**
- Nerves of the nightmind / Ontario / Springterror / Ringbearer / Silverfishes / The upper room / Does me in / The tower / Pontiac, the nightbrink / How could I abandon? / I do need saving / Pour your nighteyes.

Annie GALLUP

One of contemporary folk's leading lights, singer-songwriter ANNIE GALLUP makes easy-listening balladry into an art form that is described as 'spoke-folk'. Her silky-smooth tones have graced a raft of albums since her humble self-financed beginnings on **CAUSE AND EFFECT** (1994) {*7}. Check out 'Fight The Devil', 'Dancing With A Stranger' and the sax-laden, JONI MITCHELLish 'For Money'.

Born in Ann Arbor, Michigan, but raised in Seattle, Washington, Annie was inspired by the acoustic guitar techniques of folk-blues legends MISSISSIPPI JOHN HURT, DAVE VAN RONK and DOC WATSON, and the likes of Paul Simon, SUZANNE VEGA and Joni became her new-found heroes when she began her career at various coffee-houses and bars circa 1988/89.

Featuring her sort-of-signature tune 'The Girl With The Flyaway Hair', **BACKBONE** (1996) {*7} was her first 'folk-rap' effort for 1-800-Prime. **COURAGE MY LOVE** (1998) {*7}, the live and unaccompanied **STEADY STEADY YES** (1999) {*6} and **SWERVE** (2001) {*7} were all well promoted and worthy of the many awards she won, including the Kerrville New Folk prize.

Following a move to Santa Barbara, California in the mid-2000s, there was a lull in proceedings for the beat poet, but her well-crafted song cycle **PEARL STREET** (2005) {*7} - premiered in Ann Arbor as a one-woman show a few years before - was a splendid return. Oblique characters were often at the heart of her songs (authors Alice Munro, Margaret Atwood, Grace Paley and Stephen Dobyns were favourites), and this quirky human interest also informed her follow-up and first for Waterbug, **HALF OF MY CRIME** (2006) {*6}. **WEATHER** (2010) {*6} was another fine compositional creation, while her duo Hat Check Girl (with Peter Gallway) released their non-folk set 'Tenderness' around the same time. *MCS*

Annie Gallup - vocals, acoustic guitar

US: Flyaway Hair — UK: not issued

1994. (cd) *<none>* **CAUSE AND EFFECT**
- Fight the Devil / For money / Grandma's best china / Dancing with a stranger / You can run / So easy / As if you were there / All those fools / Steak and eggs for breakfast / There are rules / About freedom / If I loved you. *<re-iss. Sep 96 on 1-800 Prime cd/c; PCD 28 D/C>*

US: 1-800-Prime — UK: not issued

May 96. (cd/c) *<PCD 020 D/C>* **BACKBONE**
- Max / John Llewellyn / Fight the Devil / Camera / The girl with the flyaway hair / Kiss me in Rapid City / Man with a broken wing / Words / The truth about disguise / April twenty-second Somerville, Massachusetts / Real money / Easter Sunday.

Mar 98. (cd/c) *<PCD 38>* **COURAGE MY LOVE**
- It's dangerous Charlie / Oh Tom, you didn't mean that / Anything is possible / Blue dress / 100 miles from music city / A million ways / All the girls / Saint Fido / Flood / Hard work / Cowboy / Circle / Flight / Sweet good nature / Anything is possible (reprise).

Apr 99. (cd/c) *<PCD 63>* **STEADY STEADY YES**
- Howling in the distance / Three photographs / Don't go to sleep / James / Steady steady yes / Six-stone angel / If I loved you / Tiger / Jack McGraw / Hero / Circle / Anything is possible / It was you in the morning.

Apr 01. (cd) *<PCD 75>* **SWERVE**
- Money / True / What I know / Great distance / One two / My mother's daughter / Three Bills / Georgia O'Keeffe / Red hair / Absecon Bay / The sky / The end.

US: Fifty Fifty — UK: not issued

Apr 05. (cd) *<104>* **PEARL STREET**
- Down the other side / Thicker than water / Pearl street / Skinny arms / Grace / Jack / Betsi went to Jersey / Lori's long legs / I think about Richard / Tulsa / Down the other side (reprise). *[hidden tracks +=]* - [Annie interviews Annie] / The synopsis.

US: Waterbug — UK: Waterbug

Mar 06. (cd) *<WBG 70>* **HALF OF MY CRIME**
- 14 days of rain / 1917 / 3 brothers / Avalon / The contender / Third person / I rode the train / Enough / Sugar / Field of flowers / Away from the lights / Almost forgive / Faithful / Free.

Oct 10. (cd) *<(WBG 93)>* **WEATHER**
- Bird / My war / Hitchcock's thrillers / Sixty eight / All night rain / Late / Regrets / Unmapped world / India / Hound / Blacktop boardwalk / Ground zero, written in chalk.

GANDALF THE GREY

Due to its positively psychedelic bent, the studio project of singer/songwriter Chris Wilson (born at Glen Cove, Long Island) was overlooked in the first volume of this Discography. Starting out in Greenwich Village at a time when the folk scene seemed to be coming to a close or moving into other genres, Chris recorded many demos (later released as 'The Tin Angel' in 2004) at the Charles Dickens studios in New York in 1968.

Following on from his time as frontman of the Columbia act The Other Half, who worked alongside Hendrix, Springsteen and comedian/actor/promoter Bill Cosby, Chris delved into the fantasy world of J.R.R. Tolkien for inspiration and came up with GANDALF THE GREY. Recorded in his bedroom, **THE GREY WIZARD AM I** (1972) {*6} was a post-psychedelic set fusing prog and folk-rock, highlighted by the title track and 'From The Grey Havens'. Worth around $1000 mint, it earned a UK release in 1986, which is already worth a three-figure sum and could get much more expensive as the US original is still rocketing.

Wilson went into TV production work and came up with the first-ever video single in 1982; his subsequent releases are available on his wizardtv.com site. *MCS*

Chris Wilson - vocals, guitar / + **Legolas The Elf** - guitar

US: Grey Wizard — UK: not issued

1972. (lp) *<S-7>* **THE GREY WIZARD AM I**
- The grey wizard am I / My elven home / From the grey havens / Here on Eighth Street / Go and see / The Christmas song / Old town church / The home coming (the sun is down) / I don't know why the people / Mr Joe's / Sunshine down the line. *(UK-iss. 1986 on Heyoka; HEY 207) <re-iss. 2003 on Gear Fab+=; GF 202> <(cd-iss. Mar 07 +=; <cstyle:>GF 208)>* - The future belongs to the children / A young girl just died / Before tomorrow / The shadow of tomorrow / An elven song of love.

- (5-7*) compilations, others, etc.-

Dec 04. (cd) Gear Fab; *<GF 212>* **THE TIN ANGEL** [demos from 1968]
- Tin angel (part 1) / Carnival / (Yesterday comes) Before tomorrow / This is how I think of you / I wonder where they're going / What's the excuse / The sun is down / Down the stairs / Tin angel / (Yesterday comes) Before tomorrow / The shadow of tomorrow / This is how I think of you / What's the excuse (instrumental) / The shadow of tomorrow / Lavender girl / Go and see / See beyond the sea / Pocket full of dreams / Let the god of peace / I've heard it said / Beauty of the sky. *(UK-iss. Jan 10; same as US)*

2008. (cd) Grey Wizard; *<003>* **CONVERSATIONS WITH MOM (AND DAD)** [recorded November 19, 1977] — own
- Memories of the wind (Dapper's tune) / My America (Disney dreams) / Louisiana roll / True tonight / Seems that I have found / Stumble under / No free transfers / Long city nights / Leaves / (They're) Everywhere I go / Only young / The good you find in a man / Never done before / 911 - 'Take a look around' / When I was young [acoustic] / Stumble under [acoustic] / Love song / [untitled].

Laura GIBSON

Born and raised in Coquille, Oregon around the late 1970s, Portland resident LAURA GIBSON has established herself as leading the way in the country-tinged sadcore-folk scene; 1960s singer KAREN DALTON is probably her closest equivalent. Delicate and unassuming, her autumnal vocal manner and organic, close-mic'd guitar finger-picking have been recorded on a couple of solo sets for the independent Hush imprint (not including her self-financed CD-r 'Amends' of 2004).

Debut album proper **IF YOU COME GREET ME** (2007) {*6} featured the work of Norfolk & Western alumni Rachel Blumberg (drums and vibes, ex-DECEMBERISTS), Peter Broderick (strings, musical saw), Cory Gray (piano, trumpet) and co-producer Adam Selzer (electric guitar, samples). A covers EP featured two traditional songs plus Blind Lemon Jefferson's 'One Dime Blues', ELIZABETH COTTEN's 'Freight Train', Mance Lipscomb's 'One Thin Dime' and FURRY LEWIS's `Dryland Blues'.

Working alongside LAURA VEIRS's producer Tucker Martine (also her drummer), her second album, **BEASTS OF SEASONS** (2009) {*6} gave off an air of picking flowers from a grave, even if you didn't know that she apparently wrote some tracks overlooking a cemetery. 'Come By Storm', the seven-minute 'Shadows On Parade' and 'Funeral Song' were sung at a monotone JOANNA NEWSOM/slow-Bjork pace - but that's no criticism. Local experimental boffin Ethan Rose came in to help GIBSON on her dual mini-set **BRIDGE CARDS** (2010). *MCS*

Laura Gibson - vocals, acoustic guitar

US self-rel. — UK not issued

2004. (cd-r) <*none*> AMENDS
- Soul / Roll / Amends / In a constant rain / The longest day / O love.

Hush — Hush

Mar 07. (cd) <*(HUSH 064)*> **IF YOU COME GREET ME** — Nov 06
- This is not the end / Hand in pockets / Nightwatch / Broken bottle / Wintering / Small town parade / Country, country / Certainty / The longest day. *(re-iss. May 08 on Acuarela; 001)*

—— now w/ **Jason Leonard** - multi / **Mr Fantastic** (also known as M. Ward) - saw player

Mar 08. (ltd-tour;cd-ep) <*HUSH 079*> SIX WHITE HORSES: BLUES AND TRADITIONALS VOL.1
- All the pretty horses / One dime blues / Freight train / One thin dime / Black is the color of my true love's hair / Dryland blues.

Feb 09. (cd) <*HUSH 086*> **BEASTS OF SEASONS**
- Shadows on parade / Come by storm / Spirited / Postures bent / Funeral song / Where have all your good words gone? / Sleeper / Sweet deception / Glory. *<lp-iss. 2009 on Jealous Butcher; 77>*

Holocene — not issued

Feb 10. (m-cd; by LAURA GIBSON & ETHAN ROSE) <*010*> **BRIDGE CARDS**
- Introduction / Old waters / Younger / Leaving, believing / Sun / Boreas borealis / Glocken / O frailty.

Vance GILBERT

Born in Philadelphia, Pennsylvania but raised in Willingboro, New Jersey, acoustic singer-songwriter VANCE GILBERT has shaped his unique funky folk style from out of the cool jazz scene of the late 1970s and early 1980s (Stevie Wonder, George Benson, Al Jarreau, et al).

He was a schoolteacher in Boston at that time, following his graduation from Connecticut College. A SHAWN COLVIN concert inspired him to try his hand in the hectic folk business. His self-financed, self-titled debut **VANCE GILBERT** (1989) {*6} won over Philo Records, who took him on for three soulful country-folk sets kicking off with **EDGEWISE** (1994) {*7}, a storyteller-type record that revamped the Eagles's 'Lyin' Eyes' to lounge effect while introducing his politics-and-love agenda. Dave Sudbury's 'King Of Rome' was also covered.

FUGITIVES (1995) {*6} and **SHAKING OFF GRAVITY** (1998) {*7} continued in the same vein, the latter featuring covers of Jimmy Webb's 'Do What You Gotta Do' and his hero Al Jarreau's 'Could You Believe'.

Disismye Records took over his recording career, releasing first a live concert CD, **SOMERVILLE LIVE** (2000) {*7}, taken from tapes recorded in Boston's Somerville Theater a year before with his friend ELLIS PAUL; the pair released their 'Side Of The Road' album in 2003.

ONE THRU FOURTEEN (2002) {*7}, the jazz-orientated **UNFAMILIAR MOON** (2005) {*6} and **UP ON ROCKFIELD** (2008) {*6} touched on every style under the sun - it was impossible to pigeonhole his pot-pourri of folky sounds. Between these mildly celebrated sets came a homage to his heroes, **ANGELS CASTLES COVERS** (2006) {*5}, covering eleven songs by Ashford & Simpson, Todd Rundgren, Al Green, Gladys Knight, Sam Cooke, Stevie Wonder (2), Mort Shuman, JONI MITCHELL, Jimi Hendrix and SHAWN COLVIN. *MCS*

Vance Gilbert - vocals, acoustic guitar (w/ session people)

US Vance Gilbert — UK not issued

1989. (c) <*none*> **VANCE GILBERT**
- Face to face / I'm watching my heart / VW Bug / Good cup of coffee / When Jimmy falls in love / Be gone, be good, so long / Just us / Sweet freedom / Drifters love / Relentless love / Toto's tune / The nearness of you.

Philo — Philo

Feb 94. (cd/c) <*(PH 1156 CD/C)*> **EDGEWISE** — Mar 94
- When Jimmy falls in love / Your train / If these teardrops had wings / Country western rap / Good cup of coffee / Seamless life / Witness to joy / Lyin' eyes / Slip away / I'm watching my heart / Rocket to the moon / King of Rome.

Jul 95. (cd/c) <*(CDPH/CPH 1186)*> **FUGITIVES** — Aug 95
- Scene of the crime / Outside looking in / Dear Amelia / Pound of prevention / Annalee / Pablo's lights / Lightnin' rod / Jenny and the tower / Johnny / Just a mirage / Times two / Spencer the rover / Just the way it was.

Feb 98. (cd) <*(CDPH 1213)*> **SHAKING OFF GRAVITY**
- The hey lah dee dah song / Taking it all to Tennessee / Twice struck / Watching a good thing burn / Just can't go like that / House of pain / Fly / Charlene / Do what you gotta do / Icarus by night / Oh little town / Could you believe / Nothing for you.

Disismye — not issued

2000. (cd) <*003*> **SOMERVILLE LIVE** (live May 5, 1999)
- (Introduction) / Icarus by night / Watching a good thing burn / Alan Lomax's children / If these teardrops had wings / Teletubbies / I met Ellis Paul... / Taking it all to Tennessee / High rise / Utilitarian church / Could you believe? / Charlene / Why are we so cruel? / Pablo's lights / Imagination / When Jimmy falls in love.

Louisiana Red Hot — not issued

Aug 02. (cd) <*1157*> **ONE THRU FOURTEEN**
- Waiting for Gilligan / Juliana walks / Son of someone's son / Why are we so cruel? / Hard to love / I'll cry too / Don't leave a trace / Eliza Jane / If you see James / I have always loved you / Highrise / Let me know / A little bit gone / What good is that?
In 2003, ELLIS PAUL & VANCE GILBERT released the 'Side Of The Road' album

Disismye — not issued

Feb 05. (cd) <*004*> **UNFAMILIAR MOON**
- Ten thousand skies / You can go now / Leaving Avon / Unfamiliar moon / Lie to me / Gondolier / Unforgivable / Your brighter day / That front porch song / I've got a plane / Alone down here.

Aug 06. (cd) <*005*> **ANGELS CASTLES COVERS**
- Ain't nothing like the real thing / It wouldn't have made any difference / I'm so tired of being alone / Rainy night in Georgia / A change is gonna come / Until you come back to me (That's what I'm gonna do) / Save the last dance for me / A case of you / Castles made of sand / Cry like an angel / Heaven help us all.

Nov 08. (cd) <*006*> **UP ON ROCKFIELD**
- Up on Rockfield / Welcome to Lovetown / Goodbye Pluto / Old man's advice / Judge's house / Whatever Louise wants / Sweetwater / It'll never be enough / House of prayer / Some great thing / Sing me down.

Eliza GILKYSON

The daughter of folk singer and in-house Disney songwriter TERRY GILKYSON (her brother was Tony Gilkyson of X and Lone Justice) was born Elizabeth Haughton Gilkyson in 1950 in Hollywood, California. Her own career never really got under way until 1987, when she signed to Capitol/Gold Castle; for nearly two decades she had been raising a family (son Cisco Ryder, of indie favourites Knife In The Water, and daughter Delia) and only had time to issue a couple of very rare LPs, **ELIZA '69** and **LOVE FROM THE HEART** (1979).

PILGRIMS (1987) {*7}, filed under New Age, was a Tarot-related concept to judge by the cover and its contents, and hardly folk music, but tracks such as the proto-Enya 'Calling All Angels' seemed to work in the context of the production. **LEGENDS OF RAINMAKER** (1989) {*5} was another try for mainstream acceptance. Her sound, not far from Emmylou Harris and Mary Chapin Carpenter, was too often sentimental and poetically pastoral.

A change of label to Private Music brought a resurgent freshness to her subsequent albums. Comparisons with JONI MITCHELL, Rickie Lee Jones and SUZANNE VEGA were rife but not complimentary concerning the first of these, **THROUGH THE LOOKING GLASS** (1993) {*7}. It was a transitional time for Eliza, who toured with New Age artist Andreas Vollenweider, and co-wrote some songs on his album 'Eolian Minstrel', while divorcing her second husband and moving to Europe.

Times were somewhat cloudy for Eliza at this stage, and only low-key CDs such as **UNDRESSED** (1994) {*6}, **REDEMPTION ROAD** (1997) {*6} and **MISFITS** (2000) {*5} filtered through, although the latter was boosted by her reading of DYLAN's 'Chimes Of Freedom'. Moving to Red House Records, GILKYSON's career took an upswing from **HARD TIMES IN BABYLON** (2000) {*7} onwards, her country-folk style finding approval with her long-time fan base. **LOST AND FOUND** (2002) {*6} and MORE

THAN A SONG (with IAIN MATTHEWS and Ad Vanderveen in 2003) were followed by the Grammy-nominated folk set **LAND OF MILK AND HONEY** (2004) {*7}, a partly party-political protest against the Republican administration, which highlighted WOODY GUTHRIE's 'Peace Call' with backing from Mary Chapin Carpenter, Patsy Griffin and Iris DeMent. Her post-election blues were expressed on **PARADISE HOTEL** (2005) {*7}, another thought-provoking singer-songwriter classic.

For her 2007 live follow-up **YOUR TOWN TONIGHT** {*7}, Eliza delved deeper into her father Terry's work, recording an update of his 'The Bare Necessities' (from Disney's 1967 cartoon film 'The Jungle Book') and another DYLAN track, 'Jokerman', alongside some of her own personal bests. **BEAUTIFUL WORLD** (2008) {*7}, the **RED HORSE** set of 2010 {*6} (with JOHN GORKA and LUCY KAPLANSKY) and her latest solo set, **ROSES AT THE END OF TIME** (2011) {*7} might have catapulted her to international fame if they had been released a decade or so earlier. It seemed that the Americana crossover market was saturated with the many Lucindas and Emmylous out there during a hard time in a recession-torn world, a world that Eliza was doing her best, in her own literate way, to put right. *MCS*

Eliza Gilkyson - vocals, acoustic guitar

US — UK
Mont Clare — not issued

1969. (lp) *<none>* **ELIZA '69**

RCA — not issued

1971. (7"; as ELIZA GILKYSON AND THE ARK BAND) <74-0490>
GENTLY KNOW YOU NOW. / Rainmaker Sunfather

Helios — not issued

1979. (lp; as LISA GILKYSON) <HR 440> **LOVE FROM THE HEART**

Capitol — not issued

1987. (lp/c/cd) <D1/D4/D2 71307> **PILGRIMS**
- Calling all angels / Shadows and footprints / Material man / Foolish heart / Mr Mystery / Pilgrims / My baby is a universe / One heart in time / Closer. *<re-iss. May 95; same>*

Jun 89. (lp/c/cd) <D1/D4/D2 71323> **LEGENDS OF RAINMAKER**
- Song of the rainbow warrior (part 1) / Children in the wilderness / Fantasy lover / Land of skin and sorrow / Rosie strike back / Greenfields / Love will come true / Break the chain / Inspiration / Tangible things / Constant star / Song of the rainbow warrior (part 2).

Private Music — not issued

Jul 93. (cd/c) <82109-2/-4> **THROUGH THE LOOKING GLASS**
- Dionysian love / All you want / Take off your old coat / I become the moon / When we cross over / Bearing witness / Last dance / Lights of Santa Fe / Odyssey / Emmanuel / Through the looking glass.

Realizations — not issued

1994. (cd) *<none>* **UNDRESSED** — tour
- River of gold / Start / Sleeping / Roses at the end of time / Lantern / Key to Avalon / Daniel / Here comes the night / Heart of a man / Wild horse / Don't stop loving me.

Silver Wave — Silver Wave

Sep 97. (cd) <*(SD 397)*> **REDEMPTION ROAD** — Dec 98
- Pools of Eden / Unless you want me / Our time / Sleeping / Rose of Sharon / Solitary singer / Road not taken / Prayer 2000 / Her melancholy muse / Through the glass darkly / River of gold / Redemption road.

Realizations — not issued

Feb 00. (cd) <23> **MISFITS**
- Hollywood years / Mama's little baby / Sleep tonight / Father Jesus / Beautiful dreamer / Love's shadow / Bad boy - Good man / Last big thrill / Nuestra senora del Rio / Chimes of freedom.

Red House — Red House

Oct 00. (cd) <*(RHRCD 146)*> **HARD TIMES IN BABYLON** — Nov 00
- Beauty way / Hard times in Babylon / Highway / Coast / Engineer Bill / Persephone / Baby's waking / Twisted / Flatline / In my dreams / Walk away from love / Sanctuary.

Apr 02. (cd) <*(RHRCD 162)*> **LOST AND FOUND**
- Welcome back / Mama's got a boyfriend / Fall into the night / Heart of a man / Easy rider / Richmond boy / Angel and Delilah / Aphrodite's face / He'll miss this train / Riverside.

Mar 04. (cd) <*(RHRCD 174)*> **LAND OF MILK AND HONEY** — Apr 04
- Hiway 9 / Not lonely / Dark side of town / Tender mercies / Wonderland / Separated / Ballad of Yvonne Johnson / Runnin' away / Milk and honey / Peace call.

Aug 05. (cd) <*(RHRCD 187)*> **PARADISE HOTEL**
- Borderline / Paradise hotel / Man of God / Jedidiah 1777 / Bellarosa / Think about you / Is it like today? / Calm before the storm / Requiem / When you walk on.

Jul 07. (cd) <*(RHRCD 205)*> **YOUR TOWN TONIGHT** (live)
- Beauty way / Green fields (w/ intro) / Dark side of town / Tender mercies / Jokerman / Rose of Sharon (w/ intro) / Tennessee road / Angel and Delilah / Hard times in Babylon / Jedidiah 1777 / Lights of Santa Fe / Easy rider (w/ intro) / Requiem / The bare necessities.

May 08. (cd) <*(RHRCD 212)*> **BEAUTIFUL WORLD**
- Emerald street / Wildewood spring / The party's over / Great correction / Clever disguise / Dream lover / He waits for me / Runaway train / Beautiful world / Rare bird / Unsustainable.

Jul 10. (cd; by GILKYSON / GORKA / KAPLANSKY)
<*(RHRCD 233)*> **RED HORSE**
- I am a child / Scorpion / Wild horse / Promise me / Don't mind me / Sanctuary / Coshieville / Blue chalk / Forget to breathe / If these walls could talk / Walk away from love / Wayfaring stranger.

May 11. (cd) <*(RHRCD 238)*> **ROSES AT THE END OF TIME**
- Blue moon night / Death in Arkansas / Looking for a place / Roses at the end of time / Slouching towards Bethlehem / Belle of the ball / Vayan al norte / 2153 / Midnight at Raton / Once I had a home.

- (8-10*) compilations -

Oct 05. (cd) Realization; <9450-2> **RETROSPECTO**
- Beautiful dreamer / Her melancholy muse / Craggy and Belle / Last dance / Buffalo gals / Wild horse / Don't stop lovin' me / All that you want / Dionysian love / Through the looking glass / Take off your old coat / Rosie strike back / Love will come true / Closer / Talkin' to the night / Getaway / Where did I go wrong / Este salida de sol / Rainmaker / A little star came down.

Jun 07. (cd) New West; <*(NW 6121-2)*> **LIVE FROM AUSTIN, TX** (live 13th August 2001) — Oct 07
- Welcome back / Hard times in Babylon / Beauty way / Coast / Baby's waking / Easy rider / Mama's got a boyfriend / Fall into the night / Engineer Bill / Sanctuary / Love minus zero - no limit.

MORE THAN A SONG

Eliza Gilkyson *, Iain Matthews & Ad Vanderveen

Perfect Pitch — not issued

Jul 02. (cd) **MORE THAN A SONG**
- All the way / Heart of a man (*) / Rerun matinee / Home on the highway / Bird of Paradise (*) / Meaning to life / Anchor / Bottom crawl (*) / Sing sister sing / Sweet old life / Witness (*) / A beautiful lie / Fall into the night (*) / Lamb in armour / More than a song to sing.

Steve GILLETTE

Often filed under Country by many sources, the early, seminal country-folk work of southern Californian singer-songwriter STEVE GILLETTE (b. November 23, 1942) was easy for the first volume of this Discography to overlook.

His songs have been covered by many country-styled artists from Tammy Wynette to Garth Brooks, but one that stands out from the pack is 'Darcy Farrow', a minor hit for IAN & SYLVIA way back in 1966 and a track on his Vanguard classic **STEVE GILLETTE** (1968) {*8}. This album was neglected by the paying public first time around (he was a bit late for the folk train), but it contained some of his greatest songs, including 'The Erlking' (after Goethe), '2:10 Train', 'Molly And Tenbrooks' and 'The Bells In The Evening'. PAMELA POLLAND's 'Goin' Home Song' was tacked on at the end, and Disneyland workers Tom Campbell and Linda Albertano also contributed material. It was augmented by session luminaries Bruce Langhorne, Bill Lee, DICK ROSMINI and Russ Savakus.

Probably too derivative of folk contemporaries such as TIM HARDIN, TOM RUSH and TIM BUCKLEY, Steve turned to full-on Country in the 1970s, releasing three sets including one studio LP produced by Graham Nash, **A LITTLE WARMTH** (1977) {*6}.

The 1980s were of no consequence to GILLETTE except that he married multi-talented CINDY MANGSEN in 1989 and worked with her on a number of albums including a concert set, **THE LIGHT OF THE DAY** (1996) {*6}, **A SENSE OF PLACE** (2001) {*7} and the collaborative 'Fourtold' CD with ANNE HILLS and Michael Smith. **TEXAS AND TENNESSEE** (1998) {*7} was a solo comeback of sorts, featuring great tracks like 'Windows Of Heaven' and 'Cornstalk Pony'.

THE MAN (2010) {*6} is a historical concept album set in the 1920s and 1930s (his father George plays piano on some tracks), telling a semi-fictional story about a guitar player, 'Danny Murrow', in boogie-woogie, jazz, blues and folk. It's a long, long way from GILLETTE's debut over forty years ago. *MCS*

Steve Gillette - vocals, acoustic guitar / + session people

US — UK
Vanguard — not issued

Mar 68. (lp) <*VRS 9251*> **STEVE GILLETTE**
- The Erlking / Back on the street again / A number and a name / You don't know her like I do / Darcy Farrow / 2:10 train / The bells in the evening / Ten thousand times ten / Springtime meadows / Molly and Tenbrooks / Many the times / Goin' home song. *<cd-iss. Dec 93; VMD 79251>*

Outpost — not issued

1970s. (ltd-lp) *<none>* **BACK ON THE STREET AGAIN**
- Back on the street again / To be good friends / We lost the good thing we had / Ridin' on empty / I believed in you / Rhythm and blues / She's not you / Babe on babe / Sad old railroad song / Less than love / The rain / Something I said.

Regency — not issued

1977. (lp) *<REG 79002>* **A LITTLE WARMTH**
- Sweet Melinda / A little warmth / Lost the good thing we had / Babe, oh babe *[CD-only]* / You'll never be the same / Holdin' on to nothing / Ships that pass in the night / The arms of Mary *[CD-only]* / She's not you / Three lines / I believed in you / To be good friends. *<cd-iss. 2002 on Compass Rose; CRM-9>*

Sierra — not issued

1979. (lp) *<SDD-1001>* **ALONE ... DIRECT**
- Back on the street again / A number and a name / Less than love / The rain / Look at me / Goin' home song / Gamblin' man / Darcy Farrow / Sad old railroad song / 2:10 train / The bells / Molly and Tenbrooks.

Compass Rose — Brambus

1992. (cd; by STEVE GILLETTE & CINDY MANGSEN) *<CRM-2> (199231-2)* **LIVE IN CONCERT** [live at The Ark, Ann Arbor in 1991] — Oct 94
- The river / Going away / Grapes on the vine / Their brains were small and they died / Glass houses / Shake sugaree / Darcy Farrow / When I was in my prime / Corinna / Annachie Gordon / The old trail / Heartland / La guitarra / Your hopes up high / The frozen logger / Crying don't even come close / Jay Gould's daughter / Ring around the moon / Bed of roses.

1994. (cd) *<CRM-4>* **THE WAYS OF THE WORLD**
- The river / Grapes on the vine / Bed of roses / Heartland / Healing hands / Share me with Texas / La guitarra / The old trail / A little bit of solitude / The ways of the world / So close / Always on a train in my dreams.

1996. (cd; by STEVE GILLETTE & CINDY MANGSEN) *<CRM-7> (199678-2)* **THE LIGHT OF THE DAY**
- 1800 and froze to death / Johnny Appleseed / Dark of the moon / The restless wind / The bonny light horseman / Far away - The coast of France / En montant la riviere / Get up and bar the door / The unicorn / Swede-Finn medley / Right says Fred / Hole in my shoe / Song for Gamble.

Redwing — Redwing

Oct 98. (cd) *<(RWMCD 5404)>* **TEXAS AND TENNESSEE** — Feb 99
- Here's to the rocky road / Cornstalk pony / Ghost rider's medley / Railroad written all over him / 2:10 train / Two men in the building / Lorena / No ponuncias mi nombre / The windows of heaven / One door / The eye of the hurricane / The West Texas wind / If you're ever in Texas.

Feb 01. (cd; by STEVE GILLETTE / CINDY MANGSEN) *<(RWMCD 5409)>* **A SENSE OF PLACE** — Mar 01
- Tide and the river rising / Sunrise / Reel Beatrice / Eclipse / Traveler / Margery Grey / Buddy and Carol's waltz / Ou vas-tu, mon petit garcon? Point au pic.... / The architecture song / Shenandoah falls - Cincinnati rag / When the first leaves fall / Long, long trail.

—— In 2003, GILLETTE & MANGSEN (with ANNE HILLS & MICHAEL SMITH) released a harmony set, FOURTOLD

Compass Rose — not issued

May 06. (cd; by STEVE GILLETTE & CINDY MANGSEN) *<CRM-11CD>* **BEING THERE**
- Hurricane / The road through the woods / Concertina garden medley / The kid with the comic book / Odd man out / High cotton / Mr O'Reilly / Nola / J'entend le moulin - Two-step d'Armand / The Vermont waltz / Homelessness / Darkness comes.

Apr 10. (cd) *<CRM-12CD>* **THE MAN**
- Conversation on 13th Avenue / St. Louis blues - Jada / Cordovan blues / Johnny and Betty / Sunday / Sweet Lorraine - Ain't misbehavin' / Your feet's too big / Old Jim Crow / Whispering / Basie's boogie / There's a cradle in Caroline / Creole belle medley / The man who loves a train / Brother, can you spare a dime? / Good old wagon / St James infirmary blues / Let the rain decide / God is love / Wade in the water / The sunny side of the street.

Toby GOODSHANK

Anti-folk acoustic singer/songwriter, guitarist and underground visual artist TOBY GOODSHANK (formerly of The MOLDY PEACHES, on stage at least) has delivered his own take on the genre in an exhaustive series of CDs and rare CD-rs during a positive post-millennium period.

Rather than give an account of his many albums, it's simpler to recommend some great individual contributions to some mid-2000s various-artists sets, such as the Beatlesque 'Sunny Sunny Cold Cold Day' (from 'Art Star Sounds') and the Daniel Johnston cover 'Now' (from 'I Killed A Monster').

Among his solo albums, New Yorker GOODSHANK comes off best on 2004's **SAFE HARBOR** {*6} and 2007's **EVERYTHING INTERTWINGLES** {*6} - hardly folk music, more like gangsta-rap Eno.

More than prolific, Toby has moonlighted with a host of New York outfits including Double Deuce (an indie-pop Donny & Marie featuring Angela Carlucci of Baby Skins), his Olive Juice enterprise (on 2005's self-released 'Camp Candy') and The Tri-Lambs (which added Angela's sister Crystal Babyskin). *MCS*

His solo discography is partial and compiled from official CDs and CDrs.

Toby Goodshank - vocals, acoustic guitar / with friends, etc.

US Olive Music — UK not issued

2001. (cd-r) *<OJD-0005>* **LIVE @ TRASH** [live at Trash American Style in Ding]
- Lobotomy laundry / Wake up all the robots / Odd numbers / Risrbage dump / Minivan? Marsha, I need your full cooperation / Homos / Caveman soliloquy / Beautiful morning / Baby / Waiting for Jessie Minaligo / Untitled children's song.

2002. (cd-r) *<OJ-0015>* **PUT THE DEVIL WHERE YOU HANG YOUR HAT**
- Change your ways / Subz cbus / Multiply divide / By lamplight / Jackrabbit / Camp K / Straight-edge keg party / Kafka / Ride it / Barnyard matters / I'm only as good as I already am / Neither solved, nor saved.

2002. (cd-r) *<OJ-0019>* **MUSIC FOR HEROES VOLUME 1: THE DANGER VAT**
- Going down / Mutha fuckin' crazy / Russian roulette / Untitled children's song / My day off / El Spocko / Dega, I'm your father / Dragonfly / A new civilization / Liquid swords / Green tiger / Lobotomy laundry / Thumbkin / War path / Monkey troubles / Coffee of the universe / Untitled (Priest) / + thoughts / Cigarette kiss / The funky cunnilingus / Braveheart was a pussy / Pictures of brutality / Wake up all the robots / Nice cat, rotten day.

2002. (cd-r) *<OJ-0020>* **MUSIC FOR HEROES VOLUME 2: ST LENO, I HAVE NO PRAYER**
- PRO-ANTI / The age we live in / Graduation song / Untitled / I want my cherry back / Untitled / Beastiality / Get your cookies on / Auntie Victoria / Maybe you would like it / Welcome to Shinyville / Lost - Found / Reborn / We will live 4ever / Druggie / Ventura / Untitled / Another hole / Untitled / Marsha, I need your full cooperation / Hello Matthew / Welcome to Shinyville / The void / Into the unknown.

2002. (cd-r) *<OJ-0021>* **MUSIC FOR HEROES VOLUME 3: A CHRONICLE OF THE FEAR**
- The penguin / Bastards delight: A night in the fields / Thinkatron.

2004. (cd) *<OJ-0038>* **SAFE HARBOR**
- Safe harbor / I get lifted / The rainbow spring fair / Hang-up call / Wally breaks it down proper / Call me Ishmael / Take action / Student activity fee / Mistake / Ha-do-ken daddy / Me 2 hold on 2 / What I learned there / TG is burning.

2004. (cd-r) *<OJD-0073>* **COME CORRECT**
- The Lazarus pit / Dying / Another day / Bridges and balloons / The pisswater fair / Portrait of an absintheur / They say it's ok / In the morning we go to Dodgington / Store in a cool dry place / Diseased / Bonecrusher.

2005. (cd-r) *<OJD-0090>* **JYUSANGATSU**
- Mossman / Promise U / Susan B Anthony-sized / No funeral / Palom and Porom / Love theme from Romeo and Juliet (A time for us) / Black eye / Dean's dream / Shooting star / Holiday / Shining through.

Mar 06. (cd-r) *<OJ-0053>* **DI SANTA RAGIONE**
- The death of my enemies / 8" Linda / Gan signz / W/O a doubt / Hatch city / Nu grrl / Army of love / Emperor / Evil / 4 the moment / Raw peehole gospel / All goes down / Effigy.

Sep 06. (cd) *<OJD-0061>* **MOGO ON THE GOGO**
- Silver state / 1000k / Sun shards / Diamond / Very much so / PDG / Immaculate and cumbersome / Gogo / Exit thru miracles / Heidi / Midlife a / D & un-P / Crime eye.

Jul 07. (cd) *<OJD-0178>* **EVERYTHING INTERTWINGLES**
- More than one / Babylon molehill / Carry on / Strangers / Italiano / Best foot 4ward / Cyrenius booth / Oak-mot! / Bearshield / Skeleton force / No end 2 shallow / All the time / Carbombs - Confetti / Heir 2. / Minus8 / The sixth / Sunrise to sunset.

2008. (cd-r) *<OJD-0202>* **PRAY TO YOU**
- Beach / Pray to / Lost weekend / Sick of this / Walk away / Bad dream / Satanic lullaby / In this town / Opposite end / Closed casket.

2009. (cd-r) *<OJD-0262>* **UNTITLED**

John GORKA

Recognisable by his evolving beard and rich baritone voice, spiritual songwriter JOHN GORKA (b. 1958 in Edison, New Jersey) has been at the centre of contemporary country-esque blues-folk music for more than 20 years since winning top prize at the Kerriville Folk Festival in 1984.

One of the first acoustic folk artists to sign with Red House, GORKA completed his debut album **I KNOW** (1987) {*7} with the help of fellow New York folk movement artists SHAWN COLVIN and LUCY KAPLANSKY on harmony. From the dirge-like 'Branching Out' to the self-explanatory 'B.B. King Was Wrong', the album earned a good deal of praise from critics and public alike.

Subsequently shifting to Windham Hill and its offshoot High Street label, GORKA's mood changed to something more sentimental, balladeering and mainstream on the likes of **LAND OF THE BOTTOM LINE** (1990) {*6}, **JACK'S CROWS** (1991) {*5} and **TEMPORARY ROAD** (1992) {*5}, the latter a slight return roots-wise that featured backing vocals from NANCI GRIFFITH. Inevitably Nashville came calling in the person of John Jennings, who produced his follow-up, **OUT OF THE VALLEY** (1994) {*5}; guests on the set included Kathy Mattea, Mary Chapin Carpenter, LEO KOTTKE and Dave Mattacks. His storytelling prowess was almost back to its best on **BETWEEN FIVE AND SEVEN** (1996) {*6}.

John's best records had all been on Red House, and it was no big surprise when his seventh album, **AFTER YESTERDAY** (1998) {*7}, surfaced on that label. The profound **COMPANY YOU KEEP** (2001) {*4} lacked the bite of his previous efforts, although he was in good company with a star guest list of Carpenter, KAPLANSKY, PATTY LARKIN and ANI DiFRANCO.

The introspective **OLD FUTURES GONE** (2003) {*5}, **WRITING IN THE MARGINS** (2006) {*5} (featuring two rare covers, TOWNES VAN ZANDT's 'Snow Don't Fall' and STAN ROGERS's 'The Lockkeeper') and **SO DARK YOU SEE** (2009) {*6} kept GORKA in high esteem among his supporters. The last seemed a million miles away from his mildly disappointing preceding works, his deep vocals shining through on versions of Burns's 'Ae Fond Kiss', UTAH PHILLIPS's 'I Think Of You' and the bluesy jazz of old-timey pianist Richard M Jones's 'Trouble In Mind'. *MCS*

John Gorka - vocals, acoustic guitar

US Red House / UK not issued

1987. (lp) *<RHR 18>* **I KNOW**
- Downtown tonight / Winter cows / Blues palace / Love is our cross to bear / Branching out / I saw a stranger with your hair / B.B. King was wrong / Heart upon demand / I know / Out of my mind / Like my watch / Down in the milltown. *<cd-iss. Mar 92/Jul 95; RHRCD 18)>*

Windham Hill / Windham Hill

Apr 90. (cd/c) *<(WD/WT 1089)>* **LAND OF THE BOTTOM LINE**
- Land of the bottom line / Armed with a broken heart / Raven in the storm / The one that got away / Full of life / Stranger in my driver's seat / The sentinel / Dream street / Mean streak / Italian girls / Jailbirds in the big house / Prom night in Pigtown / I saw a stranger with your hair / Love is our cross to bear / That's how legends are made.

High Street / High Street

Sep 91. (cd/c) *<(72902 10309-2/-4)>* **JACK'S CROWS**
- Silence / Treasure islands / Jack's crows / Houses in the fields / The mercy of the wheels / Good / Semper fi / Where the bottles break / Night is a woman / I'm from New Jersey / My new neighborhood / The ballad of Jamie Bee / You're on your way. *<cd re-iss. 1993 on Windham Hill; 876254-2>*

Dec 92. (cd/c) *<(72902 10315-2/-4)>* **TEMPORARY ROAD** — Jan 95
- Looking forward / Baby blues / The gypsy life / Vinnie Charles is free / Gravyland / Temporary road / All that hammering / I don't feel like a train / When she kisses me / Grand larceny / If I could forget to breathe / Can you understand my joy? / Brown shirts.

May 94. (cd/c) *<(72902 10325-2/-4)>* **OUT OF THE VALLEY** — Aug 94
- Good noise / That's why / Carnival knowledge (second hand face) / Talk about love / Big time lonesome / Furniture / Mystery to me / Out of the valley / Thoughtless behavior / Always going home / Flying red horse / Up until then.

1994. (cd-ep) *<none>* MOTOR FOLKIN' — promo
- Furniture (live) / Mystery to me (remix) / Good noise (remix) / Campaign trail.

Aug 96. (cd/c) *<72902 10351-2/-4>* **BETWEEN FIVE AND SEVEN**
- Lightning's blues / Blue chalk / Can't make up my mind / The mortal groove / My invisible gun / Part of your own / Two good reasons / Airstream bohemians / Paradise, once / Campaign trail / Edgar the party man / Scraping Dixie.

Red House / Red House

Oct 98. (cd) *<(RHRCD 121)>* **AFTER YESTERDAY** — Nov 98
- When the ice goes out / Thorny patch / Cypress trees / Wisdom / Silvertown / A January floor / Amber Lee / After yesterday / When he cries / St Caffeine / Zuly / Heroes.

Mar 01. (cd) *<(RHRCD 151)>* **THE COMPANY YOU KEEP**
- What was that / A saint's complaint / Oh Abraham / When you walk in / Shape of the world / Morningside / When I lost my faith / Joint of no return / Let them in / Hank Senior moment / Around the house / Wisheries / People my age.

Sep 03. (cd) *<(RHRCD 165)>* **OLD FUTURES GONE**
- Dogs and thunder / Always / Look the other way / Outside / Trouble and care / Make them crazy / Old future / Lay me down / Shapes / Soldier after all / Poor side / War makes war / If not now / Riverside.

Jul 06. (cd) *<(RHRCD 194)>* **WRITING IN THE MARGINS**
- Chance of rain / Broken place / Satellites / Writing in the margins / Snow don't fall / Bluer state / Arm's length / The lockkeeper / I miss everyone / When you sing / Road of good intentions / Unblindfold the referee.

Oct 09. (cd) *<(RHRCD 223)>* **SO DARK YOU SEE** — Nov 09
- A fond kiss / Whole wide world / Can't get over it / Fret one / Ignorance and privilege / Utah / I think of you / Where no monuments stand / Night into day / Fret not / Live by the sword / Trouble in mind / The Dutchman / Mr Chambers / That was the year / Diminishing winds.

—— In July 2010, GORKA, ELIZA GILKYSON + LUCY KAPLANSKY issued the 'Red Horse' CD

- (5-7*) compilations, etc.-

Jun 06. (cd) Windham Hill; *<81696-2>* **PURE JOHN GORKA**
- Looking forward / Jack's crows / Blue chalk / I saw a stranger with your hair / Lightning's blues / The gypsy life / Silence / Vinnie Charles is free / Where the bottles break / That's why / Houses in the fields / When she kisses me / The ballad of Jamie Bee / I'm from New Jersey / Italian girls.

Tracy GRAMMER (⟹ CARTER, Dave &...)

GREAT LAKE SWIMMERS

A hybrid of rural indie-folk-rock and alt-country lying somewhere between NEIL YOUNG and DAMIEN JURADO, Canada's GREAT LAKE SWIMMERS (formed in Wainfleet, Toronto) looked like being their country's next big thing. Founded in 2003 and led by singer-songwriter Tony Dekker (with Erik Arnesen, Walter Kofman and Sadro Perri also integral), the lush, laid-back dynamics of the group created haunting sets such as **GREAT LAKE SWIMMERS** (2003) {*7} and **BODIES AND MINDS** (2005) {*7}, both delivered on Canadian indie outlet Misra. They later signed to Canada's leading label, Nettwerk.

Rich acoustic sadcore best describes **ONGIARA** (2007) {*7}, which included indie chartbuster 'Your Rocky Spine', which is what The Eagles or Poco might have sounded like if they had played folk. **LOST CHANNELS** (2009) {*8} fared even better critically, songs such as 'Palmistry' and 'Pulling On A Line' growing with every listen. Success may be just around the corner for Tony Dekker and his new, revolving-door line-up. *MCS*

Tony Dekker - vocals, acoustic guitar / **Erik Arnesen** - banjo / **Walter Kofman** - piano, accordion / **Sandro Perri** - cello, steel guitar

US/Can weewerk / UK/Fr Fargo

Mar 03. (cd) *<weewerk 001> (FA 20436)* **GREAT LAKE SWIMMERS** — Mar 04
- Moving pictures silent films / The man with no skin / Moving, shaking / Merge, a vessel, a harbour / I will never see the sun / This is not like home / The animals of the world / Faithful night, listening / Three days at sea (three lost years) / Great lake swimmers. *<US-iss. Apr 05 on Misra; MSR 032>*

—— **Colin Huebert** - drums; repl. Kofman

—— added **Almog Ben David** - Wurlitzer piano

Apr 05. (cd) *<weewerk 004> (FA 0055)* **BODIES AND MINDS**
- Song for the angels / Let's trade skins / When it flows / Various stages / Bodies and minds / To leave it behind / Falling into the sky / Imaginary bars / I saw you in the wild / I could be nothing / Long into the evening. *<US-iss. Oct 05 on Misra; MSR 035>*

Zunior / not issued

2006. (ltd-12" ep) *<none>* HANDS IN DIRTY GROUND — gigs
- Song for the angels (miracle version) / Hands in dirty ground / I saw you in the wild (live at Knust, Hamburg) / To leave it behind / Innocent W.Y.D. / This is not like home (live at Northsix, Brooklyn).

Nettwerk / Nettwerk

Mar 07. (cd) *<(06700 30691-2)>* **ONGIARA** — Apr 07
- Your rocky spine / Backstage with the modern dancers / Catcher song / Changing colours / There is a light / Put there by the land / I am part of a large family / Where in the world are you / Passenger song / I became awake. *<lp-iss. Sep 07 on weewerk; weewerk 009>*

Jun 07. (cd-s) *<223004>* YOUR ROCKY SPINE / Put There By The Land (live) / There Is A Light (live)

Dec 08. (m-cd; as T. DEKKER & GREAT LAKE SWIMMERS) *<none>* SONG SUNG BLUE (documentary soundtrack)
- Song sung blue / The dream / Just crushed / The depression / Awake / Old Milwaukee / Eyes on the prize / Encore / Final bow.

(above issued on weewerk Canada)

—— **Dekker** added **Mike Olsen** - cello / **Darcy Yates** - upright bass / **Greg Millson** - drums / **Julie Fader** - flute

Mar 09. (cd/lp) *<(6700 30830 27/10)>* **LOST CHANNELS** — Apr 09
- Palmistry / Everything is moving so fast / Pulling on a line / Concrete heart / She comes to me in dreams / The chorus in the underground / Singer castle bells / Stealing tomorrow / Still / New light / River's edge / Unison falling into harmony.

2009. (ltd-d 7") *<weewerk 033>* (Audiotransparent track). / SEND ME A LETTER // DON'T BE CRUEL. / (Audiotransparent track)

Apr 10. (m-cd) *<CD 30885-2>* **THE LEGION SESSIONS** [live at the Royal Canadian Legion]
-Palmistry / Everything is moving so fast / Pulling on a line / Concrete heart / She comes to me in dreams / The chorus in the underground / Stealing tomorrow / Still / New light.

—— **Bret Higgins** - upright bass; repl. Yates

Adam GREEN (⟹ The MOLDY PEACHES)

GREEN CROWN (⟹ PRYDWYN)

Stanley GREENTHAL

Although his ancestry makes his music rooted in Ireland and Scotland, singer/songwriter and mandocellist STANLEY GREENTHAL (b. April 16, 1949 in New York City) has also been creative in contemporary and traditional folk music.

Stanley arrived late on the folk scene, having spent most of the 1970s travelling the world after his wife (he was married at 21) died tragically young. He lived for a time on an island off Vancouver and settled in Seattle, Washington.

One of the first songs he wrote in the 1980s was the title track from his inspirational debut cassette album, **SONGS FOR THE JOURNEY** (1986) {*6}, a record that also incorporated instrumental jig and reel polkas with fiddler Kevin Burke, of Celtic act PATRICK STREET, and piper Micheal O Domhnaill of RELATIVITY.

His first CD release, **ALL ROADS** (1990) {*6}, also delivered on his own Madrona Ring label, was a nice and easy New Age experience that featured Mark Minkler (also on the first collection) on songs such as 'Shoal Water' and 'Walking To Watmouth'. He toured alongside ROBIN WILLIAMSON around this time.

TURNING TOWARDS YOU (1997) {*6} ended a seven-year absence, and the self-explanatory **MELODIE: BRITTANY TO THE BALKANS** (2002) {*7} - all 75 minutes of it, covering places in between including Scotland, Ireland, Bulgaria and Greece - demonstrated his love of Celtic and Balkan instrumental music. *MCS*

Stanley Greenthal - vocals, mandocello, acoustic guitar / + session people

US Madrona Ring | UK not issued

Nov 86. (c) <*MRC 001*> **SONGS FOR THE JOURNEY** ☐ ⊟
- Spring song / Song for the journey / January - After midnight polkas / Wind on the water / The rover / Song for Zoe / The shining mountains / For a woman in black / Still untitled / Markella's / Winter hymn.

Dec 90. (cd) <*MRD 002*> **ALL ROADS** ☐ ⊟
- Shoal water / Legnala Rodne / Silver madness / Sea voices / Homecoming / Arboretum kopanica / The bookbinder / All roads / Walking to Watmough.

Nov 97. (cd) <*MRD 1003*> **TURNING TOWARDS YOU** ☐ ⊟
- Light from your face / The old bridge of Mostar / Tsamiko reflections / One day / Raindance / Your bright wings / Turning towards you / Monroe / Medley from the green hill / Midnight sun / This love.

Sep 02. (cd) <*MRD 1005*> **MELODIE: BRITTANY TO THE BALKANS** ☐ ⊟
- Melodie - Person Ploergat / Gwez-kren en noz (dans en dro) / Kimiad - Calanish / Dobrudja danetz / Da li znaes, pomnis li / Oye vie - Ogham en dros / Song from Kolinda / The Bannock's march set: The battle of Waterloo - My love is the fair lad - The Bannock's march / Sonerion Bleimor / Baiduska / Razlozko kalajdzijsko horo / En dros / Syrtos argos / The lament for Limerick / Karsilamas from Thrace / Skaliotikos syrto / Rory Dall's sister's lament / Dans plinn.

Nanci GRIFFITH

The self-styled 'folkabilly' poet and singer began performing at an early age, initially with her parents in honky-tonks and later on the Texas folk circuit. Her pure, cutesy voice and girl-next-door appeal has gained her a sizeable global following.

After completing a degree in education at the University of Texas, GRIFFITH (b. July 6, 1953 in Seguin, Texas) focused wholly on music, making her recording debut a year later in 1978 with **THERE'S A LIGHT BEYOND THESE WOODS** {*5}. Released on the small independent label B.F. Deal, the album was largely self-composed, introducing her talent for vivid storytelling and snapshot vignettes.

It was another four years before she recorded a follow-up, **POET IN MY WINDOW** (1982) {*5}, which was the second release of another small label, Featherbed (the first was her ex-husband ERIC TAYLOR's 'Shameless Love', on which she sang harmony). However, it wasn't until GRIFFITH signed with folk/country label Philo that her highly original singer/songwriter style began to develop significantly.

Backed by established musicians like Irish lead (electric) guitarist Phil Donnelly and acoustic maestros such as Lloyd Green, Roy Huskey Jr. and Bela Fleck, GRIFFITH cut the acclaimed **ONCE IN A VERY BLUE MOON** (1985) {*7}. As before, the album consisted mainly of her own compositions, although there were a few fine covers including Lyle Lovett's 'If I Was The Woman You Wanted' and the exceptional Pat Alger title track. Nanci named the backing band she formed the following year, The Blue Moon Orchestra, for that song.

1986 brought the release of the Grammy-winning (Best Folk Album) **LAST OF THE TRUE BELIEVERS** {*7}, and Kathy Mattea subsequently scored a US country hit with one of its GRIFFITH-penned ballads, 'Love At The Five And Dime'. The album was the first to be released in the UK through the independently distributed Demon, and in the same year Philo re-released GRIFFITH's first two albums, her star firmly in the ascendant as she signed a new deal with MCA.

The singer made her major-label debut with **LONE STAR STATE OF MIND** (1987) {*7}. It was her most successful release thus far, featuring two of her most famous tracks, the bittersweet reminiscence of the Pat Alger/Gene Levine/Fred Koller-written title track (a minor hit) and the crystal-clear definitive reading of Julie Gold's 'From A Distance'. Other highlights included 'There's A Light Beyond These Woods (Mary Margaret)' (re-recorded from her debut) and Robert Earl Keen Jr's 'Sing One For Sister'.

LITTLE LOVE AFFAIRS (1988) {*7} marked a new songwriting maturity, GRIFFITH creating a thematic continuity on the subject of love in various contexts over the course of the album. After the live **ONE FAIR SUMMER EVENING** (1988) {*7}, Nanci moved into more AOR territory with **STORMS** (1989) {*8}, recorded in Los Angeles and produced by Glyn Johns, who has had a hand in some of the best albums in rock history. His Midas touch gave Nanci her commercial breakthrough, in the UK at least, where the record made the Top 40.

LATE NIGHT GRANDE HOTEL (1991) {*7} continued in a similar vein, employing Peter Van Hooke and Rod Argent on production duties and adding strings to her primarily acoustic-based sound. Already a major star in Ireland (she also contributed to a number of The CHIEFTAINS' releases), where she regularly plays sell-out tours, GRIFFITH finally made the UK Top 20 in 1993 with **OTHER VOICES, OTHER ROOMS** {*7}, an all-covers album that returned to her folk roots.

Among the many highlights of this tribute to her favourite songwriters were a plaintive reading of JOHN PRINE's 'Speed Of The Sound Of Loneliness' and a sensitive cover of the late TOWNES VAN ZANDT's 'Tecumseh Valley'. The record found GRIFFITH renewing her partnership with her early producer Jim Rooney, and other well-known songs included KATE WOLF's 'Across The Great Divide', RALPH McTELL's 'From Clare To Here', TOM PAXTON's 'Can't Help But Wonder Where I'm Bound', WOODY GUTHRIE's 'Do Re Mi', JANIS IAN's 'This Old Town', GORDON LIGHTFOOT's 'Ten Degrees And Getting Colder', Jerry Jeff Walker's 'Morning Song For Sally' and DYLAN's 'Boots Of Spanish Leather'.

Subsequent albums **FLYER** (1994) {*7} and **BLUE ROSES FROM THE MOONS** (1997) {*6} have seen GRIFFITH consolidate her position as one of the most respected artists in the singer/songwriter/interpreter genre alongside Emmylou Harris.

Following on from 1998's covers set **OTHER VOICES, TOO (A TRIP TO THE BOUNTIFUL)** {*7}, GRIFFITH released the ambitious and not entirely successful **DUST BOWL SYMPHONY** (1999) {*6}. A back-catalogue collection revamped with the London Symphony Orchestra, the record was a rather uncomfortable meeting of classical and country, formal and informal. The covers set was boosted by folk and country songs from RICHARD THOMPSON, SANDY DENNY, The WEAVERS, Ian Tyson and Sylvia Fricker (also known as IAN & SYLVIA), Sonny Curtis, Guy Clark, WOODY GUTHRIE, Johnny Cash, Tom Russell, STEVE GILLETTE and the great American composer Stephen Foster.

CLOCK WITHOUT HANDS (2001) {*6} found her back on more familiar if not exactly inspiring ground with her first set of wholly original material in almost five years. The live **WINTER MARQUEE** (2002) {*6} was much more heartening, a back-to-the roots concert set with Nanci in fine voice, accompanied by Emmylou Harris and Tom Russell, and covering the likes of DYLAN's 'Boots Of Spanish Leather', PHIL OCHS's 'What's That I Hear' and TOWNES VAN ZANDT's 'White Freight Liner', as well as her trademark version of 'Speed Of The Sound Of Loneliness'.

After years straddling folk and country genres, Nanci was finally invited to perform at the Grand Ole Opry in 2003, and the following year she took inspiration from the Iraq invasion and a trip to southeast Asia for 'Big Blue Ball Of War' on 2005's **HEARTS IN MIND** {*6} set.

RUBY'S TORCH (2006) {*6}, her first on the Rounder label, had only two GRIFFITH originals, the rest, including three by Tom Waits ('Grapefruit Moon', 'Please Call Me, Baby' and 'Ruby's Arms') coming from other artists. Following a three-year absence due to writer's block, Nanci completed a comeback of sorts, **THE LOVING KIND** (2009) {*6}, with help from her guitarist, the songwriter Thomm Jutz.

GRIFFITHS has covered a wide range of songs over the years, the best being 'Deadwood, South Dakota' (ERIC TAYLOR), 'Roseville Fair' (BILL STAINES), 'Heaven' (Julie Gold), 'Ballad Of Robin Wintersmith' (Richard Dobson), 'Sun And Moon And Stars' (Vince Bell), 'San Diego Serenade' (Tom Waits) and 'Gravity Of The Situation' (VIC CHESNUTT), the last a collaboration with Hootie & The Blowfish. *MCS*

Nanci Griffith - vocals, acoustic guitar

US B.F. Deal — UK not issued

Apr 78. (lp) *<BFD 6>* **THERE'S A LIGHT BEYOND THESE WOODS** [ ] [–]
- I remember Joe / Alabama soft spoken blues / Michael's song / Song for remembered heroes / West Texas sun / There's a light beyond these woods / Dollar matinee / Montana backroads / John Philip Griffith. *<re-iss. Jun 82 on Featherbed; FB 903> <re-iss. Aug 87 on Philo lp/c/cd; PH 1097/+C/CD> (UK-iss. Jul 89 on MCA; MCG/MCGC/DMCG 6052)*

Featherbed — not issued

May 82. (lp) *<FB 902>* **POET IN MY WINDOW** [ ] [–]
- Marilyn Monroe - Neon and waltzes / Heart of a miner / Julie Ann / You can't go home again / October reasons / Wheels / Workin' in corners / Trouble with roses / Tonight I think I'm gonna go downtown / Poet in my window. *<re-iss. Aug 87 & Mar 00 on Philo lp/c/cd; PH 1098/+C/CD> (UK-iss. Jul 89 on MCA lp/c/cd; MCG/MCGC/DMCG 6053) (re-iss. Oct 91 cd/c; DMCL/MCLC 1911) <(cd re-mast. Jan 02 on Philo+=; CDPH 1235)>* - Can't love wrong.

May 82. (7") *<FB 902-SA>* MARILYN MONROE - NEON AND WALTZES. / Wheels [ ] [–]

Philo — not issued

Jul 85. (7") *<4200>* ONCE IN A VERY BLUE MOON. / [ ] [–]

Dec 85. (lp) *<PH 1096>* **ONCE IN A VERY BLUE MOON** [ ] [–]
- Ghost in the music / Love is a hard waltz / Roseville fair / Mary and Omie / Friend out in the madness / I'm not drivin' these wheels (bring the prose to the wheel) / Time alone / Ballad of Richard Winter-Smith / Daddy said / Once in a very blue moon / If I were a woman you wanted / Year down in New Orleans / Spin on a red brick floor. *(UK-iss. Jul 89 on MCA lp/c/cd; MCG/MCGC/DMCG 6054) <(cd re-mast. Jan 02; CDPH 1233)>*

Dec 86. (cd/c/lp) *<CD/C+/PH 1109>* **THE LAST OF THE TRUE BELIEVERS** [ ] [–]
- The last of the true believers / Love at the five and dime / St Olav's gate / More than a whisper / Banks of the Pontchartrain / Looking for the time (workin' girl) / Goin' gone / One of these days / Love's found a shoulder / Fly by night / The wing and the wheel. *(UK-iss. Jun 88 on Rounder' lp/c/cd; REU/+C/CD 1013) (cd re-iss. Nov 96; same as US)*

MCA — MCA

Apr 87. (7") *<53008>* LONE STAR STATE OF MIND. / There's A Light Beyond These Woods (Mary Margaret) [ ] [–]

Apr 87. (lp/c) *<MCA/+C/D 5927> (MCF/+C 3364)*
LONE STAR STATE OF MIND [ ] [ ]
- Lone star state of mind / Cold hearts - Closed minds / From a distance / Beacon Street / Nickel dreams / Sing one for sister / Ford Econoline / Trouble in the fields / Love in a memory / Let it shine on me / There's a light beyond these woods (Mary Margaret). *(cd re-iss. Oct 98; MCLD 19176)*

Jun 87. (7") *<53082>* LOVE IN A MEMORY. / Trouble In The Fields [ ] [–]

Jul 87. (7") *(MCA 1169)* FROM A DISTANCE. / Sing One For Sister [–] [ ]
(cd-s) *(DMCA 1169)* - ('A') / De Lejos / Gulf Coast highway.

Nov 87. (7" ep) *<53147> (MCA 1221)* COLD HEARTS [ ] [ ]
- Cold hearts - Closed minds / Ford Econoline / Lone star state of mind.

Jan 88. (7") *<53184>* FROM A DISTANCE. / Never Mind [ ] [–]

Feb 88. (7") *(MCA 1230)* OUTBOUND PLANE. / So Long Ago [–] [ ]
(12"+=) (MCAT 1230) - Trouble in the fields.

Feb 88. (lp/c/cd) *<MCA/+C/D 42102> (MCF/MCFC/DMCF 3413)*
LITTLE LOVE AFFAIRS [ ] Mar 88 [78]
- Anyone can be somebody's fool / I knew love / Never mind / Love wore a halo (back before the war) / So long ago / Gulf Coast highway / Little love affairs / I wish it would rain / Outbound plane / I would change my life / Sweet dreams will come. *(cd re-iss.Oct98; MCLD 19211)*

Mar 88. (7") *<53306>* I KNEW LOVE. / So Long Ago [ ] [–]

Apr 88. (7") *(MCA 1240)* I KNEW LOVE. / Never Mind [–] [ ]
(12"+=) (MCAT 1240) - Lone star state of mind.

Sep 88. (7") *<53374>* ANYONE CAN BE SOMEBODY'S FOOL. / Love Wore A Halo (Back Before The War) [ ] [–]

Sep 88. (7") *(MCA 1282)* FROM A DISTANCE. / Love Wore A Halo (Back Before The War) [–] [ ]
(cd-s+=) *(DMCA 1282)* - There's a light beyond these woods (Mary Margaret).

Nov 88. (lp/c/cd) *<MCA/+C/D 42255> (MCF/MCFC/DMCF 3435)*
ONE FAIR SUMMER EVENING (live) [ ] [ ]
- Once in a very blue moon / Looking for the time (workin' girl) / Deadwood, South Dakota / More than a whisper / I would bring you Ireland / Roseville fair / Workin' in corners / Trouble in the fields / The wing and the wheel / From a distance / Love at the five and dime / Spin on a red brick floor. *(cd re-iss. Oct 98; MCLD 19388)*

Jun 89. (7") *<53700>* IT'S A HARD LIFE WHEREVER YOU GO. / From A Distance [ ] [–]

Jul 89. (7") *(MCA 1358)* IT'S A HARD LIFE WHEREVER YOU GO. / Gulf Coast Highway [–] [ ]
(cd-s+=/12"+=) (D+/MCAT 1358) - If wishes were changes.

Sep 89. (lp/c/cd) *<MCA/+C/D 6319> (MCG/MCGC/DMCG 6066)*
STORMS [99] [38]
- I don't wanna talk about love / Drive-in movies and dashboard lights / You made this love a teardrop / Brave companion of the road / Storms / It's a hard life wherever you go / If wishes were changes / Listen to the radio / Leaving the harbor / Radio Fragile. *(cd re-iss. Oct 98; MCLD 19389) (lp re-iss. Dec 98 on Alto; AA 004)*

Sep 89. (7") *<53761>* I DON'T WANNA TALK ABOUT LOVE. / Drive-In Movies And Dashboard Lights [ ] [–]

Nov 89. (7") *(MCA 1379)* YOU MADE THIS LOVE A TEARDROP. / More Than A Whisper [–] [ ]
(cd-s+=/12"+=) (D+/MCAT 1379) - Little love affairs.

Sep 91. (7") *(MCS 1566)* LATE NIGHT GRANDE HOTEL. / It's Just Another Morning Here [–] [ ]
(12"+=) (MCST 1566) - Wooden heart.
(cd-s++=) (MCSTD 1566) - From a distance.

Sep 91. (lp/c/cd) *<(MCA/+C/D 10306)>* **LATE NIGHT GRANDE HOTEL** [ ] [40]
- It's just another morning here / Late night Grande Hotel / It's too late / Fields of summer / Heaven / The power lines / Hometown streets / Down 'n' outer / One blade shy of a sharp edge / The sun, moon, and stars / San Diego serenade. *(cd re-iss. Oct 95; MCLD 10304) (cd re-iss. Oct 00; AAMCAD 10306)*

Nov 91. (7") *(MCS 1596)* HEAVEN. / Down 'N' Outer [–] [ ]
(12"+=) *(MCST 1596)* - Tumble and fall.
(cd-s+=) *(MCSTD 1596)* - Love at the Five And Dime (live).

Elektra — MCA

Feb 93. (c-s) *(MCSC 1743)* SPEED OF THE SOUND OF LONELINESS / From Clare To Here [–] [ ]
(cd-s+=) *(MCSTD 1743)* - Boots of Spanish leather.

Mar 93. (cd/c) *<61464-2/-4> (MCD/MCC 10796)* **OTHER VOICES, OTHER ROOMS** [54] Feb 93 [18]
- Across the great divide / Woman of the Phoenix / Tecumseh Valley / Three flights up / Boots of Spanish leather / Speed of the sound of loneliness / From Clare to here / Can't help but wonder where I'm bound / Do re mi / This old town / Comin' down in the rain / Ten degrees and getting colder / Morning song for Sally / Night rider's lament / Are you tired of me darling / Turn around / Wimoweh.

May 93. (c-s) *(MCSC 1771)* FROM CLARE TO HERE / Cradle Of The Interstate [–] [ ]
(cd-s+=) *(MCSTD 1771)* - De Lejos (From a distance) (Spanish version) / ('A'-extended).

Sep 94. (cd/c) *<61681-2/-4>* (MCD/MCC 11155) **FLYER** [48] [20]
- The flyer / Nobody's angel / Say it isn't so / Southbound train / These days in an open book / Time of inconvenience / Don't forget about me / Always will / Going back to Georgia / Talk to me while I'm listening / Fragile / On Grafton Street / Anything you need but me / Goodnight to a mother's dream / This heart.

Sep 94. (cd-s) *(MCSTD 2035)* ON GRAFTON STREET / These Days In An Open Book / This Heart [–] [ ]

Elektra — Elektra

Mar 97. (cd/c) *<(7559 62015-2/-4)>* **BLUE ROSES FROM THE MOONS** [ ] [64]
- Everything's comin' up roses / Two for the road / Wouldn't that be fine / I live on a battlefield / Saint Teresa of Avila / Gulf Coast highway / I fought the law / Not my way home / Is this all there is? / Maybe tomorrow / Waiting for love / I'll move along / Morning train / She ain't going nowhere.

May 97. (cd-s) *<7559-64182-2>* EVERYTHING'S COMIN' UP ROSES / Not My Way Home / Well... All Right [ ] [–]

Jul 98. (cd/c) *<(7559 62235-2/-4)>* **OTHER VOICES, TOO (A TRIP TO THE BOUNTIFUL)** [85] Sep 98 [ ]
- Wall of death / Who knows where the time goes? / You were on my mind / Walk right back / Canadian whiskey / Desperados waiting for a train / Wings of a dove / Dress of laces / Summer wages / He was a friend of mine / Hard times (come again no more) / Wasn't that a mighty storm / Deportee (plane wreck at Los Gatos) / Yarrington town / I still miss someone / Try the love / The streets of Baltimore / Darcy Farrow / If I had a hammer (the hammer song).

(below re-workings, credited with The LONDON SYMPHONY ORCHESTRA)

Sep 99. (cd/c) *<(7559 62418-2/-4)>* **DUST BOWL SYMPHONY** [ ] [ ]
- Trouble in the fields / The wing and the wheel / These days in an open book / Love at the five and dime (duet with DARIUS RUCKER) / It's a hard life wherever you go / Late night Grande Hotel / Tell me how / Not my way home / 1937 pre-war Kimball / Waiting for love / Nobody's angel / Always will / Drops from the faucet / Dust bowl reprise.

Jul 01. (cd) *<(7559 62660-2)>* **CLOCK WITHOUT HANDS** [ ] [61]
- Clock without hands / Traveling through this part of you / Where would I be / Midnight in Missoula / Lost him in the sun / The ghost inside of me / Truly something fine / Cotton / Pearl's eye view (the life of Dickey Chappelle) / Roses on

the 4th of July / Shaking out the snow / Armstrong / Last song for mother / In the wee small hours of the morning.

Rounder Rounder

Sep 02. (cd) *<11661 3220-2> (ROUCD 3220)* **WINTER MARQUEE** (live)
- Speed of sound of loneliness / I wish it would rain / Boots of Spanish leather / Two for the road / Listen to the radio / There's a light beyond these woods / Gulf coast highway / The flyer / Good night, New York / Traveling through this part of you / Last train home / I'm not drivin' these wheels (bring the prose to the wheel) / What's that I hear / White freight liner.

New Door New Door

Feb 05. (cd) *<(986 443-9)>* **HEARTS IN MIND** Oct 04
- A simple life / Angels / Heart of Indochine / Beautiful / Back when Ted loved Sylvia / Mountain of sorrow / Old Hanoi / Before / I love this town / Rise to the occasion / Love conquers all / Last train home / Big blue ball of war. *<US+=>- Our very own.*

Rounder Rounder

Nov 06. (cd) *<(116 613265-2)>* **RUBY'S TORCH**
- When I dream / If these walls could speak / Ruby's arms / Never be the sun / Bluer than blue / Brave companion of the road / Grapefruit moon / Please call me, baby / Late night grande hotel / In the wee small hours of the morning / Drops from the faucet.

Jun 09. (cd) *<(116 613275-2)>* **THE LOVING KIND**
- The loving kind / Money changes everything / One of these days / Up against the rain / Cotton / Not innocent enough / Across America / Party girl / Sing / Things I don't need / Still life / Tequila after midnight / Pour me a drink.

- (8-10*) compilations -

Oct 93. (cd/c) MCA; *<MCA D/C 10914>* **THE MCA YEARS - A RETROSPECTIVE** [-]
- (tracks as below)

Nov 93. (cd/c) MCA; *(MCD/MCC 10966)* **THE BEST OF NANCI GRIFFITH** 27
- Trouble in the fields / From a distance / Speed of the sound of loneliness / Love at the five and dime / Listen to the radio / Gulf coast highway / I wish it would rain / Ford Econoline / If wishes were changes / The wing and the wheel / Late night Grande Hotel / From Clare to here / It's just another morning here / Tumble and fall / There's a light beyond these woods (Mary Margaret) / Outbound plane / Lone star state of mind / It's a hard life wherever you go. *(UK+=)- The road to Aberdeen.*

Apr 01. (cd) M.C.A.; *<112169> (MCLD 19395)* **WINGS TO FLY AND A PLACE TO BE: AN INTRODUCTION TO NANCI GRIFFITH** Mar 00
- From a distance / I wish it would rain / Lone star state of mind / Listen to the radio / It's a hard life wherever you go / Trouble in the fields / Outbound plane / Ford Econoline / Gulf Coast highway / Love at the five and dime (live) / I knew love / Sweet dreams will come / Spin on a red brick floor / I don't want to talk about love.

Jun 02. (cd) MCA; *<(170301-2)>* **FROM A DISTANCE: THE VERY BEST OF NANCI GRIFFITH** Jul 02
- Lone star state of mind / Cold hearts - Closed minds / From a distance / Ford Econoline / Trouble in the fields / There's a light beyond these woods (Mary Margaret) / Lookin' for the time (workin' girl) (live) / I don't want to talk about love / Drive-in movies and dashboard lights / It's a hard life wherever you go / If wishes were changes / Once in a very blue moon (live) / Anyone can be somebody's fool / I knew love / Gulf coast highway / I wish it would rain / Outbound plane / Love at the five and dime (live) / It's just another morning here / Late night Grande Hotel / Hometown streets / The wing and the wheel (live).

Jun 03. (d-cd) MCA; *<044702> (170381-2)* **THE COMPLETE MCA STUDIO RECORDINGS** Jul 03
- Tumble and fall / (LONE STAR STATE OF MIND tracks) / (LITTLE LOVE AFFAIRS tracks) // Wooden heart / (STORMS tracks) / (LATE NIGHT GRANDE HOTEL tracks) / Stand your ground.

- (5-7*) compilations, etc.-

Mar 97. (cd) Universal; *<(AAMCAD 21000)>* **COUNTRY GOLD** Jan 05
- Trouble in the fields / Cold hearts - Closed minds / I knew love / Anyone can be somebody's fool / From a distance / Never mind / Once in a very blue moon / I wish it would rain / Listen to the radio / Drive-in movies and dashboard lights.

Feb 01. (cd) MCA; *<(AA88 170191-2)>* **THE BEST OF NANCI GRIFFITH: THE MILLENNIUM COLLECTION** Mar 03
- Once in a very blue moon (live) / Lone star state of mind / Trouble in the fields / From a distance / There's a light beyond these woods (Mary Margaret) / It's a hard life wherever you go / I knew love / Outbound plane / Late night Grande Hotel / Love at the five and dime (live) / The wing and the wheel.

Larkin GRIMM

Taking freak-folk music into a new, ethereal realm, Larkin drew her inspirations from her German/Afro-Caribbean/Sinti father (a fiddler) and her English/French/Cree Indian mother (a folk singer). Born September 18, 1981 into a commune (The Holy Order Of MANS, disbanded 1984) based in Memphis, Tennessee, she subsequently relocated with her parents to Dahlonega, Georgia when they severed their cultish ties.

Painting and sculpting were favourite pursuits with Larkin, and she won a scholarship to Yale, although this was interrupted for a while when she took up singing in Alaska. Returning to Yale, she began to write music for her debut album.

Recorded in dark places in Dahlonega and her new home in Providence, Rhode Island, **HARPOON** (2005) {*4} is a disjointed, experimental, back-to-nature affair that could only be described as dangling from the cliff's edge of folk music. Certainly not for the folk purist (although 'Pigeon Food' tries its damndest to be acceptable), it seems to put the listener in the presence of possessive spirits, or warped records of BUFFY SAINTE-MARIE, Yoko Ono or JANE SIBERRY. Titles such as 'I Am Eating Your Deathly Dream', 'Don't Come Down, Darkness' and 'I Killed Someone' sum up where the album's at. Plucked primal rhythms and Bjork-like shrieks of spaced-out singing fight for dominance on the longest piece, 'Future Friend', while it would be wise to dispose of any razor blades before hearing 'Touch Me, Shaping Hands' or 'Patch It Up'.

With Mother Nature as her guide in matters ecological, musical and spiritual, **THE LAST TREE** (2006) {*6} finds her making concessions to melody and rhythm, however sparse and out-there. Howling out a Danielle Dax-meets-the-banshee cascade of darkened delights, GRIMM lays bare her stripped-down, acidic freak-folk - check out the title track. From short takes 'There Is A Giant Panther' and 'The Sun Comes Up' to the 10-minute 'Little Weeper', each track weaves its way through a dense, wooded forest of musical soundscapes. Helping her out in various shapes and forms are her family, plus singer Lara Polangco (on 'The Most Excruciating Vibe' and a reading of Boudleaux Bryant's bluegrass/C&W gem 'Rocky Top') and Teppei Ozawa (on 'Into The Grey Forest, Breathing Love').

Now on the Young God label, LARKIN returned in 2008 with her best effort yet, **PARPLAR** {*7}, another eclectic album, although here she abandons freak-folk for avant-pop pastures. Accessible in most places - imagine JONI MITCHELL for 'They Were Wrong', DORY PREVIN for 'Blond And Golden Johns' and Marty Robbins's 'Ghost Riders In The Sky' for 'Ride That Cyclone') - GRIMM for once fails to live up to her name. The jauntiness of 'Dominican Rum' and 'How To Catch A Lizard' (like the one on the sleeve artwork, no doubt) are a measured counterbalance to Larkin's uniquely full-on folk. *MCS*

Larkin Grimm - vocals, dulcimer, flute, guitar / + friends

US UK
Secret Eye Secret Eye

Oct 05. (cd) *<AB-OC-18)>* **HARPOON**
- Entrance / Going out / Patch it up / Pigeon food / I am eating your deathly dreams / One hundred men / Future friend / Go gently / Harpoon baptism / I killed someone / Don't come down, darkness / Touch me, shaping hands / White water.

Oct 06. (cd) *<(AB-OC-29)>* **THE LAST TREE**
- The last tree / Into the grey forest, breathing love / I killed someone (part 2) / There is a giant panther / Little weeper / The most excruciating vibe / No moonlight / Strange creature / The sun comes up / Link in your chain / Rocky top / The waterfall.

Young God not issued

Oct 08. (cd) *<YG 37>* **PARPLAR** [-]
- They were wrong / Ride that cyclone / Blond and golden johns / Dominican rum / Parplar / Durge / Be my host / Mina minou / My Justine / Anger in your liver / All the pleasures in the world / Fall on your knees / How to catch a lizard / The dip / Hope for the hopeless.

K.C. GROVES (⟹ UNCLE EARL)

HAMELL ON TRIAL

A pivotal figure in the anti-folk movement in late-1980s New York, the musician, poet, journalist, storyteller and anarchist Ed Hamell (b. October 1, 1954 in Syracuse, New York) has racked up quite a discography in recent years, beginning as far back as 1989 when he issued the low-key LP **CONVICTION** {*6}. There were no signs of his primitive power-folk here as his Big Apple drawl and heavy CBGB attitude were summoned up on 'Another Liar', the rockabilly-esque 'Because You Should' and the slow honky-tonkin' of 'No Tradin''.

Ed subsequently moved back to Austin, Texas and set up a residency in the thriving Electric Lounge folk café, where he deliberately annoyed the patrons, who were used to gentle folk-rock, by playing grinding post-New Wave on an acoustic guitar and blurting out offensive lyrics in his half-sung, half-spoken style.

By 1994 HAMELL had accumulated a growing fan base, and people were starting to see the humorous side of his anti-folk/punk shenanigans. He signed with Austin's Doolittle imprint and issued his second set, **BIG AS LIFE** (1996) {*5}, which saw major label Mercury take an interest when they re-released it shortly afterwards. **THE CHORD IS MIGHTIER THAN THE SWORD** (1997) {*7} was delivered a year later, HAMELL having recruited a full band for his first real rock outing. Among the nods to The Stooges and The Velvet Underground, he relaxed his punk-rock austerity and wrote a touching ode to the First Beatle, 'John Lennon'.

A brief hiatus followed before he issued his first concept album, **CHOOCHTOWN** (2000) {*7}. Telling the integrated stories of various characters including 'Joe Brush', 'Uncle Morris', 'Judy' and of course 'Chooch', this was Ed at his anti-folk, acoustic-chugging, bile-spraying narrative best. Opening track 'Go Fuck Yourself' was a Travis Bickle-inspired psychotic death letter/poem to pathetic males everywhere, and 'Bill Hicks' paid tribute to the late, great comedian.

A live album, **ED'S NOT DEAD: HAMELL COMES ALIVE** (2001) {*6} (the title referred to a near-fatal car crash the singer was involved in), featured a very worthy finale of Johnny Cash's 'Folsom Prison Blues'. It was clear that Ed's stint as support to ANI DiFRANCO (his Righteous Babe label boss) was paying off, in terms of credibility at least.

Two years later, after a stint as a columnist for the British music magazine Uncut, HAMELL issued the brilliant **TOUGH LOVE** (2003) {*8}, a record that achieved cult status for his sardonic wit and lyrical prowess. Glenn Danni and Eddie Stratton were his rhythm section. Inspired by the birth of his son, Detroit, anti-folk hero HAMELL delivered his own version of punk protest on his fifth set, **SONGS FOR PARENTS WHO ENJOY DRUGS** (2006) {*6}. **TERRORISM OF EVERYDAY LIFE** (2008) was a stand-up and music set recorded in front of a favourable audience in Edinburgh. Re-credited to a solo ED HAMELL as **RANT & ROLL** {*8}, it was a truly side-splitting affair; hardly folk, but f**k was not dead by any stretch of the imagination. You have been warned.

His intentionally low profile still pleases his loyal fans, and you can download anything from his most recent project, '365 Songs A Year' (a song a day), from his website. '15 of 100' (2010) is his selection from the first hundred of these. *MCS*

Ed Hamell - vocals, guitar / with **George Rossi** - keyboards / **Rob Spagnoletti** - percussion / **Arty Lenin** - backing vocals

US Blue Wave — UK not issued

Apr 89. (lp/c) <*110*> **CONVICTION** [ ] [-]
- Looking for you / Another liar / Cocaine or me / Talking video blues / Hoo hoo song / Change of climate / When you're alone / No tradin'/ Tear at your dust / Because you should.

Mercury — not issued

Mar 96. (cd) <*314 528 829-2*> **BIG AS LIFE** [ ] [-]
- Sugarfree / Harmony / Blood of the wolf / Brother Franklin / Big as life / Pep rally / Z-roxx / Dead man's float / Piccolo Joe / In the neighborhood / Open up the gates / Get in the game / Untitled.

—— now with various band personnel

Apr 97. (cd) <*314 534 737-2*> **THE CHORD IS MIGHTIER THAN THE SWORD** [ ] [-]
- Mr Fear / No delays / The vines / Red martyr / Confess me / New world / Decisions / John Lennon / Mark don't go / In a bar / The meeting.

Such-A-Punch — Evangeline

Mar 00. (cd) <*SAPM 3001*> *(GEL 4016)* **CHOOCHTOWN** [ ] Jan 01 [ ]
- Go fuck yourself / When Bobby comes down / Hamell's ramble / I'm gonna watch you sleep / Uncle Morris / Disconnected / Nancy's got a new boyfriend / Choochtown / Shout outs / The lottery / The long drive / Judy / Joe Brush / The mall / Bill Hicks (ascension) / Bill Hicks.

—— now with **Ani DiFranco** - drums

Jun 01. (cd) <*SAPM 3002*> *(GELM 4038)* **ED'S NOT DEAD - HAMELL COMES ALIVE!** (live on tour 2000) [ ] Jan 02 [ ]
- Sugarfree / Seven seas / I hate your kid / I'm gonna watch you sleep / When Bobby comes down / Choochtown / Dead man's float / The vines / Some hearts / Disconnected / Big as life / Open up the gates / John Lennon / Hoo hoo song / The meeting / Folsom prison blues.

Righteous Babe — Righteous Babe

Aug 03. (cd) <*(RBR 033-D)*> **TOUGH LOVE** [ ] Oct 03 [ ]
- Don't kill / Halfway / When destiny calls / Hail / 95 south / Downs / All that was said / A little concerned, that's all / Everything and nothing / Tough love / Dear Pete / There is a God / First date / Worry wart / Oughta go around / Detroit lullaby.

Feb 06. (cd) <*(RBR 049-D)*> **SONGS FOR PARENTS WHO ENJOY DRUGS** [ ] Jul 07 [ ]
- Inquiring minds / Heat / Wheels (pt.1) / Pretty colors / Apartment #4 / Hey boss / Values / Maddy's (pt.1) / Jerkin' / Socializing / Maddy's (pt.2) / Coulter's snatch / Civil disobedience / Mommy's not talking today / Father's advice / Wheels (pt.2).

Jun 08. (cd+dvd; as ED HAMELL) <*RBRCD 061-D*> **RANT & ROLL: THE TERRORISM OF EVERYDAY LIFE** (LIVE IN EDINBURGH bootleg) [-] [ ]
- An attitude / John Lennon / Folk mass / When you're young / Ashes - Pete / The trough / Bands 'n' guitars / Seven seas / Crack bar / Chris and the angels / Father's kitchen - Racine - Ellicottville / Halfway / Terrors / Pussy / Parents / Father's advice / Vision - Full circle / Inquiring minds / Pledge / The meeting.

- (8-10*) compilations -

Nov 02. (cd) Evangeline: <*(GEL 4056)*> **MERCUROYALE: THE BEST OF THE MERCURY YEARS** [ ] Sep 02 [ ]
- Blood on the wolf / Sugarfree / In the neighborhood / John Lennon / Brother Franklin / Big as life / In a bar / The vines / Open up the gates / Harmony / Red martyr / Z-roxx / Dead man's float / Confess me / The meeting / Get in the game.

Butch HANCOCK

Born George Hancock, July 12, 1945 in Lubbock, Texas, singer-songwriter BUTCH HANCOCK is one of a long line of country-folk stars to emerge from the late 1970s. From his early days as a member of the legendary, Nashville-biased Flatlanders (alongside New Country giants like Jimmie Dale Gilmore and Joe Ely), Butch brought his own Hank Williams-like, GUTHRIE/DYLAN-style dustbowl drawl to a solo career that kicked off in 1978 with **WEST TEXAS WALTZES AND DUST-BLOWN TRACTOR TUNES** {*7}; 'Dry Land Farm' is one example.

Also released on his own Rainlight imprint, the double set **THE WIND'S DOMINION** (1979) {*6}, the full-band outing **DIAMOND HILL** (1980) {*7}, the live **FIRE-WATER** (1981) {*7} and **1981: A SPARE ODYSSEY** (1981) {*6} were typical of the unpolished, rootsy Americana of his early ventures. 1985's collaboration with Marce Lacouture, **YELLA ROSE** {*5}, was, as the title suggested, very Texas-orientated. In his day job he was a photographer and architect.

Cassettes were once the fashionable medium for folk and country in the US and Britain, and Butch's discography was no exception, stretching to a 14-item (140 songs, none repeated) box of his live efforts entitled **NO TWO ALIKE** (1990) {*6}. **SPLIT AND SLIDE II** (1986) {*5} and **CAUSE OF THE CACTUS** (1987) {*5} were earlier diversions, and there was a live-in-Australia collaboration with old Flatlanders comrade Dale Gilmore, released as **TWO ROADS** (1992) {*6}.

While Gilmore and Ely had stood by him on many occasions, and swapped recording sessions (including work on the musical-theatre piece 'Chippy' and a Flatlanders reunion set in 2002), HANCOCK was still prominent as a soloist with **OWN THE WAY OVER HERE** (1993) {*6} and **EATS AWAY THE NIGHT** (1994) {*7}, both on bluegrass-friendly label Sugar Hill. His Rainlight label was back in circulation for **YOU COULDA WALKED AROUND THE WORLD** (1997) {*6}, his 'Blood On The Tracks' template apparent in 'Red Blood (Drippin' From The Moon)'.

Several years in the making at his Terlingua desert-town base, **WAR AND PEACE** (2006) {*7} was his political concept album, taking on George W. Bush and his nation's vile occupation of Iraq and other countries in songs such as 'Give Them Water', 'Damage Done', etc. Butch was a true patriot American, living and fighting for his country through words some politicians couldn't even spell. *MCS*

Butch Hancock - vocals, guitars, harmonica (with session people and guests)

US Rainlight — UK not issued

1978. (lp) <*RLT-114*> **WEST TEXAS WALTZES AND DUST-BLOWN TRACTOR TUNES**
- Dry land farm / Where the west winds... have blow'd / You've never seen me cry / I wish I was only workin' / Dirt road song / West Texas waltz / They say it's a good land / I grew to be a stranger / Texas air / Little coyote waltz / Just one thunderstorm. <*cd-iss. Jan 00; same*>

1979. (d-lp) <*RLT-1644*> **THE WIND'S DOMINION**
- Sea's deadog catch / Capture, fracture and the rapture / The wind's dominion / Long road to Asia Minor / Split and slide / Smokin' in the rain / Fightin' for my life / Personal rendition of the blues / Dominoes / Once followed by the wind // Wild horses chase the wind / Own and own / Mario y Maria (Cryin' statues - Spittin' images) / Eternal triangles / Only born / The gift horse of mercy / The wind's dominion. <*cd-iss. Jan 00; same*>

1980. (lp) <*RLT-777*> **DIAMOND HILL**
- Golden hearted ways / You can take me for one / Neon wind / Diamond hill / Corona del Mar / The ghost of give-and-take avenue / Some folks call it style / Her lover of the hour / Wheels of fortune. <*cd-iss. Jan 00; same*>

1981. (lp) <*RLT-1981*> **1981: A SPARE ODYSSEY**
- Horseflies / 1981: A spare odyssey / Dawgs of transition / Two roads / Angels on the lam / 'Cause you never compromise / Sharp cutting wings / I wish you were with me tonight / Voice in the wilderness. <*cd-iss. Jan 00; same*>

1981. (lp) <*RLT-100*> **FIRE-WATER: seeks its own level**
[live at the Alamo]
- There's no hiding place down here / Like the light at dawn / Firewater (seeks its own level) / I keep wishin' for you / If you were a bluebird / One road more / Man on a pilgrimage / The wind's dominion. <*cd-iss. Jan 00; same*>

1985. (lp; by BUTCH HANCOCK & MARCE LACOUTURE)
<*RLT-1137*> **YELLA ROSE**
- Perfection in the mud / Yella rose / Like a kiss on the mouth / Ain't no mercy on the hiway / Only makes me love you more / So I'll run / Two roads / Sharp cutting wings / Tell me what you know. <*cd-iss. Jan 00; same*>

1986. (c) <*RLT-1986*> **SPLIT AND SLIDE II**

1987. (c) <*RLT-8787*> **CAUSE OF THE CACTUS**

Jul 90. (ltd; 14-c-box) <*RLT 1001-1014*> **NO TWO ALIKE** — mail-o
[six nights live at Cactus Café in February 1990]
- Little coyote / Unknown love / Only born / I wish you were here with me tonight / Long road to Asia Minor / Split and slide / Mountains of resistance / Solstice / Her personal rendition of the blues / I wish I was only working // Rawhide - Raw nerve / I played along / Coolin' down / Wheel of fortune / Just a wave / I think too much of you / Nothing of the kind / 99 holes / Stronger bonds / Her lover of the hour // There is a place to go / Golden guitar lounge / Standin' at a big hotel / Dry land farm / Tennessee is not the state I'm in / She never spoke Spanish to me / Boxcars / Row of dominoes / Suckin' on a bottle of gin / Wild horses chase the wind // Road hawg / She finally spoke Spanish to me / Voice in the wilderness / Gift horse of mercy / Sweet mother of pearl / Golden hearted ways / Eternal triangles / Angels on the lam / Once followed by the wind / Dawg of intermittent love / Seven cities of gold / Fightin' for my life / Mario y Maria / Changin' planes in Austin / Like the light at dawn / San Pedro / Sky night noon / Gently fallin' rain / Ramblin' man / Red Chevrolet // Eggs of your chickens / Man on a pilgrimage / Baby be mine / The wind's dominion / One rose alone / Own and own / Perfection in the mud / Dawgs of transition / You're so easy to touch / Some folks call it style // Banks of the Guadalupe / Stake my reputation / Capture, fracture, rapture / New Jersey lily / One kiss / 1981: a spare odyssey / Cause you never compromise / Moments of their day / Yella rose / Leo and Leona / Diamond hill / Ain't no mercy on the highway / The day my old donkey died / My mind's got a mind of its own / Already gone / Split and slide II / Sad dirty Saturday night / Battlescars / Smokin' in the rain / Baby do you love me still // Ghost of give-and-take avenue / Up times in a down town / Corona der Mar / One eternal clown / Mountains to climb / Wind's gonna blow you away / Here comes one now / Fools fall in love / In another world / Two roads // Raw Sienna / Neon wind / Like a kiss on the mouth / When will you hold me again / Big ideas now / Fire-water seeks its own level / You just tell me that / Tell me what you know / Down on the drag / Horseflies // Home is where the heart is / Little dead sweetheart #1 / Chughole / Talk of the town / They say it's a good land / Prisoner of the moon / Texas air / Where the west wind has blow'd / Just one thunderstorm / It's just a storm // Don't let go until it thunders / Real world kid / 14th street / One road more / Honky tonk tavern / Down this road and back again / The stars in my life / She had everything / You've never seen me cry / If you were a bluebird // Shadow of the moon / When the night's are cold / West Texas waltz / Wishin' for you / All my illusions / Love's transfusion / Lord of the highway / Outward bound / I grew to be a stranger / The red, white and blue // Back on the track / High noon / Another diamond hill / Deep blue eddy / Down to earth again / Only makes me love you more / Don't let the mountains down / Pal-o-mine / Roads' ends're found / Last long silver dollar.

Caroline — Virgin

Jul 92. (cd/c/lp; by BUTCH HANCOCK & JIMMIE DALE GILMORE) <*CAROL-1726-2/-4/-1*> *(CD/TC+V 2649)*
TWO ROADS [live in Australia, March 22, 1990] — Oct 90
- Hello stranger / Ramblin' man / Her lover of the hour / Tonight I think I'm gonna go downtown / Two roads / Wheels of fortune / One road more / Standin' on the corner (Blue yodel No.9) / Banks of the Guadalupe / Dallas / Already gone / Special treatment / Howlin' at midnight / Fire water (seeks its own level) / West Texas waltz.

Sugar Hill — Sugar Hill

May 93. (cd/c) <*(SHCD/SHC 1038)*> **OWN THE WAY OVER HERE**
- Talkin' about that Panama canal / Only born / Smokin' in the rain / Corona del Mar / Like the light at dawn / Gift horse of mercy / Neon wind / Perfection in the mud / Only makes me love you more / Already gone / Away from the fountain.

Oct 94. (cd/c) <*(SHCD/SHC 1048)*> **EATS AWAY THE NIGHT** — Jan 97
- To each his own / Moanin' of the midnight train / Eileen / One kiss / Pumpkineater / If you were a bluebird / Junkyard in the sun / Boxcars / Baby me mine / Welcome to the real world kid / Eats away the night.

—— In 1994/95, Butch was part of Joe Ely's ex-Flatlanders collective 'Chippy' project set.

Rainlight — not issued

Nov 97. (cd) <*RLT-37*> **YOU COULDA WALKED AROUND THE WORLD**
- Chase / Barefoot prints / Roll around / Long sunsets / Black Irish rose / Call curled up / Hidin' in the hills / Low lights of town / Red blood (drippin' from the moon) / One good time / Circumstance / Naked light of day / You coulda walked around the world.

—— In 2002 he was part of The Flatlanders' reunion album 'Now Again'.

Two Roads — not issued

Oct 06. (cd) <*TR-2006*> **WAR AND PEACE**
- Give them water / Damage done / When the good and the bad get ugly / Toast / Old man, old man / The devil in us all / The master game / Road map for the blues / Between wars / Cast the devils out / Brother won't you shake my hand? / Pot of glue / That great election day.

- (8-10*) compilations -

Oct 89. (d-lp/c/cd) Sugar Hill; <*SH+C/CD 1036*> Demon; *(D-FIEND/FIENDCD 150)* **OWN AND OWN**
- Dry land farm / The wind's dominion / Diamond hill / 1981: A spare odyssey / Firewater (seeks its own level) / West Texas waltz / Horseflies / If you were a bluebird / Own and own / Fools fall in love / Yella rose / Like a kiss on the mouth / The ghost of give-and-take avenue / Tell me what you want to know / Just a storm / Just tell me that / When will you hold me again. *(UK cd re-iss. Mar 98 on Sugar Hill; same as US)*

The HANDSOME FAMILY

Balancing on the ridge where C&W, grunge-rock and bluegrass-folk meet, The HANDSOME FAMILY (Texan songwriter Brett Sparks and his Long Island-born wife Rennie) are alt-country's answer to Gomez and Morticia, George Jones and Tammy Wynette or a distorted, updated Timbuk 3 (remember them?), although musically speaking they're miles apart from any of the others. Starting off in Chicago, Illinois in 1993, the pair were initially augmented by drummer Mike Werner.

Forged out of acute personal difficulties, The HANDSOME FAMILY's music was set against a background of strife. Brett had suffered a mental breakdown (he had been trying to write his own Bible), while Rennie was the 'school freak' who immersed herself in literature. The Greek classic The Iliad is apparently her favourite book.

From the onset the trio toured extensively, promoting their early releases and unsettling audiences in the US and Europe with their dark country tales and life-size plastic animals. Initially aided by co-producer Dave Trumfio, the renegade 'true country' duo were augmented on their first recordings by studio helpers.

ODESSA (1995) {*7} was an acerbic cocktail of Nashville-meets-GORDON LIGHTFOOT songs such as 'Arlene', the Bible-bashing 'Water Into Wine', 'Moving Furniture Around' and 'Everything That Rises Must Converge', and alt-rock numbers like the Creedence/Fogerty-styled 'Here's Hopin'', the R.E.M.-ish 'One Way Up' and 'Gorilla', and the post-grunge 'Pony', 'Claire Said' and Rennie's Hole-meet-Lydia Lunch-like 'Big Bad Wolf'. The finale was the puppy-friendly novelty 'Happy Harvest'.

MILK AND SCISSORS (1996) {*6} was arguably less inventive and inspirational ('Lake Geneva', suggestive of Leonard Cohen's 'Suzanne', testifies to that), and its accent was less on angst - more steely and Appalachian-textured, with the exception of 'Winnebago Skeletons' and their rousing rockabilly reading of trad standard 'The House Carpenter'. Werner's sole contribution was the off-kilter instrumental 'Puddin' Fingers'. Compelling tales of woe and cruel misfortune riddled the set, none more compellingly than 'The Dutch Boy' (containing the 'Milk and scissors' phrase), 'The King Who Wouldn't Smile' and 'Amelia Earhart Vs. The Dancing Bear'.

Initially released in Germany on vinyl only, **INVISIBLE HANDS** (1997) {*6} found the husband-and-wife duo (now without Werner) gaining attention outside of the confines of roots and Americana; only 'Tin Foil' (from the preceding set) had been released before. Sadly, Rennie's squeaky voice takes a back seat, rising for the moon only on the FAIRPORT-like trad number 'Barbara Allen'.

Mastered in the mobile studio of collaborator Jeff Tweedy (Wilco, Uncle Tupelo), and recorded as usual in Trumfio's living-room and bathroom, 1998's pioneering **THROUGH THE TREES** {*8} opened with the delightfully disturbing 'Weightless Again'. The track's peerless lyrics describe their despairing emotions: "This is why people OD on pills, And jump... from the Golden Gate bridge, Anything to feel weightless again." Cloaked in Brett's gothic Faron Young-meets-Neil Young vocals, The HANDSOME FAMILY's mournful tales of tragic Wild West folklore conjure up cinematic images of barren canyons and Native American ghosts dancing on General Custer's grave. Brooding vignettes and liquor-bottle ballads garnished this definitive neo-C&W set, other retro-fried highlights including 'My Sister's Tiny Hands', 'Stalled', 'Cathedrals' (also on INVISIBLE HANDS), 'The Woman Downstairs' and the explicit 'My Ghost'. Rennie's crazed, nasal hillbilly twang was most effective on the earthy 'Down In The Ground'.

Trading a little on a Johnny Cash beat, the gloomy goths returned in 2000 with the country-flavoured **IN THE AIR** {*7}. Full of whimsical murder ballads (as per usual) and recorded in the couple's living-room, the best tracks were 'A Beautiful Thing', 'When The Helicopter Comes' and the Neil Young-esque 'So Much Wine'. Some songs featured violinist Andrew Bird (ex-Squirrel Nut Zippers) and his Bowl Of Fire band, and/or guitarist Darrell Sparks.

Deliciously bleak but achingly tender, **TWILIGHT** (2001) {*6} was their first album not to be recorded in a studio - it was made on a computer at their new home in Albuquerque, apparently. However, despite the usual brilliance, there were faults within the set. Sometimes the lyrics seemed too complex for the simplicity of Brett's music, as in 'The Snow White Diner' and 'Passenger Pigeons', which are at times ruined by his bleak, foreboding croon. These issues aside, the set delivered the standard backwoods humour , 'All The TVs In Town' and 'Gravity' being particular highlights, but 'Peace In The Valley Once Again', 'No One Fell Asleep Alone' and 'Birds You Cannot See' were treading the blanket on the ground a little thin.

2002 found them taking a break of sorts, although a couple of low-key sets were issued. **LIVE AT SCHUBA'S TAVERN** {*5} was rather a good live album, initially intended for diehard fans. The self-released part-covers set, **SMOTHERED AND COVERED** {*5}, included songs by Kris Kristofferson ('Sunday Morning Coming Down'), Bill Monroe ('I Hear A Sweet Voice Calling'), The Delmore Brothers ('Trail Of Time'), The Rolling Stones ('Faraway Eyes') and two traditional cuts, 'Banks Of The Ohio' and 'Knoxville Girl'. Sadly, their reading of LEONARD COHEN's 'Famous Blue Raincoat' was reserved for the soundtrack of the 2006 Cohen documentary 'I'm Your Man'.

THE SINGING BONES (2003) {*7} was arguably richer in songwriting structure and lyrical composition, and the set contained some of the duo's best work to date. There was the eerie '24 Hour Store', the Nick Cave-like 'The Bottomless Hole', the Cash-meets-Williams number 'Dry Bones' and a pair of a cappella tracks, 'If The World Should End In Fire' and 'If The World Should End In Ice'. The latter, for some reason, sounded like Auld Lang Syne being sung by a troupe of lumberjack singers from 'Monty Python's Flying Circus'.

Choosing the somewhat safe option of back-to-basics, old-time country, **LAST DAYS OF WONDER** (2006) {*6} brought The HANDSOME FAMILY back to the fold once again. Not exactly hailed as one of their greatest, it nevertheless featured a few gothic-Americana gems in 'Tesla's Hotel Room', the Tom Waits-cloned 'These Golden Jewels', 'After We Shot The Grizzly', 'Beautiful William' and the Rennie-sung 'Hunter Green'.

Three years later and 20 years married, Brett and Rennie completed their eighth studio set, **HONEY MOON** (2009) {*7}, an eclectic record whose styles ranged over Appalachian-like tunes such as 'Little Sparrows', the doo-wop pop of 'Linger, Let Me Linger', the Hazlewood/Sinatra-style 'Wild Wood' and the peaceful, easy feelin' of 'A Thousand Diamond Rings'. *MCS*

Brett Sparks - vocals, guitar, keyboards / **Rennie Sparks** - bass, vocals / **Mike Werner** - drums, vocals

US Carrot Top — UK not issued

Jan 95. (cd) <*SAKI 005CD*> **ODESSA** [ ] [-]
- Here's hopin' / Arlene / Pony / One way up / Water into wine / Giant ant / Everything that rises must converge / Gorilla / The last / Claire said / Moving furniture around / Big bad wolf / She awoke with a jerk / Happy harvest. *(German-iss. Jan 96 on Scout; SR 1004) (UK-iss. Oct 99 & Oct 01; same as US)*

Feb 96. (cd) <*SAKI 011CD*> **MILK AND SCISSORS** [ ] [-]
- Lake Geneva / Winnebago skeletons / Drunk by noon / The house carpenter / The Dutch boy / The king who wouldn't smile / Emily Shore 1819-1839 / Three-legged dog / #1 country song / Amelia Earhart vs. the dancing bear / Tin foil / Puddin' fingers. *(German-iss. Sep 96 on Scout; SR 1011) (UK-iss. Oct 99 & Oct 01; same as US)*

—— now without Werner, who retired from music

not issued — Scout

Sep 97. (m-lp) *(SR 1012)* **INVISIBLE HANDS** [-] German [-]
- Tin foil / Cathedrals / Grandmother waits for you / Bury me here / Barbara Allen / Birds you cannot see. <*(re-iss. Oct 99 & Oct 01 on Carrot Top; SAKI 016CD)*>

Carrot Top — Vinyl Junkie

Jan 98. (cd) <*SAKI 20CD*> *(VJCD 105)* **THROUGH THE TREES** [ ] Apr 98 [ ]
- Weightless again / My sister's tiny hands / Stalled / Where the birch trees lean / Cathedrals / Down in the ground / The giant of Illinois / Down in the valley of hollow logs / I fell / The woman downstairs / Last night I went out walking / Bury me here / My ghost.

Aug 99. (7") *(MAG 025)* MY BEAUTIFUL BRIDE. / (other track by Sackville) [-] Canada [-]

(above issued on Magwheel)

Feb 00. (cd) <*SAKI 23CD*> *(VJCD 112)* **IN THE AIR** [ ] [ ]
- Don't be scared / The sad milkman / In the air / A beautiful thing / So much wine / Up falling Rock Hill / Poor, poor Lenore / When that helicopter comes / Grandmother waits for you / Lie down / My beautiful bride.

2001. (ltd-7") *(Volt 02)* (The Nineteenth Bar track). / THE HANDSOME FAMILY: I Know Who You Are [-] Ire [-]

(above issued on Volta Sounds)

Oct 01. (cd) <*SAKI 27CD*> *(VJCD 126)* **TWILIGHT** [ ] [ ]
- The snow white diner / Passenger pigeons / A dark eye / There is a sound / All the TVs in town / Gravity / Cold, cold, cold / No one fell asleep alone / I know you are there / Birds you cannot see / The white dog / So long / Peace in the valley once again.

2002. (ltd-7") *(SO 23)* (Moviola track). / The HANDSOME FAMILY: Banks Of The Ohio [ ] [-]

(above issued on Spirit Of Orr as part of the 'Quiet Weather' series)

Oct 03. (cd) <*SAKI 36CD*> *(VJCD 144)* **SINGING BONES** [ ] [ ]
- The forgotten lake / Gail with the golden hair / 24-hour store / The bottomless hole / Far from any road / If the world should end in fire / A shadow underneath / Dry bones / Fallen peaches / Whitehaven / Sleepy / The song of a hundred toads / If the world should end in ice.

Mar 06. (cd) <*SAKI 42CD*> *(VJCD 166)* **LAST DAYS OF WONDER** [ ] May 06 [ ]
- Your great journey / Tesla's hotel room / These golden jewels / After we shot the grizzly / Flapping your broken wings / Beautiful William / All the time in airports / White lights / Bowling alley bar / Hunter green / Our blue sky / Somewhere else to be.

Aug 06. (dl-s) *(VJS 7)* AFTER WE SHOT THE GRIZZLY / Eleanor Rigby [-] [ ]

Nov 07. (dl-ep) *(-)* IN THE FOREST OF MISSING AIRPLANES
- All the time in airports / Knoxville girl / The blizzard.

Apr 09. (cd) <*SAKI 50CD*> *(VJCD 185)* **HONEY MOON** [ ] [ ]
- Linger, let me linger / Little sparrows / My friend / When you whispered / The loneliness of magnets / June bugs / A thousand diamond rings / Love is like / The petrified forest / Wild wood / Darling, my darling / The winding corn maze.

- (5-7*) compilations, others, etc.-

Oct 99. (cd) Vinyl Junkie; *(VJCD 110)* **DOWN IN THE VALLEY** [-] [ ]
- Tin foil / My sister's tiny hands / Lake Geneva / Weightless again / No.1 country song / Giant of Illinois / Drunk by noon / Don't be scared / The house carpenter / Arlene / The woman downstairs / Cathedrals / Moving furniture around / The Dutch boy.

Apr 02. (cd) Handsome Family; <*(HF 001CD)*> **SMOTHERED AND COVERED** [ ] Aug 02 [ ]

- There's a city / Sunday morning coming down / Prepared piano #1 / I hear a sweet voice calling / Down in the ground (demo) / Cello #1 / Trail of time / Faraway eyes / Knoxville girl / Prepared piano #2 / The last (demo) / Banks of the Ohio / Cello #2 / Natalie Wood / #1 country song (demo) / Prepared piano #3 / Stupid bells / The weinermobile.

Jul 02. (cd) Digital Club Network; <*(DCN 1005CD)*> **LIVE AT SCHUBA'S TAVERN** (live in Chicago, December 2000)
- Amelia Earhart vs. the dancing bear / The good toothpicks / So much wine / The czar bar / Tin foil / A beautiful thing / Vienna sausage hotline / The giant of Illinois / My sister's tiny hands / Names for all his shirts / Cathedrals / Weightless again / Bony bread / Winnebago skeletons / Drunk by noon / Magic balls (introduction) / The sad milkman / Magic balls (conclusion) / I know you are there / Down in the ground / Arlene / Moving furniture around / Freebird / My ghost / The woman downstairs.

Sean HAYES

If James Blunt were an American, or indeed a soulful folkie - and don't try looking for him in this book - he might have sounded like singer-songwriter SEAN HAYES (b. August 27, 1969 in New York City and raised in North Carolina). An independent artist in the sense that he's stuck to his guns without signing a major record deal, San Francisco resident Sean has performed alongside some of roots music's top stars, including The BE GOOD TANYAS and Aimee Mann. Looking like comedian Rich Hall, but singing in a white-soul voice similar to Al Green's - for example, on 'When We Fall In', from his most recent album, **RUN WOLVES RUN** (2010) {*6} - HAYES has now delivered six above-average albums, each with a nice, horizontal, Sunday-morning appeal. **ALABAMA CHICKEN** (2003) {*6} contains a banjo-plucking rendition of DYLAN's 'Walkin' Down The Line'. *MCS*

Sean Hayes - vocals, acoustic guitar / + session band/players

US: Sean Hayes Music — UK: not issued

1999. (cd) **A THOUSAND TINY PIECES**
- A thousand tiny pieces / Candles, birds, water / Paint your face red / Mary Magdalene / When did it hit you? / Touch / This rock rolling / God's eyes / The same moon / One by one / Awake or asleep / A simple song / She is in everything / Give in. *<re-iss. Mar 08 on Snail Blue; 2767>*

2002. (cd) **LUNAR LUST**
- Hello / Mind looping / Kharma moon / For inspiration / Swim swim swim / Sea love / Smoking signals / Simple + ideal / Whalebutterfly / Greentoad / Birdcagedbird / Painted clown / Never alone / Divine. *<re-iss. Mar 08 on Snail Blue; 2766>*

Sep 03. (cd) **ALABAMA CHICKEN**
- Moonrise / Little Maggie / Here we are... / Alabama chicken / Walkin' down the line / Smoking signals / Balancing act in blue / Two big eyes / Everyday Hamlet / Diamond in the sun / The rain coming down / Rattlesnake charm (dream machine). *<re-iss. Mar 08 on Snail Blue; 2765>*

Jan 06. (cd) **BIG BLACK HOLE AND THE LITTLE BABY STAR**
- Boom boom goes the day / Feel good / 3 am / Politics / Same god / Pollinating toes / Angel / All things... / Big black hole and the little baby star / Rosebush inside (Moreese Bickham) / Fucked me right up / Calling all cars / 33 fool / Turnaroundturnmeon. *<re-iss. Mar 08 on Snail Blue; 2764>*

Jun 07. (cd) **FLOWERING SPADE**
- All for love / Midnight rounders / Time / Hip kids / Dolores Guerrero / Cool hand / Baby I do / Onion / Penniless patron / Sally Ann / Sufidrop / Elizabeth sways / Flowering spade. *<re-iss. Mar 08 on Snail Blue; 2763>*

Ambient Egg — not issued

Dec 09. (cd-s) <*none*> HONEYBEES FALLING / Jump / Day Falls Night Opens

Mar 10. (cd) <*50416*> **RUN WOLVES RUN**
- When we fall in / Open up a window / Garden / Powerful stuff / So down / Gunnin' / Shake your body / Me and my girl / One day the river / Soul shaker / Stella seed.

HEADLESS HEROES (⟹ DIANE, Alela)

HELLO, BLUE ROSES

Formed in Vancouver, Canada in 2005 by female visual artist Sydney Vermont and New Pornographers multi-instrumentalist Dan Bejar (her boyfriend), acoustic-pop folkies HELLO, BLUE ROSES have so far released one album, the well-received 2008 effort **THE PORTRAIT IS FINISHED AND I HAVE FAILED TO CAPTURE YOUR BEAUTY** {*7}.

Taking their name from a line in Tennessee Williams's play The Glass Menagerie, their album swarmed with a myriad of influences from Kate Bush to VASHTI BUNYAN and JUDEE SILL, the best tracks ranging from the almost mediaeval 'Golden Fruit' and 'Come Darkness' to the 1960s-styled sunshine pop of 'Heron Song'. Pity there's been nothing more as of mid-2011. *MCS*

Sydney Vermont - vocals, flute, acoustic guitar / **Dan Bejar** - multi-instruments, vocals (ex-Destroyer, of Swan Lake, of New Pornographers)

US: Locust — UK: Locust

Jan 08. (cd) <*(Locust 106)*> **THE PORTRAIT IS FINISHED AND I HAVE FAILED TO CAPTURE YOUR BEAUTY**
- Hello, blue roses / Scarecrow / Paquita reads by candlelight / Shadow falls / Heron song / St Angela / Coming through imposture / Golden fruit / Come darkness / Sunny skies / Mediterranean snow / Skeleton aim / Sickly star / Hymn. *(also ltd-blue-lp)*

HEM

There is an air of Celtic-folk lilt about several of HEM's songs. Whether it's their lush orchestral overtones and trad-like instrumentation, or singer Sally Ellyson's dreamy, lullaby-like readings (think Christine McVie or Margo Timmins), the ensemble pull it off in droves.

Formed in New York City in 1999 by songwriter Dan Messe and former indie-band engineer and producer Gary Maurer, they found their singer when she answered a Village Voice ad and her demo tape of children's lullabies was accepted - they'd given up hope. Guitarist, mandolinist and banjo player Steve Curtis had already answered the call, and a tight-knit backing group of Bob Hoffnar (distinctive pedal steel), Heather Zimmerman (violin), George Rush (bass) and Mark Brotter (drums) was in place for **RABBIT SONGS** (2001) {*7}. While the star of the show is the band's KALEIDOSCOPE-like take on trad standard 'The Cuckoo', others to savour were 'Half Acre', 'Stupid Mouth Shut' and 'When I Was Drinking'.

A subsequent EP, 'Talking With My Mouth' was an alt-country escapade consisting of a few covers including BILLY EDD WHEELER's 'Jackson' (included on HEM's second set, **EVENINGLAND** (2004) {*7}) and Elvis Costello's '(The Angels Wanna Wear My) Red Shoes'. Several more covers and trad songs appeared on the odds-and-ends collection **NO WORD FROM TOM** (2006) {*6}, notably R.E.M.'s 'South Central Rain', Fountains Of Wayne's 'Radiation Vibe' and Tony Joe White's 'Rainy Night In Georgia'.

The third album, **FUNNEL CLOUD** (2006) {*7}, put them in full control of production, and they seemed to be channeling Brit-folk icons The WATERSONS on 'We'll Meet Along The Way' and 'Reservoir', although most of the set was countrified in the manner of The Cowboy Junkies.

In one of their most adventurous moves (reckless, if precedents were anything to go by), HEM found themselves performing song accompaniments and Irish instrumentals on a Central Park stage production of Shakespeare's 'Twelfth Night', with a cast featuring Anne Hathaway, Audra McDonald and Raul Esparza; the resulting **TWELFTH NIGHT** (2009) {*5} wasn't exactly typical HEM (short reel pieces and a handful of songs), but it showed they were willing to try anything once. *MCS*

Sally Ellyson - vocals / **Dan Messe** - piano, accordion, glockenspiel / **Gary Maurer** - guitar, mandolin / **Steve Curtis** - guitar, banjo, mandolin / **Bob Hoffnar** - pedal steel guitar / **Heather Zimmerman** - violin / **George Rush** - bass / **Mark Brotter** - drums

US: Bar/None — UK: Setanta

Jan 01. (cd) <*BRNCD 131*> *(SETCD 094)* **RABBIT SONGS** — Sep 01
- Lord, blow the moon out please / When I was drinking / Half acre / Burying song / Betting on trains / Leave me here / All that I'm good for / Idle (the rabbit song) / Stupid mouth shut / Lazy eye / Sailor / Polly's dress / Night like a river / The cuckoo / Waltz / Horsey. *<re-iss. Jun 02 on DreamWorks; ???> <re-iss. May 05 on Rounder; 11661-3248-2>*

Sep 02. (cd-ep) *(SETCD 108)* I'M TALKING WITH MY MOUTH
- Jackson / Valentine's day / (The angels wanna wear my) Red shoes / Living without you / A dream is a wish your heart makes.

Arena Rock — not issued

Oct 04. (shared; cd-ep) <*ARE 000046*> BIRDS, BEASTS AND FLOWERS
- Half acre [live] / [The Autumn Defense track] / Pacific street [live] / [The Autumn Defense track] / St Charlene / [The Autumn Defense track].

Waveland — Liberty

Oct 04. (cd) <*7243 8 60342 2*> *(860342-2)* **EVENINGLAND** — Feb 05
- The fire thief / Lucky / Receiver / Redwing / My father's waltz / Hollow / A-hunting we will go / An easy one / Strays / Cincinnati traveler / Jackson / Dance with me now darling / The beautiful sea / Eveningland / Pacific street / Carry me home. *<re-iss. May 05 on Rounder; 11661-3240-2>*

Nettwerk Nettwerk

Sep 06. (cd) <*(6700 30605 2)*> **FUNNEL CLOUD**
- We'll meet along the way / He came to meet me / Not California / Funnel cloud / Too late to turn back now / The pills stopped working / Hotel fire / Great houses of New York / Curtains / Old Adam / The burnt-over district / Reservoir / I'll dream of you tonight / Almost home.

Jun 07. (cd-ep) <*6700 36419 2*> HOME AGAIN, HOME AGAIN
- The part where you let go / Half asleep / While my hand was letting go / The meeting place / Home again / Half acre.

Oct 09. (cd) <*(30875-2)*> **TWELFTH NIGHT** [cast soundtrack]
- Illyrian aire / Black thorn stick / One self king / The funeral / The rose in the heather / Take, o take those lips away / Take, o take those lips away / Not too fast! Soft, soft! / Full fathom five / Sebastian and Antonio / The Kerry polka / O mistress mine / Come away death / Come away death / The clock upbraids me / The little villain / To the gates of Tartar / Illyrian aire [orchestral] / Where is fancy bred? / Enter Sebastian / This is the air / The bonnie bunny / Hey Robin, jolly Robin / I am gone, sir / The bonnie bunny [orchestral] / The pests are kind / The wind and the rain / The wind and the rain [reel].

- (5-7*) compilations, others, etc.-

Feb 06. (cd) Nettwerk; <*(03770 30474 2)*> **NO WORD FROM TOM**
[outtakes, demos, live and rare] May 06
- All the pretty horses / Rainy night in Georgia / Radiation vibe / The present / Cincinnati traveler / Betting on trains / South Central rain / The Tennessee waltz / Sailor / Eveningland / Idle / Crazy arms / Oh no / All that I'm good for / The city and the traveler / Lazy eye / The beautiful sea / The golden day is dying.

Jim HENRY

Relatively unknown to many folk pundits outside the States, contemporary singer and songwriter JIM HENRY (b. December 30, 1961 in Chicago) embraces acoustic folk and country music in equal measure, although his roots lie in appearances at the Great Woods and Newport folk festivals.

Putting in time as an auxiliary member of San Franciscan cajun aces The Sundogs (probably in the 1980s) and with Celtic-countryish trio The Burns Sisters, HENRY put in some mileage for the cause, travelling and taking up residence everywhere from Kansas to New England.

1993 saw the release of his first album, **INTO THE BLUE** {*6}, a one-man-and-his-dog (as depicted on the sleeve) type of record that combined elements of cajun ('Lousiana Girl'), jazz ('The Date'), country ('I Had A Dream' and others) and folk ('These Are The Days'). A few tracks were described as something akin to JESSE COLIN YOUNG fronting PENTANGLE (best examples are 'Windy And Warm', 'Chilobi Boy' and 'Summer Blues'). Blues/folk-orientated follow-up set **JACKSONVILLE** (1995) {*7} showed his versatility and dexterity, and Jennifer Kimball, Duke Levine, ELLIS PAUL and BROOKS WILLIAMS were on the guest list.

Signing to Signature Sounds, HENRY and WILLIAMS stuck together for **RING SOME CHANGES** (1997) {*6}, a trad/covers-friendly pot-pourri of JANSCH and RENBOURN-styled acoustic tracks including versions of DAVY GRAHAM's 'Angi', Robert Johnson's 'Malted Milk', Stephane Grappelli & Django Reinhardt's 'Minor Swing' and RICHARD THOMPSON's 'Time To Ring Some Changes'.

After a seven-year period as sessionman extraordinaire to the likes of CLIFF EBERHARDT, The Weepies, MARK ERELLI and The NIELDS, JIM HENRY was back in circulation with an arsenal of instruments (Dobro, mandolin, lap-steel and all types of guitars), but first he had to help his good friend TRACY GRAMMER, whose partner DAVE CARTER had died suddenly in the summer of 2002. He almost immediately learned Dave's parts and performed with her in stage shows and on her 'Flower Of Avalon' CD.

HENRY's own show got back on the road with **THE WAYBACK** (2004) {*6}, an album that, like his further self-financed mini-sets **ONE-HORSE TOWN** (2005) {*5} and **KING OF HEARTS** (2008) {*5}, showed he could turn his hand to any style. In 2007 Jim joined the Mary Chapin Carpenter band, and he's still there as of July 2011. *MCS*

Jim Henry - vocals, guitar(s) / + session players

US own label — UK not issued

1993. (cd) <*none*> **INTO THE BLUE**
- Into the blue / One-horse town / Strange world / I had a dream / Louisiana girl / Two hands on the wheel / The date / These are the days / On a tear / Take it or leave it / Misty hills. *<re-iss. Oct 95 on Signature Sounds; SIG 1229>*

Sep 95. (cd) <*none*> **JACKSONVILLE**
- It's only business / Baby's coming home / Windy and warm / Love in the wrong direction / Pals forever dad / Chilobi boy / Louise / Till the siren blows again / Summer blues / When Maggie comes to visit / The broken man / I think it's going to work out fine / Home to me. *<re-iss. Oct 95 on Signature Sounds; SIG 1230>*

Signature Sounds — not issued

Jan 97. (cd; by JIM HENRY + BROOKS WILLIAMS)
<*SIG 1238*> **RING SOME CHANGES**
- Time to ring some changes / Are you tired of me, my darling? / I think it's going to work out fine / Minor swing / Oh what wondrous love / Gender bender / Malted milk / Angi / The second child / On the rollin' sea / Star of the county Down / When I go walkin'.

Aug 04. (cd) <*(SIG 1254)*> **THE WAYBACK**
- Drive-in movie picture show / Leaving time / Restless / Eddie and Pearl / Ruby (the girl with the flyaway hair) / Sound of the whistle blow / Texas / 1967 / Doc's rag / We think we'll keep him / Lay your head down / Last call.

Jim Henry — Jim Henry

Aug 05. (m-cd) <*none*> **ONE-HORSE TOWN**
- Deep river blues / One-horse town / St James infirmary / Quickdraw Southpaw's last hurrah / A sad farewell / This lullaby / Ruby.

Jul 08. (m-cd) <*(none)*> **KING OF HEARTS**
- Get to you / Up to me / 1952 Vincent Black Lightning / Melody of you / 28th of January / Broken man / Home on the range.

Priscilla HERDMAN

Born February 11, 1948 in Eastchester, New York, PRISCILLA HERDMAN passed the dozen-albums mark as 2008's **INTO THE STARS** {*6} reached out to her loyal audience. Not particularly prolific in the songwriting department at this stage (she's covered a great many songs in her time), Priscilla was at her rainy-day best on songs by KATE RUSBY, JOHN McCUTCHEON, ANNE HILLS, DON McLEAN, PIERCE PETTIS, Mary Chapin Carpenter and the late Mark Heard.

HERDMAN's career goes at least as far back as the 1970s, when she lived in Philadelphia and released a couple of well-received LPs. The first, for Philo, entitled **THE WATER LILY** (1977) {*7}, included one of the first versions of ERIC BOGLE's 'The Band Played Waltzing Matilda'; other tracks included Sir Walter Scott's 19th-century ballad 'Jock O'Hazeldean'.

Her gift was one part JOAN BAEZ to two parts JUDY COLLINS, at her best as an interpretive singer, as revealed on her subsequent LPs for Flying Fish, **FORGOTTEN DREAMS** (1980) {*6}, **SEASONS OF CHANGE** (1983) {*7} and **DARKNESS INTO LIGHT** (1987) {*6}. Her choice of covers embraced songs by STAN ROGERS, Randy Newman, JAMES TAYLOR, ERIC BOGLE ('No Man's Land'), Keith Sykes, Tom Waits and LUI COLLINS - and that's just on the first-named. Some of the composers named were also represented on her follow-ups, and at some point in this period she moved (with her husband, environmental activist Dick Hermans) to Pine Plains, NY, where her first daughter, Suzanna, was born in 1985.

Among her albums of the 1990s and 2000s (leaving aside her holiday/festive collaborations with ANNE HILLS and CINDY MANGSEN), 1998's simple adult-and-child set **MOONDREAMER** {*7} was the cream of the crop. Alongside three lilting lullabies by HILLS herself, there was room for songs by CHERYL WHEELER, BOB FRANKE, Peter Rowan, SI KAHN (she covered a few of his), BILL CADDICK, Bill Harley, Mary Chapin Carpenter and Billy Joel. *MCS*

Priscilla Herdman - vocals, acoustic guitar / with session people

US Philo — UK not issued

1977. (lp) <*PH 1014*> **THE WATER LILY**
- The water lily / Andy's gone with cattle / Old Wooley / The drover's sweetheart / The band played Waltzing Matilda / Jock o' Hazeldean / Do you think that I do not know / The bush girl / Reedy river / The shame of going back / Dancing at Whitsun. *<(cd+c//UK-iss. Jul 95//Aug 95; CDPH/CPH 1014)>*

Flying Fish — Flying Fish

1980. (lp) <*FF 230*> **FORGOTTEN DREAMS**
- Forty-five years / Dayton, Ohio - 1903 / Millworker / Brother, can you spare a dime? / No man's land / [*] / The coast of Marseilles / I hope that I don't fall in love with you / Turnaround / January thaw / Dreams. *(UK-iss. Mar 89; same as US) <cd/c-iss. Apr 95 +=; FF/+90/70 230>- [insert *]:* Lovers and losers / Talk to me of Mendocino.

1983. (lp) <*FF 309*> **SEASONS OF CHANGE**
- The field behind the plow / Grandfather song / Lies / Letter from May Alice Jeffers / Mothers, daughters, wives / Desaparecidos / Rice and beans / Deportees / Traveler / Thanks to Mother Mercy. *(UK-iss. Mar 89; same as US) <cd/c-iss. Sep 92; FF/+90/70 309>*

1987. (lp) <*(FF 420)*> **DARKNESS INTO LIGHT** May 88
- The faith of man / When the children come home / Old Jack Ryan / I remember

loving you / Lonesome road / The coming of the roads / Wood river / Rockin' in a weary land / From the lambing to the wool / Ain't I a woman / Turn around - The Gartan mother's lullaby / Walls and windows / Peace must come. *<cd/c-iss. Sep 92; FF 70/90 420>*

Sep 88. (lp) *<1001>* **STARDREAMER: Nightsongs and Lullabies** [children's recordings 1988]
- Waltzing with bears / Matthew, Mark, Luke and John / Autumn to May / Moon upon the left / The moon / Goodnight, Irene / Twinkle, twinkle little star / Time to sleep / Lullaby for teddy-o - Douglas mountain / First lullaby / Bush lullaby / Close your eyes (Brahms's lullaby) / The first star lullaby / Thanks a lot. *<cd-iss. Apr 94 & Oct 04 on Stardreamer>*

(above issued on Alacazam/Alcazar)

—— In 1990, HERDMAN, (Anne) HILLS and (Cindy) MANGSEN issued Voices set.

Jan 93. (cd) *<MLPD 2720>* **DAYDREAMER** [children's]
- Dreamcatcher / Branching out / Kindergarten wall / When the rain comes down / White coral bells / A fairy went a-marketing / Ticklish Tom and pickildy pie / Water from another time / Hard scrabble harvest / Love grows one by one / Apple picker's reel / What a wonderful world / Where have you been? *<re-iss. Jun 96 on Warner; 42591-2>*

(above issued on Music For Little People)

Nov 94. (cd/c) *<(FF 70/90 637)>* **FOREVER AND ALWAYS** Feb 95
- Ramblin' heart / This time of year / The first time ever I saw your face / And so it goes / When I call upon your love / Music to me / The water is wide / Ashokan farewell / Somewhere in time / I'll love you forever / Follow that road.

Gadfly — not issued

Oct 97. (cd; by PRISCILLA HERDMAN, ANNE HILLS AND CINDY MANGSEN) *<GADFLY 235>* **VOICES OF WINTER**
- Wintergrace / Snow in the street / Raise the dead of wintertime / Witch Hazel / Serving girls' holiday / Hanerot hallalu / A-roving on a winter's night / Joy health love and peace - The wren / Unto you this night / The frozen logger - Proper cup of coffee / Voices of winter - Red and green / Hot buttered rum / Mr Santa / Chickadee / More wood / Lo, how a rose.

Redwing — Redwing

May 98. (cd) *<(RWMCD 5401)>* **MOONDREAMER** Jun 98
- Howl at the moon / A velveteen love song / 1000 pairs of pajamas / Midnight round / While you sleep / Bluegrass boy / Stars on the water / John o' dreams / Moon and me / Lullabye (goodnight, my angel) / Dreamland / All through the night.

—— late in 2000, PRISCILLA HERDMAN, ANNE HILLS & CINDY MANGSEN released the festive set 'At The Turning Of The Year' for Hand And Heart records

May 03. (cd) *<(RWMCD 5412)>* **THE ROAD HOME**
- Big town / Island clay / Gentle arms of Eden / Goodnight New York / Exile / Kisangani / Prayer 2000 / Wild wind / No telling / Here.

MDZN — not issued

Dec 08. (cd) *<none>* **INTO THE STARS**
- The play / Underneath the stars / Blue boat home / Sail away / Pleiades / Satellite sky / Firefly lights / (cello intro to...) / Vincent / Comet / Ideas are like stars / The moon's song / The galaxy song.

Anne HILLS

Born in October, 1953 to American missionaries in India, but raised in Michigan, soprano ANNE HILLS has released several well-received solo albums from her base in Chicago, and her work alongside folk royalty PRISCILLA HERDMAN and CINDY MANGSEN has kept her profile even higher.

Abandoning a career in jazz after her time at the Interlochen Arts Academy, her love of folk music inspired her to open a folklore centre and run her own independent record label, Hogeye. Credited with guitarist Jan Burda, HILLS's debut release, **THE PANIC IS ON** (1982) {*5} - with friends Art Thieme, Fred Campeau and Paul Breidenbach, among others - was a nice enough start, although it would be 1985's **DON'T EXPLAIN** (1985) {*7} that made critics sit up and take notice.

Her first for Flying Fish, **WOMAN OF A CALM HEART** (1987) {*7}, took her further than her previous ventures, and her use of newbie songwriters David Roth, Simon Gregory and ILENE WEISS was commendable, given that she was hardly prolific as a composer herself; 'The Child Within' was her only original. Putting her collaborations and session work (for LIVINGSTON TAYLOR, ARTIE TRAUM, SI KAHN, Jim Post and MICHAEL SMITH) aside, Anne's solo career continued with **OCTOBER CHILD** (1993) {*6} (a collection of MICHAEL SMITH songs) and **ANGLE OF THE LIGHT** (1995) {*7}, on which she wrote or co-wrote all but two of the songs.

Redwing also gave her beautiful songs an airing on **BITTERSWEET STREET** (1998) {*6}, an innocence mission of sorts, again with only two covers, ERIC ANDERSEN's 'Close The Door Lightly' and ILENE WEISS's 'Just By Offering'. It was no surprise when HILLS and SMITH combined for the schmaltzy **PARADISE LOST AND FOUND** (1999) {*5}; check out their reading of The Beatles' 'I Will'.

The new millennium brought further joint releases in 'Under American Skies' (2001), with senior folkie TOM PAXTON, the HILLS/SMITH// MANGSEN/STEVE GILLETTE set 'Fourtold' (2003) and some sung-poems album. These marked time before her proper Appleseed Records comeback, **POINTS OF VIEW** (2009) {*6}, a mostly self-written album also highlighted by a brilliant rendition of LEONARD COHEN's 'Alexandra Leaving'. *MCS*

Anne Hills - vocals, acoustic guitar, banjo, autoharp / with various personnel

US: Hogeye — UK: not issued

1982. (lp; by ANNE & JAN HILLS BURDA) *<HOG-001>* **THE PANIC IS ON**
- Long time travelin' / The water is wide and wild geese / Dear companion / Mole in the ground / Rambler gambler / Don't let your deal go down / While you sleep / Over the mountain / Hush little baby - Father's lullaby / The panic is on.

1985. (lp) *<HOG-006>* **DON'T EXPLAIN**
- Two of a kind / Rusty old red river / Hound dog / Donna from Mobile / Rye, New Hampshire / The last day of Pompeii / Don't explain / John's wife / East Kentucky mountains / Johnson / A shadow crossing the land.

—— Later in 1985, HILLS featured alongside several artists on the festive album 'ON THIS DAY EARTH SHALL RING: SONGS FOR CHRISTMAS', re-released in 1992 on Flying Fish

Flying Fish — Flying Fish

Nov 87. (lp/c/cd) *<(FF/+90/70-464)>* **WOMAN OF A CALM HEART** Apr 89
- Woman of a calm heart / Akasha wind / No baby / Politicos / Angel in paradise / Tennessee road / Porto Limon / The child within / Manuel Garcia / Here comes that rainbow again / Light of love.

—— next with **PRISCILLA HERDMAN & CINDY MANGSEN**

Nov 90. (cd/c; by HERDMAN, HILLS, MANGSEN) *<FF 70/90-546>* **VOICES**
- Wayfaring stranger / Silken dreams / Redwing blackbird - Black burning air / Waiting for Isabella / Squalor / Adios ciudad / Katy cruel / Requiem for the giant trees / Johnny Burke / Orphans / Stars.

Sep 93. (cd/c) *<FF 70/90-621>* **OCTOBER CHILD**
- Three monkeys / Starfishes / Sister Clarissa / Disappearing heart / Paterson summer / Woman in the mirror / Rose of Sharon / Randi's birthday / Stranded in the moonlight / The Dutchman.

Nov 94. (cd; by ANNE HILLS and CINDY MANGSEN) *<(FF 70/90-638)>* **NEVER GROW OLD** Feb 95
- Where we'll never grow old / Curtains of the night / Richmond on the James / Lost Jimmy Whalen / Master Kilby / Bill Morgan and his gal / Wolves a' howlin' / McKinley's rag / Lone pilgrim / Mary Anne / The housewife's lament / Light of red and green / Pretty Sylvia / Oh my little darlin' / Railroading on the great divide / Evening shade / Where we'll never grow old.

Oct 95. (cd/c) *<(FF 70/90-648)>* **ANGLE OF THE LIGHT** Nov 95
- Yesterday's wind / Follow that road / Fighting giants / Sound of the looms / Over the bridge / Brown leaves / Dreamcatcher / Angle of the light / Lover's knot / Forget me not / Enough.

—— In 1997, PRISCILLA HERDMAN, ANNE HILLS & CINDY MANGSEN released a live set for Gadfly, 'Voices Of Winter'

Jun 98. (cd; by ANNE HILLS and CINDY MANGSEN) *<(CDFF 671)>* **NEVER GROW UP** Sep 98
- Kitty alone / Now he's sorry that he spoke / The thinnest man - Alice / Froggy went a courting / Hudson River steamboat / Wait till the clouds roll by / Chickens they're a-crowin' / The dummy line / Where did you get that hat? / The Colorado trail / Hop along Peter / Master of the sheepfold / I've got rings on my fingers / Old Blue / Watch the stars - At the gate of heaven.

Redwing — Redwing

Oct 98. (cd) *<(RWMCD 5402)>* **BITTERSWEET STREET** Feb 99
- Pleiades / Yard dreams / First day of autumn / The blur in the photography / Cloudships / Bittersweet street / Exile / Just by offering / Some boats / New companion / Wait by the river / Close the door lightly.

Aug 99. (cd; by ANNE HILLS & MICHAEL SMITH) *<RWMCD 5406>* **PARADISE LOST AND FOUND**
- Stranded in the moonlight / Paterson summer / Painted horse / Danger / Paradise lost and found / Silken dreams / Spoon river / Disappearing heart / This rain / We welcome birds / Roll me home / The Dutchman / I will.

Hand and Heart — not issued

2000. (cd; by PRISCILLA HERDMAN, ANNE HILLS & CINDY MANGSEN) *<2000>* **AT THE TURNING OF THE YEAR** [festive]
- At the turning of the year / Candlemas eve / The winter it is past / Forget-me-not / Swinton May song / Goodbye to the roses / Away ye merry lassies / Uncle Dave's grace / Solstice round / The snow / The druggist / Corn, water and wood / Years / Mississippi sawyer - Winter's come and gone.

—— In 2001, HILLS collaborated with TOM PAXTON on 'Under American Skies'; the live 1985 set 'Best Of Friends' (with TOM PAXTON and BOB GIBSON) was issued in Mar 04.

FOURTOLD

Michael Smith, Anne Hills, Steve Gillette + Cindy Mangsen

Appleseed — Appleseed

May 03. (cd) *<(APRCD 1071)>* **FOURTOLD**
- Four rode by / Molly and Tenbrooks / Pendle hill / Joshua gone Barbados / Panther in Michigan / Darcy Farrow / Ballad of Springhill / Aramalee / The nine little goblins / Two men in the building / I drew my ship / Run, come, see Jerusalem.

ANNE HILLS

Collective Works — not issued

May 06. (cd) <*0502*> **BEAUTY ATTENDS: THE HEARTSONGS OF OPAL WHITELEY**
- Blue hills / I went to look for the fairies / Potatoes / Brown leaves / Cloudships / Now it is winter / Larks of the meadow / Lichen folk / William Shakespeare / Glad for the spring / Thoughts in flowers / Song of the brook / She is dead / Interlude / Blue hills reprise.

Jun 07. (cd) <*0504*> **EF YOU DON'T WATCH OUT: ANNE HILLS SINGS THE POEMS OF JAMES WHITCOMB RILEY**
- A voice from the farm / Little orphant Annie / When the frost is on the pumpkin / The raggedy man / The lugubrious whing-whang / The little coat / Lullaby / Nine little goblins / Down on Wriggle Crick / There was a cherry tree.

Appleseed — Appleseed

Nov 09. (cd) <*(APRCD 1119)*> **POINTS OF VIEW**
- I am you / Pennsylvania / Two year winter / The farm / Alexandra leaving / My daughter and Vincent Van Gogh / A plain song / I'm nobody / The moon's song / Holy now / Gardens / Romeo and Juliet / Leaf.

- (5-7*) compilations, others, etc.-

Sep 93. (cd/c) Flying Fish; <*(FF 608 CD/C)*> **DON'T PANIC** — Apr 94
- ('DON'T EXPLAIN' + 'THE PANIC IS ON' tracks)

Doug HOEKSTRA

Despite his Nashville history and his wispy, Lou Reedish voice, Columbus, Ohio-born singer/songwriter DOUG HOEKSTRA is a folk-rock artist. Spending his Chicago-based teenage years as a member of local garage bands and alt-country outfit Bucket No.6, his C&W leanings were certainly on show on Bucket No.6's solitary set, 'High On The Hog' (1991).

Abandoning all thoughts of becoming the next Cash, Parsons or Kristofferson, acoustic guitarist HOEKSTRA delivered his debut solo album, **WHEN THE TUBES BEGIN TO GLOW** (1994) {*7}, while his follow-up, **RICKETY STAIRS** (1996) {*7}, won the Best Folk Artist in Nashville award, plus some new fans who were waiting for the next DYLAN, COHEN or DRAKE. Storytelling was his trade, and with its sparse accompaniment, that could verge on the gratingly simple at times. Best tracks are 'Matter Of Fact', 'Cottonwood Tree' and 'Dandelion Seeds'.

MAKE ME BELIEVE (1999) {*6} and the excellent **AROUND THE MARGINS** (2001) {*8} showed his prowess as a rootsy songwriter, the latter taking the honours thanks to 'Desdemona', the seven-minute 'Undone' and a retread of DYLAN's 'Isis'. The bare-bones, UK-only set **THE PAST IS NEVER PAST** (2001) {*5} featured Brecht-Weill's 'Ballad Of The Soldier's Wife'.

WAITING (2003) {*6} was another literate sadcore-folk affair reminiscent of Lou Reed and The Velvet Underground c. 1969, but excited little interest outside those in the know. A concert recording, **SU CASA, MI CASA: THE OFFICIAL LIVE BOOTLEG** (*5}, came out in 2004.

BLOOMING ROSES (2008) {*6} again strayed into the all too familiar folk/country territory of his idols, but that didn't stop 'The Best There Ever Was' (very 'All The Young Dudes' in parts), 'Acquired Taste' and 'Everywhere Is Somewhere' to shine out from this easy-on-the-ear set. *MCS*

Doug Hoekstra - vocals, guitars, mouth organ

US Back Porch — UK not issued

Jan 94. (cd) <*BP-2828*> **WHEN THE TUBES BEGIN TO GLOW**
- On the interstate / Bankrupt / The way the wind blows / Fear of heights / The home-town rule / When you return to me / Sleepin' in the front seat / Mama was a Pinkerton / Like a hummingbird / Strike up a match / Grandad's radio. *<re-iss. May 00 on Orchard; 5780>*

Jan 96. (cd) <*BP-3030*> **RICKETY STAIRS**
- Driving to Georgia / In a crowd / Slipping through the cracks / Dandelion seeds / Matter of fact / Cottonwood tree / Standing in the station / On this night / Pieces of man / Untied shoes / Greater than the gold / The list.

One Man — Round Tower

Feb 99. (cd) <*18*> *(RTMCD 98)* **MAKE ME BELIEVE** — Apr 00
- Sam Cooke sang the gospel / Shiver, bend and break / Choices / Every lover's breath / Kirkwood hotel / Here and now / Behind the shuttered blinds / Stolen gun / My father's town / Elusive dreams / Atticus / Celebrate the trance / Snowflakes / Kudzu. *<re-iss. 2000 on Orchard; 5857>*

Inbetweens — Inbetweens

Mar 01. (cd) <*IRCD 008*> **MARGINS**
- Margins / Lost among the ruins / Birmingham jail / Giving up smoking / Desdemona / Laminate man / Houses flying / That's where he was living / For the woman / Broken tower / The life we love / Isis / Undone / Black and white memories / Stranger's eyes.

Oct 01. (cd) <*(IRCD 011)*> **THE PAST IS NEVER PAST** — May 02
- She walks in beauty / Oh, Zamira / 500 miles away / Break my fall / The past is never past / Drops fell from my fingertips / If the world was blind / What's on your mind? / Staring out the window / Where I worked / The life we love #9 / Ballad of the soldier's wife / Rear-view mirror effect.

Paste — Fundamental

Aug 03. (cd) *(3 AD)* **WAITING** — Feb 04
- Blow beautiful dreams / Sunday blues / Theresa / Crawling out from under / Driftin' / In the middle of the night / Dark side of a pearl / Screwball comedy / Nighttime rain / The artesian well / Eternity / Waiting.

2004. (cd) *(5 AD)* **SU CASA, MI CASA: THE OFFICIAL LIVE BOOTLEG** (live)
- Choices / Slipping through the cracks / Pieces of man / 500 miles away / Here and now / Laminate man / Giving up smoking / Celebrate the trance / Birmingham jail / A bit of talk / Driving to Georgia / Broken tower / Theresa / The family tree / Black and white memories (radio) / Elusive dreams / Atticus / Cottonwood tree / Sam Cooke sang the gospel / A bit more talk.

WingDing — Folkwit

Aug 05. (cd-ep) <*51540*> SIX SONGS
- Diminishing returns / The bottomless pit / Snake oil / Have it all / Picture of the soul / Watercolor rose.

Feb 08. (cd) <*602*> *(FO 029)* **BLOOMING ROSES** — Oct 08
- Acquired taste / Blooming roses / The best there ever was / Naper Vegas scrabble club / Your sweet love / Instincts / Subway train / Gavin geist / Disrepair / Part of the problem, part of the solution / Everywhere is somewhere.

Jolie HOLLAND

Born September 11, 1975 in Houston, Texas, singer-songwriter JOLIE HOLLAND began her career in the all-female Canadian folk-country act The BE GOOD TANYAS, albeit for only one album, 'Blue Horse' (2001).

Taking Piedmont-styled blues as her template, although not entirely neglecting folk and old-timey country, she returned home to San Francisco, where her stark imagery and gothic-Americana solo demos were beginning to do the rounds. Signed up by Anti- Records, the demo itself surfaced as **CATALPA** (2003) {*6}, an album truly representative of her down-to-earth, back-porch approach, as illustrated by 'Alley Flowers', 'All The Morning Blues' and Hattie Hudson's 'Back Hand Blues'. 'The Littlest Birds' was a leftover from her BE GOOD TANYAS days.

Less than six months later, **ESCONDIDA** (2004) {*7} kept up the momentum, touching on every roots genre under the sun (blues, gospel, jazz and trad-folk) and revealing old-timey influences including Ma Rainey, Bessie Smith, Billie Holiday and Blind Willie McTell. Find time for 'Poor Girl's Blues', 'Sascha' and 'Old Fashioned Morphine'.

SPRINGTIME CAN KILL YOU (2006) {*7}, **THE LIVING AND THE DEAD** (2008) {*7} and her latest, **PINT OF BLOOD** (2011) {*7} - the last with The Grand Chandeliers (Shahzad Ismaily, Grey Gerstein and Marc Ribot) and featuring a cover of TOWNES VAN ZANDT's 'Rex's Blues' - continued her idiosyncratic surge towards wider acceptance. *MCS*

Jolie Holland - vocals, guitar, drums / with session people

US Anti- — UK Anti-

Nov 03. (cd) <*(8 6691-2)*> **CATALPA**
- Alley flowers / All the morning birds / Roll my blues / Black hand blues / December, 1999 / I wanna die / Demon lover improv / Catalpa waltz / The littlest birds / Wandering Angus / Periphery waltz / Ghost waltz. *(UK re-iss. Jan 09; same)*

Apr 04. (7") <*1167-7*> SASCHA. / Delia

Apr 04. (cd/lp) <*(8 6692-2/-1)*> **ESCONDIDA**
- Sascha / Black stars / Old fashioned morphine / Amen / Mad Tom of Bedlam / Poor girl's blues / Goodbye California / Do you? / Darlin' ukulele / Damn shame / Tiny idyll - Li'l Missy / Faded coat of blue. *(UK re-iss. Jan 09; same)*

May 06. (cd) <*(8 6788-2)*> **SPRINGTIME CAN KILL YOU**
- Crush in the ghetto / Mehitibell's blues / Springtime can kill you / Crazy dreams / You're not satisfied / Stubborn beast / Please don't / Moonshiner / Ghostly girl / Nothing left to do but dream / Adieu false heart / Mexican blue. *<lp-iss. Feb 06 on DBK Works; DBK 123> (UK re-iss. Jan 09; same)*

Oct 08. (cd/lp) <*(8 6952-2/-1)*> **THE LIVING AND THE DEAD**
- Mexico City / Corrido por buddy / Palmyra / You painted yourself in / Fox in its hole / Your big hands / Sweet loving man / Love Henry / The future / Enjoy yourself.

(next credited to JOLIE HOLLAND & THE GRAND CHANDELIERS)

Jun 11. (cd) <*(8 7112-2)*> **PINT OF BLOOD**
- All those girls / Remember / Tender mirror / Gold and yellow / June / Wreckage / Little birds / The devil's sake / Honey girl / Rex's blues.

HOOFBEAT, CAW & THUNDER (⟹ STONE BREATH)

HOQUIAM (⟹ JURADO, Damien)

Penelope HOUSTON

Outrageous peroxide-punk goddess turned gorgeous folkie, singer/songwriter PENELOPE HOUSTON (b. December 17, 1958 in Los Angeles) was raised in Seattle but moved back to California to front San Francisco punk outfit The Avengers, who supported the Sex Pistols on their notorious final tour of the States in early 1979. She subsequently worked with Howard Devoto and fronted the short-lived -30- (with Eric Lefcowitz, Kevin Donahue, Steve Strauss, Tom Freeman and her husband Meletios Peppas) for one acoustic-led 45, 'Full Of Wonder'.

HOUSTON brought in permanent acoustic guitarist Pat Johnson (ex-Royal Trux) and a host of folkie players to boost her first stab at a solo career, **BIRDBOYS** (1988) {*7}. Johnson wrote 'Waiting Room', and her own songs included 'Harry Dean', a tribute to actor Harry Dean Stanton. The jury is still out on her rendition of the traditional staple 'Wild Mountain Thyme'.

Passing over two rare and deleted cassette-only albums, her next positive venture was **THE WHOLE WORLD** (1993) {*6}, a kooky record credited to 'Penelope Houston And Her Band', which latter included Peppas, Strauss and guitarist Eliot Nemzer. 'Glad I'm A Girl' was one track that stood out.

KARMAL APPLE (1994) {*6} continued her trend toward the traditional, while retreads set **CUT YOU** (1996) {*6} was her major-label debut on Reprise, positioning her in the territory of Liz Phair, Aimee Mann and a hundred other female rockers; ditto the kitty-pop comeback **TONGUE** (1999) {*5}.

Bolstered by a recent Avengers reunion alongside original Greg Ingraham), **EIGHTEEN STORIES DOWN** (2003) {*7} recreated one of her old band's songs, 'Corpus Christi', with Green Day's Billie Joe Armstrong sitting in for Greg, but the other 17 numbers were revamps of songs from Penelope's folkier times. On 2003's 'Snapshots' EP, HOUSTON had no problem covering The Flying Machine's 'Maybe We've Been Loving Too Long', PENTANGLE's 'I've Got A Feeling', The BAND's 'It Makes No Difference', Shocking Blue's 'Love Machine' (with new lyrics of her own) and Colin Blunstone's 'Though You Are Far Away'.

Co-credited with old retainer Pat Johnson, **THE PALE GREEN GIRL** (2004) {*7} was another stab (and her last) at breaking into the mainstream market, Penelope assuming the role of a 1960s chanteuse. It was poignant that she should close the set with a beautiful cover of a song by Nico's erstwhile Velvet Underground colleague John Cale, 'Buffalo Ballet'. *MCS*

Penelope Houston - vocals, melodica, autoharp (with bands)

US I.D. — UK not issued

1986. (ltd-7"; by -30-) *<PH 17>* FULL OF WONDER. / Out Of My Life

Subterranean — not issued

Jan 88. (lp) *<SUB 63>* **BIRDBOYS**
- Harry Dean / Talking with you / Voices / Living dolls / Out of my life / Waiting room / Bed of lies / Wild mountain thyme / Putting me in the ground / Full of wonder / Summer of war / Stoli. *(UK-iss. Mar 91 on Round Tower cd/c/lp+=; RTM CD/MC/LP 15) (cd re-iss. Aug 99 on Normal+=; NORMAL 173CD)* - Rock 'n' roll show / All that crimson.

own label — not issued

1991. (ltd-c) *<none>* **ON BORROWED TIME: LIVE IN FRISCO**
- On borrowed time / Putting me in the ground / Honeysuckle / Father's day / White out / Fall back / Going to the Evergreen / Intro to Rock 'n' roll show / Out past Vacaville / Happy ending / Just like a man / Glad I'm a girl / Corpus Christ / Nina / Behind your eyes / Stoli.

1992. (ltd-c) **500 LUCKY PIECES** — mail-o
- Sweetheart / On borrowed time / White out / Maybe love / Qualities of mercy / Fall back / Honeysuckle / Corpus Christi / Nina / Going to the evergreen / Like I do / Glad I'm a girl.

Iloki — not issued

1992. (7") *<ISLO 104>* GLAD I'M A GIRL. / Sweetheart

1994. (7") *<ISLO 107>* TAKE CARE. / Corpus Christi

Heyday — Normal

Aug 93. (cd; as PENELOPE HOUSTON AND HER BAND) *<HEY 29> (NORMAL 153LP)* **THE WHOLE WORLD** — Mar 94
- Glad I'm a girl / On borrowed time / Sweetheart / Sugarburn / Out past Vacaville / Qualities of mercy / Father's day / Maybe love / Innocent kiss / Honeysuckle / Shadow / Behind our eyes / White out. *(UK cd-iss. Aug 99; NORMAL 153CD)*

not issued — Return To Sender

Mar 94. (ltd-cd) *(RTS 2CD)* **SILK PURSE (FROM A SOW'S EAR)** — German
- Take care / Like I do / Corpus Christi / Nina / (Going to the) Evergreen / Carol of the canyon / Fallback / Just like a man / On borrowed time / On borrowed time (live) / Water wheel / Putting me in the ground / Hillbilly head dance.

1994. (ltd-cd; as PENELOPE HOUSTON & PAT JOHNSON) *(RTS 12)* **CRAZY BABY** — German
- Another train blues / Scratch / Hold me up to the light / Mission tower / Ignition / Loners of America / Soul singers / Pale fire / Wedding waltz / No easy way down / Haight St girl.

Normal — Normal

1994. (cd-ep) *(NORMAL182CD)* RIDE / Everybody's Little Dream / Stoli / Trouble Walks By — Europe

1994. (cd; as PENELOPE HOUSTON AND HER BAND) *(NORMAL 183CD)* **KARMAL APPLE** — German
- Ride / Picturesque / New day / The mermaid / Everybody's little dream / Water wheel / Flourish / Fall back / Fall garden / Happy ending / Snakebite / Redemption / Make me. *(UK-iss. Aug 99; same)*

Reprise — East West

Jan 96. (cd-s) *(0630 13114-2)* GLAD I'M A GIRL / Scratch / Stoli / Corpus Christi

Mar 96. (cd-s) *(0630 13967-2)* SWEETHEART / Sweetheart (US remix) / Like I Do / (Going To The) Evergreen

Mar 96. (cd) *<9 46148-2> (0630 13126-2)* **CUT YOU**
- Secret sign / Sweetheart / Scratch / Locket / Fuzzy throne / Ride / Harry Dean / Waiting room / Qualities of mercy / Fall back / Pull / Glad I'm a girl / White out / Cut you.

Mar 99. (cd) *<9 47153-2>* **TONGUE**
- Grand prix / Tongue / Scum / Things / The ballad of Happy Friday and Tiger Woods / My angel lost her wings / Worm / Crushing / Hundertwasser 567 / Frankenstein heart / Dolly / Subway. *(bonus +=)- Scum (remix) / New day.*

—— now with Michael Pappenburg (guitar) and Katherine Chase (bass, guitar)

not issued — Return To Sender

Sep 01. (ltd-cd) *(RTS 34)* **LONERS, STONERS AND PRISON BRIDES** (live 1999–2000) — German
- Sweetheart / Waterwheel / Pale green girl / The ballad of Happy Friday and Tiger Woods / Walnut / Flight 609 / Pale fire / Everybody's little dream / New day / Hundertwasser 567.

Flare — not issued

Jan 04. (cd-ep) *<FRUSA-6 EP>* **SNAPSHOT**
- Maybe we've been loving too long / I've got a feeling / It makes no difference / Love machine / Though you are far away.

DBK — DBK

Mar 04. (cd; as PENELOPE HOUSTON with PAT JOHNSON) *<(DBK 110)>* **THE PALE GREEN GIRL**
- Take my hand / Hole / Bottom line / Aviatrix / Pale green girl / Flight 609 / Privilege + Gold / Walnut / Snow / Soul redeemer / Buffalo ballet.

- (8-10*) compilations -

2003. (cd) WEA; *(2564 60286-2)* **EIGHTEEN STORIES DOWN** — German
- Corpus Christi / Voices / On borrowed time / Qualities of mercy / Water wheel / Ride / Glad I'm a girl / Sweetheart / White out / Blackeyed peas / The ballad of Happy Friday and Tiger Woods / Scum / Tongue / Worm / Flight 609 / Hole / Soul redeemer / Buffalo ballet.

- (5-7*) compilations, etc.-

2000. (cd) penelope.net; *<019>* **ONCE IN A BLUE MOON** (demos and rarities from 1993–1998) — net
- Shiny knight / Another train blues / Blackeyed peas / Before you were born / Take care / Like I do / Nina / Loners of America / Soul singers / Just like a man / Hold me up to the light / (Velvet) Things / Haight Street girl / His pretty life / Ivy. *(UK-iss. Sep 04 on Interstate; IRT 5006)*

Jana HUNTER

Freak-folk, acid-folk, anti-folk, or a combination of all three? Houston, Texas-born (March 28, 1973) JANA HUNTER is part of the Gnomonsong glitterati of un-glam folk; her boss is Andy Cabic of VETIVER, a stalwart supporter of everything avant-esque. Her first recorded outing was a shared vinyl LP in 2005 with Cabic's Gnomonsong co-proprietor DEVENDRA BANHART.

Her CD debut, **BLANK UNSTARING HEIRS OF DOOM** (2005) {*7}, was as adventurous as it was musically ambiguous, covering Heath Flagvedt's 'Christmas' (Elliot Tracy supplied lyrics for the closing track, 'K') alongside original beatnik beauties including 'Farm, Ca.', 'Have You Got My Money' and 'Angels All Cry The Same'.

2007's **THERE'S NO HOME** {*7} was as beautifully bleak as its predecessor, although there were bright moments, sparsely adorned by her brother John, synth player Matt Brownlie and John Adams, such as 'Regardless', 'Sirens' and 'Pinnacle'.

The 'Carrion' EP, featuring three fresh cuts (lead track 'Paint A Babe', 'A Goblin, A Goblin' and the instrumental 'You Will Take It And Like It') and three out-takes from her preceding set, was as nice as a sadcore indie-folk record could be.

After taking a sabbatical of sorts to find her niche, HUNTER returned to the fray with Baltimore-based experimental lo-fi-folk quartet the LOWER DENS, i.e. guitarist Will Adams, bass player Geoff Graham and drummer Abram Sanders (drums). Their ethereal and twisted Krautrock/glam intricacies featured on debut Gnomonsong effort **TWIN-HAND MOVEMENT** (2010) {*7}. Check out 'I Get Nervous' and the hopefully chicken-friendly 'Two Cocks Waving Wildly At Each Other Across A Vast Open Space, A Dark Icy Tundra'. *MCS*

Jana Hunter - vocals, acoustic guitar, etc.

US Troubleman Unlimited — UK not issued

May 05. (lp; shared w/ DEVENDRA BANHART) *<TMU 153>* **JANA HUNTER / DEVENDRA BANHART**
- Black haven / A bright-ass light / Crystal lariat / That dragon is my husband / Laughing and crying / (other side by DEVENDRA BANHART).

Gnomonsong — Gnomonsong

Oct 05. (cd) *<GONG 01>* **BLANK UNSTARING HEIRS OF DOOM**
- All the best wishes / The new sane scramble / The earth has no skin / Christmas / Laughing and crying / Farm, CA. / Heatseeker's safety den / Have you got my money / Restless / The angle / Untitled (Hanging around) / Angels all cry the same / K. *<re-iss. 2006 2-cassette on Fuck It Tapes+=; FIT 025>* - The angle (live at KTRU) / Heatseeker (live at KTRU) / Songism / Death is a lonesome West Texas prairie / It's not your stereo / Untitled (Hanging around) (live at KTRU) / Have you got my money (original four-track demo) / Play the devil obsolescent.

Apr 07. (lp/cd) *<(GONG 06/+CD)>* **THERE'S NO HOME**
- Palms / Babies / Valkyries / Vultures / Movies / (Guitar) / Regardless / Bird / Pinnacle / (Guitar) / Oracle / Recess / Sirens / Sleep / There's no home.

Sep 07. (cd-ep) *<GONG 05>* CARRION EP
- Paint a babe / A goblin, a goblin / You will take it and like it / Ooh uuh [Sleep demo] / There's no home [demo] / Oracle [acoustic]. *<ltd one-sided-12" ep on Woodsist; 007>*

LOWER DENS

Jana Hunter - vocals, guitar / **Will Adams** - guitar / **Geoff Graham** - bass, vocals / **Abram Sanders** - drums

Impose — not issued

2010. (ltd-c; shared) *<IMP-016>* [Talk Normal track] / Submit

Gnomonsong — not issued

Jun 10. (7") *<GONG 16>* I GET NERVOUS. / Johnssong

Jul 10. (lp/cd) *<GONG 17/+CD>* **TWIN HAND MOVEMENT**
- Blue and silver / Tea lights / A dog's dick / Holy water / I get nervous / Completely golden / Plastic and powder / Rosie / Truss me / Hospice gates / Two cocks waving wildly at each other across a vast open space, a dark icy tundra.

Jan 11. (7") *<GONG 18>* BATMAN. / Dear Betty Baby

Sub Pop — not issued

Apr 11. (7") *<SP 927>* DEER KNIVES. / Tangiers

Lisa HUNTER

Acoustic Ann Arbor-based diva LISA HUNTER (born Ferndale, Michigan) had a steady relationship with bohemian-type folkies for several years, releasing four consistent albums kicking off in 1996 with **SOLID GROUND** {*6}. Check out 'Satisfied', 'The Party' and 'Back On Solid Ground'.

Reminiscent of SHAWN COLVIN and ANI DiFRANCO, singer/songwriter Lisa delivered more promise on her follow-up, **FLYING** (1998) {*6}, an invigorating set of twelve tracks headed by 'Faith'. **ALIVE** (2000) {*5} and her self-financed **LOVE YOURSELF JUST AS YOU ARE** (2003) {*6} could have been a springboard to greater things, had she had a bit of luck. *MCS*

Lisa Hunter - vocals, acoustic guitar / + session people

US Thursday - Swing Sister — UK Thursday - Swing Sister

1996. (cd) *<(THSS 1)>* **SOLID GROUND** — Apr 98
- Solid ground / Satisfied / The party / Breathe / The day / This road / Moonlight / Fade to black / Midnight oil / Pull from far away / Your eyes / Back on solid ground.

One Man Clapping — not issued

Jul 98. (cd) *<17>* **FLYING**
- Faith / Flying / Underground / Paralyze / Storm / River / Blue / Nowhere fast / Goodbye / Water under the bridge / Overgrown / Shine.

Spirulina — not issued

2000. (cd) *<S 7012-2>* **ALIVE**
- The very thing / Dark night / 2 truths & uh lie / Reckless / Spin / Free / Real of you / Fire / Purple hair / Ghost / Nuthin' / Faith (live).

Lisa Hunter — not issued

Jul 03. (cd) *<none>* **LOVE YOURSELF JUST AS YOU ARE**
- Love song (to myself) / Dark night / Underground / Breathing space / Spin / Free (the body image song) / Overgrown / Shine / Gold / Just as I am / The ring / Invitation / Just as I am - chant.

—— Lisa appears to have made her last record, but is believed still to be performing

HUSH ARBORS

The brainchild of singer/songwriter and guitarist Keith Wood (b. April 30, 1977 in Charlottesville, Virginia), the HUSH ARBORS could be fitted awkwardly into two genres: one experimental, in a Spiritualized/Ash Ra Tempel sort of hybrid, the other acoustic-folkie. Hence the distinctly ambiguous discography of CD-rs alongside a few proper releases.

Wood cut his teeth as a member of the late-1990s psych-punk collective Sunburned Hand Of The Man, WOODEN WAND auxiliaries The Vanishing Voice, and The Golden Oaks (with Brad Rose, alias The North Sea). Prolific, if not indeed hogging the indie party, Wood was also behind the one-off projects Ezekiel Blackouts III and The Zodiacs (as Zeke). The latter released a mini-CD, 'Gone', in 2007.

Without going too deeply into HUSH ARBORS's exotic-indie releases (Jessica Bowen featured on 2006's **LANDSCAPE OF BONE** {*6}), you can follow Wood on his Ecstatic Peace label route via psych-folk efforts **HUSH ARBORS** (2008) {*6} - a mini, not the eponymous earlier full set of glorious freak-outs - and the Justin Pizzoferrato-produced **YANKEE REALITY** (2009) {*7}, featuring retainer Leon Dufficy (guitar), Jason Ajemian (bass) and Ryan Sawyer (percussion). Among all its harder-edged moments, folk buffs might opt for 'Day Before', 'So They Say' and 'Fast Asleep'. *MCS*

Keith Wood - vocals, guitars (with guests)

US Digitalis — UK not issued

2004. (cd) *<digi 006>* **UNDER BENT LIMB TREES**
- Spirits over Mt Blanca / The forest we've been / Wooded reel / Where the black bear hides in the sky / May all your pastures now spring with herbs / Gypsy wood / Song for morning to sing / Dark mist curtains the doorway / Kudzu covered maples. *<d-cd-iss. 2007 +=; digi 037>* - Under the death tree / The valley / Brittle village / Clothed with sun / If there were spirits, let them come.

Foxglove — not issued

2004. (ltd-cd-r) *<foxglove 020>* **SINCE WE HAVE FALLEN**
- As the spring breaks (so does the heart) / Since we have fallen / The mountains will remain / Blanca peak / Spell against demons. *<lp-iss. Aug 06 on Harvest; Har 002>*

2004. (ltd-cd-r; shared) *<foxglove 027>* **SINGING THROUGH MOSS AND MIST**
- I will carry bones in my knapsack / Wasp of leaves // [The NORTH SEA tracks].

267 Lattajjaa — not issued

2005. (ltd-d-cd-r) *<LTJ-33 - digi 064>* **CLEANING THE BONE** — own
- Leaves crackling under footsteps / Hidden bone of old man / Veins of oak leaves // If there be spirits, let them come.

Barl Fire — not issued

2005. (ltd-cd-r; shared) *<BF 002>* **UNTITLED**
- Brittle village / Under the death tree // [TERRACID tracks] / [The NORTH SEA tracks].

Music Your Mind... — not issued

Aug 05. (cd-r) *<mymwly 0021>* DEATH CALLIGRAPHY. / Reconciliation... Liberation — Austra

Digitalis — not issued

2006. (cd) *<digi 021>* **HUSH ARBORS**
- Magic wood / The same tree forever / Wait for awhile / The werewolf om / Red horse / I took a watch on the sea wall / People died today / Smoke burn - Eyes so sore.

Three Lobed — not issued

Jun 06. (m-cd) *<TLR 024>* **LANDSCAPE OF BONE**
- Bones of a thousand suns / Broken bones / Oar of bone / Bones by the sea / Nine bones.

not issued Supplement — Great Pop

Feb 07. (ltd-7" shared) *(gps 13)* [VOICE OF THE SEVEN WOODS track]. / Gone On The Way To Know

May 07. (ltd-7" shared) *(gps 16)* LIGHT. / [WOODEN WAND track]

—— added **Leon Lufficy**

2008. (ltd-7" shared) *(gps 30)* [Jerusalem And The Starbaskets track]. / Mr Bones

Ecstatic Peace! — Ecstatic Peace!

Oct 08. (m-cd) *<E #100H>* **HUSH ARBORS**
- Intro / Follow closely / Rue hollow / Gone / Bless you / Sand / The light / Water II.

Oct 09. (cd) *<E #100>* **YANKEE REALITY**
- Day before / Lisbon / Fast asleep / So they say / One way ticket / Coming home / Sun shall / Take it easy / For while you slept / Devil made you high.

Meg HUTCHINSON

Born in 1978 in South Egremont, Massachusetts, the wispy, Boston-based folk-rock singer/songwriter MEG HUTCHINSON has steadily grown in stature with each release since her self-financed, self-titled {*6} debut in 1996.

Influenced by the work of JONI MITCHELL, GREG BROWN and poets including W.B. Yeats, Mary Oliver and Robert Frost, she took a liberal arts degree, majoring in creative writing, at Bard College. Meg won her first Kerriville New Folk Award in 2000, aided by her 1999 album **AGAINST THE GREY** {*7}, her first for the LRH label.

The live **ANY GIVEN DAY** (2001) {*5} and the awe-inspiring **THE CROSSING** (2004) {*8} - imagine NATALIE MERCHANT in a DAVID GRAY style - confirmed her dexterity and secured an invitation to join the bulging ranks of the Red House Records label, where GREG BROWN, JOHN GORKA and ELIZA GILKYSON were among her peers.

Whether her momentum had been lost somewhere on the way to 2008's **COME UP FULL** {*6} remains a moot point, but the long-awaited record still had its moments in 'Song For Jeffrey Lucey', 'Ready' and 'Somewhere', the latter interpolating Arlen & Harburg's 'Over The Rainbow'. **THE LIVING SIDE** (2010) {*6} provided fans and critics with at least two mini-gems, 'Hopeful Things' and 'Full Of Light'. *MCS*

Meg Hutchinson - vocals, guitar / with session band

US: unknown — UK: not issued

1996. (cd) <*none*> **MEG HUTCHINSON** □ ⊟
- Still matter / Song to Ophelia / Hunger moon / Building the ark / Sirens / Wild geese / Atlas / All day / Nothing to be grateful for / Footsteps in the hall / Only how we'll live.

US: LRH — UK: not issued

1999. (cd) <*LRH 001*> **AGAINST THE GREY** □ ⊟
- Pleasant street / Ship of fools / Neither here nor there / Always before / Lilith / Breathing lessons / Weightless / Over in a barrel / Twister / Run away / Little bit / Morning hymn / Girl's song.

2001. (cd) <*LRH 002*> **ANY GIVEN DAY** [live] □ ⊟
- When it rains / All my doors / Any given day / Paul Revere / Occam's razor / From the start / Miles / True north / Let me just / Golden mean / Heart song / Song to Ophelia / Perhaps / The promises of children / Yet to be. <*re-mast. 2009 +=; same*> - Song to Osa / True north [studio].

Jun 04. (cd) <*LRH 003*> **THE CROSSING** □ ⊟
- Coming up / Leonids / Vanishing points / San Andreas / Everything familiar / More / Sum of this / Blessed / The crossing / As the crow flies. <*re-iss. May 08 on Meg Hutchinson; none*>

2007. (cd-s) <*mp3*> TRUE NORTH □ ⊟

US: Red House — UK: Red House

Mar 08. (cd) <*(RHRCD 209)*> **COME UP FULL** □ □
- Ready / Home / Whole bird / Good day to die / America (enough) / Seeing stars / I'd like to know / Climbing mountains / Somewhere / Song for Jeffrey Lucey / Come up full / Can you tell me.

—— In 2009, she collaborated with ANTJE DUVEKOT, ANNE HEATON and NATALIA ZUKERMAN on the 'Winterbloom: Traditions Rearranged' CD.

Feb 10. (cd) <*(RHRCD 224)*> **THE LIVING SIDE** □ Mar 10 □
- Hard to change / Being happy / Gatekeeper / See me now / Hopeful things / Travel in / At first it was fun / Yea tho' we walk / Full of light / Every day / Something else.

Brian HYLAND

Who would have thought BRIAN HYLAND had ever tried his hand at folk music? Well, he did, so apologies are due for missing him out in Volume 1, an understandable omission given his track record of schmaltzy/smoochy early-1960s pop such as 'Itsy Bitsy Teenie Weenie Yellow Polka Dot Bikini', 'Ginny Come Lately and 'Sealed With A Kiss'.

However, like a few others of his ilk, headed by BOBBY DARIN and DION, Brian (b. November 12, 1943 in Woodhaven, New York) took to folk and country music like a duck to water. **COUNTRY MEETS FOLK** (1964) {*5} and **ROCKIN' FOLK** (1965) {*6} were oddities at the time, and even more so nowadays, having been shifted into the two-for-one CD market, although frustratingly not paired together, but each with other contemporary pop efforts.

The first of these LPs saw HYLAND branching out into Johnny Cash country and an itsy-bitsy sprinkle of folk by way of DYLAN ('Don't Think Twice, It's All Right'), HOYT AXTON ('Greenback Dollar') and The WEAVERS ('If I Had A Hammer'), while the follow-up brought a déjà-vu feeling with 'Blowin' In The Wind' and 'Where Have The Flowers Gone?' alongside folk staples such as 'Michael', 'Silver Threads And Golden Needles', 'Walk Right In' and 'Rock Island Line'. It's a pity in a way that Brian abandoned his folk foibles, but it was an interesting concept nevertheless. He had several subsequent minor hits, and a Top 3 smash, 'Gypsy Woman', in 1970. *MCS*

Brian Hyland - vocals, acoustic guitar / with session people, etc.

US: ABC-Paramount — UK: HMV

1964. (lp) <*ABCS 463*> *(CLP 1759)* **COUNTRY MEETS FOLK** □ □
- Act naturally / Don't think twice, it's all right / Folsom prison / The blizzard / If I had a hammer / Jamaica farewell / Candy man / Baby, what you want me to do / Give my love to Rose / Green green / Open pit mine / Greenback dollar. <*(cd-iss. Aug 07 on Beat Goes On+=; BGOCD 759)*> - HERE'S TO OUR LOVE tracks

US: Philips — UK: not issued

1965. (lp) <*PHM-200-158*> **ROCKIN' FOLK** □ ⊟
- Everglades / Michael / Blowin' in the wind / Where have all the flowers gone? / Raspberries, strawberries / Kaw-liga / Two brothers / Going to Memphis / Walk right in / Silver threads and golden needles / Jambalaya (on the bayou). <*(cd-iss. May 07 on Beat Goes On+=; BGOCD 758)*> - THE JOKER WENT WILD tracks.

—— Brian continued to work within the mainstream of music and had a few other hits

The IDITAROD

Taking their name from an Alaskan town and river, The IDITAROD (formed in 1995 by vocalist Carin Wagner and multi-instrumentalist Jeffrey Alexander in Providence, Rhode Island) were the epitome of the new breed of eerie indie-folk acts.

Debut set **THE RIVER NEKTAR** (1998) {*6} delivered a sparse and spooky mediaeval soundtrack not unlike that of IN GOWAN RING/BIRCH BOOK, but purist folkies beware - it's not for you. Other tunes recall passé grunge music from Nirvana to Radiohead, for example 'Bavaria', 'Boat' and 'Providence'.

Two songs you might recognize (but only just) are their covers of DONOVAN's 'The Lullaby Of Spring' and Eno's 'The Fat Lady Of Limbourg', obscure B-sides which appear as bonus tracks on the much-improved 2003 re-issue. Guest players included William Schaff, Margie Wienk, Miriam Goldberg, Sharron Kraus, ALEC K. REDFEARN, Matt Everett, et al.

With Everett and Wienk fully on board, joined by fellow-freak folkies FIT & LIMO and, on a few tracks, Jesse Poe, **THE GHOST, THE ELF, THE CAT AND THE ANGEL** (2002) {*7} was most definitely for the unhinged folk fan, something like Virginia Astley and/or ESPERS on speed. The eerie Indiana melancholia of 'The Falling Of The Pine' (adapted by Jeffrey from a traditional logging song) and the traditional 'Let No Man Steal Your Thyme' and 'Unfortunate Lass' displayed Carin's fragility and frailty at their most deliciously abundant - the band were beating the drum ever so slowly.

Tracks to whisk you back to mediaeval minstrel times were her 'The Roots Of The Butterfly Bush' and 'Afternoons Like This Are Hard To Come By', plus Jeffrey's 'Raga (In D#)', an instrumental inspired by Alejandro Jodorowsky's cult film 'The Holy Mountain'.

YULETIDE (2003) {*5} found them collaborating with SHARRON KRAUS before they disbanded in April 2003, bidding farewell later that year with a double-CD compilation of the same name, featuring traditional festive songs alongside a cover of The Grateful Dead's 'Mountains Of The Moon'.

Among the recordings of Alexander's subsequent project, BLACK FOREST/BLACK SEA, only their self-titled 2003 set came close to The IDITAROD's classical/ambient folk, but they were certainly a group for anyone who loves Current 93 or their ilk. *MCS*

Carin Wagner - vocals, small percussion / **Jeffrey Alexander** - guitars, dulcimer, banjo, percussion, electronics, vocals

US Hub*City — UK not issued

1998. (cd) *<H*C 003>* **THE RIVER NEKTAR**
- Meadows / Never used / Helms a-lee / Dictation and transcription / Bavaria / Gold berry white / Servants serve / Boat / East ring dell / Providence / The lorelei / Mariner / Garden. *<(re-mast. Feb 03 on Bluesanct+=; INRI 071)>* - Move / Sylvia Jean / The lullaby of spring / Boat (live version) / One minute / Children Three / The fat lady of Limbourg / Garden (original version) / Compromising.

Apr 99. (7" ep) *<BES-011>* THE EYESORES & THE IDITAROD
- The IDITAROD: Children Three / The fat lady of Limbourg / (track by The EYESORES).

(above issued on Brentwood Estates)

Oct 00. (7" clear-ep) *<HC 007>* COMPROMISING. / Boring / Moonchild

——added **Matthew Everett** - violin, vocals, percussion, guitar, recorder, viola / **Margie Wienk** - cello, wine glasses (of IN GOWAN RING, ex-Difference Engine)

Bluesanct — Bluesanct

Apr 02. (cd) *<(INRI 065)>* **THE GHOST, THE ELF, THE CAT AND THE ANGEL**
- The roots of the butterfly bush / Black strung bow / Afternoons like this are hard to come by / Raga (in D#) / Cycle circle / The falling of the pine / Ich tanzte weit / New magic in a dusty world / Let no man steal your thyme / The nameless one / Unfortunate lass.

Dutch Courage — not issued

2002. (7" ep) *<DCR-08>* JEN TURRELL / The IDITAROD: DUTCH SPLITS VOLUME ONE
- (two by JEN TURRELL) / Weaker one / Larry.

not issued — Time-Lag

2002. (ltd-7") *<Time-Lag 007>* FEEL THE BREATH OF THE WOODS UPON YOUR HEART PART ONE. / Feel The Breath Of The Woods Upon Your Heart Part Two

(above 'Terrastock 5' festival release also issued as a five-7" box with various artists: Stone Breath, Charalambides, Bardo Pond, Sonic Youth)

not issued — Elsie & Jack

Jan 03. (cd; by The IDITAROD and SHARRON KRAUS) *(eaj 014)* **YULETIDE**
- The trees are all bare / Lyke wake dirge / Gift / Winter's spell / Wintermute.

——The IDITAROD split in April 2003; Jeffrey formed BLACK FOREST/BLACK SEA; Matthew and Margie joined ESPERS

- (5-7*) compilations, others, etc.-

Apr 02. (ltd;c) *Morc; (Morc 26)* **KLEINE** — Belgium
- You are the atmosphere / 1000 years / Broadcast / Intermission / Father / Compromising, earlier on / Kleine / Closing my eyes for you / Not much time to say goodbye / Older, not wiser. *(cd-iss. Jun 07; Morc 46)*

Nov 03. (ltd;d-cd) *Camera Obscura; <CAM 063>* **YULETIDE**
- Winter suite / The snow it melts the soonest / Watch the stars - The north wind doth blow / A footprint in the ashes on new year's day / The crofter's Christmas Eve lullaby / Snow falls / The woodcutter's song / Silent carol / Trees toasted in cider / Darkness, darkness / Night's candles are burnt out / Y cwps // The trees are all bare / Scandinavian instrumental - The rowan / Draped in bardings / Mountains of the moon / In the bleak midwinter / Unspherical / Boat / The woods are lovely, dark and deep / All winter's eve / There was a pig went out to dig / Wide oak-and-iron / Thierna na oge.

BLACK FOREST/BLACK SEA

Jeffrey Alexander - guitar, banjo, Omnichord / **Miriam Goldberg** - cello, Omnichord, vocals

Last Visible Dog — not issued

Jul 03. (cd) *<LVD 036>* **BLACK FOREST/BLACK SEA**
- Sevastopol / Blackbird on gray sky / Middle song / Banjo song / Beautiful here / Sunday market / Lump in throat. *<re-iss. Jan 06 on Asphalt Duchess+=; 002>* - Sea song / Lump in throat.

Bluesanct — Bluesanct

Apr 04. (cd) *<(INRI 076)>* **FORCEFIELDS AND CONSTELLATIONS**
- Orion / Nylon 2 / These things / Kyy plays perpetual change / I'm in love... / ...With a dead man I've never met / Fish no fish / F Vs. BF/BS / Hung far lowish / Nylon 1 / The last night in Troy / Tangent universe / Jamestown.

Last Visible Dog — not issued

Jul 04. (cd) *<LVD 065>* **RADIANT SYMMETRY** (live)
- Tchai-Ovna Tearoom, Glasgow 4/20/04 / Tampere 2/03/04 / Radio Citta Del Capo, Bologna 3/21/04 / Morden Tower, Newcastle upon Tyne 4/14/04 / Bristol 4/06/04 / Tampere 2/03/04 / Morden Tower, Newcastle upon Tyne 4/14/04 / ArciBlob, Arcore 3/18/04 / Talbot Hotel, Stoke-on-Trent 4/11/04.

Time-Lag — not issued

Sep 04. (ltd-ep) *<Time-Lag 024>* CHRISTINA CARTER & BLACK FOREST/BLACK SEA
- (three by Christina Carter) / To be drunken / Ectomist / Haze of beating wings / CHRISTINA CARTER & BLACK FOREST/BLACK SEA: Orion 2.

Music Fellowship — Music Fellowship

Dec 06. (ltd-lp/cd) *<(MF 028)>* **BLACK FOREST/BLACK SEA**
- Side I / Side II.

——added **Joseph Grimm** + **Margot Goldberg**

Secret Eye — not issued

Feb 08. (ltd-10" ep) *<AB-OC-08>* PORTMANTEAU
- Gemittarius / Aquemini.

IN GOWAN RING

IN GOWAN RING was the brainchild of singer and multi-instrumentalist B'Eirth (born Bobin Jon Michael Eirth in Utah, 1964), a psych-folk pilgrim who has been the founder of many band projects, including SubCulture (in 1986/87) and Mary Throwing Stones (with future IN GOWAN player

Lincoln Lysager, C. Barry Semple and Brian Castillo). The latter group released one self-titled, limited-edition CD.

In 1992, Bee (as his friends call him) moved to London, went on tour and signed to the World Serpent label, home to fellow experimentalists CURRENT 93. After featuring in a number of various-artists compilations in the early 1990s, IN GOWAN RING, complete with a revolving-door line-up, set about combining wyrd-o mediaeval folk music with tripped-out, apocalyptic psychedelia. Imagine The INCREDIBLE STRING BAND sharing studio space with The Virgin Prunes.

LOVE CHARMS (1994) {*7} was the RING's low-key debut, B'eirth featuring on a few dozen instruments (including 'water') with gothic backing from Amber, Celise, Mary Land, Cate, Sarah G and old comrade Lincoln. From the dour lo-fi/folk opener 'Listen To Colours' and 'Of Water Wiverings' to the genius of 'Spindle Tree' and 'Dandelion Wine', the night-friendly set oozes a mystique that most folk purists will find disturbing. Be warned, it's hard listening at times; even the 'dreambox' track 'Within Rings' carries an undercurrent of subliminal, suicidal missives. The lengthy closer, 'Urn And Water', could be just the one to get you climbing the walls.

Recorded between 1994 and 1996 with the addition of various newbie recruits, the second set, **THE TWIN TREES** (1997) {*8}, abandoned most of the far-flung, off-kilter diversities of the debut, concentrating instead on neo-folk-faerie-like tracks such as the beautiful 'One Silver Ring', the darkly dream-like 'Lady Beyond The River', 'Rivertime Tome' and the jazzy title track. Things do go somewhat awry again on 'By Moss Strand And Waterspathe', although B'eirth's Celtic-folkiness gets into full retro swing on 'Cupped Hands Spell' and 'Our Rainbowed Paradox'.

A second release for BlueSanct, **ABEND THE KNURLED STITCH O'ER THE GLINTING SPADE** (1999) {*7} sadly brought IN GOWAN RING to an abrupt end. People will look back on their time as essential to the evolutionary fabrication of freak-folk. The biggies here, in terms of ritual longevity and track length, are the lush 'Cipher's String On The Tree In The Dream Of The Queen' and 'Milk Star', but it's the dreamy opener 'Two Wax Dolls' that sends shivers down your spine. It wasn't quite over, though, as the band returned for another series of CD-rs, obscure and of course hard to find.

B'Eirth, meanwhile, moonlighted with BIRCH BOOK, recording the project's debut set **BIRCH BOOK** (2005) {*7} in New England during 2002 through 2004. Spotlighting Seth Eames (Telecaster electric guitar), Annabel Lee (viola) and Moss and Victoria (chorus), the album was tinged with steely country and blues soundscapes, somewhat akin to PALACE/WILL OLDHAM. The best examples are 'Five Hundred Keys', the harmonica-driven 'Easy To Live' and the juicy jew's-harp of 'How The Hours...'. 'Coffee Morning' recalls The Velvet Underground's 'Pale Blue Eyes', 'Train To Rome' an acoustic Floyd or Zeppelin, 'Leaf Patches On Sidewalks' probably ROY HARPER or DONOVAN. If The Carpenters or Bread were still around, they'd be swiping 'Sleepless Search'.

Taking a mediaeval slant (witness more hessian-like cardboard artwork on the plaintive sleeve), BIRCH BOOK's second set, **FORTUNE AND FOLLY** (2006) {*6}, was a relatively quick follow-up. It opens and closes, like its predecessor, with light instrumentals, but elsewhere B'Eirth (on vocals and acoustic guitar) creates a hypnotic back-to-basics monotone, sombre and even horizontal on 'Young Souls', 'New Joy', 'The Carnival Is Empty' and the seven-minute 'The Trip Goes On'.

After three years in the studio, BIRCH BOOK delivered **A HAND FULL OF DAYS** (2009) {*6}, a record that veered toward psychedelia rather than folk. Released to promote an imminent tour, the limited-edition **TOMORROW'S SUN WILL RISE THE SAME** (2010) {*6} (all covers except the first and last tracks) is an interesting folk artifact to collect. B'Eirth's revamps are of Gene Clark's 'Day For Night', NICK DRAKE's 'Clothes Of Sand', Violent Femmes' 'Good Feeling', Angelo Branduardi's 'The Stag', Marc Bolan's 'Blessed Wild Apple Girl', ROGER McGUINN's 'Ballad Of Easy Rider', FRED NEIL's 'A Little Bit Of Rain', ELYSE's 'Houses', PARCHMENT's 'Corners Of My Life' and the traditional 'Silver Dagger'. *MCS*

B'Eirth - vocals, instruments, water / with **Amber** - metal flute / **Celise** - viola / **Mary Land** - chant / **Cate** - bells, bamboo flute / **Sarah G** - tinklies, toys / **Lincoln Lysager** - chapel organ, vocals

US not issued — UK World Serpent

Nov 94. (cd) *(WSCD 006)* **LOVE CHARMS**
- Listen to colours / Love charms / Spindle tree (with dreambox) / A swan song / Stone song II / Dandelion wine / Within rings (with dreambox) / Of water wiverings / Urn and water.

——**Eli Morrison** - bass, guitar; repl. Sarah
——**John Bean** - contrabass; repl. Celise
——added **Melinda Dawn** - vocals / **Lisa Oliver + E.** - singing bowl chant + **Grant J** - trumpet

not issued Musak — BlueSanct

Apr 97. (cd) *(LUNE 002CD)* **THE TWIN TREES**
- Rivertime tome / One silver ring / Stone song III / The twin trees / Lady beyond the river / By moss strand and waterspathe / Cupped hands spell / Our rainbowed paradox. *(re-iss. 2006 on Swiss label Shayo+=; 009)- Still water bonne.*

Oct 99. (cd) *(LUNE 003)* **ABEND THE KNURLED STITCH O'ER THE GLINTING SPADE**
- Two wax dolls / To thrum a glassy stem / Cipher's string on the tree / In the dream of the queen bow star / A bee at the Dolman's dell / Arrowsmith's fire / Milk star.

Oct 00. (ltd-cd) *(LUNE 000)* **COMPENDIUM 1994–2000** [compilation and rare]
- Introduction / To thrum a glassy stem / Cipher's string on the tree in the dream of the queen / Twin trees / By moss strand and waterspathe / A swan song / Dandelion wine / Urn and dreambox / Sea ritual (live) / Fifteen men on the deadman's chest / The black one (live) / The once true love / With a kiss or candle / A lullaby ere closed eyes (nap lair suite I) / Naptime cometh (nap lair suite II) / Great omniscient nap and the myriad regal mysteries therein or 'A litany to lethargy' (nap lair suite III) / Onward! Napland is at hand! (nap lair suite IV) / The wize erd and his dream (for Pscikadilik psyrkuz III).

2002. (cd) *(LUNE 004)* **HAZEL STEPS THROUGH A WEATHERED HOME**
- The orb weavers / Hazel steps / The seer and the seen / Kingdom of the shades / Morning's waking dream / A poet's lyre / Wind that cracks the leaves / Two towers.

self-rel. — not issued

Apr 02. (cd-r) *<none>* **EXISTS AND ENTRANCES - VOLUME ONE: VERNAL EQUINOX**
- Montesinho instrumental / Rosehip November / Are we lost / Bedlam boys / Winter's flowers / A spider song / Hazel steps green handed / Prospecting hazel steps / The secret heart / I went into a hazel wood / Way to blue / Montesinho revisited.

2002. (cd-r) *<none>* **EXISTS AND ENTRANCES - VOLUME TWO: AUTUMNAL EQUINOX 2002**
- Pool and leaves / Under a willow tree / Just like arcadia / Reckoner's theme \1 / Of skin and tresses / Coffee morning / The lord of man / On the butterfly's wing / Reckoner's theme \2 / Ring-o-the rascal / Jeweled jangles / Mistress of the revels / Pool and leaves - reprise. *(re-iss. Apr 09 on German label Steinklang; 58013-2)*

2003. (cd-r) *<none>* **EXISTS AND ENTRANCES - VOLUME THREE 2003: VERNAL EQUINOX**
- Vernal rising / Green grows the lily / Play for me fiddler! / A lock that ain't worth pickin' / Berzerka murzurka I / Light rays and smoke shapes / I have a friend / Spindle tree with dreambox / Urn and water / Sea ritual / The black one / A bottle of wine / Berzerka murzurka II / Vernal rising - reprise.

2003. (cd-r) *<none>* **EXISTS AND ENTRANCES - VOLUME FOUR 2003: AUTUMN EQUINOX**
- Invacation / Icarus / Elements play / Where the sun keeps shinin' / Twin trees / A single flower / In precarious flight / Li'l Sir John / Death and the maiden / The wind of change / On the setting sun / Leaf patches on sidewalks / BenterDiction.

Hand/Eye — not issued

May 05. (m-cd-r) *(h/e-moon 3)* **FULL FLOWER MOON**
- Limpid brook / Clover / Moon over ocean / Marigold / Aurora.

2006. (ltd;cd-r) *<none>* **WEBS AMONG THE DIN** (live 2005)
- Incoming - Sur le caveau 1 / Huge and luminous / Boat of the moon / Young souls / Sur le caveau 2 / Gently Johnny / Sur le caveau 3 / The seer and the seen / Morning's waking dream / The wandering boy / Mad Michael / Sur le caveau 4 / Moon over ocean / Webs among the din / Aurora / Along the straggling way / Sur le caveau 5 / Backward climbing / The vegetable man / Sur le caveau 6 / Wind the cracks the leaves / Sleepless search / Osiris / Sur le caveau - Outgoing.

Time Is A Spiral — not issued

Jul 07. (ltd;10"m-lp) *(SPIRAL 001)* **DWARS @ VPRO RADIO SESSION SERIES** — Nether
- Boat on the moon / On the stragglin' way / Morning's waking dream / The seer and the seen / Cupped hands spell / Dandelion wine.

not issued — self-rel.

Apr 08. (ltd CD-r) *(none)* **WEBS AMONG THE DIN VOL. II** (live)
- Webwork begins / Crack of the sun / Keep it with mine / Aurora / Christina's song / A Bee at the dolmen's bell / Adi shakti I / Sad song / Dandelion wine / Wheel of fortune / Nancy / Lonely prophet blues / Adi shakti II / Rumi's dance / Nature boy / Chanson de prevert / Zephyr through willows / The carnival is empty / Crack of the sun / Untitled.

Soprodasesferas — not issued

Apr 08. (enh-cd) *(sopro 000)* **IN GOWAN RING WITH MAJA ELLIOTT** (live in Portugal 2007) — Portugal
- Morning's waking dream / Zephyr through the willows / Christina's song / Dandelion wine / Boat of the moon / My lagan love / Uisneagh / Presence / Johnny's song / The wandering boy / Along the straggling way / Gently Johnny / The carnival is empty / In the dream of the queen (video).

BIRCH BOOK

Bee (B'Eirth) - voice, multi-instruments / with **Seth Eames** - electric guitar / **Annabel Lee** - viola / **Moss + Victoria** - chorus

		Lune Music	not issued
Aug 05.	(cd) *(VOL I)* **BIRCH BOOK**	[ ]	[-]

- Birch bark / How the hours... / Five hundred keys / Easy to live / Coffee morning / Eglantine / Train to Rome / Leaf patches on sidewalks / Sleepless search / Warm wind and rain / Windows / Birch bark.

		helmet rOOm	not issued
Nov 06.	(cd) *(VOL II)* **FORTUNE AND FOLLY**	[ ]	[-]

- Birch sap / New song / Whisper in the pine / Young souls / New joy / Diaspora / The wandering boy / Zephyr through willows / The trip goes on / The carnival is empty / Birch sap.

——next with **Bee + Ron Walker, Pascal Humbert + Subhadra**

		Little Somebody	not issued
Sep 09.	(cd) *<LSR 11>* **VOL. III: A HAND FULL OF DAYS**	[ ]	[-]

- Birch leaves / Feet of clay / Empty corner of the page / Left hand / Patchwork woman / Stray summer song / Hatched in stone / Sad song / Nothing more / White angel / Right hand / Life's lace / Will of the wind / Birch leaves.

		self-rel.	Les Disques Du 7eme Ciel
Mar 10.	(ltd cd-r) *<none>* **TOMORROW'S SUN WILL RISE THE SAME**	[-] own	[-]

- Tomorrow's sun arises / Day for night / Clothes of sand / Good feeling / The stag / Blessed wild apple girl / Silver dagger / Ballad of Easy Rider / A little bit of rain / Houses / Corners of my life / Tomorrow's sun sets.

May 11.	(ltd-10"+cd-ep) *(7C2)* BIRCH BOOK	[-] French	[-]

- Life's lace / Le temps de vivre / La chanson de prevert / Son du soleil / Les feuilles mortes / Vent d'automne.

INDIGO GIRLS

If arena-rockers Heart had been a folk-rock act, they might have sounded like INDIGO GIRLS. Formed in Decatur, Georgia in 1980 by singer-songwriters Amy Ray and Emily Saliers (who had been performing together since childhood), the duo have been leaders in their field of MOR acoustic-folk for more than 30 years.

The girls made their vinyl debut in the summer of 1985 with an independently-released single, 'Crazy Game', following it up with a self-titled EP and a self-financed debut album, **STRANGE FIRE** (1987) {*5}. It didn't exactly set the world on fire, but with the success of such female nu-folk artists as SUZANNE VEGA and TRACY CHAPMAN, the INDIGO GIRLS' cutesy-pie, strum-friendly acoustics became hot property. They were signed up by Epic, who almost immediately re-promoted the debut album, which featured concert favourites 'Land Of Canaan', the single 'Crazy Game' and a cover of The YOUNGBLOODS' 'Get Together'.

Featuring contributions from the likes of R.E.M., LUKA BLOOM and The Hothouse Flowers, **INDIGO GIRLS** (1989) {*8} was a strong major-label debut which had no problem crossing over from their loyal grassroots following to the pop market, where it hit the Top 30. Similar to The ROCHES, KATE WOLF or HOLLY NEAR in their social and environmental awareness, INDIGO GIRLS' harmony-laden folk-pop/rock found particular favour with the burgeoning US feminist movement, and 'Closer To Fine', 'Kid Fears' and another version of 'Land Of Canaan' brought them into the bedsitter/college-student market.

Again featuring an array of respected names, including Mary Chapin Carpenter and Jim Keltner, **NOMADS - INDIANS - SAINTS** (1990) {*7} wasn't quite so successful, although it did throw up a few thought-provoking numbers in 'Hammer And A Nail', 'Pushing The Needle Too Far' and 'World Falls'. The timing of the mini-set **LIVE: BACK ON THE BUS Y'ALL** (1991) {*4} was a little ill-advised, but it did take on the challenge of DYLAN's 'All Along The Watchtower'.

The more adventurous **RITES OF PASSAGE** (1992) {*6}, featuring Lisa Germano, The ROCHES, David Crosby, Jackson Browne and an orchestra conducted by Michael Kamen, almost made the US Top 20 and was nominated for a Grammy, though 'Galileo', 'Joking' and 'Cedar Tree' were less recognisable than their folky reading of Dire Straits' 'Romeo And Juliet'.

The latter album's more expansive approach was further developed on **SWAMP OPHELIA** (1994) {*6}, which employed Germano's violin to similarly impressive results alongside cellist Jane Scarpantoni, Canadian singer JANE SIBERRY and the acoustic bass playing of the ubiquitous DANNY THOMPSON. The record finally took the pair into the Top 10, but while that achievement was repeated with the studio follow-up **SHAMING OF THE SUN** (1997) {*6}, their success in Britain remained minimal.

Their earlier double-live effort, **1200 CURFEWS** (1995) {*6}, found space for rocking folk covers of JONI MITCHELL's 'River', BUFFY SAINTE-MARIE's 'Bury My Heart At Wounded Knee', DYLAN's 'Tangled Up In Blue', NEIL YOUNG's 'Down By The River', Gerard McHugh's 'Thin Line' and the Gladys Knight hit 'Midnight Train To Georgia'.

With its stellar cast of guests (including Sheryl Crow, Natacha Atlas, Joan Osborne, Me'Shell Ndegeocello and The BAND's Garth Hudson) and a thrillingly diverse approach, **COME ON NOW SOCIAL** (1999) {*7} was as likely as any of their past records to find them a UK audience. Featuring heads-down, Garbage-style rock ('Go'), straight-up country ('Gone Again'), Fleetwood Mac-like AOR ('Cold Beer And Remote Control') and the soulful single 'Peace Tonight', it showcased the GIRLS at the height of their art.

BECOME YOU (2002) {*6}, in contrast, was a pared-back affair, shorn of any production or guest-star excess and concentrating on the kind of obliquely personal songwriting with which the duo, now backed by Carol Isaacs, Claire Kenny and Brady Blade, had made their name. **ALL THAT WE LET IN** (2004) {*6} continued the run of Top 40 studio albums but was their last for the Epic label.

Despite their new five-album contract with Hollywood Records, the deal produced only one set, the Mitchell Froom-produced **DESPITE OUR DIFFERENCES** (2006) {*6}. Guests Brandi Carlile and Pink were the photogenic glam behind the pop-pourri of Laurel Canyon-type folk fodder.

A radical change of direction was needed, but whether **POSEIDON AND THE BITTER BUG** (2009) {*6} (their first for the rejuvenated independent Vanguard label) was the musical fuel injection that was required, maybe only time will tell. Another double-live venture, **STARING DOWN THE BRILLIANT DREAM** (2010) {*6}, which closed with the Jagger-Richards song 'Wild Horses', and a festive bluegrass set, **HOLLY HAPPY DAYS** (2010) {*5}, were nothing new from a duo who were still to make it big outside North America. *MCS*

Amy Ray (b. Apr 12 '64) - vocals, guitars / **Emily Saliers** (b. Jul 22 '63, New Haven, Connecticut) - vocals, acoustic guitar (with session people on subsequent releases)

		US	UK
		J Ellis	not issued
Jun 85.	(ltd-7") *<A 1264>* CRAZY GAME. / Everybody's Waiting (For Someone To Come Home)	[ ]	[-]
		DragonPath	not issued
Nov 86.	(ltd-12"ep) *<LMM I>* INDIGO GIRLS	[ ]	[-]

- Land of Canaan / Lifeblood / History of us / Never stop / Cold as ice / Finlandia.

		Indigo Music	not issued
Oct 87.	(lp) *<LMM II>* **STRANGE FIRE**	[ ]	[-]

- Make it easier / Walk away / Crazy game / I don't wanna know / You left it up to me / Hey Jesus / Strange fire / High horse / Left me a fool / Land of Canaan / Blood and fire. *<US re-iss. Nov 89 on Epic; EK 45427>* - Strange fire / Crazy game / Left me a fool / I don't wanna know / Hey Jesus / Get together / Walk away / Make it easier / You left it up to me / Land of Canaan. *<(cd re-iss. Oct 00 on Epic+=; 500750-2)>* - Crazy game [early 45 version] / Everybody's waiting (for someone to come home) [early 45 version].

		Epic	Epic
Jun 89.	(7") *<68912>* CLOSER TO FINE. / Cold As Ice	[52]	[-]
Jun 89.	(7") *(654907-7)* CLOSER TO FINE. / History Of Us (12"+=/cd-s+=) *(654907-5/-2)* - Center stage (live).	[-]	[ ]
Feb 89.	(lp/c/cd) *<ET/EK 45044> (463491-1/-4/-2)* **INDIGO GIRLS**	[22]	Jul 89 [ ]

- Closer to fine / Secure yourself / Kid fears / Prince of darkness / Blood and fire / Tried to be true / Love's recovery / Land of Canaan / Center stage / History of us. *<(cd re-iss. Oct 00 +=; 500751-2)>* - Land of Canaan (remix) / Center stage (live). *<d-cd-iss. May 08 on Sony-Legacy+=; 8869 72966-7>* - RITES OF PASSAGE

Sep 89.	(7") *<73003>* LAND OF CANAAN. / Never Stop	[ ]	[-]
Nov 89.	(12" ep/cd-ep) *(655135-8/-2)* CLOSER TO FINE / Closer To Fine (live). / Mona Lisas And Mad Hatters (live) / American Tune (live)	[-]	[ ]
Feb 90.	(7") *<73255>* GET TOGETHER. / Finlandia	[ ]	[-]
Sep 90.	(cd/c/lp) *<EK/ET 46820> (467308-2/-4/-1)* **NOMADS - INDIANS - SAINTS**	[34]	Nov 90 [ ]

- Hammer and a nail / Welcome me / World falls / Southland in the springtime / 1 2 3 / Keeper of my heart / Watershed / Hand me downs / You and me of the 10,000 wars / Pushing the needle too far / The girl with the weight of the world in her hands. *<(cd re-iss. Oct 00 +=; 500752-2)>* - (interview) / You and me of the 10,000 wars (live).

Oct 90.	(c-s) *<73607>* HAMMER AND A NAIL / Welcome (live)	[ ]	[-]
Jun 91.	(m-cd) *<EK 47508> (468415-2)* **BACK ON THE BUS, Y'ALL** (live)	[ ]	[ ]

- 1 2 3 / Tried to be true / You and me of the 10,000 wars / Prince of darkness / Kid fears / Left me a fool / All along the watchtower / 1 2 3 (studio version).

May 92.	(cd/c/lp) *<EK/ET 48865> (471363-2/-4/-1)* **RITES OF PASSAGE**	[21]	Jun 92 [ ]

- Three hits / Galileo / Ghost / Joking / Jonas and Ezekiel / Love will come to you / Romeo and Juliet / Virginia Woolf / Chickenman / Airplane / Nashville / Let it be me / Cedar tree. *<(cd re-iss. Oct 00 +=; 500753-2)>* - Three hits (live) / Love will come to you (live). *<d-cd-iss.+=>* - INDIGO GIRLS

Jul 92.	(c-s) *<74326>* GALILEO / (album version)	[89]	[-]
Oct 92.	(7"/c-s) *(658768-7/-4)* GALILEO. / Kid Fears	[-]	[ ]

(cd-s) *(658768-2)* - ('A') / Closer to fine / Tried to be true / Hammer and a nail.

May 94. (cd-ep) *(660340-2)* LEAST COMPLICATED / Dead Man's Hill (acoustic) / Mystery (acoustic) / Kid Fears [-] [ ]
May 94. (cd/c/lp) *<EK 057621> (475931-2/-4/-1)* **SWAMP OPHELIA** [9] [66]
- Fugitive / Least complicated / Language or the kiss / Reunion / Power of two / Touch me fall / The wood song / Mystery / Dead man's hill / Fare thee well / This train revised.
Jun 95. (c-s) *(662166-4)* CLOSER TO FINE / Rockin' In The Free World [-] [ ]
(cd-s+=) *(662166-2)* - Dead man's hill (acoustic) / Mystery (acoustic).
(cd-s) *(662166-5)* - ('A') / Kid fears / All along the watchtower (live) / Left me a fool (live).
Oct 95. (d-cd) *<EK 067229>* **1200 CURFEWS** (live) [40] [-]
- Joking / Least complicated / Thin line / River / Strange fire / Power of two / Pushing the needle too far / Virginia Woolf / Jonas and Ezekiel / Tangled up in blue / World falls / Bury my heart at Wounded Knee / Ghost / Dead man's hill // I don't wanna know / Galileo / Down by the river / Love's recovery / Land of Canaan / Mystery / This train revised / Back together again / Language or the kiss / Chickenman / Midnight train to Georgia / Closer to fine / Bury my heart at Wounded Knee (live). *<hidden track +=>* - Go go go.
Apr 97. (cd/c) *<EK/ET 067891> (486982-2/-4)* **SHAMING OF THE SUN** [7] May 97 [ ]
- Shame on you / Get out the map / Shed your skin / It's alright / Caramia / Don't give that girl a gun / Leeds / Scooter boys / Everything in its own time / Cut it out / Burn all the letters / Hey kind friend.
Sep 99. (cd/c) *<EK 069914> (495091-2/-4)* **COME ON NOW SOCIAL** [34] Oct 99 [ ]
- Go / Soon to be nothing / Gone again / Trouble / Sister / Peace tonight / Ozilline / We are together / Cold beer and remote control / Compromise / Andy / Faye Tucker. *<hidden tracks +=>* - Sister (reprise) / Philosophy of loss.
Mar 02. (cd) *<86401> (507575-2)* **BECOME YOU** [30] May 02 [ ]
- Moment of forgiveness / Deconstruction / Become you / You've got to show / Yield / Collecting you / Hope alone / Bitterroot / Our deliverance / Starkville / She's saving me / Nuevas senoritas.
Feb 04. (cd) *<92859-2> (515144-2)* **ALL THAT WE LET IN** [35] [ ]
- Fill it up again / Heartache for everyone / Free in you / Perfect world / All that we let in / Tether / Come on home / Dairy queen / Something real / Cordova / Rise up.

Hollywood Hollywood

Sep 06. (cd) *<2061-62635-2> (385470-2)* **DESPITE OUR DIFFERENCES** [44] Feb 07 [ ]
- Pendulum swinger / Little perennials / I believe in love / Three country highway / Run / Rock and roll heaven's gate (featuring PINK) / Lay my head down / Money made you mean / Fly away / Dirt and dead ends / All the way / They won't have me / Last tears (featuring BRANDI CARLILE). *<d-cd+=; 2061-62655-2>* - (live and acoustic):- Money made you mean / Last tears / Little perennials / Fly away / Pendulum swinger / Three country highway.

Vanguard Vanguard

Mar 09. (cd-s) *<79948-2>* WHAT ARE YOU LIKE? (full band version) / (acoustic version) [ ] [-]
Mar 09. (cd) *<79896-2> (79934-2)* **POSEIDON AND THE BITTER BUG** [29] [ ]
- Digging for your dream / Sugar tongue / Love of our lives / Driver education / I'll change / Second time around / What are you like? / Ghost of the gang / Fleet of hope / True romantic. *<(d-cd iss.+=; VSD 79934)>* - (acoustic sessions):- Ghost of the gang / I'll change / Sugar tongue / Love of our lives / Salty south / Digging for your dream / Second time around / What are you like? / Driver education / Fleet of hope / True romantic.
Jun 10. (d-cd) *<(78069-2)>* **STARING DOWN THE BRILLIANT DREAM** [live from 2006–2009] [ ] [ ]
- Heartache for everyone / Closer to fine / Go / Come on home / Devotion / Cold beer and remote control / Moment of forgiveness / Fill it up again / Sugar tongue / Fly away / Ozilline / Don't think twice, it's all right / Kid fears / Watershed / Shame on you // Get out the map / Salty south / The wood song / Three county highway / Digging for your dream / Rock and roll heaven's gate / I believe in love / Fugitive / Cordova / What are you like / Second time around / Love of our lives / Become you / Prince of darkness / Tether / Wild horses.
Oct 10. (cd) *<78120-2>* **HOLLY HAPPY DAYS** [festive] [ ] [-]
- I feel the Christmas spirit / It really is (a wonderful life) / O holy night / Your holiday song / I'll be home for Christmas / Mistletoe / Peace child / The wonder song / In the bleak midwinter / Happy joyous Hanukkah / Angels we have heard on high / There's still my joy.

- (8-10*) compilations -

Jul 95. (cd/c) *Epic; (480439-2/-4)* **4.5 (THE BEST OF THE INDIGO GIRLS)** [-] [43]
- Joking / Hammer and a nail / Kid fears / Galileo / Tried to be true / Power of two / Pushing the needle too far / Reunion / Closer to fine / Three hits / Least complicated / Touch me fall / Love's recovery / Land of Canaan / Ghost.
Oct 00. (cd/c) *Epic; <EK/ET 61602> (500988-2/-4)* **RETROSPECTIVE** [ ] [ ]
- Strange fire / Closer to fine / Kid fears / Watershed / Three hits / Galileo / Ghost / Reunion / Power of two / Least complicated / Shame on you / Get out the map / Go / Trouble / Devotion *[new song]* / Leaving *[new song]*.

- (5-7*) compilations, others, etc.-

Jun 98. (3xcd-box) *Epic-Sony; <65609>* **3 PAK** [ ] [-]
- (INDIGO GIRLS) // (STRANGE FIRE) // (NOMADS INDIANS SAINTS)
Jun 05. (cd) *Epic; <EK 94442>* **RARITIES** [ ] [-]
- Clampdown / I don't wanna talk about it / Mona Lisas and mad hatters (live) / Let me go easy (live) / Winthrop / Free of hope / Shed your skin (Tom Morello remix) / Never stop (1986 EP version) / Ghost (demo) / Uncle John's band / I'll give you my skin (featuring MICHAEL STIPE) / Free in you (Dave Cooley remix) / Point hope F.O.I.A. / Ramblin' round (live featuring ANI DiFRANCO) / Cold as ice (live) / Walk your valley / It won't take long / Finlandia (live).
Jan 09. (cd) *Epic-Legacy; <(8869 734334-2)>* **PLAYLIST: THE VERY BEST OF INDIGO GIRLS** [ ] [ ]
- Become you / Least complicated / Tried to be true (live) / Fill it up again / Shame on you / Closer to fine / Moment of forgiveness / Power of two / Nashville / Galileo (live) / Hammer and nail / Kid fears / Peace tonight / Midnight train to Georgia (live). *(w/ CD-rom track)*

IRON AND WINE

IRON AND WINE might seem like a peculiar combination, but it is the stage name of one Samuel Beam, which itself sounds not unlike a character from an American novel of the 1900s; his nom de guerre is taken from a dietary supplement called 'Beef Iron and Wine'. Deft folk-rock is Beam's stock in trade, and he's been plying his trade successfully since the early 2000s.

In the post-grunge fallout, Seattle label Sub Pop, struggling to find its niche again, was revived in part by the debut IRON AND WINE album, **THE CREEK DRANK THE CRADLE** (2002) {*8}. Written, recorded and produced by Beam at his home studio, the one-man-band nature of the record did not stop the energy and fragile beauty of his songs shining through, to critical acclaim. An EP, 'Sea and The Rhythm', followed in 2003, and Beam's second album, **OUR ENDLESS NUMBERED DAYS** (2004) {*7}, arrived six months later to further celebratory reviews.

The 'Woman King' EP, themed around strong, spiritual women, demonstrated his prolific writing skills and his desire to expand the IRON AND WINE sound, adding (shock! horror!) electric guitars to the mix. The EP proved a segue into another left turn for Beam, this time a collaborative recording with the Tucson, Arizona group Calexico. The band brought their dusty Tex-Mex flavours to bear on Beam's warm acoustica, to joyous effect. Calexico's Joey Burns went on to reappear on Beam's album **THE SHEPHERD'S DOG** (2007) {*8}, which enjoyed a more lush, expanded sonic palette than its predecessors. Beam also found an unlikely fan in teen-film vampire hottie Kirstin Stewart, who requested that the track 'Flightless Bird, American Mouth' be soundtracked to the prom scene in the blockbuster movie 'Twilight'.

AROUND THE WELL (2009) {*7} was an extensive compilation of unreleased and hard-to-find tracks, while Beam's fourth long player (first for new label Warner), **KISS EACH OTHER CLEAN** (2011) {*7}, was as pop as anything he had ever produced. Lead single 'Tree By The River' was a perfect example of the evolution, shooting Beam's folk style through the prism of 1970s US FM radio. *MR*

Samuel Beam (b. Jul 26 '74, Columbia, South Carolina) - vocals, acoustic guitar, slide guitar, banjo

US Sub Pop UK Sub Pop

Mar 02. (ltd-7" clear) *<SP 598>* CALL YOUR BOYS. / Dearest Forsaken [ ] [-]
Sep 02. (cd) *<(SPCD 600)>* **THE CREEK DRANK THE CRADLE** [ ] Feb 03 [ ]
- Lion's mane / Bird stealing bread / Faded from the winter / Promising light / The rooster moans / Upward over the mountain / Southern anthem / An angry blade / Weary memory / Promise what you will / Muddy hymnal. *<lp-iss. May 03 w/ free 7"+=; SP 600>* - Her tea leaves / Carissa's wierd.
Sep 03. (cd-ep) *<(SPCD 619)>* THE SEA AND THE RHYTHM [ ] Oct 03 [ ]
- Beneath the balcony / The sea and the rhythm / The night descending / Jesus the Mexican boy / Someday the waves. *<12" ep-iss. Jul 07 +=; SP 619>*
Mar 04. (lp/cd) *<(SP/+CD 630)>* **OUR ENDLESS NUMBERED DAYS** [ ] Apr 04 [ ]
- On your wings / Naked as we came / Cinder and smoke / Sunset soon forgotten / Teeth in the grass / Love and some verses / Radio war / Each coming night / Free until they cut me down / Fever dream / Sodom, South Georgia / Passing afternoon. *<lp w/ free 7"+=>* - Sinning hands / No moon. *(cd w/ free cd-ep+=)* - Cinder and smoke (demo) / Swans and the swimming / Free until they cut me down (demo) / Hickory.
Oct 04. (cd-s) *<SPCD 664>* PASSING AFTERNOON / Communion Cups And Someone's Coat / Dearest Forsaken (live @ KCRW) [ ] [-]
Feb 05. (cd-ep) *<(SPCD 655)>* WOMAN KING [ ] [ ]
- Woman king / Jezebel / Gray stables / Freedom hangs like heaven / My lady's house / Evening on the ground (Lilith's song).
Sep 05. (m-cd/m-lp; IRON AND WINE / CALEXICO) *<OC 28> (TG 290 CD/LP)* **IN THE REINS** [ ] [ ]

- He lay in reins / Prison on route 41 / History of lovers / Red dust / 16, maybe less / Burn that broken bed / Dead man's will.

(above issued on Overcoat, US & Touch And Go, UK)

Jul 06. (cd-s) <*(SPCD 724)*> SUCH GREAT HEIGHTS / Trapeze Swinger (live) / Naked As We Came (live) — Aug 06

Sub Pop — Transgressive

Jul 07. (ltd-10"/cd-s) <*SPCD 743*> *(TRANS 058 TE/CD)* Carried Home / BOY WITH A COIN. / Kingdom Of The Animals — Aug 07

Sep 07. (cd/lp) <*SPCD 710*> *(TRANSCD 59)*
THE SHEPHERD'S DOG [24] [74]
- Pagan angel and a borrowed car / White tooth man / Lovesong of the buzzard / Carousel / House by the sea / Innocent bones / Wolves (song of the shepherd's dog) / Resurrection fern / Boy with a coin / The Devil never sleeps / Peace beneath the city / Flightless bird, American mouth. *(ltd cd+=/lp+=)* - Arms of a thief / Serpent charmer.

Jun 08. (ltd-10") *(TRANS 070)* LOVESONG OF THE BUZZARD. / Arms Of A Thief / Serpent Charmer [–]

Warners — 4 a.d.

Nov 10. (7") *(AD 3102)* WALKING FAR FROM HOME. / Biting Your Tail
(US; 12"+=/cd-s+=) <*526246-0/-2*> - Summer in Savannah.

Jan 11. (lp/cd) <*526280/+2*> *(CAD 3103/+CD)*
KISS EACH OTHER CLEAN [2] [32]
- Walking far from home / Me and Lazarus / Tree by the river / Monkeys uptown / Half moon / Rabbits will run / Brother in love / Big burned hand / Glad man singing / Your fake name is good enough for me.

Daytrotter — Daytrotter

May 11. (ltd-12" ep; shared) <*(IW 001)*> DAYTROTTER SESSION
- Godless brother in love / Tree by the river / Glad man singing / Naked as we came // [The LOW ANTHEM tracks x 4].

- (5-7*) compilations, others, etc.-

May 09. (cd) *Sub Pop;* <*(SPCD 808)*> **AROUND THE WELL** [25]
- Dearest forsaken / Morning / Loud as hope / Peng! 33 / Sacred vision / Friends they are jewels / Hickory / Waitin' for a superman / Swans and the swimming / Call your boys / Such great heights / Communion cups and someone's coat / Belated promise ring / God made the automobile / Homeward, these shoes / Love vigilantes / Sinning hands / No moon / Serpent charmer / Carried home / Kingdom of the animals / Arms of a thief / The trapeze swinger.

Asa IRONS & Swaan MILLER (⟹ FEATHERS)

J

Essie JAIN

Although London-born, the pianist, acoustic guitarist and singer/songwriter ESSIE JAIN is essentially a New York girl with a sense of folk déjà-vu. Her fascination with retro late-1960s/early-1970s shadows such as VASHTI BUNYAN, LINDA PERHACS and SHELAGH McDONALD was revealed on her debut set, **WE MADE THIS OURSELVES** (2007) {*7}. Awkwardly confessional at times ('Talking', 'Give' and 'Disgrace' are prime examples), she wasn't exactly the next DORY PREVIN, but her sadcore strums and her morose monotones and piano-plunking were therapeutic for anyone ready to pour their tears into a few handkerchiefs.

The same goes for her second for Ba Da Bing, **THE INBETWEEN** (2008) {*7}, a shorter record but just as effective in the crying-game stakes; 'Eavesdrop', 'I Ask You' and 'Please' stand out from the pack. Then came her big awakening with **UNTIL THE LIGHT OF MORNING** (2011) {*6}, a mother-to-baby record that... zzz... *MCS*

Essie Jain - vocals, acoustic guitar, piano / + session people

US Ba Da Bing — UK Leaf

Feb 07. (cd) *<Bing 051> (BAY 62CD)* **WE MADE THIS OURSELVES** □ Mar 08 □
- Glory / Haze / Sailor / Talking / Indefinable / Grace / Give / Understand / Loaded / No mistake.

May 08. (cd) *<Bing 056> (BAY 66CD)* **THE INBETWEEN** □ Nov 08 □
- Eavesdrop / Here we go / I ask you / Please / The rights / Stop / Do it / Weight off me / You / Goodbye / Not yours / I remember it just like this.

not issued — Light Of Morning

Feb 11. (cd) *(LOM 01CD)* **UNTIL THE LIGHT OF MORNING** ⊟ □
- What a big wide world / Lay down / Falling asleep / I'm not afraid of the dark / O, I love you / The magic star / Top toes / Midnight starship.

Michael JERLING

Another post-1980s singer/songwriter in the long line of contemporary country-folk artists to have won a Kerriville Music Award, Illinois-born MICHAEL JERLING is further characterised by his use of rock 'n' roll and jazz in his vast repertoire.

From his debut, **ON TOP OF FOOL'S HILL** (1981) {*6}, to his five-year-spread second-album gem **BLUE HEARTLAND** (1988) {*7} and onwards to his most recent, self-released seventh set **CROOKED PATH** (2007) {*6}, the acoustic guitarist has revealed his love of everything roots. Released on Shanachie and augmented by Robin and Linda Williams, third album **MY EVIL TWIN** (1992) {*7} was easily his best, featuring picturesque ballads such as 'Before The Country Moved To Town', 'Breakdown' and 'Stranger In Your House'.

Always laid-back and unobtrusive, subsequent albums **NEW SUIT OF CLOTHES** (1994) {*6} (with a guest spot from JOHN SEBASTIAN), **IN ANOTHER LIFE** (1997) {*5} (his only release for Waterbug), and the self-financed **LITTLE MOVIES** (2002) {*5} proved JERLING to be a safe bet for a good old song, without raising the roof hootenanny-style. *MCS*

Michael Jerling - vocals, acoustic guitar / + session people

US Moonlight Magic — UK not issued

1981. (lp) *<MMR 1001>* **ON TOP OF FOOL'S HILL** □ ⊟
- On top of fool's hill / Riverboat rag / Drivin' Willy home / Mr Billy Bones / Factory town / Everybody's scared / Marry me, Mary Edwards / Kitchen two-step / Lullabye / Just a good boy tryin' to go bad.

1988. (lp) *<MMR-1003>* **BLUE HEARTLAND** □ ⊟
- Jimmy and Jerry Lee / Here we go again / Blue heartland / Water street / Roadhouse / Long black wall / I can't speak (with JOHNNY & THE TRIUMPHS) / Stupid / The only one / Man with the x-ray eyes / Quiet street.

Shanachie — Shanachie

Mar 92. (cd/c) *<SHCD/SHMC 8004>* **MY EVIL TWIN** □ ⊟
- Stranger in your house / Sorry thing to say / Breakdown / Missionary / Before the country moved to town / Things I learned from life / Pinto pony / Take me to Juarez / Fast forward / I can depend on you / My evil twin.

Apr 94. (cd/c) *<(SHCD/SHMC 8010)>* **NEW SUIT OF CLOTHES** □ Dec 94 □
- Time to begin again / This bitter taste / Shadowland / Starting tomorrow / I can't see me / Sleepwalking / Tuxedo blues / All that remains the same / Save me / Bush league hero / Songs about Georgia / Katy's stroll / Without my chains / Mercy on these blues.

Waterbug — not issued

Feb 97. (cd) *<WBG 0027>* **IN ANOTHER LIFE** □ ⊟
- In another life / How can people live like that? / Wide awake in Parsippany / Fishtrap lake / Room at the top / Bad news / Doubter's prayer / Old stones / The raven / Come away with me / Grandpa's ukulele / Whinin' at me / On the far side.

Fool's Hill — not issued

May 02. (cd) *<2001>* **LITTLE MOVIES** □ ⊟
- Dawn patrol / Old Henry's house / Angelina / Last natural man / Dirty little war / It's a wonderful life / Sweet soul music / In the middle ages / Love at a certain age / The flying lawn chair / The weather channel / These old photographs / Last plane to paradise / Only time will tell.

Sep 07. (cd) *<2002>* **CROOKED PATH** □ ⊟
- 40 days and nights / Hold on / Thousand dollar car / Cold river / Will love arise / Johnny Cash is gone / Chief Waukenon motel / Why they run the race / Through Christmastime / My acceptance speech / Preachin' to the choir / I've been feelin' better / Crooked path.

Oct 09. (cd) *<2003>* **MUSIC HERE TONIGHT: LIVE AT CAFFE LENA** □ ⊟
- Blue heartland / North country jukebox / Wide awake in Parsippany / Old Henry's house / These old photographs / In the middle ages / Old stones / Pinto pony / Jimmy and Jerry Lee / Dawn patrol / Fishtrap lake / Why they run the race / How can people live like that / The weather channel / Doubter's prayer / My evil twin / Music here tonight / Bush league hero.

- (5-7*) compilations -

Oct 98. (cd) *Waterbug; <WBG 0043>* **EARLY JERLING** (recordings 1977–1986) □ ⊟
- Here we go again / On top of fool's hill / Riverboat rag / Kitchen two-step / Drivin' Willy home / Factory town / North country jukebox / Roadhouse / Blue heartland / Stupid / Jimmy and Jerry Lee / Water street / Long black wall / The only one / Hotel DeVille.

JOHN AND MARY (⟹ 10,000 MANIACS)

Glenn JONES

Not to be confused with the American R&B and gospel singer of the same name, this GLENN JONES is the astute guitarist from indie-psych practitioners Cul De Sac, a 1990s outfit who collaborated with fingerpicking legend JOHN FAHEY on 'The Epiphany Of Glenn Jones' (1997).

Taking the Takoma Records stalwart as his template (you could also throw in ROBBIE BASHO, PETER LANG and LEO KOTTKE), disciple JONES revived the art of blues-folk in a way even his virtuoso models would be proud of. His solo debut for Strange Attractors, **THIS IS THE WIND THAT BLOWS IT OUT** (2004) {*6} paid homage to his masters, although his transcendental fluidity and distinctive jingle-jangle gentleness were apparent on 'Fahey's Car', 'One Jack Rose (That I Mean)' and his joint effort with JACK ROSE (of Pelt), 'Linden Avenue Stomp'.

His second and third albums, **AGAINST WHICH THE SEA CONTINUALLY BEATS** (2007) {*6} and **BARBECUE BOB IN FISHTOWN** (2009) {*7}, were released in a manner not unlike FAHEY's or BASHO's sporadic mid-1960s to mid-1970s release schedule. Lengthy folk mantras such as 'Freedom Raga' featured largely on AGAINST WHICH ..., while the last-named introduced fans to his new love, the banjo. His forthcoming album on Thrill Jockey, 'The Wanting', scheduled for September 2011, is eagerly awaited. *MCS*

Glenn Jones - acoustic guitars / with guests

US UK

Jul 04. (cd) *<SAAH 024>* **THIS IS THE WIND THAT BLOWS IT OUT**
- This is the wind that blows it out / Sphinx unto curious men / Friday nights with / Fahey's car / The doll hospital / Linden avenue stomp / Nora's leather jacket / One Jack Rose (that I mean).

Mar 07. (cd) *<SAAH 046>* **AGAINST WHICH THE SEA CONTINUALLY BEATS**
- Island 1 / David and the phoenix / Little dog's day / Cady / Richard Nixon orchid / Freedom raga / Against my ruin / The teething necklace (for John Fahey) / Heartbreak hill / Bill Muller on the Erie Lackawanna / Island 2.

Sep 09. (cd) *<SAAH 056>* **BARBECUE BOB IN FISHTOWN**
- Barbecue Bob in Fishtown / Keep it a hundred years / For Wendy, in her girlish days / Redwood ramble misremembered / Snowdrops (for Robert Walser) / Dead reckoning / A lark in earnest / 1337 Shattuck Avenue, apartment D / A geranium for Mano-o-mano.

Thrill Jockey Thrill Jockey

Sep 11. (cd/lp) *<(THRILL 271/+LP)>* **THE WANTING**
- [tracks as yet unadvised]

Damien JURADO

A spiritual punk rather than an urban folkie, the California-born singer/songwriter (b. November 12, 1972) has been a slow-burner on the indie scene over the past two decades or so, but many of his heartfelt songs have proved enduring. He moved to Seattle, Washington at the age of 13.

Kicking off his rootsy career with small-time labels such as the Christian-tinged Coolidge, Cupcakes, Flowermouth, Moonboy and Lo-Life, JURADO gradually acquired a local following, largely due to some self-released cassettes in the mid-1990s - 'Leaded', 'Trailer Park Radio' and 'Gasoline'. These were brought to the attention of the Sub Pop team by fan Jeremy Enigk, the frontman with Sunny Day Real Estate, and JURADO signed up and released two singles, 'Trampoline' and 'Motorbike'.

His inaugural album, **WATERS AVE S.** {*6} arrived in early 1997. A selection of 13 tracks showcased his gift for crooner-folk storytelling; some were light-hearted, some painfully inspired by his parents' recent divorce, and some were just stories.

If further confirmation of his talent as a singer/songwriter was required, then 1999's **REHEARSALS FOR DEPARTURE** {*8} provided it. Lyrical, plaintive and intimate, it painted an often bleak portrait of urban middle-class America. With instrumentation provided by friends, there was a diversity of styles and sounds - contrast the honky-tonk 'Honey Baby' and the dreamy 'Saturday'. **POSTCARDS AND AUDIO LETTERS** (2000) {*5} was an odd and audacious collection of conversations taken from tapes found in charity-shop boom-boxes and answering machines - without any music.

Returning to more conventional urban-folk with **GHOST OF DAVID** (2000) {*7}, JURADO was now attracting comparisons with artists like Tom Waits and NICK DRAKE. The album had a reflective, brooding atmosphere, courtesy of songs like 'Tonight I Will Retire', 'Medication' and 'Ghost In The Snow'. The traditional `Rosewood Casket' was just as earnest and morbidly sweet.

Forsaking his pacemaker-friendly folk for an electrified sound with backing band Gathered In Song (Eric Fisher, Andrew Myers and Josh Golden), JURADO showed he could rock with the best of them on **I BREAK CHAIRS** (2002) {*7} - think Pixies or Husker Du. His band was named for one of his earlier EPs.

He switched styles again (and labels) when he signed with Secretly Canadian, releasing **WHERE SHALL YOU TAKE ME?** (2003) {*6}, a moody, minimalist, lo-fi-folk affair highlighting original gems 'Abilene', 'Intoxicated Hands' and the GORDON LIGHTFOOT-like alt-country rocker 'Texas To Ohio'. **ON MY WAY TO ABSENCE** (2005) {*7}, **AND NOW THAT I'M IN YOUR SHADOW** (2006) {*6}, **CAUGHT IN THE TREES** (2008) {*6} and **SAINT BARTLETT** (2010) {*7} continued his mission to restore alt-country-folk to the masses and supersede his hero NEIL YOUNG in the process. *MCS*

Damien Jurado - vocals, guitars / with various back-up

US UK

Casa Recordings not issued

1994. (c) *<none>* LEADED self

1995. (c) *<none>* TRAILER PARK RADIO self

1995. (c) *<none>* GASOLINE self

Sub Pop Sub Pop

Nov 95. (7"ep) *<SP 335>* MOTORBIKE
- Motorbike / Broken chain / Farewell janitor / Bicycle.

Jul 96. (7") *<SP 364>* TRAMPOLINE
- Rollerskating queen / Trampoline / Pigtails.

Jan 97. (lp/cd) *<SP/+CD 374>* **WATER AVE S.** Nov 97
- Wedding cake / Angel of May / Treasures of gold / Yuma, AZ / The joke is over / Space age mom / Circus, circus, circus / Hell or high water / Independent / Purple anteater / Sarah / Halo friendly / Water Ave S. *<re-iss. Dec 97 on Tooth And Nail; TNCD 01>*

Summershine not issued

1997. (7"m) *<Shine-US 17>* HALO FRIENDLY. / Ocean Shores 97 / Long Distance

Tooth And Nail not issued

1997. (7" ep) *<TNV 13>* VARY
- Fall down / Frustrated / Ranier Valley / Sad boy, happy girl.

Snowstorm not issued

1998. (7" m) *<SNOWS 002>* CHEVROLET. / Simple Hello / East Virginia

Sub Pop Rykodisc

Feb 99. (cd) *<SPCD 440> (RCD 10382)* **REHEARSALS FOR DEPARTURE** Mar 99
- Ohio / Tragedy / Curbside / Honey baby / Eyes for window / Letters and drawings / Love the same / Saturday / Tornado / Rehearsals for departure.

May 99. (cd-s) *(RCD5-1059)* LETTERS AND DRAWINGS / As You Wish

Sub Pop Sub Pop

Sep 00. (cd) *<(SPCD 507)>* **GHOST OF DAVID** Oct 00
- Medication / Desert / Johnny go riding / Great today / Tonight I will retire / Ghost of David / Parking lot / Rearview / Paxil / Walk with me / December / Rosewood casket / Ghost in the snow.

Feb 02. (etched-12" ep) *<(BTV 041)>* FOUR SONGS
- Spitting teeth / How I broke my legs / The killer / Flowers in the yard.

(above issued on Burnt Toast Vinyl)

——next with **Eric Fisher** - keyboards, guitar, glockenspiel + **Andrew Myers** - drums, glockenspiel / **Josh Golden** - bass, guitar, keyboards, vocals

Feb 02. (cd; as DAMIEN JURADO AND GATHERED IN SONG) *<(SP/+CD 571)>* **I BREAK CHAIRS** Mar 02
- Paperwings / Dancing / Birdcage / Inevitable / Air show disaster / Never ending tide / Big deal / The way you look / Castles / Like Titanic / Parade / Lose my head.

Secretly Canadian not issued

Dec 02. (7") *<SC 067>* BIG LET DOWN. / Make Up Your Mind

Mar 03. (cd/lp) *<SC 84/+LP>* **WHERE SHALL YOU TAKE ME?**
- Amateur night / Omaha / Abilene / Texas to Ohio / Window / I can't get over you / Intoxicated hands / Tether / Matinee / Bad dreams.

Sep 03. (ltd-cd-ep) *(nois 035)* HOLDING HIS BREATH Spain
- I am the greatest of all liars / Oh dead art with me / Big let down / Now you're swimming / Butcher's boy.

(above issued on Acuarela Discos)

Nov 04. (cd-ep) *<SC 115>* JUST IN TIME FOR SOMETHING [live to tape]
- Smith 1972 / Motion sickness / Night out for the downer / Prices / Engine fire.

Apr 05. (cd/lp) *<(SC 88/+LP)>* **ON MY WAY TO ABSENCE** Jun 05
- White center / Lottery / Big decision / Lion tamer / Fuel / Simple hello / Sucker / I am the mountain / Night out for the downer / Northbound / Icicle / A jealous heart is a healthy heart.

Jan 06. (ltd-7") *<SC 139>* TRADED FOR FIRE. / [Dolorean]: Ghost Of David

Oct 06. (cd/d-lp) *<(SC 145/+LP)>* **AND NOW THAT I'M IN YOUR SHADOW**
- Hoquiam / Denton, TX / I had no intentions / Hotel hospital / And now that I'm in your shadow / What were the chances / Shannon Rhodes / There goes your man / I am still here / Gasoline drinks / Survived by her husband / Gas station / Montesano.

Sep 08. (cd/lp) *<(SC 175/+LP)>* **CAUGHT IN THE TREES** Oct 08
- Gillian was a horse / Trials / Caskets / Coats of ice / Go first / Sorry is for you / Last rights / Dimes / Everything trying / Sheets / Paper kite / Best dress / Predictive living.

May 10. (cd/lp) *<(SC 192/+LP)>* **SAINT BARTLETT**
- Cloudy shoes / Arkansas / Rachel and Cali / Throwing your voice / Wallingford / Pear / Kansas City / Harborview / Kalama / The falling snow / Beacon hill / With lightning in your hands. *(UK 'Amazon'-only cd w/cd-ep+=; SC 222)* - OUR TURN TO SHINE:- Josephine / Everyone a star / Three to be seen / Wyoming birds / You for a while.

- (5-7*) special recordings & compilations, etc.-

Mar 99. (cd-ep) *Made In Mexico;* <*MEX 003CD*> GATHERED IN SONG
- Chevrolet / Simple hello / Happy birthday John / East Virginia / To those who will burn... *(UK-iss. Apr 01; same as US)* <*cd re-iss. Jan 07* +=; *MEX 015*> - [demos 1999]: Tragedy / Happy birthday John / Matinee / Saturday / [4-track]: As you wish.

Jun 00. (cd) *Made In Mexico;* <*(MEX 009CD)*> **POSTCARDS AND AUDIO LETTERS** [spoken word; no music]
- Robert 1972 / Angel 1972 / Christmas 1983 / Christmas 1983 (part 2) / 'Hi Dawn, this is Phil' / Waking Dawn / At the airport / 'Our kid is getting hurt'.

2004. (ltd-lp; some white) *Burnt Toast;* <*BTV 061*> **THIS FABULOUS CENTURY** [1998 demos]
- It ain't me / Jump out the window / Headlights / Backseat Iowa / The deep end / 1988 - Remove the past / The transmitter the man [electric version] / Aberdeen / Drunk on you / The transmitter the man / Under water / Silver dollar eyes / Pushing your coffin.

HOQUIAM

Damien + Drake Durado

St Ives — not issued

Feb 10. (lp) <*SAINT 37*> **HOQUIAM**
- Zombies of the sea / Moclips / Wooden / Ocean shores / Ticket Maria / The marks / Neck bones / Fake teeth / Finish with starting / Madison / On the beach / Car keys / Hope ocean / Slow bird / Gallons / Party fell / Make it back islands.

Brenda KAHN

A difficult artist to pigeonhole, having embraced jazz, blues, country, punk and spoken word, urban singer/songwriter BRENDA KAHN (b. 1967 in Connecticut and raised in New Jersey) fits into the burgeoning New York anti-folk movement of the late 1980s and early 1990s. Alongside the likes of LACH, KIRK KELLY and ROGER MANNING, Brenda was one of the pioneers of the Lower East Side-based genre, and after a spell studying in London she was ready to record her debut set, **GOLDFISH DON'T TALK BACK** (1990) {*7}.

Minneapolis was her next port of call. Releasing the highly-regarded indie EP 'Life In The Drug War Trenches' (showcasing minor gems 'I Don't Sleep, I Drink Coffee Instead' and the DYLANesque 'Mint Juleps And Needles'), Brenda was spotted by producer David Kahne, who set up a major-label deal with Columbia subsidiary Chaos Records. **EPIPHANY IN BROOKLYN** (1992) {*8} embodied her use of New York narrative in a way Lydia Lunch would have been proud of, if she could sing. Tracks name-checking places around the world painted a portrait of her travels: 'Madagascar', 'Mojave Desert' and 'In Indiana' sat comfortably alongside her caffeine-buzz opener 'I Don't Sleep, I Drink Coffee Instead', while relationship songs like 'My Lover' and 'Lost' kept the adrenaline high.

The Chaos/Columbia cull of the mid-1990s led to KAHN being dropped, although producer Tim Patalan (and a band that included guitarist and singer Jeff Buckley, who co-wrote 'Faith Salons') kept the momentum going with the release on Shanachie of the nearly-shelved **DESTINATION ANYWHERE** (1996) {*8}. Brooding and aggressive, the record at times takes the listener into Patti Smith territory (as on 'Night'), but its disillusioned romanticism (listen to 'Spoon' and 'Yellow Sun') demonstrated her lyrical prowess.

OUTSIDE THE BEAUTY SALON (1997) {*6} found her struggling a little to maintain her street cred. Her folk-punk veered towards country-rock in several cases, but songs like 'Alice', 'Matador' and 'Heather' still ring true, though without the usual verbal vigour. Her need to be different among the crowded cacophony of run-down artists was underlined by her all-acoustic narrative recording **HUNGER** (1998) {*7}, a homage to Jeff Buckley that was accompanied only by her own guitar and the jazzy double bass of Ernie Adzentoivich. Some pieces, including the three-part 'Mexico', were written on a beach in Playa del Carmen.

Conspicuous by her recording absence as she founded the online magazine womanrock.com, KAHN returned with a download album, **SEVEN LAWS OF GRAVITY** (2010) {*6}. *MCS*

Brenda Kahn - vocals, acoustic guitar / with various session people

US / UK

Community 3 / not issued

Oct 90. (cd/lp) *<C3-1990/3906-1>* **GOLDFISH DON'T TALK BACK** □ ⊟
- The coal train blues / Third Avenue L / Eggs on drugs / Goldfish don't talk back / Sweet Marie / Winchester chimes / This land is my land / If red were blue / Waterloo Bridge / The ballad of Ridge Street / Eulogy for my next lover / Paper dragons.

Crackpot / not issued

1992. (ltd-7" ep) *<CPS 2061>* LIFE IN THE DRUG WAR TRENCHES EP □ ⊟
- I don't sleep, I drink coffee instead / Mint juleps and needles / The dollar bill blues.

Chaos / Creation

Nov 92. (cd/c) *<OK/OT 52768> (SHED 004 CD/C)* **EPIPHANY IN BROOKLYN** □ Sep 93 □
- I don't sleep, I drink coffee instead / Mojave winters / She's in love / Anesthesia / Mint juleps and needles / My lover / Sleepwalking / Lost / The great divide / Madagascar / Losing time / In Indiana.

1994. (cd-s) *<OSK 6626>* KING OF CAIRO EP □ ⊟
- Reconcile / Spoon / Faith salons.

Shanachie / Shanachie

May 96. (cd) *<(SHCD 5708)>* **DESTINATION ANYWHERE** □ Jul 96 □
- Reconcile / Terrorist / Lie / Spoon / Faith salons / Yellow sun / Too far gone / Night / No cure / Omaha.

1996. (promo-cd) *<350 504>* HEY ROMEO / Heather ⊟ ⊟

(above issued on the Koch International label)

Mar 97. (cd) *<(SHCD 5721)>* **OUTSIDE THE BEAUTY SALON** □ Apr 97 □
- Matador / Smoking in the Jane room / Heather / Wedding ring / Door locks / Alice / I believe in you (song for Thomas) / Lincoln hotel / Guillotine / Hey Romeo / The bridge / She wore red / Destination: anywhere. *<(re-iss. May 98 on Koch International; KOCCD 3326-2)>*

Rocket 99 / not issued

Oct 98. (cd) *<none>* **HUNGER** □ ⊟
- Mexico one / Messiah / Light / Hunger / Queen of distance / Mexico two / So what if I saw Jesus / Sidestep the bullet / Dictaphone / Christopher says / Mexico three.

——Brenda retired from studio work after her 'Remington' EP

Law Of Seven / not issued

2010. (dl-cd) *<none>* **SEVEN LAWS OF GRAVITY** ⊟ ⊟
- Blue room / Chipotle / New kind of day / Remington / Photograph / Regular job / Stephanie says / Dead can dance / Everything you need / Slow highway.

Cindy KALLET

Most folk fans will know the name of singer/songwriter CINDY KALLET (b. January 10, 1955 in New Rochelle, NY) through her musical partnership with shanty singer GORDON BOK. Cindy moved to Martha's Vineyard in New England, but now lives in Bloomington, Indiana.

Not only does KALLET have a delicate and relaxing vocal tone, somewhat akin to a trad-folk JONI MITCHELL, her intricate and emotional guitar playing is displayed on several instrumentals (unusual for a woman folk artist in this era) from her first two Folk-Legacy LPs, **WORKING ON WINGS TO FLY** (1981) {*6} and **2** (1983) {*7}. As with many of her contemporaries, her songs deal with war, politics, love and relationships. A set that takes the listener into her world is her long-delayed third album, **DREAMING DOWN A QUIET LINE** (1989) {*6}.

ANGELS IN DARING (1988) {*5} was recorded with Ellen Epstein and Michael Cicone, and her subsequent projects were also of the collaborative kind. **ONLY HUMAN** (1993) {*5} and **HEARTWALK** (2008) {*5} were by the same trio, and there were children's folk sets with her friends, a few albums with Grey Larsen and at least one ('Neighbors', 1996) with GORDON BOK. *MCS*

Cindy Kallet - vocals, acoustic guitar

US / UK

Folk-Legacy / not issued

1981. (lp) *<FSI-83>* **WORKING ON WINGS TO FLY** □ ⊟
- Nantucket sound / Wings to fly (crow) / Three-masted schooner / A walk down the hill / Big dark's fancy / Blackberry downs / Roll to the river / We rigged our ship / Far off the mountains / Out on the farthest range / Hey-o... / Hang in there / Come down... / Ladies come in jewels / One for the island / Shores of Africa. *<cd-iss. Dec 99; CD-83>*

1983. (lp) *<C-98>* **2** □ ⊟
- Listen, I think the rain's come / When I was now / Mystic aureole [instrumental] / Trying times / Time came down / Wolf's lullaby [instrumental] / Steamboat to the mainland / Marblehead neck / Going for the gold / If I sing / Take me to the moon / Who do you think / Mountains range / Walking on the clouds with you (only spring) / I don't have to... / Ain't no time / Come away to the sea. *<cd-iss. Jan 02; CD-98>*

Overall / not issued

1988. (c; by CINDY KALLET, ELLEN EPSTEIN, MICHAEL CICONE) *<OM-1>* **ANGELS IN DARING** □ ⊟
- Sail away ladies / Lowlands of Holland / Ready for the storm / Wings of a gull / The last leviathan / Shake these bones / Song for gale / Marblehead neck *[cd-only]* / Ferryboat serenade / When the moon shines in the evening / Macarthur's lament / Terror time / Shantyboatin' / Narrow space / Cold is the night. *<cd-iss. Sep 97; OM-01CD>*

1989. (lp/c) *<none>* **DREAMING DOWN A QUIET LINE** □ ⊟
- Glacier song / Song for Margaret / Rain night / Cherry tree carol / Before words

/ Chris' song / Seven coots / Bodies / Sarah's song / Election day / Mouse's dream / I got a heart / Together or alone / Haven't I been good / Tide and the river rising. *<cd-iss. Feb 08 on Stones Throw; STM-1>*

1993. (c; by CINDY KALLET, ELLEN EPSTEIN, MICHAEL CICONE)
<OM-2> **ONLY HUMAN**
- When the ship comes in / Roll 'er down the bay / Lucky man / I but a little girl / Sweet water / Clues / Re Gilardin / Evening falls / I'm a mammal / My Johnny was a shoemaker / Willy the waterboy / My hometown / Be like a bird - Wings / Aboard the spray / The Mhairi bhan. *<re-iss. Sep 97; OM-02CD>*

——In 1996, she teamed up with folk stalwart GORDON BOK on the album 'Neighbors'.

Stones Throw — not issued

2000. (c; as CINDY KALLET AND FRIENDS) *<STM-2>*
THIS WAY HOME
- Huckleberries / Salmon river / I used to go walking / New hymn / Them stars / Snipe it's fancy / Winter window / Shallow brown - Cargo / Nets in water / Red spruce (this way home) / Skunk don't care / Window tree / Landing / Longed so far. *<cd re-iss. Feb 08; same>*

2000. (c; as CINDY KALLET & FRIENDS) *<STM-3>*
LEAVE THE CAKE IN THE MAILBOX: Songs for Parents and Kids Growing Up
- We sail the ocean blue / The royal bloke / Handy's birthday / Old King Cole / I'm a mammal / My mama said / I got a hat / Froggy went a courtin' / Before I was two / I dread not / Izzy's toes / No - Don't wake up / Diapers by heart / Blessings / Hoosen Johnny / Woody knows nothing / Turn the glasses over - Whup jamboree. *<cd re-iss. Feb 08; same>*

Sleepy Creek — not issued

Dec 07. (cd; by CINDY KALLET & GREY LARSEN) *<SCM 105>*
CROSS THE WATER
- Courage / The humours of Trim - The moons of Jupiter - Mulhaire's jig / The eighth of January - Black mountain rag / October song / If you say yes / Playing with a full deck / I lull myself asleep / The swallowtail reel - The wind that shakes the barley - The merry harriers / Fisher's hornpipe - Old leather britches / Once / Your love / The south shore / Cross the water - Little girl.

Overall — not issued

Aug 08. (cd; by CINDY KALLET, ELLEN EPSTEIN, MICHAEL CICONE) *<OM-03>* **HEARTWALK**
- Farthest field / The shanghaied dredger / When the traffic light's red / Underneath the pines / Old Zeb / Holy now / I arise facing east / Frobisher Bay / Bonnet and shawl / Since you asked / Sally free and easy / Life comes in / My heart is ready - I'm gonna walk / Swampie's fancy - Househunting / Shine on.

Dec 10. (cd-s; by CINDY KALLET & GREY LARSEN) *<none>*
BACK WHEN WE WERE ALL MACHINES

Lucy KAPLANSKY

Coming from the well-to-do suburb of Hyde Park, Chicago, LUCY KAPLANSKY (b. February 2, 1960) abandoned further education and moved to New York, joining the burgeoning 'Fast Folk' cooperative of rising stars and supporting her art by working as a psychologist in private practice. The various-artists LPs included with 'Fast Folk' magazine featured almost a dozen of her recordings.

Staking her claim as a newbie folksinger alongside star-to-be SHAWN COLVIN and harmonising on albums by NANCI GRIFFITH, Lucy forsook a few major-label offers to earn her Ph.D from Yeshiva University, NYC, and after that signed to the Red House label. With COLVIN on production duties, Lucy's debut, **THE TIDE** (1994) {*6}, finally came ashore, but with only a handful of originals it relied on her countrified interpretations of songs by RICHARD THOMPSON ('When I Get To The Border'), BILL MORRISSEY ('Texas Blues'), Tom Russell/Greg Trooper ('The Heart'), DAVID MASSENGILL ('My Name Joe'), Robin Batteau ('Guinevere' and 'The Eyes Of My Beholder'), CLIFF EBERHARDT ('Goodnight') and Sting ('Secret Journey').

On a par with her previous effort, but with Anton Sanko at the controls (he had produced her old friend SUZANNE VEGA), **FLESH AND BONE** (1996) {*7} saw Lucy and her film-maker husband Richard Litvin combine on every track except the covers of Nick Lowe's '(What's So Funny 'Bout) Peace, Love And Understanding', Gram Parsons's 'Return Of The Grievous Angel', RICHARD THOMPSON's 'Don't Renege On Our Love' and the trad standard 'Mary And The Soldier'.

TEN YEAR NIGHT (1999) {*7} followed on from a CRY, CRY, CRY collaboration (alongside RICHARD SHINDELL and DAR WILLIAMS), her only cover on the former being her take on Steve Earle's 'Somewhere Out There'. The giant of New Country was also responsible for the track 'You're Still Standing There' on her 2001 follow-up **EVERY SINGLE DAY** {*7}, which also featured PAUL BRADY's 'Crazy Dreams', Julie Miller's 'Broken Things' and The Louvin Brothers' gospel number 'The Angels Rejoiced Last Night'.

Continuing to mix her pot-pourri of rootsy country-folk, **THE RED THREAD** (2004) {*5} and **OVER THE HILLS** (2007) {*5} were almost formulaic, except for her post-9/11 songs. Songwriters BILL MORRISSEY, James McMurtry, DAVE CARTER, Bryan Ferry, Johnny Cash, LOUDON WAINWRIGHT III, Jim Lauderdale/Buddy Miller, Julie Miller and IAN TYSON supplied the covers. Her most recent work was the shared 'Red Horse' (2010) project/album with ELIZA GILKYSON and JOHN GORKA. *MCS*

Lucy Kaplansky - vocals, acoustic guitar (w/ session people)

US Red House — UK Red House

Sep 94. (cd/c) *<(RHR CD/MC 65)>* **THE TIDE** — May 95
- The tide / When I get to the border / Texas blues / The heart / My name Joe / Somebody's home / Guinevere / Delivery truck / You just need a home / The eyes of my beholder / Secret journey / Goodnight. *<cd re-mast. Oct 05 +=; RHRCD 190)>* - Everybody knows but me / I've just seen a face.

Oct 96. (cd) *<(RHRCD 92)>* **FLESH AND BONE** — Nov 96
- Scorpion / (What's so funny 'bout) Peace, love and understanding / If you could see / Don't renege on our love / Still life / This is mine / Mary and the soldier / Love is the ride / The thief / Edges / Return of the grievous angel / Ruby.

——In 1998, KAPLANSKY, RICHARD SHINDELL and DAR WILLIAMS were the trio behind the self-titled album CRY, CRY, CRY

Mar 99. (cd) *<(RHRCD 126)>* **TEN YEAR NIGHT**
- Ten year night / End of the day / One good reason / Five in the morning / Promise me / Turn the lights back on / Just you tonight / For once in your life / Somewhere out there / A child's hands.

Sep 01. (cd) *<(RHRCD 156)>* **EVERY SINGLE DAY**
- Written on the back of his hand / Crazy dreams / Every single day / Don't mind me / Broken things / Guilty as sin / Nowhere / No more excuses / Song for Molly / You're still standing there / The angels rejoiced last night.

Feb 04. (cd) *<(RHRCD 166)>* **THE RED THREAD**
- I had something / Line in the sand / Love song - New York / This is home / Off and running / Land of the living / Cowboy singer / Hole in my head / The red thread / Brooklyn train.

Mar 07. (cd) *<(RHRCD 200)>* **OVER THE HILLS**
- Manhattan moon / Amelia / More than this / Ring of fire / Swimming song / Today's the day / Over the hills / Somewhere trouble don't go / Someday soon / The gift.

—— In 2010, (Eliza) GILKYSON, (John) GORKA + KAPLANSKY released 'RED HORSE'

Kirk KELLY

Although he's somehow become associated with the anti-folk movement of the 1980s, punkish singer-songwriter KIRK KELLY (b. 1960 in Long Island, New York) had more in common with the folk giants of his boyhood, such as DYLAN and OCHS. His political agenda was clear from the various-artists records that accompanied the 'Fast Folk' magazine - he had been a pivotal figure playing acoustic guitar and mouth-harp around Manhattan's Lower East Side - and KELLY found himself on the roster of SST Records, the label that launched the careers of Black Flag, The Minutemen and The Meat Puppets.

His solo debut, **GO MAN GO** (1988) {*7}, showed his heart was with the disenfranchised on tracks such as 'I Pity The Poor British Soldier', 'Corporation Plow' and the energy-fuelled title track. Kirk was of course a member of The Folk Brothers (alongside fellow anti-folkie LACH), but if you can find their cassette **ALL FOLKED UP WITH NOWHERE TO GO** (1985) {*5}, you should look for a Willy Wonka golden ticket as well.

Although active on the scene during the 1990s, and still a regular player to this day, KELLY managed only one more release (on his Mugsy label), the passionate and aggression-strewn **NEW CITY** (1997) {*6}. Check out 'Book Burning', 'Hooray, We Won The War', 'Service Economy' and 'Joe Doherty'. *MCS*

Kirk Kelly - vocals, acoustic guitar, harmonica / with other (first with **Lach**)

US own label — UK not issued

1985. (c; by The FOLK BROTHERS) *<none>* **ALL FOLKED UP WITH NOWHERE TO GO**

SST — SST

Dec 88. (lp/c/cd) *<(SST 223/+C/CD)>* **GO MAN GO** — Jan 89
- Go man go / Talkin' train blues / Corporation plow / Red blues / I pity the poor British soldier / Heroes of tomorrow / Haul away Joe / Last dance / California blues / Marching off to Gaul / Never more.

Mugsy — not issued

1997. (cd) *<001>* **NEW CITY**
- Service economy / Working in the vineyard / Lisa Jane / Joe Doherty / Waltz of

time / Book burning / New city / Jonah / Heart of hearts / Clubworld / Hooray, we won the war.

——Kirk is still performing live

Barbara KESSLER

Born April 7, 1962 in Boston, Massachusetts, contemporary-folk singer/songwriter BARBARA KESSLER continues to perform live, even though her most recent release, **BARBARA KESSLER** {*5}, emerged way back in 2000 - and that was after a four-year hiatus.

A former winner of the Kerriville Folk Festival songwriter award, Barbara fits nicely between JONI MITCHELL, SHAWN COLVIN and Jonatha Brooke, and she's won numerous other prizes for her autumnal and sombre take on the genre. Many fans from the New England state will know her for at least one song, 'Mary Tyler Moore', one of a dozen (including covers of LEONARD COHEN's 'Bird On A Wire' and The Eagles' 'Desperado') from her debut album, **STRANGER TO THIS LAND** (1994) {*6}, recorded live at the Kendall Café in Cambridge. Guest players included MARTIN SEXTON, CLIFF EBERHARDT, Duke Levine, Diane Ziegler and Jonatha Brooke's The STORY.

1996's session-friendly **NOTION** {*6} turned up a handful of decent songs, such as 'Sister Mary Madeline', 'Jane's Last Day' and a studio version of 'The Date (Making Mountains Out Of Molehills)', but Barbara's career couldn't rise to those of her peers VEGA, COLVIN or even PATTY LARKIN. *MCS*

Barbara Kessler - vocals, acoustic guitar (w/ session people)

US Eastern Front — UK not issued

Nov 94. (cd/c) <*90696-0104-2/-4*> **STRANGER TO THIS LAND** (live at the Kendall Café, Cambridge, Massachusetts, March 20, 1994)
- Deep country / Kathy / I can see it, Davey / Happy with you / Take a ride / Casual love / Desperado / The date (making mountains out of molehills) / Better times / The sports fan / Mary Tyler Moore / Bird on a wire.

Mar 96. (cd/c) <*90696-0110-2/-4*> **NOTION**
- That hurricane / At my age / Notion / Carolina / Me / Sister Mary Madeline / Jane's last day / The date / Kathy / Forever haunted / Big sky. <*re-iss. Aug 00 on CD Freedom; 9003*>

Purple Turtle — not issued

Aug 00. (cd) <*9004*> **BARBARA KESSLER**
- Happy / Bridge mix / Soundtrack / Kristin / Angels are crying / Red yellow blue / A perfectly good way to pray / Confession / Persephone / Grown-up love songs and other oxymorons / Baby.

Charlie KING

Born 1947 in Brockton, Massachusetts, folk singer and activist CHARLIE KING has been at the centre of protest folk since his politically-motivated independent debut with Paul Despinosa in 1976, **OLD DREAMS AND NEW NIGHTMARES** {*6}.

He had already done his bit against Nixon and the Vietnam War, and for the civil rights movement, in the heady 1960s and early 1970s, and artists old and new including PETE SEEGER, PEGGY SEEGER, CHAD MITCHELL, JUDY SMALL, ARLO GUTHRIE, HOLLY NEAR, RONNIE GILBERT and JOHN McCUTCHEON, to name but a few, have sung and recorded his socially-conscious and anti-war songs.

Flying Fish released a string of solo LPs in the 1980s and 1990s, and one that stood out from the pack was 1992's **FOOD PHONE GAS LODGING** {*7}, a record that proved he could also cover his own idols, SEEGER, GILBERT and BOB FRANKE.

A radical change of style resulted in Charlie veering into Irish country music, but his heart was always at home with his long-term partner and musical companion Karen Brandow (b. 1954 in Philadelphia). They met in the 1990s and started performing as a duo in 1998; several albums have since surfaced, including the poignant and good-humoured **I STRUCK GOLD** (2001) {*6}. *MCS*

Charlie King - vocals, acoustic guitar / with session/guests, etc.

US CW — UK not issued

1976. (lp; as CHARLIE KING with PAUL DESPINOSA) <*CK 1*>| **OLD DREAMS AND NEW NIGHTMARES**
- Do the continental walk / Talkin' whip inflation now blues / America, where did you go? / Time is a love thief / This world is one / He had a dream / The good ol' CIA / I don't feel sorry for you Mr Nixon / Ordinary love song / The rats are winning / Pour yourself out in love / The Mayaguez incident / An old and simple dream.

Rainbow Snake — not issued

1979. (lp) <*RSR 002*> **SOMEBODY'S STORY**
- The dancing boilerman / The whole world's lover / Taft-Hartley / Two good arms / Access of clams / A woman of great energy (keep on movin') / Mountains of Mourne / Who's the criminal here? / Thank you Anita / Acceptable risks / Our life is more than our work. <*cd/c-iss.+=*> - VAGUELY REMINISCENT

——next with members of **Bright Morning Star**

1982. (lp) <*RSR 005*> **VAGUELY REMINISCENT** [live in NYC]
- Song for a hobbit / The hammer has to fall / Kugelsberg bank / I'm sure that we'll find it somewhere / Paulette's song (take me as you find me) / Another Jamaica farewell / Food stamp stomp / George's trip / Vaguely reminiscent of the 60s (the story) / Vaguely reminiscent of the 60s (the song). <*c-iss. 1998 cd-iss. Apr 09 +=; none*> - SOMEBODY'S STORY

——In 1982, Charlie was part of Bright Morning Star (with Court Dorsey, Cheryl Fox, George Fulginiti-Shakar, Ken Giles and Marcia Taylor) on the LP 'Live In The US'.

——next two sets credited with **Dave & Kay Gordon**

Flying Fish — Flying Fish

1984. (lp/c) <*FF+90 349*> **MY HEART KEEPS SNEAKIN' UP ON MY HEAD**
- The news, the blues and the people / Last night Danny went sailing / Devil take the farmer / Balloons! Banners! Uber alles / Tonight, I missed Miller time again / Camerado / Trying to find a way home / Wildcards (the JROTC song) / My name Joe / Count it all joy. *(UK-iss. Mar 89; same as US)* <*(cd-iss. Oct 92; FF70 349)*>

1986. (lp/c) <*FF/+90 417*> **FEELINGS OF FIRE**
- Strugglers and diehards / Nobody ever gets killed in our house / The Corvette / Circle of love / What if the Russians don't come? / Bonnie Green owes you one / Decals / Self-storage / Whoever invented the fishstick / Eat Meese / From the lambing to the wool.

——next with **Martha Leader** - fiddle, piano, guitar

Feb 89. (lp/c; by CHARLIE KING & MARTHA LEADER) <*(FF/+90 492)*> **STEPPIN' OUT**
- I've been kissed by a communist / Marie / World turned upside down / Didn't you eat on Tuesday / Mi re do / The ballad of Crispus Attucks / Newfoundlanders / New race to run / Loon song / We just come to work here / A woman's anger / Paz y libertad. <*cd-iss. Sep 92; FF70 492*>

Sep 92. (lp/c/cd) <*(FF/+90/70 536)*> **FOOD PHONE GAS LODGING** [rec. early 1989]
- Buy, buy this American car / Hands on the switch / Lisa Kalveledge / Lost in the stars again / Food phone gas lodging / He couldn't let go / The view from Red Hook / That's the way I made my millions / A still, small voice / Charlie Armakillo / Are you now or have you ever been.

Vaguely Reminiscent — not issued

1992. (lp) <*none*> **TWO GOOD ARMS**
- New York Central line / Close to the fire / US steal / My old man / Look into the camera and lie / Ballad of Anita Hill / People like you / Two good arms (for Sacco and Vanzetti) / Are you now or have you ever been? / There is a wall / Taft-Hartley / The dancing boilerman / Our life is more than our work. <*re-iss. Apr 09; same*>

1995. (cd) <*none*> **INSIDE OUT**
- Step into the holy circle / Don't ask don't tell / If Jimmy didn't have a go / Murphy's overpass / Eight hours / Bring back the eight hour day / Wrap that rascal / The place we found for Michael / S&L so long / The war has been coming home / Video games / Step by step.

1996. (c: by CHARLIE KING with Nell McGloin-King) <*none*> **SHIP IN THE SKY**
- How Aaron got his cat / I can't find my pajama / Would you like some coffeetea / Where is the manatee / My daddy flies a ship in the sky / Did you find a red yoyo / What does the tooth fairy do with my teeth / Hey little ant / Charlie Armadillo / Sing Mandella free. <*d-cd-iss. Apr 09 +=; none*> - THE SENSELESS LAUGHTER OF WHALES

1996. (c; by CHARLIE KING with Sally Rogers) <*none*> **THE SENSELESS LAUGHTER OF WHALES**
- Nothing happened last night / The sloth / The lonely raven / Lonnie Smith and Annie Jones / Where have all the flowers gone / The sunrise on Carawan hill / Bridget Evans / Some windows / Nine gold medals (a true story) / Let us come in. <*d-cd-iss.+=*> - SHIP IN THE SKY

——next with **Len Wallace and Sharon Abreu**

Mar 00. (cd) <*800085*> **BRILLIANT: SONGS OF IRELAND**
- Muirsheen durkin / Arthur McBride / Matty / Dublin fusiliers / If anything happened to you / The sea around us / Reel in the flickering light / The man with the cap / Dicey Riley / The hot asphalt / After the ball / The bold tenant farmer / Abdul Abulbul Amir / The march ditch / St Brendan's voyage / Farewell to Sicily / The Irish rover / Daughters and sons.

CHARLIE KING & KAREN BRANDOW

Appleseed — Appleseed

Mar 01. (cd) <*(APRCD 1050)*> **I STRUCK GOLD**
- I struck gold / I cannot sleep for thinking of the children / The one that got away / Que sera de mis hermanos / Six days with the boss / Tinky winky / Dignity / Wal-Mart union gonna rise again / Barney / The ballad of Penny Evans / Yanira merino / God danced.

Vaguely Reminiscent — not issued

2002. (cd) <*none*> **PUPPET TOWN**
- Little Jewish ladies for Buchanan (2000 election song) / Deeper waters / Pequena serenata diurna / Dr Laura polka / I remember, I believe / One puppet town / The worst you've ever done (death penalty song) / Oh glory how happy I am / We are one / Terror on Sesame St / We don't need no stinking badges / Levantese companero / Pour yourself out in love / If you want peace (work for justice).

2002. (cd) <*none*> **REMEMBERING SACCO & VANZETTI: in story and song. A live performance by...**
- (introduction and reading) / Emigrant eyes / (reading) / Bread and roses / (reading) / Yaniro merino / (reading) / Brother can you spare a dime? / Out of your pocket / (reading) / Banks of marble / (reading) / I ain't marching anymore / We are one / (reading) / Facing the chair / (reading) / Sing Mandela free / (reading) / Sacco's letter to his son / (reading) / People like you / (reading) / Levantese companero / (reading) / Two good arms / Finale.

2003. (cd) <*none*> **SPARKS AND TEARS: Lively In Concert**
- (introduction) / Bound for freedom / The twelve days of invasion / If Jimmy didn't have to go / Don't pay taxes / Children of God / Homeland uber alles / Christmas in the trenches / Coming into my years / Moving day - We shall not be moved / The list / Stand up / Ain't gonna let nobody turn me around / (encore).

2006. (cd) <*none*> **ON THE JOURNEY**
- If baboons can work it out / Defenders of marriage (about gay marriage) / (intro to...) / Martin and the crooked man / La chanson Francee / (intro to...) I don't remember (about Ronald Reagan) / Trying to find a way home / Waist deep in the big muddy / Growing up and slowing down / I can't find my pajamas / (intro to...) / Goon squad / Ossie Davis / Old devil time / Soy pan, soy paz, soy mas / Break 'em on down.

2008. (cd) <*none*> **HIGHER GROUND** [with Tex LaMountain]
- The news, the blues and the people take II / If loving you were a dangerous thing / Who's gonna bail out Scooter? (for Scooter Libby) / Who will be next on the gallows? / Higher ground / La ley de gravedad / Mrs McGrath revisited / You can't buy me / King of the whole wide world / I wonder why / The freedom song / The money's gonna flow / Romero / From way up here / Our father (new, revised edition).

Dec 10. (cd) <*none*> **THE DISTANCE REMAINING**
- Open the window / Slip of the hand / You'll sing to me too / Plegarias - Prayers (reading) / Plegarias (song) / Our problems stem from our acceptance of this filthy rotten system / My one secret you never knew / I got the light of freedom / Things redux / Rigoberta / Genetically modified doxology / Sweet Thames flow softly / Trickle up / How beautiful upon the mountain.

Dana & Karen KLETTER (⟹ BLACKGIRLS)

Sharron KRAUS

There aren't many acts who can whisk you back to folk's 1960s and 1970s heydays, but American-born, English-raised SHARRON KRAUS (born March 7, 1968) does it with aplomb. Part of the school of intimate and haunting femme-folk a la ANNE BRIGGS, SHIRLEY COLLINS and VASHTI BUNYAN, Sharron left Oxford University to find favour in, of all places, Philadelphia. Initially inspired by LEONARD COHEN, Tom Waits and The Violent Femmes, KRAUS has also dabbled with other styles in various side-projects, some outside the boundaries of folk.

Recorded while she was living in Alameda, North California in the very early 2000s, her debut, **BEAUTIFUL TWISTED** (2002) {*7}, was a traditional-sounding set but featured only her own compositions. It's a long way from her ancestral-folk counterparts, but songs like the haunting 'The River's Daughter' echo her idols just a little too much. That's hardly a fault, though. With five-string banjo in hand, Sharron plucks her way through broadside and bluegrass-styled tracks such as 'Moonbathing', 'The Family Tradition', 'Death Jig' and 'Cold-Hearted Devil' (the last recalling Roxy Music's 'In Every Dream Home A Heartache', without the sexual connotations).

Follow-up **SONGS OF LOVE AND LOSS** (2004) {*7}, recorded in Oxford with a band, opened with the trad/original mash-up 'Gallows Song - Gallows Hill', and spirits of the past were filtered through 'The Frozen Lake', 'Song Of The Hanged Man' and 'Murder Of Crows'. Two collaborative sets in 2006, 'The Black Dove', with Christian Kiefer, and 'Leaves From Off The Tree' (alongside ESPERS alumni MEG BAIRD and HELENA ESPVALL) came between children's set **SONGS FOR THE TWINS** (2005) {*5} and the festive **RIGHT WANTONLY A-MUMMING** (2007) {*7}, the latter a few years on from her inclusion on The IDATAROD's 'Yuletide' effort.

Sharron's next solo set proper, **THE FOX'S WEDDING** (2008) {*6}, had all the traits of early SHIRLEY & DOLLY COLLINS, ANNE BRIGGS and MADDY PRIOR, although the whole album (give or take the odd Thomas Campion poem) was created and performed by herself alone. The **TAU EMERALD** (2008) {*6} set was a collaboration with Fursaxa, and the **RUSALNAIA** (2008) {*7} album, credited with Gillian Chadwick (of Woodwose), featured GREG WEEKS and others of the freak-folk variety.

Recorded with guests including Christophe Albertijn, **THE WOODY NIGHTSHADE** (2010) {*7} was in folk-album terms a garden of unearthly delights. Tracks that fans old and new might appreciate include the sedate and "Wicker Man"-reminiscent 'Nothing', 'Two Brothers', 'Once', 'Evergreen Sisters' and the ever-so-creepy title track. *MCS*

Sharron Kraus - vocals, guitar, five-string banjo, keyboards, low whistle / with **Amy Clay** (or) **Tracy Farbstein** - fiddle / **Ron Guensche** - upright bass / etc.

US Camera Obscura — UK Camera Obscura

Apr 02. (cd) <*(CAM 050CD)*> **BEAUTIFUL TWISTED** — May 02
- The peacock's wing / The river's daughter / Moonbathing / The family tradition / Twins / Cold hearted devil / Death jig / The wrong man / Godstow / Beautiful twisted / Song of the unfree.

—— in 2003, Kraus was credited on The IDITAROD's set 'Yuletide'

——now with band **Colin Fletcher** - bass / **Jane Griffiths** - cello, fiddle / **Jon Fletcher** - banjo, guitar

May 04. (cd) <*(CAM 065CD)*> **SONGS OF LOVE AND LOSS** — Jun 04
- Gallows song - Gallows hill / The frozen lake / The tree of knowledge / Come to me / Song and dance of the bees / The pale prisoner / Impasse / Song of the hanged man / Angelica Caraway / Still / The fastest train / Eternal love / Murder of crows.

self-rel. — not issued

Dec 05. (cd) <*none*> **SONGS FOR THE TWINS**
- Sing a song of sixpence / Herring's head / All the pretty horses / London Bridge / Brian Oalinn / Old Bangum / Tom the piper's son / Hunt the wren / Sleep, baby, sleep / Three blind mice / Uncle Rat / I saw a ship / Who killed Cock Robin? / The tree in the wood / Twinkle, twinkle little star / Daddy fox / Gaelic lullaby.

—— in Mar '06, she collaborated with Christian Kiefer on 'The Black Dove'

—— in Oct '06, KRAUS collaborated on 'Leaves From Off The Tree' with ESPERS ladies MEG BAIRD and HELENA ESPVALL.

not issued — Bo' Weavil

Jun 07. (cd) *(Weavil 25CD)* **RIGHT WANTONLY A-MUMMING:** A collection of seasonal songs and celebrations by Sharron Kraus
- Wake up, sleepers / Dargason / Welcome joyful spring / Come let us all a-Maying go / May song / Wedding song / Midsummer / The hawthorn tree / Barleycorn / Harvest time / Bacca pipes / All hallows / Sun and rose / To shorten winter's sadness.

Durtro Jnana — Durtro Jnana

Apr 08. (cd) <*(DURTROJNANA 1959)*> **THE FOX'S WEDDING** — Mar 08
- Brigid / Green man / In the middle of summer / July skies / Harvest moon / Would I / The prophet / Thrice across these oaken ashes / Robin is dead / Ruthless and alone / Made my home / Magpie child.

Strange Attractors Audio House — not issued

Sep 10. (cd) <*SAAH 063*> **THE WOODY NIGHTSHADE**
- Nothing / Two brothers / Heaviness of heart / Evergreen sisters / Once / Story / The woody nightshade / Teacher / Rejoice in love / Traveller between the worlds.

TAU EMERALD

Sharron Kraus + **Tara Burke** (of Fursaxa)

Important — Important

Feb 08. (cd) <*(IMPREC 172)*> **TRAVELLERS TWO** — Jan 08
- Travellers two / Evening wings / Stoikite / Barrowlands / Full moon / Pilgrims return / Henbane / Water divining / Bani caapi / Mermaid's call / Laureola.

RUSALNAIA

Sharron Kraus + **Gillian Chadwick** (of EX REVERIE) / augmented by **Greg Weeks** - keyboards (of ESPERS) + **Margie Wienk** - cello, double bass (of FERN KNIGHT + of ESPERS)

Camera Obscura — Camera Obscura

Mar 08. (cd) <*(CAM 082CD)*> **RUSALNAIA**
- The sailor and the siren / Shifting sands / Kindling / Rusalnaia / The ravager / Winter / Dandelion wine / Wild summer.

L

LACH

New York was at the centre of the anti-folk movement in the 1990s, and LACH was one of its pioneers. Born in Brooklyn and raised in Rockland County, NY, he spent his formative musical years in punk band Proper I.D. alongside bassist Geoff Notkin. The band were inspired by British acts such as The Clash and The Jam, but his own interests were in Lou Reed and the folk music of GUTHRIE, DYLAN and OCHS.

The anti-folk scene was jumping at the outset of the decade as ROGER MANNING and KIRK KELLY were developing their own take on the genre, and LACH became a club organizer and MC on Manhattan's Lower East Side. When Capitol offshoot Gold Castle Records came calling (just before they closed down), LACH had the opportunity to deliver his first album, **CONTENDER** (1990) {*6}. Running around half an hour, the record had its moments with 'The John Glenn Song' and 'The Edie Effect', two tracks with elements of the spaced-out. Frustrated by the lack of interest after his label sank, LACH relocated to San Francisco for a couple of years, while his 'The Hillary Clinton Song' struck up radio airplay, in all places, Arkansas.

Back in New York City, at The Fort at Sidewalk Café in East Greenwich Village, LACH and his anti-folk allies (HAMELL ON TRIAL Mr Scarecrow, The Humans, etc) performed on his 'Lach's Antihoot' set in 1996. 'Hey!', 'Ballad Of The Thinning Man' and 'Drinking Beers With Mom (Everything Is Alright)' were LACH's own contributions.

1999 saw his return of the man on a new label, Fortified. **BLANG!** {*7}, with its mock-up Action Man-figurine cover art, melded his takes on punk and folk in 'Coffee Black', 'Teenage Alcoholic' and the hard-metal homage 'Kiss Loves You'. He was accompanied on this occasion by bassist Roy Edroso (of Reverb Motherfuckers) and drummer Billy Ficca (ex-Television).

KIDS FLY FREE (2001) {*7} (featuring a minute of WOODY GUTHRIE's 'This Land Is Your Land'), **TODAY** (2004) {*6} and **THE CALM BEFORE** (2008) {*6} continued his campaign to reclaim the gap between BOB DYLAN and Jello Biafra. Most recently, LACH released his sixth set, the Song By Toad release **RAMSHACKLE HEART** (2011) {*6}. *MCS*

Lach - vocals, guitars / + session people/band

		US Gold Castle	UK not issued
Jun 90.	(cd/c) *<D2/D4 71340>* **CONTENDER**	[ ]	[–]
	- The Edie effect / Red and white / The John Glenn song / Doomed from the start / Hard times / For the money / Loisaida / Baby / Let's dive / Stephen said.		
		Fortified	not issued
Feb 99.	(cd) *<1803>* **BLANG!**	[ ]	[–]
	- Coffee black / Teenage alcoholic / Ungrateful / I love them / Jester / Blue monk / Gasoline blue / Kiss loves you / Ambition burns / Sometimes the songs / The boy who never went outside / If you break it / Dreamboat / Drinking beers with mom.		
Sep 01.	(cd) *<1805>* **KIDS FLY FREE**	[ ]	[–]
	- Holy days / Human boy / Smoking again / He wanted to talk about his art / The hesitant / I love America (but she don't love me) / This land is your land / Beautiful / Little Miss Mystery / Sally's gone blue / Secrets theme / You better be good to her / Ain't it the most / A day without me (kids fly free). *<cd-r re-iss. Dec 10 on Track; none>*		
Apr 04.	(cd) *<62874 0 71002-9>* **TODAY**	[ ]	[–]
	- Antenna / Parade / The human torch song / Junior / Do the next right thing / Love song, No.1 / Power lies within / Secrets theme II / Sixties girl / Wail away / Wendy / Let's make a movie.		
Mar 08.	(cd) *<1808>* **THE CALM BEFORE**	[ ]	[–]
	- Egg / I want to be with you / This ain't a song / I won't miss you / A quiet distance / Men don't come back / Positions of power / Oh well / Letter to Theo / George at Coney / Gone gone gone / Questions / Crazy house.		
		Song By Toad	not issued
Jul 11.	(cd/lp) *<SBTR B/A 015>* **RAMSHACKLE HEART**	[ ]	[–]
	- Another night without you / Break the day / Everyone's therapist / She's brave now / Stunned / Baby, I don't want to go / Lonesome for you / My gangster / Blue overcoat / Sensitivity.		

Ray LaMONTAGNE

In a sea of earnest singer-songwriters, RAY LaMONTAGNE (born Raymond Charles Jack LaMontagne, June 18, 1973 in New Jersey) didn't instantly stand out as one who would blaze a trail to commercial success. But he did so, off the back of a breakthrough single, 'Trouble', from the album of the same name. Perhaps it was because the world (mainly the UK and Europe, initially) was enthralled by the chinless platitudes of James Blunt at the time, but LaMONTAGNE seemed like a breath of fresh air. His songs, showing what one man and a guitar and some soul could really do, created something lush and rich yet earthy and grounded.

Inspired initially by Stephen Stills's 'So Alone' album, Ray picked up an acoustic guitar and wrote and demo'd ten songs, which he gigged extensively around the East Coast at the onset of the 2000s. These tracks made their way to Chrysalis Music's Jamie Ceretta, who helped finance LaMONTAGNE to re-record the songs for producer Ethan Johns - son of the legendary Glyn, and producer to the likes of Ryan Adams, Rufus Wainwright and Kings Of Leon. These songs became his debut album, **TROUBLE** (2004) {*8}.

It was a record of refined beauty and plaintive magic, with LaMONTAGNE's haunting tones - think Rod Stewart or Al Green minus the histrionics - firmly at the centre on tracks like 'Hold You In My Arms' and 'Narrow Escape'. There were guest appearances by members of Nickel Creek, and by Jennifer Stills, daughter of Ray's inspiration. The album sold a quarter of a million copies in the US and was played in heavy rotation on the newly re-energised Radio 2 in the UK, which led to him playing Britain's larger concert halls by the end of the year.

Following that massive success, Ray stayed true to his roots with a second set of great songs but approached them in a very different way. Johns built up layers of keyboards and swathes of lush strings around LaMONTAGNE's affecting growl, making **TILL THE SUN TURNS BLACK** (2006) {*7} a brave and successful new application of his skills. The album kept LaMONTAGNE flying high, receiving better reviews than its predecessor and entering the UK Top 40.

GOSSIP IN THE GRAIN (2008) {*6} saw the singer expand his musical range further, still in the company of Johns. The album received mixed reviews, the parping brass of 'You Are The Best Thing' and the languid Motown balladry of 'Let It Be Me' showing up a varied collection by an artist trying to push his own musical boundaries.

If boundary-pushing was the intention, the job was accomplished in earnest on **GOD WILLIN' AND THE CREEK DON'T RISE** (2010) {*8}, which saw several changes in the LaMONTAGNE camp. It was credited to Ray LaMontagne And The Pariah Dogs, the first time he'd acknowledged his regular band, and he produced the album himself without his regular collaborator Ethan Johns. Aside from the decidedly funky opener, 'Repo Man', the album was a thoroughly laid- back affair, recorded over an easy two weeks at LaMONTAGNE's home in Massachusetts. He continued to enjoy commercial success despite the changes, and the album was Grammy-nominated as folk album of the year. Stand-out track 'Beg, Steal Or Borrow' won the Grammy award for song of the year. *MR*

Ray LaMontagne - vocals, guitars, harmonica (+ accompaniment)

		US RCA		UK Echo
Sep 04.	(cd/lp) *<82876 63459-2/88697 39844-1> (ECHCD 57)* **TROUBLE**	[ ]		[ ]
	- Trouble / Shelter / Hold you in my arms / Narrow escape / Burn / Forever my friend / Hannah / How come / Jolene / All the wild horses.			
Feb 05.	(7"/cd-s) *(ECS/+CD 155)* TROUBLE. / Narrow Escape [demo]	[–]		[ ]
		RCA		14th Floor
May 06.	(7" red) *(14FLR 14V)* HOW COME. / CRAZY	[–]		[ ]
Jun 06.	(re; cd) *(82564 6 33392-2)* **TROUBLE**	[–]		[5]
Jul 06.	(7clear) *(14FLR 15V)* TROUBLE [new radio mix]. / Burn [live]	[–]		[25]
Aug 06.	(cd/lp) *<82876 83328-2/88697 39842-1> (82564 6 39032-8)* **TILL THE SUN TURNS BLACK**	[28]	Jun 07	[35]

- Be here now / Empty / Barfly / Three more days / Can I stay / You can bring me flowers / Gone away from me / Lessons learned / Truly, madly, deeply / Till the sun turns black / Within you.

Nov 06. (ltd-7") *(14FLR 17V)* HOW COME. / [acoustic mix] [–] [ ]

Feb 07. (ltd-7"white) *(14FLR 20V)* JOLENE [solo alt. mix]. / [live] [–] [ ]

Jun 07. (ltd-7") *(14FLR 23V)* BE HERE NOW. / [live] [–] [ ]

Aug 07. (7"yellow) *(14FLR 25V)* THREE MORE DAYS. / In A Station [live] [–] [ ]

Oct 08. (cd/d-lp) *<88697-32670-2/-1> (5186 5 1020-2)* **GOSSIP IN THE GRAIN** [3] [23]

- You are the best thing / Let it be me / Sarah / I still care for you / Winter birds / Meg White / Hey me, hey mama / Henry nearly killed me (it's a shame) / A falling through / Gossip in the grain.

Nov 08. (dl-s) <-> YOU ARE THE BEST THING [90] [–]

——next with band: **Eric Heywood** - guitar / **Greg Leisz** - guitar, banjo / **Patrick Warren** - keyboards / **Jennifer Condos** - bass / **Jay Bellerose** - drums

RCA RCA

Aug 10. (cd; as RAY LaMONTAGNE and the PARIAH DOGS) *<(88697-65086-2)>* **GOD WILLIN' AND THE CREEK DON'T RISE** [3] [17]

- Repo man / New York City's killing me / God willin' and the creek don't rise / Beg, steal or borrow / Are we really through / This love is over / Old before your time / For the summer / Like rock 'n' roll and radio / Devil's in the jukebox.

LAVENDER DIAMOND

There is a tendency for fresh-folk fans to clasp anything vaguely resembling the genre to their hearts, and the cutesy-pie sunshine pop of LAVENDER DIAMOND may be a prime example of this foible. Singer Becky Stark has a sweet, choirgirl-like voice verging on freak-folk or chamber-folk, in the mould of SANDY DENNY or Linda Ronstadt, and she has had some experience as a solo artist.

Moving to Los Angeles in 2003 from their original base in Providence, Rhode Island, Becky and accomplished indie-pop musicians Jeff Rosenberg (guitar), Steve Gregoropoulos (piano) and Ron Rege Jr (drums) opened their musical account with a single, 'When Are You Coming Home', in 2003, and in 2005 released an EP, 'The Cavalry Of Light'.

They toured alongside The DECEMBERISTS (having also split a 45 with Colin Meloy), and the quartet's countrified 'folk' was effective on their debut set, **IMAGINE OUR LOVE** (2007) {*7}. The lilting Stark was almost ethereal on Bacharach/David-like tracks such as 'I'll Never Lie Again', 'Open Your Heart', 'Find A Way' and 'Bring Me A Song'. In the same year, they covered Madonna's 'Like A Prayer' on the tribute album 'Through The Wilderness'. Where are they now? *MCS*

Becky Stark - vocals (ex-Solo Artist) / **Jeffrey Rosenberg** - guitar, vocals (ex-Pink & Brown) / **Steve Gregoropoulos** - piano / **Ron Rege Jr.** - drums (ex-Swirlies)

US Lavender Diamond — UK not issued

2003. (ltd-7") *<LD 0701>* WHEN ARE YOU COMING HOME? / Wild [ ] [–]

Apr 05. (cd-ep) *<LDR 001>* THE CAVALRY OF LIGHT [ ] [–]

- You broke my heart / Please / In heaven there is no heat / Rise in the springtime. *<re-iss. Jan 07 on Matador 12" ep/cd-ep; OLE 751-1/-2> (UK-iss. Jan 07 on Rough Trade; RTRADCD 365)*

Cold Sweat — not issued

2005. (ltd-7") *<CLD 004.5>* [track by The Queens Of Sheba]. / The Song Of Impossible Occurences [ ] [–]

Matador — Rough Trade

Mar 07. (ltd-7") *(RTRADS 398)* OPEN YOUR HEART. / Oh No [by Colin Meloy of The Decemberists] [–] [ ]

May 07. (cd/lp) *<OLE 752-2/-1> (RTRADCD 395)* **IMAGINE OUR LOVE** [ ] [ ]

- Oh no / The garden rose / Open your heart / Side of the Lord / I'll never lie again / Dance until tomorrow / Like an arrow / My shadow is a Monday / Bring me a song / Here comes one / Find a way / When you wake for certain.

Christine LAVIN

Funny lady and quirky folksinger, CHRISTINE LAVIN (born January 2, 1952 in Geneva, New York) has been part of the new 'Fast Folk' contingent of rising stars from the early 1980s onwards. Starting with her in-concert debut, **ABSOLUTELY LIVE** (1981) {*5}, her reputation for giving us a laugh was earned from the get-go, though it must be said that songs like 'Three Months To Live' brought storytelling and fantasy too close together for an audience without special knowledge to tell the difference. Songs about biological clocks, failed relationships and other problems would fare better in times to come, but one surprise was how well her folk take on the Petula Clark hit 'Downtown' came across.

Her first studio album, **FUTURE FOSSILS** (1984) {*8}, came out on the Philo label, and her second, **BEAU WOES AND OTHER PROBLEMS OF MODERN LIFE** (1986) {*7}, featured some of her old songs including 'Amoeba Hop', 'Prince Charles' and 'Doris And Edwin: The Movie', and a version of The Everly Brothers' 'All I Have To Do Is Dream'. Christine's time at Philo was not all plain sailing, though, and only her 1988 contemporary-folk set **GOOD THING HE CAN'T READ MY MIND** {*7} can really be recommended.

Her sideline with The FOUR BITCHIN' BABES resulted in many fine songs and laughs before she left in 1997. Meanwhile, her solo career was on the rise again with 1995's **PLEASE DON'T MAKE ME TOO HAPPY** {*7}, her best for Shanachie until twilight label Appleseed released, as well as some children's songs, the more sarcastic and ambivalent **FOLKZINGER** (2005) {*6}. Featuring her readings of DONOVAN's 'Happiness Runs', Lennon/McCartney's 'All My Loving' and some songs written with Ervin Drake (the Bush-baiting 'The Peter Principle At Work' was very poignant and no laughing matter), the set was a charming one.

In 2006, LAVIN presented a various-artists CD/'cookbooklet', 'One Meat Ball'. Her latest album, on Yellow Tail, **COLD PIZZA FOR BREAKFAST** (2009) {*6}, featured a version of Malcolm McKinney's 'Sometimes' and probably her most ambitious recording to date, The Killers' 'Human'. *MCS*

Christine Lavin - vocals, acoustic guitar (with session people)

US Lifesong — UK not issued

Nov 81. (lp) *<LS 8134>* **ABSOLUTELY LIVE** [live June 29, 1981] [ ] [–]

- Three months to live / Amoeba hop / Summer weddings / Add me to the list / The bitter end / Mistresses' lament (I'm mad) / Downtown / Getting' used to leavin' / Doris and Edmund: the movie / The air conditioner song / If I should call you / I've been living on milk and cookies (since you've been gone). *<cd-iss. Apr 00 on Winthrop+=; 1002>* - ["intros"].

Palindrome — not issued

1983. (12" ep) *<PAL 101>* HUSBANDS AND WIVES [ ] [–]

- If you want space, go to Utah / The vacation of their lives / Giant TV screen / The danger / Tidal wave / Another woman's man. *<re-iss. 1987/Aug 88 as 'ANOTHER WOMAN'S MAN' on Philo+=; PH 002EP)>* - If I could be Sonja Henie. (cd see comps)

1984. (lp) *<PAL 105>* **FUTURE FOSSILS** [ ] [–]

- Don't ever call your sweetheart by his name / Damaged goods / Cold pizza for breakfast / Rockaway / Nobody's fat in Aspen / Rituals / The big ladies' ball / Regretting what I said / Sweet Irene the disco queen / Ramblin' waltz / Artificial means / Space between rings / The Dakota. *<re-iss. Sep 85 on Philo lp/c; PH 1104/+C> <cd-iss. Oct 88 & Feb 94; CDPH 1104)>*

Philo — Philo

1986. (lp/c) *<(PH 1107/+C)>* **BEAU WOES AND OTHER PROBLEMS OF MODERN LIFE** [ ] 1988 [ ]

- Amoeba hop / Summer weddings / Prince Charles / Getting' used to leavin' / Camping / Ballad of a ballgame / Doris and Edwin: the movie / Roses for the wrong man / Air conditioner / All I have to do is dream - A summer song / Biological time bomb / The moment slipped away. *<(cd-iss. Oct 88; CDPH 1107)>*

1988. (lp/c) *<(PH 1121/+C)>* **GOOD THING HE CAN'T READ MY MIND** [ ] [ ]

- Good thing he can't read my mind / Bumblebees / The Santa Monica pier / Waltzing with him / Mysterious woman / Realities / Downtown / Never go back / 85 / Somebody's baby / Ain't love grand. *<(cd-iss. Oct 88; CDPH 1121)>*

Mar 90. (cd) *<(CDPH 1132)>* **ATTAINABLE LOVE** [ ] Jul 90 [ ]

- Attainable love / Castlemaine / Yonder blue / Sensitive new age guys / Victim - Volunteer / The kind of love you never recover from / Fly on a plane / Venus kissed the moon / Moving target / Shopping cart of love: the play.

—— In 1991, Christine and others put together their first FOUR BITCHIN' BABES album

Nov 91. (cd/c) *<CD-/C-PH 1142>* **COMPASS** [ ] [–]

- Blind dating fun / Compass / Rushcutter's bay / Replaced / You think you've got problems / Until now / High heel shoes / Prisoners of their hairdos / I bring out the worst in you / Ten o'clock in Toronto / Katy says today is the best day of my whole entire life. *(UK-iss. Mar 00; same as US)*

Nov 93. (cd) *<(CD-PH 1159)>* **LIVE AT THE CACTUS CAFÉ: WHAT WAS I THINKING?** [live at Texas University's Union Cactus Café on January 16, 1993] [ ] Jan 94 [ ]

- Prince Charles / We are the true Americans / Dear Dan / Bald headed men / What was I thinking? / I blab about celebrities I have spied on at my local health club / Doris and Edwin: the movie / Alternate endings to the above song, if the one here is too scary for sensitive you / [intermission] / The Dakota / Regretting what I said... / How the Lord helped me rewrite a troublesome line in 'Regretting what I said' / Shopping cart of love: the play / Katy says today is the best day of my whole entire life. *(bonus +=)* - What was I thinking? [the dance mix].

Shanachie Shanachie

Mar 95. (cd/c) <*(SHAN 8016 CD/C)*> **PLEASE DON'T MAKE ME TOO HAPPY** □ Apr 95 □
- Oh no / Constant state of want / Psychic / The secrets at this wedding / The sixth floor / Jane / Jagged hearts / Scatter new seeds / Waiting for the B train / Something is wrong with this picture / 69 / Please don't make me too happy / Oh no.

—— In 1996, Christine was behind two various-artists volumes of 'Laugh Tracks - two evenings of music and madness, live at the Bottom Line' on Shanachie.

Feb 97. (cd) <*(SHAN 8024)*> **SHINING MY FLASHLIGHT ON THE MOON** □ Mar 97 □
- Shining my flashlight on the moon / Two Americans in Paris / Introduction to the one-song musical 'Honey, We Have To Talk' / I want to be lonely again / Music to operate by / Happy divorce day / The polka-dancing bus driver and the 40-year-old mystery / Robert and Annie in Larchmont, New York / If I ruled the world / As bad as it gets / Snackin' / The scent of the cologne / Planet X.

Christine Lavin not issued

Sep 98. (cd) **ONE WILD NIGHT IN CONCERT** [live at the Blue Moon Coffeehouse at Wesleyan University in Bloomington, November 22, 1997] ⊟ gigs ⊟
- (and now a few words from our sponsor, Darcy Greder) / Oh no / They look alike, they walk alike... / National apology day / Flip side of fame / (creating just the right mood for the next song) / The kind of love you never recover from / (Amanda McBroom at the Rainbow and Stars Room) / Errol Flynn / (the secret fear of songwriters) / Please don't make me too happy / (the audience votes) / The voice of the relaxation tape / (visiting Dallas) / The sixth floor / (the day after a plane to California) / Great big bug.

Jan 00. (cd) **GETTING IN TOUCH WITH MY INNER BITCH** [live shows May and August 1999] ⊟ gigs ⊟
- (choice words from Dave Palmater) / Single voice / (I venture into the crowd with a spelunking lamp on my head) / You look pretty good for your age / (don't make me naughty) / What was I thinking in 1999 / (what Monica L. and Cameron D. have in common) / (it's dangerous to confide in a songwriter) / Another New York afternoon / (a late-night I.M. turns into...) / Plateau / (Gene Shay adds his voice to the low fat/no fat debate) / (happy birthday Maureen) / Harrison Ford / The polka-dancing bus driver and the 40-year-old mystery / The piper / Getting in touch with my inner bitch / (Megon McDough, one of our greats, inspires an idea) / Adjust your dreams - Shining my flashlight / Piranha women of the avocado jungle of death.

Apr 01. (cd) **THE SUBWAY SERIES** [live September 11, 2000] ⊟ gigs ⊟
- (John Platt introduces Christine) / Waiting for the B train / Doris and Edwin: the movie / (wait! Here are better endings to that frightening movie) / Good thing he can't read my mind / (good thing you couldn't read my mind when I was singing that) / (Dallas, TX '63, NYC '99, today) / The sixth floor - Moon-rising tide - We are the lucky ones / Where is the mango princess / If we had no moon / (have I got a deli man for you!) / Another New York afternoon / Shopping cart of love: the play (with new improved healthier ending) / The moment slipped away / OK, gang, one more song (snag), then it's upstairs for milk and cookies.

Redwing not issued

Aug 02. (cd) <*RWMCD 5411*> **I WAS IN LOVE WITH A DIFFICULT MAN** □ ⊟
- I was in love with a difficult man / Jack and Wanda / Strangers talk to me / Sunday breakfast with Christine (and Ervin) / Making friends with my grey hair / Wind chimes / Trade up / All you want is what you want / Three-storied life / Firehouse / For Carolyn - Something beautiful / Looked good on paper.

Appleseed Appleseed

Oct 03. (cd; as CHRISTINE LAVIN & THE MISTLETONES) <*(APRCD 1075)*> **THE RUNAWAY CHRISTMAS TREE:** favorite holiday songs and bedtime stories □ Nov 03 □
- A Christmas Kwanzaa/Solstice/Chanukah/Ramadan/Boxing Day song / Snow! Medley: Snow snow snow snow - Onward thru the snow / The runaway Christmas tree / Dona nobis pacem / Lamb and lion / The all purpose carol / Elves / Scalloped potatoes / Polkadot pancakes / Tacobel canon / A New Year's round / TH 12 DYS F CHRSTMS / Allelujah - Samen / Good night to you all.

May 04. (cd) <*(APRCD 1079)*> **SOMETIMES MOTHER REALLY DOES KNOW BEST** [live] □ □
- Strangers talk to me in Colorado Springs on a Thursday night / (Rocky Mountain... hi!) / Wind chimes / (you should have seen the frightened looks on your faces) / (what kind of ridiculous glamour trajectory am I on?) / What was I thinking? / (Martha Stewart... Victoria's secret... Bob Dylan... Pachelbel?) / The Tacobel canon / (Steve... you are so busted) / A question of tempo (when I'm under pressure) / Planet X / (Planet? Planot? Goofy?) / (who are the brainiacs in the house tonight?) / (Bernice, Carol, and tonight's crowd compete for the science prize) / You look pretty good for your age / Art Jensen, Mr. Colorado Springs, your life will never be the same / (flashback to 1956: How do you spell Cassiopeia?) / (Boston Red Sox fans: the most loyal, most tenacious, yet most troubled) / Ballad of a ballgame / The legal ramifications of a crackerjack vendor who works in Yankee Stadium / Sometimes mother really does know best.

Sep 05. (cd) <*(APRCD 1091)*> **FOLKZINGER** □ □
- Armageddon / Happiness runs / The bends / Winter in Manhattan / Moken spoken here / Chicken soup / Bad girl dreams / All my loving / One of the boys / The Peter Principle at work / (I'm a)-card-carrying bleeding-heart liberal / Surprise / Winter in Manhattan.

Yellow Tail not issued

Sep 07. (cd) <*YT 10022*> **HAPPYDANCE OF THE XENOPHOBE** □ ⊟
- The most polite city in the world / Happydance / Chocolate covered espresso beans / More than 1,000,000 Americans / Here comes hurricane season / Tom Cruise scares me / Smokers / Russina Michael / As we stumble along / Whipped cream / Why? / Reminiscing with the elusive gentle lonely boxer of love / [untitled].

Nov 08. (cd) <*YT 10023*> **I DON'T MAKE THIS STUFF UP... I JUST MAKE IT RHYME** [live at Anabel Taylor Hall] □ ⊟
- (Phil Shapiro introduces Bound For Glory) / The most polite city in the world / A shark in New York waters / Sharkman on Malta / Planet X (featuring SAL RUIBAL) / Good thing he can't read my mind [brand new dude version and dude/dudette version] / I am psychic so are you / Good thing he can't read my mind [video] / More than 1,000,000 Americans / Alone again naturally / Tacobel canon / Worst birthdays / Birthday game: Alissa vs. Andrea / Sunday breakfast with Christine / Here's the recipe - Really! / The moment slipped away / What was I thinking (1993-2007)? *[hidden tracks]*: A shark in New York water (w/ JED FORT, STEVE DOYLE & BRIAN BAUERS) / Good thing he can't read my mind [video].

Nov 09. (cd) <*YT 10024*> **COLD PIZZA FOR BREAKFAST** □ ⊟
- Cold pizza for breakfast redux / A firefly's life / The kind of love you never recover from / Sometimes (feat. ANIL MELWANI) / Here comes Caesar the dog whisperer / Too old for the national spelling bee / That elusive blue (feat. ROBIN BATTEAU) / Human (feat. ROBIN BATTEAU) / Attractive stupid people / Not me not me not me / Odds are / Mencken's pen / Bring back the bow / [Christine reads an excerpt of chapter two from her book 'Cold Pizza For Breakfast: A Mem-Wha??'] / Good thing she can't read my mind: a dude's eye view [live].

- (5-7*) compilations, others, etc.-

Jun 00. (cd) *Philo;* <*(CDPH 1220)*> **THE BELLEVUE YEARS** □ Nov 00 □
- (HUSBANDS AND WIVES EP tracks) / [interview with David Weinstein, January 22, 1984] / Cold pizza for breakfast / Music - Sport notes, 1984 / Lady knights, the Atlantic Ten and the Atavistics / Isn't this just like empty-vee? / Let's get out of here, Jody / Camping [live from the general feed and seed store with John Sandidge, June 14, 1986] / Artificial means / The moment slipped away / I want to be the first folk singer on the space shuttle [live with Trumbull & Cove, November 7, 1987] / If I could be Sonja Henie.

LES SHELLEYS (⟹ BROSSEAU, Tom)

Jeffrey LEWIS

Much of a piece with fellow anti-folk heroes The MOLDY PEACHES (for whom he designed some album sleeves), underground comix illustrator and independent singer-songwriter JEFFREY LEWIS (b. November 20, 1975 in New York City) was the product of Grateful Dead-loving parents and the post-grunge scene.

Not particularly enamoured of his anti-folk classification, Jeffrey's musical career began with several rare CD-rs, including 'When Madman Was Good - Version One' (1997) and 'Songs From Austin' (2001). Along with his playful antics at open-mic nights, these endeared him to Rough Trade, who released his brilliantly oddball debut album proper, **THE LAST TIME I DID ACID I WENT INSANE AND OTHER FAVORITES** (2002) {*8}.

Introspective, touchingly autobiographical and extremely literate, in the tradition of Lou Reed and Daniel Johnston, Jeffrey's comic-book stories were brought to life on the seven-minute, LEONARD COHEN-like 'The Chelsea Hotel Oral Sex Song', the squeaky 'The Man With The Golden Arm' and the title track. Sticking to his the theme of fractured consciousness, **IT'S THE ONES WHO'VE CRACKED THAT THE LIGHT SHINES THROUGH** (2003) {*6} was volume two of his splintered and witty narratives. 'No LSD Tonight', 'You Don't Have To Be A Scientist To Do Experiments On Your Heart' and 'Don't Let Your Record Label Take You Out To Lunch' were nothing if not heartfelt and ironic.

Upgraded to official sidekick, his brother Jack Lewis (credited alongside Anders Griffen on Jeffrey's previous set) featured prominently on several tracks on the third album, **CITY AND EASTERN SONGS** (2006) {*7}. The six rapping/ranting minutes of 'Williamsburg Will Oldham Horror', and the derivative Velvets/John Cale-style violas of 'Don't Be Upset', were far-from-easy listening, but Jeffrey at least took new directions on 'The Singing Tree', 'Art Land' and the punky 'Time Machine'.

Though too young to have been a fan when English Oi!/punk practitioners Crass were out and about at the outset of the 1980s (he discovered them in '93), LEWIS and friends including vocalist Helen Schreiner took on a whole set of the anarchists' material on **12 CRASS SONGS** (2007) {*7}. The musicians sounded twee and goofy on real anti-folk tracks 'Systematic Death', 'The Gasman Cometh', 'Do They Owe Us A Living' and 'Big A, Little A', but the originals should be heard before any judgment is made.

In another nod to New Wave/avant-rock, Jeffrey Lewis & The Junkyard (brother Jack and drummer David Beauchamp) delivered **'EM ARE I** (2009)

{*7}. Not as fast with the wordplay as before, it clearly marked a transitional period for LEWIS; highlights are 'Bugs And Flowers', 'To Be Objectified' and 'Slogans'. *MCS*

There are many unofficial EPs and CDrs of collaborations and pre-solo work

Jeffrey Lewis - vocals, guitar / with various sessioners incl. Jack Lewis

US Rough Trade / UK Rough Trade

Jul 01. (ltd one-sided 7") *(RTRADES 020)* THE CHELSEA HOTEL ORAL SEX SONG

—— In 2001/02, JEFF LEWIS teamed up with KIMYA DAWSON on a homemade CD-r.

Apr 02. (cd) <*(RTRADECD 027)*> **THE LAST TIME I DID ACID I WENT INSANE AND OTHER FAVORITES** Sep 01
- The east river / Another girl / Seattle / The Chelsea Hotel oral sex song / Amanda is a scalape (LINA & THE SCALAPES) / Heavy heart / The last time I did acid I went insane / The man with the golden arm / Springtime / Life.

May 02. (7"/cd-s) *(RTRADES 055)* BACK WHEN I WAS FOUR. / Three-quarter Moon / The Modern Age

—— In 2002, his Guitar Situations released the limited 'Musical Conduct'.

——next credited (on cover): **Jack Lewis + Anders Griffen**

Aug 03. (cd) <*(RTRADECD 099)*> **IT'S THE ONES WHO'VE CRACKED THAT THE LIGHT SHINES THROUGH** Jul 03
- Back when I was four / Alphabet / No LSD tonight / Don't let the record label take you out to lunch / Gold / Texas / Sea song / Arrow / Zaster / If you shoot the head you kill the ghoul / I saw a hippy girl on Eighth Ave. / Graveyard / You don't have to be a scientist to do experiments on your own heart.

Sep 06. (cd; as JEFFREY & JACK LEWIS) <*(RTRADECD 237)*> **CITY AND EASTERN SONGS** Jan 07
- Posters / Don't be upset / Williamsburg Will Oldham horror / Something good / The singing tree / Anxiety attack / Time machine / Moving / Art land / New old friends / They always knew / Had it all.

Oct 07. (cd) <*(RTRADECD 414)*> **12 CRASS SONGS**
- End result / I ain't thick, it's just a trick / Systematic death / The gasman cometh / Banned from the Roxy / Where next Colombus? / Do they owe us a living? / Securicor / Demoncrats / Big A, little A / Punk is dead / Walls (fun in the oven).

May 09. (7"; as JEFFREY LEWIS & THE JUNKYARD) *(RTRADS 506)* ROLL BUS ROLL. / Broken Song

May 09. (cd; as JEFFREY LEWIS & THE JUNKYARD) <*(RTRADCD 514)*> **'EM ARE I** Apr 09
- Slogans / Roll bus roll / If life exists / Broken broken broken heart / Whistle past the graveyard / To be objectified / The upside-down cross / Bugs and flowers / Good old pig gone to Avalon / It's not impossible / Mini theme: Moocher from the future.

——In 2010, Jeffrey + Jack were part of one-off project The BUNDLES alongside ex-MOLDY PEACHES frontgirl Kimya Dawson

——2010 saw the release of a collaborative album, 'Come On Board', featuring Jeffrey with Peter Stampfel (of The HOLY MODAL ROUNDERS)

- other official releases -

2008. (cd; as JEFFREY & JACK LEWIS) *Olive Juice;* <*OJ-0209*> **CITY AND EASTERN TAPES** [other sessions]
- Posters [early recording] / Don't be upset [radio session] / Williamsburg Will Oldham horror [live] / Something good [early demo] / The singing tree [radio session] / Anxiety attack [early demo] / Time machine [alt.] / Moving [radio session] / Art land [early recording] / New old friends [radio session] / They always knew [early recording] / Had it all [radio session] / Summertime called [aka Punxatawnie Phil] / Journey to the center of the earth / Chicago / Don't be scared / Flower for Fahey [acoustic instrumental] / Buy nothing day [electric instrumental].

LIGHTNING DUST

Acid-folk or acid-country (now there's a new term), east Vancouver duo LIGHTNING DUST stretched their musical barriers beyond the confines of Joshua Wells and gothic singer Amber Webber's space-rock venture Black Mountain.

Recorded in a dank cave and finished off in a bright blue house, their minimalist approach paid off on their self-titled set **LIGHTNING DUST** (2007) {*7}. The short, sharp and upbeat 'Wind Me Up' (a radio hit in Canada) was a diversion from the lo-fi Grace Slick/David Surkamp-like 'Listened On' and 'Take Me Back', and 'Jump In' was very Nick Cave 'n' Kylie. Amber's vibrato vocals were the bee's knees.

Just as trippy, in a Hazlewood-Sinatra kind of way, second album **INFINITE LIGHT** (2009) {*7} picked up where its predecessor left off, although 'I Knew' and the lilting country of 'Antonia June' were hardly folk music - acid-folk, at a push.

Amber is the twin sister of Ashley Webber, formerly the bass player with Canadian indie outfit The Organ. *MCS*

Amber Webber - vocals / **Joshua Wells** - multi (of Black Mountain)

US Jagjaguwar / UK Jagjaguwar

Jun 07. (cd/lp) <*(JAG 112)*> **LIGHTNING DUST**
- Listened on / When you go / Wind me up / Take me back / Jump in / Heaven / Castles and caves / Highway / Breathe / Days go by.

Aug 09. (cd/lp) <*(JAG 139)*> **INFINITE LIGHT**
- Antonia June / I knew / Dreamer / The times / Never seen / History / Honest man / Waiting on the sun to rise / Wondering what everyone knows / Take it home.

The LOW ANTHEM

Roll up, roll up for rootsy Americana-purveyors The LOW ANTHEM, a part indie-folk, part alt-country, part gospel-blues outfit led by classically-trained Brown University musicians Ben Knox Miller and Jeff Prystowsky. Formed in 2006 in Providence, Rhode Island, they were quick to get off their marks with their low-key, self-titled CD **THE LOW ANTHEM** (2006) {*6}.

The founding pair were joined by Jocie Adams, who replaced early member Dan Lefkowitz, on **WHAT THE CROW BRINGS**(2007) . Her introduction is more than justified by 'Coal Mountain Lullaby'. The album also featured a version of The Carter Family's 'Keep On The Sunny Side'.

The harmony-drenched **OH MY GOD, CHARLIE DARWIN** (2008) {*8} drew comparisons with FLEET FOXES and The Neville Brothers (on 'Charlie Darwin' and 'Cage The Songbird'), and even Crosby, Stills and Nash ('To Ohio'). It was no surprise that when its independent release sold out, Nonesuch (US) and Bella Union (UK) signed them up. Together with a DYLANesque cover of Tom Waits's 'Home I'll Never Be', Ben and Jeff's showpieces were 'Champion Angel' and another harmonium -friendly track, 'To The Ghosts Who Write History Books'.

Anticipation was keen in the lead-up to their Top 200 entry **SMART FLESH** (2011) {*7}, which featured multi-instrumentalist newcomer Mat Davidson and returning producer Jesse Lauter, who set them up in an deserted sauce factory in Central Falls, near their new home on Block Island. New Country rather than folk-rock dominated the set, starting with A.P. Carter's 'Ghost Woman Blues' and their own 'Apothecary Love'. The LOW ANTHEM chilled out for 'Love And Altar' and wigged out, NEIL YOUNG-like, on 'Boeing 737'. One to watch for the future. *MCS*

Ben Knox Miller - vocals, multi / **Jeff Prystowsky** - multi, vocals / early member **Dan Lefkowitz**

US Basement Project / UK not issued

May 06. (cd) <*none*> **THE LOW ANTHEM**
- Burlington / Lonely dollar / I need you / Military planes / Matchstick rafters / Bluebirds / Running weary / Take care of your own / Country wine / Don't say no / Monday's rain / Southbound train.

——added **Jocie Adams** - multi, vocals

The Low Anthem / not issued

Oct 07. (lp) <*none*> **WHAT THE CROW BRINGS** own
- The ballad of the broken bones / Yellowed by the sun / As the flame burns down / Bless your tombstone heart / This god damn house / A weary horse can hide the pain / Scavenger bird / Sawdust saloon / Keep on the sunny side / Senorita / Coal mountain lullaby.

Sep 08. (cd) <*2ed*> OH MY GOD, CHARLIE DARWIN own
- Charlie Darwin / To Ohio / Ticket taker / The horizon is a beltway / Home I'll never be / Cage the songbird / (Don't) Tremble / Music box / Champion angel / To the ghosts who write history books / OMGCD / To Ohio (reprise).

not issued / End of The Road

Feb 09. (ltd-7" m) *(EOTR 0011)* CHARLIE DARWIN. / To Ohio / Home I'll Never Be

Nonesuch / Bella Union

Jun 09. (re; cd/lp) <*519598-2/-1*> *(BELLA CD/V 202)* **OH MY GOD, CHARLIE DARWIN**

Oct 09. (ltd-7" white) *(BELLAV 215)* CHARLIE DARWIN. / Sally, Where'd You Get Your Liquor From

Feb 10. (ltd-7") *(BELLAV 231)* TO THE GHOSTS WHO WRITE HISTORY BOOKS. / Don't Let Nobody Turn You Around

Mar 10. (7"m) <*523775-7*> CHARLIE DARWIN. / Sally, Where'd You Get Your Liquor From / Don't Let Nobody Turn You Around

——(late '09) added **Mat Davidson** - multi, vocals

Feb 11. (cd/lp) <*523691-2/-1*> *(BELLA CD/V 276)* **SMART FLESH**
- Ghost woman blues / Apothecary love / Boeing 737 / Love and altar / Matter of time / Wire / Burn / Hey, all you hippies! / I'll take out your ashes / Golden cattle / Smart flesh.

LOWER DENS (⟹ HUNTER, Jana)

Samara LUBELSKI

A latecomer to the world of folk-rock music, New York-born singer/songwriter SAMARA LUBELSKI (b. around 1967) has enough experience under her belt, including a long career in session work, to justify a book to herself. The former violinist of Of A Mesh (a mid-1980s indie-goth act) and Sonora Pine, she was also part of Salmon Skin before probably her most distinguished group, Hall Of Fame (both with Dan Brown), while Tower Recordings, Metabolismus, Azalia Snail, Jackie-O Motherfucker, The Bummer Road and Thurston Moore have all required her input.

Samara's CD-r solo debut **IN THE VALLEY** (2003) {*6} is essential, though not essentially folk, but **THE FLEETING SKIES** (2004) {*6} brought the singer to the attention of fans of LINDA PERHACS, ANNE BRIGGS, VASHTI BUNYAN and 1960s psych confectioners Strawberry Alarm Clock; check out 'Waiting By The Gate', 'Follow You' and 'Keeper Of Beauty'. The same goes for their dreamy, pop/organic-folk follow-up **SPECTACULAR OF PASSAGES** (2005) {*7}, thirty-odd minutes of pleasant-valley-Sunday music with more than a nod to Belle And Sebastian on tracks such as 'Magic Winding', 'Road To Misfortune' and the excellent 'Broken Links'.

Crediting a distinguished list of accompanists including drummer Hamish Kilgour (of The Clean), **PARALLEL SUNS** (2007) {*8} was a psych masterpiece - lush, enchanting and autumnal on tracks such as 'Have You Seen The Colors', 'Snowy Meadows II' and the very ESPERS-like 'The Cloistered Palace'.

It was inevitable that Samara would turn up on the Ecstatic Peace! label (producer Thurston Moore's imprint) for her fifth album, **FUTURE SLIP** (2009) {*6}. The Sonic Youth connection is further emphasised by the appearance of drummer Steve Shelley, while solo artist PG SIX plays guitar. Highlights of the 28-minute set include the folky 'Culture King '66', the Syd Barrett-like 'Silver Hair' and 'The Evolution Flow'. *MCS*

Samara Lubelski - vocals, guitar, keyboards, violin, percussion / with session people

US: Child Of Microtones — UK: not issued

2003. (ltd cd-r) <*COM 7*> IN THE VALLEY
- Cave dweller open your door! / I love thlowth / Song of the stations / All the tired horses / Speedway of the winged shuffle to the southern hemisphere / Odyssey rider. *<ltd-lp-iss. Oct 05 on Eclipse; ECL-043>*

US: The Social Registry — UK: The Social Registry

Oct 04. (cd) <*(SR 017)*> **THE FLEETING SKIES** — Nov 04
- The fleeting skies / Keeper of beauty / Guarding the sun / Under the gaze / Waiting by the gate / Immortal design / Follow you / The boy who bought the cosmos / Now's morning's calling / Crowns and courts. *<ltd-lp-iss. 2004 on De Stijl; IND-044>*

Nov 05. (cd) <*(TSR 022)*> **SPECTACULAR OF PASSAGES**
- Lick 'n' leap / Sister silver / Snow white feathered man / Magic winding / Road to misfortune / Broken links / Caravan / Onion / Fired to / Quartered field. *<lp-iss. 2005 on De Stijl; IND-054>*

Oct 07. (cd/lp) <*(TSR 056)*> **PARALLEL SUNS**
- Have you seen the colors / Taste the candy / Meeting of the sun / Snowy meadows II / Born from the tree / The cloistered palace / Ego blossoms / Spirit of the age / Greener grass.

US: not issued — UK: Ecstatic Peace!

Sep 09. (cd) *(E 110cd)* **FUTURE SLIP**
- Culture king '66 / Empire's dream / The evolution flow / Future hold / Headships down / The trip is out / New age slip / Silver hair / Walking in the waves / Field the mine.

US: Time-Lag — UK: not issued

Oct 09. (ltd-7") <*048*> DID YOU SEE? / Spectacular Of Passages

M

Rod MacDONALD

The songs of Greenwich Village singer/songwriter ROD MACDONALD have appeared on recordings by many artists including CHRISTINE LAVIN, GORDON BOK, JEAN REDPATH, HAPPY TRAUM, SHAWN COLVIN, DAVE VAN RONK, Garnet Rogers and Jonathan Edwards, and he has released over a dozen consistently good and distinctive crossover/ mainstream-friendly sets of his own.

Born August 17, 1948 in Southington, Connecticut, MacDONALD studied law (graduating from Columbia Law School) before pursuing a career as a folk performer. A scion of New York's spreading 'Fast Folk' movement/cooperative, his bookings took him beyond the US and into Canada and Europe. His folk style was derivative of Jackson Browne, RICHARD FARINA and PHIL OCHS, and like his idols he chose subject matter that was political, anthemic and thought-provoking. 'American Jerusalem', 'The Unearthly Fire' and the epic, acappella 'A Sailor's Prayer' (all from his 1983 debut **NO COMMERCIAL TRAFFIC** {*7}) were just a taste of what was ahead.

What did follow was at least two simple but effective albums, **WHITE BUFFALO** (1985) {*7} and **BRING ON THE LIONS** (1989) {*7}, initially released only in Europe but imported by the bucketful for his loyal Village fan base. A period on Shanachie resulted in a couple of sets, **HIGHWAY TO NOWHERE** (1992) {*6} and **THE MAN ON THE LEDGE** (1994) {*6}, that reprised some of his 'Fast Folk'-era material alongside some solid, searching new songs. With a nod to his hero OCHS and his gold-lame-suit period, **LEE HARVEY, THE MICRODOTS AND ME** (1997) {*7} showed how the scathing Rod could take more than a few chances and stances. 'The Contract On America', 'Little Black Pearls' and 'The American Way' were obvious political statements on all the news that's fit (or unfit) to print.

MACDONALD has shown himself dependably more than adept at taking on the establishment within the music industry. It's just a pity that later albums such as **A TALE OF TWO AMERICAS** (2005) {*7} (featuring 'I Am Bob Dylan' and a nine-minute cover of DYLAN's 'With God On Our Side') and his most recent, **SONGS OF FREEDOM** (2011) {*6}, didn't get across to a wider audience outside the US. Rod's connection with the five-piece DYLAN tribute band Big Brass Bed surfaced in 2007 with **A FEW DYLAN SONGS** {*5} - 11 of them, including, as might be expected, 'Lay Lady Lay'. *MCS*

Rod Macdonald - vocals, acoustic guitar, harmonica, piano (w/ session people)

US Cinemagic — UK not issued

1983. (lp) *<HR 8007>* **NO COMMERCIAL TRAFFIC**
- The unearthly fire / It's goin' to take some time / Butter my bread / Something beautiful / On the road in NY town / American Jerusalem / Dear grandfather / A sailor's prayer / What I wanted / Every living thing.

not issued — Autogram

1985. (lp) *(03139)* **WHITE BUFFALO** (alt. title 'ALBUM 2 FOR SALE') German
- Song of my brothers / Cross country waltz / Ode to the pretty girls / Sanctuary / Sand castles / White buffalo / Water / The aliens came in business suits / Blues for the river / Stop the war. *<re-iss. 1987 on McDisc; ???> (cd-iss. Nov 93 on Brambus+=; BRAM 199129-2)* - A sailor's prayer / Routine day in paradise / Every living thing. *<cd-iss. Jul 96 on Gadfly; Gadfly 211>*

not issued — Brambus

1989. (cd) *(BRAM 198908-2)* **BRING ON THE LIONS** Swiss
- Saving grace / Now that the rain has gone / Love at the time / Distant radios / The coming of the snow / After the singing / Norman / Wonderin' why / The well / So many songs / South Africa / (untitled) / New man. *(UK-iss. Nov 93; same)*

Shanachie — Shanachie

1992. (cd/c) *<SHCD/SHMC 8001>* **HIGHWAY TO NOWHERE**
- Norman / Now that the rain has gone / The coming of the snow / Moonlight and fire / After the singing / So many songs / Love at the time / Distant radios / Saving grace / The well / The way to Calvary.

1994. (cd/c) *<(SHCD/SHMC 8011)>* **THE MAN ON THE LEDGE** Dec 94
- Zydeco / It's your dime / I can't see the reason / For the people (song for Czechoslovakia) / Hey, Mister President / Some things I like about America / Dallas / The man on the ledge / Up on the mountain / Women of the world / American Jerusalem / Honorable men / Auschwitz / For all the grapes on the vine.

Gadfly — not issued

Feb 97. (cd) *<Gadfly 224>* **AND THEN HE WOKE UP**
- Happy all the time / Ballad of a black haired man / On any old Sunday / And then he woke up / The death of Victor Jara / Me and Uncle Joe / I can't believe (how good you've been to me) / The last train to Pontiac / Love for all seasons / Out in the country / I'll walk in the Highlands / Keeper of the flame / Who built the bomb (that blew Oklahoma City down?) / Timothy.

Sep 99. (cd) *<Gadfly 256>* **INTO THE BLUE**
- Seven days / I have no problem with this / Best defence / Days of rain / Here's a song for you / It's a tough life / Six strings and a hole big and round / The Aucilla river song / Deep down in the Everglades / Lightning over the sea / Into the blue / Fear / Sun dancer / The cure for insomnia.

Wind River — Brambus

2002. (cd) *<4028> (BRAM 200268-2)* **RECOGNITION** 2004
- You who sleep beside me / The man who dropped the bomb on Hiroshima / Just one kiss / My neighbors in Delray / Dr Gachet / Video games / When angel gets blue / We got it good and that ain't bad / Mickey world / Dance by lightning / Ireland, Ireland / 137 executions (and not one innocent man) / The little girls love to dance / Willie Jean / Now you're talkin' baby / For the good of America / Mojo and the St Luke's flukes.

Aug 05. (cd) *<4034> (BRAM 200502-2)* **A TALE OF TWO AMERICAS** Apr 05
- Ray and Ron / Terror / Missing / The governator / Beloved enemy / Smoke / Treat you right / I'm your dad / The lucky ones / Don't let your dim light die / Sacrifice / Peace / Here I stand *[US-only]* / True love / A tale of two Americas / Love is the common ground / I am Bob Dylan / With God on our side.

Blue Flute — Brambus

Feb 09. (cd) *<none> (BRAM 200840-2)* **AFTER THE WAR** (Euro title 'THIS ONE') Sep 08
- Opening disclaimer / Stop the war / For the people / Days of rain / Two Americans / The coming of the snow / Ballerina / After the war / American Jerusalem / Soldiers / Half heaven half heartache / I'll walk in the Highlands / After the spring / White buffalo / Wings of light / Every living thing / (untitled).

May 11. (cd) *<none>* **SONGS OF FREEDOM**
- Springtime in America / Google me baby / Big money / Freedom of religion / Election night at Walmart / The belly button song / True to the blues / Learning to crawl / When you were two / One good song / Moron radio / Why it's so / Open up your world / John King / Watching the birds / Just because.

- (5-7*) compilations, others, etc.-

1997. (c) *Blue Flute; <A1>* **SOME TUNES FROM THE 1970s:** (solo studio and live on WBAI)
- Fifty one years ago / Here comes the clones / Three Russian violinists / La rue de la fortune / Look homeward boy / Baby blue / A man called Alias / Misery walks the streets tonight / Miles the frog / The face of the sun / Bury me deep / Children of paradise / All done in his name.

1997. (c) *Blue Flute; <A4>* **LIVE AT THE SPEAKEASY** (live 1983–85)
- Meet me baby (after the bombs do fall) / The unearthly fire / Ode to the pretty girls / Baby glows in the dark / Song of my brothers / American Jerusalem / Rockabilly wedding / Nothing / The man with the hired face / Real Americans / Mojo and the St Luke's flukes / (I left my heart on) MacDougal Street.

1997. (c) *Blue Flute; <A5>* **LIVE AT THE UPTOWN COFFEEHOUSE + 3** (live at WSHU-FM, February 1994)

1997. (cd) *Blue Flute; <A6>* **LEE HARVEY, THE MICRODOTS AND ME:** various recordings 1991–96
- You swallowed the lie / Hollywood movie / The ballad of Lee Harvey Oswald / Here's a pretty girl / The aliens came in business suits / The contract on America / Too much fun / Little black pearls / The American way.

2000. (cd-r) *Rod Macdonald; <none>* **HOUSE CONCERT** (live in Cadeberge, Germany, spring 1998) self
- I can't believe (how good you've been to me) / Keeper of the flame / Some things I like about America / Ballad of a black haired man / The death of Victor Jara / After the singing / A sailor's prayer / Up on the mountain / The aliens came in business suits / Dallas / Man on the ledge / I'll walk in the highlands.

2002. (cd-r) *Rod Macdonald; <none>* **THE ORIGINAL ROD MACDONALD BAND 1976–1978** self
- The night's still on our side / Ballerina / Sleepless nights / Island / Memories (ain't

what they used to be) / Somebody waiting / All of the same ole saviours / City lights / Hard times / The ballad of Ernesto Miranda / (I don't believe) You don't wanna dance.

2003. (cd-r) *Rod Macdonald; <none>* **GUILTY PLEASURES** (unreleased tracks from 1991–2000) — self —
- Now is the time / I hope you understand / The perfect stranger / The rain / My last days of Monique / So long, love / True love / Minstrel boy / I remember you / Open up your world / Maggie.

2004. (cd-r) *Rod Macdonald; <none>* **LIVE AT THE OUTPOST IN THE BURBS** (live in Montclair, NY, November 7th, 2003) — self —
- Dr Gachet / You who sleep beside me / Why I love America / Blues for the river / Dear grandfather / Sleeping on the beach / American Jerusalem / Terror / White buffalo / I am Bob Dylan / Open up your world / For the good of America / My neighbors in Delray / A sailor's prayer / Seven days.

2004. (cd-r) *Rod Macdonald; <none>* **FESTIVAL** (live at the Florida Folk Festival, May 25, 2003 // + Tucson Folk Festival, May 1, 2004) — self —
- Aucilla river song / My neighbors in Delray / Seven days / Stop the war / On the road in NY town // For the good of America / You who sleep beside me / The governor / White buffalo / I am Bob Dylan.

2004. (cd-r) *Rod Macdonald; <none>* **LIVE AT THE MAIN ST CAFÉ: HOMESTEAD, FL. 9/11/03** — self —
- Intro / You who sleep beside me / American Jerusalem / Black haired man / My beloved enemy / My neighbors in Delray / On any old Sunday / I am Bob Dylan / Deep down in the Everglades / Highlands / Stop the war / Terror / Hiroshima / For the good of America / A sailor's prayer / Victor Jara / Every living thing.

2007. (cd; as BIG BRASS BED) *Solstice; <none>* **A FEW DYLAN SONGS** — own —
- From a Buick 6 / One more cup of coffee / Subterranean homesick blues / Mississippi / Don't think twice, it's all right / She belongs to me / Ballad of a thin man / Shelter from the storm / Just like Tom Thumb's blues / Lay lady lay / Licence to kill.

Kate MacLEOD

Striking, flame-haired country/blues-folk singer/songwriter KATE MacLEOD (b. March 8, 1961 in Baltimore, Maryland) has crossed into Celtic and pop territory on more than one occasion. Moving from Washington D.C. to Salt Lake City at 19, she spent the whole of the 1980s and then some tutoring youngsters at Peter Prier's Violin Making School of America. Not only an accomplished fiddler, she was also adept on guitar and harmonica.

Early in 1995 she was given a scholarship to attend the Folk Alliance Conference in Portland, Oregon, and there she met ANDREW CALHOUN, who helped her get a recording contract. There was echoes of DYLAN, JONI MITCHELL and JEAN RITCHIE on her promising debut set, **TRYING TO GET IT RIGHT** (1995) {*7} - she covered Jean's 'None But One' - and picturesque Americana was represented by 'Alaska', 'Alabama Midwife' and 'Welfare Line'.

Her second album for Chicago's Waterbug label, **CONSTANT EMOTION** (1997) {*7}, assured listeners she was no one-trick pony; sunny-day tracks such as 'Talkin' About Good News' and 'The Red And Green House' were matched by her interpretation of BUFFY SAINTE-MARIE's 'The Piney Wood Hills'. The pattern and formula were maintained when Kate covered Mary McCaslin's 'Way Out West' on her long-awaited third album, **FEEL THE EARTH SPIN** (2001) {*6}.

As a sideline to her solo work, Kate was also a member of the Utah-based Celtic outfit Shanahy, who released three albums, 'Trip To Ballymena' (1995), 'Far Away' (1999) and 'A Fair Land Lies Before Me' (2004). The Celtic association, and her friendship with collaborator KAT EGGLESTON, continued on **DRAWN FROM THE WELL** (2002) {*7}, a beautifully crafted, trad-biased set that housed ghostly gothic gems in 'Good Ship In Order' and her own instrumental title track.

Her fourth solo album, **BREAKFAST** (2005) {*6}, with backing band The Pancakes (Mark Hazel on vocals and guitars, Barry Carter on acoustic bass and Cliff Smith on percussion), showed just why she was such an in-demand artist. The set featured covers including DYLAN's 'Time Passes Slowly' and JACK HARDY's 'Forget Me Nots', plus several trad standards including 'The Greenwood Side', 'Prodigal Son' and 'Gartan Mother's Lullaby'.

2009's **BLOOMING** {*6} followed a more compositional path, albeit with one cover, 'The Inner Man', another JACK HARDY song. Kate and KAT EGGLESTON celebrated Waterbug's 100th release with the joint effort **LOST AND FOUND** (2011) {*7}, which was steeped in American and British tradition, although just what their revamp of Abba's 'Chiquitita' was doing there was anybody's guess. Somehow it worked, though, as did the sourced tracks, their own individual compositions and Burns's 'Rantin Rovin' Robin', JEAN RITCHIE's 'None But One' and ANDREW CALHOUN's 'The Living And The Breathing Wind'. *MCS*

Kate MacLeod - vocals, guitars, fiddle, harmonica

US Waterbug — UK not issued

Jul 95. (cd) *<WBG-17>* **TRYING TO GET IT RIGHT**
- Lark in the morning / Alaska / Angels on my mind / Me and my medicine / Prairyerth / Pawn shop man / Welfare line / Alabama midwife / Play the piano with style / Some things are easy / Gospel songs / None but one.

Aug 97. (cd) *<WBG-32>* **CONSTANT EMOTION**
- Constant emotion / Talkin' about good news / Long ride home / My forsaken love / Adam / New song / A long time ago / Second chance at romance / The Piney Wood hills / The red and green house / The child / Green.

Wind River — not issued

Oct 01. (cd) *<WR 4020CD>* **FEEL THE EARTH SPIN**
- Potter's wheel / Way out west / My baby leaving / Wild birds / Cliffhanger / My unclaimed love / Shadow changes / Beautiful flowers / The annual Menhaden / Winter love / Revelation #1.

Oct 02. (cd; by KATE MacLEOD & KAT EGGLESTON) *<WR 4023CD>* **DRAWN FROM THE WELL**
- Good ship in order / Drawn from the well / The annual menhaden / Measure for measure / Kitty's rambles / Tom Egan / The beverage set: Coffey's reel - A cup of tea - The Kylebrack rambler / Go to the water / Give me your hand / Over the moor to Maggie / The two sisters / New homeland.

Waterbug — not issued

Apr 05. (cd; as KATE MACLEOD and the PANCAKES) *<WBG-63>* **BREAKFAST**
- Thirst quencher / Potter's wheel / No more cane / Forget me nots / Autumn / Love is gone / Gartan mother's lullaby / Whole world round / Handsome Molly / Prodigal son / The Greenwood side / Balmy song / Time passes slowly.

Jun 08. (dl-s) <-> WYOMING DOVE

Oct 09. (cd) *<WBG-89>* **BLOOMING**
- The day is mine / Blooming / Where the magic happens / Riding the white horse home / Road to heaven / Branded heart / Something left you living / My Teton home / Return to Rawlins / The inner man / A smile worth a million / As far as the heart can see.

Jun 11. (cd; by KATE MacLEOD and KAT EGGLESTON) *<WBG-100>* **LOST AND FOUND**
- Sometimes a sound / Rain / The cliffs of Moher / Lark in the morning / Africa / Bluehill / Rantin' rovin' Robin / None but one / My forsaken love / Cattle in the cane - The growlin' old man and the growlin' old woman / The living and the breathing wind / Out on the ocean - Willie Coleman's / History man - Sanctuary / Chiquitita.

MAJOR MATT MASON USA

This is the nom de guerre of Kansas-born Matt Roth (not to be confused with another Major Matt Mason, a rock quartet), an urban anti-folk singer/songwriter who took the name from a popular Mattel action toy figure of the 1950s. The real Matt also led two comparatively conventional indie-rock acts, Schwervon! (with girlfriend Nan Turner) and the trio Kansas State Flower (alongside Julie DeLano of The Leader and Christy Davis of Mold, etc) before recording his solo debut **ME ME ME** (1999) {*7}.

Inspired by Daniel Johnston, the prince of lo-fi indie-pop (he would cover Johnston's 'Mind Controlled' on the 2006 various-artists set 'I Killed A Monster'), Matt was already an established player on New York's Lower East Side, and his simple pop sensibility and bare-bones production echoed peers such as Jonathan Richman and Violent Femmes, rather than The MOLDY PEACHES or JEFFREY LEWIS.

Further Olive Juice recordings (it was his own imprint) were licensed to Shoeshine for release in the UK, and albums such as **HONEY, ARE YOU READY FOR THE BALLET?** (2002) {*6} and **BAD PEOPLE RULE THE WORLD** (2004) {*6} contained some wonderful song titles (if not songs), such as 'Mittens' and 'I Love Stevie Nicks'. His most recent release was the CD-r **SENILE PIE STRIVE PIP MELANCHOLY** (2007). *MCS*

Matt Roth - vocals, acoustic guitar

US HC — UK not issued

1994. (7"; as MAJOR MATT MASON) *<HC 005>* THE LOBSTER SONG. / Mr Mrs Something

Olive Juice — Shoeshine

1999. (cd) *<OJ-0004> (SHOECD 008)* **ME ME ME** — Jan 02
- Mr Softie / Budapest / Rockstar / The ballad of Danny Scheer / Inside of you / Black hole / I know you know / Rose paned glasses / Price is right / Apple sauce / I'm sorry / Goodbye southern death swing / Kicker / Krooklyn / Waitress song / Plutonium.

2001. (cd-r) *<OJ-0009>* **RIVINGTON '94 AND THE TOWER DAYS**

- Uptown / Everything / Thank you, no / Riff / Downtown / Ned the bed head / Uh / U is A / Frog legs / Telephone / Do nothing / 5th of July / Girlfriend / Tower song.

2001. (shared-7") *<OJ-0011>* THE DOG SONG. / [others by Army Of Ants + Farmer's Market]

Oct 02. (cd) *<OJ-0023> (SHOECD 014)* **HONEY, ARE YOU READY FOR THE BALLET?**
- Shark attack / Misdirected / Follow her / You're a girl / Mittens / Hunted / Pet rock / Tow the line / Lame / Surface depth / It's all you. *<US+=>* - 808 / Lost weekend / Thar she blows.

May 04. (cd) *<OJ-0037> (SHOECD 019)* **BAD PEOPLE RULE THE WORLD**
- Your biggest fan / Simone / Starbelly (slow) / Sidewalker / Good(bye) / The world is not against you / I love Stevie Nicks / Starbelly (fast) / Munich / Tower song / Animal shelter.

Jan 07. (cd-r) *<OJ/0064>* **SENILE PIE STRIVE PIP MELANCHOLY**
- Poor school / 1,000 ice creams / Ladies night / Tripping yourself / Turnstile blues (NEIL YOUNG) / Something in my eye / Moderoto / Hurting you hurting me / Caprian pervert / Way home / 333.

Dan MANGAN

NICE, NICE, VERY NICE (2009) {*7} - the title of his second set - well describes newbie folk singer/songwriter Daniel Mangan (b. April 28, 1983 in Smithers, British Columbia), the Canadian equivalent of DAMIEN RICE or BON IVER. The album itself was as autumnal as it was organic and introspective, 'Robots', 'You Silly Git' and 'Pine For Cedars' reflecting his quirky identity at the time.

His self-financed debut album, **POSTCARDS AND DAYDREAMING** (2005) {*7}, featuring backing vocals by Amy Arsenault and instrumental accompaniment by Daniel Elmes and Simon Kelly, finally achieved an official US release in 2007, and world tours boosted his fan base. At the stage his dulcet vocals and finger-picking guitar licks were very reminiscent of NICK DRAKE on tracks such as 'Unnatural Progression', 'Journal Of A Narcoleptic' and 'Western Wind'.

With numerous festival appearances set up for the summer of 2011 to promote his third album, 'Oh Fortune' (scheduled for September), he'll probably have become one of the top stars by the time you read this. *MCS*

Dan Mangan - vocals, acoustic guitar, piano / + session people/band

US/Can: Dan Mangan — UK: not issued

2003. (cd-ep) *<none>* ALL AT ONCE — Canada

Oct 05. (cd) *<DMCD 00015>* **POSTCARDS AND DAYDREAMING** — Canada
- Not what you think it is / Unnatural progression / Above the headlights / Journal of a narcoleptic / Don't listen / So much for everyone / Western wind / West 8th / Fabulous / Come down / Some place to come home to / Reason to think aloud. *<re-iss. on File Under: Music+=; FUM 001>* - Ash babe *[extended]*.

File Under: Music — not issued

Mar 09. (cd-ep) *<FUM 005>* ROBOTEERING EP — Canada
- Robots / The indie queens are waiting / Sold / Till I fall / Tragic turn of events - Move pen move.

Aug 09. (cd/lp) *<FUM 06/008>* **NICE, NICE, VERY NICE** — Canada
- Road regrets / Robots / The indie queens are waiting / Sold / Fair Verona / You silly git / Tina's glorious comeback / Et les mots croises / Some people / Pine for cedars / Basket / Set the sails. *<(cd+lp re-iss. Aug10/Nov10 on Arts And Crafts; A&C 055)>*

Roger MANNING

Not to be confused with the Roger Joseph Manning, Jr who played a part in alt-popsters Jellyfish, Imperial Drag and The Moog Cookbook, this ROGER MANNING was a 1980s/90s New York City anti-folk artist often allied with LACH and others.

Confrontational but almost amiable, political but not in-your-face, activist Roger busked the streets and subways of New York while his association with leftist punk band Missing Foundation (on his pseudonymous "Joe Folk" cassette) raged against the machine. MANNING's best and probably most creative period arrived in the late 1980s, when Black Flag's Greg Ginn signed him to his seminal hardcore-punk imprint SST, a label not known as a centre of the anti-folk movement. The **ROGER MANNING** (1988) {*7} set drew comparisons with DYLAN, but Roger's sideways haircut relayed a different prospectus. It wasn't exactly the blues, although every song had that word in its title, but 'The #14 Blues', 'The Pearly Blues' and 'The Airport Blues' stood out from the derivative pack.

Just to confuse matters, his follow-up albums were Shimmy Disc's **ROGER MANNING** (1993) {*6} (alternate title 'Soho Valley Boys') and the Moll/Shanachie LP **ROGER MANNING** (1995) {*6}. Both were misfiled in many stores as re-issues of his SST debut. However, the picture becomes clearer on listening, with real gems inside such as the trad 'Gallows Pole' and numerous variant takes of 'The Pearly Blues', 'The Driving Blues' and 'The Hitchhiker Blues'.

MANNING continues on the fringes of folk performance, albeit only as a guest player, as he spends most of his time writing books and designing websites. *MCS*

Roger Manning - vocals, acoustic guitar, snare drum

US: SST — UK: SST

Dec 88. (lp/c/cd) *<(SST 203 LP/CA/CD)>* **ROGER MANNING**
- The #14 blues / The pearly blues / The lefty rhetoric blues / The hitchhiker blues / The west valley blues / Strange little blues / The airport blues / The #16 blues / The #17 blues / Blues for the chosen few / The 1010 blues / The Sicilian train blues.

Shimmy Disc — Shimmy Disc

Aug 93. (cd/c/lp) *<(SHIMMY 067 CD/MC/LP)>* **ROGER MANNING (SOHO VALLEY BOYS)**
- The busybody blues (E. 5th St blues) / Take back the night / The #19 blues (Pearly blues #3) / The hitchhiker blues No.2 (Pearly blues No.3) / Traitors? / The radical blues / Speaker phone / The Perisa blues / Unrequited / The Waterloo blues / The subway blues No.2 / Waterloo calling - Parade account / The Pacifica blues / The Dallas blues / The serious blues (No.18 blues) / Tompkins Square blues No.99 / Gallows pole / Sub-folk.

not issued — Moll

Jan 95. (cd) *(Moll 10)* **ROGER MANNING** — German
- Grand Teton blues / The driving blues / The pearly blues #6 / Loisaida covers Billy syndrome / The Bohemia blues / The East 5th St blues #5 / The war museum blues / The driving blues #2 / The driving blues #3 / The rear view mirror blues / The pearly blues #8 / The hitchhiker blues #5 (Midnight blues) / The hitchhiker blues #4 / The projection blues / Homer's backyard / The I.O.S. blues #2 / The hitchhiker blues #3. *<(US/UK-iss. Feb 97 on Shanachie; SHANCD 5718)>*

—Roger retired from music to be a web designer

Leigh MARBLE

New England-raised anti-folk singer/songwriter and Brown University graduate LEIGH MARBLE (born around1978) ventured to Portland, Oregon with demo in hand. Aided by local producer Larry Crane (who has worked with The DECEMBERISTS, Elliott Smith, etc), Leigh's first release was a shared 7" with fellow alt-folkster ERIN McKEOWN, 'Blankets For Two'. A sidetrack with cheeky rappers The Buttery Lords took up precious time post-millennium.

Recorded in 2003, **PEEP** {*6} materialised in 2004 on his own Laughing Stock label. 'A Rock From The Sky' and 'Unwound' were arguably his best here, and a touring backing band of Ben Macy (accordion/keyboards) and Jason Russell (drums) came along for subsequent live shows. **RED TORNADO** (2007) {*7} staked his claim in the indie-folk market with a Beck-meets-freak album that fitted into the outer fringes of the genre like most modern-day folkies' records - acoustic, Americana and assorted. Typical were 'Lucky Bastards', 'On Your Way' and 'Strip The Bed'. *MCS*

Leigh Marble - vocals, guitars / + band

US: Anticipation et Denouement — UK: not issued

1999. (7" shared) *<none>* BLANKETS FOR TWO. / [Erin McKeown track]

Laughing Stock — not issued

Nov 04. (cd) *<LSR 003>* **PEEP**
- A rock from the sky / Killed instantly / Pale blue / Long overdue / Unwound / Parting shot / Five years / Focus / Peep / Two pairs / Airlift / Last chance.

Nov 07. (cd) *<LSR 005>* **RED TORNADO**
- Lucky bastards / On your way / Salt in the wound / Fast and loose / Baby Ruth / So far / Get yours / The big words / Gave it all / Stakes / Strip the bed.

Oct 08. (dl-s) <-> INEBRIATE WALTZ — net

Oct 08. (mp3) <-> **TWISTER [remixes]** — net
- Salt in the wound [alabaster variation] / On your way [math lab remix] / Strip the bed [one eyed mix] / Fast and loose [live bootleg 1966] / Lucky bastards [King County jail dub] / Gave it all [chamber dub remix].

Mar 10. (mp3; as LEIGH MARBLE + THE ASCETIC JUNKIES) <-> LEIGH & THE LOLLIPOPS — net
- On your way / Lucky bastards.

Dec 10. (mp3; as DR MARBLE) <-> REMIXES [other artists] — net

Willy MASON

One of the new breed of rootsy fringe-folk artists drawing on a range of rebellious inspirations such as DYLAN, Costello and Cobain, WILLY MASON (b. November 21, 1984 in Martha's Vineyard, MA) was discovered on a local radio show, aged 19, by Conor Oberst associate Sean Foley. Like so many alt-rockers, MASON made his performance debut in a poorly-attended gig at the South By Southwest festival in Austin, Texas, but one person in the audience, BBC Radio 1 DJ Zane Lowe, found him interesting enough to add one of his songs, 'Oxygen', to his playlist.

Released as a single for Virgin Records in the UK (and Astralwerks at home), it almost hit the Top 20, helping its parent album, **WHERE THE HUMANS EAT** (2004) {*7} to sneak a Top 40 placing - gawky geek-rock was making a comeback. Speaking of parents, his mother has performed with him on a few recordings.

Not building much on his previous set, **IF THE OCEAN GETS ROUGH** (2007) {*7} still managed to crack the UK Top 40 again. What shone through on this album were his playful melodies and harmonies, structured in many ways like blues/trad pieces of old, though all the songs were his own compositions, highlighted by 'Gotta Keep Walking', 'We Can Be Strong' and 'Simple Town'. His next release is expected in late 2011. *MCS*

Willy Mason - vocals, acoustic guitar

US: G-Ma's Basement / UK: not issued

Jul 04. (cd-ep) UNTITLED EP [–] net [–]
- Live it up / Hard hand to hold / Waiter at the station / Not lie down / Oxygen.

US: Astralwerks / UK: Virgin

Oct 04. (cd/lp) *<ASW 75377> (CD+/V 2993)* **WHERE THE HUMANS EAT** [ ] [38]
- Gotta keep moving / All you can do / Still a fly / Where the humans eat / Fear no pain / Hard hand to hold / Letter No.1 / Sold my soul / Our town / So long / Oxygen / 21st century boy. *<US cd+=>* - Oxygen [video] / So long [video]. <lp-iss.on Team Love; TL-02>

Feb 05. (ltd-etched-7") *(VS 1892)* OXYGEN [–] [23]
(cd-s+=) *(VSCDX 1892)* - Into tomorrow / Not lie down / ['A'-CD-rom].

Apr 05. (ltd-etched-7") *(VS 1898)* SO LONG [live] [–] [45]
(cd-s) *(VSCDX 1898)* - ['A'-studio] / Into tomorrow [electric] / Harvesting digital children / ['A'-video].

2005. (cd-ep) *(VSCDX 1903)* HARD TO LIE DOWN EP [–] [ ]
- Hard hand to hold / [live from Glastonbury 2005]: Wild dog blues / Live it up / Oxygen / When the river moves on.

Feb 07. (7") *(VS 1928)* SAVE MYSELF. / Baby, Why? [–] [42]
(7") *(VSX 1928)* - ['A'-live acoustic version] / Mosquitoes.
(cd-s) *(VSCDT 1928)* - ['A'] / Take control.

Mar 07. (cd) *<3 83905 2> (CDV 3029)* **IF THE OCEAN GETS ROUGH** [ ] [33]
- Gotta keep walking / The world that I wanted / We can be strong / Save myself / I can't sleep / Riptide / When the river moves on / If the ocean gets rough / Simple town / The end of the race / When the leaves have fallen.

—— next single featured KT TUNSTALL

May 07. (7") *(VS 1939)* WE CAN BE STRONG. / What's So Bad About Being Bad [–] [52]
(7") *(VSX 1939)* - ['A'-alt.] / Not enough.
(cd-s) *(VSCDT 1939)* - ['A'] / Belly of the whale.

US: Team Love / UK: not issued

2009. (mp3) *<none>* POUGHKEEPSIE SESSION EP [–] net [–]
- Hard hand to hold / Restless fugitive / One simple thing / If it's the end / Goodbye.

——rumoured to be about to release his long-awaited third set in 2011

David MASSENGILL

Many folkies may know the song 'On The Road To Fairfax County' (made famous in recordings by JOAN BAEZ and The ROCHES), but not so many will recall its writer, DAVID MASSENGILL, unless they have his first solo album, **COMING UP FOR AIR** (1992) {*7}.

Born in 1951 in Bristol, Tennessee, the singer/songwriter first came to prominence (however minor) in The Folk Brothers, a New York duo with fellow 'Fast Folk' graduate JACK HARDY. A rising star in that community, he laid down several tracks for various-artists sets, and the self-financed 'The Great American Bootleg Tape' and 'The Kitchen Tape' also surfaced in the mid-1980s. He signed a deal with Flying Fish in the early 1990s, issuing the aforementioned debut, which included great story songs such as 'My Name Joe', 'Don Quixote's Lullaby' and 'On The Road To Fairfax County'.

Adept with dulcimer as well as acoustic guitar, MASSENGILL moved to the Plump label for follow-ups **THE RETURN** (1995) {*6} and **TWILIGHT THE TAJ MAHAL** (1998) {*7}, the latter highlighting two spoken-word readings of letters by himself (as a child) and his great-grandfather.

MY HOME MUST BE A SPECIAL PLACE (2002) {*6} and **WE WILL BE TOGETHER** (2006) {*6} preceded his tribute album to one of his heroes, DAVE VAN RONK (who died in 2002), **DAVE ON DAVE** (2007) {*6}. As well as originals and trad arrangements from the VAN RONK songbook, it featured a few of MASSENGILL's own, including the affectionate 'Talkin' Dave Van Ronk Blues'. *MCS*

David Massengill - vocals, acoustic guitar, dulcimer

US: Bowser Wowser / UK: not issued

1986. (c) *<none>* THE GREAT AMERICAN BOOTLEG TAPE (live) [ ] [–]

1987. (c) *<none>* THE KITCHEN TAPE (demos) [ ] [–]

US: Flying Fish / UK: Flying Fish

1992. (cd) *<(FF 590CD)>* **COMING UP FOR AIR** [ ] Apr 94 [ ]
- My name Joe / On the road to Fairfax County / Number one in America / Coming up for air / Don Quixote's lullaby / Like a big wheel (you make me feel) / Where has my true love gone? / A notable social event - The debutantes' ball / Contrary Mary / It's a beautiful world.

US: Plump / UK: Plump

Oct 95. (cd) *<5903> (PLUCD 5)* **THE RETURN** [ ] Jun 96 [ ]
- Rider on an orphan train / Medley: Blind man - Black swan / The great American dream / Fireball's last ride / Perfect love / Wake up / The return / Sightseer / Madou / Jesus, the fugitive prince / What's wrong with the man upstairs / A girl's daring escape.

Sep 98. (cd) *<8901>* **TWILIGHT THE TAJ MAHAL** [ ] [–]
- The fugitive / Twilight the Taj Mahal / One for the loons / The whittlin' boy / Evangeline / Once upon a time in Jefferson / Our lady of Shinbone Alley / Sierra Blanca massacre / Down Derry down / Nothing / Rats and bats and the spring water / Mrs Howard's elementary waltz.

US: Gadfly / UK: not issued

Aug 02. (cd) *<Gadfly 281>* **MY HOME MUST BE A SPECIAL PLACE** [ ] [–]
- Prologue: The first time my father saw my mother / The girl from Nebraska / My first kiss / Shamas rides / The great Holston mountain rescue of 1954 / My home must be a special place / Culture hurts / Cousin Jackie and Mamaw's hedges / Mrs Credle was my first love / Aunt Fannie and the Yankees / Where did Miss Nancy Sterett go? / Frank Goodpasture had a pony / My hometown / Epilogue: Old letters in a rolltop desk.

Jul 06. (cd) *<Gadfly 293>* **WE WILL BE TOGETHER** [ ] [–]
- To climb a tree / A valentine for her highness / We will be together / Talkin' Dave Van Ronk blues / Tell old Bill / Forever love / Family reunion / Rainchild / Morgana the pirate queen / Jack and the beanstalk / Scratchee goes a-wooing / Dave Van Ronk's last cigar / Somebody else not me / A tree romance / Killer Keller's last stand / Penley at the wheel / The fairy's code / The gambler-in-chief / Used to be.

Oct 07. (cd) *<Gadfly 295>* **DAVE ON DAVE: A TRIBUTE TO DAVE VAN RONK BY DAVID MASSENGILL** [ ] [–]
- Tell old Bill / Candy man blues / House of the rising sun / Talkin' Dave Van Ronk blues / Another time and place / Green, green rocky road / The old man / Somebody else not me / The song of the wandering Angus / My good old friend / Long John / Dink's song / Dave Van Ronk's last cigar / Zen Koans gonna rise again / Honey hair / He was a friend of mine / In conditional support of beauty / Last call.

—— In 2008, as The Folk Brothers, DAVID MASSENGILL and JACK HARDY released the 'Partners In Crime' set.

Kate McDONNELL

Born in Baltimore, Maryland, singer/songwriter and upside-down-guitar player KATE McDONNELL began her career in twin duo Katie and Anne McDonnell before she broke away to form the late-1980s New England-based duo McDonnell-Tane. It's uncertain whether that act released any albums.

Working in various jobs by day and playing gigs in McDonnell-Tane at night (they opened for DYLAN, ARLO GUTHRIE, Kathy Mattea, LEO KOTTKE and SUZANNE VEGA), Kate also moonlighted in New Haven a-cappella trio Colossal Olive alongside funny girls Alison Farrell and Cara Burgarella. At a time when she was the toast of the Kerrville Folk Festival (she won it in 1995), she signed with ANDREW CALHOUN's Waterbug label, which re-released her self-financed debut of 1994, **BROKEN BONES** {*6}, in 1996. A promising start, its highlights were the easy-going 'Wishbone', 'Drink The Rain' and Dill & Wilkin's 'Long Black Veil' (better known to CHIEFTAINS fans).

NEXT (1998) {*6} featured Dewey Burns's 'Just How Long' alongside Joan BAEZ-type gems like 'Enola Gay' and 'Dong's Odyssey'. **DON'T GET ME STARTED** (2001) {*5} was released on her own Dog-Eared Discs label. **WHERE THE MANGOES ARE** (2005) {*8}, issued on twilight folk label Appleseed and her last album thus far, took her to new, rootsy horizons, her electric backing band of Marc Shulman (guitar), Scott Petito (bass), Sam Brewton (drums) and Mindy Jostyn (violin, harmonica and accordion) lifting here above the parapet of minor folk stardom. Hopefully it won't be her last, as songs like 'Tumbleweed', 'Hey Joe' (not the much-covered blues, but very close), 'Fires', 'Mercy' and the psychedelic 'Lemon Marmalade' were McDONNELL at her lyrical best. The traditional 'Railroad Bill' and a version of Steve Earle's 'Goodbye Song' were others to die for. *MCS*

Kate McDonnell - vocals, acoustic guitar (+ session players)

US own label — UK not issued

1994. (cd) <*none*> **BROKEN BONES**
- Wishbone / Anything that runs / Ordinary man / Seeking passage / Falling down / The last time Robbie called me / Long black veil / Long time / New England blues / Car broke down on memory lane / Letter from Rose Greenhow / Drink the rain. <*re-iss. Jan 96 on Waterbug; WBGCD-20*>

Waterbug — Waterbug

Feb 98. (cd) <*(WBGCD-38)*> **NEXT** — Mar 98
- If I knew / Tangerine shirt / Lines / Baltimore / Our love / Looking down for looking up / Enola Gay / Secret / Dong's odyssey / Don't fix my faucet / Just how long / I just assumed / Time and time again.

Dog-Eared Discs — Brambus

2001. (cd) <*none*> *(BRAMBUS 200142-2)* **DON'T GET ME STARTED** — Apr 05
- Don't get me started / Give it back / Gone / You're wrong / Toss it to the wind / Sticky buns / Take me home / Banks of the Ohio / Will you be leaving / What good will it do? / Back to home.

Appleseed — Appleseed

Feb 05. (cd) <*(APRCD 1085)*> **WHERE THE MANGOES ARE** — Mar 05
- Tumbleweed / Hey Joe / Go down Moses / Mercy / 5:05 / Fires / Railroad Bill / Lemon marmalade / Luis / Mayday / Goodbye song / Softhearted girl.

Megon (Megan) McDONOUGH

Though overlooked by many (as in Volume I of this Discography), Megon's contribution to folk music should never be understated, though her part in FOUR BITCHIN' BABES has given her some well-deserved time in the spotlight. Born in 1955 in Chicago, one of nine children of an Irish-Catholic family, Megan (as she was then called) released four LPs for the Wooden Nickel label, while tours supporting JOHN DENVER and Harry Chapin kept her profile reasonably high. She also branched into country-pop, most noticeably on her 1979 effort **IF I COULD ONLY REACH YOU** {*4}.

However, it was her move to New York and her name change to Megon (a fortune-teller had predicted the o would bring her success) that led to greater things. From solo albums to working with the FOUR BITCHIN' BABES and appearing as Patsy Cline in a theatre musical, the 1990s were good times for her. **AMERICAN GIRL** (1990) {*7} found a bridge between contemporary country-folk and slick MOR/showtime-pop with songs like Lennon-McCartney's 'I'm Looking Through You' and a couple by MICHAEL SMITH. McDONOUGH can turn her voice to any old standard, and it's a pity she seems to have turned her back on folk music. *MCS*

Megan McDonough - vocals, acoustic guitar (+ session players)

US Wooden Nickel — UK RCA

1971. (lp; as MEGAN McDONOUGH) <*WNS-1004*> **IN THE MEGAN MANNER**
- Pocketful / Vintage / Part I / Kevin Jane / Guitar picker / Part II / Peacemakers / Room and board / Part III / Stay in touch / Comin' down easy / On the shores of your tomorrow / Don't worry mama / Song without a story / Next.

1972. (lp; as MEGAN McDONOUGH) <*WNS-1007*> *(SF 8337)* **MEGAN MUSIC**
- Lady in love / Second avenues / No return / Eulogy for a rock 'n' roll band / California cowboy / Dark cafes / Broken guitar / All time heartbreak / Let me sing the blues / Dirty dishes / The words all around.

1973. (lp; as MEGAN McDONOUGH) <*BWL1-0145*> **KEEPSAKE**
- Love comes and love goes / Texas motel / Hold on / Daddy always like a lady / Stars / Wishing for you / Where do I go from here? / Chances R / Angry eyes / Not the same woman.

1974. (lp; as MEGAN McDONOUGH) <*BWL1-0499*> **SKETCHES**
- You've turned my head around / Empty spaces / Do me wrong, but do me / Mirror / What am I gonna do? / One woman / Delta shelter / No southern man / Jesus children of America / Rainmaker / Coming on strong.

own label — not issued

1979. (lp; as MEGAN McDONOUGH) <*none*> **IF I COULD ONLY REACH YOU**
- If I could only reach you / Never wanna see it end / I won't be comin' home / Hotline to heaven / Indelibly blue / Lady in love / Too soon to say I love you / The times I've tried / The real thing / Still feel a song comin' on.

Singing Flower — not issued

1989. (c) <*SFM 1*> **DAY BY DAY**
- Everlasting love / Serenity song / Day by day / Heavy the coat / Sunday song / Joy in the journey / Every living thing / Katy's sweet / Oh great spirit / Wake up and dream.

Sirius

Nov 90. (cd) **AMERICAN GIRL**
- American girl / Painless love / I'm looking through you / If love is a dream / Soon enough / River of wishes / But not tonight / Dreams of deep water / Big blue river / Luck of the rodeo.

— it was at this point she helped form FOUR BITCHIN' BABES (alongside PATTY LARKIN, CHRISTINE LAVIN + SALLY FINGERETT)

1993. (cd) **BLUE STAR HIGHWAY**
- Blue star highway / A woman's got her pride / Boots to glory / Denvir / The tree / House of mannequins / Never just one reason / Lesson in every goodbye / The body is a car / Danny boy. <*re-iss. Aug 06 as 'AMAZING THINGS' on In Tune*>

Shanachie — Shanachie

Oct 96. (cd) <*(SHANCD 5027)*> **MY ONE AND ONLY LOVE** — Nov 96
- That's all / Embraceable you / Piano improv / I remember / When I take my sugar to tea / Here's that rainy day / Bass improv / Gee baby, ain't I good to you / You taught my heart to sing / My one and only love / If I had you / Horn improv / A time for love / Losing my mind / Drum improv / It's a wonderful world.

Medicine Wheel — not issued

Nov 02. (cd-ep) <*none*> **4+1: Music Inspired by the Four Agreements by Don Miguel Ruiz**
- Your word is your wand / Don't take it personally / All my assumptions / Amazing things / That's what a menu's all about.

— next with Don Stiernberg

Dec 02. (cd) <*none*> **THE PATSY PROJECT** [Patsy Cline covers]
- Leavin' on your mind / Lovesick blues / Sweet dreams / I fall to pieces / Bill Bailey / Back in baby's arms / Walkin' after midnight / Crazy / Your cheatin' heart / So wrong.

—In 2006 she issued an instructional CD, 'Introductory Yoga'.

In Tune — not issued

Nov 06. (cd) <*none*> **SPIRITS IN THE MATERIAL WORLD**
- Spirits in the material world / Warmth of the sun / I will / Beatle love / The water carrier / In the end / My one and only love / Butter / Ring of fire / Amazing things / People / [Butter on i-pod].

Dec 06. (cd-s) <*none*> AMAZING THINGS / [backtrack]

Erin McKEOWN

Born in 1977 in Northampton, Massachusetts but raised in Fredricksburg, Virginia, intimate singer/songwriter ERIN McKEOWN balanced a career that ran in parallel with the indie scene while keeping a strong foothold in neo-contemporary alt-folk. She studied ethnomusicology at Brown University in the mid-1990s, and she was a semi-finalist in the Mid-Atlantic song contest around the same time.

In a transitional period of developing her talents before entering major-label-land, she started her own label, TVP, and mobilised a stellar backing crew (KATRYNA NIELDS, Beth Amsel and Ben Demerath) to record her promising debut, **MONDAY MORNING COLD** (1999) {*6}. Signature Sounds came in for her appropriately-titled second set, **DISTILLATION** (2000) {*7}, a record that blended roots music (folk, blues and country) into one melodious pot-pourri of anything-goes, featuring a cover of the Tin Pan Alley standard 'You Mustn't Kick It Around'.

The same could be said of **GRAND** (2003) {*5}, her eclectic homage to all of the above and a whole lot more besides. Disappointingly for folk fans, it seemed that the majors (Nettwerk in North America and Parlophone in Britain) had won out in terms of control. It was an different kettle of fish when Tucker Martine produced her next set, the wonderfully contemptuous **WE WILL BECOME LIKE BIRDS** (2005) {*7}, which found her working with PETER MULVEY (on 'Delicate December') and Argentinian Juana Molina (on 'The Golden Dream').

But once again Erin was guided towards nostalgia, and a whole bunch of staples and standards was released on **SING YOU SINNERS** (2006) {*6}. While it was a worthy and admirable attempt at bringing back the good old days of swing, jazz and the classics, discerning folk fans should avoid stuff like 'Paper Moon', 'Get Happy' and 'Just One Of Those Things'; only MICHELLE SHOCKED among folk singers comes to mind as ever attempting this kind of homage. **LAFAYETTE** (2007) {*4} was Erin's live interpretation of the set.

A return to something a bit more contemporary and modern-day was needed, and the answer was an alliance with ANI DiFRANCO at Righteous Babe for **HUNDREDS OF LIONS** (2009) {*6}. This comprised 11 originals firmly rooted in folk, though there was a sprightly Aimee Mann-meets-

Bacharach/David feel about highlights such as 'The Foxes', 'Santa Cruz' and 'The Lions'. Only time will tell her next direction, but whatever that is, this ambitious and talented singer will have exactly what she wants. *MCS*

Erin McKeown - vocals, guitars (with session bands)

US: Anticipation et Denouement — UK: not issued

1999. (7"-shared) <*none*> [Leigh Marble track]. / DAISY AND PRUDENCE — [–]

US: TVP — UK: not issued

Nov 99. (cd) <*TVP 2504CD*> **MONDAY MORNING COLD** — [–]
- Fast as I can [band] / Lullaby in three/four / My hips / Monday morning cold [band] / Easy baby / Softly Moses [band] / Glass / Fast as I can / How to open my heart in four easy steps / Something comes / You don't know.

US: Signature Sounds — UK: Parlophone

Oct 00. (cd) <*SIG 1262*> (*582083-2*) **DISTILLATION** — Feb 03
- Queen of quiet / Blackbirds / Didn't they? / La petit mort / The little cowboy / Daisy and Prudence / Fas as I can / You musn't kick it around / How to open my heart in four easy steps / Dirt gardener / Love in two parts.

Jan 01. (cd-ep) <*SIG 1262a*> QUEEN OF QUIET — [–]
- Queen of quiet [fancy radio mix] / Lullaby / The door / Fast as I can / Queen of quiet.

—— In 2001, Erin was part of Voices On The Verge (alongside Jess Klein, Beth Amsel and ROSE POLENZANI), a country-meets-folk-pop collaboration on the set 'Live In Philadelphia'.

US: Nettwerk — UK: Parlophone

Jun 03. (cd) <*6700 30307 2*> (*591297-2*) **GRAND** — Sep 03
- Slung-lo / Cinematic / The taste of you / Born to hum / Civilians / Envelopes of glassine / How to be a lady / A better wife / Cosmopolitans / Lucky day / An innocent fiction / James! / Starlit / Vera.

Nov 03. (cd-s) (*R 6626*) BORN TO HUM / Slung-Lo [–]

Jun 05. (cd) <*6700 30418 2*> (*330952-2*) **WE WILL BECOME LIKE BIRDS** — Sep 05
- Aspera / Air / Life on the moon / To the stars / Beautiful (I guess) / Float / We are more / White city / The golden dream (feat. JUANA MOLINA) / Bells and bombs / Delicate December (feat. PETER MULVEY) / You were right about everything.

US: Nettwerk — UK: Nettwerk

Oct 06. (cd) <*(6700 30564 2)*> **SING YOU SINNERS** [covers set]
- Get happy / Paper moon / Coucou / Melody / They say it's spring / I was a little too lonely (you were a little too late) / Sing you sinners / Rhode Island is famous for you / Something's gotta give / Just one of those things / If you a viper / Thanks for the boogie ride / Don't worry 'bout me.

US: Signature Sounds — UK: Signature Sounds

Sep 07. (cd) <*(SIG 2007)*> **LAFAYETTE** [live] — Nov 07
- (...the band takes the stage!) / Thanks for the boogie ride / To the stars / You were right about everything / Fast as I can / Melody / James! / We are more / Lullaby in 3/4 / You, sailor / Slung-lo / Blackbirds / (...the band says thank you and goodnight!).

US: Righteouss Babe — UK: Righteous Babe

Oct 09. (cd) <*(RBCD 068)*> **HUNDREDS OF LIONS** — Nov 09
- To a hammer / Santa Cruz / You, sailor / The foxes / (Put the fun back in) The funeral / The lions / All that time you missed / The boats / The rascal / 28 / Seamless.

Natalie MERCHANT

The focal point of detached folk-rock outfit 10,000 MANIACS since 1981, vegetarian NATALIE 'Whirling Dervish' MERCHANT (b. October 26, 1963 in Jamestown, New York) embarked on a solo career in 1993. Over the preceding 12 years her literate songs and distinctive vocals had made the MANIACS one of the most popular alt-rock bands in the business.

Spending over a year in the studio, MERCHANT returned in fine style with her self-produced debut album, **TIGERLILY** (1995) {*8}, an emotive and eclectic collection of songs that stayed high in the US charts for some time. Three singles were lifted from it, 'Carnival', 'Wonder' and Jealousy', all stirring up enough support for Top 30 placings. B-side covers were The Rolling Stones' 'Sympathy For The Devil', JONI MITCHELL's 'All I Want' and a medley of The Ronettes' 'Baby I Love You' with the Dusty Springfield hit 'Son Of A Preacher Man'.

Follow-up effort **OPHELIA** (1998) {*5} was more oblique and impenetrable, a thing of nocturnal beauty enhanced by support from Zairean guitarist Lokua Kanza and Tibetan devotional singer Yungchen Lihamo. Strikingly different from MERCHANT's wonderful performance on that year's WOODY GUTHRIE tribute set 'Mermaid Avenue', it made the US Top 10, but perhaps unsurprisingly, given its introspective depths, failed to make the critical or commercial impact of its predecessor.

LIVE IN CONCERT (1999) {*6} was made up largely of material from her debut, plus covers of David Bowie's 'Space Oddity', NEIL YOUNG's 'After The Gold Rush' and one from her 10,000 MANIACS repertoire, 'Dust Bowl'. She took a completely different tack with producer T-Bone Burnett on the Top 30 **MOTHERLAND** (2001) {*7}, a more solid album with arrangements that played to her vocal strengths. She took an Eastern approach on the likes of 'This House Is On Fire' and the title track, but acoustic folk songs such as 'Tell Yourself', 'I'm Not Gonna Beg' and 'The Ballad Of Henry Darger' (think SANDY DENNY) showed she had indeed returned to her roots.

MERCHANT surprised, confounded and delighted her fans in equal measure with 2003's self-financed **THE HOUSE CARPENTER'S DAUGHTER** {*7}. While long-time fans (especially those who had bought her preceding set and 'Mermaid Avenue') shouldn't have been too shocked to find her doing an album of full-blown folk covers, the arrangements allowed breathing space for her rock roots. It was still a thrill to hear those distinctive, doleful tones carry the weight of traditional songs like 'Weeping Pilgrim', 'Sally Ann' and `Poor Wayfaring Stranger' as well as covers of The CARTER FAMILY's 'Bury Me Under The Weeping Willow' and the true weeper here, FAIRPORT CONVENTION's 'Crazy Man Michael'.

She took a family-life sabbatical to get married to Malaga-based photographer Daniel de la Calle in 2003 and have a baby, Lucia, who no doubt inspired her next project, the lullaby-laden double album **LEAVE YOUR SLEEP** (2010) {*7}. Few childhood concept albums of this kind have crossed over into the mainstream or the charts, but Natalie's powerful and poetic portrayals of anonymous nursery rhymes and sourced material from bygone times produced her most satisfying release to date. And yes, it was folk music again. *MCS*

Natalie Merchant - vocals, piano (with session people)

US: Elektra — US: Elektra

Jun 95. (cd/c) <*(7559 61745-2/-4)*> **TIGERLILY** [13] [39]
- San Andreas fault / Wonder / Beloved wife / River / Carnival / I may know the word / The letter / Cowboy romance / Jealousy / Where I go / Seven years.

Jul 95. (c-s/cd-s) <*4-/2-64413*> (*EKR 203 C/CD*) CARNIVAL / I May Know The Word [10]

Nov 95. (cd-s) <*2-64376*> WONDER / Baby I Love You / Wonder [video] [20] [–]

Apr 96. (c-s/cd-s) (*EKR 217 C/CD1*) WONDER / [live medley]: Baby I Love You - Son Of A Preacher Man / All I Want [–]
(cd-s) (*EKR 217CD2*) - ['A'] / [live]:- Sympathy for the Devil / Take a look / The work song.

May 96. (cd-s) <*2-64301*> JEALOUSY / Sympathy For The Devil [live] [23] [–]

May 98. (cd/c) <*(7559 62196-2/-4)*> **OPHELIA** [8] Jun 98 [52]
- Ophelia / Life is sweet / Kind and generous / Frozen Charlotte / My skin / Break your heart / King of May / Thick as thieves / Effigy / The living / When they ring the golden bells / Ophelia (reprise).

Nov 98. (cd-s) (*E 3831CD*) KIND AND GENEROUS / Frozen Charlotte / Wonder [–]

May 99. (cd-s) (*E 3786CD*) BREAK YOUR HEART / [version] / Carnival [version] [–]

Nov 99. (cd/c) <*62444-2/-4*> (*7559 62479-2/-4*) **LIVE IN CONCERT** [at the Neil Simon Theater, New York City - June 13, 1999] [82]
- Wonder / San Andreas fault / Beloved wife / Space oddity / Carnival / Dust bowl / After the gold rush / Gun shy / The gulf of Araby / Ophelia / Seven years.

Nov 01. (cd) <*(7559 62721-2)*> **MOTHERLAND** [30]
- This house is on fire / Motherland / Saint Judas / Put the law on you / Build a levee / Golden boy / Henry Darger / The worst thing / Tell yourself / Just can't last / Not in this life / I'm not gonna beg.

US: Myth America — UK: Myth America

Sep 03. (cd) <*(MA 1026)*> **THE HOUSE CARPENTER'S DAUGHTER** — Mar 04
- Sally Ann / Which side are you on? / Crazy man Michael / Diver boy / Weeping pilgrim / Soldier, soldier / Bury me under the weeping willow / House carpenter / Owensboro / Down on Penny's farm / Poor wayfaring stranger.

US: Nonesuch — UK: Nonesuch

Apr 10. (d-cd) <*522304-2*> (*7559 79803-9*) **LEAVE YOUR SLEEP** [17] [46]
- [LEAVE YOUR SUPPER]: 1. Nursery rhyme of innocence and experience / 2. Equestrienne / 3. Calico pie / 4. Bleezer's ice-cream / 5. It makes a change / 6. The king of China's daughter / 7. The dancing bear / 8. The man in the wilderness / 9. Maggie and Milly and Molly and May / 10. If no one ever marries me / 11. The sleepy giant / 12. The peppery man / 13. The blind men and the elephant // [LEAVE YOUR SLEEP]: 14. Adventures of Isabel / 15. The walloping window blind / 16. Topsyturvey world / 17. The janitor's boy / 18. Griselda / 19. The land of nod / 20. Vain and careless / 21. Crying, my little one / 22. Sweet and a lullaby / 23. I saw a ship a-sailing / 24. Autumn lullaby / 25. Spring and fall: To a young child / 26. Indian names. (*1-cd iss; 7559 79804-2*) - [tracks 1, 8, 2, 7, 3, 17, 12, 16, 4, 5, 14, 6, 11, 10, 9, 25].

Jul 10. (dl-cd) <-> **iTUNES SESSION** [–]

- (8-10*) compilations -

Sep 05. (cd) *Rhino-Elektra*; <*(R2 73121)*> **RETROSPECTIVE 1990–2005**

- Wonder / Carnival / Jealousy / San Andreas fault / Kind and generous / Break your heart / Life is sweet / The living / Build a levee / Not in this life / Motherland / Owensboro / Sally Ann. <*(deluxe d-cd+=; R2 73122)*> - She devil / Cowboy romance / Children go where I send thee / Birds and ships (with BILLY BRAGG) / The lowlands of Holland (with The CHIEFTAINS) / One fine day / Photograph (with R.E.M.) / Party of God (10,000 MANIACS with BILLY BRAGG) / Thick as thieves / Bread and circuses / Because I could not stop for death (with SUSAN McKEOWN & THE CHANTING HOUSE) / Tell yourself / But not for me / I know how to do it / Come take a trip in my airship.

- essential boxed sets -

Dec 05. (3-cd-box) *Rhino-Elektra; (8122 73312-2)* **TRILOGY** [–] [ ]
- (MOTHERLAND) // (OPHELIA) // (TIGERLILY)

MIDLAKE [folk part]

It would be wrong to think of Denton, Texas collective MIDLAKE as a true and pure folk act, as they have also flirted with being the next Fleetwood Mac (without the girls), America and CROSBY, STILLS, NASH & YOUNG.

Formed by jazz musicians Tim Smith, Eric Pulido, Eric Nichelson and friends, their third album, **THE COURAGE OF OTHERS** (2010) {*7}, has been their only prog-folk set so far, sounding somewhat akin to ESPERS or progsters Camel. Forget previous sets 'Bamnan And Slivercork' (2004) and 'The Trials Of Van Occupanther' (2006); the new and successful MIDLAKE were now Top 20 propositions for the Bella Union stable. Tracks such as 'Acts Of Man', 'Children Of The Grounds', 'In The Ground' and 'Small Mountain' recalled the organic days of gatefold albums with mystical cover art and unfailingly cerebral music. *MCS*

Tim Smith - vocals, guitars, wind, keyboards / **Eric Pulido** - guitars, autoharp, dulcimer, percussion, vocals / **Eric Nichelson** - guitars, autoharp, percussion / **Paul Alexander** - bass, guitar, bassoon / **McKenzie Smith** - drums, percussion

US Bella Union — UK Bella Union

Dec 09. (ltd-12") *(BELLAV 228)* ACTS OF MAN. / Rulers, Ruling All Things [–] [ ]
Feb 10. (cd/d-lp) <*(BELLA CD/V 224)*> **THE COURAGE OF OTHERS** [94] [18]
- Acts of man / Winter dies / Small mountain / Core of nature / Fortune / Rulers, ruling all things / Children of the grounds / Bring down / The horn / The courage of others / In the ground.
Mar 11. (12"-shared) *(ALN12-24)* AM I GOING INSANE. / [Will Self track] [–] [ ]
(above issued on Late Night Tales)

Lynn MILES

Most Canadian folk singer/songwriters have had more than a hint of country and rock about their sound, and LYNN MILES (b. September 29, 1958 in Sweetsburg, Quebec) was no exception. Often likened to NANCI GRIFFITH, SHAWN COLVIN and LUCINDA WILLIAMS, the Ottawa-based singer cut short her stay at Carleton University to take up performing her songs at local bars and coffee-houses.

Self-financing a demo tape to circulate at gigs, MILES (a voice teacher at the Ottawa Folklore Centre at this time) produced her debut album proper, **CHALK THIS ONE UP TO THE MOON** {*6}, in 1991. Although it wasn't on the album (it may have been on her demo tape), her 'Remembrance Day' was used by her country's armed forces on a nationally televised video portraying the sadness of war.

Her multi-octave vocal range helped her win over the Philo label for two further sets, the well-received **SLIGHTLY HAUNTED** (1996) {*7} and **NIGHT IN A STRANGE TOWN** (1999) {*7}, between which she had moved from Nashville to Los Angeles. She reunited with former collaborator Ian LaFeuvre on her fourth set, **UNRAVEL** (2001) {*7}, which won the Juno prize for Best Roots And Traditional Album. This might not have been the best time to take a career break, but **LOVE SWEET LOVE** (2006) {*7} achieved another Juno nomination and was released on Red House in the US. Described by MILES as a 'road album', it marked time (as did her re-recorded songbook, 2010's **BLACK FLOWERS VOLUMES 1 & 2** {*6}) before yet another comeback with 2011's **FALL FOR BEAUTY** {*6}. *MCS*

Lynn Miles - vocals, acoustic guitar (+ session people)

US Snowy River — UK not issued

Oct 91. (cd) <*SRR-S30CD*> **CHALK THIS ONE UP TO THE MOON** [ ] [–]
- All I ever wanted / It's gone / It's hockey night in Canada / I can't tell you why / Whiskey / Roses and intentions / Nobody's angel / A little rain / It'll be here / The Venus motel / Never again / A bell will ring.

Philo — Philo

Feb 96. (cd) <*(CDPH 1190)*> **SLIGHTLY HAUNTED** [ ] Mar 96 [ ]
- You don't love me anymore / I always told you the truth / I loved a cowboy / Loneliness / I know it was love / The ghost of Deadlock / Long time coming / Last night / This heart that lives in winter / Big brown city / I'm still here.
Jan 99. (cd) <*(CDPH 1215)*> **NIGHT IN A STRANGE TOWN** [ ] Sep 98 [ ]
- Anywhere / Middle of the night / The one you're waiting for / Yeah yeah / Beautiful night / Sacre coeur / Wrong / Map of my heart / Perfect romance / Sunset Blvd / Rust.

Okra-Tone Song City — Continental

Jun 99. (cd-ep) *(CRS 9)* SUNSET BLVD [–] [ ]
- Yeah yeah / [live]: Sunset Blvd / The one you're waiting for / [+1].
Sep 01. (cd) <*4967*> *(CSCCD 1022)* **UNRAVEL** [ ] [ ]
- I'm the moon / Now I understand / Undertow / You're not coming back / Over you / When did the world / Unravel / Brave parade / Black flowers / I give up / Surrender Dorothy.
Jul 03. (cd-s) *(CRCDS 22)* UNDERTOW [–] [ ]

Red House Song City — Continental

Feb 06. (cd) <*RHRCD 193*> *(CSCCD 1035)* **LOVE SWEET LOVE** [ ] Jul 05 [ ]
- Flames of love / Love sweet love / 1000 lovers / Trying not to be sad / Never coming back / Night drive / Rainmaker / Eight hour drive / This is the night / Sweet and tender heart / Casinos el camino.

True North — True North

Feb 10. (d-cd) <*(TNCD 531)*> **BLACK FLOWERS VOLUMES 1 & 2** [acoustic re-recorded versions] [ ] Mar 10 [ ]
- A thousand lovers / I give up / Map of my heart / Night drive / You're not coming back / I'm the moon / Over you / Try not to be sad / When my ship comes in // All I ever wanted / Eight hour drive / Rust / Flames of love / Hide your heart / Last night / When did the world / I always told you the truth / Black flowers / The people you love.
Jan 11. (cd) <*(TNCD 533)*> **FALL FOR BEAUTY** [ ] Nov 10 [ ]
- Something beauty / Fearless heart / I will / Three chords and the truth / Cracked and broken / Little bird / Love doesn't hurt / Save me / Goodbye / Time to let the sun.

Bill MILLER

Like folkies BUFFY SAINTE-MARIE and PATRICK SKY before him, singer-songwriter BILL MILLER was a Native American, of Mohican and German parentage. Nature, spirit, God and land combined in his hymnal, New Age music.

Born January 23, 1955 on the Stockbridge-Munsee reservation in Wisconsin, Bill (native name Fush-Ya Heay, meaning "bird song") picked up his first guitar when he was 12, and was part of bluegrass and folk bands influenced by PETE SEEGER. His other inspirations ranged from The Beatles to The BYRDS, the latter group probably the reason why he moved to Nashville in 1984.

Tori Amos, a rising star at the time, subsequently invited him to support her on a nationwide tour, and bluegrass legend Peter Rowan teamed up with MILLER on the song 'Tumbleweed' on Rowan's 1990 set 'Dust Bowl Children'. This encouraged Bill, a master of the Native American flute, to serve up his third and fourth sets, **THE ART OF SURVIVAL** (1990) {*5} and **LOON, MOUNTAIN, AND MOON: NATIVE AMERICAN FLUTE SONGS** (1991) {*6}, in quick succession. His early long-players, **NATIVE SONS** (1982) {*5} and **OLD DREAMS AND NEW HOPES** (1987) {*5}, had gone virtually unnoticed.

To promote his touring career MILLER released the live **RESERVATION ROAD** (1992) {*6}, a country-folk record highlighted by his versions of Johnny Cash's 'Folsom Prison Blues', The Allman Brothers' 'Melissa' and Michael Martin Murphy's 'Geronimo's Cadillac'. Rowan was in his band along with Darrell Scott and John Flanagan.

Reprising 'Tumbleweed' for his major-label debut, **THE RED ROAD** (1993) {*6}, Bill also pushed through two albums reflecting different sides of his Mohican heritage, **RAVEN IN THE SNOW** (1995) {*7} and the daring **NATIVE SUITE: CHANTS, DANCES AND THE REMEMBERED EARTH** (1996) {*5}, the latter a shared effort with Robert Mirabel.

Formerly home to his aforementioned influences SKY and SAINTE-MARIE, the Vanguard label was a natural choice for MILLER, who was beginning to sound more Springsteen than Springsteen on his follow-up set, **GHOSTDANCE** (1999) {*7}. Sadly, apart from re-issues of older material, this was his only album on Vanguard, and his subsequent sets were independently released. **SPIRIT RAIN** (2002) {*7} was the pick of the bunch. *MCS*

Bill Miller - vocals, guitar, flute, drums, harmonica (with session people)

US Windspirit / UK not issued

1982. (lp) <*WSM-101*> **NATIVE SONS**
- Let it rain / Paintings / Whirlwind / Two places at once / Eagle song / Lessons / Hard earned love / Mother and child.

1987. (c) <*WSM-102*> **OLD DREAMS AND NEW HOPES**
- Westwind / Legends never die / Some of Shelly's blues / I'll wait for you / Old dreams and new hopes / Borderline / No one else but you / Dance the blues away / Billy Ray / Under one roof.

Rosebud / not issued

1990. (cd) <*RR-102*> **THE ART OF SURVIVAL**
- Ordinary man / I could fall all over and over again / Reservation road [live] / Forever ride / Night chase / The art of survival / As long as the grass will grow / Broken bottles / The road home / Wind spirit. *<re-iss. Jul 00 on Vanguard; VCD 79569>*

1991. (cd) <*RR-103*> **LOON, MOUNTAIN, AND MOON: NATIVE AMERICAN FLUTE SONGS**
- Loon, mountain, and moon / Canyon dance / White road, red heart / Mohican lullabye / Night chase II / The Little Bighorn march / Beyond the battle / Three tribes / Amazing grace. *<re-iss. Jul 00 on Vanguard; VCD 79567>*

1992. (cd) <*RR-105*> **RESERVATION ROAD: BILL BILLER - LIVE**
- Reservation road / Different drum / Tumbleweed / Street of dreams / Folsom Prison blues / Ordinary man / Orphan child / Still on the run / Melissa / Geronimo's Cadillac. *<re-iss. Jul 00 on Vanguard; VCD 79568>*

Warner Western / not issued

Aug 93. (cd/c) <*9 45324-2/-4*> **THE RED ROAD**
- Dreams of Wounded Knee / Praises / Two hawks / Reservation road / Tumbleweed / Faith of a child / Many trials / Trail of freedom / Inter-tribal pow-wow song / Kokopelli's journey / My people.

Reprise / not issued

Oct 95. (cd/c) <*9 45991-2/-4*> **RAVEN IN THE SNOW**
- River of time / Brave heart / In every corner of the forest (part 1) / Listen to me / Red bird, yellow sun / After the storm / Raven in the snow / Pile of stones / In every corner of the forest (part 2) / The final word / Eagle must fly free / This kind of love / In every corner of the forest (part 3).

——next credited featuring BILL MILLER, Robert Mirabel and the Smokey Town Singers

Feb 96. (cd/c) <*9 45858-2/-4*> **NATIVE SUITE: CHANTS, DANCES AND THE REMEMBERED EARTH**
- Into the twilight / Embrace and betrayal / [two tracks by Robert Mirabel].

Vanguard / not issued

May 99. (cd) <*VCD 79565*> **GHOSTDANCE**
- Prelude (the sun is gonna rise again) / Every mountain I climb / The reason / Ghostdance / Forgive / The vision / There is you / The last stand / Blessing wind / Waiting for the rain / The sun is gonna rise.

Integrity / not issued

Oct 00. (cd) <*???*> **HEAR OUR PRAYER**
- I see the Lord / All creatures of our God and King / Holy lands / Praises / Hear our prayer / Bird song [instrumental] / Father / Listen to me / Prayers from the forest [instrumental] / I believe in you / Ain't gonna let nobody turn me around.

Good Cop Bad Cop / not issued

Jan 01. (cd) **HEALING WATERS**
- I believe / Hanging on a memory / River and the rain / Sundog / You're the rain / Healing waters / Voice of love / Faith / Red sky red heart / Ghost dance prelude / Ghost dance / Prayers for the truth.

Paras / Paras

Jul 02. (cd) <*(PRC 1126-2)*> **SPIRIT RAIN** — Aug 02
- Approaching thunder / You are the rain / Rain down your love / Never too far / Red sky red heart / Face the blues / I believe / Love sustained / Sun dog / Prayers for the truth / 1st dream / The promise / Little brother (spirit rain) / Underneath the blue sky.

Sep 02. (cd) <*(PRC 1130-2)*> **A SACRED GIFT [festive]** — Nov 02
- Sacred gift / Joy to the world / Oh holy night / I saw the star of Bethlehem / What child is this? / Christmas morning / Silent night / Cedar, sweet grass, and sage / The first noel.

Apr 04. (cd) <*PRC 1142-2*> **CEDAR DREAM SONGS**
- Unspoken prayer / Faith of fire / Prophecy / Pathway to dreams / Blood brothers / Dsacred ground / Birds of the air / Peace offering / Calling the rain.

——In Nov '06, Sacred Earth featured BILL MILLER on the single 'Wind Of The West'.

Big Yellow Horse / not issued

Jul 09. (mp3) <*-*> **SPIRIT WIND NORTH**
- Birds of pray / Together as one / High eagle prayer / Lost canyon / Vision quest / Tranquil fire / Journey into prayer / Amazing grace / Reconciliation prayer.

Cool Springs / not issued

Jun 10. (cd) <*none*> **CHRONICLES OF HOPE**
- Dark river / Hurricane / Eagle / Time / Waitin' on the Lord / You can't hide / Fly away / Keep it holy / Blind faith / Eternal / Last breath / Chasing birds.

Sep 10. (cd) <*none*> **SPIRIT WIND EAST**
- Where the water never still / Eastern woodland / Nighthawk / Evergreen / The river / Greyhawk / Morning bird / Prayer stones / Sacred secrets / Flight of the soul / Bird of spring / Eagles' wings / Founding brothers.

- (8-10*) compilations -

Mar 04. (cd) *Vanguard; <(VCD 79729)>* **SPIRIT SONGS: THE BEST OF BILL MILLER** — May 04
- Dreams of Wounded Knee / Praises / Faith of a child / Listen to me / Ghostdance / The sun is gonna rise / Every mountain I climb / Reservation road / Tumbleweed / Geronimo's Cadillac / The art of survival / Wind spirit / Never too far / You are the rain / Love sustained / Underneath the blue sky.

Anais MITCHELL

Although she's not a freak-folk artist by any stretch of the imagination, ANAIS MITCHELL's kooky, childlike vocal style has an odd similarity to JOANNA NEWSOM, SHAWN COLVIN and indeed Tori Amos. Born in 1981 on a farm in Vermont, Anais (pronounced "uh-nay-is") found her vocation early and was writing songs at the age of 17. She studied at Middlebury College and took a degree in global politics, travelling throughout Europe and the Middle East.

Released on her own label, **THE SONG THEY SANG... WHEN ROME FELL** (2002) {*5} won praise from everyone who had the chance to hear it, and Waterbug were impressed enough by this set and her subsequent Kerrville Folk Festival appearance to let her express her confessional art on **HYMNS FOR THE EXILED** (2004) {*6}. The title track was a song from the previous set.

She needed a boost from somewhere, and this came in the shape of ANI DiFRANCO and her Righteous Babe label, obviously enthralled by her recordings so far; her folk opera Hadestown, based on the Greek myth of Orpheus and Eurydice, was toured around New England. **THE BRIGHTNESS** (2007) {*7}, however, was her first album on her new label. Introspective, meditative and a little autumnal, her moods could switch at the drop of a hat. 'Hades And Persephone' and 'Your Fonder Heart' led the way from either end of her emotional spectrum.

A farm girl at heart, her collaborative 'Country' EP with Rachel Ries marked time until the epic one-hour **HADESTOWN** (2010) {*8} was released. Showcasing a stellar cast of friends and associates (MITCHELL played Eurydice), her mythical masterwork realised a lifetime's ambition. BON IVER (Justin Vernon) was Orpheus, GREG BROWN was Hades, ANI DiFRANCO was Persephone, The LOW ANTHEM's Ben Knox Miller was Hermes and the Haden triplets (Petra, Tanya and Rachel) were the Fates. Death, despair and desire were given equal prominence on tracks such as 'Epic', the jazzy 'Our Lady Of The Underground' and 'How Long'. In a few years Anais may well emerge from folk's underworld and become much better known . *MCS*

Anais Mitchell - vocals, acoustic guitar

US own label / US not issued

2002. (cd) <*none*> **THE SONG THEY SANG... WHEN ROME FELL**
- The calling / Parking lot nudie bar / Make it up / Hymn for the exiled / Work makes free / Deliberately / The routine / Orleanna / The song they sang when Rome fell / Hold this. *(bonus+=)* - Go fuck yourself (live).

Waterbug / not issued

Sep 04. (cd) <*WBGCD 58*> **HYMNS FOR THE EXILED**
- Before the eyes of storytelling girls / 1984 / Cosmic American / The belly and the beast / Orion / Mockingbird / I wear your dress / Quecreek flood / A hymn for the exiled / Two kids / One good thing. *<(re-iss. May08/Feb 09 on Righteous Babe; RBR 060CD)>*

Righteous Babe / Righteous Babe

Feb 07. (cd) <*(RBR 053CD)*> **THE BRIGHTNESS** — Apr 07
- Your fonder heart / Of a Friday night / Namesake / Shenandoah / Changer / Song of the magi / Santa Fe dream / Hobo's lullaby / Old-fashioned hat / Hades and Persephone / Out of pawn.

Sep 08. (cd-ep; by ANAIS MITCHELL & RACHEL RIES) <*RBR 58CD*> COUNTRY EP
- O my star! / Mgd / Come September / Grace the day / When you fall.

Mar 10. (cd) <*(RBR 070CD)*> **HADESTOWN** — Apr 10
- Wedding song / Epic (part one) / Way down Hadestown / Songbird (intro) / Hey, little songbird / Gone, I'm gone / When the chips are down / Wait for me / Why we build the wall / Our lady of the underground / Flowers (Eurydice's song) / Nothing changes / If it's true / Paper (Hades finds out) / How long? / Epic (part two) / Lover's desire / His kiss, the riot / Doubt comes in / I raise my cup to him.

The MOLDY PEACHES

The most prominent of the anti-folk glitterati, The MOLDY PEACHES were formed by Adam Green and his partner Kimya Dawson in Mount Kisco, New York around the mid-1990s. After they met somewhere on the Lower East Side, the pedigree lo-fi champions began writing material when Kimya fell in love with Adam's childish post-grunge songs. Extra guitarists Toby Goodshank and Jack Dishel, bass player Steve Mertens and drummer Strictly Beats were on hand as auxiliary live members.

Falling under the spell of the burgeoning New York City anti-folk movement, Rough Trade (who had just signed The Strokes) offered to issue a Greatest Hits album (not, in fact, a best-of) before the irresistibly cheesy **MOLDY PEACHES** {*7} hit the shops in April 2001. Embarrassingly lo-fi, the set consisted of songs recorded mostly on a four-track. The opener 'Lucky Number Nine' was reminiscent of a hip, folky Velvet Underground (that kept the New York connection intact), and the immature but poignant 'Jorge Regula' adapted War's 'Low Rider' to bizarre and astounding effect.

Among the other gems were 'Downloading Porn With Davo', a faux-bebop track with jangly pianos and very rude lyrics indeed; 'Who's Got The Crack?' (an NME Single of the Week); and 'Lazy Confessions', which could have been lifted straight from Beck's 'One Foot In The Grave' set. The lyrics were a bit childish (not to mention the costumes), and the music a tad loose, but The MOLDY PEACHES proved that content-over-style was more interesting than a polished, hyper- produced record with no soul.

The four cover versions (The Four Seasons' 'Big Girls Don't Cry', Grateful Dead's 'Friend Of The Devil', Hulk Hogan & The Boot Band's 'I Wanna Be A Hulkamaniac' and The Spin Doctors' 'Two Princes') on their double collection, **UNRELEASED CUTZ AND LIVE JAMZ 1994-2002** (2003) {*4}, are generally considered a non-event.

Kimya and Adam maintained their indie cool without once washing the grime from under their fingernails. With the duo taking a brief sabbatical in 2002 as The White Stripes took the world by storm, ADAM GREEN found time to put together his self-titled solo debut, released in the US as **GARFIELD** (2002) {*5}. Anti-folk and at times romantically punk, his album struck a mellower, reflective mood that was reminiscent of the heyday of TIM HARDIN, LEONARD COHEN and PHIL OCHS.

Meanwhile, KIMYA DAWSON made her break for it with a twee solo collection, **I'M SORRY THAT SOMETIMES I'M MEAN** (2002) {*6}, a reet-petite DIY delivery of riot-grrrl stuff and nonsense that was as angst-ridden as it was cathartic and witty.

While Kimya continued on her quest to rid the world of production techniques on a handful of unmemorable sets, she found her 15 minutes when she contributed several songs to the award-winning and chart-topping soundtrack of the 2007 cult film 'Juno'. Three goofball albums for the legendary K label maintained her profile; **HIDDEN VAGENDA** (2004) {*6} and **REMEMBER THAT I LOVE YOU** (2006) {*7} probably found fans among dysfunctional, giggle-happy girls about to inject more than just fun into their lives.

ADAM GREEN was a different kettle of funny fish, grating on and jarring his bedsitter audience on the quirky, indie/cabaret-type **FRIENDS OF MINE** (2003) {*6}, **GEMSTONES** (2005) {*7}, **JACKET FULL OF DANGER** (2006) {*7}, the nostalgia-styled **SIXES AND SEVENS** (2008) {*6} and his first Fat Possum delivery, the stylish, Lou Reed-cloned **MINOR LOVE** (2010) {*6}.

Throughout the past decade GREEN has released the following covers on flipsides: The Beach Boys' 'Kokomo' (Ben Kweller sang this double-A), The Libertines' 'What A Waster', Bruce Springsteen's 'Born To Run', The Velvet Underground's 'I'll Be Your Mirror', Buddy Holly's 'Crying, Waiting, Hoping' and Sam Cooke's 'Cupid'. *MCS*

Adam Green (b. May 28 '81, Mt. Kisco, NY) - vocals, guitars / **Kimya Dawson** (b. Nov 17 '72, Bedford Hills, NY) - vocals (a semi-member initially): + stage guitarists **Toby Goodshank** + **Jack Dishel** plus **Steve Mertens** - bass + **Strictly Beats** - drums

US Average Cabbage / UK not issued

1996. (ltd-7" ep) <???> X-RAY VISION [ ] [–]
- Rap sux! / Little bunny Foo Foo / On top / I wish I was Ben Lee / Flea circus / Moldy Peaches in da house / Punching bag.

1999. (ltd-c/cd) <???> **MOLDY PEACHES 2000: FER THE KIDS // LIVE 1999** (live) [ ] [–]
- Nothing came out / Bleeding heart / Greyhound bus / Lucky number nine / What went wrong / D2 boyfriend / Secret tongues / Shame / Wake up / These burgers / I forgot / Lazy confessions / It's hard / Lucky charms // What went wrong / Lazy confessions / D2 boyfriend / Crazy burgers / Where is mankind? / Big girls don't cry / Goodbye song / Little bunny Foo Foo / Greyhound bus / Shame / Secret tongues / Lucky number nine / Bleeding heart / Nothing came out.

—the duo added various friends/guests **Brian Piltin** - bass, vocals / **Jack Dishel** - guitar, drums, vocals / **Steve Espinola** - piano / **Drew Blood** - piano, vocals / **Chris Barron** - guitar / **Kurt Feldman** - drums / **Denise Koleda** - bass / **Adam Goldstein** - vocals / **Hollis Smith** - vocals

Sanctuary / Rough Trade

Apr 01. (one-sided 7") *(RTRADES 016)* WHO'S GOT THE CRACK? / NYC's Like A Graveyard [–] [ ]

Sep 01. (cd/lp) *<06076-83200-2> (RTRADE CD/LP 014)* **THE MOLDY PEACHES** [ ] May 01 [ ]
- Lucky number nine / Jorge Regula / What went wrong / Nothing came out / Downloading porn with Davo - All I ever think about is drowning / These burgers / Steak for chicken / On top / Greyhound bus / Anyone else but you / Little bunny Foo Foo / The ballad of Helen Keller and Rip Van Winkle / Who's got the crack? / Lucky charms / D2 boyfriend / I forgot / Lazy confessions / NYC's like a graveyard / Goodbye song.

Apr 02. (cd-s) *(RTRADESCD 047)* COUNTY FAIR / RAINBOWS [–] [ ]

—split on a temporary basis...

Mar 03. (d-cd) *<06076-83217-2> (RTRADECD 076)* **MOLDY PEACHES 2000: UNRELEASED CUTZ AND LIVE JAMZ 1994-2002** [compilation] [ ] [ ]
- Moldy Peaches in da house / Answering machine #1 / Answering machine #2 / Nothing came out (original recording) / Shame / Secret tongues / (live '99):- What went wrong / Bleeding heart / Times are bad / Lucky charms (original recording) / (live '99):- D2 boyfriend / MP2K / Bunny Foo Foo / Shame / Big girls don't cry / I think I'm in love / These burgers / Lucky \9 / Bunny Foo Foo / Lach's intro / Greyhound bus / Witty banter / Lazy confessions / On top / Friend of the devil / Rap sux / (live '00):- Jorge Regula / Downloading porn with Davo / I forgot / County fair / Steak for chicken (acoustic) / NYC's like a graveyard // I wanna be a Hulkamaniac / (live '01):- Who's got the crack / Steak for chicken / These burgers / I forgot / Nothing came out / On top / Helen Keller / Jorge Regula / One good turn / D2 boyfriend / County fair / Rainbows / Who's got the crack / Goodbye song / (live '02):- V-PRO intro / Downloading porn with Davo / Steak for chicken / Anyone else but you / Lucky charms / Two princes / Lucky \9 (video) / Cheese.

—The MOLDY PEACHES returned for the 'Juno' OST (2007) promo Anyone Else But You'

ADAM GREEN

with various augmentation

Sanctuary / Rough Trade

Apr 02. (cd) *(RTRADECD 051)* **ADAM GREEN** [–] [ ]
- Apples, I'm home / My shadow tagg on behind / Bartholemew / Mozzarella swastikas / Dance with me / Computer show / Her father and her / Baby's gonna die tonight / Times are bad / Can you see me.

Oct 02. (cd) *<06076-83206-2>* **GARFIELD** [ ] [–]
- (as 'ADAM GREEN') <+=> - *(EP versions)*:- Dance with me / Bleeding heart / Computer show.

Nov 02. (cd-s) *(RTRADESCD 062)* DANCE WITH ME / Bleeding Heart / Computer Show [–] [ ]

Jul 03. (cd/lp) *<06076-83223-2> (RTRADE CD/LP 107)* **FRIENDS OF MINE** [ ] Mar 04 [ ]
- Bluebirds / Hard to be a girl / Jessica / Musical ladders / The prince's bed / Bunnyranch / Friends of mine / Frozen in time / Broken joystick / I wanna die / Salty candy / No legs / We're not supposed to be lovers / Secret tongues / Bungee.

Aug 03. (cd-ep) *<06076-83228-2>* JESSICA / Friends Of Mine / Don't Smoke - The Bronx Zoo 1989 / What A Waster / Kokomo [ ] [–]

Mar 04. (7") *(RTRADES 112)* JESSICA. / KOKOMO [–] [63]
(cd-s+=) *(RTRADESCD 112)* - Don't smoke - The Bronx zoo 1989.

Aug 04. (7") *(RTRADS 171)* FRIENDS OF MINE. / Born To Run [–] [ ]
(cd-s+=) *(RTRADSCD 171)* - I wanna die (home demo).

Rough Trade / Rough Trade

Jan 05. (cd/lp) *<RTA 30050-2> (RTRAD CD/LP 194)* **GEMSTONES** [ ] [ ]
- Gemstones / Down on the street / He's the brat / Over the sunrise / Crackhouse blues / Before my bedtime / Carolina / Emily / Who's your boyfriend / Country road / Choke on a cock / Bible club / Chubby princess / Losing on a Tuesday / Teddy boys.

Feb 05. (7") *(RTRADS 213)* EMILY. / What A Waster [–] [ ]
(cd-s) *(RTRADSCD 213)* - ('A') / The rotary shakes / Crackhouse blues (alt. take) / ('A'-version).

Aug 05. (7") *(RTRADS 249)* CAROLINA. / Morning After Midnight / I'll Be Your Mirror [–] [ ]
(cd-s+=) *(RTRADSCD 249)* - Heart and soul / ('A'-video).

Apr 06. (cd/lp) *<34692932> (RTRAD CD/LP 293)* **JACKET FULL OF DANGER** [ ] [ ]
- Pay the toll / Hollywood Bowl / Vultures / Novotel / Party line / Hey dude / Nat King Cole / C-birds / Animal dreams / Cast a shadow / Drugs / Jolly good / Watching old movies / White women / Hairy women.

May 06. (7") *(RTRADS 308)* NAT KING COLE. / Crying, Waiting, Hoping / Cupid [–] [ ]
(cd-s+=) *(RTRADSCD 308)* - Bleeding Heart (02/15/96).

Mar 08. (cd) *<34694322> (RTRADCD 432)* **SIXES AND SEVENS** [ ] [ ]
- Festival song / Tropical island / Cannot get sicker / That sounds like a pony /

Morning after morning / Twee twee dee / You get so lucky / Getting led / Drowning head first / Broadcast beach / It's a fine / Homelife / Be my man / Grandma Shirly and Papa / When a pretty face / Exp. 1 / Leaky flask / Bed of prayer / Sticky Ricki / Rich kids.

Jan 10. (cd) *(RTRADCD 532)* **MINOR LOVE** ⊟ ☐
- Breaking locks / Give them a token / Buddy Bradley / Goblin / Bathing birds / What makes him act so bad / Stadium soul / Cigarette burns forever / Boss inside / Castles and tassles / Oh shucks / Don't call me uncle / Lockout / You blacken my stay.

not issued — Contraphonic

May 10. (lp) *(CON 086)* **MUSIK FOR A PLAY** ⊟ ☐
- Gallop / Sailor shirts / Big lips / Lazy dog / Twins / Ellington / Lasers / Sticky Ricki [remix] / Ron Asheton / [demos]:- Sailor shirts / Big lips / Gallop.

KIMYA DAWSON

with a handful of session people

own label — not issued

2001. (cd-r; by KIMYA DAWSON and JEFF LEWIS) *<none>*
ANTI FOLK COLLABORATIONS ⊟ ⊟
- A common chorus / Pirates declare war / Shamrock glamrock / Ishalicious (Ish finds his family). *<cd re-iss. 2002 on Olive Juice+=; OJD 0082>* - (tracks by DIANE CLUCK & JEFFREY LEWIS).

Sanctuary — Rough Trade

Nov 02. (cd) *<06076-83208-2> (RTRADECD 052)* **I'M SORRY THAT SOMETIMES I'M MEAN** ☐ Jun 02 ☐
- Trump style / Reminders of then / Everything's alright / Rocks with holes / Talking ernest / Wandering daughter / Eleventeen / Hold my hand / Stinky stuff / Sleep / So far to go.

Important — Important

Sep 03. (cd) *<(imprec 018)>* **KNOCK-KNOCK WHO?** ☐ ☐
- Nobody's hippie / Great crap / My bike / Jest's birthday / Time to think / The sound of Ataris / So nice so smart / For boxer / I'm fine / Stink mama / Red white and blue dream / Once upon a time. *<lp-iss. Aug 04; imprec 032>*

Sep 03. (cd) *<(imprec 019)>* **MY CUTE FIEND SWEET PRINCESS** ☐ ☐
- Chemistry / Velvet rabbit / Hadlock padlock / Being cool / Anthrax / The beer / Will you be me? / Everything's alright / For Katie. *<lp-iss. Aug 04; imprec 031>*

K — K

Oct 04. (lp/cd) *<(KLP 165/+CD)>* **HIDDEN VAGENDA** ☐ Nov 04 ☐
- It's been raining / Fire / Viva la persistence / Lullaby for the taken / I will never forget / Singing machine / Moving on / Blue like nevermind / My heroes / Parade / Five years / Anthrax (powerballad version) / You love me / Angels and seagulls.

Feb 06. (7" split) *<IPU 107>* KIMYA DAWSON: My Mom / [other by Matty Pop Chart] ☐ ⊟

——In 2006, Kimya augmented the children's band/album project 'Antsy Pants'.

May 06. (lp/cd) *<(KLP 175/+CD)>* **REMEMBER THAT I LOVE YOU** ☐ ☐
- Tire swing / My mom / Loose lips / Caving in / Better weather / Underground / I like giants / The competition / France / I miss you / 12-26 / My rollercoaster.

——In 2007, Kimya supplied several tracks ('My Rollercoaster', 'Tire Swing', 'Loose Lips', 'Sleep', 'So Nice So Smart', 'Tree Hugger' (with Antsy Pants) and 'Anyone Else But You' (with The MOLDY PEACHES) to the US No.1 soundtrack of the cult teen movie 'Juno' on the Rhino label.

Sep 08. (lp/cd; as KIMYA DAWSON AND FRIENDS) *<(KLP 193/+CD)>* **ALPHABUTT** ☐ ☐
- Little monster babies / Alphabutt / Bobby-O / Louie / Smoothie / I like bears / Seven hungry tigers / Happy home (keep on writing) / Wiggle my tooth / I love you sweet baby / Pee-pee in the potty / Uncle Hukee's house / We're all animals / Little panda bear / Sunbeams and some beans.

The BUNDLES

Kimya Dawson - vocals, keyboards / **Jeffrey Lewis** - vocals, guitar / **Jack Lewis** - bass, vocals / **Karl Blau** - piano, sax, vocals / **Anders Griffen** - drums, percussion, vocals

Mar 10. (cd,white-lp) *<KLP 214>* **THE BUNDLES** ☐ ⊟
- A common chorus / Pirates declare war / Klutter / Shamrock glamrock / Over the moon / Ishalicious / In the beginning / Desert bundles / Metal mouth / Be yourself.

Ruth MOODY (⟹ The WAILIN' JENNYS)

Bill MORRISSEY

Born November 25, 1951 in Hartford, Connecticut, BILL MORRISSEY was initially inspired by the folk blues of MISSISSIPPI JOHN HURT, the pure C&W of Hank Williams and the Kansas City jazz-swing of Count Basie. With a voice that could rasp and croak with the best of them - Kris Kristofferson, Leon Redbone and Kurt Wagner included - he turned pro and delivered his self-titled debut, **BILL MORRISSEY** (1984) {*5}. A move to the Philo label followed for the man-of-the-people singer/songwriter.

The introspective NORTH (1986) {*8} was his first album proper, an observational set about life seen through the eyes of mill-town people in narrative songs such as 'Married Man', 'He Drinks Alone', and 'Night Shift'. **STANDING EIGHT** (1989) {*7} and **INSIDE** (1992) {*6} showed his line of storytelling could go further than just bar-room blues recitals, as **NIGHT TRAIN** (1993) {*7} and **YOU'LL NEVER GET TO HEAVEN** (1996) {*6} would further testify.

Similar in many respects, and both big names on the folk-blues circuit, BILL MORRISSEY and GREG BROWN teamed up for what was almost an all-covers set, **FRIEND OF MINE** (1993) {*7}, which worked well on songs like the traditional title track and borrowings from acts including The Rolling Stones, Willie Dixon, Chuck Berry, Danny O'Keefe and Big Joe Williams. MORRISSEY's next musical project was **SONGS OF MISSISSIPPI JOHN HURT** (1999) {*6}. In 1996 he published his first novel, 'Edson'.

All his ghostly, Hemingwayesque characters took their place at the bar once again on 2001's **SOMETHING I SAW OR THOUGHT I SAW** {*6}, his final set for Philo/Rounder, and Bill bowed out in grand style with what turned out to be his swansong set, **COME RUNNING** (2007) {*6}, on Turn And Spin.

Sadly, Bill died of heart disease on July 23, 2011 in Dalton, Georgia, while on tour. A second novel, 'Imaginary Runner', had been completed just before his death. *MCS*

Bill Morrissey - vocals, acoustic guitar, harmonica (w/ session people)

US — UK

Shoot The Cat — not issued

1977. (7") *<STC 001>* LIVE FREE OR DIE. / Trailer Park ☐ ⊟

Reckless — not issued

1984. (lp/c) *<RK 1917>* **BILL MORRISSEY** ☐ ⊟
- Barstow / Small town on the river / Darlin' Lisa / Oil money / Morrissey falls in love at first sight / Texas blues / My baby and me / The Packard company / A problem with logic / Run you through the mill / Grizzly bear / Rosie. *<(re-iss. Apr 86 on Philo lp/c; PH 1105/+C)> <(cd-iss. Feb 94/Mar 00 + 're-recorded February 27, 1991' +=; CDPH 1105)>* - Little bit of whiskey / Live free or die (w/ TRIGGER COOK) / Amnesia (w/ NICK KLAUS).

Philo — Philo

May 86. (lp/c) *<(PH 1106/+C)>* **NORTH** ☐ 1988 ☐
- Pantherville / It's dangerous out there / Night shift / Married man / (w/ Cormac McCarthy) / Ice fishing / My old town / North / She moved through the fair / He drinks alone / Snow outside the mill / Fishing a stream I once fished as a kid. *<(cd-iss. Feb 94/Mar 00; CDPH 1106)>*

1989. (lp/c) *<PH 1123/+C>* **STANDING EIGHT** ☐ ⊟
- Handsome Molly / Love song - New York, 1982 / Party at the UN / Last day of the last furlough / Motels and planes / Up on the the CP line / Summer night / She's that kind of mystery / Girls of Santa Fe / The driver's song / Car and driver / John Haber / She's your baby now / These cold fingers. *<(cd-iss. Feb 94/Mar 00; CDPH 1123)>*

Jan 92. (cd/c) *<PH 1145 CD/C>* **INSIDE** ☐ ⊟
- Inside / Everybody warned me / Off-white / Gambler's blues / Long gone / Man from out of town / Rite of spring / Robert Johnson / Hang me, oh hang me / Chameleon blues / Sister Joe / Casey, Illinois. *(UK cd-iss. Mar 00 & Nov 09; CDPH 1145)*

May 93. (cd/c; by BILL MORRISSEY & GREG BROWN) *<(PH 1151 CD/C)>* **FRIEND OF MINE** ☐ ☐
- Ain't life a brook / Little red rooster / He was a friend of mine / Memphis, Tennessee / The road / You can't always get what you want / Duncan and Brady / Tom Dula / Summer wages / I'll never get out of this world alive / Fishing with Bill / Baby, please don't go. *(UK cd re-iss. Mar 00; CDPH 1151)*

Sep 93. (cd/c) *<(PH 1154 CD/C)>* **NIGHT TRAIN** ☐ Jan 94 ☐
- Night train / Sandy / Birches / Cold, cold night / Letter from heaven / Ellen's tune / So many things / Love arrives / Blues in the morning / Broken waltz time / Walk down these streets / Time to go home.

Apr 96. (cd/c) *<PH 1194 CD/C>* **YOU'LL NEVER GET TO HEAVEN** ☐ ⊟
- When summer's ended / You'll never get to heaven / Married for money / As long as the sun / Ashes, grain and sand / Winter laundry / Waiting for the rain / Different currency / Hills of Tuscany / Closed-down mill / Turn and spin / Big leg Ida. *(UK cd-iss. Mar 00; CDPH 1194)*

Feb 99. (cd) *<(PH 1216CD)>* **SONGS OF MISSISSIPPI JOHN HURT** ☐ ☐
- If you don't want me / Avalon blues / Shake that thing / Louis Collins / First shot missed him / Big leg blues / Hey, honey, right away / Joe Turner blues / I'm satisfied / Beulah land / Funky butt / Coffee blues / Monday morning blues / Good morning, Carrie / Hot times in the old town.

Apr 01. (cd) *<(CDPH 1227)>* **SOMETHING I SAW OR THOUGHT I SAW** ☐ May 01 ☐
- Twenty-third street / Harry's last call / Just before we lost the war / Winter song / Moving day / Buddy Bolden's blues / St Valentine's day / Traveling by cab / Fix your hair the way you used to / Judgment day / Mobile / Will you be my rose?

Turn & Spin — not issued

May 07. (cd) *<1125>* **COME RUNNING** ☐ ⊟
- I ain't walking / Thirty years / Dangerous way / Holden's blues / He's not from Kansas City / Summer's jumped all over me / By the grave of Baudelaire / Canal street / I was a fool / Death letter / Victory at sea / New walking blues / Johnny's tune.

- (8-10*) compilations -

Jun 04. (cd) *Rounder;* <*(ROUCD 11595)*>
THE ESSENTIAL COLLECTION
- Barstow / Inside / Robert Johnson / Fifty / These cold fingers / Ice fishing / Just before we lost the war / Avalon blues / Letter from heaven / Handsome Molly / Different currency / Cold, cold night / Small town on the river / You'll never get to heaven / Birches / Long gone / Twenty-third street / Joe Turner blues / Just today / Boston eyes.

The MOUNTAIN GOATS

It's hard to say what makes California singer/songwriter John Darnielle's outfit 'folk' - apart from the strumming of an acoustic guitar and sounding like a cross between MIKE SCOTT and Daniel Johnston with a cold - but he was certainly an indie/lo-fi alternative to the plethora of derivate roots acts.

While working as a psychiatric nurse and studying at Pitzer College, Claremont, John subsidised his income by playing for numerous acts. As The MOUNTAIN GOATS (with Rachel Ware and a few more disciples) he issued two cassette-only mini-albums for the tiny label Shrimper, **TABOO VI: THE HOMECOMING** (1991) {*5} and **THE HOUND CHRONICLES** (1992) {*5}. As the years progressed Darnielle, now something of a Daniel Johnston figure in terms of his prolific release schedule, produced further cassette albums and 7" singles, all recorded on a crude ghetto-blaster and all displaying his intricate guitar and vocal work.

His first CD album, **SWEDEN** {*7}, was delivered in 1995 to critical acclaim. Again entirely recorded on his stereo, it introduced what would become classic MOUNTAIN GOATS motifs in the 'Going To...' and 'Songs For...' sets of songs. An outstanding version of Steely Dan's 'FM' was the first of many oddball cover songs to come.

ZOPILOTE MACHINE {*6} was released the year before, containing a host of brilliant tracks including 'Alpha Sun Heat' and the wonderful 'Going To Georgia'. Maintaining the raw DIY production, reminiscent of Beck's 1995 set 'One Foot In The Grave', it helped push the lo-fi envelope further into the 1990s; Grandaddy, NEUTRAL MILK HOTEL and Pavement were certainly taking note.

Darnielle and musical buddies Peter Hughes and Allen Callachi moved into the studio for the mini-album **NINE BLACK POPPIES** (1995) {*7}, though some of these tracks were still home-recorded. Featured tracks included the simple ballad 'I Know You've Come To Take My Toys Away' and a cover of Refrigerator's 'Lonesome Surprise', sung as a duo with Callachi, who may literally have phoned in his vocal.

It was hard to keep up with the outfit, but 1996 and 1997 saw The MOUNTAIN GOATS turn moody with **NOTHING FOR JUICE** {*6} (co-written and sung with Rachel Ware and issued on Ajax) and the slightly disappointing **FULL FORCE GALESBURG** {*5}, a meditative, melancholic album that was followed by a three-year hiatus

Darnell returned in 2000, with members of Lullaby For The Working Class and BRIGHT EYES on the sleeve, for the brilliant, scatterbrain **THE CORONER'S GAMBIT** {*7}, another cathartic and rambling GOATS special (it was back to the ghetto-blaster again). Darnielle made sure that his songs were given the proper treatment, with the background tape hiss making a welcome reappearance. Also revived was his side project, the legendary Extra Glenns, with Nothing Painted Blue's Franklin Bruno; they played San Francisco's Noise Pop Festival and delivered the album 'Martial Arts Weekend', which had apparently been in the pipeline for ten years.

In 2001/2002 The MOUNTAIN GOATS released a ton of material, beginning with **ALL HAIL WEST TEXAS** {*7} (check out the hilarious 'The Best Ever Death Metal Band In Denton'), and three excellent compilations, **PROTEIN SOURCE OF THE FUTURE... NOW!** {*6}, **BITTER MELON FARM** {*7} and **GHANA** {*7}. There was also a freshly recorded studio album, **TALLAHASSEE** {*7}, their first for the 4 a.d. label.

The MOUNTAIN GOATS were a different proposition by this time - more lush, more polished and everything they were against when John started off. **WE SHALL BE HEALED** (2004) {*6}, the folky **GET LONELY** (2006) {*6}, **HERETIC PRIDE** (2008) {*6} and **THE LIFE OF THE WORLD TO COME** (2009) each sold better than the one before, and the last-named biblical road trip actually bubbled under the Top 100 for a few weeks. Surfacing on the Merge label, Darnielle and co's umpteenth set, **ALL ETERNALS DECK** (2011) {*7}, was another concept piece, this time taking the Tarot cards for inspiration. *MCS*

John Darnielle (b. Mar 16 '67, Bloomington, Indiana) - vocals, guitar, tapes / **Rachel Ware** - vocals, bass / with p/t **Amy, Rosanne + Sara**

US Shrimper — UK not issued

1991. (m-c) <*SHR 27*> **TABOO VI: THE HOMECOMING**
- Running away with what Freud said / Ice cream, cobra man / Move (Chicago 196?) / This magic moment / Don't take the dogs away / One winter at Point Alpha Privative / Solomon revisited / Going to Alaska / I'm so lonesome I could cry / Eleven bands.

1992. (c) <*SHR 33*> **THE HOUND CHRONICLES**
- The garden song / Going to Wisconsin / Spilling toward Alpha / Alpha negative / Torch song / Ape (Be quiet) / The cow song / (Untitled) / Going to Chino / Standard bitter love song \4 / Going to Mexico / Lab rat blues / Going to Kansas / The water song / Going to Spain / Keep it on your mind.

1992. (7"ep) <*SHR 705*> SONGS FOR PETRONIUS
- The bad doctor / Alpha double negative - Going to Catalina / Pure intentions / The lady from Shanghai / Pure love.

Ajax — not issued

1993. (7" ep) <*ajax 028*> CHILE DE ARBOL
- Night of the mules / Going to Malibu / Billy the Kid's dream of the magic shoes / Fresh berries for you / Alphabetizing.

Sonic Enemy — not issued

1993. (c-ep) <*???*> TRANSMISSIONS TO HORACE
- Going to Cleveland / Early spring / Historiography / No, I can't / Alpha desperation march / Going to Monaco / Star dusting / Teenage world / Going to Santiago / Sail on.

Shrimper — not issued

1993. (c) <*SHR 45*> HOT GARDEN STOMP
- Pure milk / Ice blue / Water song II / Sun song / Going to Japan / Are you cleaning off the stone? / The hot garden stomp / Love hymn to Aphrodite / Beach house / Hello there Howard / Going to Norwalk / Fresh cherries in Trinidad / Feed this end / 15-1 / Thanks for the dress / Tell me on a Sunday.

Ajax — not issued

1994. (cd) <*ajax 36*> **ZOPILOTE MACHINE**
- Alpha incipiens / Azo tle Nelli in Tlalticpac? / Alpha sun hat / The black ice cream song / Sinaloan milk snake song / We have seen the enemy / Standard bitter love song \7 / Quetzalcoatl eats plums / Orange ball of love / Orange ball of hate / Bad priestess / Going to Bristol / Young Caesar 2000 / Going to Lebanon / Grendel's mother / Song for Tura Santana / Alpha in Tauris / Going to Georgia / Quetzalcoalt is born. <*re-iss. Mar 05 on Three Beads Of Sweat; 3BOS 1006.2*>

Theme Park — not issued

1994. (7"ep) <*TP 04*> PHILYRA
- Third snow song / The monkey song / Love cuts the strings / Pure honey.

Car In Car Disco — not issued

1994. (c-ep) <*???*> TAKING THE DATIVE
- Orange ball of peace / Standard bitter love song \8 / Chino love song 1979 / Wrong! / Going to Jamaica / Alpha Gelida.

Sing, Eunuchs! — not issued

1994. (7"ep; shared) <*eunuch 13*> WHY YOU ALL SO THIEF?
- Going to Tennessee / Pure heat / (other two by Simon Joyner)

Oska — not issued

1994. (c-ep) <*???*> YAM, THE KING OF CROPS
- Seed song / Quetzalcoatl comes through / Omega blaster / Coco-yam song / Alagemo / Two thousand seasons / Chinese rifle song / Yam, the king of crops.

Walt — not issued

1994. (7" ep; with ALASTAIR GALBRAITH) <*Walt 005*>
ORANGE RAJA, BLOOD ROYAL
- Blood royal / The only thing I know / Raja vocative / Hatha hill.

——added **Peter Hughes** - vocals

Sonic Squid — not issued

1995. (ltd-7" ep;some red) <*MZG 1585*> SONGS FOR PETER HUGHES
- Short song about the 10 freeway / No, I can't / Song for Dana Plato / The sign.

Emperor Jones — Emperor Jones

Oct 95. (m-cd) <*(EJ 02CD)*> **NINE BLACK POPPIES** — Nov 95
- Cubs in five / Going to Utrecht / Cheshire county / Chanson du bon chose / Pure money / I know you've come to take my toys away / Nine black poppies / Stars fell on Alabama / Lonesome surprise (live).

Cassiel — not issued

1995. (7"ep) <*Cassiel 2B*> SONGS ABOUT FIRE
- Pure gold / Papagallo / Songs for John Davis / Stars around her.

Shrimper — not issued

1995. (lp/cd) <*SHR 68/+CD*> **SWEDEN**
- The recognition scene / Downtown Seoul / Some Swedish trees / I wonder where our love has gone / Deianara crush / Whole wide world / Flashing lights / Sept 19 triple X love! love! / Going to Queens / Tahitianambrosia maker / Going to Bolivia / Tollund man / California song / Snow crush killing song / Send me an angel / Neon orange glimmer song / FM / Prana ferox / Cold milk bottle. *(UK-iss. Dec 96; same as US)*

Jan 96. (10" m-lp/m-cd) <*SHR 99/+CD*> **BEAUTIFUL RAT SUNSET** (rec.1993)
- Itzcuintli-Totzli days / New star song / Song for Cleomenes / Sendero luminoso verdero / Song for Mark and Joel / Going to Maryland / Seeing daylight / Resonant bell world. *(UK-iss. Dec 96; same as US)*

Ajax — not issued

Aug 96. (cd) <*ajax 056-2*> **NOTHING FOR JUICE**

- Then the letting go / Heights / Alpha double negative: Going to Catalina / Hellbound on my trail / Blueberry frost / Alabama nova / Moon and sand / I will grab you by the ears / It froze me / Full flower / Million / Going to Bogota / Orange ball of pain / Going to Kansas / Waving at you / Going to Reykjavik / Corinthians 13: 8-10 / Going to Scotland. *<re-iss. Mar 05 on Three Beads Of Sweat; 3BOS 1007.2>*

Little Mafia — not issued

1997. (7" ep; shared w/ FURNITURE HUSCHLE) *<???>* TROPICAL DEPRESSION (rec. 1994)
- (Furniture Huschle tracks) / Anti-music song / Going to Hungary / Earth air water trees.

Emperor Jones — Emperor Jones

Jun 97. (lp/cd) *<(EJ 11/+CD)>* **FULL FORCE GALESBURG** — Nov 97
- New Britain / Snow owl / West Country dream / Masher / Chinese house flowers / Ontario / Down here / Twin human highway flares / Weekend in western Illinois / Us mill / Song for the Julian calendar / Maize stalk drinking blood / Evening in Stalingrad / Minnesota / Original air-blue-gown / It's all here in Brownsville.

YoYo — not issued

1998. (etched-12" ep) *<???>* NEW ASIAN CINEMA
- Cao Dai blowout / Korean bird paintings / Narakaloka / Golden jackal song / Treetop song.

2000. (etched-12" ep) *<???>* ISOPANISAD RADIO HOUR
- Abide with me / Born ready / Cobscook Bay / Dutch orchestra blues / Pseudothyrum song / The last limit of Bhakti.

——now with **Simon Joyner + Lullaby For The Working Class**

Absolutely Kosher — Absolutely Kosher

Oct 00. (cd/lp) *<(AK 012/+1)>* **THE CORONER'S GAMBIT** — Jan 01
- Jaipur / Elijah / Trick mirror / Island garden song / The coroner's gambit / Baboon / Scotch grove / Horseradish road / Family happiness / Onions / 'Blue jays and cardinals' / Shadow song / There will be no divorce / Insurance fraud #2 / The Alphonse mambo / We were patriots.

Nursecall — not issued

2001. (3" cd-ep) *<NC.006>* ON JUHU BEACH
- Hotel road / Bad waves / Transjordanian blues / Burned my tongue / World cylinder.

YoYo — not issued

2001. (etched-12"ep) *<YOYO-LP 20>* DEVIL IN THE SHORTWAVE
- Crows / Genesis 19: 1-2 / Yoga / Dirty old town / Commandante.

Emperor Jones — Emperor Jones

Nov 01. (cd) *<(EJ 41CD)>* **ALL HAIL WEST TEXAS** — Feb 02
- The best ever death metal band in Denton / Fall of the star high school running back / Color in your cheeks / Jenny / Fault lines / Balance / Pink and blue / Riches and wonders / The mess inside / Jeff Davis county blues / Distant stations / Blues in Dallas / Source delay / Lithops effect.

——**Darnielle** still retained **Hughes**

4 a.d. — 4 a.d.

Nov 02. (7") *(AD 2208)* SEE AMERICA RIGHT. / New Chevrolet In Flames
(cd-s+=) *(BAD 2208CD)* - Design your own container garden.

Nov 02. (cd) *<72215> (CAD 2215CD)* **TALLAHASSEE** — Jan 03
- Tallahassee / First few desperate hours / Southwood plantation road / Games shows touch our lives / The house that dripped blood / Idylls of the king / No children / See America right / Peacocks / International small arms traffic blues / Have to explode / Old college try / Oceanographer's choice / Alpha rats' nest.

2003. (ltd-7") *(br 002)* SOFT TARGETS. / (other by John Vanderslice)
(above issued on Bedside Recordings)

2003. (7") *(AD 2306)* PALMCORDER YAJNA. / Butter Teeth
(cd-s+=) *(BAD 2306CD)* - Snakeheads.

Feb 04. (lp/cd) *<72401> (CAD 2401/+CD)* **WE SHALL ALL BE HEALED**
- Slow west vultures / Palmcorder Yajna / Linda Blair was born innocent / Letter from Belgium / The young thousands / Your Belgian things / Mole / Home again garden grove / All up the seething coast / Quito / Cotton / Against pollution / Pigs that ran straightaway into the water, triumph of.

Apr 04. (7") *(AD 2410)* LETTER FROM BELGIUM. / Nova Scotia
(cd-s+=) *(BAD 2410CD)* - Attention All Pickpockets.

Apr 05. (d-ls) *(EAD 2506S)* DILAUDID / This Year / Collapsing Stars / Dilaudid (Marrtronix mix)

May 05. (cd) *<72508> (CAD 2508CD)* **THE SUNSET TREE**
- You or your memory / Broom people / This year / Dilaudid / Dance music / Dinu Lipatti's bones / Up the wolves / Lion's teeth / Hast thou considered the tetrapod / Magpie / Song for Dennis Brown / Love love love / Pale green things. *(ltd-lp as 'COME, COME TO THE SUNSET TREE'; CAD 2508)*

Aug 06. (lp/cd) *<72614> (CAD 2614/+CD)* **GET LONELY**
- Wild sage / New monster avenue / Half dead / Get lonely / Maybe sprout wings / Moon over Goldsboro / In the hidden places / Song for lonely giants / Woke up new / If you see light / Cobra tattoo / In Corolla.

——**Darnielle + Hughes** added **Jon Wurster** - percussion

Feb 08. (lp/cd) *<72801> (CAD 2801/+CD)* **HERETIC PRIDE**
- Sax Rohmer #1 / San Bernadino / Heretic pride / Autoclave / New Zion / So desperate / In the craters on the moon / Lovecraft in Brooklyn / Tianchi lake / How to embrace a swamp creature / Marduk T-shirt men's room incident / Sept 15, 1983 / Michael Myers resplendent.

Oct 09. (lp/cd) *<72932> (CAD 2932/+CD)* **THE LIFE OF THE WORLD TO COME**
- 1 Samuel 15:23 / Psalms 40:2 / Genesis 3:23 / Philippians 3:20-21 / Hebrews 11:40 / Genesis 30:3 / Romans 10:9 / 1 John 4:16 / Matthew 25:21 / Deuteronomy 2:10 / Isaiah 45:23 / Ezekiel 7 and the permanent efficacy of grace.

Merge — Merge

Mar 11. (cd) *<(MRG 405)>* **ALL ETERNALS DECK**
- Damn these vampires / Birth of serpents / Estate sale sign / Age of kings / The autopsy garland / Beautiful gas mask / High hawk season / Prowl great Cain / Sourdoire Valley song / Outer scorpion squadron / For Charles Bronson / Never quite free / Liza forever Minnelli.

- (8-10*) compilations, etc.-

Apr 02. (cd) *Three Beads Of Sweat; <(3BOS 1001)>* **PROTEIN SOURCE OF THE FUTURE... NOW!** — Aug 02
- Going to Tennessee / Pure heat / Hand ball / The window song / Night of the mules / Going to Malibu / Billy The Kid's dream of the magic shoes / Fresh berries for you / Alphabetizing / Third snow song / The monkey song / Love cuts the strings / Pure honey / Duke Ellington / Seed song / Quetzalcoatal comes through / Omega blaster / Coco-yam song / Alagemo / Two thousand seasons / Chinese rifle song / Yam, the king of crops / Alpha Omega.

Apr 02. (cd) *Three Beads Of Sweat; <(3BOS 1002)>* **BITTER MELON FARM** (early recordings) — Aug 02
- Noche del guajolote / Going to Bangor / Against Agamemnon / Going to Cleveland / Early spring / Historiography / No, I can't / Alpha desperation march / Going to Monaco / Star dusting / Teenage world / Going to Santiago / Sail on / Black Molly / Rain song / The bad doctor / Alpha double negative: Going to Catalina / Pure intentions / The lady of Shanghai / Pure love / Song for an old friend / Snow song / Faithless bacchant song / Short song about the 10 freeway / No, I can't / Song for Dana Plato / The sign.

Apr 02. (cd) *Three Beads Of Sweat; <(3BOS 1003CD)>* **GHANA** — Aug 02
- Golden boy / Pure gold / Papagallo / Song for John Davis / Stars around her / Going to Port Washington / Blood royal / The only thing I know / Raja vocative / Hatha hill / Going to Kirby Sigston / Please come home to Hamngatan / The last day of Jimi Hendrix's life / Orange ball of peace / Standard bitter love song \8 / Chino love song 1979 / Wrong! / Alpha Gelida / Wild Palm City / The Anglo-Saxons (live) / Flight 717: Going to Denmark / The admonishing song / Anti music song / Going to Hungary / Earth air water trees / Creature song / Pure sound / Going to Maine / Noctifer Birmingham / Leaving home.

EXTRA GLENNS

John Darnielle + Franklin Bruno (of Nothing Painted Blue)

Absolutely Kosher — Absolutely Kosher

Feb 02. (cd) *<(AK 017)>* **MARTIAL ARTS WEEKEND**
- Baltimore / All rooms cable a/c free coffee / Ultra violet / Twelve hands high / The river song / Somebody else's parking lot in Sebastopol / Memories / Going to Morocco / Going to Michigan / Terminal grain / Malevolent seascape Y / Going to Marrakesh.

MOUNTAIN HOME

This fringe freak-folk duo may, sadly, have been just be a one-off enterprise for San Diego-based songwriters Joshua Blatchley and Kristin Sherer. Although there was plenty of help from the likes of Ilya Monosov, FERN KNIGHT's Margie Wienk, Greg Weeks of ESPERS and MARISSA NADLER (anonymous vocals, apparently), the self-titled **MOUNTAIN HOME** (2007) {*6} didn't quite live up to expectations.

On the plus side, there was the gothic, 'Eerie, Indiana' air of 'The Sparrow' and 'Comes, The Winter', but the mournful detachment of the two unrecognisable trad tracks ('Omie Wise' and 'Nottamun Town') and the overstretched 10-minute 'Battle, We Were' could be a little dull and cold. Good try, though, and anything involving their famous guests has to be worth a listen. *MCS*

Joshua Blatchley - acoustic guitar, harmonium / **Kristin Sherer** - dulcimer / **Ilya Monosov** - banjo, acoustic guitar, hurdy-gurdy (of Shining Path) / **Margie Wienk** - acoustic cello (of FERN KNIGHT) / **anonymous (Marissa Nadler)** - vocals / **Greg Weeks** - vocals, guitar, harmonium (of ESPERS)

US Language Of Stone — UK not issued

Sep 07. (cd) *<LOS-002>* **MOUNTAIN HOME**
- The sparrow / Battle, we were / Comes, the winter / Omie wise / Nottamun town.

MOURNING CLOAK (⟹ STONE BREATH)

MOXY FRUVOUS

This troupe of political satirists from Thornhill, Ontario was formed by former college classmates Jian Ghomeshi, Murray Foster and Mike Ford in

1989, almost immediately adding David Matheson to busk with them on the streets of Toronto. Coming from somewhere between The KINGSTON TRIO and Barenaked Ladies, the theatrical barbershop quartet signed a deal with Atlantic Records after an early single, 'King Of Spain', hit No.1 in Canada.

BARGAINVILLE (1994) {*6} didn't quite live up to expectations, but the guys seemed to be enjoying themselves with giddy abandon on songs such as the Fresh Prince-like folk-rap of 'B.J. Don't Cry' and the doo-wop 'My Baby Loves A Bunch Of Authors'. The joke was over by the release of their more serious second set, **WOOD** (1996) {*7}, an earnest but uneasy transition into alt-rock; check out 'Horseshoes', 'Fly' and 'On Her Doorstep'. It was given a British release only and the band were dropped by Atlantic.

Released on Velvel, **YOU WILL GO TO THE MOON** (1997) {*7} was another departure of sorts, taking in contemporary styles on 'Michigan Militia' (a true gem), The Beatles-like 'Get In The Car' and a funky cover of the Bee Gees' 'I've Gotta Get A Message To You'. Their arrangements, often unaccompanied in the early days, continued to become more instrumentally conventional on their subsequent studio records, **THE B ALBUM** (1998) {*7}, the Don Dixon-produced **THORNHILL** (1999) {*6} and their back-to-bawdy-basics fun set **THE C ALBUM** (2000) {*7}.

MOXY FRUVOUS had a reputation as an outstanding live band, and the 1998 concert set **LIVE NOISE** (1998) {*7} captures their hoedown humour intact on all their best tracks, varied with choice covers of Talking Heads' 'Psycho Killer', Tom Waits's 'Jockey Full Of Bourbon' and LEADBELLY's 'The Drinking Song'. *MCS*

Mike Ford - vocals, acoustic guitar, accordion / **David Matheson** - vocals, acoustic guitar, accordion, piano / **Murray Foster** - vocals, bass / **Jian Ghomeshi** - vocals, drums, percussion, tin whistle

US/Can Moxy Fruvous — UK not issued

1992. (c-ep) <*MF 292*> MOXY FRUVOUS ⊟ Canada ⊟
- The king of Spain / My baby loves a bunch of authors / B.J. don't cry / The Gulf War song / Green eggs and ham / The drinking song [live].

Atlantic — East West

Feb 94. (cd/c) <*(4509 93134-2/-4)*> **BARGAINVILLE** □ Apr 94 □
- River valley / Stuck in the 90s / B.J. don't cry / Video Bargainville / Fell in love / The 1 lazy boy / My baby loves a bunch of authors / The drinking song / Morphee / King of Spain / Darlington darling / Bittersweet / Laika / Spiderman / Gulf War song.

Feb 96. (cd/c) *(0630 10616-2/-4)* **WOOD** ⊟ □
- Down from above / Horseshoes / Fly / The present tense tureen / Poor Mary Lane / On her doorstep / Misplaced / It's too cold / Bed and breakfast / Nuits de reve / Sad today.

Bottom Line — not issued

Mar 97. (cd/c) <*63440-47301-2/-4*> **YOU WILL GO TO THE MOON** ⊟ Canada ⊟
- Michigan militia / Get in the car / I've gotta get a message to you / Lazlo's career / Sahara / Lee / No no Raja / The incredible medicine show / Your new boyfriend / Kick in the ass / Boo time / Love set free / You will go to the moon. *<US-iss. 1997 on Velvel; 97301-2>*

May 98. (cd) <*none*> **LIVE NOISE** [live] ⊟ Canada ⊟
- Michigan militia / Jockey full of bourbon / Intra-Pennsylvania rivalry / Horseshoes / Good date band? / Fly / Boo time / Kirk King intro / King of Spain / Lowest highest point - improv / BJ don't cry / Johnny Saucep'n / Nature sounds / I've gotta get a message to you / My baby loves a bunch of authors / Naked puppets / No no Raja / Video Bargainville / Kasparov vs. Deep Blue / Psycho killer / Losers / King of Spain [cranky monarch version] / The drinking song. *<re-iss. Jun 09; same>*

Oct 98. (cd) <*CD 14187*> **THE B ALBUM** ⊟ Canada ⊟
- Big fish / Jenny Washington / The greatest man in America [live] / Ash hash / I love my boss / Gord's gold / Johnny Saucep'n / The ballad of Cedric Fruvous / Entropy / The kids' song [live].

Aug 99. (cd) <*79301 82849-2*> **THORNHILL** ⊟ Canada ⊟
- Half as much / Sad girl / You can't be too careful / I will hold on / Earthquakes / When she talks / Splatter splatter / Independence day / Downsizing / Hate letter / If only you knew / My poor generation.

Consolidated Fruvous — not issued

May 00. (cd) <*MF 500*> **THE C ALBUM** ⊟ Canada ⊟
- Welcome to C / Pisco bandito / The Norbals! / Video disco Bargainville / Beware the killer tents / Heatseeker boy / The mitosis waltz / Jared (the wild boy) / Bad Jim / The good judge / The Norbals! (reprise) / Pork tenderloin / Guinea-pig.

—disbanded soon after above; Murray joined Great Big Sea and Great Atomic Power (with Matheson)

Heidi MULLER

The name of Heidi always conjures up images of hillsides, and rambling-minstrel mountain dulcimer player HEIDI MULLER (b. November 29, 1953 in New Jersey) fits that vision perfectly. Raised by talented parents who loved music and poetry, and inspired by an East German-born uncle who was adept on the zither, she took a degree in psychology and began to perform in a coffee-house folk duo alongside Gail Rundlett, who went on to release a couple of albums, 'Farther Along' (1989) and 'Full Circle' (1995).

The Seattle-based singer/songwriter's first solo album was the cassette-only **BETWEEN THE WATER AND THE WIND** (1985) {*6}, a record that was strong on traditional style but also featured country-style covers of songs by BILL STAINES, Guy Clark and Bob Blue.

MATTERS OF THE HEART (1989) {*7} won the Folk Album Of The Year award of the Northwest Area Music Association, highlighted by 'Good Road', the theme to the Northwest Inland Radio Folk show, and MULLER appeared as a finalist at the annual Kerrville Folk Festival. Further self-financed albums **CASSIOPEIA** (1992) {*5}, **GIVING BACK** (1996) {*5}, **GYPSY WIND** (2002) {*5} and her Bob Webb collaboration **SEEING THINGS** (2005) {*5} were recorded in between day gigs as a mountain dulcimer tutor and a teacher of business skills to budding musicians in Seattle. *MCS*

Heidi Muller - vocals, acoustic guitar, mountain dulcimer

US Cascadian — UK not issued

1985. (c) <*CM 101*> **BETWEEN THE WATER AND THE WIND** □ ⊟
- Honey in my tea / All the diamonds / You're the sun / River affair / The ballad of Erica Levine / The oak and the ash / Lone Star hotel cafe / River / All of me / Paradise and Puget Sound.

1989. (cd) <*CM 102*> **MATTERS OF THE HEART** □ ⊟
- Matters of the heart / Between the lines / Jesse's carol / Sandwood down to Kyle / Whitebark / Sometime next summer / Distant trains / Dark side of the moon / Rising dawn / Where the coho flash silver / The children draw guns / Keep that dream / Good road.

1992. (cd) <*CM 103*> **CASSIOPEIA** □ ⊟
- Looking for you / Long way to another friend / Cassiopeia / Winter goodbye - Snow on the buds / Average woman / Swing on down to Texas / Campfire in my guitar / Sing to the baby / Kitchikan / Palouse lullaby / Where dear friends will never part / I don't drive that road anymore / All that is gold.

1996. (cd) <*CM 104*> **GIVING BACK** □ ⊟
- Arrowhead / My old cat / Lost and found / The edge / Talk a little Texan / Groundhog / Whiskey before breakfast - Over the waterfall / November / I like baseball / Don't let me come home a stranger (with DAN MAHER) / You're the sun / Lowlands of Holland / Last one to go.

Oct 02. (cd) <*CM 105*> **GYPSY WIND** □ ⊟
- This much I know / Big ideas / Lie easy / Real change / Acres of clams - Rosin the beau / Voice of love / The Methow suite: Twisp river jig - Ray's good garlic - Leaving the Methow / Mama you're always there / Love has a life of its own / Stitchery song / Winter's turning / Gypsy wind.

Nov 05. (cd; by HEIDI MULLER & BOB WEBB) <*CM 106*>
SEEING THINGS □ ⊟
- Seeing things / Snowdance / Elk river blues - West Virginia hills / Highway is calling / Ghost stories / I will / From an earlier time / Snowdrops / Bach's old coat (cello prelude - Greasy coat) / My barista / Waltz for Susan / Sycamore / Sacred ground.

Peter MULVEY

American urban-folk singer-songwriter PETER MULVEY (b. September 6, 1969) fell into the music scene after playing an impromptu gig for his visiting brother and friends. He busked in subways after he lost his day job, and his new vocation was sealed when he won the 1994 Boston Acoustic Underground competition. He had already circulated two self-financed CDs, **BROTHER RABBIT SPEAKS** (1992) {*4} and **RAIN** (1994) {*5}, both re-issued later on Signature Sounds.

With his gruff, deep-fried, bluesy vocals, **RAPTURE** (1996) {*5} (featuring a live subway version of The WATERBOYS' 'The Whole Of The Moon') and **DEEP BLUE** (1997) {*6}, highlighted by CHRIS SMITHERS' 'Every Mother's Son' and Tom Waits's 'Clap Hands', continued his surge toward a small kind of stardom. More bluesy and funky than folk-rock at this stage, he was accompanied by Groovasaurus alumni David Goodrich (guitar) and Mike Piehl (drums).

Not content with a solo career, Peter resurrected his band Big Sky (with Milwaukee guys Joe Panzetta and Dave Janssen), a roots-rock/Americana outfit with four early-1990s albums to their credit including 1997's 'Lately' (credited to Little Sky). This Big Sky are not to be confused with the CAPERCAILLIE offshoot of the same name.

If one thing was clear, it was MULVEY's ability to play guitar with astonishing technique while singing in a contemporary roots style. This asset was in abundance on his most accomplished and polished set to date, **THE TROUBLE WITH POETS** (2000) {*7}, which co-credits Goodrich on most of the titles.

Like most singer-songwriters, MULVEY had a yen to pay tribute to his roots and influences with a covers album, and **TEN THOUSAND MORNINGS** (2002) {*6} was the result. Only very slightly tinged with folk-rock, his revamped and re-imagined versions of songs by Paul Simon, Marvin Gaye, DYLAN, Randy Newman, Elvis Costello and Lennon-McCartney were interesting rather than exceptional, but God loves a trier. DAR WILLIAMS' 'The Ocean', LEO KOTTKE's 'Running Up The Stairs' and the Gillian Welch gem 'Caleb Meyer' were more of the rootsy variety.

Before his participation in 2003 with KRIS DELMHORST and JEFFREY FOUCAULT in the REDBIRD album project (officially released in 2005), **KITCHEN RADIO** (2004) {*6} and **THE KNUCKLEBALL SUITE** (2006) {*5} added to his CV without causing much fuss outside his loyal fan base. The latter featured his unrecognisable cover of U2's 'The Fly'.

The re-recordings of **NOTES FROM ELSEWHERE** (2007) {*6} and the jazzier **LETTERS FROM A FLYING MACHINE** (2009) {*7} expressed a deeper and cooler manifesto. Likes all his lyrically astute albums, they are worth more than a cursory inspection. *MCS*

Peter Mulvey - vocals, acoustic guitar

US self-rel. / UK not issued

1992 (cd) <*none*> BROTHER RABBIT SPEAKS [–] [–]
- The tree / Rain dog / Black rabbit / Train bound for Evermore / The moon of the geese losing their feathers / Midwife / The weremoose / Juda / Rain song / Imamu / The voice / September dawn. <*re-iss. 2002; ???*> <*re-iss. Jun 07 on Black Walnut+=; ???*>*- RAIN*

1994. (cd) <*none*> RAIN [–] [–]
- The tree / November / Little foot / Birgit / No wonder / All in good fun / The prince / No one else / The dreams / The way that I love you / September dawn. <*re-iss. 2002; ???*> <*re-iss.+=*> - BROTHER RABBIT SPEAKS

Eastern Front / not issued

Jan 96. (cd) <*EFR 109*> **RAPTURE** [ ] [–]
- Rapture / On the way up / Question mark / Smell the future / The voice / So much more / If love is not enough / The whole of the moon / Half the time / Black rabbit / Dog talk / The dreams / The whole of the moon [live subway recording] / Aurora borealis.

May 97. (cd) <*EFR 112*> **DEEP BLUE** [ ] [–]
- Grace / Smoke / Midwife / Take this / No sense of humor / Deep blue / Every mother's son / Birgit / Out here / Clap hands / Forever night shade Mary. *(re-iss. Aug 03 on Peter Mulvey; 2)*

1997. (cd-ep) <*none*> GOODBYE BOB [ ] [–]
- Sign o' the times / If love is not enough / Deep blue / On the way up [live] / The dreams [live].

Black Walnut / not issued

Jan 00. (cd) <*003*> **GLEN CREE** [live] [–] tour [–]
- The trouble with poets / Tender blindspot / A better way to go / Ithaca / Hard times come again no more [feat. Juliet Turner] / Brand new '64 Dodge / Stephen's green / Smoke / If I were [feat. Juliet Turner] / Stretched on your grave.

Signature / Signature

Apr 00. (cd) <*SIG 1258*> **THE TROUBLE WITH POETS** [ ] [–]
- The trouble with poets / Words too small to say / Check me out (hey hey hey) / Every word except goodbye / Wings of the ragman / You meet the nicest people in your dreams / Eyes front (see through you) / All the way home / Bright idea / Tender blindspot / Home. *(UK-iss. Aug 04; same as US)*

Aug 02. (cd) <*SIG 1274*> **TEN THOUSAND MORNINGS** [ ] [–]
- Stranded in a limousine / Inner city blues (make me wanna holler) / Comes love / Two Janes / Running up the stairs / Mama, you been on my mind / Caleb Meyer / In Germany before the war / Oliver's army / For no one / Rain and snow / The ocean. <*(re+UK-iss. Apr 04 on Acoustic Roots; AR 004)*>

Mar 04. (cd) <*(SIG 1283)*> **KITCHEN RADIO** [ ] Aug 04 [ ]
- Road to Mallow / Shirt / 29 cent head / Falling / Charlie / Denver, 6 am / Rise / Bloomington / Me and Albert / You / Thirty / Toad / Sad, sad, sad, sad (and faraway from home).

——In 2005 the REDBIRD set (with KRIS DELMHORST + JEFFREY FOUCAULT) was issued on Signature Sounds, having been independently delivered in late 2003

Apr 06. (cd) <*(SIG 1297)*> **THE KNUCKLEBALL SUITE** [ ] [ ]
- Old Simon Stimson / The fly / Girl in the hi-tops / You and me and the ten thousand things / Horses / Thorn / Lila blue / Marty and Lou / Brady Street stroll / The knuckleball suite / The fix is on / Coda: Ballymore.

Nov 07. (cd) <*(SIG 2008)*> **NOTES FROM ELSEWHERE** [re-recordings] [ ] [ ]
- Shirt / Better way to go / The dreams / Old Simon Stimson / Rapture / The trouble with poets / Grace / Black rabbit / If love is not enough / The knuckleball suite / Every word except goodbye / Charlie / Tender blindspot / On the way up / Wings of the ragman / Words too small to say / Little foot.

Aug 09. (cd) <*(SIG 2023)*> **LETTERS FROM A FLYING MACHINE** [ ] [ ]
- Kids in the square / Some people / Letters from a flying machine / Windshield / What's keeping Erica? / ...Plus the many inevitable fragments / Dynamite Bill / Shoulderbirds (you know me) / Bears / Vlad the astrophysicist / On a wing and a prayer / Coda: Love is here to stay.

N

Marissa NADLER

The music of singer/songwriter and multi-instrumentalist MARISSA NADLER (b. April 5, 1981 in Washington, D.C.), close freak-folk kin to JOSEPHINE FOSTER, ALELA DIANE, JOANNA NEWSOM and FAUN FABLES, was not exactly a walk in the park.

BALLADS OF LIVING AND DYING (2004) {*6} is the title of her debut album. There was a sense of foreboding on this record, which boasted timeless, dreamy delights such as 'Box Of Cedar', 'Stallions' and 'Days Of Rum'. Also issued on the Eclipse imprint, **THE SAGA OF MAYFLOWER MAY** (2005) {*6} harked back to the halcyon days of Brit-folk with a serving of Celtic-style narrative. She was accompanied by producer Brian McTear (on Hammond organ) and guest NICK CASTRO for the delicate 'The Little Famous Song'. Intimate and otherworldly, Marissa delivered lilting warbles on some great cuts such as 'Calico', 'Under An Old Umbrella' and 'Mr. John Lee (Velveteen Rose)'.

2007 was a pivotal year. A third album (her first for Kemado), **SONGS III: BIRD ON THE WATER** {*7}, found her in good freak-folk company with ESPERS people Greg Weeks (production and distorted guitar licks), Helena Espvall (cello), Otto Hauser (percussion) and ORION RIGEL DOMMISSE (mandolin and harp). The recommended playlist is 'Diamond Heart', 'Silvia', 'Mexican Summer', 'Feathers' and a cover of LEONARD COHEN's 'Famous Blue Raincoat'. If you want more, find a copy with the free EP that contains her take on NEIL YOUNG's 'Cortez The Killer'.

Following sideline roles as the anonymous vocalist on MOUNTAIN HOME's self-titled 2007 album, and as part of the choir on one-man metal act Xasthur's 2010 set 'Portal Of Sorrow', she surfaced again with **LITTLE HELLS** (2009) {*8}, a record that escapes from her folk roots on a handful of tracks. Nevertheless, 'Ghosts And Lovers', 'Heartpaper Lover' and 'Mistress' can be recommended.

Dropped by Kemado, she released the self-titled and self-financed **MARISSA NADLER** (2011) {*7}, which was closer to Margo Timmins or Hope Sandoval than the Brit-folk/freak-folk acts she had been compared with in the past. Featuring session people Carter Tanton (bass), Jim Callan (pedal steel), Ben McConnell (percussion) and DOMMISSE (synths), the whole approach of the set was languid and lo-fi, and its highlights were 'Baby, I Will Leave You In The Morning' (a proposed single), 'Alabaster Queen' and 'Daisy, Where Did You Go?'. *MCS*

Marissa Nadler - vocals, guitars, banjo, dulcimer, organ

US Eclipse / Happiness — UK Beautiful

2004. (cd/lp) <*ECL-036*> *(HAPP 005)* **BALLADS OF LIVING AND DYING** — Feb 05
- Fifty five falls / Hay tantos muertos / Stallions / Undertaker / Box of cedar / Bird song / Mayflower May / Days of rum / Virginia / Annabelle Lee. *(bonus+=)* - Day when the rain came. <*lp re-iss. Jan 09 on Mexican Summer; MEX 005*>

Jul 05. (cd/lp) <*ECL-044*> *(HAPP 007)* **THE SAGA OF MAYFLOWER MAY** — Jan 06
- Under an old umbrella / The little famous song / Mr John Lee (velveteen rose) / Damsels in the dark / Lily, Henry, and the willow trees / Yellow lights / Old love haunts me in the morning / My little lark / In the time of the lorry low / Calico / Horses and their kin.

not issued — My Kung Fu

May 06. (7") *(MYFUNGFU 16)* DIAMOND HEART. / Leather Made Shoes

Kemado — Peacefrog

Feb 07. (7"/cd-s) *(PFG 095/+CD)* DIAMOND HEART. / Dying Breed

Feb 07. (cd) <*KEM 055*> *(PFG 096)* **SONGS III: BIRD ON THE WATER** — Mar 07
- Diamond heart / Dying breed / Mexican summer / Thinking of you / Silvia / Bird on your grave / Rachel / Feathers / Famous blue raincoat / My love and I / Leather made shoes. <*US to download +=*> - Conjuring spirit worlds / Daisy and Violet / Honey bear / Cortez the killer.

Kemado — Kemado

Mar 09. (cd/lp) <*(KEM 085/086)*> **LITTLE HELLS**
- Heartpaper lover / Rosary / Mary comes alive / Little hells / Ghosts and lovers / Brittle, crushed and torn / The hole is wide / River of dirt / Loner / Mistress. *(w/ free cd-ep at Rough Trade shops +=)* - River of dirt / River of dirt [alt.] / Conjuring spirit worlds [out-take] / Daisy and Violet / Honey bear / Cortez the killer.

Box Of Cedar — Box Of Cedar

Jun 11. (cd) <*(BOC 001CD)*> **MARISSA NADLER**
- In your lair, bear / Alabaster queen / The sun always reminds me of you / Mr John Lee revisited / Baby, I will leave you in the morning / Puppet master / Wind up doll / Wedding / Little king / In a magazine / Daisy, where did you go?

Lau NAU

Laura Naukkarinen and her trio LAU NAU can be safely filed under Finnish freak-folk. Born 1980 in Helsinki, Finland, the free-spirited Laura spent her formative years helping to create a handful of live, improvised scores for cult silent films including Vertov's 'Man With A Movie Camera', Christensen's 'Haxan' and Dreyer's 'La Passion de Joan d'Arc'.

With her partner, Antti Tolvi (they had a son, Nuutti, in 2005), Pekko Kappi and Tomas Regan, the band produced the demos of **KUUTARHA** (2005) {*5}. The word means 'moon garden'. The demos found their way to Chicago's Locust Music label. Though certainly not for the uninitiated or the folk purist, the set evokes the warmth of a campfire with eclectic layers of song and soundscape, featuring banjo and other exotic instrumentation. Track nine, 'Kivi Murenee Jolla Kavelee', stems from a Nepalese traditional song (imagine the sound of tribes of Inuit washing pots and pans), but it's 'Kuula', 'Johdattaja-Joleen' and 'Kuljen Halki Kuutarhan' that steal Laura's lo-fi-folk show.

NUKKUU (2008) {*7}, nine cosmic lullabies for the Clangers generation (the word means 'sleeps'), picked up where her debut left off. Somewhat reminiscent of Mother Gong (Gilli Smyth) or My Bloody Valentine-meets-The Residents on Diazepam, the set literally cries out for some co-ordination. 'Lahtolaulu' is the catalyst, using fuzz guitars over dizzy, discordant echoes of Lau's pixieish vocals.

Maybe closer attention might lead the listener to her musical garden of Eden, but too many times (as on 'Maapahkinapuu' and 'Mooste') the tearful tracks meander and fight to get out from under a needle on a scratched 78. Trying to caress the listener into submission, the hymnal 'Vuoren Laelle' (written by Herra Kirsikka) sparks fiery images of 'The Wicker Man' juxtaposed with Dreyer's 'Joan Of Arc'. *MCS*

Laura Naukkarinen - vocals, multi / with **Pekko Kappi** - strings / **Tomas Regan** - double bass, banjo / **Antti Tolvi**

US Locust — UK Locust

Feb 05. (cd/lp) <*Locust 66*> **KUUTARHA**
- Jos minulla olisi / Kuula / Plakkikanteletar / Tulkaa! / Puuportti rautaportilta / Johdattaja-Joleen / Hunnun / Kuljen halki kuutarhan / Kivi murenee jolla kavelee / Sammiolimnut.

——**Mari Kalkun** repl. Tomas

May 08. (cd/lp) <*(Locust 111)*> **NUKKUU**
- Lue kartalta / Painovoimaa, valoa / Ruusosuu / Rubiinilasia / Lahtolaulu / Maapahkinapuu / Mooste / Jouhet / Vuoren laelle.

NEUTRAL MILK HOTEL

The brainchild of singer/songwriter and multi-instrumentalist Jeff Mangum, the Athens, Georgia-based NEUTRAL MILK HOTEL (originally with William Cullen Hart and Bill Doss, who bailed out to form Olivia Tremor

Control) were at the top of the Elephant 6 Collective heap that surfaced in the early 1990s. Robert Schneider (an Apples In Stereo recruit) was also a member, and he had been a friend of Jeff since their formative days growing up in Rushton, Los Angeles.

Mangum got NEUTRAL MILK HOTEL properly under way after false starts as Cranberry Life Cycle and the pre-Olivia Tremor Control outfit Synthetic Flying Machine, releasing a series of obscure singles and demos before Cher Doll released the single 'Everything Is' in 1994.

The Merge label took over for **ON AVERY ISLAND** (1996) {*7}, a record apparently recorded on Schneider's bedroom four-track. It was released in the UK on the Fire label. The record itself - think Beach Boys and Sonic Youth - faced inevitable comparisons with Olivia Tremor Control's 'Dusk At Cubist Castle', if only for its fantastical concept strangeness. Not as overtly psychedelic as the latter album, but rampantly experimental, the album was a collision of seemingly spontaneous, barely formed musical ideas, samples and sound effects, grounded in a frazzled pop genius and executed with delirious abandon.

Mangum continued to indulge his passion for conceptual weirdness with 1998's **IN THE AEROPLANE OVER THE SEA** {*9}, a truly inspiring fuzz-folk set of lo-fi acid trips with Mangum emotive and creative in equal degrees of greatness. The three-parter 'The King Of Carrot Flowers' challenged the very nature of what folk music really was. The band of Jeremy Barnes (before his A HAWK AND A HACKSAW days), Scott Spillane and Julian Koster was continuously cohesive on other gems such as 'Two-Headed Boy', 'Holland, 1945' and the eight-minute 'Oh Comely' - the missing link between DYLAN and Nirvana. *MCS*

Jeff Mangum - vocals, multi / with initially **Robert Schneider** - xylophone, etc / **Hilarie Sidney** - multi (of Apples In Stereo, of Secret Square) / **Aaron Reedy** - multi / **Rick Benjamin** - trombone / **Lisa Janssen** - bass (of Secret Square)

US Elephant 6 — UK not issued

1991. (c-ep) *<none>* INVENT YOURSELF A SHORTCAKE ☐ ⊟

1992. (c-ep) *<none>* BEAUTY ☐ ⊟

1993. (c) *<none>* **HYPE CITY SOUNDTRACK** ☐ ⊟
- Up and over we go / Wood guitar / Tuesday moon / April 1st / Tea-time - Bombdrop / Gardenhead - Leave me alone / Biscuit / Los Angeles / Piggy / Engine.

Cher Doll — not issued

Nov 94. (7") *<Cher 002>* EVERYTHING IS. / Snow Song pt. one ☐ ⊟

——Cher Doll Records also issued a few split singles which included the tracks 'Up And Over' and 'Invent Yourself A Shortcake'

Merge — Fire

Jul 95. (7") *(BLAZE 79)* EVERYTHING IS. / Snow Song pt. one ⊟ ☐
(cd-s+=) (BLAZE 79CD) - Aunt Eggma blowtorch. *<US re-iss. Oct 01 as cd-ep on Orange Twin+=; OTR 05CD>* - Tuesday moon.

Mar 96. (cd) *<MRG 53> (FIRECD 53)* **ON AVERY ISLAND** ☐ Sep 96 ☐
- Song against sex / You've passed / Someone is waiting / A baby for Pree / Marching theme / Where you'll find me now / Avery Island - April 1st / Gardenhead - Leave me alone / Three peaches / Naomi / April 8th / Pree-sisters swallowing a donkey's eye. *(UK+=)* - Everything is / Snow song pt.1. *(lp re-iss. 2011 +=; FF 053R)*

——now without Janssen

——**Mangum** was joined by **Jeremy Barnes** - drums, organ / **Julian Koster** - accordion, saw, etc / **Scott Spillane** - brass

Merge — Blue Rose

Feb 98. (cd) *<MRG 136CD> (BRRC 1019-2)* **IN THE AEROPLANE OVER THE SEA** ☐ Jun 98 ☐
- The king of carrot flowers (pt. one) / The king of carrot flowers (pts. two and three) / In the aeroplane over the sea / Two-headed boy / The fool / Holland, 1945 / Communist daughter / Oh comely / Ghost / (untitled) / Two-headed boy (part 2). *(UK re-iss. Nov 00; same as US) (re-iss. Sep 05 on Domino cd/lp+=; REWIG CD/LP 21)*

Oct 98. (7") *(BRRC 1023-7)* HOLLAND, 1945. / Engine ⊟ ☐

——after the split, Mangum released the solo 'Live At Jittery Jo's' in 2001; Barnes formed A HAWK AND A HACKSAW

Carrie NEWCOMER

Born, of Quaker stock, on May 25, 1958 in Dowagiac, Michigan, the folk singer and songwriter CARRIE NEWCOMER has been around the 'Fast Folk' scene since her days fronting the Indiana-based outfit STONE SOUP alongside fellow acoustic guitarist Larry Smeyak and percussionist Dennis Leas. The pop-folk trio released two self-financed albums, **LONG FIELDS** (1984) {*5} and **OCTOBER NIGHTS** (1987) {*6}.

VISIONS AND DREAMS (1991) {*6}, featuring L.J. Booth's 'The Boogie Man', was likewise delivered on her own Windchime label. Philo subsequently signed her on the strength of this safe, MOR country/blues-tinged folk record, and kept faith until moving her along the corridor to Rounder Records for her latest, Appalachians-moving effort, **BEFORE AND AFTER** (2010) {*6}. However, it was albums such as her spiritual Philo sets **AN ANGEL AT MY SHOULDER** (1994) {*7} and **THE BIRD OR THE WING** (1995) {*6} that made folk fans take note.

She tours supporting good friends like Mary Chapin Carpenter and Alison Kraus, and if it were necessary to recommend only one of her folk albums, 2002's Joni MITCHELLish **THE GATHERING OF SPIRITS** {*6} would be it.

She toured India in 2009, and with classical/world music sarod master Amjad Ali Khan (and his sons Ayaan and Amaan) she found time to produce an album's worth of spiritual folk material, 2011's **EVERYTHING IS EVERYWHERE**. Released in India initially, it will be an exciting project for fans in the US to get to grips with when released there in October 2011. Carrie now lives in Elkhart, Indiana.*MCS*

STONE SOUP

Carrie Newcomer - vocals, acoustic guitar / **Larry Smeyak** - acoustic guitar, vocals / **Dennis Leas** - percussion

US Windchime — UK not issued

1984. (lp) *<RC-101/S>* **LONG FIELDS** ☐ ⊟
- Survivors / Waiting / Leaves / Long fields / Alternatively / Under the tree / San Isidro / Weather top.

1987. (cd) *<RC-102-2>* **OCTOBER NIGHTS** ☐ ⊟
- October nights / A piece of the truth / Winter / Links in the chain / Windows and doors / Jack / All around the shoreline / Iowa / Baby's a train / True to you.

CARRIE NEWCOMER

Windchime — not issued

1991. (cd) *<RC-103-2>* **VISIONS AND DREAMS** ☐ ⊟
- Visions and dreams / 1000 miles away / I'm on your side / A whole lot of hope / Another thunder / I don't want to fight today / Birds on a telephone wire / Just what it is / Something true to believe in / Sounds of the morning / Some kind of grace / Lead me on / Right brain born (in a left brain world) / Situations like lightning / The boogie man. *<re-iss. Oct 95/Nov 95 on Philo; CDPH 1193>*

Philo — Philo

Apr 94. (cd/c) *<(CDPH/CPH 1163)>* **AN ANGEL AT MY SHOULDER** ☐ ☐
- Only one shoe / Streamline / It goes both ways / Hold on / Love like an immigrant / An angel at my shoulder / My mamma said it's true / In the city / Playing with matches / Meet you on a Monday / Three women / A safe place / Take one step / Who have you been (and who are you now).

Feb 95. (cd/c) *<(CDPH/CPH 1183)>* **THE BIRD OR THE WING** ☐ May 95 ☐
- Holy ground / The bird or the wing / Nomads / Tenderly with you / The love letter / The yes of yes / Wisdom is watching / Under your skin / I'm not going to let you break my heart / Closer to home / Looking for something / The prelude / Distance. *<cd re-iss. Nov 09; same>*

Sep 96. (cd) *<(CDPH 1203)>* **MY FATHER'S ONLY SON** ☐ Oct 96 ☐
- Crazy in love / Tracks / These are the moments / You can choose / My father's only son / I'm not thinking of you / Up in the attic / Closer to you / Bearing witness / The madness you get used to / The rooms my mother made / Amelia almost 13.

Mar 98. (cd) *<(CDPH 1223)>* **MY TRUE NAME** ☐ ☐
- I should've known better / When one door closes (another one opens wide) / What kind of love is this / This long / The moon over Tucson / The razor's edge / Take it around again / My true name / Something worth fighting for / Just a little hand / One good turn / Close your eyes / The length of my arms.

Aug 00. (cd) *<(CDPH 1226)>* **THE AGE OF POSSIBILITY** ☐ Sep 00 ☐
- When it's gone it's gone / Tornado alley / Thread / Love is wide / All I know / Bare to the bone / Anything with wings / Just like downtown / Sparrow / Seven dreams / It's not ok / One great cry / This too will pass.

Jul 02. (cd) *<CDPH 9901>* **BARE TO THE BONE** [live] ☐ ⊟
- (introduction) / Sparrow / Just like downtown / I'm on your side / Bare to the bone / Hold on / The moon over Tucson / Three women / When one door closes / My father's only son / The yes of yes / Anything with wings.

Sep 02. (cd) *<(CDPH 1243)>* **THE GATHERING OF SPIRITS** ☐ ☐
- Holy as a day is spent / Straight to the point / I'll go too / The gathering of spirits / The fisher king / Little earthquakes / There and back / Silver / I'm still standing / I heard an owl / The things I've gone and done.

Aug 05. (cd) *<(CDPH 1247)>* **REGULARS AND REFUGEES** ☐ ☐
- Angels unaware / Be true / Nothing's ever wasted / I fly / Alice and Roy / Arthur B and Bob / Five years on / La paloma / All saints' day / Below the waves / There is a spirit / A coal red sky / Before the fall / Betty's diner [remix].

Feb 08. (cd) *<(CDPH 1253)>* **THE GEOGRAPHY OF LIGHT** ☐ ☐
- There is a tree / The clean edge of change / A map of shadows / Geodes / Two toasts / Where you been / Biscuits and butter / A mean kind of justice / Leaves don't drop (they just let go) / You'd think by now / One woman and a shovel / Lazarus / Throw me a line / Don't push send.

Rounder Rounder

Feb 10. (cd) <*(ROUCD 3276)*> **BEFORE AND AFTER**
- Before and after / Ghost train / I do not know its name / Stones in the river / If not now / A small flashlight / I meant to do my work today / A simple change of heart / Hush / Coy dogs / Do no harm / I wish I may, I wish I might / A crash of rhinoceros.

Available Light The Times Of India

Oct 11. (cd; by CARRIE NEWCOMER & AMJAD ALI KHAN) <*(none)*> **EVERYTHING IS EVERYWHERE** Aug 11
- Breathe in breathe out / Everything is everywhere / We were sleeping / I believe / Shine / Dreaming / Air and smoke / May we be released / Fountain of love.

- (8-10*) compilations -

Jan 04. (cd) *Philo;* <*(CDPH 1245)*> **BETTY'S DINER: THE BEST OF CARRIE NEWCOMER** Feb 04
- Toward the horizon / Betty's diner / Bowling baby / I'll go too / Bare to the bone / When it's gone it's gone / Love is wide / The gathering of spirits / Hold on / I should've known better / The moon over Tucson / When one door closes / Threads / The yes of yes / Only one shoe / Straight to the point / My father's only son / Three women.

Harris NEWMAN

Canadian finger-picking guitarist HARRIS NEWMAN (b. 1974 in Montreal, Toronto) might be best known to fans of indie stalwarts Sackville, or even Triple Burner, his post-millennium duo with Bruce Cawdron (percussionist of Godspeed You Black Emperor!).

Inspired by the likes of folk-blues guitar legends JOHN FAHEY and ROBBIE BASHO, and playing in the same ballpark as indie-folkies GLENN JONES, STEFFEN BASHO-JUNGHANS and SEAN SMITH, Harris and Bruce deliver improvised ramblings that would make any of those maestros proud. NEWMAN's debut CD for Strange Attractors, **NON-SEQUITURS** (2003) {*7}, created a myriad of tremulous and dynamic soundscapes, none more organic than the 15-minute 'Forest For The Trees', though that's probably not the best example. His second album, **ACCIDENTS WITH NATURE AND EACH OTHER** (2005) {*7}, took a more Eastern and experimental approach; highlights here were the bluesy 'A Thousand Stolen Blankets To Warm You At Night' and 'The Butcher's Block'.

Honouring the spirit of FAHEY and company once more, his third official album, **DECORATED** (2007) {*7}, crossed ambient, New Age and neo-folk boundaries in 'The Malarial Two-Step', 'Opera House Stomp' (written with drummer Eric Craven) and the sombre 'Anamnesis', very like Mogwai in acoustic mode. *MCS*

Harris Newman - guitars, bass (with **Bruce Cawdron** - percussion)

US Strange Attractors UK Strange Attractors

Oct 03. (cd) <*(SAAH 18CD)*> **NON-SEQUITURS**
- Around about thirty-six / Bitten / The bullheaded stranger / Sometimes a bad attitude is all it takes / Feral blues / The pyramids / Trick question / God is in the details / I fought the lottery / Forest for the trees / Throwing the goat.

Feb 05. (cd) <*(SAAH 29CD)*> **ACCIDENTS WITH NATURE AND EACH OTHER**
- The butcher's block / Cloud city / Continental drift / It's a trap (part I) / Lake Shore drive / A thousand stolen blankets to warm you at night / Lords and ladies / Out of sorts / It's a trap (part II) / Accidents / Stopgap measure / Driving all night with only my mind.

Sep 07. (cd/lp) <*SAAH 52 CD/LP*> **DECORATED**
- Our cavalcade of sightless riders / Anamnesis / Decorated / The malarial two-step / Blues for Vilhelm / Golden valleys as seen from the east / We return to Black Wolf mountain / Opera house stomp / A quarter to call the ambulance.

not issued own label

Feb 09. (cd-r; by IGNATZ & HARRIS NEWMAN) *(none)* **BRING YOU BUZZARD MEAT** Belg
- Political song for Carla Bruni to sing (with synthesizer) / I will bring you buzzard meat / Rise while you fall / Under the reef of cloud / Stray dog.

- (5-7*) others, etc.-

Jun 06. (ltd-cd) *(KD 011)* **DARK WAS THE NIGHT** [live at Atalante, Goteberg, Sweden, February 13, 2006] Sweden
- Anamnesis / Decorated / The malarial two-step / The butcher's block / Stopgap measure / Out of sorts / Museum dweller / The wherewithal / A thousand stolen blankets to keep you warm at night / Cloud city / Sometimes a bad attitude is all it takes.

May 07. (ltd-lp) *Glasvocht; (GVLP 01)* **HARRIS NEWMAN // Mauro Antonio Pawlowski** Belg
- Early-onset Tourette's / Sit down, stay down / Son of Ichabod // [other artist tracks].

Joanna NEWSOM

Coming from a rich musical background (her father was a guitarist, her mother a concert pianist), Joanna played piano and Celtic harp from an early age. Her neighbour was the avant-garde composer Terry Riley. Born January 18, 1982, in Nevada City, California, the influences that surrounded her were Appalachian old-timey folk music (KAREN DALTON, TEXAS GLADDEN), Venezuelan and West African rhythms, New Wave (Blondie, Television, Patti Smith, etc) and jazz (Billie Holiday).

During the early 2000s Joanna was a member of two alt-rock outfits, The Pleased (alongside likeminded guitarist turned folk producer NOAH GEORGESON) and indie supergroup Nervous Cop, featuring Greg Saunier of Deerhoof and Zach Hill of Hella. Issued around the same time as her self-released solo sets, WALNUT WHALES and YARN AND GLUE, these bands delivered a few records featuring the classically-trained NEWSOM, The Pleased with 'One Piece In The Middle' (2002) and 'Don't Make Things' (2003), and Nervous Cop with a self-titled effort in 2003.

With support slots for WILL OLDHAM and indie chanteuse Cat Power, NEWSOM found her way on to the Drag City label, which almost immediately released her debut album proper, the Noah Georgeson-produced **THE MILK-EYED MENDER** (2004) {*7}. One thing that hits you, apart from her graceful harp playing and songwriting, is her squeaky, innocent vocals; you can't help thinking of Shirley Temple or Rickie Lee Jones.

Integrating Appalachian and bluegrass folk music with quirky, lighthearted ballads and fairytales, the album is in parts endearing, in others nauseating. Tracks include 'Bridges And Balloons', 'Sprout And The Bean', the six-minute 'Sadie', the harpsichord-infused 'Peach, Plum, Pear' and the sole trad rendition, the 'Dirty Old Town'-like 'Three Little Babes'. To promote the set, she toured supporting DEVENDRA BANHART, while her session work included a stint on Smog's 'A River Ain't Too Much To Love'.

Towards the autumn of 2006, a second official album, **YS** {*8} (pr. 'ease', featuring guitarist Grant Geissman, percussionist Don Heffington, bassist Lee Sklar and an orchestra arranged and conducted by co-producer Van Dyke Parks), was released. Mixed by Jim O'Rourke and recorded in part (harp and vocals) by legendary engineer Steve Albini, it consisted of five lengthy tracks spanning almost an hour. More ambitious than its predecessor, the set weaves its magic through fairytales of mythical imagery on the concept of a transfigurative, Hollywood-like musical base. The complex arrangements and plot twists are at first hard to grab hold of, but after some consecutive listens to lilting songs such as 'Emily', 'Monkey And Bear' and the 17-minute 'Only Skin', the album unfolds like nature itself.

As an addendum to this organic and elegant set, she released a tour-souvenir EP, 'Joanna Newsom & The Ys Street Band', a fleeting nod to Bruce Springsteen. As well as the new song 'Colleen', the record featured two of her oldies, 'Clam Crab Cockle Cowrie' (from her debut) and the 13-minute 'Cosmia' (from YS).

After a three-year hiatus, Joanna made amends with a two-hour, three-disc album, **HAVE ONE ON ME** (2010) {*6}, in which she took on detached, Laurel Canyon-meets-chamber-pop music rather than unfurling her deepest and darkest tales of the unexpected. It certainly had its moments, but most tracks went on long past their sell-by dates. 'Kingfisher', 'Baby Birch', 'In California', 'Autumn' and the title track all ran eight minutes and more. Worth a few listens if you've got time on your hands. *MCS*

Joanna Newsom - vocals, harp, piano, harpsichord / + session people

US self-rel. UK not issued

2002. (cd-r) <*none*> WALNUT WHALES
- Erin / Cassiopeia / Peach, plumb, pear / Clam crab cockle cowrie / Flying a kite / The fray / En gallop! / The book of right-on.

2003. (cd-r) <*none*> YARN AND GLUE
- Sprout and the bean / This side of the blue / Yarn and glue / What we have known / Bridges and balloons.

Drag City Drag City

Mar 04. (cd) <*(DC 263CD)*> **THE MILK-EYED MENDER** May 04
- Bridges and balloons / Sprout and the bean / The book of right-on / Sadie /

Inflammatory writ / This side of the blue / 'En gallop' / Cassiopeia / Peach, plum, pear / Swansea / Three little babes / Clam crab cockle cowrie.

Nov 04. (cd-s) *<(DC 287CD5)>* SPROUT AND THE BEAN / What We Have Known / Sprout And The Bean (video)

Nov 06. (cd/d-lp) *<(DC 303 CD/2xLP)>* **YS**
- Emily / Monkey and bear / Sawdust and diamonds / Only skin / Cosmia.

Apr 07. (cd-ep/12" ep) *<(DC 336 CD/12)>* JOANNA NEWSOM & THE YS STREET BAND E.P.
- Colleen / Clam crab cockle cowrie / Cosmia.

Mar 10. (3-lp/3-cd-box) *<(DC 390/+CD)>* **HAVE ONE ON ME**
- Easy / Have one on me / '81 / Good intentions paving company / No provenance / Baby birch // On a good day / You and me, Bess / In California / Jackrabbits / Go long / Occident // Soft as chalk / Esme / Autumn / Ribbon bows / Kingfisher / Does not suffice.

The NIELDS

Raised in Washington, D.C, native New Yorkers Nerissa Nields and her younger sister Katryna were brought up singing (taught by their father), so it was no surprise that after graduating from Yale and Trinity College, Hartford respectively they went on to perform as a duo. At college Nerissa met and subsequently married guitarist David Nields, who took her surname and joined the band.

The acoustic trio were soon playing coffee-houses from Windsor, Connecticut (where they were temporarily based) to Massachusetts, self-distributing two low-key sets along the way, **66 HOXLEY STREET** (1992) {*6} and **LIVE AT THE IRON HORSE MUSIC HALL** (1993) {*5}. Expanding the trio format, The NIELDS brought in a couple of outsiders, although rhythm section Dave Chalfont and Dave Hower (at first only a guest) were more than just auxiliaries. Chalfont produced the group's transitional third set, **BOB ON THE CEILING** (1994) {*6}.

Better was to come with **GOTTA GET OVER GRETA** (1996) {*7}, which first came out on Razor & Tie, but did better when Capitol re-promoted it in 1997 {*8} with three extra tracks, including a solid cover of Lennon/ McCartney's 'Lovely Rita'.

Verging ever so close to Country, The NIELDS delivered **PLAY** (1998) {*6}, an ambitious and ethereal attempt at a concept theatrical work that was mainly down to Nerissa. The back-to-basics **IF YOU LIVED HERE, YOU'D BE HOME NOW** (2000) {*7}, highlighted by Hank Williams's 'I'm So Lonesome I Could Cry', wrapped up the family band until a few comeback sets, made for children, were released later in the decade.

NERISSA & KATRYNA NIELDS stuck together for a couple of countrified rock ventures, **LOVE AND CHINA** (2002) {*5} and **THIS TOWN IS WRONG** (2004) {*5}, the latter borrowing its title from an old NIELDS song. *MCS*

David Nields (born David Jones) - vocals, acoustic guitar / **Nerissa Nields** (b. Jun 2 '67) - acoustic guitar, vocals / **Katryna Nields** (b. Apr 30 '69) - vocals, tambourine

US own label — UK not issued

1992. (cd) *<none>* **66 HOXLEY STREET**
- The king is falling / Shaking / I would have done the same for you / This happens again and again / Travel onward / Sharing the wealth / I'll be your song / Full midwestern moon / Tripping the light fantastic / Paul Klee / Superhero soup.

1993. (cd) *<none>* **LIVE AT THE IRON HORSE MUSIC HALL** [live in Northampton, MA]
- Jordi speaks / This is my life / I would have done the same for you / Shaking / Fade to black / Sweet holy grail / Just like Christopher Columbus / Blue room / The talking / Julia (not Julia) / Ash Wednesday / Full midwestern moon / I'll be your song / This happens again and again / The king is falling.

——added **Dave Chalfant** (b. Jan 31 '68, Barcelona) - bass, vocals

Peter Quince — not issued

1994. (cd) *<none>* **BOB ON THE CEILING**
- Be nice to me / If this were a movie / James / Ash Wednesday / Black boys on mopeds / Merry Christmas, Mr Jones / Memory leaves town / Boys will be boys / Where did it go? / Just like Christopher Columbus.

——added (formerly guest) **Dave Hower** (b. Jan 8 '67, New York) - drums, percussion (of WINTERPILLS)

1995. (cd-ep) *<none>* ABIGAIL
- Happy ever after afternoon / Cowards / Alfred Hitchcock / Waco lake / Goodnight, Irene.

Razor & Tie — not issued

Feb 96. (cd) *<RT 2822-2>* **GOTTA GET OVER GRETA**
- [*] / I need a doctor / Best black dress / Gotta get over Greta [track 2 re-] / Bulletproof / I know what kind of love this is / King of the hill / [**] / Blind / Fountain of youth / Cowards / Goodbye / All my pretty horses. *<re-iss. May 97 on Guardian Angel-Capitol+=; 56711-2>* - Taxi girl [insert *] / Einstein's daughter [insert **] / Lovely Rita [insert ***].

Zoe — Zoe

Jan 98. (cd) *<none>* **MOUSSE**
- Daddy's little girl / The trade / I'll meet you in the sky / Cary / Giving them back to Susan / Living it up in the garden / Stainless steel / Monster / Einstein's daughter [live] / Cool in the backseat / Dictator / Kamikaze / I hate MCI / 39 Orange Street / Waco lake / Blind / Julia (not Julia) / Superhero soup [live].

Sep 98. (cd) *<01143-1002-2> (ZOE 1002)* **PLAY** — Oct 98
- Easy people / Georgia I / In the hush before the heartbreak / Snowman / Art of the gun / Negehtfortra / Last kisses / Friday at the Circle K / Check it out / Nebraska / Train / Jennifer falling down / Innertube / Tomorrowland.

Mar 00. (cd) *<01143-1007-2>* **IF YOU LIVED HERE, YOU'D BE HOME NOW**
- Jeremy Newborn Street / Wanting / This town is wrong / Maybe it's love / May day café / Caroline dreams / Poem / One hundred names / Mr Right now / Jack the giant killer / I'm so lonesome I could cry / Mercy house / Keys to the kingdom / Forever / I still believe in my friends.

2001. (d-cd) *<none>* **LIVE FROM NORTHAMPTON** [live]
- Intro (The difference) / Jack the giant-killer / Taxi girl / Snowman / I need a doctor / May day café / 100 names / Bulletproof / Your wish is my command / Alfred Hitchcock / The train / Easy people / Keys to the kingdom // This town is wrong / Strawberry girl / Georgia O / I know what kind of love this is / Gotta get over Greta / Best black dress / Jennifer falling down / I'll meet you in the sky / Check it out / Living it up in the garden.

——the group split for a time

Mar 02. (cd; by NERISSA & KATRYNA NIELDS) *<01143-1025-2> (ZOE 1025)* **LOVE AND CHINA**
- Ticket to my house / Yesterday's girl / Love me one more time / Tailspin / I haven't got a thing / The sweetness / He loves the road / Love and China / Christmas carol / This happens again and again / All these years / Heading home / Eulogy for Emma / New state of grace.

Jan 04. (cd; by NERISSA & KATRYNA NIELDS) *<01143-1042-2> (ZOE 1042)* **THIS TOWN IS WRONG**
- The day I let glory steer / Glow in the dark plastic angel / This is the work that we do / When I let you into my closet / Haven't I been good / Clairman town / Paris / Sara, with your ring / When I'm here / If I wanted to / Kiss me to the moon / This town is wrong.

2004. (cd-ep; by NERISSA & KATRYNA NIELDS) *<none>* SONGS FOR AMELIA [children's]
- Amelia's little red dog / Amelia's big red dog / Howl at moon / Amelia / The enemy called pants / ABC / The caterpillar song / Suite for washcloth puppets / Crazy duck / If you're happy and you know it / One more song / Dragon unicorn / The caterpillar song (subversive) / Pants remix.

Mercy House — not issued

Jul 07. (cd; by NERISSA & KATRYNA NIELDS) *<none>* **SISTER HOLLER**
- Leave that trouble alone / The endless day / Eloise / Give me a clean heart / Who will shoe my pretty foot? / Moonlighter / Ain't that good news / The soldier at your door / That's my ship / This train / Abington sea fair / The right road (the sweetness, part 2) / We'll plant an oak.

Peter Quince — not issued

Apr 07. (cd) *<014>* **ALL TOGETHER SINGING IN THE KITCHEN** [family album]
- Going to the zoo / The fox / The unicorn / Red, red robin / Oh, Mary don't you weep / John, the rabbit / Anna, kick a hole in the sky / Night rider's lament / Shoes: farewell my pants / Aikendrum / Hop up ladies / He's got the whole world in his hands / Planting an even row / Hi, ho the rattlin' bog / Irish rover / Toes / All together singing in the kitchen.

Oct 08. (d-cd) *<016>* **ROCK ALL DAY // ROCK ALL NIGHT** [children's]
- Going to Boston / With catlike tread / The muffin man / Come and go with me / Who are you not to / Shine / Organic farm / Percy on Pluto / When the saints / Old grey bonnet / Dog on a ball / ABC / Mango walk / Allouette / Molly / My favorite color / Superhero soup / The enemy called pants / Sweet Rosyanna // Hobo's lullaby / Sylvie / Harvest table / In the bleak midwinter / May day carol / Wild mountain thyme / Sumer is a cumen in / Michael row the boat ashore / One man shall mow my meadow / Don't take too long / Ball for baby / I will bow and be / Simple / Easy people / Rise and shine / Sweet Rosyanna.

NORTHAMPTON HARMONY (⟹ CORDELIA'S DAD)

NOVEMTHREE

Founded in Takoma, Washington by bearded singer-songwriter and multi-instrumentalist Pythagumus Olaf Marshall and friends, the improvisional NOVEMTHREE was born out of the psych-folk of similar outfits IN GOWAN RING, ESPERS and STONE BREATH.

Shared CD-rs seem to have been the essence of NOVEMTHREE's existence, and one in particular, alongside ARROWWOOD (companion and musical associate Chelsea Robb), extracted all the goodness of their musical forest in **ARROWWOOD / NOVEMTHREE** (2007) {*7}. Blair Witchy tracks such as the haunting 'Beneath The Hemlock, Within The Grove', 'To Breathe In The Trees', 'Stones Of Blood' and 'Scythe To The Grass - Reworked' were an eerie, cinematic soundtrack that needed no horror film to draw the pictures. Another record that might raise the hairs on the back of your neck is the CD-r **MEANDERING IN STREAMS OF REFLECTION** (2009) {*6}, shared with The Joy Of Nature and setting the poetry of Hermann Hesse to music on some of the tracks. Not to be listened to at night in a rural log cabin; you have been warned. *MCS*

Pythagumus - vocals, multi-instruments / + guests

US self-rel. — UK not issued

2004. (ltd-cd-r) <*none*> FOG AND LEAVES [–] [–]
- Silence / Fog and leaves / Thicket / Floating / Gone.

2005. (ltd-cd-r) <*none*> **A PARLIAMENT OF OWLS** [–] [–]
- A brilliance of starling / Notebook / Specks / 73 drops into a rusty bucket / My intentions are thus / Play / All of the little forest animals shed their winter coats, gather together, feast and dance for the spring equinox.

Jan 06. (ltd-cd-r) <*none*> A WOODLAND FABLE [–] [–]
- At the feast, Mr Badger warns of impending doom... / This comes as a shock, as Mrs Fox protects her younglings... / All of the otters, both of them, begin to argue... / The squirrels scatter amongst the firs, but the rest stay to listen... / Even the birds stay alert, though high up in the trees... / Just then, Ms Grizzly buries her head in her paws as she hears it approach... <*also on shared C-30 on Hand Panther+=; HP 016*> - Metcha: Elegy Twenty Four.

Little Somebody — not issued

Jun 06. (ltd-cd-r) <*LSR 4*> **OF MY MOTHER'S WEARY WANDERINGS** [–] [–]
- Prey / A celebration / Waxing gibbons / Gedwolmann / Drifting / A mother's wish / Lying down asleep in her hair.

——added guest **Kelly Wyse** - (classical) piano, (harmony) vocals

Dec 07. (d-m-cd-r) <*LSR 8*> **Arrowwood // NOVEMTHREE** [–] [–]
- [ARROWWOOD tracks] // Scythe to the grass [reworked] / Stones of blood / Beneath the hemlock, within the grove / Winding away through the thicket / To breathe in the trees / Vespers.

Feb 09. (d-m-cd-r) <*LSR 9*> **The Joy Of Nature: Auguries Of Innocence // MEANDERING IN STREAMS OF REFLECTION** [–] [–]
- [The Joy Of Nature cd] // Reaching the summit at nightfall / The first flowers / We all must die / Gathering wildflowers / How heavy the days / Meadow song / We choose to lie calm.

Midnight — not issued

Jun 10. (ltd-7"green) <*MN 010*> FROM THESE ASHES... [ ] [–]
- Ashes / Cloister garden.
(ltd-7"+cd-r+=) <*same*> - Within the candlelit chamber / Meandering / The hidden grotto / Owlet / Meadow song (the fawn and the cedar) / The black forest / Magpie upon a mossy stem / Blood red bird.

- (8-10*) compilations -

2008. (cd-r) *Novemthree;* <*none*> **COLLECTED WORKS VOL.1** [–] [–]
- Silence / Fog and leaves / Floating / 73 drops into a rusty bucket / Specks / My intentions are thus / Play / The squirrels scatter amongst the firs, but the rest stay to listen... / Even the birds stay alert, though high up in the trees... / Drifting / A celebration of / Gedwolmann / A mother's wish / Lying down asleep in her hair / Harvest dance / Old year's feast / Scythe to the grass / Stones of blood / Dust of ages.

Will OLDHAM / BONNIE "PRINCE" BILLY (⟹ Great Country Discography)

Tom OVANS

Born June 8, 1953, near Boston, Massachusetts, streetwise singer-songwriter TOM OVANS resembles, in his gritty vocal style, a mature DYLAN or a hard-rocking fusion of Steve Earle and Joe Ely. This is reflected in the fact that Tom used to live in Nashville and now lives in Austin, Texas with his artist wife Lou Ann Bardash.

From his Americana-friendly debut album **INDUSTRIAL DAYS** (1991) {*7} to his most recent report cards, **PARTY GIRL** (2007) {*8} and the live-in-the-studio **GET ON BOARD** (2009) {*8}, OVANS has been one of many plying their trade on the same busy market stall. Britain and Europe, and the UK magazine 'Uncut', have taken him on board, releasing CDs that American labels have shunned.

Not exactly a dyed-in-the-wool folkie, the prolific writer OVANS nevertheless takes the ethos of DYLAN, GUTHRIE and OCHS (he was a good friend of Ochs and of TIM HARDIN) and gives it a kind of timeless rebirth, as though the 1970s, 1980s and 1990s never happened. Tom has released around a dozen decent albums, and good places to start, apart from the bookends already mentioned, would be **THE BEAT TRADE** (1999) {*7}, **STILL IN THE WORLD** (2001) {*6}, **TOMBSTONE BOYS, GRAVEYARD GIRLS** (2003) {*6} and the double set **HONEST ABE AND THE ASSASSINS** (2005) {*6}. *MCS*

Tom Ovans - vocals, guitar (+ session people)

US North Star / UK Survival

1991. (cd) <*nsr 4765-2*> **INDUSTRIAL DAYS**
- Wild wind blowing / Little child / Sad streets / Gonna be missing you / Hallelujah child / Lay down by my side / True love travels a rocky road / Those days have passed us by / Early one morning / Why do you treat love this way / Crazy. *(UK-iss. Feb 95; same as US)*

1993. (cd) <*nsr 4766-2*> **UNREAL CITY**
- Whatcha doing / High stake gambling town / Concrete love / Need I say more / Ballad of the rockabilly trash / Never fell from love the easy way / When things get tough / Back road blues / Tallahassee baby / Don't quit / Say a prayer / Gone to Mexico / Honey honey honey (how we need some money) / Just have a go / River girl. *(UK-iss. Feb 95; same as US)*

Feb 95. (cd) <*nsr 4767-2*> *(SUR 437CD)* **TALES FROM THE UNDERGROUND** — May 95
- Let it rain / Mr Blue / Uncle Joe / Dance with me girl / The sailor / Angelou / Echoes of the fall / Lucky to be alive / Brakeman's blues / The real Bono / Nine below zero / Waiting on you.

not issued / Demon

Jun 96. (cd) *(FIENDCD 783)* **NUCLEAR SKY** (re-recordings)
- High stake gambling town / Concrete love / Never fell from love the easy way / Hallelujah child / Sad streets / Early one morning / Those days have passed us by / Crazy / Whatcha doin / Need I say more / I'm going down / Angelou / Dance with me girl / The sailor / Mr Blue

Jun 97. (cd) *(FIENDCD 797)* **DEAD SOUTH**
- Killing me / James Dean coming over the hill / 1945 / Here she comes / The folksinger / Rita, Memphis and the blues / Exile / Better off alone / Real television / Pray for me / In the rain / Drowning man.

not issued / Floating World

Nov 99. (cd) *(fw 004)* **THE BEAT TRADE**
- The monkeys have landed / What about you? / Going someplace / Hey Woody Guthrie / Salvation / Tell me babe / Rebel roadside / Just to be with you / Can't blame her none / Bozo world / There are times / Where the moon shines bright. *<(re-iss. Oct 02/Aug 02; FWM 7017)>*

Mar 01. (cd) *(GEL 4019)* **STILL IN THE WORLD**
- Mama went to Arkansas / Cool daddy / Let my spirit fly / I see you there / Dark road / Sixth avenue / Underground train / Meeting on the road / Living in this town / The night I saw the Devil / I got a feeling for you.

(above issued on Evangeline)

May 03. (cd) *(fw 021)* **TOMBSTONE BOYS, GRAVEYARD GIRLS**
- Before I'm dead / Blues for Lenny / It's hard / Great big lie / Revolution / Tombstone boys, graveyard girls / Walking back to Tupelo / Standing in the rain / South to Alabama / Maria / Racine.

Nov 05. (d-cd) *(fw 029)* **HONEST ABE AND THE ASSASSINS**
- Bakersfield tonight / Hey Miss Lucy / Free your mind / Sunday afternoon in Austin / Soul street shuffle / Send a picture / In memory of Benny (2) / Song for the homeless / In my grave / My home city / Pack of lies / Blow man blow / A love song / So far behind / Innocent man // Midnight eclipse / Nashville blues / Sister's farm / Love and trust / Lovers in the night / Alright / Code of the west / Look out / I got a feeling / In memory of Benny (1) / New Orleans / Brownsville tonight / Trains go by / Jackson / Light travels with Buddha / There's a line.

Oct 07. (cd) *(fw 032)* **PARTY GIRL**
- Party girl / Whiskey jar / Sugar mama / I'll be seeing you / Hole in my shoe / Ain't no river / Both sides of the night / Nobody knows / Ooh baby / I keep on hoping / Rosalie / Somebody told me / West Texas blues.

Nov 09. (cd) *(fw 036)* **GET ON BOARD**
- Get on board / Rainbows / Breakdown and cry / Candy lane / Every single one / Taken with you / Honorable mention / Never been in love / On my way / Night train / Western plains blues / What I saw / Too late now.

- (5-7*) compilations, others, etc.-

Jul 02. (cd) *Floating World; (FWM 7014)* **15 UNRELEASED** (recorded from 1985...)
- Sun city / Angelou / Wild wind blowing (live) / Dance with me girl (live) / Brakeman's blues (live) / Out here on the farm / Honey, honey, honey / Rita, Memphis and the blues - James Dean coming over the hill (live) / Reputation (live) / Little child (live) / These days / Back road blues / New York City / Killing me (live) / River girl.

P

PANDA BEAR (⟹ ANIMAL COLLECTIVE)

Ellis PAUL

A leading light on Boston's effervescent and thriving contemporary folk scene, literate singer/songwriter ELLIS PAUL (b. Paul Plissey, January 14, 1965 in Aroostook County, Maine) has been a national treasure for the past 20 years or so. To mark his twentieth year in the business that has honoured him with award after award, the mayor of Boston proclaimed July 9, 2010 as 'Ellis Paul Day in Boston'.

Inspired in his formative years by DYLAN, GUTHRIE and (James) TAYLOR, Ellis has climbed in among folk-star friends and peers such as JOHN GORKA, BILL MORRISSEY, SHAWN COLVIN and VANCE GILBERT, becoming a headliner in his own right. His passionate and emotive vocals beam out of the speakers in such a cool and laid-back way that the listener could be in the studio with him. Nora Guthrie, Woody's daughter, is a big fan; she asked PAUL to perform at an all-star Woody Guthrie tribute show in September 1996.

Among his many albums, **URBAN FOLK SONGS** (1990) {*6} and **AM I HOME** (1990) {*5} are a good gauge of his early sound, while his well-polished debut CD proper, **SAY SOMETHING** (1993) {*7}, featuring BILL MORRISSEY on production and PATTY GRIFFIN and The STORY on harmonies, carried him on to greater things.

For many years PAUL was on the Philo label, reeling off several studio albums from 1994's **STORIES** {*7} to 2005's **AMERICAN JUKEBOX FABLES** ,{*6}, although **TRANSLUCENT SOUL** (1998) {*7} was arguably his most intimate and near-the-knuckle set, as he had just come through the breakdown of his marriage. In the 2000s he moved to the Black Wolf label, which also became his literary imprint. ELLIS PAUL's most recent musical narratives appear on **THE DAY AFTER EVERYTHING CHANGED** (2010) {*6}, inspired by the recession and Hurricane Katrina. Some of the songs were written with Kristian Bush (of Sugarland) in Nashville. *MCS*

Ellis Paul - vocals, acoustic guitar, piano (w/ session people)

US End Construction — UK not issued

1990. (c) *<none>* **URBAN FOLK SONGS**
- Ashes to dust / Photograph / Urban girl / Broke and hungry / Clock / Father to son / My gold mine / Jester fool / Raven and scarecrow / The love remains / Worn out pretention / Lonely man. *<cd-iss. Oct 00 on Black Wolf; ellispaul 4>*

1990. (c) *<none>* **AM I HOME**
- Angel / This old car / Fireflies / Am I home / Poet fool / Traffic / City song / New light on your halo / Town crier / Friday night. *<cd-iss. Oct 00 on Black Wolf; ellispaul 5>*

Eastern Front — not issued

Feb 93. (cd) *<501>* **SAY SOMETHING**
- Conversation with a ghost / Look at the wind blow / Just the jester fool / Angel / Thin man / Washington D.C. 5/91 / New light on your halo / Friday night / Blizzard / Jumpin' a train / Say something. *<re-iss. May 02 on Black Wolf; BW 9653>*

Philo — Philo

Apr 94. (cd/c) *<(CDPH/CPH 1181)>* **STORIES** — Oct 95
- All things being the same / 3000 miles / Here she is / Autobiography of a pistol / River / Last in the table / Last call / Who killed John Lennon? / King of Seventh Avenue / Looking for my friends / Don't breathe / (untitled). *<cd re-iss. 2002 on Black Wolf; BW 9654>*

Jun 96. (cd) *<(CDPH 1191)>* **A CARNIVAL OF VOICES** — Jul 96
- Midnight strikes too soon / Paris in a day / Trolley car / Deliver me / The ball is coming down / Weightless / All my heroes were junkies / Lay your wager down / Never lived at all / Self portrait / Change / Ghosts.

Sep 98. (cd) *<(CDPH 1120)>* **TRANSLUCENT SOUL** — Oct 98
- Take me down / I'm the one to save / Seven / She loves a girl / Bring me backwards / Did I ever know you? / Live in the now / The world ain't slowin' down / Angel in Manhattan / I won't cry over you / Translucent soul. *<+ bonus untitled track>*

Mar 00. (d-cd) *<(CDPH 1229)>* **LIVE** (live at the Somerville Theater, Massachusetts, etc.) — Jul 00
- (introduction) / Take me down / Conversation with a ghost [solo] / Look at the wind blow / Airplane pilot dead head [story] / Here she is / Tornado girl [poem] / Marty's lounge / Maria's beautiful mess / New York City evening out [story] / Angel in Manhattan // (intro: mosh pit) / 3000 miles / Did Galileo pray? / Last call / Harmony [poem] / Conversation with a ghost / Seize the day / Changing your name / When we begin / All things being the same / Autobiography / Never lived at all / Love's too familiar a word [poem] / The world ain't slowin' down / Weightless.

Nov 01. (cd) *<802035>* **SWEET MISTAKES** — fan club
- Kristian's song / Sweet mistakes / New Orleans / Seventeen Septembers / Independence day / 3000 miles (remix) / The martyr's lounge / Roll away bed / The art of distance / Medicine / The 20th century is over / Beautiful world.

(above demo release issued on Orchard)

Sep 02. (cd) *<(CDPH 1242)>* **THE SPEED OF TREES**
- Maria's beautiful mess / Give in, give up / Eighteen / If you break down / The ballad of Chris McCandless / Sweet mistakes / Words / Roll away bed / Breaking through the radio / When we begin / God's promise / The speed of trees.

Sep 03. (cd; by ELLIS PAUL & VANCE GILBERT) *<(CDPH 1239)>* **SIDE OF THE ROAD** — Oct 03
- The only way / Side of the road / Citizen of the world / Comes a time / May I suggest / What do I want what do I need / Gentle arms of Eden / This morning I am born again / Alone down here / Comfort you.

Apr 05. (cd) *<(CDPH 1246)>* **AMERICAN JUKEBOX FABLES**
- Blacktop train / Kiss the sun / Take all the sky you need / Time / Goodbye Hollywood / Marc Chagall / Jukebox on my grave / Home / Alice's champagne palace / She was / Bad, bad blood / Mystified / Clarity.

Black Wolf — Black Wolf

2006. (cd) *<none>* **LIVE AT CLUB PASSIM - NEW YEAR'S EVE 2005** (live) — benefit
- Maria's beautiful mess / intro... / Take all the sky you need / Alice's champagne palace / 3,000 miles / intro... / Jukebox on my grave / The martyr's lounge / (New Year's eve - spoken celebration) / Two bends in the road / intro... / Home / Snow in Austin / The night the lights went out on Christmas / Sweet mistakes.

Jan 08. (cd) *<BW 2290>* **THE DRAGONFLY RACES**
- Wabi-sabi / Because it's there / Abiola / Road trip / The dragonfly races / The bed song / The little red rose / I lost a day to the rain / I like to swing / Million chameleon march / Pinwheel / The star inside the apple / Nine months to fix the world / You are my sunshine.

Apr 09. (ltd-cd) *<(BW 0007)>* **A SUMMER NIGHT IN GEORGIA** (live from Eddie's Attic)
- (Eddie's intro) / Hurricane angel / (banter) / Maria's beautiful mess / Homer story / Alice's champagne palace / (banter) / The world ain't slowin' down / (banter) / 3000 miles / (banter) / Waking up to you / (banter) / Once upon a summertime / (banter) / Brant's birthday song / intro... / Alice in Manhattan / intro... / Road trip / Black top train / intro... / Calendar man / (thanks to Eddie's) / Take all the sky you need.

Jan 10. (cd) *<(BW 0010)>* **THE DAY AFTER EVERYTHING CHANGED**
- Annalee / Rose tattoo / River road / The day after everything changed / The lights of Vegas / Hurricane angel / Heaven's wherever you are / Dragonfly / Sometime, someplace / Once upon a summertime / Waking up to me / Walking after midnight - Change / The cotton's burning / Paper dolls / Nothing left to take.

- (8-10*) compilations -

Oct 06. (d-cd) *Philo; <(CDPH 1250)>* **ESSENTIALS** — Aug 08
- Take me down / Eighteen / Paris in a day / Home / If she's the one / Take all the sky you need / Maria's beautiful mess / The only way / Conversation with a ghost / The world ain't slowin' down / Angel in Manhattan / If you break down / Words / intro... / Snow in Austin (live) / Did Galileo pray? / Jukebox on my grave (live) // Sweet mistakes / 3000 miles / Blacktop train / Seventeen Septembers / Autobiography of a pistol / The martyr's lounge / Midnight strikes too soon / Alice's champagne palace / Roll away bed / All things being the same / Deliver me / Welcome home to Maine / She loves a girl / She was / The speed of trees (live) / intro... / God's promise.

Elvis PERKINS

First there was Elvis Presley, then there was Elvis Costello, and now we have ELVIS PERKINS, the son of the late, great cult actor (and Presley fanatic) Anthony Perkins, who played Norman Bates in the film 'Psycho'. Often compared to COHEN and DYLAN, singer/songwriter Elvis (b. February 9, 1976 in Manhattan, NY) was raised in Los Angeles and New York. His mother died on Flight 11, one of the planes flown into the World Trade Center, New York City in the 9/11 terrorist attacks in 2001.

Spurred on by the tragic deaths of his parents (his father had died of AIDS-related complications in 1992), PERKINS played guitar in various rock bands, tutored by Prescott Niles of The Knack. In 2004 he formed the band that would subsequently become ELVIS PERKINS IN DEARLAND, although it would be as a solo artist that he really arrived in the business.

ASH WEDNESDAY (2007) {*7}, the title referring to what he was left with after the untimely deaths of his parents, was a record of introspection, loneliness and heartache, but also about survival and hope. 'While You Were Sleeping', 'All The Night Without Love' and the Lennonesque title track stood out from one hell of a debut album.

Complemented by a full band (Wyndham Boylan-Garnett, Brigham Brough and Nicholas Kinsey), **ELVIS PERKINS IN DEARLAND** (2009) {*7} goes on another rustic charm offensive, the best tracks as before being the deeply-felt ones, such as 'Shampoo', 'Send My Fond Regards To Lonelyville', 'I'll Be Arriving' and the DYLANesque (weren't they all?) 'How's Forever Been Baby?'. The solemn and funereal 'Doomsday' made a second appearance on 'The Doomsday EP', alongside a version of the traditional standard 'Gypsy Davy'. *MCS*

Elvis Perkins - vocals, acoustic guitar / with session people

US XL — UK XL

Feb 07. (cd/lp) <*40206-2*> (*XLCD/XLLP 262*) **ASH WEDNESDAY** — Jul 07
- While you were sleeping / All the night without love / May day / Moon woman (part 2) / It's only me / Emile's Vietnam in the sky / Ash Wednesday / The night and the liquor / It's a sad world after all / Sleep sandwich / Good Friday.

May 07. (7") (*XLS 258*) ALL THE NIGHT WITHOUT LOVE. / The Dumps

Jul 07. (7") (*XLS 282*) WHILE YOU WERE SLEEPING. / Counterclockwise

ELVIS PERKINS IN DEARLAND

added **Wyndham Boylan-Garnett** - keyboards, guitar / **Brigham Brough** - double bass (from previous set) / **Nicholas Kinsey** - drums

Mar 09. (cd/lp) <*40401-2*> (*XLCD/XLLP 401*) **ELVIS PERKINS IN DEARLAND**
- Shampoo / Hey / Hours last stand / I heard your voice in Dresden / Send my fond regards to Lonelyville / I'll be arriving / Chains, chains, chains / Doomsday / 123 goodbye / How's forever been baby?

Apr 09. (7") <*XLS 416*> LORRAINE, LOOKOUT. / I'll Be Arriving

Apr 09. (7") (*XLS 423*) HEY. / SHAMPOO

Oct 09. (cd-ep) <*40459-2*> (*XLCD 459*) THE DOOMSDAY EP
- Doomsday / Gypsy Davy / Stay zombie stay / Stop drop rock and roll / Weeping Mary / Slow doomsday.

PETER AND THE WOLF

Eclectic, experimental and organically earthy, PETER AND THE WOLF (not to be confused with the Liverpool folk outfit) is the creation of lo-fi Americana folkie Red Hunter (Brian Redding Hunter). Launching the project in and around Austin, Texas in 2004, the singer/songwriter self-released a couple of low-key CD-rs. Before that, he had made his mark performing his acoustic 'Order of the Owl' show in graveyards, on islands accessible only by boat, and at Austin's South by Southwest festival.

PETER AND THE WOLF's first album proper, **LIGHTNESS** (2006) {*6}, was accompanied as before by his fellow fringe-folkie and jazzman Dana Falconberry, who shines a light on Red's nocturnal vocals. A precursor to BON IVER, FLEET FOXES et al, the 16-track set, released on the small indie label The Workers' Institute, has elements of Ry Cooder and Will Oldham ('The Ivy') and a jug-band HANDSOME FAMILY ('The Bonsai Tree'), but 'Safe Travels' is obviously the best song.

Subsequently released on Whiskey And Apples, **THE IVORI PALMS** (2007) maintained Hunter's lo-fi profile. *MCS*

Red Hunter (b. Brian Redding Hunter) - vocals, acoustic guitar / **Dana Falconberry** - vocals, mandolin (+ session people)

US self-rel. — UK not issued

2005. (cd-r) <*none*> PETER AND THE WOLF — mail-o
- Time flies / Fireflies / A race around the earth / Images / Balloon voyage / Island rose / Henry D / Palace in the sun / Spanish absinthe / The wind.

2006. (cd-r) <*none*> EXPERIMENTS IN JUNK — mail-o
- Strange machines / Anna Maria (live on KVRX) / Paint the town / Alexander and Diogenes / Snake charmer / Brother (live on KVRX) / Miss Caroline / Chinatown / Fata Morgana / The window / Black saltwater / Electrical tape / (interview live on KVRX) / Jaywalkin' / Sayonara suckers / Mad love / To kill a moose.

The Workers' Institute — not issued

Oct 06. (cd) <*twi-6*> **LIGHTNESS**
- Midnight train / The ivy / Safe travels / My grey overcoat / The highway / The owl / Anna Maria / The bonsai tree / The apple tree / Canada / Dear old Robyn / Captain Dan / Black saltwater / Holy water / Silent movies / Lightness.

Whiskey And Apples — not issued

Sep 07. (cd) <*none*> **THE IVORI PALMS**
- Where summer goes / Scarlet and grey / Check out the river / Ghost sandals (live) / Waiting for a train / Southern moon / The bike of Jonas / The ivori palms / A hundred days / The lighthouse / Better days / The beggars' waltz / The traveler and the county boys / Sparks (live).

Sep 08. (cd-r) <*none*> **MELLOW OWL**

Pierce PETTIS (⟹ Great Country Discography)

P.G. SIX

New York-born singer/songwriter Patrick Gubler was the moving spirit behind P.G. SIX, a single-handed neo-folk venture that translated the spirit of Brit-folk legends like BERT JANSCH and JOHN RENBOURN into the 21st century.

Almost Celtic in atmosphere, the beautiful **PARLOR TRICKS AND PORCH FAVORITES** (2001) {*8} took many pundits by surprise. Gubler's sedate and sombre, INCREDIBLE STRING BAND-like reading of ANNE BRIGGS's 'Go Your Way' (more than eight minutes long) was one of its many highlights, along with 'Letter To Lilli St Cyr', the mediaeval, fuzz-driven 'When I Was A Young Man' and the BUFFALO SPRINGFIELD-like 'The Shepherd'. Multi-percussionist Tim Barnes was on hand with essential backing.

THE WELL OF MEMORY (2004) {*7} explored the more ethereal and experimental end of the multi-instrumentalist's dark spectrum. Guest vocalist Helen Rush sang with Gubler on 'The Weeping Willow', 'Crooked Way' and the almost traditional 'Come In - The Winter It Is Past'. In similar vein to the last-named, 'Old Man On The Mountain' (after the Child ballad 'The Cherry Tree Carol') made 'calm' the new in-word in folk.

It's impossible to recommend the improvisional collection **THE SHERMAN BOX SERIES** (2006) {*5} (1994-2005), a record that folk buffs should avoid. There are other sets that might pique a new disciple's interest, some of them including a handful of decent covers such as 'I Saw The World' (TOM RAPP), 'High, Low And In Between' (TOWNES VAN ZANDT), 'My Name Is Death' (ROBIN WILLIAMSON) and 'Til Dreams Come True' (JUDEE SILL).

Sheltering unusual indie acts has been something of a specialty for the Drag City label, which released P.G. SIX's **SLIGHTLY SORRY** (2007) {*6}. Filled with arcane delights, and with Helen Rush again in tow (on 'The End Of Winter'), the record delivered a handful of good tracks including 'Sweet Music', 'Not I The Seed' and the sourced 'Lily Of The West'. As we go to press, Gubler's much-anticipated fourth album, **STARRY MIND** (2011), is hitting the shops.

Splinter act The Tower Recordings (Gubler, Matt Valentine, Marc Wolf, Helen Rush and Scott Freyer) pushed the limits of avant-folk too far for the scope of this Discography, but their recordings are listed below for the sake of completeness. *MCS*

Patrick Gubler (b. Feb 21 '69, The Bronx, New York) - vocals, multi

US Superlux — UK not issued

1995. (7") <*LUX 005*> THE BOOK OF RAYGUNS. / [continued]

——added guest **Tim Barnes** - drums, percussion (of Essex Green, of Jim O'Rourke)

Amish — Amish

Mar 01. (cd) <*(AMI 014)*> **PARLOR TRICKS AND PORCH FAVORITES** — Jul 04
- Introduction (Letter to Lilli St Cyr) / When I was a young man / The divine invasion / Unteleported man / Quiet man for SK / The shepherd / Go your way /The fallen leaves that jewel the ground / Letter to Lilli St Cyr. <*lp-iss. on Perhaps Transparent; none*>

2003. (7") *<AMI 017-7>* OLD MAN ON THE MOUNTAIN. / High, Low And In Between

Apr 04. (cd) *<(AMI 019)>* **THE WELL OF MEMORY** Jul 04
- Well of memory part I / Come in - The winter it is past / Old man on the mountain / A little harp tune / Evening comes / Crooked way / Considering the lateness of the hour / Three stages of a band / Well of memory part II / The weeping willow. *<lp-iss. on Perhaps Transparent; none>*

Sep 06. (cd) *<(AMI 024)>* **music from THE SHERMAN BOX SERIES and other works** [part compilation]
- For wire-strung harp with echo / For prepared wire-strung harp with tremolo pedal / For bray harp / For two wire-strung harps / For two bray harps / For wire-strung harp with slide / For bray harp with echo and flanged reverb / The book of rayguns for six electric guitars / Cartographies for piano and electronics.

——now with some session people incl. **Debby Schwartz** - bass

Drag City Drag City

Feb 07. (lp/cd) *<(DC 305/+CD)>* **SLIGHTLY SORRY** Jan 09
- Untitled micro mini / The dance / Strange messages / Cover art reprised / The end of winter / I've been traveling / Bless these blues / Not I the seed / Lily of the west / Sweet music.

Aug 11. (lp/cd) *<(DC 480/+CD)>* **STARRY MIND**
- January / Letter / Days hang heavy / Palace / Talk me down / Wrong side of yesterday / Crooked way / This song.

- others, etc.-

2004. (cd-r) *Perhaps Transparent; <none>* **LIVE TONIC 6-11-00** [live in NYC]
- Fallen leaves that jewel the ground I / In silence - The crooked way / Old man on the mountain / When I was young - Deserter / I saw the world - Divine invasion / Cover art - The shepherd - Winter it is past / Fallen leaves that jewel the ground II.

2005. (cd-r) *Perhaps Transparent; <none>* **LIVE GLADTREE FESTIVAL 4-10-04** [live at Hampshire College]
- Intro - Old man on the mountain / When I was a young man - Lake of beer / High, low and in between / The shepherd / The divine invasion / My name is Death / Crooked way - Winter it is past / Bray harp improvisation.

2007. (ltd-7" ep) *Abaton Book Company; <lost lathe>* P.G. SIX & THE FLAMING MANHOLES
- The black grocery gang soundscrape / I took a ride / I'm waitin' on the SBHotM, man! / You know the signs.

PHRANC

Born Susan Gottlieb, August 28, 1957 in Santa Monica, California, the uncompromising Jewish, lesbian folk singer changed her name to PHRANC in the mid-1970s and subsequently fell in with the notorious early-1980s Los Angeles punk/hardcore scene, playing guitar with the likes of Castration Squad and Catholic Discipline. The last-named (with Claud Bessy on shared vocals, Robert Lopez on keyboards, Ricke Jaffe on bass and Craig Lee on drums) had a few tracks on the various-artists albums 'San Francisco Punks' and 'The Decline Of The Western Civilization'.

Eventually tiring of the scene's insularity and relentless negativity, she retraced her folk roots and in 1985 released a debut album, **FOLKSINGER** {*7}, for retro specialist Rhino Records. A characteristically candid and honest exploration of politics, both sexual and otherwise, the record, which featured the singalong 'Female Mudwrestling' and a version of DYLAN's 'The Lonesome Death Of Hattie Carroll', was heartily received by the more radical critics and increased her small but loyal band of fans.

PHRANC signed to Island at the end of the 1980s and released a belated follow-up set, **I ENJOY BEING A GIRL** (1989) {*7}. The title track was the Rodgers & Hammerstein & Rodgers number from the show 'Flower Drum Song', and Tin Pan Alley was also represented by Burke & Van Heusen's 'Moonlight Becomes You'. The task of bringing PHRANC to a wider audience proved too great a challenge even for a label as eclectic as Island, and they parted company after 1991's **POSITIVELY PHRANC** {*5}. A pity, as she had demonstrated her wide-ranging appeal with covers of The Beach Boys' 'Surfer Girl' and Jonathan Richman's 'Pablo Picasso' (as 'Gertrude Stein'), and by supporting Morrissey on his UK tour the same year.

Her cult indie credentials stayed intact in the mid-1990s courtesy of two releases, the single 'Bulldagger Swagger' and the 'Goofyfoot' EP, for the seminal Riot Grrrl imprint Kill Rock Stars, both featuring members of Olympia (Team Dresch), headed by Donna Dresch. The EP showcased Herman's Hermits' 'Mrs Brown You've Got A Lovely Daughter' and Bobbie Gentry's 'Ode To Billie Joe'.

Her comeback was complete with the long-awaited **MILKMAN** (1998) {*5}, with backing from Anna Waronker, Steve McDonald and a few seasoned auxiliaries to beef up the likes of trad cuts 'The Handsome Cabin Boy' and 'Tzena, Tzena'. Sadly, this was to be her last release. *MCS*

Phranc - vocals, acoustic guitar

US Rhino UK Stiff

Nov 85. (7") *(BUY 233)* AMAZON. / El Salvador
(12"+=) *(BUYIT 233)* - Charlotte.

Nov 85. (lp) *<RNDA 856> (SEEZ 60)* **FOLKSINGER** Jan 86
- One o' the girls / Noguchi / Mary Hooley / Ballad of the dumb hairdresser / Caped crusader / Female mudwrestling / The lonesome death of Hattie Carroll / Amazons / Liar liar / Handicapped / Carolyn / Lifelover. *<cd/c-iss. 1990 on Island+=; 846358 cd/cs>* - Everywhere I go (I hear The Go-Gos).

Mar 86. (7") *(BUY 247)* THE LONESOME DEATH OF HATTIE CARROLL. / El Salvador

Island Island

Aug 89. (cd/c/lp) *<A2-/A4-/A1-91259> (CID/ICT/ILPS 9940)* **I ENJOY BEING A GIRL**
- Folksinger / I enjoy being a girl / Double decker bed / Bloodbath / Individuality / Rodeo parakeet / Take off your swastika / Toy time / M-A-R-T-I-N-A / Myriam and Esther / The ballad of Lucy + Ted / Moonlight becomes you.

Mar 91. (cd/c/lp) *<848-282-2> (CID/ICT/ILPS 9981)* **POSITIVELY PHRANC** Jul 91
- I like you / I'm not romantic / '64 Ford / Hitchcock / Tipton / Dress code / Why? / Gertrude Stein / Surfer girl / Outta here.

Jun 91. (7") *(868666-7)* I'M NOT ROMANTIC. / I Enjoy Being A Girl
(12"+=/cd-s+=) *(868666-6/-2)* - Outta here.

Kill Rock Stars Kill Rock Stars

Aug 94. (7") *<(KRS 230)>* BULLDAGGER SWAGGER. / Hillary's Eyebrows

Aug 95. (12" ep/cd-ep) *<KRS 233 12/CD>* GOOFYFOOT
- Surferdyke pal / Mrs Brown, you've got a lovely daughter / Bulldagger swagger / Ode to Billie Joe / Goofyfoot.

Phancy not issued

Nov 98. (cd) *<pha-1>* **MILKMAN**
- Twirly / The handsome cabin boy / Ozzie and Harriet / Yer the one / They lied / Where were you? / Gary / Cuffs / Lullaby / Tzena, Tzena.

——Phranc has since retired from studio recordings

The PINES

The Red House label rarely recruits rootsy folk groups, but boss GREG BROWN decided to break the mould after hearing The PINES, a duo (multi-instrumental singer-songwriters David Huckfelt and Benson Ramsey) based in Minneapolis by way of Iowa and a meeting in a Mexican barrio in Arizona. Inspired by SPIDER JOHN KOERNER (to whom they had attributed their 'Roll On John'), The PINES first surfaced locally on Trailer Records (US) with **THE PINES** (2004) {*6}, their blend of folk, blues and well-crafted indie-rock winning over audiences wherever they performed.

SPARROWS IN THE BELL (2007) {*7} opened their account with Red House, and was named among the best roots releases of the year by Q magazine. 'Careless Love' was the only trad number here.

The duo later covered songs by KOERNER ('Skipper And His Wife') and MISSISSIPPI JOHN HURT ('Spike Driver Blues') on 2009's **TREMOLO** (2009) {*6}. They could be ones to watch out for, with folk-blues and alt-country (BON IVER, The DECEMBERISTS and FLEET FOXES) getting their fair share of chart action in the 2010s. *MCS*

David Huckfelt - vocals, multi / **Benson Ramsey** - vocals, multi

US Trailer US not issued

Oct 04. (cd) *<38>* **THE PINES**
- Moon where the cherries turn black / Bound to fall / Make a run / Different clothes / Wishing well waltz / Pale white horse / Bella / Black train / Too far gone / It wasn't you / Stevenson motel breakdown / Absaroka instrumental / Roll on John.

Red House Red House

Jun 07. (cd) *<(RHR 201)>* **SPARROWS IN THE BELL**
- Horse and buggy / Don't let me go / Without a kiss / Throw me in the river / Let's go / Circle around the sun / Light under the door / Careless love / Midnight sun / Goin' home.

Aug 09. (cd) *<(RHR 222)>* **TREMOLO**
- Pray tell / Heart and bones / Shine on moon / Lonesome tremolo blues / Meadows of dawn / Skipper and his wife / Spike driver blues / Behind the time / Avenue of the saints / Shiny shoes.

Wally PLEASANT

Uniting anti-folk, rock 'n' roll and the punk ethos (think of Jonathan Richman or Violent Femmes), Detroit-raised singer/songwriter WALLY PLEASANT (b. Wallace Martin Bullard, August 29, 1967) is a rare breed indeed. A performer since he first armed himself with an Reo Speedwagon songbook and a guitar bought for him by his parents, Wally soon began writing his own material, which grew to over 150 songs, and he filled a 90-minute cassette with some of them at his local radio station's request.

Encouraged by good sales of that tape at various college and other venues, he self-financed his debut CD, **SONGS ABOUT STUFF** (1992) {*7}. A quick-fire series of follow-ups produced an overwhelming response from dysfunctional-type college kids around the Michigan area, where he was and remains based. **WELCOME TO PLEASANTVILLE** (1993) {*5} and **HOUSES OF THE HOLY MOLY** (1994) {*7} carried on in the same droll and quirky line, and the latter set produced a regional smash hit, 'Alternateen'.

WALLY WORLD (1996) {*7} (namechecking pop-culture references including Ted Nugent, Elvis, baseball legend Ty Cobb and TV detective 'Quincy ME') and **HOEDOWN** (2000) {*5}, featuring a reading of DAVE GUARD's 'Scotch And Soda', provided more amiable slacker fun before a six-year silence that ended with **MUSIC FOR NERDS AND PERVERTS** (2006) {*6}. A new album is due for release in 2011, and most recently he contributed his version of 'Helen Of Troy' to the various-artists Robert Plant tribute album 'Plant Waves' in 2007. *MCS*

Wally Pleasant - vocals, guitars

US Miranda — UK not issued

1992. (cd) <*WP 91490*> **SONGS ABOUT STUFF**
- Small time drug dealer / Bad haircut / That's evolution / Ode to Detroit / First love / Lost weekend Las Vegas / She's in love with a geek / Cool guy with a car / Psycho roommate / Hippies' lament / (I wanna be a) Pop star / If I were / Restless college years / Dead rock 'n' roll stars.

1993. (cd) <*WP 91491*> **WELCOME TO PLEASANTVILLE**
- She's addicted to clothes / Merry Christmas time again / I hate cops / I've got a garden / Rock-n-roll yard sale / How I got lost on the road less traveled but then got instant karma on I-96 / Only everything / I was a teenage Republican / Farmhand a go-go / Rock song / Man with a tan / It's a beautiful day / Smoking / I was a teenage Republican [George Bush mega-mix].

1994. (cd) <*???*> **HOUSES OF THE HOLY MOLY**
- Out on the road / Postgraduate overeducated out of work blues / Stupid day job / Sons of Bob Dylan / Dysfunctionally yours / Alternateen / Denny's at 4:00 am / Cat came back / I'm nice / Toxic waste block party / Wonderful sex / Raindrops.

1996. (cd) <*2913*> **WALLY WORLD**
- The day Ted Nugent killed all the animals / Bigger than Elvis / Let's play life / I want a stalker / Hardcore man / Quincy / Mojo? / The ballad of Ty Cobb / Love is... (overproduced 1980s soundtrack mix) / Bingo addicted grandma / Amusement park death song / Rumble at the karaoke bar. *(bonus +=)* - Sunday morning.

2000. (cd) <*???*> **HOEDOWN**
- Chrysler Cordoba / Two for one coupon / Wreck of the old 486 / VH1 song / New action hero / Bad kids show host / Java jonesin' / Home sweet home on wheels / Folk singer manifesto / Stock market bop / Cleopatra / Scotch and soda.

Spat! — not issued

May 06. (cd) <*006*> **MUSIC FOR NERDS AND PERVERTS**
- Buffet paradise / Plan B / Get with your girl / My Hole tribute band / Captain Marvel / I wanna rock you to death / Barista / Hey Georgie / Backyard wrestler guy / Olde time beer / Nightclub of our discontent / Handyman special / Let's go bowling tonight / This town.

Rose POLENZANI

Coming across as a countrified NICK DRAKE or LEONARD COHEN - we're in bedsitter-blues land here - singer/songwriter ROSE POLENZANI (born March 7, 1975 in Waukesha, Wisconsin) has been on tour with SHAWN COLVIN, JONATHA BROOKE and INDIGO GIRL Amy Ray.

From honor student to art school graduate, from open-mic sessions in Chicago to appearing at the Newport Folk Festival and Lilith Fair in 1998, POLENZANI finally put together her debut set, **DRAGERSVILLE** (1998) {*7}. Reminiscent of Edie Brickell and country-folk artist CATIE CURTIS, Rose was backed by Geoff Benge, Jordi Kleiner and ANDREW BIRD. 'Olga's Birthday' tells the story of lesbian lovers who split up when one of them gets religion.

Upping the ante by going electric (even more so on her third set), **ANYBODY** (1999) {*6} and **ROSE POLENZANI** (2001) {*6} continued along her organic folk-rock path. As an integral part of the Voices On The Verge collective (alongside ERIN McKEOWN, Jess Klein and Beth Amsel), she appeared on the Rykodisc concert set 'Live In Philadelphia'.

On her fourth record, **AUGUST** (2004) {*6}, the NICK DRAKE/SCOTT APPEL influence was apparent again (it was released on Parhelion, who had published the latter), and although Rose has since settled in Boston, Massachusetts, she has found time to front ROSE POLENZANI with SESSION AMERICANA on their one-off bluegrass/old-timey effort, **WHEN THE RIVER MEETS THE SEA** (2008) {*6}. The title track is a Paul Williams song, and 'She Is A Rainbow' is from the pen of Sharon Lewis of POOKA.

August 2011 will bring a new, live-in-the-studio solo CD, **THE RABBIT** {*6}. *MCS*

Rose Polenzani - vocals, guitar (+ some piano)

US self-rel. — UK not issued

Aug 98. (cd) <*polenzani 2*> **DRAGERSVILLE**
- You don't know / Olga's birthday / Allah / The chalice / Mercy / Or / Ramon / The necklace / Jesus loves me like a bird / In the middle / Molly's lily. <*re-iss. 2000 on Parhelion; 6026-2*>

Daemon — not issued

Jul 99. (cd) <*19022*> **ANYBODY**
- Shake through to ugly / Molly's lily / Or / Abalin / Olga's birthday / Omen / Chalice / Angel / Ditty to surround a bell / Look no hands / Parhelion.

Jun 01. (cd) <*19029*> **ROSE POLENZANI**
- Fell / Whatever remains / Bad dreams / The flood / Mary Lee / Sacramento avenue / The llama / Polliwog's lament / Orange crush / Thorn II.

——in 2001/02 she was part of the folk-meets-country touring ensemble Voices On The Verge (one set was issued, 'Live In Philadelphia')

Parhelion — not issued

Oct 04. (cd) <*7921-2*> **AUGUST**
- Blue angel / How shall I love thee? / Girl / Rolling suitcase / And these hands / The first time / You used to ease my mind / Explain it to me / Easter hymn / Married man / Hardest hurt / Sometimes.

CDBaby — not issued

Oct 08. (cd; as ROSE POLENZANI with SESSION AMERICANA) <*none*> **WHEN THE RIVER MEETS THE SEA**
- Queen Anne's lace / Song of the stars / Some way / Sarsaparilla / The soft parts / When the river meets the sea / If I could hit you / Push me if I snore / Paying a visit / You were drunk / She is a rainbow.

Aug 11. (cd) <*none*> **THE RABBIT**

POPCORN BEHAVOIR (⟹ AMIDON, Sam)

Willy PORTER

Singer/songwriter WILLY PORTER (b. 1969 in Wisconsin), who combines soulful acoustic folk with easy-on-the-ear blues, was a viola player until he picked up the guitar, influenced by finger-picking six- and 12-string master LEO KOTTKE. New Age maestro Michael Hedges was also an early inspiration.

The hard-to-come-by cassette **LEAVING TOMAH HOME** (1988) has to be taken on trust, but the innovative and wonderfully dexterous **THE TREES HAVE SOUL** (1990) {*7} had emotion and passion galore. From the co-written duet 'Reach' with CARRIE NEWCOMER and 'Moonbeam' with L.J. Booth, to conceptual New Age instrumentals 'Zak's Tale' I & II, the set had a nice balance and strength.

Going mainstream with **DOG EARED DREAM** (1994) {*6}, PORTER realised his potential, albeit a little too late and independently to break through to America's pop-rock market. 'Angry Words' and revamps of 'Cool Water' and 'Moonbeam', from his previous set, were the obvious draws. Re-released a year later on Private Music, PORTER promoted it on support slots with Tori Amos, The Cranberries, Rickie Lee Jones and Jethro Tull - he's great friends with Tull guitarist Martin Barre.

Disillusioned with major-label demands, he took a long sabbatical before reappearing in 1999 with his independent pop-rock comeback, **FALLING FORWARD** {*6}. The Six Degrees label also delivered two further efforts, **WILLY PORTER** (2002) {*6} and **HIGH WIRE LIVE** (2003) {*7}, the latter a concert set recorded in places from England to Los Angeles and featuring a cover of RICHARD SHINDELL's 'You Stay Here'. Switching to Weasel Records, Willy kept his profile high and his loyal fan base happy with studio sets **AVAILABLE LIGHT** (2006) {*6} and **HOW TO ROB A BANK** (2009) {*6}. *MCS*

Willy Porter - vocals, guitars (with session people)

US own label / UK not issued

1988. (c) <*none*> **LEAVING TOMAH HOME** — self —

——next credited WILLY PORTER with PAUL PERRONE

1990. (lp) <*none*> **THE TREES HAVE SOUL** — self —
- Cool water / Draw the time / Zak's tale part I - Zak at home / Moonbeam / Lines of age / Fullerton express / Undertow / The trees have soul / Reach / Zak's tale part II - Zak at the bar / Southwind. *<cd-iss. Nov 96 on Don't; 1021>*

Don't / not issued

Nov 94. (cd) <*(1002)*> **DOG EARED DREAM**
- Angry words / Rita / Jesus on the grille / Boab tree / Watercolor / [*] / Cool water / Be here now / Flying / Glow / Cold wind / Out of the blue. *<(re-iss. Feb 95/Feb 96 on Private; 01005 82134-2)> <cd re-iss. Jun 05 on Six Degrees+=; 65703 6 1114-2>* - Moonbeam [insert *]

Six Degrees / Six Degrees

Aug 99. (cd) <*(65703 6 1016-2)*> **FALLING FORWARD** — Mar 00
- Mystery / Cut the rope / The line / Paper airplane / Infinity / Sister / Road bone / Sowelu / Tribe / Hard / Anonymous caller / Somebody else. *(UK-iss. Feb 03; same)*

Jul 02. (cd) <*(65703 6 1073-2)*> **WILLY PORTER** — Mar 03
- Breathe / If love were an airplane / Unconditional / Everything but sorry / Dirty movie / Big yellow pine / All fall down / How did you know? / Dandelion on the minefield / Blue light / Dishwater blonde.

Sep 03. (cd) <*(65703 6 1094-2)*> **HIGH WIRE LIVE** [live] — Nov 03
- Tribe / Angry words / Unconditional / Breathe / Dishwater blonde / Jesus on the grille / Paper airplane / You stay here / Mystery / Road bone.

Weasel / Weasel

Sep 06. (cd) <*(928315-2)*> **AVAILABLE LIGHT**
- Available light / Loose gravel / Still doing time / Set yourself free / Sleepy little / Reveal / Me and my old man / Hairball / One more September / Where are my keys?

Jun 09. (cd) <*612681-2*> **HOW TO ROB A BANK**
- Learning the language / Colored lights / I didn't bring it up / Hard place / The lemon tree / Wide open mind / How to rob a bank / Too big to sell / Fear only fear / Psychic vampire / Barefoot reel.

Nov 10. (cd; as WILLY PORTER & CARPE DIEM) <*WSL 1001*> **LIVE AT BOMA** [live March 12-13, 2010]
- Moonbeam / Dishwater blonde / Breathe / Big yellow pine / Paper airplane / Hard place / Watercolor.

Jim POST

Overshadowed by the plethora of singer/songwriter folk stars around in the 1970s and 1980s, and lately pigeonholed as a children's entertainer, JIM POST (b. October 28, 1939 in Houston, Texas) was better known to bubblegum/acid-folk fans as the other half of Cathy Post (b. Catherine Conn, May 30, 1945 in Chicago, Illinois) in hitmakers FRIEND & LOVER.

Formed in Alberta, Canada in 1965 and based in and around New York, the husband-and-wife team created a stir when the Nashville-recorded 'Reach Out Of The Darkness' soared into the Top 10 in the summer of 1968 at a time when America was still grieving for the assassinated Martin Luther King, Jr. To mark 40 years of flower power, a solo JIM POST (looking like Einstein, or David Crosby's twin brother) revamped the song at a San Francisco 'Summer of Love' concert on September 2, 2007.

By the time FRIEND & LOVER got around to producing their one and only long-player, **REACH OUT OF THE DARKNESS** (1969) {*5}, music had moved on, as Jim and Cathy were about to. Cathy remarried twice, and is now a proud grandmother living in the mountains of New Mexico.

JIM POST, who had some musical history with early-1960s folk outfit The Rum Runners, continued to write songs and signed up with Fantasy in the early 1970s, inspired by the Chicago-based talent around him such as JOHN PRINE, STEVE GOODMAN, BONNIE KOLOC, Fred Holstein and the late Tom Dundee (d. 2006).

From 1972 to 1974 POST delivered four fair-to-middling LPs in **SLOW TO 20** {*6}, **LOOKS GOOD TO ME,** {*6}, **COLORADO EXILE** {*6} and **RATTLESNAKE** {*6}. He contributed a song, 'You're The Only Girl (I Ever Really Loved)', to the label's soundtrack album of underground cartoonist Ralph Bakshi's 1972 animated film 'Fritz The Cat'.

Bluegrass and folk were always underlying elements in Jim's music, and when country-rock came into vogue his two LPs for Mountain Railroad, **BACK ON THE STREET AGAIN: LIVE** (1977) {*6} and **I LOVE MY LIFE** (1978) {*6}, rolled along with the bandwagon, but not as profitably as other acts in the same line, such as Poco and The Eagles.

The Flying Fish label maintained his affiliation with country-folk through a trio of sets, among which the live **MAGIC: IN CONCERT** (1979) {*6} and **SHIP SHAPE** (1980) {*6} were somewhat overshadowed by his traditional/covers album **JIM POST & FRIENDS** (1987) {*7}. The last-named album featured material such as 'Golden Slippers', 'Sixteen Tons' and his own 'Oh Galena'.

Moving to Galena, Illinois (where he still lives), he dedicated a self-released set, **GALENA ROSE** (1987), to the city's history and culture. With his wife Janet as storyteller, the curious **THE HEART OF CHRISTMAS** (1989) {*5} launched a Mississippi raft of festive, family and children's CDs, one of which, **MARK TWAIN AND THE LAUGHING RIVER** (1997) {*6}, has also given rise to a DVD of the original stage show.

For POST's finest moments, look no further than 1984's **THE CROONER FROM OUTER SPACE** {*7}. His most recent work, **REACH OUT TOGETHER** (2009) {*7} - the title comes from his 1968 hit, mashed up here with The YOUNGBLOODS' 'Get Together' - includes some re-recorded gems, with backing from new bluegrass buddies Jerry Miller, Randy Sabien and Andy Steil. *MCS*

FRIEND & LOVER

Jim Post - vocals, acoustic guitar / **Cathy Post** - vocals

US Verve Forecast / UK Verve Forecast

Apr 68. (7") <*KF-5069*> *(VS 1515)* REACH OUT OF THE DARKNESS. / Time On Your Side (You're Only 15 Years Old) — 10 — May 68

Aug 68. (7") <*K-F5091*> IF LOVE IS IN YOUR HEART. / Zig-Zag — 86

Jan 69. (lp) <*FTS 3055*> **REACH OUT OF THE DARKNESS**
- Boston is a lovely town / I'm a woman, I'm a man / Zig-zag / Saturday's hero / Room to let (to Rowena with love) / Reach out of the darkness / A wise man changes his mind / Ode to a dandelion / If love is in your heart / The weddin' march (I feel groovy) / The way we were in the beginning. *<(cd re-mast. Dec 05/Feb10 on Collectors' Choice; CCM 610-2)>*

JIM POST

Fantasy / Fantasy

Jul 72. (lp) <*F-9408*> **SLOW TO 20**
- Let the boy boogie / Sing / Move back in sweet mama / Homemade music / Woman in Chicago / Jazz man / Sara / Boys in the band / Tell old Bill.

Jan 73. (lp) <*F-9401*> **COLORADO EXILE**
- Look over yonder / Once you were a rock / Ride, Rita, ride / High up on the ridge / Colorado exile / Turn around (Bambu Lou) / Louella rainwater / Simple life / Dancing in the wind / I love you / One more day.

Nov 73. (lp) <*F-9425*> **RATTLESNAKE**
- Bicycle wheel / Payday / Jenny / Sister Liza Bookman / Santana winds / Love has no foundation / Silver engine / The ballad of Rattlesnake / The wild man / Sunday morning in the mountains.

Jan 74. (7") *(FTC 112)* PAYDAY. / Bicycle Wheel

Nov 74. (lp) <*F-9451*> **LOOKS GOOD TO ME**
- Your daddy's an engineer / Jenny Lynn / Goin' up the river / Homemade music time / Buzzy and Jimmy / Old funky song / Dance gypsy / Light up my lady / Michael and Adrienne / I walk the line / Let the time roll by.

Mountain Railroad / not issued

1977. (lp) <*MR 52778*> **BACK ON THE STREET AGAIN: LIVE**
- Back on the street again / Windego / Hello babe / Walk on the water - An old story / Woman in Chicago / Goodbye to Tennessee / Medley: Light of life and love - Don't look for love - If my life were a... / Bicycle wheel.

1978. (lp) <*MR 52784*> **I LOVE MY LIFE**
- Hot summer night / I love my life / Comfortable feeling / Crystal ocean tides / Billie Jean Rose / Stanley and Henry / My dreams never come true / Grab your life and run / Waterfall dream / One blessed hour.

Flying Fish / Flying Fish

1979. (lp) <*FF-216*> **MAGIC: IN CONCERT** [live]
- Silver engine / Brain damage / Light up my lady / No nukes / Let the sun shine / I'd do it again / Lord I want to go back to California / Get off, lay back / Three soft touches / Rachael's song / The waves roll in on Oregon. *(UK-iss. Mar 89; same as US)*

1980. (lp) <*FF-240*> **SHIP SHAPE** [live at Charlotte's Web, Rockford, IL]
- Hot summer night / With love from Alberta / Marblehead morning / The legend of Jack Dawson / Dance, gypsy, dance / Engineer's dream tune / Angel of the lighthouse / Snowshoe / Woodland dream / Blow, December winds. *(UK-iss. Mar 89; same as US)*

1984. (lp) <*01905*> **THE CROONER FROM OUTER SPACE**
- Lonely heart, don't abandon me / The galaxy lighten up / This morning I came down with love / Magnolia, I'm coming home / I hate to waste a full moon / Sugar rush / Phenomenon of love / First teardrop on the moon / Yours / Wake up and dream lighten up (reprise).

(above issued on Freckle)

1987. (lp) <*(FF-419)*> **JIM POST & FRIENDS** ☐ 1988 ☐
- Pallet on your floor / Sixteen tons / Shenandoah / Golden slippers / Lilywhite / Oh Galena / Star of the County Down / Wildwood flower / Handsome Molly / Preacher went a-hunting. <*cd-iss. 1993; FF-70419*>

own label | not issued

1987. (cd) <*none*> **JIM POST'S GALENA ROSE** ☐ ⊟
- Galena Rose / This is my new home / The man from the moon / Enough of nothing / White dress / Thank God for whiskey / Riverboat man / James Duncan / O Galena / Run Indians / Sir Reginald / Riverboat honeymoon.

Chicago Master Works | not issued

1989. (cd; by JIM POST and JANET POST) <*CM-1263*>
THE HEART OF CHRISTMAS [festive / w/interludes] ☐ ⊟
- Heart of Christmas / Jagget's gonna get ya / Thank you for the child / My boy / List song / Chief Red Wing / Riverboat Christmas / Jagget's gonna get ya reprise / A child is born / Twelfth month / I can hear the bells a-ringing / Christmas chantey / Deck the halls / Angels we have heard on high / Joy to the world / Whoa back buck.

——next with **Jerry Miller** (of Moby Grape), **Randy Sabien** + **Andy Steil**

own label | not issued

Nov 09. (cd) <*#1*> **REACH OUT TOGETHER** ☐ ⊟
- The paradise bar / Rag time love / Live by a river / Reach out together / City of New Orleans / Apple picking time / Daddy drive 'em / Boozoo man / Back on the street / Jack Dawson / Dusty road back home / Silver engine / For the children / Beautiful city.

- (5-7*) children's/family albums -

1997. (cd) *Woodside Avenue*; <*WA-006-2*> **MARK TWAIN AND THE LAUGHING RIVER** ☐ ⊟
- Mighty big river / Uncle John's farm / Hannibal / Riverboat man / Huckleberry Finn / Naked little boy / Riverboat honeymoon / Cat in the box / Steamboat's comin' / Elegy / Jubilee music / Live by a river.

2000. (cd) <*none*> **FROG IN THE KITCHEN SINK** ☐ ⊟
- Frog in the kitchen sink / Mabel the milk cow / Giggle song / Cowboy Joe / Color of the rainbow / Scritchin' 'n' scratchin' / If I were a grasshopper / Big brown bear / Alfred the earthworm / Addle, addle, addle (silly song) / Jelly fish jamboree / Clouds are dreams.

(all released on Breaking The Sounds Barrier)

Oct 01. (cd) <*jimpost 1*> **QUEENS AND QUARTERBACKS** ☐ ⊟
- QU Rap / Don't be afraid to ask questions / X rap / Excuse me / C rap / Come to the circus / Short I rap / Izzie the inchworm / Short E rap / The echo song / Short-vowel rap / The short-vowel song / The consonant rap / Celebration of the children / All of the children of the world / Annie alligator ate apples.

Oct 01. (cd) <*jimpost 2*> **PURPLE PIG** ☐ ⊟
- P phoneme rap / Purple pig song / B phoneme rap / Big brown bear song / PB phoneme rap / P and B rap song / T phoneme rap / Toes, toes song / D phoneme rap / Delbert the dinosaur song / TD phoneme rap / Dakota Indian rap song / K phoneme rap / Kink in my link song / G phoneme rap / Giggle song / KG phoneme rap / Komodo dragon rap song / CH phoneme rap / Chick-a-dee song / J phoneme rap / Jelly jamboree song / JCH phoneme rap / Cha cha cha rap / Annie alligator ate apples.

Oct 01. (cd) <*jimpost 3*> **FROG TOWN BAND** ☐ ⊟
- F phoneme rap / Frog town band / V phoneme rap / Vegetables, vegetables song / FV phoneme rap / Vroom, vroom, it's the traveling tune / TH phoneme rap / Luther the cowboy / Short A phoneme rap / Never argue with an ant / TH game rap / Thimble, thimble, game / Singing all the sounds in the USA / Z phomeme rap / Lallapalooza rap / SZ phoneme rap / Secret, secret, I've got a secret / SH phoneme rap / Shhhhhhh, there's a shark going by / Short O phoneme rap / You oughta be an otter / Annie alligator ate apples.

Oct 01. (cd) <*jimpost 4*> **OODLES AND LOADS AND LOTS OF THINGS** ☐ ⊟
- L phonemerap / Oodles and loads and lots of things / R phoneme rap / Oh red is a rousing color! / M phoneme rap / Mabel the mild cow / N phoneme rap / Everyone has a name! / Name game song / NG phoneme rap / Yesterday, today and tomorrow / W phoneme rap / A wish is something wonderful / H phoneme rap / Hippo song / Y phoneme rap / Yellow jump rope rap / Short U phoneme rap / Bugs, bugs, bugs! / Annie alligator ate apples.

May 05. (cd) *Orchard*; <*100794*> **ALPHABET SONGS** ☐ ⊟
- Never argue with an ant / Big brown bear / Come to the circus / Delbert the dinosaur / An echo will come back to you! / Frog town bear / It's great to have a giggle / Hazel the hippo / Izzie the inchworm / Jellyfish jamboree / I've a kink in my link / Oodles and loads and lots of things / Mabel the milk cow / Name, name, everyone has a name! / Oh! you oughta be an otter! / Purple pig / Don't be afraid to ask questions / Red is a rousing color! / Singing all the sounds / Toes, toes, we all have toes / Ugh! It's a bug! / Vegetables, vegetables / A wish is a wonderful thing / Excuse me! / Yellow jump rose / Lallapalooza zoo / CH song, chick-a-dee song / TH song, Luther the cowboy.

PRENTICE & TUTTLE

Unfortunately omitted from Volume I, Bostonians PRENTICE & TUTTLE (Steve and Stephen) issued two very rare and collectable albums in 1971-72, **PRENTICE & TUTTLE** (1971) {*5} and **EVERY LOVING DAY** (1972) {*6}, the latter a country-tinged folk recording that has since been re-issued on CD. Fragile folk in the manner of America or CSN&Y, its highlights were 'The Devil Be Your Lord', 'Old Man Taylor', 'Jacob's Tree' and the title track. Session musicians on the set were David Cain and John Gerbron. *MCS*

Steve Prentice - vocals, acoustic guitar / **Stephen Tuttle** - vocals, acoustic guitar

US R.P.C. | UK not issued

1971. (ltd-lp) <*AZ-59501*> **PRENTICE & TUTTLE** ☐ ⊟

1972. (ltd-lp) <*RPC 50172*> **EVERY LOVING DAY** ☐ ⊟
- The river song / Old man Taylor / This downhill walk / Jacob's tree / It's getting mighty cold / Deep blue affection / Like a midnight crier / Just how you feel / The Devil be your lord / It isn't going to rain this day / Ring them bells / Every loving day. *(cd-iss. Jan 00 on French label Underground Masters; UM 001-2)*

PROPINQUITY (⟹ SCIAKY, Carla)

PRYDWYN

Prydwyn Olvardil Piper (his real name, apparently) is a pagan-folk multi-instrumentalist who accompanies his singing on harp, lute, cittern and a host of other mediaeval instrument. Over the span of 20 years or so, PRYDWYN has released a string of solo albums as well as appearing as GREEN CROWN and as half of STONE BREATH. While the last-named have their own entry, the acid-folk of solo PRYDWYN sounds like a Celtic-styled Wicker Man festival. Four traditional tunes including 'The Death Of Young Andrew' were featured on his first official release, **AT THE FEET OF MARY MOONCOIN** (1995) {*6}.

As for GREEN CROWN (also featuring Jim 'Barleycorn' Brewster, Diana McFadden, White Deer and Sherry Gibson), their only studio outing, **WASHED IN HER BLOOD** (1998) {*7}, was a delight, containing covers of 'Pat's Song' (COUNTRY JOE McDONALD) and 'Three Is A Green Crown' (The INCREDIBLE STRING BAND). Highlights of their live album **IN PRINCIPIO** (2000, recorded 1997) include versions of the above-mentioned songs, as well as 'See Emily Play' (Pink Floyd), 'Lady With A Fan' (The Grateful Dead) and Jethro Tull's 'My God'.

Fresh from his time with STONE BREATH, PRYDWYN and his Quickthorn consort of minstrels slowed the pace down somewhat with a kind-of-comeback set of oddball items, **SOLITUDE OWES ME A SMILE** (2009) {*6}, definitely one for the connoisseur of psych-folk meanderings. Readings included Peter Green's 'Showbiz Blues', The Velvet Underground's 'Venus In Furs' and DYLAN's 'Girl From The North Country'. *MCS*

Prydwyn - vocals, harp, guitar, lute, cittern, mandolin, flute

US self-rel. | UK not issued

1991. (ltd-c) <*none*> **PSYCHOLOGY STIFLES THE PROPHET** ☐ ⊟
- Annie Jerboa / Too well / Goibniu's tippler / Can't hurt you / Somewhere / For a while / Twenty years away / Siren / So hard to see / Ages past.

Lordly Nightshade | not issued

Nov 95. (cd/c) <*LNCD/LNCS 7021*> **AT THE FEET OF MARY MOONCOIN** ☐ ⊟
- Naked beauty / A maid walked slow / The nobleman's wedding / In the darkness / Sleep awhile / The death of young Andrew / Fhir a' bhata / Tha thid' agam eirigh / Somewhere / Attis and Cybele / Pentre, even - The great man's gift.

Green Crown | not issued

1997. (c; by OLVARDIL PRYDWYN & DIANA McFADDEN) <*GCCS 0012C*> **THE WITCH IN THE WELL** ☐ ⊟
- John Barleycorn / Midsummer faire / Lady with a fan / Isle of Islay / Porpoise mouth / Pat's song / See Emily play (Games for May) / The witch in the well.

——it was at this point that Prydwyn became part of STONE BREATH

GREEN CROWN

Prydwyn with **Jim 'Barleycorn' Brewster** - fiddle, bass, drums, percussion / **Diana McFadden** - cello, percussion / **White Deer** - percussion, drums / **Sherry Gibson** - percussion, harmonium

Harvest Queen | not issued

1998. (cd) <*HQCD 001G*> **WASHED IN HER BLOOD** ☐ ⊟
- Another day / Washed in green / Spirit waltz / New song / Pat's song / Three is a green crown / Mistress moon - Selene / Untitled / John Barleycorn / Midsummer faire / The witch in the well / Sleep a while.

Rockdreamer | not issued

2000. (cd-r) <*none*> **IN PRINCIPIO: Live At The 1997 Pagan Spirit Gathering** ⊟ ⊟

- John Barleycorn / Lady with a fan / See Emily play / Pat's song / A maid walked slow / Cuckoo's nest / My God / Mistress moon / Three is a green crown / Band introductions / Fhir a' bhata.

Harvest Queen — not issued

2002. (cd-r) <*none*> **WITH WITCH TO FEED THE FAIRIES: 1997–2001 - THE FIRST FIVE LIVE** [–] [–]
- Witches reel / Cuckoo's nest / Tir na nog / Season of the witch / Enchanted gypsy / Bedlam boys - Break on through / Willow's song / Legend of a mind - White rabbit / Tourdion / The end.

PRYDWYN (with QUICKTHORN)

Prydwyn with **Kira** - vocals / **Yashi** - zuk / **Wye** - classical guitar, harpsichord / **Koivulaanista** - recorder consort

Hand/Eye — not issued

Jul 09. (cd-ep) <*h/e 044a*> THIS TOO SHALL PASS [live September 2005 // outtake] [ ] [–]
- Showbiz blues / Venus in furs / Girl from the north country // Winter is blue.

Aug 09. (cd;) <*h/e 044*> **SOLITUDE OWES ME A SMILE** [ ] [–]
- Ashling / Shotgun down the avalanche / Cornfield / Grantchester meadows / A leaf must fall / Arthur McBride / Closing my eyes / Curragh of Kildare / The darkling maid / Untitled.

QUINN / VERDURE (⟹ The SKYGREEN LEOPARDS)

REDBIRD (⟹ FOUCAULT, Jeffrey)

Ann REED

Although she's been a well-kept secret in folk circles for the past 30 years or so, singer/songwriter ANN REED (b. 1954 in Minneapolis, Minnesota) has worked hard to fill as many as 20 albums with her bright and breezy folk music. Compared to JONI MITCHELL for her song structures as well as her voice, Ann is also adept at strumming her custom-made 12-string guitar to her many beautifully crafted originals. Inspired by her older brothers' and mother's large folk, rock and jazz record collection, REED was inspired by the likes of MARY TRAVERS, PETE SEEGER, Ella Fitzgerald and of course Joni.

Her first set, **CARPEDIEM** {*5}, came out in 1981, while more recently appearances on Garrison Keillor's radio show 'A Prairie Home Companion' and ABC TV's 'Good Morning America' have kept her profile high. The width and breadth of North America has been the unassuming troubadour's performance playground, from clubs to concert venues and festivals.

For some years now she has been donating a significant percentage of her concert earnings to women's and children's charities, but aside from being a worthy human being, it's her folk-message music that has won her one music award after another, mainly in her home state. All her many albums are extremely pleasant and politically correct, but her best time seems to have been her spell on the Red House label, for which she made the albums **JUST CAN'T STOP** (1986) {*7} and **TALK TO ME** (1990) {*7}.

That's not to say her other work is weak. For a taste of some of her best, try the live double-CD **TELLING STORIES** (2006) {*7}, the second half of which features traditional material like 'Loch Lomond' and 'Clementine' alongside a Rodgers & Hammerstein number, Lennon/McCartney's 'You've Got To Hide Your Love Away' and LEADBELLY's 'Goodnight, Irene'. *MCS*

Ann Reed - vocals, 12-string acoustic guitar / + session people

US Vivid — UK not issued

1981. (lp) *<2169>* **CARPEDIEM**
- Can't be easy / Jessie / Looks like you / Slimy cat / Swing tune / Carpediem / It might happen / Next time / Melinda / Milwaukee / Lisa C's song. *(UK cd-iss. Jun 09 on Big Pink; 11)*

Iceberg — not issued

1984. (lp/c) *<ICE-213/+C>* **ROOM AND BOARD**
- Jaynie / Call it friends / Love in the first place / Swan's song / Family of strangers / Room and board / The woman you'd love / Willow weep for me / Carry me.

Red House — not issued

1986. (lp) *<RHR 11>* **JUST CAN'T STOP**
- Stumblin' through / The thought of you / Who's tellin' who / Still be missing you - For Jane / If you are / Lonely heart / Feels so right / All my life without you / Just can't stop / Every long journey (the expedition song). *<cd-iss. 1992; RHRCD 11>*

Apr 90. (lp) *<RHR 24>* **TALK TO ME**
- Talk to me / Once bitten / Just out of reach / Nothing to say / Autumn rain / Complications to a simple life / Ghosts / I want to believe / True romance / I would love to dance. *<cd/c-iss. Mar 92; RHR CD/C 24>*

Turtlecub — not issued

Nov 90. (cd/c) *<TC 001>* **BACK AND FORTH**
- The woman you'd love / Jessie / Willow weep for me / Family of strangers / Swing tune / It might happen / Jaynie / Love in the first place / Carry me / What made you love her / Where the hell is Boston / Push the river / Next time. *<re-iss. Jul 94 on A Major Label cd/c; R-01-AR-0990-2/-4>*

1991. (cd/c) *<1007-2/-4>* **ROAD OF THE HEART**
- Told you so / Anybody else but you / Used to be / So glad / Maybe it's you / Love's a long road home / Temporary low / Second chance / I know what I know / Road of the heart / If you were mine. *<re-iss. Jun 94 on A Major Label cd/c; WR-02-AR-0991-2/-4>*

A Major Label — not issued

Jun 92. (cd) *<AM 1>* **BY REQUEST** (live)
- Styrofoam / Money / Every long journey / Easy street / The fair / Lisa's song / 2 & 2 together / Last dollar bill / Oh, baby I love to dance / Prairie wind / I would love to dance / Deep fat frying / I hope you.

1993. (cd/c) *<AM 2>* **HOLE IN THE DAY**
- Too much trouble / Hindsight / Some hearts / Miles home to you / What a pity / Somethin' to do with you / Tired old world / I don't like it / No road to Juneau / Heroes / Even in reunion. *<cd re-iss. Jun 94; 11008>*

Jun 94. (cd/c) *<AM 4>* **LIFE GETS REAL**
- Life gets real / Lost and found / Pieces of dreams / Roll on by / Love online / Walk / Good friends / Hard on y'self / Fading away / God is sleeping - You've got to be carefully taught.

Jul 96. (cd/c; as ANN REED & PHYLLIS GOLDIN) *<AM 3>* **STRINGS ATTACHED**
- Perpetual emergency (REED solo) / (two by PHYLLIS) / Women's room / I'll keep my hat (REED solo) / Bid you farewell / Frog call / Piano response / Spring thaw / Sadie / Piano response / Ancestry dance.

Ladyslipper — not issued

May 97. (cd/c) *<075578 1101-26>* **TIMING IS EVERYTHING**
- Love like this / I write a letter / Martha / Dark, the outhouse and the creatures on either side / Can't sleep / Eye-wuh / US ranger / Power tools / No parking / I will be there for you / Say goodbye / Watching over you.

Turtlecub — not issued

Aug 01. (cd) *<TC 12>* **THROUGH THE WINDOW**
- Light of the moon / No time like the present / Dream / Carolyn's party (solstice) / Keep on walkin' / Mailman cometh / Afterlife / I 'E' / Look at her go / Northern star / One waltz.

Nov 02. (cd) *<TC 14>* **NOT YOUR AVERAGE HOLIDAY CD** (festive)
- I saw three ships - The first noel / O come, o come, Emmanuel / O little town of Bethlehem / Away in a manger / Good King Wenceslas / We three kings / O Christmas tree / Christmas songs / Masters in the hall - Bring a torch, Jeanette Isabelle / Coventry carol / Silent night / Joy to the world - Jingle bells / Dona nobis pacem.

Nov 02. (cd) *<TC 15>* **GIFT OF AGE**
- Saying hello / Gift of age / Get outta my kitchen / This year I sing / Walkin' my puppy / Please, Mr Ashcroft / Marching back to school / You never know / The busker / Meals on wheels / Two trees / Leap of faith.

Apr 04. (cd) *<TC 16>* **THE VALENTINE COLLECTION**
- Miles home to you / Love like this / So glad / Still be missing you / Northern star / Second chance / Love online / Anybody else but you / Two trees / I will be there for you / No time like the present / All of my life without you / Love at the fair / I hope you / Pieces of dreams / If you were mine / Somethin' to do with you / Just out of reach / Maybe it's you / It might happen / Watching over you. *<re-iss. Feb 08; same>*

Apr 06. (d-cd) *<TC 25>* **TELLING STORIES** (live April–October 2005)
- Forgot my shoes / Walk with you / My grateful heart / Holiday lake / Cassiopeia / Like you / Dropped down in the water / Racing tortoise (instrumental) / If there's a room / Stay that way / One more minute // Life gets real / Every long journey - Road of the heart / Plane travel - Girl scouts / You've got to hide your love away / Loch Lomond / Dad - Holiday lake / Meeting Joan / Stay that way / Willow weep for me / Clementine / I'll keep my hat / Leap of faith / God is sleeping - You've got to be carefully taught - Heroes / Haiku / Goodnight, Irene / Taxes - Crazy / Fair story - The fair.

Jun 08. (cd-ep) *<none>* **THE STATE FAIR SONGS**
- The fair / My Minnesota state fair / One fair fair / Love at the fair / Somewhere at the fair.

Nov 08. (cd-s) *<none>* GOODBYE GEORGE

Nov 08. (cd) *<TC 2008>* **SONGS FOR MINNESOTA**
- Hey, Minnesota / My Minnesota state fair / Marching back to school / Try lutefisk / Love at the fair / Hole in the day / Northern star / One fair fair / Betty Crocker / Where the earth is round / Somewhere at the fair / I love my state / The fair.

Dec 09. (cd) *<TC 2009>* **WHERE THE EARTH IS ROUND**
- Not some far-away place / Where the earth is round / Coffee tasted better when you were here / Pink guitar / How did I? / Space 'neath the sky - Softly and tenderly / Loons on Lake Calhoun / Good thing I bounce / If you forget / A song for the end of the day / We will / Friendsong.

- (8-10*) compilations, etc.-

Feb 08. (cd) *Turtlecub; <none>* **EVERY LONG JOURNEY: SONGS FOR WELLNESS**
- Dropped down in the water / Carry me / I hope you / I will be there for you / Life gets real / No time like the present / Every long journey / Family of strangers / Lisa's song / Watching over you / Northern star / Leap of faith / My grateful heart.

Dan REEDER

Born 1954 in Louisiana, singer/songwriter Dan REEDER was almost 50 before getting any product into retail, but the whimsical, homespun blues-folk on his self-titled debut **DAN REEDER** (2004) {*7} shows that JOHN PRINE was right to give the big grizzly bear his break.

The son of a minister, Dan grew up in southern California and attended Santa Ana College before studying art at Cal State Fullerton, where he met his German-born wife, with whom he has relocated to Germany, where he was making his living as an artist when his demo tape was discovered, SEASICK STEVE-like, by the great PRINE and his Oh Boy independent. Dan's critically acclaimed debut, on which he plays every home-made instrument, is full of sass and audacity in titles such as 'Food And Pussy' and the gospel-like 'My Little Bitty Pee Pee'; ditto 'Work Song', in which he tells the listener he's got "all the fucking work I need".

SWEETHEART (2006) {*6} continued his devotion to the good things in life, but tracks like 'I Drink Beer' and a few more 'pussy' songs are sure to divide opinion, though he plays safe with his closing cover of Procol Harum's 'A Whiter Shade Of Pale'. Reminiscent of John Lurie and his 'Marvin Pontiac' alter-ego, or indeed JOHN PRINE and storyteller Randy Newman, third album **THIS NEW CENTURY** (2010) {*6} was another record rich in anecdotes and observational vignettes, although all too many of the 20 songs seem too short. 'The Walk To The God House' and 'Everybody Wants A Cookie' are ones to check out. *MCS*

Dan Reeder - vocals, acoustic guitar, etc.

US Oh Boy — UK Oh Boy

Mar 04. (cd) <*CDOBR 027*> **DAN REEDER**
- Three chords / No one will laugh / The tulips on the table / Food and pussy / Fight my way out / Shackles and chains / Here in the kitchen / My little bitty pee pee / Work song / Po po dancing / The day is over / These are a few of my favorite things / The coolest blues ever / Havana burning / Dr Gunter / The world's slowest blues song / The brain is not the mind / Clean Elvis.

Sep 06. (cd) <*(CDOBR 036)*> **SWEETHEART**
- Waiting for my cappuccino / Just a tune / You'll never surf again / I drink beer / Bach is dead and gone / You should have wrote a book / Shoot me to the moon / 99 friends of mine / Beautiful / Cowboy song / Pussy titty / Pussy heaven / I don't really want to talk to you / All my money / Just leave me alone today / A whiter shade of pale.

Feb 10. (cd) <*CDOBR 041*> **THIS NEW CENTURY**
- Bitch nation / James Brown is dead and gone / Brain the doon (part 1) / Brain the doon (part 2) / Beachball / Angels may / Long ago / The walk to the God house / I've been hiding / Everybody wants a cookie / Fireball / Angels, brain cells / Breathe in on the G / She won't even blow / Weather is a dead man / Troubled soul / Maybe / It feels so good / This new century / Two songs that I know.

RIO EN MEDIO

Nothing could fit the freak-folk or acid-folk bill better than Danielle Stech-Homsy's RIO EN MEDIO and her ever-changing line-up of musicians. Born in northern New Mexico and living in New York, she befriended Sierra Casady of indie/electro duo CocoRosie , which led to a meeting with DEVENDRA BANHART, who almost immediately signed her to his Gnomonsong label.

Delicate and almost detached from pop music, Danielle's off-kilter approach (reminiscent of VASHTI BUNYAN, LINDA PERHACS and JOANNA NEWSOM) was evident on her debut set, **THE BRIDE OF DYNAMITE** (2007) {*6}. Bathed in ethereal soundscapes and trippy instrumentation (she plays baritone ukulele), most of the songs are settings of prose and poetry by the likes of Ellen M.H. Gates (eerie opener 'You Can Stand'), William Blake ('Europe A Prophecy'), Paul Eluard (the French-sung 'Liberte'), Freya Stark ('The Baghdad Merchant's Son') and John Ashbery ('Girls On The Run'). Oddball and wispy, Stech-Homsy's shy vocals have an air of ghostly parallels with ancient mountain chanters, although most of her spooky songs (except for 'Joe Was On The Plane', 'Everyone Is Someone's' and 'I See The Star') are out there on another planet.

Not one to be pigeonholed, Danielle discreetly recorded two disco songs - Earth Wind And Fire's 'Let's Groove' and the Bee Gees' 'Staying Alive' - in a Montreal hotel room, later releasing them on a limited-edition 45.

Released initially on vinyl only, **FRONTIER** (2008) {*7} again combined her folksy whispers with folktronica atmospherics. The opener, 'Heartless', combined oblique techno meanderings with pop sensibilities - think Goldfrapp on folk pills - but what stole the show was the lo-fi-folk acoustics of 'Ferris', 'Standing Horses' and the title track. Forget the 'Another Green World'-style antics of the eight-minute closing track, 'The Visitor'. *MCS*

Danielle Stech-Homsy - vocals, baritone ukulele / with Tim Fite (electronic percussion), Andy Cabic (guitar, synths and vocals), David Coulter (percussion, etc), Francis Hahn (cello), Thom Monahan (wurlitzer) + Sierra Casady (some vocals)

US Gnomonsong — UK Gnomonsong

Feb 07. (cd) <*(GONG 03)*> **THE BRIDE OF DYNAMITE**
- You can stand / Heaven is high / Tiger's ear / Everyone is someone's / Europe a prophecy / Girls on the run / Kill the messenger / Joe was on the plane / Friday / I see a star / The Baghdad merchant's son / Liberte.

Seven Inch — not issued

2008. (ltd-7") <*Seven-005*> LET'S GROOVE. / Staying Alive

——now with Christian Lee (guitar), Justin Riddle (drums), Nicholas Toll (keyboards and percussion) + Vlad Kromatika (keyboards, etc.)

Manimal Vinyl — not issued

Oct 08. (lp) <*MANI 012*> **FRONTIER**
- Heartless / Ferris / The umbrella / The diamond wall / Venus of Willendorf / Standing horses / The last child's tear / Frontier / Fall up / Stars are / Nameless / Never get you / The light house / The visitor. <*(cd-iss. Mar 09; MV 012CD)*>

Josh RITTER

A big hit in Ireland, like some American cultural exchange for DAMIEN RICE, folk singer/songwriter JOSH RITTER took his cue from the likes of DYLAN, Cash and COHEN. Born October 21, 1976 in Idaho, he went to Oberlin College, Ohio and followed his dream of becoming the next Ryan Adams by performing at venues (including favourite spot Club Passim) in and around the Boston area.

Initially self-distributed at these gigs and others, albums **JOSH RITTER** (2000) {*7} and **GOLDEN AGE OF RADIO** (2002) {*7} deservedly found their way to the hearts and minds of Signature Sounds and Bob DYLAN, both of whom invited Josh to join them. Opening for DYLAN in Ireland caused a minor stir, and tracks such as 'You've Got The Moon', 'Me And Jiggs' (a Top 40 hit there) and 'Golden Age Of Radio' were particular audience-pleasers.

Recorded in under a fortnight in a rickety French farmhouse with Curtis Mayfield's sound equipment, the introspective and literate **HELLO STARLING** (2003) {*8} fared even better critically, showcasing the DYLANish 'Kathleen', 'You Don't Make It Easy Babe', 'Wings' and 'Snow Is Gone'.

Taking time to reflect after signing to the V2 label, RITTER released **THE ANIMAL YEARS** (2006) {*7}, which looked with a serious eye on delicate matters such as the Iraq war and the rollercoaster ride between things hellish and heavenly. 'Girl In The War', 'Lillian Egypt' and 'In The Dark' matched the almost-10-minute Velvet Underground/'Heroin' buzz of 'Thin Blue Flame'.

Live albums aside (there were a few, released for Irish consumption), follow-up **THE HISTORICAL CONQUESTS OF JOSH RITTER** (2007) {*7} was RITTER's 'Subterranean Homesick Blues' album, mostly motormouth (like 'To The Dogs Or Whoever') but tempered slightly by lighter, SIMON & GARFUNKEL-like pieces such as 'The Temptation Of Adam'. It was his last major-label release, but US Top 50 set **SO RUNS AWAY THE WORLD** (2010) {*7} continued his SUFJAN STEVENS-meets-Kerouac-meets-Twain road trip. Pick of the bunch here were 'Change Of Time', 'Lark' and the MISSISSIPPI JOHN HURT-inspired 'Folk Bloodbath'. *MCS*

Josh Ritter - vocals, acoustic guitar, piano (+ session people)

US Orchard — UK not issued

Apr 00. (cd) <*2089-2*> **JOSH RITTER**
- Leaves and kings / Beautiful night / Hotel song / Paint your picture / Angels on her shoulders / Morning is a long way down / Potter's wheel / Letter from Omaha / Last ditch effort (see you try) / Paths will cross / Pretty Polly / Horrible qualities. *(hidden track +=)* - Stuck to you.

Signature Sounds — Signature Sounds

Jan 02. (cd) <*SIG 1269*> **GOLDEN AGE OF RADIO**
- Come and find me / Me and Jiggs / You've got the moon / Lawrence, KS / Anne / Roll on / Leaving / Other side / Harrisburg / Drive away / Golden age of radio / Song for the fireflies. *(UK-iss. Feb 04 on Setanta; SETCD 234)* <*lp-iss. Nov 04; SIG 1282*> <*cd re-iss. Apr 09 w/cd-ep+=; SIG 1282CD*> - Come and find me [newly recorded mix] / Other side [Jackdrag remix] / Chelsea hotel #2 / Me and Jiggs / Other side.

Signature Sounds — Setanta

Sep 03. (cd) <*SIG 1280*> *(SETCD 138)* **HELLO STARLING**
- Bright smile / Kathleen / You don't make it easy babe / Man burning / Rainslicker

/ Wings / California / Snow is gone / Bone of song / Baby that's not all / The bad actress. *<(re-iss. Jan 05 on V2; VVR 103044-2)> (d-cd-iss. Mar 05 on V2+=; VVR 103134-2)* - [solo acoustic equivalents] / [live]:- Kathleen / Golden age of radio / You don't make it easy babe / Snow is gone.

May 04. (cd-s) *(SETCD 139)* HELLO STARLING (SNOW IS GONE) / Tonight You Belong To Me / ['A'-version]

Feb 05. (cd-ep) *<63881-27239-2>* FOUR SONGS LIVE [live]
- Kathleen / Golden stage of radio / You don't make it easy babe / Snow is gone (hello starling).

V2 V2

Apr 06. (cd) *<63881-27296-2> (VVR 103698-2)* **THE ANIMAL YEARS** Mar 06
- Girl in the war / Wolves / Monster ballads / Lillian, Egypt / Idaho / In the dark / One more mouth / Good man / Best for the best / Thin blue flame / Here at the right time. *<d-cd-iss. Feb 11 on Sony+=; B004HLO8OM>* - [solo acoustic equivalents] / Blame it on the Tetons / Harbortown / Peter killed the dragon / Monster ballads [early version].

Dec 06. (cd-ep) *(VVR 104401-2)* GIRL IN THE WAR
- Girl in the war / Blame it on the Tetons / Harbortown / Peter killed the dragon / Monster ballads [early version] / In the dark [acoustic demo] / Girl in the war [acoustic demo].

Dec 06. (7") *<63881-27852-7>* GIRL IN THE WAR. / Peter Killed The Dragon

Sony V2

Aug 07. (cd) *<88697-12256-2> (VVR 104862-8)* **THE HISTORICAL CONQUESTS OF JOSH RITTER** 79 Oct 07
- To the dogs or whoever / Mind's eye / Right moves / The temptation of Adam / Open doors / Rumors / Wait for love / Real long distance / Next to the last romantic / Moons / Still beating / Empty hearts / Wait for love (you know you will). *<US w/ EP+=>* - Wildfires / Spot in my heart / Naked as a window / Labelship down.

not issued self-rel.

Feb 08. (cd+dvd) *<none>* **IN THE DARK: LIVE AT VICAR STREET // IN GOOD COMPANY: A CONCERT MOVIE** Ire
- Idaho / Good man / Me and Jiggs / Harrisburg / Wings / One more mouth / Lillian, Egypt / (intro to...) / Kathleen / Best for the best / Girl in the war / Thin blue flame / Snow is gone / Leaving // [DVD tracks].

Victor not issued

Apr 08. (cd-ep) *<29483-2>* **LIVE AT THE 9:30 CLUB** [live in Washington DC in October 2007]
- Mind's eye / To the dogs or whoever / Rumors / The temptation of Adam / Right moves / Real long distance / Lawrence, KS / Next to the last true romantic [featuring OLD SCHOOL FREIGHT TRAIN].

Pytheas Pytheas

Apr 10. (cd/lp) *<(CD-/LP-PYTH 001)>* **SO RUNS THE WORLD AWAY** 41 May 10
- Curtains / Change of time / The curse / Southern Pacifica / Rattling locks / Folk bloodbath / Lark / Lantern / The remnant / See how the man was made / Another new world / Orbital / Long shadows.

Feb 11. (cd-ep) *<CD-PYTH 002>* TO THE YET UNKNOWING WORLD: B-sides, Demos and Remixes from SO RUNS THE WORLD AWAY
- Galahad / Tokyo! / Wild goose / Lantern / The remnant / Rattling locks / [+ 2 videos].

Sally ROGERS

Born September 19, 1954 in Michigan, crystal-clear singer SALLY ROGERS is probably better known for her award-winning children's albums and her MOR-folk style than her early trad/contemporary-folk material of the late 1970s onwards.

THE UNCLAIMED PINT (1979) {*6} (featuring a youthful CLAUDIA SCHMIDT on dulcimer and vocals) and **IN THE CIRCLE OF THE SUN** (1982) {*6} were two such easy-listening LPs, while her work with her husband, Howie Bursen, kicked off with their **SATISFIED CUSTOMERS** (1984) {*6} set. The children's and family-orientated sets were of course steeped in folk tradition: **PEACE BY PEACE** (1988) {*7} was aimed at children aged three seven, while 1989's **GENERATIONS** {*7} filled the gap between Celtic and Americana roots music. SI KAHN's title track is a favourite, and JEAN RITCHIE's 'Peace Round', BONNIE KOLOC's 'I'll Still Be Loving You' and TOM PAXTON's 'Mother' were other minor gems.

Sadly, it seems that the spiritual **WE'LL PASS THEM ON** (1995) {*6} will be her last outing; she is now, to give her her full title, a Master Teaching Artist for the Connecticut Commission on Culture and Tourism. *MCS*

Sally Rogers - vocals, acoustic guitar, dulcimer, banjo / with session people

US UK
Wheatland not issued

1979. (lp) *<005>* **THE UNCLAIMED PINT**
- I go numb / Dive into the pool of love / On Blonde Street / When you love somebody / (Just like) Romeo and Juliet / Wall around your heart / The king of Tonga / Picasso played a blue guitar / Italian rain / Let your heart remember / When love was grand / Separate lives / R's theme. *<re-iss. 1982 on Thrushwood; TH 001> <re-iss. 1986 on Flying Fish; FF 409> (UK-iss. Mar 89; same as US) <cd-iss. 1993 + Aug 09 +=; FF70 409>* - IN THE CIRCLE OF THE SUN

Thrushwood not issued

1982. (lp) *<TH 002>* **IN THE CIRCLE OF THE SUN**
- Circle of the sun / En revenant des noces / The kissing song / Planxty Fanny Power / Lady Margaret / I wish I had someone to love me / Where the coho flash silver / I'm going home to Georgia / Ecstasy / Old father fall / A little man on my own / Fall is here / Thanksgiving eve. *<(re+UK-iss. 1986 on Flying Fish; FF 413)> <cd-iss.+=>* - THE UNCLAIMED PINT *<(cd/c-iss.2002; FF70/FF90 413)>*

1984. (lp; by SALLY ROGERS & HOWARD BURSEN) *<TH 003>* **SATISFIED CUSTOMERS**
- Milwaukee St Paul / Small business blues / Way down the road / If I were a featherbed / The magpie / King's peak - Cattle in the cane / Take me home / Nancy - Paddy on the railroad / Jack Orion / The gentle Earl / Abelard and Eloise / Beggars to God. *<re-iss. 1985 on Flying Fish; FF 381> (UK-iss. Mar 89; same as US)*

Flying Fish Flying Fish

Nov 85. (lp) *<(FF 365)>* **LOVE WILL GUIDE US** Apr 86
- The old blue suit / Suzanna Martin / Farmer in Florida / Stacy's catch - Spotted pony / Some little bug is gonna find you someday / Some have fathers gone to glory / The mother song / Turn around / The Keewenaw light / Forever / Love will guide us. *<cd-iss. Nov 92; FF70 365>*

Nov 87. (lp; by SALLY ROGERS & CLAUDIA SCHMIDT) *<(FF 425)>* **CLOSING THE DISTANCE** May 88
- Begone dull care / Are you tired of me, my darling? / Gentlemen of distinction in the army / Come thou font of every blessing - Mountain field / Come take a trip in my airship / Quetico / Ezekiel saw the world / Blessing / Appalachian round / Mama, I miss you tonight / Lovely Agnes / Hey hey Watenay - I walk in beauty / Some fathers have gone to glory / Circle of the sun / I wish I had someone to love me / Way down the road. *<(cd/c-iss. Sep 92; FF70/FF90 425)>*

Nov 89. (lp) *<(FF 493)>* **GENERATIONS**
- Prayin' for rain / Seven long years / Testimony of Patience Kershaw / Blue lion suite / I'll be there / Who can sail / Generations / The ballad of Sojourner Truth / Valse de jouets (Waltz for the toys) / I'll still be loving you / Mother / Peace round / Dead girl of Hiroshima. *<cd-iss. Sep 92; FF70 493>*

Nov 90. (cd/c; by SALLY ROGERS & HOWIE BURSEN) *<(FF70/FF90 538)>* **WHEN HOWIE MET SALLY** 1992
- A chat with your mother / Plastic rap / Our children / Katie's choice / The last paycheck - The Martin house / Testing / Cordova / The dove - The cuckoo - Give the fiddler a dram / Names / The good in living - Speed the plough - Flying cloud / Ain't life (like a wide, wide load on a narrow road) / It's a pleasure to know you.

——In 1991, ROGERS teamed up with CLAUDIA SCHMIDT on the album 'While We Live'.

Red House Red House

Aug 95. (cd) *<(RHRCD 71)>* **WE'LL PASS THEM ON**
- Across the blue mountains / Le bouvier / Virginia's Alders (friends and neighbors) / Home again / There is no place / Gone to the dogs / In the name of all of our children / Mother Courage / A dozen years / Black is the color / My little doney gal - The cuckoo / Black Jack Davey / Hard work / We'll pass them on.

——In 1996, Sally was credited on CHARLIE KING's CD 'The Senseless Laughter Of Whales'

——In 1998, Sally Rogers and friends put together 'Heritage Corridor' CD for schools

- children's albums -

1988. (c) *Golden Music; <41042>* **PEACE BY PEACE**
- I've got a song / I wanna be somebody / Magic penny / I can be anything / Lambeth children / Dear Mr President / Don't you push me / It's a miracle / I can't imagine / I'm so lucky / Hands / Study war no more / Mur... peace.

Nov 90. (cd) *Round River; <RRCD 301>* **PIGGYBACK PLANET: Songs for a Whole Earth**
- Hello, ladybug / Over in an endangered meadow / The rain round - What have they done to the rain? / K'ang ting song / La tierra es mi madre / Whale song / Garbage / Junk round / The recycle song / I walk in beauty / What did the dinosaurs say? / This land is your land. *<re-iss. Dec 10 on cd-r Thrushwood Kids; none>*

1992. (c) *Round River; <none>* **WHAT CAN ONE LITTLE PERSON DO?**
- What can one little person do? / Amelia Earhart / Billy Magee Magaw / The stoplight / I care for joy / Where do the animals put all their trash? / Migratin' / No one / It all turned blue / Piri-miri-dictum domini / Fifty states / 1492 / P is for peace. *<cd-iss. Dec10 on cd-r Thrushwood Kids; 571521>*

Jan 94. (cd) *Alcazar; <AL-113CA>* **AT QUIET O'CLOCK**
- Kitty alone / Bye'm bye / I gave my love a cherry / Ride ride ranke / One man shall mow my meadow / Hush little baby / Sleepy sleep / I see the moon / Round my lullay / Baby's boat / Dance to your daddy.

Jack ROSE

Similar in many ways to former Cul De Sac finger-picker GLENN JONES, and also from an indie/alt-rock background, versatile guitarist JACK ROSE (from 1990s drone-mongers Pelt) echoed his idol JOHN FAHEY and others such as ROBBIE BASHO and SANDY BULL.

Jack (b. February 16, 1971 in Richmond, Virginia) didn't abandon Pelt altogether to go solo, but maintained a parallel career in which he could fire off the odd group/trio set aside from his solo folk-meets-bluegrass outings. Here we'll be sticking to his post-millennium discography.

America has strength in depth when it comes to roots artists such as ROSE, but his next-generation difference is that he imbues the sentiment of old-timey tradition with a ragtime and cajun/country feel, taking the music beyond the confines of Folkways and Takoma aficionados. A good introduction for genre greenhorns might be **TWO ORIGINALS OF JACK ROSE** (2004) {*8}, which encompasses two older limited-edition LPs, **RED HORSE, WHITE MULE** (2002) {*6} and **OPIUM MUSICK** (2003) {*6}), or 2005's **KENSINGTON BLUES** {*7}. The last-named featured his rendition of FAHEY's 'Sunflower River Blues'.

Released either side of his untimely death on December 4, 2009 were two definitive projects, the public-domain-biased **JACK ROSE & THE BLACK TWIG PICKERS** (2009) {*7} and the posthumous solo set **LUCK IN THE VALLEY** (2010) {*7}, with GLENN JONES, Harmonica Dan and Hans Chew in tow. The latter contains renditions of Blind Blake's 'West Coast Blues', W.C. Handy's 'St. Louis Blues' and Rob Summers's 'Everybody Ought To Pray Sometime'. *MCS*

Jack Rose - guitars, vocals / (+ guests)

US Eclipse — UK not issued

2002. (ltd-lp) *<ECL-012>* **RED HORSE, WHITE MULE**
- Red horse / Dark was the night, cold was the ground / White mule (part 1) / White mule (part 2) / Hide the whiskey (blues for the colonel). *<cd-iss. Mar 04 as TWO ORIGINALS OF JACK ROSE on VHF+=; VHF #81> (UK cd-iss. Mar 04 on Beautiful Happiness+=; HAPP 001CD)* - OPIUM MUSICK

2003. (ltd-lp) *<ECL-026>* **OPIUM MUSICK**
- Yaman blues / Linden Ave stomp / Mountaintop lament / Black pearls. *<(cd-iss.+=)>* - RED HORSE, WHITE MULE

VHF — VHF

Jun 04. (cd) *<(VHF #85)>* **RAAG MANIFESTOS** (live)
- Black pearls from the river / Tower of Babel / Hart Crane's old boyfriends / Tex / Crossing the great waters / Road / Blessed be the name of the Lord. *<lp-iss. Jan 06 on Eclipse; ECL-039>*

VHF — Beautiful Happiness

Aug 05. (cd) *<VHF #92> (HAPP 006CD)* **KENSINGTON BLUES**
- Kensington blues / Cross the north fork / Cathedral et Chartres / Rappaharock river rag (for William Moore) / Sunflower river blues / Now that I'm a man full grown II / Flirtin' with the undertaker / Calais to Dover. *<lp-iss. Apr 08 on Tequila Sunrise; TS-12001>*

2006. (ltd-cd) *<archive 28>* **SELF TITLED**
- Levee / Revolt / St Louis blues / Miss Mary's place / Gage blues / Spirits in the house / Dark was the night. *<ltd lp-iss. May07 on Tequila Sunrise; TS-12006>*

(above issued on Archive) (below on Tequila Sunrise)

2006. (ltd-7") *<TS-7002>* UNTITLED (Part I). / Untitled (Part II)

2007. (ltd-7"; shared) *<ff 015>* HOW GREEN WAS MY VALLEY / Buckdancer's Choice. / (other track by Silvester Anfang) — Belg

(above on Funeral Folk)

Tequila Sunrise — Beautiful Happiness

Mar 08. (cd) *<TS-5006> (HAPP 010)* **DR RAGTIME & PALS**
- Miss Mary's place / Revolt / Song for the owl / Bells / Knoxville blues / Fishtown flower / Dusty grass / Soft steel piston / Linden Ave stomp / Blessed be the name of the Lord / Walkin' blues / Buckdancer's choice. *<w/ free cd+=; TS-5007>* - (SELF TITLED album tracks). <lp-iss. Sep 08; TS-12007R>

JACK ROSE & THE BLACK TWIG PICKERS

not issued Supplement — Great Pop

2008. (7"; as JACK ROSE and THE BLACK TWIGS) *(GPS 28)*|
REVOLT. / Soft Steel Piston

2009. (7") *(GPS 49)* SHOOTING CREEK. / Rappanhanock River Rag

VHF — VHF

Jul 09. (cd) *<(VHF #116)>* **JACK ROSE & THE BLACK TWIG PICKERS**
- Little Sadie / Sail away ladies - I shall not be moved / Hand me down my walking cane / Soft steel piston / Some happy day / Ride old Buck / Revolt / Kensington blues / Special rider / Bright sunny south / Goodbye booze. *<lp-iss. on Klang Industries; 008>*

JACK ROSE

Thrill Jockey — Thrill Jockey

Feb 10. (cd) *<(CDTHRILL 22)>* **LUCK IN THE VALLEY**
- Blues for Percy Danforth / Lick mountain ramble / Woodpiles on the side of the road / When tailgate drops, the bullshit stops / Moon in the gutter / Luck in the valley / St Louis blues / Tree in the valley / Everybody ought to pray sometime / West Coast blues.

——Jack died in December 2009

- (5-7*) compilations, others, etc.-

Mar 08. (ltd; cd/lp) *Three Lobed; <TLR 049>* **I DO PLAY ROCK AND ROLL** (live November 13, 2004 & December 1, 2006)
- Calais to Dover / Cathedral et Chartres / Sundogs.

Apr 09. (ltd-lp) *Three Lobed; <TLR 066>* **THE BLACK DIRT SESSIONS**
- Dusty grass / Cross the north fork / Fishtown flower / Song for the owl / Box of pine / The world has let me down.

David ROVICS

It's important to put one's impartial hat on when assessing the political folk of confrontational activist DAVID ROVICS (b. April 10, 1967 in New York City, raised in Wilton, Connecticut), a musical rebel not too far removed from the late, great PHIL OCHS. Whether David's work has been intentionally trampled underfoot by government oppressors, or he's simply been protecting the anti-commercial ethos of his DIY/punk-folk, is for the man himself to explain. His country and his maker will make their judgment one day on whether he really is an enemy of the people or an atheist martyr for the cause. His initial inspiration is said to have come from the fatal shooting of a close friend by a gang.

If music be the food of love, ROVICS (once a Boston busker) serves up a seven-course deal of trad-based tunes and political poetry, and it's been said he's cracked more than a few eggs to make his omelette. From his low-key, cassette-only covers effort of 1996, **MAKE IT SO** {*5}, to his bombardment of website downloads in 2010/11, he gets his point of view across in many media. One album in particular, **THE COMMONS** (2007) {*8}, finally got his message across in Britain when unleashed on ROBB JOHNSON's Irregular Records.

A glance at ROVIC's titles in the mainly {*6} discography should be more than enough to see where the man is coming from. Essential tracks that should bait the red, white and blue of the US without the breaking down of doors are the 'people's songs' 'If I Die Tomorrow', 'New Orleans', 'Operation Iraqi Liberation', 'Minimum Wage Strike' and 'Behind The Barricades', all of them live favourites. *MCS*

David Rovics - vocals, acoustic guitar / + session players, etc.

US David Rovics — UK not issued

1996. (c) *<none>* **MAKE IT SO**
- The Boston burglar / Make it so / People used to / If you love the water, let it rain / Vigilante man / Song of the rail / The bicycle song / Field of summer's gold / In the eyes of Hollywood / In the heat of the summer / The bluegrass fiddler of London / Me and my uncle / Only our rivers run free / Talkin' union / Enola Gay / Whiskey-drinkin' mama / Ghost dance lullaby / Big rock candy mountain.

1998. (cd) *<none>* **WE JUST WANT THE WORLD**
- Minimum wage strike / We just want the world / The death of David Chain / Judi Bari / Cannabis café / Parking lots and strip malls / Song for Boxcar Betty / Contras, kings and generals / Henry Ford was a fascist / Song for Hugh Thompson / T-stop café / Too proud to beg / Glory and fame / If I die tomorrow. *<re-iss. Apr 04; same>*

2000. (cd) *<CLUB PASSIM 03>* **LIVE AT THE CLUB PASSIM** [live]
- Song for the big mountain / (intro to...) / Song for the BBB / Song for my broken heart / (intro to...) / The alligator song / Terror in the skies / (intro to...) / Henry Ford was a fascist / Song for Eric / Cannabis café / (intro to...) / Deadhead in prison / Song for the SOA / Minimum wage strike / (intro to...) / Morning at Minnehaha / Song for Boxcar Betty / Pray for the dead and fight like hell for the living / (intro to...) / The flag desecration rag / Hobo's lullaby. *<re-iss. Apr 04; same>*

2001. (cd) *<01>* **LIVING IN THESE TIMES**
- The dying firefighter / From Kabul to Khartoum / St Patrick battalion / Who will tell the people / The rinky dink song / Shut them down / Behind the barricades / Song for Basta / International terrorists / Trading with the enemy / No one is illegal / My daughter / I remember Warsaw / Children of Jerusalem / D.U. / Polyamory song / The jewel of Bucharest. *<re-iss. Apr 04; same>*

—— next credited **Allie Rosenblatt**

2002. (cd) *<none>* **HANG A FLAG IN THE WINDOW**
- The next attack / Hang a flag in the window / Drink of the death squads / The village where nothing happened / Bomb ourselves / Jenin / Good Kurds, bad Kurds / Song for Basra / I have seen the enemy / One night in Greece / The pirate radio song / Ballad of a cluster bomb / Vanguard / Mi amor / Sit down to piss / By the time they nuke DC / Song for the ELF / Outside agitator / In one world / We are everywhere / Behind the barricades. *<re-iss. Apr 04; same>*

Ever Reviled — not issued

Sep 03. (cd) *<none>* **RETURN**

- After the revolution / Palestine / Occupation / The death of Rachel Corrie / So many years ago / Resistance / Reichstag fire / Promised land / Times gone by / Strike a blow against the empire / Song for Ana Belen Montes / Hiroshima / The key / Return.

Apr 04. (cd) *<ER 0007-2>* **SONGS FOR MAHMUD**
- Miami / Operation Iraqi liberation / Face of victory / Song the songbird sings / They're building a wall / Who would Jesus bomb? / Evening news / Here at the end of the world / Used to be a city / More gardens song / Butcher for hire / Trafalgar Square / Song for the SOA #2 / All the ghosts that walk this earth / Korea / I wanna go home / Moron / War is over / Battle of Blair Mountain / Oppositional defiant disorder / What if you knew.

YoYo not issued

Mar 05. (cd) *<YOYO 027>* **FOR THE MOMENT**
- After we torture our prisoners / Falluja / The draft is coming / Berlin / Song for Hugo Chavez / Guantanamo Bay / Spanish journalist strike / They're building a wall / The scar upon your face / Saint Patrick battalion / Unknown soldier / Like I think about you / Mi amor / More gardens song / My daughter / I wanna go home / Whoever wins in November / After the revolution / Every minute of the day.

High Times not issued

Sep 06. (cd+dvd) *<HTR 121>* **HALLIBURTON BOARDROOM MASSACRE**
- Crashing down / How far is it from here to Nuremberg / New Orleans / Tsunami / Halliburton boardroom massacre / When Johnny came marching home / RPG / Four blank slates / Song for Cindy Sheehan / Waiting for the fall / Paul Wolfowitz / Life is beautiful // [DVD tracks].

David Rovics not issued

Sep 08. (cd) *<none>* **HAR, HAR, HAR: SONGS ABOUT PIRATES, PENGUINS AND PUNK ROCK BABIES** [children's/family]
- Walking on the ceiling / Roller coaster train / Punk rock baby / The fruit that got away / The pirate song / Fly around the world / Boogers / Tappety tippety / Two mommies and two daddies / Bullies / I'm gonna fly / Daddy's camper van / Don't fall into the toilet / I'm running away / Owl dream / Together.

Jan 10. (cd) *<none>* **TEN THOUSAND MILES AWAY**
- Travelodge / In the name of God / Song for the Eureka stockade / Brad / Floating down the river / Now that you're gone / Berkshire hills / Atif and Sebastian / Pirates of Somalia / Lebanon / John Brown / Luis Posada / Guanajuanto / Free / East Tennessee / Land of the midnight sun / I know a man / Santiago / Song for Ginger Goodwin / Song for Al Grierson / World of broken dreams.

—— his website has since released a string of download CDs including 'Troubadour: People's History In Song' (2010), 'Ten New Songs' (2011) and 'Big Red Sessions' (2011).

- (8-10*) compilations, others, etc.-

Dec 03. (cd) *AK PRESS - Daemon; <AKA 038CD - DAM 19041>*
BEHIND THE BARRICADES: THE BEST OF DAVID ROVICS
- Shut them down / Drink of the death squads / Saint Patrick battalion / We are everywhere / Minimum wage strike / Hang a flag in the window / Jenin / In one world / Behind the barricades / Song for the Earth Liberation Front / (intro to...) / Song for the BBB / I remember Warsaw / (intro to...) / Henry Ford was a fascist / If I die tomorrow / (intro to...) / The flag desecration rag / Who would Jesus bomb? / Operation Iraqi liberation / I wanna go home.

Nov 07. (cd) *Irregular; (IRR 067)* **THE COMMONS**
- Operation Iraqi liberation / Falluja / New Orleans / I'm a better anarchist than you / Halliburton boardroom massacre / Oppositional defiant disorder / Who would Jesus bomb? / Burn it down / Jenin / Black flag flying / The cannabis café / The St Patrick's battalion / They're building a wall / Life is beautiful / The commons / Behind the barricades / After the revolution.

RUSALNAIA (⟹ KRAUS, Sharron)

S

SAMAMIDON (⟹ AMIDON, Sam)

Claudia SCHMIDT

If you can imagine JONI MITCHELL backed by It's A Beautiful Day, or BARBARA DICKSON in Tin Pan Alley mode, you might grasp the dexterous and vocally agile talents of folk singer/songwriter CLAUDIA SCHMIDT. Born 1953 in New Baltimore, Michigan, she has flitted in and out of folk, jazz and blues at the drop of a hat, and was audacious and eclectic enough to integrate her diverse musical territories on several of her albums.

Her debut for Flying Fish, **CLAUDIA SCHMIDT** (1979) {*6}, was one example, a charismatic and earnest introduction to her own compositions and works by the likes of MICHAEL SMITH ('Spoon River') and Buddy Johnson ('Since I Fell For You'), Arlen & Harburg's 'If I Only Had A Brain' (from 'The Wizard Of Oz') and two traditional tracks, 'Horse Thief' and 'Farewell To Tarwathie'.

The multi-instrumentalist's formative acoustic years had seen her become a fixture on Garrison Keillor's radio show 'A Prairie Home Companion', while she had also befriended Chicago's best-known folk artists, STEVE GOODMAN, BOB GIBSON and JIM POST.

Albums two to four seemed to repeat the originals-and-covers prescription. **MIDWESTERN HEART** (1981) {*7} took on SMITH's 'Vampire', the traditional 'Farewell My Friends' and ALISTAIR ANDERSON's 'The Darkening'. The semi-concept **NEW GOODBYES, OLD HELLOS** (1983) {*5} found room for no less than six reinterpretations: BOB FRANKE's 'Hard Love', PETE SEEGER's 'Old Devil Time', Larry Penn's 'I'm A Little Cookie', BRUCE COCKBURN's 'For The Birds', Bill Withers' 'Grandma's Hands' and Eric Kaz's 'River Of Tears'. 1985's **OUT OF THE DARK** (1985) {*7} stepped back in time with staples 'Skylark' (Hoagy Carmichael) and 'Beginning To See The Light' (Duke Ellington). Tom Waits's 'San Diego Serenade' was a more recent borrowing.

Either side of her first two efforts for Red House (**BIG EARFUL** (1987) {*5} and **ESSENTIAL TENSION** (1991) {*7}) came a couple of fine collaborative sets with SALLY ROGERS, the second of which, **WHILE WE LIVE** (1991) {*7} saw them cover MALVINA REYNOLDS's 'I Wish You Were Here' and Cathy Fink's 'Sewing A Name'. Her solo covers on 'Big Earful' were Charlie Hollins's 'Make It Across The Road', Percy Mayfield's 'Danger Zone', and Alan Bergman & Michel LeGrand's 'You Must Believe In Spring'.

Described as her back-to-basics album, and like her preceding solo set fully original, **IT LOOKS FINE FROM HERE** (1994) {*6} tackled bittersweet romance and death in a way only JONI MITCHELL and her jazz-infused 'Blue' album had previously handled. Claudia's 12-string acoustics and dulcimer were effectively augmented by Dean Magraw (guitar) and Marc Anderson (percussion). Although delivered over six years later, **WINGS OF WONDER** (2000) {*6} was another intense and genre-busting set of classy songs.

Further post-millennium product from SCHMIDT has found her at a transitional time in her life, her self-financed albums flirting between spoken-word, jazz and funk - very Joni. *MCS*

Claudia Schmidt - vocals, guitars, dulcimer, harmonium / with session people

US Flying Fish — UK Flying Fish

1979. (lp) *<FF 066>* **CLAUDIA SCHMIDT**
- Drinking buddy / If I only had a brain / Spoon river / Old woman lament / Lady / Fuzzy / Horse thief / Since I fell for you / Whale song - Farewell to Tarwathie. *(UK-iss. Mar 89; same as US) <(cd/c-iss. Sep 92; FF 70/90 066)> <cd re-iss. Nov 08 on New Rounder; none>*

1981. (lp) *<FF 241>* **MIDWESTERN HEART**
- Give me some / Man who visits me / The darkening / Vampire / Broken glass / Farewell my friends / Alley dancer / Coming home to you / Afternoon on a woodpile / Dolphin story / This is the hour. *(UK-iss. Mar 89; same as US) <(cd/c-iss. Sep 92; FF 70/90 241)>*

1983. (lp) *<FF 305>* **NEW GOODBYES, OLD HELLOS**
- Hard love / Skin gangsters / Tired [*] / Old devil time / I'm a little cookie / Beaver Island jubilee - For the birds - Replenish / Ashleyville / Stairs / Grandma's hands / Old friend [*] / Passing [*] / River of tears. *(UK-iss. Mar 89; same as US) <cd see+=>* - OUT OF THE DARK

1985. (lp) *<(FF 361)>* **OUT OF THE DARK** — Apr 86
- Happy hearts / Let me in / Hip to be homeless / Birdwings - Skylark / Can't be cool / Gather you in / I'm beginning to see the light / Fanfare for Forsythia / Dulcimer interlude / San Diego serenade / We hold back / Love is the strongest thing. *<cd-iss. Sep 93 +=; FF70 361>* - NEW GOODBYES, OLD HELLOS [except *].

—— In 1987, Claudia collaborated with SALLY ROGERS on LP 'Closing The Distance'.

Red House — Red House

1987. (lp) *<RHR 19>* **BIG EARFUL**
- Bend in the river / Pretty at the end / Herds of words / You can call me baby / Make it across the road / Rock that sucker / Danger zone / You must believe in spring / Novembering / The last snow / Roads. *<cd/c-iss. Mar 92; RHR CD/C 19>*

Mar 91. (cd/c) *<RHR CD/C 38>* **ESSENTIAL TENSION**
- Racer / Black crow / Coming clear / New Beltane boogie / Gotta get down (to get up) / Persephone's song / Right from the start / Anniversary / Want to shine / Visitor on solstice eve / Tired of going / Invitation to the weep.

Nov 91. (cd/c; by CLAUDIA SCHMIDT & SALLY ROGERS) *<RHR CD/C 45>* **WHILE WE LIVE**
- Tree of life / Going by / Sewing a name / Mortal friend / I wish you were here / O, little children / Grampa Johnson / Song for Dave / Love is a song / I had an old coat / Mr Fox / I see the moon / The garlic waltz / While we live.

Apr 94. (cd) *<(RHRCD 64)>* **IT LOOKS FINE FROM HERE** — Jul 95
- Banana moon / We don't know / Mowin' at Owen's / Another kind / Postcard from Andrea / Miss Eulalia Thomas / Waltzing at the 45th parallel / Winter love / These stars / Quiet hills / You can't stop / Rising.

Sep 00. (cd) *<(RHRCD 144)>* **WINGS OF WONDER**
- Wings of wonder / It all depends / Peter and Lois go round and round / Remember / Friday the loveteenth / Chamada / Stop to rest / My one and only love / Somebody else's restaurant / Wayfaring stranger / The moon winked at Hale-Bopp / Livingstone's farewell.

—— In 2000, she self-released (with the Jump Boys) the jazz-blues set LIVE AT THE OLD RECTORY PUB: Beaver Island, Michigan. I THOUGHT ABOUT YOU (a jazz collection - also with the Jumpboys) and LIVE AT THE DAKOTA were her second and third jazz offerings

Independent — not issued

2003. (cd) *<none>* **ROADS** [spoken word and poetry]
- Roads [poem] / Red winged blackbird / June 23 AM / Skin gangsters / Basic hygiene / Folding sheets / Winter invocation / Thank you note / Pie / One blue chip / The vowels / Let us give thanks / Wild strawberries [poem] / Terminal hors d'oeuvre / Without wings / Garden party [poem] / A taste of life.

2006. (cd) *<none>* **SPINNING**
- Quiet way / Spinning / Too late for breakfast / Chickadee blues / O waly waly / Trailhead / Waiting / The moment they knew / Here comes joy / Be nice / Christmas Eve / Coyote / God's gift to women.

Feb 10. (cd; as CLAUDIA SCHMIDT and her FUNTET) *<none>* **PROMISING SKY**
- Can't get yourself out of love / Missy ma'am / What luck's been up to / Ubumama / I don't know / Meelie's waltz / Wisconsin country / Sea of love / If all goes well / Tree of dreams / Promising sky / Make peace / We'll be together again.

Danny SCHMIDT

Born October 7, 1970 in Austin, Texas, the stylish singer-songwriter DANNY SCHMIDT takes his deep-rooted inspirations from the Appalachian mountains, NEIL YOUNG, BOB DYLAN, JOHN PRINE and all aspects of Piedmont blues.

Not to be confused with the 1980s blues artist of the same name, SCHMIDT was a late starter in songwriter terms, finding his vocation at the age of 25 after time spent in the Blue Ridge mountains of Virginia, via the Ozarks and a meeting with fellow songwriter DEVON SPROULE. Making

Charlottesville, Virginia his home in the late 1990s, Danny's first release was a low-key concert set, **LIVE AT THE PRISM COFFEEHOUSE** (2000) {*6}.

His post-millennium period had its fair share of ups and downs while he worked on other media projects (film and video production), meanwhile surviving a battle with cancer. These difficult times nevertheless brought forth three good, solid, self-financed albums in **ENJOYING THE FALL** (2001) {*6}, **MAKE RIGHT THE TIME** (2003) {*6} and **PARABLES AND PRIMES** (2005) {*6}. He went on to win the New Folk award at the Kerrville Folk Festival in 2007.

The Waterbug label was the first to show interest in the country-folk troubadour. **LITTLE GREY SHEEP** (2008) {*6} courted controversy with its cover art of a black sheep on top of a white one, but Danny's music spoke louder with 'Go Ugly Early', 'The Drawing Board' and 'Emigrant, MT'. Whether his future country-blues and old-timey recordings with Red House were actually folk music was a puzzle for purists, but **INSTEAD THE FOREST ROSE TO SING** (2009) {*7} and **MAN OF MANY MOONS** (2011) {*6} housed some of his most accomplished work to date, including the NEIL YOUNG-cloned 'Little White Angels' and the LOUDON WAINWRIGHT III-like 'Guilt By Association Blues'. *MCS*

Danny Schmidt - vocals, acoustic guitar

US The Orchard — UK not issued

Mar 00. (cd) *<2278>* **LIVE AT THE PRISM COFFEEHOUSE: April 25 - 1999** — self
- Intro / Cliff song / The donut song / Three chords and cloud of dust / Intro to Sassafras; or Danny manages to say 'um' 19 times in 1:19 minutes / Waiting on Sassafras / Anarchy for a night rag / Chapter thirteen / Lucky / Last night / Sad songs walking / Belief? / McCreary's pipes / Heaven / Canyon walls. *<re-iss. May 02 on Live Once; X 0895>*

Live Once — not issued

Nov 01. (cd) *<B00314 0 5102-2>* **ENJOYING THE FALL**
- God's love of man / These ain't Tynan's blues / Girlwhiskey / Sometimes a friend / Tennee, Mama and Desiree / Blue railroad train / Drunk at the Biltmore / Oaxacan vacation / McCreary's pipes / Ten penny nails / Columbine / Not unlike water / (untitled).

May 03. (cd) *<none>* **MAKE RIGHT THE TIME**
- Make right the time (part 1) / Tick tock / Today / Sunny days / Cleopatra / Boils down to blood / The winds / Anarchy for a night rag / Closing time / Already done / Make right the time (part two).

Jul 05. (cd) *<none>* **PARABLES AND PRIMES**
- This too shall pass / Neil Young / Dark-eyed prince / Happy all the time / Riddle and lies / Esmee by the river / Stained glass / Ghosts / Beggars and mules / A circus of clowns / Parables and primes. *(UK-iss. Nov 07 on Tin Angel; 004)*

Waterbug — not issued

Feb 08. (cd) *<WBG 79>* **LITTLE GREY SHEEP**
- Leaves are burning / Drawing board / Go ugly early / Cliff song / Around the waist / Adios to Tejasito / Tales of sweet Odysseus / Emigrant, MT / California's on fire / Song for Judy and Bridget / Company of friends / Trouble comes calling.

Red House — Red House

Mar 09. (cd) *<RHRCD 216>* **INSTEAD THE FOREST ROSE TO SING**
- Better off broke / Swing me down / Grampa built bridges / Southland street / Two timing bank robber's lament / Firestorm / Serpentine cycle of money / Oh bally ho / Accidentally daisies / The night's beginning to shine.

Feb 11. (cd) *<(RHRCD 232)>* **MAN OF MANY MOONS**
- Houses sing / Little white angels / Man of many moons / Buckets of rain / Ragtime ragtime blues / Guilt by association blues / Almost round the world / Two guitars / On abundance / I've mostly watched / Know thy place.

Carla SCIAKY

Inspired by her mother, a nursery-school teacher and counsellor and an adept classical pianist, child piano prodigy Carla (b. 1954, Brooklyn, NY, raised in Boulder, Colorado) added to her talents by learning to play the guitar at a summer camp in Oaxaca, Mexico with her grandmother. Few of her peers had combined higher education with numerous day jobs and fronting a folk-rock outfit, but Carla was an exceptional life student, and her band recorded one LP, the self-titled **PROPINQUITY** (1973) {*5}.

Abandoning her educational workshops and her postgraduate activities with the Dufay Consort, SCIAKY's solo career moved centre-stage from the early 1980s onwards. Her solo debut, **TO MEET YOU** (1982) {*6}, and two further self-financed LPs, **IN BETWEEN** (1985) {*7} and **UNDER THE QUARTER MOON** (1988) {*5}, promised much without popping any corks.

Another decade and another direction showed that SCIAKY (pr. 'see-ah-kee') could adapt to any folk style and step away from her Fast Folk foundations. Normally more at home with Celtic connections, the Green Linnet label produced three contemporary-meets-trad CDs, 1992's **THE UNDERTOW** {*7}, 1993's wholly-sourced **SPIN THE WEAVER'S SONG** {*7} and 1995's **AWAKENING** {*6}, all very much about the female perspective since time immemorial.

Of late Carla has concentrated on bringing up her children (when they were very young she delivered the one-off children's set **WISHES AND DREAMS** (1997) {*6}), but she's had something of a resurgence through appearing on albums by The Mother Fockers, The Folkaltones and the latter's offshoot act, The Trifolkals (alongside Miriam Rosenblum and Hal Aqua). *MCS*

Carla Sciaky - vocals, acoustic guitar, piano, multi / with several guest musicians

US Propinquity — UK not issued

1982. (lp) *<PR 1001>* **TO MEET YOU**
- Harmonies / Coo coo / Llorona / Joker / Lakes of Pontchartrain / Douce dame jolie / Adjustment / Aunque mis ojos perdieron / Foggy dew / Why do you bob your hair girls / To meet you.

1985. (lp) *<PR 1002>* **IN BETWEEN**
- Some like it hot / Slipping away / Searching for lambs / Aquel cavalelero, madre / Keoka coffee / The foggy dew / Billy Grimes / Charmer blues / Urge for going / Farewell lovely Nancy - Blackbirds and thrushes / Norwegian waltz / Sjala moma ran bosilek / And I will sing.

1988. (lp) *<PR 1004>* **UNDER THE QUARTER MOON**
- Drive this drought away / Propinquity / Sprig of thyme / The foggy dew / Peregrina / The yuppie of Denver / The hills of Glenshee / Under the quarter moon / Evermore / Tristan's lament / Pretty crowin' chicken / Woman's been after man ever since / Fathers, now our meeting is over.

Green Linnet — Green Linnet

Jan 92. (cd/c) *<GLCD/CSIF 2103>* **THE UNDERTOW**
- This deep love / Late in the day / The undertow / The whole world 'round / Rolling in the dew / Everybody's strange but me / Home is where the heart is / I'm a wimp / Focus on the road / Celia / Listen to the thunder / There is a war a-raging / Song from the heart.

Jan 93. (cd/c) *<GLCD/CSIF 2106>* **SPIN THE WEAVER'S SONG**
- Sheep shearing toast [vocal version] / Sheep shearing toast / The sheep shearers / Sheep shearing / Click, click, that's how the shears go / Shearing the sheep / The band of shearers / The flax in bloom / Jog along till shearing / Spinn spinn - La filadora / Snosti e dobra dotsna sedela / Pukala Sam Lenek / Viragos kenderem / The spool / Song for the spinning wheel / Spinning wheel song / La tejedora de nanduti / Cotton picker's rag / The weaver's glee / I can weave linen / The weaver is handsome / Paddy the weaver / The weaver / The weaver's march - Gallant weaver / The weaver's daughter / The weaver and the chambermaid / Sweet Becky at the loom / Waulking song / Song of the sky loom / Weaving lilt.

Jan 95. (cd/c) *<(GLCD/CSIF 2115>* **AWAKENING** — Feb 95
- Awakening / For a long time to come / Is this water? / These awkward days / Gladys and Harley / Insomnia blues / The song that bird sings / There are three reasons / Once I had a sweetheart / I cannot tell you / Icarus / Aunt Sue / Hope the hermit / There are many roads.

Alacazam — not issued

Sep 97. (cd/c) *<Alcazar 2006>* **WISHES AND DREAMS:** songs composed with kids, for kids
- Wishes and dreams / A rainy day / Hacky sack / The hundred dollar bill / The trip to the ice cream parlor / A good friend / School lunch / Sing, sing, sing / The future / There's a hornet in our classroom / Seasons / Nighttime / I want to know why / Growing up / Tesseract / Colorado skiing / Halloween (pt. II) / We're going to miss you, Mrs Sciaky / Wynken, Blynken, and Nod.

—— she retired from the music scene for a decade...

—— next with **Miriam Rosenblum** + **Hal Aqua**

own label — not issued

2008. (cd-ep; by The FOLKALTONES) *<none>* TUNING UP
- I'll dance with you / The deluded lover / Jig medley (Brother Gildis', tell her I will, tell her I am) / Hard rock bottom / One door opens - Reels (Boys of the lough - The new fashioned habit) / All is quiet.

- (5-7*) compilations, others, etc.-

2008. (cd) *self-rel.; <none>* **REWIND:** the vinyl years
- Some like it hot / Bouncing back (Adjustment) / The foggy dew / The foggy dew / Under the quarter moon / Triatian's lament / Sprig of thyme / Joker / Pretty crownin' chicken / The lakes of Pontchartrain / Urge for going / Aquel cavallero, madre / Evermore / The hills of Glenshee / To meet you / Fathers now our meeting is over.

PROPINQUITY

Carla Sciaky - vocals, guitar, violin, bass / **Jason Potter** - vocals, guitar / **Pat Hubbard** - vocals, guitar, piano / **Mel Stonebraker** - vocals, bass, guitar / **Jeff Harper** - drums, percussion

Owl — not issued

1973. (lp) *<Owl 23>* **PROPINQUITY**
- People come / And I a fairy tale lady / Tappan Square / You don't have to hurry / Standing in the doorway / Dorian: 240 lament / Window / Binghamton / I'll be here in the morning / Ohio / Miles before sleeping / Sea song. *<cd-iss. Oct 07 on Asterisk+=; ASTERISK 003CD>* - Suite for windy spring / Child / Where I'm bound / Chermaine.

SEASICK STEVE

There are other examples of artists finally hitting paydirt after years of obscurity, but the tale of SEASICK STEVE (Steven Gene Wold, b. 1941 in Oakland, California) is a joy to behold. After 45 years on the fringes and beyond, he finds himself the toast of the critics, appearing on TV and having hit albums.

Steve plied his gruff, blues-storytelling trade around America from the 1960s to the 1980s, rubbing shoulders with the likes of Janis Joplin and Kurt Cobain. Much has been made of his life as a hobo, travelling WOODY GUTHRIE-style around America's railroads in search of work, but in truth he's spent more time as a recording engineer. He produced US indie outfit Modest Mouse's 1996 debut album.

Steve says his three-string guitar, the 'Trance Wonder', may be haunted, and he attributes much of his success to it. After playing around the US for decades but never making any official recordings, he decamped to Paris and then on to Norway in the early 2000s, and there he recorded his first album, **CHEAP** (2004) {*6}, credited with the Level Devils. The result was seriously lo-fi, complete with phoned-in vocal sound and arrangements of nodding, stripped-down blues.

His solo debut, **DOG HOUSE MUSIC** (2006) {*7}, took things even further back to basics. Steve's slide guitar playing sounds as though it could have been recorded 70 years ago, especially on stand-out tracks like the almost GUTHRIE-esque 'Fallen Off A Rock', the ZZ Top/Joe Satriani-like 'Dog House Boogie' and the spartan but expressive love song 'Shirly Lou'. This album caught the attention of BBC TV's musical magpie Jools Holland, who booked Steve for his British TV debut as part of Jools's 2006 Hogmanay Hootenanny special.

Steve's star began to rise in earnest at this time, and 2008's **I STARTED OUT WITH NOTHIN AND I STILL GOT MOST OF IT LEFT** {*8} was his major-label debut, by which time he was filling big theatres in the UK and Europe and audiences were marvelling at the Trance Wonder. The title track is as sweet-humoured and warm as the man himself, while the chugging 'St Louis Slim' employs a funky beat to great effect. The album was more upbeat and sonically cleaner than its predecessors but no less compelling, Steve's itchy guitar playing and soulful rumble rarely needing or benefiting from accompaniment. The album and his ensuing fame earned Steve two consecutive Brit Awards nominations for International Solo Male Artist, and he cut a novel shape among the rap show-offs, Photo-fit popsters and strutting indie boys who were also nominated. The UK Top 10 album was quickly followed by the equally successful **MAN FROM ANOTHER TIME** (2009) {*6}, which aped its predecessor but lacked some of the fizz of old.

He took to hanging with rock royalty again, and Led Zeppelin's John Paul Jones contributed to **YOU CAN'T TEACH AN OLD DOG NEW TRICKS** (2011) {*8}, as did Steve's son Paul, who showed up on drums. Dirty, cruddy stompers like 'Back In The Doghouse', the smouldering creep of 'Burnin' Up' and the swaggering title track showed Steve back at his energised best. A singular talent, he continued to win friends at numerous summer festivals and gained gold record status for all but one of his albums, something all the more marvellous when you consider that he gained recognition without changing or compromising on one note of his music. *MR*

Seasick Steve - vocals, acoustic guitar, steel guitar

US: There's A Dead Skunk — UK: Vinyl Junkie

2004. (cd; as SEASICK STEVE & THE LEVEL DEVILS) *<none>* *(VJCD 159)* **CHEAP** [ ] Jul 05 [ ]
- Cheap / Rockin' chair / Hobo blues / Story #1 / Sorry Mr. Jesus / Love thang / Dr Jekyll and Mr Hyde / Story #2 / 8 ball / Christmas prison blues / Levi song / Rooster blues. *(<re-iss. May 07/Aug 09 on Bronzerat; BR 05>)*

US: Skycap — UK: Bronzerat

Nov 06. (cd/lp) *<3012136-2/-1>* *(BR 04)* **DOG HOUSE MUSIC** [ ] [ ]
- Yellow dog / Things go up / Cut my wings / Fallen off a rock / Dog house boogie / Save me / Hobo low / Shirly Lou / My Donny / The dead song / Last po' man / Salem blues / I'm gone. *<cd re-iss. Aug 09 on +1; 005>*

Jun 07. (7") *(BR 06)* IT'S ALL GOOD. / Thunderbird [–] [ ]
cd-s+=) *(BR 006CD)* - The jungle / Last po' man.

US: Warners — UK: Warners

Sep 08. (cd) *<(8 2564 69415 37)>* **I STARTED OUT WITH NOTHIN AND I STILL GOT MOST OF IT LEFT** [ ] [9]
- Started out with nothin / Walkin man / St Louis Slim / Happy man / Prospect lane / Thunderbird / Fly by night / Just like a king / One true / Chiggers / My youth. *(UK+=)* - The log cabin. *(lp-iss. 2008 on Bronzerat+=; BR 07LP) - Roll and tumble blues. (d-cd-iss.++=; 2564 69411 1)* - Train / Story / Breakfast / Heart attack / Lunch / Laughin' to keep from cryin'.

Nov 08. (dl-s) *(-)* WALKIN MAN [–] [ ]

Jan 09. (re; cd/lp) *(BR 04/+LP)* **DOG HOUSE MUSIC** [–] [36]

Feb 09. (dl-s) *(-)* HAPPY MAN / St Louis Slim (live at the Astoria) [–] [ ]

US: Rykodisc — UK: Warners

Nov 09. (cd) *<RCD 11006>* *(5186 56158-2)* **MAN FROM ANOTHER TIME** [ ] Oct 09 [4]
- Diddley Bo / Big green and yeller / Happy (to have a job) / The banjo song / Man from another time / That's all / Just because I can / Never go west / Dark / Wenatchee / My home (blue eyes) / Seasick boogie - I'm so lonesome I could cry.

US: P.I.A.S. — UK: P.I.A.S.

Jun 11. (cd) *<(PIAS 515 CD/LP)>* **YOU CAN'T TEACH AN OLD DOG NEW TRICKS** [ ] [6]
- Treasures / You can't teach an old dog new tricks / Burnin' up / Don't know why she love me but she do / Have mercy on the lonely / Whiskey ballad / Back in the doghouse / Underneath a blue and colorless sky / What a way to go / Part / Days gone / It's a long, long way / Levee camp blues (write me a few of your lines).

- (5-7*) compilations, etc.-

Jan 10. (m-cd) *Atlantic; (657631-2)* **...SONGS FOR ELISABETH** [–] [33]
- 8 ball / Walkin' man / My Donny / Dr Jekyll and Mr Hyde / Just like a king / My home (blue eyes) / Ready for love.

Martin SEXTON

With his soulful, blues-folk trademark style, contemporary singer/songwriter MARTIN SEXTON (b. March 2, 1966 in Syracuse, New Jersey) has been truly awe-inspiring since his days playing coffeehouses, open-mic gigs and street corners in and around the Boston area.

Raised in a family of fourteen, the self-taught guitarist and husky singer had it tough until Eastern Front gave him his first break by releasing his almost autobiographical second set, **BLACK SHEEP** (1996) {*7}. His debut was the cassette-only **IN THE JOURNEY** (1992) {*7}, recorded in a friend's attic and sold from a suitcase as he played to passers-by on the streets. Both records drew comparisons with the likes of Al Green, Lenny Kravitz, Aaron Neville and VAN MORRISON, any of whom SEXTON could mimic.

A gruelling concert schedule, and the National Academy of Songwriters' Artist of the Year Award in 1994, helped Martin win over Atlantic Records. His talent could cross over into many genres, and country, gospel, R&B, jazz and grunge loomed large in his following raucous and rootsy efforts, **THE AMERICAN** (1998) {*7} and **WONDER BAR** (2000) {*6} - hardly folk music per se, but defiantly on the fringes.

After marking time with a concert double-set, **LIVE WIDE OPEN** (2002) {*7}, featuring extended versions of 'Gypsy Woman' (over 16 minutes) and 'Black Sheep', and another self-financed album, the festive **CAMP HOLIDAY**(2005) {*5}, he released the comeback set **SEEDS** (2007) {*7}.

Why he needed another live set, only Martin knows, but **SOLO** (2008) {*6} had its one-man moments, and there was room for mainstream covers of Ray Charles's 'Hard Times', Lennon-McCartney's 'With A Little Help From My Friends' and Prince's 'Purple Rain'. If there were any remnants of his folk credentials remaining, 2010's funky, jazz-country **SUGARCOATING** {*6} left no doubt where his loyalties lay. That isn't to say he'd sold out; like many artists before him, he had moved on. *MCS*

Martin Sexton - vocals, acoustic guitar (with session people)

US: own label — UK: not issued

1992. (ltd-c) *<none>* **IN THE JOURNEY** [–] [–]
- The way I am / In the journey / 13 step boogie / Beautiful baby (variation on a theme) / Things to come / 13 step (reprise) / My faith is gone / Silence now. *<(cd-iss. Nov 00 on Koch+=; KOCD 8170)>* - Women and wine / So long Suzanna. *<cd re-iss. Apr 04 on Kitchen Table; KTR-002>*

US: Eastern Front — UK: not issued

May 96. (cd) *<111>* **BLACK SHEEP** [ ] [–]
- Black sheep / Glory bound / Diner / Freedom of the road / Caught in the rain / Love keep us together / Over my head / Gypsy woman / Candy / Can't stop thinking about you / America the beautiful. *<(re-iss. Nov 00 on Koch; KOCD 8169)>* *<re-iss. Apr 04 on Kitchen Table; KTR-003>*

US: Atlantic — UK: Atlantic

Oct 98. (cd) *<(83143-2)>* **THE AMERICAN** [ ] [ ]
- Glory bound / The American / Station man / My Maria / Candy / The beast in me / Where it begins / Young and beautiful / Animal song / Love keep us together / Diggin' me / Way I am.

Oct 00. (cd) *<(83405-2)>* **WONDER BAR** [ ] [ ]
- Angeline / Real man / Elephant's memory / Faith on the table / Casino foundation / Where did I go wrong with you / She cries and sings / Things you do to me / Hallelujah / Free world / Golden road.

Kitchen Table — Kitchen Table

Apr 02. (d-cd) *<KTR-001>* **LIVE WIDE OPEN** [live April 9, 2000]
- In the journey / Angeline / Beast in me / Freedom of the road / Hallelujah / Things you do to me / Women and wine / Where did I go wrong / 13 step boogie / Gypsy woman / Can't stop / Wasted / Black sheep / Ice cream man / Amazing grace.

Nov 05. (cd) *<KTR-CD004>* **CAMP HOLIDAY** [festive]
- I'll be home for Christmas / Holly jolly Christmas / Blue Christmas / Little drummer boy / White Christmas / Silent night / Do you hear what I hear / O Christmas tree / Welcome to the camp / Silver bells / Auld lang syne / Let there be peace on earth. *(UK-iss. Dec 10; same as US)*

Apr 07. (cd) *<KTR-CD005>* **SEEDS**
- Happy / Thought I knew ya / Wild angels / Will it go round in circles / Goin' to the country / I'm here / There go I / Right where you belong / Marry me / Failure / Still think about you / How far I've come / Wild angels (reprise). *(hidden +=)* - Keep it simple.

Oct 08. (cd) *<KTR-CD006>* **SOLO** [live]
- Intro / How far I've come / There go I / Happy / Diner / So long Suzanna / Diggin' me / Candy / Failure / Caught in the rain / Will it go round in circles / Hard times / Wishes from Michigan / With a little help from my friends / Purple rain. *(bonus +=)* - Failure / Animal song. *(w/ free dvd extras+=)*

Apr 10. (cd/d-lp) *<(KTR/+LP 007)>* **SUGARCOATING** — Nov 10
- Found / Boom sh-boom / Always got away / Livin' the life / Sugarcoating / Stick around / Long haul / Shane / Wants out / Friends again / Easy on the eyes / Alone / Just to be alive. *(d-lp+=)* - Beast in me / There go I / Diner / Glory bound / Sugarcoating [acoustic].

Jon SHAIN

An all-rounder in terms of genres, having played psych-bluegrass in Flyin' Mice, alt-country in Wake and folk-rock as a solo artist, singer/songwriter and guitarist JON SHAIN (b. Jonathan Bruce Shain, November 18, 1967, Haverhill, Massachusetts) has been versatile, to say the least. From a new base in Durham, North Carolina, he played electric guitar with bluesman Richard 'Big Boy' Henry on 'Big Boy Henry & The Slewfoot Blues Band' in 1988, and performed alongside post-flower-power stars Jorma Kaukonen and DAVID GRISMAN.

The Flyin' Mice released a couple of sets, 'So Hi Drive' (1991) and 'Brighter Day' (1994), before he and drummer Mark Simonsen enlisted Kirsten O'Rourke (vocals) and Stu Cole (bass) to form Wake and record a one-off, self-titled CD in 1997.

SHAIN began his solo career not long after Wake split. **BRAND NEW LIFETIME** (1999) {*6}, featuring 14 originals and a cover of DYLAN's 'Meet Me In The Morning' , promised much, as did 2001's **FOOLS AND FINE LADIES** {*6}. Going his own way and staying his own man, he carried on producing his own CDs, releasing **NO TAG, NO TAIL LIGHT** (2003) {*6}, **HOME BEFORE LONG** (2005) {*6}, **ARMY JACKET WINTER** (2007) {*6} - featuring a version of Tom Petty's 'Time To Move On' and a couple of songs dedicated to his wife Maria Bilinski and their daughter Johanna - and his most recent work, **TIMES RIGHT NOW** (2009) {*6}. *MCS*

Jon Shain - vocals, acoustic guitar

US Flyin' — UK not issued

Sep 99. (cd) *<FR 002>* **BRAND NEW LIFETIME**
- New Year's Eve / Light still shines / Virginia city girl / Brand new lifetime / New Orleans '88 / Sapphire sky / Come on down / Porcupine bag / Song for Joe / Loan me a year / The captain's song / Child of tomorrow's summers / Armchair warrior / Summer is over / Meet me in the morning.

Jun 01. (cd) *<FR 003>* **FOOLS AND FINE LADIES**
- Like the ocean / Fine ladies / Pawnshop girl / Govinda's in the rain / Luck don't come easy / Chincoteague chick-a-dee / Mountain tune / Sherry Ann / Drunken horses / Fools / Laughter fades away.

Jun 03. (cd) *<FR 004>* **NO TAG, NO TAIL LIGHT**
- Worried messenger / Getaway car / Philly girl / Give my regards to brother Ray / Get what you deserve / The deep freeze / Ka-ching ka-ching / Only the blues / Merrimack / Second chance blues / Whistle blower / Charade.

Apr 05. (cd) *<FR 005>* **HOME BEFORE LONG**
- Poetry and sin / Ten days / Broken white line / Pretty Peggy-o / Johnson city detour / Buck up baby / Joe Turner ridin' down Main St / Full bloom / Empty vessels / Scratch card Sally.

May 07. (cd) *<FR 006>* **ARMY JACKET WINTER**
- Time to move on / Silvertone / Another month of Mondays / Cornershops and subway trains / Pictures from the past / Lucy don't you see / To rise again / Song for Maria / Song for Jojo / In real time / Dyehouse blues / Slowdance / Flat earth crowd / Throne of gold.

Nov 09. (cd) *<FR 007>* **TIMES RIGHT NOW**
- James Alley blues / Mr Snakeoil! / Spinning compass / Something new / Clementine / Driving them crazy / Careless love / Ooncha ooncha music / Midnight snack / Louise, Louise / Song for Dara / Little flower / Yadkin river blues.

Richard SHINDELL

Richard's voice has an uncanny resemblance to that of R.E.M. icon Michael Stipe, and some might add that of Eddie Vedder (without the grungy histrionics) or ERIC ANDERSEN. Born in 1960 in Lakehurst, New Jersey, singer/songwriter RICHARD SHINDELL first came to the attention of the 'Fast Folk' magazine/label in the mid-1980s, having spread the word by performing with a young JOHN GORKA in the Razzy Dazzy Spasm Band.

Starting with one's best album can be a hard act to follow, but **SPARROWS POINT** (1992) {*8}, his first of three for Shanachie, was all it promised and more. Augmented by a Celtic/country backing, the pick of the songs are 'Are You Happy Now?', the blue-collar trucking song 'The Kenworth Of My Dreams', 'The Courier' and 'On The Sea Of Fleur De Lis'.

BLUE DIVIDE (1994) {*6}, his pivotal political set, didn't shy away from thorny subjects, with songs such as 'Arrowhead', 'Fishing' and 'The Ballad Of Mary Magdalen' showing Richard could stir it with the best of them. **REUNION HILL** (1997) {*6} was another step in the right direction, although his choice of covers (JESSE COLIN YOUNG's 'Darkness, Darkness' and TOWNES VAN ZANDT's 'I'll Be Here In The Morning') was over-ambitious. There was a whole raft of covers on his 1998 side project, CRY CRY CRY (with DAR WILLIAMS and LUCY KAPLANSKY), but he might have been better at revamping R.E.M.'s 'Fall On Me' than Dar was.

Switching labels to Signature Sounds, **SOMEWHERE NEAR PATERSON** (2000) {*6} had more of a contemporary alt-country feel, as on his cover of Buddy & Julie Miller's 'My Love Will Follow You', with harmonies from Dar and Lucy. Producer and guitarist Larry Campbell had DYLAN sessions and tours to his credit. It was a nice collection, SHINDELL's poignant character portraits never better than in 'Confessions', 'You Stay Here' and 'Abuelita'.

Recorded in concert a year earlier with his band (John Putnam on electric guitar, bassist Lincoln Schleifer and drummer Denny MacDermott) plus guests Lucy and Larry, **COURIER** (2002) {*7} was the bees' knees, featuring powerful retreads of old songs, some new ones and covers of Little Feat's 'Willin'' and SPRINGSTEEN's 'Fourth Of July, Asbury Park'.

Although in 2000 he moved to Buenos Aires, and still lives there with his wife and children, albums such as the Latinesque **VUELTA** (2004) {*8} and the Americana covers set **SOUTH OF DELIA** (2007) {*7} kept his profile high in the States. The latter's tracks were 'Acadian Driftwood' (The BAND), 'Senor (Tales Of Yankee Power)' (DYLAN), 'The Humpback Whale' (Harry Robertson), the near-unrecognisable 'Born In The USA' (Bruce Springsteen), 'Mercy Street' (Peter Gabriel), 'The Storms Are On The Ocean' (A.P. Carter), 'Northbound 35' (JEFFREY FOUCAULT), 'Sitting On Top Of The World' and 'Texas Rangers' (trad), Deportee (Plane Wreck At Los Gatos)' (WOODY GUTHRIE), 'Solo Le Pido A Dios' (Leon Gieco) and 'Lawrence, KS' (JOSH RITTER).

Back on Signature Sounds ('Vuelta' was on Koch and 'South Of Delia' on his own label), **NOT FAR NOW** (2009) {*6} was only his third fresh studio release in nine years. It paid homage to the late DAVE CARTER with 'The Mountain' and Silvio Rodriguez's 'Que Hago Ahora?' alongside his usual character studies, 'A Juggler Out In The Traffic', 'Get Up Clara' and 'Balloon Man'. *MCS*

Richard Shindell - vocals, guitars (w/ session people)

US Shanachie — UK Shanachie

Mar 92. (cd/c) *<SHANCD/SHMC 8002>* **SPARROWS POINT**
- Are you happy now? / Castaway / The courier / Sparrows point / The Kenworth of my dreams / On a sea of fleur de lis / Memory of you / You again / Nora / Howling at the trouble / By now. *(UK cd-iss. Oct 99; same as US)*

Sep 94. (cd/c) *<(SHANCD/SHMC 8014)>* **BLUE DIVIDE** — Dec 94
- A summer wind, a cotton dress / Fishing / The ballad of Mary Magdalen / Lazy / The things that I have seen / TV light / A tune for nowhere / Arrowhead / Ascent / Blue divide.

Aug 97. (cd) *<(SHANCD 8027)>* **REUNION HILL**
- The next Best Western / Smiling / May / I saw my youth today / Reunion hill / Beyond the iron gate / Darkness, darkness / Money for floods / Easy streets / The weather / I'll be here in the morning.

—— 1998, Shindell was part of CRY CRY CRY (one self-titled set) alongside DAR WILLIAMS and LUCY KAPLANSKY

Signature Sounds — Signature Sounds

Feb 00. (cd) *<SIG 1256>* **SOMEWHERE NEAR PATERSON**
- Confessions / Abuelita / You stay here / My love will follow you / Spring / Wisteria / Waiting for the storm / The grocer's broom / Merritt parkway, 2 am / Transit / Calling the moon. *(UK-iss. Aug 04; same as US)*

Feb 02. (cd) *<SIG 1270>* **COURIER** (live February 2, 2001) –
- The courier / Memory of you / Next Best Western / Willin' / The Kenworth of my dreams / Nora / Arrowhead / Reunion hill / Fishing / A summer wind, a cotton dress / On a sea of fleur de lis / The ballad of Mary Magdalen / Are you happy now? / Transit / Fourth of July, Asbury Park. *(UK-iss. Aug 04; same as US)*

Koch — not issued

Aug 04. (cd) *<KOC-CD 9538>* **VUELTA** –
- Fenario / Waist deep in the big muddy / The island / Hazel's house / Che Guevara T-shirt / Cancion sencilla / There goes Mavis / So says the whipporwill / The last fare of the day / Gray green.

Richard Shindell — Richard Shindell

May 07. (cd) *<1809>* **SOUTH OF DELIA**
- Acadian driftwood / Senor (tales of Yankee power) / The humpback whale / Born in the USA / Mercy street / The storms are on the ocean / Northbound 35 / Sitting on top of the world / Texas rangers / Deportee (plane wreck at Los Gatos) / Solo le pido a dios / Lawrence, KS.

Signature — Signature

Apr 09. (cd) *<(SIG 2020)>* **NOT FAR NOW** May 09
- Parasol ants / A juggler out in traffic / Gethsemane goodbye / Que hago ahora? / Bye bye / Mariana's table / State of the union / One man's Arkansas / Get up Clara / The mountain / Balloon man.

own label — not issued

2009. (cd-ep) *<none>* MARIANA'S EP: ALT VERSIONS AND NO SHOWS FROM NOT FAR NOW – own –
- Get up Clara [alt.] / Balloon man [alt] / Mariana's table [alt] / State of the union [demo] / I am / Hideous grin.

Michelle SHOCKED

With echoes of iconic folk stars JOAN BAEZ and dustbowl troubadour WOODY GUTHRIE, urban singer/songwriter MICHELLE SHOCKED (born Karen Michelle Johnston, February 24, 1962 in Gilmer, East Texas) had finger-picking cool and a lyrical prowess that was forged in her teenage years.

After a childhood spent moving around army bases with her stepfather, Michelle experienced a turbulent adolescence that included a spell in a psychiatric hospital (committed by her fundamentalist Mormon mother) and a stint as a radical anarcho-punk squatter in San Francisco - all grist for the songwriting mill, and the source of her adopted name. Having journeyed from Texas to New York via Amsterdam, Michelle's break came in 1986 when she was talent-spotted at the Kerrville Folk Festival by Englishman Pete Lawrence, founder of the Cooking Vinyl label, who taped an informal round-the-campfire set on a Walkman. It was a break that SHOCKED was initially unsure about, and understandably she was suspicious of the machinations of the music industry, like her hero WOODY GUTHRIE.

The recordings were eventually released in late 1986 as **THE TEXAS CAMPFIRE TAPES** {*7}, and Michelle found herself at the top of the UK indie charts. She premiered the majority of the set at London's Queen Elizabeth Hall, including classy songs like '5 AM In Amsterdam', 'Down On Thomas St' and 'Fogtown', complete with authentic crickets. The CD featured versions of Paul Simon's 'Stranded In A Limousine' and LEADBELLY's 'Goodnight, Irene'.

With much trepidation, she assented to a major-label deal with Polygram that would put her next few records on the London label in Britain and Mercury in the US. In keeping with her fiercely-held beliefs and constant striving for integrity, SHOCKED reportedly made sure that she retained some creative control, encouraged by the critical and commercial success of her debut album.

Produced by Pete Anderson, the Nashville-styled **SHORT SHARP SHOCKED** (1988) {*8}, with sleeve art depicting Michelle in a policeman's stranglehold, was a defiant rabble of engaging protest songs that combined roots folk with rock and pop accessibility. Among the highlights were the rootsy 'When I Grow Up', the lilting 'Anchorage' and the affecting 'Graffiti Limbo', an elegy for Michael Stewart, the young New York graffiti artist who died following his arrest in 1983. She also covered JEAN RITCHIE's 'The L&N Don't Stop Here Anymore'.

Although the long-player made the UK Top 40 and picked up a groundswell of support, her follow-up album, **CAPTAIN SWING** (1989) {*5}, was way off the mark, moving away from her lone acoustic-folk approach in favour of more ambitious Western-swing arrangements. While SHOCKED was criticised in some quarters for political preaching, her more hardcore fans thought the record wasn't radical enough.

Casting these complaints aside, SHOCKED went off on a musical pilgrimage of sorts, touring America WOODY GUTHRIE-style and recording with an array of respected roots musicians including Taj Mahal, Hothouse Flowers, Pops Staples, DOC WATSON, The Red Clay Ramblers, Clarence 'Gatemouth' Brown, Levon Helm and Garth Hudson, and the brilliant Uncle Tupelo. The results were issued in 1991 as **ARKANSAS TRAVELER** {*7}, and the star-studded set reclaimed some of her lost critical ground, although it failed to make much of an impact on the charts except in Britain. The finale was a revamp of GUTHRIE's 'Woody's Rag'.

Unhappy with the way she was being treated by her record label, SHOCKED sued the company and self-financed her next album, **KIND HEARTED WOMAN** {*6}, recorded in 1992 but not receiving an official release until 1994. Going independent with sets like the label-baiting **ARTISTS MAKE LOUSY SLAVES** (1996) {*4} (a collaboration with Hothouse Flowers' Fiachna O Braonain) and **GOOD NEWS** (1998) {*7}, Michelle stayed indie for post-millennium sets on Mighty Sound from **DEEP NATURAL** (2002) {*6} to her most recent rootsy, bluegrass-meets-gospel deliveries, **TO HEAVEN U RIDE** (2007) {*6} (live from 2003) and **SOUL OF MY SOUL** (2009) {*6}, the former featuring covers of Sister Rosetta Tharpe's 'Strange Things Happening Every Day' and The BAND's 'The Weight'.

In the summer of 2005 she released three albums simultaneously, the rootsy pot-pourri **DON'T ASK DON'T TELL** {*6}, the Disney-sanctioned **GOT NO STRINGS** {*6} and the Latin-American blues collision **MEXICAN STANDOFF** {*5}. *MCS & BG*

Michelle Shocked - vocals, acoustic guitar / + session people

US Mercury — UK Cooking Vinyl

Nov 86. (lp/c/cd) *<834581-1/-4/-2> (COOK/+C 002)*
THE TEXAS CAMPFIRE TAPES
- 5 am in Amsterdam / The secret admirer / The incomplete image / Who cares? / Down on Thomas St / Fogtown / Steppin' out / The hepcat / Necktie / (Don't you mess around with) My little sister / The ballad of Patch Eye and Meg / The secret to a long life (is knowing when it's time to go). *(cd-iss. Apr 88 +=; COOKCD 002)* - The chain smoker / Stranded in a limousine / Goodnight Irene. *(re-iss. Nov 93 cd/c; same as US) (cd re-iss. Apr 99 on Mooncrest+=; CRESTCD 039) <(d-cd re-mast. Apr 03 as THE TEXAS CAMPFIRE TAKES on Mighty Sound+=; MS 02)>* - 5 am in Amsterdam / Fogtown / 4-4 troubadour / Steppin' out / Hold me back / Fool for cocaine / Down on Thomas St / Hardly gonna miss him / The hepcat / Necktie / My little sister / Patcheye and Meg / Secret to a long life / When I grow up / Ghost town / Secret admirer / Black widow / Chain smoker / Old time feeling / Stranded in a limousine / Contest coming / Lagniappe. (bonus +=)- (untitled).

Jun 87. (7") *(FRY 002)* DISORIENTATED. / If Love Was A Train –
(12"+=) *(FRY 002T) <cstyle>* - Chain smoker / Stranded in a limousine / Goodnight Irene.

Mercury — London

Aug 88. (cd)(lp/c) *<(834924-2)>(CV LP/MC 1)*
SHORT SHARP SHOCKED 73 — 33
- When I grow up / Hello Hopeville / Memories of East Texas / (Making the run to) Gladewater / Graffiti limbo / If love was a train / Anchorage / The L&N don't stop here anymore / V.F.D. / Black widow. *(hidden +=)* - Fogtown. *<(d-cd re-mast. Sep 03 on Mighty Sound++=; MS 03)>* - When I grow up (demo) / Memories of East Texas (live) / Yamboree queen (live) / Strawberry jam / Graffiti limbo (demo) / If love was a train (alt. take) / Anchorage (radio version) / The L&N don't stop here anymore (alt. take) / V.F.D. (live) / Black widow (alt. take) / Leaving Louisiana in broad daylight / Disorientated / Lovely Rita / Ballad of Penny Evans / Remodeling the Pentagon / Fred's winter song / Prince of darkness (with The MEKONS) / One piece at a time / 5 am in Amsterdam / Campus crusade / Goodnight Irene.

Sep 88. (7") *(LON 193)* ANCHORAGE. / Fogtown – 60
(10"+=) *(LONT 193)* - Remodeling the Pentagon / Ballad of Penny Evans (live).
(12"+=/cd-s+=) *LON X/CD 193)* - Strawberry jam (live) / Ballad of Penny Evans (live).

Nov 88. (7") *<870611>* ANCHORAGE. / ('A'-live) 66 –

Dec 88. (7") *(LON 212)* IF LOVE WAS A TRAIN. / Memories Of East Texas – 63
(12"+=) *(LONX 212)* - Graffiti limbo (live).
(cd-s+=) *(LONCD 212)* - V.F.D. / Yamboree queen.

Feb 89. (7") *(LON 219)* WHEN I GROW UP. / 5 am In Amsterdam (live) – 67
(12"+=) *(LONX 219)* - Goodnight Irene.
(cd-s+=) *(LONCD 219)* - Campus crusade.

Oct 89. (lp/c/cd) *<(838 878-1/-4/-2)>* **CAPTAIN SWING** 95 — Nov 89 31
- God is a real estate developer / On the greener side / Silent ways / Sleep keeps me awake / The cement lament / (You don't mess around with) My little sister / Looks like Mona Lisa (smells like tuna fish) / Too little, too late / Streetcorner ambassador / Must be luff. *<(cd re-mast. Mar 04/Jul 04 on Mighty Sound+=; MS 1005)>* - Russian roulette / Must be luff / Sleep keeps me awake / Cement lament / Silent ways / Streetcorner ambassador / Early morning Saturday / God is a real estate developer /

Too little, too late / Barefootin' (live) / Garden salad diplomacy (live) / Poll tax song (live) / The Titanic / Old paint / Worth the weight (live) / Fairy tales (live).
Nov 89. (7"/c-s) *(LON/+CS 245)* ON THE GREENER SIDE. / Russian Roulette [–] [ ]
(12"+=/cd-s+=) *(LON X/CD 245)* - The Titanic / Old Paint.
Feb 90. (c-s) *(LONCS 251)* (YOU DON'T MESS AROUND WITH) MY LITTLE SISTER / Russian Roulette [–] [ ]
(12"+=) *(LONX 251)* - Waters wide.
Oct 91. (cd/c/lp) *<(512 189-2/-4/-1)>* **ARKANSAS TRAVELER** [ ] Apr 92 [46]
- 33 RPM soul / Come a long way / Secret to a long life / Contest coming (Cripple Creek) / Over the waterfall / Shaking hands (soldier's joy) / Jump Jim Crow - Zip-a-dee-doo-dah / Hold me back / Strawberry jam / Prodigal daughter (Cotton-eyed Joe) / Blackberry blossom / Weaving way / Arkansas traveler / Woody's rag. *<(cd re-mast. Sep 04 on Mighty Sound+=; MS 1006)>* - Worth the weight (live) / Come a long way / Blackberry blossom (live) / Weaving way / Down in the Arkansas (live) / Introducing dollar bill (live) / C-H-I-C-K-E-N (the way to spell chicken) (live).
Mar 92. (7"/c-s) *(LON/+CS 316)* COME A LONG WAY. / Over The Waterfall (live) [–] [ ]
(cd-s+=) *(LONCD 316)* - Contest coming (cripple creek) / Jump Jim Crow.
(cd-s+=) *(LOCDP 316)* - Worth the weight (live) / Shaking hands (soldier's toy) (live).
May 92. (7") *(LON 321)* 33 R.P.M. SOUL. / Blackberry Blossom (live) [–] [ ]
(cd-s+=) *(LONCD 321)* - Over the waterfall (live) / ('A'-live).

Michelle Shocked — not issued

Mar 94. (cd) *<MS 001>* **KIND HEARTED WOMAN** [–] mail-o [–]
- Stillborn / Homestead / Winter wheat / Cold comfort / Eddie / A child like grace / Fever breaks / Silver spoon / Hard way / No sign of rain. *<(re-iss. Nov 96 on Private Music cd/c; 01005 82145-2/-4)>*

(was a collaboration with Fiachna O Braonain of Hothouse Flowers)

self-rel. — not issued

Jul 96. (cd; by MICHELLE SHOCKED & FIACHNA O BRAONAIN) *<#0001>* **ARTISTS MAKE LOUSY SLAVES** [–] tour [–]
- Laundry day / Drip dry / Soul searching / New Orleans / Groove baby's lullaby / Last love / Can you see it in me / Only a prayer / Live and learn / Carrickfergus - The water is wide.

—— next with the Anointed Earls

Mood Swings — not issued

Mar 98. (cd) *<162044-4WI-8049>* **GOOD NEWS** [ ] [–]
- Good news / Can't take my joy / Forgive to forget / Little Billie / What can I say? / Why do I get the feeling? / No wonder / You take the cake / Tabloid / Crying shame. *(+= hidden track)*

Mighty Sound — Mighty Sound

Apr 02. (cd) *<(YTY 10012)>* **DEEP NATURAL** [ ] Sep 02 [ ]
- Joy / What can I say? / Why do I get the feeling? / Good news / Forgive to forget / That's so amazing / Peachfuzz / I know what you need / Can't take my joy / Little Billie / If not here / Moanin' dove / House burnin' down / Psalm / Go in peace. *(w/ free cd+=)* - DUB NATURAL - Go dub / I know what you dub / Match burns dub / DOD dub / House burns dub / Forget to dub / Why do I dub? / Draughts of Dublin / What dub? / Peachfuzz / Can't take my dub / Fat Brown snake dub / F2F dub.
Jun 05. (cd) *<(MS 1007)>* **DON'T ASK DON'T TELL** [ ] [ ]
- Early morning Saturday / How you play the game / Don't ask / Used car lot / Hardly gonna miss him / Evacuation route / Fools like us / Elaborate sabotage / Don't tell / Goodbye / (Hi skool).
Jun 05. (cd) *<(MS 1008)>* **GOT NO STRINGS** [ ] [ ]
- To be a cat / Give a little whistle / Got no strings / Spoonful of sugar / Spectrum / Wish upon a star / Baby mine / A dream is a wish / The bare necessities / On the front porch.
Jun 05. (cd) *<(MS 1009)>* **MEXICAN STANDOFF** [ ] [ ]
- Lonely planet / La cantina el gato negro / Wanted man / Picoesque / Match burns twice / Mouth of the Mississippi / Bitter pill / 180 proof / Weasel be poppin' / Blackjack heart.
Sep 07. (cd) *<(MS 1014)>* **TO HEAVEN U RIDE** (live at The Telluride Bluegrass Festival in 2003) [ ] [ ]
- Introductions / Strange things happening every day / The weight / Quality of mercy / God bless the child / Good news / Cancer alley rap / Wade in the water / Uncloudy day / Study war no more / Blessed / Psalm / Answered prayer rap / Can't take my joy.
May 09. (cd) *<(MS 1016)>* **SOUL OF MY SOUL** [ ] [ ]
- Love's song / Other people / Liquid prayer / Ballad of the battle of the ballot and the bullet part 1: Ugly American / Waterproof / Paperboy / Giant killer / Heart to heart / Pompeii / True story.

- (8-10*) compilations -

Nov 96. (cd/c) *London; <(532960-2/-4)>* **MERCURY POISE: 1988–1995** [ ] [ ]
- On the greener side / Anchorage / Come a long way / Quality of mercy / Streetcorner ambassador / Too little, too late / If love was a train / When I grow up / Prodigal daughter / Over the waterfall / Holy spirit / Stillborn.

- essential boxed sets -

Jun 05. (3-cd-box) *Mighty Sound; <(MS 3333)>* **THREESOME** [ ] [ ]
- (MEXICAN STANDOFF) // (DON'T ASK DON'T TELL) // (GOT NO STRINGS).

Jane SIBERRY

Flitting between experimental Kate Bush/JONI MITCHELL-type jazz-pop and fringe folk music, singer/songwriter JANE SIBERRY (b. October 12, 1955 in Toronto) was writing operatic music from an early age and gained a degree in microbiology at Ontario University.

It was all a bit low-budget for SIBERRY in the early 1980s, when to finance her debut LP **JANE SIBERRY** (1981) {*6} she worked extra hours as a waitress for the tips. This album revealed the influences of Joni and the pop-fuelled harmonies of Kate Bush.

NO BORDERS HERE (1983) {*6} was typical 1980s new-wave fodder, but it did include her excellent college hit 'Mimi On The Beach'. The record was produced by her long-time friend and colleague John Switzer. **THE SPECKLESS SKY** (1986) {*7}, her only Top 200 Billboard entry, confirmed the ethereal singer's promise, tracks like 'One More Color', the seven-minute 'Vladimir, Vladimir' and 'The Taxi Ride' pointing to some arty soundscape formerly the territory of Laurie Anderson.

SIBERRY progressed even further into experimental pop for her first Reprise album, **THE WALKING** (1988) {*7}, which represented her off-kilter and pop-sensibility sides in equal measure. 'Ingrid The Footman' and 'The Bird In The Gravel' could easily stand alongside the songs Sinead O'Connor was recording at the time.

Jane attempted a more commercial approach for 1989's **BOUND BY THE BEAUTY** {*6} and **WHEN I WAS A BOY** (1993) {*6}, the latter featuring Brian Eno and Michael Brook, but it was far from folk music. So was 1995's jazz-inflected **MARIA** {*6}, her last effort for a major label.

The underrated **TEENAGER** (1996) {*6} comprised songs that she had written when she was a teenager herself, revamped as a kind of postscript to her time at Reprise. The Joni-esque 'The Squirrel Crossed The Road' was quite folky, and the only downside was the largely unnecessary introductions. It was her first recording on her own Sheeba label.

Subsequent 'Live at The Bottom Line' sets saw SIBERRY singing traditional festive songs on **CHILD** (1997) {*5}, followed by two self-explanatory titles from the same nights, **TREE: MUSIC FOR FILM AND FORESTS** (1999) {*6} and **LIPS: MUSIC FOR SAYING IT** (1999) {*6}.

Her first real stab at something territorially folk in nature was **HUSH** (2000) {*5}, a deliberate attempt to tone down her experimental side with nine traditional songs, from 'As I Roved Out' to 'The Water Is Wide', plus the Kern/Hammerstein Broadway standard 'Ol' Man River'. SIBERRY has a curious talent, and her worldly approach to all aspects of her music has attracted a loyal fan base, though at the sacrifice of a wider global appeal. Right up to the odds-and-ends **CITY** (2001) {*5} and her most recent work as ISSA/JANE SIBERRY, one has to admire her ambition and dexterity. *MCS*

Jane Siberry - vocals, piano, acoustic guitar, accordion (with session people)

US Street — UK not issued

Feb 81. (lp) *<SR 002>* **JANE SIBERRY** [–] Canada [–]
- Marco Polo / This girl I know / The sky is so blue / The mystery at Ogwen's farm / The magic beads / Writers are a funny breed / The strange well / Above the treeline / In the blue light. *<(UK/US cd-iss. Nov 97 & Jul 00 on Street; SRCD 002-2)>*

Open Air — Reprise

Dec 83. (lp/c) *<OD/OT 0302>* **NO BORDERS HERE** [ ] [–]
- The waitress / I muse aloud / Dancing class / Extra executives / You don't need / Symmetry (the way things have to be) / Follow me / Mimi on the beach / Map of the world (part I). *<(cd-iss. Jul 00 on Duke Street; DSBD 31006)>*
May 86. (lp/c) *<OD 0305> (9-25578-1/-4)* **THE SPECKLESS SKY** [ ] Jun 87 [ ]
- One more color / Seven steps to the wall / The very large hat / Vladimir - Vladimir / Mein bitte / The empty city / Map of the world (part II) / The taxi ride. *(UK+=)* - Mimi on the beach. *<(cd-iss. Nov 97 on Duke Street; DSBD 31019)>*

Reprise — Reprise

Jan 88. (lp/c/cd) *<(25678-1/-4/-2)>* **THE WALKING** [ ] Apr 88 [ ]
- The white tent the raft / Red high heels / Goodbye / Ingrid and the footman / Lena is a white table / The walking (and constantly) / The lobby / The bird in the gravel. *<(cd re-iss. Nov 97 on Duke Street; DSBD 31040)>*
Aug 89. (cd)(lp/c) *<(K 25942-2)>(WX 293/+C)* **BOUND BY THE BEAUTY** [ ] [ ]
- Bound by the beauty / Something about trains / Hockey / Everything reminds me of my dog / The valley / The life is the red wagon / Half angel half eagle / La jalouse / Miss Punta Blanca / Are we dancing now? (Map III). *<(cd-iss. Dec 97 on Duke St; DSBD 31058)>*
Apr 92. (7"/c-s) *(W 0097/+C)* THE LIFE IS THE RED WAGON. / Bound By The Beauty [–] [ ]
(12"+=/cd-s+=) *(W 0097 T/CD)* - Everything reminds me of my dog.

Jul 93. (cd/c) *<(7599 26824-2/-4)>* **WHEN I WAS A BOY**
- Temple / Calling all angels (with k.d. LANG) / Love is everything / Sail across the water / All the candles in the world / Sweet incarnadine / The gospel according to darkness / An angel stepped down (and slowly looked around) / The vigil (the sea) / At the beginning of time / Love is everything (harmony version).

Aug 93. (cd-ep) *<41174>* TEMPLE (five mixes) / An Angel Stepped Down (And Slowly Looked Up)

Aug 95. (cd/c) *<(7599 45915-2/-4)>* **MARIA**
- Maria / See the child / Honey bee / Caravan / Lovin' cup / Begat begat / Goodbye sweet pumpkinhead / Would you go? / Mary had a little lamb / Oh my my.

Oct 95. (cd-s) *<17742>* LOVIN' CUP / (album version)

Sheeba Sheeba

Oct 96. (cd) *<(SHEEB 1)>* **TEENAGER** Feb 97
- (Introduction) / The squirrel crossed the road / Let's not talk now / Song to my father / Broken birds / Puppet city / Oh my sister / The long pirouette / Bessie / We should be there by morning / Viking heart / When spring comes / Angel voyeur / Trumpeter swan.

Nov 97. (d-cd) *<(SHEEB 2)>* **CHILD: Music For The Christmas season** (live at The Bottom Line)
- She's playing the taxidriver / Caravan / Wildwood carol / A bitter Christmas / What is this fragrance softly stealing? / Quoi, ma voisine, es-tu fachee? / Shir amami / Mary's lullaby / An angel stepped down (and slowly looked around) / Silent night / You will be born / O holy night / In the bleak midwinter / Christmas mass / The Christmas song / Maria wanders through the thorn / What child is this? / The valley / Hockey / The twelve days of Christmas / Are you burning, little candle?

Sep 99. (cd) *<SHEEB 06>* **TREE: Music For Films And Forests** (live at The Bottom Line 1996)
- Slow tango / Burning ship / When last I was a fisherman / It can't rain all the time / I paddle my canoe / Adam and Eve / Up the loggin' road / Goin' down the river / At the beginning of time.

Sep 99. (cd) *<SHEEB 07>* **LIPS: Music For Saying It** (live at The Bottom Line 1996)
- First word / Valley of the dolls / Freedom is gold / Hotel room 417 / Foecke / I will survive / Flirtin' is a flo-thing / Say it (excerpt) / Grace hospital / You say I say / Mimi speaks / Last word / Say it / Barkis is willin'.

Sheeba Sounds True

Sep 00. (cd) *<SHEEB 008> (STAMM 00121D)* **HUSH** Oct 00
- Jacob's ladder / All through the night / Pontchartrain / Streets of Laredo / As I roved out / False false fly / The water is wide / Swing low, sweet chariot / Ol' man river / O Shenandoah - Sail away.

Nov 03. (cd) *<SHEEB 0011>* **SHUSHAN THE PALACE: HYMNS OF EARTH** (live festive)
- How beautiful are the feet / Sheep may safely graze / A star shall rise up out of Jacob / I know that my redeemer liveth / Lo, how a rose e'er blooming / In the bleak midwinter / Jesus Christ the apple tree / Break forth, O beauteous heavenly light / If God be for us.

Dec 08. (cd; as ISSA) *<none>* **DRAGON DREAMS**
- A train is coming [a cappella excerpt] / Wilderness wheel / Superhero dream / Even as we fall from grace / Oui allo? / I pick up the phone (and I don't call you) / You never know (who you're talking to) / You had a good thing (and you blew it) / When we are queen / A train is coming / Send me someone to love.

Dec 09. (cd) *<none>* **WITH WHAT SHALL I KEEP WARM?**
- Eden (can't get this body thing right) / Hide not your light / This is not the way / Phoenix (for teenagers) / In my dreams / Further in the garden (interlude) / Take me to my tent / Tiny lies are killing me / Then we heard a shout / Mama hereby / Walk on water.

- (8-10*) compilations -

Apr 92. (cd) *Reprise; (7599 26936-2)* **SUMMER IN THE YUKON**
- My life is the red wagon / Miss Punta Blanca / Calling all angels (with k.d. LANG) / Above the treeline / In the blue light / Seven steps to the wall / Mimi on the beach / The walking (and constantly) / The very large hat / The lobby / Red high heels / Map of the world (part II) / The taxi ride.

Mar 95. (cd) *Duke Street; <(DSBD 31093)>* **A COLLECTION 1984-1989** Dec 97
- I muse aloud / Mimi on the beach / The waitress / You don't need / One more color / Map of the world (part II) / The taxi ride / Seven steps to the wall / The walking (and constantly) / Red high heels / Ingrid and the footman / The life is the red wagon / Miss Punta Blanca / Bound by the beauty.

Apr 02. (d-cd) *Rhino; <(8122 78277-2)>* **LOVE IS EVERYTHING: THE JANE SIBERRY ANTHOLOGY** May 02
- In the blue light / Bessie / The mystery at Ogwen's farm / You don't need / The taxi ride / One more color / The walking (and constantly) / Red high heels / The lobby / Bound by the beauty / Everything reminds me of my dog / The life is the red wagon / Calling all angels / Love is everything (harmony version) / Sail across the water // Temple / Goodbye sweet pumpkinhead / Maria / The squirrel crossed the road / Peony / Mimi on the beach / Mimi speaks / Barkis is willin' / Are you burning, little candle? / All through the night / The water is wide / Map of the world (part I) / Map of the world (part II) / Map of the world (part III): Are we dancing now? / Map of the world (part IV): The pilgrim.

- (5-7*) compilations, etc.-

Aug 97. (cd) *Sheeba; <SHECD 002>* **A DAY IN THE LIFE**
- Yoga class / Jane's message / Coming up for air (with PATTY LARKIN) / When I think of Laura Nyro (with LAURA NYRO) / Microsoft - Riff 'Peony' / The bridge (with JOE JACKSON) / The Bottom Line / Oh, Shenandoah (with DAROL ANGER) / Solar blast / Hain't it funny (with k.d. LANG) / The end of the day / In my dream / Moon.

Oct 01. (cd) *Sheeba; <SHEEB 009>* **CITY** (collaborations and film music)
- My mother is not the white dove (with PETER GABRIEL) / Harmonix - I went down to the river (with PETER GABRIEL) / It can't rain all the time (from 'The Crow') / Shir amami (with FRANK LONDON) / The bridge (with JOE JACKSON) / She's like a swallow (with HECTOR ZAZOU) / When I think of Laura Nyro / Calling all angels (with k.d. LANG) / Nut brown maid (with MICHAEL GREY) / All the pretty ponies (from TV's 'Barney and Friends') / Spade and sparrow (with TAKAFUMI SOTOMA) / Narrow bridge (with MORGAN FISHER) / Slow tango (from 'Faraway, So Close') / The kiss (with GHOSTLAND).

SILVER SUMMIT

Formed by Brooklyn-based multi-instrumentalists David Shawn Bosler and Sondra Sun-Odeon, SILVER SUMMIT were one of several rising freak-folk acts who briefly adorned the creation of GREG WEEKS and his wife Jessica's label Language Of Stone. Distinguished company included ORION RIGEL DOMMISSE, MOUNTAIN HOME, EX REVERIE, NOA BABAYOF and SHARON VAN ETTEN.

While there were echoes of Dead Can Dance and CURRENT 93 on their self-titled debut of 2008, **SILVER SUMMIT** {*7} extracted the best elements of Brit-folk exotica with eclectic Eastern instrumentation such as saz, gong and Tibetan singing bowls. Strong structures and meditative mantras were the order of the day on several tracks, none more powerful and effective than the EX REVERIE-meets-ESPERS-like 'Awaken', 'The Door', 'Acadia' and 'In-Between Place'. For the semi-purist, there was a revamp of BERT JANSCH's 'Wishing Well'. Please, can we have some more? *MCS*

Sondra Sun-Odeon - vocals, multi / **David Shawn Bosler** - multi, vocals

US Language Of Stone — UK Language Of Stone

Jun 08. (cd/lp) *<(LOS-007)>* **SILVER SUMMIT** Jul 08
- Music in the afterlife / The door / Awaken / In-between place / Apple tree / Water's edge / Acadia / Fool's love / Wishing well / The bridge.

Mariee SIOUX

Some knowledgeable folkies out there may recall her guest-vocalist contributions to ALELA DIANE's 'Songs Whistled Through White Teeth' and 'The Pirate's Gospel' sets; others will know she's worked with JOANNA NEWSOM and her Ys Street Band. The singer/songwriter was born Mariee Sioux Sobonya, February 4, 1985 in Humboldt County, California and raised in Nevada City.

It might be hard to find anyone who has heard the earliest of her limited-edition CD-rs, **PRAY ME A SHADOW** (2004) {*5} and **A BUNDLED BUNDLE OF BUNDLES** (2006) {*6}, but acoustic-friendly collectors may have stumbled across a single, 'Two Tongues At One Time', c/w 'Buried In Teeth', two tracks from the Native American-orientated nightingale's album **FACES IN THE ROCKS** (2007) {*7}. Where is she now? *MCS*

Mariee Sioux - vocals, acoustic guitar

US self-rel. — UK not issued

2004. (cd-r) *<none>* **PRAY ME A SHADOW**
- Icarus eye / Axemen / Patagonia / Silent be the way / Gray whale winter / Friendboats / Twin song / You were my missing elements / Ghosts in my heart.

Sep 06. (cd-r) *<none>* **A BUNDLED BUNDLE OF BUNDLES**
- Bravitzlana Rubakalva / Wizard flurry home / Fists 'n' seagulls / Wild eyes / Buried in teeth / Bundles.

—— added **Gentle Thunder** - flute / **Gary Sobonya** - mandolin

Grass Roots — Grass Roots

Oct 07. (cd) *<(15)>* **FACES IN THE ROCKS**
- Wizard flurry home / Buried in teeth / Friendboats / Wild eyes / Bravitzlana Rubakalva / Two tongues / Bundles / Flowers and blood.

Dec 07. (7") TWO TONGUES AT ONE TIME. / Buried In Teeth

SIX ORGANS OF ADMITTANCE

Psychedelic folk comes no more effervescent or wigged-out than Ben Chasny's indie outfit SIX ORGANS OF ADMITTANCE. Formed in 1998 as a side project to his rather louder Plague Lounge, the ORGANS soon became the Californian one-man-show from Santa Cruz's primary project. However, he would continue to jam and record with Comets On Fire (from 2003 onwards), Badgerlore, CURRENT 93, Magik Markers and Rangda, the last-named alongside SIR RICHARD BISHOP (of Sun City Girls) and SOoA sidekick Chris Corsano.

Without having explored every avenue of Ben's myriad releases (initially on his own Holy Mountain imprint), it can be said that his raga-style excursions had enough hypnotic structure to render them listenable. **SIX ORGANS OF ADMITTANCE** (1998) {*6} opened the proceedings, notable for one track, 'Sum Of All Heaven', that ran all of 17 minutes and was very flower-power-era JEFFERSON AIRPLANE.

DUST AND CHIMES (2000) {*7}, **NIGHTLY TREMBLING** (2000) {*7} and the mini-set **THE MANIFESTATION** (2000) {*6}, with an added side-length piece featuring Jennifer Juniper Stratford and Utrillo Kushner (percussion, electronics), came along in quick succession, Chasny's guitar finger-picking taking on the mantle of a modern-day BASHO, BULL or FAHEY. **DARK NOONTIDE** (2002) {*8} took this one step further, a masterwork of perfection headed by 'Khidr And The Mountain', `Spirits Abandoned' and the title track. Ben's Tibetan/Buddhist eastern influences were integral to the design and were his template for the follow-on works **FOR OCTAVIO PAZ** (2003) {*6} and **COMPATHIA** (2003) {*6}.

No label could understand better than Drag City the meaning of Chasny's free-folk sketches, and that's who released SOoA's experimental **SCHOOL OF THE FLOWER** (2005) {*7}, with Corsano (on organ and percussion) supplying a great deal of the ambience. Check out the cover of GARY HIGGINS's 'Thicker Than A Smokey'.

The group recording (without Corsano) **THE SUN AWAKENS** (2006) {*8} took freak-folk to new levels and probably beyond its own far-flung boundaries; 24 minutes of 'River Of Transfiguration' was the ultimate proof. Solo outing **SHELTER FROM THE ASH** (2007) {*7} re-defined Chasny's sense of acoustic purity, which was laid out from the get-go on the FAHEY-like 'Alone With The Alone'. **LUMINOUS LIGHT** (2009) {*7} and **ASLEEP ON THE FLOODPLAIN** (2011) {*7} stretched Chasny out even further, recorded while he worked between his new homes in Seattle and San Francisco. *MCS*

Ben Chasny - vocals, acoustic guitar, autoharp, percussion, turntables (ex-Plague Lounge, of Comets On Fire, of Badgerlore)

US UK
Pavillion not issued

Dec 98. (ltd-lp) <*PVL-001*> **SIX ORGANS OF ADMITTANCE**
- Maria / Sum of all heaven / Shadow of a dune / Harmonice Mundi LL / Race for Vishnu. <*(cd-iss. May 03 on Holy Mountain; 121964)*> - Invitation to the SR for supper / Don't be afraid.

2000. (ltd-8") <*none*> INVITATION TO THE S.R. FOR SUPPER / Don't Be Afraid

2000. (ltd-cd-r) <*PVL-003*> **DUST AND CHIMES**
- Stone finders verse I / Assyria / Hollow light severed sun / Tukulti will burn / Blue sun chiming / Oak path / Black needle rhymes / Sophia / Journey through Sankuan path / Stone finders verse II / Dance among the waiting. <*(cd-iss. Jun 04 on Holy Mountain; HOLY 1165)*>

2000. (ltd-lp) <*PVL-004*> **NIGHTLY TREMBLING**
- Redefinition of being (featuring creation aspects fire, air, water) / Creation aspect fire (reprise) / Creation aspect earth. <*ltd-re-iss. 2003 on Time-Lag; Time-Lag 013*>

Warm Freedom Of Tongue not issued

2000. (ltd-7" m) <*WFOT-6*> SOMEWHERE BETWEEN. / Sum Of All Heaven / Dead Flowers

Ba Da Bing! not issued

2000. (etched-12"m-lp) <*SD 82200*> **THE MANIFESTATION**
- The manifestation. <*(cd-iss. Sep 04 on Strange Attractors Audio House+=; SAAH 026)*> - The six stations.

Time-Lag not issued

2001. (ltd-lp; shared w/ CHARALAMBIDES) <*Time-Lag 002*> **SONGS FROM THE ENTOPTIC GARDEN VOLUME TWO**
- As voyage, in voyage - Bury dreams - Resurrection song - The gardener (for Hildebrand) / Her breath, a prayer // (track by CHARALAMBIDES).

Holy Mountain Holy Mountain

Feb 02. (cd,lp) <*(HOLY 1240)*> **DARK NOONTIDE**
- Spirits abandoned / Regeneration / On returning home / Dark noontide / This hand / Awaken / Khidr and the fountain / A thousand birds.

Mar 02. (cd-ep) <*TLR 004*> YOU CAN ALWAYS SEE THE SUN
(above issued on Three Lobed Recordings)

Sep 03. (cd) <*(HOLY 21852)*> **FOR OCTAVIO PAZ** May 04
- Fire on rain / When you finally return / Memory, memory, memory / The night knows nothing at all / Elk river / They fixed the broken windmill today / Rain on fire / The acceptance of absolute negation. <*ltd-lp-iss. 2004 on Time-Lag; Time-Lag 014*>

Oct 03. (cd) <*(HM 82614)*> **COMPATHIA** Jun 04
- Close to the sky / Run! / Wind in my palm / Somewhere between / Compathia / Gone astray / Hum a silent prayer / Only the sun knows.

not issued Durtro

2004. (7") *(ORGANS 7V)* IT WAS WRITTEN. / (other track by STEPHANIE VOLKMAR)

—— added **Chris Corsano** - organ, percussion

Drag City Drag City

Jan 05. (cd/lp) <*(DC 282 CD/LP)*> **SCHOOL OF THE FLOWER**
- Eighth cognition - All you've left / Words for two / Saint Cloud / Procession of cherry blossom spirits / Home / School of the flower / Thicker than a smokey / Lisboa.

—— added **Noel Jon Harmonson** - drums / **Tim Green** - tone generator / **John Connell** - Persian ney

Jun 06. (lp/cd) <*(DC 312/+CD)*> **THE SUN AWAKENS**
- Torn by wolves / Bless your blood / Black wall / The desert is a circle / Attar / Wolves' pup / River of transfiguration.

Jul 06. (7") <*HOLY 331761*> (track by OM). / ASSYRIAN BLOOD
(above issued on Holy Mountain) (below on Manhand)

2006. (ltd-cd-r) <*40*> **DAYS OF BLOOD**
- Noise / Procession of cherry blossom spirits / Awaken / A thousand birds / All you've left / Elk river / Words for two / Redefinition of being / Hum a silent prayer / Redefinition of being / All cats / A thousand birds. <*ltd-lp-iss. 2008 on Hash; HASH-01*>

Nov 07. (lp/cd) <*(DC 348/+CD)*> **SHELTER FROM THE ASH**
- Alone with the alone / Strangled road / Jade like wine / Coming to get you / Goddess atonement / Final wing / Shelter from the ash / Goodnight.

Aug 09. (lp/cd) <*(DC 409/+CD)*> **LUMINOUS LIGHT**
- Actaeon's fall (against the hounds) / Anesthesia / Bar-nasha / Cover your wounds with the sky / Ursa minor / River of heaven / The ballad of Charlie Harper / Enemies before the light.

Feb 11. (lp/cd) <*(DC 453/+CD)*> **ASLEEP ON THE FLOODPLAIN**
- Above a desert I've never seen / Light of the light / Brilliant blue sea between us / Saint of fisherman / Hold but let go / River of my youth / Poppies / S/word and leviathan / A new name on an old cement bridge / Dawn, running home.

- compilations, others, etc.-

Jan 09. (d-cd) *Drag City;* <*DC 383CD*> **RTZ**
- [SONGS FROM THE ENTOPTIC GARDEN VOLUME TWO tracks] / Warm earth, which I've been told / You can always see the sun / Punish the chasms with wings: Keep the cold - Last lantern to be seen from / [NIGHT TREMBLING tracks].

The SKYGREEN LEOPARDS

Formed in San Francisco in 2001 by singer/songwriters and multi-instrumentalists Donovan Quinn and Glenn Donaldson, experimental psych-folk duo The SKYGREEN LEOPARDS were the Bay Area's bright young things, an update of The BYRDS, Syd Barrett and The INCREDIBLE STRING BAND. Hardly innovative, then.

A stalwart of the indie-psych-folk scene, Glenn was also part of oblique experimentalists Badgerlore, Thuja, The Birdtree, Blythe Sons and his most prominent offshoot outfit, The FRANCISCAN HOBBIES, while his Jewelled Antler labelmate Donovan was equally active with his own venture, VERDURE.

Jewelled Antler were responsible for the pair's earliest CD-rs, including SKYGREEN's limited and rare 'I Dreamt She Rode On A Pink Gazelle And Other Dreams' (2001) and 'The Story Of The Green Lamb And The Other Jerusalem Priestess Of Leaves' (2002). 2003's **ONE THOUSAND BIRD CEREMONY** {*6} was issued on Soft Abuse, and they tempted the Jagjaguwar label to give **LIFE AND LOVE IN SPARROW'S MEADOW** (2005) {*7} and the vinyl-only, old-timey-styled **CHILD GOD IN THE GARDEN OF IDOLS** (2005) {*6} a chance. A mini-set, **JEHOVAH SURRENDER** {*5}, completed a prolific year for the pair. With more than a nod to the jingle-jangle of The BYRDS c. 1965-1967), their syrupy horizontal psychedelics were in full flow again on **DISCIPLES OF CALIFORNIA** (2006) {*7} and **GORGEOUS JOHNNY** (2009) {*7}.

Weaving between VERDURE and solo releases (one with his 13th Month colleagues Jason Quever, Helene Renaut, Karl Bauer and Jess Roberts), the DYLANesque QUINN was behind at least five extra-curricular sets. There was **THE TELESCOPE DREAMPATTERNS** (2004) {*7} and another Verdure album, **CROSS AND SATELLITE STATION** (2008) {*6}, plus the solo **OCTOBER LANTERNS** (2007) {*7}, **DONOVAN QUINN & THE 13TH MONTH** (2008) {*6} and **YOUR WICKED MAN** (2010) {*6}.

Breaking slightly from the folk-rock mould, DONALDSON continued making his own colourful neo-psych albums under an assortment of these names. Note that there are a few off-kilter, folk-orientated titles among them that some pundits might more than likely call freak-folk. *MCS*

Donovan Quinn - vocals, instruments / **Glenn Donaldson** - vocals, instruments

US UK
Jewelled Antler not issued

2001. (cd-r) *<none>* I DREAMT SHE RODE ON A PINK GAZELLE AND OTHER DREAMS

2002. (cd-r) *<none>* THE STORY OF THE GREEN LAMB AND THE JERUSALEM PRIESTESS OF LEAVES

Soft Abuse not issued

Nov 03. (cd) *<SAB 005>* **ONE THOUSAND BIRD CEREMONY**
- Summer alchemy / Morning of gulls (A dream of waters, part one) / Let me grow in your meadow / Walk with the golden cross / All our plagues were rainbows / One thousand birds / Hello to all your rain / The heron (A dream of waters, part two) / Tambourine, play it slow / Seaflowers (A dream of waters, part three) / Lost in the shadow arms of lust / Where do songs come from? / Parallel shadows / A breeze of pine blows through me / Summer pharmacy. *(UK-iss. Jan 06; same as US)*

Jagjaguwar Jagjaguwar

Feb 05. (cd/lp) *<(JAG 82 CD/LP)>* **LIFE AND LOVE IN SPARROW'S MEADOW**
- Mother the sun makes me cry / Belle of the woodman's autumn ball / Egyptian Rosemarie / Clouds through sparrows eyes / Tents along the water / Careless gardeners (of Eden) - Sparrows of Eden (Eden fading) - Drunken gardeners dance (Paradise lost sweetly) / Come down off your mountain, Moses / Minotaur (burn a candle for love) / Labyrinth windows / The supplication of fireflies / A child adrift.

Mar 05. (ltd-lp) *<JAG 84>* **CHILD GOD IN THE GARDEN OF IDOLS**
- Parasols thro' the moors / Butterfly dance / Hill-dwelling bride / The orchard daughter / Christ-child dances / Hobo sparrow's dream / Woodman's dance / Parallel shadows (part II) - Mad lion (part VII) / Child god.

Oct 05. (m-cd) *<(JAG 92CD)>* **JEHOVAH SURRENDER** Nov 05
- Jehovah I surrender / Julie-Anne, patron of thieves / Play for the spring / Apparition of suns (also known as The ferryman's long arms) / Let the lion be swallowed by a dove / I was a thief.

Oct 06. (cd/lp) *<(JAG 104 CD/LP)>* **DISCIPLES OF CALIFORNIA**
- Disciples of California / Places west of Shawnapee / Sally Orchid / Egyptian circus / Marching band / William and the sacred hammer / Golden pilgrim / Jesus was Californian / I remember Sally Orchid / Silvery branches / Hollow tree. *(UK-iss. Aug 08 on Cosmo)*

Jul 09. (cd/lp) *<(JAG 147 CD/LP)>* **GORGEOUS JOHNNY**
- Johnny's theme / Margery / Dixie cups in the dead grass / SGLs et al / Can go back / Goodnight Anna / Jehovah will never come / Gorgeous Johnny / Inland towns / Nine car train for Fremont / Robber's lace / If our love fails / Paid by the hour.

DONOVAN QUINN

Camera Obscura not issued

Jun 04. (cd; as VERDURE) *<CAM 66CD>* **THE TELESCOPE DREAMPATTERNS** Australia
- Into the blacktrees / The coffin splits in two / The greentrees / Moon landing / Seeing the telescope dreampatterns / Birds that come back again / Softly, the embers / Fluttering pastures / The sea funeral / Ash-Wednesday / Graveyard porchlight.

Puissant not issued

2007. (ltd-cd-r) *<PUI 005>* **OCTOBER LANTERNS**
- October lanterns / Blackbird headchamber / The guttering flame / At the tent revival / One thousand matchsticks / Saw a ghost on the water / The crooked smile of a jack-o-lantern / Along the hollies / Miner / October lanterns.

Lexicon Devil not issued

Aug 08. (cd; as VERDURE) *<LEXDEV 011CD>* **CROSS AND SATELLITE STATION**
- Crystal glass / Cross and satellite theme / Everything's dancing / Looking for the ocean / Trick with two mirrors / Pope Innocent X / France eats / Anonymous 1917 / Suns gonna come take over my sky / Hot air balloon / Paints.

—— next with band: **Jason Quever** - guitar, keyboards, vocals / **Helene Renaut** - piano, violin / **Karl Bauer** - drums / **Jess Roberts** - backing vocals

Soft Abuse not issued

Jun 08. (7"; as DONOVAN QUINN & THE 13TH MONTH) *<SAB 027>* SISTER ALCHEMY. / The Rabbit Tracks

Sep 08. (cd; as DONOVAN QUINN & THE 13TH MONTH) *<SAB 028>* **DONOVAN QUINN & THE 13th MONTH**
- October's bride / Horror and fear / Sister alchemy / Patterns on a summer dress / The wind at her craft / Quarantine / They're going to pick us apart / Take the cross off the mantle / Hallowed candles / 'Moose Indian' / Holy agent / Dark motel / Heathen honeymoon / I have seen the season change.

Shrimper Shrimper

Aug 10. (cd) *<(SHR 157)>* **YOUR WICKED MAN**
- Winter in a rented room / Mom's house / Your wicked man / April tenth / Street fighting girls / The door locks itself / Leave like you came / Silvia and the gremlins / Red corona / Open flame. *<ltd-lp-iss. on Soft Abuse; SAB 040>*

GLENN DONALDSON

Jewelled Antler not issued

2001. (cd-r; as The BLYTHE SONS) *<#4>* **WAVES OF GRASS** [live]
- Sun and rocks - The constant leaf / Waves of grass / I know you forever / Season / Direction / Summer blazes / Tree-lined road.

2001. (cd-r; as GLASSINE) *<#5>* **BIRDS ARE THE LIFE OF THE SKY 1995-1997**
- Lyca / Above the wing is heaven / Orchard / Birds are the life of the sky / Kingfisher / Dust is falling / White sands / Blight / Doorways.

2001. (cd-r; as The BIRDTREE) *<#13>* **ORCHARDS AND CARAVANS**
- White sundials faced the sun / Pillar of clouds / Animals of the summit / Red midnight raven / The marsh / Black rainbows (parts 1 & 2) / Everyone of us a new leaf / Mary Ann / Scorpions and lions / The bluish vapor of tall eucalyptus trees / The lost sun / Raven returns - The uppermost forest / Sleeper under a tree / Leaffish. *<cd re-iss. 2003 on Last Visible Dog; LVD 041>*

—— next with **Loren Chasse, Greg Bianchini, Kerry McLaughlin, Rob Reger**, etc.

2002. (cd-r; as The FRANCISCAN HOBBIES) *<#49>* **CATERPILLARS OF THE OAK BEAUTY**
- Caterpillars of the oak beauty / The secret forces / Paralysed by a grey dust / Magic matched against magic / Green moss / Boats / Antiphons / Illusionist without an illusion / The dawn of belief / Festival of sticks and grasses.

—— added **Buffy Vice Sick** + **Christine Boepple**

not issued PseudoArcana

2002. (cd-r; as The FRANCISCAN HOBBIES) *(PA 027)* **AT THE WORLD'S END** NewZ
- Omens from birds / Centaur envy / The black chimes / Seekers in darkness / The unicorn murders / False-hearted love / Echippus / Table of figures / Secret of the rose window.

Soft Abuse not issued

2003. (cd; as The FRANCISCAN HOBBIES) *<SAB 002>* **MASKS AND MEANINGS**
- A preordained sequence / Wasp embodiment / Withered spring / The animal performers / Plough drawn by toads / Apprehension of reality / The matchless phenomenon. *<re-iss. Oct 06; same>*

—— (no Buffy) added **Allan Horrocks, Jason Honea** + **Bryan De Roo**

Music Fellowship not issued

Oct 04. (cd; as The FRANCISCAN HOBBIES) *<MF 013>* **WALLS ARE STUCK**
- The modern revival / Elijah the stone / Satan crystals / Empty hands / Goat with the dolphin face / The happy burial / Placing of the flowers / Asmodeus / Lake of holy fishes / Death music / The etheric double.

—— **Glenn** now with **Shayde Sartin** - guitars, bass + drums

Soft Abuse not issued

2007. (cd; by GIANT SKYFLOWER BAND) *<SAB 019>* **BLOOD OF THE SUNWORM** [rec. 2005]
- Oh Mary Green / Starbeams / Time won't sing a song for you / Feast of blood / Rainbows and dreams (with worms singing) / Bitter wild rabbit - Builds the bone / All of us (you and me) / Lice of rainbows / The arcangel (hurray for the beast) / Meditations on Christ and the Magi.

Fred SMALL

Born Frederick Emerson Small, November 6, 1952 in Plainfield, New Jersey, the grand-nephew of artist, painter and harmonica player Thomas Hart Benton, the Yale law graduate and singer/songwriter FRED SMALL is old-school folk, one of the artists inspired by the revivalists and protest singers of the 1960s. PETE SEEGER once called Fred "one of America's best songwriters".

Deciding to desert his post as an attorney in an established Boston law firm after a concert at New York's Battery Park in 1978, Fred went from coffee-house attraction to theatre draw in the space of a few years, although with limited resources at hand initially, only one independent cassette surfaced, **LOVE WILL CARRY US** (1981) {*6}. When Rounder Records came calling, the LPs **THE HEART OF THE APPALOOSA** (1984) {*7} and **NO LIMIT** (1985) {*6} set the ball rolling.

Moving along the corridor to Flying Fish, more examples of his witty humour and activist seriousness came along with **I WILL STAND FAST** (1988) {*6}, **JAGUAR** (1991) {*6} and the in-concert set **EVERYTHING POSSIBLE** (1993) {*7}, the latter with a backing band that included fiddler JOHNNY CUNNINGHAM, mandolinist John Curtis and harmony singer Catherine David.

Around 1996 Fred took on a ministerial role at the First Parish Church in Cambridge, Massachusetts, where he had been a member for some time, and only one set, **ONLY LOVE** (2001) {*5}, has since emerged, though he of course works music into his pastoral calling. *MCS*

Fred Small - vocals, acoustic guitar

US Aquifer — UK not issued

1981. (c) *<AQU 1001>* **LOVE'S GONNA CARRY US**
- Love's gonna carry us / Lifeboat / Gonna get a grant / Fifty-nine cents / A modest proposal (the long underwear song) / Stand up / Three Mile Island / The hug / The dancing light / Letter from May Alice Jeffers / I lost that pretty little girl of mine (to title IX) / Housewarming.

Rounder — Rounder

Jan 84. (lp) *<(ROU 4014>* **THE HEART OF THE APPALOOSA**
- The heart of the Appaloosa / Talking wheelchair blues / Willie's song / Face at the window / Peace is / Annie / Death in disguise / Dig a hole in the ground, or, how to prosper during the coming nuclear war / No more Vietnams / Larry the polar bear. *<(c-iss. Aug 88; ROUC 4014)> <(cd-iss. Jan 94 & Mar 00; ROUCD 4014)>*

Sep 85. (lp) *<(ROU 4018)>* **NO LIMIT**
- Big Italian rose / Jimmy come lately / Scrambled eggs and prayers / Everything possible / Cranes over Hiroshima / Peace dragon / Leslie is different / Father's song / No limit. *<(c-iss. Aug 88; ROUC 4018)> <(cd-iss. Jan 94 & Mar 00; ROUCD 4018)>*

Flying Fish — Flying Fish

Nov 88. (lp/c/cd) *<(FF+/90/70 491)>* **I WILL STAND FAST** — Feb 89
- The hills of Ayalon / Diamonds of anger / I will stand fast / At the Elbe / If I were a moose / Every man / Scott and Jamie / Denmark, 1943 / This love.

Aug 91. (cd/c) *<(FF70/FF90 570)>* **JAGUAR** — May 93
- Jaguar / Simple living / Warlords / Gravity / The last time I had autumn / I didn't know / Survivors / Light in the hall / The distance / Mistaken identity / All the time in the world.

Nov 93. (cd/c) *<(FF70/FF90 625)>* **EVERYTHING POSSIBLE: FRED SMALL IN CONCERT** [live March 26, 1993] — Dec 93
- (introduction by Susan Wilson) / Guinevere and the fire / (intro...) / The other side of the wood / (intro...) / Hot frogs on the loose / Smile when you're ready / Simple living / (intro...) / Rodney King's blessing / The hug song / (intro...) / Friends first / (intro...) / Too many people / If I were taken now / The marine's lament, or, the pink peril / (...outro) / Everything possible / Peace is.

Aquifer — not issued

Jul 01. (cd) *<AQU 2001CD>* **ONLY LOVE**
- A dream in the light / Nobody's beauty / Not in our town / Only love / Buddha behind the wheel / The weed / Roger and Phoebe / Reverie's end / Don't take moderation to excess / The great green earth / My roving days.

—— Small continued his work as a pastor/minister but hasn't released anything since

Debi SMITH

Born December 30, 1953 in Philadelphia and raised in Falls Church, Virginia, three-octave singer/songwriter and multi-instrumentalist DEBI SMITH has been at the heart of folk music, albeit with more than a hint of country and Celtic, since her 1980s days with older sister Megan in the DOC & Merle WATSON-produced duo The SMITH SISTERS.

Releasing five albums in the space of 10 years, four of them on Flying Fish, the sisters produced some relaxing and soothing contemporary sounds on **BLUEBIRD** (1984) {*6} and **MOCKINGBIRD** (1986) {*6}, the latter featuring covers of JUDY COLLINS's 'Since You Asked', JOAN BAEZ's 'Diamonds And Rust' and JAMES TAYLOR's 'Walking Man'. These were followed by **ROADRUNNER** (1989) {*5} and **A CANARY'S SONG** (1993) {*7}. Their swansong effort (after the 1991 children's set **I SEE THE MOON** {*6}) housed a handful of Bobby Mondlock songs, including the title track, co-written with Garth Brooks.

Replacing Julie Gold in the comedy-folk act FOUR BITCHIN' BABES, where she's still a member as of 2011, DEBI SMITH took full flight as a solo folk star with 1994's **IN MY DREAMS** {*6}. She moved to Shanachie for her second and third solo albums, **MORE THAN ONCE** (1998) {*6} and her tribute to her father, **RED BIRD RED** (2001) {*6}. From the last-named, check out her TOM PAXTON collaborations 'Marry Me Again' and 'Slipping Away'. 2004's **CUPID** {*5} and 2007's **THE SOPRANO** {*6} were basically exercises for her wide vocal range and not much to do with her country-folk roots. *MCS*

The SMITH SISTERS

Debi Smith - vocals, acoustic guitar / **Megan Smith** (b. Dec 29 '58) - vocals, bass

US Flying Fish — UK Flying Fish

1984. (lp) *<FF 328>* **BLUEBIRD**
- The traveler / Airport / Leatherwing bat / Tuileries / Mountain child / Are you mine / The back door / My Johnny / Hello stranger / Summer sky / Bluebird / Sunny side. *(UK-iss. Mar 89; same as US)*

1986. (lp) *<FF 370>* **MOCKINGBIRD**
- Little girl's heart / Since you asked / Tell me more / I got, you got / Medley / Diamonds and rust / Baby don't go / Walking man / Stargazing / The fair / Mockingbird / Sweet sunny south. *(UK-iss. Mar 89; same as US)*

1989. (cd) *<(FF70 496)>* **ROADRUNNER** — 1992
- The river and the moon / Dancyville road / Crazy over you / River roll on / Fire of change / Virginia / French broad river waltz / All through throwing good love after bad / Closer now than ever / The bramble and the rose.

1991. (c) *<AM-C-111>* **I SEE THE MOON: Folk Songs For Children**
- I've been working on the railroad / On top of Old Smoky / Billy boy / Frere Jacques / Kookaberra / The day the bass players took over the world / I see the moon / The prune song / Goober peas / Stone in the shoe / One bottle of pop / Michael the lion / Simon songs / Ladies and jellyspoons / Take me for a ride in your car / Web footed friends.

(above issued on American Melody)

1993. (cd) *<FF70 616>* **A CANARY'S SONG**
- Rappahanock / Blues song for sopranos in A minor / My father was a quiet man / Solid ground / In my dreams / The bramble and the rose / Hard times (come again no more) / Pampa, Texas / Arrow / Leaving train / Distant thunder / Rhythm of love / A canary's song / Fire of change / A new day / Amazing Grace.

DEBI SMITH

Debi Smith - vocals, acoustic guitar, piano, bodhran (w/ session people)

Amerisound — not issued

Nov 94. (cd) *<AMR-1-977-303>* **IN MY DREAMS**
- One horse town / My father was a quiet man / Where Sam was born / Straight for a fall / Canary's song / In my dreams / Pampa, Texas / The mirror knows / Nothing new / Haunted / Higher ground / To the angel in my arms.

Shanachie — Shanachie

May 98. (cd) *<(SHANCD 8032)>* **MORE THAN ONCE** — Jun 98
- Virginia - Shenandoah / Mother's hands / Hang the moon / Life outside this town / Snowbound / Everyone's got a story / Old river / Sleep / Intertwined / First choice / More than once / Out to forget / He doesn't work on love / Italy and France.

Oct 01. (cd) *<(SHANCD 8037)>* **RED BIRD RED** — Mar 04
- Red bird red / God help us / If you don't listen / Niagara Falls / Kiss the clouds / Marry me again / Chevy Impala / Slipping away / I will always / Myrta and Emory / Angels calling / O mio bambino Caro.

Degan Music — not issued

Dec 04. (cd) *<none>* **CUPID**
- Shadow / Pass it on / Pie / Cupid / Water is wide / Drivin' / Whatever you do / My kinda man / Let's go away / Nothin' / Get a hold / Over the rainbow.

Sep 07. (cd) *<none>* **THE SOPRANO**
- Barcarolle: Belle nuit o nuit d'amour / Wild mountain thyme / Shenandoah / Ave Maria / Bluebird / Habenera / Come all ye fair and tender ladies / Jock of Hazeldine / Bob Dylan's poetry / Amazing grace / Italy and France / O mio bambino Caro / In my dreams / Ebben?... ne andro lontana / Star spangled banner / Greensleeves (what child is this) / From the hills of Bethlehem / O holy night / A baby cries / Patapan / Silent night / What wondrous love is this / Ave Maria / God's own / Lord's prayer / Amen.

Elliott SMITH

ELLIOTT SMITH (b. Steven Paul Smith, August 6, 1969 in Omaha, Nebraska) was for many a fringe figure in folk, though rooted in post-grunge sadcore, lo-fi and indie-acoustic pop. Many fans and critics mourned his untimely death.

Raised from an early age by his father in Portland, Oregon, after his parents divorced, the singer/songwriter relocated to university digs in Brooklyn, New York, playing in noisy mid-1990s alt-rock band Heatmiser. In four years they made three albums, 'Dead Air' (1993), 'Cop And Speeder' (1995) and 'Mic City Sons' (1996), but SMITH meanwhile had opted for a more sedate solo career.

After his debut, the mini-set **ROMAN CANDLE** (1994) {*7}, he delivered two very well received albums for the Kill Rock Stars imprint, **ELLIOTT SMITH** (1995) {*8*} and **EITHER/OR** (1997) {*9}, all licensed in 1998 to the UK arm of the Domino label before he signed up with DreamWorks. These were two of the best albums of the era, and the songs 'Needle In The Hay' (very Kurt Cobain), 'Between The Bars', 'Ballad Of Big Nothing' and the Eric Matthews-like 'Say Yes' are regarded as classics.

His appearance at the 1998 Oscars ceremony was much praised, playing his 'Miss Misery' contribution to the soundtrack of Gus Van Sant's 'Good Will Hunting', which had been nominated as Best Song. His unfashionable approach (especially his taste in clothing and headgear) was slightly reminiscent of SIMON & GARFUNKEL, NICK DRAKE, Big Star (he covered their 'Thirteen') and the lo-fi Richard Davies of The Cardinal.

Elliott's fourth album, **XO** {*8}, hit the shops later in 1998, pick of the bunch being the minor UK hits 'Waltz #2 (XO)' and 'Baby Britain', 'Sweet Adeline' and 'Independence Day'.

Sounding very much at home in his new big-budget environment, **FIGURE 8** (2000) {*6} found SMITH taking the opportunity to imbue his songwriting with the luxurious feel of classic Beatles-meet-CS&N-meet-Beach Boys while never relinquishing his Skid Row wisdom. Check out 'Son Of Sam', 'Pretty Mary K' and 'Somebody That I Used To Know'.

Elliott was still in the process of recording his next album when he died from stab wounds to the chest in Los Angeles on October 21, 2003. What may have been a suicide note was found, but post-mortem evidence was inconclusive as to whether he died by suicide or by foul play.

FROM A BASEMENT ON THE HILL {*8} was posthumously collated and mixed by his longtime producer Rob Schnapf and former girlfriend Joanna Bolme (of Minders and Stephen Malkmus & The Jicks) and released in October 2004. While there was controversy over the fact that producer David McConnell wasn't involved with the record, despite having presided over the sessions prior to Elliott's death, the end result was generally well received by fans and critics. Darker and harder-edged than anything he'd previously released, the record (which reached the US Top 20) inevitably attracted comment focused on the lyrics and their supposed relevance to SMITH's fate. *MCS*

Elliott Smith - vocals, drums, bass, saxophones, etc / with session band

US Slo-Mo — UK not issued

1994. (ltd-7"; by ELLIOTT SMITH & PETE KREBS) <*SM 001*>
NO CONFIDENCE MAN. / Shytown [ ] [-]

Cavity Search — not issued

Dec 94. (m-cd/m-c) <*CSR 13-2/13*> **ROMAN CANDLE** [ ] [-]
- Roman candle / Condor Ave / No name #1 / No name #2 / No name #3 / Drive all over town / No name #4 / Last call / Kiwi maddog 20-20. *(UK-iss. Mar 98 on Cavity Search; same as US) (UK re-iss. Aug 98 & Dec 04 on Domino cd/lp; REWIG CD/LP 002) (UK cd/lp re-mast. Apr 10 on Domino; REWIG CD/LP 75) <lp re-iss. Apr 10 on Kill Rock Stars; KRS-523>*

Kill Rock Stars — Kill Rock Stars

Feb 95. (7"m) <*KRS 239*> NEEDLE IN THE HAY. / Alphabet Town / Some Song [ ] [-]

Jul 95. (lp/cd) <*KRS 246/+CD*> **ELLIOTT SMITH** [ ] [-]
- Needle in the hay / Christian brothers / Clementine / Southern belle / Single file / Coming up roses / Satellite / Alphabet town / St Ides heaven / Good to go / The white lady loves you more / The biggest lie. *(UK-iss. Mar 98; same) (re-iss. Aug 98 & Dec 04 on Domino cd/lp; REWIG CD/LP 001)*

Oct 96. (7" m) <*KRS 266*> SPEED TRIALS. / Angeles / I Don't Think I'm Ever Gonna Figure It Out [ ] [-]

Mar 97. (lp/cd) <*(KRS 269/+CD)*> **EITHER/OR** [ ] [ ]
- Speed trials / Alameda / Ballad of big nothing / Between the bars / Pictures of me / No name No.5 / Rose parade / Punch and Judy / Angeles / Cupid's trick / 2:45 am / Say yes. *(UK-iss. Jun 98 & Dec 04 on Domino cd/lp; WIG CD/LP 51)*

1997. (7"/cd-s) <*(S-005/+CD)*> DIVISION DAY. / No Name #6 [ ] May 00 [ ]
(above issued on Suicide Squeeze)

Jun 98. (7") *(RUG 74)* BALLAD OF BIG NOTHING. / Some Song / Division Day [-] [ ]
(cd-s+=) *(RUG 74CD)* - Angeles.

DreamWorks — DreamWorks

Aug 98. (cd/c) <*(DRD/DRC 50048)*> **XO** [ ] [ ]
- Sweet Adeline / Tomorrow tomorrow / Waltz #2 (XO) / Baby Britain / Pitseleh / Independence day / Bled white / Waltz #1 / Amity / Oh well, okay / Bottle up and explode! / A question mark / Everybody cares, everybody understands / I didn't understand. *<(lp-iss. Jun 00 on Bongload; BL 35)> <white-lp re-iss. 2008 on Plain; plain 126>*

Dec 98. (7") *(DRMS 22347)* WALTZ #2 (XO). / Our Thing [-] [52]
(cd-s+=) *(DRMCD 22347)* - How to take a fall.

Apr 99. (7") *(DRMS7 50953)* BABY BRITAIN. / Waltz #1 [demo] [-] [55]
(cd-s+=) *(DRMDM 50950)* - The enemy is you.
(cd-s) *(DRMDM 50951)* - ['A'] / Some song [alt] / Bottle up and explode! [early].

Jan 00. (7"/cd-s) <*CSR 40 - 0044-59037-2*> HAPPINESS. / Son Of Sam [ ] [-]
(above 7"-only issued on Cavity Search)

Apr 00. (cd) <*(4 50225-2)*> **FIGURE 8** [99] [37]
- Son of Sam / Somebody that I used to know / Junk bond trader / Everything reminds me of her / Everything means nothing to me / LA / In the lost and found (honky Bach) - The roost / Stupidity tries / Easy way out / Wouldn't mama be proud? / Color bars / Happiness - The gondola man / Pretty Mary K / I better be quiet now / Can't make a sound / Bye. *<(lp-iss. Jul 00 on Bongload; BL 48)> <red-d-lp iss. 2008 on Plain; plain 127>*

Jun 00. (7") *(450949-7)* SON OF SAM. / A Living Will [-] [55]
(cd-s+=) *(450949-2)* - Figure 8.

Suicide Squeeze — Domino

Aug 03. (ltd-7") <*S-028*> *(RUG 195)* PRETTY (UGLY BEFORE). / A Distorted Reality Is Now A Necessity To Be Free [ ] Dec 04 [ ]

—— Smith died October 21, 2003 - final recordings below

Anti — Domino

Oct 04. (cd/d-lp) <*86741-2/-1*> *(WIG CD/LP 147)*
FROM A BASEMENT ON THE HILL [19] [41]
- Coast to coast / Let's get lost / Pretty (ugly before) / Don't go down / Strung out again / A fond farewell / King's crossing / Ostrich and chirping / Twilight / A passing feeling / The last hour / Shooting star / Memory lane / Little one / A distorted reality is now a necessity to be free. *<d-lp re-iss. Apr 10 on Kill Rock Stars; KRS 524>*

- (8-10*) compilations, others, etc.-

May 07. (d-cd/d-lp) *Kill Rock Stars; <KRS 455> Domino; (WIG CD/LP 198)* **NEW MOON** [24] [39]
- Angel in the snow / Talking to Mary / High times / New monkey / Looking over my shoulder / Going nowhere / Riot coming / All cleaned out / First timer / Go by / Miss misery [early version] / Thirteen // Georgia, Georgia / Whatever (folk song in C) / Big decision / Placeholder / New disaster / Seen how things are hard / Fear city / Either/or / Pretty Mary K [other version] / Almost over / See you later / Half right.

Nov 10. (cd/lp) *Kill Rock Stars; <KRS 541> Domino; (WIG CD/LP 265)*
AN INTRODUCTION TO... [ ] [ ]
- Ballad of big nothing / Waltz #2 (XO) / Pictures of me / The biggest lie / Alameda / Between the bars / Needle in the hay / Last call / Angeles / Twilight / Pretty (ugly before) / Angel in the snow / Miss Misery [early version] / Happiness [single version].

- essential boxed set + tidbits -

Oct 01. (3-cd-box) *Domino; (WIG 105)* **ROMAN CANDLE // ELLIOTT SMITH // EITHER/OR** [-] [ ]

Nov 10. (ltd-7") *Domino; (RUG 381)* BALLAD OF BIG NOTHING. / Division Day [-] [ ]

Michael (Peter) SMITH

Born Michael Peter Smith, September 7, 1941 in South Orange, New Jersey (and not to be confused with a few other artists called Michael Smith), this SMITH is one of the genre's star singer/songwriters, and his songs have become hot property with many rising folk singers.

His career began in the rock trio Juarez (with his first wife, Barbara Barrow, and Ron Kickasola), who delivered one LP for Decca around the late 1960s before the couple, credited as Michael & Barbara Smith, recorded the 1970s rock and roll set 'Mickey And Babs Get Hot', on which Barbara plays a solo piano version of Michael's much-covered song 'The Dutchman'. Their privately-issued live album 'Zen' and 1981's Jet Band set 'Empty Handed' could not be further removed from Michael's subsequent folk projects.

'The Dutchman' was written in 1968, at which time he'd never been to Amsterdam, where the story of devotion and conditional love was set. Many artists have since covered the song, none more gracefully than STEVE GOODMAN (on his 1973 LP 'Somebody Else's Troubles'), country star Suzy Bogguss and ANNE HILLS. David Soul's may be the least essential of numerous other versions.

Over the years SMITH has written a number of classics covered by a wide range of artists, among them 'Spoon River', 'Last Day Of Pompeii', 'Crazy Mary' and 'Dead Egyptian Blues', which are also to be found on his first two solo albums on Flying Fish, **MICHAEL SMITH** (1986) {*7} and **LOVE STORIES** (1988) {*7}.

With fellow folk star ANNE HILLS at the controls, **TIME** (1994) {*6} was a comeback of sorts. HILLS would later combine with SMITH on the spiritual/religious 'Paradise Lost And Found' (1999), and the collective 'Fourtold' CD (2003) alongside CINDY MANGSEN and STEVE GILLETTE.

Between these albums Michael was busy writing songs and music for various stage production, and the official CD release of 1993's autobiographical stage musical **MICHAEL MARGARET PAT & KATE** in 2000 {*6} was an award-winning achievement in itself. Respected by his peers and fans in equal measure, Michael has continued to record and release numerous post-millennium projects, including live recordings, theatre projects and songs for children. *MCS*

Michael Smith - vocals, acoustic guitar / + session people

US Flying Fish — UK Flying Fish

Nov 86. (lp) <*FF-404*> **MICHAEL SMITH** [ ] [-]
- Panther in Michigan / Demon lover / Spoon river / The Dutchman / Ballad of Dan Moody / Last day of Pompeii / Vampire / Coleen's song. *<cd-iss. Sep 92 +=; FF70-461>- LOVE STORIES <cd re-iss. Nov 07 by MICHAEL PETER SMITH as SONGS FROM BIRD AVENUE; same>* - LOVE STORIES

Feb 88. (lp) <*(FF-461)*> **LOVE STORIES** Jul 89
- Come away Anita / Sister Clarissa / Loretta of the rivers / Move over Mr Gauguin / Crazy Mary / Three monkeys / Dead Egyptian blues / One blessed hour. <*cd-iss.+=*> - MICHAEL SMITH

May 94. (cd) <*(FF70-613)*> **TIME** Nov 94
- Time is moving in the hallway / The ballad of Elizabeth Dark / Hawkins Falls / Lady Susquehanna / I brought my father with me / Lily and the blackwater / This here mandolin / Gracie / Altoona waltz / 25th century blues / Lee Remick / Gamble's guitar / We become birds.

— In 1997, Jamie O'Reilly & MICHAEL SMITH (with Katrina O'Reilly) released the Winter Theater Festival recording 'Songs Of The Spanish Civil War 1936–1939' for Bird Avenue

— In 1999, ANNE HILLS & MICHAEL SMITH released 'Paradise Lost And Found'.

Wind River — not issued

Apr 00. (cd) <*MSI 4006D*> **MICHAEL MARGARET PAT & KATE**
[the 1994 theatre musical]
- (spoken intro) / Five angels / Star of the County Down / Looking for Maureen / Sister Clarissa / Palamino Pal / Sweet Sue / Belmar / Little falls / Patricia's song (63 Wilmore Road) / Five angels / Coffeehouse days / Kilgarry mountain / The ballad of Elizabeth Dark / Somethin' about big twist / I brought my father with me / (spoken closing) / Five angels / Begin the beguine.

— In 2000, the 'Weavermania!' CD was by SMITH, Barbara Barrow, Tom Dundee & Mark Dvorak

Oct 02. (cd) <*MSI 4022D*> **THERE**
- Alexandria / There / Painted horse / Hole in the sky / Kill the buddha / Hey kid / Rainy season again / Caribbean snow / Memory of August / Look look.

— In 2003, SMITH, HILLS, STEVE GILLETTE & CINDY MANGSEN issued 'Fourtold'.

Beechwood — not issued

May 03. (cd; by MICHAEL SMITH & JAMES LEE STANLEY) <*none*>
TWO MAN BAND TWO [recorded 2000]
- Stranded / There / Only one lonely one / Keep me in mind / Somewhere in between / Saving my heart / Train / Rain (in the key of D) / Long way from home / Soon enough / Saving grace.

Bird Avenue — not issued

Nov 03. (cd; by MICHAEL SMITH & JAMES O'REILLY) <*none*>
THE GIFT OF THE MAGI [part-festive]
- We three kings / Narration I / I wish someone would take me dancing / Nineteen and five / Gotta like a guy / Long-haired woman / Madame Sofronie / Troika ride / Pawnbroker's lullaby / I heard the bells on Christmas Day / The Magi / Narration II / On our own / Silent night / A wanderer am I.

own label — not issued

2004. (cd; as MICHAEL PETER SMITH) <*none*> **LIVE AT DARK-THIRTY** [live March 2, 2003]
- Tom mix blues / Sister Clarissa / The princess and the frog / The Dutchman / October child (Rondi's birthday) / Spoon river / Gamble's guitar / Such things are finely done / Palomino pal / Starfisher / Crazy Mary / Vampire / Dialing / Zippy.

— In 2005, MICHAEL P. SMITH collaborated with John McDermott on 'Just Plain Folk'

Tales From The Tavern — not issued

Aug 06. (cd) <*019*> **SUCH THINGS ARE FINELY DONE: Michael Smith Live at Tales From the Tavern**
[live Feb. 28, 2003 at Mattei's Tavern in Los Olivos, California]
- (introduction) / Sister Clarissa / The ballad of Elizabeth Dark / The princess and the frog / Famous in France / The Dutchman / I brought my father with me / Move over Mr Gauguin / Four jokes / There / Something about big twist / Zippy / Honey to the hive / Such things are finely done.

Nov 08. (cd) <*none*> **LOVE LETTER ON A FISH: Michael Smith Live at Tales From the Tavern Too**
- (intro) / Dead Egyptian blues / Rondi's birthday / Tom Mix blues / Palomino pal / Spoon river / Barbara Dodd / Panther in Michigan / Vampire / Tom Dundee / We become birds / Love letter on a fish / Bees bees bees bees bees bees bees / Crazy Mary (from Londonderry) / Teenage heaven.

Bird Avenue — not issued

2009. (cd) <*none*> **THE SELFISH GIANT** [from Chicago's Children's Theater] mail-o
- Everyone's a giant / This particular giant / No kids allowed / Kid free / Imaginary guitars / Us birds / Bee knees / Winter all year / Not about to go back there / Giant winter / Like it much better this way / I get the picture now / A good long life / A beautiful story.

- (5-7*) compilations, etc.-

2005. (cd; as MICHAEL PETER SMITH) *Bird Avenue*; <*none*>
ANTHOLOGY ONE mail-o
- Fun house / What's the sea done to the sailor / Panther in Michigan / The Dutchman / Portrait of Isabel / Dead Egyptian blues / Lavallette / Keep me in mind / Blazin' guns / Portland fancy.

Sean SMITH

Definitely not to be confused with the popular jazz-rock bassist of the same name, San Franciscan finger-picker SEAN SMITH (born 1980) wears the mantle of folk-blues greats FAHEY, BULL, BASHO, KOTTKE, et al, while he's also been lumped in with Cul De Sac's GLENN JONES and Sackville's HARRIS NEWMAN. Sean guested for Dead Oceans indie-rock act Citay on their 2010 set 'Dream Get Together'.

The self-titled **SEAN SMITH** (2004) {*7} spread his name as fast as his finger-picking fretwork, instrumentals like 'Silver Ships On Plasmic Oceans' and the lengthy 'Someone Somewhere Has Sensed That I Am A Frightened Man' taking the set beyond the commonplace and into forefathers-of-folk land.

While the follow-up, **SACRED CRAG DANCER, CORPSE WHISPERER** (2006) {*6}, relied on the same formula, Eastern influences came into the mix on , **ETERNAL** (CD 2010, limited LP release 2008) {*6}, and also in 2010 he released a festive set, **CHRISTMAS** {*5}. His second set for Strange Attractors, **HUGE FLUID FREEDOM** (2011) {*7}, is by all accounts very freewheeling and indiefied - think SIX ORGANS OF ADMITTANCE. *MCS*

Sean Smith - guitars / with session people

US — UK
Sailor On The Riverbed — not issued

2004. (ltd-7" split) <*SOTR 001*> (track by Matthew Baldwin). /
RAILROAD BILL / CRAWDAD HOLE

Isota — Isota

Jan 05. (cd) <*(sody 027-2)*> **SEAN SMITH** Oct 04
- Silver ships on plasmic oceans / Ride the bus to the library / Alice Street waltz / Someone somewhere has sensed that I am a frightened man / Birds / Window light blues / I can't wait for winter / Love always beautiful / Such a small and closely. <*also issued on Plain; pla 014*>

Sep 06. (cd) <*sody 037-2*> **SACRED CRAG DANCER, CORPSE WHISPERER**
- Extrance / Sacred crag dancer, corpse whisperer / Some men are born posthumously / Late lunch / Another beautiful day, again / Prasanna / Kill that owl / Jeweled escapement / Nachtmystium / The real.

Tompkins Square — Tompkins Square

Aug 06. (cd/lp; shared) <*TSQ 5252*> **BERKELEY GUITAR**
- The augur of deviation / What once was will be / Die until tomorrow sleep / [tracks by Adam Snider] / [tracks by Adam Baldwin].

Feb 08. (ltd-lp+cd-r) <*GNM-006*> **ETERNAL**
- Topinambour / Palak Paneer / Goat seer / The real / Holly / Prompter of conscience / Greetings death love (excerpt). <*cd-iss. Apr 10 on Strange Attractors+=; SAAH 059CD*> - Yellow grey / Indian forgiven.

(above originally issued on Gnome Life)

Nov 10. (cd) <*(TSQ 2486)*> **CHRISTMAS** [festive]
- The first noel / Good King Wenceslas / Little drummer boy / Joy to the world / Silent night, holy night / We three kings / Hark! the herald angels sing / Christmas morning (improvisation I) / Christmas eve (improvisation II) / Christmas time is here, a meditation / O Tannenbaum / O come all ye faithful / Deck the halls / It came upon a midnight clear / Twelve days of Christmas / Auld lang syne.

Strange Attractors — not issued

Aug 11. (cd/lp) <*SAAH 069 CD/LP*> **HUGE FLUID FREEDOM**
- I know you are tired, but come. This is the way / The real / Ourselves when we are real / Huge fluid freedom.

The SMITH SISTERS (⟹ SMITH, Debi)

SOMETYMES WHY

Formed in 2004 as Sometimes Why (not to be confused with the outfit of a similar name who released the set 'Keepsake' in 2005), the all-female neo-traditionalists SOMETYMES WHY came to the fore through the dexterity and panache of core members Kristin Andreassen, Aoife O'Donovan and Ruth Ungar-Merenda, all from various alt-country acts such as Crooked Still, UNCLE EARL, etc.

Taking LUCINDA WILLIAMS and Alison Krauss as their influences, they showed where they were coming from on songs like 'Clover', 'Middle' and 'The Seasick Dawn' from their debut album, **SOMETIMES WHY** (2005) {*6}, and they covered Concrete Blonde's 'Joey' on their Nashville-meets-Britfolk follow-up for Signature Sounds, **YOUR HEART IS A GLORIOUS MACHINE** (2009) {*7}. While there is a hint of The Dixie Chicks about the record, the old-timey folk-blues of 'Slow Down' and 'Glorious Machine' wins through. *MCS*

Kristin Andreassen - vocals, harmonica, acoustic guitar, glockenspiel, tambourine (of UNCLE EARL, of Jolly Bankers) / **Aoife O'Donovan** - vocals, ukulele, piano, Wurlitzer, glockenspiel (of Crooked Still, Wild Band Of Snee, Wayfaring Strangers) / **Ruth Ungar-Merenda** - vocals, fiddle, ukuleles, acoustic guitar, glockenspiel (of Mammals, of Jay Ungar)

US | UK
Sometimes Why | not issued

Jul 05. (cd; as SOMETIMES WHY) *<none>* **SOMETIMES WHY** [ ] [-]
- Middle / I'm tryin' to remember what city I know you from / Hush child / Clover / The rearview mirror / Let down / Too repressed / Shell game / The seasick dawn / Hallowell.

Signature Sounds | not issued

Mar 09. (cd) *<SIG 2019>* **YOUR HEART IS A GLORIOUS MACHINE** [ ] [-]
- Aphrodisiaholic / Slow down / My crazy / Joey / Shine it / Diamond / The stupid kiss / Cold feet blues / Glorious machine / The sound asleep.

SONS OF THE NEVER WRONG

Like a modern-day PETE SEEGER and The WEAVERS or PETER, PAUL & MARY, Chicago-based country-folkies SONS OF THE NEVER WRONG (formed 1992) sounded as though they'd been transported from the harmony-fuelled 1950s and 1960s through a time-warp all of their own. Singers and musicians Bruce Roper (their main songwriter), Sue Demel and Nancy Walker could dip a toe into any genre at the drop of a hat.

The Waterbug releases **THREE GOOD REASONS** (1995) {*6} and **CONSEQUENCE OF SPEECH** (1997) {*6} were prime examples of what they could achieve, popping in and out of styles from the cod-reggae 'Sun Song' to the acoustic post-grunge-meets-calypso 'Waiting'. Imagine The Connells trying to rid themselves of their one-hit-wonder tag.

Folk music has had its elements of surprise over the years, but SONS OF THE NEVER WRONG (now with Deborah Lader replacing Nancy) took ambiguity and diversity to another plateau on their third album, **ONE IF BY HAND** (2000) {*5}. This was not to say that the trio weren't up to scratch, but albums like **4 EVER ON** (2002) {*5} and **NUTHATCH SUITE** (2005) {*5} seemed to be going in too many directions, and they polarised opinion as strongly as Marmite. A switch back to Waterbug from Gadfly resulted in the comeback album **ON A GOOD DAY... I AM** (2009) {*6}. *MCS*

Bruce Roper - vocals, acoustic guitar, accordion, banjo, keyboards / **Sue Demel** - vocals, acoustic guitar, percussion / **Nancy Walker** - vocals, acoustic guitar, mandolin / + session people

US | UK
Waterbug | not issued

Sep 95. (cd) *<WBG 18>* **THREE GOOD REASONS** [ ] [-]
- Three good reasons / Dead on the highway / Alone in the wake (songbird) / Guitar song / Set all God's children free / Tiny blue flowers / Tattoo / Place / Doin' what I like to do / Falling / Lovin' ground / Door of love / Carpenter song / With or with.

Jul 97. (cd) *<WBG 30>* **CONSEQUENCE OF SPEECH** [ ] [-]
- Demi-overture / Maybe, just maybe / #253 in the red book - Bridge over troubled water / Reprise / Small bird / I I I love you / Consequence of speech / Modern dating / Sun song / In your dreams / Reprise / Girl shanty / Waiting / All that I've known / Over? sure!

—— **Deborah Lader** - vocals, guitar, mandolin, slide banjo; repl. Nancy

Gadfly | not issued

Aug 00. (cd) *<GADFLY 268>* **ONE IF BY HAND** [ ] [-]
- Madame Butterfly / Comet / Jonah / My last boyfriend / One simple question / Hallelujah for the getaway / No 1-4 me / Getting better / Secrets / Magnetic poetry / Teva / Home hymn / Sleeping bag.

Aug 02. (cd) *<GADFLY 282>* **4 EVER ON** [ ] [-]
- Way to go / Witness / Looks like Illinois / Mobile / Everybody's gotta / Queen of today / If you come to take me / Toast / Italy (goodnight Lorenza wherever you are) / Frankie / Pocket / Sister / Variations / Forever on.

Aug 05. (cd) *<GADFLY 291>* **NUTHATCH SUITE** [ ] [-]
- Too many / Good for her / Wind - Tree / Tea tale / Here we go babe 1-2-3 / 'Stylish Sue' / Standin' in the dust / Crazy dog / Beside you / Stylish man / Weed / 'Stylish Bruce' / If I knew then / When I was little / Talk to me darlin' / 'Stylish Deb' / Little brown puppy.

Waterbug | not issued

Sep 09. (cd) *<WBG 88>* **ON A GOOD DAY... I AM** [ ] [-]
- I am / I saw sorrow / Intrada / Say goodbye / Pass it on / All in a song / Head over heels / Twiggy little bird / Leona / On a good day / Prodigal son / Interlude / Order in my house / Other things / Pablo Neruda / Intermezzo / Painting the boat / And Intheend.

The SPECTRAL LIGHT & THE MOONSHINE FIREFLY SNAKEOIL JAMBOREE (⟹ STONE BREATH)

Regina SPEKTOR

Female folk singer/songwriters whose main instrument was piano have between few and far between (only JANIS IAN and JONI MITCHELL come to mind), but REGINA SPEKTOR was firmly planted in the anti-folk movement. Born February 19, 1980 in Moscow, her life was turned upside down from the age of nine when she emigrated with her Jewish family to the Bronx, New York. Although she for the most part fitted into the east coast US culture, Regina's first love was the classical piano, which she mastered at the State University of New York Purchase Conservatory.

Inspired by blues, jazz and folk artists including Billie Holiday, JONI MITCHELL and Fiona Apple, Regina showed plenty of promise on two of her earliest self-financed works, **11:11** (2001) {*6} and **SONGS** (2002) {*6}. Her first big break came when They Might Be Giants drummer Alan Bezozi passed her material to Strokes producer Gordon Raphael. Both of them worked on her third set, **SOVIET KITSCH** (2004) {*7}, an inspired record that found a global audience when it was released on Sire Records. Songs like the punky 'Your Honor' (with British band Kill Kenada), 'The Flowers', 'Ode To Divorce' and 'Somedays' found favour with a new generation of disaffected folk fans.

BEGIN TO HOPE (2006) {*8} took her into the mainstream and the charts, its glossy theatrical leanings at their most whimsical and quirky on 'Fidelity' (a minor US hit), the one-that-got-away 'On The Radio' and 'Better'. But was it folk?

She came back with a vengeance on her third Sire album, the over-polished but Top 3 career-best **FAR** (2009) {*6}, though **LIVE IN LONDON** (2010) {*7}, recorded at the Hammersmith Apollo, was much more representative of her earlier style. *MCS*

Regina Spektor - vocals, piano / with session people

US | UK
own label | not issued

Jul 01. (cd) *<none>* **11:11** [-] [-]
- Love affair / Rejazz / Back of a truck / Buildings / Marry Ann / Flyin' / Wasteside / Pavlov's daughter / 2.99 cent blues / Braille / I want to sing / Sunshine.

Feb 02. (cd) *<none>* **SONGS** [-] [-]
- Samson / Oedipus / Prisoners / Reading time with pickle / Consequence of sounds / Daniel Cowman / Bon idee / Aching to pupate / Lounge / Lacrimosa / Lulliby / Ne me quitte pas.

not issued | Shoplifter

Jun 04. (7") *(SLRV 003)* YOUR HONOR. / THE FLOWERS [-] [ ]

Aug 04. (cd) *(SLR 005)* **SOVIET KITSCH** [-] [ ]
- Ode to divorce / Poor little rich boy / Carbon monoxide / The flowers / Us / Sailor song / *** / Your honor / Ghost of corporate future / Chemo limo / Somedays. *<US re-iss. Sep 04 on Sire cd+=/lp; 48953-2/-1>- [DVD stuff]. (UK-iss. Mar 07 on Sire; 9362 49352-2)*

Sire | Transgressive

Sep 05. (cd-ep) *<49459-2>* LIVE AT BULL MOOSE [live at the record store in Portland, Maine] [ ] [-]
- Ain't no cover / Carbon monoxide / Pound of flesh / The noise / My man (medley).

Nov 05. (7") *(TRANS 012)* CARBON MONOXIDE. / Uh-merica [-] [ ]

Jan 06. (cd) *(TRANS 019)* **MARY ANN MEETS THE GRAVEDIGGERS AND OTHER SHORT STORIES** [-] [ ]
- Oedipus / Love affair / Poor little rich boy / Sailor song / Mary Ann / Prisoners / Consequence of sounds / Daniel Cowman / Lacrimosa / Pavlov's daughter / Chemo limo / Us // [DVD tracks].

Feb 06. (cd-s) *(TRANS 018CD)* US / Scarecrow and Fungus [-] [ ]
(7" m+=) *(TRANS 018)* - December.

Sire | Sire

Jun 06. (dl-s) <-> FIDELITY [51] [-]

Jun 06. (cd) *<(9362-44112-2)>* **BEGIN TO HOPE** [20] Jul 06 [53]
- Fidelity / Better / Samson / On the radio / Field below / Hotel song / Apres moi / 20 years of snow / That time / Edit / Lady / Summer in the city. *<(cd w/cd-ep+=; 9362 44315-2)>* - Another town / Uh-merica / Baobabs / Dusseldorf / Music box. *<d-lp iss. Apr 09 ++=; 517761-1>* - Better [piano and voice] / Better [radio recut] / Hero / Bartender.

Jul 06. (7") *(W 718)* ON THE RADIO. / Ain't No Cover [-] [ ]
(7") *(W 718X)* - ['A'] / 20 years of snow [live].
(cd-s) *(W 718CD)* - ['A'] / Dusseldorf.

Feb 07. (cd-ep) *<101250-2>* LIVE IN CALIFORNIA 2006 EP [live at The Avalon, LA] [ ] [-]
- Fidelity / Field below / Sailor song / Ghost of corporate future.

Mar 07. (7"/cd-s) *(W 737/+CD1)* FIDELITY. / Music Box [-] [ ]
(cd-s+=) *(W 737CD2)* - December / ['A'-video].

Aug 07. (7") *<7-261884>* BETTER [radio recut]. / Better [piano and voice] [ ] [-]

May 09. (dl-s) <-> LAUGHING WITH / BLUE LIPS [ ] [-]

Jun 09. (cd-ep) *<520219-2>* LAUGHING WITH ...[EP]... [ ] [-]
- Laughing with / Folding chair / The call / The noise [live].

Jun 09. (cd) *<519396-2> (9362 49746-5)* **FAR** [3] [30]
- The calculation / Eet / Blue lips / Folding chair / Machine / Laughing with / Human of the year / Two birds / Dance anthem of the 80s / Genius next door / Wallet / One more time with feeling / Man of a thousand faces. *<cd w/dvd+=; 519748-2>* - Time is all around / The sword and the pen // [DVD tracks].

Nov 10. (cd+dvd/d-lp) *<525512-2/-1>* **LIVE IN LONDON**
[live December 4, 2009]
- On the radio / Eet / Folding chair / Blue lips / Apres moi / Dance anthem of the 80s / Silly eye-color generalizations / Bobbing for apples / Wallet / Ode to divorce / That time / The calculation / Machine / Laughing with / Man of a thousand faces / Hotel song / Us / Fidelity / Samson / The call / Love, you're a whore // [DVD tracks].

SPIRES THAT IN THE SUNSET RISE

Taking freak-folk to new extremes, the Spires are the musical equivalent of the Blair Witch Project, fusing oblique, apocalyptic sounds with dark, uneasy, off-kilter psychedelics. Formed in 2003 in Decatur, Illinois by vocalists and multi-instrumentalists Kathleen Baird, Taralie Peterson and Georgia Vallas, the trio soon relocated to nearby Chicago. Inspired by Lydia Lunch, Danielle Dax, CURRENT 93 and COMUS, they almost immediately conjured up their debut set, the self-titled **SPIRES THAT IN THE SUNSET RISE** (2003) {*4}.

Experimental to the nth degree, this album (featuring guest Anne Fritz on cello and violin) involves some serious listening. Those who prefer melody over tortured chaos might want to try 'Leader Of Change And The Leader Of Within', 'No Fate' (very Slits/Raincoats) and 'I Follow You Follow Me'.

With the addition of Tracy Peterson, **FOUR WINDS THE WALKER** (2005) {*6} was a marked improvement, albeit in a Yoko Ono-meets-Godz kind of way. Whether it was ESP-Disk eclecticism or sheer musical pandemonium, it was certainly free-form folk or jazz laid bare in an unprecedented way. The eight-minute 'This Ain't For Mama' just about says it all.

The solo KATHLEEN BAIRD was an altogether more moderate freak-folk proposition. **LULLABY FOR STRANGERS** (2006) {*6} - her earliest recordings from 2000-2001 - had a more soothing and calm effect, while as TRAVELING BELL, under which name she released **SCATTER WAYS** (2005) {*6}, she could sound like the new NICO.

The SPIRES rose again on **THIS IS FIRE** (2006) {*6}, a strident blend of detached, self-indulgent acid-folk that might wake the dead. Appealing to a probable fan base of Ouija-boarders and LARKIN GRIMM fans, it has plenty of tracks to blow your mind, while 'Bee Forms', 'Desert Mind' and Morning Song' might at a stretch be described as their most accessible material.

Reverting to a trio (without sister Tracy, but with GREG WEEKS of ESPERS at the desk), **CURSE THE TRACED BIRD** (2008) {*7} propelled the trio across the fluctuating border between psych-folk and indie improv. There were still uneasy pickings to be had, as on the nine-minute 'Party Favors', but the album showed fluidity in 'Java Pop' and the banjo-plucking 'Pouring Mind'. The SPIRES now reside in Madison, Wisconsin. *MCS*

Kathleen Baird - vocals, spike fiddle, guitars, harmonium, organ, banjo, drums, percussion / **Taralie Peterson** - vocals, slide guitar, violin, lap harp, spike fiddle, bowed banjo, guitars, zither / **Georgia Vallas** - autoharp, recorder, harmonium, zither, lap/slide guitar, drums, percussion, vocals

US / UK
Galactic Zoo - Eclipse / not issued

2003. (lp) *<GZD - ECL-01>* **SPIRES THAT IN THE SUNSET RISE**
- I am sewn / Birds of paradise / Crooked spine / Rattlesnake / Leader of change and the leader of within / Tampico / No fate / I follow you follow me / Moonhouse / Bells don't ring at night. *<cd-iss. Dec 04 on Graveface; grave 11>*

—— added **Tracy Peterson** - percussion, guitar, cello, washboard, drums, little harp, vocals

Secret Eye / not issued

Jul 05. (cd) *<AB-OC-17>* **FOUR WINDS THE WALKER**
- Four winds / Wide awake / Little for a lot / Sheye / Sort sands / Ong song / This ain't for mama / Shining / No matter / Imaginary skin / Serum / The May ham / Born in a room / The walker.

2005. (ltd-shared-7" purple) *<NIHIL 32>* LITTLE FOR A LOT. /
[other by Panicsville]

(above issued on Nihilist)

Oct 06. (cd) *<AB-OC-28>* **THIS IS FIRE**
- Spike fiddle song / Clouds / Sleeplike / Morning song / Sea shanty / Let the crows fly / Bee forms / Desert mind.

—— now a trio when Tracy departed

Feb 08. (cd/lp) *<AB-OC-38>* **CURSE THE TRACED BIRD**
- Black earth / Java pop / Party favors / Equus haar / Underscore / Red fall / Pouring mind.

KATHLEEN BAIRD

solo on all vocals and instruments

Secret Eye / not issued

May 05. (cd; as TRAVELING BELL) *<AB-OC-15>* **SCATTER WAYS**
- Scatter ways / Untitled / Calm in trees / Song for Eno / Treasures and griefs / Indecision song / Solving, dissolving forces / You are my blood / Through my sleeves / Fog of the dust / Let you go / Dark fair / Claims (ferry song).

Apr 06. (m-cd) *<AB-OC-23>* **LULLABY FOR STRANGERS**
(rec. 2000–2001)
- Traps / Breaking the roofs / Morning song #1 / Myself as the shore / The last word / Lost anchors / Morning song #2 / With which these waters swarm / Bury deeper / Storms stay fine.

Devon SPROULE

Girl-next-door Canadian singer/songwriter DEVON SPROULE (b. April 23, 1982 in Kingston, Ontario) has made her base in Charlottesville, Virginia, having spent a lot of her alternative childhood in the eco-village community of Twin Oaks. She is married to fellow country-folk-blues artist PAUL CURRERI, who paid homage to her on 'Songs For Devon Sproule' (2003).

While still at high school she decided on a music career, and at 17 she embarked on a nationwide tour and released her debut album, **DEVON** (2000) {*6}. Her second set, **LONG SLEEVE STORY** (2001) {*6}, took her further, winning plaudits from the likes of the 'Village Voice'. Her Gibson ES-125 'jazz' guitar certainly brought a distinctive flavour to her sound.

UPSTATE SONGS (2003) {*7} (a favourite of 'Rolling Stone' magazine) and **KEEP YOUR SILVER SHINED** (2007) {*7} brought other, timeless elements to the table, and the inclusion of old-timey songs was a definite feather in her cap. By the time she released her third CD for Tin Angel, **I LOVE YOU, GO EASY** (2011) {*6} (the first two were **DON'T HURRY FOR HEAVEN** (2009) {*6} and **LIVE IN LONDON** (2010) {*6}), her numerous awards included the prestigious ASCAP Foundation Sammy Cahn Prize (shared with newcomer Oren Lavie) of 2009. *MCS*

Devon Sproule - vocals, guitars / + session band

US / UK
Three Word / not issued

Jan 00. (cd) *<001>* **DEVON**
- Rain song / Hysterically / Survive alone / Montreal waltz / New song / Generic love song / Deeply you / Appreciate me.

Nov 01. (cd) *<002>* **LONG SLEEVE STORY**
- 25 mph / Sleep satisfied / What I'm used to / Fast statue / Better at night / Keep light / Way up there / She's not here / Let me in on it / Long sleeve story / Swamp love / Bird feeder.

City Salvage / not issued

Jun 03. (cd) *<CSR 06>* **UPSTATE SONGS**
- Plea for a good night's rest / Come comet or dove / Farewell, seasick suffering! / Tristan and Isolde / Should have been snow / You aren't really here, it isn't really light out / White kite at Georgetown Green / My baby just cares for me / Last summer's lifeguard / Country sun. *<(re-iss. Jan 09 on Tin Angel; TAR 002)>*

Apr 07. (cd) *<CSR 16>* **KEEP YOUR SILVER SHINED**
- Old Virginia block / Keep your silver shined / 1340 Chesapeake St / Let's go out / The well-dressed son to his sweetheart / Eloise and Alex / Does the day feel long? / Dress sharp, play well, be modest / Stop by anytime / The weeping willow. *<also iss. on Waterbug; WBG 75> <(re-iss. Dec 08 on Tin Angel; TAR 001)>*

Tin Angel / Tin Angel

May 09. (cd) *<(TAR 010)>* **DON'T HURRY FOR HEAVEN**
- Ain't that the way / Julie / Healthy parents, happy couple / You need a Maria / Don't hurry for heaven / Good to get out / The easier way / Bowling green / Sponji reggae / A picture of us in the garden. *<re-iss. Mar 10 on Black Hen'; BHCD-060>*

Sep 10. (cd+dvd) *<(TAR 018)>* **LIVE IN LONDON**
[live at Queen Elizabeth Hall]
- Julie / The weeping willow / Sponji reggae / One eye open / Come comet or dove / Plea for a good night's rest / Old Virginia block / Stop by anytime / Ain't that the way / Steady and true. // [+ DVD tracks].

May 11. (cd/lp) *(TAR 024/+LP)* **I LOVE YOU, GO EASY**
- If I can do this / I love you, go easy / The unmarked animals / Monk/monkey / Runs in the family / The warning bell / The evening ghost crab / The faulty body / Body's in trouble / Now's the time.

Sufjan STEVENS

Few pop/rock artists have made music in as many genres as SUFJAN (pr. 'suifjain') STEVENS. Born July 1, 1975 in Detroit but raised from the age of nine in nearby Petoskey, Michigan, the singer/songwriter and multi-instrumentalist (guitar, bass, sitar, banjo, xylophone, piano, French horn, recorder, vibraphone, oboe, drums, etc) cut his teeth with Marzuki, a folk band named for his brother, a famous marathon runner.

While attending Hope College, Holland, Michigan, Sufjan and his stepfather founded the Asthmatic Kitty imprint in 1999, the outlet that would release STEVENS's debut set **A SUN CAME!** (2000) {*8}. Reflecting his upbringing listening to ethnic folk musics from the Middle East (his name is Persian and means 'comes with a sword'), the record is a hotchpotch of global folk sounds.

Recorded on a four-track, this superb debut opens with three gems, 'We Are What You Say', 'A Winner Needs A Wand' and the whispering 'Rake' (sometimes called 'You Are The Rake'). However, the album starts to take a different - grungy, Sonic Youth - direction by track five, 'Demetrius' (also on 'The Oracle Said Wander'), while 'Dumb I Sound' and 'Wordsworth's Ridge' receive a Celtic-rock twist. By track nine, an unrecognisable cover of the Jeff Beck Group's 'Rice Pudding', things go a little haywire and Daniel Johnston-like. Turning his back on folk in favour of electronica and indie-pop, STEVENS becomes impossible to pigeonhole on 'A Loverless Bed (w/out Remission)', 'Super Sexy Woman', 'Happy Birthday' and 'Jason'.

For the last three numbers, 'Kill', 'Ya Leil' and the title track, STEVENS returns to folky singer-songwriter mould. This notably disparate set lasts for more than an hour, the re-issue with bonus tracks even longer.

ENJOY YOUR RABBIT (2001) {*7} was a radical departure from his pan-ethnic folk debut as this time around, taking the Chinese zodiac as his theme, he opted for ambitious knob-twiddling with playful blips and bleeps. From 'Year Of The Monkey' to the 13-minute 'Year Of The Horse', everything here could best be described as Oldfield-esque or Tomita-like. Accompanied by Liz Janes (occasional voice) and Tom Eaton (trumpet), this is Sufjan taking his first of many musical excursions. Check out 'Year Of The Snake' at least.

Paying homage to his home state, **GREETINGS FROM MICHIGAN: THE GREAT LAKE STATE** (2003) {*7} was an enterprising display of rustic folk that edged into the gap between Jim O'Rourke and Stereolab without going entirely AWOL from its home genre, and The Danielson Famile (Daniel, Megan and Elin) added their mantra-minstrel harmonies to great effect. Harking back to SIMON & GARFUNKEL (a big influence no doubt), 'Say Yes! To M!ch!gan!' and 'Holland' are just superb.

The Danielson Famile-produced **SEVEN SWANS** (2004) {*7} continued STEVENS's progress toward folk stardom. His ambitious musical road trip continued with the prog-folk-like **COME ON FEEL THE ILLINOISE** (2005) {*7}, a part-orchestral set closer to The Polyphonic Spree than shape-shifting folk music. Hot on its heels came 2006's **THE AVALANCHE** {*6}, which was made up of out-takes from his preceding double album.

Word of mouth spread rapidly, and his next projects, **THE AGE OF ADZ** (2010) {*7} and the accompanying 59-minute **ALL DELIGHTED PEOPLE EP** {*6}, found Sufjan riding high in the Top 30. Folk music might have had been sacrificed for conceptual electro-orchestral manoeuvres in the studio, but he was the master of musical exorcism. *MCS*

Sufjan Stevens - vocals, multi

US Asthmatic Kitty / UK not issued

Jun 00. (cd) *<AKR 001>* **A SUN CAME!** [ ] [–]
- We are what you say / A winner needs a wand / Rake / Siamese twins / Demetrius / Dumb I sound / Wordsworth's ridge / Belly button / Rice pudding / A loverless bed (w/out remission) / Godzuki / Super sexy woman / The oracle said wander / Happy birthday / Jason / Kill / Ya leil / A sun came / Satan's saxophones. *<(re+UK-iss. Jul 04 on Asthmatic Kitty+=; AKR 009CD)>* - Joy! joy! joy! [rec. Brooklyn 2001] / You are the rake [rec. 2004]

Sep 01. (cd) *<AKR 003CD>* **ENJOY YOUR RABBIT** [ ] [–]
- Year of the asthmatic cat / Year of the monkey / Year of the rat / Year of the ox / Year of the boar / Year of the tiger / Year of the snake / Year of the sheep / Year of the rooster / Year of the dragon / Enjoy your rabbit / Year of the dog / Year of the horse / Year of our Lord. *(UK-iss. Jun 04; same as US) <(re-mixed cd/lp Nov 09 by OSSO diff. track order; AKR 049/+LP)>*

Jul 03. (cd) *<AKR 007CD>* **GREETINGS FROM MICHIGAN: THE GREAT LAKE STATE** [ ] [–]
- Flint (for the unemployed and underpaid) / All good naysayers, speak up! or forever hold your peace! / For the widows in paradise, for the fatherless in Ypsilanti / Say yes! to M!ch!gan! / The upper peninsula / Tahquamenon Falls / Holland / Detroit, lift up your weary head! (rebuild! restore! reconsider!) / Romulus / Alanson, crooked river / Sleeping Bear, Sault Saint Marie / They also mourn who do not wear black (for the homeless in Muskegon) / Oh God, where are you now? (in Pickeral Lake? Pigeon? Marquette? Mackinaw?) / Redford (for Yia-Yia and Pappou) / Vito's ordination song. *<d-lp-iss. Jul 03 on Sounds Familyre; SF 010> (UK re-iss. Jun 04 on Rough Trade+=; RTRADCD 170)- Marching band / Pickeral Lake.*

Sounds Familyre / Rough Trade

Mar 04. (7") *(RTRADS 169)* THE DRESS LOOKS NICE ON YOU. / Borderline [–] [ ]

Mar 04. (cd) *<SF 013> (RTRADCD 162)* **SEVEN SWANS** [ ] Apr 04 [ ]
- All the trees of the field will clap their hands / The dress looks nice on you / In the Devil's territory / To be alone with you / Abraham / Sister / Size too small / We won't need legs to stand / A good man is hard to find / He woke me up again / Seven swans / The transfiguration. *<lp-iss. Mar 04 with Burnt Toast Vinyl; btv 058> <lp-iss. Jan 07 w/7"+=; SF 018>- I Went Dancing With My Sister. / Waste Of What Your Kids Won't Have*

Asthmatic Kitty / Rough Trade

Jul 05. (cd) *<AKR 014CD> (RTRADCD 250)* **COME ON FEEL THE ILLINOISE** [ ] [ ]
- Concerning the UFO sighting near Highland, Illinois / The Black Hawk war, or, how to demolish an entire civilization and still feel good about yourself in the morning, or, we apologize for the inconvenience but you're going to have to leave now, or, 'I have fought the Big Knives and will continue to fight them until they are off our lands!' / Come on! feel the Illinoise! Part 1: The world's Columbian exposition, Part 2: Carl Sandburg visits me in a dream / John Wayne Gacy, Jr / Jacksonville / A short reprise for Mary Todd, who went insane, but for very good reasons / Decatur, or, round of applause for your stepmother! / One last 'whoo-hoo!' for the Pullman / Chicago / Casimir Pulaski day / To the workers of the Rock River Valley region, I have an idea concerning your predicament / The man of Metropolis steals our hearts / Prairie fire that wanders about / A conjunction of drones simulating the way in which Sufjan Stevens has an existential crisis in the Great Godfrey maze / The predatory wasp of the Palisades is out to get us! / They are night zombies!! They are neighbors!! They have come back from the dead!! ahhhh! / Let's hear that string part again, because I don't think they heard it all the way out in Bushnell / In this temple as in the hearts of man for whom he saved the Earth / The seer's tower / The tallest man, the broadest shoulders Part 1: The great frontier, Part 2: Come to see me only with playthings now / Riffs and variations on a single note for Jelly Roll, Earl Hines, Louis Armstrong, Baby Dodds and the king of swing, to name a few / Out of Egypt, into the great laugh of mankind, and I shake the dirt from my sandals as I run.

Jul 06. (cd) <AKR 022CD> (RTRADCD 350) **THE AVALANCHE** (outtakes and extras from the 'Illinoise' album) [71] [ ]
- The avalanche / Dear Mr Supercomputer / Adlai Stevenson / The Vivian Girls are visited in the night by Saint Dargarius and his squadron of benevolent butterflies / Chicago (acoustic version) / The Henney Buggy band / Saul Bellow / Carlyle Lake / Springfield, or Bobby got a shadfly caught in his hair / The mistress witch from McClure (or, the mind that knows itself) / Kaskaskia river / Chicago (adult contemporary easy listening version) / Inaugural pop music for Jane Margaret Byrne / No man's land / The Palm Sunday tornado hits Crystal Lake / The pick-up / The perpetual self, or 'what would Saul Alinsky do?' / For Clyde Tombaugh / Chicago (multiple personality disorder version) / Pittsfield / The undivided self (for Eppie and Popo).

Nov 06. (5-cd-ep-box) *<AKR 028CD> (RTRADCD 450)* **SONGS FOR CHRISTMAS SINGALONG** (festive compilation) [ ] [ ]
- NOEL (2001) VOL.1:- Silent night / O come O come Emmanuel / We're goin' to the country! / Lo! how a rose e'er blooming / It's Christmas! Let's be glad! / Holy holy, etc. / Amazing grace // HARK! (2002) VOL.II:- Angels we have heard on high / Put the lights on the tree / Come thou fount of every blessing / I saw three ships / Only at Christmas time / Once in Royal David's city / Hark! the herald angels sing! / What child is this anyway? / Bring a torch, Jeanette, Isabella // DING! DONG! (2003) VOL.III:- O come, O come Emmanuel / Come on! let's boogie to the elf dance! / We three kings / O holy night / That was the worst Christmas ever! / Ding! dong! / All the king's horns / The friendly beasts // JOY! (2005) VOL.IV:- The little drummer boy / Away in a manger / Hey guys! It's Christmas time! / The first noel / Did I make you cry on Christmas Day? (well, you deserved it!) / The incarnation / Joy to the world // PEACE (2006) VOL.V:- Once in Royal David's city / Get behind me, Santa! / Jingle bells / Christmas in July / Lo! how a rose e'er blooming / Jupiter winter / Sister winter / O come O come Emmanuel / Star of wonder / Holy, holy, holy / The winter solstice.

Oct 09. (cd/d-lp) *<AKR 278/+LP> (RTRAD CD/LP 550)* **THE BQE** (film music suite) [ ] [ ]
- Prelude on the Esplanade / Introductory fanfare for the Hooper heroes / Movement I: In the countenance of kings / Movement II: Sleeping invader / Interlude I: Dream sequence in subi circumnavigation / Movement III: Linear tableau with intersecting surprise / Movement IV: Traffic shock / Movement V: Self-organizing emergent patterns / Interlude II: Subi power waltz / Interlude III: Invisible accidents / Movement VI: Isorhythmic night dance with interchanges / Movement VII (finale): The emperor of centrifuge / Postlude: Critical mass / The original cinematic suite in widescreen triptych display.

(above is crossover-classical music) (below are not entirely folk releases)

Asthmatic Kitty / Asthmatic Kitty

Oct 10. (cd/d-lp) <*(AKR 077/+LP)*> **THE AGE OF ADZ** [7] [30]
- Futile devices / Too much / The age of Adz / I walked / Now that I'm older / Get

real get right / Bad communication / Vesuvius / All for myself / I want to be well / Impossible soul.

Dec 10. (cd) *<(AKR 075/+LP)>* **ALL DELIGHTED PEOPLE EP** [27]
- All delighted people [original version] / Enchanting ghost / Heirloom / From the mouth of Gabriel / The owl and the tanager / All delighted people [classic rock version] / Arnika / Djohariah.

STONE BREATH

Formed over 1995 to 2006 by vocalist and multi-instrumentalist Timothy Renner, whom many folk buffs will know from MOURNING CLOAK, a one-off apocalyptic folk act that delivered **IN DREAMS YOU SEE** (1996) {*6}. This was basically just a project (featuring Stone Breath alumni Paul Chavez and Alison Renner, Timothy's wife) that led up to the one under discussion here, and you can hear aspects of CURRENT 93, Dead Can Dance and The INCREDIBLE STRING BAND on exotic tracks like 'The Space Between Everything' and 'Honey Mushrooms And The Nature Of Darkness'.

Timothy meanwhile had set up his own imprint, Hand/Eye, with Alison while developing the more experimental STONE BREATH. Located somewhere between space-rock and acid-folk, and initially issued on the Camera Obscura label, **SONGS OF MOONLIGHT AND RAIN** (1997) {*6} was out there in a ghost garden of unearthly delights, exemplified by the CURRENT 93-esque 'Perched Upon The Temple Bell, The Butterfly Sleeps' and 'Seven Things Placed In A Hollow Tree'.

For the follow-up, **A SILVER THREAD TO WEAVE THE SEASONS** (2000) {*7}, Timothy recruited another multi-talented solo artist, PRYDWYN (Piper), and there was also room on board for Sarada (Holt) and R.A. Campbell.

Definitely folk on the fringes of freaky, as was **LANTERNA LUCIS VIRIDITATIS** (2000) {*6}, which mixed original material with a raft of covers (and more when re-issued later) including 'It's Hard To Dance With The Devil On Your Back' and 'Bitter Was The Night' (SYDNEY CARTER), 'Solomon's Song' and 'Osiris' (CLIVE PALMER), 'A Soldier's Dream' (DONOVAN), 'Love Song' (DERROLL ADAMS) and 'Man Should Surrender' (Pailhead).

Although some of Renner's work has yet to reach the ears of this discography, STONE BREATH's work with PRYDWYN and Sarada on **THE SILVER SKEIN UNWOUND** (2003) {*7} certainly sounded the part - mediaeval, mythical, magical and macabre. 2008's **KNOTWORK** {*6} was also cool.

For Renner's BLACK HAPPY DAY project he teamed up with Tara Vanflower, who had issued an ambient shoegazer set, 'This Womb Like Liquid Honey' (1999), before completing her work with Mike VanPortfleet (her colleague in the gothic/darkwave Lycia) on the mini-set 'The Time Has Come And Gone' (2000). While Lycia delivered several albums in the 1990s and 2000s, Tara took time to record a second solo outing, 'My Little Fire-Filled Heart' (2005). **THE GARDEN OF THE GHOSTFLOWERS** (2006) {*6} had at least four barely recognisable trad tracks, namely 'The Leaves Of Life', 'Edward', 'A Lyke Wake Dirge' (made famous by PENTANGLE) and 'Be Thou My Vision'.

Among his numerous other guises, Jenner's most traditional and sourced set was SPECTRAL LIGHT's **SCARECROW STUFFING** (2002) {*6}. In 2007-2008 he worked with A.E. Hoskin on a series of mystical ritual/psychedelic/dub-folk recordings (see discography) under the avant-garde banner of Crow Tongue. *MCS*

MOURNING CLOAK

Timothy Renner - vocals, instruments / **Paul Chavez** (of Tranquil) / **Alison Renner**

UK Hand/Eye — US not issued

1995. (ltd-7" m) *<h/e 001>* STARGAZER. / Runecast Heartflower / The Starlit Night Of Waking Dreams

Minefield — not issued

1996. (cd) *<MindCD 01>* **IN DREAMS YOU SEE**
- Honey mushrooms and the nature of darkness / Darkened day's memory / The secret path / Chrysalis repose / Mistbreather / Butterfly sleeping wind / Incantation / Entelekia / The space between everything / Dreamlines / Moth's wing / The eleventh letter / Bright.

—— **P.J. Dorsey** - guitars, sitar, synths; repl. Chavez

Ichor — not issued

1999. (cd) *<ich 002>* **BEYOND**
- Stargazing / The dreaming mask / Sidereal shadows / Words on petals / The prayer of St Francis...

STONE BREATH

Timothy Renner plus **Alison Renner** - multi instruments and vocals

Hand/Eye — not issued

Oct 96. (ltd-7"clear-ep) *<h/e 002>* STRANGE FAMILIARS EP
- Seven things placed in the heart of a tree / Footprints of a ghost girl / My ghost / The strength to face the stars again / Will o' wisp (honey mushrooms and the nature of darkness).

Camera Obscura — not issued

1997. (cd) *<CAM 001CD>* **SONGS OF MOONLIGHT AND RAIN**
- The ghosts of sounds long dead / Seven things placed in a hollow tree / Pennies (stolen from the eyes of a dead man) / Wisdom on the moth's wing / Perched upon the temple bell, the butterfly sleeps / Flowers on your grave / Earthlights / The sound of ghosts long dead / Words written on petals / Willowisp / The strength to face the stars above / To cull undying flowers / The flight of the black swan / Long lost friend / Snaketooth vision. *<(UK+re-iss. Oct 07 on Hand/Eye+=; h/e 031)>* - Footprints of a ghost girl / My ghost / Leafwalker / Funeral gifts / Rain song / Snaketooth vision (birth) / Seal of seasons / Will-o-Wisp [feat. FIT & LIMO] / The long lost friend (cobweb'ed).

—— **Timothy** added **Prydwyn Piper** - vocals, whistle, flute, harmonium, bull-fiddle, bouzouki, percussion / **Sarada (Holt)** - vocals, guitar drones + **R.A. Campbell** - bass, mastering

Apr 00. (cd) *<(CAM 010CD)>* **A SILVER THREAD TO WEAVE THE SEASONS**
- Seed / The silver thread / The rainbow-gilded leaves of autumn / Peppermint and clover honey / The clouds of red twilight / Evening air / Summer's night / My heart is an acorn buried in the black earth / Odalisque / Fleance / Rain of days / Listen, listen, listen / Leaves about our feet, we reached for the moon / Devotional one / Devotional two. *<(d-cd UK+re-iss. Feb 08 on Hand/Eye+= w/ The SPECTRAL LIGHT AND MOONSHINE FIREFLY SNAKEOIL JAMBOREE tracks*; h/e 033)>* - Through the trees (a prophecy) / The bone collector (*) / Path of nails (*) / Dark globe / Black horse ride (*) / The song of the scarecrow (*) / Golden hair / Stealing the fire from heaven (*) / Thirteen (*) / Red twilight [feat. FIT & LIMO] / Listen listen [Agape mix] / Devotional three (always all one, all ways alone).

Hand/Eye — not issued

Oct 00. (ltd-7" ep; shared) *<h/e 005>* THE SILENCE OF A MILLION TONGUES
- Treehugger - Decay / [two FIT & LIMO tracks] / The unbinding string (epistle to Prydwyn).

Nov 00. (cd) *<h/e 006>* **LANTERNA LUCIS VIRIDITATIS**
- Sunshine in the eyes of death / The eyelit path / Sword baptismal / Solomon's song / The way of the green Osiris / John Barleycorn / The red cross knight / It's hard to dance with the Devil on your back / Sleep then, with the incense of orchids around you / The face of God / Estampie / Moongazer / The lantern of the greening light. *<d-cd-iss. Nov 08 +=; h/e 042>* - Osiris / The blood of the woven-vine / A soldier's dream / The song of the last / Of bloody wings and sleep's death / Love song / Footprints filled with rain / Treehugger - Decay / The unbinding string (epistle to Prydwyn) / Man should surrender / [live]:- The eyes of death [feat. FIT & LIMO] / A bottle of breath / The heart and star of scared memory / The house carpenter / The lantern of the greening light.

Time-Lag — Vauva

2002. (ltd-7"; in shared V/A box) *<Time-Lag 008>* EPHRATA (LET WATER PASS ABOVE ME). / The Passing Of The River Waltz / Bitter Was The Night

2002. (7") *(VAUVA-04)* GREEN SHROUDS FOR DEAD GODS... GREEN SWADDLING FOR GODS REBORN
- The dead-leaf relics / A dream of you in the garden of Gethsemane.

not issued — September Gurls

2003. (cd; as BREATHE STONE) *(???)* **HEX THISTLE** — German
- A thread in the silver skein / Candle, corpse and bell / Ophelia / Funeral masque, funeral mask / The song of the thrones at the lantern / Down in yon forest.

Hand/Eye — not issued

2003. (cd-ep; shared) *<h/e 012>* [The Does: Sleep Deprivation Blues] / CROW OMENS
- [The Does tracks] / Rara avis / Crow omens / Maria walks amid the thorn.

Camera Obscura — Camera Obscura

Nov 03. (cd) *<(CAM 061CD)>* **THE SILVER SKEIN UNWOUND**
- [*] / Wasp-sting, thorn, and arrowhead / A bottle of breath / The prayer of the circling birds / Last lost love song / Secrets bound in skin / Through the trees again / Bless the lily, bless the rose / Ephrata sacred heart / Midgard for a dreamless sleeper - The false bird / The hidden heart / For those with ears to hear us / Let the towers fall / Arrowhead, thorn, and wasp-sting. *<re-iss. Jun 09 +=; h/e 045>* - Veil of tears [insert *].

—— next with added guests: **B'Eirth, Michael Anderson, Margie Wienk, Matt Everett**

Hand/Eye — not issued

Mar 05. (ltd-cd-r) *<h/e-moon 1>* **REVELATION MOON**
- Revelation.

Dec 07. (cd-s) *<hew 03>* THE HOLLY CROWN. / Christmastime Will Soon Be Over

Nov 09. (c/lp) *<h/e 046>* **THE SHEPHERDESS AND THE BONE-WHITE BIRD**
- The song of the bone-white bird / The vision of the face in the well / In a breath: one thousand years / Even the dead shall sing / The shepherdess of the fiery wheels.

- (5-7*) compilations, etc.-

Jan 04. (cd) *Perun; (Run 0404)* **THE LONG LOST FRIEND: A PATCHWORK** Poland
- (Stones Breathed): Long lost friend [cobweb'ed version] / Leafwalker / Footprints of a ghost girl / My ghost / Through the trees (a prophecy) / The song of the last / Footprints filled with rain / Treehugger - Decay / The unbinding string (epistle to Prydwyn) / (Stones Gathered): Listen, listen [Agape mix] / Osiris / On that long ago lazy day / Dark globe / Golden hair / Man should surrender / (Stones Cast): The heart and star of sacred memory / The house carpenter / The lantern of the greening light / The long lost friend.

Nov 08. (cd) *Hand/Eye; <h/e 043>* **KNOTWORK**
- The passing of the river waltz / A silver crown song / A dream of you in the garden of Gethsemane / Bitter was the night / The dead-leaf relics / Where the holy ghosts haunt the forest gods / Ring thing / Sacco's last letter / The lily and the heron / Shine on harvest moon / Christmastime will soon be over / The holly crown.

The SPECTRAL LIGHT AND MOONSHINE FIREFLY SNAKEOIL JAMBOREE

Timothy Renner

Dark Holler not issued

Jul 02. (cd) *<Hollr 991>* **SCARECROW STUFFING**
- God bless the moon / Tom Dula / Path of nails / Black horse ride / Cold rain and snow / The song of the scarecrow / Walkin' in the parlor / A conversation with death / The bone collector / The cuckoo / Stealing the fire from heaven / Little Margaret / House carpenter / Thirteen / Satan, your kingdom must come down / Untitled. *<d-lp-iss. Jul 04 on Acony Bell+=; none>* - BURNING MILLS:- The rolling mills are burning down / Little Matty Grover / The two magicians / Gallows pole / The three dead boys / O the dreadful wind and rain / Gypsy Davey / The witch mother / Sleep baby sleep...

2003. (cd-ep) *<Hollr 232>* THE GRAVEDIGGER'S LAMENT AND THE UNQUIET DEAD
- Sweet Nora Lee - June apple / Two white horses / Dark holler blues / In the pines / Death letter / The unquiet grave.

MOTH MASQUE

Timothy, Revelator - vocals, banjo + **Alicia** - vocals (of Funeral)

Hand/Eye not issued

2005. (cd-r) *<h/e 016>* **UNTITLED**
- Hope beneath the stars / Beneath wing shadows / Flutter / Kindred moth / Staring into the stars / A moth history - Moon under moon / Wisdom on the moth's wing / The dance / Moth rest / Skeletonizer / Moth angel chant / More symbols thrown.

TIMOTHY, REVELATOR

Hand/Eye not issued

2005. (m-cd) *<h/e 017>* **BENEATH THE BLEEDING MOON: LOST GOSPEL MUSIC VOLUME ONE**
- The weeping eye of God / Petals on the arms of the wind / On the still surviving marks of our saviour's wounds / Blessed of the holy trees / In silence and in shadow keep / Upon the infant martyrs / Song upon the bleeding crucifix / Within your halo / A song / Angel of the first dream / Another eye.

Insurrection not issued

2007. (ltd-cd; as TIMOTHY) *<#013>* **PRIMITIVE RECORDINGS**
- Angeline / Little Sadie / The queen of all gypsies / Dyin' bed / Pretty Polly / Haunted road blues / The valley / Summer's night / Lazy farmer / Friday morning / Satan your kingdom must come down / The cuckoo bird / Curtains of night / Two white horses.

BLACK HAPPY DAY

Timothy with **Tara Vanflower** - vocals (ex-Estraya, of Lycia)

Silber Silber

Sep 06. (cd) *<(silber 053)>* **IN THE GARDEN OF THE GHOSTFLOWERS** Apr 07
- The leaves of life / In the garden of the ghostflowers / Whore / Edward / Of the wind and loneliness / How they weep and moan! / A lyke wake dirge / How many hours 'til the spider's work is done? / Wolf and hare / Hand in hand / Be thou my vision.

HOOFBEAT, CAW & THUNDER

Timothy, Revelator + Shane Speal + Sarada

Jun 07. (cd) *<h/e 024>* **HOOFBEAT, CAW & THUNDER**
- I / II / III / IV / V / VI / VII / VIII / IX.

CROW TONGUE

Timothy plus **A.E. Hoskin** - tabla

2007. (m-cd-r) *<h/e 027>* **DITCH MIX VOLUME TWO**
- Wake Nicodemus / Prayers for the dead / Chant revolution / The red hand mark.

2007. (m-cd-r) *<h/e 029>* **DITCH MIX VOLUME THREE**
- Crowskull chapel.

2008. (cd) *<h/e 034>* **GHOST: EYE: SEEKER**
- Ghost eye gaze: Ghost eye see - Brightless gaze, the true vision - The silverspun web - Cloud eye sight - Beneath wings, above wind / Seeker: Seeker chant - Dream asleep, pray awake / Candle, corpse and bell.

2008. (m-cd) *<h/e 036>* **THE RED HAND MARK**
- The red hand mark / Ghost seeds / Osiris / Ypres / Sixteen hooves / The prophets' dream.

2008. (cd-r) *<h/e 036>* **PROPHECIES AND SECRETS (The Red Hand Mark In Dub)**
- Undead voices / Four horses ride / Calling to the ancient ears / Owl eyes / Evergreenman / Patchwork men / Dreamer prophets / Untitled / Corpse candle.

AntiClock not issued

Oct 08. (7") *<RCr 001>* [Language Of Light track]. / WIND CHANT

STONE SOUP (⟹ NEWCOMER, Carrie)

The STORY

Although this harmony-fuelled folk-pop duo from Amherst, Massachusetts made only two sets together, it's worth pointing out that both records were of the highest production quality. The pity was that similar folkies SUZANNE VEGA, SHAWN COLVIN and the INDIGO GIRLS were already saturating the market, and Jonatha Brooke (the main songwriter) and Jennifer Kimball might have been better marketed than as a folk act anyway.

Formed as Jonatha and Jennifer as far back as 1981, the Amherst College girls performed regularly throughout the Boston area. Their first big break came several years later, when their tape 'Over Oceans' encouraged the Green Linnet label to sign them. Folk music had branched out in so many directions in this period that jazz, torch, nostalgia and just about everything else had crept into the genre. The STORY's self-titled debut of 1991 was a prime example of post-1980s production techniques and top-notch session dexterity from Duke Levine (guitar), Alain Mallet (keyboards), Mike Rivard (bass) and producer Ben Wittman (drums). It was no surprise then that Elektra Records signed up The STORY, re-releasing their debut under the title of **GRACE IN GRAVITY** (1991) {*6}. While one can't help thinking of Sting, Enya and several other mainstream artists, the album had its funky-folk moments in the acappella 'Over Oceans', 'Damn Everything But The Circus' and 'Just One Word'.

Turning their direction towards feminist and spiritual values, the duo released a second album, **THE ANGEL IN THE HOUSE** (1993) {*6}. For folk aficionados the saving graces of the album were the Celtic-ish 'In The Gloaming' and the Joni MITCHELL-like 'Amelia' (not to be confused with Joni's own song of that name on 'Hejira').

Describing Kimball as the Andrew Ridgeley of the duo was probably unfair, but it was Brooke who sang lead, wrote the songs and played acoustic guitar, and it was only a matter of time until someone at the label would notice this. Subsequently billed as JONATHA BROOKE & THE STORY (Jennifer had gone), the band continued with **PLUMB** (1995) {*7}, mystifying for its inclusion of Jerry O'Sullivan's Celtic-inspired 'Andrew Duffy's Jig' after the Suzanne VEGA-type song 'Charming'.

KIMBALL finally got her own solo career under way with 1998's **VEERING FROM THE WAVE** {*5} - **OH HEAR US** (2006) {*6} was a tad better - but BROOKE looked to be on the downslide when MCA dropped her after 1997's **10 CENT WINGS** {*6}, her effort to be the next Sheryl Crow or Sarah McLachlan. The self-explanatory **LIVE** (1999) {*6}, on the Bad Dog label, was not universally acclaimed, but despite its mail-order status it sold better than its major-label studio predecessor.

Jonatha maintained her independence with **STEADY PULL** (2001) {*6}, **BACK IN THE CIRCUS** (2004) {*7}, **LIVE IN NEW YORK** (2006) {*6} and **CAREFUL WHAT YOU WISH FOR** (2007) {*5}, the last giving more prominence to co-writer Eric Bazilian (ex-Hooters). From the second album, covers of JAMES TAYLOR'S 'Fire And Rain', The Beach Boys' 'God Only Knows' and The Alan Parsons Project's 'Eye In The Sky' only arguably qualified as 'folk', but all brought Jonatha a great deal of respect from her peers and loyal fans.

THE WORKS (2008) {*6} was Jonatha's answer to BILLY BRAGG & Wilco's WOODY GUTHRIE-infused `Mermaid Avenue' of a decade before. Like her folk-meets-country predecessors, she took unrecorded lyrics from Woody's lately discovered archive and, with her co-producer Bob Clearmountain, revamped each song in Sheryl Crow or Rickie Lee Jones fashion - but at least it was folk music. *MCS*

Jonatha Brooke (b. Jan 23 '64, Illinois) - vocals, acoustic guitar / **Jennifer Kimball** (b. Fort Knox, Kentucky) - vocals / with **Duke Levine** - guitar / **Alain Mallet** - keyboards / **Mike Rivard** - bass / **Ben Wittman** - drums, producer

US Green Linnet / UK not issued

Mar 91. (cd/c) *<GLCD/CSIF 2104>* **THE STORY** — -

Elektra / Elektra

Nov 91. (cd/c) *<(7559 61321-2/-4)>* **GRACE IN GRAVITY** [debut re-issued] — Jun 92
- Grace in gravity / The perfect crime / Always / Damn everything but the circus / The alarm is on love / Easier than sorry / Just one word / And our faces, my heart, brief as photos / Dog dreams / Over oceans / Love is more thicker than forget.

Aug 93. (cd/c) *<(7559 61471-2/-4)>* **THE ANGEL IN THE HOUSE**
- So much mine / Missing person afternoon / The gilded cage / When two and two are five / At the still point / The angel in the house / Mermaid / The barefoot ballroom / In the gloaming / Fatso / Love song / Amelia / Fatso, part 2: Yo estoy bien asi.

JONATHA BROOKE & THE STORY

retained **Mallet**

Blue Thumb / Blue Thumb

Aug 95. (cd/c) *<(BTD 7003-2/-4)>* **PLUMB** — Feb 96
- Nothing sacred / Where were you? / Inconsolable / No better / West Point / War / Made of gold / Is this all? / Full-fledged strangers / Paris / Charming / Andrew Duffy's jig. *(cd re-iss. Mar 03 on Universal; AABTD 7003)*

Dec 95. (cd-s) *(BTR 5207-2)* NOTHING SACRED / War / West Point — -

JONATHA BROOKE

with session people

Refuge-MCA / Refuge-MCA

Nov 97. (cd/c) *<(11706-2/-4)>* **10 CENT WINGS**
- Secrets and lies / Crumbs / Because I told you so / Blood from a stone / Glass half empty / The choice / Last innocent year / Shame on us / Genius or a fool / 10 cent wings / Landmine / Annie. *(cd re-iss. Mar 03 on Universal; AAMCAD 11706)*

Bad Dog / Instant Karma

Feb 99. (cd) *<BDR 60201-2>* **LIVE** (live) — -
- Annie / West Point / Always / Is this all? / At the still point / 10 cent wings / Because I told you so / Blood from a stone / Where were you? / In the gloaming.

Feb 01. (cd) *<BDR 60301-2>* **STEADY PULL** — -
- Linger / How deep is your love? / Walking / Red dress / Room in my heart / Steady pull / Your house / New dress / Digging / Out of your mind / I'll take it from here / Lullaby.

Feb 04. (cd) *<00017540-2> (DHARMACD 6)* **BACK IN THE CIRCUS** — Apr 05
- Back in the circus / Better after all / It matters now / Sleeping with the light on / Fire and rain / Everything I wanted / God only knows / Less than love is nothing / Sally / No net below / Eye in the sky.

Sep 06. (cd+dvd) *<BDR 60606-2>* **LIVE IN NEW YORK** [live at the Anspacher Theatre in March 04] — -
- Damn everything but the circus / Sally / Better after all / Crumbs / Red dress / Love is more thicker than forget / Deny / Because I told you so / Room in my heart / Steady pull / Inconsolable / Landmine.

Apr 07. (cd) *<BDR 60703-2>* **CAREFUL WHAT YOU WISH FOR** — -
- Careful what you wish for / Beautiful girl / Keep the river on your right / I'll leave the light on / Baby wait / Hearsay / Forgiven / Je n' peux pas te plaire / Prodigal daughter / After the tears / Never too late for love.

Aug 08. (cd) *<BDR 60808-2>* **THE WORKS** — -
- My sweet and bitter bowl / You'd oughta be satisfied now / All you gotta do is touch me / My flowers grow green / Madonna on the curb / There's more true lovers than one / Sweetest angel / My battle / Little bird / Taste of danger / New star / Coney Island intro / King of my love.

JENNIFER KIMBALL

Imaginary Road / not issued

Aug 98. (cd/c) *<314 558 081-2/-4>* **VEERING FROM THE WAVE** — -
- Meet me in the twilight / Kissing in the car / Fall at your feet / Gagna's song / It's a long way home / An ordinary soldier / Take one step / The revelations / (This is) My new vow / World without end / Veering from the wave / Lullaby.

Epiosse / not issued

Jan 06. (cd) *<1094>* **OH HEAR US** — -
- Can't climb up / Don't take your love away / Eternal father / Is he or isn't he? / The wheel / Last ride home / When I was lost / East of Indiana / Lightning bugs / Ballad #61 / Wrap your troubles in dreams.

SUPPERBELL ROUNDUP (⇒ VIKING MOSES!)

T

Holly TANNEN

Singer and dulcimer player HOLLY TANNEN (b. 1947, New York City) is something like an updated JEAN RITCHIE. She sings traditional ballads from both sides of the Atlantic, from Scotland to the States. Her first recorded appearance was on a various-artists long-player, 'Berkeley Farms', on Folkways in 1972.

Holly has been associated as much with magic (she was ordained as a priestess in 1984) as with reviving magical songs of a bygone past. Time in Britain resulted in a one-off set, co-credited with fiddler PETE COOPER, **FROSTY MORNING** (1979) {*6}, which also featured guest guitarist MARTIN SIMPSON and producer Nigel Pegrum. On this mainly traditional set there was room for the covers 'Conversation With Death' (DOCK BOGGS), 'Halleluja, I'm A Bum' (Harry McClintock) and 'Shall I Sue?' (John Dowland).

The Kicking Mule-released **INVOCATION** (1983) {*6} and the independently issued **BETWEEN THE WORLDS** (1984) {*7} could and should have attracted more attention from what was then a largely redundant folk scene. One comparison that rings true is that if JUNE TABOR had been born American, she'd have sounded like Holly - check out the latter's versions of 'The Unquiet Grave', 'Bird In The Bush' and the acappella 'Malpas Wassail'.

Folklorist TANNEN made a study of the nomadic travellers of northern Scotland, writing a thesis for Berkeley University. She became an associate professor of anthropology at the College of the Redwoods, California, for several years from the late 1980s onwards, and lectured on magic at other universities including Yale.

Her release schedule curtailed by her busy academic life, the new century saw her put on a one-woman show, 'Practical Alchemy', at the Helen Schoeni Theater in Mendocino, which was turned into her comeback set, **CRAZY LAUGHTER: SEVEN YEARS WITH THE SPIRIT OF ARTHUR RIMBAUD** (2008) {*6}, inspired by the works of the French poet. **RIME OF THE ANCIENT MATRIARCH** (2009) {*6} was her Americana-based follow-up, taking in folk, country, bluegrass and doo-wop plus the fresh TANNEN originals 'Online Romance', 'Lily Of The Net' and the Celtic-fuelled 'Suburban Shaman' (sung by CARNAHAN, CASWELL & MORRIS). *MCS*

Holly Tannen - dulcimer (+ some guests, etc.)

US not issued / UK Plant Life

Sep 79. (lp; by HOLLY TANNEN & PETE COOPER) <*PLR 015*> **ROSTY MORNING** ☐ ☐
- Frosty morning - Sheep shell corn by the rattle of his horn / The soldier and the lady / Prince William - Pant Corlan yr wyn / Jack o' Diamonds / Muddy roads - Cuffey / Conversation with death / Halleluja, I'm a bum / Little rabbit / Rolling of the stones / Shall I sue? - The butterfly / Polly Vaughn / Young Collins.

Kicking Mule / not issued

1983. (lp) <*KM 236*> **INVOCATION** ☐ ☐
- Open the door softly / The bunch of rushes / Morris dances: Bobby and Joan / William and Nancy / George Campbell / A swallow song / King Orfeo / Spirits, Cutty Wren / All among the barley / Waltzes: Star of the County Down / Devin Keegan's waltz / A strange affair.

unknown / not issued

1984. (lp) <*none*> **BETWEEN THE WORLDS** ☐ ☐
- Bury me not on the lone prairie / The unquiet grave / The heretic heart / Through all the world below / Tam Lin / The nine points of roguery - The merry sisters / Bird in the bush / Dark island / Malpas wassail / The rainmaker (also known as Medicine hat) / Gone gonna rise again. <*cd-iss. Apr 09 on Gold Leaf; ???*>

Gold Leaf / not issued

Jan 08. (cd) <*103*> **CRAZY LAUGHTER: SEVEN YEARS WITH THE SPIRIT OF ARTHUR RIMBAUD** ☐ ☐
- Crazy laughter / The edge between / Marie Laveau / Bonobo wannabee / Brownies for breakfast / Dawn / La femme du berger / Are you sleepin', Maggie / Painted toenails / Lay this body down / The drunken boat / Sleeping rough / The soul knows its own / Alembic (the boy with the tortured heart).

Apr 09. (cd) <*none*> **RIME OF THE ANCIENT MATRIARCH** ☐ ☐
- High and lonesome / Lily of the net / Victim of them / Online romance / Death and the maiden / Fair Margaret and young whatshisname / Humboldt wassail / Suburban shaman (sung by CARNAHAN, CASWELL & MORRIS) / Ballad of the white seal maid / Traveler unknown / Wailing wall wail / Rime of the ancient matriarch.

TAU EMERALD (⟹ KRAUS, Sharron)

Eric TAYLOR

Gruff-voiced singer/songwriter ERIC TAYLOR (b. September 25, 1949 in Atlanta, Georgia) has had his fair share of the blues, despite his affiliation with some of the greats of country and folk.

A friend of Guy Clark and TOWNES VAN ZANDT since their formative Texas days at the start of the 1970s, the Vietnam veteran also nurtured the young NANCI GRIFFITH, whom he married in 1976. Some of TAYLOR's songs featured on her initial sets 'There's A Light Beyond These Woods' and 'Poet In My Window' (the latter for the Featherbed label), but he had drink and drugs problems and they divorced in 1982. They have remained good friends, and she appears on TAYLOR's latest recording, 2011's 'Live At The Red Shack', alongside his old country-rock friend Lyle Lovett, among others.

His own Featherbed imprint released what many thought would be his only album, **SHAMELESS LOVE** (1981) {*8}, though that would be to disregard his previous cuts for the 'Fast Folk' magazine and the Kerrville Folk Festival, where he won Best Songwriter in 1978. He was assisted by GRIFFITH on several tracks, and 'Only Lovers' and 'East Texas Moon' are prime southern-blend beauties.

Although not entirely neglecting his talents (he sang backing on Nanci's 1988 live album 'One Fair Summer Evening'), Eric let music take a back seat in his life, qualifying as a psychologist and spending time counselling in a half-way house for recovering addicts. It was only when Lyle Lovett (now a star in his own right) invited him to play support on his coffee-house tour of Texas that TAYLOR felt the urge to get his music career going again.

With the aid of a publishing deal with Polygram and a recording contract with Watermelon Records, his comeback was complete with the IAIN MATTHEWS-produced **ERIC TAYLOR** (1995) {*7} set. Songs that stood out from the pack were 'Deadwood' (fans of GRIFFITH might recall it as 'Deadwood, South Dakota'), 'Dean Moriarty' and 'Shoeshine Boy', all minor masterpieces echoing the likes of PRINE and VAN ZANDT.

RESURRECT (1998) {*6} and **SCUFFLETOWN** (2001) {*7} continued his musical resuscitation in leaps and bounds, his songwriting prowess intact, and on the latter set there was room for two inspired covers from the repertoire of his recently deceased old friend VAN ZANDT, 'Nothin'' and 'Where I Lead Me'. The last-named song also featured on his **THE KERRVILLE TAPES** (2003) {*5}, and VAN ZANDT's 'Highway Kind' was among the covers (alongside the trad 'Rally 'Round The Flag' and Susan Lindfors's 'A Matter Of Degrees') on Eric's most recent studio outing, **HOLLYWOOD POCKETKNIFE** (2007) {*6}.

THE GREAT DIVIDE (2005) {*7} was Eric's first set on his own Blue Ruby label, another brilliant country-folk album that again revisited his time as songwriter-in-chief for Nanci with his revamp of 'Storms'. *MCS*

Eric Taylor - vocals, acoustic guitar (+ guests on session)

US Featherbed / UK not issued

1981. (lp) <*FB 901*> **SHAMELESS LOVE** ☐ ☐

- Only lovers / Game of hearts / Hey little ryder / East Texas moon / Joseph Cross / Featherbed / Shermann Karmann / Cowgirl's heel / Charlie Ray McWhite / Shameless love. *<cd-iss. 2004 on Blue Ruby+=; 001>* - Dollar bill Hines / Half moon hotel.

——Taylor almost retired from music, qualifying as a psychologist

Watermelon | not issued

Sep 95. (cd) *<CD 1040>* **ERIC TAYLOR** □ ⊟
- Dean Moriarty / Prison movie / Hey little ryder / Deadwood / Mission door / Tractor song / Visitors from Indiana / All so much like me / Whooping crane / Hemingway's shotgun / All day Saturday / Shoeshine boy.

Koch Int. | not issued

Aug 98. (cd) *<KOC-CD 8026>* **RESURRECT** □ ⊟
- Walkin' back home / Louis Armstrong's broken heart / Sweet sunny south / Texas, Texas / Two fires / Birdland / Strong enough for two / Four great white fathers / Comanche / Resurrect / Depot light.

Eminent | not issued

Mar 01. (cd) *<EM-26001>* **SCUFFLETOWN** □ ⊟
- Happy endings / Where I lead me / All the way to heaven / Chicken pie / Blue piano / White bone / Delia - Bad news / Your god / Bread and wine / Game is gone / Nothin'.

Silverwolf | not issued

Jun 03. (cd) *<1031>* **THE KERRVILLE TAPES** (live at the Kerrville Folk Festival) □ ⊟
- Sweet sunny south / Texas, Texas / Where I lead me / Prison movie / Walkin' back home / Louis Armstrong's broken heart / Hemingway's shotgun / Two fires / Birdland / Strong enough for two.

Blue Ruby | not issued

Mar 05. (cd) *<002>* **THE GREAT DIVIDE** ⊟ mail-o ⊟
- The great divide / Big love / Whorehouse mirrors and pawnshop knives / Mickey Finn / Ain't but one thing give a man the blues / Just short of the line / Manhattan mandolin blues / Storms / Shoes / Brand new companion - Lulu's back in town - Dirty dirty / Bonnie & Avery.

Oct 07. (cd) *<003>* **HOLLYWOOD POCKETKNIFE** ⊟ mail-o ⊟
- Hollywood pocketknife / Carnival Jim and Jean / Highway kind / Jail widow's walk / Better man / Olney's poison and the Houston blues / A matter of degrees / Postcards, three for a dime / Peppercorn tree / Rally round the flag.

10,000 MANIACS

Part post-New Wave, part jangly folk-rock and at times part cod-reggae - it seems an unlikely combination, but 10,000 MANIACS (named in honour of the cult 1964 horror film 'Two Thousand Maniacs!') were all that and more besides. Formed in 1981 in Jamestown, New York by singer and lyricist Natalie Merchant and guitarist/songwriter J.C. Lombardo, the group was completed by lead guitarist Robert Buck, bassist Steven Gustafson, keyboard player Dennis Drew and drummer Jerry Augustyniak.

After a series of gigs the sextet debuted in 1982 with the 12" EP 'Human Conflict Number Five', although trying to find a copy at the time was a bit of a chore. A UK re-pressing found its way out a few years later.

Much could be said for band's **SECRETS OF THE I-CHING** (1983) {*5}, a full set which scaled the UK indie chart in the summer of 1984 and won praise from Radio One DJ and guru John Peel. In hindsight its success was down to just one song, the already-available classic 45 'My Mother The War'.

On the strength of their promise and the swirling dervish Natalie, with her unique elasticated vocal cords, the group secured an international deal with Elektra. Produced by veteran folk legend Joe Boyd (responsible for NICK DRAKE, The INCREDIBLE STRING BAND, etc.), **THE WISHING CHAIR** (1985) {*7} saw the band develop their incisive, rootsy sound, and there was yet another take of 'My Mother The War', which had been promoted on the British TV music show The Tube.

Alongside the traditional 'Just As The Tide Was A-Flowing', the excellent one-that-got-away single 'Can't Ignore The Train' and another flop 45, 'Scorpio Rising', the remainder of the set had a few ups and downs - the ups being 'Lily Dale', 'Grey Victory' and 'Back O' The Moon', the downs 'Arbor Day' and the calypso/reggae 'Daktari'. When things calmed down a little, Lombardo took his leave to form JOHN AND MARY with vocalist Mary Ramsey - and it wasn't the last we would hear of either.

By 1987 things had opened up for 10,000 MANIACS, and they were now touring alongside R.E.M.; Michael Stipe was Natalie's beau for a while. Produced by pop legend Peter Asher (of Peter & Gordon fame, among other things), third album **IN MY TRIBE** (1987) {*8} let them reap some commercial rewards to match their growing critical acclaim. The record had a graceful sound along with sharpened songwriting that emphasised Merchant's hypnotically plangent vocals, and the group had minor US hits with 'Like The Weather' and 'What's The Matter Here?'. A cover of CAT STEVENS's 'Peace Train' failed to chart (it was omitted from later pressings following comments by the Muslim convert, now Yusef Islam, on the fatwa against novelist Salman Rushdie), but there was consolation in mini-gems such as 'Hey Jack Kerouac', 'Don't Talk' and 'Verdi Cries'.

Follow-up set **BLIND MAN'S ZOO** (1989) {*6} took a more political stance, though the enigmatic Merchant stopped short of preaching. Reaching the Top 20 in the US and Britain, it was a letdown compared to its predecessor, although there were highlights in 'Eat For Two', `'Trouble Me' (a Top 50 hit) and 'Poison In The Well'.

Following the accompanying tour, the band took a brief sabbatical, returning in September 1992 with another adventurous transatlantic-Top 40 set, **OUR TIME IN EDEN** {*7}. Three minor hits, 'These Are Days', 'Candy Everybody Wants' and 'Few And Far Between', complemented poignantly thought-provoking songs such as 'I'm Not The Man', about an innocent man awaiting execution. Yes, it was that sort of record.

By the release of the ubiquitous, languorous **MTV UNPLUGGED** (1993) {*6} set (whence came the near-Top 10 cover of SPRINGSTEEN's 'Because The Night'), MERCHANT was disillusioned with the group and left soon afterwards for a lucrative solo career.

10,000 MANIACS replaced Natalie with ex-member Lombardo and new frontwoman Mary Ramsey (of JOHN AND MARY), but the group had lost its focal point. Minus Merchant, 10,000 MANIACS carried on regardless, releasing the sorry folk-rock set **LOVE AMONG THE RUINS** (1997) {*4}, on which Jules Shear co-wrote a few songs. Although it would be unfair to dismiss the record entirely, the fire was all but extinguished when their version of Bryan Ferry's 'More Than This' reached the US Top 30. It was to be their penultimate album, as the independently released **THE EARTH PRESSED FLAT** (1999) {*5} also failed to generate much interest. Guitarist Robert Buck died on December 19, 2000 of complications of liver disease, aged 42.

JOHN & MARY, who had issued a couple of sets in the early 1990s - the Mitch Easter-produced **VICTORY GARDENS** (1991) {*5} and **THE WEEDKILLER'S DAUGHTER** (1993) {*6}, featuring a cover of MARIANNE SEGAL's 'Fly Me To The North' - continued as a duo, releasing **PINWHEEL GALAXY** (2003) {*5} and **PEACE BRIDGE** (2007) {*5}, with The Valkyries co-credited on the last-named.

10,000 MANIACS' B-side cover versions included 'Hello In There' (JOHN PRINE), 'Wildwood Flower' (A.P. Carter), 'Don't Call Us' (Thomas-Blanch), `From The Time You Say Goodbye' (Leslie Sturdy) , 'I Hope That I Don't Fall In Love With You' (Tom Waits), 'These Days' (Jackson Browne), 'Starman/ Moonage Daydream' (David Bowie), 'Everyday Is Like Sunday' (Morrissey), 'Sally Ann' (Dick Powell), 'Don't Go Back To Rockville' (R.E.M.), 'To Sir With Love' (a hit for Lulu) and 'Let The Mystery Be' (Iris DeMent). *MCS*

Natalie Merchant (b. Oct 26 '63) - vocals / **Robert Buck** (b. Aug 1 '58) - lead guitar, mandolin, pedal steel / **John 'J.C.' Lombardo** (b. Sep 30 '52) - rhythm guitar, bass (ex-Still Life) / **Steven Gustafson** (b. Apr 10 '57, Madrid, Spain) - bass, guitar / **Dennis Drew** (b. Aug 8 '57, Buffalo, NY) - organ, piano, accordion / **Jerry Augustyniak** (b. Sep 2 '58, Lackawanna, NY) - drums

US | UK

Mark - Christian Burial | not issued

Sep 82. (12" ep) *<MC 20247>* HUMAN CONFLICT NUMBER FIVE □ ⊟
- Tension / Planned obsolescence / Orange / Groove dub / Anthem for doomed youth. *(UK-iss. Jun 84 on Press; P 2010) <(for CD see comps)>*

Nov 83. (lp) *<MC 20389>* **SECRETS OF THE I-CHING** □ ⊟
- Grey victory / Pour de Chirico / Death of Manolette / Tension / Daktari / Pit viper / Katrina's fair / The Latin one / National education week / My mother the war. *(UK-iss. Aug 84 on Press; P 3001) <(for CD see comps)>*

not issued | Reflex

Mar 84. (12" m) *(RE 1)* MY MOTHER THE WAR. / Planned Obsolescence / National Education Week ⊟ □

Elektra | Elektra

Jun 85. (7") *(EKR 11)* CAN'T IGNORE THE TRAIN. / Daktari ⊟ □
(12"+=) *(EKR 11T)* - Grey victory / The colonial wing.

Nov 85. (lp/c/cd) *<9 60428-1/-4/-2> (EKT 14/+C)*
THE WISHING CHAIR □ □
- Can't ignore the train / Scorpio rising / Just as the tide was a-flowing / Lilydale / Back o' the moon / Maddox table / The colonial wing [*] / Grey victory / Among the Americans / Everyone a puzzle lover / Cotton alley / Daktari [*] / My mother the war / Tension makes a tangle / Arbor day. *(UK cd re-iss. 1989 += *; 960 428-2)*

Jan 86. (7") *(EKR 28)* SCORPIO RISING. / Arbor Day ⊟ □

——trimmed to a quintet when Lombardo departed to form JOHN AND MARY

Aug 87. (7") *<7-69457> (EKR 61)* PEACE TRAIN. / The Painted Desert □ □

Aug 87. (lp/c)(cd) *<9 60738-1/-4/-2> (EKT 41/+C)(960738-2)*
IN MY TRIBE [37] □
- What's the matter here? / Hey Jack Kerouac / Like the weather / Cherry tree / The painted desert / Don't talk / Peace train [*] / Gun shy / My sister Rose / A campfire

song / City of angels / Verdi cries. (initial copies cont. Elektra sampler with X / The CALL; SAM 390) *<US cd re-iss. 1989 w/out *>*

Nov 87. (7") *(EKR 64)* DON'T TALK. / City Of Angels [–] [ ]
(12"+=) *(EKR 64T)* - Goodbye (tribal chants).

Mar 88. (7") *(EKR 71)* WHAT'S THE MATTER HERE? / Verdi Cries [–] [ ]
(12"+=/cd-s+=) *(EKR 71T)* - Like the weather [live] / Gun shy [live].

Apr 88. (7") *<7-69418> (EKR 77)* LIKE THE WEATHER. / A Campfire Song [68] Jul 88 [ ]
(12"+=/12"w-poster) *(EKR 77T/+W)* - Poison in the well [live] / Verdi cries [live].

Aug 88. (7") *<7-69388>* WHAT'S THE MATTER HERE? / Cherry Tree [80] [–]

May 89. (lp/c)(cd) *<9 60815-1/-4/-2> (EKT 57/+C)(960815-2)* **BLIND MAN'S ZOO** [13] [18]
- Eat for two / Please forgive us / The big parade / Trouble me / You happy puppet / Headstrong / Poison in the well / Dust bowl / The lion's share / Hateful hate / Jubilee.

Jun 89. (7"/c-s) *<7-69298> (EKR 93)* TROUBLE ME. / The Lion's Share [44] [ ]
(12"+=/3"cd-s+=/3"s-cd-s+=) *(EKR 93 T/CD/CDX)* - Party of God (with BILLY BRAGG).

Sep 89. (cd-ep) *<9-66669-2>* YOU HAPPY PUPPET [ ] [–]
- You happy puppet / Gun shy [acoustic] / Wildwood flower / Hello in there.

Nov 89. (7"ep) *(EKR 100)* EAT FOR TWO [–] [ ]
- Eat for two / Wildwood flower / Don't call us / From the time you say goodbye.
(12"/12" w/poster/3" cd-s) *(EKR 100 T/TW/CD)* - [1st & 2nd tracks] / Gun shy [acoustic] / Hello in there.
(10") *(EKR 100TE)* - [1st & 4th tracks] / What's the matter here? [acoustic] / ['A'-acoustic].

Sep 92. (7"/c-s) *<4-64700> (EKR 156/+C)* THESE ARE DAYS. / Circle Dream [66] [58]
(cd-s+=) *(EKR 156CD)* - I hope that I don't fall in love with you.
(cd-s) *(EKR 156CDX)* - ['A'] / Medley: Starman - Moonage daydream / These days.

Sep 92. (cd/c/lp) *<(7559 61385-2/-4/-1)>* **OUR TIME IN EDEN** [28] [33]
- Noah's dove / These are days / Eden / Few and far between / Stockton gala days / Gold rush brides / Jezebel / How you've grown / Candy everybody wants / Circle dream / If you intend / I'm not the man. *(cd+=)* - Tolerance.

Feb 93. (c-s) *<4-64665>* CANDY EVERYBODY WANTS / I Hope That I Don't Fall In Love With You [67] [–]
(cd-s) *<2-66342>* - ['A'] / Everyday is like Sunday / Sally Ann / Don't go back to Rockville.

Mar 93. (7"/c-s) *(EKR 160/+C)* CANDY EVERYBODY WANTS. / Everyday Is Like Sunday [–] [47]
(cd-s+=) *(EKR 160CD1)* - Don't go back to Rockville (with MICHAEL STIPE) / ['A'-MTV version].
(cd-s) *(EKR 160CDX)* - ['A'] / [live]:- Eat for two / Hey Jack Kerouac / My sister Rose.

Aug 93. (cd-ep) *<2-66296>* FEW AND FAR BETWEEN [95] [–]
- Few and far between / Candy everybody wants / To sir with love / Let the mystery be.

Oct 93. (7"/c-s) *(EKR 175/+C)* BECAUSE THE NIGHT [live]. / Stockton Gala Days [live] [–] [65]
(cd-s+=) *(EKR 175CD)* - Let the mystery be [live] / Sally Ann.

Oct 93. (7"/c-s) *<7-/4-64595>* BECAUSE THE NIGHT [live] / Eat For Two [live] [11] [–]

Oct 93. (cd/c) *<(7559 61569-2/-4)>* **MTV UNPLUGGED** [live] [13] [40]
- These are days / Eat for two / Candy everybody wants / I'm not the man / Don't talk / Hey Jack Kerouac / What's the matter here? / Gold rush brides / Like the weather / Trouble me / Jezebel / Because the night / Stockton gala days / Noah's dove.

——10,000 MANIACS split when NATALIE MERCHANT went solo; the remainder re-formed in 1995 and added ex-original **John Lombardo** and his (JOHN AND MARY) partner **Mary Ramsey** - vocals, violin

Geffen Geffen

Jun 97. (cd) *<(GEFD/GED 25009)>* **LOVE AMONG THE RUINS** [ ] Oct 97 [ ]
- Rainy day / Love among the ruins / Even with my eyes closed / Girl on a train / Green children / A room for everything / More than this / Big star / You won't find me there / All that never happens / Shining light / Across the fields. *(re-iss. Jul 02; 425009-2)*

Jul 97. (c-s) *<4-19411> (GFSC 22284)* MORE THAN THIS / Beyond The Blue [25] Sep 97 [ ]
(cd-s+=) *(GFSTD 22284)* - ['A'-Tee's radio mix] / Time turns.
(12") *(GFST 22284)* - ['A'-mixes: hard club / Airways 12" vocal / Tee's frozen dub / Tee's radio].

Bar/None Bar/None

Apr 99. (cd/c) *<(BARNONE 106)>* **THE EARTH PRESSED FLAT** [ ] May 99 [ ]
- The Earth pressed flat / Ellen / Once a city / Glow / On and on (mercy song) / Somebody's heaven / Cabaret / Beyond the blue / Smallest step / In the quiet morning / Time turns / Hidden in my heart / Who knows where the times goes? *(cd+=)* - Rainbows.

——sadly, Buck died of liver failure in 2000; group split but re-formed infrequently

Sony Sony

Jun 09. (cd) *<(A 747059)>* **EXTENDED VERSIONS** [live at the Seneca Niagara Casino, Niagara Falls, NY April 7–8 2006] [ ] May 09 [ ]
- What's the matter here? / Candy everybody wants / Trouble me / Eden / Don't talk / City of angels / Stockton gala days / These are days / My sister Rose / Hey Jack Kerouac.

- (8-10*) compilations -

Feb 04. (d-cd) *Rhino-Elektra; <(R2 73900)>* **CAMPFIRE SONGS: THE POPULAR, OBSCURE AND UNKNOWN RECORDINGS** [ ] [ ]
- Planned obsolescence / My mother the war / Tension / Scorpio rising / Like the weather / Don't talk / What's the matter here? / Hey Jack Kerouac / Verdi cries / Trouble me / Poison in the well / You happy puppet / Eat for two / Stockton gala days / Candy everybody wants / These are days / Because the night // Poppy selling man / Can't ignore the train [demo] / Peace train / Wildwood flower / Hello in there / To sir with love / Everyday is like Sunday / These days / I hope that I don't fall in love with you / Starman / Let the mystery be / Noah's dove [demo] / Circle dream [alt. lyrics demo] / Eden [alt. lyrics demo].

- essential boxed sets -

Dec 05. (3-cd-box) *Rhino-Elektra; (7559-60815-2)* **TRILOGY** [–] [ ]
- (BLIND MAN'S ZOO) // (IN MY TRIBE) // (OUR TIME IN EDEN).

- (5-7*) compilations, others, etc.-

Oct 90. (cd)(lp/c)(cd) *Elektra; <(7599 60962-2)> (EKT 79/+C)* **HOPE CHEST: THE FREDONIA RECORDINGS 1982–1983** [ ] [ ]
- Planned obsolescence / The Latin one / Katrina's fair / Pour de Chirico / Grey victory / National education week / Death of Manolete / Orange / Tension / Anthem for doomed youth / Daktari / Groove dub / Pit viper / My mother the war.

JOHN AND MARY

Lombardo - vocals, bass, guitars / **Ramsey** - vocals, keyboards, violin, viola / with **Buck** + **Augustyniak**

Rykodisc Rykodisc

Jul 91. (cd) *<(RCD 10203)>* **VICTORY GARDENS** [ ] [ ]
- Red wooden beads / Azalea festival / Piles of dead leaves / We have nothing / Rags of flowers / I became alone / Open window / July 6th / Pram / Canadien errant.

—— now with guests:- Alex Chilton, Mary Margaret O'Hara, Andrew Case, Bob Wiseman, Scott Miller, David Kane, Joanne Ramsey + Buck

Mar 93. (cd) *<(RCD 10259)>* **THE WEEDKILLER'S DAUGHTER** [ ] [ ]
- Two worlds parted / Angels of stone / Your return / Clare's scarf / Cemetery ridge / Nightfall / I wanted you / One step backward / Fly me to the north / Clouds of reason / Maid of mist / Poor murdered woman.

Pinwheel Galaxy not issued

Jul 03. (cd) *<2002>* **THE PINWHEEL GALAXY** [ ] [–]
- A brighter day / Beyond love / Lilies of the valley / Summer street / The drone / Gaze / Halo of stars / Lady Margaret and Sweet William / Five weeks in a ballroom / Vacant chair / In a little while / My shattered illusions.

own label not issued

Aug 07. (cd; as JOHN & MARY & THE VALKYRIES) *<none>* **PEACE BRIDGE** [ ] [–]
- Poppy / Easter / Shudder girl / The gift of life / Goodbye Stan / Triumph / 23 days / Johnny and Mary / Autumn in Rio / This time alone / That's where I went wrong / Billy and Shelley / Time hard.

J. TILLMAN

Whether you call him alt-country or folk-rock, bearded singer/songwriter Joshua Tillman (b. May 3, 1981 in Seattle, Washington) will be best known for being a recent recruit (late in 2008) to FLEET FOXES, as their drummer. His other bands, Stately and Saxon Shore (the latter are the American equivalent of Mogwai) have been on the go since the early 2000s.

As a solo artist J. TILLMAN's flame was kindled by the moody textures of NICK DRAKE, Ryan Adams and DAMIEN JURADO, the last-named inviting him as a backing musician (and later solo support act) on his mid-2000s tour. His recordings at this stage were of the cd-r variety, but **I WILL RETURN** (2005) {*6} and **LONG MAY YOU RUN, J. TILLMAN** (2006) {*6} were surprisingly polished, while finding a sense of fragility and tenderness all of their own.

Albums three and four, **MINOR WORKS** (2006) {*7} and **CANCER AND DELIRIUM** (2007) {*6}, arrived in quick succession and from different outlets, more country swagger than folk music. While FLEET FOXES scurried up the charts with their debut album, TILLMAN's fresh solo sets, **VACILANDO TERRITORY BLUES** (2009) {*6} and **YEAR IN THE KINGDOM** (2009) {*6}, were giving him his own independence, albeit with the backing of Robin Guthrie's Bella Union imprint. In the States, Western Vinyl were behind these releases, as they were with his vinyl-only follow-up, **SINGING AX** (2010) {*6}. *MCS*

Josh Tillman - vocals, acoustic guitar / + session people

US Keep / UK not issued

Jan 05. (ltd; cd-r) <*KR 18*> **I WILL RETURN** [−] [−]
- Lilac hem / Your mother's ghost / This jealous blood / I will return / Cecille, my love / A hit play / Golden string for your nest / Trailing white / Occurrence at the Jordan river. *(d-cd-iss. May 07 on Fargo (French)+=; 339-0093-2)* - LONG MAY YOU RUN, J. TILLMAN

Jan 06. (ltd;cd-r) <*KR 24*> **LONG MAY YOU RUN, J. TILLMAN** [−] [−]
- Two years on film / Casualties / House arms built / My waking days / Jamestown bridge / Fireworks / Wayward glance blues / Seven states across / Before we retire / Ties, that bind / Trouble's always free. *(d-cd-iss.+=)* - I WILL RETURN

not issued / Fargo

Nov 06. (lp/cd) *(339-0087-1/-2)* **MINOR WORKS** [−] French [−]
- Darling night / Jesse's not a sleeper / Crooked roof / With wolves / Minor works / For an hour with you / Take care / Relentless / Now you're among strangers.

Yer Bird / not issued

Apr 07. (cd) <*YB 005*> **CANCER AND DELIRIUM** [ ] [−]
- Visions of a troubled mind / Milk white air / Evans and falls / A fine suit / Ribbons of glass / Under the sun / If I get to the borderline / When I light your darkened door / How much mystery.

Western Vinyl / Bella Union

Jan 09. (cd) <*WEST 056*> *(BELLACD 186)* **VACILANDO TERRITORY BLUES** [ ] Mar 09 [ ]
- All you see / No occasion / Firstborn / Vessels / James blues / Steel on steel / Laborless land / Barter blues / New imperial grand blues / Master's house / Someone with child / Above all men / Vacilando territory.

Sep 09. <lp>(cd) <*WEST 068*>*(BELLACD 212)* **YEAR IN THE KINGDOM** [ ] [ ]
- Year in the kingdom / Crosswinds / Earthly bodies / Howling light / Though I have wronged you / Age of man / There is no good in me / Marked in the valley / Light of the living.

Feb 10. (ltd-7") <*WEST 069*> WILD HONEY NEVER STOLEN. / Borne Away On A Black Barge [ ] [−]

Western Vinyl / Western Vinyl

Sep 10. (lp) <*(WEST 078)*> **SINGING AX** [ ] [ ]
- Three sisters / Diamondback / Love no less worthy / One task / Our beloved tyrant / Tillman's rag / Mere ornaments / Singing ax / Madness on the mountain / Maria / A seat at the table.

TIMOTHY, REVELATOR (⟹ STONE BREATH)

James Jackson TOTH (⟹ WOODEN WAND)

Ed TRICKETT

Professor of psychology by day, renowned song interpreter and hammered-dulcimer player in his own time - many folk buffs will have discovered his gentle performances on collaborative album projects alongside GORDON BOK and Ann Mayo Muir. Born in the early 1940s, TRICKETT (a friend of fellow New Golden Ring member SARA GREY, with whose solo debut he helped in 1970) also delivered a number of solo sets after his time in the 1960s folk-pop collective The GOLDEN RING, which was basically Ed, Sara, Gordon, Caroline and Sandy Paton, Ann Mitchell, Joe Hickerson, Neal MacMillan, John Dildine and George Armstrong.

While this college of harmony-fuelled singers were a nice enough addition to folk's old school, their material was hardly groundbreaking. TRICKETT's solo material, however, was more in line with the sounds of the 1970s, though with at least one foot in the past. His best albums (see discography) are his first two, **THE TELLING TAKES ME HOME** (1972) {*6} - featuring two from BRUCE 'UTAH' PHILLIPS, 'The Goodnight-Loving Trail' and the title track - and **GENTLY DOWN THE STREAM OF TIME** (1977) {*6}. His last solo CD, the Celtic/seafarers'/trad **ECHO ON THE EVENING TIDE** (2000) {*6}, was also typical TRICKETT, sentimental and nostalgic. *MCS*

Ed Trickett - vocals, acoustic guitar, hammered dulcimer [solo sets only]

US Folk-Legacy / UK not issued

1972. (lp) <*FSI-46*> **THE TELLING TAKES ME HOME** [ ] [−]
- The telling takes me home / Hark of all / Sea fever / You gotta talk my language / Just as the evening sun / Finger ring / Before they close the minstrel show / Searching for home / The blooming bright star of Belle Isle / The goodnight-loving trail / Home, dearie, home / Yea ho, little fish / Brave boys / Come fare away. *<cd-iss. Oct 10; CD-46>*

——In 1975, Ed guested on Joan Sprungs's Folk-Legacy LP 'Ballads And Butterflies'.

1977. (lp) <*FSI-64*> **GENTLY DOWN THE STREAM OF TIME** [ ] [−]
- A la rorro, nino / Bonny love / Calico pie / Craney hill / Eyes are blue / The fit / Gently down the stream of time / Grandfather's clock / Hymn song / January man / Only an hour until morning / Tear old Wilson down / Wild horse / Will you love me when I'm old. *<cd-iss. Oct 10; CD-64>*

—— In 1978, Ed augmented Bob Zentz on his LP 'Beaucatcher Farewell'.

—— In 1981, Ed augmented Lorre Wyatt on the LP 'Roots and Branches'.

1982. (lp) <*FSI-92*> **PEOPLE LIKE YOU** [ ] [−]
- Cold winter is coming / Sweet freedom / Old wing / Dry Cardrona / River of the big canoe / Cotton mill blues / Rock the cradle / Joe / People like you / The lover's return / Kitty and I / Clayton Boone / Ashes on the sea. *<cd-iss. Apr 11; CD-92>*

——In 1985 and 1987, Ed guested on Folk-Legacy LPs by Ann Mayo Muir ('So Goes My Heart') and Caroline & Sandy Paton ('New Harmony')

—— a list of albums as/by GORDON BOK ⟹, Ann Mayo Muir & Ed Trickett (all on Folk-Legacy): 'Turning Toward The Morning' (1975), 'The Ways Of Man' (1978), 'A Water Over Stone' (1980), 'All Shall Be Well Again' (1983), 'Fashioned In The Clay' (1985), 'Minneapolis Concert' (1987), 'And So Will We Yet' (1990), 'Language Of The Heart' (1994) and 'Harbors Of Home' (1998).

Azalea / not issued

Apr 00. (cd) <*9901*> **ECHO ON THE EVENING TIDE** [ ] [−]
- Broken hand / Annie Laurie - Bad half hour / Booze yacht / The Vance song / Ferrybank piper / We danced / Never never land / Diamond Joe / Henry in his boat / Row on / Lonesome robin / Who's gonna buy you ribbons / Joe Hill's will / Old songs - Piano.

GOLDEN RING

basically a collective of musicians incl. **Ed Trickett, Sara Grey, Gordon Bok, Caroline & Sandy Paton, Ann Mitchell, Joe Hickerson, Neal MacMillan, John Dildine, George Armstrong**

Folk-Legacy / not issued

1964. (lp; by GOLDEN RING) <*FSI-16*> **A GATHERING OF FRIENDS FOR MAKING MUSIC** [ ] [−]
- The blind man's song / Jesse James / Nonesuch / The hound dog song / Captain Kidd / Dipper of stars / When Jesus wept / Simple gifts / Rollin' a-rollin' / One man shall mow my meadow / Howie's breakdown / Barbara Ellen / Golden ring around my Susan girl / The holly bears a berry / Babe of Bethlehem / This old world. *<cd-iss. Oct 96; CD-16>*

Apr 71. (lp; by The NEW GOLDEN RING) <*FSI-41*> **FIVE DAYS SINGING: Volume I** [ ] [−]
- Waterbound / The waters of Tyne / World of misery / Benjamin Bowmaneer / Over the waterfall / Ginny's gone to Ohio / Leaning on the everlasting arms / Lord Bateman / The rolling hills of the border / D composition in C / Poor Howard / Sundown / Temperance reel / It soon be done. *<cd-iss. Oct 96; CD-41>*

Apr 71. (lp; as NEW GOLDEN RING) <*FSI-42*> **FIVE DAYS SINGING: Volume II** [ ] [−]
- Rolling home / Angeline the baker / Sammy's bar / The kangaroo song / Few days / Calvary / Mortality / Ah, robin / Over the water to Charlie / Sam gone away / Jute mill song / The Galveston flood / First covered mountains / Goodbye, fare you well. *<cd-iss. Oct 96; CD-42>*

——Ed Trickett & Harry Tuft / Cathy Barton & Dave Para / Caroline, David & Sandy Paton

1992. (cd; by GOLDEN RING) <*CD-121*> **FOR ALL THE GOOD PEOPLE: A Golden Ring Reunion** [ ] [−]
- Singer's request / Grandma's song - The reindeer song / Springtime brings on the shearing / Richmond - Last letter home / Damned ol' piney mountains / Goodbye to the Lowlands / Devil in the garden / Stoney's waltz / When you and I were young, Maggie / Weaver's reverie / Little creek / Early / Napoleon crossing the Rhine / Dark island / Golden years / The last wagon / Last train to glory / All the good people.

William TYLER

Formerly of Nashville electro duo Hands Off Cuba, and a part-timer with off-kilter alt-country ensemble Lambchop, virtuoso prog-folk guitarist WILLIAM TYLER's first act was The Paper Hats, a one-off project that spawned the beautiful **DESERT CANYON** (2008) {*7} set. Graced by three 11-minutes-plus instrumental explorations in 'Man Of Oran', 'Parliament Of Birds' and 'Crystal Palace, Sea Of Glass', this record was like ROBBIE BASHO or JOHN FAHEY at their best.

Willy T, as he is known in the trade, was an unusual acquisition for New York's Tompkins Square imprint, although others such as Brit-based JAMES BLACKSHAW had been recent recruits. **BEHOLD THE SPIRIT** (2010) {*7} was definitely in line with the BERT JANSCH/Jimmy Page school of tuning (DADGAG). Impressive opener 'Terrace Of The Leper King' and 'The Cult Of The Peacock Angel' were finger-picking favourites. *MCS*

William Tyler - guitars / + session people on solo set

US not issued / UK Apparent Extent

Oct 08. (cd, lp; as The PAPER HATS) *(AE 005)* **DESERT CANYON** [−] German [−]
- Man of Oran / Parliament of birds / The green cigar kept smiling / The sleeping prophet / Hermit kingdom / Waltz of the circassian beauties / Crystal palace, sea of glass.

Tompkins Square / Tompkins Square

Nov 10. (cd/lp) <*(TSQ 2431 CD/LP)*> **BEHOLD THE SPIRIT** [ ] Dec 10 [ ]
- Terrace of the leper king / Missionary ridge / Oahspe / To the Finland station / The cult of the peacock angel / Tears and saints / Signal mountain / The green pastures / Ponotoc.

U + V

UNCLE EARL (⟹ Great Country Discography)

The VALERIE PROJECT (⟹ ESPERS)

Sharon VAN ETTEN

New Jersey-born, Brooklyn-based folk singer/songwriter SHARON VAN ETTEN's distinctive, lazy alto drawl echoes a few impassioned vocalists of bygone days, such as Judie Tzuke, Neko Case and JOSEPHINE FOSTER. Surfacing from Middle Tennessee State University, her career in indie-folk-based music was initially mentored by Kyp Malone of TV On The Radio.

Language Of Stone released her lo-fi debut album **BECAUSE I WAS IN LOVE** (2009) {*7}, a fragile, lilting and unemotional set that was occasionally filled out with sparse backing; check out 'I Wish I Knew', 'For You' and 'Tornado'. Augmented by a full band and delivered on the Ba Da Bing! independent, **EPIC** (2010) {*7} comprised seven more-upbeat songs that broke free of the confines of folk at one bound. The alt-rock 'Peace Signs' is matched by the country twang of 'Save Yourself'.

Two effective songs, recorded with GREG WEEKS (of ESPERS), that escaped her earlier sessions were 'I'm Giving Up On You' and 'You Didn't Really Do That'. They were issued as a double-header 7" shortly afterwards, and a deal with indie major Jagjaguwar (BON IVER, etc) looked possible. She's definitely a star in the making. *MCS*

Sharon Van Etten - vocals, acoustic guitar / + session people

		US	UK
		own label	not issued
2007.	(ltd-7") <*none*> MUCH MORE OF THAT. / Over Your Shoulder	–	–
2008.	(ltd-cd) <*none*> UNTITLED	–	demo –
	- I wish I knew / For you / It's not like / Holding out / Keep / Tornado / Have you seen / I can't breathe / Carry on / Where is my love / Damn right.		
		Language Of Stone	Language Of Stone
May 09.	(cd/lp) <*(LOS 011)*> **BECAUSE I WAS IN LOVE**		Jun 09
	- I wish I knew / Consolation prize / For you / I fold / Have you seen / Tornado / Much more than that / Same dream / Keep / It's not like / Holding out.		
		Ba Da Bing!	Ba Da Bing!
Sep 10.	(cd/lp) <*(BING 072)*> **EPIC**		
	- A crime / Peace signs / Save yourself / DSharpG / Don't do it / One day / Love more.		
		Polyvinyl	Polyvinyl
Sep 10.	(7") <*(PRC-206)*> I'M GIVING UP ON YOU. / You Didn't Really Do That		Nov 10

VANDAVEER

The sideline project of Ohio-born, Kentucky-raised multi-instrumentalist frontman Mark Charles Heidinger (who heads The Apparitions and plays bass for These United States), Washington D.C.'s VANDAVEER have a tendency to sound like VIC CHESNUTT or DAVID GRAY. His backing musicians are VANDAVEER stalwarts Justin Craig (guitar), drummer Robby Catholic, percussionist Robby Cosenza and clarinettist and ukulele player Chris Sullivan.

GRACE AND SPEED (2007) {*7} marked a promising independent start for Heidinger and friends. Tracks such as 'Marianne, You've Done It Now...', 'Crooked Mast' and 'However Many It Takes' were exceptional, though firmly rooted in the past.

Enlisting the help of high-harmony singer Rose Guerin, **DIVIDE AND CONQUER** (2009) {*7} and **DIG DOWN DEEP** (2011) {*7} unearthed still more positive critical responses as the collective reached the 500-gig mark.

Surprisingly, they are not unknown in France, where their carousel chamber-pop (exemplified by 'Resurrection Mary', 'A Mighty Leviathan Of Gold' and 'Turpentine', all from 1909) was particularly popular. *MCS*

Mark Charles Heidinger - vocals, acoustic guitar, multi / with **Justin Craig** - guitar / **Chris Sullivan** - clarinet / **Robby Cosenza** - percussion / + live: **Rose Guerin** - vocals + **Robby Catholic** - drums

		US	UK
		Gypsy Eyes	Alter K
Mar 07.	(cd) <*GYP 004*> **GRACE AND SPEED**		–
	- However many it takes / Marianne, you've done it now... / Grace and speed / The streets is full of creeps / Out past the moat / Crooked mast / Different cities / Second best / Parasites and ghosts / Roman candle. *(French-iss. May 08 on Alter K; none)*		
May 09.	(ltd-7") *(none)* TURPENTINE. / Woolgathering	–	French –
		Supply & Demand	not issued
Aug 09.	(cd) <*SAD 005*> **DIVIDE AND CONQUER**		–
	- Divide and conquer / Fistful of swoon / Resurrection Mary / A mighty leviathan of old / Woolgathering / Turpentine / Before the great war / Long lost cause / The sound and the fury / Beverly Cleary's 115th dream. *(French-iss. Apr 09 on Alter K diff.order; none)*		
Sep 10.	(cd-ep) <*???*> A MINOR SPELL		–
	- The waking hour (A minor spell) / Everything is spinning / Good morning / All together for the taking / Ways and means.		
Apr 11.	(cd) <*SAD 011*> **DIG DOWN DEEP**		–
	- Dig down deep / Concerning past and future conquests / Beat, beat, my heart / The great Gray / As a matter of fact / The nature of our kind / Spite / Pick up the pace / AOK / The waking hour.		

Suzanne VEGA

Demure singer/songwriter SUZANNE VEGA (b. Suzanne Nadine Peck, July 11, 1959 in Santa Monica, California) was probably the most left-field and stylishly autumnal among the 1980s femme-folk cohort that included TRACY CHAPMAN, SHAWN COLVIN and MICHELLE SHOCKED,

Renamed SUZANNE VEGA after her jazz-guitarist mother got divorced and married Puerto Rican novelist Ed Vega, she was brought up in the Spanish Harlem neighbourhood of Manhattan and New York's Upper West Side. Studying dance at the High School of Performing Arts, the songwriting prodigy spent her spare time gaining valuable musical experience in the folk clubs of Greenwich Village, inspired by the likes of COHEN, DYLAN, Lou Reed and BAEZ.

Hooking up with managers Ron Fierstein and Steve Addabbo, VEGA eventually secured a contract with A&M, and Addabbo and Lenny Kaye (ex-Patti Smith Group) produced her self-titled debut album, **SUZANNE VEGA** (1985) {*7}.

Critically acclaimed, this starkly compelling folk set saw VEGA hailed as the new JONI MITCHELL, with some observers drawing comparisons with JANIS IAN and even DORY PREVIN. Highly intelligent and acutely observed, VEGA's musings were reminiscent of LEONARD COHEN, although she possessed a distinctive lyric style with a hushed, delicately understated vocal to match.

Buoyed by the UK success (on its second release) of the single 'Marlene On The Wall', the album almost made the Top 10, although it struggled to penetrate the US Top 100. A couple of months later she scored another UK Top 40 with the moodily intense 'Left Of Center', written for the soundtrack of cult 1980s teen movie 'Pretty In Pink' and featuring New Wave jazz aficionado Joe Jackson on piano.

VEGA finally broke through in her home country with 'Luka', a poignant character portrait of an abused child that made it all the way to No.3 in the US charts. The accompanying album, **SOLITUDE STANDING** (1987) {*8}, consolidated VEGA's standing as one of the most promising young talents in the new singer-songwriter movement. One track, the acappella 'Tom's Diner' (only a minor UK hit on its original release in 1987), was later reworked by the dance act DNA, its success prompting a re-mixed UK Top 5 version.

A third album, **DAYS OF OPEN HAND** (1990) {*6}, met with mixed reactions, its more ambitious jazz arrangements (co-produced by her keyboard player and boyfriend Anton Sanko) and enigmatic lyrics contrasting with the economical simplicity of her earlier work. No hit singles were forthcoming, although the success of 'Tom's Diner' kept VEGA's career on the commercial straight and narrow.

No doubt inspired by the rhythmic innovation of the re-mix of that track, her fourth set, **99.9 F** (1992) {*6}, produced by husband-to-be Mitchell Froom, found VEGA experimenting with all manner of sound effects. The result was arguably her most consistent set since the debut, the likes of 'Blood Makes Noise' and 'Fat Man And Dancing Girl' fastening spiky rhythmic structures on to VEGA's trademark sound, while the more traditional 'When Heroes Go Down' showed she could still write affecting folk-pop. In 1996 she was back with her most accessible work to date **NINE OBJECTS OF DESIRE** {*6}, another record that went beyond the boundaries of folk.

While her 1990s were characterised by experimentalism, largely due to the influence of husband/producer Mitchell Froom, their subsequent divorce made for rich songwriting material and a back-to-basics approach on the Rupert Hine-produced **SONGS IN RED AND GRAY** (2001) {*6}. Very much a return to the spare, confessional style that made her name back in the 1980s, the record analysed the breakdown of her marriage in oblique yet emotionally loaded style. After six years in the musical wilderness (during which time she married again, suffered the loss of her artist brother Timothy Vega and changed labels), Suzanne was, for many critics, back to her very best on her contemporary comeback set **BEAUTY AND CRIME** (2007) {*7}. *MCS*

Suzanne Vega - vocals, acoustic guitar (with session band)

US A&M / UK A&M

Jun 85. (lp/c/cd) *<75021-5072-1/-4/-2> (AMA/AMC/CDA 5072)*
SUZANNE VEGA [91] Jul 85 [11]
- Cracking / Freeze tag / Marlene on the wall / Small blue thing / Straight lines / Undertow / Some journey / The queen and the soldier / Knight moves / Neighborhood girls. *(cd-iss. Mar 93; CDMID 177) (lp re-iss. Apr 00 on Vivante; VPLP 006)*

Aug 85. (7") *<2759> (AM 275)* MARLENE ON THE WALL. / Neighborhood Girls [ ] [ ]

Jan 86. (7") *(AM 294)* SMALL BLUE THING. / The Queen And The Soldier [–] [65]
(d7"+=) *(DAM 294)* - Some journey / Black widow station.

Feb 86. (7") *<2834>* SMALL BLUE THING. / Left Of Center [ ] [–]

Mar 86. (7") *(AM 309)* MARLENE ON THE WALL. / Small Blue Thing [–] [21]
(10"+=) *(AMY 309)* - Neighborhood girls / Straight lines (live).

May 86. (7") *(AM 320)* LEFT OF CENTER. / Undertow [–] [32]
(10"+=) *(AMX 320)* - ('A'-live) / Freeze tag (live).
(cd-s+=) *(CDQ 320)* - Cracking.
——(above single featured Joe Jackson on piano)

Oct 86. (7") *(AM 349)* GYPSY. / Cracking (live) [–] [ ]
(12"+=) *(AMY 349)* - Knight movies (live).

May 87. (lp/c/cd) *<75021-5136-1/-4/-2> (SUZ LP/MC/CD 2)*
SOLITUDE STANDING [11] [2]
- Tom's diner / Luka / Ironbound - Fancy poultry / In the eye / Night vision / Solitude standing / Calypso / Language / Gypsy / Wooden horse (Caspar Hauser's song) / Tom's diner (reprise).

May 87. (7") *<2937>* LUKA. / Night Vision [3] [–]

May 87. (7") *(VEGA 1)* LUKA. / Straight Lines (live) [–] [23]
(12"+=) *(VEGA 12)* - Neighborhood girls.
(10"+=/c-s+=) *(VEGA 10/C10)* - Cracking (alt. mix).

Jul 87. (7") *(VEGA 2)* TOM'S DINER. / Left Of Center [–] [58]
(10"+=/12"+=) *(VEGA 210/212)* - Luka (live).
(cd-s+=) *(VEGCD 2)* ('A'-live).

Aug 87. (7") *<2960>* SOLITUDE STANDING. / Tom's Diner [94] [–]

Nov 87. (7") *<2888>* GYPSY. / Left Of Center [ ] [–]

Nov 87. (7"/c-s) *(VEGA/+C 3)* SOLITUDE STANDING. / Luka [–] [ ]
(12"+=) *(VEGA 3-12)* - Ironbound - Fancy poultry.
(10"/cd-s) *(VEG A3-10/CD 3)* - ('A') / Marlene on the wall (live) / Some journey (live).

Apr 90. (cd/c/lp) *<75021-5293-2/-4/-1> (CDA/AMC/AMA 5293)*
DAYS OF OPEN HAND [50] [7]
- Tired of sleeping / Men in a war / Rusted pipe / Book of dreams / Institution green / Those whole girls (run in grace) / Room off the street / Big space / Predictions / Fifty-fifty chance / Pilgrimage. *(cd re-iss. May 95; 395293-2)*

Apr 90. (7"/c-s) *(AM/+MC 559)* BOOK OF DREAMS. / Big Space [–] [66]
(cd-s+=) *(AMCD 559)* - Marlene on the wall (live) / Ironbound (live).
(10"++=) *(AMX 559)* - Fancy poultry (live).

Jun 90. (7") *(AM 565)* TIRED OF SLEEPING. / Those Whole Girls (Run In Grace) [–] [ ]
(10"+=/cd-s+=) *(AM X/CD 565)* - Left of center / Room off the street.

Sep 90. (7"/c-s; DNA featuring SUZANNE VEGA) *<1529>* *(AM/+MC 592)* TOM'S DINER. / ('A'-version) [5] Jul 90 [2]
(12"+=/cd-s+=) *(AM X/CD 592)* - (two other DNA mixes).

Sep 90. (7"/c-s) *(AM/+MC 584)* MEN IN A WAR. / Undertow (live) [–] [ ]
(12"+=/cd-s+=) *(AM X/CD 584)* - ('A'-live).

Aug 92. (7"/c-s) *(AM/+C 0029)* IN LIVERPOOL. / Some Journey [–] [52]
(cd-s+=) *(AMCD 0029)* - The queen and the soldier / Luka.

Sep 92. (cd/c/lp) *<314-540005-2/-4/-1> (540012-2/-4/-1)* **99.9 F** [86] [20]
- Rock in this pocket (song of David) / Blood makes noise / In Liverpool / 99.9 F / Blood sings / Fat man and dancing girl / (If you were) In my movie / As a child / Bad wisdom / When heroes go down / As girls go / Songs of sand. *(UK cd bonus +=)* - Private goes public. *(cd re-iss. Sep 97; same)*

Oct 92. (7"/c-s) *(AM/+C 0085)* 99.9 F. / Men Will Be Men [–] [46]
(cd-s+=) *(AMCD 0085)* - Rock in this pocket (acoustic) / In Liverpool (acoustic).
(cd-s) *(AMCDX 0085)* - ('A') / Tired of sleeping / Straight lines / Tom's diner (all live).

Dec 92. (7"/c-s) *(AM/+C 0112)* BLOOD MAKES NOISE. / Tom's Diner [–] [60]
(cd-s) *(AMCD 0112)* - ('A') / Neighborhood girls / Predictions / China doll.
(12") *(AMY 0112)* - ('A') / ('A'-Mitchell Froom remix) / ('A' house mix) / ('A'-master mix).

Feb 93. (7"/c-s) *(AM/+C 0158)* WHEN HEROES GO DOWN. / Knight Moves (live) [–] [58]
(cd-s+=) *(AMCD 0158)* - Men in a war (live) / Gypsy (live).
(cd-s) *(AMCDX 0158)* - ('A') / Marlene on the wall / Luka / Left of center.

Sep 96. (cd/c) *<(540583-2/-4)>* **NINE OBJECTS OF DESIRE** [92] Feb 97 [43]
- Birth-day (love made real) / Headshots / Caramel / Stockings / Casual match / Thin man / No cheap thrill / World before Columbus / Lolita / Honeymoon suite / Tombstone / My favorite plum.

Feb 97. (c-ep/cd-ep) *(581869-4/-2)* NO CHEAP THRILL / Luka / Marlene On The Wall / Tom's Diner [–] [40]

Jun 97. (c-s) *(582269-4)* BIRTH-DAY (LOVE MADE REAL) / Women On A Tier [–] [ ]
(cd-s) *(582267-2)* - ('A') / Caramel / Small blue thing / Blood makes noise.
(cd-s) *(582269-2)* - ('A') / Casual match / World before Columbus.

A&M / Universal

Sep 01. (cd) *<10493-2> (493111-2)* **SONGS IN RED AND GRAY** [ ] [ ]
- Penitent / Widow's walk / (I'll never be) Your Maggie May / It makes me wonder / Soap and water / Songs in red and gray / Last year's troubles / Priscilla / If I were a weapon / Harbor song / Machine ballerina / Solitaire / St Clare.

Blue Note / EMI

Jul 07. (cd) *<68270-2> (3973422)* **BEAUTY AND CRIME** [ ] Jun 07 [ ]
- Zephyr and I / Ludlow Street / New York is a woman / Pornographer's dream / Frank and Ava / Edith Wharton's figurines / Bound / Unbound / As you are now / Angel's doorway / Anniversary.

- (8-10*) compilations -

Dec 99. (cd/c) *A&M; <(540945-2/-4)>* **THE BEST OF SUZANNE VEGA: TRIED AND TRUE** [ ] Oct 98 [46]
- Luka / Tom's diner (DNA featuring SUZANNE VEGA) / Marlene on the wall / Caramel / 99.9 f / Small blue thing / Blood makes noise / Left of center (featuring JOE JACKSON on piano) / In Liverpool / Gypsy / Book of dreams / No cheap thrill / World before Columbus / When heroes go down / The queen and the soldier / Book and a cover / Rosemary.

Apr 03. (cd) *Universal; <AA69 493670-2> (9808884)*
RETROSPECTIVE: THE BEST OF SUZANNE VEGA [ ] Jul 03 [27]
- Luka / Tom's diner (DNA featuring SUZANNE VEGA) / Marlene on the wall / Caramel / 99.9 f / Tired of sleeping / Small blue thing / Blood makes noise / Left of center / (I'll never be) Your Maggie May / In Liverpool / Gypsy / Book of dreams / No cheap thrill / Calypso / World before Columbus / Solitude standing / Penitent / Rosemary / The queen and the soldier (live) / Woman on the tier (I'll see you through). *(d-cd-iss. Nov 03 +=; 9812889)* - Caramel (live) / Widow's talk (live) / Solitude standing (live) / Blood makes noise (live) / In Liverpool (a short reading from The Passionate Eye) / In Liverpool (live) / Anniversary (demo) / Tom's diner (original).

- (5-7*) compilations, others, etc.-

Oct 88. (cd-ep) *A&M; (AMCD 912)* COMPACT HITS [–] [ ]
- Luka / Left of center / Neighbourhood girls / The queen and the soldier.

Sep 91. (cd/c/lp; Various Artists) *A&M; (395363-2/-4/-1)*
TOM'S ALBUM [–] [ ]
- (contained reworkings by other artists of the track TOM'S DINER)

Feb 10. (cd) *Amanuensis; <69851 9 2501 2 4> Cooking Vinyl; (COOKCD 521)* **CLOSE-UP: VOL.1, LOVE SONGS** [ ] Jun 10 [ ]
- Small blue thing / Caramel / (If you were) In my movie / Gypsy / Marlene on the wall / (I'll never be) Your Maggie May / Harbor song / Headshots / Songs in red and gray / Stockings / Some journey / Bound.

Oct 10. (cd) *Amanuensis; <69851 9 2502 2 4> Cooking Vinyl; (COOKCD 522)* **CLOSE-UP: VOL.2, PEOPLE & PLACES** [ ] [ ]
- Luka / Zephyr and I / New York is a woman / In Liverpool / Calypso / Fat man and dancing girl / The queen and the soldier / Rock in this pocket (song of David)

/ Angel's doorway / Ironbound - Fancy poultry / Neighborhood girls / Tom's diner / The man who played God.

Jul 11. (cd) *Amanuensis; <69851 9 2503 2 4> Cooking Vinyl; (COOKCD 523)* **CLOSE-UP: VOL.3, STATES OF BEING** ▭ ▭
- Undertow / When heroes go down / My favourite plum / Solitude standing / Cracking / Last year's troubles / Solitaire / Blood makes noise / 50-50 chance / Penitent / Straight lines / Pornographer's dream / Instant of the hour after.

Laura VEIRS

Introspective neo-country-folkie LAURA VEIRS (b. October 24, 1973 in Colorado Springs, Colorado) has steadily risen from the ranks of kooky singer/songwriters, earning a New York Times 'Critics' Choice' nod for her wondrous fifth album, **YEAR OF METEORS** (2005) {*8}. Her second release for Nonesuch, it mapped out her intimate vignettes and her romantic and poetic visions like a modern-day SUZANNE VEGA or Sheryl Crow. Sample her wordplay and banter on 'Galaxies', 'Secret Someones', 'Parisian Dreams' and 'Magnetize'. She was backed by her Tortured Souls band of Steve Moore, Karl Blau and boyfriend/producer Tucker Martine of Modest Mouse.

Several years back, her self-financed, self-titled debut, **LAURA VEIRS** (1999) {*5}, was a live set that reflected her coffeehouse status at the time, and her clear, girly vocals and polite pronunciations trademarked VIERS from the get-go. **THE TRIUMPHS AND TRAVAILS OF ORPHAN MAE** (2001) {*7} let the listener wander into her mythical memoirs, sung with passion, on 'Up The River', 'Jailhouse Fire' and 'Blue Ink'.

Accompanied by jazz musicians Bill Frisell (guitar), Amy Denio (sax) and Fred Chalenor (bass), among others, her lyricism went beyond the realm of folk on the following set, **TROUBLED BY THE FIRE** (2003) {*7}, her first for the UK's Bella Union imprint, re-issued on Kill Rock Stars in 2006. Her first album on Nonesuch, **CARBON GLACIER** (2004) {*8}, put Laura on the critical map; check out 'Ether Sings', 'The Cloud Room', 'Lonely Angel Dust' and 'Riptide'.

Her sixth album, **SALTBREAKERS** (2007) {*7}, was her most assured record thus far, and tracks like 'Ocean Night Song', 'To The Country' (featuring the great Frisell again) and the title track expanded her appeal. A subsequent covers EP comprised MISSISSIPPI JOHN HURT's 'Spike Driver's Blues', A.P. Carter's 'Wildwood Flowers', CLARENCE ASHLEY's 'The Coo Coo Bird', ELIZABETH COTTEN's 'Freight Train' and Mike Dumovich's 'Wasps Of Rain', showing that there was more than one string to her bow.

Back to basics, and away from the control of a major record company, **JULY FLAME** (2010) {*7} found her free to expand her horizons in any direction she desired. Her best-selling record by far (it bubbled under the Top 100), it definitely had an air of her halcyon folky days. While FLEET FOXES had made it possible for Americans to buy into the burgeoning nu-folk scene, her best compositions here ('Sun Is King', 'I Can See Your Tracks' and 'Where Are You Driving?' took their own turn. *MCS*

Laura Veirs - vocals, guitars, banjo, bass / with session people

US: Raven Marching Band — UK: Bella Union

1999. (cd)*<RMB 001>* **LAURA VEIRS** [live] ▭ ⊟
- Green cowgirl / Dirty sheep / Blackbird pie / Tangerine / Marianas trench / I miss you / Outside Bud's Jazz Records / American way / Toe / Look out the window / Motorcycle man / Star panties / Hummingbird.

2001. (cd) *<RMB 002>* **THE TRIUMPHS AND TRAVAILS OF ORPHAN MAE** ▭ ⊟
- Jailhouse fire / Up the river / John Henry lives / Black-eyed Susan / Orphan Mae / Blue ink / Montague road / Through December / Raven marching band / Movin' along. *(UK-iss. Feb 05 on Bella Union; BELLACD 88) <re-iss. Jul 06 on Kill Rock Stars; KRS 475> <cd/red-lp-iss. May 11; RMB 002 CD/LP>*

Mar 03. (cd) *<RMB 003> (AKA 02)* **TROUBLED BY THE FIRE** ▭ Apr 04 ▭
- Lost at Seaflower cove / Bedroom eyes / The ballad of John Vogelin / Song my friends taught me / Cannon fodder / Tom Skookum road / Tiger tattoos / A shining lamp / Ohio clouds / Devil's hootenanny / Midnight singer. *<re-iss. Jul 06 on Kill Rock Stars; KRS 476>*

Nonesuch - Warners — Bella Union

Mar 04. (cd-s) *(BELLACD 62)* THE CLOUD ROOM / Shadow Blues ⊟ ▭

Aug 04. (cd) *<7559 79854-2> (BELLACD 52)* **CARBON GLACIER** ▭ Apr 04 ▭
- Ether sings / Icebound stream / Rapture / Lonely angel dust / The cloud room / Wind is blowing stars / Shadow blues / Anne Bonny rag / [*] / Snow camping / Chimney sweeping man / Salvage a smile / Blackened anchor / Riptide. *<lp-iss. Nov 07 on Jealous Butcher+=[*]; JB 064>* - Cliff driver.

Sep 04. (cd-s) *(BELLACD 84)* RIPTIDE / Rave Marching Band / Cliff Driver ⊟ ▭

Nonesuch - Warners — Nonesuch - Warners

Aug 05. (cd) *<(7559 79893-2)>* **YEAR OF METEORS** ▭ ▭
- Fire snakes / Galaxies / Secret someones / Magnetized / Parisian dream / Rialto / Through the glow / Cool water / Spelunking / Black gold blues / Where gravity is dead / Lake swimming. *(w/ untitled track) <lp-iss. Jan 06 on Kill Rock Stars; KRS 447>*

Oct 05. (ltd-7" blue) *(NS 003 - 7559 79931 7)* GALAXIES. / Magnetized ['punk' version] ⊟ ▭
(cd-s) *(7559 79929 2)* - ['A'] / ['A'-Kotos The Rock Thrower].

Mar 06. (ltd-7") *(NS 005)* SECRET SOMEONES. / Heart Of 17 [demo] ⊟ ▭

Mar 07. (ltd-7" blue/cd-s) *(NS 009 - 7559 79989 6/79988 1)* DON'T LOSE YOURSELF. / Bright Glittering Gifts ⊟ ▭

Apr 07. (cd) *<(7559 79993-5)>* **SALTBREAKERS** ▭ ▭
- Pink light / Ocean night song / Don't lose yourself / Drink deep / Wandering kind / Nightingale / Saltbreakers / To the country / Cast a hook in me / Phantom mountain / Black butterfly / Wrecking. *<lp-iss. Oct 07 on Film Guerrero; FG 26>*

Jul 07. (ltd-7" green) *(NS 012 - 7559 79971 1)* SALTBREAKERS. / Shape The Swarm ⊟ ▭

Raven Marching Band — Bella Union

2009. (cd-ep) *<RMB 005>* TWO BEERS VEIRS ⊟ tour ⊟
- Spike driver's blues / Wildwood flower / The coo coo bird / Freight train / Wasps of rain.

Jan 10. (cd/lp) *<RMB 006> (BELLA CD/V 220)* **JULY FLAME** ▭ ▭
- I can see your tracks / July flame / Sun is king / Where are you driving? / Life is good blues / Silo song / Little deschutes / Summer is the champion / When you give your heart / Sleeper in the valley / Wide-eyed, legless / Carol Kaye / Make something good. *(also digi-cd; BELLACD 220X)*

VERDURE (⟹ The SKYGREEN LEOPARDS)

VETIVER

An associate and friend of lo-fi folkie DEVENDRA BANHART (with whom he founded the label Gnomonsong), San Francisco-based Andy Cabic is best known for his own project, VETIVER. In the 1990s he had led out indie noisemongers The Raymond Brake (from Greensboro, North Carolina), who were responsible for a few EPs and an album, 'Piles Of Dirty Winters' (1995).

Cabic relocated to the west coast to study at the San Francisco Art Institute, and there he made friends with Devendra and other rising freak-folk stars such as JOANNA NEWSOM. Named after an Asian type of lemongrass used in the making of perfumes, VETIVER was born.

With backing from Jim Gaylord (violin), Alissa Anderson (cello) and BANHART on additional guitar, with guests Hope Sandoval of Mazzy Star and Colm O'Ciosoig of My Bloody Valentine, the Thom Monahan-produced **VETIVER** (2004) {*7} was unleashed. Devendra was Cabic's writing partner on two Tyrannosaurus Rex-like, mantra-meets-minstrel tracks, 'Amour Fou' and 'Los Pajaros Del Rio', while 'Oh Papa', 'Amerilie' and 'Luna Sea' were effectively emotional.

VETIVER and Cabic overhauled the band with incoming Noah Georgeson (guitar), Kevin Barker (guitar, ukulele, vocals) and Otto Hauser (drums, keyboards) for the subsequent odds-and-ends EP 'Between' - five songs including Fleetwood Mac's 'Find Me A Place' - and their second set, **TO FIND ME GONE** (2006) {*6}. The lovely song 'Maureen' featured on both records, and there was also a country tint on 'I Know No Pardon' and 'Down At El Rio'. Not content with his VETIVER activities, Cabic contributed to RIO EN MEDIO's 'The Bride Of Dynamite' set in 2007, which was far from his only outside work.

Their heritage lineage was taken further afield on VETIVER's next project, the covers set **THING OF THE PAST** (2008) {*7}, with Sanders Trippe (guitar) and Brent Dunne (bass) now in place. This eclectic collection saddled up a dozen covers of songs by country, folk and other rootsy artists, and here's the list: 'Houses' (ELYSE Weinberg), 'Roll On Babe' (DERROLL ADAMS), 'Sleep A Million Years' (VASHTI BUNYAN), 'Hook And Ladder' (Norman Greenbaum), 'To Baby' (Biff Rose), 'Road To Ronderlin' (IAIN MATTHEWS), 'Lon Chaney' (Garland Jeffreys), 'Hurry On Sundown' (Hawkwind), 'The Swimming Song' (LOUDON WAINWRIGHT III), 'Blue Driver' (MICHAEL HURLEY), 'Standin" (TOWNES VAN ZANDT) and 'I Must Be In A Good Place' (Bobby Charles).

Signing up wih Sub Pop (Bella Union in Europe), Cabic and his cosmic crew reunited for a fresh set of classic-rock-meets-AOR-folk, **TIGHT KNIT** (2009) {*7}, a slick record that demanded only the easiest of listening on tracks like 'Rolling Sea', 'Through The Front Door' and 'At Forest Edge' -

pass the Bread around! The same goes for the luscious and layered **THE ERRANT CHARM** (2011) {*6}. *MCS*

Andy Cabic - vocals, guitar, banjo / **Jim Gaylord** - violin / **Alissa Anderson** - cello / added **Devendra Banhart** - guitar

US DiCristina Stair Builders — UK DiCristina Stair Builders

Mar 04. (lp/cd) <*(STEP 02/+CD)*> **VETIVER** — May 04
- Oh papa / Without a song / Farther on / Amour fou / Los pajaros del Rio / Amerilie / Arboretum / Angels' share / Luna sea / Belles / On a nerve.

——**Noah Georgeson** - guitar; repl. Gaylord

——added **Kevin Barker** - guitar, ukulele, vocals / **Otto Hauser** - drums, keyboards

DiCristina Stair — Fat Cat

2005. (cd-ep) <*STEP 05CD*> BETWEEN
- Been so long / Save me a place / Busted (Brokedown version) / Maureen (live in Bolinas) / Belles (live at WMBR).

Jun 06. (d-lp/cd) <*STEP 07/+CD*> *(FAT LP/CD 43)* **TO FIND ME GONE**
- Been so long / You may be blue / No one word / Idle ties / I know no pardon / Maureen / The porter / Double / Red lantern girls / Lost and found *[d-lp only]* / Won't be me / Busted *[d-lp only]* / Down at El Rio.

——**Cabic, Anderson, Barker + Hauser** added **Brent Dunn** - bass / **Sanders Trippe** - guitar, vocals

Gnomonsong — Fat Cat

Jan 08. (12") <*GONG 10*> YOU MAY BE LONG (Neighbors remix). / Been So Long (Neighbors remix)

May 08. (lp/cd) <*GONG 11*> *(FAT LP/CD 75)* **THING OF THE PAST** — Jun 08
- Houses / Roll on babe / Sleep a million years / Hook and ladder / To baby / Road to Ronderlin / Lon Chaney / Hurry on sundown / The swimming song / Blue driver / Standin' / I must be in a good place now.

Sub Pop — Bella Union

Feb 09. (cd/lp) <*SPCD/SPLP 795*> *(BELLACD 194)* **TIGHT KNIT** — Mar 09
- Rolling sea / Sister / Everyday / Through the front door / Down from above / On the other side / More of this / Another reason to go / Strictly rule / At forest edge.

Jun 11. (cd/lp) <*SPCD/SPLP 936*> *(BELLA CD/V 291)* **THE ERRANT CHARM**
- It's beyond me / Worse for wear / Can't you tell / Hard to break / Fog emotion / Right away / Wonder why / Ride ride ride / Faint praise / Soft glass.

VIKING MOSES!

This was the brainchild of Brendon Massei of Tunas, Missouri, who had begun his GUTHRIE-driven dustbowl campaign with the solo effort **AT STATION FOUR** (1999) {*6} under the guise of SUPPERBELL ROUNDUP. Before that he had released cassettes as Spork.

A musically talented high-school dropout, his first port of call as an indie entertainer was playing support to the likes of Ted Leo, DEVENDRA BANHART, Cat Power and Will Oldham. Not an easy fit into the folk music category, VIKING MOSES got under way with debut album **CROSSES** (2005) {*6}, initially a double set split with Spenking, also known as Spencer Klingman. Taking in neo-traditionalist ideals and a freak-folkish ethos, the album was best served by 'Still My Home' (very LEONARD COHEN's 'Hallelujah'), 'Little Emma's Smile' and the title track.

'Crosses' and 2008's **THE PARTS THAT SHOWED** {*6} demonstrated that Brendon had only a marginal interest in emo-folk; he was unhappy with any kind of pigeonholing or association. His most interesting recordings, although certainly not his best, are on the 2007 EP 'Swollen And Small: The Songs Of Neutral Milk Hotel', a fully-fledged homage to the latter band. Massei has been a little conspicuous by his absence of late. *MCS*

SUPPERBELL ROUNDUP

Brendon Massei - vocals, acoustic guitar, banjo

US Happy Christ — UK not issued

1996. (c) <*none*> EVERYTHING HAPPENED SO FAST, WHERE'D IT ALL GO WRONG?

Recycled Carbon — not issued

Aug 98. (cd-ep) <*none*> MATCHBOOK SORROWS

SideOneDummy — not issued

Mar 99. (cd) <*1211*> **AT STATION FOUR**
- Playing the old banjo / Lord knows, I need my own place to stay / Where you'd end up / Come in through the side door / The night before you had to leave / Things aren't the same as they used to be / Riding the bus back home / Where'd it all go wrong / Springfield / O babe, it ain't no lie / Leaving town.

BRENDON MASSEI

No Town Sound — not issued

2000. (cd) <*MDISTRO 001*> **NO MORE SAD EYES**
- Get me away, and get me back strong / The way and the will to do so / Las Vegas town / I can't hang / Those who have helped me / The ones most valued / I know where I'll go, where we'll all go / No more sad eyes, and have you less fear / If you've no one to see, I'd love you to go out with me / They call me what they will.

VIKING MOSES!

Massei - vocals, instruments (w/ occasionally Spencer Klingman + Kate Urcioli)

Nightpass — not issued

Sep 04. (3"cd- ep) <*none*> SANDSTORMS EP
- Sandstorms / In servitude / No blessing as fine as this.

Natrix — not issued

Nov 04. (c) <*none*> LIVE AT CHEZ BIPPY (live)

Marriage — Poptones

Feb 05. (d-cd; split) <*MAR 009*> **CROSSES / Spenking**
- (tracks below + eight further tracks by Spenking [Spencer Klingman])

Sep 05. (7" split) <*FT 003*> The Aum Rifle (2). / VIKING MOSES!: The Chinese Pavillion

(above issued on Folk Tales)

May 06. (7") *(mc 5108s)* SANDSTORMS. / I Will Always Love You

Aug 06. (cd) *(mc 5112cd)* **CROSSES**
- Still my home / Little Emma's smile / Country gown / Georgia / My husband's hand / Dancing by the water day / Carolina / Crosses / Wet stones at both my sides / Virginia / Little arms / Fingernail moon / Delighted / Home.

Nov 06. (7") *(mc 5123s)* WEREWOLVES IN THE CITY. / Threshold Of Man

not issued — Fire

Mar 07. (cd-ep) *(FIRECD 103)* SWOLLEN AND SMALL: THE SONGS OF NEUTRAL MILK HOTEL
- You've passed / Gardenhead - Leave me alone / Where you'll find me now / Holland 1945.

——**Massei + Klingman** added **John McCauley III** - guitar (of Deer Tick) / **Cody Brant** - bass / **Jacob Soto** - drums (of Flashar)

Epiphysis — Poptones

Nov 08. (cd/col-lp) <*none*> *(MC 5125)* **THE PARTS THAT SHOWED** — Mar 07
- Lucky numbers / Old buck knife / One arm around the sinner / Sole command of the day / Jones boys / On and one in sunsets / Life empty eyes / Little bows / Under the soda sky / Ma Moses / Belly down / Pa Moses.

The WAILIN' JENNYS

Formed in Winnipeg, Manitoba in 2002, Canadian harmony group The WAILIN' JENNYS were not, despite basing their name on Waylon Jennings, a country act. Although their roots were firmly planted in that genre, it was neo-folk and bluegrass that they relied on, at least initially - a pleasant surprise indeed.

With three multi-talented singers and not a Dixie Chick in sight, Cara Luft (alto), Nicky Mehta (mezzo-soprano) and ex-Scruj MacDuhk member Ruth Moody (soprano) worked their way up the musical ladder after a semi-impromptu performance at their local Sled Dog Music guitar shop. Ruth had already self-released her 'Blue Muse' set in 2002, and Nicky Mehta had issued 'Weather Vane' a year earlier.

The combination was too hard to resist for the Red House label, which almost immediately set about recording their debut album, **40 DAYS** (2004) {*7}, later a Juno Award winner. Mixing sea shanties 'Saucy Sailor' and the acappella 'The Parting Glass' with their own originals (including Luft's similar 'Come All You Sailors') and covers of NEIL YOUNG's 'Old Man' and John Hiatt's 'Take It Down', the trio had all the harmonies of Heart, The Corrs and the INDIGO GIRLS.

When Luft left for a solo career, the equally harmonious Annabelle Chvostek brought a sweet country taste to the table on their second album, **FIRECRACKER** (2006) {*7}, which had one sourced track, 'Long Time Traveler', and otherwise shared songwriting duties around the group. But just as the trio had settled, cracks appeared once again as Annabelle opted to leave. Heather Masse, from Maine, joined in time for the 2008-recorded concert set **LIVE AT THE MAUCH CHUNK OPERA HOUSE** (2009) {*6}. Featuring Emmylou Harris's 'Deeper Well', LEADBELLY's 'Bring Me Li'l Water Silvy', Gillian Welch's 'One More Dollar', Ella Jenkins's 'Racing With The Sun', JANE SIBERRY's 'Calling All Angels', Heather Moose's 'Driving', George Gershwin's 'Summertime' and trad cuts 'Bold Riley' and 'Motherless Child', it offered an eclectic and rootsy crossover for their growing fan base. Named after a traditional song, **BRIGHT MORNING STARS** (2011) {*7} was another seamless melding of effortless originals that sounded like perennials of a bygone age; check out 'Bird Song', 'Swing Low Sail High' and 'Across The Sea'. *MCS*

Cara Luft - vocals, acoustic guitar / **Nicky Mehta** - vocals, multi / **Ruth Moody** - vocals, multi (ex-Scruj MacDuhk)

US Maple — UK not issued

2003. (cd-ep) *<001>* THE WAILIN' JENNYS [–] own [–]
- Come all you sailors / Deeper well / Sun's gonna rise / Row him home / Bring me li'l water, Silvy / Bring 'em all in.

Red House — Jericho Beach

Aug 04. (cd) *<RHRCD 177> (JMB 0403)* **40 DAYS** [ ] Dec 04 [ ]
- One voice / Saucy sailor / Arlington / Beautiful dawn / [untitled] / This is where / Old man / Heaven when we're home / Ten mile stilts / Come all you sailors / Take it down / Something to hold onto / The parting glass.

——(late 2004) **Annabelle Chvostek** - alto vocals, guitar; repl. Luft; she released a solo set in 2007, 'The Light Fantastic'

Jun 06. (cd) *<RHRCD 195> (JMB 0605)* **FIRECRACKER** [ ] Jul 06 [ ]
- The Devil's paintbrush road / Glory bound / Begin / Things that you know / Swallow / Starlight / Apocalypse lullaby / This heart of mine / Long time traveler / Avila / Some good thing / Prairie town / Firecracker.

——(2007) **Heather Masse** - alto vocals, upright bass (ex-Heather & The Barbarians; one set, 'Tell Me Tonight') repl. Chvostek

Red House — Red House

Aug 09. (cd) *<(RHRCD 220)>* **LIVE AT THE MAUCH CHUNK OPERA HOUSE** [live August 30, 2008] [ ] [ ]
- Deeper well / Summertime / (intro to...) / Driving / Bold Riley / (intro to...) / Glory bound / Arlington / Bring me li'l water Silvy / One more dollar / Racing with the sun / Paint a picture / (intro to...) / Begin / Motherless child / Calling all angels / (intro to...) / One voice.

Red House — True North

Jan 11. (cd) *<RHRCD 234> (TND 543)* **BRIGHT MORNING STARS** [ ] Feb 11 [ ]
- Swing low sail high / All the stars / Bird song / Away but never gone / Storm comin' / Mona Louise / Bright morning stars / Across the sea / Asleep at last / What has been done / Cherry blossom love / You are here / Last goodbye.

RUTH MOODY

Red House — Red House

Jul 10. (cd) *<(RHRCD 230)>* **THE GARDEN** [ ] [ ]
- The garden / Cold outside / Travelin' shoes / We can only listen / Within without you / Never said goodbye / Winter waltz / Nest / We could pretend / Tell me / Valentine / Closer now.

—— Heather Masse released a solo set, 'Bird Song' (2010)

Lucy WAINWRIGHT ROCHE

Being born 1981 in the hub of NY's perennial folk fountain of Greenwich Village probably had its perks, but having two celeb folk parents LOUDON WAINWRIGHT III and SUZZY ROCHE definitely had more advantages than most. That's not to say she used any of her pop pedigree as a crux, Lucy - like her half-siblings Rufus and Martha - wanted to experience a world outside her musical appendenges before deciding; for Lucy it was a matter of teacher-training and garnering a masters degree before thinking musical glory.

By the mid-00s though, she'd all but abandoned her classroom exploits to turn singer for brother Rufus. To boost interest in her revived love of the biz, WAINWRIGHT ROCHE toured supporting Neko Case, DAR WILLIAMS, etc. Finally, without much of a bugle sound, her first album **LUCY** (2010) {*6} surfaced. Compared to the likes of JONI MITCHELL, Tori Amos and INDIGO GIRLS, there were a few top tunes here by way of `Early Train' and the Snow Patrol-esque `Open Season', while two covers appeared through SIMON & GARFUNKEL's `America' and ELLIOTT SMITH's `Say Yes' (the latter a hidden track). *MCS*

Lucy Wainwright Roche - vocals, acoustic guitar / + session people

US Strike Back — UK not issued

Oct 10. (cd) *<SB 130>* **LUCY** [ ] [ ]
- Once in / Open season / Early train / The worst part / October / Statesville / I-35 / Accident & emergency (for S.J.C.) / Mercury news / Starting square / America. *(hidden track +=)* - Say yes.

Martha WAINWRIGHT

If you're going to be a folk singer, it can't be too bad if your parents are LOUDON WAINWRIGHT III and KATE McGARRIGLE, plus an equally famous older sibling, Rufus Wainwright - not forgetting aunt SLOAN WAINWRIGHT. Nevertheless, Martha (b. May 8, 1976 in Montreal, Quebec) was reluctant at first to follow her musical dynasty, although it was clear from early on that she had an abundance of talent.

Gaining confidence through her drama studies at Montreal's Concordia University, she slowly began to write the occasional song, and those who saw her perform at coffee-houses and bars (she produced a demo tape, 'Ground Floor', in 1997) encouraged her to take a more serious approach. Brother Rufus enlisted her as a backing singer on his stage shows, and she took a part in the stage musical 'Largo'. Her first official release was a self-titled EP in 1999.

Moving to New York, she met producer Brad Albetta, who worked with her on her debut album, also entitled **MARTHA WAINWRIGHT** (2005) {*7}, and married him in September 2007. Although the record bore traces of her mother Kate (of KATE & ANNA McGARRIGLE fame), Martha's dramatic, folky, show-tunes manner shone through on gems like 'Bloody Mother Fucking Asshole' (her first single), 'Factory', 'These Flowers', 'Don't Forget' and the climactic reworking of Vaughan Williams's 'Whither I Must Wander'. In 2006 Martha featured on Snow Patrol's hit 'Set The Fire...', a slight indie-pop diversion but a useful addition to her eclectic CV.

I KNOW YOU'RE MARRIED BUT I'VE GOT FEELINGS TOO (2008) {*7} put the spotlight on her VEGA-meets-Cyndi Lauper life portraits, her skill at defining relationships in graceful vignettes coming to the fore on 'Bleeding Over You', 'Comin' Tonight' and 'The George Song'. The tacked-on karaoke covers of Pink Floyd's 'See Emily Play' and Eurythmics' 'Love Is A Stranger' were a tad ill-advised.

2009's self-indulgent and showbizzy **SANS FUSILS, NI SOULIERS, A PARIS: MARTHA WAINWRIGHT'S PIAF RECORD** {*6} stamped her passport with a whole set of songs associated with Edith Piaf covers.

Martha's mother, KATE McGARRIGLE, died on January 18, 2010. *MCS*

Martha Wainwright - vocals, acoustic guitar / + session players

Can/US Querbes Service — UK not issued

1999. (cd-ep) *<QS 902>* MARTHA WAINWRIGHT [-] Canada [-]
- Lolita / G.P.T. / You've got a way / Laurel & Hardy / Jimi (takes so much time) / Don't forget.

Zoe — Drowned In Sound

Jan 05. (cd-ep) *<01143 2007-2> (DiS 0009)* BLOODY MOTHER FUCKING ASSHOLE [ ] Nov 04 [ ]
- Bloody mother fucking asshole / I will internalize / When the day is short *[not on UK rel.]* / It's over / How soon.

Mar 05. (cd-ep) *(DiS 0010)* FACTORY [-] [ ]
- Factory / Car song / Bye bye blackbird (live) / New York, New York, New York.

Apr 05. (cd) *<01143 1063-2> (DiS 0011)* **MARTHA WAINWRIGHT** [ ] [63]
- Far away / G.P.T. / Factory / These flowers / Ball and chain / Don't forget / This life / When the day is short / Bloody mother fucking asshole / TV show / The maker / Who was I kidding? / Whither must I wander. *(re-iss. May 05 +=; DIS 0011X)* - Bring back my heart (feat. RUFUS WAINWRIGHT) / Baby / Dis, quand reviendras-tu?

Aug 05. (cd-s) *<01143-1063-2 SI01> (DiS 0012)* WHEN THE DAY S SHORT / New York, New York, New York / I Was In The House When The House Burned Down (live) [ ] [ ]

Nov 05. (cd-ep) *<MRCD 6452>* I WILL INTERNALIZE [-] Canada [-]
- I will internalize / Baby / Bring back my heart / New York, New York, New York / Dis, quand reviendras-tu?

(above issued on MapleMusic)

May 08. (7") *(DiS 0038)* BLEEDING ALL OVER YOU. / Love Is A Stranger [-] [ ]

Jun 08. (cd) *<431116> (DiS 0039)* **I KNOW YOU'RE MARRIED BUT I'VE GOT FEELINGS TOO** [ ] [29]
- Bleeding all over you / You cheated me / Jesus and Mary / Comin' tonight / Tower song / Hearts club band / So many friends / In the middle of the night / The George song / Niger river / Jimi / See Emily play / I wish I were / Love is a stranger.

V2 — V2

Nov 09. (cd/lp) *<(VVR 723067/723882)>* **SANS FUSILS, NI SOULIERS, A PARIS: MARTHA WAINWRIGHT'S PIAF RECORD** (live at Dixon Place Theatre, NY) [ ] [ ]
- La foule / Adieu mon coeur / Une enfant / L'accordeoniste / Le brun et le blond / Les grognards / C'est toujours la meme histoire / Hudsonia / C'est a Hambourg / Non, la vie n'est pas triste / Soudain une vallee / Marie Trottoir / Le metro de Paris / Le chant d'amour / Les blouses blanches. *(w/free DVD)*

Sloan WAINWRIGHT

If country-blues is folk music, then singer/songwriter SLOAN WAINWRIGHT (b. 1957, younger sister of sardonic folkie LOUDON WAINWRIGHT III) can take her place with the best of latter genre in history. Her smoky, multi-octave voice can be compared with the likes of Joan Armatrading and Beverly Craven, with a tinge of TIM BUCKLEY thrown in. While she was raising two children, her first taste of the limelight came through composing songs for children's theatre and dance projects, and she entered open-mic competitions at the Town Crier Café in Pawling, NY in 1990.

By the mid-1990s the SLOAN WAINWRIGHT band had come together, comprising Steven Murphy (guitar), ex-Skatalites jazz player Cary Brown (keyboards), Doug Wray (bass) and Greg Burrows (percussion). She signed a contract with the Waterbug label, releasing the album **SLOAN WAINWRIGHT** {*6} in 1996. With a dozen songs, there was room for a cover of the Grateful Dead's 'Box Of Rain', and her version of The Beatles' 'Across The Universe' boosted her second set, **FROM WHERE YOU ARE** (1998) {*6}.

THE SONG INSIDE (2002) {*5} disappointed the critics a little, although lyrically she still possessed a good deal of insight and rootsy passion, as heard on 'Bridgeburner'. **COOL MORNING** (2004) {*6} was a self-financed release.

ON A NIGHT BEFORE CHRISTMAS (2005) {*5}, **LIFE GROWS BACK** (2006) {*7} and **REDISCOVERY** (2008) {*6} had their high and low moments. The last-named was a covers set taking in NICK DRAKE's 'Time Of No Reply', Johnny Cash's 'Ring Of Fire', NEIL YOUNG's 'After The Gold Rush', BOB DYLAN's 'Meet Me In The Morning' and 'Every Grain Of Sand', George Harrison's 'All Things Must Pass', Marvin Gaye's 'Mercy Me - The Ecology', PHIL OCHS's 'There But For Fortune', John Lennon's 'Love' and Jimmy Cliff's 'Sitting Here In Limbo'.

The WAINWRIGHT family's loss of Loudon's ex-wife KATE McGARRIGLE (mother of Sloan's nephew Rufus and niece Martha) in January 2010 followed fast on the death of Sloan's husband of three decades, George McTavey, in December 2008. Her eighth album, **UPSIDE DOWN AND UNDER MY HEART** (2011) {*6}, paid homage to him. *MCS*

Sloan Wainwright - vocals, acoustic guitar (w/ session people)

US Waterbug — UK Waterbug

Aug 96. (cd) *<(WBG 0023CD)>* **SLOAN WAINWRIGHT** [ ] [ ]
- Hey girl / Unseen guide / Box of rain / Steal my thunder / Poison television / On a windy day (baretrees) / Daddy's water / Without / Arm's length / Our love / Stand / I'm only listening.

Sep 98. (cd) *<(WBG 0042CD)>* **FROM WHERE YOU ARE** [ ] Oct 98 [ ]
- Mountain of sense / I eye the lady / Psycho pondering / Don't go / Here comes the rain / For my pride / My new car / Lament / I guess I can / Unravel / Across the universe / From where you are. *(bonus +=)* - Untitled.

Farkie Music — not issued

Apr 02. (cd) *<7017>* **THE SONG INSIDE** [ ] [-]
- Too nice for too long / You are the feast / Wavelength / Bridgeburner / Falling backwards / The song inside / Less is more / Fall with me / Freedom / Martha / Steven Leif / I stand up / Unseen guide.

Derby Disc — not issued

Aug 04. (cd) **COOL MORNING** [ ] [-]
- Cool morning / Word of the day / Good day to live / Illinois / Where the streets have no name / Illuminate / I spied you / Ready or not / From where you are / Summertime.

Nov 05. (cd; as SLOAN WAINWRIGHT and Friends) **ON A NIGHT BEFORE CHRISTMAS** (live) [ ] [-]
- Illuminate / 2000 miles / River / Blue Christmas / How beautiful are the feet / Thank God it's Christmas / Silver bells / O come, o come Emmanuel / We three guitarists / A soalin' / Search the sky / Christmas is the time to say I love you / Silent night.

Jun 06. (cd) **LIFE GROWS BACK** [ ] [-]
- When I walk away / Tired of wasting time / Between the lines / Wild in this world / Bad for her / These are the days / The baby and the bathwater / Meet the sun halfway / Out of her hands / Viking tree / Something that comes close.

Oct 08. (cd) **REDISCOVERY** [ ] [-]
- Time of no reply / Ring of fire / After the gold rush / Meet me in the morning / All things must pass / Mercy me - The ecology / There but for fortune / Every grain of sand / Love / Sitting here in limbo.

Jun 11. (cd) **UPSIDE DOWN AND UNDER MY HEART** [ ] [-]
- Living out the best of your life / Upside down and under my heart / Here I am / I can see now / Today / My song / I wear the ring / Holland / Little bit right / I am free.

Abigail WASHBURN

Neo-traditionalist singer/songwriter ABIGAIL WASHBURN (b. November 10, 1979 in Evanston, Illinois) has maintained a Chinese connection since her first visit in 1996, having been an East Asian Studies major at school.

Coming home and moving to Nashville via Vermont, she discovered bluegrass music and the banjo, later taking lead vocals with her friends The Cleary Brothers - she had been singing at festivals since she was a child - as they continued to tour post-millennium. Abigail's love of old-timey, folk and country led to an invitation to join femme folkies UNCLE EARL, although her tenure was all too brief, featuring only on their 2005 album, 'She Waits For Night'. On the strength of coming second with her song 'Rockabye Dixie' at the Chris Austin Songwriting Contest at the MerleFest trad festival in North Carolina, she signed a solo deal with the Nettwerk label.

WASHBURN was accompanied by a diverse line-up, including Collective Soul's Ryan Hoyle, Bela Fleck and Jason McConnell of The Duhks, on her off-kilter, Appalachian-inspired debut **SONG OF THE TRAVELING DAUGHTER** (2005) {*6}. Led Zeppelin fans should steer clear of her version of the trad song 'Nobody's Fault But Mine'.

After visiting China again (and also Tibet) on a US government-funded tour with the Sparrow Quartet (alongside Bela Fleck on banjo, Casey Driessen on fiddle and Ben Sollee on cello), she released a whole album of east-meets-west songs, **ABIGAIL WASHBURN & THE SPARROW QUARTET** (2008) {*7}. Featuring some Chinese lyrics and the double-banjo attack of Bela and Abigail, it proved the trip had been worthwhile. In 2009 she released the commendable trip-folk EP 'Afterquake', proceeds going to help survivors of the Sichuan Province earthquake.

With an impressive session list including Bill Frisell, Viktor Krauss, Wu Fei and fiddlers Jeremy Kittel and Rayna Gellert, **CITY OF REFUGE** (2011) {*7} was as contemporary, from a roots angle, as could be. Writing most of the songs with Kai Welch, WASHBURN and band cruised along on everything from country/gospel to dustbowl folk-blues. Check out 'Bring Me My Queen', 'Dreams Of Nectar' and the trad song 'Bright Morning Stars'. *MCS*

Abigail Washburn - vocals, banjo (ex-UNCLE EARL) / + session players

US Nettwerk — UK Nettwerk

Aug 05. (cd) *<30423-2>* **SONG OF THE TRAVELING DAUGHTER** — Feb 06
- Sometimes / Rockabye Dixie / Coffee's cold / Red and blazing / Single drop of honey / Eve stole the apple / Who's gonna shoe / Backstep Cindy - Purple bamboo / The lost lamb / Nobody's fault but mine / Halo / Song of the traveling daughter / Deep in the night / Momma.

May 08. (cd) *<30792-2>* **ABIGAIL WASHBURN & THE SPARROW QUARTET**
- Overture / A fuller wine / Strange things / Great big wall in China / Taiyang chulai / Oh me, oh my / Captain / A Kazakh melody / Banjo pickin' girl / Kangding qingge - Old-timey dance party / Sugar and pie / It ain't easy / Journey home.

(next presented by ABIGAIL WASHBURN and the Shanghai Restoration Project)

Afterquake — not issued

May 09. (cd-ep) *<none>* AFTERQUAKE — -
- Quake / Tibetan wish / Sala / Dream seek / Chinese recess / Song for mama / Little birdie.

Foreign Children — Rounder - Decca

Jan 11. (cd) *<15465-2> <6 13289-2>* **CITY OF REFUGE**
- Prelude / City of refuge / Bring me my queen / Chains / Ballad of treason / Last train / Burn thru / Corner girl / Dreams of nectar / Divine bell / Bright morning stars.

Linda WATERFALL

With a name that embodies part of nature itself, New Age folk singer/songwriter LINDA WATERFALL (b. 1950 in north Illinois) turns poetical works into music in transcendental creations on her many albums.

She was in fact of Swiss ancestry, the family name originally being Wassenfallen. Although Linda was classically trained in piano and adept at guitar, she was encouraged to take up the visual arts rather than become a professional musician. She graduated from Stanford University in 1971, moving to Seattle in the mid-1970s.

Following in the tradition of JOAN BAEZ, JUDY COLLINS, JONI MITCHELL and their ilk, her first recordings appeared in 1974 on a four-track EP by Entropy Service (alongside Peter Langston, J.B. White and Judith Cook-Tucker), to which she contributed 'Over The Mountain'. **MARY'S GARDEN** (1977) {*6} and **MY HEART SINGS** (1979) {*6} helped get her solo career off the ground, and on her fourth LP, **EVERYTHING LOOKS DIFFERENT** (1983) {*6}, she was joined by guitar maestro Scott Nygaard. Her third set, **BANANALAND** (1981) {*5}, was the last of her first group of recordings for her own Trout label.

She acknowledged her classical grounding with the 'Clear Day Of Grace' set with the Mt. Madonna Choir in 1992, but returned to her folksy roots with **BODY ENGLISH** (1987) {*6} and **A LITTLE BIT AT A TIME** (1991) {*5}, the former based on six poems by Walt Whitman. Later surviving breast cancer, Linda delved into the more spiritual aspects of music. 1998's **IN THE PRESENCE OF THE LIGHT** {*6} was again inspired by Whitman and his 'Leaves Of Grass' poem cycle. *MCS*

Linda Waterfall - vocals, guitar, keyboards, synths

US Windham Hill — UK not issued

1977. (lp) *<WH 1002>* **MARY'S GARDEN** — -
- Country bar / Mary's garden / Song for Elizabeth / The spell / Gary / Grandma's crumbcake / Cherry tomato / The bird song / Lullaby / All alone tonight. *<re-iss. 1977 on Trout; TR 1977>*

Trout — not issued

1979. (lp) *<TR 1979>* **MY HEART SINGS** — -
- Clarity / My name is Maya / Country lullaby / Promises / Blue moon. / My heart is gonna break / My heart sings / La cigale et la fourmi / Promises / Blue moon.

——next with band: **Donnie Teesdale, Dudley Hill + Greg Pecknold**

1981. (lp) *<TR 1981>* **BANANALAND** — -
- Bananaland / Out to lunch / That's all I need / Comin' across the blues / Stand up to you / Wyoming boys / Poison arrow / Eye of the cyclone / My heart is gonna break / I saw him go / Long hard road.

1983. (lp; by LINDA WATERFALL & SCOTT NYGAARD) *<TR 1983>* **EVERYTHING LOOKS DIFFERENT** — -
- Everything looks different / April 22nd / I can't talk about it / The light / Raspberries / The whale song / A squirrel's ear / Love song / Song like a roar.

Flying Fish — Flying Fish

1987. (lp/c) *<(FF/+90 439)>* **BODY ENGLISH** — 1988
- Run it like a business / It's getting closer to me / Body English / Going to the water / Fourth of July / You and I are waiting / Leaves of grass / Waves / Song for Erin. *<cd-iss. 2005 on Trout; none>*

1991. (cd/c) *<FF70/FF90 565>* **A LITTLE BIT AT A TIME** — -
- Low rider / I like to look at you / Love your Mother Earth / Something that we already know / A little bit at a time / Mirage / Coconut milk / I'll take care of you tonight / Twice as shy / Make it your own idea.

Trout — not issued

1994. (cd) *<TR 94>* **FLYING TIME** — -
- Love out of nowhere / Mother's love / Piece of stone / Away ye merry lassies / Flying time / For the moment / I need to know / Tree / Climbing to the high country / Om kara shiva / Balance.

Jun 98. (cd) *<TR 98>* **IN THE PRESENCE OF THE LIGHT** — -
- Drawing down the moon / Reception / Cool touch / In the presence of the light / Kalalau / Escape velocity / Waiting for your luck to change / Mango mouth / Leaves of grass: Press close, bare bosom'd night - I bequeath myself to the dirt - You lingering sparse leaves - Allons, the road is before us.

——next w/ University of Washington Chamber Singers; Geoffrey Boers

2002. (cd) *<none>* **THAT ART THOU: SONGS FROM THE VEDAS** — -
- Creation hymn / The two full of butter / Firestick / Arrow / That art thou, Sventaketu.

2006. (cd) *<none>* **PLACE OF REFUGE** — -
- Place of refuge / Capacitor / The prodigal son / The word of the prophet / A little flash of light / Let all mortal flesh keep silence / I'm only sleeping / Cielito Lindo / Se de noche vez que brillan / The carpenter / Lewiston factor girls / Ponderosa pine / Reaching out for life.

——next performed by The ESOTERICS: ERIC BANKS FOUNDING DIRECTOR

2007. (cd) *<none>* **SONGS FROM THE DAO DE JING** — -
- Dao - The way / Zhan zheng - War / Jing - Essence / Gu shen - Valley spirit / Xing yu da dao - I'll travel my way.

Greg WEEKS (⟹ ESPERS)

The WEEPIES

With their inoffensive, sugar-coated folk-pop and unadulterated 1970s-style acoustic soft-rock (think The Carpenters, Bread, Paul Simon, etc), the Cambridge, Massachusetts-based husband-and-wife duo Steve Tannen and Deb Talan could, to refrain from anything too derogatory, bring a tear to many an eye.

Raised in Australia, Canada and New York, Steve had already released an album, 'Big Senorita' (2000), before The WEEPIES took shape in 2001. Deb Talan had been the leader of 1990s Portland punks Hummingbird.

Kicking off with a vanity-pressing mini-set, **HAPPINESS** (2003) {*6}, their sunny-day music was made for looks-only TV shows like 'Dawson's Creek' and 'Felicity', The Rembrandts and Sixpence None The Richer having split years before. The Nettwerk label booked them a rented cottage in Pasadena to record their follow-up set, the schmaltzy **SAY I AM YOU** (2006) {*6}.

The latter, like US Top 40 albums **HIDEAWAY** (2008) {*6} and **BE MY THRILL** (2010) {*6}, seemed to appeal to the beachwear brigade somewhere in the US. Song titles 'Be My Honeypie', 'They're In Love, Where Am I?' and 'I Was Made For Sunny Days' should convey an idea of their pillow-soft folk; you have been warned. *MCS*

Deb Talan (b. Jan 27 '68) - vocals, acoustic guitar / **Steve Tannen** (b. 1968, New York City) - vocals, acoustic guitar / with session band

US own label — UK not issued

Nov 03. (m-cd) *<1320>* **HAPPINESS** — -
- Happiness / All that I want / Vegas baby / Somebody loved / Jolene / Simple life / Dating a porn star / Keep it there.

Nettwerk — Nettwerk

Mar 06. (cd) *<(50377 0 3 0466 2 7)>* **SAY I AM YOU**

- Take it from me / Gotta have you / World spins madly on / Citywide rodeo / Riga girls / Suicide blonde / Painting by Chagall / Nobody knows me at all / Not your year / Living in twilight / Stars / Love doesn't last too long / Slow pony home.

Apr 08. (cd) *<5 03770 3 0777 2 0>* **HIDEAWAY** 31

- Can't go back now / Orbiting / Hideaway / Wish I could forget / All good things / Little bird / Antarctica / How you survived the war / Not dead yet / Old coyote / Just blue / Lighting candles / Takes so long / All this beauty.

Aug 10. (cd/lp) *<06700 3 0890 2 0>* **BE MY THRILL** 34

- Please speak well of me / When you go away / Red red rose / I was made for sunny days / They're in love, where am I? / Add my effort / Be my thrill / Be my honeypie / Hummingbird / Hard to please / Not a lullaby / How do you get high? / Hope tomorrow / Empty your hands.

Ilene WEISS

Very much a singer/songwriter in the 'Fast Folk' mould, Philadelphia-born New Yorker ILENE WEISS (b. August 16, 1955) has had a number of her compositions covered by folkies including ANNE HILLS, Cathy Fink and Robin Flower.

Not far removed from the sound of SUZANNE VEGA or Carole King, Ilene's best-known songs appeared on her often humorous debut set **OUTSIDE AND CURIOUS** (1992) {*7} - 'Woman Of A Calm Heart', 'I Came, I Saw, I Squirmed' and 'Crush On The Boss'. It's a pity there was no room for her 'Fast Folk' magazine/album tracks such as 'Somebody To Do That For' and 'Nowhere With Nothing And No One'.

OBLIVIOUSLY (1996) {*6} continued her surge towards bigger things (she was nominated for a BMI award), but even very good songs such as 'Healing Place', 'Joined In Laughter' and the title track couldn't lift her above the parapet and into major-label stardom.

Although she presumably felt she had to prove herself by writing almost all the material, her festive set **WEISS CHRISTMAS** (1997) {*6} was in fact too schmaltzy for some. Despite its covers-friendly subject, there were only two non-originals, 'Santa Claus Is Coming To Town' and The Isley Brothers' 'Harvest For The World'.

Ilene later found her vocation as a clown with the music-centred Big Apple Circus Clown Care, with which she had been subsidising her mainstream career since 1992, and has set up children's summer camps. Recently she has been a member of the BMI Lehman Engel Musical Theater Workshop, honing her skills as a lyricist and collaborating with 'serious' composers. *MCS*

Ilene Weiss - vocals, acoustic guitar

US Gadfly — UK Gadfly

Feb 92. (cd/c) *<Gadfly 159>* **OUTSIDE AND CURIOUS** — -

- Outside / In the name of lust / 4 am / This part of the world / Crush on the boss / Just by offering / I came, I saw, I squirmed / No baby / Please be my umbrella / These fearful times / Curious / Woman of calm heart.

Aug 96. (cd) *<Gadfly 216>* **OBLIVIOUSLY** — -

- Make you disappear / Healing place / Answer to come / I wanna be his... / Get out now / Joined in laughter / Waiting around for love / A discovery / Taking the long way home / Out of luck / Somebody (to do that for) / Obliviously.

Oct 97. (cd) *<Gadfly 236>* **WEISS CHRISTMAS** [festive] — -

- It's that time again / Talkin' to the wrong guy / His initials / Tree / Santa Claus is coming to town / The Santa rap / Christmas at the South Pole (tonight) / A minute after midnight / No room at the inn / Take it all away / Another funky Christmas / The day a baby was born / Harvest for the world.

Cheryl WHEELER

Primarily a country-folk artist, New England-based singer/songwriter CHERYL WHEELER (b. July 10, 1951 in Timonium, Maryland) has had much of her repertoire covered by country stars such as Garth Brooks, Suzy Bogguss, Kathy Mattea and Juice Newton, although folkies like MELANIE, HOLLY NEAR and PETER, PAUL & MARY have also endorsed her work.

Cheryl, whose discography now runs into double figures, has gone from playing small venues in Rhode Island, Baltimore and Washington D.C. in the mid-1970s to becoming an occasional member of the FOUR BITCHIN' BABES and subsequently a star of the Rounder Records roster. Long before that, in 1983, she released her first record, the EP 'Newport Songs'. It was sponsored by the sports promoter Franz Kneissl to promote his company, 'Newport Is Sports', which is the title of the lead track.

She became a protégé of country singer/producer Jonathan Edwards and signed to North Star Music, which released her debut set, **CHERYL WHEELER** {*7}, in 1986. Tracks included a cover of Clint Ballard's 'Game Of Love' (a 1960s chart-topper for Wayne Fontana & The Mindbenders) and her own 'Addicted', which was covered by Dan Seals. With Edwards behind her all the way, Cheryl completed a series of nice sets in **HALF A BOOK** (1989, Cypress/A&M) {*5}, **CIRCLES AND ARROWS** (1990, Capitol) {*7} and her first release for the Philo label, **DRIVING HOME** (1993) {*6}.

MRS PINOCCI'S GUITAR (1995) {*6}, **SYLVIA HOTEL** (1999) {*6} and **DEFYING GRAVITY** (2005) {*6}, the last featuring Jesse Winchester's title track, continued to embrace her innermost feelings in song. She was certainly not afraid to take on difficult subjects such as death and soured relationships, though her own life had taken an upswing after she married her partner, Cathleen, in 2004.

POINTING AT THE SUN (2009) {*6} was a return to independence, with producers Ben Wisch and Kenny White and guitar maestro Duke Levine on hand to guide her along the way. *MCS*

Cheryl Wheeler - vocals, acoustic guitar / with session people

US own label — UK not issued

1983. (7" ep) *<none>* NEWPORT SONGS — -

- Newport is sports / Headed for a heartache / On the beach / Summer fly.

North Star — not issued

Jan 86. (lp) *<W 0001>* **CHERYL WHEELER** — -

- Gimme the right sign / Invisible lady / Addicted / Lethal detective / Behind the barn / Paradise in troubled waters / Your radio's up too loud / Game of love / Quarter moon / Same old game / Arrow. *<cd/c-iss. Sep 92; W 0001 CD/C>*

Cypress — not issued

Feb 89. (cd) *<14166-0107-2>* **HALF A BOOK** — -

- Emotional response / I don't have the time / I don't reach you anymore / Tell him goodbye / In your heart / Rainin' / Half a book / I see your eyes / Thinkin' of leavin' / Summer fly / Piper. *<cd re-iss. Sep 92 on North Star; W 0005CD>*

Capitol — Capitol

May 90. (cd) *<CDP 792 063-2>* **CIRCLES AND ARROWS** — Sep 90

- I know this town / Hard line to draw / Aces / Estate sale / Don't wanna / Northern girl / Soon as I find my voice / Miss you more than I'm mad / Moonlight and roses / When you're gone / Arrow. *<(re-iss. May 95 on Philo; CDPH/CPH 1162)>*

Philo — Philo

Oct 93. (cd/c) *<(CDPH/CPH 1152)>* **DRIVING HOME** — Jan 94

- Driving home / Silver lining / Music in my room / Frequently wrong but never in doubt / Don't forget the guns / Act of nature / 75 Septembers / Spring / Bad connection / When fall comes to New England / Orbiting Jupiter / Almost.

Oct 95. (cd/c) *<(CDPH/CPH 1192)>* **MRS PINOCCI'S GUITAR** — Nov 95

- Mrs Pinocci's guitar / Does the future look black / School girls / TV / The rivers / Further and further away / Is it peace or is it Prozac? / Howl at the moon / The storm / So far to fall / Makes good sense to me / Piper / Time taketh away / One love.

Jan 99. (cd) *<(CDPH 1212)>* **SYLVIA HOTEL**

- His hometown / But the days and nights are long / If it were up to me / Right way to do the wrong thing / All the live long day / Sylvia hotel / Unworthy / Rainy road into Atlanta / Lighting up the mighty Mississippi / Potato / Meow / Who am I foolin'?

Feb 05. (cd) *<(CDPH 1240)>* **DEFYING GRAVITY**

- Since you've been gone / Little road / Must be sinking now / Beyond the lights / Summer's almost over / Defying gravity / Clearwater, Florida / Here come Floyd / Alice / This is me / It's the phone / On the plane / Blessed.

Dias — Dias

May 09. (cd) *<(DIAS 1001)>* **POINTING AT THE SUN**

- Holding on / Summer fly / Pointing at the sun / One step at a time / Grey and green / You know you will / Praise the lord and life is grand / Underbrush / White cat / Cat accountant / My cat's birthday.

- (8-10*) compilations -

Jan 03. (cd) *Philo; <(CDPH 1217)>* **DIFFERENT STRIPE** — Mar 03

- Northern girl / Arrow / Walk around downtown / Moonlight and roses / Gandhi - Buddha / When fall comes to New England / Quarter moon / Aces / Hard line to draw / Almost / Addicted / So far to fall / Don't wanna / Miss you more than I'm mad / Sylvia hotel / Who am I foolin'? / 75 Septembers / Further and further away / One love.

Erica WHEELER

Inspired as much by Appalachian protest folk-singer HAZEL DICKENS as JUDY COLLINS or JOAN BAEZ, Erica began to write and perform her own songs as she progressed through high school and Hampshire College, Massachusetts before becoming a wildlife field biologist.

Born October 24, 1961 in Silver Spring, Maryland, WHEELER was raised in Chevy Chase, Maryland and Washington D.C, and eventually shared stages from Boston to Berkeley and beyond with the likes of GREG BROWN, INDIGO GIRLS and SHAWN COLVIN. While she could easily adapt to folk, country and bluegrass, her songs were pure roots Americana, richly expressive and with a warmth that endeared her to many an audience that cracked up at her witty stage banter. Erica is also a speaker, educator and conservation advocate, training people to "find a sense of place", as she writes in her e-book 'Seven Soulful Ways to Connect to Place'.

On the music front, she got off her mark in 1989 with a cassette-only independent release, **STRONG HEART** {*5}, a rare recording that was deleted by the time her second set, **FROM THAT FAR** {*7}, went retail in 1992. 'I Know You Rider' was of course a traditional piece, the other nine her own originals including choice cuts 'Beautiful', 'Amanda Crazy Wolf' and the Joni-esque title track. The Signature Sounds label came on board for her next pair of literate New Country/contemporary folk CDs.

THE HARVEST (1996) {*7}, featuring a cover of CLAUDIA SCHMIDT's 'Quiet Hills', and the Steven Miller-produced **THREE WISHES** (1999) {*7}, with BILL MORRISSEY and JAMES McMURTRY covers, caught her voice and her songwriting at their best on tracks like 'Frozen River', 'January Wind' and 'Angels'. The concert set **ALMOST LIKE TONIGHT** (2005) {*7} captured the essence of her popular shows, and her comeback studio set, **GOOD SUMMER RAIN** (2008), {*6} kept her star high. *MCS*

Erica Wheeler - vocals, acoustic guitar

US Blue Pie — UK not issued

1989. (c) <*BP 100*> **STRONG HEART**

1992. (cd) <*BP 200*> **FROM THAT FAR**
- Beautiful / Boston song / Amanda Crazy Wolf / Car with no brakes / From that far / Back burner blues / Rivers / I know you rider / Down river / No one else. *<c-iss. Jul 96; BP 200C> <cd re-iss. Apr 01; BP 200CD>*

Signature Sounds — not issued

Nov 96. (cd) <*SIG 1237*> **THE HARVEST**
- The harvest / Spirit lake / Arrowheads / Colorado town / Goodnight moon / Quiet hills / Maryland country road / The mystery / Sober Harley guys / Hot / Autumn. *(UK-iss. Aug 04; same as US)*

Apr 99. (cd) <*SIG 1250*> **THREE WISHES**
- Onward from here / January wind / Jack's tavern / Frozen river / Layin' it down / Angeline / Solace of a prayer / Nowhere to go / Casey, Illinois / Angels / Saturday. *(UK-iss. Aug 04; same as US)*

Blue Pie — not issued

Apr 05. (cd) <*BP 300*> **ALMOST LIKE TONIGHT** [live]
- Angeline / Saturday / Back burner blues / Downriver / (intro...) / Maryland County road / (intro...) / I can see your aura / The first sunset / Onward from here / Autumn / Crazy love / (intro...) / The harvest / Quiet hills / (intro...) / Sober Harley guys / (intro...) / My pretty kitty / KPIG intro / Spirit lake / Quiet night.

Mar 08. (cd) <*BP 400*> **GOOD SUMMER RAIN**
- As the crow flies / Good summer rain / Apache motel / Brand new starts / Endless pines / Muddy waters / Lucky in love / The first sunset / Harold / Elk song / To deep water.

Emily Jane WHITE

There's been an affinity between folk music and the cello since the heady days of NICK DRAKE and a few others, and California girl EMILY JANE WHITE gives it its latest expression. At first influenced by traditional blues and folk, but coming across as the next Hope Sandoval, Chan Marshall or Nina Nastasia, the Fort Bragg-raised Emily developed her whispering vocal style in the early 2000s, having abandoned her aspiration to front a punk-metal outfit. Her first real band was Diamond Star Halos.

A spell in France led to a contract with the Talitres imprint, and while she was promoting her first album, **DARK UNDERCOAT** (2007) {*8}, in San Francisco, the album was charting in France. Produced by Wainwright Hewlett, the record was a million miles away from her Santa Cruz College punk days, and her sadcore dramas were best served by 'Bessie Smith', 'Hole In The Middle' and 'The Demon'. Her song 'Wild Tigers I Have Known' was lifted for the soundtrack (released for CURRENT 93's Durtro label) to Cam Archer's film of the same name,

Augmented by celloist Jen Grady, violinist Carey Lamprecht and pedal steel player Henry Nagle, Emily echoed the gothic brooding of her debut with **VICTORIAN AMERICA** (2010) {*7}. Haunting and spooky, the album took on a darker country aspect. 'Never Dead' (a lament for a suicidal friend), the equally forlorn 'Stairs' and the finale, 'Ghost Of A Horse', might easily have been by Nick Cave.

Released in 2011 (2010 in France), **ODE TO SENTIENCE** {*6} was her third cello-fuelled album. 'Oh Katherine', 'I Lay To Rest (California)' and 'The Preacher' kept her dour, experimental side to the fore alongside an invasion of country-orientated songs. She seems intent on taking her music in various directions, which is commendable, and hopefully it will be fruitful in the future. *MCS*

Emily Jane White - vocals, guitar, piano, percussion / + session people

US Double Negative — UK/Fra Talitres

Nov 07. (cd) *<006> (TAL 039 CD/LP)* **DARK UNDERCOAT** — Apr 08
- Bessie Smith / Hole in the middle / Dark undercoat / Dagger / Time on your side / The demon / Sleeping dead / Blue / Wild tigers I have known / Two shots to the head. *(UK-iss. Oct 08; same as French) <US lp-iss. 2008 on Saint Rose; SR 001> <US cd-iss. Apr 09 on Important+=; imprec 242>* - Robotic arms.

Milan — Talitres

Apr 10. (cd/d-lp) *<M2/DOTO 36484> (TAL 050 CD/LP)*
VICTORIAN AMERICA — Oct 09
- Never dead / Stairs / Victorian America / The baby / Frozen heart / The country life / Liza / The ravens / Red serpent / Red dress / A shot rang out / Ghost of a horse.

Nov 10. (cd/lp) *(TAL 056 CD/LP)* **ODE TO SENTIENCE** — French
- Oh, Katherine / The cliff / Black silk / The black oak / I lay to rest (California) / Clipped wings / The preacher / The law / Requiem waltz / Broken words. *(UK-iss. Feb 11; same as French)*

Simone WHITE

Not to be confused with the Afro-Mystik rapper of the same name, this SIMONE WHITE is an altogether different artist in a folk-country vein. Born February 7, 1970 in Oahu, Hawaii, she lived in London between 1994 and 2000 before New York became her residence of choice.

Accompanied in places by her friend Frank Bango and her songwriting partner Richy Vesecky, her David Domanich-produced debut set, **THE SINCERE RECORDING CO. PRESENTS** (2003) {*6}, was a joint effort of sorts, Simone's soft, pastel voice often compared to SUZANNE VEGA. It contained one outsider cover, Goffin-King's 'I Didn't Have Any Summer Romance', which was reprised as the opening track on her second set.

Following a trip to Nashville, Tennessee and an alliance with alt-country knob-twiddler Mark Nevers, **I AM THE MAN** (2007) {*8} surfaced on the Honest Jon's branch of the EMI conglomerate. A favourite with many trendy music magazines including 'Mojo' and 'Q', the album was boosted by 'The Beep Beep Song', a short, Laurie Anderson-like track that was used in an Audi TV commercial.

In a similar vein, and as always featuring a handful of Bango-Vesecky songs, her third set, **YAKIIMO** (2009) {*7}, provided another TV ad soundtrack, 'Bunny In A Boiler Suit', for the Omega Ladymatic watch campaign. Other splendid tracks on the folk-blues album were 'Candy Bar Killer', 'Let The Cold Wind Blow' and her smoky reading of W.C. Handy's 'St. Louis Blues'. She now lives in Los Angeles. *MCS*

Simone White - vocals, acoustic guitar (+ session people)

US Sincere — UK not issued

Sep 03. (cd) <*SR 002*> **THE SINCERE RECORDING CO. PRESENTS...**
- America in '54 / Candy bar killer / Wrong about you / Mary Jane / Train song / Soldier soldier / I didn't have a summer romance / 66 bell / Shots / Roses are not red / Blueprint / Olivia 101.

Honest Jon's — Honest Jon's

Jun 07. (cd/lp) *<(HJR CD/LP 28)>* **I AM THE MAN**
- I didn't have any summer romance / Worm has wood / The beep beep song / The American war / Roses are not red / Great imperialist state / Mary Jane / You may be in the darkness / Sweetest love song / We used to stand so tall / Why is your raincoat always crying? / Only the moon / I am the man.

Aug 07. (7" m) *(HJSW 001)* THE AMERICAN WAR. / The Beep Beep Song / Black Dog

Nov 07. (7") *(HJSW 002)* CHRISTMAS MAKES ME BLUE. / Blueprint

Nov 09. (cd/lp) *<(HJR CD/LP 44)>* **YAKIIMO** — Jun 09
- Bunny in a bunny suit / Candy bar killer / Victoria Anne / Baby lie down with me / Yakiimo / A girl you never met / Without a sound / Train song / Your stop / Olivia 101 / Let the cold wind blow / St Louis blues.

WHITE MAGIC

A strange one is Brooklyn's WHITE MAGIC, a psychedelic-folk-rock trio of considerable pedigree originally consisting of singer and musician Mira Billotte (ex-Quix*o*tic), Miggy Littleton of Ida (drums and bass) and Andy MacLeod of California Speedway (guitar and drums).

Following a splendid performance at the All Tomorrow's Parties festival, the haunting freak-folk of mini-set **THROUGH THE SUN DOOR** (2004) {*6} was a powerful start to their eerie repertoire. Billotte's inspired alto range drew comparisons with Grace Slick and KAREN DALTON, the best songs being 'Keeping The Wolves From The Door', 'Apocalypse' and the William Burroughs setting 'Plain Gold Ring' (fans of Nina Simone and Nick Cave might recognise the last one).

Subsequently joined by guitarist 'Sleepy' Doug Shaw and a few guests (Tim DeWitt of Gang Gang Dance was one), Mira and a revised WHITE MAGIC unleashed the mediaeval cabaret-folk of **DAT ROSA MEL APIBUS** (2006) {*6}. For freak-folk fans only one track stands out, the traditional song 'Katie Cruel'. Billotte, Shaw and guest drummer Jim White (of the Dirty Three, and a friend of Nick Cave) gave their listeners another treat with the acid-folk, country-blues four-track EP 'Dark Stars' in 2007. Apart from an appearance in the DYLAN bio-pic 'I'm Not There' and the live title track of the EP 'New Egypt', WHITE MAGIC have since been conspicuous by their absence. *MCS*

Mira Billotte - vocals, guitar, piano (ex-Quix*o*tic) / **Miggy Littleton** - drums, bass (of Ida, of Blood On The Wall) / **Andy MacLeod** - guitar, drums (of California Speedway)

US Drag City — UK Drag City

May 04. (m-lp/m-cd) *<(DC 265/+CD)>* **THROUGH THE SUN DOOR** [ ] Jun 04 [ ]
- One-note / Don't need / Keeping the wolves from the door / The gypsies came marching after / Plain gold ring / Apocalypse.

2005. (m-cd; split) *<Ouch! 5>* SONGS OF HURT AND HEALING [ ] [-]
- [tracks by The American Analog Set] / Day / Twilight / Night.

(above issued on the Ouch! label)

——**'Sleepy' Douglas Shaw** - guitar; repl. Littleton + MacLeod

Nov 06. (cd-s) *<DC 328CD>* KATIE CRUEL / Hold Your Hand In The Dark [ ] [-]

Nov 06. (d-lp/cd) *<(DC 293/+CD)>* **DAT ROSA MEL APIBUS** [ ] [ ]
- The light / Hear my call / Childhood song / What I see / All the world wept / Dat rosa mel apibus / Sun song / Hold your hand in the dark / Katie cruel / Sea chanty / Palm and wine / Song of Solomon.

——added **Jim White** - drums (ex-Dirty Three)

Oct 07. (ltd; 12" ep/cd-ep) *<(DC 350/+CD)>* DARK STARS [ ] [ ]
- Shine on heaven / Very late / Poor Harold / Winds.

not issued — Latitudes

Jun 08. (cd-ep/12" ep) *(GMT 0:13/+V)* NEW EGYPT. / Tpyge Wen [-] [ ]

David WILCOX

Not to be confused with the Canadian blues-rocker of the same name, this jazzy folk singer/songwriter was born in 1958 in Mentor, Ohio. Learning the guitar at Antioch College in Yellow Springs, he graduated from Warren Wilson College in Asheville, North Carolina in the early 1980s. Playing residencies at the club and bar McDibbs, he quickly developed his guitar technique from listening to JOHN MARTYN and JAMES TAYLOR. His first album was the charming, self-financed **THE NIGHTSHIFT WATCHMAN** (1987) {*6}.

Spotted by A&M execs at Nashville's Blue Rock Café, he was given a lucrative deal that produced three well-equipped sets, **HOW DID YOU FIND ME HERE** (1989) {*7}, **HOME AGAIN** (1991) {*7} and his only Top 200 appearance, **BIG HORIZON** (1994) {*5}. The last one featured covers of John Waite's 'Missing You' and the Four Tops hit 'It's The Same Old Song'.

Dropped unceremoniously by A&M, WILCOX thought it the right time to deliver a live album, **EAST ASHEVILLE HARDWARE** (1996) {*7}, showcasing previously unrecorded live favourites including his hilarious rendition of CHUCK BRODSKY's 'Blow 'Em Away', BOB FRANKE's 'For Real' and Freddy Bradburn's 'Barbie'. His comical turn continued on his comeback studio album **TURNING POINT** (1997) {*6}.

One of several artists taken on by the revamped Vanguard imprint, WILCOX in all his lyrical pith and glory released two further albums, **UNDERNEATH** (1999) {*6} and **WHAT YOU WHISPERED** (2000) {*5}, backed on the latter by acoustic-rock act Jars Of Clay.

A journeyman through and through, WILCOX succumbed to releasing another concert disc, **LIVE SONGS AND STORIES** (2002) {*7}. A veteran of countless intimate gigs, he'd always been suited to this medium. Studio set **INTO THE MYSTERY** (2003) {*6} saw him collaborating on a couple of songs with Pierce Pettis and Maia Sharp, and it seemed his laid-back slow-burners were back in vogue. 2005's 'songs for peace' project album, **OUT BEYOND IDEAS** {*6} - a collaboration with Nance Pettit - found inspiration in sacred poetry, while four solo studio sets for What Are? - **VISTA** (2006) {*6}, **AIRSTREAM** (2008) {*6}, **OPEN HAND** (2009) {*7} and **REVERIE** (2010) {*7} - kept his profile high among his brigade of loyal fans. *MCS*

David Wilcox - vocals, acoustic guitar (w/ session people)

US Song Of The Woods — UK not issued

1987. (c/cd) *<SOTW 1087 CD/C>* **THE NIGHTSHIFT WATCHMAN** [ ] [-]
- The nightshift watchman / Frozen in the snow / Daddy's money / That's why I'm laughing / Come away to sea / It's almost time / Gone to Santa Fe / Golden key / Do I care? / Hugh hill / Sunshine on the land. *<cd-iss. Feb 96 on Fresh Baked-Koch Int.; KOC-CD 7921>*

A&M — not issued

Oct 89. (lp/c/cd) *<5275-1/-4/-2>* **HOW DID YOU FIND ME HERE** [ ] [-]
- Eye of the hurricane / Language of the heart / Rusty old American dream / How did you find me here / Leave it like it is / Saturday they'll all be back again / Jamie's secret / It's almost time / Just a vehicle / Common as the rain / The kid. *(UK cd-iss. Mar 03 on Universal; AA75021 5275-2)*

Aug 91. (cd/c) *<5357-2/-4>* **HOME AGAIN** [ ] [-]
- Burgundy heart-shaped medallion / Farther to fall / (You were) Going somewhere / Wildberry pie (for my sweetie pie) / Let them in / Distant water / Top of the roller coaster / Covert war / Advertising man / Last chance waltz / She's just dancing / Chet Baker's unsung swan song / Mighty ocean. *(UK cd-iss. Mar 03 on Universal; AA75021 5357-2)*

Nov 91. (m-cd) *<7241-2>* **MOSTLY LIVE AUTHORIZED BOOTLEG** (live except opener) [ ] [-]
- (You were) Going somewhere / Four-lane dance/ (spoken intro) / Saturday they'll all be back again / Daddy's money / Johnny's Camaro / Chet Baker's unsung swan song.

Feb 94. (cd/c) *<0060-2/-4>* **BIG HORIZON** [ ] [-]
- New world / Someday soon / That's what the lonely is for / Show the way / Block dog / Break in the cup / It's the same old song / The farthest shore / Strong chemistry / Make it look easy / Please don't call / Big mistake / All the roots grow deeper when it's dry / Hold it up to the light / Missing you. *(UK cd-iss. Mar 03 on Universal; AA31454 0060-2)*

Koch Int. — Koch Int.

Feb 96. (cd) *<KOC-CD 7920>* **EAST ASHEVILLE HARDWARE** (live) [ ] [-]
- Blow 'em away / Johnny's Camaro / East Asheville hardware / Top of my head / Dangerous / Roadside art / You should see the way it feels / Cold / Catch me if I try / Down inside yourself / For real / Mango story / Mango / Levi blues / Carpenter story / Fearless love / Boob job / Barbie / After your orgasm / Golden day.

May 97. (cd/c) *<(3 7942-2/-4)>* **TURNING POINT** [ ] Dec 97 [ ]
- Show me the key / Silent prayer / Western ridge / Glory / Kindness / Spin / Tattered old kite / Right now / Human cannonball / Secret church / Turning point / Waffle house.

Vanguard — not issued

Feb 99. (cd) *<VSD 79528-2>* **UNDERNEATH** [ ] [-]
- Underneath / Never enough / Down here / Spirit wind / Prisoner of war / Hometown / All my life / Guilty either way / Leaving you - Leaving you (reprise) / Young man dies / Slipping through my fist / Home within your heart - Home within your heart (reprise) / Sex and music.

Aug 00. (cd) *<VSD 79564-2>* **WHAT YOU WHISPERED** [ ] [-]
- What you whispered / This tattoo / Deeper still / Start with the ending / In the broken places / The inside of my head / The whisper of the wheels / On your way back down / Rule number one / When you're ready / Step into your skin / Guitar shopping / Soul song.

What Are? — not issued

Apr 02. (cd) *<WHARE 60053>* **LIVE SONGS AND STORIES** (live) [ ] [-]
- Rusty old American dream / The terminal tavern / Show the way / Impact... / Eye of the hurricane / Two roads diverge / Hold it up to the light / Waffle house / Start with the ending / Get it out of the way / Moe / Shiny ride / Spin / No far away / Traveling companion / Words alone / Appreciating the differences / Good together / Metaphorical reasons / That's what the lonely is for / Kindness.

Feb 03. (cd) *<WHARE 60063>* **INTO THE MYSTERY** [ ] [-]
- If it wasn't for the night / Rise / Last one gone / Out of the question / In this stream / Radio men / On to the next / City of dreams / Apple a day / Blue horizon / Ask for more / Native tongue / Fall away.

Sep 05. (cd; by DAVID WILCOX & NANCY PETTIT) *<WHARE 60073>* **OUT BEYOND IDEAS** [ ] [-]
- How did the rose ever open / The breeze at dawn / Slicing potatoes / On a day when the wind is perfect / Absolutely clear / No one knows his name / Some seeds / Farsi intro / Out beyond ideas / You who knew me / Elephant story / Midnight / This we have now / Trembling with joy / Shell trick / Three things / Awake my dear.

Jun 06. (cd) *<WHARE 60077>* **VISTA** [ ] [-]
- Get on / Party of one / Into one / Same shaker / Vista / Wilford Brandon Hayes / No doubt about it / Good man / The hard part / Let it go / Grateful for her beauty / Miracle / Everywhere / Coming alive / Great big world.

Mar 08. (cd) *<WHARE 60090>* **AIRSTREAM**
- Right on time / Forever now / Perfect storm / Three brothers / Plain view / The reason / Reaper sweepstakes / Falling for it / To love / Little white lie / This old car / Never change / No telling where / The crossings.

Apr 09. (cd) *<WHARE 60102>* **OPEN HAND**
- Dream again / Red eye / Open hand / How long / Winter at the shore / Modern world / Outside door / Vow of silence / Captain wanker / Beyond belief / Not from here / River run dry.

Nov 10. (cd) *<WHARE 60107>* **REVERIE**
- End of the world (again) / Shark man / Cast off / Dynamite in the distance / One way to find out / Little fish / Ireland / Reverie / Buster / Stones of Jerusalem / Piece of me / We call it freedom / Let the wave say / Angeline.

- (8-10*) compilations -

Oct 01. (cd) *Universal; <(AA69 493141-2)>* **THE VERY BEST OF DAVID WILCOX**
- Eye of the hurricane / Language of the heart / Rusty old American dream / How did you find me here / Leave it like it is / Johnny's Camaro (live) / Saturday they'll all be back again / The kid / Daddy's money (live) / Farther to fall / Top of the roller coaster / Covert war / Advertising man / Last chance waltz / Chet Baker's unsung swan song / Strong chemistry / New world / That's what the lonely is for / Break in the cup / Farthest shore.

- (5-7*) compilations, etc.-

Jun 07. (cd) *Vanguard; <VCD 73173>* **VANGUARD VISIONARIES**
- What you whispered / Never enough / This tattoo / Guitar shopping / Soul song / Down here / Start with the ending / Rule number one / Deeper still / The inside of my head.

Brooks WILLIAMS

Born November 10, 1958 in Statesboro, Georgia, contemporary folk-blues singer/songwriter BROOKS WILLIAMS first got the call in 1987 after listening to acoustic-blues starlet Rory Block at a club in upstate New York. While he sounded a little like JAMES TAYLOR, his inspirations came from further afield, by way of Robert Johnson and Muddy Waters.

NORTH FROM STATESBORO (1990) {*7} began his career in fine style; his steady instrumentals and settings of poems by Robert Frost (including 'Acquainted By The Night') were lauded in some circles, as was his follow-up, **HOW THE NIGHT-TIME SINGS** (1991) {*7}.

Switching from the Red Guitar Blue label to Green Linnet, **BACK TO MERCY** (1993) {*5} took Brooks into other territories, such as jazz ('Dancer's Delight'), GROSSMAN-style finger-picking ('Before Coffee') and traditional/Celtic ('Old Blue'). **INLAND SAILOR** (1994) {*6}, **KNIFE EDGE** (1995) {*6} and **SEVEN SISTERS** (1997) {*7} repeated the formula, while another label switch, to Signature Sounds, brought forth a varied handful of crossover cover versions - Buddy Miller's 'My Love Will Follow You', John Spillane's 'All The Ways You Wander', Ted Hawkins's 'The Good And The Bad' and Lennon/McCartney's 'I Will' - on album number seven, **HUNDRED YEAR OLD SHADOW** (1999) {*5}.

Reggae is hardly a branch of folk music, but WILLIAMS's cover of The Maytals' '54-46 (Was My Number)' was one of the inspired choices on his next album, the instrumental **LITTLE LION** (2000) {*7}, among others including Beethoven's 'Joyful, Joyful' and Hot Tuna's 'Water Song'. **SKIFFLE-BOP** (2001) {*6} gathered another eclectic bunch of originals and covers, and his interpretations of Pat Metheny's 'Travels', The Blue Nile's 'Love Came Down', T-Bone Burnett's 'Libera Me' and Jerry Ragavoy's 'Ring Bell' displayed his artistry to good advantage. **NECTAR** (2003) {*7} once again extended the boundaries of folk, taking in Roddy Frame's 'Birth Of The True', Memphis Slim's 'Mother Earth', DOUGIE MACLEAN's 'She Loves Me (When I Try)' and JOHN MARTYN's 'May You Never'.

BLUES AND BALLADS (2004) {*6} broke free from the shackles of folk music and was his first set to get totally back to basics. The blues, bossa nova, jazz, nostalgia and classical were part of the make-up of **GUITAR PLAYER** (2005) {*7}; Luiz Bonfa, J.S. Bach and Leonard Bernstein all played their part here. *MCS*

Brooks Williams - vocals, acoustic guitar

US Red Guitar Blue Music — UK not issued

Jul 90. (cd) *<RGBM-8901>* **NORTH FROM STATESBORO**
- Faces of light / Frenzy at the feeder / Acquainted with the night / Good man down / Postcard from gulfside / On the rollin' sea / Big blue wonder / Jericho / Promises - What the builder left behind / Pavillions (until the time is right) / We will dance someday / Over the hill / Geography / Bush pilot / Engulfed / Blues to stay.

1991. (cd) *<RGBM-9102>* **HOW THE NIGHT-TIME SINGS**
- Blues is first / Jubilee / How the night-time sings / Los padres / Happy all the time / Hard love / What do I need to do / Look what the cat dragged in / Railwalker / Dusty road / The Monte Vista / Streets of heaven / Reina's lullaby / When I reach / Weather the storm / Great dream of heaven.

Green Linnet — Green Linnet

Jan 93. (cd/c) *<GLCD/CSIF 2108>* **BACK TO MERCY**
- Search for you / All that is gold / If I never / Boy's first thaw / Mason-Dixon line / Stormy weather / Dancer's delight / Before coffee / Tulips in the spring / Mercy Illinois / Old Blue / Minutes to midnight. *(UK cd-iss. Mar 00; same as US)*

Jan 94. (cd/c) *<(GLCD/CSIF 2114)>* **INLAND SAILOR** — Apr 94
- Inland sailor / Springfield mountain / Navigator / Won't you meet me? / Big change / This time / Home by dawn / Through the darkening night / Light of day / Seasons of the year / Promises revisited / Narrow boat / Vancouver.

Aug 95. (cd/c) *<(GLCD/CSIF 2121)>* **KNIFE EDGE**
- Belfast blues / You don't know my mind / Late night train / Monterey pines / Knife edge / Lee's highway / From Boston to Dublin / Rotterdam bar / Caves of Missouri / Quiet days / Wanderer's song / When the dentist dreams / Night fears / Someone else to blame / Goodbye Walker Percy / This world is not my home.

——In Feb 97, Jim Henry & Brooks Williams released 'Ring Some Changes'

Aug 97. (cd/c) *<(GLCD/CSIF 2125)>* **SEVEN SISTERS** — Sep 97
- Seven sisters / Mother Earth / Rich tonight / Nothing at all / Hello heartbreak / Minor maybe / Jane / Miles away / Winter moon / Threadbare soul / Some fine day.

Signature Sounds — not issued

Feb 99. (cd) *<SIG 1248>* **HUNDRED YEAR SHADOW**
- Darker kind of blue / My love will follow you / House of truth / Mockin' bird hill / All the ways you wander / Willie Mae Browne / Kar-kar / Monkey / The good and the bad / Songs my brother taught me / I will. *(UK-iss. Aug 04; same as US)*

Jan 00. (cd) *<SIG 1255>* **LITTLE LION**
- O leaozinho / Frenzy at the feeder / Only for a moment / Joyful, joyful / Goodbye Walker Percy / Lizard logic / Water song / Belfast blues / Asa Branca / Meesa kaibash / What wondrous love / Magpie / 54-46 was my number. *(UK-iss. Aug 04; same as US)*

Apr 01. (cd) *<SIG 1264>* **SKIFFLE-BOP**
- Love came down / Ring bell / Author / Travels / Restless / Mountain / Zoe / Weary of the moon / Chasin' the groove / Libera me / Liberation waltz. *(UK-iss. Aug 04; same as US)*

Feb 03. (cd) *<SIG 1275>* **NECTAR**
- Birth of the true / Forget about him / Singing in the dark / Half the grace / May you never / Yellow hummingbird / Unexpected rose / Great big sea / Mother Earth / She loves me (when I try). *(UK-iss. Feb 04 on Acoustic Roots; 008)*

Red Guitar Blue Music — not issued

Apr 04. (cd) *<RGBM-0501>* **BLUES AND BALLADS**
- Weeping willow blues / In the evening / Shady grove / All blues / Doesn't get around much any more / Love in vain / Ten penny bit / Honey babe / Watch the stars / Peacemaker's hornpipe / One day I walk / Take my hand precious lord / Trouble in mind.

Solid Air — not issued

Mar 05. (cd) *<2049>* **GUITAR PLAYER**
- Bakerloo / Gentle rain / Working dog / The bright field / Jaguar / Happy chappy / Some other time / The drowsy bee / Triangular situations (Sitaucoes triangulares) / All that is gold / Jesu, joy of man's desiring / Aguinaldo Jibara / Far away / In Christ there is no east or west / South hill / I bid you goodnight.

Red Guitar Blue Music — not issued

Apr 06. (cd) *<RGBM-0401>* **LIVE SOLO** (live)
- Chasing the groove / Dancer's delight / Knife edge / Belfast blues / Mountain / Mercy Illinois / Kar kar / Restless / How the night-time sings / Singing in the dark / Half the grace / Weary of the moon / Old Blue / Joyful, joyful.

Jan 08. (cd) *<RGBM-0801>* **THE TIME I SPEND WITH YOU**
- The time I spend with you / Rich tonight / 61 highway / Everywhere / You don't know me / Johnny's farewell / Lightning (going back to Texas) / Statesboro blues / Beaumont rag / Martha / How long (till I'm in my baby's arms) / Vagabond blues / Same ol' me.

Apr 10. (cd) *<RGBM-1001>* **BABY O!**
- Frank Delandry / Grinnin' in your face / Walk you off my mind / All been said / Last chance love / Baby O / Amazing grace / Louis Collins / Moon on down / Devil's punchbowl / Sugar sweet / I got it bad (and that ain't good).

- (8-10*) compilations -

Feb 01. (cd) *Silent Planet; <1301>* **DEAD SEA CAFE (1992–1997: A BEST OF)**
- Mystery / Seven sisters / Wanderer's song / Late night train / Caves of Missouri / When the dentist dreams / We will dance someday / Winter moon / If I never / Inland sailor / Jane / Before coffee / Tulips in the spring (live) / Happy all the time.

- (5-7*) compilations, others, etc.-

Apr 06. (cd) *Red Guitar Blue Music; <none>* **ACOUSTIC BEGINNINGS: 1990–1991**
- Railwalker / What do I need to do / Jubilee / On the rolling sea / Los padres / Postcard from the gulfside / How the night-time sings / Promises - What the builder left behind / Faces of light / Great dream of heaven / Look what the cat dragged in / When I reach / Reina's lullabye.

Dar WILLIAMS

A child prodigy who was playing guitar at the age of nine and writing her first song soon after that, folk singer/songwriter DAR WILLIAMS (b. Dorothy Snowden Williams, April 19, 1967 in Mount Kisco, New York) was raised in a well-to-do household in Chappaqua, with liberal parents who were educated at Yale and Vassar. From directing plays, earning her B.A. and stage-managing the Opera Company of Boston, she was eventually encouraged to take up singing in clubs and coffee-houses around the east coast.

After handing out her self-financed demo cassettes at gigs, WILLIAMS came to the attention of the Waterbug label, who saw possibilities in the third of them, **THE HONESTY ROOM** (1993) {*6}, and issued it on CD. Entirely self-written, the record was somewhat pop-infused, but it included one of her best-known numbers, 'When I Was A Boy', and her Kerrville Festival favourite, 'The Babysitter's Here'.

There was always a certain amount of humour in Dar's mischievous lyrics (think Alanis Morissette), as in 'The Christians And The Pagans' and 'The Pointless, Yet Poignant, Crisis Of A Co-Ed' from her follow-up album, **MORTAL CITY** (1996) {*7}. **END OF THE SUMMER** (1997) {*7} was certainly her slickest and most raucous, featuring an electric band and a cover of The Kinks' 'Better Things'.

Her next project was CRY CRY CRY, with LUCY KAPLANSKY and RICHARD SHINDELL, though only for one self-titled covers set {*6} in 1998. The acts whose songs they covered were R.E.M., James Keelaghan, Ron Sexsmith, Buddy Mondlock, Robert Earl Keen, GREG BROWN, Julie Miller, CLIFF EBERHARDT, Leslie Smith and The NIELDS.

Her fourth solo album, **THE GREEN WORLD** (2000) {*7}, raised the bar higher and became her second Top 200 entry. Her freewheeling, jingle-jangle folk continued with **OUT THERE: LIVE** (2001) {*7}, featuring concert favourites including 'I Won't Be Your Yoko Ono', 'Are You Out There' and 'The Babysitter's Here', complete with fun intros. Studio albums **THE BEAUTY OF THE RAIN** (2003) {*7} (featuring The BAND's 'Whispering Pines') and **MY BETTER SELF** (2005) {*7} (with Pink Floyd's 'Comfortably Numb' and NEIL YOUNG's 'Everybody Knows This Is Nowhere') showed she could do more than just create a jaunty rock-pop ballad.

Her first Top 100 entry, **PROMISED LAND** (2008) {*6}, was even more evidence of where she'd taken her blend of introspective folkish meditations. **MANY GREAT COMPANIONS** (2010) {*7} was a double set revisiting her own back pages with guests including New Country stars Mary Chapin Carpenter, Patty Larkin and Gary Louris (of The Jayhawks). *MCS*

Dar Williams - vocals, acoustic guitar / + session people

US Burning Field — UK not issued

1990. (m-c) <*none*> I HAVE NO HISTORY — self
- Crossing the field / How do I work / No more troubles / No revolution here / Charlie Frye / I have no history / Ireland / Terrarium.

1991. (m-c) <*none*> ALL MY HEROES ARE DEAD — self
- All my heroes are dead / For everyone / Stop smoking / Mark Rothko song / Calamity John / Flinty kind of woman / Anthem / Arrival / When it gets that way.

Nov 93. (c) <*none*> **THE HONESTY ROOM** — self
- When I was a boy / Alleluia / The great unknown / When Sal's burned down / The babysitter's here / You're aging well / Traveling again (Traveling I) / In love but not at peace / Mark Rothko song / This is not the house that pain built / I love, I love (Traveling II) / Flinty kind of woman / Arrival. *<cd-iss. Sep 94 on Waterbug; WBG 0010> <cd/c re-mixed & re-iss. Feb 95 on Razor And Tie+=; 82816-2/-4>* - Flinty kind of woman / Arrival.

Razor And Tie — Grapevine

Dec 95. (cd-s) <*none*> THE CHRISTIANS AND THE PAGANS / Traveling Again (live acoustic) / Nora

Jan 96. (cd/c) *<82821-2/-4> (GRA CD/MC 212)* **MORTAL CITY** — Feb 96
- As cool as I am / February / Iowa (Traveling III) / The Christians and the pagans / This was Pompeii / The ocean / Family / The pointless, yet poignant, crisis of a co-ed / The blessings / Southern California wants to be western NY / Mortal city. *(re-ltd d-cd/d-c iss. Nov 96 +=; GRCDX/GRMCX 211)* - THE HONESTY ROOM

Mar 96. (cd-s) *(CDGPS 207)* AS COOL AS I AM / When I Was A Boy (live) / This Was Pompeii (live)

Razor And Tie — Razor And Tie

Jul 97. (cd) *<(82830-2)>* **END OF THE SUMMER** — Sep 98
- Are you out there / Party generation / If I wrote you / What do you hear in these sounds / The end of the summer / Teenagers, kick our butts / My friends / Bought and sold / Road buddy / It's a war in there / Better things.

——WILLIAMS' next set was a collab. w/ LUCY KAPLANSKY & RICHARD SHINDELL

Oct 98. (cd; as CRY CRY CRY) *<(82840-2)>* **CRY CRY CRY** — Mar 99
- Fall on me / Cold Missouri waters / Speaking with the angel / The kid / Shades of gray / Lord, I have made you a place in my heart / By way of sorrow / Memphis / Northern cross / Down by the water / I know what kind of love this is / The ballad of Mary Magdalen.

Aug 00. (cd) *<(82856-2)>* **THE GREEN WORLD**
- Playing to the firmament / And a god descended / After all / What do you love more than love / Spring street / We learned the sea / I won't be your Yoko Ono / Calling the moon / I had no right / It happens every day / Another mystery. *(re-iss. Oct 01 on East Central One+= hidden track; RTIECD 001)* - O Canada girls.

Razor And Tie — East Central One

Sep 01. (cd) *<82871-2> (RTIECD 002)* **OUT THERE LIVE** (live November 18–21, 2000) — Nov 01
- As cool as I am / If I wrote you / Spring street / (intro)... / I won't be your Yoko Ono / February / The ocean / Better things / Iowa / End of the summer / We learned the sea / (intro)... / Are you out there / When I was a boy / What do you hear in these sounds / After all / (intro)... / The babysitter's here / The Christians and the pagans.

Razor And Tie — Evangeline

Feb 03. (cd) *<82886-2> (GEL 4062)* **THE BEAUTY OF THE RAIN**
- Mercy of the fallen / Farewell to the old me / I saw a bird fly away / The beauty of the rain / The world's not falling apart / The one who knows / Closer to me / Fishing in the morning / Whispering pines / Your fire your soul / I have lost my dreams. *(UK cd/dvd-iss. Jun 05 on Silverline+=; 284133-2)* - [DVD tracks].

Sep 05. (cd) <*82944-2*> **MY BETTER SELF**
- Teen for God / I'll miss you till I meet you / Echoes / Blue light of the flame / Everybody knows this is nowhere / Two sides of the river / Empire / Comfortably numb / So close to my heart / Beautiful enemy / Liar / You rise and meet the day / The Hudson. *(UK-iss. Aug 08 on Zoe; ZOE 1079)*

Razor And Tie — Razor And Tie

Sep 08. (cd) *<(82996-2)>* **PROMISED LAND** — 95
- It's alright / Book of love / The easy way / The tide falls away / Buzzer / The business of things / You are everyone / Go to the woods / Holly tree / Troubled times / Midnight radio / Summerday.

Oct 10. (d-cd) *<(83112-2)>* **MANY GREAT COMPANIONS** [acoustic revisited // compilation]
- Calling the moon / If I wrote you / Spring street / I'll miss you till I meet you / The Christians and the pagans / What do you hear in these sounds / The one who knows / The babysitter's here / As cool as I am / You rise and meet the day / Iowa / When I was a boy // It's alright / Are you out there / As cool as I am / If I wrote you / February / Mercy of the fallen / The easy way / The one who knows / Teen for God / After all / Book of love / The beauty of the rain / The babysitter's here / Better things / Spring street / The ocean / Closer to me / Empire / The end of the summer / When I was a boy.

Lucinda WILLIAMS

Born January 26, 1953 at Lake Charles, Louisiana, LUCINDA WILLIAMS has gone from cult country-blues starlet to universally accepted folk-rock visionary. The daughter of an English Literature professor and poet, WILLIAMS's childhood was spent in locations as diverse as Texas, Mexico City and the Chilean capital, Santiago. Influenced primarily by the literature and music of the deep South, in her teens WILLIAMS began to play the clubs around Houston, where the likes of TOWNES VAN ZANDT and Guy Clark had founded a burgeoning folk-country scene, and Austin.

By the release of her debut album, **RAMBLIN' ON MY MIND** (1979) {*5}, she was already on the way to becoming a seasoned performer, and the record's trad country-blues standards - mainly borrowed from Robert Johnson, A.P. Carter, Hank Williams and Memphis Minnie - reflected her apprenticeship. Smithsonian-Folkways subsequently re-promoted the LP as 'Ramblin'' in the early 1990s, having signed Williams to their label in the 1980s.

In contrast, the following year's **HAPPY WOMAN BLUES** {*7} comprised entirely original material backed up by a full acoustic band. After a brief flirtation with the Greenwich Village folk scene and a further period down south, WILLIAMS eventually settled in Los Angeles, where she concentrated on writing, performing and building up a permanent band.

Deflecting regular major-label offers, WILLIAMS's insistence on full creative control finally led her to a deal with UK indie Rough Trade, who issued the long-awaited **LUCINDA WILLIAMS** (1988) {*7}. While the music married the unmistakable influence of Los Angeles' rock 'n' roll heart with her trademark take on rootsy Americana, many of the lyrics centred on her recent divorce (from Greg Sowders of The Long Ryders), and the likes of 'Passionate Kisses' and 'The Night's Too Long' made for compelling listening. The former track was later covered by Mary Chapin Carpenter, while Patty Loveless took the latter into the country charts.

WILLIAMS sold her work by the sheer hard graft of touring rather than any singles success, although her stock with critics and roots fans had never been higher. The collapse of Rough Trade certainly didn't help raise her profile, however, and after a doomed dalliance with RCA she signed to another indie label, Chameleon. The result was 1992's **SWEET OLD WORLD** {*8}, a roots-rock masterclass that managed to be both accomplished and inventively diverse, even pulling off a NICK DRAKE cover, 'Which Will'.

When her new label went bust, WILLIAMS moved on to Rick Rubin's American Recordings imprint before settling at Mercury. She had also based herself in Nashville, and 1998's acclaimed **CAR WHEELS ON A GRAVEL ROAD** {*9} was arguably the best thing to come out of Music City in a good few years. Grittier than the likes of Sheryl Crow and certainly a lot more credible than Shania Twain, the record was roundly praised by both rock and country camps, cropping up in many end-of-year polls and enjoying a prolonged stay in 'Mojo' magazine's playlist.

While her profile remained lower than it really should have been, WILLIAMS's unquestionable musical integrity continued to endear her to critics and roots aficionados alike. That integrity was perhaps even more evident on **ESSENCE** (2001) {*7}, a much more personal, delicate record that explored human frailty and possibility with a keenness and sympathy rarely witnessed on record. It was a brave step after the forthright country-rock of 'Car Wheels ...', but one that long-time fans will relish.

WORLD WITHOUT TEARS (2003) {*7}, meanwhile, was probably an even braver step, as raw and visceral a statement as she'd yet put together. Sonically stark, and roughly split between brooding balladry and driving, cathartic country/blues-rock, the record made no concessions whatever to either commercial considerations or the expectations, given her career path thus far, of at least some of her fans. Lyrically unflinching in its dissection of love's destructive power and obsessional dark side, the likes of 'Those Three Days' laid bare her soul as never before.

Having marked time with a live set, **LIVE @ THE FILLMORE** (2005) {*7} - recorded over three nights at the San Francisco venue - her third studio album for Lost Highway, **WEST** (2007) {*6}, took her all the way into the Top 30 in both the US and Britain. The Eric Liljestrand/Tom Overby-produced **LITTLE HONEY** (2008) {*6} fared even better and careered into the Top 10, a record that was rooted in electric Americana from blues to country and folk to rock. Ditto **BLESSED** (2011) {*7}, produced by Don Was with Liljestrand and Overby, whom she had married in 2009. *MCS & BG*

Lucinda Williams - vocals, acoustic guitar / with **John Grimaudo** - guitar

US: Heartbeat — UK: not issued

1979. (lp) *<HB 3507>* **RAMBLIN' ON MY MIND** [ ] [–]
- Ramblin' on my mind / Me and my chauffeur blues / Motherless children / Malted milk / Disgusted / Jug band music / Stop breaking down / Drop down daddy / Little darlin' pal of mine / Make me a pallet on the floor / Jambalaya (on the bayou) / Great speckled bird / You're gonna need that pure religion / Satisfied mind. *<(cd/c-iss. 1991 & UK Dec 94/Dec 98 as RAMBLIN' on Smithsonian-Folkways; SFW CD/MC 40042)> <(cd re-iss. Aug 09 on Retroworld; FLOATM 6019)>*

——she was now backed by a full band

US: Folkways — UK: not issued

Nov 80. (lp) *<FTS 31067>* **HAPPY WOMAN BLUES** [ ] [–]
- Lafayette / I lost it / Maria / Happy woman blues / King of hearts / Rolling along / One night stand / Howlin' at midnight / Hard road / Louisiana man / Sharp cutting wings (song to a poet). *(UK cd-iss. Oct 90 on Network; NETCD 12) <(cd/c-iss. 1990 & UK Dec 94/Dec 98 on Smithsonian-Folkways; SFW CD/MC 40003)> <(cd re-iss. Aug 09 on Retroworld; FLOATM 6020)>*

US: Rough Trade — UK: Rough Trade

Nov 88. (lp/c/cd) *<ROUGHUS 47/+C/CD> (ROUGH/+C/CD 130)*
LUCINDA WILLIAMS [ ] Jan 89 [ ]
- I just wanted to see you so bad / The night's too long / Abandoned / Big red sun blues / Like a rose / Changed the locks / Passionate kisses / Am I too blue / Crescent city / Side of the road / Price to pay / I asked for water (he gave me gasoline). *<re-iss. 1992 on Chameleon cd/c; 61387-2/-4> (cd re-iss. Jul 94 +=; R 316-2) (cd re-iss. Jun 98 & May 03 on Koch Int.+=; 38005-2)* - (live): - Nothing in rambling / Disgusted / Side of the road / Goin' back home / Something about what happens when we talk / Sundays.

Apr 89. (7"/12") *(RT/+T 224)* I JUST WANTED TO SEE YOU SO BAD. [–] [ ]

Aug 89. (7"/12") *(RT/+T 232)* PASSIONATE KISSES. / Side Of The Road [–] [ ]
(cd-ep+=) *<ROUGHUS 66CD> (RT 232CD)* - Nothing in rambling (live) / Goin' back home (live) / Disgusted (live).

US: Chameleon -WEA — UK: Chameleon -WEA

Aug 92. (cd/c) *<(3705 61351-2/-4)>* **SWEET OLD WORLD** [ ] Jan 93 [ ]
- Six blocks away / Something about what happens when we talk / He never got enough love / Sweet old world / Little angel, little brother / Pineola / Lines around your eyes / Prove my love / Sidewalks of the city / Memphis pearl / Hot blood / Which will.

US: Mercury — UK: Mercury

Jun 98. (cd) *<(558338-2)>* **CAR WHEELS ON A GRAVEL ROAD** [65] Jul 98 [ ]
- Right in time / Car wheels on a gravel road / 2 kool 2 be 4-gotten / Drunken angel / Concrete and barbed wire / Lake Charles / Can't let go / I lost it / Metal firecracker / Greenville / Still I long for your kiss / Joy / Jackson. *<d-cd-iss. Oct 06 on Mercury+=; 7378-2>* - Down the big road blues / Out of touch / Still I long for your kiss (alt.) // (WXPN LIVE AT THE WORLD CAFE):- Pineola / Something about what happens when we talk / Car wheels on a gravel road / Metal firecracker / Right in time / Drunken angel / Greenville / Still I long for your kiss / 2 kool 2 be 4-gotten / Can't let go / Hot blood / Changed the locks / Joy.

US: Lost Highway — UK: Lost Highway

Jun 01. (cd) *<(088 170197-2)>* **ESSENCE** [28] [63]
- Lonely girls / Steal your love / I envy the wind / Blue / Out of touch / Are you down / Essence / Reason to cry / Get right with God / Bus to Baton Rouge / Broken butterflies.

Apr 03. (cd/d-lp) *<(088 170355-2/-1)>* **WORLD WITHOUT TEARS** [18] [48]
- Fruits of my labor / Righteously / Ventura / Real live bleeding fingers and broken guitar strings / Over time / Those three days / Atonement / Sweet side / Minneapolis / People talkin' / American dream / World without tears / Words fell.

May 05. (d-cd) *<00023680-02> (9862123)* **LIVE @ THE FILLMORE**
(live November 20–22, 2003) [66] [ ]
- Ventura / Reason to cry / Fruits of my labor / Out of touch / Sweet side / Lonely girls / Overtime / Blue / Changed the locks / Atonement / I lost it / Pineola / Righteously / Joy / Essence / Real live bleeding fingers and broken guitar strings / Are you down / Those three days / American dream / World without tears / Bus to Baton Rouge / Words fell.

Feb 07. (cd) *<B0006938-02> (1723563)* **WEST** [14] [30]
- Are you alright? / Mama you sweet / Learning how to live / Fancy funeral / Unsuffer me / Everything has changed / Come on / Where is my love? / Rescue / What if / Wrap my head around that / Words / West.

Oct 08. (cd/d-lp) *<B0011434-02/-01> (1785915)* **LITTLE HONEY** [9] [51]
- Real love / Circles and Xs / Tears of joy / Little rock star / Honey bee / Well well well / If wishes were horses / Jailhouse tears / Knowing / Heaven blues / Rarity / Plan to marry / It's a long way to the top. *(UK+=)* - Jailhouse tears (early alt. version).

Mar 11. (cd/d-lp) *<B0015189-02/-01> (2759591)* **BLESSED** [15] [53]
- Buttercup / I don't know how you're livin' / Copenhagen / Born to be loved / Seeing black / Soldier's song / Blessed / Sweet love / Ugly truth / Convince me / Awakening / Kiss like your kiss. *<deluxe d-cd+=; B0015240-02>* - [THE KITCHEN TAPES versions].

Victoria WILLIAMS

A veteran of the US music scene but still relatively unknown, the enigmatic singer/songwriter VICTORIA WILLIAMS (b. December 23, 1958 in Shreveport, Louisiana) began playing professionally on the Los Angeles club circuit in the late 1970s. The following decade saw her marry Peter Case, formerly of the Plimsouls, before signing with Geffen after an earlier recording deal had come to naught.

Released in 1987, **HAPPY COME HOME** {*6} was produced by Anton Fier and Stephen Soles, and Van Dyke Parks handled the arrangements - a case of maverick talent nurturing new maverick talent - as WILLIAMS demonstrated her bizarre, squealing vocals (think MARIANNE FAITHFULL or KAREN DALTON) and her pithy, offbeat and quirkily observational but enchanting worldview. While her brand of off-kilter folk-pop may have been too much of an acquired taste for the average alternative fan, WILLIAMS attracted an impressive fan club of fellow artists and songwriters who admired her highly original approach.

Moving from major-label status back to the independent sector (Mammoth in the US, Rough Trade in the UK) for 1990's **SWING THE STATUE!** {*8}, she again received critical plaudits for what many observers have rated as her best album. Co-produced by Tom Waits, it featured the evocative brilliance of 'Summer Of Drugs', a song that in live performance she would interpolate with The Beatles' 'Dear Prudence'.

'Summer Of Drugs' was covered by Soul Asylum for the 1993 tribute album 'Sweet Relief: A Benefit For Victoria Williams'. The singer had been diagnosed with multiple sclerosis the year before, and the album was aimed at raising funds for her spiralling medical bills. Lou Reed, Matthew Sweet and The Jayhawks were among those giving their support by interpreting their favourite songs from her back catalogue.

WILLIAMS returned to the studio for 1994's **LOOSE** {*7}, another star-studded collection, featuring covers of Sam Cooke's 'What A Wonderful World' and Spirit's 'Nature's Way' alongside a duet with future husband Mark Olson (ex-Jayhawks). She also duetted with VIC CHESNUTT on 'God Is Good' for his 1996 tribute album, and her next studio set, **MUSINGS OF**

A CREEK DIPPER (1998) {*7}, was written and recorded on the remote desert ranch she shared with Olson.

Released a few years before and recorded with her backing outfit The Loose Band (David Mansfield, Tim Ray, Calexico's Joey Burns and the brothers David and Andrew Williams - not Lucinda's brothers), **THIS MOMENT: LIVE IN TORONTO** (1995) {*6} showcased a handful of covers including the INCREDIBLE STRING BAND title track and back-to-back pop staples 'Imagination' and 'Smoke Gets In Your Eyes'. In 2002 Victoria released a full set of Tin Pan Alley standards, **SINGS SOME OL' SONGS** {*5}.

Apart from that nostalgic outing, her most recent studio set was **WATER TO DRINK** (2000) {*7}, featuring Antonio Carlos Jobim's title track and two other standards, 'Young At Heart' and 'Until The Real Thing Comes Along'. For further listening, there is her extra-curricular work with Mark Olson's side-project The Original Harmony Ridge Creekdippers. *MCS & BG*

Victoria Williams - vocals, piano / with session people

US Geffen / UK Blanco Y Negro

Jun 87. (lp/c) *<GHS/M5G 24140> (BYN/+C 10)*
HAPPY COME HOME
- Shoes / Frying pan / Merry-go-round / Happy / TC / I'll do his will / Big fish / Animal wild / Main road / Lights / Opalousas / Statue of a bum / Poetry. *<cd-iss. Jan 94 on Geffen; GFLD 19239>*

Mammoth / Rough Trade

Apr 90. (lp/c/cd) *<MR 075> (R 140/+C/CD)* **SWING THE STATUE!**
- Why look at the moon / Boogieman / Clothesline / Tarbelly and Featherfoot / On time / Holy spirit / Summer of drugs / I can't cry hard enough / Wobbling / Vieux amis / Weeds / Lift him up. *(re-iss. May 94 on Mammoth cd/c; MR 075-2/-4) <cd re-iss. Nov 98 on Universal; 559253-2>*

Mammoth - Atlantic / Mammoth - Atlantic

Oct 94. (cd/c/lp) *<(7567 92430-2/-4/-1)>* **LOOSE** Jan 95
- Century plant / You R loved / Harry went to heaven / Crazy Mary / When we sing together / Polish those shoes / Love / What a wonderful world / Waterfall / Nature's way / Sunshine country / Happy to have known Pappy / My ally / Hitchhikers smile / Get away / Psalms.

Feb 95. (7"/c-s) *(A 8266/+C)* CRAZY MARY. / Polish Those Shoes
(cd-s+=) *(A 8266CD)* - ('A'-mixes).

——In Aug 95, WILLIAMS and SHAWN COLVIN were credited on Julie Miller's Myrrh Records album, 'He Walks Through Walls'.

——next with The Loose Band: **David Williams** (vocals), **Andrew Williams** (guitar), **Tim Ray** (keyboards), **Joey Burns** (bass, vocals) + **David Mansfield** (violin, mandolin, steel guitar, Dobro)

Nov 95. (cd) *<(7567 92642-2)>* **THIS MOMENT IN TORONTO WITH VICTORIA WILLIAMS & THE LOOSE BAND**
(live 29th March 1995) Jan 96
- This moment / Graveyard / Harry went to heaven / Waterfall / Polish those shoes / Hitchhikers smile / Crazy Mary / Summer of drugs / Imagination / Smoke gets in your eyes / Can't cry hard enough / Sunshine country / Love.

——In 1997, WILLIAMS, MARK OLSON (ex-Jayhawks) and multi-instrumentalist Mike 'Razz' Russell recorded their first of a handful of country-rock sets under the name of The Original Harmony Ridge Creekdippers - the self-titled set was followed by 'Pacific Coast Rambler' (1998), 'Zola And The Tulip Tree' (1999) and 'My Own Jo Ellen' (2000).

Atlantic / Atlantic

Jan 98. (cd) *<(7567 83072-2)>* **MUSINGS OF A CREEK DIPPER** Mar 98
- Periwinkle sky / Rainmaker / Kashmir's corn / Train song (demise of the caboose) / The last word / Nature boy / Tree song (eucalyptus lullabye) / Let it be so / Allergic boy / Humming bird / Grandpa in the cornpatch / Blackbirds rise.

Aug 00. (cd) *<(7567 83361-2)>* **WATER TO DRINK**
- Grandma's hat pin / Gladys and Lucy / Water to drink / Light the lamp Freddie / Claude / Joy of love / Until the real thing comes along / Lagniappe / Junk / Little bird / Young at heart / A little bit of love.

Dualtone / Dualtone

Aug 02. (cd) *<1126> (IDLCD 018)* **SINGS SOME OL' SONGS** Sep 02
- Moon river / Blue skies / And roses and roses / Over the rainbow / My funny valentine / Keep sweeping cobwebs off the moon / I'm old fashioned / As time goes by / Someone to watch over me / Mongoose / Do you know what it means to miss New Orleans?

——Williams has recently been conspicuous by her absence on the solo front, although she has guested on sets by M. Ward and Christopher Rees

- (5-7*) compilations, etc.-

Jul 07. (cd-ep) *Rhino-Atlantic; <???>* RHINO HI-FIVE
- Nature boy / Crazy Mary / What a wonderful world / Water to drink / Periwinkle sky.

WOODS

A side-project of Brooklyn alt/indie outfit Meneguar, Jeremy Earl and Christian DeRoeck's WOODS first came to light through their 2005 double-cassette release **HOW TO SURVIVE IN + IN THE WOODS** {*7}. Re-released on CD a few years later, it had all the folky hallmarks of BON IVER (or Daniel Johnson, or Sebadoah) in shape and sound, although they were in fact precursors to BON IVER rather than followers. 'Silence Is Golden', 'Broke' and 'Holes' come off best. **AT REAR HOUSE** (2006) {*6} was virtually part two of its predecessor, once again with the high-pitched quiver of Earl at its squeakiest.

Adding Meneguar multi-instrumentalist Steven Justin Taveniere and tape-effects man G. Lucas Crane (Kevin Morby played bass), the structure of the group took a more experimental standpoint on the **WOODS FAMILY CREEPS** (2008) {*6} semi-side-project.

SONGS OF SHAME (2009) {*7} was WOODS taking folk-rock music to new levels, but where the jam-packed, nine-minute wig-out of 'September With Pete' (featuring Pete Nolan of The Magick Markers) fitted in was a mystery. Their version of Graham Nash's classic 'Military Madness' was timely, and indirectly it gave Earl his NEIL YOUNG connection. **ECHO LAKE** (2010) {*7} and **SUN AND SHADE** (2011) {*7} continued with Earl and Taveniere's newfound BYRDS-meet-Grateful Dead approach; the West Coast was reborn in a setting one foot past Death Valley. *MCS*

Jeremy Earl - vocals, guitar / **Christian DeRoeck** - multi

US FuckItTapes / UK not issued

2005. (ltd-d-c) *<FIT 016>* **HOW TO SURVIVE IN + IN THE WOODS**
- Holes / Kid's got heart / How to survive in / 8-5 5-10 / Silence is golden / Keep it on / God hates the faithless / Angel's trumpet / Broke / I get by / In the woods / Make time for kitty / Holier than no one. *<cd/lp-iss. Nov 07 on Shrimper; SHR 152>*

2006. (ltd-7" white) *<GGGR-003>* RAM. / Woods Children / Do They Smoke Cigarettes In Heaven

(above issued on Gilgongo)

2006. (ltd-c) *<FIT 037>* **AT REAR HOUSE**
- Don't pass on me / Hungover / Keep it on / Be still / Woods children (part 2) / Ring me to sleep / Night creature / Walk the dogs / Love song for pigeons / Bone tapper / Picking up the pieces. *<cd-iss. Jan 07 on Shrimper; SHR 150> <ltd-lp-iss. Nov 07 on Woodsist; woodsist 004> <re-lp iss. 2007 on Troubleman; TMU 123>*

2008. (ltd-C40) *<FIT 048>* TOUR TAPE w/ Religious Knives tour
- [below tracks + 'untitled' track by Religious Knives].

2008. (ltd-C20) *<FIT 055>* FROM THE HORN / To See tour

——added **Steven Justin Taveniere** - multi (of Meneguar) / **G. Lucas Crane** - tape-effects / plus **Kevin Morby** - bass

Time-Lag / not issued

Mar 08. (ltd; cd/red-lp; as WOODS FAMILY CREEPS) *<TLR-RR-002>*
WOODS FAMILY CREEPS
- End to end / Creeps collage / Twisted tongue / Family / Howling on howling / Diamond days / Spike / Sleep sleep sleep / The creeps. *<re-iss. 2009; Time-Lag 049>*

Woodsist / Woodsist

Apr 09. (lp) *<woodsist 025>* **SONGS OF SHAME**
- To clean / The hold / The number / September with Pete / Down this road / Military madness / Born to lose / Echo lake / Rain on / Gypsy hand / Where and what are you? *<cd-iss. Apr 09 on Shrimper; SHR 156>*

Jul 09. (one-sided-12" ep; as ACOUSTIC FAMILY CREEPS) *<none>*
PLAY LIVE IN THE WOODS EP
- Rain on / Twisted tongue / To clean / The number.
two on Half Machine and Captured Tracks, above on own-label 12")

Aug 09. (7") *(HMR 015)* TO CLEAN. / Rain On [live on WVKR]

Nov 09. (ltd-7") *<CT-004>* SUNLIT. / The Dark

Feb 10. (ltd-7") *<woodsist 041>* I WAS GONE
- Days gone by / I was gone / Hang on.

May 10. (cd/c/lp) *<(woodsist 040)>* **ECHO LAKE**
- Blood dries darker / Pick up / Suffering season / Time fading lines / From the horn / Death rattles / Mornin' time / I was gone / Get back / Deep / Til the sun rips.

Jun 11. (cd/lp) *<(woodsist 053)>* **SUN AND SHADE**
- Pushing onlys / Any other day / Be all be easy / Out of the eye / Hand it out / To have in the home / Sol y sombra / Wouldn't waste / Who do you think I am? / What faces the sheet / White out / Say goodbye.

Sacred Bones / not issued

Jul 11. (ltd-7") *<SBR-060>* FIND THEM EMPTY. / Be There

Y

Jenny Owen YOUNGS

Born November 22, 1981 in Montclair, New Jersey, alt-folk-rocker JENNY OWEN YOUNGS made quite a promising start to her career, albeit a tad controversially, with her radio-unfriendly 'Fuck Was I', a record that has since had further exposure on the TV drama 'Weeds'.

Lifted from her independently-delivered debut set, **BATTEN THE HATCHES** (2005) {*7}, it also prompted some re-promotion from her new Canadian label, Nettwerk. Drawing comparisons with Liz Phair, ERIN McKEOWN and her anti-folk counterpart REGINA SPEKTOR (whom she supported on tour in 2005), the album was not quite typical of its large peer group of nu-folk by girly waifs. Tracks that shone were 'From Here', 'Woodcut' and the new addition, 'Drinking Song'.

TRANSMITTER FAILURE (2009) {*6} resumed her folk-pop career, omitting the barbs and bruises of her now forgotten debut set in favour of pop sentimentality and buoyant, bubbly diversions. If she carries on in the same direction, her next album will sound like the new Avril Lavigne. Ah, major labels; don't we all love their control? *MCS*

Jenny Owen Youngs - vocals, guitar, etc / + session people

		US own label	UK Gravity Dip
Nov 05.	(cd) <*none*> **BATTEN THE HATCHES**		–
	- Porchrail / From here / Fuck was I / Lightning rod / Voice on tape / P.S. / Bricks / Drinking Song [*] / Woodcut / Coyote / Keys out lights on. <*(re-iss. Apr 07/Dec 08 on Nettwerk+= [*]; 06700 30648 2 8)*> - Woodcut [the Age of Rockets remix] / F-ck was I [child-friendly radio edit].		
Apr 07.	(ltd-10" clear-ep) <*DIP-037*> Dave House // JENNY OWEN YOUNGS split	–	
	- [Dave House tracks] // Fuck was I / Hot in here.		
2009.	(ltd-7") <*none*> LAST PERSON. / [Jukebox The Ghost track]		–
		Nettwerk	Nettwerk
May 09.	(cd) <*(06700 30840 2 8)*> **TRANSMITTER FAILURE**		
	- First person / Led to the sea / Dissolve / Here is a heart / Clean break / If I didn't know / What beats within / Secrets / No more words / Last person / Nighty night / Transmitter failure / Start and stop.		